CANADA'S POP ~~~~~~ IN A GLOBAL CONTEXT

AN INTRODUCTION TO SOCIAL DEMOGRAPHY

FRANK TROVATO

OXFORD
UNIVERSITY PRESS

OXFORD
UNIVERSITY PRESS

70 Wynford Drive, Don Mills, Ontario M3C 1J9
www.oupcanada.com

Oxford University Press is a department of the University of Oxford.
It furthers the University's objective of excellence in research, scholarship,
and education by publishing worldwide in

Oxford   New York

Auckland   Cape Town   Dar es Salaam   Hong Kong   Karachi   Kuala Lumpur   Madrid
Melbourne   Mexico City   Nairobi   New Delhi   Shanghai   Taipei   Toronto

With offices in

Argentina   Austria   Brazil   Chile   Czech Republic   France   Greece
Guatemala   Hungary   Italy   Japan   Poland   Portugal   Singapore
South Korea   Switzerland   Thailand   Turkey   Ukraine   Vietnam

Oxford is a trade mark of Oxford University Press
in the UK and in certain other countries

Published in Canada
by Oxford University Press

Library and Archives Canada Cataloguing in Publication

Trovato, Frank, 1951–
Canada's population in a global context : an introduction to social
demography / Frank Trovato.

Includes bibliographical references and index.
ISBN 978-0-19-541907-8

1. Canada—Population.   2. Demography—Canada.   I. Title.

HB3529.T695 2008   304.60971   C2007-907248-8

Cover image: Yamada Taro/Getty Images

1 2 3 4 – 12 11 10 09
This book is printed on permanent (acid-free) paper ∞.
Printed in Canada

Contents

Tables, Figures, and Boxes

Tables

Figures

Boxes

Chapter 2

Chapter 3

Chapter 4

Chapter 5

Chapter 6

Chapter 7

Chapter 8

Chapter 9

Chapter 10

Chapter 11

Chapter 12

Preface

Canadian Population in a Global Context: An Introduction to Social Demography

Since the early 1970s, generations of Canadian college and university students have learned about the demography of this country from a select number of excellent textbooks. Notable among these are the several editions produced by the late Warren Kalbach and his collaborator Wayne McVey (Kalbach and McVey, 1971, 1979; McVey and Kalbach, 1995). The works of Beaujot and McQuillan (1983) and of Beaujot and Kerr (2004) deserve mention here as well. But although these introductory texts have provided a foundational understanding of the demographic trends and patterns of Canadian society, they give limited attention to the broader global aspects of population as a field of study and as a comparative discipline. The present textbook, which shares many features with its predecessors, is designed to complement these excellent textbooks on Canadian population by incorporating a global perspective as well as coverage of the fundamental concepts, theories, and perspectives of demography and population studies.

For a Canadian textbook such as this to adopt an international perspective seems particularly important today, given the intense interest among scholars and the public at large in the phenomenon of globalization. The pervasive diffusion of Western values, ideas, and economic practices has had a homogenizing effect on many countries. Paradoxically, there are, at the same time, widespread socioeconomic gaps between countries, with poverty an ongoing reality in many parts of the globe. In terms of demographic development, it is clear that while some developing countries have, or nearly have, caught up to the industrialized countries' stage

of demographic transition, many others continue to lag far behind. In the light of these divergent demographic and socioeconomic patterns affecting countries worldwide, it seems no longer useful to examine Canadian population in isolation of the broader global context.

This textbook identifies issues at the heart of demography as a scientific field and covers areas of population studies typically included in introductory university courses, including population history and theories of population change; the relationship of population to environment and resources; fertility, mortality, and nuptiality; migration and urbanization; age and sex composition; and population policy. The text's twelve chapters are organized in five parts. Part I deals with the concepts and theories of population studies, including data sources and population history. Part II covers demographic composition, focusing primarily on age and sex structure and nuptiality. Part III is devoted to the central demographic processes of fertility and mortality, while Part IV focuses on the other key demographic process: migration. Finally, Part V examines the interconnection of population with urbanization, the interconnection of population with resources, and the interconnection of population change with policy concerns, each of these treated as a separate chapter. Together, these five parts provide a framework for addressing some fundamental questions, such as the following:

- What roles do individuals play in the production of demographic phenomena?
- How do culture and social structure influence individual demographic action?
- Why did the human population begin growing at such explosive rates so recently? What important demographic and non-demographic factors are responsible for this?

- Why is the human population distributed unevenly across the world's geographic regions? Why are birth and death rates so low in some parts of the world and relatively high in others?
- Why do some nations discourage population growth and others encourage it?
- How do the demographic histories of Canada and other countries of the industrialized world differ from those of today's developing nations?
- What accounts for the different trajectories of population growth for developing nations versus industrialized societies?

Both reader and instructor will find that this text places strong emphasis on conceptual and theoretical frameworks of demographic phenomena. Wherever possible, figures and schematic representations are offered to clarify key concepts and theories. In over two decades of teaching, I have found illustrations of this kind extremely useful in helping students grasp complex ideas. I have also tried to situate, wherever possible, current and historical Canadian demographic trends as either varying from or conforming to patterns elsewhere in the world, an approach that will, I hope, help instill in the beginning student a strong appreciation of the universality of demographic concepts, measures, and theories.

Another feature that distinguishes this text from others in the field is its use, where appropriate, of techniques of demographic analysis, which are frequently minimized in or omitted from introductory textbooks. Technical matters are not avoided here, although the techniques featured are kept at an introductory level appropriate for beginning students. I believe it is necessary and beneficial to include technical rudiments of demographic analysis as long as these are presented in an accessible manner. Each chapter, at its conclusion, offers exercises and questions for further study designed to help reinforce substantive and technical material covered in the main text. Instructors are encouraged to incorporate new data as they become available to complement the study questions and the corresponding data laid out in this part of the book. Each chapter also includes a list of additional readings for the interested reader, as well as some useful websites for those who wish to pursue further exploration of topics on their own.

A note about notation in this book. I have simplified the notation in formulas to make them as accessible as possible to the beginning student without compromising their inherent structures. Throughout the text the subscript 'x' is used to denote a given age group or category. For example, in the presentation of the age-specific fertility rate, the formula $f_x = B_x/W_x$ is used. This formula says that the fertility rate (f_x) for women aged x is equal to the number of births to women of that age (B_x) divided by the number of women of that age (W_x). As applied in this textbook, the symbol 'x' can represent either single years of age or grouped age categories, most frequently five-year age groups (e.g., 0–4, 5–9, 10–14, . . . or 0, 1–4, 5–9, 10–14, . . .). In the formal treatment of grouped age-specific rates, the convention is to represent an age interval symbolically as '$x, x + n$', where 'x' is the beginning age in the interval, and 'n' is the number of years in the interval. Demographic rates are typically computed for a specific period of time, most often a calendar year; in such cases, unless otherwise indicated, the population at risk (the denominator) is always the mid-year population.

As with any introductory textbook on population, much of the information used has come from published vital statistics and census materials from Canada and from international statistical agencies, most notably the United Nations and the World Health Organization. Fortunately, there is an abundance of data on population. However, one drawback of this is that new data are always being published, making it virtually impossible for any writer to keep abreast of all the latest statistics. In producing the many tables and graphs in this book I was able to make wide use of information from the 2001 Canadian census made public by Statistics Canada and from newly released 2006 census data. I expect that by the time this book is published, more data from the 2006 census will have become available. While recognizing this characteristic feature of the field, I have tried to emphasize the enduring and foundational principles of demographic analysis and population studies in the hope that instructors will feel confident relying on the text as a source for the presentation of basic concepts, theories, and methods to their students, in spite of the availability of newer data.

Demographic trends can never occur in isolation of the social, cultural, and institutional contexts of society. The substantive orientation of this textbook is sociological. In particular, I assume that since all societies are, by definition, populations, and since populations are dynamic bodies that are constantly changing, the systematic study of population, to a significant extent, necessarily implies the study of social change. Society cannot be understood in isolation of demography, nor can demography be fully appreciated without knowledge of how sociological structures and processes affect people's actions toward such things as marriage, divorce, having children, or moving. Furthermore, demographic change is thought to be both a cause and a consequence of social, institutional, and cultural processes, operating through their effects on individuals' decisions and actions. A systematic appreciation of how populations change in size, distribution, and composition over time, and how these in turn relate to societal processes, is a prerequisite for anyone seriously interested in gaining a fundamental understanding of how societies are structured, how they change, and how they function.

The interconnectedness of demographic and societal change can be illustrated with numerous examples. How is it possible to fully understand the current baby dearth in Canadian society (and in most other industrialized countries today) without first knowing about the baby boom of the post-war years, between 1946 and 1966? How is it possible to properly appreciate the current low fertility pattern without knowing about the successive boom and bust trends in the marriage rate between the 1950s and the early 1980s? On a different note, most readers are acutely aware that over the past three decades or so, Canadian society has been transformed into an increasingly multiracial nation. Is international migration partly or mainly the cause? What has been the role of changing immigration patterns in this phenomenon?

It is my wholehearted belief that such questions are best answered through an interdisciplinary approach. Demography is a field that overlaps greatly with many other disciplines in the natural and social sciences. So, even though the substantive emphasis in this textbook is mainly sociological, many of the theoretical perspectives presented are contributions by scholars from diverse fields, including biology, economics, geography, history, mathematics, anthropology, political science, public health, epidemiology, and statistics, among others. This interdisciplinarity is, in my view, an essential feature of demography as a scientific discipline.

Acknowledgements

Like the author of any work of this nature, which requires extensive effort and time commitment, I am indebted to many individuals for their support, assistance, and encouragement. I have been fortunate to work with the editorial team at Oxford University Press. In particular, special thanks are due to Euan White and Megan Mueller, who first read and approved my proposal for this work. Their professionalism reinforced my confidence to take on the challenge of writing this textbook. I am also indebted to others at Oxford Press, particularly Lisa Meschino, Roberta Osborne, Rachael Cayley, Jennifer Charlton, Sally Livingston, Eric Sinkins, and Janice Evans for their diligent and skillful organizational and editorial work. Their insightful queries often led me to rethink aspects of my writing, thereby rendering the work more accessible without compromising its essential features. I appreciate their wisdom and patience, and if in places throughout the book I have remained obdurate it is of no fault of their own.

The University of Alberta's sociology department provided the facilities and proper environment necessary to complete this work. I would like to acknowledge my colleagues for their unwavering encouragement and willingness to assist when needed. David Odynak of the Population Research Laboratory took time off his busy schedule on numerous occasions to help me solve some complicated data and programming problems. The encouragement and assistance I have received from Niranna Lalu, Parameswara Krishnan, and Wayne McVey Jr is also gratefully noted. I would be remiss if I failed to acknowledge the insightful contributions of the many students I have taught at the University of Alberta, whose penetrating questions contributed to the development of some important ideas for this textbook.

My gratitude goes also to the three anonymous reviewers of the first draft of this book. Their constructive criticisms and comments proved especially important for subsequent revision. I thank them most gratefully but do not hold them responsible for any errors or omissions that may have remained in the final product. There are others who in various ways helped me to bring this work to fruition whose names are forgotten but whose contributions were very helpful. Lastly, no adequate homage can fully acknowledge one's indebtedness to his family. I am deeply thankful to Frances, Laura, and Cathy for their dedicated and unflagging support throughout the duration of this project.

Frank Trovato
Edmonton, 25 July 2008

To my parents, Vito and Rosina,
for loving me unconditionally.

PART ONE

Population as a Scientific Discipline

Chapter 1

The Study of Population

Demography is commonly perceived by the layperson as a discipline whose principal concern is the rapid growth of human population. This is certainly one aspect of the field. The 'population problem' receives much attention in the literature and continues to stimulate important scholarly inquiry. Interest reached a peak during the 1960s and 1970s, when the global population was growing faster than at any other time in history. The threat of 'overpopulation', with its dire implications for the future of a world with runaway population growth, became a frequent topic of discussion in the popular media and academic circles, stoked by influential books like Paul Ehrlich's *The Population Bomb* (1968) that warned of looming disaster. This anxiety was also reflected in *The Limits to Growth* (Meadows et al., 1972), a study grounded on a massive simulation model of the world system. It projected, among other things, that the continued exponential growth of humans would have a devastating effect on environmental quality, renewable and non-renewable resources, and industrial output. Pondering the results of their simulation models, the study's authors concluded that if the growth trends in world population, industrialization, pollution, food production, and resource depletion were to continue unchanged, the limits to growth on the planet would be reached sometime in the twenty-first century, resulting most probably in a sudden, uncontrollable decline in both population and industrial capacity (23).

Just three decades later, the prevailing concern in the industrialized countries is a very different one. The trouble on the horizon may be tied not to explosive growth but to below-replacement birth rates coupled with annual rates of population growth close to zero—into negative figures for some countries. The 'overpopulation crisis' that threatened industrialized countries in the 1960s and 1970s has given way to fears over depopulation and increased levels of population aging (Teitelbaum and Winter, 1985). Even the developing countries, which have population growth rates above the world average, are seeing these growth rates decline.

Less evident, perhaps, to the beginning student is the fact that the subject matter central to demography is based on some common experiences we all share. Consider this: all of us were born and will someday die, and between these two fateful occurrences we will experience a host of formative events, which might include graduation, a first full-time job, marriage, parenting, divorce, remarriage, widowhood, numerous changes of residence, and so forth. The *timing* and *intensity* of these events—when in life they occur, and how frequently in the population—is an important subject of investigation. *Demographers*—those who study population dynamics—investigate what we call *aggregate manifestations* of such behaviours among broadly defined groups of people.

An example of an aggregate measure is the birth rate. It summarizes the extent to which individual women in the population have given birth during a specified period. Similarly, the death rate can tell us how many members of a particular group, on average, died over a particular time interval. Aggregate measures such as these also mirror aspects of population change. In particular, whether a population will grow, decline, or remain stable in real numbers will depend on shifting rates of *fertility*, *mortality*, and *migration*—the three fundamental variables of demographic analysis.

While fertility, mortality, and migration are central to population change, other variables play an indirect role by acting on these. Two examples are age and sex. At the individual level, age and sex are biological facts: every one of us is born male or female, and we measure our age in years. In the aggregate, age and sex are used to characterize the composition of an entire population, so that a population may be described as having a relatively young or relatively old age structure, and a balanced or distorted sex composition. Age and sex are so important in population analysis that they merit their own chapter.

'Population analysis' sounds like an occupation reserved for specialized academic study, yet a look through any of our major daily newspapers reveals that demography is a topic we encounter frequently in the popular press. For example, a headline in the 18 July 2007 edition of the *Globe and Mail* announces 'The economic challenge of age'. The ensuing story, based on Statistics Canada's recent release of 2006 census data on age and sex, outlines fears that with Canada's aging baby boomers steamrolling into retirement, there soon won't be enough young people to replace those leaving the work force. Clearly, the ramifications for Canadian society of an aging population are of interest not just to the public but also to policy officials responsible for planning in the areas of labour force, education, and health care.

Another *Globe* headline warns: 'We have seen the future, and its sprawl and emissions' (16 March 2007). This article, also reporting on 2006 census data, confirms what many of us knew or suspected: that the world's second largest land mass is a predominantly urban country, with most of its population living in large and expanding metropolitan areas. Urban expansion is gobbling up agricultural land at an alarming rate, with outlying suburban areas growing much faster than urban centres themselves. The unfortunate consequence of urban sprawl is a greater reliance on automobiles to commute longer distances to work, which

results in more greenhouse gas emissions and more pollution. In this case, population growth is an indirect contributor to the problem.

A final example is based on a cover story in the 28 May 2007 issue of *Maclean's* magazine: 'Hey Lady! What will it take to make you breed?' This provocative headline speaks to another important population issue facing Canada and most other high-income nations today: baby dearth. Over the last four decades the birth rate has been falling and currently sits at its lowest point in Canadian history. The average Canadian woman in her childbearing years has just 1.5 children; in some countries this figure is even lower. The demographic implications of very low fertility are far-reaching, and it is the role of the demographer to discover the causes and consequences. We shall discuss this matter in greater detail later in this textbook.

Newspaper coverage of issues like Canada's aging workforce, urban sprawl, and baby dearth is proof that these issues are of interest to all Canadians. Demographers, as we shall learn throughout this textbook, play an important role in shedding light on these and other issues of vital importance to society.

Population Defined

We have already noted that demography is concerned with the study of population, but before we proceed much further we should clarify that term. In general, a population is a group of people: students, workers, physicians, parents—each one may be considered a population. To a demographer, however, 'population' refers specifically to a collectivity of people coexisting within a prescribed geographic territory, such as a country, a province, or a state, at a given point in time (Pressat, 1985: 176). In modern times the census is the tool that allows us to count the number of persons present in a given area at a specified time (Clarke, 1997: 13–14; Petersen, 2000: 1).

Because human populations are constantly changing in size and composition, temporal continuity must also be introduced as another element in our definition. The notion of temporal continuity recognizes that people living today are descendants of many earlier generations (Ricklef, 1990). Ryder (1965) refers to the succession of generations in a population as 'demographic metabolism'—a continuing process of societal renewal through fundamental demographic processes (birth, death, and in- and out-migration).

A human population, then, is a dynamic aggregate existing within a defined geographic boundary and continuously changing as a result of the complementary processes of *attrition* (losses through deaths and emigration) and *accession* (gains through births and immigration). A national population exists through time and can be projected using mathematical procedures guided by sound assumptions concerning the direction and magnitude of changes in fertility, mortality, and migration (Preston, Heuveline, and Guillot, 2001: 1).

As McNicoll observes (2003b: 731), there are always challenges in delimiting the boundaries of a population. 'Consider', he writes, 'the population of a city. . . . Even if there are agreed physical boundaries, the number of legal residents may differ greatly from the number of *de facto* residents. . . . The actual number of people within a city's defined borders varies greatly by time of day, day of the week, and season.' We can add, to this challenge, the fact that for any national population, the census can identify three subsets of the overall population: the civilian population, the total resident population, and the total population living abroad (including nationals who are military personnel, tourists, professionals of various types, missionaries, students, employees of voluntary organizations, and so forth). As a result, it is seldom possible for the census to trace and enumerate every living citizen of a country, and so there will always be varying degrees of census undercount of population. In Canada, the census undercount is usually in the range of 2 to 4 per cent of the population total (Statistics Canada, *The Daily*, 2003a).

One of the challenges in delimiting populations is that even those within agreed physical borders can be quite heterogeneous along racial, ethnic, and linguistic lines (McNeill, 1984; Petersen, 2000). To meet these challenges, researchers often develop composite populations based on some arbitrarily defined set of criteria. For instance, someone undertaking a study of ethnic differences in home ownership in Toronto must first establish some criteria of inclusion and exclusion with regard to the ethnic groups. Should all or only certain groups be included? Perhaps only the largest ethnic populations? Are recent immigrants to be excluded? A researcher may opt to restrict his or her analysis to, say, the five largest ethnic populations in the city, and then interview only household heads who have been residents of the city for at least 10 years. These types of specifications are driven by the study objectives.

Formal Demography and Population Studies

The term *demography* derives from the Greek words *demos,* meaning 'people', and *graphia,* meaning 'the study of'. Demography, then, is the scientific study of population and how population is affected by births, deaths, and migration. Pressat (1985: 54) suggests that most demographic work focuses on three core areas:

1. the size and makeup of populations according to diverse criteria (age, sex, marital status, educational attainment, spatial distribution, etc.)—in short, pictures of a population at a fixed moment;
2. the different processes that bear directly on population composition (fertility, mortality, nuptiality, migration, etc.); and
3. the relationship between these static and dynamic elements and the social, economic, and cultural environment within which they exist.

This last point identifies sociology (and by extension, the social sciences) as an important vehicle towards a proper understanding of population phenomena. Keyfitz (1996c: 1) is explicit in his acknowledgement of this, calling demography '. . . a branch of sociology [that] uses birth and death rates and related statistics to determine the characteristics of a population, discover patterns of change, and make predictions.' The social sciences figure prominently in *population studies*, one of two principal branches of demography customarily recognized in introductory courses. The other branch is commonly known as *formal demography*. While it would be misleading to suggest there is consensus on whether and how to differentiate population studies from formal demography, the division is helpful, particularly in a text of this kind. These two branches are explained in the sections that follow.

Formal Demography

The statistical and mathematical aspects of the field constitute what is commonly called *formal demography*. Formal demography deals with the quantitative study of population in terms of growth, distribution, and development (or change). As David Yaukey (2001: 1) neatly puts it, formal demography is concerned with finding out 'how many people, of what kind, are where.' The first part of this question, *how many?*, highlights the accounting aspect of demographic analysis involved in determining or estimating, for example, the size of a population and its change over time. The question *of what kind?* draws attention to population composition, the statistical analysis of the distribution of a population in terms of specific demographic characteristics, particularly age, sex, and marital status. Some of the other characteristics subject to this kind of analysis are racial and ethnic origin, language, religion, employment status, income, and occupation. The final part of the question, *where?*, refers to formal demography's concern with the geographic dimension of population analysis—the distribution and concentration of the population across geographic space, and its mobility across borders.

Population Studies

Demography is an interdisciplinary science. This means that demographers usually expand their analyses beyond the formal methodologies of the discipline to include perspectives, models, and theories drawn from diverse fields, including sociology, economics, geography, history, anthropology, biology, ecology, epidemiology, and medicine, among others. Likewise, specialists from these and other disciplines frequently rely on demography in their work. An economist, for instance, would use demography to study the interrelation of demographic and economic variables across human populations; ecologists study human (and animal) populations to see how they develop and change in the context of varying conditions in their natural environment; sociologists and the other social scientists investigate demographic change in terms of underlying social forces; geographers look at spatial dimensions of demographic development; medical scientists and epidemiol-

Achille Guillard, a French political economist, coined the term *demography* in his *Elements de statistique humanine, ou demographie comparee* (1855). Petersen (2000: 4) observes that

earlier writings about birth and deaths, the growth in numbers, and the relation of population to other social processes went by different names: 'political arithmetic' (used to denote the pioneer efforts of such mercantilist writers as the English professor of anatomy William Petty, who coined the phrase); 'political economy' (the term current at the time of Thomas Robert Malthus to designate the study of population, among other topics); and 'human statistics' or simply 'statistics' (used particularly by German analysts of the early modern period).

ogists focus on the demographic bases of population health; and so on. In short, scientists from these different fields, though they approach the study of population from the perspectives of their respective disciplines, share a common appreciation of and reliance on formal demographic methods and their proper application to the analysis of population problems. The interplay between demography and these other disciplines makes up the bulk of demography's second branch, *population studies* (also known as *social demography*).

Central to population studies is its emphasis on identifying *determinants* and *consequences* (broadly speaking) of demographic change. Whereas formal demography is concerned with statistics and finding out 'How many people, of what kind, are where?', population studies has, as its core questions, 'How come?' and 'So what?' (Yaukey, 1985: 1). Implicit in the first of these questions is the importance of specifying the causal mechanisms responsible for population change—in other words, the social and demographic determinants of demographic change. The term 'social' here is used in its broadest sense to encompass environmental and societal factors (political, cultural, psychological, etc.) of potential relevance. The 'So what?' question points to the consequences of population change for both the individual and society (for instance, social policy issues that derive from current and projected demographic developments). Table 1.1 reviews the core questions of formal demography and population studies.

The demarcation of formal demography and population studies provides a neat division that helps the beginning student gain a basic understanding of the field, but in actual practice, it should be noted, this distinction is often a matter of degree; the two aspects are seldom separate in true demographic study. The scientific analysis of population usually involves the use of both principles or methods of formal demography and substantive conceptual frameworks of population studies. Seldom does a demographer

rely on a formal technique or methodology for purely technical motives. Rather, formal methods are typically developed and applied in the context of some clearly specified theoretical groundwork. This is the case even in applied demography (where formal techniques are applied to, say, business), though in such cases the theoretical context may be subordinate to the technical application.

This text is premised on the view that formal demography and population studies represent complementary rather than separate aspects of population analysis. For this reason, a statistical description of demographic trends is usually followed by substantive sociological analysis. In fact, we support Burch's argument (2002a, 2002b) that many technical methods thought of as 'formal' and thus separate from population studies are in fact theoretical descriptions of demographic processes. We may ask questions such as *Is the population increasing or decreasing?*, *Is the change in population over some period of time due to a rise or a decline in fertility?*, *Is change solely accounted by migration?* But once answered, these questions typically lead us to *how?*, *why?*, and *so what?* type queries.

The Nature of Demographic Change

The study of population phenomena may be approached from either a *static* or a *dynamic* perspective. A static analysis would focus on demographic conditions at a fixed point in time. By contrast, a dynamic analysis would study the change in demographic conditions over a period of time. This kind of analysis might emphasize *process variables*—variables that reflect human behavioural processes, such as fertility, mortality, and migration. Fertility can be treated as a process variable because it presupposes the existence of couples, in heterosexual unions, undergoing sequential stages of the fertility process: conception, gestation, and parturition. Mortality

Table 1.1 Typology of the two traditional domains in the scientific study of population

Domain	Central questions	Analytical approaches	Principles implied in the question
Formal demography	How many people, of what kind, are where?	• Quantitative accounting of demographic processes and phenomena • Formulation and application of mathematical and statistical models of population processes and dynamics • Planning and collection of demographic data (census, vital registration, surveys) • Detection and adjustment of errors in demographic data • Estimation and projection of population, and demographic parameters	'How many people?' implies: Population size and its change over time (i.e., growth, stability, decline) 'Of what kind?' implies: The distribution (i.e., composition) of the population in accordance with specific characteristics (esp. age, sex, and marital status) and change over time in these distributions 'Are where?' implies: The distribution and concentration of population with respect to geographic space (e.g., urban/rural, province/state, etc.), and change over time in distribution and concentration
Population studies	How come? (i.e., why, how, where, when, who) So what? (implications)	• Development and application of substantive theories/models from the social sciences and other sciences, to describe and explain systematically micro- and macro-level population phenomena (models based approach) • Application of multi-variate methods for analysis (formal demographic methods and models)	'How come?' implies: How and why population processes occur and change over time; where and when is change occurring? (past; current; future) Who (what part of the population) is/are involved in the phenomenon? (The whole population? One or more subset of the population? Etc.) 'So what?' implies: What are the sociological implications of population change for the present and the future? What policy interventions, if any, are needed to address the current and projected implications of demographic change?

can be described as a process because a variety of causal mechanisms and conditions can operate over a period to cause the death of an individual. Consider, for example, that over 20,000 Canadians die each year of ischemic heart disease (World Health Organization, 1998), a disease that, in the majority of cases, occurs over many years, starting as early as childhood; for some, there may be a genetic predisposition to the disease, while for others, poor diet and a host of lifestyle-related problems (smoking, stress, lack of exercise, and so on) may be responsible. Migration is also a dynamic process. In most cases, geographic relocation involves a conscious decision by an individual, but the move is not instantaneous. The person will have to make arrangements to leave his or her place of residence and arrangements to take up residence elsewhere; all of these aspects of migration presuppose a process of decision-making and adjustment on the part of the individual. In the population as a whole, these three demographic processes—fertility, mortality, and migration—take place continuously.

Change in Population Size

We can measure the change in the size of a population between two points in time by examining the natural processes of fertility and mortality, as well as net migration (the net difference between the number of incoming and outgoing migrants). This principle is illustrated by the *demographic components equation*, also known as the *demographic balancing equation*:

$$P_{t2} - P_{t1} = (B_{t1,\,t2} - D_{t1,\,t2})$$
$$+ (IN_{t1,\,t2} - OUT_{t1,\,t2})$$

P_{t1} and P_{t2} represent, respectively, the population at the beginning and the population at the end of some specified interval. The numerical change in population over the interval ($P_{t2} - P_{t1}$), can be expressed as a function of the difference in births and deaths ($B_{t1,\,t2} - D_{t1,\,t2}$) plus the net exchange in the numbers of immigrants ($IN_{t1,\,t2}$) and emigrants ($OUT_{t1,\,t2}$). The compo-

nent $B_{t1,\,t2} - D_{t1,\,t2}$ is called *natural increase,* and the term $IN_{t1,\,t2} - OUT_{t1,\,t2}$ is *net migration.* Therefore, we may rewrite the demographic equation as shown below:

$$P_{t2} = P_{t1} + (\textbf{natural increase}_{t1,\,t2})$$
$$+ (\textbf{net migration}_{t1,\,t2})$$

Figure 1.1 displays the demographic balancing equation in graphic form for Canada for the period 1996–2001. During this interval, births in Canada exceeded deaths by a notable margin, and immigrants greatly outnumbered emigrants. However, as the figure shows, the net effect of migration was much greater than the effect of natural increase and played a much larger role in population growth over this period. In proportionate terms, natural increase accounted for 44 per cent of population growth, while net migration accounted for 56 per cent. This phenomenon is the result of continued low fertility coupled with generally rising international immigration.

Linear, Geometric, and Exponential Models of Population Growth

We can study variations in population size over time without referring directly to the demographic processes of fertility, mortality, and migration (though these are always implied). Instead, we can look at the pattern of population change as it is plotted on a graph. To illustrate, in 1901 the total population of Canada was 7,207,000; in 1991, the population had grown to 31,111,000 (Statistics Canada, 2003g). What is the growth trend between these two points? What was the average annual rate of growth during this interval? To answer these questions, we can consider four mathematical models: the linear, the geometric, the exponential, and the logistic. Figure 1.2 shows what each of these models looks like in graphic form and provides a description of each model's elemental characteristics.

In graphic form, the *linear model* (also knows as the *arithmetic model*) assumes a straight-line

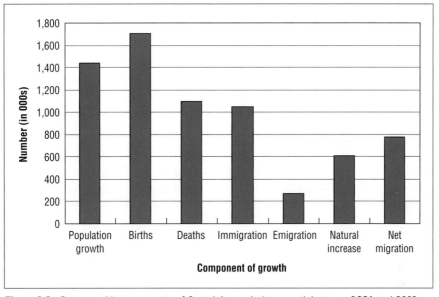

Figure 1.1 Demographic components of Canada's population growth between 1996 and 2001

Source: Statistics Canada website, http://www.statcan.ca/english/Pgdb/demo03.htm.

progression of change over time. The rate of change in this progression is constant, as the quantity of one variable (in this case, population) increases in line with the second variable (in this case, years). Though the linear model of growth can be used to characterize population growth over short periods, it is an unrealistic description of long-term population growth (Rowland, 2003: 48). In most human populations, the historical trajectory of growth up to the present time corresponds closely to the geometric and exponential models.

Geometric and *exponential models* are based on a common principle, that growth follows a non-linear trend over time. That is, population rises gently at first, and then gradually picks up momentum, producing an increasingly large increment of population numbers over time. Whereas a linear progression takes the form *1, 2, 3, 4, 5, 6, 7* . . . a geometric progression would be *1, 2, 4, 8, 16, 32, 64, 128* . . . . This pattern of growth is similar to the effect of compound interest, to use a financial analogy. Assuming geometric principles, a person who invests $100

Table 1.2 The interaction of demographic components in population change

Natural increase is:		Net migration is:		
		Positive (In > Out)	Negative (In < Out)	Zero (In = Out)
Positive	(B > D)	(1) IDS	(2) D	(3) D
Negative	(B < D)	(4) IDS	(5) IDS	(6) I
Zero	(B = D)	(7) I	(8) D	(9) S

Note: The letter 'I' means increase in population size; 'D' means decrease in population size; and 'S' indicates stability in population size. 'IDS' means any one of these three outcomes can occur.

Source: Goldscheider (1971): 10.

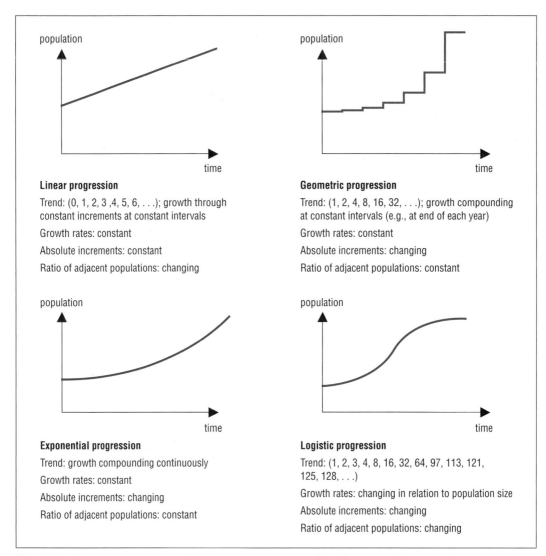

Linear progression

Trend: (0, 1, 2, 3 ,4, 5, 6, . . .); growth through constant increments at constant intervals

Growth rates: constant

Absolute increments: constant

Ratio of adjacent populations: changing

Geometric progression

Trend: (1, 2, 4, 8, 16, 32, . . .); growth compounding at constant intervals (e.g., at end of each year)

Growth rates: constant

Absolute increments: changing

Ratio of adjacent populations: constant

Exponential progression

Trend: growth compounding continuously

Growth rates: constant

Absolute increments: changing

Ratio of adjacent populations: constant

Logistic progression

Trend: (1, 2, 3, 4, 8, 16, 32, 64, 97, 113, 121, 125, 128, . . .)

Growth rates: changing in relation to population size

Absolute increments: changing

Ratio of adjacent populations: changing

Figure 1.2 Graphic representations of linear, geometric, exponential, and logistic population growth
Source: Adapted Rowland (2003): 47, 50.

at 10 per cent interest over a period of five years will, at the end of the first year, have $110; by the end of year two, her investment of $100 will have grown to $121, and by the fifth year, she will have $161. In the exponential model, compounding occurs continuously. If we were to apply geometric growth to the same example, the compounding would take place at a fixed interval, such as the end of each year. Therefore it fol-

lows that for a given period and a fixed rate of interest, an investor would gain more over a long term through exponential compounding than through geometric compounding. The same conclusion would also apply to population growth if it were to follow an exponential progression. In true demographic analysis the geometric growth model is applied frequently because population data are typically not available on a continuous basis, but rather on a periodic basis (such as once a year or every five years).

On a global level, indefinite geometric/exponential population growth cannot be sustained without the population at some point exhausting its ecological limits (Coale, 1974). Recognition of the impossibility of indefinite exponential growth led demographers to develop the *logistic model* of population growth (Pearl and Reed, 1920; Verhulst, 1838). A variation of the exponential model, the logistic model assumes that a human population undergoing prolonged exponential growth will eventually experience insupportable levels of *population density*, which will impose strains on resources and the environment. Under such conditions a society would be compelled to implement measures to curtail population growth or face increased rates of mortality. The logistic model therefore supposes that the rate of population growth varies depending on the size of population: when the population is small and population density is low, the rate of growth will increase, gradually at first but with greater intensity as population increases; then, once the population growth has reached a maximum point, the growth rate will begin to decline gradually toward zero. The upper tail of the logistic curve in Figure 1.2 reflects continued population growth at progressively reduced rates of change.

There is to date no evidence of any human population having conformed fully to the logistic model of growth (Cowgill, 1971). In the early twentieth century, Pearl and Reed (1920) predicted that the population of the United States would follow a logistic growth pattern. Their extrapolations of the US population to 1940, based on the logistic equation computed with population counts from 1790 to 1910, proved fairly accurate: the model provided a very close fit to the observed population counts obtained from American censuses. However, extensions of the logistic model beyond the 1940s produced population estimates well below the figures observed in the censuses (Ricklefs, 1990: 328; Rowland, 2003: 54). Never-

theless, it would be hasty to abandon the logistic model altogether. Besides its wide applicability to a variety of scientific areas (for instance, the statistical study of epidemics) it represents one of several possible (though hardly the most desirable) patterns of growth over the long term future of the global population (Coale, 1974). This point will be discussed further in Chapter 3, which looks at the history and future of the human population.

Compositional Change

Populations are also subject to *compositional change*, or change in the distribution of key population characteristics, such as age, sex, marital status, education, and occupation. 'Distribution' here refers to either *absolute* or *relative frequencies* of people across categories of age, sex, marital status, and so on. An example we will consider in Chapter 4 is the age–sex pyramid, which is a graphic representation of the distribution of the population in terms of age and sex. As we will see, the age and sex compositions of populations can change as a result of any one of a number of demographic mechanisms. One mechanism is sex-selective migration, a process in which a large influx or exodus of either men or women alters the gender balance of a population. Sex-selective mortality is another factor that can alter the gender balance of a population (men typically have higher death rates than women do). Significant change in fertility is a major factor explaining change in the age distribution of a population.

Individual Behaviour and Demographic Processes

Demography is principally interested in aggregate population phenomena. At the same time, however, demographers recognize the importance of studying ways in which individual action helps 'produce' phenomena at the population (macro) level. Individual behaviour is strongly conditioned by our responses to, and our perception of, situations in the broader social environment. Demographic change at the macro level must therefore arise through the expression of individual behaviors guided by cultural values, norms, and institutional structures. While the study of aggregate phenomena remains the overarching concern of this textbook, we will stop here briefly to touch on a point generally neglected in introductory population texts: the importance of individual action to demographic phenomena.

Individual State Transitions as Demographic Behaviour

Individuals in a population occupy multiple statuses that are socially defined and that carry certain responsibilities and obligations. For example, consider the intersecting statuses of a divorced man, aged 45, who is a father of two children, and who is currently employed as a bank manager. In demographic analysis, the intersection of these statuses constitutes a *multistate classification*. Individuals can move in and out of such states, making what Hazelrigg (1999) terms *interstate transitions*, or simply *state transitions*. Some transitions are *repeatable*. For instance, the move from 'single' to 'married' status is a common repeatable transition, since one may marry, divorce, remarry, divorce again, and so on. Death, as it can occur only once, is the most common example of a *non-repeatable transition* (also referred to as an *absorbing state*).

Hazelrigg (1997) makes an important point regarding the variability of state transitions when he says that 'Both the probability of a transition and the duration of a transition may be variably sensitive to the preceding state duration, as well as to other factors' (99). State transitions are probabilistic occurrences, since there is a varying probability attached to any particular movement between given states. The probability varies in accordance with the characteristics of the individual—age, education background, length of time spent in the *exiting state* (the state being left)—as well as a multitude of conditions external to the person (culture, social structure, environment).

Figure 1.3 sketches four models of state transition. Diagram (a) illustrates the processes of birth, death, and migration from the demographic balancing equation, which we reviewed on page 8. Diagram (b) illustrates a single non-repeatable state transition (alive to dead). Diagram (c) shows one kind of repeatable state transition, becoming a parent. The arrows pointing to 'dead' are there to show the continuous presence of some probability of death, which exists for the person regardless of his or her status as a parent. Finally, diagram (d) displays a multistate situation with respect to marital statuses and mortality. Marital statuses are repeatable states, since a person may become married, divorced, or widowed more than once. Death is a non-repeatable event, but since the probability of death exists regardless of a person's marital state, there are several arrows pointing to death.

Individual state transitions account, in varying degrees, for change in certain compositional characteristics of a larger population. Consider marital status as an example: the greater the number of adults in a population exiting the single state to enter the married state, the greater the proportion of married persons to single persons in the population. Students of population dynamics who are interested in analyzing aggregate measures of demographic processes, including the birth rate, the death rate, the migration rate, and the marriage rate, are wise to keep in mind that such demographic rates are aggregate manifestations of individual state transitions.

Individual State Transitions and Demographic Rates

The concept of *rate* is central to demographic analysis. A rate is a dynamic, quantifiable measure of risk given exposure to some specific event. For example, the death rate is a measure of the risk of death for the average person in the population during a given period. This example illustrates two related ideas. First, a rate is based in part on the sum of a specific event that has actually occurred during a defined interval (this is the numerator). Second, it implies the exist-

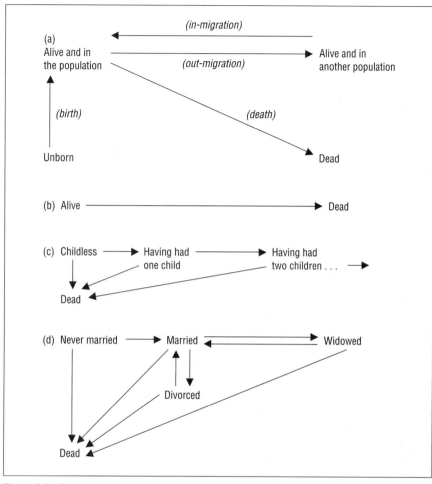

Figure 1.3 Four representations of state transitions

(a) the demographic balancing equation as a multistate classification

(b) state transition involving a non-repeatable event (death)

(c) state transitions involving a repeatable event (childbearing)

(d) multistate transitions involving both repeatable and non-repeatable events

Source: Adapted from Hinde (1998): 2, 3, 78.

ence of a population that is exposed to the risk of experiencing the event in question during the specified time period (this is the denominator). Thus,

$$\text{rate} = \frac{\text{number of events in a given time interval}}{\text{number of persons in the interval exposed to the risk of experiencing the event}}$$

We can think of the death rate as an aggregate representation of individual state transitions in the population (from living to dead) as depicted in model (b) of Figure 1.3. Thus, generally speaking, a high (or low) rate of a particular demographic event (such as birth, or marriage) implies a greater (or lower) incidence of a corresponding state transition among individual members of the population. The concept of 'rate' is sketched out in Figure 1.4. A clear understanding of rate is essential as demographic analyses are often based on the computation and investigation of rates of some type of event.

It is customary in demographic analysis to make the denominator the midpoint population for a given interval, whether that interval is one year, five years, or some other length of time. In many applications, the time interval is one year, so the exposed population at risk is the population at the midway point of the year. Two examples are the crude death and birth rates:

$$\frac{\text{crude birth}}{\text{rate (CBR)}} = \frac{\text{number of births in given year}}{\text{mid-year population in given year}} \times 1,000$$

$$\frac{\text{crude death}}{\text{rate (CDR)}} = \frac{\text{number of deaths in given year}}{\text{mid-year population in given year}} \times 1,000$$

The numerical value of a rate depends not just on the intensity of the event in question (the frequency with which the event occurs in the population—i.e., the numerator) but also on the size of the population exposed to the risk of experiencing the event (i.e., the denominator). For this reason, a constant number of events in a population compared over two different intervals may result in two different rates because the denominator may change from one point in time to the other: it could increase (owing perhaps to natural increase and/or net migration) or it could decline. In either of these conditions, a constant numerator will derive two different rates. This principle is sketched out in Figure 1.5.

Table 1.3 presents a typology that illustrates how individual action relates to state transitions and to demographic rates. A typology is an attempt to classify (but not necessarily explain in causal terms) a phenomenon. The typology in Table 1.3 makes use of two concepts discussed earlier: the concept of 'state' (a status occupied by an individual at a given point in time) and the notion of 'state transition' (a change of status between two specified points in time). The hypothetical scenarios concern the childbearing status and pregnancy status of women of childbearing age observed over two points in time. Let us denote t_1 as the start of the interval and t_2 as the end point. At the start of the observation

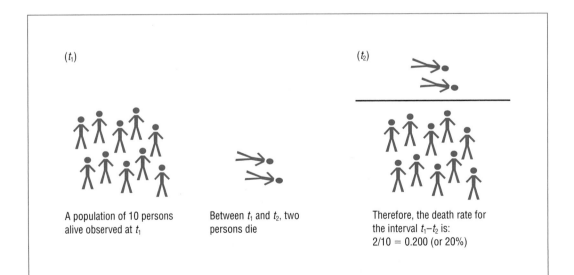

(t_1)

(t_2)

A population of 10 persons alive observed at t_1

Between t_1 and t_2, two persons die

Therefore, the death rate for the interval t_1–t_2 is: 2/10 = 0.200 (or 20%)

Figure 1.4 Schematic representation of the death rate

t_1

number of events = 10
population exposed = 100
rate = 0.10 (or 10 per 100 population)

---

t_2(a): the population at risk increases but the numerator remains the same

events = 10
exposures = 200
rate = 0.05 (or 5 per 100 population)

---

t_2(b): the population at risk decreases but numerator remains the same

events = 10
exposures = 75
rate = 0.133 (or 13.3 per 100 population)

Figure 1.5   Rate under varying populations at risk but same number of events

period some women were in the state of 'childless', while others were in the state of 'mother', meaning they had given birth to at least one child as of time point t_1. Cells C and D in the table represent two different state transitions: cell C involves women who were childless at time t_1 and who became mothers in the interval between t_1 and t_2; cell D concerns women who were already mothers at time t_1 and who had an additional child during the interval between t_1 and t_2. Cells A and B represent static conditions: the women described in these cells occupied the states of 'childless' or 'mother' at time t_1 and remained in their separate states over time.

From the information in Table 1.3 we can derive aggregated counts of all the state transitions involving the individual women during the interval t_1 to t_2. For example, by dividing cell H by cell I, we can obtain the birth rate for women of childbearing age (15 to 49) for the interval t_1 to t_2. Alternatively, we could measure the rate of childbearing for first-time mothers—cell C divided by cell I. Though hypothetical, these scenarios reflect a demographic process in real populations. Demographers observe the aggre-

Table 1.3   Typology of the relationship between states and state transitions and demographic aggregates; women of childbearing ages

Pregnancy status occupied by women at time t_2	Childbearing status occupied by women at time t_1		aggregated totals for time t_2
	childless	mother	
not pregnant	(A) childless women at t_1 who remained childless between t_1 and t_2	(B) mothers at t_1 who did not bear children between t_1 and t_2	(G) total number of women at t_2 who did not bear children between t_1 and t_2
have given birth	(C) childless women at t_1 who became mothers between t_1 and t_2	(D) mothers at t_1 who gave birth between t_1 and t_2	(H) total number of women at t_2 who gave birth between t_1 and t_2
aggregated totals for time t_1	(E) = (A) + (C) total number of women who were childless at t_1	(F) = (B) + (D) total number of women who were mothers at t_1	(I) = (G) + (H) = (E) + (F) total number of women at t_2 who were either childless or mothers at t_1

gated sums of state transitions like these and calculate corresponding rates to measure the intensity and extent of the behaviour in question. Observed over time, this kind of data can help establish the occurrence of either upward or downward trends in certain demographic rates.

Reclassification Processes

Another way that a population can experience change in the distribution of some of its characteristics is through *reclassification*. Reclassification is similar to state transition, though as we shall see there are some key differences between these two processes. The following example will help to illustrate the meaning of reclassification in the context of demographic change. In Canada, the census asks people to record their ethnic background and country of birth, as well as a number of other social and economic characteristics; this information tells us how many members of the population identify themselves as belonging to a given ethnicity. A change in distribution of ethnic identification between census periods would imply, among other things, the occurrence of some degree of reclassification in the population. In fact, over the last several censuses in Canada demographers have noted a great deal of *ethnic mobility*—shifts in the distribution of ethnic self-identification beyond what can be attributed to natural increase and net migration.

The underlying reasons for the phenomenon of ethnic mobility are complex, but one important factor is the high rates of marriage involving persons of varied ethnic origins and the tendency for the children of these 'mixed' marriages to vary their ethnic identification from one census to the next (Krotki, Odynak, and Reed, 1990; Krotki, 1997). For example, the child of an Italian-born mother and a French Canadian father may identify herself on the census as 'French Canadian' or 'Italian' or both, or possibly also 'Canadian'. In a subsequent census, she may or may not list the same ethnic affiliation she identified previously, depending on her sense of ethnic identity at the time of the census. Ethnic

mobility is generally more frequent among the second and subsequent generations of immigrants.

A similar phenomenon has been observed among Canadian Aboriginal peoples. Over the last several censuses, the growth rate for Canada's Aboriginal population has been greater than would be expected based on natural increase (birth and death rates) or immigration (there is little international in- or out-migration among the Aboriginal peoples). How, then, can we account for the Aboriginal growth rate? One explanation has to do with the increasing tendency among Aboriginal Canadians to declare their First Nations ancestry on the census. Another explanation involves recent changes to the Indian Act, which have broadened the definition of 'Aboriginal', making the category more inclusive that it was. Thus, the greater-than-expected growth of the Aboriginal population in Canada can be attributed, at least in part, to these reclassification processes (Guimond, 1999).

Another example of reclassification is explored in the urbanization literature. Consider a village that is reclassified so that it becomes a town, or a town that becomes reclassified as a city. In such cases, the decision to reclassify the settlement is not in any way linked to individual behaviour. Rather, the reclassification is an administrative process based on specific criteria, such as the settlement's population size. This type of reclassification helps explain, in part, the growth of settlements of varying population size categories between periods within a country.

These examples highlight an important distinction between the concepts of 'state transition' and 'reclassification': while state transitions involve a behavioural change on the part of an individual (for instance, a person exits the state of singlehood by getting married), reclassification can involve a change in identification by individuals. The example of ethnic mobility reflects this idea.

Demographic Change and Social Change

If demographic rates are aggregate manifestations of individual state transitions, it follows that social change, broadly speaking, must somehow be associated with demographic change in society. It is not always possible to establish in causal terms where social change originates: does demographic change lead to social change or is demographic change brought about by changes in the social system? In many instances demographic shifts are conceptualized as 'social change'. Consider, for instance, the commonly held view that the divorce revolution of recent decades in the industrial nations (a *demographic fact*) represents a radical shift in orientation (a *social-psychological fact*) about the permanency of the family institution (a *sociological fact*). In fact, this is something of a chicken-and-egg scenario, as it is seldom possible to establish, unambiguously, the temporal order between changes in the demography of a society and change in the social system (Moore, 1974).

The complexities surrounding the study of social change have prompted one sociologist, commenting on the difficulty of defining social change, to wonder 'How much does something have to change to call it change?' (Charon, 1998: 182). Generally, we say that social change has occurred when a social pattern (or structure, or culture, or institution) is significantly different from what it has been in the past. The question we then need to ask is: What causes social patterns to change?'

In addressing this question, Charon (1998: 182) lists, among other things, 'acts of individuals' and 'changes in population' as agents of social change, while recognizing that new technologies can often engender significant changes in society. He also observes that in many cases, 'change in one social pattern affects other social patterns' (182). Some social change can be seen as a manifestation of demographic change, and alterations in the social system can in some cases influence individual behaviour. Davis and van

den Oever (1982: 495) reflect on this point while discussing the interrelationship between demographic changes and one of the most important social movements in the recent history of the Western world:

> . . . [D]emographic changes in advanced industrial societies—changes such as increased longevity, widening sex differences in mortality, aging populations, and low fertility— . . . give rise to new circumstances between men and women. . . . This in turn brings forth [new] ideological developments such as the feminist movement. It is not that the demographic trends are perceived by each individual and thus consciously adapted to, but rather that they arise spontaneously in advanced societies and alter the conditions of life.

Social change may be brought about by the behaviour of individuals in cases where, for instance, a novel behaviour develops into a widespread social phenomenon. Once widely adopted, the behaviour may become *normative*, meaning that it becomes a standard form of behaviour. The current widespread preference among young Canadian couples to form co-habiting unions may be cited as an example of a demographic development towards a behaviour that in earlier times was thought of as non-normative. Diffusion of new ideas and behaviours such as cohabitation become widespread in society through the process of imitation (people imitating what others are doing), and through the action of the mass media (the transmission of new ideas to the masses via television and other media). Both processes play a crucial role in social change (Carlson, 1966; Kohler, 2000).

The historian David Herlihy (1997) offers a fascinating account of the complex interconnection between demography and social change in *The Bright Side of the Plague*. Herlihy suggests that the Black Death, the epidemic that devastated populations across Asia, Europe, and northern Africa during the fourteenth and fifteenth centuries, was indirectly responsible for the development of European nationalism and the establishment of several national European universities. Herlihy argues that many wealthy Europeans bequeathed their fortunes to new centres of higher learning that were being established as alternatives to the ancient universities of Bologna and Padova in Italy and of Paris in France. Many teachers in the new universities, because they were unfamiliar with Latin— the language of higher learning at the time, used vernacular languages in their teaching. Consequently, Hirlihy surmises, instructors and students developed strong nationalistic loyalties. In this way, he argues that a demographic phenomenon—the sustained rise of mortality due to the Black Death—brought significant structural and cultural transformations in European society.

Age, Period, and Cohort: The Mechanisms of Demographic Change

The aggregate actions of individuals in society, we have seen, help produce demographic phenomena. We have also seen that the translation of individual demographic action into aggregate demographic change occurs through individual behaviour (i.e., state transitions) in the context of social and cultural forces. These relationships suggest a series of related facts:

1. Individual action necessarily implies individual reaction to societal forces of significance to the individual.
2. All individuals experience *biological aging*, the passage through life from birth to death.
3. All individuals experience *chronological aging*, the passage through biological and calendar time simultaneously.
4. Individuals in a society who are born during a specified time interval form a unique birth cohort, whose members pass through biological and chronological time together.
5. Every member of the population belongs to a distinct birth cohort, whose members generally experience formative life course events and transitions at similar points in time.

These postulates indicate an interconnectedness among three key variables: age, calendar time ('period'), and cohort (the intersection of age and period). Age, period, and cohort are involved in all demographic phenomena (Ryder, 1965), so it is important to gain an understanding of how they are interconnected. Figure 1.6 sketches the relationship among age, period, and cohort, and shows how these three variables are linked to hypothetical individual lifelines during a two-year period represented by the quadrant LNMO. In this figure, age and calendar year are cross-classified: exact age as of last birthday (indexed by the symbol x) is represented on the vertical axis, and calendar year, indexed by the symbol t, is represented on the horizontal axis. Thus, x denotes the age of a person who is living during the two-year interval t_1 through t_3. The symbol $x+1$ denotes the age of a person one year older than x. To make this concrete, assume that x = age 30; then $x-1$ = age 29; $x+1$ = age 31, and $x+2$ = age 32. The diagonals in Figure 1.6 capture three different birth cohorts: C, $C-1$ and $C+1$. If we let C be the cohort of focus for our purposes, then $C-1$ is a neighbouring cohort made up of individuals born one year earlier than the members of cohort C. Similarly, $C+1$ is made up of individuals born one year later than those in cohort C. Within the quadrant LNMO are three separate parallelograms, each focusing on a different cohort. For instance, TRUS corresponds to the segment of cohort C that is in the intersection of age x to $x+1$ and period t_1 to t_3. Notice that there are two members of cohort C within this age–time space: we identify these individuals as persons 0_2 and 0_3. Both individuals are the same age, though it is clear in the figure that 0_3 is somewhat older than 0_2. The hypothetical past and future lifelines of these individuals are also shown, represented by the solid and hatched lines, respectively.

The parallelograms MWUV and QPRN encompass members of cohorts $C+1$ and $C-1$, respectively. The lifeline of individual 0_1, who is one year younger than individual 0_3 in cohort C, is depicted in MWUV; the lifeline of individual

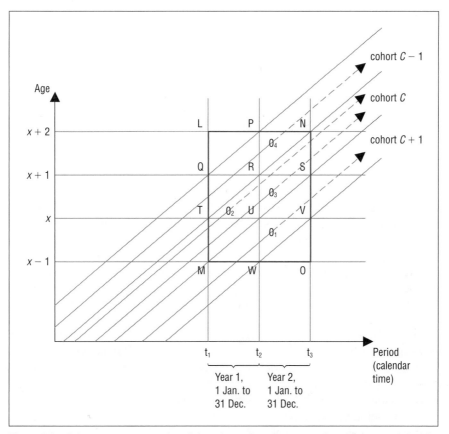

Figure 1.6   Schematic representation of the relationship of age, period, and cohort, and the life-line of individuals extending through age and time

Legend:

O_1 lifeline of a member of cohort $C+1$

O_2 lifeline of a member of cohort C

O_3 lifeline of another member of cohort C

O_4 lifeline of a member of cohort $C-1$

L, N, M, O = quadrant encompassing two calendar years: t_1 to t_3

———— = lifeline of an individual from birth to the present

– – – – = projected lifeline of an individual into the future

x = exact age of an individual as of last birthday (e.g., x may be age 20 at last birthday; therefore $x-1$ would be age 19 at last birthday, age $x+1$ would be age 21 at last birthday, etc.)

O_4, who is one year older than individual O_3, is in QPRN. Note that the three hypothetical individuals—O_1, O_3, and O_4—all experience their birthdays on the same day but are different ages and, as a result, are members of three different birth cohorts.

The significance of Figure 1.6 for our understanding of demographic processes cannot be overstated. Members of birth cohorts tend to experience similar sets of life conditions and circumstances, including important events such as graduation, entry into the labour force, mar-

The demographic experience of cohorts can vary significantly depending on the historical conditions (political, economic, social) under which different cohorts come into being or develop. Even cohorts that experience the same historical events often vary greatly in their reaction to them. For instance, a cohort entering the labour force during a prolonged economic depression would fare less well in life than the members of a cohort entering the labour force under booming economic conditions (Hardy and Waite, 1997). Winsborough (1978) found that *war cohorts* (cohorts whose members were born early in the century and passed through youth and young adulthood during World War II and the Korean War) experienced high rates of school disruption and thus a shorter duration of schooling. In comparison to individuals of more recent cohorts, members of the war cohorts entered the labour force relatively late in life and waited longer on average to marry.

Traumatic episodes like war and economic depression may become deeply engrained in the mentality of a cohort (Ryder, 1965: 851), and it is possible for cohorts to autonomously develop countercultures. The countercultural movement of the 1960s may be cited as an example of 'autonomous cultural dynamics brought on by the baby boom generation' (Lesthaeghe and Surkyn, 1988).

riage, home ownership, childbearing, relocation, and family disruption. The timing (i.e., the age at which these events occur) and *intensity* (i.e., the number of persons involved) of such events can be ascertained from summary measures specific to a cohort (or across cohorts): the average age at which members of a cohort experience an event, the proportion of the cohort that have experienced an event by a given age, the rate at which the cohort undergoes a specific state transition, and so forth.

What accounts for the uniformity among members of a cohort is a matter best approached from a social science perspective. Why, for instance, should so many members of the cohort experience a given event at more or less the same juncture in life? As we have learned, aggregate demographic phenomena result from the combined action of individuals. Winsborough (1978: 234) has made some important observations on this point as it relates to the cohort concept. A cohort experiences similar conditions at similar life cycle stages as it moves through its lifetime, and it is this sharing of experiences that sets a cohort off both objectively and subjectively from others. Objective circumstances can encourage the members of a cohort to marry early or late, which can affect subsequent nuptial, fertility, or even labor force behaviour of the cohort. Subjectively, a cohort's shared experiences (such as having lived through a major economic depression or a war) may create unique sentiments and even a unique world view among its members that the members of other cohorts may find difficult to appreciate. For this reason, it is important to understand that the population of a society at any given point in time is really a set of unique birth cohorts.

How Do We Know the Facts of Demography?

Almost three decades ago, Nathan Keyfitz (1975) asked: 'How do we know the facts of demography?' Keyfitz was hoping to demonstrate that demographic phenomena, for the most part, could not be fully explained by direct observation of data or statistical relationships among variables. Rather, he argued, observation of statistical relations could only be a starting point to explanation: the analyst must have in mind a model of the causal mechanisms governing the phenomenon he or she is trying to understand. 'No model,' he wrote, 'no explanation.' The data by themselves are insufficient basis for causal explanation of phenomena.

Like any scientific discipline, demography places emphasis on describing and explaining phenomena, not just observing and measuring them. We have noted on several occasions in this chapter that relying solely on quantitative trends provides an insufficient account of *why* and *how* social phenomena develop. An important part of explanation is the formulation of *theory*, a systematic attempt to describe and explain phenomena in a way that clearly sets out, or *predicts*, the conditions under which a phenomenon is expected to occur.

Philosophers of science point out that there are three kinds of models that scientists use or develop in their work: physical scale models, visual (diagrammatic) models, and theoretical models (Giere, 1999: 5). Physical models are concrete representations, such as a small-scale model of a building; visual models are pictorial representations of some abstraction of the real world. Theoretical models are verbal statements, propositions that are logically interconnected, that attempt to explain some aspect of the real world—in Giere's words, 'Abstract objects, imaginary entities whose structure might or might not be similar to aspects of objects and processes in the real world' (5). Throughout this book we will look at a variety of models and theories (making no real distinction between the two) that are instrumental to population studies.

That demography is a purely quantitative discipline devoid of any concern for theory is an antiquated and, frankly, incorrect perception. Demographers and other population scholars, whether their preoccupations may be formal methodologies or substantive analysis, are primarily concerned with explaining real-world situations and how populations behave under different social and ecological conditions. In other words, population scientists are inherently interested in developing and applying models of demographic action or processes in order to gain a better understanding of population dynamics. It should be no surprise, then, that a great deal of material in this book involves theories or models of demographic processes and phenomena.

The models of demographic phenomena presented in this book are mostly visual, since rigorous mathematical models are simply beyond the scope of an introductory text. As a result, mathematical treatment of population dynamics and processes is kept to a minimum, though certainly not avoided when necessary, and, wherever possible, concepts have been illustrated in diagrammatic form. Finally, following the discussion earlier in this chapter, we have left behind the traditional demarcation of 'formal' demography and 'population studies'. Instead, this book is guided by the principle that the scientific study of population involves the development and application of sound models in conjunction with formal methodologies, which are inherently theoretical and should not be treated as different from substantive demographic theory (Burch, 2002a, 2002b).

Micro and Macro Models of Demographic Phenomena

As we have seen, the aim of population studies is to explain aggregate demographic phenomena, which are the products of individual action, or *micro-level phenomena*. Demography, then, relies on *micro-level models*, models of individual decision-making and behaviour, as well as *macro-level models*, which examine the behaviour of entire populations.

Micro Models of Human Action: Rational Actor, Normative, and 'Drift'

One class of micro models is the *rational actor model* (also called the *microeconomic model*), which describes actors as *maximizing agents*. In this conceptualization, the individual is seen as attempting to minimize perceived costs associated with an intended action (for example, to have a baby) while at the same time attempting to maximize the benefits to be derived from the intended action. Burch (1979) presented a synthesis of rational actor models that can be summarized under the theme 'human decision-making (and therefore action) as driven by maximizing principles'. Processes such as marriage, divorce, migration, changing residence, and having children can all be explained by elemental microeconomic and social-psychological principles: an individual forms rational decisions based on perceived gains (material and psychological) and losses (material and psychological) from some anticipated action.

Rational action seldom occurs in the absence of normative considerations by the individual. This point leads us to a second model of human action: the *normative model*. The fundamental premise of this model is that individual behaviour is conditioned by two sets of factors: rational microeconomic principles, as outlined above, and normative considerations. Normative considerations are based on perceptions of how a significant other (or significant others) would react to an intended action. Significant others include spouses, children, extended family members, co-workers, peers, and others who would be expected to exert varying degrees of influence on the individual (Burch, 1979).

The normative and the microeconomic rational models of human action are essentially complementary explanations of behavioural intentions, both based on the premise that behavioural intentions are highly correlated with actual behaviour (Fishbein, 1972). Implicit in this formulation is the idea that the individual is always consciously involved in the decision-making process, fully aware of the motives, goals, and constraints to any intended behaviour. Critics have questioned whether this conceptualization can accurately capture the complex nature of the human decision-making process (e.g., Leibenstein, 1982; Field, 1984). Is human behaviour always rational? Are individuals always perfectly aware of the potential costs and benefits of an intended course of action? Are there some aspects of human behaviour that cannot be fully explained by maximizing principles or normative principles alone?

Questions such as these lie behind an alternative conceptualization proposed by Day (1985), who argues that most human action is guided by what he calls 'drift principles'. Day envisions a continuum of behaviour: at one pole

is the microeconomic model, which describes an individual who coolly calculates the gains and losses to be anticipated from available possibilities; at the opposite pole is the normative model, depicting an individual who constantly conforms to normative expectations. Day's drift principles lie somewhere between these poles, governing decisions about a range of important life matters—whether to have a child; when to have a child; whether or not to marry, to divorce, to move out—that are seldom executed in the narrow, calculative, and precise manner dictated by the microeconomic model or in automatic adherence to normative constraints as implied by the normative model.

In reality, people make conscious choices within a broad range of normative options that are themselves under limits imposed by society. Society's broad normative framework sets out what behaviour is considered appropriate under given circumstances and also sets the boundaries for the means one can use to realize certain goals (Field, 1984; Liebenstein, 1982). In this sense, conscious choice exists only if one thinks of conscious choice as being a matter of degree rather than something in absolute terms. The 'drift' model assumes that behaviour arises almost by accident at one or another point within a limited range of socially allowable choices, and then is gently (but not necessarily inexorably) guided by underlying influences toward its conclusion in a manner largely imperceptible to the person doing the acting (Day, 1985: 196). Obviously, not all behaviour is like this, and the degree to which conscious choice governs particular behaviours differs according to the particular psychological and social milieux occupied by individual actors. Nevertheless, argues Day, the 'drift' model is an accurate representation of a very high proportion of human behaviour.

While the 'drift' model may not be antagonistic to utility and normative perspectives, Day's central point is that human action is mostly contingent on emergent properties of interaction, habit, and even unconscious motivation (see also Field, 1984; Leibenstein, 1982; Miller and Godwin, 1977). Friedman and colleagues (1994), arguing along these same lines, suggest that certain demographic behaviours—having a child, changing residence, getting divorced, and so on—are often driven by an unconscious need on the part of individuals to reduce uncertainty in life. For example, a teenaged couple deciding to have a child may appear as an irrational and self-defeating outcome, but having a baby will set a predictable pattern in the life of the parents.

Micro models of human action are instructive because they help us to get beyond the macro-level explanations frequently found in demography and population studies. It is important to understand how micro processes relate to phenomena at the societal level. And while it may not always be possible to specify how individual-level models of behaviour apply to observed macro-level phenomena, we can at the very least remind ourselves that there are alternative realities operating at the level of the individual actor, and that aggregate phenomena are manifestations of individual action.

Macro Models of Demographic Change

Macro models of demographic phenomena attempt to describe and explain population change in the context of structural changes in society. A cornerstone of demographic theorizing is the *demographic transition theory*. Though it will be discussed in greater detail later in the text, Kirk's sketch of the theory (1996: 361) will be helpful here: 'Stripped to essentials [the theory] states that societies that experience modernization progress from a pre-modern regime of high fertility and high mortality to a post-modern one in which both are low'. Thus, the demographic transition is a description of long-term shifts in a society's vital rates, from a primitive stage of high birth and death rates (and thus very low rates of population increase), to an intermediate stage of declining mortality

and high fertility (and therefore very high rates of population growth), to a final stage of low fertility and mortality levels (hence a return to very low growth rates).

Even in this elemental form, it is clear that the demographic transition is but one of several transformations a society may experience as it moves from a primitive type of social organization based on an agrarian or feudal economy to an urban-industrial complex social system (Moore, 1974). Associated with this transformation are radical shifts in other aspects of society:

- political change, from disparate monarchic or feudal forms of governance to democratic government
- scientific-technological revolution, as modern science replaces traditional folkways of understanding nature
- institutional complexity, as life becomes increasingly organized and compartmentalized under different sectors of the social system (for example, children's education is taken out of the home and into the academic institutions)
- industrialization, as work shifts away from the family farm and into the industrial economy

Spengler (1974: 153) identifies a number of structural indicators of modernization: 'the fraction of a country's labor force that is engaged in agriculture' (the higher the percentage engaged in non-agricultural work, the greater the degree of modernization); the percentage of the population living in urban, as opposed to rural, areas (a larger percentage of urban dwellers implies greater modernization); and rising incomes, as reflected in the gross national product (GNP).

Beyond structural change, modernization implies a social-psychological transformation of the society, or a cultural shift. As Spengler (1974: 153) explains, 'modernization consists of a variety of changes describable as changes in the 'content of the mind'. That is, there occurs a diffusion of secular-rational norms and values in the culture system; there is greater personal freedom of expression.' Spengler then cites the six dimensions of individual modernity identified by Inkeles and Smith (1974):

(1) openness to new experiences; (2) increasing independence from traditional authority figures and a shift of allegiance to public leaders; (3) a belief in the efficacy of science and medicine to solve human problems as opposed to a belief in nonrational means such as magic and witchcraft; (4) the development of achievement and social mobility aspirations; (5) a strong desire to participate in civic life; (6) a strive to attain general as opposed to localized knowledge about social life and world events. (cited in Spengler 1974: 153)

This brief outline of modernization theory is intended to give only a general overview of what is a very complex and varied literature concerning the historical experiences that modernization implies for a society. Clearly, there are many discontinuities in the process of modernization (Gusfield, 1967; Hoogvelt, 1976). Not all societies pass through the stages of development in exactly the same way or even in the same sequence. For instance, some contemporary societies that are modernizing economically are characterized by non-democratic systems of government (consider, for instance, some of the oil-rich countries in the Middle East). Conversely, some of the relatively recent democracies (for example, countries in Latin America) are lagging in their economic development as compared to the Western industrial societies. In other words, modernization is not necessarily a unilinear process (Gusfield, 1967). Only in the most general sense can one claim that, in the long term, all societies pass through the various stages of social, economic, and cultural change. The conditions and factors that account for modernization can vary from society to society. As part of this large-scale change, societies undergo demographic transition.

As one of the most important conceptual models in population studies, the demographic transition receives special attention in parts of this book. Revisions to demographic transition theory have been proposed in recent years, and these will be examined later in the text. In essence, as we have already mentioned, the demographic transition is a theory about fertility change, mortality decline, and population growth in a context of massive societal transformations. In actuality, the demographic transition theory subsumes sub-theories of fertility change and mortality change.

Macro-level theories of demographic change are part and parcel of a larger theoretical framework: modernization theory. These theories range from economic (e.g., population growth and economic development theories) to ideational ones (i.e., the role of ideas and innovations and their diffusion in society). Finally, there are theoretical formulations we shall see that focus on the broader question of the causal relevance of population to environment and resources. In this class of theories we shall examine the works of Malthus, Marx, and their contemporaries. Though stated in macro terms, these theories have clear implications not just for society as a system but for the individual as well.

Conclusion

A human population is a collectivity—a community of people bound by common beliefs or interests—coexisting within a geographic area at a certain point in time. The concept of population also entails time continuity, as the people who make up a population are descendents of those who made up the population in the past.

Populations renew themselves through fundamental demographic processes (births, deaths, in-migration, and out-migration).

The scientific study of population is broadly divided into formal demography and population studies. Formal demography is primarily concerned with the quantitative aspects of the field, while population studies (also called social demography) aims to explain the sociological causes and consequences of demographic change and development. Although the division represents an effective way to examine the field, in reality, formal demography and population studies are inseparable: they are complementary rather than separate aspects of population analysis.

The natural processes of fertility and mortality combined with net migration account for the difference in population size between two points in time. These components of demographic change are represented neatly in the demographic balancing equation. Other mathematical models used to study trends in population growth include the linear, the geometric, the exponential, and the logistic models.

Demographers study numerical changes in population, but they also examine compositional change—shifts in age and sex distributions of a population as well as changing trends associated with other important characteristics, such as marital status, education, and occupation.

A society is necessarily a population organized under the umbrellas of culture and social structure. Individual behaviour is conditioned by these features of the social world. Therefore, aggregate demographic phenomena must, to a large extent, reflect the sum of individual behaviours in accordance with the norms, values, and institutional structure of the society. In this regard, it is individual state transitions that help produce many macro-level demographic phenomena. State transitions occur whenever a person undergoes a change in status, from single to married, for example, or even from living to dead. Individual state transitions are reflected in demographic rates for the greater population.

Three important mechanisms of demographic change are age, period, and cohort. These variables are interrelated: it is impossible to extricate any one from the others. The intersection of aging with time is something we all experience as individuals going through life, from birth to death. People who are born at roughly the same time and who advance through the life course together make up a birth cohort. New cohorts emerge in a society as old ones exit through death. Cohorts differ in their social and economic circumstances: for example, some cohorts reach their formative years in prosperous economic times while others come of age during economic downturns or times of war. Cohorts, as collectivities, can be important agents of social as well as demographic change.

It is often stated that the primary concern of population studies is to explain aggregate demographic phenomena. While this is true to an extent, understanding micro-level dynamics is also essential in order to gain a complete appreciation of demographic phenomena. Several models of individual action are reviewed in this chapter: the rational actor model, the normative model, and the 'drift' model. Of the three, the 'drift' model places the greatest emphasis on the subconscious and therefore less rational features of human behaviour.

Macro models of demographic phenomena attempt to describe and explain population change in the context of structural changes in society. One of the most important macro models of demographic change is the demographic transition theory. Though not a theory in the true sense of the word, it is a useful generalization of the demographic shifts that occur as part of a society's large-scale transformations during socioeconomic modernization. One of the most important conceptual models in population studies, the demographic transition theory subsumes sub-theories of fertility and mortality change.

Exercises

1. Table 1.4 below gives data for Canada and Sweden for 1988–9. Use the demographic balancing equation to estimate the values left blank in the table.

Table 1.4 Population data for Canada and Sweden, 1988–9

	Canada	Sweden
Population at beginning of 1988	26,449,888	8,416,599
Population at end of 1989	26,798,303	8,461,554
Growth during period		
Births during period	384,035	112,080
Deaths during period	188,408	96,756
Natural increase during period		
In-migration during period	178,152	51,092
Out-migration during period	25,364	21,461
Net migration during period		

Source: Adapted from Preston, Heuveline, and Guillot (2001) and Statistics Canada (2003d): 22–3.

2. From the data in Table 1.4, calculate the crude birth rate (CBR) and the crude death rate (CDR) for Canada and for Sweden, and also the two countries' rates of natural increase (RNI). Record your results in Table 1.5, on the next page. The population denominators for these rates can be derived by adding the respective population counts for the beginning and the end of the period and then dividing by two. (This is necessary because these rates require the denominators to be the mid-year populations.) The rate of natural increase (RNI) is:

$$\text{RNI} = \frac{\text{births} - \text{deaths}}{\text{mid-year population}} \times 100$$

Alternatively, this measure can be computed as,

$$\text{RNI} = \left[\frac{\text{CBR}}{1,000} - \frac{\text{CDR}}{1,000} \right] \times 100$$

Table 1.5 Crude birth and death rates and rates of natural increase for Canada and Sweden, 1988–9

	Canada	Sweden
Estimated mid-year population		
Crude birth rate per 1,000		
Crude death rate per 1,000		
Crude rate of natural increase per 100		
Annual rate of population growth between 1988 and 1989 (%)		

3. The growth rate of population can be expressed in various ways. One approach is the average annual rate of growth formula:

$$r = \frac{\left[\frac{P_2 - P_1}{P_1} \times 100\right]}{n}$$

where r = the growth rate, P_2 = population at the end of the interval, P_1 = population at the beginning of the interval, and n = the number of years in the interval.

Use the data in Table 1.4 to compute the growth rate for the two populations. (Note: Dividing the percentage change by n gives the average annual rate of population growth during a specified time interval. Since in the present case the interval is one year, dividing by n would give the same result as that obtained by the percentage change formula above.)

4. Write a short essay explaining how demographic phenomena can be understood as both micro-level and macro-level processes.

Additional Reading

Demeny, Paul, and Geoffrey McNicoll, eds. 2003. *Encyclopedia of Population*, vols 1 and 2. New York: Macmillan Reference USA/Thomson–Gale.

Heer, David M., and Jill S. Grigsby. 1992. *Society and Population*. Englewood Cliffs, NJ: Prentice Hall.

Kammeyer, Kenneth C.W., and Helen Ginn. 1986. *An Introduction to Population*. Chicago: Dorsey.

Matras, Judah. 1977. *Introduction to Population: A Sociological Approach*. Englewood Cliffs, NJ: Prentice-Hall.

Nam, Charles B. 1994. *Understanding Population Change*. Itasca, IL: F.E. Peacock.

Petersen, William. 1975. *Population*, 3rd edn. New York: Macmillan.

Poston, Dudley L., and Michael Micklin. 2003. *Handbook of Population*. Hingham, MA: Klewer.

Riley, Nancy E., and James McCarthy. 2003. *Demography in the Age of the Postmodern*. Cambridge: Cambridge University Press.

Stycos, Mayone. 1989. *Demography as an Interdiscipline*. New Brunswick, NJ: Transaction.

Weeks, John R. 2002. *Population: An Introduction to Concepts and Issues*. Belmont, CA: Wadsworth.

Web Resources

A useful, though not recent, resource is the guide to population websites prepared by Zuali H. Malsawma ('A Guide to Population-Related Home Pages on the World Wide Web', *Population Today*, October 1996: 4–5). See also recent issues of *Population Today* for updates on new websites, or visit the website of the Population Reference Bureau: www.prb.org/Home.aspx.

The Population Reference Bureau also issues a series of excellent publications on a regular basis, including *Population Bulletin*, and the annual *World Population Data Sheet*, which can be obtained from this site: www.worldpop.org/datafinder.htm.

The World Health Organization's *World Health Statistics Annual* contains deaths by cause, age, and sex for a large number of countries. WHO publishes these tables on a yearly basis: www.who.int/publications/en.

Published annually, the *United Nations Demographic Yearbook* contains a wealth of demographic information by country. Another product from the United Nations is its *Human Development Report*: www.unpopulation.org.

The World Bank is an excellent source of population and socioeconomic data for the world's countries: www.worldbank.org.

The United States Census Bureau is one of the best sources of demographic information for the United States and other countries. Check out their population clock, which gives continuous updates on the population of the world: www.census.gov/main/www/popclock.html.

The RAND Corporation publishes important population research on a number of topics, including aging, labour force, and family. RAND has a number of programs related to these areas of study, including the Center for the Study of Aging: www.rand.org/centers/aging; the Population Research Center: www.rand.org/centers/population; and the Center for the Study of the Family in Economic Development: www.rand.org/centers/family.

An important online bibliographic database on population research and related topics is POPLINE, at Johns Hopkins University: http://db.jhuccp.org/ics-wpd/popweb/basic.html.

Princeton University's Office of Population Research is one of the most important demographic centres in the world. Their website offers many links to other major demographic institutes. You can also access *Population Index*, a leading database of bibliographic sources on population: http://opr.princeton.edu/resources.

Chapter 2

Population Data: Their Sources and Nature

Introduction

It is generally agreed that census and vital statistics are the most important data sources for demographic research and analysis. Population surveys and administrative databases (such as health records or tax files) provide additional information that is useful for the study of population. This chapter surveys the two principal systems of data collection: census and vital statistics registration.

The Population Census

The term 'census' derives from the Latin verb *censere*, which means 'to assess'. Since ancient times societies have been listing and counting the population within their territories. Censuses are said to have been taken as early as 3800 BCE in Babylon and 2000 BCE in ancient China (Statistics Canada Census Operations Division, 1997: 7). But as Petersen (2000) notes, the counting of population was an uncommon practice until fairly recently. In the distant past, counts of the population were closely connected to the collection of taxes, the recruitment of conscripts for the military, and other state interests. It is doubtful that these early censuses were comprehensive enough to account for all citizens. It was not before the middle part of the eighteenth century that European countries started to undertake regular censuses (Petersen, 2000); prior to that time, listing and counting the population must be assumed to have been not only irregular but also highly inaccurate

and incomplete (Coale, 1974: 15; Petersen, 2000: 10; Yaukey, 2001: 17).

According to Coale (1974: 15), the first series of modern censuses taken at regular intervals of no more than 10 years was begun by Sweden in 1750; decennial enumerations were begun in the United States in 1790 and in France and England in 1800, and have been conducted ever since. Yet Coale (1974: 15) also indicates that it was not until the nineteenth century that the census became widespread among the more developed countries, and the practice has spread slowly to other parts of the world. India's population has been enumerated at decennial intervals only since 1871, and a number of Latin American populations have been counted, mostly at irregular intervals, only since the late nineteenth century. The first comprehensive census of Russia was not conducted until 1897, and the population of most of Tropical Africa remained uncounted until after World War II.

A Brief History of the Canadian Census

In 1608, some 70 years after Jacques Cartier travelled up the St Lawrence River and established France's claim to North America, a small number of French settlers led by Samuel de Champlain set foot in present-day Quebec and thus helped found the colony of New France. Half a century later, Jean Talon was entrusted by the French king Louis XIV to oversee the development of the fledgling colonies and help them become self-sufficient producers of goods required 'for the growth of French industry' (Statistics Canada Census Operations Division,

1997: 7). As part of his mandate, Jean Talon in 1666 organized and directed the colony's first census, considered by some the first systematic modern census (Beaujot, 1978: 5). The 1666 count set the total population of New France at 3,215, of which 2,034 were men and 1,181 were women. The census also determined that 1,019 persons were married, and that there were 528 families (Statistics Canada Census Operations Division, 1997: 7). It is important to point out that the tally did not include Aboriginal inhabitants or members of the military stationed in the colony.

Between 1666 and the early part of the twentieth century, periodic censuses were taken in Canada at irregular intervals and with varying degrees of coverage. A complete history of the modern census would require a separate volume; therefore, only a brief sketch is given here. (For additional information on the history of the Canadian census see Wargon (2002) and the Statistics Canada website, www12.statcan.ca/english/census01/Info/history.cfm.) It was not until the mid-1800s that legislation was passed to provide regular and complete counts of the population in Canada, beginning in 1851, and it was not until 1905 that a permanent Census and Statistics Office was established in Ottawa; this became the Dominion Bureau of Statistics in 1918, renamed Statistics Canada in 1971.

During the French regime, covering the period from 1608 to 1759, no fewer than 36 censuses were conducted. Under British rule, the first census of Canada's population was carried out in 1765. It was during this time that questions concerning race, ethnicity, religion and place of birth first began to appear in the census questionnaires. During the early 1800s, censuses of the populations of the Atlantic colonies, Upper (Quebec) and Lower (Ontario) Canada, and Manitoba were taken sporadically. All of this changed with Confederation in 1867, when the Constitution Act (formerly the British North America Act) stipulated that an official count of the population would be undertaken every ten years, beginning in 1871 (Wargon, 2002). In 1956 the interval between censuses was changed from 10 to 5 years to make up-to-date information on Canada's rapidly changing population more readily available (Statistics Canada Census Operations Division, 1997).

Table 2.1 outlines milestones in the history of the Canadian census. Canada's 2001 census marks 335 years of population counting; over this time, the country has grown from the 3,215 people documented in Jean Talon's 1666 census to a nation of 31 million-plus inhabitants, who coexist in a rapidly changing social, economic, and demographic environment.

Contemporary Population Censuses

A modern census provides a complete account of a country's population at a point in time, including its size and geographic distribution as well as its demographic and socioeconomic characteristics. It is, as some have described it, a 'snapshot of the population'—a statistical portrait of a country and its people at one point in time.

Most of the world's countries, except the very poorest ones, have formal statistical agencies responsible for planning and administering demographic data collection and dissemination. Statistics Canada is this country's statistical bureau, in charge of conducting the census and collecting vital statistics, among other responsibilities. Since the registration of births, deaths, marriages, divorces, and fetal deaths is a provincial function, these vital records are collected by provincial government bureaus and then passed on to the central statistical agency for assessment, processing, and dissemination. The same principle applies in the United States, where the US Census Bureau is the organization entrusted with planning and executing the census, while the National Center for Health Statistics (NCHS) oversees the vital registration system with files supplied through state-operated registration systems (Siegel, 2002: 88–9). In other industrial countries, such as France, the United Kingdom, the Netherlands, and Italy, national

Table 2.1 Milestones in the history of the Canadian census

1666	First census in New France. The total population was 3,215, excluding Aboriginal people and royal troops.
1739	Last census under French rule.
1767	The Census of Nova Scotia adds religion and ethnic-origin variables.
1817	The Census of Nova Scotia adds place-of-birth variable.
1831	The first census in what would become Western Canada is taken in the Assiniboine.
1851	With the enactment of legislation requiring censuses in 1851, 1861, and every tenth year thereafter, the decennial census is born.
1870	First Census of British Columbia and Manitoba.
1871	First Census of Canada after Confederation. The questionnaire was produced in both English and French, as it has been in every census since.
1905	The census office becomes a permanent part of the government.
1906	A quinquennial census is taken in Manitoba, Saskatchewan, and Alberta.
1911	The census is moved from April to June to avoid poor weather and road conditions and to improve the accuracy of crop acreage data.
1918	The Dominion Bureau of Statistics is established with the enactment of the 1918 Statistics Act.
1941	The census is moved for this year only to 14 June to avoid conflicting with the first Victory Bond campaign. Sampling is used for the first time; the questions concern housing.
1956	The first nationwide quinquennial census is conducted.
1971	For the first time, most respondents complete the questionnaire by themselves (self-enumeration). The Dominion Bureau of Statistics becomes Statistic Canada. A new Statistics Act requires that a census of population and agriculture be conducted every five years.
1986	The census contains a question on activity limitations, which is later used to form a sample for the first postcensal survey on activity limitations.
1991	The question on common-law status is asked for the first time.
1996	For the first time the census collects information about unpaid housework and mode of transportation to work.
2001	For the first time the census collects information about common-law couples of the same sex, as well as information on language of work.

Source: Adapted from Statistics Canada publication *2001 Census Handbook, Reference*. Catalogue no. 92-379-XIE, p. 27.

agencies devoted to census and vital statistics systems perform similar functions.

A national census is very costly and requires extensive preparations and planning. For these reasons, most national governments find it efficient to conduct a complete enumeration of their populations at periodic intervals, usually every five (as in Canada) or ten (as in the US) years. In an effort to help achieve a standard set of practices that would make it easier to compare census data across countries, the United Nations proposed a number of guidelines for population counting, including the following four:

1. A census should be based on individual responses to predetermined questions regarding specific demographic data, including age, sex, marital status, and a wide array of secondary traits (e.g., education, occupation, income).

2. It should be universal in scope, in order to include all members of the population.
3. It should be conducted throughout a nation's territory on a predetermined date.
4. It should be carried out at regular intervals; those countries taking censuses at ten-year intervals should do so on the years ending in zero. (Shryock and Seigel, 1976; Yaukey, 1985: 19)

Taking censuses at regular intervals helps make the results consistent and easier to compare across nations. Encouraging countries to monitor changes in demography at regular intervals also makes computing intercensal estimates of the population easier and more accurate.

Censuses can be conducted on either a *de jure* or a *de facto* basis. With the *de jure* method of enumeration, people are counted at their usual place of residence, not wherever they happen to be living or staying at the time of the census. In the case of *de facto* census, the respondent is counted as a resident of the address where he or she happens to have stayed on the night preceding the day of the census, regardless of whether the respondent is temporarily away from his or her usual residence. In Canada, where the *de jure* census is used, students attending university away from home are enumerated with their parents even though they live elsewhere most of the year. If the Canadian census were based on the *de facto* method, a student who usually resides in Halifax but who is studying at the University of Montreal at the time of the census would be counted as a resident of Montreal. Similarly, Canadian residents living temporarily in a motel or seasonal work lodging at the time of the census receive separate questionnaires and are asked to provide their usual place of residence. In addition to Canada, the United States and a large number of European countries have adopted the *de jure* method, while France, the United Kingdom, Greece, and Russia are a few of the countries that still favour *de facto* censuses.

Census data are extremely useful for a wide range of purposes. They can alert governments

It is worth noting that the comparability of two ostensibly *de facto* totals or two ostensibly *de jure* totals is often undermined by the fact that, simple as the two concepts appear, strict conformity to either of them is rare. To give a few examples, some *de facto* counts do not include foreign military, naval, and diplomatic personnel present in the country or region on official duty, nor their accompanying family members and servants; some do not include foreign visitors in transit through the country or region. On the other hand, they may include merchant seamen and fishermen who are out of the country or region working at their trade (United Nations Department of Economic and Social Affairs Population Division, 2002c: 4). And the Canadian census, although it is conducted on a *de jure* basis, has since 1991 collected information on non-permanent residents (students from abroad, workers with visas, etc.); these data are not, however, reported in published population totals.

to demographic shifts that could pose challenges without proper advanced planning. A rapidly growing child population, for example, should signal the need for new schools as well as recruitment and training programs for additional teachers. A central government uses census data as an objective basis for distributing funds to its constituent parts—provinces, territories, states. In Canada, for example, a key criterion for allocating government transfer payments is a province's population size: the larger the province's population, the greater the share of funds it receives to cover the costs of delivering social programs, building new hospitals, maintaining roads, establishing daycare facilities, and improving transit systems. Census counts are also used for establishing and revising electoral boundaries, since the number of government seats allocated to each territory depends on its proportionate share of the total population (Statistics Canada Census Operations Division, 2003a). Of course, it is not just governments that use population figures and other census data. Businesses frequently scrutinize census data to discover population trends that will help them target potential markets.

A national census typically covers a wide array of questions on several key topics. The Canadian census, for example, asks questions on the following categories:

- *demographic characteristics*, e.g., name, relationship of household members to the person filling out the census questionnaire, date of birth, sex, marital/common-law status
- *sociocultural characteristics*, e.g., place/country of birth, citizenship, landed immigrant status, racial and ethnic origin, Aboriginal status, year of immigration, knowledge and use of the two official languages (English and French)
- *socioeconomic characteristics*, e.g., education, occupation, employment status, income, number of hours worked during the previous year; home ownership
- *geographic characteristics*, e.g., place of residence, place of work, mobility status

A national census may introduce new questions on topics of importance to the government of the day. For instance, recent Canadian censuses have covered topics pertaining to health and disability. The Canadian census also includes a section on agriculture. A detailed list of questionnaire items found on Canadian censuses since Confederation is provided in the Appendix on page 556.

The Census: A Reflection of Its Time

Over the years some questions have been dropped from the Canadian census and others added. Some items dropped from an earlier census are reinstated in a subsequent census, while certain questions are asked only every tenth year. None of this is as arbitrary as it sounds. Changes to the census questionnaire largely mirror sociological change in the population. As new social trends begin to emerge, questions pertaining to these trends are proposed and then carefully evaluated for inclusion on the census question-

naire. McVey and Kalbach (1995a: 12) identify three general criteria used by census authorities to assess the suitability of new questions:

1. *practical value to the nation broadly speaking*, including government departments at all levels, business, industry, the research community, and citizens
2. *public acceptance of a question*: the question must be socially acceptable so that people will be willing to answer honestly
3. *comparability with previous censuses*: new questions must be similar in wording and presentation to questions asked in previous censuses

Once a question has been screened and assessed, it must be officially approved by the federal government before it is allowed a place on the census questionnaire.

The topic of common-law relationships illustrates how sociological changes in the population are reflected in the census. Unions of men and women living together but not legally married had become increasingly common in Canada since the 1970s, and by the 1980s it had become apparent that the trend would continue and needed to be studied systematically. Census planners could not avoid including a question on such an important trend, and finally added the item in the 1991 census. A similar development was the addition in 2001 of a question regarding same-sex unions, a topic that in earlier times would have been viewed as too controversial or socially unacceptable but by the start of the twenty-first century had sufficient popular support to warrant inclusion.

Space limitations and the costs involved in including and tabulating items in the census often mean that adding a new item to the questionnaire requires the removal of another. From 1941 to 1991, every decennial census included a question about 'children ever born'. Adult women respondents were asked to declare the number of children they had ever had, including children from previous marriages, children born outside of marriage, and children who were deceased.

When it was introduced in the mid-twentieth century, the question on 'children ever born' was seen as an important way to track fertility among Canadian women, and the data it yielded was used in important analytical studies on changing fertility patterns in pre- and post-war Canada (see, for instance, Balakrishnan, Ebanks, and Grindstaff, 1979; Charles, 1948; Henripin, 1972). But by the end of the century Canadian fertility had stabilized at below-replacement levels, and variations in fertility rates across subgroups—groups from different regions, say, or representing different ethnic backgrounds—had practically converged to the national level. So a question on completed fertility seemed secondary in importance to emerging issues of greater social and economic significance.

One of the issues demanding greater attention is the issue of unpaid work—caring for children and seniors, preparing family meals, doing housework and home maintenance—and how this relates to the rising trend in women's participation in the labour force. As a result of changing priorities, the fertility question was removed and an item on unpaid work was added in the 2001 census. It is interesting to note that the general consensus among Canadian demographers today is that in the light of persisting low fertility, a question on fertility is now all the more important and should be reinstated in the census of 2011.

Ethnicity is another topic that has garnered increasing coverage in recent censuses. In 1981, respondents could for the first time declare more than one ethnic origin, and the 1986 census included detailed instructions to guide respondents in filling out the multiple ethnicity question. Both additions reflect an acknowledgement on the part of Canada's census planners that the country's multicultural makeup and growing ethnic diversity need to be properly studied. In 2001, the census included a question about parents' place of birth, a topic that had been treated in earlier censuses before being removed in 1976. In this case it was the research community that pressured Statistics Canada to put the item

back on the census form. This data, they argued, was key to assessing the socioeconomic progress of first- and second-generation immigrants.

Political changes can also lead to changes in the census. In 1985, the federal government amended provisions of the Indian Act of Canada that caused Native women to relinquish their Indian status if they married a non-Indian. The 1985 amendments allowed these women, as well as their children, to regain their Indian status, which led to a dramatic increase in the population of registered Indians. Between 1985 and 1993 the number of registered status Indians in Canada rose by over half a million (553,559), or 54 per cent. Particularly striking is the growth, over the same period, of the off-reserve Indian population, from 104,455 to 226,872—a change of 117 per cent. In 1991, Statistics Canada added a question about registered Indian status to the census questionnaire. While this addition no doubt reflects growing awareness of and interest in Aboriginal issues, it can almost certainly be tied to the 1985 Indian Act amendments, which were largely responsible for the sudden growth of Canada's Native population.

The Use of Sampling in the Census

In recent years, survey sampling has been made an integral part of the Canadian census. Statistics Canada distributes the so-called 'short-form' questionnaire, which contains seven questions, to 80 per cent of all households enumerated, and the 'long-form' questionnaire, which contains an additional 52 items, to the remaining 20 per cent. Information from the long-form questionnaire is generalized to the entire population, generating an accurate set of data in a manner that is both more efficient and more cost-effective than distributing the long-form survey to the entire population.

Census Undercoverage

In theory, a national census is supposed to obtain a complete enumeration of the population. In truth, this is seldom the case, as there is always some level of undercounting. Statistics Canada officials have taken steps to reduce this discrepancy; for instance, census takers are dispatched to remote areas and Native reserves to complete some household questionnaires in person (Statistics Canada Census Operations Division, 2003b). But despite such efforts, the reality is that certain segments of the population are particularly difficult to track, including transient populations and the homeless, as well as people living in distant and remote rural locations. McVey and Kalbach (1995a: 16) have noted that the extent of census undercount in Canada tends to be highest among men between the ages of 20 and 24 and lowest among women aged 45-54. In their analysis of the 1991 census (McVey and Kalbalch, 1995a: 16), they indicate that the segments of the population that were most difficult to locate for enumeration were

- residents of the Yukon Territory (3.83 per cent) and Ontario (3.64 per cent),
- people who had never been married (5.98 per cent),
- divorced men (7.11 per cent),
- people who rented rather than owned a home (5.09 per cent), and
- those who had lived outside of Canada one year prior to the census (19.91 percent).

Commenting on this problem, Petersen (2000: 11) observed that

more generally, sectors at a society's periphery—not only the homeless but casual laborers, criminals, and near-criminals—are always the most difficult to count and therefore the most likely to be overlooked. There is also the problem of people who refuse to participate in the census, though they are legally bound to do so. Enumerators have occasionally been denied entrance to Native reserves, contributing to the undercounting of the Aboriginal population. In the 1991 census, 78 reserves—home to an estimated 38,000 people— were incompletely enumerated; this actually marks an improvement over the 1986 census, when 136

Anderson and Fienberg (1999: 108) documented the US Census Bureau's first-ever attempt to enumerate the homeless population for the 1990 census. On 20 March 1990, dubbed 'Street and Shelter Night' or simply 'S-Night', around 23,000 census enumerators were dispatched across American cities to locate and count the homeless. It was a well-publicized event, as members of the news media followed enumerators in their search for homeless people at shelters, in parks, under bridges, and anywhere else they might be sleeping. Unofficial estimates of America's homeless population had been in the range of 3 million people; however, the S-Night enumeration indicated a national homeless population of less than a quarter of a million. The process angered advocates for the homeless, who argued that the enumeration badly undercounted the homeless population and failed to accurately represent the problem of homelessness in the US.

reserves, representing approximately 44,733 residents, were incompletely enumerated (Kastes, 1993: 67–8).

Census bureaus throughout the world often exclude (or, at best, enumerate with less precision) such marginal sectors of the population as illegal immigrants, residents of the shantytowns that ring the cities of less developed countries, the indigenous population of some South American jungle regions, or the nomads in some countries of northern Africa.

Post-enumeration Surveys

Once completed, a national census is typically followed by a post-enumeration survey, which helps determine the extent of undercount in the census. The objective is to obtain, from a representative survey of the population, an estimate of the population size that should correspond to the population count obtained through the census. In most industrialized nations with a long history of census counting, the mechanisms for carrying out the census are well established and subject to rigorous checks; underenumeration rates in these countries seldom exceed 2 or 3 per cent. The 2001 Census of Canada, for example, missed 3.1 per cent of the population, which is a little higher than the 1996 rate of 2.4 per cent (Statistics Canada, *The Daily*, 2003a: 11). The largest degree of undercoverage occurred in the Northwest Territories (8.1 per cent), the Yukon Terriroty (4.7 per cent) and Nunavut (4.5 per cent). Prince Edward Island and Newfoundland and Labrador had the lowest rates of under-count, at 1.0 per cent and 1.8 per cent, respectively (Statistics Canada, *The Daily*, 2003a: 11).

Intercensal Estimates of Population

Population surveys are useful for calculating population estimates in *intercensal* years—years between censuses. Population estimates, normally classified by age, sex, and marital status, are developed routinely and revised periodically in accordance with incoming data from the latest census (Statistics Canada, 1999a: 1; Statistics Canada Census Operations Division, 2003b: 1). These estimates form the basis of population projections. For example, Statistics Canada recently calculated population projections to the year 2026. These were prepared using the 2000 preliminary population estimates, which were in turn developed from the 1996 census figures (George et al., 2001: ii).

Specialized Population Surveys

National statistical agencies frequently conduct sample surveys of the population to obtain demographic information that is not typically asked for in a census. In Canada and the United States, for example, surveys of the labour force are taken routinely to monitor employment and unemployment trends and other economic indicators. The US Census Bureau, on behalf of the Bureau of Labor Statistics, carries out a monthly survey of around 50,000 households; known as the Current Population Survey or CPS, it is designed to obtain information about the

employment status of respondents and their families (Anderson, 2003: 122). Statistics Canada, meanwhile, is currently involved in a longitudinal study of children and youth. The National Longitudinal Survey of Children and Youth (NLSCY), which began in 1994 with a large sample of families and children aged between infancy and four, is designed to collect information about factors influencing a child's social, emotional, and behavioural development and to monitor the impact of these factors over time. The children, as well as their families, will be asked to participate in follow-up interviews every two years until they are 18. The information from the NLSCY, which includes data on children's health, physical development, learning, and social environment, will be used by officials at all levels of government as well as academic researchers (Statistics Canada, 2003h).

The NLSCY is just one of a number of specialized surveys that Statistics Canada is involved in. Two other important population surveys are the Aboriginal Peoples' Survey and the National Population Health Survey. Both are typically taken shortly after a census and are based on random selection from the census returns.

Vital Statistics

In the Western world, vital statistics were first compiled by churches (Petersen, 2000: 10). In England, the clergy was required as early as the sixteenth century to keep records of christenings, marriages, and burials, and similar records began to be kept by the clergies of France, Italy, and Spain during the seventeenth century. As a result, many historical records about early modern populations come from the parish registers, which, especially in the case of the earliest records, suffer serious deficiencies concerning their accuracy and completeness.

In North America, the clergy and government officials in the colonies began to record vital statistics in the seventeenth century. On a national level, the United States government started publishing annual records of deaths in 1900 and of births in 1915 (*Columbia Encyclopedia*, 2003). In Canada, the publication of annual vital statistics for the country and the provinces began in 1921, although, as we have seen, the history of census taking in what would become Canada dates back to the early seventeenth century (see Table 2.3).

Early Investigations of Vital Records and the Origins of Population Studies

The modern foundations of population studies as a discipline are closely connected to a number of scholars who conducted early investigations of one form of vital statistics: mortality. The English economist and clergyman Thomas Malthus (1766–1834) is often cited as the 'father of modern demography'. It is certainly fair to say that he was one of the founding fathers, but perhaps not the only one. Others who, along with Malthus, contributed to the early development of the discipline include pioneer demographers John Graunt (1620–74) and William Petty (1623–87). Graunt is credited with having produced, in 1662, the first known (though very crude) life table based on the death records of the city of London, known as the Bills of Mortality. Rowland (2003: 14) neatly summarizes the historical context surrounding Graunt's work:

> After the fourteenth century Black Death killed at least a quarter of the population of Europe, and around 50 million in Europe and Asia overall, there followed centuries with further devastating epidemics of bubonic plague. Early in the sixteenth century, an ordinance required parish priests in London to compile weekly lists of deaths from plague, called the Bills of Mortality. These were intended initially to identify outbreaks and areas for quarantine. Later, other causes of death were included, as well as weddings and christenings and the collection was extended to cover all English parishes. Disastrous plagues struck London in 1603 and again in 1625. In the latter year an estimated one quarter of the population of London died. Interest in population at the time centred on the effects of epidemics on population numbers, together with the new field of 'political arithmetic' concerned with estimating national wealth.

This context of epidemic mortality may have influenced Graunt to write his *Natural and Political Observations Made upon the Bills of Mortality*.[1] In assessing this work and its impact on the study of population, Philip Kreager (2003: 472) describes Graunt as 'the author of the first quantitative analysis of human populations'. Graunt explored some of the essential measures of demographic analysis—simple ratios, proportions, odds, and rates—and calculated basic measures of mortality, including rates of infant and child mortality, sex ratios, and crude death and birth rates. But his most enduring legacy was his invention of the life table. According to Kreager (2003),

> Graunt's estimate of the 'number of fighting men' (i.e. for London's defense) relied on a hypothetical table of mortality by age. Mathematicians interested in the nascent calculus of probabilities, such as . . . Christian Huygens, astronomer Edmund Halley, and philosopher and mathematician Gottfried Leibnitz (1646–1716), quickly recognized in his reasoning a more general logic for calculating life expectancy. Although Graunt had not employed his table for that purpose, their analyses gave rise to the first abstract model of population: the life table. (Kreager, 2003: 473)

---

[1] The full and unwieldy title of Graunt's book is *Natural and Political Observations Mentioned in a Following Index, and Made upon the Bills of Mortality, with Reference to the Government, Religion, Trade, Growth, Air, Diseases and the Several Changes of the Said City.*

William Petty, a contemporary and close acquaintance of Graunt's, is considered the originator of national accounting systems. Petty regarded population dynamics 'as an integral part of social accounting' (McNicoll, 2003a: 729). He made important contributions to population analysis with his early (and crude) estimates of mortality and population size for major cities. Petty presented his ideas on population in his book *Political Arithmetic*. McNicoll (2003a: 729) points to Petty's early survey of Ireland as the basis for that country's first census, in 1659. Petty's work helped lay the foundations for the more systematic analyses of social and economic statistics by subsequent scholars such as Gregory King (1648–1712) and Edmond Halley (1656–1742), both of whom went on to expand on the work of Graunt by refining the life table as a mathematical construct (Rowland, 2003: 267). Halley, like Graunt, based his work on his analysis of the Bills of Mortality, *but in his case* for the city of Breslau, Germany. His contribution in this area, argues Rowland, is especially noteworthy, as it is a 'foreshadowing [of] methods used today' (Rowland, 2003: 267).

Another early demographer who is worth mentioning here is Antoine Deparcieux (1703–68), whose importance is outlined by Pressat (1985: 55–6). Like Halley, Deparcieux was an astronomer who developed further extensions of the life table. He is responsible for introducing the concept of 'exposure to risk' in mortality analysis, in addition to helping refine the process for computing life expectancy. Deparcieux published one of the earliest modern studies on the life table, *Essay on the Probabilities of the Length of Human Life*, in 1746.

Modern Vital Statistics Systems

Unlike the census, which is a periodic undertaking, the registration of vital events is a continuous activity. The main purpose of a national *vital statistics system* is to collect, compile, and process statistical information on all vital events that take place in the population on a daily basis. Grindstaff summarizes these events as 'the entrance to and exit from life, and the civil statuses that are acquired along the way' (1981b: 47). Like the census, vital registration systems are institutionalized legal administrative institutions that form an integral part of the governmental bureaucracy.

A vital statistics system must be continuous and complete. It must also satisfy the following four requirements, identified by Grindstaff:

1. Vital events must be officially recorded within a short period of time, as specified by the legal authorities. (In Canada, this period usually ranges from 5 to 15 days.)
2. Events must be recorded at the geographic place (the city, town, municipality, and so on) where they occur.
3. The registration of an event (a marriage, for instance) is free, or has only a nominal cost.
4. Registration is compulsory. (Grindstaff, 1981b: 46)

As members of a population, we are all part of a vital statistics system, and as we go through life, we are at times required to register vital events. Each of us has a birth certificate; each of us will also, someday, have a death certificate. Many of us will at some point submit a marriage certificate to the vital statistics registry, and if we should dissolve that marriage, we would be bound to declare the divorce with the registration system. From birth to death, we are involved in the legal observance and recording of many such facts of life, or vital events; in most industrialized countries, including Canada, our participation in this process is compulsory. The box on the following page lays out what an average day in Canada is like in terms of vital events.

The list of vital events that must be reported by law varies from country to country. For example, according to the United Nations Department of Economic and Social Affairs Population Division (2002c: 6), in some countries and territories, only births and deaths are registered, and with varying degrees of accuracy and

On an Average Day in Canada in 1996 . . .

428 couples married (including non-residents marrying in Canada)

- 317 unions were solemnized by religious officials; 111 were civil ceremonies
- 282 marriages took place between couples where both parties were marrying for the first time
- in 56 marriages, both spouses were foreign-born
- in 2 marriages, both were teenagers

195 divorces were finalized

- 148 divorces were granted to couples where both spouses were in their first marriage
- 15 divorces took place between couples who had both been divorced at least once before
- in 52 divorces, both spouses were in their thirties
- in 5 divorces, both spouses were at least 65 years old or both were younger than 25

1,001 babies were born

- 514 were boys and 487 were girls
- 283 offspring had unmarried mothers (122 in Quebec)
- 60 were born to teenage mothers
- 57 had a low birthweight
- 43 were pre-term
- 117 were born to women aged 35–39; 17 were born to women 40 years or older
- 24 were in multiple-birth sets
- 6 infants died; another 6 were stillborn

582 persons died

- 305 were male, 277 were female
- 51 men and 92 women were 85 years or older
- 10 men and 5 women were under 25 years of age
- 217 deaths were due to diseases of the circulatory system, including 158 deaths from heart diseases and 43 deaths from cerebrovascular disease
- 162 deaths were due to cancer, including 43 to lung cancer, 17 to colorectal cancer, 14 to breast cancer, and 10 to prostate cancer
- 52 deaths were due to diseases of the respiratory system, including 26 deaths from chronic obstructive pulmonary diseases and 20 deaths from pneumonia and flu
- 37 deaths resulted from unintended injuries or violence, including 11 deaths from suicide, 8 deaths from motor vehicle accidents, and 1 death from homicide
- 7 deaths were due to Alzheimer's disease, 5 deaths were directly attributable to alcohol, and 4 resulted from HIV infection

Source: Adapted from Statistics Canada publication *Vital Statistics Compendium 1996*. Catalogue no. 84-214-XPE.

completeness. In Canada, the following information must be reported by law:

- live birth
- death
- fetal death
- marriage
- divorce
- legal separation
- annulment
- adoption

Annual published vital statistics usually include births, deaths, marriages, and divorces.

In an effort to collect information on vital events for each country, the United Nations (2002c: 7) established a set of standard definitions for vital events (see p. 41).

Unfortunately, these definitions are not applied uniformly across all countries. For example, in some countries an infant must survive for at least 24 hours before it can be inscribed in the live-birth register; in other jurisdictions, an infant born alive who dies before registration is considered a late fetal death. Such cases might not be counted either as births or as deaths, and without proper adjustments, accurate comparative studies of birth and death rates are difficult to achieve.

Marriage and divorce can pose even greater difficulties, for as the United Nations (2002c: 7) points out, 'Unlike birth and death, which are biological events, marriage and divorce are defined only in terms of laws and custom and as such are less amenable to universally applicable statistical definitions.' Marriage laws in particular vary widely. The most broadly applied requirement is a minimum legal age, but there are often other requirements that must be met (for instance, in some countries, parental consent may be required for a marriage to be official). Divorce is also highly regulated. In some countries the dissolution of marriage is strictly prohibited, while in many others there are many grounds for the granting of divorce. Again, to the extent that such practices and customs vary

from society to society, there will be a varying degree of discrepancy in the statistics.

One obstacle faced by vital statistics systems is how to address the *underregistration* of vital events. Underregistration may happen for a number of reasons. Rural and isolated areas may not possess the infrastructure required to monitor and enforce prompt reporting, while some countries are home to nomadic populations that are constantly mobile. The result, in either of these cases, can be a considerable lag between the time an event occurs and the time it is registered, if it is registered at all.

It is important to note that underregistration occurs even in the industrialized countries of the world. For example, in 1994, Statistics Canada received late information from the provinces on 280 deaths and 1,720 live births, which were consequently excluded from the 1994 published tabulations (Statistics Canada Health Statistics Division, 1999: xiv). Information that is reported on a voluntary basis is also subject to underregistration. In Canada, listing 'country of birth' on a death certificate is optional; as a result, this information has been reported sporadically over the years by the provinces.

Population Registers

Some countries maintain what is called a *population register*, in which change of residence, in addition to births, deaths, marriages, and divorces, must be declared to the authorities (Plane and Rogerson, 1994: 94; Rogers and Willekens, 1986: 22; Shryock and Siegel, 1976: 23–4). This kind of register is common only in small developed countries, such as Switzerland, the Netherlands, and the Scandinavian countries (Overbeek, 1980: 3), and in certain Asian countries, including Taiwan, Israel, Japan, and China (Shryock and Siegel, 1976: 23–4). Shryock and Siegel point out that the primary purpose of population registers is usually not demographic; rather, they are a means to keep track of citizens from birth to death, in a sense an institutionalized form of identification and control. In China, for instance, citizens must report their

UN Standard Definitions for Vital Events

Live birth is complete expulsion or extraction from its mother of a product of conception, irrespective of the duration of pregnancy, which after such separation breathes or shows any other evidence of life such as beating of the heart, pulsation of the umbilical cord, or definite movement of voluntary muscles, whether or not the umbilical cord has been cut or the placenta is attached; each product of such a birth is considered live-born regardless of gestational age.

Death is the permanent disappearance of all evidence of life at any time after live birth has taken place (postnatal cessation of vital functions without capability of resuscitation). This definition therefore excludes fetal deaths.

Fetal death is death prior to the complete expulsion or extraction from its mother of a product of conception, irrespective of the duration of pregnancy; the death is indicated by the fact that after such separation the fetus does not breathe or show any other evidence of life, such as beating of the heart, pulsation of the umbilical cord, or definite movement of voluntary muscles. Late fetal deaths are those of twenty-eight or more completed weeks of gestation. These are synonymous with the events reported under the pre-1950 term stillbirth.

Abortion is defined, with reference to the woman, as any interruption of pregnancy before 28 weeks of gestation with a dead fetus. There are two major categories of abortion: spontaneous and induced. Induced abortions are those initiated by deliberate action undertaken with the intention of terminating pregnancy; all other abortions are considered as spontaneous.

Marriage is the act, ceremony, or process by which the legal relationship of husband and wife is constituted. The legality of the union may be established by civil, religious, or other means as recognized by the laws of each country.

Divorce is a final legal dissolution of a marriage, that is, that separation of husband and wife which confers on the parties the right to remarriage under civil, religious, and/or other provisions, according to the laws of each country.

Source: United Nations Department of Economic and Social Affairs Population Division (2002c).

relocations to the police, who submit the information to the register (Yaukey, 2001: 18). In Canada and the United States, change of residence does not have to be reported by law.

Monitoring Migratory Movements

The discussion of population registers brings us to an important question: If in many countries there is no system to keep track of the movements of it citizens, how is migration studied?

Most countries have established procedures for processing foreigners crossing their borders, and migration into a country is monitored and recorded systematically by appropriate government agencies. Counting the number of people leaving a country is a much more difficult task, however. Normally this aspect of population counting is incomplete and must be estimated based on partial information. Canada, for example, has an official agreement with the United States, the United Kingdom, and some other countries to record and exchange information about individuals travelling between these partner nations. Clearly, since not every country is involved in these types of arrangements, data on emigration are incomplete.

What about the movement of people *within* a country where a continuous recording of changes of residence is not kept? In such cases internal migration is monitored using administrative databases. In Canada, this kind of monitoring is done through such data sources as tax files, which all adults must submit to the government at the end of each taxation year. Since the respondent must indicate his or her address on the tax return, migration between cities or provinces, signified by change in address from one year to the next, is easily discovered. The census is another valuable source of migration statistics. Usually, one or more questions on the census will ask about residential moves during the previous five years; this information gives a reliable indication of the extent of internal migration during a five-year interval. The Canadian census also includes a question on one-year mobility to get information on moves made in the year preceding the census).

Indirect Estimation of Vital Events

In some poor countries censuses are rarely taken and vital statistics collected only sporadically. Typically the problem is a lack of both the necessary infrastructure and the funds to support institutions responsible for continuous registration of vital events. For settings in which a census is not possible, and where registration systems are lacking or are deficient, demographic parameters such as births and deaths must be estimated. Often these estimates are based on incomplete information. Demographers have developed specialized techniques to handle such problems; a brief hypothetical illus-

China has a long history of household registration (Yaukey, 2001: 18–19), yet before 1982, the country was not able to conduct a complete census. Under the current registration system, established in 1955, all Chinese are by law required to 'register their household addresses with local authorities'. Each person over 15 is expected to have an identity card stating his or her name, birth date, and authorized place of residence (Yaukey, 2001: 18). China had conducted partial censuses in 1953 and 1964, but these were impossible to evaluate for their accuracy (Coale, 1974: 15).

The main complication for Chinese authorities is the large segment of its population that lives in remote rural areas that are difficult to access. The 1982 census was successful largely because of the Chinese officials' strong determination to complete an accurate census. China also benefited from significant international assistance and expertise provided by the United Nations Fund for Population Activities (UNFPA), the United States Census Bureau, and the Japanese government (Yaukey, 1985: 18).

tration is given in the box entitled 'Indirect Estimation of Vital Events'.

Canadian Vital Statistics: Background and Overview

Prior to 1921, when the Canadian vital statistics system was launched, each province ran its own registration of vital events. Although church authorities in Quebec had been registering baptisms, burials, and marriages since 1610, there was little standardization across the provinces in the way the data were collected and processed. It was with an eye to correcting these inconsistencies that the federal government initiated the national registration system.

Founded in 1918, the Dominion Bureau of Statistics (known by its current name, Statistics Canada, since 1971) organized two planning conferences to discuss the establishment of a standardized system of registration and reporting.

Indirect Estimation of Vital Events: Dual Records-Matching Method

In a country where a registration system exits but is flawed, demographers will sometimes apply what is known as a *dual record estimation procedure* to obtain a credible estimate of the population count or some other parameter (such as births or deaths). Table 2.2 below illustrates how the number of births may be estimated through a dual record check in a setting in which there is strong suspicion that the registration system is not working well.

Table 2.2 Example of dual record estimation of births in a hypothetical setting

Sample survey of mothers who report their births	Registration system		Total
	In	Not in	
Births reported	(C) Births counted in both the registration system and the sample survey	(N2) Births not found in the registration system but recorded in the sample survey	(S) Total number of births in the survey
No births reported	(N1) Births listed in the registration system, but not listed in the sample survey	(X) Births *not* listed in the registration system *and not* listed in the sample survey	Number of births not reported in the survey
		(unknown)	**(unknown)**
Total	(R) Total number of births in the registration system	Total number of births not listed in the registration system	(N) Total births
		(unknown)	**(unknown)**

Skipping many of the complexities of this methodology, it suffices to say that under the assumption of independence between two separate systems of data collection, probability theory allows us to derive an estimate of the total number of events—in this case, births—matching records of one system with records of the other. Imagine that there is a registration system in place for a given area. We take a representative sample of birth records from this registration system. We also take a random sample of households and interview women who have had children. We ask the women how many children they have had.

Once we have collected all the data, we then try to match all the birth records obtained from the survey with those in the registration system. The matching process would result in the outcomes shown in the cells of Table 2.2. Note the various cell designations: C, N1, N2,

X, S, R, N. Each of these represents a unique combination of the two possible conditions of being 'in' or 'not in' either of the two collection systems. So, for example, 'C' denotes births counted in both the registration system and the sample survey; N1 contains births listed in the registration system but not in the sample survey; N2 contains the births not found in the registration system but recorded in the sample survey; and X is an unknown, which must be estimated: it is the number of births *not* listed in the registration system *and not* listed in the sample survey. The key is to come up with an estimate of the unknown quantity X. Once this value is obtained, then it is a simple matter to compute the other unknown values and the overall total, N. An estimate of X is: $N1 \times N2/C$. Therefore $N = C + N1 + N2 + X$ (Marks, Seltzer, and Krotki, 1974).

Under the legislative purview of the Canada Vital Statistics Act, the Bureau would supply all provinces with standard forms for recording vital events, and the provinces would forward to the Bureau transcripts of their vital statistics certificates each year. The Bureau would check and then process the data, which would be published in an annual report. The practice is very much the same today. The provinces and territories supply microfilm or machine-readable copies of registration forms to Statistics Canada in Ottawa. Two provinces—Alberta and British Columbia—send vital statistics information to Ottawa in real time: once a birth is registered, the information is transmitted electronically to Statistics Canada. The real-time procedure is expected to soon become common practice across all other jurisdictions in Canada (Haugrud, 2007).

The first vital statistics report, issued in 1923, reported on data taken in 1921 on births, deaths, and marriages for Canada and the eight provinces (Canada Dominion Bureau of Statistics, 1923).[2] Quebec joined the system in 1926, and Newfoundland joined in 1949. Data for the Yukon Territory and the Northwest Territories were first included in the annual publications in 1950 (Statistics Canada Health Statistics Division, 1999: x), and Nunavut was added to the annual publications in 2000.

Officially, the mandate of the Canadian vital statistics system is 'to obtain and preserve such documentary evidence as is necessary to protect the legal rights of the individual' (Statistics Canada, 1990: iv). The data is available to the public, so that at any time after registration, an individual may refer to his or her own family's records to verify facts concerning a birth, marriage, or death. However, the data are also used extensively by researchers and health professionals. At the national level, the data is used for population estimates and projections, demographic trend analyses, health surveillance, and epidemiological research (Statistics Canada, 1990: v–vi). The process involved in reporting vital statistics is outlined in Figure 2.1, which is based on a sketch by McVey and Kalbach (1995a: 19).

---

[2]Specifically, the table of contents of the 1921 *Vital Statistics of Canada* lists the following items: births, infant mortality, general mortality, mortality by causes of death, and marriages. Divorces were not included in the publications until 1944, and it was not until 1969, after the passage of the Divorce Act, that statistics on divorce for Canada and the provinces and territories began to appear regularly in vital statistics publications.

Table 2.3 Highlights of the development of national vital statistics in Canada, 1605–1945

1605	Priests enumerate 44 settlers in the colony of New France.
1608	Quebec City is founded by Samuel de Champlain.
1617	Louis Hébert and his family, the first colonists, settle in Quebec.
1665–6	Jean Talon enumerates 3,215 inhabitants in the first census of the colony of New France.
1847	The Census and the Statistics Act of 1847 is passed, providing for a decennial census and the registration of births and deaths in the United Provinces of Upper and Lower Canada.
1867	The British North American Act creates the Dominion of Canada through the union of Ontario, Quebec, Nova Scotia, and New Brunswick.
1871	The first census of the Dominion of Canada is conducted. Published results include the compilation of vital statistics on the French Roman Catholic population of Quebec from 1608 to 1871.
1879	The Dominion of Canada's first Census and Statistics Act provides for the decennial census of 1881, and for the collection, abstraction, and tabulation of vital, agricultural, commercial, and other statistics.
1881	Census takers are required to take an oath of secrecy.
1898	An American Public Health Association meeting in Ottawa recommends the adoption of the *International Classification of Causes of Death* by registrars of Canada, the United States, and Mexico.
1905	Canada's first permanent Census and Statistics office is established.
1915	The office of the Dominion Statistician is created.
1918	The Statistics Act of 1918 is passed, creating the Dominion Bureau of Statistics (DBS).
1919	An Order-in-Council detailing the establishment of a national system of vital statistics is approved by the dominion government.
1921	The first detailed report on vital statistics is published by DBS, covering eight provinces.
1926	A national vital statistics report covering all of Canada (i.e., nine provinces plus the Yukon and Northwest Territories) is published.
1935	Improvements are made to registration techniques and procedures (e.g., revision of the medical certificate of death).
1938	The fifth revision of the *International List of Causes of Death* is adopted.
1940	The *Vital Statistics Handbook* and *Physician's Pocket Reference* are prepared.
1944	National tabulations on births and deaths begin to be reported by place of residence, in addition to place of event.
1945	The national scheme of Family Allowances is implemented on July 1.

Source: Martha M. Fair, 'The Development of National Vital Statistics in Canada: Part I, From 1605 to 1945', *Health Reports* 6 (3): 336–57.

The Use of Census and Vital Statistics Data in Population Analysis

Researchers interested in computing basic demographic measures for a population typically draw the data for these computations from vital statistics and the census. Consider, for example, the computation of crude birth and death rates for a census year. In 2001, there were 334,080 births in Canada; the mid-year population from the 2001 census (adjusted for undercoverage) was 31,110,565 (Statistics Canada Health Statistics Division, 2003: 1, 19). That same year 219,538 deaths were recorded (Statistics Canada, *The Daily*, 2003a: 9). The corresponding crude birth and death rates computed with these figures are 10.74 and 7.06 per 1,000 population, respectively.

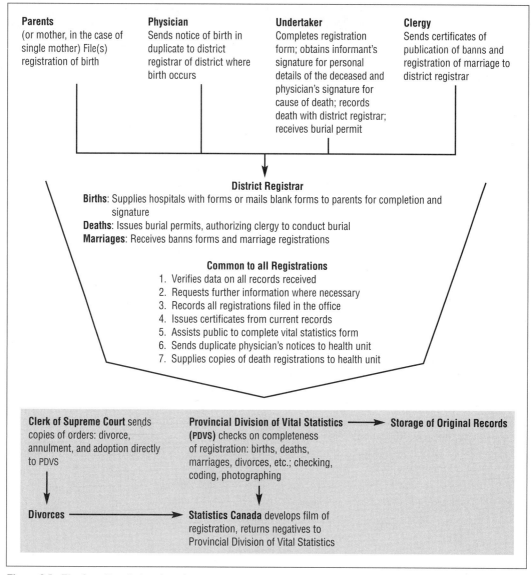

Figure 2.1 The Canadian vital registration process
Source: Adapted from McVey and Kalbach (1995a): 19.

How, then, are such rates computed for off-census years? The numerator for this kind of calculation would be available annually from the vital statistics system, since it is continuous. To obtain the denominator (i.e., the mid-year population) for a year in which a census is not taken the researcher would have to rely on a *postcensal population estimate*. This is an estimate of the population based on information from the most recent census. Government statistical agencies routinely provide these population estimates between censuses. So, for example, the 2002 mid-year population estimate of 31,413,990 provided by Statistics Canada was derived from the 2001 census population figure plus data concerning the components of population change between 2001 and 2002, namely births, deaths, and net migration (Statistics Canada Demography Division, 2003: 21).

Many other demographic measures are calculated the same way, using vital statistics data as numerators and population data (actual or estimated) as denominators. Various such computations will be introduced throughout this book.

Conclusion

This chapter looked at the two principal sources of data for demographic analysis: the census and vital statistics. The census is a one-point-in-time accounting of the population with respect to a variety of demographic, geographic, social, and economic characteristics. It provides a realistic indication of the demographic, social, and economic state of the population at a point in time. The vital statistics registration system is an ongoing process in which citizens of a country are required by law to register births, deaths, marriages, and divorces. In some countries there are population registers, where change of residence is recorded on a continual basis in addition to these other vital occurrences. In countries like Canada and the United States that

do not have population registers, data on migration are obtained from other sources, including administrative records and censuses.

Other sources of population data include postcensal surveys and special demographic sample surveys. Several of these surveys are taken routinely in Canada; examples include the Labour Force Survey, the General Social Survey, and the National Longitudinal Survey of Children and Youth. All advanced societies have similar types of surveys to supplement data gathered from their censuses and vital statistics systems. One important function of a postcensal survey is that it allows for an estimate of the degree of census undercoverage, which in Canada has generally ranged from 2 to 4 per cent.

The history of population studies is closely connected to early studies of vital statistics. The study of death records for the city of London by John Graunt in 1662 is considered the first systematic analysis in demography. His work based on the Bills of Mortality set the foundations for the life table, a staple of demographic analysis. While population counting of various sorts and extensiveness has been practised since antiquity, the census is a fairly recent invention, initiated by the Scandinavian countries in the mid-1700s.

Many demographic measures require the use of vital statistics and census population. Vital statistics data are usually used as the numerators, census population, the denominators. For years in which a census of the population is not taken, population estimates are used.

Exercises

1. Locate a copy of the United Nations' latest *Demographic Yearbook* at your library or on the United Nations website (www.un.org). Read the 'Introduction' of this publication (available at: http://unstats.un.org/unsd/demographic/products/dyb/dyb2004 /DYB2004_Introduction_E.pdf). Also, visit the Population Reference Bureau website (www.prb.org) and download their latest *World Population Data Sheet* (available at: http://prb.org/Publications/Datasheets/2006/2006WorldPopulationDataSheet.aspx). Read the 'Notes, Sources, and Definitions' section of the data sheet.

Identify in these two data sources the following data and coverage issues and discuss them briefly:

  a) problems associated with the extent of coverage of demographic information across countries
  b) problems associated with variations in data sources across countries
  c) problems associated with the standardization of measures across countries

2. Refer to the Appendix (on page 556) and examine the census questionnaire for the 2006 census of Canada. Write a short essay to describe how the information obtained from the questions in the census form could be used for social demographic research. What kinds of research topics would you propose? Describe your examples.

3. Sample copies of vital statistics forms for birth, death, and marriage for Alberta are provided in the Appendix (on page 572). In these forms some questions are asked consistently throughout, while others are not. Identify the 'common' questions. Why do you think these common questions are necessary?

4. Having familiarized yourself with the census questionnaire and the vital statistics forms, describe how the information contained in these two sources can be used to compute demographic rates for a population. For example, think about how the information on the birth and death forms can be used along with census data to compute such measures as birth and death rates for the population as a whole, and possibly for different subsets of the population. What other demographic measures can be computed from the information contained in the vital statistics and the census forms? Give at least ten examples along with a brief explanation of each.

5. Looking at the census and vital statistics forms, think of possible errors that could arise in the actual collection of vital and census information with the use of these forms, and also as a result of other possible complication in the process of data collection. Write a short essay on this topic.

Additional Reading

Curtis, Bruce. 2001. *The Politics of Population: State Formation, Statistics, and the Census of Canada, 1840–1875*. Toronto: University of Toronto Press.

Demeny, Paul, and Geoffrey McNicoll, eds. *Encyclopedia of Population*, vols 1 and 2. New York: Macmillan Reference USA/Thomsom–Gale.

Emery, George. 1993. *Facts of Life: The Social Construction of Vital Statistics, Ontario 1869–1952*. Montreal and Kingston: McGill–Queens University Press.

Levitas, Ruth, and Will Guy, eds. 1996. *Interpreting Official Statistics*. London and New York: Routledge.

Petersen, William, and Renee Petersen. 1986. *Dictionary of Demography—Terms, Concepts, and Institutions*, vols 1 and 2. New York: Greenwood.

Pressat, Roland. 1985. *The Dictionary of Demography*. Christopher Wilson, ed. Oxford: Basil Blackwell.

Rees, Philip, David Martin, and Paul Williamson, eds. 2002. *The Census Data System*. Chichester: Wiley.

United Nations. 1998. *Draft Principles and Recommendations for Population and Housing Censuses—Revision 1*. E.98.XVII.8. New York: United Nations.

United Nations. 2001. *Principles and Recommendations for a Vital Statistics System—Revision 2*. E.01.XVII.10. New York: United Nations.

Worton, David A. 1998. *The Dominion Bureau of Statistics: A History of Canada's Central Statistical Office and Its Antecedents, 1841–1972*. Montreal and Kingston: McGill–Queen's University Press.

Web Resources

The Vital Statistics Council of Canada publishes an interesting and informative newsletter called *Vital News*. It usually contains the latest information on trends in health and mortality for Canada and for the provinces and territories. Occasionally, it also features international vital statistics news and trends: www.vscouncil.ca.

Statistics Canada's *Census Handbooks* can be obtained online. These make an excellent resource for the background and planning of the Canadian census. Statistics Canada also publishes *Health Reports*, which contains valuable analytical articles on a wide range of population health topics. Electronic versions of the articles are available for download. Various other annual vital statistics publications are available from Statistics Canada (e.g., births, deaths, marriages, and divorces shelf tables): www.statcan.ca.

Population health information on Canadians can be found at the Health Canada website: www.hc-sc.gc.ca/.

Located in Paris, France, the Institut National d'Études Démographique (INED) is one of the premiere demographic institutions in the world: www.ined.fr/.

Also found on the INED's website is a list of their current research reports and key publications. Their Population Society bulletin is particularly useful: www.ined.fr/en/resources_documentation/publications/pop_soc.

The Netherlands Interdisciplinary Demographic Institute (NIDI) is a research body of the Royal Netherlands Academy of Arts and Sciences (KNAW) engaged in the scientific study of population. The NIDI, through its research, aims to contribute to the description, analysis, explanation, and prediction of demographic trends in the past, the present, and the future. It also studies the determinants and consequences of these trends for society in general and policy in particular. NIDI research is characterized by its interdisciplinary approach and international orientation: www.nidi.nl/.

NIDI's website also provides links (over 500!) to other demographic institutes throughout the world: www.nidi.nl/links/nidi6000.html.

The National Center for Health Statistics is the United States' vital statistics office: www.cdc.gov/nchs.

The United States Census Bureau is one of the best sources of demographic information for the United States and other countries: www.census.gov/index.html.

An important source of international mortality and population data is the *World Health Organization Statistics Annual*. This publication contains deaths by cause, age, and sex for a large number of countries. WHO publishes these tables on a yearly basis: www.who.int/home-page.

The premiere population centre for demographic training and research is the Office of Population Research at Princeton University. Their website offers many links to other major demographic centres and resources of relevance to population and demography: http://opr.princeton.edu/resources.

Chapter 3

Population: Past, Present, and Futures

Introduction

This chapter is divided into two parts. The first part begins with an examination of the world population situation in 2006, and then looks at the historical growth of the human population from ancient times to the present before turning to future projections for both industrialized and developing countries. Part two provides an overview of the demographic history of Canada and some of the more important social demographic transformations that have taken place in this country over the past 150 years or so.

Population History

World Population Today

At 6.55 billion, the population of the world in 2006 was the largest ever recorded in the history of humanity. The difference between the crude birth and death rates—21 and 9 per 1,000 population, respectively—produces an annual rate of natural increase of 1.2 per cent (Population Reference Bureau, 2006). If this rate of growth were to remain constant, the world's population would grow by approximately 79 million persons annually and double in roughly 58 years. Population growth is not uniform throughout the regions. As Table 3.1 shows, the more developed countries have an overall rate of natural increase of only 0.1 per cent, while the rest of the world is growing substantially faster, with rates somewhere between 1.5 and 1.8 per cent (depending on whether China is included in the calculations). Growth rates in some industrialized nations, including Germany, Italy, and Japan, have even fallen slightly below zero in recent years; by contrast, countries such as

Nigeria, Ethiopia, Congo, and Guatemala are growing at rates well above 2 per cent (Population Reference Bureau, 1995, 2001, 2006).

Together, the less developed countries today account for roughly 81 per cent of the world's total population; if China is excluded this proportion falls to 61 per cent. The vast majority of the earth's people endure a standard of living far below that enjoyed in the developed countries. Indeed, the average income in the more developed countries is almost six times greater than that in the less developed world. Compounding this disparity is the high population density in the less developed world. The combination of rapid population growth, relatively low income, and high population density suggests that the resources available to the average citizen in these countries will continue to diminish. It's important to note that the population densities listed in Table 3.1 are calculated on the basis of total area, including regions that are not arable, such as lakes, rivers, mountains, and deserts. A more accurate reflection of living conditions is provided by a measure called 'nutritional density'—the ratio of total population to total arable area in a country (Trewartha, 1969: 74).

Table 3.1 also shows regional patterns of population size, variability in growth rates, birth and death rates, income, and population density. The highest birth rates in the world are found in Africa—especially the sub-Saharan region, where the crude birth rate of 40 per 1,000 population is substantially higher than in Western and South Central Asia, the regions with the next highest birth rates (26 and 25 per 1,000, respectively). Europe, North America, and East Asia have the lowest birth rates, ranging between 10 and 14 per 1,000. Crude death rates show little variation across regions but are highest in Africa,

Table 3.1 Demographic data for the world and more developed and less developed regions, 2006

Area	Population mid-2006 (millions)	% of world total population	Births per 1,000 population	Deaths per 1,000 population	Rate of natural increase	Population doubling time (years)	GNI PPP per capita 2005 (US$)	Population per square mile
World	6,555	100.0	21	9	1.2	58	7,160	122
MDCs[1]	1,216	19.0	11	10	0.1	700	27,790	61
LDCs[2]	5,339	81.0	23	8	1.5	47	4,950	167
LDCs (excl. China)	4,028	61.0	27	9	1.8	39	4,410	142
Africa	924	**14.1**	38	15	2.3	30	2,480	66
Sub-Saharan	767	11.7	40	16	2.4	29	1,970	82
Northern	198	3.0	26	6	2.0	35	4,350	60
Western	271	4.1	43	17	2.6	27	1,270	114
Eastern	284	4.3	41	16	2.4	29	1,090	116
Middle	116	1.8	44	16	2.8	25	1,310	45
Southern	54	0.8	24	19	0.5	140	11,460	52
North America	332	**5.1**	14	8	0.6	117	40,980	43
Latin America/Carib.	566	**8.6**	21	6	1.5	47	7,950	71
Central	149	2.3	24	5	1.9	37	8,640	156
Caribbean	39	0.6	20	8	1.2	58	—[3]	433
South	378	5.8	21	6	1.4	50	8,210	55
Asia	3,968	**60.5**	20	7	1.2	58	5,960	324
Asia (excl. China)	2,657	**40.5**	23	7	1.6	44	5,640	310
Western	218	3.3	26	6	2.0	35	7,500	119
South Central	1,642	25.0	25	8	1.7	41	3,330	395
Southeast	567	8.6	21	6	1.4	50	4,530	326
East	1,544	23.6	12	7	0.5	140	9,050	340
Europe	732	**11.2**	10	12	-0.1	-700[4]	21,120	82
Northern	97	1.5	12	10	0.2	350	31,570	143
Western	187	2.9	10	9	0.1	700	30,690	437
Eastern	296	4.5	10	14	-0.5	-140[4]	10,640	41
Southern	152	2.3	10	10	0.1	700	23,090	300
Oceania	34	**0.5**	17	7	1.0	70	22,180	10

Note: GNI PPP per capita 2005 (US$) is gross national income in purchasing power parity (PPP) divided by mid-year population. This measure makes it possible to compare the quantities of goods and services that the average person in each country could afford to buy, based on that country's GNP.

[1]more developed countries; [2]less developed countries; [3]data not available; [4]the negative value implies that the population will decrease to half its current size in this number of years, given this constant negative rate of natural increase.

Source: Population Reference Bureau (2007).

reflecting the devastating impact of HIV/AIDS in recent decades.

The regional gaps in these two vital rates determine regional differences in natural increase. With the exception of South Africa, where the rate of natural increase is 0.5 per cent, African countries all have growth rates of 2 per cent or above. One way to determine how fast a population is growing is to compute its doubling time—the number of years it would take for the population to double if its current rate of growth were to remain unchanged. In the case of Africa, the doubling time is only about 29 years. (See the Notes for Further Study, on page 82, for a detailed discussion of doubling time.) With a growth rate of 2.8 per cent, Middle Africa would experience an even faster doubling—24 years. This is the highest rate of natural increase in any of the world's major regions.

In sharp contrast, European growth rates are on the order of −0.1 to 0.1 per cent; if the negative growth rates in some countries were to remain constant, those populations would eventually become extinct. Under current demographic conditions it would take roughly 700 years for Europe as a whole to reach half its current size. Growth rates in North America and East Asia, at around 0.6 or 0.5 per cent, are also well below the world average. The situation in Asia depends on whether China is included in the computations: 1.6 per cent with China, 1.3 per cent without. Within Asia, the Western sub-region is the fastest-growing area, at 2 per cent. Oceania (which includes Australia and New Zealand) had a growth rate of 1.0 per cent in 2006.

From Gradual to Explosive Growth

To understand the current and possible future state of the world's population it is necessary to look at the broader context of human history. The farther back we go, however, the less certain our estimates are; before about 1750 we are essentially reduced to making educated guesses (Coale, 1974; Trewartha, 1969). Long-term future projections suffer from uncertainty as well. The reasonableness of our estimates regarding the distant past depends on the quality of the assumptions we introduce into our calculations regarding mortality and fertility. The same is true of future projections: informed assumptions can produce reasonable projections, especially over the short term (less than 25 years into the future), but the picture becomes increasingly uncertain over longer periods.

Coale (1974) divides population history into two broad segments: the first, from the beginning of humanity to around 1750 CE, was a very long era of slow population growth; the second—extremely brief in historical terms, from c. 1750 to the present—is one of explosive increases. The estimated average annual growth rate between 8000 BCE and 1 CE was only 0.036 per cent per year. Between 1 CE and 1750 the average rate rose to 0.056 per cent; and from 1750 to 1800 it increased to 0.44 per cent. By the 1950s growth rates had reached approximately 1.5 per cent per year. And during the 1960s and early 1970s they soared to their historic maximum of just over 2 per cent (Coale, 1974). Figure 3.1 offers a long-view perspective on human population from prehistory to the present. As it shows, the growth since roughly 1750 CE has been exponential.

Although the graph suggests a smooth progression over the millions of years leading up to 1750, in fact population change has been irregular through most of human history. Until the advent of the Agricultural Revolution (between the tenth and fifth centuries BCE) and throughout the medieval and modern periods, cycles of population growth, decline, and recovery were common, reflecting periods of 'crisis' mortality followed by birth deficits and subsequent population surges (Biraben, 2003b; Cipolla, 1962; Coale, 1974; Diamond, 1999; Herlihy and Cohn, 1997; Livi-Bacci, 1997; Wrigley, 1969; Wrigley and Schofield, 1981a).

The evidence also suggests that the human population has gone through periods of abrupt increases (see Figure 3.2). Biraben (1979, 2003a,

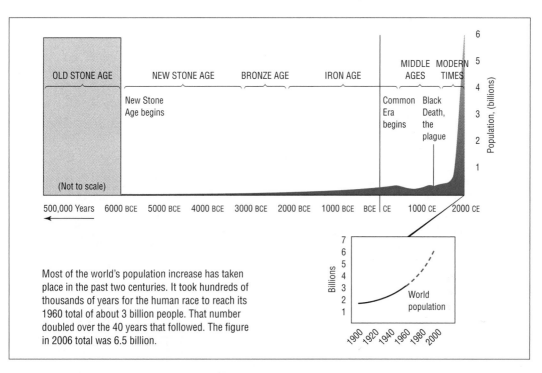

Most of the world's population increase has taken place in the past two centuries. It took hundreds of thousands of years for the human race to reach its 1960 total of about 3 billion people. That number doubled over the 40 years that followed. The figure in 2006 total was 6.5 billion.

World population growth through broad historical periods and projections

Period	Estimated population	Estimated average annual growth rate (%)	Years to add 1 billion
1 million–8000 BCE	8 million	0.010[1]	
8000 BCE–1 CE	300 million	0.036[1]	
1 CE–1750	800 million	0.056[1]	
1804	1 billion	0.400[1]	all of human history
1927	2 billion	0.540[1]	123
1950	2.5 billion	0.800[1]	—
1960	3 billion	1.7–2.0[2]	33
1974	4 billion	2.0–1.8[2]	14
1987	5 billion	1.8–1.6[2]	13
1999	6 billion	1.6–1.4[2]	12
2013 (projected)[4]	7 billion	1.04[3]	14
2028 (projected)[4]	8 billion	0.90[3]	15
2050 (projected)[4]	9 billion	0.57[3]	22

Figure 3.1 Population of the world through history

[1]Estimated average population or average rate of growth at the end of the period.

[2]Range of growth rates between specified periods.

[3]Estimated.

[4]Projections based on the 2004 revision of the UN's World Population Prospects, medium variant (United Nations, 2006).

Sources: Figure adapted from Trewartha (1969): 29. Table based on Coale (1974); Trewartha (1969); Bongaarts and Bulatao (2000); Population Reference Bureau (various years).

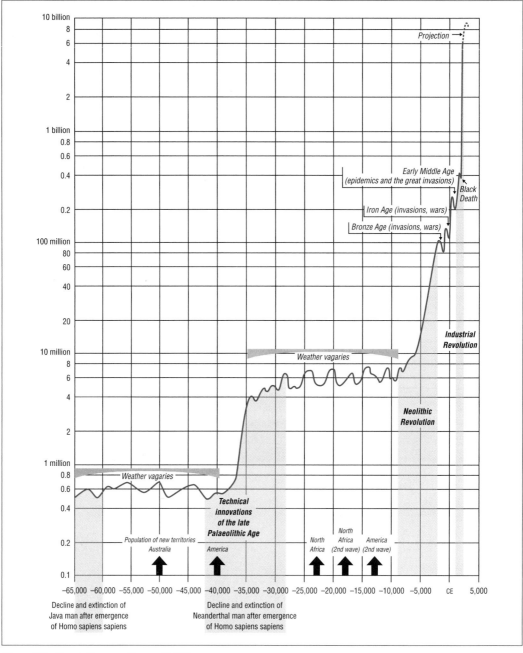

Figure 3.2 Population growth over 65,000 years

Source: Biraben (2003a): 3. Reprinted by permission of the publisher.

2003b) counts three great population surges, each associated with a major technological revolution that made humans less vulnerable to the vagaries of nature and increased their control over their environment. The first of these revolutions was the acquisition of clothing, along with hunting and fishing tools, in the Upper Paleolithic period (*c*.30000–10000 BCE). The second was sedentarization and the development of agriculture, animal husbandry, and maritime navigation in the Neolithic period (*c*.8000–5000 BCE). The most recent was the Industrial Revolution, which began in the eighteenth century and is now coming to its end as we move into the post-industrial era.

From 400 BCE to 1 CE population seems to have increased across all the regions of the world. Since that time, however, some regions have experienced cycles of depopulation and recovery during certain periods. As Table 3.2 shows, a notable instance of crisis mortality occurred between 1300 and 1400, when the global population is estimated to have been reduced by 65 million, from roughly 429 million in 1300 to about 364 million a century later. The decline seems to have been especially marked in China, India, and Europe. The plague, which spread throughout continental Europe between 1347 and 1351 (and reappeared intermittently over the next three centuries), killed between one-quarter and one-third of the European population (between 20 and 35 million people) (Cohn, 2003; Porter, 1997: 123).

The Demographic Transition

As we noted above, the human population has undergone repeated cycles of rising and falling growth rates. The most recent such cycle, which began in western Europe about 150 years ago, is generally known as the demographic transition. It is usually described as occurring in three stages, beginning with high rates of both births and deaths, moving through a transitional phase of high birth and declining death rates, and concluding with low rates of both fertility and mortality. (Some authors divide the second stage into two periods; for instance, Trewartha [1969] identifies 'early expanding' and 'late expanding' phases within stage two; see Figure 3.3.) It was only about two centuries ago that developments in medicine, sanitation, and nutrition began to achieve significant increases in human life expectancy. Until that time mortality rates were very high. The same was true of fertility rates in the days before the development of modern contraceptive techniques. Since both rates were high, however, rates of natural increase remained very low for most of human history.

In the pre-transition decades around 1700 total fertility rates in Europe were between 4 and 6.5; life expectancy at birth ranged from 20 to 35; and population growth remained near zero (Coale, 1974, 1986: 23). Today, long after the completion of the transition, fertility rates in western Europe are quite low by historical standards, falling somewhere between 1.3 and 2.1 births per woman; life expectancy at birth is close to 80 years; and rates of population growth are once again close to zero (in some cases even negative). The change from pre- to post-transitional status is clear in the second

It is generally agreed that the disease known variously as the plague, Black Death, or Great Pestilence originated in China. In 1346 it travelled to India and parts of Russia, and in the fall of 1347 it reached Europe, entering through the city of Messina, Sicily. By 1351 the epidemic had crossed the continent, even reaching as far north as Greenland. Although it had more or less disappeared from Europe by the end of the seventeenth century, outbreaks of a similar, though less virulent, strain have been identified as recently as the early 1920s. For more details on the history of the plague in Europe, see Cohn (2003), Livi-Bacci (1997), and Porter (1997).

Table 3.2 World population estimates, by region, selected dates, 400 BCE–2000 CE (millions)

Region	400 BCE	0	500 CE	1000	1300	1400	1500	1700	1800	1900	2000
China[1]	19	70	32	56	83	70	84	150	330	415	1,273
India[2]	30	46	33	40	100	74	95	175	190	290	1,320
Southwest Asia	42	47	45	33	21	19	23	30	28	38	259
Japan	0.1	0.3	2	7	7	8	8	28	30	44	126
Rest of Asia	3	5	8	19	29	29	33	53	68	115	653
Europe[3]	32	43	41	43	86	65	84	125	195	422	782
North Africa	10	13	12	10	9	8	8	9	9	23	143
Rest of Africa	7	12	20	30	60	60	78	97	92	95	657
North America	1	2	2	2	3	3	3	2	5	90	307
Latin America[4]	7	10	13	16	29	36	39	10	19	75	512
Oceania	1	1	1	1	2	2	3	3	2	6	30
World total	**152**	**250**	**205**	**257**	**429**	**374**	**458**	**682**	**968**	**1,613**	**6,062**

						% distribution					
Region	400 BCE	0	500 CE	1000	1300	1400	1500	1700	1800	1900	2000
China[1]	12.5	28.1	15.3	21.8	19.3	18.7	18.3	22.0	34.1	25.7	21.0
India[2]	19.7	18.5	15.8	15.6	23.3	19.8	20.7	25.7	19.6	18.0	21.8
Southwest Asia	27.6	18.9	21.5	12.8	4.9	5.1	5.0	4.4	2.9	2.4	4.3
Japan	0.1	0.1	1.0	2.7	1.6	2.1	1.7	4.1	3.1	2.7	2.1
Rest of Asia	2.0	2.0	3.8	7.4	6.8	7.8	7.2	7.8	7.0	7.1	10.8
Europe[3]	21.0	17.2	19.6	16.7	20.0	17.4	18.3	18.3	20.1	26.2	12.9
North Africa	6.6	5.2	5.7	3.9	2.1	2.1	1.7	1.3	0.9	1.4	2.4
Rest of Africa	4.6	4.8	9.6	11.7	14.0	16.0	17.0	14.2	9.5	5.9	10.8
North America	0.7	0.8	1.0	0.8	0.7	0.8	0.7	0.3	0.5	5.6	5.1
Latin America[4]	4.6	4.0	6.2	6.2	6.8	9.6	8.5	1.5	2.0	4.6	8.4
Oceania	0.7	0.4	0.5	0.4	0.5	0.5	0.7	0.4	0.2	0.4	0.5
World total	**100**	**100**	**100**	**100**	**100**	**100**	**100**	**100**	**100**	**100**	**100**

[1]China includes the Korean Peninsula.

[2]India includes Pakistan, Bangladesh, and Sri Lanka.

[3]Europe includes the former Soviet Union.

[4]Latin America includes the Caribbean.

Source: Biraben, 'World Population Growth', in *Encyclopedia of Population*, 2nd edn, by Paul George Demeny and Geoffrey McNicoll (Eds), 2003. Reprinted with permission of Gale, a division of Thomson Learning: www.thomsonrights.com. Fax 800-730-2215.

part of Figure 3.4, which shows how fertility and life expectancy in European societies have changed since the pre-modern period.

During the second stage of the demographic transition, death rates typically decline first, while fertility rates remain high for some time. In Europe this period of imbalance in the two vital rates extended from the mid-1800s through the early 1900s. The unprecedented rates of natural increase caused by this demographic imbalance, according to McKeown (1976), were responsible for the modern rise of population. Gradually, as European societies attained greater levels of modernization and socioeconomic development, birth rates began to fall, and by 1930 both mortality and fertility

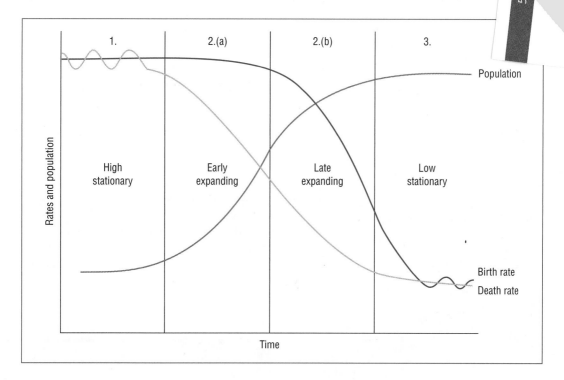

	1.	2.(a)	2.(b)	3.
	High stationary	Early expanding	Late expanding	Low stationary

Figure 3.3 The classic demographic transition model

Source: Adapted from Trewartha (1969): 45, 47.

Stage	Fertility	Mortality	Population growth	Economy
1. Pre-industrial	High, fluctuating	High, fluctuating (low life expectancy)	Static to very low	Primitive or agrarian
2. Early industrial	High	Falling	High, explosive	Mixed
3. Modern urban industrial	Controlled: low to moderate to sub-replacement levels	Low (high life expectancy)	Low to moderate to negative	Urban industrial to post-industrial

in most Western nations were the lowest they had ever been. As a consequence the rate of natural increase once again fell. This time the decline in population growth rates was attributable to humans' increasing control over nature: industrialization, urbanization, economic growth, modern science and medicine, and widespread use of contraception to regulate family size, all of which helped to bring down the death rate to historically low levels.

Extensive research into the fertility component of the transition across Europe led Coale (1973, 1986) to conclude that the timing and the societal preconditions for long-term fertility decline varied widely. He therefore argued that an all-encompassing theory was not possible. How-

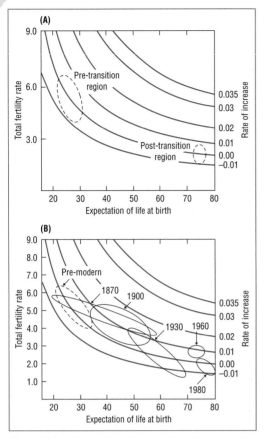

Figure 3.4 Expected trajectory of fertility, mortality, and natural increase for societies moving from pre- to post-demographic transition regimes (A), and actual trajectory of European populations across the stages of the demographic transition (B)

Note: The ellipses represent groups of countries.

Source: Adapted from Coale (1986): 23, 27.

ever, his observations suggested three general preconditions for fertility decline (Coale, 1973):

1. Fertility must be within the 'calculus of conscious choice'. Potential parents must consider it acceptable to balance advantages and disadvantages before deciding to have another child—unlike, for example, most present-day Hutterites or Amish, who do not practise birth control and would consider any such calculation immoral.

2. Social and economic circumstances must be such that individual couples will perceive reduced fertility as advantageous in some way.

3. Effective techniques of fertility reduction must be available. Techniques that will in fact prevent conception or birth must be known, and there must be sufficient communication between spouses, to use those techniques successfully.

Unless all three of these preconditions are present, fertility is likely to remain high. This is the case in some contemporary developing countries, where social norms still favour large families. Thus even though family planning may be available and accessible, pronatalist norms prevent the widespread use of birth control.

There has been some debate over whether the demographic transition model qualifies as a 'theory' (Kirk, 1996). Strictly speaking, a theory should both explain and predict phenomena in the real world. But while the demographic transition account explains in a general sense the historical shifts in birth and death rates in the context of socioeconomic modernization, it has had some difficulty specifying what conditions must prevail in a society, and at what intensity, in order to provoke sustained mortality and fertility declines. Prediction is another area of admitted weakness. In the case of the Western countries, for example, the model could not have predicted the baby boom that followed the Second World War. These weaknesses notwithstanding, the demographic transition still offers a solid account of macro-level change across societies, and it should be regarded as one of the mainstays in demographic theorizing and research. See, for example, Cleland and Wilson (1987); Coale (1969, 1973); Coale and Watkins (1986); Davis (1945); Landry (1934, 1945); Notestein (1945, 1953); Thompson (1929, 1944).

Moreover, in highly insecure socioeconomic environments, children represent a form of security for parents, and large families are therefore highly desirable.

The Demographic Transition in the Industrialized Countries

Although the classical formulation of the demographic transition theory suggests that all societies will experience this transition in much the same way, the timing and intensity of mortality and fertility declines have in fact varied widely. Figure 3.5 charts the demographic transitions of England and Wales, France, Sweden, Finland, and Japan. The first graph, depicting England and Wales, shows the classic pattern, with mortality beginning its decline first (Chesnais, 1992) and the birth rate rising before it starts to fall. A pre-decline rise in fertility has characterized every case of demographic transition, Western or otherwise (Dyson and Murphy, 1985). The mechanisms responsible for this rise are changes associated with modernization. First, as the living standard improves, so does the health of the population, causing natural fertility levels to rise; then fertility rates increase accordingly until the practice of contraception becomes widespread (Romaniuk, 1980). As the graph for France shows, however, the increase in fertility is not always large. Another respect in which the French experience differed from the British was that French birth and death rates declined at a similar pace, with the result that the rate of natural increase did not rise substantially.

Both Sweden and Finland experienced several intense temporary rises in mortality during their pre-transitional stages, reflecting periods of famine, epidemic disease, and wars. In fact, all five of the graphs in Figure 3.5 clearly show the patterns associated with major wars: a rise in mortality and a decline in fertility, followed by a fertility surge and a return to low mortality soon after the cessation of conflict. Finally, Japan's demographic transition closely resembles the classic western European type, with the important exception that it took place over a much shorter period of time. The same is true of some contemporary developing countries, where first mortality and then fertility have declined rapidly.

Mechanisms of Transition: Western and Japanese Experiences

Different societies have followed different combinations of social, cultural, economic, and demographic paths towards completion of their demographic transitions (Casterline, 2001; Caldwell, 1976, 2001; Caldwell and Caldwell, 1997; Cleland, 2001; Matras, 1965). Focusing mostly on the fertility side of the equation, and drawing on examples from both Europe and Japan, Davis (1963) has proposed a 'multiphasic response theory'. This theory assumes that widespread fertility declines in a society occur in a context of rising socioeconomic opportunities, coupled with sustained high rates of natural increase (as during stage two of the European demographic transition). Under such conditions, individual members of the population will eventually recognize that a large family is an impediment to upward mobility, but how they respond will depend on their culture. In Ireland, for example, population pressure during the second stage of demographic transition meant that family land had to be subdivided into smaller and smaller plots for the increasing number of adult children. Meanwhile, as parents lived longer, the children had to wait longer to inherit family property. The Irish responded in various ways to these conditions: mass migration from the rural areas to the cities, out-migration to the Americas, delayed marriage, and increased celibacy. These responses had the effect of relieving population pressure and also reducing fertility. Japan experienced similar conditions and responses. However, the Japanese also adopted abortion as a way of controlling family size. Generally, populations will adopt the responses that are least inconvenient and least threatening to their cultures. Though abortion would not have been an 'available' response to the Catholic Irish, it was widely 'available' and practised by the Japanese (Davis, 1963).

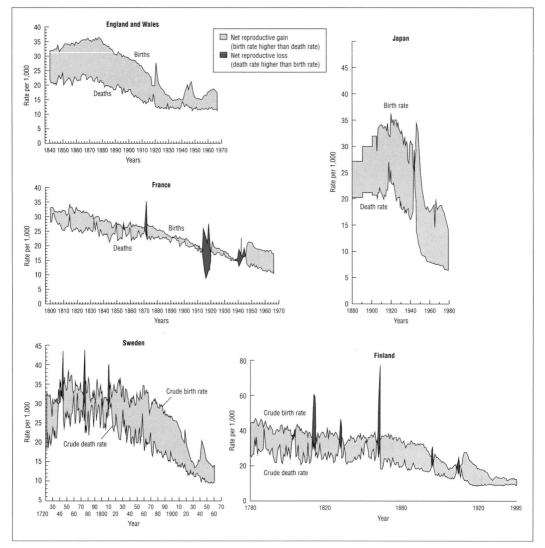

Figure 3.5 Demographic transitions of England and Wales, France, Sweden, Finland, and Japan

Sources: For Sweden: Bogue (1969): 59; reprinted by permission of the author. For England/Wales and France: Kosinski (1970): 26, 28 (Figures 9 and 10); copyright © Pearson Education Limited. For Finland: Kannisto, Nieminen, and Turpeinen (1999): 22 (Figure 1); reprinted by permission of the authors. For Japan: Chesnais (1992): 246 (Figure 8.4); reprinted by permission of Oxford University Press.

Demographic Transition of Developing Countries

Teitelbaum (1975) has pointed out a number of important differences in the demographic histories of the West and the developing countries:

1. *The pace and sources of mortality decline.* In Europe mortality declined gradually, whereas in developing nations the pace of decline has been quite rapid. Furthermore, whereas the technologies and public health

measures responsible for the improvements in the West were largely endogenous (developed within the society), in the developing countries they have been mainly exogenous (imported from outside—e.g., public health and family planning programs).

2. *Fertility levels before the decline.* In contemporary developing nations fertility rates are generally higher to begin with than they were at the corresponding point in western Europe.

3. *Rate of population growth.* European nations undergoing the demographic transition rarely experienced doubling times of less than 50 years. In contrast, doubling times in some developing nations can be as low as 30 years. At no point in their transitions did European nations experience the growth rates found in many contemporary developing countries, which can reach 3 per cent or more.

4. *Momentum for further growth.* As a result of the relatively high fertility and youthful age structures in developing nations, the poten-

tial for further significant population growth exceeds that of the industrialized nations by a wide margin.

5. *International migration as an outlet to relieve population pressure.* Western Europe was able to export tens of millions of its citizens to colonies in the Americas, Oceania, and elsewhere. Such outlets are extremely limited for the contemporary developing countries.

These observations are clearly reflected in Figure 3.6, which highlights the contrasting situations of Sweden (representative of the Western classical model) and Mexico (representative of many contemporary developing countries). Notice the considerably higher levels of birth and death rates for Mexico in the early stage of its transition as compared to Sweden between 1750 and 1800. The vital rates in Mexico in 1900—at the time of stage one—were between 35 and 45 per 1,000 population. Also clear in this graph is how much more precipitous the

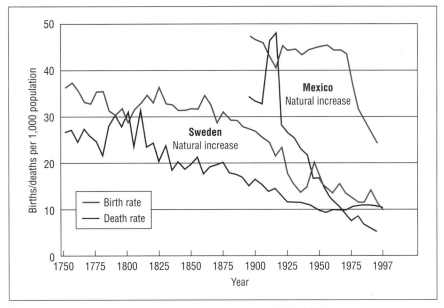

Figure 3.6 Demographic transition in Sweden and Mexico, 1750–1997
Source: Gelbard, Haub, and Kent (1999): 6 (Figure 2).

drop in Mexico's death rate was, compared to Sweden's. A third point to note is the relatively short time span in which Mexico moved from the first to the later part of the second stage of the demographic transition. In Sweden it took roughly 120 years—from about 1810 to 1930— to move from stage 1 to late stage 2. In Mexico, the same developments have taken only about 75 years. Perhaps even more striking is the rapid pace of Mexico's mortality decline; the crude death rate dropped from over 40 per 1,000 population in 1925 to below 20 per 1,000 in 1950; and by 2000 it had declined to about 9 per 1,000—just below Sweden's current rate. Finally, the difference in the rate of natural increase between Sweden and Mexico at similar stages of demographic evolution is significant. Historically, Mexico's growth rate has been approximately twice that of Sweden; this is symptomatic of the very different demographic experiences of Western and non-Western countries (see also Figures 3.7 and 3.8).

Transitional and Delayed Transition Societies

Developing countries can be distinguished by the progress they have made towards completion of the demographic transition. In broad terms there are two sets of developing countries: those that are currently approaching the end of the demographic transition, and those where this process has only recently begun. Since in most cases mortality has been declining since the 1950s or earlier, the crucial factor determining how far a society has progressed into its demographic transition would appear to be the pace of fertility decline. Among the places that began their fertility transitions relatively early, in the 1960s and 1970s, are Singapore, Taiwan, Thailand, Hong Kong, Malaysia, South Korea, Mexico, and many countries in Latin America and the Caribbean (the exceptions are Bolivia, Peru, Nicaragua, Honduras, and Haiti, which are in the delayed transition group). Between the 1950s and the late 1970s, total fertility (a measure of average fertility for a society) in Singapore, Taiwan, China,

Hong Kong, and South Korea had dropped by between 50 and 70 per cent (Coale, 1983). The 1990s saw further significant declines in these populations. These countries now have fertility rates that approximate those of the industrialized countries, and have in essence completed the demographic transition.

By the early 1970s, China had entered the transition. Its total fertility rate (the average number of children per woman) was 5.5 in 1953. By 1978 this measure had declined by 56 per cent to 2.4, and by 2000 China had a fertility rate of only 1.8—a drop of 25 per cent since 1978. A large part of this change can be attributed to the vigorous family planning regime in place since the late 1970s. But the initiation of the fertility decline may be attributable to other factors, notably rapid urbanization, increased education, and industrialization (Lavely and Freedman, 1990).

India, too, has joined the transitional group. Though still high, its birth rates have been declining steadily over the past two decades. According to Coale (1983) India's total fertility rate in 1951–60 was 6.2; in 1970 it was 4.9; and by 2000 it had declined to 3.3. These changes represent declines of 21 and 33 per cent, respectively. Egypt and other parts of Northern Africa (e.g., Morocco) and some areas of the Middle East (e.g., Turkey) have also experienced significant fertility declines since the 1980s.

All the countries that have made significant headway have had vigorous family planning programs in place for several decades (Robey, Rutestein, and Morris, 1993; Potts, 2006). Another important factor is female education. Birth rates are lower in countries where female literacy is relatively high, because education makes it possible for women to access and use effective contraceptives (Robey, Rutestein, and Morris, 1993; Westoff, 1990; Cleland and Hobcraft, 1985).

As Figures 3.7 and 3.8 show, the latecomers to the demographic transition—the *delayed transition societies*—typically have high rates of natural increase (2 per cent or more). Most of them

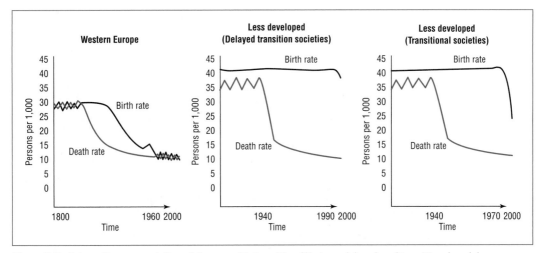

Figure 3.7 Schematic representation of demographic transition: Western, delayed, and transitional models
Source: Adapted from Trewartha (1969): 45, 47.

are located in sub-Saharan Africa. Although birth rates in this region have declined over the past two decades, the changes have been relatively small. Meanwhile, many of these countries have experienced rising death rates as a result of HIV/AIDS. Another region that includes a number of delayed transition countries is South Central Asia (Afghanistan, Pakistan, Bangladesh, and Nepal).

What Accounts for Delayed Development?

In order to understand the demography of developing countries it is essential to look at the reasons behind their delayed development. A full answer to this question would require not only a detailed historical review of European colonialism from roughly 1500 to the 1930s but an examination of economic relations and exchanges between the European powers and the colonies from 1500 to the present. What follows is only a brief overview of some of the essential aspects of the question.

Part (though only part) of the answer lies in the developing countries' experience with European *colonialism*. In the discussion on page 65, attention is directed first to economic, cultural, and geographic dimensions of the question, and then to the nature of economic exchanges between the developing countries and the advanced capitalist societies.

One of the most fundamental puzzles in economics was posed by Adam Smith: 'What determines some nations to be wealthy and others poor?' (1776 [1904]). A long list of economic historians have wrestled with the same question, from Karl Marx, Max Weber, and Emile Durkheim to Arnold Toynbee, Oswald Spengler, Fernand Braudel, and more recently Paul Kennedy and Immanuel Wallerstein, among others. Economic success is closely connected to the ability to industrialize and innovate technologically (Kuznets, 1955). According to Easterlin (1999), the differences in industrialization and technological innovation between western Europe and the developing countries have helped to further the economic growth of the West. Imperialistic exploitation of the New World colonies enabled the European economies to maintain their advantage in world affairs and thus to broaden the economic gap between themselves and the developing countries. Only since the 1960s have some parts of Asia, Latin America, and Northern Africa managed to enter the industrialization process with any degree of

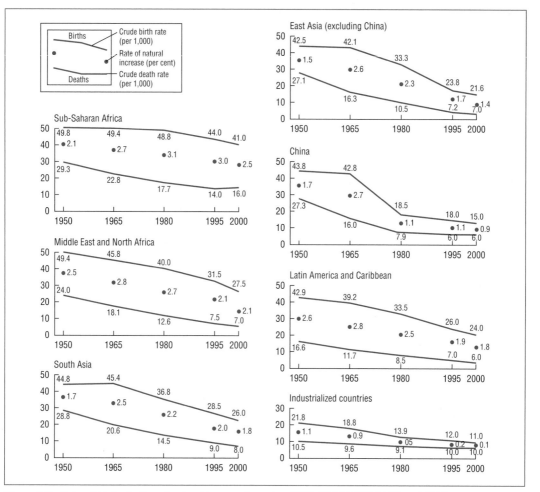

Figure 3.8 Rates of birth, death, and natural increase by region, 1950, 1965, 1980, 1995, and 2000

Note: In each case the upper line shows the crude birth rate per 1,000 and the lower line the crude death rate per 1,000; the numbers in the middle of each graph show the percentage rate of natural increase.

Sources: Donaldson (1991): 12 (Figure 1.1); Population Reference Bureau World Population Data Sheets (1995, 2000).

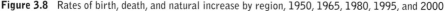

success. The economic advantage of the Western countries can also be attributed to their success in developing the institutional structures necessary to promote the innovation and technological change that spurs further economic growth. This suggests that culture may facilitate economic expansion, insofar as it predisposes a society to seek technological innovation.

The role of culture in economic development is emphasized in Landes (1999), *The Wealth and Poverty of Nations*. Indeed, Landes essentially argues that culture determines the wealth of nations. In his view, the economic success of the West over the past two centuries is the product of ideologies that at least since the fifteenth century—possibly since the tenth—have promoted a culture of freedom for the individual and encouraged the development of institutions to safeguard that freedom. For instance, the introduction of property rights helped to establish the sense of security necessary for the individual to explore new possibilities while encouraging

The damage done by European colonialism around the world is undeniable. Nevertheless, colonialism does not explain all the problems that developing countries face. For instance, a UN-sponsored report on human development in the Arab world (United Nations Development Programme, 2002b), drafted by a group of Middle Eastern intellectuals, acknowledges that many of the socioeconomic problems facing the Arab world have been largely self-created. Among the factors cited by the report are the subjugation of women; political autocracy that ensures censorship, stifles creativity, and promotes corruption; limited use of the Internet; high rates of emigration among talented scientists; high population growth; and a general 'freedom deficit' for a large segment of the region's population.

In a significant number of other developing countries today, social and economic development is constrained by corrupt despotic regimes (Bhagwati, 2000, 2002; Diamond, 1993; *The Economist*, 2003: 28 June–4 July; Harms and Ursprung, 2002). According to Held et al. (1999: 46–7), the largest concentration of authoritarian regimes today is in sub-Saharan Africa. Thousands of people in Congo, Sierra Leone, Sudan, and Liberia have died and millions more have been forced to flee their homes as a result of protracted civil war and unrest (*The Economist*, 2003a, 2003b: 17 May; Stremlau, 2000). Compounding the plight of many of these countries is their vulnerability to natural disasters such as drought. Ethiopia, for example, has endured recurring droughts and famines as well as political instability and conflict: between 1970 and 1980 an estimated 1 to 1.5 million lives were lost as a direct result of war and famine (Lindstrom and Berhanu, 1999: 248; Hill, 2003; Nolen, 2002a, 2002b). Outside Africa, North Korea was devastated by a massive famine caused in part by floods and in part by the withdrawal of aid from the Soviet Union and China beginning in the early 1990s. Although it is difficult to know for certain, it has been estimated that famine-related deaths in North Korea between 1995 and 2000 numbered between 600,000 and 1 million (Goodkind and West, 2001: 220).

the development of the entrepreneurial spirit. As early as the tenth century people in European city states had the freedom to move to other areas of the continent; they could own private property, engage in trade and commerce, accumulate wealth, and create wealth through specialized economic activities. And the rise of commerce and trade in Europe as far back as the Middle Ages set the stage for the Industrial Revolution. Meanwhile, the exploration and colonization of new lands beginning in the fifteenth century brought new wealth to the European empires, stimulating further economic growth at home. From this point of view, Western values are the keys to economic success, and nations that lack or fail to promote those values are doomed to failure.

Of course, a country's natural endowments, its location and environment, also help to determine its economic success. As Diamond (1999: 25) argues, 'history followed different courses for different peoples because of differences among peoples' environments, not because of biological differences among them.' How does geographic location influence a nation's wealth? Landes (1999) suggests that Europe's geography gave it a number of important natural advantages. In addition to a temperate climate, warm winds from the Gulf Stream, gentle rains, water in all seasons, and low rates of evaporation—conditions that favoured dense forests, good crops, and large livestock, all of which contributed to economic growth and the accumulation of wealth—Europeans benefited from navigable rivers, natural seaports, and plentiful mineral resources.

Sachs, Mellinger, and Gallup (2001) attribute international differences in wealth to a series of complex interrelationships between geo-graphic location, climate, and access to sea routes—something that Adam Smith himself suggested. Among the causal mechanisms involved are the influence of climate on disease exposure and prevalence in a geographic area, and the consequences of disease for economic production. For instance, nations in tropical zones generally experience higher rates of infectious diseases such as malaria and lower agricultural productivity than their counterparts in temperate zones. The very poorest regions in the world, these authors say, are those saddled with a tropical or desert environment and without easy access to maritime trade.

Coastal countries with temperate climates such as Germany, these authors note, have lower transportation costs and higher farm productivity than landlocked tropical countries (e.g., Uganda). Among the high-income economies of the world, only Hong Kong, Singapore, and part of Taiwan are in the tropical climate zone. In addition, as Sachs, Mellinger, and Gallup (2001) note, almost all the temperate-zone countries have either high-income economies (North America, western Europe, South Korea, Japan) or middle-income economies burdened by socialist policies in the past (eastern Europe, the former Soviet Union). In some cases there is a strong temperate–tropical divide within countries that include both climate types. Most of Brazil, for example, lies within the tropical zone, but the richest part of the nation—the south—is in the temperate zone (Sachs, Mellinger, and Gallup, 2001: 73). These researchers also point to the influence of geography and climate on food production, noting that tropical environments are plagued by pests and parasites that can devastate both crops and livestock.

Finally, as Sachs, Mellinger, and Gallup (2001) recognize, environmental variables and geographic location together determine both the resources available and a country's ability to exploit them. Access to plentiful resources allows nations to develop the institutions that bolster social well-being and productivity: free markets, equitable tax laws, private property rights, universal education, and health care.

Marxist-oriented writers, by contrast, have seen underdevelopment as a function of European colonization and exploitation and the resulting unequal political and economic relations and exchanges between peripheral and advanced economies (Held et al., 1999; Hoogvelt, 2001; Skartein, 1997). In addition, according to Myrdal (1957), internal economic conditions such as the unequal spread of trade-induced growth from a relatively small export sector (i.e., an urban economy) to a large traditional sector (i.e., a rural economy) increases the income gap between the two sectors and further impoverishes a developing country.

Myrdal's argument associates him with what has come to be known as the *dependency school*. Another proponent of this perspective was Andre Gunder Frank (1969, 1984, 1991) who argued that the developed countries (the centre), through their dominant position in the world economy, have created a chronic situation of dependency among the developing countries (the periphery). Exchange relations between industrialized and developing countries reinforce the development of underdevelopment. For example, direct foreign investment by the centre in the peripheral economy favours the centre, which in addition to surplus profits gains increasing control over the 'satellite' economy, thus aggravating its poverty. Thus, even if foreign investment does raise living standards for the less developed countries, it increases those countries' dependence on the centre. Furthermore, wealth generated by foreign investment is usually not distributed equitably; thus the few rich get richer while the many stay poor—a perfect formula for economic stagnation.

Wallerstein (1974, 1980) took a similar view, seeing peripheral countries as disadvantaged by the 'core' nations (what Frank called 'the centre'). A key difference, however, is that whereas the early dependency theorists focused on specific developing countries or regions, Wallerstein takes a much broader view, focusing on the evolution of the global economy from the six-teenth century to the present and how Western capitalism became the dominant system. For Wallerstein, dependency can be understood only in the context of long-term multinational economic and political interactions. Wallerstein sees the world as consisting of core, semi-peripheral, and peripheral regions, each of which is made up of individual countries con-nected by economic and political exchanges in which the strong core states exercise *hegemonic power* over the dependent states. The intermedi-ate or semiperipheral regions, according to Wallerstein, serve as an economic and political buffer between the core and the periphery, and help to perpetuate the capitalist hegemony by allying themselves with the more politically and economically influential core states while main-taining relations with the peripheral nations.

Like Frank, Wallerstein believes that the unequal trade exchanges between the core and the periphery have created a stratified economy on the world scale. Where the two differ is in their proposed solutions. In Frank's view, the periph-ery should cut all ties with the imperialist centre and develop an anti-bourgeois socialist system of economic production and relations. For Wallerstein, however, the situation is not so straightforward, because the periphery nations are not independent entities; they are a part of a larger system—a world system—consisting of interdependent parts linked and integrated under a system of economic production and exchange. The peripheral nations cannot simply pull out of such a system without endangering themselves economically. Wallerstein's argument seems all the more relevant in the twenty-first century. Contrary to the predictions of the early dependency theorists, some developing coun-tries have benefited significantly from globaliza-tion: witness China, India, the 'Asian Tiger' economies, and some Latin American countries (Stiglitz, 2002, 2003). Notwithstanding the financial crises that countries such as Argentina and Mexico faced in the 1990s, economic and social conditions for many people in the de-veloping world have improved significantly (Firebaugh, 2003; Fischer, 2003; United Nations Development Programme, 2003a, 2003b).

The developing countries recognize that they must participate in the global economy if they wish to raise their standards of living. Unfortu-nately, many of them face multiple challenges, from epidemics such as HIV/AIDS to natural disasters, droughts, famines, and in some cases political instability. At the same time, they must find work for bulging youth populations mov-ing into the prime labour force years. Therefore developing countries, with the help of the de-veloped countries, must do all they can to create jobs and help increase the wealth and prosperity necessary for social development to take place. It is generally agreed among economists (even those who express concerns about globalization) that international trade liberalization, to the extent that it is practised fairly—and this is not always the case—can help poor nations lift themselves out of poverty (Bhagwati, 2002, 2000; Stiglitz, 2002, 2003).

The World Trade Organization (WTO), the International Monetary Fund (IMF), and the World Bank can help in this effort. The failure of past policies such as the structural adjustment programs introduced in the 1980s in parts of Africa and Southeast Asia, as well as Argentina and other countries in Latin America, should serve as lessons to those institutions in their efforts to help poor countries move towards economic stability and social development. One hopeful step in this direction is the pro-gram of debt relief for the poorest countries introduced by the IMF and the World Bank in 1996 (United Nations Development Pro-gramme 2003b: 152).

Mechanisms of Demographic Transition: Western and Non-Western Cases

The forces that sparked the demographic transi-tion in western Europe were endogenous to European society, the cumulative effects of inno-vations and structural changes that, by improv-ing living conditions over a long period of time, served to gradually reduce mortality (i.e., increased food supply, better nutrition, rapid urbanization and industrialization, improvements in hygiene, public health, and modern medicine). By contrast, the causes of the widespread mortality declines in the developing countries since the 1950s have been largely exogenous, the product of outside intervention in the form of aid and assistance from the industrialized countries. Preston (1980) points to the West's introduction of public health programs (e.g., anti-malaria and immunization campaigns) as a major factor in the reduction of mortality in the developing countries, beginning around 1930. Family planning programs have also played an important part. The resulting mortality declines have, in general, been considerably more precipitous than was the case in Europe.

A multitude of social, cultural, and economic factors contributed to the massive downturn in western Europe's fertility rates between the mid-1800s and the first three decades of the 1900s. Some demographic scholars—*innovation theorists*—have emphasized the role played by new contraceptive technologies and new ideas emphasizing small families (Bulatao, 2001; Carlson, 1966; Cleland and Wilson, 1987; Caldwell, 1976; Lesthaeghe, 1983). Others—known as *adjustment theorists*—have suggested that new socioeconomic opportunities in a context of industrialization and urbanization made large families less desirable than they had been in the past (Davis, 1963; Friedlander, 1969; Becker, 1960).

According to innovation theorists, the idea of limiting family size was foreign to most people before the mid-1800s and spread only gradually, beginning with the upper classes and the urban population. Van de Walle has suggested that 'the perception of a particular family size as a goal' (1992: 490) was generally non-existent prior to the nineteenth century. The invention of modern birth control, then, can be seen as a product of growing demand for an effective way of achieving the desired family size. Ariès (1980) has argued that the emergence of the small-family ideal reflected the desire of parents in the nineteenth century to do all they could to ensure that their progeny would have the best possible life. Having fewer children made it possible to devote more time, care, and resources to each child.

Adjustment theorists, on the other hand, maintain that different methods of family limitation, most notably coitus interruptus, have been known throughout human history; what was lacking until the nineteenth century was the motivation for most couples to apply that knowledge. With socioeconomic modernization, however, couples began to see the advantages of curtailing their fertility through whatever means might be available, including the use of modern contraceptives. According to this theory, then, the fertility transition in western Europe emanated not from a novel idea or technology (i.e., modern birth control), but from an adjustment process, whereby adults began to see tangible advantages in having fewer children.

In the case of western Europe, innovation and adjustment may both have contributed to the fertility transition (Knodel, 1977). As Europeans came to enjoy better standards of living, many structural changes were introduced to promote the well-being of the individual. With the introduction of mandatory education, for instance, society began to see the child as something more than an extra set of hands to work on the family farm. As the costs of raising children increased, parents began to look for ways to prevent unwanted births. As already suggested, the development of modern birth control during the later part of the 1800s was largely a consequence of this ideational shift along with new attitudes toward the importance of the child. The child became the centre of the family (Ariès, 1980), and the ideal of the small family gradually diffused throughout Western society. The result was a long-term decline in the birth rate, beginning around 1850. (We will return to this topic in Chapter 6.)

Explanations for the fertility transition in developing countries also point to a wide range of factors, cultural, social, economic, and demographic (Cleland and Wilson, 1987; Hirschman, 1994; Mason, 1997a; Caldwell, 1976; Easterlin, 1983). The central factors, however, appear to be the rapid spread of Western ideas and a change in the way parents and society think about children. With modernization, the nuclear family takes priority over the extended family; couples move away from the larger family constellation and set up independent households (Caldwell, 1976). In the course of this nucleation process, the child in particular becomes the focus of attention in the family. Compulsory education further elevates children's status in the society, and the intergenerational flow of wealth (i.e., money, time, and resources) shifts so that children are no longer seen primarily in terms of their economic contributions to the family; rather, parents come to see them as persons in whom it is worth investing time and resources to promote their well-being and development. Eventually, as in the West, this change in the way children are perceived leads parents to desire fewer children. For Caldwell, these structural and ideational shifts in developing societies are necessary conditions for the fertility transition to begin.

Another effect of socioeconomic modernization is a decline in infant and child mortality. As childhood survival rates improve, couples adjust their ideal family size to favour fewer children. And as traditional norms and values erode, couples will increasingly resort to modern contraceptives and family planning methods. Improvements in the status of women through education and increased access to economic independence can also contribute to rapid changes in fertility rates (Robey, Rutestein, and Morris, 1993).

What differentiates the countries that have embarked on the transition from those that have not is the degree to which (1) couples are emotionally nucleated and (2) the child occupies a central place in the family and society. As the economic value of children falls, their value to parents increasingly lies in the realm of emotions. On a broader level, the transitional societies undergoing these types of social-

psychological and economic changes tend to enjoy greater access to health and family planning programs, and have governments strongly committed to family planning. Thus institutional factors also play an important role (Ross and Mauldin, 1996; Berelson et al., 1990).

Demographic Transition and World Population Growth

A number of generalizations about population history can now be laid out. First, the prime cause of the world population explosion was the dramatic decline in death rates in Europe starting in the eighteenth century, at a time when fertility rates remained high. Declining mortality coupled with persistently high fertility fuelled a 'population explosion' that began around 1750 and picked up steam over the following century and a half (McKeown, 1976). Second, now that the Western nations, Japan, and other industrialized countries are well into the post-transition stage they are experiencing very low growth—with the result that developing countries still undergoing the transition now account for most of the world's population growth.

World Population Futures

The global population growth rate has been declining steadily for three decades. This trend is expected to continue into the foreseeable future. By 2050 the rate may even fall below 0.5 per cent (Bongaarts and Bulatao, 2000: 20; Eberstad, 1997; Lutz, 1994; United Nations Department of Economic and Social Affairs Population Division, 1999, 2003b, 2006e). This remarkable reduction will come about as a result of anticipated declines in fertility and mortality over the next half century.

Population Projections

A *population projection* is a computational exercise intended to determine a future population's size and age–sex distribution (Haub, 1987: 7), based on anticipated changes over a specified period in rates of birth, death, and, where appropriate, migration (projections for a specific country or region would consider migration, whereas projections for the world as a whole would not). Typically, historical data are used to create statistical models depicting temporal trends in fertility, mortality, and migration; then the parameter values from those models are used to extrapolate further changes in these variables over the specified time of the projection. Separate projections are prepared for fertility, mortality, and migration; then those results are combined to compute the projected population. Usually, several projections are prepared for a given target date, based on different sets of assumptions. For instance, the United Nations (2006e) projections of the world's population to 2050 were based on low, medium, and high variant assumptions regarding the timing, degree, and direction of change in fertility and mortality over the projection period. The base population for the projections is usually obtained from the latest census or population estimates. What is considered a 'low', 'medium', or 'high' scenario depends on the analyst's own understanding of why and how fertility and mortality rates change historically. Much also depends on the ability to anticipate circumstances or conditions in society between the present and the future that could cause fertility and mortality (and migration where applicable) to increase or decrease. Thus the calculation of population projections requires historical data analysis as well as a strong appreciation of demographic theory. Although demographers take great care in determining the assumptions they will use, projections are very sensitive to changes in fertility, which can be an unpredictable variable. Even small changes in fertility can have dramatic effects on the projected population.

Typically, the 'medium variant' (or 'central') projection is considered the most realistic one. According to the central projection in Table 3.3, the world's population in 2050 will likely reach just over 9 billion. But the high variant scenario produces a total of more than 10 billion, and the 'constant' model—which assumes that fertility will remain at its present level—projects a population of more than 11 billion in 2050.

Figure 3.9 depicts these possible futures in graphic form. Of particular note is the 'low variant' possibility of a downswing beginning around 2030, which would produce a population in 2050 of just under 7.5 billion. But this is still a gain of approximately 1.2 billion over the 2006 total of 6.5 billion. Why is continuing growth until the third decade of this century considered unavoidable?

Population Momentum

As a legacy of past high fertility, the proportion of the world's population in the reproductive ages today is still growing and will continue to grow over the next several decades. What makes this inevitable is *population momentum* (Bongaarts and Bulatao, 2000; Cohen, 2003; Lutz, 1994). Underlying the concept of population momentum (to be discussed in greater detail in Chapters 4 and 6) is the fact that for any population the demography of the future is inseparable from the demography of the past. As an illustration, suppose that fertility rates around the world were to fall overnight to replacement level—2.1 children per woman (the extra '.1' allows for low to moderate mortality among women of childbearing age)—while mortality remained constant: despite this new fertility regime, the total population would ultimately number more than the current population. The difference between the two population sizes would reflect population momentum: the amount of unavoidable growth that is built into the current age structure of the population. The reason for this effect is that high fertility levels in the past have produced a largely young population that has yet to reach the childbearing years. As this population gradually progresses through the childbearing years, it will produce many offspring and, as a result, the population will expand beyond its current size.

In theory, population momentum can also operate in the opposite direction (negative

Table 3.3 Population estimates and projections, 1950, 2005, and 2050, based on different variants

Region	Estimated population (millions)		Projected population (millions) in 2050, by type of variant			
	1950	2005	Low	Medium	High	Constant
World	**2,519 (100)**	**6,465 (100)**	**7,680 (100)**	**9,076 (100)**	**10,646 (100)**	**11,658 (100)**
More developed regions	813 (32.2)	1,211 (18.7)	1,057 (13.8)	1,236 (13.8)	1,440 (13.6)	1,195 (10.3)
Less developed regions	1,707 (67.6)	5,253 (81.3)	6,622 (86.2)	7,840 (86.2)	9,206 (19.1)	10,463 (89.7)
Least developed countries	201	759	1,497	1,735	1,994	2,744
Other less developed countries	1,506	4,494	5,126	6,104	7,213	7,719
Africa	224(8.9)	906 (14.0)	1,666 (21.7)	1,937 (21.7)	2,228 (21.3)	3,100 (26.6)
Asia	1,396 (55.4)	3,905 (60.4)	4,388 (57.1)	5,217 (57.1)	6,161 (57.5)	6,487 (55.6)
Europe	547 (21.7)	728 (11.3)	557 (7.2)	653 (7.2)	764 (7.2)	606 (5.2)
Latin America/ Caribbean	167 (6.6)	561 (8.7)	653 (8.5)	783 (8.5)	930 (8.6)	957 (8.2)
Northern America	172 (6.8)	331 (5.1)	375 (4.9)	438 (5.6)	509 (4.8)	454 (3.9)
Oceania	13 (0.5)	33 (0.5)	41 (0.5)	48 (0.5)	55 (0.5)	55 (0.5)

Notes: Numbers in parentheses are percentages. The sum of least developed and other less developed countries is the total population for the less developed countries. The sum of the six regions is the overall world total population.

The United Nations (2003: xiv) counts as 'less developed regions' the regions of Africa, Asia (excluding Japan), Latin America and the Caribbean, as well as Melanesia, Micronesia, and Polynesia. The 'more developed' regions are Australia/New Zealand, Europe, Northern America, and Japan. The least developed countries are 49 nations: Afghanistan, Angola, Bangladesh, Benin, Bhutan, Burkina Faso, Burundi, Cambodia, Cape Verde, Central African Republic, Chad, Comoros, Democratic Republic of the Congo, Djibouti, Equatorial Guinea, Eritrea, Ethiopia, Gambia, Guinea, Guinea–Bissau, Haiti, Kiribati, Lao People's Democratic Republic, Lesotho, Liberia, Madagascar, Malawi, Maldives, Mali, Mauritania, Mozambique, Myanmar, Nepal, Niger, Rwanda, Samoa, Sao Tome and Principe, Senegal, Sierra Leone, Solomon Islands, Somalia, Sudan, Togo, Tuvalu, Uganda, United Republic of Tanzania, Vanuatu, Yemen, and Zambia.

Source: United Nations Population Division (2006e): vol. 3, xviii. Reprinted with the permission of the United Nations.

momentum). For example, if a population experienced a prolonged period of below-replacement fertility—say three or more decades—and then suddenly saw an increase to the replacement level of 2.1 children per woman, the 'ultimate' population would be smaller than the current actual population. So, in this case, momentum translates into population decline despite a fertility increase. The reason for this effect is the prolonged period of below-replacement fertility in the past, which has produced a population made up largely of older people, with relatively few people in the younger age groups. As these smaller cohorts pass through

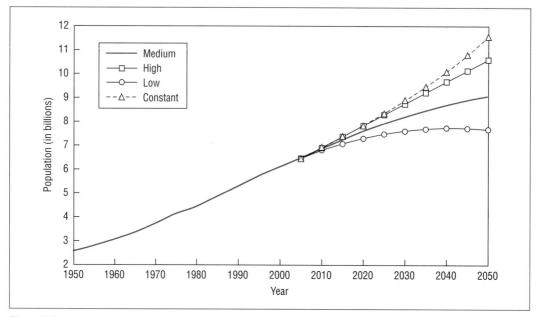

Figure 3.9 Estimated and projected population of the world by projection variant, 1950–2050

Source: United Nations Department of Economic and Social Affairs Population Division (2006d): 8 (Figure I.2). Reprinted with the permission of the United Nations.

their childbearing years, they will produce relatively few children and, ultimately, a smaller population.

Some Demographic Certainties for the Future

However uncertain population projections may be, there are some demographic trends that seem beyond doubt. In some of the industrialized countries, sustained sub-replacement fertility rates coupled with demographic aging are bound to produce a demographic implosion (Bongaarts and Bulatao, 2000; Eberstadt, 1997; Lutz, 1994; Teitelbaum and Winter, 1985). Most population growth over the next half century will take place in the least developed countries, where rates of natural increase today generally range between 1.6 and 2.5 per cent a year. Africa's share of the world's population will increase despite the ravages of HIV/AIDS; in fact, the region that has been hit hardest could still see its population more than double over the next 50 years (United Nations Department of Economic and Social Affairs Population Division, 2006a).

Over the course of this century all populations will become older, but the effect will be most pronounced in the countries where fertility reductions have been most rapid and sustained. According to some estimates, 16 per cent of the world's population in 2050 will be over the age of 65. Seniors will account for almost 26 per cent of the population in the industrial countries, and 15 per cent in the developing world as a whole (Bongaarts and Bulatao, 2000: 23). Worldwide, seniors are likely to number some 1.9 billion in 2050 (United Nations Population Division, 2003: 16). In the parts of the world where population aging is most advanced, Europe and Japan, 35 per cent of the populations will likely be over 60 in 2050. Among the transitional countries where the senior population is expected to increase substantially are Armenia, the Czech Republic, Estonia, Latvia, and Singapore. Africa will continue to have the youngest population overall, though the proportion of elderly people there will increase as well.

Finally, only one industrialized country is expected to be among the top 10 populations in 2050. The most populous countries will likely be the following (in order of projected population): India (1.6 billion); China (1.4 billion); the United States (420 million); Nigeria (299 million); Pakistan (295 million); Indonesia (285 million); Brazil (260 million); Bangladesh (231 million); the Democratic Republic of Congo (183 million); and Ethiopia (145 million) (Population Reference Bureau, 2006).

The Distant Future

The United Nations has recently published a series of long-term projections for the world and its regions to the year 2300, using a variety of assumptions (United Nations Department of Economic and Social Affairs Population Division, 2004). In 2300 the global population could number anywhere from 2.31 (low variant) to 36.44 billion (high variant). The medium-variant projection works out to 8.97 billion—approximately 2.3 billion more than in 2007.

Canadian Population History: An Overview

As one of the world's most advanced nations, Canada enjoys exceptionally favourable natural, social, economic, and demographic conditions. Birth and death rates are among the lowest in the world, and the annual rate of natural increase is currently less than 1 per cent. Its approximately 32 million people (as of 2006) are concentrated in a relatively narrow strip of the geographic landmass: along the Atlantic seaboard, down the St Lawrence River system to the Great Lakes region, then along the 49th parallel to the Pacific coast (see Figure 3.10). Only a small proportion of Canadians (mainly Aboriginal) live in the northern regions of

Nunavut, Yukon, and the Northwest Territories. The 10 provinces are predominantly urban: more than two-thirds of Canadians live in the three largest Census Metropolitan Areas (Toronto, Montreal, and Vancouver). Low rates of fertility since the mid-1970s have caused the average age of the population to climb steadily, from 22 in 1921 to 37.3 in 2001, and 39.5 in 2006 (Statistics Canada, 2007: 4). Today Canada's population growth depends more largely on immigration and than on natural increase.

Figure 3.11 shows the contributions of natural increase and net migration to population growth. Until very recently, natural increase was the driving force behind Canada's population growth, contributing most of the total gains between census periods from 1851 to 2001. Before the mid-1980s, the effect of net migration on overall population growth was, in general, substantially lower than that of natural increase. The only exception was during the decade from 1901 to 1911, when more than 1.5 million newcomers, mainly from eastern and northwestern Europe, took up the Laurier government's offer of free land in the Prairie West. To this day, that wave of immigration remains the largest in Canada's history. The contribution of net migration to total population growth was negative between 1851 and 1901, largely as a result of heavy emigration from Canada to the US, where economic opportunities were greater. A period of very low immigration was 1931–41, when the Great Depression brought immigration to almost a halt.

Since the end of World War II—and particularly from the middle part of the 1960s onwards—immigration has accounted for an increasing share of population growth: from almost 29 per cent of the total in 1951–6 to more than 50 per cent in 1996–2001. The importance of immigration to the maintenance of Canada's population over the long-term future is underlined by the fact that, overall, the average annual rates of population increase have been falling ever since the mid-1950s, when the post-war baby boom reached its height.

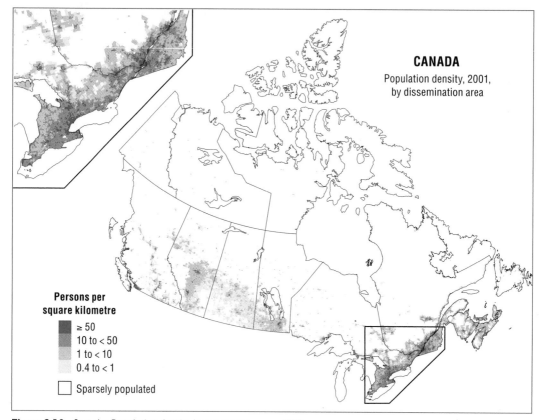

Figure 3.10 Canada: Population density by geographic area, 2001

Source: Adapted from Statistics Canada publication *Census of Canada 2002*.

Demographic Conditions in the Frontier Society

The demography of Canada has changed significantly over the past century and a half. At the time of Confederation, in 1867, the country consisted of Lower Canada (Quebec), Upper Canada (Ontario), Nova Scotia, and New Brunswick. Although demographic data for Quebec is available as far back as 1608, and the populations of the Maritime provinces and Upper Canada were enumerated at various times before Confederation, the country did not establish a national statistics system until 1921, and it is only since 1949, when Newfoundland entered Confederation, that we have had a full demographic account of Canada as it exists today.

The Demographic Transition in Quebec and Canada

From the founding of Quebec in 1608 through the end of the French regime in 1760, detailed records of marriages, baptisms, and burials were kept both by the French authorities and by local parish priests. Demographers at the University of Montreal have used these records to construct a picture of the demographic realities of the frontier society (e.g., Charbonneau, 1973, 1975; Charbonneau et al., 2000; Gauvreau, 1991; Henripin, 1954; Henripin and Péron, 1972; Pelletier, Legare, and Bourbeau, 1997; Trudel, 1973).

From a handful of settlers in 1608, the population of New France mushroomed to 50,000 in 1750. Remarkably, most of this growth was

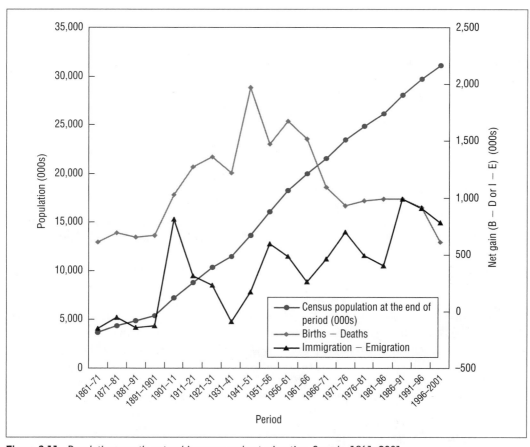

Figure 3.11 Population growth, natural increase, and net migration, Canada, 1861–2001

Source: Based on Statistics Canada data available at www.statcan.ca/english/Pgdb/demo03.htm (accessed 9 Sept. 2003).

the result of natural increase. Charbonneau et al. (2000: 106–11) estimate that New France received fewer than 25,000 immigrants. The overwhelming majority of these people were men: soldiers, indentured workers, clerics, even some prisoners. During the 1660s, however, the French Crown subsidized the immigration of hundreds of young women of marriageable age. Known as the 'filles du roi' (the king's daughters), they helped to balance the sex ratio.

The demographic success of New France can be attributed to three key factors: (1) high marriage rates and early entry into marriage, (2) exceptionally high fertility, and (3) death rates that were somewhat lower than might be expected for a frontier society (Henripin, 1994; Livi-Bacci, 1997: 63). Data assembled by Henripin and Péron (1972) suggest that from 1711 to 1760, crude death rates generally fluctuated between about 20 and 27 per 1,000 population. By the end of this period, however, the death rate had risen to almost 40 per 1,000. From around 30 per 1,000 in the mid-1760s, the crude death rate then began a gradual—if irregular—descent that continued through the early 1800s, when a more precipitous and sustained drop began (see Figure 3.13). By 1951 crude death rates in Quebec had reached modern levels (8 to 10 per 1,000 population); birth rates, however, stayed in the vicinity of 30 per 1,000.

The Aboriginal Population of the St Lawrence Valley: From Near-Extinction to Recovery

Beginning in the sixteenth century in and around the St Lawrence Valley, the demographic history of Canada's Aboriginal peoples was profoundly affected by the arrival of Europeans. We know that Aboriginal populations were devastated over the centuries that followed by (among other things) exposure to new diseases against which they had no natural immunity; warfare with Europeans and European-inspired conflict among themselves; European weaponry; and famines resulting from the Europeans' appropriation of their lands. Determining the extent of that devastation, however, remains a challenge because it is so difficult to estimate the size of pre-contact populations.

According to Dickinson and Young (2003: 5), at the beginning of the sixteenth century (circa 1500) the main Aboriginal groups in the eastern part of what is now Canada and the northeast United States were the Algonquin and the Iroquois. These authors estimate their combined population to have been about 270,000: 170,000 Algonquin (70,000 in central and eastern Canada and 100,000 in New England) and 100,000 Iroquois (in the Chesapeake Bay area, the Lower Great Lakes, and along the upper St Lawrence Valley). To the north the Inuit numbered perhaps 25,000 in total, of whom 3,000 were settled in Quebec and Labrador. In the region of French settlement along the St Lawrence, the Aboriginal population fell so dramatically that the Europeans were in the majority by 1650 (Dickinson and Young, 2003: 20).

On the broader scale, Thornton (2000: 11) suggests that the Aboriginal population of the Western Hemisphere as a whole at the time of first contact was probably about 75 million. The population decline that began at that time continued for roughly four centuries. Figure 3.12 shows the birth-rate trajectories for the Aboriginal population and New France–Canada from 1650 to 2006. The drop in Aboriginal birth rates following European contact is clear, starting in the early 1700s and reaching its lowest point in the 1820s and 1830s. Aboriginal population numbers began to recover around the turn of the twentieth century, and the recovery continues to this day. High rates of natural increase in the Aboriginal population reflect both persistently high fertility—attributable to social isolation, poverty, and possibly also a pronatalist culture—and substantial declines in death rates. A number of factors associated with socioeconomic modernization helped to delay the peak of the baby boom among Canada's Aboriginal people by roughly a decade (Jaffe, 1992; Romaniuk, 1980, 2008). One such factor was the decision of many Aboriginal mothers to abandon breast-feeding for bottle-feeding. Since breast-feeding serves as a natural contraceptive, this change meant that many became pregnant again sooner than they would have in the past. Consequently, Aboriginal fertility increased in the early 1960s. Fertility eventually began to decline as modern contraception became widely available to Aboriginal women (Romaniuk, 1980).

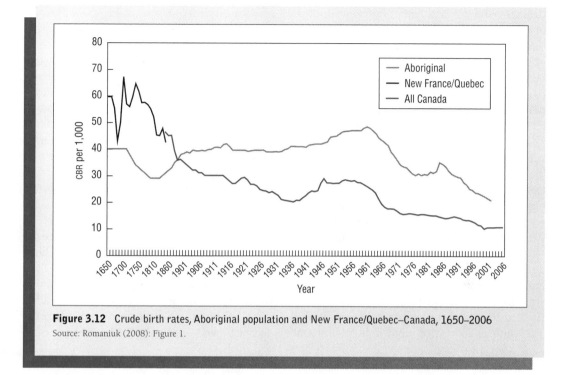

Figure 3.12 Crude birth rates, Aboriginal population and New France/Quebec–Canada, 1650–2006
Source: Romaniuk (2008): Figure 1.

Infant mortality in the first half of the eighteenth century remained very high, perhaps reaching 246 per 1,000 births (Henripin and Péron, 1972: 225), and did not fall below 100 per 1,000 births until the early 1920s (Beaujot, 2000: 211). The crude birth rate in New France was always considerably higher than the crude death rate, ranging between 51 and 56 per 1,000 population between the periods of 1711–15 and 1756–60. At that point it began to decline, picking up speed after the 1820s and reaching a low of about 30 births per 1,000 population by the early 1950s. The large difference in the two vital rates between the late 1770s and 1951 produced very high rates of natural increase—in the range of 2.5 per cent per annum on average (Charbonneau et al., 2000: 131).

McVey and Kalbach (1995: 36) point out that Quebec did not follow the typical pattern for the Western demographic transition, in which a permanent and progressive decline in death rates

preceded a decline in fertility: rather, in Quebec 'both birth and death rates appear to have been decreasing at approximately the same pace since 1770 or 1780, with birth rates beginning to decline more rapidly after the year 1850.'

Marriage was practically universal in colonial French Canada. Charbonneau and colleagues (2000: 116) calculated that in the 1600s the average age at marriage was 28 for men and 19 for women. In about 13 per cent of all cases a single male married a widow (large numbers of widows reflecting the higher mortality of males). Under the prevailing mortality conditions, widowhood occurred on the average around age 51 for men and 47 for women. Roughly 60 per cent of marriages in the colony of the St Lawrence Valley would have been broken by the death of the husband; about 36 per cent of widows, and 50 per cent of widowers, would remarry. These figures improved slightly in the following century, when fewer marriages were ended by the death of the husband and fewer weddings involved a single man and a widowed woman (see Table 3.4).

As women married relatively early in life, most were probably in their late teens or early twenties when they first gave birth. Children must have been closely spaced, the only limits on conception being postpartum amenorrhea, spontaneous abortion, natural sterility, infant mortality, and widowhood. In a context of 'natural fertility' conditions—i.e., a general absence of conscious family limitation (Bongaarts, 1978)—childbearing would have continued until fairly late in a woman's life (Charbonneau et al., 2000: 118–19).

Estimates by Henripin and Péron (1972: 220) for the period from 1711 to 1886 indicate an average family size of 7.1 for French Canadians. Birth rates in Quebec remained well above the Canadian average until the early 1960s. Then, in the context of rapid industrialization and urbanization known as the 'Quiet Revolution', the Liberal government of Premier Jean Lesage removed the Church from its traditional position of authority, especially with respect to education (Dickinson and Young, 2003). The profound changes associated with the 'Quiet Revolution' set in motion a massive fertility decline as the 'revenge of the cradle' strategy—by which the francophone minority had sought to maintain itself by sheer force of numbers—gave way to a new ethos of individualism and secularism in a context of newly emerging socioeconomic opportunities for the people of Quebec.

Demographic conditions in the rest of Canada have also changed considerably since the days of the frontier. Before the mid-1800s, birth and death rates here, as elsewhere, would have risen and fallen in response to unpredictable social and environmental conditions (Jaffe, 1992), although the crude death rate when the decline began was only about 15 per 1,000 popu-

Table 3.4   Selected demographic parameters for the French-Canadian population of the St Lawrence Valley (New France), c.1608–1760

Variable	Nuptiality		Fertility	Mortality
	17th century	18th century	1608–1760	1608–1760
Average age at marriage: Male	28.1	27.0		
Average age at marriage: Female	18.9	22.2		
% marriages broken by death of husband	61.8	54.8		
Average age at widowhood: Males	50.8	50.0		
Average age at widowhood: Females	47.3	49.8		
Fertility rate at age 30 (per 1,000, all ages at marriage)			479	
Duration of the interval (average number of months) between marriage and the first birth (women married at age 20–24)			14.3	
Average age at birth of last child (women married before age 20)			40.1	
Completed fertility for women married before age 20 (average number of children)			11.8	
Infant mortality rate (per 1,000 births)				225
Life expectancy at birth (both sexes)				35.5

Source: Adapted from Charbonneau et al. (2000): 116, 123, 126.

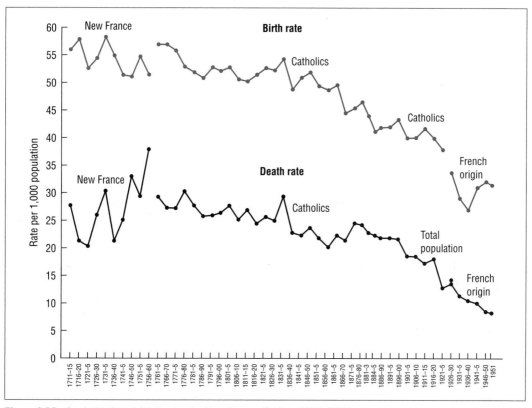

Figure 3.13 Crude birth and death rates for New France–Quebec, 1711–1951

Note: Due to limited availability of data, the series pertain to different sections of Quebec's population at different points in history.
Source: Henripin and Peron (1972): 224.

lation—a rate that in Europe was not generally seen until well into the twentieth century. The mortality decline that began in the 1850s has continued ever since and, except during the baby boom period (1946–66), has been accompanied by a parallel decline in the birth rate.

As a result of large-scale reductions in mortality and fertility over the last century, life course events that were 'expected' in early Canadian society, such as the early loss of a spouse or the death of a child, are now relatively rare (see Table 3.5). Life has become more 'predictable' for the average person, and death has become increasingly removed from day-to-day personal experience. In 1851, some 20 per cent of infants would fail to reach their first birthday; today, infant mortality is just above 5 per 1,000

births (Beaujot and McQuillan, 1982; Population Reference Bureau, 2007). Parents today can be almost certain that their offspring will survive to adulthood. Consequently, the typical couple has only one or two closely spaced children (Grindstaff, 1995, 1994; 1975; Ram and Rahudry, 1993).

Gee (1994) has constructed a statistical portrait of the typical life course for different birth cohorts of Canadian women. Women born between 1831 and 1840 married for the first time around the age of 25 and bore their first and last children at ages 27 and 41, respectively. Women born in the decade before 1900 tended to marry slightly earlier, at age 23.4; they bore their first and last children earlier as well, at ages 25.4 and 33.9. Among more recent cohorts,

Table 3.5 Demographic parameters for Canada, selected periods, 1851–2001

Variable	1851	1891	1901	1921	1931	1946	1951	1981	1991	2001
% married, age 30–54: Males				77.7	78.2		83.4	85.9	73.3	71.5
% married, age 30–54: Females				80.5	80.9	78.6	82.7	84.5	74.0	74.9
% married population 15+	54.8	53.0		62.0	59.0		64.2			59.5
Average age at marriage: Brides		23.8	24.6	25.5		24.1	23.8	25.7	28.8	31.2
Marriage rate per 1,000 population				7.9	6.4	10.9	9.2	7.8	6.4	5.1
Common-law unions as % of all unions								5.6	9.9	16.0
Crude birth rate	46.2		29.8		23.2	27.2	15.3	15.3	14.0	10.7
Crude death rate	22.2		14.4	11.6	10.5	9.4	10.1	7.0	6.9	7.3
Total fertility rate	7.030		4.009		3.200	3.360	3.503	1.704	1.710	1.510
Life expectancy at birth (both sexes)	41.1	45.2	50.2	59.7	62.1	66.8	70.8	79.0	77.8	79.7
Infant mortality rate (per 1,000 births)			139	102.2	86.0	47.8	39.0	9.0	6.4	5.3
Median age of mother at first birth						24.2	23.5	24.7	25.8	27.4

Sources: Basavarajappa and Ram (1983): A110–153; Beaujot (1995): 38; Beaujot and McQuillan (1982a); Bélanger (2002): 16–19; McInnis (2000b): 547, 596–9; McVey and Kalbach (1995): 225, 245; Peron and Strohmenger (1985): 115, 202; Statistics Canada (various).

these formative events have generally been 'compressed' into fewer years. Thus women born between 1951 and 1960 typically married at age 22.5, bore their first child at age 25.4, and completed their childbearing by age 26.3, according to Gee (1994).The median age of mothers at the birth of their first child has changed significantly since 1946, when it was 24.2; by 1981 it was to 24.7, and by 2001 it had risen to 27.4.

Gee's (1994) analysis of female cohorts at the end of their childbearing years indicates that the percentage of ever-married women without children declined from 12.8 per cent for the cohort born between 1861 and 1876 to just 7.2 per cent for the 1932–36 cohort. Among more recent cohorts, however, particularly those born after 1945, the percentage of women still childless at the end of their childbearing years (age 50) is likely to increase; although the cause in some cases will be involuntary (e.g., sterility), most of the increase is likely to reflect voluntary decisions. In fact, the proportions of ever-married women who have remained childless from census to census since 1961 have clearly increased over time. This can be explained by the tendency to delay marriage and childbearing, which has the effect of raising the incidence of childlessness (Grindstaff, 1995).

What will the demographic future hold for Canada? The population dynamics of highly industrialized countries such as Canada, the United States, the United Kingdom, France, Australia, and New Zealand have converged significantly since the early 1950s. But despite their similarities in fertility and mortality, they show substantial differences in their age distributions (Keyfitz, 1987). Part of the variation can be attributed to differences in immigration patterns, and part to the different trajectories that the declines in their birth rates have followed. Historical events such as wars also help to explain differences in age distribution and associated birth deficits among certain age cohorts. In 1987 Keyfitz predicted that by the second decade of the twenty-first century Canada would see a near doubling of its population aged 50 and older, and a decline of 10 per cent or more in its population around the age of 20. Consistent with this prediction, the 2006 census confirmed that the senior population (aged 65 and older) has been increasing steadily since 1951, and that the population aged 15 and under has been declining since 1966, so that the two trends can be expected to converge by 2015 or thereabouts, at which point seniors will begin to outnumber youth (Statistics Canada, 2007b).

The long-term demographic destiny of any population is largely a function of its fertility levels and trends. Today, however, the future for countries like Canada also depends heavily on international migration. If Canada's current low fertility rates remain stable, the median age of the population will continue to rise and the crude death rate will increase, with the result that natural increase will turn negative in the near future. Under these demographic conditions, the only realistic way to maintain population growth will be through increased immigration.

Recent medium-variant projections released by Statistics Canada (Belanger, Martel, and Caron-Malenfant, 2005) suggest that Canada's population could reach 39 million by 2031 and approach 43 million by 2056. By about 2010, however, the number of deaths each year in Canada will likely exceed the number of births. Thus immigration will become more important than ever for the maintenance of population growth. Finally, seven trends seem destined to intensify as we approach the second decade of the twenty-first century:

1. *Reliance on immigration from non-European countries*. At present Canada receives approximately 200,000 new immigrants each year. Until the 1960s most newcomers came from Europe and the United States. Since the liberalization of immigration policy in the 1970s, however, the majority have come from Asia, Latin America, and Africa.

2. *Ethnic diversity and emphasis on multiculturalism*. The traditional French–British cultural and linguistic dichotomy will certainly continue, but Canadians' conception of the country increasingly reflects its cultural diversity.

3. *Concentration of immigrants in Toronto and Vancouver*. Toronto and Vancouver are the most diverse metropolitan areas in the country and attract the majority of newcomers. As of 2001, immigrants made up 47 and 38 per cent of the populations of Toronto and Vancouver, respectively (Parkin, 2003: 6).

4. *Mixing of ethnicities*. Recent censuses have found more and more Canadians reporting more than one ethnicity. This trend suggests that ethnic intermarriage is also increasing (Krotki and Odynak, 1990; Krotki, 1997).

5. *Growth of the Aboriginal population*. Having undergone periods of severe decline in the past, the Aboriginal population has been growing significantly in recent years, and its rates of natural increase are well above the national average. In the 2001 census 3.4 per cent of Canadians (1.3 million) reported having some Aboriginal ancestry; some part of this increase may also reflect a growing willingness to claim Aboriginal identity (Parkin, 2003: 4). Future projections indicate that the proportion of Canadians reporting Aboriginal ancestry will likely reach 4.1 per cent by 2017 (Statistics Canada, *The Daily*, 2005d).

6. *Growth of the female labour force*. Women have been entering the paid labour force in increasing numbers since the late 1950s. In 1951 about 20 per cent of Canadian women in the working ages were members of the

paid labour force; in 1999 this figure was close to 60 per cent (Statistics Canada, 1999). The demographic ramifications of this trend are already being felt (e.g., delayed marriage, fewer children).

7. *Growing diversity of family configurations*. Canadians are becoming increasingly accepting of non-traditional family forms. Cohabitation is now common, accounting for 16 per cent of all unions in Canada in 2001. In 2005, the Civil Marriage Act made same-sex marriage legal across the country. The 2006 census counted 43,345 same-sex couples in Canada (Statistics Canada, 2007d).

Conclusion

In addition to surveying the overall growth of the human population from ancient times to the present, this chapter has looked at projections for the near-term future. Much of the discussion centred on the demographic transition as a generalized pattern of change in vital rates that all societies can expect to undergo as they move into the modern industrial age. Particular attention was directed to the social, cultural, and economic factors that have typically delayed the onset of the demographic transition in the developing world. Societies described as transitional have made significant economic and demographic progress in recent decades and are now either very close to completing their transitions or have recently completed the transition. By contrast, a number of societies—mostly in sub-Saharan Africa and parts of Asia—have experienced significant delays in their demographic transitions and have only recently begun to show sustained fertility declines. While death rates have been reduced over time, some of these countries have been severely affected by HIV/AIDS, with the result that in some cases mortality rates have once again started to rise. Nevertheless, a significant portion of the anticipated growth in human numbers to the year 2050 will take place in the poorest regions of the world.

Meanwhile, the industrialized countries that have completed their transitions are now experiencing significant demographic aging. Eventually, as birth rates everywhere decline, the average age of all the world's people will inevitably rise.

The second part of this chapter looked at Canada's demographic history, with a particular focus on Quebec. The demographic transitions of Quebec and Canada were also examined and compared to the typical western European pattern.

Four years after Confederation, the 1871 census counted a total population of roughly 3.7 million people. As recently as 1931 Canadian society was still predominantly rural. Today, by contrast, Canada is an overwhelmingly urban, industrial—some would say postmodern—society of more than 32 million people. Though its birth rate is now one of the lowest in the world, the population is expected to continue growing as immigrants continue to arrive from all over the world.

Notes for Further Study

Population Growth Models and Doubling Time

In the absence of migration, a population will grow if the birth rate exceeds the death rate. The difference between these two rates is the rate of natural increase (RNI), commonly expressed as $RNI = (CBR/1,000 - CDR/1,000) \times 100$. RNI can be used to calculate the *doubling time* of population. The greater the value of RNI, the shorter the time it will take a population to double its size—assuming that RNI remains constant and there is no in- or out-migration. The lower the value of RNI, the longer the doubling time. A simple formula for calculating doubling time is the *law of seventy*: doubling time = 70/RNI. If RNI is 2 per cent, therefore, the doubling time will be approximately 70/2.0 = 35 years. If the RNI is 1.5 per cent, the doubling time will be approximately 47 years. When RNI is negative, we can expect population to decline. As the following table shows, there is an inverse non-linear relationship between the rate of natural increase and the doubling time.

RNI (%)	Doubling time (years)
0.5	140
1.0	70
2.0	35
3.0	23
4.0	17
5.0	14
7.0	10
10.0	7

Geometric and Exponential Growth

If we observe two population counts at the beginning (P_1) and the end (P_2) of some interval, a simple measure of the *change* in population over this interval is:

$$\% \text{ change between } t_1 \text{ and } t_2 = \frac{P_2 - P_1}{P_1} \times 100$$

When the time interval is greater than one year, this formula should be modified to obtain the *average annual % change* over the interval:

$$r = \text{average annual \%} \atop \text{change between } t_1 \text{ and } t_2 = \left[\frac{P_2 - P_1}{P_1} \times 100 \right] / n$$

where P_1 and P_2 represent the populations at time points 1 and 2, respectively; n is the number of years in the interval; and r is the average annual % change—i.e., the average growth rate over the interval.

(Note: as this example illustrates, the *growth rate* is not the same as the *rate of natural increase*.)

Geometric Growth Model

Two important mathematical models applicable in the analysis of population growth are the *geometric* and the *exponential*. Letting P_1 represent population size at some initial point in time; P_2 population size at some later point; n the interval of time in years between these two populations, and r the average rate of growth, as defined above (note that this is not the RNI), we will first consider the simplest case, where the time interval is one year (i.e., $n = 1$). The population at the end of the first year will be

$$P_2 = P_1 + rP_1$$

The population at time point 2 is equal to the population at the beginning of the interval, plus the growth that has occurred between the two time points (rP_1). More generally, this formula is:

$$P_2 = P_1 (1 + r)$$

If the time interval is extended beyond one year, however, the formula is modified as follows:

$$P_2 = P_1 (1 + r)^n$$

And this is the geometric growth model. If r is positive, there is population growth; if r is negative, there is population decline. This model assumes that population change occurs at discrete time points within a given interval between t_1 and t_2. For example, compounding may take place halfway through the interval, or perhaps at the beginning or at the end, but not continuously. Let us work out a hypothetical example using this model. Let

P_1 = 100,000, the population at the beginning of the interval

P_2 = population size at the end of the interval

r = 0.02 (i.e., 2% annual rate of growth) during the interval

n = 5 (an interval of 5 years)

Then:

$$P_2 = 100,000 (1 + 0.02)^5$$
$$= 100,000 (1.02)^5$$
$$= 100,000 (1.10408080)$$
$$= 110,408$$

Assuming geometric growth of 2 per cent per year over this five-year interval, the population would grow to 110,408.

The geometric formula can be rearranged to determine initial population size P_1, given knowledge of P_2, the length of the time interval n, and the rate of growth r:

$$P_1 = \frac{P_2}{(1 + r)^n}$$

And if we wanted to find the interval of time n, between two population counts, the formula can be written as:

$$n = \frac{\log \frac{P_2}{P_1}}{\log(1 + r)}$$

where 'log' means base 10 logarithm.

The *doubling time* of the population, defined here as n, is obtained by

$$n = \frac{\log 2}{\log(1 + r)}$$

To see how this formula works, let us use it to calculate the doubling time of the Canadian population on the basis of its rate of natural increase. In the year 2000 the rate of natural increase was 0.40 per cent (i.e., $r = 0.004$) (Population Reference Bureau, 2000). Assuming that this rate of growth remained constant, and there was no migration either in or out, how many years would it take the population to double? We need to find n, such that $P_2 - P_1 = 2P_1$. Therefore:

$$n = \frac{\log 2}{\log(1 + 0.004)}$$

$$= \frac{1.30103}{\log 1.004}$$

$$= \frac{1.30103}{0.001734}$$

$$= 174 \text{ years}$$

The 'law of 70' formula gives: $70/0.40 = 175$ years. Note that we do not need to know the actual populations to work this out.

Exponential Growth Model

In actuality, population growth is a continuous process. At any given moment there are some people being born and others dying; and there are people entering and leaving the population through immigration and emigration. *The exponential model* accounts for this important principle—that growth is a continuous process. The exponential growth formula is

$$P_2 = P_1 e^{rn}$$

where e is the base of the system of natural logarithms, having the approximate numerical value of $2.71828\ldots$; r is the growth rate; and n is the number of years. Let us work out a hypothetical example using this model. Let

$P_1 = 100,000$, the population at the beginning of the interval

$P_2 =$ population size at the end of the interval

$r = 0.02$ (i.e., 2% annual rate of growth) during the interval

$n = 5$ (an interval of 5 years)

Given this information, under the exponential model of growth, the population at the end of five years will be 110,517:

$$P_2 = 100,000 \ e^{.02 \ (5)}$$

$$= 100,000 \ (1.10517)$$

$$= 110,517$$

Geometric and Exponential Rate of Growth

Both the geometric and exponential models can be applied to determine the rate of population growth between any two points in time. Assuming a *geometric* progression, the rate of growth over some interval n can be computed by

$$1 + r = \left[\frac{P_2}{P_1}\right]^{1/n}$$

And the growth rate can be solved by rearranging the terms as follows:

$$r = \left[\frac{P_2}{P_1}\right]^{1/n} - 1$$

Let us apply this formula. Suppose that

$P_2 = 150,000$

$P_1 = 109,000$

$n = 10$ years (the time interval between t_1 and t_2)

Then the rate of growth, r, is

$$r = \left[\frac{150,000}{109,000}\right]^{1/10} - 1$$

$$= (1.37614679)^{1/10} - 1$$

$$= 1.032443 - 1$$

$$= 0.032443$$

The average rate of growth under the geometric model is about 3.24 per cent per year during this ten-year interval.

Another way to solve for r using the geometric model is to apply base 10 logarithms as follows:

$$r = exp\left[\frac{\log P_2 - \log P_1}{n}\right] - 1$$

where '*exp*' means to take the exponent (i.e., the antilog) of the quantity in the brackets.

Let us apply this formula using the same assumed figures as before. Then:

$$r = exp\left[\frac{\log 150,000 - \log 109,000}{10}\right] - 1$$

$$= exp\left[\frac{5.176091 - 5.037426}{10}\right] - 1$$

$$= exp\,(0.013866) - 1$$

$$= 1.032443 - 1$$

$$= 0.032443$$

The result is identical to the one found before (i.e., 3.24 per cent growth rate).

As we have already noted, the *geometric growth formula* assumes that population change occurs at discrete points in time. If one assumes *continuous change*, the *exponential formula* should be used to compute the rate of growth:

$$r = \left[\frac{\ln P_2 - \ln P_1}{n}\right]$$

where ln means 'natural logarithm'.

Applied to the same data used in the previous example, the exponential model gives an average rate of growth of 3.19 per cent per year:

$$r = \left[\frac{\ln 150,000 - \ln 109,000}{10}\right]$$

$$= \left[\frac{11.91839 - 11.599103}{10}\right]$$

$$= \frac{0.319287}{10}$$

$$= 0.031929$$

$$= 3.193\%$$

Table 3.6 shows computations based on data from selected countries over different time intervals. Notice the differences and similarities in the results. In comparing columns (7) and (8), for instance, it is clear that the exponential model requires a slightly lower rate of growth than the geometric to attain the same amount of growth over an equal time interval. The difference reflects the power of continuous compounding in the exponential model.

As for computing doubling time with the exponential model, we may use the same example as applied earlier in the case of the geometric model, which assumed that $r = 0.004$. As before, the question is this: assuming that this rate of natural population growth remained constant, and there were no migration, how many years would it take the population to double its

Table 3.6 Measures of population change for selected countries over two points in time

Country (periods in parentheses)	Population at t_1	Population at t_2	Number of years between t_1 and t_2	% change between t_1 and t_2	Average annual % change between t_1 and t_2	Average annual % rate of growth between t_1 and t_2, Geometric Model	Average annual % rate of growth between t_1 and t_2, Exponential Model
(1)	(2)	(3)	(4)	(5)	(6)	(7)	(8)
China (1982, 1990)	1,003,913,927	1,130,510,638	8	12.61	1.580	1.496	1.485
Benin (1975, 1995)	3,112,000	5,408,463	20	73.79	3.690	2.800	2.764
Canada (1971, 1991)	21,568,310	27,296,860	20	26.56	1.330	1.185	1.177
Mexico (1979, 1990)	69,381,104	81,249,645	11	17.11	1.560	1.450	1.440
Sweden (1980, 1993)	8,310,473	8,745,109	13	5.23	0.402	0.393	0.392
Bulgaria (1980, 1992)	8,761,535	8,540,272	12	2.53	−0.210	−0.213	−0.213
Japan (1975, 1995)	111,933,800	125,570,246	20	12.18	0.609	0.576	0.575
Italy (1974, 1998)	55,179,995	57,563,354	24	4.32	0.180	0.176	0.176

Source: *United Nations Demographic Yearbook* (various years).

size? We need to find n, such that $P_2 - P_1 = 2P_1$. The formula in this case is

$$n = \frac{\ln 2}{r}$$

where n = the number of years for the population to double; ln means natural logarithm, and r is the rate of natural increase.

Therefore:

$$n = \frac{0.693}{0.004}$$

$$= 173.3 \text{ years}$$

What if the vale of r is negative? How would this change our calculation of doubling time? In actuality, a negative r would imply population decline, and in such cases we speak not of the doubling time but rather of the number of years

for the population to decline to half its current size (i.e., its half-life). Using the exponential model, the formula to compute the number of years it would take for a population experiencing a constant negative rate of growth to reach half its current size would be:

$$n = \frac{\ln 0.5}{-r}$$

Here we take the natural logarithm of 0.5 because instead of doubling we are concerned with halving the population (i.e., $(½)P_1 = (0.5)P_1$). Let us use the same value of r as before, only this time we'll assume it is negative (i.e., $r = -0.004$). The formula says to take the natural logarithm of 0.05, which is −0.69315. Dividing this by −0.004 gives a half-life time of approximately 173 years. The 'law of 70' formula gives the value of n as $-70/-r(100) = 175$ years. The two results are very close.

Exercises

1. Table 3.7 contains demographic and non-demographic data for selected countries over two points in time, 1975 and 2000. For each of these countries, calculate (1) the rate of natural increase; and (2) the corresponding doubling time, using the exponential formula. Interpret your computations and discuss their underlying assumptions.

2. The same table contains Human Development Index (HDI) values for 1975 and 2000 for different countries. Use Excel or some other spreadsheet to plot the values of HDI for 1975 against those of 2001. What can you conclude from this graph? How representative is this sample? Would a complete list of all the countries give similar results?

   Construct separate plots of HDI for 1975 against values in 2000 of Crude Birth Rate (CBR), Crude Death Rate (CDR), and RNI, respectively. Describe these relationships. To which of these demographic measures is HDI more strongly correlated? Is social development a determinant of demographic conditions in a country, or is social development a consequence of demographic conditions?

3. Using the population figures for 2000 for each of the countries in Table 3.7 and the corresponding rates of natural increase, compute the following: (a) the projected population in 25 years' time (using the geometric growth formula) and (b) the projected population in 25 years' time (using the exponential growth formula). Do these two formulas produce different results? If so, what explains the difference? What do these computations implicitly assume?

Additional Reading

Anderson, Michael, ed. 1996. *British Population History: From the Black Death to the Present Day*. Cambridge: Cambridge University Press.

Barro, Robert J. 1997. *Determinants of Economic Growth: A Cross-Country Empirical Study*. Cambridge, MA: MIT Press.

Brown, Craig, ed. 2002. *The Illustrated History of Canada*. Toronto: Key Porter.

Clarke, John I. 1997. *Predictions: The Future of Population*. London: Phoenix.

Hinde, Andrew. 2003. *England's Population: A History since the Domesday Survey*. New York: Oxford University Press.

Howard, Michael, and William Roger Louis. 2002. *The Oxford History of the Twentieth Century*. New York: Oxford University Press.

McBeth, Helen, and Paul Collinson, eds. 2002. *Human Population Dynamics: Cross-Disciplinary Perspectives*. Cambridge: Cambridge University Press.

Perkins, Dwight H., Steven Radelet, and David L. Lindauer. 2006. *Economics of Development*, 6th edn. New York: W.W. Norton.

Wenke, Robert J. 1990. *Patterns in Prehistory: Humankind's First Three Million Years*, 3rd edn. New York: Oxford University Press.

Wrigley, E.A., R.S. Davies, J.E. Oeppen, and R.S. Schofield. 1997. *English Population History from Family Reconstitution 1580–1873*. Cambridge: Cambridge University Press.

Table 3.7 Demographic indicators and Human Development Index values, selected countries, 1975 and 2000

Country	Mid-year population (millions)		CBR per 1,000		CDR per 1,000		RNI %		Doubling time (years)		HDI[2]	
	1975	2000	1975	2000	1975	2000	1975	2000	1975	2000	1975	2000
Egypt	37.5	68.3	37.8	26	12.8	6					.433	.642
Benin	na[1]	6.4	na	45	na	17					.286	.420
Gambia	0.5	1.3	43.3	43	24.1	19					.271	.405
Nigeria	62.9	123.3	49.3	42	22.7	13					.326	.462
Kenya	13.3	30.3	48.7	35	16	14					.442	.513
Cameroon	6.4	15.4	40.4	37	22	12					.407	.512
Rwanda	4.2	7.2	50.0	43	23.6	20					.334	.403
Niger	4.6	10.1	52.2	54	25.5	24					.234	.277
Sierra Leone	3.0	5.2	44.7	47	20.7	21					na	.275
South Africa	24.7	43.4	42.9	25	15.5	12					.648	.695
Canada	22.8	30.8	18.6	11	7.7	7					.867	.940
USA	213.9	275.6	16.9	15	9.4	9					.861	.939
Mexico	52.9	99.6	42.0	24	8.6	4					.688	.796
Argentina	25.4	37.0	21.8	14	8.8	8					.784	.844
Bolivia	5.4	8.3	43.7	19	18	10					na	.653
Brazil	109.7	170.1	37.1	30	8.8	6					.641	.759
Iraq	11.1	23.1	48.1	21	14.6	10					na	na
Kuwait	1.1	2.2	47.1	38	5.3	2					na	.813
Turkey	39.9	65.3	39.4	24	12.5	7					.592	.742
Bangladesh	73.7	128.1	49.5	22	15.7	8					.332	.478
India	613.2	1,002.1	39.9	27	15.6	9					.406	.577
Iran	32.9	67.4	45.3	27	15.6	6					.556	na
Pakistan	20.6	150.6	47.4	21	16.5	11					.343	.499
Indonesia	136.0	212.2	42.9	39	16.9	8					.467	.684
Malaysia	12.1	23.3	38.7	24	9.9	5					.614	na
Philippines	44.4	80.3	43.8	25	15.5	7					.649	.754
Singapore	2.2	4.0	21.2	29	5.2	5					.719	.885
China	822.8	1,264.5	26.9	13	10.3	6					.522	.726
Japan	111.1	126.9	19.2	15	6.6	8					.851	.933
Denmark	5.0	5.3	14.0	12	10.1	11					.866	.926
Norway	4.0	4.5	16.7	13	10.1	10					.856	.942
Sweden	8.3	8.9	14.2	10	10.5	11					.862	.941
UK	56.4	59.8	16.1	12	11.7	11					.839	.928
France	52.9	59.4	17.0	13	10.6	9					.846	.928
Germany	na	82.1	na	9	na	10					na	.925
Bulgaria	8.8	8.2	16.2	8	9.2	14					.760	.775
Russian Fed.	na	145.2	na	8	na	15					na	.781
Italy	55.0	57.8	16.0	9	9.8	10					.827	.913
Australia	13.8	19.2	21.0	13	8.1	7					.842	.939
New Zealand	3.0	3.8	23.2	15	8.3	7					.846	.917

[1]Information not available.

[2]Human Development Index.

Sources: United Nations Development Programme (2001); Population Reference Bureau (various).

Web Resources

The following sites of the United Nations Population Fund (UNFPA) provide a wealth of information on world population:

Interactive Population Center : www.unfpa.org/intercenter/.

The Day of 6 Billion: www.unfpa.org/6billion/index.htm.

The State of the World Population: www.unfpa.org/swp/swpmain.htm.

The United Nations Population Division (www.unpopulation.org/) has an important database on the world's population: http://esa.un.org/unpp/index.asp.

US Census Bureau International Programs Center (www.census.gov/ipc/www/), contains valuable demographic information on the state of the world. It also offers an international database, where you can find, among other things, age–sex pyramids for every country in the world: www.census.gov/ipc/www/idb/.

For continuous updates on the population of the United States and the world see the United States Census Bureau population clock: www.census.gov/main/www/popclock.html.

Canada has its own population clock: www.statcan.ca/english/edu/clock/population.htm.

For a population profile of Canada visit: www.statcan.ca/english/Pgdb/popula.htm.

The Population Reference Bureau (PRB) is one of the leading demographic institutions in the world. It publishes, among other things, the annual *World Population Data Sheet*. The PRB's websites have been redesigned, expanded, and merged into a powerful database, giving instant access to the latest data and analysis on population, health, and environmental issues. Reports, articles, data sheets, and policy briefs are now cross-referenced by topic, geographic region, and type of information. There are new Web sections on HIV/AIDS, the environment, reproductive health, and population trends, with articles and in-depth data and reports. Sections for educators and journalists highlight material of interest to these groups. New email services from PRB also provide users with easy access to information, and an email newsletter is offered in English. You can subscribe to the newsletter at www.prb.org/EmailSignup.aspx or by sending an email to listserv@listserv.prb.org with the text SUBSCRIBE NEWS in the body of the message.

You can receive publications free of charge through an automated email service called E-Library, which saves you the trouble of downloading documents from the Web. To view a list of publications available through E-Library, email documents@prbdocs.org with the document code LIST in the body of your message. A full list will be sent to you immediately. If you wish to become a member of PRB, more information is available at: www.prb.org/Join.aspx.

An excellent resource for those interested in globalization is the *Polity Global Transformations* site, devised by David Held and Anthony McGrew: www.polity.co.uk/global/.

Harvard University's Center for International Development is an excellent source of information about development and related concerns. The centre's website also offers research papers and data on issues of geography and development: www.cid.harvard.edu.

For reports on human rights by Human Rights Watch visit: www.hrw.org/.

Freedom House is an organization that studies political trends throughout the world. One of its recent reports, available on the web, looks at democratization trends: www.freedomhouse.org.

Demographic Composition

Chapter 4

Age and Sex Structure

Introduction

Unlike individuals, populations can both age and grow young (Sanderson and Scherbov, 2005). This capacity to change is one of the features that make age composition so important in demographic analysis. All demographic phenomena are either directly or indirectly determined in some respect by age. The processes of birth, death, and migration—the three key demographic processes—are all age-dependent. The probability of experiencing these demographic events varies strongly with age (though not in a simple linear fashion). Age is also a determining factor in the incidence of other demographic events, including cohabitation, marriage, divorce, remarriage, widowhood, labour-force activity, and unemployment.

Another recognizable feature of all demographic phenomena is that they are conditioned by sex. For instance, females enjoy lower death rates than males in most circumstances; the chances of long-distance relocation are usually greater for males than for females; widowhood is more prevalent among females than among males; men are generally more likely than women to remarry, and so forth. The sociological importance of these two characteristics explains our society's preoccupation with the collection of information on the basis of people's age and sex. Not only are age and sex data important markers of social and legal status for individuals in society, but they are highly relevant in the occurrence of various types of social and demographic behaviour. It is difficult, if not impossible, to envision any behavioural phenomenon in the social world that is not related, directly or indirectly, to age and sex.

This chapter will examine age and sex composition in the context of demographic analysis, specifically with regard to fertility, mortality, and migration. The term 'composition' in this case refers to the distribution of the population in accordance with the intersecting characteristics of age and sex. Thus in some contexts age and sex characteristics will be discussed together, as when we speak of the age–sex distribution of a population. In other contexts the focus will be on one of the two, without any direct reference to the other. Wherever the main emphasis falls, however, the underlying assumption is that the two are so interrelated that in reality they cannot be separated.

Principles of Age and Sex Composition

Population Age Distribution

In demographic analysis, population data are usually arrayed according to age and sex. Regarding age, demographers are typically (though not exclusively) interested in three segments of the population: those under 15, those aged 15–64, and those aged 65 and older. These broad age groups represent, respectively, youth, who typically are not engaged in full-time economic activity and consequently require basic services such as education from the society; those of working age, who make up most of the labour force and therefore are the ones who pay the taxes that the government uses for societal maintenance; and the post-retirement component of society.

These designations are only rough approximations of the realities they purport to reflect. Not all persons aged 65 and older, for example, are retired from the labour force. Nor are all individuals aged 15–64 working full-time; some may be unemployed or out of the labour force altogether. Similarly, in some countries many children and youth do not attend school but participate virtually full-time in family work activities. What, then, is the usefulness of these three broad age categories? By looking closely at these three demographic sectors, social scientists can get a sense of the economic 'dependency' burden in a given society. By taking the ratio of youth plus old-age dependents to the working age population, we obtain a measure of a society's overall dependency on the workers, who must provide for those not in the labour force. There are three associated measures of dependency: total, youth, and old age.

The total dependency ratio is expressed as follows:

$$\text{total dependency ratio (TDR)} = \frac{P_{0-14} + P_{65+}}{P_{15-64}} \times 100$$

This ratio can be broken down into its two component parts:

$$\text{youth dependency ratio (YDR)} = \frac{P_{0-14}}{P_{15-64}} \times 100$$

$$\text{old-age dependency ratio (ODR)} = \frac{P_{65+}}{P_{15-64}} \times 100$$

A dependency ratio greater than 100 would indicate the presence of more dependents than workers in the population: the higher the ratio, the greater the dependency 'burden' on the working population. And a ratio below 100 would signify the opposite situation. The overall dependency ratio is the sum of the youth and old-age dependency ratios. Typically, if a society has a high youth dependency ratio, its old-age dependency ratio will be relatively low, and vice versa. In some situations, however, the youth and old-age components of the dependency ratio can be roughly equal. These three measures are shown in Table 4.1 for a number of selected countries and for the world as a whole, the more developed countries, and the less

developed countries, obtained from the United Nations' *World Population Ageing, 1950* (United Nations Department of Economic and Social Affairs Population Division, 2001). The ratios are expressed as per 100. The table also shows the percentage distributions for three age categories: <15, 15–59, and 60+ (note that the age categories used in this table are slightly different from the standard age categories).

The values of the dependency ratios in Table 4.1 are closely related to a population's age distribution; they reflect the percentage distribution of the population by age. In Nigeria, for instance, almost half (45.1 per cent) of the total population consists of youths below age 15, and only 4.8 per cent is aged 60 and older. The situation is similar in the Palestinian Occupied Territory, where the proportion of the population below age 15 is even higher (46.4 per cent). Given these large youth components, we would expect the youth dependency ratios to be high as well, and they are: 86.8 per 100 in Nigeria, and 92.8 in the Occupied Palestinian Territory. These figures suggest that there are almost as many youths as persons of working age in these societies. Unsurprisingly, the old-age dependency ratios in these two populations are quite low (5.9 and 7.1, respectively). By contrast, countries like Japan, Italy, Spain, and Sweden have relatively high old-age dependency burdens and low youth dependency ratios. In these populations the youth components account for between 21 and 22 per cent of the total, while the old-age components—in the range of 25 to 27 per cent—are among the largest in the world.

Of course it is also possible to examine population distribution across a more detailed age classification. This usually involves observing absolute and relative frequencies of population by age and sex. As an illustration, the age–sex distribution of Canada in 2001 is shown in Table 4.2. Note that the distribution starts with the age group 0–4, followed by 5–9, 10–14, and so forth, up to 85+. Population frequencies are given for males and females separately as well as the total age-specific counts summed across sex.

Table 4.1 Distribution of population by age, dependency ratios, and median age in 2000; the world, development regions, and selected countries

Country	Age group (%)			Dependency ratio (per 100)			Median age (years)
	<15	15–59	60+	Youth	Old age	Total	
World	30.0	60.0	10.0	47.5	10.9	58.4	26.5
More developed regions	18.3	62.3	19.4	27.1	21.2	48.3	37.4
Less developed regions	32.8	59.5	7.7	52.9	8.2	61.1	24.3
Least developed countries	43.1	52.0	4.9	80.2	5.8	86.0	18.2
Specific regions							
Africa	42.6	52.3	5.1	78.7	6.0	84.7	18.4
Eastern	45.3	50.3	4.5	87.3	5.5	92.8	17.1
Middle	47.2	48.0	4.9	94.9	6.3	101.1	16.3
Northern	35.6	58.1	6.2	59.2	6.8	65.9	21.7
Southern	35.0	59.4	5.7	56.9	5.8	62.7	22.1
Western	44.8	50.4	4.7	85.9	5.8	91.8	17.3
Asia	30.2	61.0	8.8	47.3	9.2	56.5	26.2
Eastern	23.9	64.9	11.3	34.9	11.3	46.2	30.8
South Central	35.2	57.8	7.1	58.3	7.6	65.9	22.6
Southeastern	32.4	60.5	7.1	51.5	7.4	58.9	23.9
Western	35.9	57.0	7.1	60.5	8.0	68.5	22.1
Europe	17.5	62.3	20.3	25.8	21.7	47.4	37.7
Eastern	18.1	63.3	18.6	26.2	18.7	44.9	36.5
Northern	18.9	60.7	20.4	28.8	23.6	52.4	37.7
Southern	15.8	62.4	21.8	23.3	24.2	47.4	38.2
Western	17.0	61.3	21.7	25.4	23.9	49.3	39.0
Latin America & Caribbean	31.5	60.5	8.0	50.0	8.6	58.6	24.4
Caribbean	29.5	60.6	9.9	46.4	10.8	57.2	26.5
Central America	34.9	58.5	6.7	57.5	7.5	65.0	22.4
South America	30.4	64.3	8.2	47.6	8.8	56.4	25.4
Northern America	21.5	62.3	16.2	32.4	18.6	51.0	35.6
Oceania	25.4	61.2	13.4	39.2	15.2	54.5	30.9
Australia & New Zealand	20.9	62.9	16.2	31.3	18.2	49.4	35.0
Melanesia	39.3	56.2	4.5	67.8	4.6	72.4	19.8
Micronesia	38.7	54.4	6.8	6.8	0.8	76.1	21.1
Polynesia	35.0	58.2	6.8	57.9	7.3	65.2	22.1
Selected countries							
China	24.8	65.0	10.1	36.4	10.0	46.4	30.0
Israel	28.3	58.6	13.2	45.6	15.9	61.6	27.9
Occupied Palestinian Territory	46.4	48.7	4.9	92.8	7.1	99.9	16.8
Nigeria	45.1	50.2	4.8	86.8	5.9	92.7	17.2
Brazil	28.8	63.4	7.8	43.6	7.8	51.4	25.8
India	35.5	58.9	7.6	54.4	8.1	62.5	23.7
Mexico	33.1	59.9	6.9	53.3	7.6	60.9	23.3
United States	21.7	62.1	16.1	32.9	18.6	51.5	35.5
Canada	19.1	64.2	16.7	28.0	18.5	46.5	36.9
Sweden	18.2	59.4	22.4	28.3	27.1	55.3	39.7
Russian Federation	18.0	63.5	18.5	25.8	18.0	43.8	36.8
Japan	14.7	62.1	23.2	21.6	25.2	46.8	41.2
Italy	14.3	61.7	24.1	21.1	26.7	47.8	40.2

(continued)

Table 4.1 (*continued*)

Country	Age group (%) <15	15–59	60+	Dependency ratio (per 100) Youth	Old age	Total	Median age (years)
Spain	14.7	63.5	21.8	21.5	24.8	46.4	37.7
France	18.7	60.7	20.5	28.7	24.5	53.2	37.6
Germany	15.5	61.2	23.0	22.8	24.1	46.9	40.1
United Kingdom	19.0	60.4	20.6	29.1	24.1	53.2	37.7

Source: United Nations Department of Economic and Social Affairs Population Division (2002e). Reprinted with the permission of the United Nations.

Table 4.2 Age and sex distribution and associated summary measures, Canada, 2001

Age	Number of persons Males	Females	Total	% Males	Females	Total
0–4	868,075	828,205	1,696,280	2.9	2.8	5.7
5–9	1,011,460	964,670	1,976,130	3.4	3.2	6.6
10–14	1,051,455	1,001,665	2,053,120	3.5	3.3	6.8
15–19	1,052,145	1,001,180	2,053,325	3.5	3.3	6.8
20–24	982,285	973,530	1,955,815	3.3	3.2	6.5
25–29	935,510	962,690	1,898,200	3.1	3.2	6.3
30–34	1,031,255	1,065,490	2,096,745	3.4	3.6	7.0
35–39	1,244,995	1,277,860	2,522,855	4.2	4.3	8.4
40–44	1,271,725	1,307,040	2,578,765	4.2	4.4	8.6
45–49	1,151,155	1,182,375	2,333,530	3.8	3.9	7.8
50–54	1,033,365	1,052,395	2,085,760	3.4	3.5	7.0
55–59	789,205	805,035	1,594,240	2.6	2.7	5.3
60–64	621,570	652,210	1,273,780	2.1	2.2	4.2
65–69	543,830	589,800	1,133,630	1.8	2.0	3.8
70–74	461,780	547,430	1,009,210	1.5	1.8	3.4
75–79	338,820	474,850	813,670	1.1	1.6	2.7
80–84	192,645	323,495	516,140	0.6	1.1	1.7
85+	125,580	290,325	415,905	0.4	1.0	1.4
Total	14,706,855	15,300,245	30,007,100	49.0	51.0	100.0
Broad age groups						
<15	2,930,990	2,794,540	5,725,530	9.8	9.3	19.1
15–64	10,113,210	10,279,805	20,393,015	33.7	34.3	68.0
65+	1,662,655	2,225,900	3,888,555	5.5	7.4	13.0
Total	14,706,855	15,300,245	30,007,100	49.0	51.0	100.0
Summary measures						
YDR			28.08			
ODR			19.07			
TDR			47.15			
Median age			37.52			
Sex ratio (m/f) × 100			96.00			

Note: YDR = youth dependency ratio; ODR = old-age dependency ratio; TDR = total dependency ratio. Author's computations.
Source: Adapted from Statistics Canada publication *Age and Sex for the Population of Canada, 2001 Census*. Catlogue no. 95F0300XCB01004.

Age–sex-specific relative frequencies (percentages) are shown in the table, expressed on the basis of the total population. These relative frequencies are useful for a variety of reasons, but especially because they can be graphed to create a population age pyramid.

Age Pyramids

Age–sex percentages can be plotted on graph paper to produce an *age pyramid*: a pictorial representation of the age and sex composition of the population. A population pyramid displays the percentage distributions of males and females separately on opposite sides of the graph. For each age–sex intersection, we compute a corresponding percentage by using the total population size as the denominator. To illustrate, Table 4.2 indicates that there were 1,051,455 males aged 10–14 in Canada in 2001, and that the total population was 30,007,100. The corresponding percentage for males aged 10–14 is therefore 1,051,455 / 30,007,100 × 100 = 3.50 per cent. There were 1,001,665 females aged 10–14; and the corresponding percentage is 1,001,665 / 30,007,100 × 100 = 3.34 per cent. These computations are executed independently for all the age–sex groups in the population, starting with age 0–4 through 80–84 and finally 85+. Thus:

$$\frac{\% \text{ males in}}{\text{age group } x} = \frac{\text{number of males in age group } x}{\text{total population}} \times 100$$

$$\frac{\% \text{ females in}}{\text{age group } x} = \frac{\text{number of females in age group } x}{\text{total population}} \times 100$$

Using the information in Table 4.2, the dependency ratios for Canada in 2001 have been worked out as 28.1 (youth) and 19.1 (old age). The overall dependency ratio is the sum of these two values (47.2). This table includes another important statistic computable from the age distribution: the *median age*. This is the age that divides the distribution in half, so that half the population is above the median and half is below it (see Notes for Further Study on page 129).

Canada's Age Pyramid in 2006

Figure 4.1 shows the population age pyramid of Canada in 2006 (Statistics Canada, 2007). A number of interesting features may be outlined. The most obvious feature in this pyramid is the bulge associated with the baby boom generation, born between 1946 and 1965, who in 2006 were aged 41 to 60. This is the largest segment of the population, accounting for nearly one in three Canadians. Near the top of the age pyramid are the parents of the baby boomers, aged 68 to 84 in 2006, who were born between 1922 and 1938. This older generation has been gradually losing its members (in 2006, it accounted for less than 10 per cent of Canadians). Near the bottom of the age structure are the boomers' children, born between 1975 and 1995, who were aged 11 to 31 in 2006. There is a slight bulge in this part of the age pyramid—a reflection of an 'echo' effect of the baby boom and the impact of higher fertility in the early part of the 1990s. In 2006 this cohort represented 27.5 per cent of Canadians. There are two other smaller cohorts (smaller because they include fewer years of births): the Second World War cohort, born between 1939 and 1945, who in 2006 were between 61 and 67; and the 'baby bust' cohort, born between 1966 and 1974, in the period of rapid fertility decline that followed the baby boom. The first of these two cohorts represented 6.4 per cent of the population in 2006; the second, 12.4 per cent (Statistics Canada, 2007: 12–13).

The 2006 census showed that the proportion of the population aged 65 and over had increased in every province and territory since 2001, while the proportion under 15 had shrunk. Between 1956 and 2006 the percentage aged 65 and over grew from 7.7 to 13.7, while the percentage under 15 dropped from 32.5 to 17.7 (Statistics Canada, 2007: 14). The aging of the population implied by these trends can be readily seen in the median ages of the Canadian population from 1956 to 2006 (Statistics Canada, 2007a: 14):

Year	1956	1961	1966	1971	1976	1981	1986	1991	1996	2001	2006
Median	27.2	26.3	25.4	26.2	27.8	29.6	31.6	33.5	35.3	37.6	39.5

Typology of Age Pyramids

Canada's age structure is very similar to that of most other highly industrialized countries today. The shape of the distribution deviates somewhat from that of a true pyramid in the geometric sense. The base is narrow, there is a noticeable bulge in the ages between 35 and 55, and the top of the pyramid—representing those over the age of 65—is fairly wide. This age pyramid contrasts sharply with that of contemporary developing countries. This point is highlighted in Figure 4.2, which includes the age distributions of the more developed regions, the least developed countries, and the other less developed countries.

Age distributions change as a society's birth and death rates shift in the process of demographic transition (Birg, 1995; Golini, 2003). Hinde (2002a: 27) has proposed three proto-

typical types of age pyramids that reflect different fertility and mortality conditions, and therefore population growth rates; these are shown in Figure 4.3. Rapidly growing population pyramids (Type A) are characterized by a wide base and a narrow top. Such populations can have growth rates in the range of 2 per cent or more. In the contemporary world, nations fitting this description include many in sub-Saharan Africa (e.g., Nigeria, Ethiopia, Republic of Congo, Angola, Benin), some in Asia (e.g., Afghanistan, Nepal; Pakistan; Occupied Palestinian Territory); and some in Central America (e.g., Guatemala) (United Nations Department of Economic and Social Affairs Population Division, 2002e).

In recent decades some developing countries have been gradually moving away from the Type A form and taking a more triangular shape as the part of the distribution corresponding to

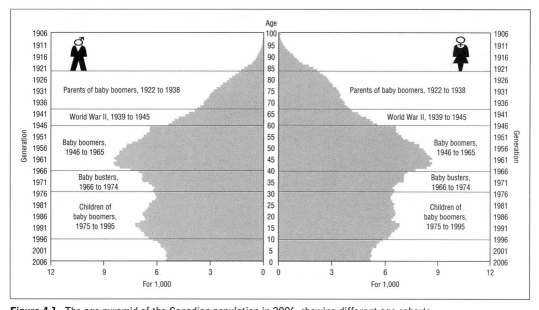

Figure 4.1 The age pyramid of the Canadian population in 2006, showing different age cohorts

Source: Adapted from Statistics Canada publication *Portrait of the Canadian Population in 2006, by Age and Sex, 2006 Census*. Catalogue no. 97-551-XIE, p. 12.

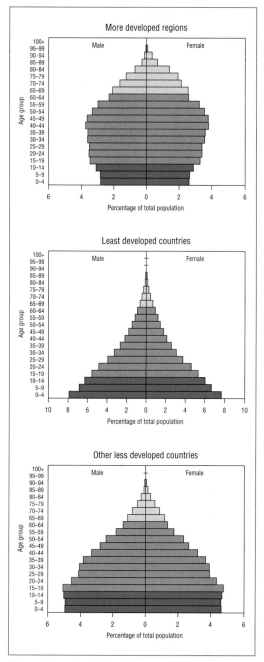

Figure 4.2   Population pyramids of more developed regions, the least developed countries, and other less developed countries, 2005

Source: United Nations Department of Economic and Social Affairs Population Division (2006e): 23 (Figure II.1). Reprinted with the permission of the United Nations.

the reproductive ages, roughly 15 to 50, grows wider. Not surprisingly, these populations are growing rapidly. This type of age composition can be seen in countries such as Turkey, Bangladesh, Egypt, India, Malaysia, the Philippines, Israel, Kenya, Ghana, Mexico, and Panama—transitional populations in which both mortality and fertility are declining rapidly, but the difference between these vital rates remains substantial. Another set of countries with similar age distributions includes China, Brazil, Thailand, Venezuela, Indonesia, and Vietnam. In these populations the bottom of the age pyramid is visibly narrowing as a result of sustained declines in fertility in recent years.

In Type B populations the age structure remains constant indefinitely. As we will see, this type represents a stationary population with constant age-specific birth and death rates, and therefore a constant rate of growth. Although no actual population fits this description exactly, some contemporary populations are approximating it. Their more or less stable age structures reflect low birth and death rates and thus low rates of natural increase. In populations that have long completed the demographic transition, fertility and mortality levels have more or less stabilized at levels around zero. This is essentially the situation in much of western Europe, as well as Canada, Japan, South Korea, Singapore, and Taiwan (Population Reference Bureau, 2006).

A subset of this group of nations is now moving towards a third type of age structure, Type C. In this scenario, envisioned for the most advanced countries in the not so distant future, the age distribution is top-heavy and the base is narrow. These countries are expected to lose population every year as a result of more or less stable negative growth rates (fewer births than deaths). Among the countries now approximating this scenario are Italy, Estonia, Latvia, Lithuania, Germany, Belarus, Bulgaria, the Czech Republic, Hungary, Romania, the Russian Federation, and Ukraine (Population Reference Bureau, 2006).

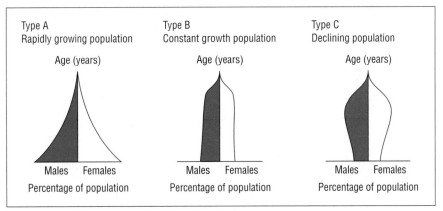

Figure 4.3 Typology of population age pyramids

Source: Hinde (1998): 163 (Figure 13.3). Copyright © 1998 Andrew Hinde. Reproduced with the permission of Edward Arnold (Publishers) Ltd.

Determinants of Age Composition

Shifts in age composition are produced mainly by changes in fertility and (to a lesser degree) mortality. While migration can also play an important role in some circumstances, its overall contribution is in general relatively minor (Preston, Heuveline, and Guillot, 2001). A comprehensive account of the demographic dynamics that determine whether a population is aging or growing younger was developed by Coale (1957a, 1957b, 1964, 1972), who found fertility to be the major determinant of changes in age composition. A young population is produced by high fertility rates. Under sustained high fertility conditions there will be a relatively high proportion of people under the age of 15, and the median age of the population will be relatively low compared to that of a population with a smaller proportion under 15. Declining fertility rates, if sustained over a long period, produce an aging population, with a smaller proportion of people under 15 and a growing proportion over 65. Mortality plays a much less important role in changing the age distribution of a population. These differential relationships can be demonstrated with the use of stable popu-

lation models. Because the stable population model is so important in demographic analysis, the section below will look at that model in some detail before examining the differential contributions of changes in fertility and mortality to population age distribution.

Stable and Stationary Populations

What would happen to the age structure of a population if its age-specific birth and death rates remained constant over a long period—say, 70 years or more? This is the fundamental question that underlies one of the most important constructs in demographic analysis: the stable age distribution. Under such conditions both the age distribution of the population and its rate of growth would be constant. Despite its name, a *stable population* can be either increasing or decreasing in size, as long as the rate of change remains constant; what is 'stable' is the shape of the age distribution (Newell, 1988: 120). A special kind of stable population is known as the *stationary population*. In this model the rate of growth is zero: neither the size of the population nor its age structure changes from year to year (Pollard, Yusuf, and Pollard, 1981: 102–3). This is the only case in which the total number of people in the population and the number and

Stable population theory can be traced back to Leonhard Euler (1707–83), who first proposed that a set of constant age-specific death rates and a constant number of births per unit time in all generations would produce a stable population. More than a century later, Alfred Lotka (1880–1949) developed an equation (the 're-newal equation') that made it possible to calculate 'the rate of increase implied by a [given] regime of birth and death rates' (Keyfitz, 2003: 322). Lotka also formulated stable population equations for the *intrinsic birth rate* (the rate at which mothers bear their daughters in a stable population, deter-mined by a set of constant age-specific birth rates) and the *intrinsic death rate* (the death rate in the stable population, determined by a set of constant age-specific death rates): the difference between these two rates determines the *intrinsic growth rate* of the stationary population, which can be posi-tive, negative, or even zero (as in the case of a stationary population). The stable population therefore will also have a corresponding life table and life expectancy function.

One other important parameter developed by Lotka is the *mean length of a generation*: the average age at which mothers in the stable popu-lation bear their daughters. In most applica-tions the stable population is computed for females only, but extension to both sexes is pos-sible (Pollard, 1973; Preston, Heuveline, and Guillot, 2001). Lotka's contributions to stable population theory (1907 [1977]) laid the foundations for many aspects of formal demo-graphic analysis. Coale (1955, 1957a, 1957b, 1972) has worked out short-cuts to Lotka's formulas that make it easier to calculate the parameters of a stable population.

percentage of the population within each of the age categories all remain constant.

At present no population in the world ac-tually fulfills *all* the restrictive criteria of the stable population model, though (as we have seen) some countries are moving in that direction.

Nevertheless, the stable population model is useful because it allows analysts to develop 'what if' scenarios. For example, a researcher might want to assume constant age-specific birth and death rates in a real population over a specified number of years into the future so as to ascertain how this situation would affect age dis-tribution. Other possible uses of the model would be to hold current age-specific fertility rates constant while varying the age-specific death rates (i.e., raising or lowering them) or to hold mortality rates constant while alter-ing fertility rates. Such experiments can help researchers anticipate future scenarios in actual populations.

The Relative Importance of Fertility and Mortality

The relative importance of fertility and mortality in determining age composition can be illus-trated with a simulation. Table 4.3 shows stable age distributions derived by combining different fertility and mortality levels. The indicator of mortality is life expectancy at birth—a measure of survival determined by a population's age-specific mortality rates; the higher the life expectancy, the better the survival conditions in a society. The index of fertility is the gross repro-duction rate (GRR), which measures the average number of daughters born to a woman, given a prevailing schedule of age-specific fertility rates; the greater the GRR, the higher the fertility. The table shows six panels, each reflecting a certain level of mortality (expectation of life at birth, e_0) and fertility (the gross reproduction rate, GRR). The percentages of the population across three broad age categories are shown in each panel.

It should be noted that varying mortality while holding fertility constant has very little effect on age distribution. For example, in panel 1 of the table life expectancy is just 20, whereas in panel 6 it is 70. Yet when fertility is kept con-stant at GRR = 1.00, the proportion aged <15 changes by only 4 percentage points: from 15 per cent in panel 1 to 19 per cent in panel 6. By contrast, the proportions within each age class

Table 4.3 Stable population age distributions derived by varying combinations of mortality and fertility rates

Mortality and fertility levels		% distribution in the stable population			Mortality and fertility levels		% distribution in the stable population		
		0–14	15–59	60+			0–14	15–59	60+
Mortality	Fertility				Mortality	Fertility			
Level 1. $e_0 = 20$	GRR				Level 4. $e_0 = 50$	GRR			
	1.0	14.8	68.3	16.9		1.0	17.8	60.7	21.5
	2.0	28.9	64.0	7.1		2.0	34.2	57.2	8.6
	3.0	38.5	57.6	3.9		3.0	44.6	50.9	4.5
	4.0	45.2	52.4	2.4		4.0	51.5	45.8	2.7
Level 2. $e_0 = 30$	GRR				Level 5. $e_0 = 60.4$	GRR			
	1.0	16.3	65.0	18.7		1.0	18.7	59.4	21.9
	2.0	31.4	60.9	7.7		2.0	35.6	55.8	8.6
	3.0	41.3	54.5	4.1		3.0	46.0	49.6	4.4
	4.0	48.2	49.2	2.6		4.0	52.9	44.4	2.7
Level 3. $e_0 = 40$	GRR				Level 6. $e_0 = 70.2$	GRR			
	1.0	17.0	62.6	20.4		1.0	19.5	58.6	21.9
	2.0	32.9	58.8	8.3		2.0	36.8	54.7	8.5
	3.0	43.1	52.5	4.4		3.0	47.3	48.4	4.3
	4.0	50.0	47.3	2.7		4.0	54.1	43.3	2.6

Source: Adapted from United Nations Department of Economic and Social Affairs Population Division (1973): 274. Reprinted with the permission of the United Nations.

change dramatically as fertility varies from a GRR of 1.00 to a GRR of 4.00. These results, based on stable population distributions derived by varying the combination of fertility and mortality rates, are consistent with Coale's (1964) calculations showing that fertility is the key determinant of change in the age composition, and that mortality plays a much smaller role.

Even so, declining mortality can in some circumstances help to shift a population's age distribution, making it younger or older. As Coale (1964) showed, mortality affects the age distribution much less than fertility does, and in the opposite direction from what most of us would expect. Prolonging life by reducing death rates makes the population somewhat younger, even though a reduction in the death rate increases the average age of death and therefore the num-

ber of old people in the population. Coale explained this paradoxical effect as follows:

It is true that as death rates fall, the average age at which people die is increased. But the average age of a population is the average age of living persons, not their average age at death. It is also true . . . that as death rates fall the number of old persons in a population increases. What we do not so readily realize is that reduced mortality increases the number of young persons as well. More persons survive from birth to ages 1, 10, 20, and 40, as well as more living to old age. Because more persons survive to be parents, more births occur' (Coale, 1964: 49–50).

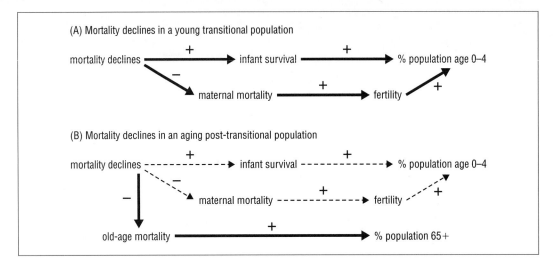

Figure 4.4 Differential effects of mortality improvements in (A) a young transitional population and (B) an aging post-transitional population

Note: Solid arrows denote strong effects; hatched arrows denote very weak effects. A 'plus' sign means that the effect serves to increase the level of a variable; a 'minus' sign means the opposite.

In developing societies in the early stages of the demographic transition, mortality improvements do not generally take place uniformly throughout the age structure. Improvements tend to occur first among infants, children, and women of reproductive age. It is only later in the transition process that other segments of the age structure begin to experience reduced death rates and thus enhanced survival probabilities (Omran, 1971). Sustained mortality reductions in the younger age groups help to increase the numbers of persons in the reproductive-age cohorts, which will eventually go on to bear children when they reach parental age. This has the effect of making the population's age structure *younger* (see Figure 4.4).

In populations that have passed through the demographic transition and are now in the post-transition stage, mortality rates in infancy, childhood, and the reproductive ages are already very low, and it is the over-60 age segment that experiences major improvements in survival probabilities (Olshansky and Ault, 1986; Manton, 1991). Thus in infancy, childhood, and young adulthood, further mortality declines are bound to be less dramatic than in the past (Stone and Fletcher, 1994). Improved survival probabilities in the older age groups amplify demographic aging (see Figure 4.4). It has been shown using stable population models that, in general, when mortality declines are concentrated in infancy and early childhood the effect will be to make the population younger. If, on the other hand, survival improvements are concentrated in the ages above 45, the effect will be to age the population (Coale, 1957a, 1957b, 1964, 1972; Preston, Heuveline, and Guillot, 2001: 160–1).

Crude and Intrinsic Growth Rates

The stable population model can also be meaningfully applied in the comparative analysis of population rates of natural increase. Typically, the rate of natural increase (RNI) is reported as the difference between the crude birth and death rates for a given population. Since the crude birth and death rates do not take into account age composition, the resulting rate of natural increase is a crude measure of the rate of growth. But a net rate of natural growth can be computed; this is called the *intrinsic rate of*

Historically, declines in mortality tended to lower rather than raise the average age of populations. The reason is that for most of human history life expectancy was very short and mortality very high, particularly in infancy and childhood. The improvements in living conditions that came with modernization dramatically reduced the death rate in the youngest age groups, with the result that the population as a whole became younger. Once a population reaches a life expectancy of about 65, however, further reductions in mortality will tend to be concentrated in the older age groups, raising the average age of the population. In the advanced societies today, where life expectancy at birth is well above 65, reductions in mortality affect mainly those over age 50, with the result that populations are clearly aging (Preston, Heuveline, and Guillot (2001: 160).

growth. It is possible to derive for any real population the underlying stable population that would result if its *current* age-specific schedules of fertility and mortality were to hold constant indefinitely. The stable population that results is called the *stable equivalent population*. The intrinsic rate of growth based on a population's equivalent stable population (i.e., the difference between the intrinsic birth and death rates) represents the rate of growth of the population *without* the confounding effects of age composition.

It is quite possible for a contemporary population to show a positive rate of natural increase even if its intrinsic growth rate is negative. Indeed, if one were to make this calculation for the industrialized countries today, many of them would show negative intrinsic growth rates. The reason has to do with persistently low fertility (below replacement level) in a context of very low death rates. The reason these populations are showing positive crude rates of natural increase—albeit very low ones—at present is that their age compositions reflect, in varying

degrees, the long-term effects of higher fertility rates in the past (e.g., the post-war baby boom).

Effects of Migration on Age–Sex Structure

The effects of migration on age structure at the national level tend to be negligible compared to the effects of fertility and mortality change (Preston, Heuveline, and Guillot, 2001). Nevertheless, there are cases in which migration can have a visible impact on the age composition of an entire society. In the case of out-migration, the impact on the 'sending' society may be noticeable if the numbers leaving are large and concentrated in a specific age category—typically the prime labour-force years—and gender. The longer the out-migration continues, the greater the impact on the age and sex structure of the sending population will be.

Immigration may also affect the age and sex composition of the receiving population in parallel ways. Immigration's effects on the host population's age structure will largely depend on the size of the age categories into which immigrants are moving, the numbers of immigrants entering those age categories, the gender composition of the immigrants, and the intensity of immigration over time. Again, because of selectivity the age composition of the immigrant group is generally quite different from that of the host population. In the Canadian case the age pyramid of the immigrant population is shaped more like a diamond than a pyramid: there are relatively few immigrants below the age of 15, and relatively few over 65. This means that most immigrants are concentrated in the prime labour-force ages of 20 to 64 (Bélanger and Dumas, 1998: 94). The impact of immigration on Canada's median age is minor because the average age on arrival is around 30, after which immigrants age along with the rest of the population (Statistics Canada, 2007a).

In some cases the effect of migration on the age structure of the receiving population may be visible on only one side of the age pyramid—either the male or the female. Some of the oil-producing countries in the Middle East have visibly distorted age structures on the male side as a result of large-scale immigration of male workers. This is clearly the case in the age pyramids of the United Arab Emirates, Saudi Arabia, Qatar, Oman, Kuwait, Guam, and Bahrain (United Nations Department of Economic and Social Affairs Population Division, 2002e). In some other cases, large-scale out-migration of females in the labour-force ages shows up as a noticeable gap in the female side of the pyramid; two examples of this pattern are Samoa and East Timor (United Nations Department of Economic and Social Affairs Population Division, 2003b). Such an imbalance would tend to affect the age distribution in these countries in two ways: first, it would shift the overall sex ratio of the population in favour of either males or females, depending on which sex is most affected by either in- or out-migration; second, sex ratios in the affected age groups would be distorted, with an oversupply of either males or females.

Age Distribution as Demographic Memory

A fundamental principle of stable population theory is that two populations with radically different age structures will converge to identical age compositions if the two populations have identical age-specific birth and death rates over 70 years or more (Coale, 1972: 3; Lopez, 1961). Age distributions gradually 'forget' their past. Consider two populations with very different age compositions in 1960: Sweden and Sri Lanka. Sweden's age distribution in 1960 was typical of an industrialized post-transitional population, while Sri Lanka's reflected a young, rapidly growing population that had not yet completed its demographic transition. Pollard and colleagues (1981) conducted a simulation in which they used Sweden's age-specific birth and death rates from 1960 as the set of constant age-specific rates to be applied to these two different populations over a period of 10 decades—1960 to 2060 (migration was not

considered). As Figure 4.5 shows, these two age structures start out very differently—as would be expected—but eventually converge, assuming identical shapes in the last decade. This principle of stable population theory has been called the *ergodic property* of populations: the tendency to eventually 'forget' their initial age distributions (Coale, 1972: 3; Keyfitz, 1968: 90).

It takes roughly a century for a population's age structure to change completely (Preston, Heuveline, and Guillot, 2001: 1). During this time, significant sociological information remains visible in the shape of the population's age pyramid. For instance, extreme irregularities in a population's age structure can sometimes be traced to major historical events that have affected birth and death rates over the long term, and are reflected in the shape of its age pyramid. In Figure 4.6, for example, the French and German pyramids are typical of the European nations that endured two world wars, while the distortions apparent in the Chinese pyramid can be linked directly to government policies (Yongping and Peng, 2000).

Population Momentum

As we saw in Chapter 3, a certain amount of growth is built into the current age structure of any population. The basic question behind the concept of population momentum is this: If a country could reduce its fertility rate to replacement level overnight, by how much would its population continue to grow before growth actually stopped? If mortality remains constant and there is no in- or out-migration, such a population will in the long run reach a stationary state with an unchanging age distribution and zero growth rate (see the box on pages 108–9). Various ways of estimating population momentum have been proposed by authors including Keyfitz (1985), Li and Tuljapurkar (1999), and Preston, Heuveline, and Guillot (2001). The basic approach is to estimate the ratio of the stationary population that will eventually be produced under the new fertil-

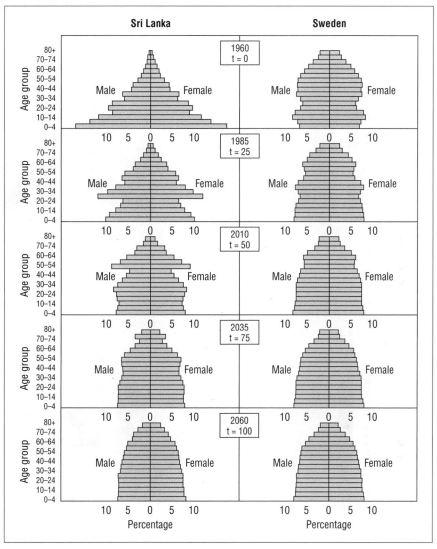

Figure 4.5 Hypothetical evolution of Sri Lankan and Swedish age pyramids over a century, given Sweden's (1960) fertility and mortality rates (t = years after 1960)

Source: Pollard, Yusuf, and Pollard (1981), 102 (Figure 7.1).

ity regime (i.e., constant fertility at the replacement level of 2.1 children per woman) to the population size when the fall in fertility occurs:

$$M = \frac{\text{size of the stationary population}}{\text{size of the initial population}}$$

Appropriate population projection methods are applied to determine the size of the stationary population. A country's population is projected for 100 years assuming replacement fertility, constant mortality at the level for the initial year, and no migration (Rowland, 2003: 331).

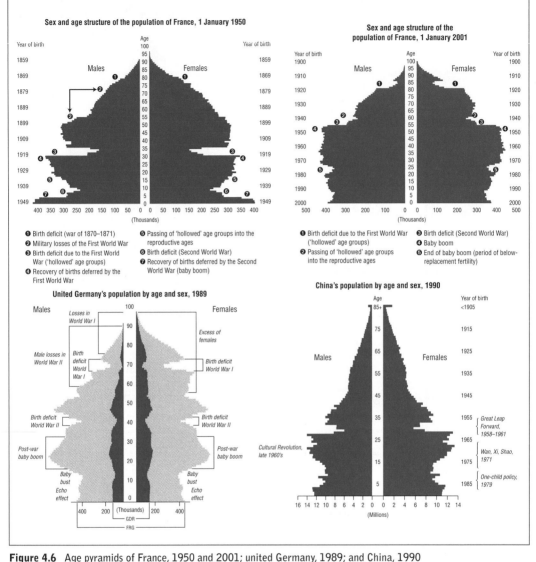

Figure 4.6 Age pyramids of France, 1950 and 2001; united Germany, 1989; and China, 1990

Sources: France: Pison (2001), reprinted by permission of the publisher; Heilig, Buttner, and Lutz (1990): 8 (Figure 2); United Nations Department of Economic and Social Affairs Division (1973): 279 (Figure 2), reprinted with permission of the United Nations; China: Yongping and Xizhe (2000): 65 (Figure 6.1).

A value of *M* greater than 1 would indicate that the population would grow as a result of momentum generated by the youthful age structure of the population. A value of 1 would imply no momentum (i.e., stationary population), while a value below 1 would mean population decline (i.e., negative momentum).

Values of *M* calculated by Preston, Heuveline, and Guillot (2001: 164) illustrate the range of variation in population momentum across regions and countries in 1997:

A shortcut formula for deriving the growth factor that represents population momentum has been worked out by Keyfitz (1985):

$$M = \frac{b\,e_0}{1,000\,\sqrt{NRR}}$$

where M is momentum, b is the population's crude birth rate, e_0 is its life expectancy at birth, and NRR is the net reproduction rate of the population before the drop in fertility to the replacement level. Thus if a population has a crude birth rate of 35, a life expectancy at birth of 65, and a net reproduction rate of 2.5, it would grow by a factor of 1.439 before it leveled off:

$$M = \frac{35 \times 65}{1,000\,\sqrt{2.5}} = 1.439$$

Region or country	Population momentum
Africa	1.56
Eastern Asia	1.22
South Central Asia	1.47
Southeastern Asia	1.48
Western Asia	1.56
Europe	0.98
Latin America and the Caribbean	1.48
Northern America	1.10
Austria	0.96
Russia	0.94
Italy	0.91
Germany	0.88
World total	1.35

If in 1997 fertility in all these countries had declined to the replacement level and mortality remained constant, the populations of Africa and western Asia would grow the most—by a factor of 1.56 (i.e., 56 per cent)—because of their youthful age compositions. In sharp contrast, the population of Europe as a whole would decline by 2 per cent (i.e., $1 - 0.98 = 0.02$). The populations of Austria, Russia, Italy, and Germany would decline, as they all had momentum factors below 1. These cases demonstrate that there can be a momentum to population decline (*negative population momentum*) as well as to population growth (Preston, Heuveline, and Guillot, 2001: 164). The eventual stationary populations in these cases would be smaller than the populations at the time at which replacement fertility is imposed. Worldwide, a population momentum factor of 1.35 implies considerable, unavoidable growth.

The analysis of population momentum is useful for planning purposes. If a society with a rapidly growing population wishes to reduce its rate of growth, it must be prepared to look far into the future. The magnitude of population momentum will depend on whether a population decides to stop growing now or at some point in the future. The difference can be quite significant. A growing population that abruptly reduces its fertility to replacement level and maintains it there will still grow for two generations or so. This residual growth will be even larger if the decline to replacement fertility takes place gradually (as is the case in reality) rather than instantaneously (Li and Tuljapurkar, 1999).

NRR is a measure of population reproductivity—that is, the extent to which mothers replace themselves by bearing daughters. NRR is approximately one-half the value of the total fertility rate (TFR). Thus a TFR of 2.1 means that women on average are bearing one daughter each. If the TFR is less than 2.1, then the number of daughters being born is less than one per woman. If the TFR is greater than 2.1, then on average women are bearing more than one daughter each. Therefore an NRR of 1 is consistent with zero population growth in the long run.

Population Momentum

The impact of population momentum on future population levels can be illustrated by the following example of two families. The first generation of each family consists of one man and one woman. Each woman has four children over her reproductive life. This second generation includes four females and four males.

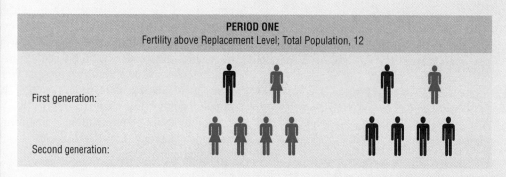

PERIOD ONE
Fertility above Replacement Level; Total Population, 12

First generation:

Second generation:

In period two, the first generation dies and everyone in the second generation marries. Each woman in the four resulting couples has two children, producing a third generation of four males and four females. Even though the second generation reaches replacement levels of fertility, population momentum causes a 33 per cent increase in total population, from 12 to 16, between period one and period two.

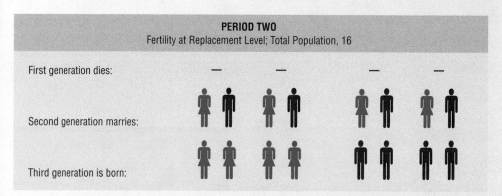

PERIOD TWO
Fertility at Replacement Level; Total Population, 16

First generation dies:

Second generation marries:

Third generation is born:

The process is repeated in period three. The second generation dies; the third generation marries and produces a fourth generation. If the third generation remains at replacement levels of fertility, the total population stabilizes. The size of the steady-state population in the final period is the result not only of the fertility decisions of the second and third generations, but of those of the first generation as well.

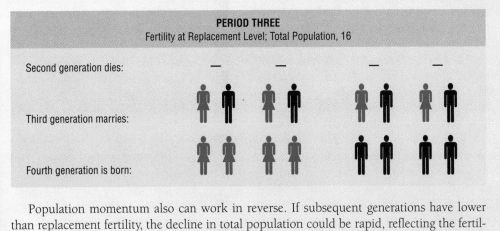

Population momentum also can work in reverse. If subsequent generations have lower than replacement fertility, the decline in total population could be rapid, reflecting the fertility decisions of both current and previous generations.

Source: Box 7.2, 'Population Momentum', from *Economics Of Development*, 6th edn, by Dwight H. Perkins, Steven Radelet, and David L. Lindauer. Copyright © 2006, 2001, 1996, 1992, 1987, 1983 by W.W. Norton & Company, Inc. Used by permission of W.W. Norton & Company, Inc.

Generalizations about Age Structure

The preceding paragraphs suggest several important generalizations:

1. Rapidly growing populations typically have high fertility rates, which manifest themselves in broad-based age pyramids. The age group 0–4 reflects the births that have occurred between year *t* and *t*–5 years ago. The more babies are born, the wider the base of the age pyramid will be. Thus the wider base of the age pyramid of less developed countries is the result of sustained high fertility rates.

2. The proportion of people at the upper end of the age pyramid diminishes with advancing age. The higher the age, the fewer the people still living. The increasing intensity of mortality translates into a narrowing of the age pyramid with advancing age. Generally, the narrower the upper part of the age distribution, the higher the death rate in the population.

3. Since the sum of the percentages across age and sex must be 100, a pyramid with a wide base will necessarily have a narrow top. In general,

the higher the median age of a population, the wider the top of the age pyramid will be. Populations with a relatively low median age characteristically have a larger proportion under 15 and a relatively small proportion over 65.

4. As a population experiences sustained reductions in fertility, the base of its age pyramid will constrict. If this condition persists over a long time, the result will be a transformation in shape from a true pyramid to an inverted pyramid: narrowest at the base and widest at the top. In that case a large percentage of the population will be older than 65 and the population will be declining.

Sex Ratios

Basic Principles

The sex ratio reflects the numerical balance between males and females in a population:

$$\text{sex ratio} = \frac{\text{number of males}}{\text{number of females}} \times 100$$

The computation of this measure can be easily illustrated with actual data. The 2001 Census of Canada counted 14,706,850 males and 15,300,245 females. Thus the sex ratio was 96.1 males for every 100 females. This indicates the presence of about 4 per cent more women than men. All things being equal, the sex ratio of a population should be close to 100 males per 100 females (i.e., equal proportions of males and females), though in fact a value in the range of about 96 to 98 is typical of most populations. Why is this ratio not exactly 100? In order to answer this question, we need to distinguish between three types of sex ratios. The *primary sex ratio* is the ratio of males to females at conception; the *secondary sex ratio* is the ratio at birth; and the *tertiary sex ratio* is the ratio at ages beyond infancy.

Sex Ratio at Conception

It is widely recognized that human populations typically conceive more males than females (Brian and Jaisson, 2007; Cavalli-Sforza and Bodmer, 1971; Chahnazarian, 1988; Clark, 2003; Croll, 2000; James, 1987a, 1987b; Teitelbaum, 1972). A reasonable estimate of the sex ratio at conception appears to be in the range of 115 to 120 males for every 100 females (McMillen, 1979; Perls and Fretts, 2002).

The literature in this area suggests that many variables may have an influence on sex at conception. For example, the chances of conceiving a male appear to increase if conception takes place at either the beginning or the end of the menstrual cycle; some researchers have speculated that this may explain why the percentage of baby boys has usually increased after major wars, since the frequency of intercourse is likely to increase at such times (James, 1997; Mealey, 2000). There is also some evidence that younger fathers may be more likely than older ones to produce sons. Birth order also seems to matter: the more children the woman has already borne, the greater the chance of her conceiving a male. In addition, a shorter interval between births may

Recent decades have seen reports of an apparent decline in sex ratios at birth in a number of countries, including Canada (Allan et al., 1997; Davis et al., 1998; Dodds and Armson, 1997; Faitosa and Krieger, 1992; Marcus et al., 1998; Ulizzi and Zonta, 1993; Vartiainen, Kartovaara, and Tuomisto, 1999). Environmental pollution is thought to be one possible cause: high exposure to certain chemicals (e.g., pesticides) may be interfering with males' ability to produce sperm cells with the Y chromosomes necessary to conceive boys. Studies based on human and animal populations suggest that the action of some toxins may be similar to hormonally induced ovulation, and this is hypothesized to cause an excess of female conceptions (Allan et al., 1997). Toxins in pesticides may also interfere with prenatal development, causing a disproportionate number of miscarriages among the frailer male embryos. Since XY embryos require hormonal stimulation to produce masculine genitalia, the unborn males are likely more vulnerable to hazardous chemicals (Albert, 1998).

increase the likelihood of bearing a male. There is also some evidence that the month of conception and the sex of earlier births to the same parents can make a difference, though empirical support for these relationships has been inconsistent (Tremblay, Vezina, and Houde, 2003).

What accounts for the preponderance of male conceptions remains unclear. However, we know that males are at greater risk of death than females throughout the life cycle. Perhaps, then, the tendency to conceive more males is a way of compensating for their greater innate vulnerability (Kramer, 2000; Perls and Fretts, 2002).

Sex Ratios at Birth and in Early Childhood

The secondary sex ratio also favours males: across human populations, roughly 105 boys are born for every 100 girls; in percentage terms, these proportions mean that just under 49 per cent of all births in a given year will be girls and just over 51 per cent will be boys. But the imbalance at this stage is much smaller than it was at conception. Even though in general more boys are conceived, substantially more male than female fetuses are lost to spontaneous abortion or stillbirth; as a result, the sex ratio at birth is reduced to about 105. (Leridon, 1976; McMillen, 1979; Perls and Frets, 2002; Clark, 2003).

The fact that sex ratios in some regions of the world—notably parts of South Asia, East Asia, the Middle East, and North Africa—are highly distorted in favour of boys in early childhood reflects a combination of cultural and social structural factors (e.g., level of economic development, differences in family form, rules of primogeniture and inheritance, rules for the care of the elderly, and marriage customs) that predispose parents to desire sons over daughters (Bhat and Halli, 1999; Goody, 1996; Lavely, Li, and Li, 2001; Leone, Matthews, and Dalla Zuanna, 2003; Sen, 2003). Now that screening technologies make it possible to determine sex before birth, some parents will choose to abort a fetus of the 'wrong' sex (Coale, 1991; Banister and Coale, 1994; Goodkind, 1996; Klasen, 2003; Croll, 2000; Junhong, 2001; Yount, 2001). Throughout history, however, many human societies have probably practised sex-selective infanticide, neglect, or abandonment under certain circumstances (e.g., conditions of severe food scarcity) (Hrdy, 1999; Johnson, 1996; Scrimshaw, 1978, 1984; Sen, 2003). In China especially, son preference and, more recently, the practice of sex-selective abortion has resulted in a serious shortage of women (Tuljapurkar, Li, and Feldman, 1995). The number of 'missing women' around the world has been estimated at between 89 and 95 million (Klasen and Wink, 2002).

Sex Ratios in Adulthood and Old Age

Age-specific sex ratios in adulthood are almost entirely determined by gender-based differences in mortality, though (as we have seen) migration can also play an important role in some circumstances. In virtually all societies females have lower age-specific death rates than males, and on average they live longer than men (Kramer, 2000; Perls and Frets, 2002). On the basis of the sex mortality differential alone, we could expect the ratio of males to females in the population to decline gradually with age. Indeed, in the industrialized countries the balance in the numbers of males to females begins to approach parity around the age of 30; and it favours females disproportionately after about 60. As Figure 4.7 shows, in the older age groups there may be fewer than 25 males for every 100 females in countries such as Canada, the United States, Japan, and Italy.

Deviations from this general pattern are noticeable. In Saudi Arabia, for example, there is a very irregular sequence of age–sex ratios between the ages of 20 and 65. It is likely that sex-selective migration is a contributing factor here: Saudi Arabia attracts many male temporary workers. In addition, high rates of maternal mortality may contribute to the high sex ratios from the age of 15 through 49.

Age–sex ratios in the Russian Federation fall below 100 relatively early in life, around age 35, and drop noticeably thereafter. This is largely a reflection of the sex differential in mortality in Russia. A female born in 1970 could expect to live, on average, 10.53 years longer than a male, and by 1992 the gap had expanded to 11.80 years (Shkolnikov, Mesle, and Vallin, 1997: 52). In 2007, the sex difference in life expectancy had grown to 13 years (Population Reference Bureau, 2007).

The patterns of age-specific sex ratios in China and India are also atypical. At age 0–4, the Chinese sex ratio is 111.3, whereas in other societies it is in the range of 103 to 106. In most cases the sex ratio declines after birth and gradually approaches parity somewhere between puberty and age 40 or so (Ulizzi and Zonta, 1993). But in China the point of convergence is

Table 4.4 Sex ratios at birth and at age 0–4, and percentages of male and female births for selected countries and periods

Country	Period	Sex ratio at birth	% Male births	% Female births	Sex ratio at age 0–4[1]	Period
Benin	1992	1.023	0.506	0.494	1.023	2000
Egypt	1998	1.065	0.516	0.484	1.050	1996
Libya	1996	1.085	0.520	0.480	1.036	1991
Mauritius	1999	1.054	0.513	0.487	1.023	1999
Morocco	1999	1.047	0.511	0.489	1.043	2000
Canada	1997	1.055	0.513	0.487	1.052	1998
Cuba	1998	1.094	0.523	0.477	1.068	1998
El Salvador	1999	1.067	0.516	0.484	1.042	1999
Nicaragua	1999	1.064	0.515	0.485	1.038	2000
Puerto Rico	1999	1.066	0.516	0.484	1.038	2000
USA	1991	1.046	0.511	0.489	1.046	1998
Brazil	1996	1.045	0.511	0.489	1.046	1998
Chile	1999	1.048	0.512	0.488	1.038	2000
Paraguay	1991	1.058	0.514	0.486	1.038	1999
Uruguay	1999	1.037	0.509	0.491	1.044	1999
Bahrain	1995	1.060	0.515	0.485	1.071	2000
Brunei Darussalam	1992	1.036	0.509	0.491	1.071	1992
China[2]	1996	1.162	0.537	0.463	1.200	1996
Hong Kong	1999	1.087	0.521	0.479	1.068	2000
India	—	—	—	—	1.051	2000
Indonesia[2]	1995	1.060	0.515	0.485	1.050	1995
Iran[2]	1996	1.058	0.514	0.486	1.055	1996
Israel	1998	1.056	0.514	0.486	1.055	2000
Japan	1999	1.056	0.514	0.486	1.052	1999
N. Korea	1993	1.050	0.512	0.488	1.055	1993
S. Korea	1999	1.096	0.523	0.477	1.134	1995
Kuwait	1999	1.052	0.513	0.487	1.040	1998
Malaysia	1998	1.071	0.517	0.483	1.061	1991
Pakistan	1997	1.077	0.519	0.481	1.040	1998
Philippines	1993	1.087	0.521	0.479	1.064	1995
Saudi Arabia[2]	1992	1.043	0.511	0.489	1.064	1992
Singapore	2000	1.092	0.522	0.478	1.072	2000
Sri Lanka	1996	1.039	0.510	0.490	1.037	1998
Thailand	1999	1.066	0.516	0.484	1.069	2000
Austria	1999	1.048	0.512	0.488	1.050	1999
Belarus	1999	1.065	0.516	0.484	1.060	2000

(*continued*)

Table 4.4 (*continued*)

Country	Period	Sex ratio at birth	% Male births	% Female births	Sex ratio at age 0–4[1]	Period
Belgium	1992	1.049	0.512	0.488	1.045	1999
Bulgaria	1997	1.081	0.519	0.481	1.054	1997
Czech Republic	1999	1.050	0.512	0.488	1.055	1999
Denmark	1999	1.048	0.512	0.488	1.055	2000
Estonia	1997	1.078	0.519	0.481	1.055	1997
Finland	1998	1.041	0.510	0.490	1.039	1998
France	1997	1.055	0.513	0.487	1.048	1998
Germany	1997	1.055	0.513	0.487	1.055	1999
Greece	1998	1.063	0.515	0.485	1.056	1991
Hungary	1999	1.069	0.517	0.483	1.059	1999
Iceland	1998	1.040	0.510	0.490	1.055	1997
Ireland	1999	1.064	0.516	0.484	1.058	1996
Italy	1995	1.064	0.516	0.484	1.059	1999
Netherlands	1998	1.050	0.512	0.488	—	—
Norway	1999	1.057	0.514	0.486	—	—
Poland	1999	1.058	0.514	0.486	—	—
Portugal	1997	1.057	0.514	0.486	—	—
Romania	1998	1.052	0.513	0.487	—	—
Slovakia	1999	1.044	0.511	0.489	—	—
Slovenia	1999	1.067	0.516	0.484	—	—
Spain	1997	1.063	0.515	0.485	1.069	1999
Sweden	1999	1.053	0.513	0.487	1.052	1999
Switzerland	1998	1.050	0.512	0.488	1.052	1998
United Kingdom	1999	1.056	0.514	0.486	1.052	1999
Australia	1999	1.048	0.512	0.488	1.054	1999
New Zealand	2000	1.062	0.515	0.485	—	—
Averages		1.061	0.515	0.485	1.056	

[1]Sex ratios for age group 0–4 based on population estimates or actual census counts for this age category.

[2]Sex ratios for infancy and corresponding proportions based on population estimate (rather than vital statistics) for ages 0–1 and 1–4, respectively.

Source: United Nations Department of Economic and Social Affairs Population Division (2002c). Reprinted with the permission of the United Nations.

much later, at age 60. One cannot rule out the possibility that data errors are at least partly responsible for the apparent distortion in sex ratios by age (this is also the case with Saudi Arabia). In India, the male-to-female ratio starts out high (106:100 at ages 0–4) and rises to 110 between ages 15 and 24; it then declines gradually to 103 at age 50–54, and finally drops

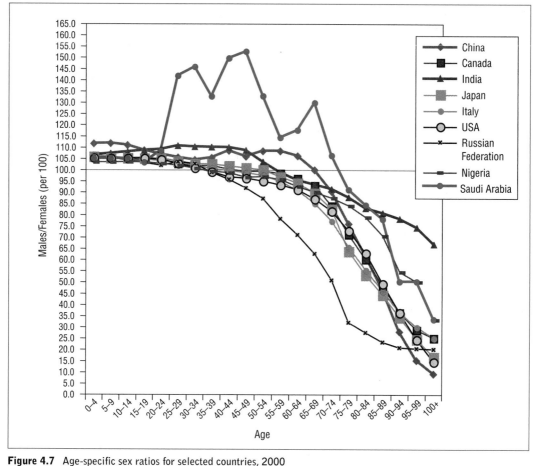

Figure 4.7 Age-specific sex ratios for selected countries, 2000

Source: United Nations Department of Economic and Social Affairs Population Division (2003b): vol. 2. Reprinted with the permission of the United Nations.

below 100 at 55–59. In the older age groups the sex ratios are all below 100.

Societal Ramifications of Change in Age–Sex Composition

Sex Ratio Effects

The balance of men and women in human populations is not uniform across all age groups; in some age groups the ratios can be severely distorted in favour of one sex or the other. Heavy in- or out-migration of one sex or the other in adulthood can also distort the sex ratio, either increasing or decreasing the gender balance. In some contexts high male death rates coupled with large-scale out-migration of males in the prime marriageable ages can contribute to a female surplus in these ages (Guttentag and Secord, 1983a; Messner and Sampson, 1991).

A severe imbalance can have a variety of important sociological effects. One illustration is given by Messner and Sampson (1991), who conducted a study of 153 large cities in the

United States in order to ascertain how unbalanced sex ratios might affect the incidence of violent crime and family disruption for black and white populations. Their statistical results showed that for both black and white populations a surplus of males between the ages of 15 and 59 was correlated with relatively low levels of family disruption (as measured by the percentage of households headed by a female) and high rates of violent crime (as indexed by robbery and homicide rates). Not surprisingly, they also found that higher rates of family disruption were strongly correlated with higher rates of violent crime (the higher the percentage of female-headed families, the higher the violent crime rate in cities). By contrast, in cities characterized by low sex ratios (i.e., where there was a deficit of males in relation to women in the ages of 15–59) the level of violent crime was relatively low, but family disruption levels were high. These relationships held after controls for a number of relevant variables had been introduced into the multivariate analysis. Messner and Sampson (1991: 705–7) concluded that their results generally support a 'model of countervailing direct positive effects of the sex ratio on rates of criminal violence and negative indirect effects via family disruption.' Thus distorted sex ratios can produce two separate structural problems. First, a high sex ratio (more men than women) generates a large demographic group that is at risk of committing violent offences; second, a low sex ratio (fewer men than women) is associated with reduced commitment to family and marriage by young men and women alike, and therefore higher levels of family instability.

Research based on *The Sex Ratio Question* (Guttentag and Secord, 1983a) has shown that in certain contexts an increased risk of divorce can be partly explained by sex ratio imbalances in the prime marriageable ages (Lichter et al., 1992; Messner and Sampson, 1991). One such study, by South and Lloyd (1992), found that the risk of marital dissolution was highest where either wives or husbands encountered an abun-

dance of spousal alternatives—for instance, in places with high rates of labour force participation among unmarried women. In other words, areas with a surplus of either gender in the young adult age groups are likely to have higher rates of divorce than areas with a more balanced gender distribution. 'In this sense, marital dissolution is, in part, a product of the demographic opportunities embedded in the social structure' (South and Lloyd, 1992: 33).

Another effect of imbalanced sex ratios may be what has been called a 'marriage squeeze' affecting either men or women in the prime marriageable ages. The causes of this phenomenon are partly demographic, involving abrupt changes in fertility rates, and partly cultural, based on the notion that husbands should be two or three years older than wives. When fertility rates increase suddenly after a prolonged period of low fertility, a marriage squeeze will develop a couple of decades later for some of the young women born during the first few years of the fertility boom, as these women will be unable to find husbands born during the last few years of the low-fertility period. Subsequent cohorts of women will not be affected in this way because the sex ratios will soon stabilize once the high-fertility regime is established.

A second marriage-squeeze scenario can be expected to develop a couple of decades after fertility rates drop, as at the end of a baby boom, when young men born near the end of the high-fertility period will find insufficient numbers of women two to three years younger than themselves. As in the first scenario, subsequent cohorts of young men should not be affected in this way. Both types of marriage squeeze are temporary, caused by abrupt changes in fertility in conjunction with cultural norms regarding the appropriate age difference between spouses (Guttentag and Secord, 1983a; Schoen, 1983; Veevers, 1994).

A serious marriage squeeze is currently in the making in China, where state policy has combined with culture and demography to create a severe shortage of marriageable young

Spousal Alternatives and Marital Dissolution

South and Lloyd (1992) used survey data from the United States to test the proposition that the quantity and quality of potential marital partners available in the local marriage market can have an impact on the rate of marital dissolution at the local level. They looked at individual-level determinants of divorce (e.g., gender, age at first marriage, years of schooling, home ownership, number of children, work status, and income) as well as contextual factors at the community level (e.g., the sex ratio of men to women, percentages of females and males employed or in school, the rate of geographic mobility in the area, and the median monthly rent in the community). Their tabular analysis showed that among male respondents, 41 per cent said that their wives had been involved with someone else just before the marriage ended. Among the women, approximately 42 per cent said that their husbands had been involved with someone else. These findings indicated that a substantial number of divorces in the communities studied were caused by marital infidelity.

Their multivariate analysis considered all the mentioned determinants at both the individual and the community level. The most important individual-level determinants of divorce risk were found to be years of schooling, home ownership, number of children, number of weeks the husband worked, and husband's income. All of these had a negative effect on divorce—that is, the higher the levels on these variables, the lower the risk of divorce. Among the most important marriage market characteristics at the community level were the ratio of men to women (negative effect on divorce risk); the percentage of females employed or in school (positive effect); the rate of geographic mobility in the community (positive effect); and the sex ratio squared (positive effect). The inclusion of the latter made it possible to estimate the effect of change in the sex ratio on change in the risk of divorce. When the sex ratio is 105 men to 100 women in a community, the risk of dissolution is about 8 per cent higher than would be expected on average. When the sex ratio imbalance increases to higher levels the risk decreases, but only up to a certain point; then it rises again. To illustrate, when the sex ratio imbalance is 115 men to 100 women, the chance of divorce is 2.6 per cent; when the sex ratio is 127, the chance of divorce drops to zero. But if the sex ratio rises to 137, then the risk of marital break-up goes up to 2.6 per cent; and if the sex ratio rises to 162, the risk increases to 13.2 per cent. Presumably, when the sex ratio imbalance is so large, the number of alternative sexual partners for women increases, thus contributing to marital instability. South and Lloyd argued that the risk of marital dissolution is highest where either wives or husbands encounter an abundance of spousal alternatives, and that increased labour force participation among unmarried women, and high geographic mobility rates in the local area increase marital instability. They concluded that 'many persons remain open to alternative relationships even while married, and that the supply of spousal alternatives in the local marriage market significantly increases the risk of marital dissolution' (21).

Reference
Scott J. South, and K.M. Lloyd (1995), 'Spousal Alternatives and Marital Dissolution', *American Sociological Review* 60: 21–35.

women. The one-child policy introduced in the late 1970s restricts couples to one child. In combination with a strong cultural preference for sons, this policy has led to the widespread practice of sex-selective termination of female pregnancies. As Tuljapurkar, Li, and Feldman (1995) have shown, over time this situation has created a severe distortion in the balance of the sexes for the male cohorts now in the prime marriageable ages (i.e., 18–34).

Demographic Aging: A Crisis in the Making?

Population aging is expected to have significant consequences not only in the industrialized economies but also in some newly emerging economies. Among the anticipated effects are labour force shortages and increasing pressures on health care and public pension systems (Bongaarts, 2004; Day, 1978, 1992; De Santis, 2003; Easterlin, 1961b, 1978, 1987; Frejka and Ross, 2001; McDonald and Kippen, 2001; Organisation for Economic Co-operation and Development, 1998, 2004; Teitelbaum and Winter, 1985; United Nations Department of Economic and Social Affairs Population Division, 2002e; World Bank, 1994). Compounding the challenge that social security systems will face is the trend towards early retirement (Costa, 1998). Retiring boomers will swell the size of the retired population for two decades, and they will be collecting benefits for a long time (Gendel, 2002: 2). Other ramifications of population aging may include changes in popular ideas about what it means to be 'old', and possibly even rethinking of intergenerational obligations within families. Increased longevity in general, and among the elderly in particular, means that interaction between children, parents, grandparents, and related family members has the potential to continue over a considerably longer stretch of time than was the case in the past (Burch, 1987; Day, 1992; Traphagan and Knight, 2003; Uhlenberg, 1996, 1980; Watkins, Menken, and Bongaarts, 1987). As a consequence, new intergenerational living arrangements may be needed to help young families cope with the increasing costs of looking after aging parents as well as their own growing households. At the same time, as aging societies must increasingly depend on immigration to supplement their dwindling supply of native-born labour, their social fabric is likely to become increasingly multicultural and multiracial (Lutz, Kritzinger, and Skirbekk, 2006).

Japan faces a similar situation, though perhaps even more extreme. Its total population—127 million—changed hardly at all between 2004 and 2005. The number of births, however, declined by approximately 48,000 from the previous year (Fox News, 2006), while the number of deaths—1.077 million—was the highest recorded since 1947. In fact, these two trend lines crossed in 2005 and the population has started to shrink (*The Economist*, 8 Jan. 2004; Population Reference Bureau, 2005). Japan has both the highest average age on the planet (42.9 in 2005) and the highest proportion of elderly people, with 21 per cent of its population over the age of 65. Assuming current birth and death rates and no major change in immigration policies, the 2007 population of 127.7 million is expected to decline to approximately 119 million in 2025 and 95 million in 2050, and to keep falling thereafter (United Nations Department of Economic and Social Affairs Population Division, 2007: 65; Population Reference Bureau, 2007).

For Japan, the fact that this shrinking population is also becoming more elderly will have an increasingly powerful impact on everything from demand for goods and services to public finances to the structure of the workforce. The consequences are likely to be especially dramatic for the labour force, as the population of 15- to 64-year-olds has been falling since 1995. Japan's labour force in 1995 was 87 million. If current demographic conditions remain constant, the future labour force is expected to shrink to 70 million in 2030, while the post-retirement population (65 and over) will soar from less than one-fifth of the total population

Sex Ratio Imbalances and the Marriage Squeeze in China

China battles army of unmarried men

Fearing explosion of social unrest, country vows sex-selection crackdown

BEIJING—Fearing an explosion of social unrest from a growing army of unmarried men, China is vowing a crackdown on the rising epidemic of abortions of female fetuses.

China will face an excess of 30 million men of marriageable age, compared with the number of marriageable women, if the trend continues to the end of the next decade, the latest projections show.

Because of China's limit of one child to a family, combined with traditional preferences for boys, a growing number of couples are aborting their babies when an ultrasound reveals it is a girl.

Chinese authorities are increasingly alarmed by the trend. 'People who conduct illegal gender testing of fetuses and sex-selective abortions should face serious punishment,' China declared yesterday in a joint statement by its government and the ruling Communist Party.

The gender imbalance, which continues to grow worse, is 'a hidden danger' that will 'affect social stability,' the statement warned.

Among newborn babies in China, there were 118 boys for every 100 girls in 2005. The ratio has dramatically worsened since 2000, when the ratio was 110 boys for every 100 girls. In some regions of China, there are as many as 130 boys for every 100 girls. (By comparison, the ratio in industrialized countries is between 104 and 107 boys for every 100 girls.)

The growing sophistication of medical technology has allowed Chinese families to take action on their traditional preference for boys—a preference based on rural ideas that men are the family breadwinners and inheritors of the family line.

In the announcement yesterday, China promised to improve its protection of baby girls. Anyone who kills, abandons or injures an infant girl should be 'severely punished,' the authorities said.

The government also promised to tighten its supervision of medical institutions where ultrasound technology and abortions are available.

China has already banned the use of ultrasound technology to determine the sex of a fetus, and it prohibits the use of abortions for sex-selection reasons.

But the current penalties are relatively mild. The government did not give details of the new penalties that would be imposed under the latest policy.

The Chinese authorities have long been worried about the social consequences of the gender imbalance. 'The increasing difficulties that men face in finding wives may lead to social instability,' the government said in a report this month.

Despite the gender imbalance, China vowed that it would 'firmly' continue its one-child policy, which has been in place for 33 years and has prevented an estimated 400 million births. Since the beginning of the policy, China has created a generation of 'only' children who now number about 90 million.

In its latest statement, the government says the one-child policy is essential because of the 'huge challenges' of the growing population. China has pledged to limit its population to 1.45 billion by 2020, compared with 1.3 billion today.

The government acknowledged this month that 60 per cent of Chinese couples would prefer to have more than one child. But it said it has no intention of relaxing the one-child limit. It said the policy has helped boost China's economic development.

The one-child policy, however, has also provoked controversy and resentment in many quarters of the country. There is widespread anger and outrage, for example, that some wealthy Chinese citizens have been allowed a second child, because they have paid a fine or submitted forged documents. A survey on a Chinese website found that 61 per cent of respondents believe that is unfair.

'How can they violate the national policy just because they have more money?' one person asked on the website.

Zhai Zhenwu, a professor at the Population and Development Studies Centre at Renmin University in Beijing, said the ability of the wealthy to have a second child could worsen the social conflicts in China.

'If the rich are not deterred by fines, no other methods exist to prevent them from having more children,' he said.

Source: Geoffrey York (2007), 'China Battles Army of Unmarried Men: Fearing Explosion of Social Unrest, Country Vows Sex-Selection Crackdown', *The Globe and Mail* (23 Jan.): A3. Reprinted with permission from *The Globe and Mail*.

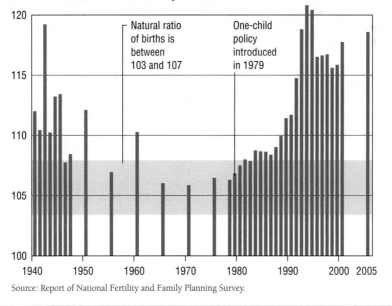

It's a Man's Man's Man's World

The Chinese traditionally favour male children, and the ratio of male to female children born each year has risen steadily since the one-child policy was introduced in 1979.

Number of males born in China for every 100 females

Source: Report of National Fertility and Family Planning Survey.

to one-third over the next several decades (*The Economist*, 8 Jan. 2004).

Industrialized countries around the world are looking for ways to reduce the risk of a social security crisis (De Santis, 2003; *The Economist*, 27 March 2004, 3 April 2004). Bongaarts (2004) has concluded that all the G-7 nations (Canada, United States, Britain, Italy, France, Germany, Japan) will see a substantial rise in old-age dependency ratios between 2000 and 2050, with Japan and Italy facing the most severe increases and the United States the least. As the pensioner-to-worker ratio increases, the average value of public pension benefits declines. The severity of the public pension crisis may be mitigated if governments can persuade older workers to delay retirement; continuing labour force activity on the part of the elderly would increase the government revenues available to fund the system. First, though, governments will have to ensure not only that jobs are available but that they are sufficiently attractive in terms of salary, hours, and so on. The latter may not be easy, given the options (travel, hobbies, etc.) available to retirees today (*The Economist*, 27 March 2004). Any solution is also likely to entail reducing the benefits that pensioners will receive. Bongaarts (2004) suggests that even though OECD countries have been trying to reform their public pension systems so as to avert impending difficulties, it is likely that 'today's workers will have to save more, work longer, retire later, receive less generous benefits, and perhaps pay more taxes' (21).

Alternative solutions are possible: governments could try to boost fertility rates, increase the legal retirement age, or require workers to make larger contributions to the pension plan. But persuading voters to accept these solutions could be difficult. Hence the growing importance of immigration. The immigration solution is deeply problematic for countries such as Japan, however, which—unlike Canada, the United States, and Australia—has never seen itself as a country of immigrants.

For countries like Canada and the United States, which experienced large baby booms in the two decades following the end of World War II, the greatest pressure on the public pension system is expected to occur between 2011 and 2036, when the baby boom generations reach retirement age. In Canada, Stone and Fletcher (1994: 96) indicate that by 2031 seniors will account for 7.5 million people, or roughly 23 per cent of the total population. Assuming that life expectancy at age 65 is in the range of 25 years, public pension payments for these boomer generations are bound to be very costly. And this problem is compounded by the increasing tendency among workers to retire early and begin drawing on the public pension system even before reaching the age of 65. In the long term, the pressure on the public pension system may ease as the large baby boom cohorts pass through old age and die off, sometime after mid-century. Subsequent generations of seniors will be smaller numerically because they will represent the low-fertility baby bust cohorts born after the mid-1960s. However, as shown by Stone and Fletcher (1994) for Canada, by Manton and Soldo (1992) for the United States, and by Kannisto et al. (1994) for other advanced societies, recent generations of elderly people tend to be healthier than previous cohorts of seniors and therefore to live longer on the average. This implies that the senior citizen population in the future may prove to be larger than current projections suggest (Suzman, Willis, and Manton, 1992).

Though most seniors can expect to enjoy relatively good health for some time (Fries, 1980), a longer life for more people must ultimately mean a rise in serious chronic disabilities (Manton, 1982). The increase in disability is expected to be greatest for the oldest group (i.e., 85 and over), which is the fastest-growing segment of the over-65 population (Olshansky and Ault, 1986; Schneider, 1999; Stone and Fletcher, 1994). Population aging can be expected to increase the costs of health care in most societies because older age groups tend to need more care (Kinsella and Vlekoff, 2001: 45). In 2021 the first of the baby boomers will turn 75—the age at which health care costs start to escalate (Schneider, 1999: 796).

Not all views on these matters are so pessimistic. One emerging perspective maintains that population aging in itself is not the main factor in many of the future 'crises' envisioned by some analysts. Proponents of the 'anti-apocalyptic demography' perspective (Gee and Gutman, 2000; Chappell et al., 2003; Day, 1992) assume that demographic aging is inextricably connected to the socioeconomic situation in which it occurs and cannot be understood apart from the broader social context. Thus they argue, for example, that diseases associated with aging (e.g., Alzheimer's) may be overdiagnosed, and that governments may use the aging paradigm to justify policy changes (e.g., increases in immigration levels or cutbacks to education) that may in fact be made for other reasons. The society creates images and ideas of aging, then scientists and policy makers work towards solving the 'problems' of an aging society within the paradigms established by these images. In this way the aging paradigm takes on a reality of its own, as a self-fulfilling prophecy—a prophecy that comes true not because it was true all along, but because people acted as if it were true. Furthermore, when we invoke population aging as the cause of shifting markets, the aged welfare burden, and increased health care costs we may miss the mark as to the real causes of the problem. For example, politicians may erroneously attribute the depletion of pension funds to population aging when in fact the pension system itself is poorly designed or badly managed. Similarly, overemphasis on the demographics of aging encourages us to think of the health care burden as an unsolvable problem rather than one that can be managed through the development of appropriate policies.

A balanced perspective between these contrasting paradigms—the demographic crisis and the 'anti-apocalyptic'—would incorporate elements of both schools of thought in the assessment and implementation of policies associated with population aging. The demographic-crisis perspective hinges on the premise that population projections have a reality of their own. The 'anti-apocalyptic' perspective suggests that the demographic weight of seniors on society, though real, is blown out of proportion by governments and certain sectors of academe. Perhaps the truth lies somewhere in between. We can expect an aging population to put significant demographic pressures on a society, but the severity of its impact will depend on other conditions, such as the nation's economic health and its ability to absorb increasing costs. If the rate of economic growth exceeds the rate of cost increases incurred by population aging, the problems posed by the latter may not be as severe as many have predicted. The costs of providing health care to a growing senior population may be offset to some extent by a decline in the youth dependency ratio resulting from low fertility (Denton and Spencer, 1975).

The Developing Countries: Demographic Windfall vs Poverty Trap

The societal implications of changing age composition for the developing countries depend to a large extent on how far they have progressed through the demographic transition (Ahlburg, Kelley, and Oppenheim Mason, 1996; Birdsall, Kelly, and Sinding, 2001; Bloom, Canning, and Sevilla, 2003; Cincotta and Engelman, 1997; Kinsella and Vlekoff, 2001; Macunovich, 1999, 2002). A country nearing the end of this process can move ahead economically by capitalizing on its demographic windfall in the form of a large and vigorous youthful labour force. But one that is lagging behind will have serious difficulty meeting the social and economic demands of a rapidly growing youth population.

The nature and impact of the demographic transition in a given country depend on many factors: how rapidly the birth rate falls after a period of sustained high fertility; the impact of past fertility on the size of the current labour force; the economic conditions prevailing at the time when the youths born in earlier periods

The Population of the World Will Be Older

According to the 2006 Revision of World Population Prospects, by 2045 the number of older persons in the world (those aged 60 years or over) will likely surpass, for the first time in history, the number of children (i.e., persons under age 15). This crossover is the consequence of the long term reductions in fertility and mortality that are leading to the steady ageing of the world population (Figure 1).

Today, the major areas find themselves at very different stages in the path to population ageing. Ageing is most advanced in Europe, where the number of persons aged 60 or over surpassed the number of children in 1995. By 2050, Europe will have twice as many older persons as children. In fact, in Europe only the older population is expected to increase in the future, whereas the population under age 60 is expected to decrease (Figure 2). This combination of a declining population of children and a declining population in the working ages (15 to 59) leads to very rapid population ageing and poses major challenges for the social and economic adaptation of societies.

Northern America has a quite different pattern of population ageing than Europe. Contrary to Europe, the population in main working age between 15 and 59 will continue to grow during the next 45 years. Other than Europe, Northern America still has a larger number of children then elderly. Only after 2015 the number of people aged 60 and above will become larger than the number of children aged 15 and below. And other than in Europe, the number of children age 15 and below will not decline but grow between 2005 and 2050 (see Figure 6).

Among the developing regions, population ageing is accelerating in Asia and in Latin America and the Caribbean. In Asia, the number of persons aged 60 or over will surpass the number of children by 2040. At about the same time, the population aged 15 to 59 is expected to reach a maximum and begin a slow decline (Figure 3). Similar trends are expected for the population of Latin America and the Caribbean, where the number of

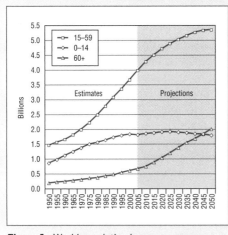

Figure 1 World population by age groups, 1950–2050

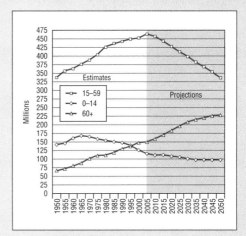

Figure 2 Europe's population by age groups, 1950–2050

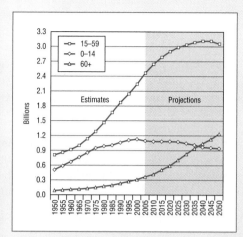

Figure 3 Asia's population by age groups, 1950–2050

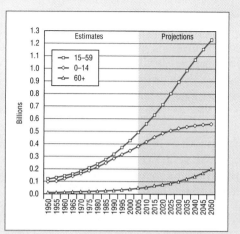

Figure 4 Africa's population by age groups, 1950–2050

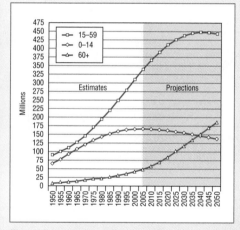

Figure 5 Latin America's population by age groups, 1950–2050

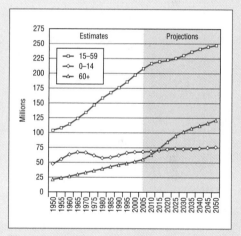

Figure 6 Northern America's population by age groups, 1950–2050

children is expected to fall below the number of older persons in 2040 and the population of working age is expected to stop growing at about the same time (Figure 5).

Africa stands out as the only major region whose population is still relatively young and where the number of elderly, although increasing, will still be far below the number of children in 2050 (Figure 4). In fact, the number of children in Africa is projected to rise from half a billion in 2050 to over 1.2 billion in 2050, a number larger than the number of children that India has today.

For further information please visit our website at: www.un.org/esa/population/unpop.htm

Source: United Nations Department of Economic and Social Affairs (DESA), Population Division, Population Estimates and Projections Section (2007). *World Population Prospects: The 2006 Revision—The Population of the World Will be Older*. Fact Sheet Series A. 7 March 2007. New York: UN. Available at: www.un.org/esa/population/publications/wpp2006/FS_ageing.pdf. Reprinted with the permission of the United Nations.

enter the labour force; and the extent to which the government is willing and able to meet the demographic challenge of an expanding labour force by investing effectively in education and job creation (Birdsall and Sinding, 2001). Together, these structural conditions can create a window of opportunity for a developing country to leap forward economically. How long this window remains open, however, will depend on the rapidity of the fertility decline. The more concentrated the decline, the less time a government will have to take advantage of its demographic windfall.

Figure 4.8 illustrates the connection between stage of demographic transition, population growth rates, and lagged shifts in the age structure of the working population. Notice how the peak in the population's growth rate coincides with the point in the demographic transition where birth and death rates are farthest apart (i.e., stage 2). Also note how the working population progresses through time in relation to the growth rate curve: the peak in the working population comes in the latter part of the transition process, when rates of population growth are low and therefore manageable from the point of

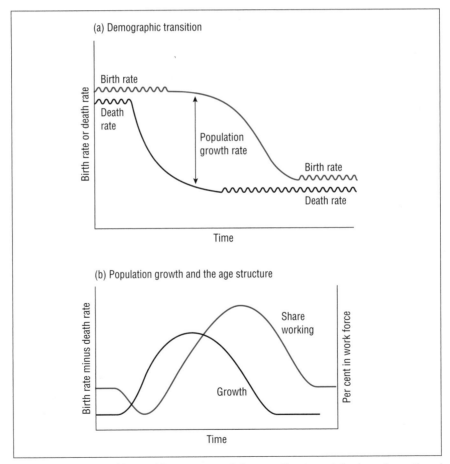

Figure 4.8 Demographic transition stage, population growth rate, and the lagged growth and decline of the working-age population

Source: Bloom and Williamson (1998). Copyright © by The World Bank. Reprinted by permission of Oxford University Press.

view of government planning and intervention. These coincident conditions will favour economic growth if 'the period of the window of opportunity is characterized by (1) more workers producing more total output, if they are productively employed; (2) greater accumulation of wealth, if savings occur and are productively invested; and (3) a larger supply of human capital, if appropriate investments are made in its formation (Birdsall and Sinding, 2001: 9).

The 'Asian Miracle' countries (South Korea, Taiwan, Singapore, Indonesia, Malaysia, and the former Hong Kong Territory) attained success because all these structural factors operated in concert. That is, the 'demographic bonus' arrived at a time of fiscally disciplined government, relatively open and competitive markets, substantial investment in education and training, success in attracting foreign investments, increased saving by the working population and also increased spending by consumers, as well as technological innovation and development in the industrial and manufacturing sectors (Bloom and Canning, 2001; Crenshaw, Ameen, and Christenson, 1997; World Bank, 1993). The relatively high degree of political stability in these societies has also been important (Barro, 1997). The 'Asian Miracle' was partly a demographic miracle, but demography was not the only cause. Also significant was the success of the governments in question in developing institutions, namely education and social safety net programs (e.g., social security, employment insurance, etc.), and in promoting investments in technology while gradually liberalizing trade with other nations (Birdsall and Sinding, 2001).

Canada's Age–Sex Composition: Change and Challenges

From the late nineteenth century until about the third decade of the twentieth, Canada's age structure reflected the youth of the country. In 1881 the median age was only 20.1 years (McVey and Kalbach, 1995a: 60), and this figure rose only gradually over the following decades. Not until the 1950s did the median age rise to just over 27. The fertility surge that followed World War II—caused by a combination of economic prosperity and a host of sociological conditions that together boosted marriage rates among young Canadian men and women—pulled the median age back to 26.3 by 1961, but it started rising again as fertility rates dropped after the baby boom, and by 1976 it had regained the level reached in the early years of the boom. The years following 1980 have seen the population age dramatically. In 2001 the median age was just under 38 years, and five years later it had reached 39.5 (Statistics Canada, 2007c). The effect of the large boomer generation born between 1946 and 1966 is clearly visible in the Canadian age pyramids beginning in 1951 (see Figure 4.1 on page 97 and Figure 4.9 on page 126). With the passage of time, the bulge in the age pyramid that reflects the boomer generation shifts upward as its members grow older.

As we saw in our discussion of the 'stable population' model, the ergodic theorem says that under certain specific demographic conditions a population will eventually 'forget' its past. In other words, disturbances in the age pyramid resulting from past increases or decreases in vital events (e.g., increased mortality, fertility deficits, and recoveries associated with war) eventually dissipate as the generations affected by such events die off. But this takes a long time. In Canada's case, the boomer bulge should finally disappear around 2060, when most of the boomers will have died. Thus the social demographic impacts of the boom generation on Canadian society will be felt for decades to come (Foot and Stoffman, 1998; Kettle, 1980; Owram, 1996).

Looked at over time, dependency ratios can help us predict changes in the dependency burden facing the working-age population. Current dependency ratio values indicate that even though our population is aging, the youth com-

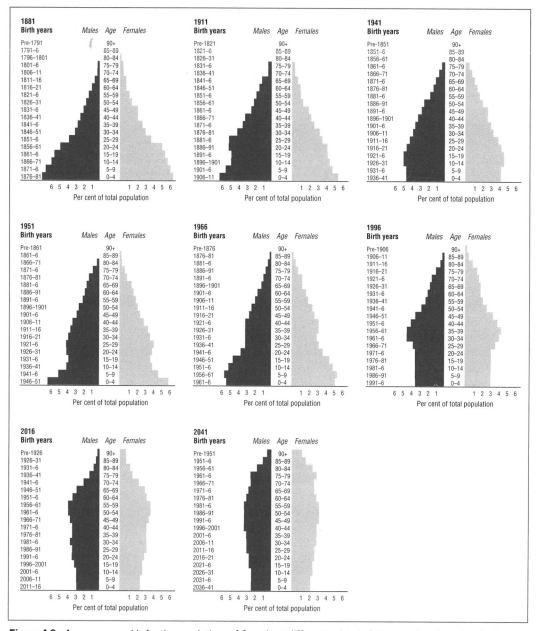

Figure 4.9 Age–sex pyramids for the populations of Canada at different points in history and projected to the future

Sources: Adapted from Grindstaff (1981b): 134–5 (Figure 6); George et al. (2001): 179, 181 (Table A3); Denton, Feaver, and Spencer (2000): 48–9 (Figure 3.1).

ponent actually represents a greater dependency burden than does the older population. McVey and Kalbach (1995a: 73) have calculated these three measures for Canada as far back as 1881. As Figure 4.10 shows, the youth dependency ratio declined from 67.7 per 100 in 1881 to 42.4 in 1941. It increased during the baby boom period, peaking at 57.6 in 1961, and then, as fertility rates fell, declined to 25.7 in 2006. The old-age dependency ratio has been rising gradually for the most part, from 7.2 in the late 1800s to 17.3 in 1991 and 20.0 in 2006.

As the median age of the population continues to rise, however, the old-age component will account for an increasing portion of overall dependency. The crossover point will probably arrive around 2015, when those aged 65 and above are expected to outnumber those aged 15 and under in Canada (Denton, Feaver, and Spencer, 2000; Statistics Canada, 2007a).

The overall sex ratio in Canada favoured males (Figure 4.11) from 1881 until the early 1970s, when the ratio of males to females fell to just about 100; its peak was 112.9, in 1911. Since 1971 the ratio has been declining; from 98.3 in 1981 to 97.2 in 1991 and 95.9 in 2006 (Statistics Canada, 2007a). The high sex ratios around the turn of the century can be explained by sex-selective migration to Canada, which was predominantly male. The declines in recent decades may in part reflect the increase in female migration to Canada. However, the more important factor is the survival advantage of women over men. Because of the much higher death rates of males in old age, the sex ratio in the age groups above 65 favours females disproportionately.

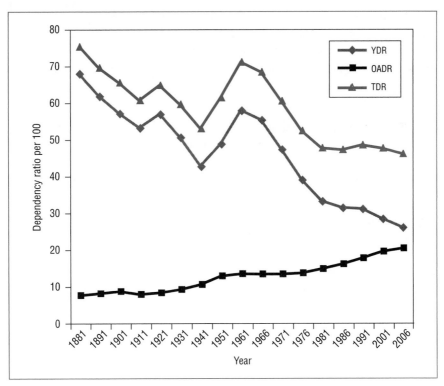

Figure 4.10 Youth, old-age, and total dependency ratios for Canada, 1881–2006

Sources: McVey and Kalbach (1995a): 73; Statistics Canada (2002h); Statistics Canada (2007c).

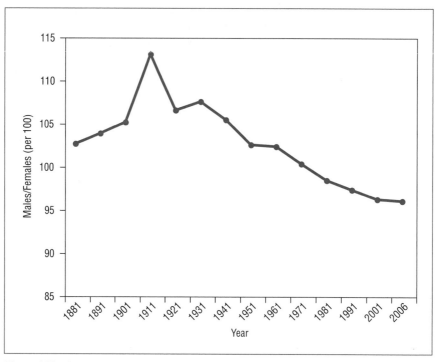

Figure 4.11   Change in overall sex ratios, Canada, 1881–2006

Sources: McVey and Kalbach (1995a), 57; Statistics Canada (2002h); Statistics Canada (2007c).

The population of Canada will continue to grow older over the course of the twenty-first century. The first of the boomers will turn 65 in 2011, and before long those over 65 will, for the first time, outnumber those under 15—the next generation of workers about to enter the labour force. The ratio of 15–24-year-olds to 55–64-year-olds has been declining since 1970, from 2.3 to just 1.1 in 2006 (Statistics Canada, 2007a). These demographic realities pose some important challenges for the country, from a shortage of young workers to higher health care costs and increasing pressure on the publicly funded pension system. The fact that there will be fewer workers paying income tax in the near future will have important implications because it is those workers who will have to support the growing population of retirees. The expected

shortage of workers will increase the need for immigrants in the prime working ages. In this context, the 'old-old' component of the Canadian population (ages 85 and older) is expected to increase significantly as the survival prospects for seniors are bound to continue improving. The 2006 census showed that the population aged 80 and over experienced the second largest increase in population since 2001 (the largest increase was among those aged 55 to 64). The number of people aged 80 and over grew by 25 per cent, to 1.16 million. Never before has Canada had so many very elderly people. Moreover, in 2006 Statistics Canada counted 4,635 people over the age of 100—an increase of more than 22 per cent since 2001—and this number is expected to triple by 2031 (Statistics Canada, 2007a, 2007b). As a prosperous advanced society, Canada should be able to more than adequately meet the challenges of demographic aging, but it will need to ensure that plans are in place sooner rather than later.

Conclusion

This chapter has looked at the demographic determinants of age and sex composition, with special attention to the societal ramifications of changes in that composition and the contrasting situations of the developed and the developing countries with regard to the process of demographic transition. Clearly, population aging is a worldwide phenomenon. The greying of the population is bound to play a critical role in shaping the collective futures of both developed and developing societies. Among the many challenges for the industrial societies are the following:

- growing pressures on the public pension system
- the need for health care reform to take into account the additional needs of a growing elderly population
- increasing economic demands on a shrinking working-age population
- significant projected growth of the population over the age of 85
- rising immigration pressures as the proportion of native-born workers in the prime working ages shrinks to unprecedented levels

In addition to all this, persisting low birth rates may make it impossible for the developed world to maintain the large military forces necessary to meet international security commitments (Kennedy, 1993a; MacKellar, 2000; Peterson, 1999; Raymond, 2003; Rowstow, 1998; Wallace, 1999).

As for the developing countries, some have taken advantage of the 'demographic bonus' associated with past changes in fertility and have prospered economically as a consequence.

Unfortunately, another subset of developing countries is still caught in a 'poverty trap' that may be difficult to break out of.

Notes for Further Study

- In notational form, the median age (Md) of population is defined as:

$$Md = l_{Md} + \frac{\frac{P}{2} - \sum P_x}{P_{Md}} i$$

where
l_{Md} = the lower limit of the age group containing the median;
P = total population;
$\sum P_x$ = the population in all age groups preceding the age group containing the median;
P_{Md} = population in the age group containing the median; and
i = the width of the age interval containing the median.

- The arithmetic average is highly sensitive to extreme values; for this reason the median is preferred as a measure of average age. The arithmetic average age of population is defined as

$$\bar{x} \text{ age} = \frac{\sum_{x=0-4}^{X=85+} m_i \cdot P_x}{\sum_{x=0-4}^{X=85+} P_x}$$

where
$\bar{x}$ age = average age;
m_i = the midpoint of a given age category (e.g., for age 0–4, it is 2.5; for age 5–9, it is 7.5, etc; and for age 85+, it is 87.5);
P_x = the population in a given age category (age = 0–4, 5–9, . . . , 85+); and
$\sum P_x$ = the sum of the population across all age groups (i.e., the total population).

Table 4.5 shows the range of variation between the median and the arithmetic average age of population for 1950 and 1990 for several countries. The differences between these two measures range from relatively small to substantial. Note that in all cases the median is smaller than the arithmetic average. Why is this the case?

- To construct a population pyramid with Excel, follow the following steps:

  1. Compute all the male and female percentage columns.
  2. Place a '−' sign next to the female percentages (this is necessary in order for Excel to work).

3. Highlight age, % male and % female columns; click on the chart wizard icon and then click on the 'bar graph' option.
4. Then click on 'series' and assign male and female labels. Click 'finish.'
5. Point to the pyramid and right-click.
6. Select 'format data series' and click on 'options'.
7. Set 'gap width' to 0 and 'overlap' to 100, then click 'OK'.
8. Point cursor to a blank space on the chart and right-click; select 'chart options'.
9. Give a title to the graph, and specify the X and Y labels.

Table 4.5 Average and median age of population for selected countries, 1950 and 1990, with differences between arithmetic averages and medians

Country	1950			1990		
	Average	Median	Average − Median	Average	Median	Average − Median
Brazil	22.88	18.87	4.01	26.21	22.66	3.55
Bangladesh	25.66	21.60	4.06	22.23	17.72	4.51
Mexico	22.94	18.16	4.78	24.47	20.33	4.14
Nigeria	21.62	17.06	4.56	20.74	15.74	5.00
Canada	30.45	27.71	2.74	35.24	33.31	1.93
USA	32.09	30.18	1.91	33.98	30.01	3.97
UK	35.32	34.63	0.69	37.84	35.76	2.08
Sweden	34.95	34.26	0.69	40.09	39.32	0.77
France	35.26	34.51	0.75	36.78	34.81	1.97
Japan	26.63	22.28	4.35	37.32	37.21	0.11

Source: Keyfitz and Flieger (1990). © University of Chicago Press.

Exercises

1. Go to the United Nations website* (see instructions below) and choose two countries; then compute the corresponding age–sex pyramids for two points in time (e.g., the early 1970s and the most recent period available). Use a spreadsheet program such as Excel to plot the corresponding age–sex pyramids.
2. Calculate the following demographic measures for the two countries for both periods:
   a) the median age of population (the median for grouped data)
   b) the arithmetic average age of population (the mean for grouped data)
   c) the youth dependency ratio
   d) the old-age dependency ratio
   e) the overall dependency ratio
   f) the total sex ratio
   g) all age-specific sex ratios
   h) the sex ratio of males aged 25–29 to females aged 20–24
   i) the average annual growth rate between periods (apply the geometric formula)
3. Analyze the results of the above computations. Describe how your chosen populations have changed demographically between the two points of observation.
4. Visit the Population Reference Bureau website (www.prb.org) and download the latest *World Population Data Sheet*. Select the following indicators for your two countries: (1) GNI PPP per capita; (2) RNI; (3) per cent of population <15; per cent of population 65+. Compare the two countries on these measures. What conclusions can you draw from this information? Explain how your analysis of age composition relates to these variables for the two countries.
5. Table 4.6 shows crude birth rates, life expectancy at birth, and net reproductive rates for selected countries, *c.*1950 and 1985. Use Keyfitz's formula to calculate the population momentum (M) for each country between the two points of observation.
6. Graph the values of M and interpret your results. How have these values changed over time? What explains this change?
7. Obtain the most recent CBR and life expectancy data for the same countries from the Population Reference Bureau's *World Population Data Sheet* (calculate approximate NRR values by dividing the TFR by half). Now calculate M values for the most recent period available. Compare these new values with the ones computed in question 5. How have M values changed?

---

*Go to http://esa.un.org/unpp/ and click on 'Panel 2, Detailed Data'. Then select (1) from the 'variable' option 'population by five-year age group and sex', and (2) from the 'region/country' option the country of your choice. Then click on 'display'. The data are expressed in thousands. Copy the data into the spreadsheet.

Table 4.6 Crude birth rates, life expectancy at birth, and net reproductive rates,
selected countries, c.1950 and 1985

Country (actual year)	1950				1985			
	CBR	e_0	NRR	M	CBR	e_0	NRR	M
Canada (1951; 1985)	27.24	68.5	1.61		14.82	76.4	0.80	
USA (1950; 1985)	23.93	68.1	1.43		15.75	74.9	0.88	
Mexico (1950; 1983)	46.56	50.8	2.43		34.96	68.8	2.14	
Somalia (1950; 1985)	49.34	33	1.70		50.81	45	2.20	
Egypt (1950; 1985)	48.6	42.5	2.07		35.96	60.7	1.98	
China (1950; 1985)	43.6	40.8	1.89		20.51	69.8	1.08	
India (1950; 1985)	44.08	38.7	1.63		32.05	57.9	1.67	
Japan (1951; 1985)	25.64	61.1	1.39		11.41	78.3	0.82	
Denmark (1951; 1985)	18.05	70.7	1.18		10.51	74.3	0.74	
France (1951; 1985)	19.83	66.8	1.3		13.93	75.5	0.87	
W. Germany (1950; 1985)	15.96	66.6	0.93		9.61	74.9	0.62	
Italy (1951; 1983)	18.59	65.6	1.05		10.59	74.7	0.71	
Spain (1950; 1983)	20.07	61.1	1.02		12.71	76.1	0.85	
Sweden (1950; 1983)	16.64	71.4	1.08		11.79	76.8	0.83	
United Kingdom (1950; 1985)	15.88	69.3	1.02		13.26	74.6	0.86	

Source: Keyfitz and Flieger (1990): 64–101 (summary table).

Additional Reading

Blackburn, Robin. 2002. *Banking on Death: Or, Investing in Life: The History and Future of Pensions*. London: Verso.

Creedy, John. 1998. *Pensions and Population Ageing: An Economic Analysis*. Cheltenham, UK: Edward Elgar.

Denton, Frank T., Deborah Fretz, and Byron G. Spencer. 2000. *Independence and Economic Security in Old Age*. Vancouver: UBC Press.

Economist, The. 2004. 'Forever Young: A Survey of Retirement'. 27 March: 3–18 (a feature insert in the regular issue).

Gonnot, Jean-Pierre, Nico Keilman, and Christopher Prinz. 2002. *Social Security, Household, and Family Dynamics in Ageing Societies*. Dordrecht, Netherlands: Kluwer Academic.

Harding, Ann, and Anil Gupta. 2007. *Modelling Our Future—Population Ageing, Social Security and Taxation*. Amsterdam: Elsevier.

Laslett, Peter. 1996. *A Fresh Map of Life: The Emergence of the Third Age*, 2nd edn. Houndsmills and London: Macmillan.

Lee, Ronald D., W. Brian Arthur, and Gerry Rodgers, eds. 1988. *Economics of Changing Age Distributions in Developed Countries*. Oxford: Clarendon.

Low, Bobbi S. 2000. *Why Sex Matters*. Princeton: Princeton University Press.

Mason, Andrew, and Georges Tapinos, eds. 2000. *Sharing the Wealth: Demographic Change and Economic Transfers Between Generations*. Oxford: Oxford University Press.

Mullan, Phil. 2000. *The Imaginary Time Bomb: Why an Ageing Population Is Not a Social Problem*. New York: I.B. Tauris.

Williamson, John B., Diane M. Watts-Roy, and Eric R. Kingson, eds. 1999. *The Generational Equity Debate*. New York: Columbia University Press.

Web Resources

The online version of *The Economist* magazine presents many special surveys on varied topics, including social and economic aspects of population aging: www.economist.com/surveys.

An important source of age and sex population data (along with mortality data by age and sex) is the World Health Organization's *Statistics Annual*: www.who.int/publications/en.

The *United Nations Demographic Yearbook* contains a wealth of demographic information by age, sex, and country. The UN's Population Prospects Revision series (latest is for 2006) can be accessed at: www.unpopulation.org.

The Population Reference Bureau issues a series of excellent publications on a regular basis, including Population Bulletin, and the annual World Population Data Sheet: www.worldpop.org/datafinder.htm.

The Central Intelligence Association (CIA) of the United States has a website that provides, among other things, useful demographic data by country: www.cia.gov/library/publication/the-world-factbook/index.htm.

Check out the 'Population Pyramid' simulator at the Institut National d'Études Démographiques (INED) website. This easy-to-use program allows one to see at a glance how a population is distributed by age and sex, and how the population changes under varying fertility and mortality assumptions: www.ined.fr/en/everything_about_population/animations/age_pyramid.

The INED website also features a population simulator that shows future population trends of the whole world or of individual countries, based on United Nations projections. You can make your own simulations by adjusting fertility, life expectancy, and sex ratio at birth: www.ined.fr/en/everything_about_population/play_population/population_simulator/.

Chapter 5

Nuptiality

Introduction

Falling marriage and rising divorce rates suggest that the industrialized countries today are in the midst of a 'marriage bust'. At the same time, the family as an institution is confronting challenges that would have been unimaginable half a century ago. The marriage boom that followed the Second World War lasted for nearly two decades. Since the early 1970s, however, Western countries in general have experienced not only significant increases in divorce but a growing rejection of traditional marriage in favour of alternative conjugal arrangements, especially among younger people. In Canada, the rate of marriage is the lowest it has ever been; the average age at first marriage has been rising steadily; and the chance of divorce among those currently married is approaching 40 per cent (Bélanger, 2006: 67).

Historically, marriage rates have declined from time to time, but the reasons typically involved external circumstances such as famine, war, or economic crisis. What is different today is that the decision not to marry is a matter of personal choice. Whereas in the past marriage was virtually compulsory for the formation of a long-term sexual relationship and the raising of children, now individuals have the option of living together without commitment to matrimony. Common-law relationships now account for an increasing share of all first conjugal unions in Western societies (United Nations Department of Economic and Social Affairs Population Division, 2003a). Single-parent and same-sex households are now widely accepted in Western societies; and growing numbers of children today are born to single mothers and common-law couples.

What these trends signify sociologically is open to debate. Does the decline in marriage mean that the traditional Western nuclear family is no longer considered as important as it once was? The answer depends in part on whether you see the growing diversity in family forms as a positive or a negative development. Many welcome the shift away from traditional marriage as allowing greater freedom and flexibility; for example, women can now combine family and career much more readily than they could in earlier times. Others, however, fear that growing up in a non-traditional family structure may in the long run be detrimental to children's development and well-being (Cherlin, 2003; Blankenhorn, 2007).

All things considered, current nuptiality trends do seem to suggest that the traditional form of the family is no longer the central institution it once was in Western society. Perhaps the single most important evidence for this view is the fact that the traditional marriage is no longer the only socially acceptable context for reproduction (Cherlin, 2003, 2004). That said, it would be extremely premature to proclaim the demise of traditional marriage, as large numbers of men and women are still choosing matrimony: almost 150,000 marriages were celebrated in Canada in 2006 alone (Statistics Canada, 2008b).

Nuptiality in Social Demographic Analysis

Strictly speaking, 'nuptiality' refers to the frequency or incidence of marriage in a population. The demographic study of nuptiality, however, encompasses all aspects of family formation and dissolution, including divorce, widowhood, and remarriage, as well as alternatives to traditional marriage, such as common-law cohabitation and same-sex marriage. As a demographic factor, nuptiality does not directly affect population numbers in the way that mortality, fertility, and migration do. Yet marriage (or the equivalent) is indirectly relevant to these demographic processes as the socially sanctioned context for reproduction and the raising of children. Even though cohabitation without marriage (also known as common-law or consensual union) is becoming more common in the West, the majority of children are still born to married couples. Thus while 45 to 65 per cent of all births in Denmark, Norway, Sweden, and Iceland now take place within non-marital unions, in Japan, Greece, and Italy this is true in only 1 to 9 per cent of cases (Wolfe, 2003).

Whether birth rates rise or fall is in many ways determined by the average age at which women marry or enter a similarly socially accepted form of conjugal relationship, whatever the society (Bongaarts, 1978; Davis and Blake, 1956). Thus, demographic analysis has focused mainly on marriage, with particular emphasis on first marriage, since subsequent unions have much less impact on fertility from a societal perspective (Pressat, 1985: 165). A case can be made that marriage is also a factor in mortality and health (see, for example, Gove, 1973) as well as migration (see, for example, Bielby and Bielby, 1992).

Since demographic phenomena mirror sociological processes, trends in family formation and dissolution can serve as indicators of socioeconomic conditions in society. Historically, marriage rates have risen during periods of prosperity and fallen in periods of economic decline (Kirk, 1960). There is additional evidence that during times of war or other major social disruption couples tend to postpone or even forgo marriage altogether (Easterlin, 1969; Ermisch, 1981). Finally, it can be argued that nuptiality trends reflect a society's attitudes towards marriage and the importance of the family institution in general (Cherlin, 2003, 2004; Westoff, 1978).

Nuptiality as a Demographic Process

Nuptiality can be understood as the demographic process in which individuals move between various marital states (Cherlin, 1981). Figure 5.1 illustrates the relationships between marital statuses and possible transitions between them. From birth to young adulthood people are in the *never married* state (i.e., single). Then at some point most young adults will enter formal marriage or some other socially recognized equivalent such as cohabitation, and the first such union can be either *first marriage* or *first cohabitation*. Eventually every union will come to an end, whether through separation, divorce, or the death of one partner (i.e., widowhood). Clearly, as Figure 5.1 shows, there are a number of possible transitions—back and forth—between the various conjugal states. The chance that any one of these events will occur depends on many factors, including age, gender, education, income, and the duration of the union. In the event of divorce, either or both parties may re-enter the married state (i.e., remarry); those who are widowed may also remarry.

Note that because of the possibility of transitions between states in both directions (back and forth) it is also possible to conceive of broader marital status categories. For example, in Figure 5.1, the *married* state would contain those who are married for the first time and those who have remarried. In this case, demographers would speak of such individuals as being in the *currently married* state. Similarly, the *nonmarried* cat-

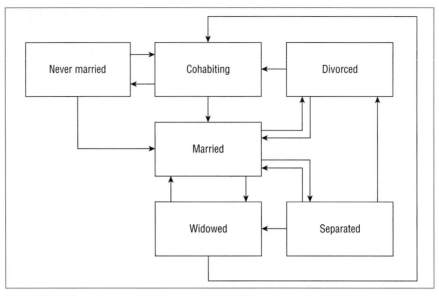

Figure 5.1   Schematic structure of marital states and transitions

Source: Hinde (1998): 258. Copyright © 1998 Andrew Hinde. Reproduced with the permission of Edward Arnold (Publishers) Ltd.

egory includes those who have never married as well as those who have been divorced or widowed. *Formerly married* covers both divorced and widowed people, while *ever married* includes the currently married, plus the divorced and widowed. Finally, *marital dissolution* encompasses both separation/divorce and mortality.

Measures of Nuptiality

The most fundamental measure of marriage in a given population is the *crude marriage rate* (CMR):

$$\text{CMR} = \frac{M}{P} \times 1{,}000$$

where M represents the total number of marriages (including both first marriages and remarriages) that take place in a given year, and P is the mid-year population.

Similarly, the *crude divorce rate* (CDivR) is defined as

$$\text{CDivR} = \frac{D}{P} \times 1{,}000$$

where D stands for the number of divorces in a given year, and P is the mid-year population.

Table 5.1 shows crude marriage and divorce rates for Canada in 2002, as well as the total numbers of marriages and divorces that year, and the mid-year population used in the computation of rates.

Even though they are used widely in the literature, these two measures are not really satisfactory. The main problem is that the denominator (P) in each case includes some people who by definition do not belong to the relevant risk set: that is, persons under the age of 15 (too young to marry) and, in the case of divorce, people who have never been married in the first place, as well as those who have been widowed. Sometimes, if the appropriate data are available, it is possible to refine the denominator first by narrowing the risk set to the mid-year population aged 15 years of age and older and then by specifying the sex of that population (typically

Table 5.1 Marriages, divorces, and corresponding crude rates, Canada, 2002

Mid-year population	Marriages	Divorces	Crude marriage rate per 1,000 population	Crude divorce rate per 1,000 population
31,372,600	146,738	70,155	4.677	2.36

Source: Adapted from Bélanger (2006): 7, 62, 68.

the denominator consists of females 15 and over). Thus the *general marriage rate* (GMR) and the *general divorce rate* (GDivR) can be expressed as follows:

$$GMR = \frac{M}{P^f_{15+}} \times 1,000$$

$$GDivR = \frac{D}{P^f_{15+}} \times 1,000$$

where P^f_{15+} is the number of females aged 15 and older at mid-year.

These two general rates are usually expressed 'per 1,000' population and give a more meaningful indication of the extent of marriage or divorce in the adult population over a specified time interval, usually one year. Table 5.2 displays these rates for Canada in 2002.

Further refinements can be achieved by including in the denominator the female population at mid-year that is married (for the divorce rate) or single, widowed, or divorced (for the marriage rate). The *refined marriage rate*

(RMR) and refined divorce rate (RDivR) would be determined as follows:

$$RMR = \frac{M}{P^f_{s,d,w}} \times 1,000$$

$$RDivR = \frac{D}{P^f_{mar}} \times 1,000$$

where, $P^f_{s,d,w}$ is the single, divorced, and widowed female population at mid-year, and P^f_{mar} is the married female population at mid-year.

Although these more precise measures are obviously preferable to the less refined ones, the information required to compute them may not be readily available. Table 5.3 shows the refined marriage and divorce rates for Canada in 2002.

First-Marriage Rate
Order-specific marriage rates are of particular interest for demographic analysis because, in general, first marriages are more strongly correlated with the birth rate than are second or higher-order marriages (Faust, 2004). The *first-*

Table 5.2 Marriages, divorces, and corresponding general rates by sex and overall, Canada, 2002

Sex	Mid-year population 15+	Marriages	Divorces	General marriage rate per 1,000 population	General divorce rate per 1,000 population
Male	12,575,391	146,738	70,155	11.669	5.579
Female	13,029,854	146,738	70,155	11.262	5.384
Overall	25,605,242	146,738	70,155	5.731	2.740

Source: Adapted from Bélanger (2006): 7, 62, 68; Statistics Canada (2003b): 51.

Table 5.3 Marriages, divorces, and corresponding refined rates by sex and overall, Canada, 2002

Denominator	Mid-year population 15+	Marriages	Divorces	Refined marriage rate per 1,000 population	Refined divorce rate per 1,000 population
Males (S+W+D)	5,098,854	146,738	70,155	28.779	
Males (Mar)	7,476,537	146,738	70,155		9.383
Females (S+W+D)	5,488,261	146,738	70,155	26.737	
Females (Mar)	7,541,595	146,738	70,155		9.302
Overall (S+W+D)	10,587,115	146,738	70,155	13.860	
Overall (Mar)	15,018,132	146,738	70,155		4.671

Note: S = single; W = widowed; D = divorced; Mar = married.
Sources: Adapted from Bélanger (2006): 7, 62, 68; Statistics Canada (2003b): 168–369.

marriage rate (FMR) is defined as the number of first marriages divided by the mid-year never-married (single) population:

$$FMR = \frac{M_1}{P_{15+_{nm}}} \times 1,000$$

where M_1 is marriages of order 1 (i.e., first marriages), and $P_{15+_{nm}}$ is the mid-year never-married population aged 15 and older.

Second-order marriage rates can be computed in the same way, by making the numerator the number of second marriages, and the denominator the population aged 15 and older that is widowed or divorced. Table 5.4 shows the first-marriage rates for men and women and for Canada overall in 2002. The first-marriage rate for single men in 2002 was 22.55 per 1,000 population aged 15 years or older, and for single women it was 27.15 per 1,000. Obviously, the number of single men getting married was not identical to the number of single women entering marriage for the first time. If we combine the men and the women marrying for the first time, the rate turns out to be 24.64 per 1,000. One important question here is what to use as the appropriate numerator for the overall first-marriage rate. Should it be the sum of male and female first marriages (as in Table 5.5, on page

Table 5.4 First marriages and corresponding first-marriage rates for males and females, Canada, 2002

Sex	Mid-year single population 15+, 2002	Number of men and women who married for the first time	First-marriage rate per 1,000
Males	4,878,843	109,992	22.545
Females	4,085,186	110,895	27.146
Overall	8,964,029	220,887	24.641

Note: Another way to calculate the overall first-marriage rate would be to take the number of couples married for the first time as the denominator. Data for 2002 were not available, but in 2000, 65.3 per cent out of a total of 157,395 marriages were first-time couples (Statistics Canada, Marriages 2000: 11; Cat. No. 84F0212XPB). If we were to apply this proportion to the 2002 total marriages, the estimated number of first-time married couples would be 0.653 × 146,738 = 95,814. If we were to use this as the numerator, the overall first-marriage rate for 2002 would be 10.689 per 1,000.
Sources: Adapted from Bélanger (2006): 7, 62, 68; Statistics Canada (2003b): 271, 272.

141) or the number of couples in which both bride and groom married for the first time? For 2002, the overall rate calculated using the latter denominator gives a first-marriage rate of 10.69 per 1,000 single people. We can get around this problem either by computing the first-marriage rate for males and females separately (as in Table 5.5), or simply by sticking with one of the two sex-specific rates (usually the female).

Additional measures of marriage and divorce incidence are possible. We shall outline four important ones here: the *age-specific marriage rate*, the *total marriage rate*, the *duration-specific divorce rate*, and the *total divorce rate*. The total marriage rate is obtained from the sum of age-specific marriage rates. The total divorce rate is obtained from the sum of duration-specific divorce rates ('duration' meaning duration of marriage). Both these 'total' rates reflect the average number of events (i.e., marriage or divorce) for a fictitious cohort exposed to the prevailing age or duration-specific marriage and divorce rates respectively in an actual population.

Age-Specific Marriage and Divorce Rates

As in the cases of mortality and fertility, the age composition of a population can affect the incidence of marriage and divorce within it. Computing age-specific rates makes it possible to focus on trends within each specific age category while controlling for the size of the population in each age group. Since few people marry after the age of 50, age-specific marriage rates are usually computed only for the population aged 15–49. (Age-specific rates in general can be computed for either single years of age categories or five-year age groups.) The general form of the *age-specific marriage rate* (MR$_x$) can be expressed as

$$MR_x = \frac{M_x}{Px_{nm}} \times 1,000$$

where the subscript x signifies a given age category (either single years of age or grouped age categories), M_x is the number of marriages to those in the age category x occurring in a given year, and Px_{nm} is the number of never-married persons aged x at mid-year.

This measure can be computed for males and females separately by altering the numerator and denominator accordingly. Analogous age-specific rates can be computed for divorce—that is to say *age-specific divorce rates* (DivR$_x$):

$$DivR_x = \frac{D_x}{Px_m} \times 1,000$$

where subscript x signifies a given age category, D_x is the number of divorces in a given year to persons in age category x, and Px_m is the number of married persons aged x at mid-year.

This measure as well can be computed for males and females separately by altering the numerator and denominator accordingly.

Figure 5.2 shows age-specific marriage and divorce rates for males and females in Canada for 2001 (marriages) and 1998 (divorces). Each set of rates follows a distinct pattern. Although marriage rates are higher for females than males at ages 15–19, in both cases the rates are exceptionally low. They rise sharply thereafter, however, peaking in the 25–29 age category. Beyond this point they fall off precipitously. As for divorce, males face the greatest risk in two age groups: 15–19 and especially 25–29. For females, the peak in divorce risk occurs at age 20–24. Beyond these maxima the rates drop off gradually, though nowhere near as rapidly as marriage rates do.

Total Marriage Rate

The age-specific marriage rates in a given period can be summed to obtain a total marriage rate (TMR) for the period. The TMR represents the average number of marriages occurring in a given period in the population aged 15 and older. Total marriage rate can be computed for either males or females separately, as the varia-

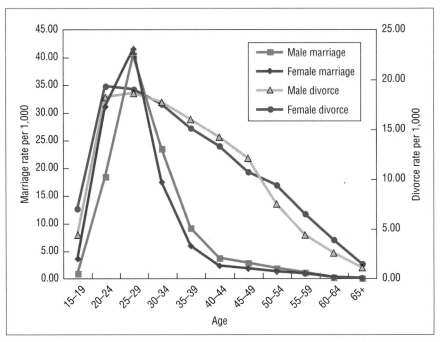

Figure 5.2 Age-specific first-marriage rates (in 2001) and divorce rates (in 1998) for men and women, Canada

Sources: Adapted from Statistics Canada publication *Current Demographic Analysis 2003* and *2004* by Alain Bélanger. Catalogue no. 91-209-XIE, pp. 70–1.

tion in the chance of marriage is different for the sexes (men tend to marry at an older age than do females). The female total marriage rate (TMR^f) can be written as

$$\text{TMR}^f = \sum_{x=15}^{\omega} \frac{M^f_x}{P^f_x} \times 1{,}000$$

where M^f_x is the number of marriages in a given year to females aged x, and P^f_x is the female population at age x at mid-year.

(The Greek letter Σ, 'sigma', is the symbol for summation, in this case summation of all the age-specific rates beginning with age 15 to the last age category, denoted by the Greek symbol omega, ω.)

Another way of interpreting the total marriage rate is to think in terms of a hypothetical cohort. Thus TMR^f tells us that if a hypothetical

cohort of women aged 15 at time t were followed though life and experienced the prevailing age-specific marriage rates at time t, they would end up having the marriage rate computed with the above formula. This measure makes it possible to predict what the future marriage rate would be *if* the current age-specific rates continued indefinitely. It is also possible to compute the same measure for first marriages—that is to say, the *total first-marriage rate*.

The total divorce rate can be computed in a similar way. In this case, age-specific divorce rates in the population for a given year t are calculated first, and then these rates are summed to obtain the total divorce rate. The *total divorce rate* for females (TDR^f) is

$$\text{TDR}^f = \sum_{x=15}^{\omega} \frac{D^f_x}{P^f_x} \times 1{,}000$$

where D^f_x is the number of divorces in a given year to women aged x, and P^f_x is the mid-year population of women aged x.

The total divorce rate parallels the total marriage rate in two ways. First, it is a period measure of the average number of divorces per 1,000 females aged 15 and older in the population at time t. Second, it can be interpreted as the divorce rate that would obtain in a hypothetical cohort of women who married at age 15 and throughout their lives were exposed to the age-specific divorce rates prevailing in the population at time t. Table 5.5 displays computed total first-marriage and divorce rates for men and women in Canada for 2001 and 1998, respectively. (Note that in order to derive the total marriage and total divorce rates in Table 5.5, the corresponding sums of age-specific rates have been multiplied by 5 to take into account the fact that age has been grouped into five-year age categories.)

Average Age at Marriage

The average age at marriage is an important measure, frequently used in the demographic literature. Typically it is computed separately for men (grooms) and women (brides). When the data are grouped into age categories, the midpoints of the age categories must be multiplied by the corresponding number of marriages in each age group. The sum of products is then divided by the total number of marriages to compute the average age at marriage:

$$\text{average age at marriage} = \frac{\sum\limits_{x=15}^{\omega} M_x \times m_i}{\sum\limits_{x=15}^{\omega} M_x}$$

where M_x is the number of marriages in a given age category, and m_i is the age-specific midpoint. The numerator is the sum of products, and the denominator is the total number of marriages.

Table 5.5 Age-specific male and female first-marriage rates in 2001 and divorce rates in 1998, Canada (rates per 1,000 population)

Age	Marriage (2001)		Divorce (1998)	
	Males	Females	Males	Females
15–19	0.91	3.6	4.4	7.0
20–24	18.44	31.1	18.2	19.3
25–29	40.40	41.5	18.6	19.0
30–34	23.46	17.4	17.7	17.5
35–39	9.15	5.9	16.0	15.1
40–44	3.75	2.3	14.2	13.3
45–49	2.85	1.8	12.1	10.7
50–54			7.5	9.4
55–59			4.4	6.5
60–64			2.6	3.9
65+			1.1	1.5
Sum of rates	98.96	103.6	122.5	117.5
Total first marriage (TFMR) or total divorce rate (TDivR)	494.8	518.0	612.5	587.5

Note: Since the data are grouped into five-year age categories, the total marriage and total divorce rates were derived by summing the age-specific rates and then multiplying the sum by 5.

Source: Statistics Canada Health Statistics Division (2000); Statistics Canada (2003b): 195.

Table 5.6 Computation of average age at marriage for grooms and brides, Canada, 2001

Age	(1) Grooms	(2) Brides	(3) Age mid-point	(4) Products: (1) × (3) [grooms]	(5) Products: (2) × (3) [brides]
<20	976	3,674	17.5	17,080	64,295
20–24	19,912	32,479	22.5	448,020	730,778
25–29	43,787	45,073	27.5	1,204,143	1,239,508
30–34	30,309	25,056	32.5	985,043	814,320
35–39	18,172	14,550	37.5	681,450	545,625
40–44	11,308	9,481	42.5	480,590	402,943
45–49	7,580	6,728	47.5	360,050	319,580
50+	14,574	9,577	52.5	765,135	502,793
Total	146,618	146,618		4,941,510	4,619,840
Average age at marriage				33.7	31.5

Note: The 50+ age category for grooms includes 64 'age unknown' cases; the 50+ category for brides contains 29 'age unknown' cases. The data pertain to marriages of all orders. The average ages at marriage involving only first marriages would differ from the averages computed in this table.

Source: Adapted from Statistics Canada publication *Annual Demographic Statistics 2003*.Catalogue no. 91-213, p.196.

Table 5.6 illustrates the computation of this measure. It shows the average age at marriage for brides and grooms in Canada in 2001. These figures do not distinguish first marriages from subsequent (higher-order) ones. In 2001 the average age of grooms was 33.7; of brides, 31.5.

The Probability of Divorce among the Currently Married

A problem with the total divorce rate as explained above is that it does not take into account how long marriages last before they break up. In other words, the chance of divorce depends heavily on marital duration (Festy, 2006). In Canada the risk of divorce tends to peak after about five years of marriage and decline gradually thereafter (Bélanger, 2006). Pressat (1974) devised an index to measure the probability of divorce among the currently married, based on the divorces that take place in a given year t distributed by marital duration. These duration-specific divorces are then related to the corresponding number of marriages that occurred in past years t-n, where n represents the number of years between the current year t and the calendar year of marriages contracted in previous years (i.e., the duration of marriage in years). For example, the divorces of duration 0 in year t would belong to the marriages contracted in year t itself, whereas the divorces of duration 1 would belong to the marriages contracted one year earlier (at time $t - 1$); the divorces of duration 2 would belong to the marriages contracted two years earlier (at time $t - 2$), and so forth. By dividing the divorces in each duration category by the corresponding marriages we can obtain duration-specific divorce rates. The sum of these rates is the total divorce rate for a fictitious cohort of marriages contracted in year t and exposed to the duration-specific divorce rates in year t.

Thus, this measure can be interpreted as indicating the probability of divorce for a fictitious cohort of marriages taking place in year t.

Using this method, Bélanger (2006) determined that in 2003 the TDivR in Canada was 3,654 per 10,000 marriages, which corresponds to a probability of divorce of roughly 37 per cent. We can interpret this to mean that about 37 per cent of marriages contracted in 2003 could be expected to end in divorce if the 2003 duration-specific divorce rates remained unchanged indefinitely. Figure 5.3 shows that the overall probability of divorce among the currently married has increased from about 31 per cent in 1976 to 37 per cent in 2003. In fact, however, the 2003 risk represents a significant decline from the 1987 figure of almost 48 per cent. The spike that occurred in 1987 reflected a legislative change in 1985 that made divorce easier to obtain. The backlog in divorce proceedings accounted for the sharp rise in 1987.

The advantage of the duration-specific measure over the usual TDivR is that it more realistically captures the probability of divorce as a function of marital duration. It does not take into account mortality (i.e., widowhood) and

remarriage as factors that affect the population exposed to the risk of divorce. However, as Pressat (1974) emphasizes, in general we can assume these influences to be relatively minor, especially in the case of mortality since death rates in the advanced societies today are quite low. Though clearly refined measures based on these demographic processes are preferred, a comparison of the Pressat method with more complex ones that do take into account mortality and remarriage indicated that in the Canadian context the difference in probabilities of divorce is not large (Trovato, 2000).

It is interesting to note that when the measures described in this overview are applied to Canada, they all point to similar trends. In other words, when looked at over time, the more refined measures correlate strongly with the crude measures (McVey and Kalbach, 1995a). For instance, the crude marriage and divorce rates for Canada in 2002 were 4.7 and 2.7 per 1,000, respectively, while the general marriage and divorce rates were not appreciably different,

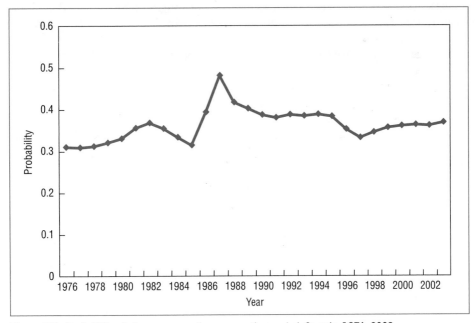

Figure 5.3 Probability of divorce among those currently married, Canada, 1976–2003

Source: Bélanger (2006): 70–1.

at 5.7 and 2.7 per 1,000, respectively. Obviously, more refined measures will produce different values than crude ones because they take into account age composition and are also more precise in limiting the denominator to the population actually subject to the events in question. The important point for analytical purposes is that the various measures should all point to the same general trend over time. The actual values of the indices will vary, but their overall direction should be consistent.

Nuptiality Trends: Cross-national Overview

Industrialized Countries

First-Marriage Rate

Table 5.7 shows first-marriage rates per 1,000 females across a large number of industrialized countries between 1960 and 2000. With a few exceptions, those rates dropped significantly from the highs recorded in 1960 and (in some cases) 1970. In fact, the 1960 and 1970 rates in some cases exceeded 1,000, because of high volumes of marriages combined with a decline in the age at marriage. This combination of demographic conditions can produce a total marriage

rate greater than 1,000. The trend towards declining marriage rates across countries did not occur uniformly, of course. The first signs of decline in northern and western Europe appeared after 1965–70; in southern Europe after 1975; and in eastern Europe after 1990 (United Nations Department of Economic and Social Affairs Population Division, 2003a). The decline was quite abrupt in western Europe, where the rate fell from around 900 per 1,000 females to only about 600 in a matter of 20 to 25 years. The fall was particularly steep in southern Europe (Greece, Italy, Portugal, and Spain), where it started about a decade later. In eastern Europe the decline between 1960 and 1980 was slight, but it increased considerably by 2000; today total first-marriage rates in this region tend to be somewhat lower than anywhere else in Europe.

According to the United Nations (Department of Economic and Social Affairs Population Division, 2003a), despite differences in the timing and pace of change, the various trends have converged in recent years to produce an average rate of roughly 600 first marriages per 1,000 females. In fact, with the exception of eastern Europe, in the year 2000 the inter-country variation across Europe was low.

Table 5.7 Total first-marriage rates per 1,000 females by country, 1960–2000

Region and country	Year									% change			
	1960	1965	1970	1975	1980	1985	1990	1995	2000	1960–70	1970–80	1980–90	1990–2000
Western Europe													
Austria	1,030	1,000	913	753	675	597	578	555	538	−11.4	−35.3	−16.8	−7.4
Belgium	—	—	983	890	772	652	723	567	518	—	−27.3	−6.8	−39.6
Denmark	1,010	990	817	668	534	573	595	653	727	−19.1	−53.0	10.3	18.2
Finland	960	930	940	702	672	584	580	571	621	−2.1	−39.9	−15.9	6.6
France	1,030	999	920	859	707	537	564	497	624	−10.7	−30.1	−25.4	9.6
Germany	1,060	1,110	978	806	693	627	640	562	582	−7.7	−41.1	−8.3	−10.0
West Germany	—	—	972	767	658	598	643	597	625	—	−47.7	−2.3	−2.9
East Germany	—	—	983	922	814	737	637	402	467	—	−20.8	−27.8	−36.4

(continued)

Table 5.7 *(continued)*

Region and country	Year									% change			
	1960	1965	1970	1975	1980	1985	1990	1995	2000	1960–70	1970–80	1980–90	1990–2000
Iceland	—	—	—	788	552	521	448	509	698	—	—	−23.2	35.8
Ireland	930	870	1,097	945	839	688	700	587	—	18.0	−30.8	−19.9	—
Luxembourg	—	—	876	801	661	562	639	556	551	—	−32.5	−3.4	−16.0
Netherlands	1,050	1,130	1,065	829	676	573	658	529	594	1.4	−57.5	−2.7	−10.8
Norway	1,040	870	956	795	651	569	578	543	—	−8.1	−46.9	−12.6	—
Sweden	950	950	625	629	525	528	553	442	528	−34.2	−19.0	5.1	−4.7
Switzerland	960	900	872	654	662	668	744	636	641	−9.2	−31.7	11.0	−16.1
United Kingdom	1,040	1,000	1,040	875	761	662	627	541	—	0.0	−36.7	−21.4	—
England & Wales	—	—	1,037	873	759	655	617	532	—	—	—	−36.6	−23.0	—
Northern Ireland	—	—	—	978	789	761	696	599	—	—	—	−13.4	—
Scotland	—	—	1,069	882	777	690	657	575	—	—	−37.6	−18.3	—
Greece	790	1,190	1,049	1,159	867	829	730	753	521	32.8	−21.0	−18.8	−40.1
Italy	980	1,030	1,009	945	779	673	691	631	—	3.0	−29.5	−12.7	—
Portugal	940	1,040	1,211	1,382	889	794	876	768	725	28.8	−36.2	−1.5	−20.8
Spain	—	—	1,010	1,046	763	642	687	601	612	—	−32.4	−11.1	−12.3
Eastern Europe													
Bulgaria	1,050	930	971	1,004	970	961	903	546	516	−7.5	−0.1	−7.4	−75.0
Czech Rep.	1,040	900	914	991	899	911	1,017	503	497	−12.1	−1.7	11.6	−104.6
Hungary	1,000	980	967	997	894	856	774	557	491	−3.3	−8.2	−15.5	−57.6
Poland	—	—	908	932	903	887	911	672	628	—	−0.6	0.9	−45.1
Romania	1,140	970	841	975	1,016	893	916	728	638	−26.2	17.2	−10.9	−43.6
Slovakia	1,010	880	866	941	874	903	961	583	518	−14.3	0.9	9.1	−85.5
Russia	1,180	1,090	1,061	1,032	959	967	1,003	750	—	−10.1	−10.6	4.4	—
Estonia	—	—	1,040	940	940	880	790	455	639	—	−10.6	−19.0	−23.6
Other													
Canada	915	919	923	812	695	641	631	553	546	0.9	−32.8	−10.1	−15.6
United States	—	—	—	804	808	776	—	—	—	—	—	—	—
Australia	—	—	—	754	696	675	661	—	—	—	—	−5.3	—
New Zealand	—	—	—	883	724	610	—	—	—	—	—	—	—

Note: Blank lines denote data not available.

Source: Sardon (2002): 111–56; United Nations Department of Economic and Social Affairs Population Division (2003a): 35; Wadhera and Strachan (1992): 30; Statistics Canada Health Statistics Division (2003b): 24.

Some of the decline in total first-marriage rates can be attributed to the tendency to postpone marriage until later in life and some to the rejection of formal marriage; unfortunately, it is not possible to separate these two explanations.

Whatever the cause, the same pattern can be observed not only in Europe (eastern and western) but also in Japan and the United States. While statistics on total first-marriage rates for Japan are not available, and for the United States are limited to earlier years, it is possible to gain a sense of nuptiality trends by examining the proportions of women aged 20–24 and 25–29 who have never married. The larger the percentage of singles in these age groups, the lower the incidence of marriage (Hajnal, 1965).

According to a United Nations report published in 2003 (*Partnership and Reproductive Behaviour in Low-Fertility Countries*), the proportions of never-married women aged 20–24 increased in the last quarter of the twentieth century, by almost 20 percentage points in Japan, 35 points in the US, and almost 40 points in western Europe. The proportions of single women aged 25–29 also reached new heights, ranging from about 40 per cent in the United States to 60 per cent in western Europe as a whole (see Figure 5.4). These figures indicate that the proportion of women in the countries with established market economies who had not married by the age of 30 increased from roughly one-quarter in 1975 to more than half in 2000. In some societies where cohabitation is still relatively rare (e.g., Southern Europe and Eastern Asia) the postponement of marriage became 'really extreme, pushing age at marriage beyond prime reproductive ages' (34).

Eastern Europe has also seen increases in the proportions of single women between the ages of 24 and 29, especially since 1990, though to a lesser extent. Nevertheless, the average proportion of never-married women in the 25–29 age

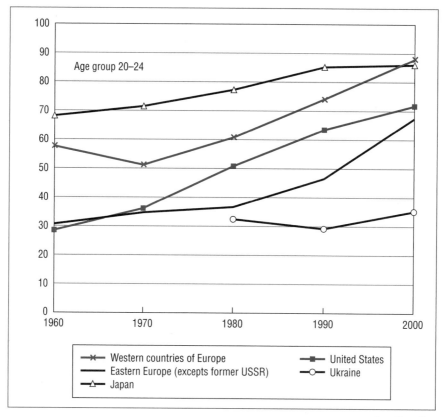

(*continued*)

Figure 5.4 Regional differences in the percentages of never-married women in age groups 20–24 and 25–29, 1960–2000

group is more than 30 percentage points lower in eastern Europe than in the west. This means that women in eastern Europe have tended to marry in large numbers before reaching age 30. Indeed, for the countries that made up the former USSR, nuptiality levels were high and stable until very recently.

Divorce and Cohabitation

Divorce

It has been estimated that between one-third and one-half of all marriages in the United States, Australia, Canada, and most of Europe today will end in divorce. The highest probability—in the range of 55 per cent—is found in the United States (Locoh, 2006). Divorce is still relatively uncommon in Southern Europe and Eastern Asia, but its incidence has been rising lately. Much of the variation in divorce rates across societies can be traced to differences in the laws

governing the legal dissolution of marriages and how long it has been since those laws were liberalized. In Italy, for example, divorce became legal only in 1971. For this reason Italy's divorce rate remains one of the lowest in the industrialized world. Divorce has also been relatively uncommon in Greece, Portugal, and Spain, but the rates in all four countries have been going up, especially since the mid-1990s (see Table 5.8).

In most western European countries, however, it appears that divorce rates may have peaked in the 1990s and have since stabilized. The recent slowdown in divorce rates can be largely attributed to the decline in formal marriage over recent years, since a couple who were not married in the first place don't need a divorce in order to dissolve their union.

Cohabitation

As with marriage and divorce trends, there are regional differences in the incidence of cohabita-

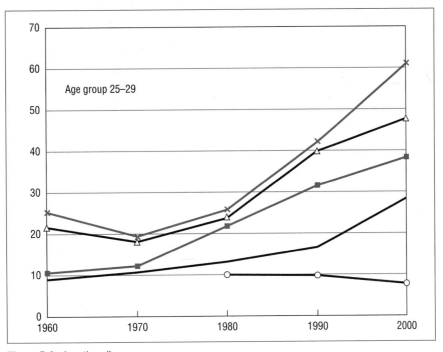

Age group 25–29

Figure 5.4 (*continued*)

Source: Adapted from United Nations Department of Economic and Social Affairs Population Division (2003a).

Table 5.8 Total divorce rates (per 1,000 marriages) by country, 1960–2000

Region and country	Year									% change			
	1960	1965	1970	1975	1980	1985	1990	1995	2000	1960–70	1970–80	1980–90	1990–2000
Western Europe													
Austria	14	14	18.2	19.7	26.2	30.8	32.8	38.3	43.4	30.0	30.5	25.2	32.3
Belgium	—	—	9.7	15.8	20.7	26.8	31.1	54.9	—	—	53.1	50.2	—
Denmark	19	18	25.1	36.5	39.9	46	43.8	41.2	44.5	32.1	37.1	9.8	1.6
Finland	11.1	13	16.9	25.5	27.7	27.6	42.4	48.3	51.2	52.3	39.0	53.1	20.8
France	9	11.1	12	17.3	22.3	30.4	32.1	38.2	—	33.3	46.2	43.9	—
Germany	12	13	16.6	25.1	25.2	33.6	29.4	32.8	—	38.3	34.1	16.7	—
West Germany	—	—	15	22	22.8	32	31.4	38	—	—	34.2	37.7	—
East Germany	—	—	19.1	30.1	31.9	39	23.7	18.4	—	—	40.1	−25.7	—
Iceland	—	—	18	25.8	28.2	35.6	33.6	33.9	39.5	—	36.2	19.1	17.6
Luxembourg	—	—	9.7	10.2	25.8	30.5	36.1	33.2	47.4	—	62.4	39.9	31.3
Netherlands	7	7	10.9	19.3	25.3	35.2	30.4	36.4	38.3	55.7	56.9	20.2	26.0
Norway	9	10	13.3	20.5	25	32.6	43.1	45.4	—	47.8	46.8	72.4	—
Sweden	16	18	23.3	49.8	42.4	45.1	44.5	51.6	54.9	45.6	45.0	5.0	23.4
Switzerland	12	13	15.3	20.8	27.3	29.4	33.2	37.8	25.5	27.5	44.0	21.6	−23.2
United Kingdom	—	—	16	28.4	34.9	38.7	37.5	39.7	—	—	54.2	7.4	—
England & Wales	—	—	16.2	32.2	39.3	43.8	42.5	45	—	—	58.8	8.1	—
Northern Ireland	—	—	—	—	—	15.1	17.6	22.2	—	—	—	—	—
Scotland	—	—	—	18.3	25.7	34.1	—	—	—	—	—	—	—
Greece	—	—	5	4.9	9.7	11	9.1	17.3	—	—	48.5	−6.2	—
Italy	—	—	5	2.8	3.2	4.1	7.7	7.9	26.2	—	−56.3	140.6	240.3
Portugal	1	—	0.7	2.2	7.5	11.3	11.8	16.2	—	−30.0	90.7	57.3	—
Spain	—	—	—	—	—	7.5	10.1	14.8	—	—	—	—	—
Eastern Europe													
Bulgaria	10	—	14	15	18	21	17	18.5	21.1	40.0	22.2	−5.6	24.1
Czech Rep.	16	—	26	30	31	36	38	38.4	43.3	62.5	16.1	22.6	13.9
Hungary	18	—	25	28	29	33	31	33.8	37.5	38.9	13.8	6.9	21.0
Poland	—	—	14	15	14	17	15	14	17.3	—	0.0	7.1	15.3
Romania	20	—	4.6	21.1	19.6	19	19	20.3	19.1	−77.0	76.5	−3.1	0.5
Slovakia	—	—	—	—	—	22.2	24.3	23.8	26.9	—	—	—	10.7
Russia	17	—	33.7	37.9	42.4	40.7	40	50.3	—	98.2	20.5	−5.7	—
Estonia	—	—	—	—	—	49	46	66.4	52.9	—	—	—	15.0
Other													
Canada	—	—	—	29.3	32.8	31.2	38.4	—	46.7	—	—	17.1	21.6
United States	—	—	—	54.8	58.9	54.8	—	—	—	—	—	—	—
Japan	—	—	0.9	—	1.2	—	1.3	1.6	—	—	25.0	8.3	—

Note: Blank lines denote data not available.

Source: Sardon (2002): 111–56; United Nations Department of Economic and Social Affairs Population Division (2003a): 31.

tion. This type of conjugal union is rare in southern and eastern Europe but very common in Nordic countries, particularly Sweden, Denmark, Norway, Finland, and Iceland; although Estonia and Latvia are culturally similar to their Scandinavian neighbours, their cohabitation rates are closer to those found in northern and western Europe. This suggests that attitudes towards cohabitation are rooted in different cultural and socio-historical traditions. The wide acceptance of cohabitation in the Scandinavian countries, for instance, has been facilitated by the region's historical tendency to see marriage as a contract between two individuals; by contrast, cohabitation is generally discouraged in societies that have traditionally seen marriage primarily as a contract between families, as is the case in southern Europe, for example (United Nations Department of Economics and Social Affairs Population Division, 2003a: 23).

Sociologists interpret the 'destandardization' of family forms as a reflection of the increasing emphasis on personal choice among the younger generations with respect to sexuality, mate selection, and conjugal relationships: 'Cohabitation can thus be seen as one component in the process in which individual behavior is becoming less determined by tradition and institutional arrangements and more open to individual choice' (Bernhardt, 2003: 154). Japan is closer to southern than northern Europe in this respect. Cohabitation without marriage is still very rare—less than 2 per cent of Japanese adults cohabit—and there is no evidence yet of a major trend towards cohabitation as a precursor to marriage among young adults (United Nations Department of Economics and Social Affairs Population Division, 2003a: 28).

Patterns of cohabitation can be gauged by examining the proportions of women who by age 25 have entered a cohabiting union as their first conjugal relationship (see Table 5.9). The data are arranged according to the respondent's

Table 5.9 Percentages of females, by birth cohort, reporting cohabitation as their first conjugal relationship by age 25, selected countries

Country	Birth cohort					% change 1950–55 to 1960–65
	1945–50 %	1950–55 %	1955–60 %	1960–65 %	1965–70 %	
Estonia	29	47	49	61	64	29.8
Hungary		7	15	18		157.1
Poland	3	3	4	4		33.3
Latvia	16	24	25	29	40	20.8
Norway	9	26	44	58		123.1
Sweden	68	74	76	74		0.0
Italy	1	3	3	5	5	66.7
Spain	2	3	5	7	10	133.3
Austria	22	38	45	55	58	44.7
France	15	21	35	46	60	119.0
Netherlands		18	28	45	50	150.0
Switzerland	18	33	45	51	51	54.5
Canada	7	20	32	42		110.0

Note: Blank lines denote data not available.

Source: Adapted from United Nations Department of Economic and Social Affairs Population Division (2003a): 24–5.

Six Degrees of Cohabitation

In an analysis of industrialized nations, Heuveline and Timberlake (2004) classified the countries they studied according to six distinct types of cohabiting regime:

1. *marginal cohabitation*   This is the arrangement in countries where cohabitation is rare and socially discouraged (e.g., Italy, Spain, Poland). In these countries, the incidence and duration of adult cohabitation is low, and children's exposure to this kind of living arrangement is even lower.
2. *prelude to marriage*   In countries including Belgium, the Czech Republic, Hungary, and Switzerland, cohabitation tends to be a prelude to marriage, akin to a trial marriage. The period of unmarried cohabitation in these societies is typically short, and relatively few children are born into cohabiting unions of this kind.
3. *stage in the marriage process*   In countries like Austria, Finland, Germany, Latvia, and Slovenia, cohabitation is seen not as a prelude to marriage but as a stage in the marriage process. Cohabiting couples in these countries typically do not feel strongly about the order and timing of childbearing and marriage, and children are often born before the marriage is formalized. However, since the period of this kind of cohabitation tends to be brief, children's exposure to cohabitation is also short.
4. *alternative to living single*   Partners who wish to postpone getting married but would rather live together than separately during courtship belong to this model of cohabitation, which is typical of New Zealand and the United States. The commitment of these partners is more characteristic of a dating relationship; the period of cohabitation is usually brief and often ends in separation rather than marriage.
5. *alternative to marriage*   In some societies, such as those of Canada (particularly Quebec) and France, couples choose to cohabit instead of marrying, and form families as married couples would.
6. *indistinguishable from marriage*   In societies like Sweden where cohabitation is widely accepted, with plenty of institutional supports for unmarried parents, couples may opt for cohabitation not because they view it as an alternative to marriage but because they are simply indifferent to the idea of marriage, which offers no tangible benefits. Compared with countries where cohabitation is seen as an alternative to marriage, this societal context, where there is cultural approval and institutional support for children born out of wedlock, will see a greater number of children born to cohabiting parents. However, the duration of cohabitation is still fairly short (with or without children) because many of these unions eventually transition to formal marriage.

Given the diversity of cohabitation regimes today, it probably makes sense to think of different countries as sitting at different points along a continuum with respect to the incidence of this type of union and the extent to which it approximates the traditional family ideal.

birth cohort. A number of conclusions are possible from this data. First, in all the countries selected, younger generations have been much more likely than their predecessors to cohabit without marriage. Second, there are sharp differentials in the intensity of the cohabitation phenomenon. For example, among the women born between 1960 and 1965 the proportions reporting cohabitation as their first union were 74 per cent in Sweden, 58 per cent in Norway, and 61 per cent in Estonia. At the other end of the spectrum were Italy (5 per cent), Spain (7 per cent), and Poland (4 per cent). Third, the bastions of cohabitation are Sweden, where the level was roughly 75 per cent across cohorts, and Norway, which started at only 9 per cent among the 1945–50 cohort but has seen significant increases with subsequent cohorts. Fourth, even in Italy, Spain, and Hungary cohabitation has increased across the birth cohorts. Perhaps not surprisingly, in the countries where rates of cohabitation are generally low, cohabiting couples are very likely to marry within five years, whereas in countries where rates of consensual unions are high, this tendency is generally minor. In Italy, for example, more than 60 per cent of cohabiting unions become marriages, as compared to only about 12 per cent in Sweden.

Developing Countries: Nuptiality Patterns

Marriage in some form or other continues to be nearly universal across human societies. Even so, the developing countries, too, have seen some change in nuptiality patterns in recent decades. The changes are not uniform, of course, and there are regional variations in the prevalence of different conjugal forms. Polygyny, for example, is common in Africa but rare elsewhere, while in other regions—Latin America is a notable example—consensual unions and formal marriage have coexisted since long before the rise of cohabitation in the industrialized world. This section will provide an overview of nuptiality trends in the developing world, specifically Africa, Asia, and Latin America.

According to the UN's *World Fertility Report 2003* (United Nations Department of Economic and Social Affairs Population Division, 2005b), it is not just in the industrialized world that age at first marriage (or the equivalent) has been rising. In the developing world, the median proportion of women single at ages 25–29 increased from 15 per cent in the 1970s to 24 per cent in the 1990s, indicating that women and men in the developing countries are marrying or entering consensual unions later than they did in the 1970s. The implications of this trend are far-reaching, since later marriage usually leads to reductions in fertility and a more rapid progression through the demographic transition (Westoff, 2003). With respect to divorce, the UN report concluded that rates of family dissolution in the developing world are on the increase. Among those countries for which data are available, the median rate of divorce increased between the 1970s and 1990s from 7 to 12 divorces per 100 men, and from 5 to 15 divorces per 100 women, indicating that, as in the more developed countries, marital instability is on the rise in developing countries (United Nations Department of Economic and Social Affairs Population Division, 2005b).

As beneficial as the increase in the median age at marriage in sub-Saharan Africa may be, Bongaarts (2006a) has pointed out that this is likely to increase the period of premarital sexual activity (during which partner changes are relatively common) and hence increase the risk of exposure to HIV infection. Using ecological data for 33 countries in Africa, as well as individual-level data from Demographic Health Surveys, Bongaarts found a significant positive correlation between HIV prevalence and the median age at first marriage, and between HIV prevalence and the interval between first sexual activity and first marriage.

Africa

Judging from Table 5.10, marriage or some similar form of conjugal union is widespread in Africa. The percentage of women married or cohabiting with a man ranges between 41 and 84 per cent, the average being approximately 65 per cent. Although this table does not differentiate between marital and non-marital unions, Westoff's (2003) analysis of Demographic Health Survey countries found that informal non-marital cohabitation is quite prevalent in some regions of Africa.

Table 5.10   Nuptiality statistics for developing countries included in Demographic Health Surveys in the 1990s and early 2000s

Country/region	% never married	% married/ cohabiting	% divorced/ separated	Median age at first marriage, women 25–49
Sub-Saharan Africa				
Benin 2001	21.7	73.4	3.1	18.8
Burkina Faso 1998–9	16.9	80.4	1.0	17.6
Cameroon 1998	23.4	66.9	6.6	17.4
Central African Republic 1994–5	19.5	69.4	9.1	17.3
Chad 1996–7	13.7	78.2	5.0	15.8
Comoros 1996	39.0	53.6	6.3	18.5
Côte d'Ivoire 1998–9	30.4	61.3	6.2	18.7
Eritrea 2002	23.3	65.5	7.4	18.3
Ethiopia 2000	24.0	63.7	8.7	16.0
Gabon 2000	32.6	54.1	12.1	19.7
Ghana 1998	23.7	64.6	9.9	19.1
Guinea 1999	13.9	82.4	2.2	16.4
Kenya 1998	30.1	61.4	4.9	19.2
Madagascar 1997	23.4	62.8	11.6	18.5
Malawi 2000	17.0	71.5	8.0	17.8
Mali 2001	13.5	83.5	1.8	16.5
Mauritania 2000–1	28.6	58.8	10.8	17.1
Mozambique 1997	15.1	74.4	9.3	17.1
Namibia 1992	51.3	41.6	5.5	24.8
Niger 1998	11.2	84.2	3.1	15.1
Nigeria 1999	26.0	70.1	2.2	17.9
Rwanda 2000	34.1	48.5	9.5	20.7
Senegal 1997	26.9	68.1	4.1	17.4
South Africa 1998	48.3	43.2	6.1	24.2
Sudan 1990	39.8	55.5	2.7	17.8
Tanzania 1999	23.4	65.8	7.6	18.1
Togo 1998	24.9	67.9	4.8	18.8
Uganda 2000–1	20.1	67.4	9.2	17.8

(*continued*)

Table 5.10   (*continued*)

Country/region	% never married	% married/ cohabiting	% divorced/ separated	Median age at first marriage, women 25–49
Zambia 2001–2	24.8	61.3	9.3	17.8
Zimbabwe 1999	27.7	61.1	7.0	19.3
Northern Africa/Western Asia/Europe				
Armenia 2000	28.8	64.1	3.8	20.5
Egypt 2000	31.9	62.8	1.8	19.5
Jordan 2002	45.6	51.7	1.2	21.8
Morocco 1995	42.4	52.2	3.4	20.2
Turkey 1998	27.7	69.0	1.5	19.5
Yemen 1997	28.3	67.4	2.4	16.0
Central Asia				
Kazakhstan 1999	25.3	62.9	8.8	21.2
Kyrgyz Republic 1997	21.5	69.5	6.5	20.4
Turkmenistan 2000	32.4	61.7	3.6	21.5
Uzbekistan 1996	24.9	70.2	3.0	20.1
Southern/Southeastern Asia				
Bangladesh 1999–2000	17.3	76.2	2.9	14.7
Cambodia 2000	31.8	59.1	3.1	20.0
India 1998–9	19.9	75.1	1.6	16.9
Indonesia 1997	25.3	69.7	2.5	18.6
Nepal 2001	17.9	78.5	1.2	16.7
Pakistan 1991–5	24.2	74.2	0.4	18.6
Philippines 1998	36.4	59.6	2.3	22.1
Vietnam 1997	33.5	62.7	2.0	21.3
Latin America/Caribbean				
Bolivia 1998	33.4	59.4	5.7	20.9
Brazil 1996	30.6	60.1	7.7	21.1
Colombia 2000	34.0	51.2	12.7	21.5
Dominican Republic 2002	23.0	59.8	16.6	19.0
Ecuador 1999	32.1	58.0	8.5	
El Salvador 1998	29.6	55.8		
Guatemala 1998–9	26.2	65.8	6.5	19.3
Haiti 2000	31.4	58.7	8.3	20.5
Nicaragua 2001	25.8	56.8	16.5	18.2
Paraguay 1995–6	30.1	62.3	6.7	20.9
Peru 2000	35.8	56.1	6.6	21.4

Source: Adapted from Westoff (2003): 2–3, 25.

Early marriage is most prevalent in sub-Saharan Africa and least common in North Africa (Singh and Samara, 1996). Across the continent the median age at first marriage (see Table 5.10) is still relatively low (about 19); only in Namibia and South Africa is the median over 20. Even so, that age has been rising in recent years: Westoff (2003) reports that this trend can be seen in 21 of the 30 countries surveyed in sub-Saharan Africa. Thus a major nuptiality transition seems to be under way. After a long period of no real change in the age at first marriage for women, sub-Saharan Africa is now experiencing notable increases in this indicator—a trend that should help to accelerate the fertility transition in the region. Westoff's (2003) analysis indicates that the proportion of women married for the first time before the age of 20 has declined in Niger, Nigeria, Malawi, Senegal, Mauritania, Gabon, Eritrea, Zimbabwe, and Kenya, among others; however, no such trend is evident in Burkina Faso, Uganda, Mozambique, the Central African Republic, Togo, or Guinea.

Among the cultural factors that help to explain regional variations in marriage in Africa are differences in the rules governing things like property succession and dowry, and the norms aimed at controlling female sexuality. These cultural traditions tend to erode with increasing urbanization and all the other social, psychological, and economic changes typically associated with modernization (Caldwell, 1982; Zuberi et al., 2003). In their cross-national analysis, Singh and Samara (1996) found that a woman who has attended secondary school is likely to marry later than one who has not. This suggests that one of the most powerful agents of change in marriage timing in Africa and other developing countries is formal schooling for girls, because education opens up options that otherwise are not readily available (Mason, 1993).

Asia

Asia is not only vast but highly diverse, both demographically and culturally. Although marriage remains almost universal, there are notable cross-country variations. At one extreme, women in the Indian subcontinent have historically married very early (Hajnal, 1965). Thus, the median age at first marriage for Indian women is estimated to be roughly 17, and the figures are similar for Pakistan, Bangladesh, and Nepal. At the other extreme, marriage patterns in Japan, South Korea, Taiwan, and China are closer to the western European pattern of late average entry into marriage. With a few exceptions (e.g., Kazakhstan, the Kyrgyz Republic, and Uzbekistan), the median age at first marriage has been rising in the Middle East and western Asia, and there has been a corresponding general decline in the proportions of women marrying before the age of 20 (Westoff, 2003).

Latin America

The period from 1950 through the 1970s was one of relative economic prosperity for Latin America. Beginning in the 1980s, however, the region was afflicted by debilitating economic stagnation and restructuring, resulting in very high levels of income inequality by the late 1990s. Women's education and employment levels have increased significantly over time. But nuptiality levels have remained remarkably stable over the past 50 years. In their overview of nuptiality patterns in Latin America between 1950 and 2000, Fussell and Palloni (2004) draw attention to three noteworthy trends in the region:

1. Marriage or the equivalent consensual union is nearly universal and still occurs relatively early in life for women (between the ages of 20 and 25).
2. The proportion of the population entering into marriages or consensual unions increased over the 50-year period from already very high levels (in 2000, the proportion of women aged 45–49 who were single ranged between only 1 and 15 per cent).
3. Rates of divorce and separation, though increasing slightly, are still low.

Also interesting is the fact that although rates of union formation remain high, this region has seen rapid fertility declines since the late 1960s. This may seem paradoxical because fertility decline is usually associated with declining marriage rates. In fact, the fertility transition started earlier in countries where the average age at marriage for women has been relatively high (e.g., Argentina, Chile) than in countries characterized by low age at marriage. Nonetheless, fertility dropped rapidly in the 1970s throughout Latin America, irrespective of early marriage. This aspect of the Latin American fertility transition reflects the widespread use of contraception. Apparently, people adjusted to changing social and economic conditions by lowering fertility within marriage rather than delaying or forgoing marriage itself.

According to Fussell and Palloni (2004), consensual (i.e., non-marital) unions constitute a large proportion of all unions in Central America and the Caribbean (e.g., in El Salvador, Guatemala, Honduras, Nicaragua, Panama, and the Dominican Republic) but are relatively rare in the more economically advanced countries (Argentina, Brazil, Chile, Costa Rica, Mexico, and Uruguay). The Andean countries (Bolivia, Colombia, Ecuador, Paraguay, Peru, and Venezuela) are in the middle range. Countries where consensual unions were common in the past tend to follow the same pattern today. Countries where consensual unions were less common have seen only slight increases in this type of union.

Explanations of Nuptiality Change

This section will examine a variety of perspectives on the question of how the Western world's current nuptiality patterns became established. Although the main focus of the discussion will be the period since the end of the Second World War, we will begin with Hajnal's historical study of the European marriage pattern. In his extensive analysis, Hajnal (1965: 101) noted that,

The marriage pattern of most of Europe as it existed for at least two centuries up to 1940 was, so far as we can tell, unique or almost unique in the world. There is no known example of a population of non-European civilization which has had a similar pattern. The distinctive marks of the 'European pattern' are (1) a high age at marriage and (2) a high proportion of people who never marry at all. The 'European' pattern pervaded the whole of Europe except for the eastern and southeastern portion.

Hajnal proposed that the extent of marriage in a society can be measured by the percentage single in the ages 20–24 and 25–29 (the higher the percentage single in these age categories, the lower the proportion married) and that the level of permanent celibacy can be estimated by the proportion of men and women who are single at 45–49, since beyond this age range very few people actually marry (the higher the percentage single, the higher the level of celibacy). Using these indicators, Hajnal showed, for example, that in Belgium and Sweden in 1900, 85 and 92 per cent of men aged 25–29 were single; the comparable figures for women were 71 and 80 per cent. At 45–49, the proportion single in these two countries ranged between 13 and 19 per cent for men and women, respectively. These high levels of singlehood and celibacy were quite common throughout western Europe during the nineteenth century. By contrast, in eastern Europe, Asia, and parts of southern Europe (e.g., Greece, Serbia) marriage was generally early and universal well into the twentieth century.

Locating the exact origins of the western European marriage pattern proved difficult in the absence of verifiable historical records prior to the mid-1600s; however, based on a variety of historical sources, Hajnal (1965: 134) concluded that the distinctive western European marriage pattern can be traced as far back as the sixteenth century among groups such as the

British peerage and the ruling families of Geneva. One factor that Hajnal thought might account for this pattern was the cultural expectation that before marrying, a man should secure a livelihood sufficient to support a family. A second factor was the rule of succession under which family landholdings passed to the eldest son upon the death of the patriarch. This rule of primogeniture meant that other sons had no prospect of inheriting an independent source of economic security, which reduced their chances of marriage from the start. A clear example of this situation occurred in nineteenth-century Ireland, which had exceptionally high levels of celibacy (over 20 per cent) and exceptionally low marriage rates (see Kennedy, 1973). In fact, even an eldest son might have to wait a long time before marrying, especially as declining death rates would have translated into a longer life for the family patriarch.

Writing in the 1960s, Hajnal could not have foreseen the changes in nuptiality patterns—notably the declining marriage rates and rising incidence of divorce and cohabitation—that became evident in the 1970s. The rest of this section will look at some of the more prominent theories on these developments, focusing in particular on economic factors and the changing roles and status of women in society. Although most scholars have identified women's increased autonomy and economic independence as the key factors in the 'flight from marriage' in industrialized countries (Becker, 1991; Macunovich, 2002), some disagree, arguing that the primary cause was the decline of economic opportunities open to men, who, as a result, could not afford to enter into marriage (Easterlin, 1980; Oppenheimer, 1994, 1997).

The 'Flight from Marriage': Theoretical Explanations

No single explanation can account for the 'flight from marriage' that has become apparent since the 1970s: the sociological causes are complex and multifaceted. It is widely accepted, however, that contemporary family patterns in the West are at least in part the result of profound changes set in motion by the Industrial Revolution. In the agrarian economy the family was the primary unit of economic production: all family members contributed their labour to the growing of food, the making of tools, and so on. At the same time the family was the primary social institution, responsible for everything from the education and socialization of children to the care of the elderly. With modernization the family was gradually displaced from many of these traditional functions. In the process of shifting the locus of economic production from the farm to the factory, industrialization created the 'male breadwinner' system, in which the man of the family became the sole earner and provider and the woman specialized in domestic affairs. Meanwhile, the introduction of mandatory formal schooling displaced the family from its educational function, and in time the care of the infirm and elderly was increasingly delegated to external institutions as well. Today, the nuclear family may still be the primary unit for (1) reproduction, (2) common residence, (3) economic co-operation, (4) the socialization of children, and (5) the satisfaction of adults' sexual needs (Leslie and Korman, 1989: 14). But it is certainly not the only setting for the performance of these functions.

Although economic co-operation remains an important feature of the modern nuclear family, the nature of that co-operation has changed radically since industrialization made women economically dependent on male breadwinners. The options available to women expanded briefly during the Second World War, when their productive activity was crucial to the war effort. But those options quickly contracted again once the war ended and the baby boom began. This was the period described by Betty Friedan in her book *The Feminine Mystique* (1963), in which women were generally expected to devote themselves exclusively to family life and their husbands' economic success.

The decline of the male breadwinner system began gradually in the 1950s and early 1960s, when women started seeking alternatives to marriage and total commitment to reproduction and childrearing (Davis, 1984a). Entry into the labour force has meant that women no longer need to rely on matrimony for economic security. For many scholars this shift was a primary cause of family change in the industrialized countries (Davis and van den Oever, 1982; Goldscheider and Waite, 1986, 1991; Westoff, 1983). Indeed, as early as 1978 Westoff (70) proclaimed that the steady decline since 1960 in the proportion of women marrying at ages 20–24 marked the beginning of a radical change in the family. Today the median age at first marriage continues to rise, and increasing numbers of people are choosing not to marry at all.

The 'Second Demographic Transition' Perspective

The structural changes associated with modernization have been accompanied by changes in societal values regarding marriage and the family. Some scholars have described this phenomenon as a 'second demographic transition'. At the core of this perspective is the idea that in postmodern societies tradition has largely ceased to function as a guiding principle in people's lives: in its place an ethos of individualism, complemented by secularism and materialism, is leading growing numbers of young people to choose alternative lifestyles, especially in the areas of sexuality and conjugal behaviour (Lesthaeghe, 1995; van de Kaa, 1987). According to Roussel (1985: 233), the two distinguishing features of the current system are high 'marital mobility' (resulting from the increasing prevalence of divorce) and growing diversity of household models. For the second demographic transition theorists, all these trends—late marriage, divorce, cohabitation, same-sex unions—are part of the same shift in values away from the family and towards the individual. According to van de Kaa (1987: 6–7) these tendencies—pervasive among young people in postmodern societies—stem from two sources: a personal desire for greater self-fulfillment, and a growing tolerance of diversity in other individuals' lifestyles.

Some of the theorists in the second demographic transition school (e.g., Lesthaeghe, 1995; Lesthaehge and Surkyn, 1988; Lesthaeghe and Neels, 2002) have identified a 'post-materialist' tendency among young people to reject the conventional, materialistic aspirations of the bourgeoisie in favour of emotional intimacy, or what Giddens (1992) refers to as the 'pure relationship'. In relationships of this kind external criteria (i.e., traditional norms) are irrelevant: the relationship exists purely for the sake of what it can give the persons involved. As Giddens points out, such a relationship is by nature unstable and impermanent, since it can be terminated more or less at will by either party at any time. To the extent that the 'pure relationship' has come to represent the primary model of intimacy for young people, it serves to undermine traditional marriage by promoting nontraditional alternatives (i.e., living together without marriage) and encouraging a mindset in which impermanence is the norm. Proponents of the 'second demographic transition' theory would argue that the 'pure relationship' is a reflection of the growing importance of postmaterial values in a society where traditional conventions are increasingly relegated to secondary status (see also Simons, 1980).

Demographic Theory

In the early 1970s, Dixon (1971) proposed that the timing and extent of marriage in society are determined by three factors:

1. the availability of potential mates (i.e., sex ratios in the prime marriageable ages)
2. the feasibility of marriage (i.e., young adults' economic circumstances)
3. the desirability of marriage (i.e., social attitudes and orientation towards marriage)

With respect to the first factor, Dixon (1971: 22) hypothesized that masculinity ratios (i.e., the ratio of males to females) 'should be positively correlated with marital delays among men and with bachelorhood, and negatively correlated with marital delays among women and with spinsterhood.' In other words, an oversupply of males would mean, on average, longer waits for men and shorter waits for women before marriage, while an oversupply of females would mean the reverse.

We noted in Chapter 4 that there is a cultural preference in the West for women to marry men who are a little older than themselves; the difference is usually about two or three years. This *mating gradient* can play an additional role in the way sex ratios affect marriage markets (Akers, 1967; Davis and van den Oever, 1982). Thus women born at the beginning of the baby boom, immediately after the Second World War, would have faced a marriage squeeze, since the cohort of appropriately aged men would have been born during the low-fertility war years. These women would have been in their prime marriageable ages in the mid- to late 1960s. As it happens, however, marriage rates were on the rise in those years; and by the time those rates began to decline, in the early 1970s, there was no longer a shortage of suitably aged male partners.

A more complex theory regarding the consequences of skewed sex ratios has been proposed by Guttentag and Secord (1983a), who argued that discrepancies in the numbers of men and women in the prime marriageable ages at the macro level can lead to profound changes in what they call 'dyadic power' between the sexes at the micro level. According to these authors, a surplus of males would typically result in intense competition for female partners. Under these conditions, gender roles would be governed by 'traditional' norms and expectations, and the sexual division of labour would conform to the male breadwinner pattern. In this context women might lack 'structural power' (i.e., economic and social power), but they would enjoy significant influence with their male partners. The family in this social context would be stable, divorce rates would be low, and

no significant alternatives to traditional marriage would be available. Pioneer societies of the past conformed to this pattern. By contrast, a surplus of females would mean a wider selection of partners for young men to choose from. Women under these conditions would be less highly valued and therefore their dyadic power would be reduced. In this scenario marriage rates would be low, since men would not need to commit to matrimony in order to find sexual partners, and rates of family dissolution would be high.

Both of these scenarios have prevailed at different times in history. The contemporary situation in the industrialized world does not conform to either pattern, however. Through formal education and large-scale participation in the labour force, women have for the first time in history acquired both structural power and economic independence from men. Under these conditions imbalanced sex ratios no longer matter, because women now see marriage as just one among a number of possible options. Thus Guttentag and Secord would suggest that the decline of marriage and the rise both of divorce and of common-law relationships in the advanced societies is mainly attributable to changes in the status of women.

The Economic Opportunities Thesis

Not all scholars agree with the emphasis on women as the principal actors in family change. Easterlin (1980, 1969), for example, proposed that the decline in marriage in the West is primarily a function of the economic opportunities available to young men rather than women's reduced desire for matrimony. Oppenheimer (1997, 1994, 1988) concurs, remarking that the social demographic literature must 'bring men back' into the explanation of family change. For Easterlin and Oppenheimer, both the post-war marriage boom and the marriage bust of the period since the 1970s can be best understood as reflections of the economic prospects that different cohorts of young adult men have faced and hence their ability to afford marriage and family building.

From this perspective the increase in marriage rates after the Second World War was a function not only of economic prosperity but also of the fact that opportunities for young male workers were relatively numerous because the cohorts entering the labour force after the war had been born in the 1930s—the time when birth rates had reached their lowest level in history. According to Easterlin (1980) members of small cohorts generally enjoy several advantages over members of larger cohorts, including less competition for entry-level jobs, easier advancement in the workplace, and higher average wages.

In the same way these scholars interpret the marriage bust that began in the late 1970s as a reflection of the relative economic deprivation faced by the large cohorts of young male baby boomers, beginning with increased competition for entry-level positions. These structural conditions are seen as discouraging to early marriage, and may have led some men to avoid matrimony altogether. To make matters worse, the world has seen several recessions since the 1973 oil crisis, and in recent years economic globalization has intensified competition for consumer markets and profits. The need to cut costs has led to job losses as a result of restructuring, and many manufacturing jobs have been lost to the developing countries where labour costs are lower.

More recent entry-level cohorts, born in the low-fertility regimes of the 1980s and 1990s, have certainly been smaller in size, but they too have faced less than optimal labour market conditions, which have been reflected in declining marriage rates. In short, the key problem, for Easterlin and Oppenheimer, is the erosion of economic security among young men.

Rising divorce rates and the rise of alternative family forms can also be interpreted as consequences of the declining socioeconomic fortunes of young men, since economic instability leading to financial difficulties would tend to intensify marital tensions and ultimately increase the likelihood of divorce. The trend towards cohabitation can also be viewed as a consequence of economic insecurity, on the assumption that young men might see common-law arrangements as less costly than marriage.

The 'Gains to Marriage' Thesis

As we have seen, Dixon (1971) proposed that marriage propensities in a society are affected not only by the feasibility of marriage and the supply of potential partners, but also by the extent to which young adults consider marriage desirable. The more alternatives to matrimony become available, the less desirable marriage itself will become. The economist Gary Becker (1991, 1973, 1974) has developed a thesis that elaborates on this proposition. His 'gains to marriage' thesis explains how the gains associated with traditional marriage have waned since 1960, especially for women. In the past, under the male breadwinner system, the husband specialized in market work and the wife in home production. The wife traded domestic services, including childbearing and -raising, to the husband in exchange for economic security provided through his income. Today, however, women who have gained economic independence are less accepting of a traditional division of labour in the home. The decline in the 'gain' associated with marriage is reflected not only in rising divorce rates and growing numbers of unmarried couples living together, but in the increasing numbers of families headed by women, and to some degree also the trend towards childbearing outside of traditional marriage.

From Becker's perspective, women are the principal agents of family change in contemporary industrial society. Similarly, Becker would attribute the rise of divorce as a further manifestation of women's rising status in society. In general, marriages dissolve because the gains that women today can expect from divorce outweigh the gains they can expect from staying married (Becker, Landes, and Michael, 1977; Grossbard-Schechtman, 1995; Hess, 2004). In other words, women who are capable of economic self-sufficiency have little reason to stay in an unrewarding marital relationship. Together, therefore, rising wages and labour force participation among women, especially married women, have probably also contributed significantly to the growth in divorce rates.

A number of other studies are consistent with these ideas. In his study of England and Wales, Ermisch (1981) found that the downturn in marriage at most ages is attributable to the growing economic opportunities for women. Preston and Richards (1975) found that in the United States improved economic opportunities for women have been influential in reducing the proportion of women ever married in the age group 20–24. And some researchers have found wives' economic resources to be positively associated with the risk of divorce (Booth et al., 1984; Hiedemann, Suhomlinova, and O'Rand, 1998).

Others, however, have found wives' economic resources to be negatively associated with the risk of divorce. Yet another set of findings shows that the risk of divorce is lowest when the two partners' resources are similar (Coltrane, 1996; Ono, 1998; Risman and Johnson-Sumerford, 1998). Rogers (2004) confirmed that wives' income shows a positive association with the risk of divorce, but that this relationship is contingent on the quality of the marriage and the size of the difference between the two spouses' financial contributions. Rogers surmises that divorce is more likely to occur when spouses have similar economic resources, which he interprets to mean that in this type of situation 'there is less [role] specialization and spousal interdependence in the marriage' (71). But it is also possible that similar economic resources may make it easier for either spouse to initiate a divorce because 'their economic obligations to each other are low, and also because they may be confident that their spouses can provide for themselves economically' (72–3). Thus, according to Rogers (2004), the chance of divorce seems to depend on both the quality of the marriage (how happy each spouse is with the marriage) and the balance of resources between spouses, a view that is not inconsistent with Becker's 'gains to marriage' perspective

Towards a Synthesis of Explanations

There is no overarching theory that can explain completely the causes of the changes in nuptiality observed over the last half century or so (Seltzer et al., 2005). In Dixon's (1971) cross-national analysis, the sex ratio thesis showed the weakest correlation with marriage rates, leading her to conclude that 'Overall, delayed marriage and celibacy are most highly correlated with indicators of the desirability of marriage, less so with feasibility, and least with availability' (225). Sex ratio imbalances in the prime marriageable age groups obviously affect the availability of eligible partners; but culture and social structure seem to have more influence on nuptiality change. The Easterlin/Oppenheimer thesis focuses on how men's socioeconomic prospects affect their marriage probabilities and divorce. Becker's 'gains to marriage' explanation emphasizes changes in the status of women as the central factor in marriage and family change. On the other hand, it is possible that Becker is mistaken in assuming that declines in marriage indicate that women are abandoning marriage altogether: many women may simply be postponing marriage to older ages.

A complete explanation of nuptiality change would likely have to take into account not only changes in the status of women in society but also changes in the lives of men, broadly speaking. It is true that the behaviour of both young men and young women today is conditioned to some extent by their economic prospects, but other factors are also important, among them value shifts, or ideational change; the breakdown of tradition and the rise of secular society; the diminished desirability of marriage among the younger generations; the trend towards greater symmetry in gender roles; the multiplicity of lifestyles available to people; and increasing societal acceptance of alternatives to traditional marriage (Lesthaeghe and Neels, 2002; Goldscheider and Waite, 1986, 1991).

Canadian Nuptiality Trends and Patterns

From the Early 1920s Onwards

The Canadian vital statistics system was not established until 1921; hence our knowledge of nuptiality trends before that time is limited. However, it seems that marriage rates in Canada in the second half of the nineteenth century were somewhat higher than was the case in western Europe (McInnis, 2000a, 2000b; Merten, 1976).

Change in the Marriage Rate

Industrialized countries became fully urban and completed the demographic transition in the first half of the twentieth century—a period that also included two major World Wars and the Great Depression. As might be expected, the Canadian marriage rate declined in response to these events, but in each case it recovered once

the disruption came to an end. Figure 5.5 shows the long-term trends in crude marriage and divorce rates in Canada from 1921 to 2006, while Figures 5.6 and 5.7 show provincial variations in marriage and divorce rates. The marriage rate in 1921 stood at 7.9 per 1,000; eleven years later, in 1932, it had declined to 5.9—one of the lowest levels ever recorded in Canadian history. Such a low rate would not be seen again in Canada until the early 1990s. Higher marriage rates in the early to mid-1940s, according to McVey and Kalbach (1995a: 228), were stimulated by a combination of social, economic, and demographic influences, especially (1) the economic recovery sparked by Canada's involvement in the Second World War; (2) the increased employment levels and rising prosperity that continued into the post-war period; and (3) the fact that people who had had to postpone marriage because of the Depression or the War were finally able to wed. As a consequence of these developments, Canada reached its peak

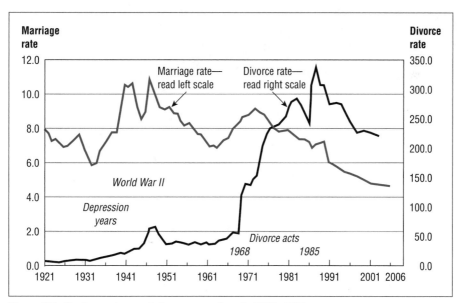

Figure 5.5 Crude marriage and divorce rates, Canada, 1921–2006

Note: Rates are per 1,000 population in the case of marriage; per 100,000 in the case of divorce.

Source: Adapted from McVey and Kalbach (1995a): 230. Additional sources for years after 1991: Bélanger (2006): 64, 69; Statistics Canada (2003j): 4; Statistics Canada (2002j): 2. Marriage rates for 2003–6 were calculated with data from Statistics Canada (2007e, 2007f: 20).

crude marriage rates of 10.6 and 10.9 per 1,000 in 1942 and 1946, respectively.

The marriage rate then began a prolonged decline that lasted until 1963, when it reached 6.9 per 1,000. The main reason for this trend was the fact that the cohorts born during the Depression and reaching marriageable age in the 1950s were unusually small. In fact, the proportion of people aged 15–25 who were marrying for the first time actually increased between 1941 and 1961, as did the married proportion of the total population 15 years of age and older. But these increases were insufficient to overcome the negative effects on overall marriage rates of the small Depression-era cohorts. The fact that Canada was experiencing an economic recession in the early 1960s may also have con-

tributed to the decline in the crude marriage rate (McVey and Kalbach, 1995a: 229).

After 1963 the marriage rate began to rise again, peaking in the early 1970s, but it never again reached the heights attained immediately after 1945. This more recent marriage surge can be attributed mainly to the coming of age of the cohorts born during the early years of the baby boom. As Figure 5.5 clearly shows, marriage rates fell precipitously after 1972, though they have stabilized at around 4.7 per 1,000 population in recent years. This is the lowest level recorded in Canadian history. No doubt part of the reason for these low marriage rates is the demographic effect of declining fertility beginning in the early 1960s and the consequent declines over the course of the last several

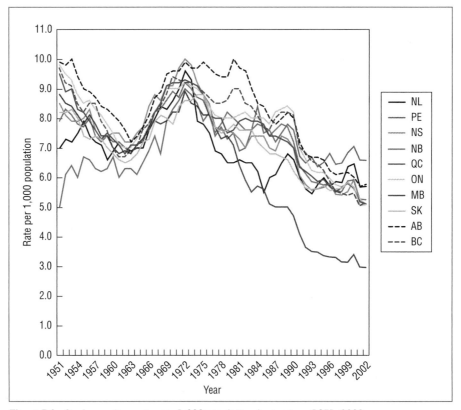

Figure 5.6 Crude marriage rates per 1,000 population, by province, 1951–2002

Sources: Wadhera and Strachan (1992): 17–18; Bélanger (2006: 64, 2003: 106).

decades in the size of cohorts of young men and women of marriageable age (McVey and Kalbach, 1995a: 229). Among the other factors that could be mentioned are changes in the economy and the impact of such changes on the economic prospects of young people. For instance, the additional education and training demanded of entry-level workers by today's economy means that many young men and women are staying in school longer and therefore marrying later than earlier generations did. But this is not the whole story. Values have changed as well. For many people today marriage does not appear to be the central institution it once was, and society is much more tolerant of alternative living arrangements.

Change in the Divorce Rate

Before 1968, when the laws were liberalized, a Canadian couple wishing to dissolve their marriage required a Private Act of Parliament in order to obtain a divorce decree (McVey and Kalbach, 1995a: 231). For this reason, Canadian divorce rates until the late 1960s remained quite low. In Figure 5.5 we can identify three distinct waves of divorce in Canada between the end of the Second World War and 2003. The first, between 1946 and 1951, largely reflected the disruptive effects of separation during the war. The dramatic spike that began in the late 1960s and continued until 1982 was the result of the liberalizing reforms that passed into law in 1968. Having peaked in 1982 at 285.9 divorces per 100,000 population, the rate declined slightly and then rose again, reaching an all-time high of 345.2 per 100,000 in 1987 (McVey and Kalbach, 1995a: 232). This third wave followed the passage of the 1985 Divorce Act, which further relaxed the legal restrictions. Under the revised Act, the evidence required to support a claim of marriage breakdown was reduced considerably, making a divorce even easier to obtain than had been the cases under the 1968 act. Consequently there was a spike in the divorce rate in 1987. Since then, however, the rate of marital dissolution has actually been declining, both in the country as a whole and across the provinces (see Figure 5.7). The rate in 2003—roughly 223 per 100,000—was close to the rates recorded in the early 1970s. The declining trend through the 1990s was in part a reflection of the decline in marriage rates beginning in the early 1970s. If marriage rates continue their downward trend, divorce rates can be expected to drop further in the future as the risk set of potential divorcees becomes progressively smaller over the years.

But demographic changes are not the only factors that may help to explain the recent reductions in the incidence of divorce. Society in the 1960s witnessed radical sociological shifts, two of the most relevant being the counter-culture movement's rejection of traditional values, including marriage, and the social changes that made it easier for women to enter (or re-enter) the labour force; these shifts allowed many unhappily married women to make the transition to divorced status with greater ease and confidence than before (McVey and Kalbach, 1995a: 232).

It may be argued that in addition to the recent gains made by women, the divorce revolution of the 1970s reflected a general shift in social attitudes regarding the permanency of the marital institution. Since the early 1960s, society has come to take a much more relaxed view of family break-up. In the past, people who had been divorced might well face social ostracism. Today, by contrast, the individuals involved can return to the life of singlehood without facing any social penalty. And if singlehood is unsatisfactory they can find new partners either to marry or to live with. Perhaps the most fundamental change in regard to both marriage and divorce since the early 1970s, then, has been a change in mentality whereby a growing proportion of the society has come to regard marriage as less important than it once was.

Over time, marriage and divorce rates alike have shown a fair degree of uniformity across the provinces (see Figures 5.6 and 5.7). In 2003, the highest and lowest marriage rates were recorded by Prince Edward Island and Quebec, respectively; the highest and lowest divorce rates, by Alberta and Newfoundland. The general similarity of these trends across the country suggests similar underlying conditions (Goyder, 1993). One common factor in the decline of divorce, for example, is the demographic effect of the growing tendency to choose cohabitation rather than formal marriage: the more couples opt for cohabitation, the lower the marriage rate; and fewer marriages mean fewer divorces.

Trends in Remarriage and Common-Law Unions

For individual people remarriage represents a quest to re-establish a marital bond. For a society a trend towards remarriage could indicate that marriage as an institution is in better shape than high divorce rates would suggest. In recent years approximately one-third of Canadian marriages have involved at least one previously divorced or widowed spouse. The number of such marriages in 2002 was 49,814 out of 146,738 marriages in total (Bélanger, 2006: 62). The proportion of remarriages in which both spouses had been previously married has actually increased since the early 1980s, from almost 41 per cent in 1981 to nearly 46 per cent in 2002 (see Table 5.11). In fact, estimates indicate that between two-thirds and three-quarters of divorced Canadians do eventually remarry (Wu and Schimmele, 2005). About 4 per cent of Canadian women and 6 per

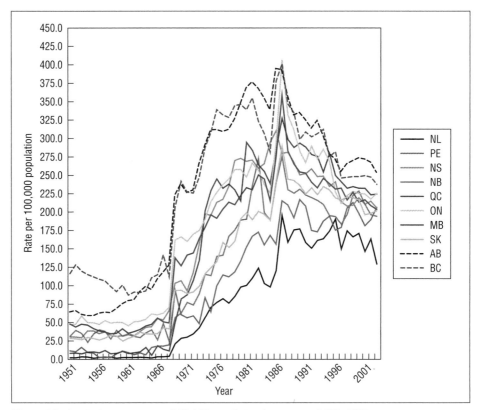

Figure 5.7 Crude divorce rates per 100,000 population, by province, 1951–2003

Sources: Statistics Canada (1983, 1979); Bélanger (2003): 28.

Table 5.11 Marriages, first marriages, and remarriages in Canada, 1981–2002

Year	Number of marriages	Number of first marriages		Number and proportion of marriages in which at least one spouse has been previously married		Number and proportion of remarriages in which both spouses have been previously married	
		Men	Women	Number	%	Number	%
1981	190,082	151,978	154,506	52,340	27.5	21,340	40.8
1986	175,518	137,665	138,523	52,678	30.0	22,170	42.1
1991	172,251	131,996	118,285	55,278	32.1	23,644	42.8
1996	156,691	117,574	110,281	53,481	34.1	24,042	45.0
2001	146,618	109,917	110,895	50,144	34.2	22,894	45.7
2002	146,738	109,992	110,895	49,814	33.9	22,775	45.7

Source: Adapted from Statistics Canada publication *Current Demographic Analysis 2003* and *2004*, by Alain Bélanger. Catalogue no. 91-209-XIE, p. 62.

cent of men remarry within three years of marital dissolution. After five years these proportions rise to 7 per cent for women and 12 per cent for men. And after 10 years they reach 14 and 20 per cent for women and men, respectively (Wu and Schimmele, 2005: 222). One possible interpretation of these trends in remarriage is that the high rates of divorce seen in Canada have less to do with declining respect for marriage as an institution than with desire for a 'good' marriage and low tolerance for one that is unhappy and unrewarding.

Yet a look at remarriage rates over time casts doubt on the notion that remarriage represents a reassertion of faith in marriage. Remarriage rates (as measured by the number of remarried persons per 1,000 of those previously married) actually declined after the late 1960s and stayed low throughout the 1990s (Wu and Schimmele, 2005). On the other hand, remarriage rates do not necessarily tell us very much because it seems likely that a large proportion of the divorced people who do not remarry still form new common-law relationships. In fact, common-law unions have accounted for a rising proportion of relationships in recent decades (see Table 5.12). Between 1976 and 2001 the proportion of women aged 30–34 living in com-

Table 5.12 Percentage of couples in common-law unions by age of woman, Canada, 1996 and 2001

Age group	1996	2001	% change 1996–2001
15–19	75.4	77.6	2.2
20–24	50.6	58.4	7.8
25–29	27.7	33.4	5.7
30–34	17.8	21.5	3.7
35–39	13.4	17.2	3.8
40–44	10.6	14.2	3.6
45–49	8.4	11.7	3.3
50–54	6.7	9.2	2.5
55–59	4.6	7.1	2.5
60–64	3.0	4.7	1.7
65+	1.8	2.5	0.7

Source: Adapted from Statistics Canada publication *Current Demographic Analysis 2003* and *2004*, by Alain Bélanger. Catalogue no. 91-209-XIE, p. 62.

Would You Live Common Law?

Who is likely to live in a common-law union? To answer this question, Milan (2003) analyzed data from the Canadian General Social Survey for 2001 concerning the willingness of
unmarried people (both never-married and previously married) who had never lived common law in the past to do so in the future. The data revealed some interesting results:

1. Just under half of the respondents (48 per cent) said they could live common law at some
   future time; 52 per cent said they could not.
2. More men than women were willing to live common law (62 per cent to 36 per cent).
3. Willingness to live common law declined as respondents' age rose; agreement was typically lower for women at each age category.
4. Willingness to live common law was conditioned by education and labour force status.
   Those with more education were more likely to take a favourable view of common law
   arrangements than were those with less education. In addition, those in the labour force
   were more likely to consider living common law than were those still attending school.
5. Residents of Quebec were more willing than people elsewhere in Canada to live common
   law. More than three-fifths (61 per cent) of unmarried people in Quebec who had never
   lived common law said they would consider this type of relationship, compared with
   about two-fifths (39 per cent) of those in Ontario and the Prairie provinces (41 per cent).
   In both the Atlantic provinces and British Columbia, just over half (51 per cent) of the
   unmarried population would cohabit without legal marriage.
6. Respondents born outside Canada were less likely than others to accept common-law
   unions. About 52 per cent of the Canadian-born were willing to live common law, compared with 30 per cent of the foreign-born.
7. Those reporting regular attendance at religious services were less willing than others to
   live in common-law unions. Among respondents aged 15–29, only 27 per cent of the
   'very religious' took a favourable view of common-law arrangements, compared to 81 per
   cent among the non-religious.
8. Family experience appeared to influence attitudes towards common-law relationships.
   Men and women who had lived with both their parents until the age of 15 were less willing to live common law than those who had experienced the disruption of their own parents' marriages, whether through divorce, separation, or death.
9. People with conservative family attitudes tended to opt for marriage, while those with
   liberal views were more likely to choose a common-law union. Some 43 per cent of those
   who perceived marriage to be important or very important for a happy life indicated that
   they could live in a common-law union, as compared with 57 per cent of those who perceived marriage as not very or not at all important. Among individuals who described a
   lasting relationship as very important or important for a happy life, 53 per cent indicated
   they could live common law compared with 36 per cent for whom a lasting relationship
   was not important.

Source: Based on Milan (2003), 2–6.

mon-law unions increased from 18 to 22 per cent; for women aged 25–29 the increase was from just under 28 to 33.4 per cent over the same period. Unfortunately, common-law unions are not very stable. One reason for this that is mentioned in the literature is that the people attracted to common-law arrangements tend to be less than fully committed to a long-term conjugal relationship (Budinski and Trovato, 2005; Hall and Zhao, 1995; Le Bourdais, Neill, and Turcotte, 2000; Wu, 2000).

The instability of all types of conjugal unions, marital and common law, in Canada today suggests that increasing proportions of adults may be spending a significant part of their lives living alone or in short-term relationships. This is particularly likely to be the case among younger cohorts, where break-up rates tend to be high, especially for those whose first and second unions have been common law. Indeed, the proportion of women who had experienced at least two conjugal unions—marital or common law—was nearly three times as great for women in their thirties (39 per cent) as for those in their sixties (14 per cent) (Le Bourdais, Neill, and Turcotte, 2000). Another study by Statistics Canada (2002a), confirmed these tendencies.

What has changed, of course, is the nature of the first union. Young people today are significantly more likely than earlier generations to report that their first conjugal union was a common-law relationship (as opposed to matrimony). In a recent survey, when never-married or previously married people were asked if they were willing to live in a common-law union, there was a clear age gradient in affirmative responses: the younger the respondent, the greater his or her willingness to accept this type of relationship (Milan, 2003).

The Case of Quebec

Until the Quiet Revolution of the late 1950s and early 1960s, marriage rates in Quebec were generally high and people tended to marry early.

Today Quebec has both the lowest marriage rate in the country and the highest incidence of non-marital unions; census data for 2001 indicated that approximately 30 per cent of all couples in the province were living common law. The comparable figure for the rest of Canada was just under 12 per cent. The 2006 census enumerated 611,900 common-law couple families in Quebec—an increase of just over 20 per cent from 2001. Common-law unions accounted for 34.6 per cent of all couples in the province. This is a much higher proportion than any other province in Canada. On a national level, in 2006, Quebec accounted for 44.4 per cent of all common-law couples in the country. The closest other province was Ontario (25.5 per cent of the national total) (Statistics Canada 2007d: 35). Even by international standards, the level of cohabitation in Quebec is unusually high, exceeding the figures for Sweden (25.4 per cent), Finland (23.9 per cent), New Zealand (23.7 per cent), and Denmark (22.2 per cent) (Statistics Canada, 2007d: 35). Whereas 59 per cent of women in other provinces aged 30–39 reported their first conjugal union to have been a marriage, this is the case for only 25.6 per cent of women in Quebec (Statistics Canada, 2002b).

According to Henripin (2003: 185), the era of 'paperless marriage' in Quebec began in the 1970s, and all the relevant indicators—declining marriage rates, rising age at first marriage, high rates of both divorce and cohabitation—suggest that it is now well established. In the rest of Canada cohabitation is usually a precursor to marriage, but this is not the case in Quebec: the chance that cohabiting women will eventually marry is 33 per cent lower in Quebec than in other provinces (Wu, 2000). As Henripin (2003: 187) notes, it appears that cohabitation in Quebec is not primarily a kind of trial marriage for young couples, or even an alternative to traditional marriage: rather, it appears to be evolving into a new type of family form. In 2006, Statistics Canada (2007d: 39) estimated

Fewer Quebeckers Choosing to Marry

Edna Langis and Pierre Charbonneau of Montreal have all the trappings of modern married life—a home, a car, two teenage kids and a commitment to stay together through good times and rocky times.

What they don't have is a marriage certificate, a fact that places them in good company in Quebec. If the two most common words between Quebec couples used to be 'I do,' they have now become 'What for?'

'Marriage wouldn't have made our relationship any stronger,' said Mr Charbonneau, a 45-year-old freelance photographer who has lived with Ms Langis for 26 years. 'Our feeling is, "Why tamper with success?"'

Quebec has joined Sweden, that laboratory for all things liberal and liberated, as the champion of unmarried couples in the world. . . . The up-and-coming generation in Quebec may even be making the institution of marriage extinct: nearly two in three Quebeckers under 35 who live together didn't bother walking down the aisle.

'Quite simply, Quebeckers aren't getting married any more,' said Josée Martel, a demographer with Statistics Canada. 'And marriage is no longer a prerequisite to having children.'

The Charbonneau-Langis household in Montreal's Notre-Dame-de-Grâce district is typical. The couple moved in together in the mid-1970s when Mr Charbonneau was still in school and Ms Langis had just started working.

Over the years, they watched several friends and family members get married, sometimes after living together for many years. Yet many of the marriages broke up.

Ms Langis's seven brothers and sisters all tied the knot. Today, only one is still married.

'After so many years together, I asked myself, "why do it? What would it bring us?"' Ms Langis asked. 'A piece of paper isn't going to strengthen our commitment.'

Source: Ingrid Peritz (2002), 'Fewer Quebeckers Choosing to Marry', *The Globe and Mail* (23 Oct.): A9.

that almost 15 per cent of children aged 0–14 in Canada lived with common-law parents. Of all the provinces, Quebec led the way in this tendency, with nearly 30 per cent of children in that age group living in common-law families.

Future Outlook

If current trends in nuptiality continue, the Canadian family could look quite different by the end of the twenty-first century than it does today. Data from the 2006 census (see Figure 5.8) show that traditional marriage is in decline while common-law unions and single-parenthood are on the rise. The number of married couples counted in 2006 was just over 6.1 million, but although this constituted the largest group of all census families (68.6 per cent), the proportion of married couples has been sliding steadily since the 1960s. Between 2001 and 2006, the rise in the number of married couples represented an increase of just 3.35 per cent; by comparison, over the same period the total number of common-law unions (1.38 million in 2006) and lone-parent families (1.4 million) grew by 19 and 7.8 per cent, respectively. In 2006, for the first time since data on marriage began being collected in this country, more than half of the adult population aged 15 and older were unmarried—that is, they had either never been married or they were divorced, separated,

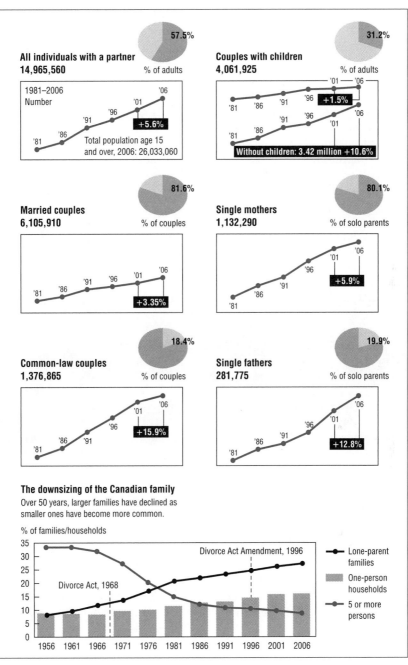

Figure 5.8 Family change in Canada

Note: The percentages in each of the pie charts for married and common-law couples are based on the number of individuals with a partner (14,965,560). Percentages in the pie charts for single fathers and single mothers are based on total couples with children (4,061,925).

Source: Audette (2007): A2. Material reprinted with the express permission of 'Edmonton Journal Group Inc.', a CanWest Partnership.

widowed, or living common law (Statistics Canada, *The Daily*, 2007c).

Another indication that the traditional Canadian family is changing is the diminishing proportion of married couples with children. In 1986, married-couple families with children aged 24 and under made up nearly 50 per cent of all family households; as of 2006, just 34.6 per cent of all family households included married couples with children, and over the same 20-year interval, the proportion of couples without children has risen from nearly 31 per cent to 34 per cent. Other noteworthy trends include the continued rise in the numbers of single mothers (over 1.1 million in 2006) and single fathers (nearly 282,000), the decline in families with five or more members, and the dramatic growth of one-person households. Taken together, these trends strongly suggest that Canadian society is unlikely to turn back the clock to the more traditional family models of earlier times, as the momentum behind these trends seems much too strong.

Conclusion

Nuptiality occupies a central place in demographic analysis because it is an important precursor to fertility: the overall fertility of a population depends to a significant extent on the timing of a woman's first sexual union, whether that union is traditional marriage or some other socially accepted form. Analysis of marriage, divorce, cohabitation, and other aspects of nuptiality can also be viewed as areas of independent sociological study in and of themselves because to a large extent changes in these variables are

Same-Sex Couples in Canada

Of the 45,300 same-sex couples enumerated in 2006, more than 80 per cent lived in urban areas, most of them in the country's three largest cities. Toronto, Montreal, and Vancouver respectively were home to 18.4, 21.2, and 10.3 per cent of all same-sex couples across the nation.

In Montreal and Vancouver, same-sex couples represented 1.0 per cent of all couples. In Toronto that proportion was slightly lower (0.8 per cent of all couples), but still above the national average (0.6 per cent). The proportions of same-sex couples were also above average in Halifax, Moncton, the Ontario cities of Guelph and Kingston, Ottawa–Gatineau, Quebec City, and Victoria.

The first provinces to legalize same-sex marriage were Ontario and British Columbia, both in 2003; Quebec followed suit the next year. The proportions of same-sex couples who had taken advantage of the opportunity to marry were also above the national average (16.5 per cent) in the census metropolitan areas of Toronto (24.8 per cent) and Vancouver (18.9 per cent). In Montreal, however, only 10.5 per cent of same-sex couples were legally married—likely reflecting the higher propensity of all couples in Quebec to prefer common-law unions.

Within census metropolitan areas, same-sex couples were much more likely to live in central than in peripheral municipalities (77.4 per cent vs 22.6 per cent). The corresponding proportions for opposite-sex couples were 56.3 and 43.7 per cent, respectively.

Source: Based on Statistics Canada (2007d), 46.

necessarily a function of broader cultural and social structural changes in society.

In this chapter we examined the basic concepts and measures of nuptiality and looked at the trends in marriage, divorce, and cohabitation across the developed and the developing regions of the world. Our broad overview suggests that in the developed countries marriage has been declining, and cohabitation without marriage increasing, since the 1970s. This pattern reflects profound changes in the way young adults think about marriage and the institution of the family in general. To say that the Western family is on the decline might be too extreme, but marriage, as an important part of the Western family model, certainly appears to be less central for younger generations than it was for their predecessors. Even in countries like Italy, Spain, Greece, and Poland—the last bastions of traditional marriage in the industrialized world—the average age at first marriage continues to increase, and rates of cohabitation without marriage are on the rise. Divorce rates have generally increased in the industrialized countries and, although this trend has been levelling off in recent years, this likely reflects the decline in marriage rates. In the developing countries age at first marriage has generally increased since the early 1970s, and divorce is becoming more common. In time, with increasing levels of urbanization and especially improvements in the status of women, age at first marriage can be expected to increase further. As urbanization, globalization of the economy, and the spread of Western values continue throughout the world, nuptiality patterns are bound to become increasingly similar across the regions (Goode, 1970; McDonald, 1985).

In the Western world, what the future holds for marriage and the family as an institution remains uncertain. But it seems clear that the social barriers to diversity in family form have weakened considerably and are likely to weaken further. People now have a plethora of options: they can remain single; marry or cohabit; divorce and form new relationships, with or without marriage; bear and raise children with or without a partner of either sex. Some experts (e.g., Blankenhorn, 2007) openly express reservations about these trends, while others welcome the new options, irrespective of the uncertainty they may pose for the future of the family (Stacey, 1990; Lapierre-Adamcyk and Charvet, 2000; Heuveline and Timberlake, 2004; Seltzer et al., 2005).

Exercises

1. Discuss how the following factors might have contributed to the rise in divorce rates in Western countries over the past four decades:

   (a) increasing numbers of families in which both partners have jobs
   (b) increasing geographic mobility
   (c) decreasing attachment to religion and religious institutions
   (d) increasing economic independence for women
   (e) increasing economic insecurity in families

   Are there any other factors you can think of that might also have played a part in the rise of divorce?

2. Discuss the proposition that cohabitation is replacing marriage in Western countries today. What evidence is there to support this proposition? Is there any evidence that seems to contradict it? To what extent is cohabitation a precursor to marriage rather than an alternative to it?

3. Explain why marriage rates in the Western world have declined since the early 1970s. What is the future of marriage in the Western world?

4. Describe how the family institution is changing in the developing countries. Is there any evidence that nuptiality trends in the less developed countries are approximating Western patterns?

5. Do alternative family forms such as same-sex marriage pose a serious challenge to the institution of the family in the Western world?

Additional Reading

Bianchi, Suzanne, John P. Robinson, and Melissa A. Milkie. 2006. *Changing Rhythms of American Family Life*. Chicago: University of Chicago Press and Russel Sage Foundation.

Blossfeld, Hans-Peter, and Andreas Timm, eds. 2003. *Who Marries Whom? Educational Systems as Marriage Markets in Modern Societies*. Dordrecht: Kluwer Academic.

Burguière, André, Christiane Klapisch-Zuber, M. Segalen, and F. Zonabend, eds. 1996. *A History of the Family*. 2 vols. Cambridge, MA: The Belknap Press of Harvard University Press.

De Beer, Joop, and Fred Deven, eds. 2000. *Diversity in Family Formation: The 2nd Demographic Transition in Belgium and the Netherlands*. Dordrecht: Kluwer Academic.

Jacobs, Jerry A., and Kathleen Gerson. 2004. *The Time Divide: Work, Family, and Gender Inequality*. New York: Harvard University Press.

National Research Council and Institute of Medicine. 2005. *Growing Up Global: The Changing Transitions to Adulthood in the Developing Countries*. Panel on Transitions to Adulthood in Developing Countries. Ed. Cynthia B. Lloyd. Committee on Population and Board on Children, Youth, and Families. Division of Behavioral and Social Sciences and Education. Washington, DC: The National Academies Press.

Presser, Harriet B. 2003. *Working in a 24/7 Economy: Challenges for American Families*. New York: Russell Sage Foundation.

Waite, Linda J., and Maggie Gallagher. 2000. *The Case for Marriage: Why Married People Are Happier, Healthier, and Better off Financially*. New York: Broadway Books.

Wu, Lawrence L., and Barbara Wolf, eds. 2001. *Out of Wedlock: Causes and Consequences of Nonmarital Fertility*. New York: Russell Sage Foundation.

Zimmerman, F. Klaus, and Michael Vogler, eds. 2003. *Family, Household and Work*. Berlin: Springer.

Web Resources

The Vanier Institute of the Family is a non-profit organization dedicated to promoting the well-being of Canadian families. It conducts research and analysis on a variety of issues concerning families and is an excellent source of information. http://www. vifamily.ca/about/about.html.

The Child and Family Research Institute is committed to world-class research on a wide range of children's and women's health concerns. It is the largest research institute of its kind in Western Canada: www.bcricwh.bc.ca/.

The UCLA Center on Everyday Lives of Families is an interdisciplinary institution where anthropologists, applied linguists, education specialists, and psychologists study how working parents and their children balance the demands of work, school, and family life: www.celf.ucla.edu/.

The Policy Research Initiative (PRI) conducts research on a variety of topics of interest to Canadian policy-makers. One of its units, the Population, Work, and Family Policy Research Collaboration (PWFC), specializes in research in the areas of the labour market, population change, and the life course: www.policyresearch.gc.ca/.

PART THREE

Demographic Processes I: Fertility and Mortality

Chapter 6

Fertility

Introduction

Compared to migration and mortality, fertility receives inordinate attention in population studies. This is because it is the variable most responsible for population growth and the main factor determining change in age composition of a population. Although inherently a biological process, human fertility is strongly influenced by societal and cultural factors that make it a collective as well as an individual matter. A society's survival depends on its fertility, and for this reason all societies possess elements of culture that promote and encourage some level of reproduction. A population's fertility is therefore the product of biological, social, and behavioural factors.

Basic Concepts and Measures

Fecundity and Fertility

Fecundity describes the physiological ability of a woman, a man, or a couple to reproduce. Logically, fecundity depends on a sequence of events: the female must produce an egg capable of being fertilized; the male must produce sperm that can fertilize the egg; fertilization must occur; the fertilized egg must survive to implant in the uterus; and, once implantation has occurred, the pregnancy must result in a live birth (Trussell, 2003: 397). The opposite of fecundity is *infecundity*—the total inability to reproduce (in other words, *sterility*). For some individuals, infecundity may be the result of a lifelong genetic or biological condition that prevents them from conceiving or bringing about conception. For others, sterility may develop as a result of some acquired disease that damages

the reproductive system (McFalls, 1979: 4). *Subfecundity* is the term used to describe the condition of couples incapable of having children because of impairments in any of the biological aspects of reproduction. These impairments include

- *coital inability*, the temporary or permanent inability to perform normal heterosexual intercourse because of physical or psychological disease;
- *conceptive failure*, the diminished ability to conceive or to bring about conception; and
- *pregnancy loss*, the involuntary termination of a pregnancy before a live birth, including spontaneous abortion, late fetal death, and stillbirth, but neither induced abortion nor neonatal mortality. (McFalls, 1979, 1990)

The extent of subfecundity can vary, from situations where both partners have chronic reproductive impairments to cases in which one partner suffers from an impairment that is medically treatable.

The realization of fecundity is referred to as fertility. Fertility is the actual reproductive output of a woman, a man, or a couple, as measured by the number of offspring. At the aggregate level, this term implies some summary measure of reproduction for a population.

Measures of Fertility

Generally speaking, *period measures* of fertility are computed on the basis of current information, usually for a given year or some other specified interval, while *cohort measures* are derived from information on specific generations of women (for example, the cohort of women born between 1900 and 1905). Cohort measures are based on the completed childbearing experience of a woman at the end of the cohort's reproductive lifespan.

The following sections outline some common period and cohort measures of fertility. As we will see, some of the period measures, like the total fertility rate and the gross and net reproduction rates, can also be computed for cohorts. However, while the methods of calculating period and cohort measures are essentially the same, their data requirements and the implications of their results will, of course, differ.

Crude Birth Rate

The crude birth rate (CBR) measures the number of births over a specified period per 1,000 population:

$$CBR = \frac{B}{P} \times 1,000$$

where B represents the number of births in a given time period (usually a year), and P is the corresponding mid-year population.

In 2005, the world's crude birth rate was 21 per 1,000 population. In the more developed countries, the CBR was only 11 per 1,000 population, while in the less developed countries it was 24, or about 14 per cent above the world rate. Africa stands out for its high birth rates (Middle Africa, for instance, has a rate of 44 per 1,000), while the lowest CBRs are in Europe. The rates for western, southern, and eastern Europe seldom exceed 10 per 1,000 (see Figure 6.1).

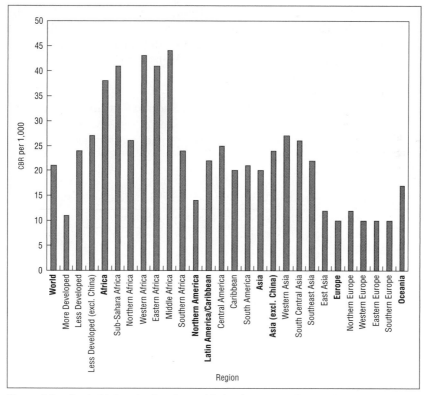

Figure 6.1 Crude birth rates for the world, development regions, and major geographic regions in 2005

Source: Population Reference Bureau (2005).

A number of drawbacks with the CBR make it impractical for comparative analysis. First, it overlooks the effect of age on fertility. As we shall see later, women's fertility varies with age, and since the CBR does not account for age differences, it is all but useless for comparing the birth rates of two or more populations. Second, the mid-year population used in the denominator includes not just women of childbearing age but also children, the elderly, and men— segments of the population that have no direct relationship to the risk of childbearing. For these reasons in particular, relying solely on the crude birth rate can invite misleading conclusions about cross-national variations in fertility. As a result, analysts prefer other period measures that are based on age-specific data for women in the reproductive ages.

General Fertility Rate

The simplest age-limited measure of fertility is the general fertility rate (GFR), which represents the number of births per 1,000 women between the ages of 15 and 49 (which is generally considered the reproductive age span for women):

$$\text{GFR} = \frac{B}{P^f_{15-49}} \times 1,000$$

The numerator is the total number of births in a given period in the population, and the denominator corresponds to the mid-year population of females (signified by the superscript f) aged 15–49. Note that in many applications of this formula for industrialized countries, the upper age is set at 44, since few women in these societies bear children past this age.

Table 6.1 shows Canada's GFR for 2004 based on the two denominators, 15–49 and 15–44. The derived figure of 41.02 based on the first of these denominators indicates that in 2004 there were roughly 41 births for every 1,000 women of childbearing age (15–49). The second computation, based on the shorter childbearing span typically used for industrialized countries (15–44), gives a higher rate of 49.21. We may gain a sense of how Canadian fertility rates have changed over time by comparing these two calculations with rates from earlier in the twentieth century. In 1957, the Canadian GFR$_{(15-49)}$ was 118.0, and the GFR$_{(15-44)}$ was 129.8. These are the highest recorded GFRs for Canada since 1921.

Age-Specific Fertility Rates

Age-specific fertility rates get around some of the problems associated with the crude birth

Table 6.1 Number of live births by age of mother, female population, and calculated age-specific fertility rates and general fertility rate, Canada, 2004

Age of mother	Number of live births	Female population	Rate per 1,000
15–19	14,075	1,027,372	13.7
20–24	55,383	1,085,941	51.0
25–29	103,743	1,065,123	97.4
30–34	105,705	1,103,392	95.8
35–39	48,130	1,200,249	40.1
40–44	9,376	1,358,841	6.9
45–49	413	1,376,667	0.3
Total	337,072	8,217,586	
GFR$_{15-49}$			41.02
GFR$_{15-44}$			49.21

Note: Computed rates do not include data for age <15 or age not stated, which in total accounted for 247 births.
Source: Adapted from Statistics Canada (2006d).

rate. The formula for an age-specific fertility rate can be written as

$$f_x = \frac{B_x}{W_x} \times 1{,}000$$

where f_x symbolizes the age-specific fertility rate, B_x is the number of births in a given year to women aged x, and W_x is the mid-year female population aged x.

Thus, this formula calculates the number of births to women of a given age group in a given period for every 1,000 women in the same age group.

If we were to plot age-specific fertility rates on a graph we would notice a distinct pattern across age: rates tend to be relatively low for women aged 15–19 but rise steeply for those aged 20–24 and 25–29 before levelling off and declining. In populations with high overall fertility, birth rates are usually highest in the age group 20–24. In the developed countries, where women are more inclined to have children later in life, the peak age group is usually 25–29 or (especially in recent years) 30–34. In general, fertility rates fall precipitously after the mid-thirties, approaching zero as women reach their mid- to late forties. Figure 6.2 illustrates the age-specific fertility pattern of American Hutterite women in the early 1920s, in comparison with the rates for women from other populations. The Hutterites are thought to be the most fertile group in history (Coale, 1969; Eaton and Meyer, 1953; Henry, 1961).

Total Fertility Rate

An advantage of age-specific fertility rates is that they can be used to compute other important indexes of reproduction. One of these is the total fertility rate (TFR), which is a summary measure of the total reproductive output for a given population during a specific interval (usually a year). As a single index of fertility, the TFR

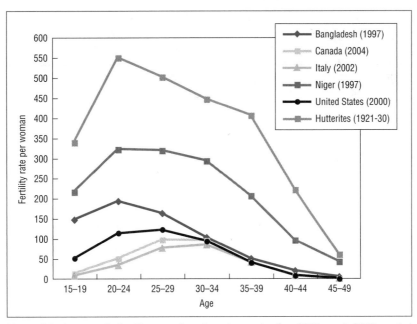

Figure 6.2 Age-specific fertility rates for selected countries, late 1990s–early 2000s, and of Hutterite women from South Dakota married between 1921 and 1930

Sources: Henry (1961); Statistics Canada (2006d); United Nations Department of Economic and Social Affairs, Population Division (2005b).

has the advantage of being easily computable and interpretable. It is a pure fertility measure that is not affected by age composition, and it is one of the few aggregate-level period measures of fertility that can be interpreted in terms of the number of children expected to be born to an individual woman over the course of her childbearing years. In other words, the TFR represents the expected average number of children ever born to a randomly selected woman who survives to the end of her reproductive span (usually menopause or some suitably advanced age, such as 50 years), given that the current age-specific fertility rates in the population remain constant (Wood, 1994: 27). We can think of a hypothetical cohort of 1,000 women who start reproducing at age 15, and who will eventually end their childbearing once they reach age 50. If this hypothetical cohort were to bear children in accordance with the age-specific fertility rates of a real population, then at the end of their child-bearing years these hypothetical women would end up with a certain average number of children. That eventual average is the TFR.

In terms of how it is calculated, the TFR is the sum of age-specific fertility rates for women aged 15 to 49, and can be expressed as follows:

$$\text{TFR} = \sum_{15}^{49} f_x$$

where f_x represents age-specific fertility rate *per woman*.

In most applications, the data are grouped into five-year age categories, and the formula is expressed slightly differently. The sum of the rates must be multiplied by 5 to take into account the five-year age interval, so the formula becomes:

$$\text{TFR} = 5 \times \sum_{15-19}^{45-49} f_x$$

In Table 6.2, the sum of age-specific fertility rates is 305.2. Multiplying this value by 5 gives a

Table 6.2 Computation of TFR, GRR, and NRR using Canada's age-specific fertility rates for 2004

(1)	(2)	(3)	(4)	(5)
Age of mother	Age-specific fertility rate per 1,000	Age-specific fertility rate per woman	Life table female survival ratio	Products of columns (2) and (4)
15–19	13.7	0.0137	4.96455	0.068014
20–24	51.0	0.0510	4.95651	0.252782
25–29	97.4	0.0974	4.94828	0.481962
30–34	95.8	0.0958	4.93893	0.473149
35–39	40.1	0.0401	4.92505	0.197495
40–44	6.9	0.0069	4.90384	0.033836
45–49	0.3	0.0003	4.87100	0.001461
Totals	305.2	0.3052		1.508701
TFR	1,526	1.526		
GRR	741.6	0.7416		
NRR	733.2	0.7332		

Note: The TFR, GRR, and NRR are expressed as both per 1,000 women aged 15–49 and as *per woman* 15–49. The proportion for the sex ratio at birth—i.e., the proportion of newborn baby girls—applied to the GRR and NRR is 0.486.
Source: Statistics Canada (2006d, 2006e).

TFR of 1,526 children per 1,000 women of reproductive age, or approximately 1.53 children *per woman*. Another way of stating this is to say that a hypothetical woman aged 15 in 2004, if she were exposed to the age-specific fertility rates of Canada in 2004, would by the age of 50 have borne 1.53 children.

Demographers frequently attempt to determine whether a population is growing fast enough to replace itself, and the total fertility rate is useful in this exercise. The fertility level required for a population to replace itself varies depending on mortality conditions up to the end of the childbearing ages. It has been calculated that if a population has a life expectancy at birth of 25 years, the TFR needed for replacement is 5.21 children per woman. With a life expectancy at birth of 45 years, a population would require a TFR of 3.08 for replacement. A TFR of 2.1 coincides with a life expectancy at birth of 75 years. Since many countries have attained this life expectancy, a TFR of 2.1 is usually regarded as replacement-level fertility (Coale and Demeny, 1983).

Table 6.3 shows the TFRs for selected countries and the corresponding age-specific fertility

Table 6.3 Age-specific fertility rates (per 1,000 women) and total fertility rates for selected countries (year of observation in parentheses)

Country (year)	15–19	20–24	25–29	30–34	35–39	40–44	45–49	TFR (per woman)
Bangladesh (1997)	147	193	163	103	50	20	5	3.4
Canada (2004)	13.7	51	97.4	95.8	40.1	6.9	0.3	1.5
Italy (2002)	7	33	76	84	40	8	0	1.2
Niger (1997)	216	322	319	293	206	96	42	7.5
Sweden (2001)	7	47	104	103	44	8	0	1.6
United States (2000)	49	112	121	94	40	8	0	2.1
Japan (2000)	5	39	98	91	31	4	0	1.3
Denmark (2001)	8	51	126	115	43	7	0	1.7
France (1999)	10	61	133	105	42	8	0	1.8
Spain (2000)	9	26	67	95	43	7	0	1.2
Germany (2000)	13	57	93	79	30	5	0	1.4
UK (2000)	29	69	95	88	40	8	0	1.6
Afghanistan (1973)	168	359	355	307	235	137	81	8.2
China (2001)	3	108	115	40	9	2	1	1.4
India (1997)	54	226	188	109	55	26	8	3.3
Israel (2000)	17	117	187	162	86	21	2	3.0
Palestine Territory (1970)	55	242	340	343	330	129	56	7.5
Australia (2000)	17	56	107	110	49	9	0	1.7
New Zealand (2000)	29	78	116	116	53	10	0	2.0
Brazil (1994)	88	153	126	81	45	16	3	2.6
Mexico (1996)	75	146	144	102	56	19	3	2.7
Argentina (2000)	66	117	127	106	60	18	2	2.5

Sources: United Nations Department of Economic and Social Affairs, Population Division (2005b)—reprinted with the permission of the United Nations; Statistics Canada (2006d).

rates. Although these rates do not pertain to one uniform time period, it is clear that some countries have fertility levels well above the 2.1 replacement level. A notable case is Niger, where in 1997 women had on average 7.5 children. Age-specific fertility rates in this country are unusually high by today's standards, especially among 15–19-year-olds (216 births per 1,000 women), which suggests that, relatively speaking, women in Niger enter sexual unions and start reproducing earlier than women in other parts of the world, and consequently have large families.

A measure related to the TFR is the total marital fertility rate (TMFR). It is identical to the TFR except that it relates specifically to *married* women of childbearing age. Because the majority of births in most populations are to married women, the TMFR gives a better picture of fertility in the population. The difference between the TMFR and the TFR for a given population provides a measure of the effect of marriage on overall fertility.

Gross Reproduction Rate

As mentioned earlier, demographers frequently use the total fertility rate to assess whether or not a population is growing fast enough to replace itself in the long term. It is important to understand, however, that replacement fertility really has to do with the average number of *female* offspring that women produce. The measure that addresses this important feature of a population's reproductivity is the gross reproduction rate (GRR), which is obtained by multiplying the computed TFR by the proportion of female births in the population:

$$GRR = TFR \times \pi$$

where the symbol π is used to represent the proportion of all newborns in a given year that are female.

In most populations the proportion of female to male newborns does not vary significantly from one year to the next. It typically fluctuates around a proportion value 0.49, based on the fact that in most populations there are 105 boys born for every 100 girls; expressed as a proportion, this ratio is 100/105, which equals 0.4878, or 0.49 when rounded. In Canada between 1961 and 2004, the proportion of female newborns averages out to 0.4860.

In 2004, the Canadian total fertility rate was 1.526, and the gross reproduction rate for that year works out to 0.745. This is the expected number of female children a woman will have assuming that she survives through the childbearing ages and has children according to the age-specific fertility rates prevailing in the population. If the computed GRR is below 1—as it is in this case—it means that on average, mothers are having less than one daughter. Over the long term, this level of reproductivity is insufficient to ensure that the population will replace itself; any value greater than 1 is generally considered to be above replacement fertility. Gross reproduction 1 would be consistent with zero population growth in the long run, meaning that each woman in the population would essentially be replacing herself with one female.

Note the close connection between gross reproduction rate and total fertility rate: it is clear that total fertility rates around 2 will also imply zero population growth in the long run, since in most populations approximately half of all births are male and half are female.

Net Reproduction Rate

The gross reproduction rate is useful in predicting whether a population will grow or decline over time, but to get an even more accurate view of a population's prospects for long-term growth, we need to account for the possibility that some of the women of childbearing age who are exposed to the chance of giving birth may not survive through the childbearing age groups. The net reproduction rate (NRR) represents the average number of female births to women after the effect of mortality to women in the reproductive ages has been taken into account. Stated differently, the NRR is in actuality the gross reproduction rate (GRR) adjusted for mortality to women in the childbearing ages. So if, for instance, the GRR is computed to be exactly 1, we would expect the NRR to be somewhat lower than 1 because of mortality to women in their childbearing years. In fact, the NRR will always be smaller than the computed GRR because in any population there will be some level of mortality, however low, to women in the childbearing years.

In order to derive the NRR we need the age-specific survival ratios for women between the ages of 15 and 49, which can be obtained from an appropriate female life table. Life tables will be explained in detail in Chapter 7. At this point it suffices to say that a life table reflects the mortality experience of a hypothetical cohort of newborns, followed through life as the cohort ages. At each age there will be deaths and survivors according to a schedule of age-specific mortality rates taken from an actual population. Male and female life tables are calculated separately because men's and women's mortality rates differ substantially. In our case here, our objective is to use the female life table to derive age-specific survival ratios for women in each age group, from 15–19 to 45–49. Since the life table begins with a hypothetical cohort of 100,000 newborns, the age-specific survival ratios will be calculated by dividing the number of person-years lived by the cohort at a given age by 100,000. So, the female age-specific survival ratios (SR$_x$) would be computed as follows:

$$SR_x = \frac{L_x}{100,000}$$

where L$_x$ represents the number of person-years lived by the life table cohort for those in age group x. The value of 100,000 is a constant based on the size of the life table cohort at birth.

According to the Canadian female life table for 2001, women aged 15–19 together lived a total of 496,455 person-years. The survival ratio

(SR$_x$) for this age category is therefore 496,455/ 100,000 or 4.96455. In practical terms, this tells us that a woman in this age category would live almost the full five years of the age interval. Expressed as a probability, the chance of surviving through this five-year interval would be 99.3 per cent (i.e., 4.96455/5 = 0.9929 × 100 = 99.3 per cent). Once we've calculated the survival ratios, we can apply them to the corresponding age-specific fertility rates. The sum of the products multiplied by the proportion of female births will give the net reproduction rate (NRR):

$$NRR = \left[\sum_{15}^{49} f_x \, SR_x \right] \times \pi$$

The net reproduction rate is a key indicator of long-term potential population growth. A net reproduction rate greater than 1 means population growth without limit in the long run. A net reproduction rate less than 1 will lead, in the long run, to the population becoming extinct. Keeping in mind the close relationships among TFR, GRR, and NRR, there is a fine line between long-term growth and decline for a population: less than around 2 children per woman will lead to extinction in the long run; 3 children per woman will lead, over the long term, to exponential growth without limit.

This interpretation must be accepted with a note of caution. Since populations do not have stable population growth rates over very long periods of time, the NRR cannot be used as a definitive predictor of a population's ultimate fate. Rather, the NRR provides an *indication* of where a population is headed with respect to long-term growth or decline. The qualifier 'in the long run' is very important. A net reproduction rate equal to 1 will lead to zero population growth only if it should prevail *in the long run*.

Table 6.2 (page 180) outlines the steps involved in computing the period TFR, GRR, and NRR. The input data are the 2004 age-specific fertility rates for Canadian women, and the corresponding survival ratios are computed with the data in the female life table for 2001. The worked-out NRR is 0.7332. Since it is below 1, it reinforces the idea that current fertility in Canada is substantially below replacement levels. Not taking into account the possibility of migration, if this level of fertility were to remain indefinitely, the population of Canada will, in the long run, reach extinction.

Cohort Fertility Rate

Fundamentally, the period TFR reflects fertility only for the period for which it is calculated. It would be risky to interpret the period TFR as the fertility rate of the future since period TFR can fluctuate considerably from one year to the next. How, then, can we gain a more accurate sense of future fertility?

The answer lies in assembling retroactive information for generations of women who have already passed through their reproductive lifespans, and using this information to compute the average completed family size for specific generations of women. The input data for this would be period age-specific fertility rates for each over a number of years, beginning as far back as data are available and ending with the

most recent year of observation. For instance, in Canada, vital statistics data are available from 1921. The age-specific fertility rates for each of the years since 1921 can be assembled into a matrix that juxtaposes age and calendar year. The diagonal elements in this matrix would represent the age-specific fertility rates of different cohorts of women born at different points in time. For each cohort, we could compute the average completed fertility in the same manner we calculated the period TFR.

The formula for the average completed fertility rate for cohort k (CFR_k) is shown below:

$$\text{CFR}_k = \sum_{15}^{49} f_x$$

The formula says to sum all the age-specific fertility rates for women in cohort k. If the data are grouped into five-year age categories, the formula should be modified accordingly, as described earlier in connection with the period TFR.

Table 6.4 is a matrix of age-specific fertility rates for Canadian women from 1960 to 2000. Note that there is complete information for just

Table 6.4 Age-specific fertility rates (per 1,000) by period for Canadian women, showing period TFR, cohort TFR, and the period of birth of three completed cohorts of women

Year t	15–19	20–24	25–29	30–34	35–39	40–44	45–49	Period TFR, year t	Cohort completed fertility in year t	Period of birth of cohort completing fertility in year t
2000	16.3	56.1	97.9	89.9	35.5	6.1	0.3	1.552	1.966	1951–1955
1995	24.5	70.6	109.7	86.8	31.3	4.8	0.2	1.640	2.095	1946–1950
1990	26.9	85.4	140.2	87.5	28.6	3.9	0.1	1.863	2.413	1941–1945
1985	23.7	85.3	125.3	74.6	21.8	3.0	0.1	1.669		
1980	27.6	100.1	129.4	69.3	19.4	3.1	0.2	1.746		
1975	35.3	112.7	131.2	64.4	21.6	4.8	0.4	1.852		
1970	42.8	143.3	147.2	81.8	39.0	11.3	0.9	2.332		
1965	49.3	188.6	181.9	119.4	65.9	22.0	2.0	3.146		
1960	59.8	233.5	224.4	146.2	84.2	28.5	2.4	3.895		

Column group header spanning 15–19 through 45–49: **Age of women**

Source: Statistics Canada (2002i, 1997); Wadhera and Strachan (1993).

three cohorts: those for 1941–5, 1946–50, and 1951–5 (see also Table 6.16 in the exercise section at the end of this chapter). For ease of identification the diagonals for the corresponding age-specific fertility rates have been bolded. The shaded bottom triangle of the matrix is truncated, as it contains incomplete information for cohorts born before 1941. The shaded triangle at the upper left-hand corner pertains to younger cohorts born after 1955, for which there is insufficient data to compute a cohort completed average family size. Period TFRs for 1960 through 2000 are also shown in this table to help clarify the difference between cohort and period fertility. It is clear that CFRs for the women that completed their childbearing in 1990, 1995, and 2000 differ from the period TFRs for these three years. In fact, period and cohort rates are rarely the same, as the two measures are computed from different input data.

It is interesting to note that on the basis of the period TFRs alone, it would appear that fertility in Canada has been below replacement since the mid-1970s. However, values for cohort completed fertility declined below 2.1 starting with the post-war generation of 1951–5. The generations of women born before had completed family sizes above 2.1. As this example shows, period and cohort rates can provide very different—and equally important—perspectives on the reproductive patterns of a population.

Mean Age at Childbearing

Closely connected to both period and cohort fertility is the mean age at childbearing, or MAC, a measure of the average age at which women bear children. An increasing trend in the MAC reflects a *postponement effect*, which sees women putting off childbirth until later in life, and correlates closely with total fertility: a greater degree of postponement translates into a higher MAC and a lower period TFR. This principle applies to cohorts as well: to the extent that generations postpone having children, the average age at maternity for the cohort will increase.

From age-specific fertility rates we can derive the average age at childbearing of mothers (MAC):

$$\text{MAC} = \frac{\sum\limits_{15}^{49} f_x m_i}{\sum\limits_{15}^{49} f_x}$$

where m_i is the midpoint for a given age group and f_x is the age-specific fertility rate.

To illustrate the use of this formula, here is how the information in Table 6.4 was used to derive the period MAC of 29.02 for the year 2000:

$$\frac{16.3 \times 17.5 + 56.1 \times 22.5 + 97.9 \times 27.5 + 89.9 \times 32.5 + 35.5 \times 37.5 + 6.1 \times 42.5 + 0.3 \times 47.5}{16.3 + 56.1 + 97.9 + 89.9 + 35.5 + 6.1 + 0.3}$$

When considering the relationship between period TFR, cohort completed fertility (CFR), and average age at childbearing (MAC), it is important to bear in mind that situations that are unfavourable to early childbearing—war, economic depression, and so on—would be reflected in an older average age at childbearing, while comparatively favourable socioeconomic conditions would have the opposite effect. These factors would have a bearing on period TFR and possibly cohort completed fertility.

Postponed fertility in today's low-fertility populations mostly reflects planned behaviour by young couples striving to establish themselves economically as they pass through their prime childbearing years. This translates into low period TFRs, producing what Ryder (1965, 1980) would call a *tempo effect*, since it concerns the late timing of childbearing, as reflected in older average age of childbearing. (Ryder also described a *quantum effect*, which concerns the quantity of childbearing as reflected in the average number of children born to cohorts). Postponed fertility necessarily implies the birth of fewer children on an annual basis, and so period TFRs have remained low—in many cases, below replacement levels. It is also the case that some postponed fertility actually turns into foregone fertility, and therefore cohort completed fertility rates would be lower than estimated.

Recently demographers have begun to make adjustments to the period TFR for tempo distortions due to the postponement effect (see, for instance, Bongaarts and Feeney, 1998; Frejka and Calot, 2001; Frejka and Sardon, 2004; Kohler, Billari, and Ortega, 2002; Schoen, 2004; Sobotka, 2004; Billari, and Kohler, 2004). In most cases, adjustments made for tempo effects raise the period TFR, though in most cases the adjusted rates still remain well below 2.1 (Vienna Institute of Demography, 2007).

Population Momentum as a Cohort Phenomenon

Population momentum is a term used to describe the principle that abrupt 'period' changes in the components of population change (i.e., fertility or mortality, or both) tend to have delayed effects on population growth through change in population age structure. According to this principle, a prolonged period of population growth will not end immediately or even very quickly if fertility falls abruptly to replacement level. Similarly, a population that has had fertility below replacement level for some time cannot expect immediate population growth when its total fertility rises abruptly to 2.1.

Population momentum explains why, even though fertility rates have dropped significantly in the industrialized countries since the 1970s, natural population growth (natural increase) has for the most part been positive. In countries that experienced the post-war baby boom, the 'echo' effect has ensured a high number of births annually in spite of low birth rates. On a yearly basis births have exceeded deaths, but in time the 'echo' effect will diminish because newer generations have been smaller than those that preceded them. In some countries that experienced the post-war baby boom, including Japan, Germany, and Italy, rates of natural increase have already reached zero or negative levels (Population Reference Bureau, 2006).

It is important to recognize that population momentum is a cohort phenomenon. This is evident in an example provided by Hinde (2002a). Table 6.5 charts a population in which fertility falls abruptly to replacement level. The fall takes place over a period of time but affects different cohorts of women at different ages. Some of the cohorts that are of childbearing age in this period will have had many of their children in previous years. For example, those women who are aged 35–39 when fertility falls to replacement level will have been bearing children for 20–25 years at the previous, higher fertility rates and will have just 10–15 years left to bear children at replacement-level fertility. Their average completed family size will, therefore, largely reflect the earlier, higher fertility rates and will be greater than replacement levels. Only when fertility has been at replacement level for long enough for a cohort to spend all its childbearing years experiencing age-specific fertility rates corresponding to replacement level will that cohort produce a generation that is the same size as the cohort itself, that is, having an NRR of 1.0.

Even when a population has an NRR of 1.0, it will still be subject to population momentum, for the current age structure influences the future development of the population. At the point when the NRR reaches 1.0, the people born in earlier periods, when the NRR was greater than 1.0, will still be alive. Before the abrupt fall in fertility, the population was growing, so its age structure will be youthful. In the years after the decline in fertility, these young people will grow older, producing a relatively large proportion of the population who will be of childbearing age. This will inflate the number of children born relative to the total population, thus raising the birth rate and delaying the arrival of 'zero population growth'. Eventually, of course, the age structure of the population will stabilize, but this is likely to take some time.

Society and Fertility: Social–Biological Interactions

Human fertility can be understood as a product of interactions between biological and societal

Table 6.5 Illustration of population momentum using age-specific fertility rates for women by period and cohort (hypothetical)

Period t	Age of women at period t							TFR, period t	Cohort TFR completed in period t	Period of birth of women completing fertility in period t
	15–19	20–24	25–29	30–34	35–39	40–44	45–49			
2030–4	0.045	0.135	0.136	0.069	0.026	0.008	0.001	2.10	2.1000	1983–7
2025–9	0.045	0.135	0.136	0.069	0.026	0.008	0.001	2.10	2.2125	1978–82
2020–4	0.045	0.135	0.136	0.069	0.026	0.008	0.001	2.10	2.5500	1973–7
2015–19	0.045	0.135	0.136	0.069	0.026	0.008	0.001	2.10	2.8900	1968–72
2010–14	0.045	0.135	0.136	0.069	0.026	0.008	0.001	2.10	3.0625	1963–7
2005–9	0.045	0.135	0.136	0.069	0.026	0.008	0.001	2.10	3.1275	1958–62
2000–4	0.045	0.135	0.136	0.069	0.026	0.008	0.001	2.10	3.1475	1953–7
1995–9	0.0675	0.2025	0.204	0.1035	0.039	0.012	0.0015	3.15	3.1500	1948–52
1990–4	0.0675	0.2025	0.204	0.1035	0.039	0.012	0.0015	3.15	3.1500	1943–7
1985–9	0.0675	0.2025	0.204	0.1035	0.039	0.012	0.0015	3.15	3.1500	1938–42
1980–4	0.0675	0.2025	0.204	0.1035	0.039	0.012	0.0015	3.15	3.1500	1933–7
1975–9	0.0675	0.2025	0.204	0.1035	0.039	0.012	0.0015	3.15	3.1500	1928–32
1970–4	0.0675	0.2025	0.204	0.1035	0.039	0.012	0.0015	3.15	3.1500	1923–7

Note: The period TFRs are synthetic measurements that denote the average completed family size that would be obtained by a group of women who, at each age, had the age-specific fertility rates for that period. In this example, fertility falls abruptly on 1 January 2000 to a TFR of 2.1 (replacement level). Estimates of the completed fertility of birth cohorts are obtained from the age-specific fertility rates by summing diagonally. Thus, for example, the 1953–7 birth cohort was aged 15–19 in 1970–4, 20–24 in 1975–9, and so on, and so its completed fertility may be estimated by summing the relevant diagonal elements and multiplying by five (because we are using five-year age groups). The resulting cohort TFRs for successive cohorts are shown in the shaded part of the table. The bold numbers for the diagonal elements correspond to those cohorts that complete their fertility during periods that occur after there has been a drop in fertility to the replacement value of 2.1 (the boxed number for the period 2000–4). Note that not until the 1983–7 birth cohort, which completes its childbearing in 2030, is replacement-level fertility reached.

Source: Adapted from Hinde (2002b): 31.

factors, broadly speaking. This can be illustrated with a number of examples that we will review in the sections that follow.

Age at Menarche and Age at First Birth

In a cross-national study, Udry and Cliquet (1982) found that variation in age at menarche,

or first menstruation, influences the timing of first sexual intercourse, first marriage, and first birth among women. Early onset of menstruation in girls is highly correlated with early sexual intercourse and a young age at first marriage, both of which in turn correlate strongly with having a first birth relatively early in life.

The Demographic Study of Sexual Intercourse

Surprisingly, sexual intercourse has received little systematic attention in the demographic literature. Recently, though, demographers have been exploring the question of gender differences in the initiation of sexual intercourse. This is an important topic because early sexual initiation can often lead to early pregnancy and, possibly, early entry into marriage or cohabitation.

Bozon (2003) looked at cross-country variations in the median age at first sexual intercourse for men and women born around 1950 and around 1970–5. A portion of his analysis for selected countries is reproduced in Table 6.6. His data reveals three models of sexual initiation in the cohorts born in 1950:

1. Societies where women and girls are pressured by family to enter into sexual relationships and conjugal unions—typically with much older men—as close to puberty as possible. This model characterizes countries of sub-Saharan Africa (e.g., Mali, Senegal, Ethiopia) and the Indian subcontinent (e.g., Nepal). Men in these societies are free to engage in premarital sexual activity without any real social sanctions.
2. Societies where social controls are exerted to delay young women's union formation and sexual activity. In these societies, a woman is under considerable pressure to preserve her virginity as long as possible to avoid dishonouring herself, her family, and her prospective spouse. Young men, on the other hand, are encouraged to prove their manhood early, either with prostitutes or with older women, so they experience sexual initiation at a younger age than women do. Societies fitting this model include countries of southern Europe (e.g., Greece, Portugal, Italy, Spain), Latin America (e.g., Brazil, Chile), and Asia (e.g., Thailand).
3. Societies in which the timing of first sexual intercourse is similar for men and women. Examples include Singapore, Sri Lanka, China, and Vietnam. In these societies there is usually later marriage and strict supervision of the conduct of young people. In fact, some countries in this category—Poland and Lithuania, for example—are seeing a trend toward later sexual initiation for both men and women. In contrast, in many European countries—notably those of Scandinavia, but also Germany and the Czech Republic—sexual initiation occurs at a comparatively young age, though it remains 'gender-equal' in its timing.

Among the younger cohorts—those born in the 1970s—Bozon (2003) observed a narrowing of the gap in timing for men's and women's sexual initiation. In general, almost all men and a lower, though growing, number of women in this cohort experienced sexual initiation before first union (i.e., marriage, or cohabitation), reflecting an increasing level of personal freedom among young people worldwide. Bozon (2003: 4) concluded that for women in societies where contraception is not widely used, the traditional connection between first sexual intercourse and entry into reproductive and conjugal life still exists. However, even in societies where contraception is prevalent, sexual initiation is still a gender-differential event: men view it as a relatively non-committal experience, but women place much importance on the choice of first partner—typically older and more experienced—with whom they will likely form a relationship.

Table 6.6 Median ages at first sexual intercourse for men and women (selected countries), by approximate age at time of survey and cohort

Population and year of survey	Cohorts born around 1950 (approximate age at time of survey: 45–49)		Cohorts born around 1970 (approximate age at time of survey: 20–24)	
	Female	Male	Female	Male
Africa				
Benin (1969)	17.2	18.7	17.2	17.5
Ghana (1998)	17.3	19.4	17.4	19.5
Niger (1997)	15.0	20.9	15.5	20.3
Nigeria (1999)	18.1	20.4	18.1	19.8
Kenya (1998)	15.9	17.4	17.2	15.9
Zimbabwe (1999)	18.5	19.9	19.1	19.1
Latin America/Caribbean				
Bolivia (1997)	18.8	17.9	19.5	17.0
Brazil (1996)	20.5	17.1	18.6	16.2
Peru (1996)	18.6	16.9	19.6	17.4
Asia				
Japan (1999)	21.3	19.8	19.5	19.6
Nepal (2001)	16.6	19.2	16.9	17.8
Europe and USA				
Hungary (1993)	19.1	18.5	18.5	18.0
Poland (1996)	20.9	21.7	19.6	19.7
West Germany (1990)	18.6	18.4	17.7	17.7
Denmark (1989)	18.3	18.2	16.7	17.4
Spain (2001)	20.1	18.5	19.1	18.2
United Kingdom (1991)	19.5	18.3	17.4	17.1
Italy (1995)	20.6	18.6	20.3	18.4
United States (1994)	19.1	18.6	17.6	17.1

Source: Bozon (2003): 3.

The main biological factor at play in this causal relationship is the production of hormones that affect the timing of puberty and increase 'readiness' for early sexual intercourse: the earlier a woman enters puberty, the greater her fecundity and therefore the greater the probability of early sexual experience, marriage, and conception. The sociocultural aspect of this phenomenon is the way the development of secondary sexual characteristics increases attractiveness to males: girls who develop early are more likely to attract boys at an earlier age and hence experience first sexual intercourse earlier than late-maturing women. Another important societal factor to consider is the set of norms surrounding female sexual behaviour and the ideal timing of marriage for women, which varies from culture to culture.

Moral Codes Toward Sexuality, Contraception, and Abortion

One of the most influential modern scholars to fully examine the interplay of biological and societal factors affecting human sexuality and fertility was Sigmund Freud. In *Civilization and Its Discontents* (1930 [2005]) Freud argued that our collective unhappiness is connected to the way society controls our lives, including our sexual instincts. The individual, in Freud's view, is caught in an irreparable conflict between natural instincts and the social institutions that inexorably seek to suppress or regulate them. Because sex is such a powerful natural instinct, society must constantly control it through mores and legal proscriptions. This is civilization. More recently, Barash and Lipton, in *The Myth of Monogamy* (2001), have supported Freud's view in arguing that monogamy is but a social invention designed to control our natural sexual urges. Noting that 'extra-pair' sex is the most common form of sexual arrangement in the animal kingdom, they argue that monogamy does not truly exist even among humans.

Throughout much of history, the key agent of social control over sexuality and fertility has been organized religion. In the Christian church, sex-uality is associated with the 'original sin' of Adam and Eve. Potts and Short (1999: 296–7) contend that the early religious leaders erred in viewing the sexual act as a sin rather than the basis of adult love: '[B]y claiming that sexual intercourse was licit only if it was associated with the possibility of procreation, they categorized women as dogs, where copulation does indeed coincide with ovulation and sex is limited to procreation.' This contempt for sex except for procreation helps to explain the Church's position against abortion and contraception. Saint Augustine (354–430) and Thomas Aquinas (1225–74) are among the early theologians whose writings served as the moral basis for state-implemented penal codes with severe punishments for those resorting to contraception or abortion (Potts and Short, 1999: 296).

In recent times there have been many challenges to religiously based codes, and the idea that sexual intercourse is sinful—justifiable only to conceive a baby—is no longer a widely held view. Laws about sexuality, contraception, and abortion have been liberalized to allow greater freedom to the individual in such matters, and contraception today is accepted widely in the developed countries and increasingly in the developing world (Bongaarts, 2003; Spinelli et al., 2000). Similarly, the prevalence of abortion today is widespread (Dalla Zuanna, 2006; David and Skilogianis, 1999; Henshaw, 2003). The relaxing of these societal controls over contraception and abortion has had a significant depressing effect on fertility rates. Couples have greater means to prevent or abort an unplanned and unwanted pregnancy. With this 'freedom' comes a certain responsibility: the onus lies squarely on the individual to make important decisions about the proper timing of childbearing based on personal socioeconomic considerations.

Seasonality of Conceptions and Births

While humans, unlike other mammals, are sexually active throughout the year and do not have a defined breeding season, there is evidence of seasonal patterns of conceptions among different human populations. This seasonality may have biological (i.e., hormonal), ecological, social, and even behavioural dimensions to it (Campbell and Wood, 1994; Potts and Sellman, 1978; Wood, 1994).

Historical demographers have studied the seasonality of births and deaths across a variety of populations of the past. Wrigley and Schofield (1981a), after examining reconstituted parish records for England dating back to the 1500s, discovered a distinct seasonal pattern that appeared fairly consistently from the sixteenth century though the late eighteenth century. They found that the number of conceptions was highest in the late spring and early summer (April to July) and lowest in the late summer and autumn (August to November). According to the two authors, the annual seasonal pattern of conceptions reflected biological and social factors (Wrigley and Schofield, 1981a: 291–2). The fall in conceptions between August and November occurred during the crop-gathering months for northwestern Europe. Whether the people recognized it or not, their sexual activity appears to have been conditioned by the agricultural cycle.

More recently, researchers have reported a preponderance of births occurring during the spring and early summer (March to July), with a secondary peak in births for the month of September. This pattern has been identified in the United States (Seiver, 1985), in Canada (Trovato and Odynak, 1993), and in a number of other national settings (Lam and Miron, 1991; Wood, 1994). In general, there is a trough in births during the late fall and the winter months (coinciding with conceptions in January through May). And although the intensity of the spring effect in births varies considerably from country to country, in virtually all settings examined there is unmistakable evidence of a secondary peak in births occurring in September, a trend that has been observed in both northern and southern hemispheres (Lam and Miron, 1991, 1996).

A comprehensive analysis of Canadian birth records from 1881 to 1989 revealed that there has been a shift in the seasonal distribution of births (Trovato and Odynak, 1993). The earlier pattern, which lasted from 1881 through the early twentieth century, is characterized by a trough of births during the spring, with most babies born in the months of January, February, and March. The more recent pattern, from the early 1920s on, has remained fairly constant, with most births occurring between the spring and early summer and a deficit through fall and winter. These characteristic features of the 'contemporary' pattern are seen across the Canadian provinces, and over the course of the twentieth century the seasonal pattern of births in the Territories has been converging with that of the general Canadian pattern (see Figure 6.3). Wrigley and Schofield's (1981a) interpretation of the western European case likely applies here as well: the seasonal variation in Canadian births seems to follow the rhythm of life as governed to a large extent by such factors as the agricultural cycle in the past, and holiday cycles today.

There are many other interpretations of the spring/summer effect in birth probabilities. Scholars have identified factors ranging from the biological (seasonal fluctuations in sex hormones) to the sociological (preference for having children in the spring and summer) and the cultural (the influence of seasonal customs on birth timing motivation) (Bobak and Gjonca, 2001; Cummings, 2003; Greksa, 2003; Lam and Miron, 1996; Panter-Brick, 1996; Rojansky, Brzezinski, and Schenker, 1992; Seiver, 1985; Trovato and Odynak, 1993; Wood, 1994). The current tendency for many couples in Canada and other industrialized countries to have children in the spring and summer likely reflects the conscious decision to avoid giving birth during the harsh winter months; most couples would prefer to have a child in the spring and summer, when mother and baby can enjoy the warmth and comfort of milder weather. To this end, couples discontinue the use of birth control, taking a step that Miller and colleagues call *proception* (Miller, 1986; Miller, Severy, and Pasta, 2004). It would appear that most couples 'procept' dur-

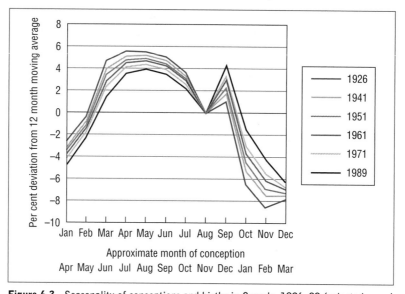

Figure 6.3 Seasonality of conceptions and births in Canada, 1926–89 (selected years)
Source: Frank Trovato and Dave Odynak (1993), 'The Seasonality of Births in Canada and the Provinces, 1881–1989: Theory and Analysis', *Canadian Studies in Population* 20 (1): 1–41.

ing the peak summer months, resulting in the large number of births from March to July. The September spike in births may reflect the influence of winter holidays—particularly Christmas/New Year's—on rates of sexual activity (Seiver, 1985; Trovato and Odynak, 1993; Lam and Miron, 1991). Wrigley and Schofield (1981a: 293) recognized this phenomenon for the historical populations in Europe: '[t]he greater con-

viviality of this time of year may have led to an increase in the frequency of sexual activity, producing a surge of births in the following September.'

Natural and Human-Made Disasters and Fertility

Demographers have identified several links between traumatic events—such as war, terrorism, or natural disasters—and fertility. We know that the fertility rate usually drops significantly during major wars, famines, and epidemics, partly because such events prevent large numbers of couples from marrying, but also because they are associated with conditions that can adversely affect fecundability, including poor nutrition and health, increased rates of involuntary fetal loss, forced separation of couples, and reduced coital rates (Agadjanian and Prate, 2002; Cai and Feng, 2005; Hill, 2004; Lindstrom and Berhanu, 1999; Mamelund, 2004).

However, a period of devastation can also engender a temporary surge in the birth rate,

It is interesting to note that in class discussions about the seasonality of births, the vast majority of students, when asked, said they would prefer to have a child in the spring or summer, supporting the notion of a preferential norm for having children during this part of the year. In which season or month would you choose to give birth, assuming you would be in a situation in your life to adequately consider this event? What are the reasons for your preference?

once the disruption has ended and 'normal life' resumes. A notable instance of this phenomenon, which has been observed in a number of historical and contemporary contexts, is the baby boom that occurred throughout Europe, North America, and Australia and New Zealand following the end of the Second World War. Although the causes of the baby boom are multivariable and complex, it has been suggested that one causative mechanism was a strong impulse to celebrate life in the wake of such a devastating event. Having children is, after all, a natural way to recognize the value of human life. A similar baby boom occurred in Sarajevo following the civil war that shattered the former Yugoslavia in the 1990s. Between the end of hostilities in 1993 and Christmas 1994, there was reportedly a 50 per cent rise in the number of births in the city (*Il Nuovo Mondo*, 1995).

War can also spark a less celebratory, more pragmatic approach to fertility. In the Chechen Republic, which has been embroiled in a costly military conflict with Russia since declaring its independence in 1991, many Chechens have expressed the feeling that 'they have to replace all the men that are dying' (Canadian Broadcasting Corporation, 2004). Traumatic acts of terrorism may have a similar effect on fertility. Rodgers, St John, and Coleman (2005) studied fertility rates in the state of Oklahoma following the Oklahoma City bombing that claimed 195 lives—many of them children—in April 1995. They discovered that in the 10-year period following the event, fertility rose in Oklahoma County (though not in the state's other nine counties). In attempting to explain this change, the study's authors suggested that there had been an unconscious motivation among the people of the community most affected by the bombing to replace the children and other loved ones who had perished in the tragedy.

Devastating acts of nature may engender a similar effect. A *Globe and Mail* report with the headline 'Indonesia Prepares for Baby Boom' (25 April 2005) described the anticipated rise in the country's birth levels in the wake of the December 2004 tsunami. The article quoted an aid worker who speculated, based on her experience with similar situations, that Aceh province, which had been particularly hard hit by the tsunami, would experience an unusual rise in births by the end of the year. '[W]hat we know from a lot of other emergencies where there are a lot of deaths is that populations right themselves, they get themselves sorted out again. . . . We have to be prepared for a lot of pregnancies.'

It is not uncommon to find media reports of mini baby booms nine months after severe storms in the developed world. Consider, for example, the following segment from a story that appeared in the *Globe and Mail* following the January 1998 ice storm that crippled parts of Ontario and Quebec:

'We're seeing an increase in births right now [in October] due to the ice storm,' Ms St-Jacques said. [Charles Lemoyne Hospital] staff estimated that births are 40 per cent above average at the hospital for this time of year.

October is normally a slow month for babies in Quebec. Parents like to have their children born in April, when the days are getting longer and warm summer months lie ahead. The Quebec Bureau of Statistics said births in the province peak in the spring and decline until December. That leaves one possible explanation for Charles Lemoyne Hospital's October baby boom: love can bloom in a very cold and unpleasant climate.

'People are telling us . . . "there were more opportunities to make babies because they had more leisure time",' Ms St-Jacques said. . . . 'Women,' she added, 'often forgot their birth-control pills. . . . The upheaval also played tricks with their ovulation cycles. At a time when people's routines were disrupted, some pregnancies were unplanned too.'

This kind of anecdotal evidence hasn't always been easy to substantiate. Udry (1970), who studied the baby boom that supposedly followed New York City's great blackout of 1965, dismissed this type of explanation after finding that there was no real increase in births. Yet perhaps the case of the ice storm is different.

The causal process for a mini baby boom nine months after a severe storm is thought to involve a spontaneous rise in sexual activity during a time of temporary disruption in the routine activities of people's lives. Couples in industrialized societies are typically in pregnancy-avoidance mode and rely on birth control accordingly (Tsui, de Silva, and Marinshaw, 1991). However, it is safe to assume that at any given time there is a significant number of couples trying to conceive their first child. Many of them may be having difficulty conceiving, in part because of the amount of stress in their lives (McFalls, 1979). Therefore, an unexpected break in routine activities—including work—prolonged over a period of days or even weeks brought on by a major natural disaster may in actual fact produce conditions favourable to a rise in conception probabilities.

The ice storm of 1998 was of such severity that it disrupted the everyday routines of many people for an entire month, and even longer in some exceptional cases. It is not inconceivable, then, that this disaster could have had a much greater bearing on conception probabilities than a brief disruption like the New York blackout.

Proximate Determinants of Fertility

Davis and Blake Framework
According to Davis and Blake (1956), social structure and culture affect fertility indirectly through a series of intermediate variables. These variables fall into three sets of factors:

1. variables that affect exposure to intercourse
2. variables that affect exposure to conception

3. variables that affect gestation and successful parturition of pregnancies (see Figure 6.4)

The premise of the Davis and Blake framework is that change in the level of fertility observed for a population is the result of change in one or more of the intermediate variables. For example, an increase in the use of contraceptives (an intermediate variable that affects exposure to conception) will cause a decrease in fertility, assuming of course that the other intermediate variables remain constant.

This principle of a direct effect on fertility does not apply to background societal factors. For example, if there has been an overall increase in income in a society, any impact of this change on fertility will be made indirectly through one or more of the intermediate variables. Similarly, any difference in fertility rates within and across populations can always be traced to variations in one or more of the intermediate variables (Bongaarts, 2003: 412).

Bongaarts' Proximate Determinants
Bongaarts (1978) reformulated the Davis and Blake model to make it quantifiable. He began by showing that virtually all fluctuations in fertility rates could be attributed to four proximate variables:

1. the extent of marriage
2. the extent of contraceptive use
3. the extent of induced abortion
4. the extent and duration of breastfeeding (a proxy for postpartum amenorrhea) (Bongaarts, 1975, 1978; Bongaarts and Potter, 1983)

Other proximate variables, listed under the category of 'natural marital fertility factors', were shown to play a relatively minor role in explaining fertility variations (Bongaarts, 2003; Leridon, 2006). These 'natural fertility' factors include the frequency of intercourse, sterility, spontaneous intrauterine mortality, and duration of the fertile period.

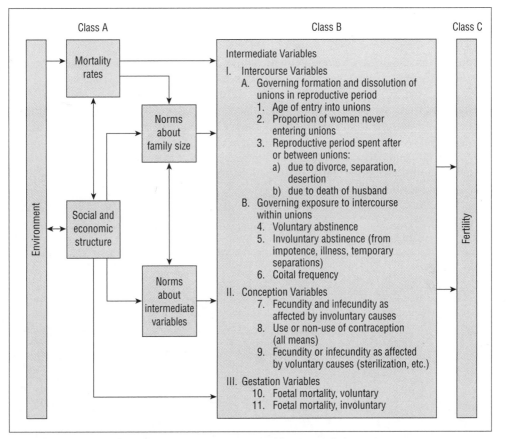

Figure 6.4 The Davis and Blake intermediate framework of fertility analysis

Source: David Yaukey (1969), 'Theorizing About Fertility', *The American Sociologist* 4 (May): 100–4; reprinted with kind permission of Springer Science and Business Media.

Natural Fertility Populations

Louis Henry (1961) coined the term 'natural fertility' to describe the behaviour of couples in earlier populations who did not plan their family size or alter their reproduction habits depending on how many children they already had. This type of procreative pattern differs radically from that of contemporary developed societies, where contraception is widely practised and where couples adjust their childbearing to achieve the desired family size, the desired spacing of children, and even the desired timing of each birth.

The most prolific of the various natural fertility populations is the Hutterites, an Anabaptist religious sect, originally from Europe, that in the 1880s settled in parts of the United States (South Dakota and Montana) and Canada (Manitoba, Saskatchewan, and Alberta). The Hutterite belief system prohibits the use of any kind of birth control. According to Coale

(1969: 4), in the 1920s, the average number of children born to Hutterite women in South Dakota, who married at age 15, was 12.6. Few populations have come close to this level of reproduction: the Cocos-Keeling Islanders achieved a rate of just over 8 children per woman in 1938–46 (Smith, 1960); the Islanders of Tristan Da Cunha achieved a total fertility rate of nearly 9 in the 1830s; and married French-Canadian women of the seventeenth and eighteenth centuries attained completed fertility levels nearly the same as those of the Hutterites during the 1920s (Henripin, 1954; Henry, 1961; Charbonneau, 1977).

Table 6.7 below contrasts Hutterites with the Cocos-Keeling Islanders and the Islanders of Tristan Da Cunha with respect to the historical, natural, environmental, social, and demographic conditions under which these populations developed and how these conditions influenced their fertility.

Table 6.7 Three natural fertility societies: Interactions of historical, cultural, social, and demographic conditions

Dimension	Hutterites	Cocos-Keeling Islanders	Islanders of Tristan da Cunha
Background	The Hutterites are an Anabaptist religious sect, originating in Zurich in 1525, with a history of persecution and flight to different parts of western and eastern Europe due to widespread antagonism to their belief in communal property and the wish to be separate from Catholicism and Protestantism. In 1874, the group fled to the United States and settled in North and South Dakota, later in Montana and parts of Canada (Manitoba, Saskatchewan, and Alberta).	The Cocos-Keeling Islands are 27 small islands located in the Indian Ocean, southwest of Indonesia. The nearest land is Kiritimati Island, about 800 km away. They were discovered (uninhabited) in 1825 by John Clunies-Ross, a Scottish explorer. A plantation economy was established (coconuts and coconut oil).	Tristan da Cunha is a tiny volcanic island in the south Atlantic, 700 miles from Cape Town and 1,900 miles from South America. The nearest land is the island of St Helena, 1,500 miles northeast of Tristan da Cunha. The tiny settlement originated at the time of Napoleon's exile to St Helena. A garrison was stationed on Tristan da Cunha to prevent Napoleon's escape. In 1817, the garrison was recalled by the British, but three of the original settlers decided to stay. Later, sailors from various countries and women from St Helena joined this small group and formed a small population.
Demography	In 1880, the population was only 443; by 1950, it had reached 8,542, with a growth rate of 4.1 per cent per year. During this period, Hutterite women who had entered marriage at age 18 and lived with their husbands throughout their reproductive years (i.e., to age 50) bore on average 12.6 children. Mortality rates were very low, and 50 per cent of the Hutterites were below the age of 15.	The Cocos-Keeling islands were populated by labour migrants from Malaysia, many of whom stayed permanently. By 1888, the population had reached 500, growing to 1,800 by 1947. Fertility was very high, but not as high as that of the Hutterites. On average, a Cocos Malay woman would bear 8 children. The population was young, with an almost equal balance of men and women. Mortality rates were relatively high (higher than in the Hutterite population).	At the time of the study in the late 1960s there were 270 islanders. Their fertility was very low. There was an imbalance in the age composition of the population, with many more young than old. Although mortality rates were relatively low, they were higher than those of the Hutterites.

(continued)

Table 6.7   (*continued*)

Dimension	Hutterites	Cocos-Keeling Islanders	Islanders of Tristan da Cunha
Belief system	Private property is considered sinful. All property is shared by the community. All members must be baptized, but not before adulthood.	The main religion of the population is Islam, but it is not strictly adhered to. There is belief in the spirit world—that the spirits of the dead are constantly present and watching the living, especially at night. There are no proscriptions against birth control, premarital sex, or abortion.	Tristan islanders do not follow a particular religious belief system. The culture is based on simple principles of co-operation and survival. The island is bleak, and there is little suitable land for agriculture. People live off the sea by fishing, and raise sheep and cattle.
Individual and society	Individuals are encouraged to conform to the Hutterite belief system. Birth control and abortion are strictly prohibited, as is premarital sex. Consequently, fertility is very high. Marriage occurs only after a person has been baptized, which must take place once one reaches adulthood and not before. Mortality rates are as low as in any industrialized population, largely because of prohibitions against alcohol and tobacco, as well as the existence of strong communal supports. Once the population of a community reaches 100, a new community is formed (planned migration).	The individual is not restricted by any religious value system. Behaviour is dictated by rational considerations in relation to personal desires and needs. In the social and economic context of the Cocos-Keeling islands, large families would not be undesirable. Infant mortality is high, so parents will try to have lots of children to ensure that some will survive to adulthood. Marriage occurs early, and most women marry by age 20. Divorce and separation are rare.	Behaviours such as premarital sex and abortion are neither encouraged nor discouraged. Family limitation is not a moral issue. Average fertility in 1830 was 8.8 children per woman; by 1920 this had declined to 3.7, indicating that some form of family limitation was practised. Compared with the Hutterites and the Cocos-Keeling Islanders, marriage among the Tristans occurs relatively late because of isolation and the scarcity of suitable mates. This may explain a large part of the fertility decline over time. As a consequence of isolation, there has been a high degree of inbreeding among the Islanders, resulting in a relatively high prevalence of certain genetic disorders.

Adapted from: Eaton and Mayer (1953): 256–62; Lewis, Roberts, and Edwards (1972); Smith (1960).

Bongaarts estimated that the maximum average fertility for a population is about 15.3 births per woman (Bongaarts, 1975, 1978; Bongaarts and Potter, 1983). This level of fertility can be achieved only by a rare combination of conditions:

1. There is continuous exposure to the risk of conception between menarche and meno-pause, meaning that a woman is in a steady sexual relationship throughout her entire reproductive lifespan.

2. There is complete avoidance of any method of birth control, including natural methods of avoiding conception, during a woman's entire reproductive lifespan.

3. There is no reliance on abortion or any

action that could cause a spontaneous miscarriage.

4. There is no practice of breastfeeding. (Hill, 1990: 146)

Women in natural fertility societies (i.e., populations that do not consciously practise any form of family limitation) could not achieve this maximum average fertility because they would be pregnant for only about one-sixth of their reproductive years; they would spend the remainder of these potential childbearing years in states that do not produce children, such as the unmarried state, the sterile state for those who are infecund, and postpartum anovulatory periods after a birth (Bongaarts and Potter, 1983).

Bongaarts (1978) concluded that the gap between maximum potential fertility and actual fertility achieved by 'high fertility' populations today arises from the inhibiting effects of the proximate determinants on total fecundity. Bongaarts' (1978) formula below helps us to understand this principle by breaking down the observed TFR of a population into the contributions of the four principal proximate determinants, each ranging in value between 0 and 1:

$$\text{TFR} = C_m \times C_c \times C_a \times C_i \times TF$$

where

C_m is the *index of nuptiality* (1 = all women of reproductive age are married; 0 = there is no marriage);

C_c is the *index of contraception* (1 = no contraception; 0 = all fertile women use a method that is 100 per cent effective);

C_a is the *index of abortion* (1 = no abortion; 0 = all pregnancies are aborted);

C_i is the *index of postpartum nonsusceptibility* (1 = no woman breastfeeds and there is no abstinence from coitus; 0 = the duration of infecundability is infinite—i.e., all women breastfeed and there is complete abstinence from sexual intercourse after a birth); and

TF is total fecundity (i.e., maximum total fertility), which is fixed at 15.3 children per woman.

A population that scores exactly 1 on all four proximate determinants will end up with a total fertility rate of 15.3 (i.e., $1 \times 1 \times 1 \times 1 \times 15.3$ = 15.3). However, depending on the extent to which the values deviate from 1, the observed TFR will be below 15.3. Thus, the effect of the proximate determinants is to inhibit total fecundity, bringing this maximum rate down to the observed TFR. The relative importance of the proximate determinants is summarized in Table 6.8.

We can illustrate how the proximate framework is applied by drawing on Islam and colleagues' (2003) analysis of Bangladesh, where between 1975 and 1999 the total fertility rate fell from just over 6 to roughly 3 children per woman. Over the same period, total fecundity actually increased, due to improved socioeco-

Bongaarts's estimate of the maximum average fertility—15.3 births per woman—is not to deny that some women can produce more than 15 children. Anecdotally, the *Guinness Book of Records* cites an eighteenth-century Russian woman who allegedly gave birth to 69 children from 27 pregnancies! While this staggering figure defies belief, Petersen (2000: 51) reports on the anomalous cases of babies born to mothers as young as 6 and as old as 59. In contemporary society, aided by new reproductive technologies, women well past the 'normal' age of childbearing are now capable of having children. An interesting case is that of the Romanian professor Adriana Iliescu, who on 17 January 2005, at the age of 66, gave birth to a baby girl, thus becoming the world's oldest recorded mother (Radio Free Europe Radio Liberty, 2005). As further advances in reproductive health and technology enable women to produce offspring well beyond the normal period of a woman's fecundity, it is reasonable to expect more cases of this kind in the future—though it is highly unlikely that any woman will ever have as many as 69 children!

Table 6.8   Rating of proximate determinants with respect to sensitivity of fertility and variability among populations

Proximate determinants	Sensitivity of fertility to the determinant	Variability among populations	Overall rating
1. Onset of cohabitation and union disruption	OOO	OOO	OOO
2. Onset of permanent sterility	OO	O	O
3. Postpartum infecundability	OO	OOO	OOO
4. Fecundability	OO	OO	OO
5. Contraception	OOO	OOO	OOO
6. Spontaneous abortion	O	O	O
7. Induced abortion	OO	OOO	OOO

Note: OOO = high; OO = medium; O = low or absent.

Source: John Bongaarts (2003), 'Fertility, proximate determinants', in Paul George Demeny and Geoffrey McNicoll, eds, *Encyclopedia of Population*, 2nd edn. Reprinted with permission of Gale, a division of Thomson Learning: www.thomsonrights.com. Fax 800-730-2215.

nomic conditions and health in the population. Therefore, the drop in the TFR between these two time periods must have been caused by the inhibiting effects on total fecundity of the proximate determinants, a conclusion supported by the evidence. The index of nuptiality had a 15 per cent inhibiting effect on fertility in 1975 but just 14.2 per cent in 1999; in other words, there was little change in the proportion of unmarried women, and the inhibiting effect of non-marriage on fertility changed only slightly. The inhibiting effect of contraceptive use rose from nearly 10 per cent in 1975 (i.e., an index value of 0.90) to over 58 per cent in 1999 (i.e., an index value of 0.42), contributing greatly to the reduction in TFR during this time interval. The inhibiting effect of postpartum *infecundability*—the inability of a breastfeeding woman to become pregnant (breastfeeding acts as a natural contraceptive)—was relatively minor in 1975 but by 1999 had become more pronounced, with the value of this index falling from nearly 0.75 to just under 0.28 over the period. This suggests that the interval between births widened, contributing to a modest inhibiting effect on total fecundity. Islam and associates (2003) did not calculate the index of abortion

because the relevant data was not available (it's safe to assume that due to cultural prohibitions induced abortion in Bangladesh is non-existent).

The proximate determinants can also be analyzed for a specific point in time. If we look at 1999 only, it is clear that early marriage is the most important variable accounting for high fertility in Bangladesh, since the inhibiting effect of nuptiality on total fecunditiy is relatively small (only 0.14). Contraceptive use, on the other hand, is the strongest inhibiting variable, with an effect on total fecundity of around 0.42. Postpartum infecundability, which relates to the spacing of births, accounted for an almost 28 per cent inhibiting effect on total fecundity. So Bangladesh's 1999 TFR of about 3 can be explained by examining the countervailing effects of these three proximate determinants: the high marriage rate and relatively young age at which women were entering into sexual unions (which, together, raise potential fertility) versus increasing contraceptive use and widening birth intervals (both of which act to reduce fertility). Given the relative importance of nuptiality and contraception, we can conclude that if more women were to marry later and adopt modern contraceptives, Bangla-

Proximate Determinants of Fertility in Canada

To see how the proximate determinants work in explaining observed total fertility rates in a population, consider Henripin's (2003) sketch for Quebec in 1896, Canada in 1900, and Canada in 2000. As we've seen, the estimated maximum fecundity for human populations is about 15 births per woman, and there are essentially four key proximate determinants that limit this maximum level to the observed birth rate in a population: the extent of abortion; the prevalence of contraception; the level of temporary sterility due to breastfeeding; and the duration of marriage as determined by age at entry into conjugal unions by women.

Figure 6.5 indicates that in Quebec in 1896, the maximum fertility rate of 15 was reduced by 2 to a value of 13 due to the inhibiting effect of temporary sterility. Relatively short marriage duration due to early death of a husband further inhibited this level by 6 points, bringing the fertility rate to 7, which was the total fertility observed in Quebec in 1896. For Canada as a whole, the diagram shows that between 1900 and 2000, the observed TFR dropped from 4.2 children per woman to 1.7. Over time, the inhibiting effect of contraceptive use has gained strength (from an effect of 2.4 in 1900 to 4.5 in 2000). By comparison, the effect of temporary sterility was stronger in 1900, and today this variable plays a relatively minor role in explaining Canada's observed TFR. The inhibiting effect of marriage duration has intensified over time, from an impact of 7.2 in 1900 to 8 in 2000. Stated differently, today's relatively low TFR is explained primarily by the inhibiting effects on maximum fertility of marriage duration (shorter duration due to later entry into marriage) and the widespread use of contraception. Abortion and sterility play smaller roles compared to these other two variables.

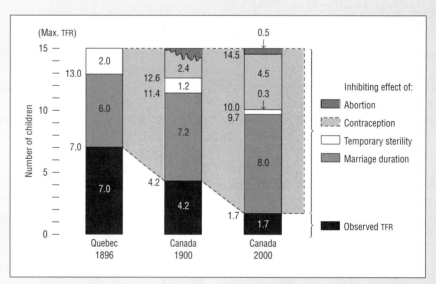

Figure 6.5   Average number of births averted due to the inhibiting effects on maximum biological fertility of 4 proximate determinants for 3 points in time in Canada

Source: Jacques Henripin (2003), *La métamorphose de la population canadienne*, Montreal: Les Éditions Varia, p. 168; reprinted by permission of the publisher.

deshi fertility would be substantially lower than it is today.

Fertility Transition

European Fertility Transition

The low fertility in the developed world today is the culmination of a century-long period of change that demographers have called the *fertility transition*. In the past, when people did not have knowledge of or recourse to effective measures of family limitation, fertility was largely a matter of chance. As Western society became more modern and standards of living improved, death rates declined and, some time later, birth rates also fell. In the period between the fall in death and birth rates there were unprecedented increases in natural population growth. A third stage followed, characterized by low birth rates as well as low death rates, which brought the low rates of natural increase we see today.

The trouble with the sweeping picture of birth rate movement in western Europe as presented by the classical version of the demographic transition theory (Thompson, 1929; Davis, 1945; Notestein, 1945, 1953) is that it overlooks many national and sub-national variations and the fact that fertility declines took place under a wide variety of social, economic, and demographic conditions (Kirk, 1996). Based on his extensive research on the European fertility transition, Coale (1969, 1973) showed that not all countries started their transitions at the same time in history, nor did they all complete it in unison. In many historical settings fertility rates actually increased before embarking on a sustained pattern of decline, indicating that a temporary rise in fertility was, and is, a precondition for the fertility transition (Dyson and Murphy, 1985).

Additional research in Europe (for instance, Knodel and van de Walle, 1979) revealed other unexpected relationships. First, in contradiction to the classical version of demographic transition theory, socioeconomic modernization did

not always precede the decline in fertility. In some cases (France and Hungary, for example) fertility declined prior to industrialization. Second, evidence from the European project indicated that family planning had been practised in some pre-transition populations, particularly among the nobility in France, Italy, and England, the bourgeoisie of Geneva, and the Jews in Italian cities. The original formulation of the demographic transition assumed a complete absence of family limitation before the late nineteenth century. Third, while a drop in mortality usually preceded the decline in fertility, in some cases (most notably France) the order of these two events was reversed. Finally, there was evidence that marriage rates prior to the decline in fertility were not uniformly high, as anticipated by the early version of the theory. Recall that Hajnal (1965) drew attention to the unique western European pattern of nuptiality, characterized by high age at marriage and a high proportion never marrying—a pattern that held for most of modern history up until World War II (see also Coale, 1969, 1973; Coale and Watkins, 1986; Demeny, 1968; Goldscheider, 1971; Knodel and van de Walle, 1979; Livi-Bacci, 1986).

Having noted the impossibility of incorporating the varied historical experiences of European countries into a coherent overarching theory of fertility transition, Coale (1973) concluded that three preconditions must be met for a fertility transition to occur:

1. Fertility decisions must be within the calculus of conscious choice; that is, beliefs and norms should not forbid family planning, nor should they favour large families.
2. Reduced fertility must be viewed by couples as economically advantageous.
3. Effective methods of fertility control must be known and be available to couples. (Coale, 1973)

The first precondition refers to the belief among those in the distant past that they had very little control over their lives and environment. Fertility was regarded as a matter of fate. Today, people recognize that they have the ability to make their own decisions about the number of children they wish to have and when to have them.

When considering the second precondition, it is important to bear in mind that in pre-industrial contexts, having large families was considered advantageous for many reasons. For one thing, having more children meant a greater likelihood that at least one or two would survive to adulthood to extend the family lineage, in spite of high mortality conditions. Also, more children meant more hands to contribute to work and family chores. In this sense, children were economic assets. Finally, large families provided support and security to parents in their old age or in the event they became incapable of looking after themselves because of injury or illness. The situation today is different. Modern society's mortality rates are low, and the state provides plenty of security for the average citizen. The cost of raising and educating children can be very high, and so it's reasonable that people today would desire fewer children than in the past.

The third precondition surrounds the issue of fertility regulation and when methods of family planning became widely known and available. Demographers are divided into two camps on the question of whether people in pre-transitional societies actually knew about birth control. Proponents of the *adjustment theory* (Carlson, 1966; Davis, 1963; Friedlander, 1969; McLaren, 1984; Mosher, 1980) argue that various methods of birth control, however primitive, were known and available, but that there was not the motivation to use them. Adjustment theorists believe that once the motivation for reducing family size exists, people will choose whatever means are available to help realize their fertility plans. These means might include the practice of abortion (as in Japan), massive emigration and rural-to-urban migration (as in Ireland), and late marriage and non-marriage (as in western Europe) (Davis, 1963).

The *innovation-diffusion thesis* (Ariès, 1960; Cleland and Wilson, 1987; Lesthaeghe and Wilson, 1986; Shorter, 1975; van de Walle, 1992) posits that family limitation emerged as a novel idea in the mid-nineteenth century as part of the social-psychological transformation that accompanies socioeconomic modernization, urbanization, and secularization. These phenomena changed the way people felt about themselves and their social environment, and in this case what they considered to be an ideal size of family. Innovation-diffusion theorists believe that once the idea of the small family diffused from the urban areas to the countryside, from the wealthy to the less wealthy, from the educated to the uneducated, family limitation became widespread. This, they argue, was the key factor in the transition from a high and uncontrolled fertility regime to low and controlled fertility.

Ultimately, it seems likely that both adjustment and innovation processes were responsible for the European fertility transition. Indeed, Knodel's (1977) analysis of European and Asian societies is compelling: he concluded that family limitation is both a type of innovative behaviour and an adjustment to changing structural conditions in society during the course of socioeconomic development.

The State of Fertility Transition Today

While Japan and countries of the West have already passed through the fertility transition (interrupted briefly by the post-World War II rise in the birth rate), most of the world's populations have begun to undergo fertility transition only since the end of the Second World War. The late 1960s and early 1970s were watershed points in the demographic histories of most developing countries (outside of sub-Saharan Africa, which has lagged considerably in this process), where fertility has fallen since about that time to between 2 and 3 children per woman. Birth rates remain high in Africa, at around 4 children per woman, and in certain less developed countries, such as Bangladesh, Afghanistan, and Myanmar, where total fertility lies in the range of 2.5 to 3 or higher. Since the early 1970s, rapid fertility declines have been noted in some developing countries, including Macao, South Korea, Tunisia, Hong Kong, Iran, Mongolia, Albania, Kuwait, Vietnam, and China (see Table 6.9).

Table 6.9   Ten countries and areas with largest declines in total fertility (percentage), by development group, 1970–5 to 2000–5

Rank	Country or area	Total fertility rate		Change 1970–5 to 2000–5	
		1970–5	2000–5	Difference	Percentage
A. More developed countries					
1	Spain	2.86	1.27	−1.59	−55.6
2	Slovakia	2.51	1.20	−1.39	−52.2
3	Republic of Moldova	2.56	1.23	−1.33	−52.0
4	Romania	2.62	1.26	−1.36	−51.9
5	Albania	4.66	2.29	−2.37	−50.9
6	Bosnia and Herzegovina	2.63	1.32	−1.31	−49.8
7	Ireland	3.82	1.94	−1.87	−49.0
8	TFYR Macedonia	2.96	1.53	−1.43	−48.3
9	Ukraine	2.16	1.12	−1.04	−48.1
10	Czech Republic	2.21	1.17	−1.04	−47.1
B. Least developed countries					
1	Myanmar	5.75	2.46	−3.29	−57.2
2	Bangladesh	6.15	3.25	−2.91	−47.3
3	Cape Verde	7.00	3.77	−3.23	−46.1
4	Solomon Islands	7.23	4.33	−2.90	−40.1
5	Maldives	7.00	4.33	−2.67	−38.1
6	Sao Tomé and Principe	6.52	4.06	−2.46	−37.7
7	Lesotho	5.74	3.65	−2.09	−36.4
8	Nepal	5.79	3.71	−2.08	−35.9
9	Sudan	6.67	4.45	−2.23	−33.4
10	Vanuatu	6.11	4.15	−1.96	−32.1
C. Other less developed countries					
1	Macao, China SAR	3.20	0.84	−2.36	−73.8
2	Republic of Korea	4.28	1.23	−3.06	−71.5
3	Tunisia	6.21	2.00	−4.21	−67.8
4	Hong Kong, China SAR	2.89	0.94	−1.95	−67.5
5	Iran	6.40	2.12	−4.28	−66.9
6	Mongolia	7.33	2.45	−4.89	−66.7
7	Algeria	7.38	2.53	−4.85	−65.7
8	Kuwait	6.90	2.38	−4.52	−65.5
9	Vietnam	6.70	2.32	−4.37	−65.2
10	China	4.86	1.70	−3.16	−65.0

Source: United Nations Department of Economic and Social Affairs, Population Division (2006e): 43. Reprinted with the permission of the United Nations.

As recently as 2004, a number of countries still showed no sign of even beginning the fertility transition (see Table 6.10). These 12 countries represented almost 25 per cent of the population living in the least developed areas of the world. In 22 other less developed countries, some fertility decline has occurred, but the average number of children per woman remains high at more than 5. These countries account for 8.8 per cent of the population of the less developed world and 48.2 per cent of the population of Africa. Presently, the majority of the developing world's population lives in 70 countries where total fertility levels range from 2.1 to 4 children per woman. These countries make up over 40 per cent of the world's total population (United Nations Department of Economic and Social Affairs Population Division, 2006e).

All together, more than 42 per cent of the population in Asia, three-quarters of the population in Oceania, and nearly all of the population of Europe and North America live in countries where fertility levels are below replacement levels. Of particular interest is the fact that almost 30 per cent of the population in the less developed regions has achieved below-replacement fertility levels similar to those in more developed countries (see Table 6.11).

Theories of Fertility Change

The significant declines in reproductive levels worldwide since the 1970s requires some explanation. Why is fertility below replacement levels in some countries and close to 8 children per

Table 6.10   Countries and areas where the fertility transition had not begun by 2000–5

| Major area or country | Total fertility (children per woman) | | | | |
	1950–5	2000–5	Maximum level during 1950–2005	2000–5 per cent decline from maximum	Reference period of maximum level
Africa	7.70	7.91	8.20	3.6	1975–2000
Niger	6.90	7.10	7.10	—	1965–2005
Uganda	5.58	7.10	7.10	—	1970–2005
Guinea-Bissau	7.11	6.92	7.56	8.4	1970–1985
Burundi	6.80	6.80	6.80	—	1950–2005
Liberia	6.45	6.80	6.90	1.4	1965–1995
Angola	7.00	6.75	7.40	8.8	1960–1970
Dem. Rep. of the Congo	6.00	6.70	6.70	—	1980–2005
Chad	5.77	6.65	6.66	0.1	1970–2005
Sierra Leone	6.09	6.50	6.50	—	1975–2005
Congo	5.68	6.29	6.29	—	1970–2005
Equatorial Guinea	5.50	5.89	5.89	—	1985–2005
Asia					
Afghanistan	7.70	7.48	8.00	6.5	1990–2000

Note: Countries are ordered by total fertility in 2000–5 and, where that is equal, by total fertility in 1950–5.

Source: United Nations Department of Economics and Social Affairs Population Division (2006e): 39. Reprinted with the permission of the United Nations.

Table 6.11 Stages of the fertility transition, by development group and major area, 2000–5

Development group or major area	No transition	Incipient decline[1]	Decline to levels between 4 and 5 children per woman	Decline to levels between 3 and 4 children per woman	Decline to levels between replacement level[2] and 3 children per woman[3]	Decline to levels at or below replacement level[2]	Total
				Number of countries[4]			
World	13	22	21	26	45	65	192
More developed regions	—	—	—	—	1	43	44
Less developed regions	13	22	21	26	44	22	148
Least developed regions	12	18	12	5	1	—	48
Other less developed countries	1	4	9	21	43	22	100
Africa	12	19	8	9	4	2	54
Asia	1	3	7	9	16	14	50
Europe	—	—	—	—	1	38	39
Latin America and the Caribbean	—	—	1	7	20	7	35
Northern America	—	—	—	—	—	2	2
Oceania	—	—	5	1	4	2	12
				Percentage of population			
World	3.0	7.2	5.2	23.6	18.2	42.8	100.0
More developed regions	—	—	—	—	0.3	99.7	100.0
Less developed regions	3.7	8.8	6.4	29.1	22.4	29.7	100.0
Least developed regions	24.7	36.2	8.7	23.7	6.7	—	100.0
Other less developed countries	0.1	4.2	6.0	30.0	25.0	34.7	100.0
Africa	17.9	48.2	9.1	11.1	12.4	1.3	100.0
Asia	0.8	0.7	6.0	35.6	14.9	42.1	100.0
Europe	—	—	—	—	0.4	99.6	100.0
Latin America and the Caribbean	—	—	2.2	6.6	85.1	6.1	100.0
Northern America	—	—	—	—	—	—	100.0
Oceania	—	—	21.0	0.3	4.6	74.0	100.0

[1]Fertility has declined but is still more than 5 children per woman.
[2]Replacement level assumed to be TFR of 2.1.
[3]Including Argentina and Uruguay, which had experienced an early transition to low fertility but had not reached levels at or below replacement level by 2000–5.
[4]Figures pertain to the 192 countries for which information on fertility is available.

Source: United Nations Department of Economic and Social Affairs Population Division (2006e): 35–6. Reprinted with the permission of the United Nations.

woman in others? Why has fertility fallen rapidly in certain cases and very little in others? Hirschman (1994) observed that although the demographic literature contains an abundance of theories aimed at explaining the fertility transition of Europe and most of the developing countries, not one has really provided a single exhaustive explanation of the causes. The theories span a host of causative mechanisms, from the Malthusian idea that fertility levels are determined by sexual passion and the moral restraints imposed to control them (an idea we'll examine at length in Chapter 11) to the notion that mortality declines and growing socioeconomic pressures prompt individuals at the household level to adopt means of reducing their family size (Davis, 1963; Hirschman, 1994).

Theories of fertility change fall under a number of different headings—economic, sociological, social-psychological, anthropological, and even evolutionary. Some fertility theories are macro-level explanations, while others are aimed at explaining micro processes at the household or individual level. For our purposes it's best to focus on several macro-level theories that have gained widespread attention in the demographic literature. Some of these highlight economic forces, while others emphasize sociological determinants. Others still combine economics and sociological concepts to produce integrated explanations. Some of these theories apply to fertility change strictly in the industrial countries while others consider developing societies now undergoing socioeconomic modernization. In spite of the many different angles on fertility change, you will undoubtedly notice a certain amount of overlap among the various perspectives.

We begin our review with the theory of Gary Becker, who specified the economic conditions for a fertility transition from a traditional regime of high birth rates to modern low birth rates, based largely on the experience of the United States and other high-income countries.

Becker's Theory

Central to economic theories of the family are the rising material and nonmaterial costs of parenting in contemporary society. Here the concepts of supply and demand take centre stage. Prices in the market are based on the supply and demand of consumer goods: if demand is high and supply is limited, prices for a given good will be high; if demand is low and supply is plentiful, prices will be low. Becker's (1960; 1991) idea about fertility is in essence a demand-based theory. The 'demand' for children—that is, the number of children desired by parents—is conditioned by rational evaluations. Parents desire the best-quality goods subject to their ability to afford them. The amount and quality of a good is therefore determined by the

Blake (1968) rejected the idea of children being consumer durables. Human fertility, Blake argued, is governed by 'coercive pronatalism' (elements of society that promote, reinforce, and regulate childbearing). Once born, a child cannot be returned for a refund like most purchased products; it cannot be substituted or exchanged for something else, unlike a common market good. Blake (1968) also disputed that parents have control over the quality of their children, as Becker assumed, since child 'quality' may depend on uncontrollable genetic factors and not just on the amounts of parental care and investment in the child.

Becker (1991) later clarified his ideas on the substitutability of children for consumer goods. He has since argued that although children and goods are not perfect substitutes as such, time-intensive children and goods-intensive commodities are in fact indirectly substitutable.

What do you make of Becker's analogy between children and consumer goods? Do you find it far-fetched and irrelevant, or do you accept it as useful in spite of the imperfections Becker acknowledged?

utility of the good to the individual and the buyer's budgetary constraints (i.e., affordability). Becker's theory treats children as a special type of consumer durable for which quality considerations figure prominently.

Becker made the important observation that during the process of socioeconomic modernization, fertility falls as income increases (see Figure 6.6). He found this counterintuitive, since it suggested that children are an inferior 'good', purchased only when, in relation to other goods, they are less costly; as a result, it would seem, parents would 'acquire' more children only if their income were to fall. Becker (1960) reasoned that, on the contrary, based on basic economic principles, with rising income should come a corresponding increase in the number of children born to parents, since children, like consumer goods, become more affordable. So why is the empirical evidence at odds with the expectation? Why is the statistical association of income with fertility inverse?

Becker (1991) reasoned that parents do not necessarily translate more of their rising incomes into having more children. Instead, they are likely to invest more in ensuring the quality of their children. In general, it is fair to assume that people always desire the best possible product, regardless of whether it is a car, a house, or some other item. The factors that limit one's ability to get the best possible item (including children) are budgetary constraints and time constraints. The latter, as it applies to children, relates to how much time parents can devote to their children, given their other obligations (to work and career, for instance) and preferences (for leisure activities, personal pastimes, and so on). With children, quality is attained through investments of time and money in the child's human capital, especially through education, nurturing talents and skills, and so forth. Parents will opt for smaller families and invest more in each child, thus balancing their family size preferences with aspirations for child quality.

For Becker, this substitution of child quality for child quantity explained the usually observed inverse association between income and fertility in the empirical literature. He theorized (1960, 1991) that parents will try to 'produce' the best possible child, given the household's budgetary and time constraints. Children who have more resources spent on them are considered 'higher quality' children (though Becker was quick to caution that 'higher quality' in no way implies 'morally better', as morality is a completely different matter). In short, if parents voluntarily spend more on a child, it is because they obtain additional satisfaction through the child from the additional expenditure; thus, parents choose the best com-

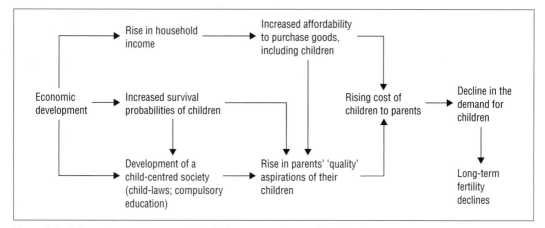

Figure 6.6 Schematic representation of Becker's economic theory of fertility change

bination of the number of children, their desired quality, and the parents' own standard of living subject to the lifetime income of the parents and the prices that they face in life toward maintaining a household. Should the parents' income increase, there would be an increase in both the quantity and the quality of children; however, in view of the tendency for parents to increase the quality of most consumer durable goods proportionately much more than the quantity of such goods when their income increases, Becker argued that this is also likely to be the case for children (Ermisch, 2003: 110; Willis, 1987; Robinson, 1997).

Applied to today's industrialized societies, Becker's theory would imply that low fertility is the result of parents investing in fewer children of greater quality. In the modern context, children are no longer economic assets as they were in the past—in fact, they are, for the most part, economic liabilities for their parents. Instead, their utility to parents is of an inherently non-material nature, manifest in such intangible benefits as self-fulfillment, pleasure, prestige, extension of the self, and so on (Fawcett, 1983; Hoffman and Hoffman, 1973).

Easterlin's Cyclical Theory

The economist Richard Easterlin carried out a landmark study of fertility change in the United States, which produced results and a theory that may be broadly applied to other industrialized countries. After the end of World War II, birth rates in western Europe, Japan, Canada, the United States, Australia, and New Zealand rose unexpectedly, following a period of low fertility that had lasted through the 1930s. In the countries with the most pronounced baby booms (the US, Canada, Australia, New Zealand), the surge in births lasted approximately two decades, from 1946 through the mid 1960s, and was followed by a protracted 'baby bust', characterized by long-term fertility declines that have culminated in the sub-replacement birth rates characteristic of most high-income nations today. This pattern can be seen in Table 6.12,

which includes data on the 13 countries that experienced a post-war baby boom. The peak birth rates occurred at different times for the 13 countries, all between 1957 and 1964 (1957 for the US, 1959 for Canada, and between 1961 and 1964 for the others), but by 1975, fertility had plummeted across all of the nations. Even so, there are some notable variations. For instance, Australia showed a TFR of 2.20 in 1975, while the other 12 countries had by this time seen their birth rates fall to below replacement levels, with West Germany showing the lowest rate at 1.45 births per woman. By 1995, fertility rates had declined beyond 1975 levels in all countries except for the United States, whose TFR in 1995 was just above 2.0.

As Figure 6.7 shows, the 1930s fall in the birth rate followed by the post-war rise and then decline since the mid-1960s represents a cyclical pattern of change. Easterlin (1969, 1980) attributes this pattern to the combined influences of demographic, sociological, and economic factors, including

- the state of the economy and how well young adults have been able to realize their material aspirations;
- the proportion of young workers to older workers (relative cohort size); and
- the type of socialization that cohorts experienced during their childhood and adolescence.

The 1930s were a period of unprecedented low fertility, and the cohorts born during this decade were numerically small. As these generations began to enter the labour force in the 1950s and 1960s, this aspect of their background proved highly advantageous, for as Easterlin argued, small cohorts have better access to jobs and employment opportunities. The 1930s were also marked by the Great Depression and socioeconomic hardship, another factor that, according to Easterlin, contributed to the rise in fertility rates. This part of Easterlin's argument relates to his belief that the desired standards of

Table 6.12 Total fertility rates for selected low-fertility countries, 1930s–2005

Country	Post-WWII (1930s)	Pre-WWII (Early 1950s)	Baby boom peak	Baby bust (1975)	Contemporary levels		
					1985	1995	2005
Australia	2.16	3.09	3.51	2.20	1.89	1.83	1.80
	(1933)	(1950–2)	(1961)				
Austria	1.65	2.07	2.81	1.83	1.47	1.40	1.40
	(1933–4)	(1950–2)	(1963)				
Belgium	1.96	2.37	2.69	1.74	1.51	1.55	1.60
	(1933–7)	(1948–52)	(1964)				
Canada	2.69	3.53	3.93	1.83	1.64	1.65	1.50
	(1936–40)	(1950–2)	(1959)				
Denmark	2.13	2.53	2.63	1.92	1.45	1.80	1.80
	(1936)	(1950–2)	(1963)				
United Kingdom	1.83	2.15	2.88	1.81	1.80	1.71	1.80
	(1933)	(1950–2)	(1964)				
Germany (West)	2.03	2.06	2.54	1.45	1.28	1.34	1.30*
	(1934)	(1951–3)	(1964)				
France	2.07	2.85	2.86	1.93	1.82	1.70	1.90
	(1934–8)	(1949–53)	(1964)				
Netherlands	2.63	3.17	3.19	1.66	1.51	1.53	1.70
	(1933–7)	(1948–52)	(1961)				
Norway	1.84	2.6	2.96	1.98	1.68	1.87	1.80
	(1934–5)	(1951–5)	(1964)				
Sweden	1.7	2.31	2.49	1.78	1.74	1.74	1.80
	(1933–7)	(1948–52)	(1964)				
Switzerland	1.75	2.34	2.66	1.61	1.52	1.48	1.40
	(1937)	(1950–2)	(1964)				
United States	2.04	3.08	3.76	1.78	1.84	2.03	2.0
	(1934–6)	(1949–51)	(1957)				

*2005 figure is for united Germany.

Source: Adapted from Morgan (2003b); Population Reference Bureau (2006).

living and material aspirations of young adults are shaped by the living standards they experienced during their childhood and adolescence. Children raised in a prosperous socioeconomic environment should, as adults, develop strong aspirations for material comfort and expect a standard of living commensurate with the standards of living they experienced early in life in the parental household. On the other hand, the expectations of individuals who have grown up in the context of economic hardship and restraint will be different. On the whole, these individuals are likely to have much more modest expectations regarding their future standard of living. All of this led Easterlin to surmise that fertility among young adults is heavily determined by the extent to which they are able to actualize their material aspirations.

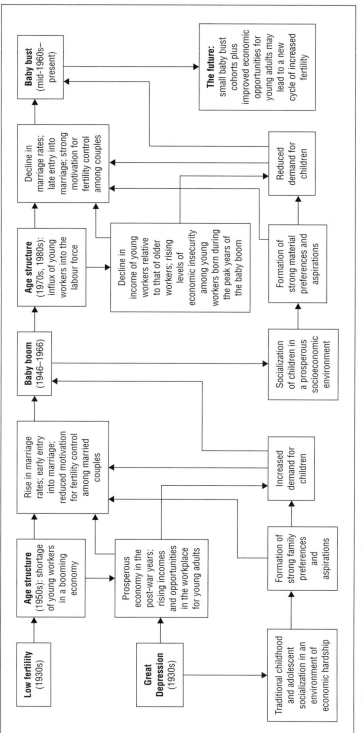

Figure 6.7 Schematic representation of Easterlin's cyclical theory of fertility change in industrialized countries

Easterlin's thesis implies that the post-war boom in fertility can be attributed to the generations of adults born in the 1920s and 1930s, whose childhood and adolescent socialization took place in the hard days of the Great Depression when the economy had collapsed. Moreover, their social values were strongly shaped by tradition and adherence to strong family norms. Given this combination of social and economic conditions, the generations of the 1930s developed strong preferences for early marriage and family building.

During the 1950s and 1960s, in the aftermath of the Second World War, the economies of industrialized countries underwent a period of rapid growth, and the demand for workers was intense. For young men entering the labour force, this situation presented a fortuitous combination of circumstances: jobs were plentiful, and opportunities for advancement in the workplace were better than ever. The favourable state of the economy, combined with this generation's traditional childhood socialization experience and its small numerical size, produced a setting highly conducive to early matrimony and parenting. These young adults could realize their material aspirations while at the same time conforming to traditional expectations to marry young and have plenty of children.

For Easterlin, the drop in birth rates across industrialized countries after the 1960s can be explained by the same sets of forces attributed to the baby boom period. In this instance, however, the socioeconomic conditions for young adults entering the labour force during the 1970s, 1980s, and 1990s were less favourable to early marriage and childbearing. These young adults had been raised in the very prosperous socioeconomic environment of the 1950s and 1960s, which helped instill strong materialistic aspirations. The factors affecting the fertility rate among the 'baby boomers' of this generation—especially the large cohorts born at the peak of the baby boom (the late 1950s to mid-1960s)—can be summarized as follows:

- These cohorts, born during a period of very high fertility, are numerically large.
- The material aspirations of this generation are very strong, because as children these individuals were raised in a context of economic prosperity.
- The new economy since the 1970s has made job and career prospects for young adults more tenuous than was the case for the generations that preceded them.

This unfavourable conjunction of demographic, sociological, and economic conditions, according to Easterlin, has fostered a sense of socioeconomic insecurity in today's young adults, especially young men (Macunovich, 2002; Oppenheimer, 1994, 1997). Under such conditions, young people are reluctant to commit to matrimony, and among those who are married, the insecurity generated by this set of circumstances has led many couples to postpone having children and perhaps avoid having children altogether.

The cyclical theory does not rule out a possible return to above-replacement fertility in the near future, but it would depend on two important conditions. The first of these—that the current 'baby bust' generation be numerically small—has been satisfied already. The product of low fertility since the early 1970s, this generation should experience a relatively favourable labour force situation on the basis of this factor alone (Kohler, Billari, and Ortega, 2002). But in order for fertility rates to rise, the economic prospects for these young adults would have to improve appreciably in order for them to gain a strong sense of security and confidence about long-term socioeconomic prospects. Unfortunately, this latter condition may be difficult to satisfy.

To review briefly the two fertility change theories we've seen so far, Easterlin argues that today's low fertility stems from young adults' struggles to satisfy their material aspirations because of economic insecurity, which is compounded by the large size of their generation;

these factors lead to a general flight from marriage on the one hand and to postponed parenthood on the other. Becker, in contrast, emphasizes the declining desire by parents to have large families because they prefer to meet the increasing costs of raising children by investing in quality over quantity. Unlike Easterlin's theory, which allows for the possibility of a return to higher fertility in the future, Becker's view suggests that low fertility is likely to continue indefinitely, since the cost—in time and money—of raising high-quality children continues to rise, together with parents' preference for quality over quantity.

Butz and Ward's Countercyclical Explanation

Butz and Ward (1979a, 1979b), following many of Becker's postulates, proposed a countercyclical explanation of fertility change, which challenges Easterlin's view of a possible return to higher fertility levels. In particular, Butz and Ward take aim at what they view as important limitations in Easterlin's formulation, most notably the changing role and status of women in society since the 1960s, the consequent rise of women's economic independence, and the expanded range of role options women now

enjoy beyond marriage and motherhood (see Figure 6.8).

Unlike Easterlin, whose theory focuses mainly on how the economic prospects of young men affect marriage and procreation, Butz and Ward (1979a, 1979b) make a distinction between men's and women's incomes and how each of these in turn affects fertility. They suggest that, all other things being equal, a rise in men's income would have the effect of increasing the number of children a couple would have. Thus, the baby boom can be understood as a response to rising male income after the war. However, since the 1960s, women have improved their economic situation significantly through increased levels of education and labour force participation. In their empirical analysis, Butz and Ward (1979a, 1979b) determined that a rise in women's earnings would have a *depressing* effect on reproduction. Any increase in a woman's average wage would raise the household income but would simultaneously raise the cost of having children by the amount of earnings lost while an employed woman takes time off work to have and raise children. While showing that increased male income raises a couple's fertility, Butz and Ward determined that the negative impact of women's opportunity costs on

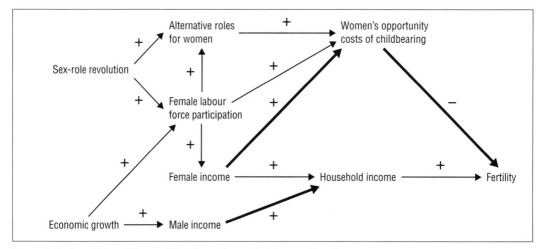

Figure 6.8 A rendition of Butz and Ward's countercyclical theory of fertility

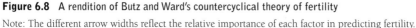
Note: The different arrow widths reflect the relative importance of each factor in predicting fertility.

fertility is significantly stronger, thus producing a negative net effect on fertility.

Bearing children affects women's opportunity costs in three ways:

1. There is an immediate effect on women's employment.
2. There are long-term effects on earning power.
3. There will be, as a result, a loss in terms of future pension coverage.

Although many women today combine child-rearing and employment, the estimated loss of gross earnings associated with motherhood remains substantial in most cases (Davis, Joshi, and Peronacci, 2000). There are also psychological costs associated with having children, including the stress associated with having to take care of children while maintaining a job or career and the restriction on personal freedom as a consequence of being a parent. Butz and Ward conclude that low fertility in the industrialized world is largely a function of women's rising opportunity costs associated with motherhood, and they predict that as long as women's roles in society do not change radically from what they are today, birth rates are bound to remain low.

Sociological Theories

Sociological theories of fertility change typically consider macro-structural changes in society as the key agents of value shifts and behavioural changes. For many sociological theorists, the root cause of today's low birth rate is the inherent nature of postmodern culture, whose contemporary values, attitudes, and lifestyles seem incompatible with marrying early and raising large families. The traditional sources of authority in matters of family and procreation—religion, community, extended family—have weakened considerably, supplanted by an ethos of individualism. Consequently, many of the pronatal forces of the past have receded to near insignificance.

In explaining low fertility, sociological theorists point to the traditional family form's apparent loss of centrality as a source of self-fulfillment for young men and women, as alternative family forms are increasingly accepted (Ariès, 1980; Keyfitz, 1986; Preston, 1986; Simons, 1980; Westoff, 1986). In this general context, it is no longer seen as unusual for young couples to consciously avoid having children or for individuals to forgo matrimony in favour of less committed conjugal relationships, such as cohabitation (Bourgeois-Pichat, 1986; Rindfuss, 1991). We can also note the breakdown of the traditional 'breadwinner system' of gender roles, its obsolescence hastened by the rise of female participation in the paid economy (Davis, 1984a, 1986; Davis and van der Oever, 1982). Such changes to social values, when combined with modern contraceptive technology and legalized abortion, make it easy to understand today's very low fertility rates (Westoff, 1983: 101). For the sociological school, the prognosis is quite clear: since none of these changes seems likely to be reversed, a continuation of low fertility should be expected.

Second Demographic Transition Perspective

Broadly speaking, the *second demographic transition* refers to a situation in countries that have long passed through the first demographic transition and are now experiencing significant change in several key social demographic dimensions. These changes include

- a pluralization of living arrangements among young adults, accompanied by a pervasive tendency to postpone marriage in favour of cohabiting unions;
- declining marriage rates;
- increased divorce probabilities;
- very high levels of contraceptive use;
- very low fertility rates;
- increased proportion of couples remaining childless; and
- an increasing tendency among couples for childbearing outside of traditional marriage.

Proponents of this theoretical school view this configuration of social demographic trends as fuelled by a completely separate set of factors than those involved in the first demographic transition of the nineteenth and early twentieth centuries. They argue that current trends in family formation and procreation are inherently supported by a mindset characterized by a generalized skepticism toward established institutions and traditional sources of authority. The earlier transition was sparked by an enormous sentimental and financial investment in the child by parents; in this context, smaller families were much better suited to enhancing parents' ability to properly look after their children (Ariès, 1960, 1980). In contrast, the contemporary 'birth dearth' has been provoked by a diametrically opposed attitude: the days of the 'child king' as the central purpose of marriage and family has given way to the self-actualization of the individual, or the 'queen couple'. Theorists in this school of thought (e.g., Van de Kaa, 1987, 1999, 2003, 2004a, 2004b; Lesthaeghe, 1995; Lesthaeghe and Surkyn, 1988) point to the importance of postmodernity, post-materialism, and associated values that centre on the ethos of individualism—freedom, self-expression, personal search for a better way of life (self-actualization), and detachment from traditional values, institutional authority, and group ethics enshrined in religion.

If all of this is true, then what has helped engender these post-materialist values among the young? According to Inglehart (1997: 110) affluence and material security have played a major role. Post-war generations have enjoyed greater levels of material security and resources than did earlier generations who lived through the depression and world wars. Having their material needs satisfied is a principal nonphysiological, or post-materialist, goal among today's young adults. What this growing individualism means in terms of marriage and procreation is that family formation is now seen as being of secondary importance to personal development.

For van de Kaa (1999: 31) this shift in value orientation provides a perfect explanation for the many demographic changes in the Western world beginning in the second half of the twentieth century. It is consistent with an individualistic lifestyle in which people feel free to have children within or outside marriage, alone or with a partner, early or late in life; a lifestyle where it is understood that sex and marriage are no longer closely related, and that contraception is interrupted only to have a self-fulfilling conception. Also common to postmodern societies is the reflexive nature of the individuation process—a process of self-questioning and self-confrontation by prospective parents. Couples typically ask themselves if having children will enrich their lives. In many cases today, the answer appears to be 'no'. But once a couple decide that they do want a child, they will do everything possible to realize their desire, even if it means seeking medical assistance through such means as in vitro fertilization, surrogate motherhood, and adoption (van de Kaa, 2004b).

The Individuation Thesis of Lesthaeghe and Surkyn

Lesthaeghe and Surkyn (1988) proposed a sociological theory that incorporates the kinds of changes described by the second demographic transition perspective with elements of Easterlin's theory (see Figure 6.9). In essence, they argue that when a generation feels satisfied with the institutions of family, economy, government, and religion, young adults tend to marry and raise families fairly early in life, and marriage and fertility rates are generally high. However, whenever there is widespread disenchantment with the major social institutions, young people see marriage and family formation as less desirable, and they look for alternative family forms that are incompatible with high fertility.

Each generation comes equipped with values acquired through the experience of childhood and adolescent socialization in the parental home. These values change as new generations

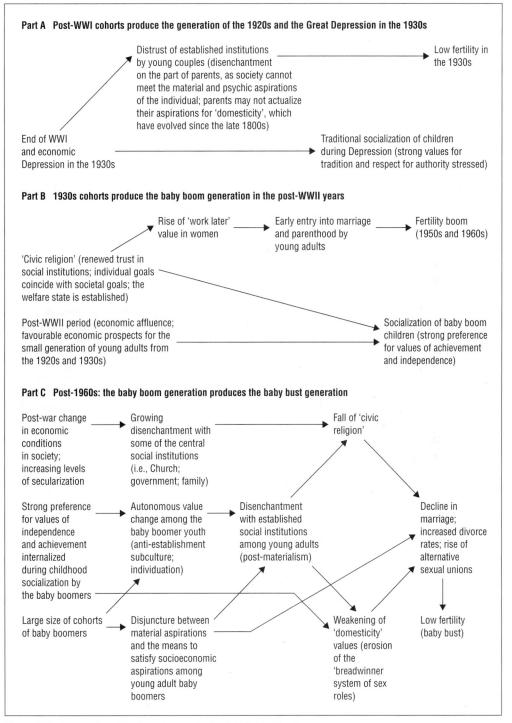

Figure 6.9 A rendition of Lesthaeghe and Surkyn's individuation thesis

challenge some of the values they learned as children. A generation's unique socio-historical experiences of events such as war, economic depression, or technological revolution can also cause value shifts by provoking new attitudes and ideas (i.e., autonomous value change).

The classic example of this, described by Ariès (1980), is the countercultural movement of the 1960s and 1970s, often referred to as the 'hippie movement'. While questioning and rejecting many traditional values, the youthful members of this movement also introduced new ideas—free love, communal living, rock music, mod fashions, and so forth. The hippie counter-culture was inherently skeptical of tradition as a guide to life, and questioned and rejected many traditional sources of regulation and authority, including institutional religion. It also instilled alternative conceptions of family, intimacy, sexuality, and commitment to marriage; indeed, it may be argued that the rise of cohabitation and the generalized rejection of traditional marriage among today's young adults had its genesis in the counter movement of the 1960s.

Lesthaeghe and Surkyn (1988) use the term 'embourgeoisment' to describe the tendency for societies to adopt as 'normal' ideas that when originally introduced may have been viewed as threatening. Of course, not all new ideas become widely accepted, nor do all accepted ideas persist indefinitely; some are rejected outright, while others become adopted only gradually, first by fringe countercultural groups and eventually by society at large (witness, for example, the case of cohabitation, which was once viewed by society as deviant but is now widely accepted).

Lesthaeghe and Surkyn suggest that the generations born after World War II are characterized by high levels of disenchantment with established social institutions, and this has provoked the diffusion of 'post-material values' (made easier by the spread over this period of communication technologies—radio, television, film, the Internet). The profusion of post-material and postmodern values reflects an increasingly individualistic orientation to life, which can only mean a continuation of low marriage and fertility rates—the legacy of ideational shifts brought on by the 'rebellious' generations of the 1960s and 1970s. Not all social demographic change should be ascribed to the rebellious generations, however. The generation that preceded the baby boomers themselves questioned certain entrenched traditional values. The divorce boom of the early 1970s, for instance, was mainly a product of that generation's growing disenchantment with marriage and the family institution.

Wealth Flow Theory

The theories of fertility change that we've seen so far have all been based on the experience of industrialized countries. Caldwell (1976, 1982) presented a theory that attempts to describe the process of fertility transition in developing countries as they undergo socioeconomic modernization. Caldwell's theory hinges on the fundamental assumption that individual reproductive behaviour is economically rational but modified by non-economic factors—particularly physiological, social, and psychological factors—to produce the level and pattern of fertility that is observed in a society. Caldwell (1982: 157) also asserted that fertility behaviour in both pre-transitional and post-transitional societies is economically rational, though bounded by biological and social cultural factors. Clearly, no society has a fertility rate of zero, nor is there a society in which fertility reaches the maximum attainable rate (recall that Bongaarts [1978] had estimated the biological maximum level of fecundity to be 15.3 children per woman). Culture and social structure impose mechanisms that promote some level of fertility, while biological constraints ensure against the attainment of maximum fertility.

Caldwell distinguished two types of societies: one of stable high fertility, where there would be no net economic gain accruing to the family from lowered fertility levels, and one in which economic rationality alone would dictate a low level of reproduction. The former is characterized by 'net wealth flow' from younger to older generations, and the latter by 'flows' in the opposite direction. By 'wealth flow' Caldwell means monetary and other benefits and services that one family member provides for another. In traditional societies, the predominant flow of wealth is from children to parents. Examples of monetary and other benefits provided by children to their parents include the following:

- the provision by working children to their parents of a portion or most of their wages
- care for aging parents
- survival of the family name through child-bearing
- performance of necessary religious services for deceased ancestors
- help and security given to the immediate and extended family in times of need or devastation (e.g., famine, natural disasters, war)
- the provision of labour, so that an aging parent may be relieved of a workload

In societies where wealth flows predominantly from the parents to the children, children can expect to benefit from a similar range of material and non-material goods and services: protection, care, and the provision of education and other necessities until the child reaches adulthood.

According to Caldwell, the divide between high- and low-fertility regimes will be bridged by a modernizing country when

1. there is a sustained infusion of Western values into the society (which, Caldwell maintains, can occur even in relatively underdeveloped countries), and
2. there is a shift in the intergenerational flow of wealth, from a traditional regime characterized by wealth flowing from child to parents, to an arrangement in which wealth flows primarily from parents to the children.

Figure 6.10 shows that the two main conditions hastening these developments are the 'Western-

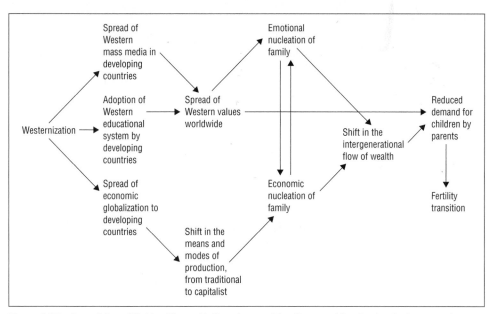

Figure 6.10 A rendition of Caldwell's wealth flow theory of fertility transition for developing countries

Source: Excerpted with permission from John C. Caldwell, 'The Globalization of Fertility Behavior', from Rodolfo A. Bulatao and John B. Casterline, eds, *Global Fertility Transition*, supplement to vol. 27 of *Population and Development Review* (New York: Population Council, 2001): 95.

ization' of values and ideas (especially through Western mass media) and the increasing recognition by parents and society at large of the integrity and uniqueness of the child, leading to the establishment of child-protection laws guaranteeing mandatory education and freedom from abuse and exploitation.

Central to the change in how children are viewed in developing countries is a process known as the *nucleation* (both economic and emotional) *of the family*. In the economically nucleated family, parents direct their resources to their immediate household in the same manner that nuclear families of the industrialized countries do. The parents' principal financial obligation is to their children and then to themselves and their household; the financial needs of the extended family are a secondary priority. As a result, the material value of children to parents declines, and the costs of raising children increase significantly. The child becomes the focal point of the family, and the primary force that binds family members is love and affection (i.e., emotional nucleation). In an argument reminiscent of Becker's (1960), Caldwell theorizes that in this type of social context, it is rational for parents to opt for small families, because as the parental aspirations for child quality increase, the material costs of having and raising children rise significantly.

Applied to sub-Saharan Africa, where fertility transition lags behind trends of other modernizing countries, Caldwell's wealth flow thesis would suggest that the economic and emotional nucleation of families has not yet occurred on a grand scale. There are many social forces unique to Africa that promote high fertility and therefore slow the course of fertility transition. These include the importance of family lineage and the cultural adherence to ancestor worship, polygyny, and cultural views regarding sexuality (see Caldwell and Caldwell, 1990). As well, many parts of Africa are plagued by crisis, from widespread famine to civil wars, economic meltdowns, and the devastating HIV/AIDS epidemic (Zuberi et al., 2003). In spite of these factors that

operate against fertility transition in sub-Saharan Africa, there is evidence of very recent fertility declines, which suggest that the changes Caldwell outlined may have begun to take hold.

Some critics have raised questions about the general applicability of Caldwell's wealth flow theory to other parts of the developing world. Thandani (1978), for example, contends that structural changes—notably economic growth and urbanization—must reach a certain threshold before Western values can spread in a modernizing society. Cain (1982, 1983) has disputed Caldwell's premise that high fertility is always economically rational in pre-transitional settings. Moreover, Cain's research in Bangladesh suggests that Caldwell may have exaggerated the economic utility of children to parents in conditions of extreme poverty. The real value of children in poor societies, he argues, may be in the assistance they can provide to parents in the event of environmental disasters (e.g., floods and crop failures) and protection against physical harm from others, especially those who might make aggressive attempts to take over the family property.

In response to these criticisms and the evidence accumulated during three decades of research in developing countries, Caldwell (2006) has recently updated his theory along four specific areas:

- the role of children's labour inputs and consumption in farming communities in the years preceding fertility transition
- the mode of production that defines the different cultures of work in traditional society
- the role of children as 'insurance' to parents
- the conditions of fertility transition

For the most part, Caldwell's interpretation of the evidence confirms the wealth flow theory. He finds that in the pre-transition stage, before the advent of mandatory schooling, children's work comes close to compensating for their consumption, and that even when their consumption levels exceed their work input, their insurance value to parents makes up for the disparity, making the child primarily a production agent. A child's value as a production agent varies according to the mode of production that predominates in a pre-transitional society. In nomadic hunting-gathering societies, there is less time spent working because families produce only enough food for daily subsistence, and frequent movement makes storing food impractical. In this setting—as compared, for instance, with an agricultural context—children represent a fairly limited value as production agents, and as a result, fertility among hunter-gatherers would be lower than among farmers. A lifestyle based on agriculture is typically sedentary and requires a greater accumulation of material possessions (e.g., permanent housing, tools for farming, storage for excess food, family land). Under these conditions, children are seen as an important source of labour and a source of insurance for parents in their old age. Grown children can also protect the family and its property. As for the conditions of fertility transition in the developing countries, Caldwell (2006: 103–4) neatly summarizes his argument thus:

> [F]ertility transition began when a series of conditions were met by, in succession, colonial governments, preparing for independence and newly independent governments enthusiastically preparing for the future by a huge increase in educational capacity; the replacement of colonial officials by indigenous ones, usually with a significant growth in the bureaucracy; the realization by parents that they could safely invest in the education of children in contrast to simply in their number; a steep decline in infant and child mortality led by international efforts; urbanization providing new jobs in the private sector; a continuing rise in per capita incomes (except recently in sub-Saharan Africa); and independent governments being in a better position than colonial ones to urge and offer family planning. Cumulatively, these changes finally reversed the wealth flow, and fertility fell.

The Synthesis Framework

In his synthesis theory of fertility change in a modernizing society, Easterlin (1975, 1978a, 1983) incorporates the concepts of *supply of children* and *demand for children*. Supply of children refers to the number of children parents would have if they made no attempt at controlling fertility; demand for children refers to the number of surviving children parents would want if fertility control were costless. A third factor in the synthesis framework is *regulation costs*, or the costs to parents of intentionally limiting family size.

Part (a) of Figure 6.11 outlines the synthesis framework, in which background modernization factors (such as improved education and health and living standards, urbanization, and the introduction of new goods into society) and cultural factors that promote traditional norms (especially ethnicity and religion) affect regulation costs (Rc), the demand for children (Cd), and the supply of children (Cn). These three factors in turn influence the proximate determinants of fertility, including deliberate fertility control variables (such as the use of modern contraception). Ultimately, in this three-stage model, the number of children born is a direct function of the proximate determinants and the effects of the other factors on fertility being indirect through the proximate determinants.

Part (b) of Figure 6.11 lays out the temporal process of change in Cn, Cd, and actual family size (C), as society passes through the modernization process. On balance, modernization lowers the demand for children and the costs of fertility regulation. At the same time, however, the potential supply of children rises: since modernization improves the health of the population and helps lower mortality, potential family size increases because couples can potentially have more surviving children. Therefore, since modernization raises natural fertility (i.e., Cn), a temporary rise in the birth rate may be observed

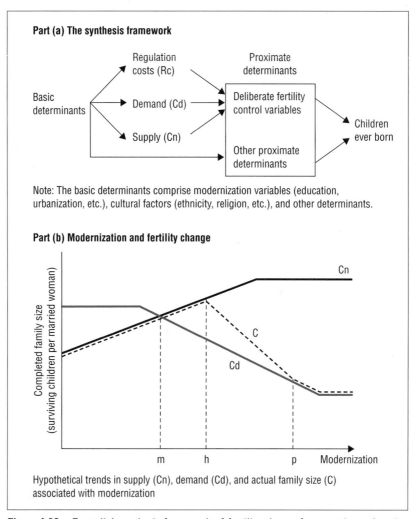

Part (a) The synthesis framework

Note: The basic determinants comprise modernization variables (education, urbanization, etc.), cultural factors (ethnicity, religion, etc.), and other determinants.

Part (b) Modernization and fertility change

Hypothetical trends in supply (Cn), demand (Cd), and actual family size (C) associated with modernization

Figure 6.11   Easterlin's synthesis framework of fertility change for countries undergoing socioeconomic modernization
Source: Easterlin (1984): 566, 574.

during the early stages of the modernization process before the population adopts widespread use of birth control.

Easterlin (1983: 573–6) explains that as modernization occurs and the excess of supply over demand grows, the prospective number of unwanted children increases, generating a corresponding growth in the motivation to limit family size. Moreover, regulation costs and, thus, the obstacles to limiting family size decline, and

at some point the balance between the motivation for and cost of regulation tips in favour of the former. At this point, individuals take deliberate actions to limit family size, and actual family size starts to fall below potential supply, though it still exceeds demand. Motivation for regulation continues to rise and the costs of regulation continue to fall until eventually the population reaches a point at which actual family size corresponds to demand.

Easterlin's synthesis thesis attempts to show that countries that have passed through the fertility transition did so because they successfully promoted a shift in motivation for fertility control in a context of rising potential fertility brought forth by modernization. It also helps us understand how a region such as sub-Saharan Africa has been delayed in its fertility transition. In this case the psychic costs of fertility regulation remain high for couples because of strong norms that encourage the demand for children while at the same time discouraging widespread adoption of family limitation.

Social Interaction Perspective on Contemporary Fertility Transitions

As we have seen, there are various explanations for the fact that more developed countries tend to have lower fertility rates than less developed countries. Bongaarts and Watkins (1996) offer an explanation of fertility transition that relies heavily on the concept of social interactions. Their thesis attempts to shed light on why fertility is high in pre-transitional settings, why it declines with the onset of socioeconomic modernization, and why the timing and onset of fertility transition vary across societies.

After observing statistical correlations between the United Nations' Human Development Index (HDI) and the total fertility rate for 69 developing countries between 1960 and 1990, Bongaarts and Watkins (1996) discovered a number of trends that could not be readily explained by cross-national variability development. Among their findings are the following:

- in pre-transition societies, fertility is at first unresponsive to the level of socioeconomic development, so that there are significant delays in the onset of fertility transition
- once a few countries in a macro-region embark on the fertility transition, other countries in the same region tend to follow sooner than expected
- as time passes, the onset of fertility transition occurs at ever lower levels of socioeconomic development
- once a fertility transition is underway, fertility changes more rapidly than expected as a result of changes in socioeconomic development alone
- the pace of fertility decline is not related to the pace of socioeconomic development, but to the level of socioeconomic development when the transition began

To explain these unexpected findings, Bongaarts and Watkins proposed a social interaction explanation of fertility change. Their explanation keys in on the role of personal networks in transmitting new ideas about fertility control and family planning throughout the territorial communities, the nation, and groups of nations. For instance, at the local level individuals transmit new knowledge to others in their social networks, and behaviour within those networks is conditioned by social influence—people are more likely to follow network figures that have status and prestige. At the broader level, people from neighbouring communities would exchange information about new methods of family limitation, their interactions facilitated by such communication channels as transportation routes and new communication technologies. To the extent that people have access to radios and televisions, they are also connected to the global community and are thus influenced by what they hear and see in other parts of the world, which could lead to the adoption of innovative behaviours and their subsequent diffusion to others.

The social interaction thesis attributes high fertility in pre-transition settings to the combined effects of low socioeconomic development, norms that promote large families, limited knowledge of birth control, and the absence of penalties for parents who 'overproduce'. In this high-fertility context, personal networks are likely to be homogeneous, with few new ideas to challenge the status quo. Even when new information is introduced, community leaders might denounce it as inappropriate, thereby constraining innovative behaviour. Underdeveloped settings also feature fewer structural channels —communication and transportation systems— that promote increased social interaction across communities. All this slows the onset of fertility transition.

Fertility transition begins when the costs associated with having and raising children increase while the material value of children decreases. Easterlin (1978a, 1984), though, has argued that in the initial stages of modernization, fertility could actually increase temporarily. Once again, Bongaarts and Watkins' social interaction thesis can help explain these phenomena. They argue that at the earliest stage of fertility change there is uncertainty among prospective parents about the appropriateness of using fertility control to achieve a desired number of children. Individuals do not assess their options in isolation; rather, they rely on their social networks to gather as much information as possible before modifying their reproductive and family planning habits. In many cases, the shift from large to smaller families could take some time because not all members of an individual's social network are favourable to the new behaviours. With time, however, as more influential members modify their family planning practices, others are influenced and take up the use of modern contraception. The process often spreads through family members, relatives, friends and acquaintances, and eventually the society at large.

When it comes to cross-national variation in the pace of fertility transition, the level of socioeconomic development is again important, but not in isolation of social interaction processes. Bongaarts and Watkins argue that the level of development influences the demand for children but can also stimulate or hinder social interaction. Where levels of development are high at the onset of a transition, fertility change can occur fairly rapidly because demand for smaller families is typically widespread and most couples have ready access to contraceptives. In these contexts, socioeconomic development is associated with 'a multiplication of the channels through which information, ideas, and social influence flow' (Bongaarts and Watkins, 1996: 668). This may explain why the pace of fertility decline is strongly associated with the level of development at the onset of a fertility transition rather than to the pace of subsequent socioeconomic development. Uneven development within and across developing countries can affect the extent to which effective channels of communication are available to help influence change in family planning behaviours.

Bongaarts and Watkins' social interaction thesis does not supersede the important role of socioeconomic development in the start of fertility transition in developing countries. Instead, their perspective provides a complementary explanation that emphasizes processes assumed to operate at the level of social networks and communities: the exchange of new ideas and information—as conditioned by the level of socioeconomic development—that could lead to the adoption of new behaviours, in this case family planning behaviours. By implication, the social interaction thesis suggests that as globalization (economic and ideational) spreads rapidly throughout the developing regions, there will be an opening up of global channels of interaction (e.g., the Internet and television), and that as a result, very few developing countries will fail to undergo the fertility transition over the next few decades.

Women's Autonomy and Fertility Transition in Developing Countries

Throughout the chapter we have touched on the role of gender structure, and the difficulty women face in balancing family and work responsibilities has been mentioned on several occasions. Theories of fertility transition in the developing countries implicitly recognize gender relations. Caldwell, for instance, in his wealth flow theory, suggests that in a high-fertility regime, the patriarchal extended family is inherently pronatalist. Senior men have power over women and children, and they benefit from their labour; therefore, high fertility is advantageous to the patriarch in the extended family system. The shift to a low-fertility regime occurs when this traditional family system is undermined and the balance of power within nucleated families becomes more equitable. In the emotionally nucleated family, women's control over reproduction is a fundamental force behind fertility transition because they are the ones who are best able to actualize their fertility desires (Mason, 1988).

Cain (1982, 1983, 1993) has written about women's economic dependence on male family members in poor countries like Bangladesh. For women in these harsh and unpredictable settings, having many children is a strategy to enhance their survival and well-being in the face of an institutionalized patriarchal system that promotes male control of women. Unable to own property or gain economic independence, women have children as a form of security or, as Cain would argue, as a form of risk insurance and support in old age. In this situation, sons are preferred over daughters, since sons afford greater security. (Men, too, may be motivated to have sons because daughters typically do not contribute economically to the household.) Thus, this gender role structure promotes high fertility. Presumably, fertility decline occurs only when this gender role regime is destabilized and women gain greater economic independence from males.

Economic theories of fertility and the family tend to depict the household as a partnership in which husbands and wives have equal interests and are bound by a single utility function. This view of the family and household power relations has been challenged by feminist social scientists, including Folbre (1983, 1988) and Mason (1988, 1993, 1997b), among others (e.g., Jeffery and Jeffery, 1997; Riley, 1999, 2005; Watkins, 1993). Folbre (1983) in particu-

lar advocated the need to 'bring in' women as active agents in theories of family change, in order to frame a more realistic perspective of how families and households behave, given the differential power and gender role hierarchies that usually exist in families. An influential study of gender and fertility was carried out by Mason (1993); some of her findings are outlined in the box on page 224.

Search for Underlying Uniformities

Low Fertility in Industrialized Countries

As we have seen, the world's industrialized countries have become a region of low fertility, with some showing TFRs below 1.5. In 2001, for instance, no country in western Europe showed a replacement-level TFR of 2.1. Japan's TFR was just 1.3. As reported by Sardon (2004: 291–2), the 2001 average birth rate for the original 15 European Union countries was 1.50 children per woman, with rates as low as 1.25 for some countries (Italy, Greece). As far as eastern Europe is concerned, countries such as Albania, Croatia, Bulgaria, Poland, Romania, Belarus, Ukraine, Azerbaijan, and Georgia—all of which had TFRs well above 2 in the 1970s—had by 2001 witnessed precipitous declines in fertility to rates in the range of 1.14 (Poland) to 1.60 (Azerbaijan) (Sardon, 2004: 291–2).

The cross-national evidence presented by Frejka and Sardon (2004: 2) concerning long-term trends in period and cohort completed fertility rates points to the conclusion that below-replacement fertility is likely to be a permanent condition in most European countries. A return to fertility rates beyond 2.1 seems highly unlikely, they argue, given that women who were still in their mid-twenties at the turn of the new millennium would have to have unusually high completed fertility when they eventually reach the end of their childbearing years. These

Mason on Women's Role in Fertility Transition

In her review and critique of the established demographic literature on matters regarding gender and fertility, Mason (1993) concluded that regular demographic survey approaches could not possibly provide sufficient insight into the ways in which gender relations and power imbalances between men and women affect fertility. She recommended the use of multi-level comparative studies of how women's position affects fertility, to be carried out at both the community and the national level. From her review of the literature, Mason (1993: 30–1) identified seven key ideas that bear on women's role in fertility transition.

1. An increase in women's autonomy will facilitate the postponement of marriage and hence the decline of fertility by reducing the need to control unmarried women's sexuality through early marriage.
2. In family systems that give all rights of women's labour to the husband's family, women's economic independence will facilitate the postponement of marriage and hence the decline of fertility; in other family systems, the effects of women's economic independence on marriage are indeterminate.
3. Because it channels the rewards of children disproportionately to men and the costs of rearing them disproportionately to women, patriarchal family structure encourages high fertility; egalitarian family structure facilitates fertility decline.
4. Women's economic dependency on men produces strong son-preferences among both women and men, and hence relatively high fertility desires for purposes of risk insurance and old-age security; in conjugally oriented family systems, women's economic independence facilitates fertility decline.
5. The extent of women's autonomy and economic dependency determine women's dependency on the maternal role for legitimacy, security, and satisfaction, and hence the opportunity costs of having children and the motivation to limit fertility.
6. Women's autonomy influences their access to modern knowledge and modes of action and hence their propensity to engage in innovative behaviour, including fertility limitation within marriage.
7. Social equality and emotional intimacy between husbands and wives tend to influence fertility by affecting the role that the wife's health and well-being plays in fertility decision-making, and by influencing the likelihood or effectiveness of contraceptive use. (Mason, 1993: 30–1)

These ideas are interrelated in that they concern the impact of women's autonomy on their age at entry into marriage and on their motivation to limit fertility within marriage. Mason (1993, 1997b) notes that although the empirical evidence in support of these propositions is often indirect, the literature is generally consistent with them.

Source: Based on Mason (1993). Used by permission of Oxford University Press.

very low-fertility countries may have fallen into what Lutz, Skirbekk, and Testa (2006) refer to as a 'low fertility trap', in which women postpone childbearing longer than expected, and in time a new norm emerges emphasizing the one-child family. There is evidence that this may be happening in Italy, Spain, Germany, and Russia (*The Economist*, 2007: 4).

In spite of this, recent findings indicate that in Europe, two distinct patterns of fertility are emerging. The examples below, based on a select number of countries, show the period TFR and the corresponding TFR adjusted for tempo distortions (i.e., the effect of postponed fertility on the period TFR), as calculated by the Vienna Institute of Demography (2007):

Country	TFR	Adjusted TFR
Denmark	1.78	2.00
Finland	1.80	1.88
France	1.91	2.02
Germany	1.36	1.51
Greece	1.29	1.49
Italy	1.33	1.41
Iceland	1.93	2.22
Ireland	1.93	2.22
Norway	1.83	2.07
Sweden	1.75	1.91
Spain	1.32	1.33
United Kingdom	1.63	1.85
Latvia	1.24	1.36
Russia	1.31	1.47
Japan	1.29	1.39
United States	2.05	2.15

Source: Vienna Institute of Demography (2007).

Indeed, from Scandinavia to France, fertility rates appear to have increased, in some cases even breaching the 2.1 mark. In 2005, for example, Sweden, Denmark, France, and Ireland all had close to replacement-level fertility. There appear to be no obvious uniformities to account for these rising birth rates, although observers have pointed to pronatalist measures—baby bonuses, extended parental leaves, generous daycare subsidies, and so on (Rindfuss et al., 2007)—and to growing populations of some immigrant groups that traditionally favour large families (*The Economist*, 2007).

On the other hand, in the Mediterranean region and in eastern Europe, low to very low fertility seems an entrenched reality (Lutz, Skirbekk, and Testa, 2006). Research by Billari and Kohler (2004) shows that the 'lowest-low' fertility countries are heterogeneous and cluster into two distinct patterns. On the one hand, lowest-low fertility countries in southern Europe, especially Italy and Spain, exhibit late home-leaving behaviour, a limited spread of non-marital cohabitation, a low proportion of extramarital births, a limited diffusion of divorce, and a relatively low proportion of women participating in the labour force; at the same time, they also exhibit a more marked postponement of first births and less recuperation of fertility at higher ages. The low-fertility countries in central and eastern Europe, on the other hand, are characterized by earlier household independence and union-formation among young people. They

Whether the rising trend in fertility in some parts western Europe and in the United States is but a temporary phenomenon remains to be seen. The higher fertility of the United States may be linked to a constellation of factors that are generally conducive to replacement-level fertility. For instance, access to fairly affordable childcare makes it possible for women to combine motherhood and work (Morgan, 2003b; Rindfuss et al., 2007). High poverty rates among blacks and Hispanics, two large minority groups, may be playing a role as well. The US also has a high prevalence of unplanned pregnancies, especially among teens (Frejka, 2004: 90). All of these factors may play a role in rising fertility rates in the United States.

also have higher extramarital fertility and higher divorce rates, and first births in these countries take place earlier than in the lowest-low fertility countries of southern Europe. Billari and Kohler (2001: 171–2) also observe that there is remarkably little convergence in many behavioural patterns characteristic of lowest-low fertility countries. This suggests that many of the characteristic features of lowest-low fertility countries may be products of unique socio-historical experiences and are thus likely to persist, at least over the near and medium-term future.

Is there then no overall generalization to account for the pervasive low-fertility pattern in eastern Europe and the Mediterranean countries on the one hand, and the modest rise in birth rates for other European countries? Caldwell and Schindlmayr (2003) have argued that a common underlying force behind all fertility transitions is 'the creation of a world economic system where children are of no immediate economic value to their parents' (257). Society rewards women who work outside the home, and this, coupled with the many temptations of the modern consumer society, promotes a desire for material possessions that is stronger than the desire for children.

As a general explanation this covers a great deal of ground, but some critics argue that it may be too sweeping. Van de Kaa (2004b) asserts that the global pattern of fertility decline identified by Caldwell and Schindlmayr is less uniform than these authors maintain. Japan and countries in eastern Europe, for example, began to achieve low fertility before modern contraception became widely available, and well before globalization became a significant movement. Fertility was already declining when modern methods of family limitation became available.

An interesting alternative explanation for low fertility is Aarssen's (2005) suggestion that it is the manifest outcome of evolutionary principles, stemming from a relaxation of innate selective processes for high fertility. Specifically, Aarssen argues that the empowerment of women that

leads to reduced fertility is an evolutionary consequence of selection that reflects an inherent preference for lower fertility in females. This has allowed random genetic drift to take place, producing an increased frequency of innate behaviours that at the same time promote low fertility and a discontentment with large families. On the other hand, while low fertility seems a permanent condition in many societies, it is unlikely that birth rates will drop to levels much below what they are today because social norms ensure that the majority of women will want to bear at least one child (Foster, 2000).

McDonald (2000) has advanced an explanation emphasizing the gender system of advanced societies as a central force in fertility change, which may at the same time explain why some industrialized countries are seeing a rise in fertility while others are not. McDonald (2000) distinguishes between 'gender equity in individual-oriented institutions' and 'gender equity within the family and family-oriented institutions'. These two types of gender equity may not necessarily coincide. A society may have a high degree of gender equity in individual-oriented institutions (translating into equal access to higher education and careers in the paid economy) but low equity in the family-oriented institutions. This is the case even in some advanced societies, where in spite of the gains women have made in individual-oriented institutions, the family institution still maintains a relatively traditional gender role structure, where women are expected to take care of the children and perform the usual household chores of cooking, cleaning, and so forth, even while holding full- or part-time jobs (Fuwa, 2004; Torr and Short, 2004).

According to McDonald, this disjuncture between the two types of gender equity systems, which is especially characteristic of Mediterranean countries, is likely to lead to very low fertility because women are less able to cope with the dual demands of work and family. In societies where family-oriented institutions as well as individually based institutions are equitable, fertility rates are typically higher (though they might still fall short of replacement level). Examples of societies that meet both gender equity conditions are the Scandinavian countries and, to some extent, the United States (Engelhardt, Kogel, and Prskawetz, 2004; Frejka, 2004). The key factor in ensuring equity in family-oriented institutions seems to be family-friendly state policies that support and ease parenthood for couples. This implies that if institutions were made to be more family-friendly, birth rates would likely rise (Gauthier and Hatzius, 1997; Hobcroft, 2004).

Generalizations about Fertility Transition in Developing Countries

During the 1970s and 1980s many developing nations—Taiwan, Indonesia, Thailand, China, and several Latin American and Caribbean countries, to name just a few—embarked on a period of sustained fertility decline; others have recently begun their fertility transitions. But the pattern of fertility transition experienced in these developing countries is different from the changes experienced in western Europe, where declining birth rates followed long-term economic growth and improvements in living conditions. Important findings from surveys carried out in developing nations indicate that access to methods of birth control, changes in cultural values favouring the small-family ideal, and rising female education and independence, all in conjunction with socioeconomic development, have been some of the key driving forces behind fertility decline (Caldwell, 2001; Robey, Rutstein, and Morris, 1993). Theories of fertility transition in the developing countries encompass these factors as well as additional ones. Bulatao (2001: 2–3) provides a useful summary of some of the most important propositions concerning fertility decline associated with fertility transition in developing countries. These propositions, which have received substantial support in the literature, emphasize the interaction of cultural, economic, sociological, and demographic factors in fertility transition. They are outlined in the box on page 228.

Canadian Fertility Trends and Patterns

Back when Canada was a frontier society, the fertility of its people was much higher than what it is today. We know that in the mid-1800s, for instance, the Canadian crude birth rate was around 45 per 1,000 (Wadhera and Strachan, 1993). Before that time, it must have been even higher. If we were to look at the long-term trend in the crude birth and death rates for French Canada and Canada, taken together, from the early 1700s all the way to the present (Figure 6.12), we would notice six broad stages of fertility change in Canada:

- *Stage One* (1711–15 to 1756–60) is characterized by fairly stable high fertility and rising

---

Henripin's (1954: 39) data for French Canada between 1661 and 1770 show crude birth rates fluctuating between 50 and 65 births per 1,000 population. These early French-Canadian birth rates exceed crude birth rates found in most developing countries today.

1661–70	50.6
1671–80	52.5
1681–90	47.3
1691–1700	54.2
1701–10	56.4
1711–20	56.9
1721–30	54.2
1931–40	58.1
1741–50	59.0
1751–60	61.8
1761–70	65.2

Bulatao's Seven Propositions on Fertility Change in Developing Countries

1. In virtually all cases long-run declines in mortality eventually instill a lagged response for long-term fertility reductions. This is so because reducing infant and childhood deaths lowers the need among parents to produce a given desired number of surviving children.

2. In modernizing societies, once children are viewed as economic burdens, fewer children are desired by parents. In other words, fertility is high when children earn income or contribute materially to the household, and it is low when they do not. Related to this, the introduction of institutionalized social security systems should lower fertility by reducing the need for parents to depend on their children for support in old age.

3. As rearing children interferes with adult activities, the opportunity costs of having children increases. Fertility should fall when there is an increase in opportunities for women to work in jobs that are relatively incompatible with childbearing, which essentially means work outside the home.

4. As societies modernize, the shift to fewer births accompanies a transformation in the institution of the family, from a multigenerational concern with clear lines of authority to a small conjugal unit, focused on the individual needs of the members. In such contexts the parents devote more time and resources to the child as compared to a traditional regime.

5. As societies undergo socioeconomic modernization, traditional norms favouring large families eventually erode, and individuals opt for smaller families.

6. Greater access to modern contraceptives through family planning programs greatly accelerates the fertility transition.

7. As women increasingly obtain education and participate more in the labour force, there occurs significant delays in marriage among women, and this helps fertility to decline.

8. The diffusion of contraceptive knowledge through the mass media, the education system, other communication systems, and through personal interactions of the small-family ideal, facilitates a widespread process of fertility decline.

Source: Excerpted with permission from Rodolfo A. Bulatao, 'Introduction', in Rodolfo A. Bulatao and Jon B. Casterline, eds, *Global Fertility Transitions*, supplement to vol. 27 of *Population and Development Review* (New York: Population Council, 2001): 1–14.

death rates, with rates of natural increase fluctuating between 1.4 and 3.6 per cent per year.

- *Stage Two* (1761–5 to 1831–5) is marked by sustained declines in both fertility and mortality, with the death rate declining somewhat faster than fertility. In this stage, average annual growth rates never declined below 2 per cent and in some cases went up as far as 3 per cent.

- *Stage Three* (1836–40 to 1891–1900) saw fertility decline rapidly. Mortality, despite being on a declining trend overall, showed some increase between 1871 and 1881. The rates of natural increase during Stage Three were still high by most standards, but towards the start of the twentieth century, they began to decline from almost 3 per cent to about 1.6 per cent on average (with some exceptions).

- *Stage Four* (1901 to 1941) is characterized by very rapid declines in both vital rates, with rates of natural increase in the vicinity of 2 per cent.

- *Stage Five* (1941 to 1966) saw both Quebec and Canada experience a general upturn in fertility following the Second World War.
- *Stage Six* (1966 to today) is characterized by a general convergence in birth and death rates. In both Quebec and Canada as a whole, very low crude birth and death rates have produced very low rates of natural increase.

From Baby Boom to Baby Bust

By the early 1930s, the period of fertility transition in Canada had pretty much come to an end, with the birth rate reaching historic lows of about 20 per 1,000. As we have already seen, the low fertility of the 1930s was a common phenomenon in the industrial nations of western Europe and the United States. As the Great Depression of the 1930s unfolded, fertility rates,

while remaining low, increased gradually leading up to the Second World War. The outbreak of war helped to end the economic depression and at the same time stimulated a surge in the marriage rate, consequently also the birth rate. By 1943, the crude birth rate had risen to 24 per 1,000 (McInnis, 2000b). This increase turned out to be a prelude to what would be an unprecedented surge in the Canadian birth rate immediately after World War II.

The trend in Canada's total fertility rate through the twentieth century and into the twenty-first is shown in Table 6.13. From the Depression until the eve of the Second World War, the TFR declined, falling to below 3 children per woman for 1936 and 1941. The decline can actually be traced to 1933, when the recorded rate was 2.86. These values remained

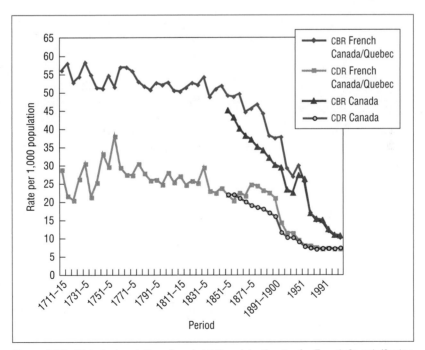

Figure 6.12   Historical evolution of crude birth and death rates for French Canada/Quebec (1711–15 to 2004) and Canada (1851–5 to 2004)

Sources: Bureau de la Statistique du Quebec (1997): 149, 132, 135; Henripin (1972): 18; Henripin and Peron (1972): 230; McVey and Kalbach (1995a): 184; Nagnur (1986b): 45; Pelletier, Legare, and Bourbeau (1997): 95; Statistics Canada (2006a): 218, (1993b): 9, 15, 32–3, 39–40; Urquhart (1983): A1–14.

Table 6.13 Number of live births, total and gross reproduction rates, Canada, 1921–2004

Year	Number of live births	Total fertility rate
1921	264,879	3.536
1926	240,015	3.357
1931	247,205	3.200
1936	227,980	2.696
1941	263,993	2.832
1946	343,504	3.374
1951	381,092	3.503
1956	450,739	3.858
1961	475,700	3.840
1966	387,710	2.813
1971	362,187	2.187
1976	359,987	1.825
1981	371,346	1.704
1986	372,913	1.672
1991	402,533	1.799
1996	366,200	1.630
2001	333,744	1.530
2004	337,072	1.526

Sources: Bélanger (2006): 31; McVey and Kalbach (1995a): 270; Statistics Canada (2006d).

below 3 until 1943, when the fertility rate reached 3.04 children per woman, and in the ensuing 19-year period, from 1946 to 1965, the total fertility rate remained above 3. In fact, some of the highest-ever Canadian fertility rates were recorded during that period, including the 1952 TFR of 3.64, which was then the highest birth rate achieved since 1921. This level would ultimately be surpassed when, in 1959, the country recorded a total fertility rate of almost 4 (3.93), marking the apex of the baby boom. In that year, 479,275 children were born in Canada, setting a record yet unmatched in the country's history.

The year 1966 marked the end of the baby boom (Foot and Stoffman, 1998) and the start of the precipitous decline in the birth rate known as the 'baby bust' (Grindstaff, 1975, 1985; Romaniuk, 1984). In 1972, Canada saw its total fertility rate fall below the 2.1 replacement level, and the trend since then has been, on the whole, downward. There have been minor upward perturbations, but the rate has never re-established itself at replacement level, and currently stands at around 1.5.

Explanations for the Baby Boom and Baby Bust in Canada

The rise and fall of fertility in Canada after World War II can be attributed to social, cultural, demographic, and economic factors. The end of hostilities in 1945 brought unprecedented economic prosperity to Canada, stimulating a marriage boom. Jobs were abundant, and Canadian men and women married at younger ages than they had in earlier generations. As a result, couples started their families earlier and had more children on average (Romaniuk, 1984). All of this was facilitated by the abundance of jobs available to young men following the war, as Easterlin (1969, 1980) has argued. Low fertility in the 1930s meant that roughly two decades later, in the 1950s and 1960s, there were fewer entry-level workers seeking jobs. The small cohorts of the 1930s could gain employment relatively easily and enjoy a sense of security and excellent prospects for the future thanks to the booming economic conditions of the time. For that generation of Canadians material aspirations could be actualized even with a household of three or more children. At the same time, governments were enhancing the welfare state in order to provide better social and economic security for Canadians by means of universal health care and education, employment insurance, and so on. Once these developments are considered together, it seems unsurprising that young couples would commit fairly early to the institution of marriage and family.

Against this socioeconomic backdrop, the traditional gender role system that prevailed until the 1960s, which cast the man of the house as the 'breadwinner', helped promote higher fertility. This system would later be displaced by a more egalitarian arrangement of gender roles, brought on to a large extent by the efforts of the women's emancipation movement of the 1960s. But before this time, traditional values about family and marriage were strong, and the Church exercised considerable influence in people's lives (Clark, 2003). In this social context, young people saw value in the institutions of marriage and family, reinforced by religion and society at large, and married in large numbers. Moreover, for many young people in the 1950s, early marriage was seen as a route to personal freedom from the authority of parents; for older couples, especially those whose family-building desires had been frustrated by the war, this was an opportunity to have children and raise a family. All of this, again, contributed to higher rates of marriage and fertility.

In many respects, the same factors responsible for the baby boom were also involved in the baby bust. If the high fertility of the baby boom period was partly attributable to the traditional system of gender roles, then declining birth rates during the baby bust were also determined by gender roles, but in this case it was the breakdown of the traditional breadwinner system that mattered. The traditional values that had encouraged couples to marry early and have many children became supplanted by new modern ideas about the desirability of small families. The centrality of marriage in people's lives began to wane in the 1960s, and the new generations of Canadians born during the baby boom would eventually explore alternative family arrangements, first noticeable with the rise of cohabitation and common-law unions beginning in the early 1970s. The legacy of these new ideas is in

evidence today, as Canada and other post-industrial societies are now in the midst of the 'second demographic transition' (Lesthaeghe, 1995; van de Kaa, 1987, 1999, 2003, 2004a, 2004b).

Today, late marriage and non-marriage are the most important proximate determinants of Canada's low birth rate, with contraceptive use a distant second (Henripin, 2003: 168). The probability of a Canadian woman experiencing marriage as her first union has fallen significantly, a trend that is more pronounced among the younger cohorts of Canadian women (Wu, 2000). The Canadian marriage rate, which in 1971 was just over 9 per 1,000 population, has declined to just below 5 per 1,000 (Wilson, 2005: 156). Meanwhile, the total divorce rate, which in 1969—immediately after the liberalization of divorce laws—stood at close to 150 per 1,000 marriages, had risen to about 400 per 1,000 marriages by the year 2000. (Wu and Schimmele, 2005: 213). Rates of remarriage have been on a downward trend since the late 1960s (Wu and Schimmele, 2005: 223), and the rise of cohabitation has not translated into increased fertility rates. In fact, cohabiting unions are generally not the most prolific (Le Bourdais and Lapierre-Adamcyk, 2004; Mills and Trovato, 2001; Turcotte and Bélanger, 1997; Wu and Balakrishnan, 1995).

As a result of their growing involvement in the paid labour force and enhanced education and occupational training, an increasing number of women today draw earnings equal to or exceeding those of their husbands. During the early 1970s, this distribution of household income was evident in just 6 per cent of working couples. By the late 1990s, the number of couples in which the wife earned the same as or more than the husband had grown to 25 per cent (Gunderson, 1998; Grindstaff and Trovato, 1990; Little, 2000). This means that working women today must consider the 'opportunity costs' of having children, including delayed advancement in the workplace and forgone

Between the early 1980s and 2000, the proportion of babies born outside of marital unions in Canada increased from about 1 in 6 to about 1 in 3. This is largely attributable to babies born in common-law unions, a trend that is especially pronounced in Quebec (where currently about half of all births are to cohabiting parents). In the rest of Canada, only about 15 per cent of all births occur to common-law couples (Kerr, Moyser, and Beaujot, 2006).

earnings (Drolet, 2003; Grindstaff, Balakrishnan, and Dewit, 1992). These opportunity costs increase with women's education and professional status. This must be considered an important factor in the recent downturn in fertility in Canada, as young couples adjust to the demands of modern living by having children later in life in order to accommodate career and work aspirations with family goals (Ram and Rahim, 1993).

It is also important to recognize the growing difficulty young people face in getting a start in today's labour market. There have been recessions in recent decades, and unemployment rates for young workers have not been favourable (Crompton and Vickers, 2000; Morissette and Johnson, 2005). Young men are earning less than older workers (Bélanger and Ouellet, 2002; Romaniuk, 1984: 80)—in fact, the real earnings of young men in Canada were actually lower at the end of the 1990s than they had been in the early 1980s. This situation could not have fostered among young adults a strong desire for marriage and family building.

Differential Fertility

Regional
The long-term trend in the TFR of Canada as a whole and its constituent regions has been fairly uniform over the twentieth century. Following the low fertility of the 1930s, all parts of Canada witnessed the post-war baby boom and subsequent baby bust. In general, the past three decades have seen the TFRs for the provinces move increasingly toward convergence around 1.5, with some relatively minor annual fluctuations (see Figure 6.13). In 2004, provincial TFRs ranged from 1.31 (Newfoundland and Labrador) to 1.81 (Manitoba). The two regions that stand out for their unusually high birth rates are Nunavut and the Northwest Territories. Geographic isolation, regional underdevelopment, and, perhaps most important, the large percentage of Aboriginal inhabitants in these regions are factors that all help to account for the unusually high fertility of the two territories.

Religion and Ethnicity
Religion and ethnicity have long been of interest to demographers who study fertility trends and differentials in Canada (e.g., Burch, 1966; Charles, 1948; Henripin, 1972; Hurd, 1965; Tracey, 1941). Until midway through the 1970s Catholics had higher birth rates than did Protestants, and some variability in fertility by urban/rural residence and by ethnic origin were still noticeable (Balakrishnan, Ebanks, and Grindstaff, 1979; Beaujot, Krotki, and Krishnan, 1978; Halli, 1990; Trovato and Grindstaff, 1980). However, by the 1990s, ethnic and religious differences in fertility had receded almost to insignificance (Balakrishnan, Krotki, and Lapierre-Adamczyk, 1993; Henripin, 1972, 2002), except among a few numerically small religious groups (Mormons, Mennonites, Hutterites), Aboriginal peoples, and some immigrant visible minorities (Arabs, West Asians, South Asians) (Malenfant and Bélanger, 2006).

Among Canada's Native people, fertility rates have been declining for some time, though they are not likely to converge with rates for the rest of the country until the mid-twenty-first century. It is interesting that the long-term fertility decline among Canadian Aboriginal people,

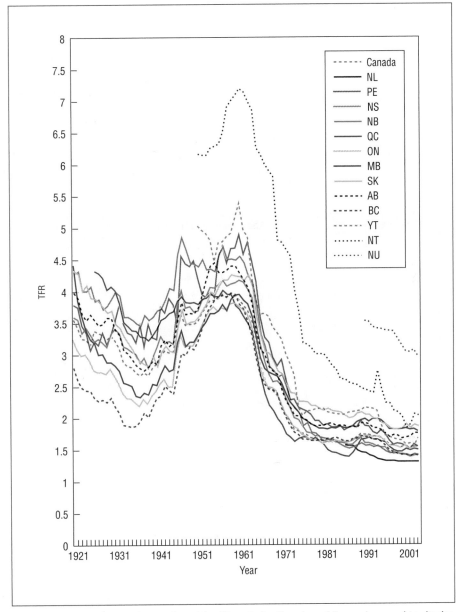

Figure 6.13   Historical evolution of total fertility rate for Canada and its provinces and territories, 1921–2004

Note: Data for Newfoundland and Labrador (NL) available only after 1981. Nunavut (NU) came into being in 1989.

Sources: Statistics Canada: 2006d; 1993b; *Births 1991* and *1992* (Cat. 84-210 Annual, Table 17); *Births and Deaths, 1994* (Cat. 84-210.XPD, Table 3.4); *Births and Deaths, 1995* (Cat. 84-210.XPD, Table 3.5); *The Daily* (1998). Data for 1921–82: Roamniuk (1984); data for 1986–99: Bélanger (2002): Table A6; data for 2000–3: Bélanger (2006): 31.

which began in the early 1960s, coincides with fertility transitions among other indigenous populations, including those of the United States, Australia, and New Zealand (Caldwell, 2001: 95). As of the late 1990s and early 2000s, the total fertility rate for Canada's Native people as a whole was about 70 per cent above the national average (see Table 6.14). The TFR is highest for the Inuit, reaching an estimated rate of 3.21 in 1996–2001. The Métis have the lowest TFR, at around 2.15. In many respects, these variations reflect differences in geographic and socioeconomic marginalization from the mainstream Canadian society.

Among the various theories proposed to explain the divergent trends in fertility among disadvantaged sub-populations is *the characteristics assimilation thesis*, which states that minority groups have high fertility because of their disadvantaged socioeconomic position in relation to the larger society. Lower education levels, lower income, and greater rates of unemployment in

Table 6.14 Three perspectives on Canadian Aboriginal fertility: By year, 1974–2001; by age, 1966–2001; and by age and sub-group, 1996–2001

Year	Registered Indians	All Canadians	Ratio: Indians/Canada
1974	4.42	1.88	2.35
1975	4.16	1.81	2.30
1976	3.95	1.79	2.21
1977	3.74	1.76	2.13
1978	3.62	1.71	2.12
1979	3.52	1.70	2.07
1980	3.41	1.69	2.02
1981	3.33	1.66	2.01
1982	3.33	1.64	2.03
1983	3.29	1.62	2.03
1984	3.27	1.62	2.02
1985	3.24	1.61	2.01
1986	3.18	1.59	2.00
1987	3.03	1.57	1.93
1988	2.92	1.60	1.83
1989	2.86	1.65	1.73
1990	2.83	1.71	1.65
1991	2.85	1.71	1.67
1992	2.87	1.71	1.68
1993	2.86	1.68	1.70
1994	2.80	1.68	1.67
1995	2.76	1.67	1.65
1996	2.73	1.62	1.69
1996–2001	2.60	1.56	1.67

(continued)

Table 6.14   (*continued*)

Age group	Age-specific fertility rates (all Aboriginal peoples) by period				
	1966–71	1976–81	1986–91	1991–6	1996–2001
15–19	120.4	112.3	115.5	116.2	99.9
20–24	297.5	203.9	183.1	181.7	168.4
25–29	251.6	160.7	143.8	145.5	131.4
30–34	189.6	85.3	89.3	81.6	74.2
35–39	153.3	51.4	54.3	35.2	33.3
40–44	79.2	24.4	10.5	10.2	11.6
45–49	11.9	2.7	1.3	1.7	1.0

Age group	Age-specific fertility rates (Canada and Aboriginal sub-groups), 1996–2001				
	Canada	North American Indian	Registered Indian	Métis	Inuit
15–19	20.3	114.2	110.3	72.5	100.0
20–24	64.2	182.3	173.6	142.3	179.0
25–29	103.7	136.7	128.5	119.6	156.9
30–34	85.5	78.5	73.9	63.1	101.0
35–39	32.9	36.8	35.7	25.4	57.4
40–44	5.3	13.7	13.6	5.5	41.0
45–49	0.2	1.0	1.0	0.7	6.6
TFR	1.5605	2.816	2.683	2.1455	3.2095

Sources: Adapted from: Loh and George (2003): 122; Ram (2004): 191.

The long-term fertility decline among Canada's Aboriginal populations began in the early 1960s. This point also marks the onset of fertility transition among indigenous populations of the United States, Australia, and New Zealand. Caldwell (2001: 95) prepared the table below to show the similar timing of fertility transition among these indigenous groups.

Indigenous minority	Onset of decline	+5% decline	+10% decline
American Indians	1960	1961	1962
Canadian Indians	1962	1964	1966
New Zealand Maoris	1963	1964	1966
Australian Aborigines	1971	1972	1973

relation to others all contribute to diminished socioeconomic status, which is believed to contribute to relatively high fertility rates (Johnson, 1979; Trovato, 1987). Another explanation suggests that certain minority groups possess a *particularized ideology* that promotes high fertility. For example, fertility among Catholics at one time surpassed the rate for Protestants, presumably in part because of the Catholic Church's opposition to birth control (Burch, 1966; Day, 1968; Van Heek, 1956).

Certain minority populations, including North Americans of Chinese, Japanese, and Jewish background, also manifest below-average fertility levels (Chui and Trovato, 1989; Johnson and Lean, 1985; Tang, 2006). Goldscheider and Uhlenberg (1969), articulating the *minority status insecurity thesis*, suggested that these groups suffer social-psychological insecurities associated with their minority status, which is the underlying cause of their low fertility. They further explain that these minority groups typically have a history of prejudice and discrimination, and share strong aspirations for socioeconomic assimilation. They typically have no particularized ideology prohibiting the use of birth control, so having a small family may be viewed as part of a conscious strategy by minority couples to achieve and maintain socioeconomic success.

If we were to apply these theories to Canada's Native people, we might conclude that high Aboriginal fertility results from the marginalizing effects of discrimination and prejudice this group has experienced for centuries, and their difficulty achieving socioeconomic parity with the larger society. In empirical analyses, such demographic variables as education and income explain in large part the variation in birth rates between Aboriginal people and others. This suggests that socioeconomic improvements in this subpopulation could indeed lead to significantly lower birth rates among Native people. However, empirical evidence shows that these variables do not completely account for the fertility differential between Aboriginal people and others. This suggests that there may be a particularized ideology in the Native population promoting high fertility (Trovato, 1981, 1987).

Other Differentials

In the general Canadian population today, the most influential of the variables that differentiate between above- and below-average fertility are women's education and labour force status, each exerting strong negative effects on fertility (Balakrishnan, Ebanks, and Grindstaff, 1979; Balakrishnan, Krotki, and Lapierre-Adamczyk, 1993; Hou et al., 1996; McVey and Kalbach, 1995a). Higher income has in the past been shown to have negative effects on fertility (Charles, 1948; Tracey, 1941), but more recent analyses indicate that once social demographic factors such as residence, education, and labour force status are taken into account, the net influence of income

on number of children born is weak (Balakrishnan, Krotki, and Lapierre-Adamczyk, 1993). McVey and Kalbach (1995a: 290) have pointed out that over time the relationship 'has been shifting to a positive one in which fertility increases with increasing income.' It would not be surprising if the data showed low-income and upper-income couples with above-average fertility, and middle-income Canadians with below-average fertility. High-income couples may have larger families because they are able to afford children without compromising their household's overall living standards. The low fertility of the middle classes, which are most heavily burdened by taxes and general household expenses, can be explained by their greater degree of economic insecurity. Higher fertility among low-income couples may be explained in part by lack of knowledge about (and ability to purchase) effective birth control, though clearly other factors must also be involved.

Future Prospects

Cohort fertility trends can help us to visualize other dimensions of the changes in the Canadian birth rate in a historical context. As we have already noted, the period TFR measures period fertility as it changes from year to year, while cohort fertility considers the completed family size of generations of women who, in each given calendar year, have reached the end of their reproductive lifespan at age 50. Cohort information allows us to discover the average number of children different generations of women have borne during their reproductive lives. As Figure 6.14 shows, the turn to below-replacement fertility, when looked at from a cohort perspective, took place in the middle part of the 1970s, with the generation of mothers born in 1946. For subsequent cohorts of women there is a declining average completed family size below 2.1, much in line with the general trend of the period TFR. The time trend in completed fertility for the most recent cohorts is based on incomplete data, since women born after the mid-1970s have yet to reach the age of 50. Nevertheless, the indication from Figure 6.14 is quite clear: the trend in completed family size is downward. In strictly demographic terms, the future of the Canadian population is precarious, as the pattern of reproduction reflected in both the period and the cohort fertility rates implies eventual depopulation over the long term.

This scenario can, of course, be offset by increased immigration, but the number of immigrants required to maintain a stable rate of population growth indefinitely would be much larger than many Canadians might consider desirable. Evidence presented by Bélanger (2006), based on cohort age-specific fertility rates, shows that women born between 1955 and 1980 have experienced a notable deficit in fertility compared to women born in 1946. Although more recent generations tend to show a tendency

toward higher fertility rates at ages above 30, this is really insufficient to make up for their substantially lower fertility between ages 15 and 29. In other words, as Frejka and Sardon (2004) have concluded in their extensive study of period and cohort completed fertility in industrialized countries, young Canadian female cohorts cannot make up for the lag established during their twenties with increased fertility in their thirties and forties. Bélanger (2006: 30) points out a particularly astonishing feature of this phenomenon: judging from the fertility patterns of the cohort born in 1980 (who were 23 years of age in 2003), it seems likely that their fertility rate at age 25 may turn out to be even lower. If this is true, then unless there is a significant rise in fertility after age 30, the completed fertility rate of this cohort could end up being the lowest of all. The drop in fertility observed

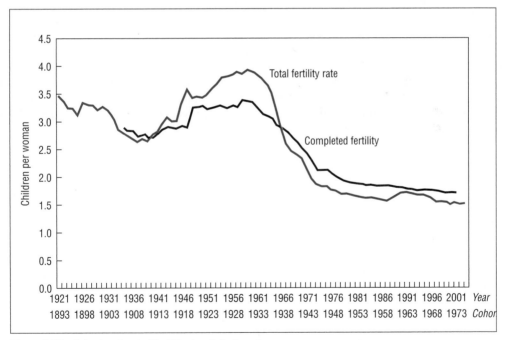

Figure 6.14 Cohort and period fertility trends in Canada

Note: the cohort completed fertility rates have been shifted forward by 28 years, since this is the average age at maternity in Canada over the past three decades (Bélanger, 2006: 30).

Source: Adapted from Statistics Canada publication *Report on the Demographic Situation in Canada 2003* and *2004*, by Alain Bélanger. Catalogue no. 91-209-XIE, p. 30.

for recent cohorts would consequently result in a drop in the number of children and not merely a postponement of childbearing.

Examined through the lenses of period and cohort fertility trends, Canada during the postwar years has moved from what Henripin (2003) calls 'a period of abundance' in terms of reproductive levels to 'one of deficit'. We may at this point offer a concluding statement about the reasons behind the reduced childbearing of the baby bust period. As we have seen with our overview of theories, lower fertility has resulted from a combination of sociological, economic, and cultural factors, including the following:

- an unprecedented sense of social and economic freedom among women
- the widespread movement of women into the paid labour force (which has increased the opportunity costs of bearing and raising children)
- higher household living standards and material aspirations that compete with childbearing
- the postponement of childbearing as women juggle the demands of work, career, and family
- the tendency for many to postpone or forgo marriage, and a growing preference among recent generations of young adults for cohabitation over traditional marriage
- the decreasing influence of tradition and religion as guides to family planning and reproduction
- the ever-increasing cost of living and raising children
- the widespread availability of effective birth control methods, surgical sterilization, and abortion

Finally, we cannot overlook the role of childlessness as a component of the low-fertility pattern described for Canada (Ram, 2000). During the high-fertility period of the 1950s, less than 10 per cent of married women in Canada were without children; by 1981, the percentage was close to 20 per cent, and this is likely to be even higher today (McInnis, 2000b: 581).

Data on contraceptive use in Canada indicates that the birth-control pill is the most widely used method of birth control among women aged 15–29. Women past age 30 are increasingly willing to opt for surgical sterilization, which is the most common method (Bélanger, 2002:123). At the same time, abortion rates have increased steadily since the mid-1970s, from 0.3 abortions per woman in 1976 to about 0.5 in 1997. The annual number of therapeutic abortions in Canada now ranges well above 100,000 per year. In 2002, there were 105,154 abortions, with just over two-thirds of those occurring in Ontario (over 38,000) and Quebec (over 31,000) (Statistics Canada, *The Daily*, 2005a).

Conclusion

In this chapter we examined the basic concepts and measures of fertility before discussing the social/biological determinants of fertility. We also looked at various theories of fertility change to try to discover why the secular pattern of fertility over the past two centuries has followed its observed trajectory. Economic theories of fertility transition emphasize changes in the value of time for parents and the rising costs of raising children. Sociological theories tend to focus on the declining influence of tradition and the increasing secularization that usually accompanies urbanization and socioeconomic modernization. Demographers such as Caldwell (1976, 1982) and Easterlin (1975, 1978a, 1983) have attempted to explain how modernization in developing societies produces a fertility transition. Although Caldwell's wealth flow theory has been challenged recently (see Bulatao and Casterline, 2001), its essential ingredients appear to remain relevant to Africa and to other high-fertility societies in the developing world.

Among the many other explanations of why fertility changes, the dominant perspective in recent decades has been the microeconomic rational model of decision-making advanced by Becker and other economists from the University of Chicago. This model assumes that the decision to have a child is a rational choice that is, in principle, no different from the decision one makes when buying a car or a house. Parents weigh the perceived costs and values of having a child in the context of their budgetary constraints. Parents will usually have the number of children they believe they can afford, given their income, their preferences for material comfort, and how much they feel they must invest in the 'quality' of children they raise. For most couples in industrialized countries today, this typically means opting for no more than one or two children on average.

We concluded our examination of fertility by taking a close look at the fertility trends and

patterns in Canada, with particular attention to the long-term decline in the birth rate, the interruption of this pattern by the post-war baby boom, and the resumption of low fertility that continues to this day. Changes in the proximate determinants, particularly the flight from traditional marriage and the increased reliance on birth control and abortion, together with the postponement of childbearing to older ages explains virtually all of the drop in the TFR to its current below-replacement levels. We note, however, that sociological factors—particularly socioeconomic change and value-shifts away from traditionalism in favour of postmaterialism—have had considerable indirect bearing on the proximate determinants of fertility in Canada.

Exercises

Table 6.16 (on page 241) contains age-specific fertility rates for Canadian women spanning quinquennial intervals from 1895–9 to 2000–5. Use the data in this table to complete the following exercises.

1. Compute all period TFRs.
2. For each period, compute all gross reproduction rates (assume the proportion of baby girls at birth is 0.4860).
3. For each period, compute the corresponding net reproduction rates. Assume the age-specific female survival ratios (SRs) provided in Table 6.15. For the period 1895–1915, apply the SR values for 1891–1911.

Table 6.15 Age-specific female survival ratios, 1891–2000

Life table period	SR$_{15-19}$	SR$_{20-24}$	SR$_{25-29}$	SR$_{30-34}$	SR$_{35-39}$	SR$_{40-44}$	SR$_{45-49}$
2000	4.96455	4.95651	4.94828	4.93893	4.92505	4.90384	4.87100
1995	4.95814	4.94995	4.94135	4.93054	4.91527	4.89142	4.85382
1990	4.95419	4.94528	4.93571	4.92419	4.90792	4.88380	4.84477
1985	4.94567	4.93555	4.92529	4.91279	4.89700	4.87177	4.82934

(continued)

Table 6.15 (*continued*)

Life table period	SR_{15-19}	SR_{20-24}	SR_{25-29}	SR_{30-34}	SR_{35-39}	SR_{40-44}	SR_{45-49}
1980	4.93283	4.92141	4.90922	4.89513	4.87557	4.84430	4.79499
1975	4.91044	4.89714	4.88396	4.86821	4.84498	4.80942	4.75166
1970	4.88610	4.87219	4.85776	4.83942	4.81303	4.77290	4.71275
1965	4.86059	4.84761	4.83329	4.81518	4.78929	4.74996	4.68806
1960	4.84208	4.82907	4.81389	4.79535	4.76878	4.72839	4.66534
1955	4.81279	4.79868	4.78108	4.75895	4.72957	4.68538	4.61490
1950	4.76163	4.74081	4.71638	4.68676	4.64647	4.58867	4.50338
1945	4.69453	4.65983	4.61953	4.57454	4.51971	4.45083	4.35638
1940	4.62030	4.58022	4.52878	4.47018	4.40177	4.31824	4.21233
1935	4.41604	4.36386	4.30412	4.23838	4.16149	4.06813	3.94650
1930	4.44672	4.38412	4.30609	4.22133	4.12888	4.02497	3.90412
1925	4.43176	4.36540	4.28809	4.20880	4.11797	4.01507	3.89812
1920	4.38358	4.31338	4.22852	4.13778	4.03470	3.92058	3.79327
1911	4.07329	3.98891	3.88645	3.77469	3.65787	3.53371	3.39365
1901	3.85443	3.75676	3.64004	3.51483	3.38635	3.25283	3.10602
1891	3.53690	3.53690	3.40946	3.27470	3.13853	2.99955	2.84977

Sources: for 1891–1911, Bourbeau, Légaré, and Émond (1997); for 1920–81, Nagnur (1986b); for 1981–2000, Statistics Canada (various years).

4. Explain how TFR, GRR, and NRR are interrelated, and then interpret their computed values.
5. Compute all possible cohort completed fertility rates.
6. Graph the cohort completed fertility rates and the period TFRs.
7. Explain why cohort completed fertility and period TFRs differ.
8. Estimate the completed fertility of the cohorts who would end their childbearing in 2010 and 2015. To do this, first consider the time trend in observed age-specific fertility rates, then estimate the future completed fertility of these cohorts. Clearly spell out your assumptions and approach for the estimations. Interpret your results from the point of view of the future of fertility in Canada.
9. Compute the average age at childbearing (MAC) for each of the cohorts in Table 6.16. How has MAC changed across cohorts? What is the relationship between change in MAC for cohorts and cohort completed fertility? Graph this relationship.

Table 6.16   Age-specific fertility rates per 1,000 Canadian women, 1895–9 to 2000–5

Year t	Age 15–19	20–24	25–29	30–34	35–39	40–44	45–49	TFR year t	GRR year t	NRR year t	Cohort fertility	Cohort MAC	Period of birth of cohort
2015													1966–70
2010													1961–5
2005	13.7	51.0	97.4	95.8	40.1	6.9	0.3						1956–60
2000	16.3	56.1	97.9	89.9	35.5	6.1	0.3						1951–5
1995	24.5	70.6	109.7	86.8	31.3	4.8	0.2						1946–50
1990	26.9	85.4	140.2	87.5	28.6	3.9	0.1						1941–5
1985	23.7	85.3	125.3	74.6	21.8	3.0	0.1						1936–40
1980	27.6	100.1	129.4	69.3	19.4	3.1	0.2						1931–5
1975	35.3	112.7	131.2	64.4	21.6	4.8	0.4						1926–30
1970	42.8	143.3	147.2	81.8	39.0	11.3	0.9						1921–5
1965	49.3	188.6	181.9	119.4	65.9	22.0	2.0						1916–20
1960	59.8	233.5	224.4	146.2	84.2	28.5	2.4						1911–15
1955	54.2	218.3	215.1	153.8	89.8	32.3	2.9						1906–10
1950	46.0	181.3	200.6	141.3	87.9	30.8	3.0						1901–5
1945	31.6	143.3	166.8	134.3	90.3	33.5	3.7						1896–1900
1940	29.3	130.3	152.6	122.8	81.7	32.7	3.7						1891–5
1935	26.5	112.5	148.5	128.6	92.6	37.3	4.9						1886–90
1930	30.5	143.0	176.0	148.0	106.7	46.6	5.5						1881–5
1925	33.6	138.8	167.5	139.6	99.3	42.5	5.5						1876–80
1920	38.0	165.4	186.0	154.6	112.3	55.5	6.6						
1915	38.2	180.3	225.3	190.3	150.1	68.4	9.0						
1910	37.3	195.2	255.0	215.3	165.7	71.5	10.0						
1905	31.5	190.1	260.1	230.3	170.7	73.2	10.5						
1900	27.0	175.0	270.4	235.3	175.5	78.3	11.1						
1895	26.0	170.4	285.9	270.2	180.3	80.4	12.2						

Note: The fertility rates shown for 1920 are actually those for 1921, and the fertility rates for 2005 are actually for 2004. The diagonal elements represent age-specific fertility rates for a specific birth cohort of women; the row elements are age-specific fertility rates for a given period. Figures up to and including 1985 exclude Newfoundland and Labrador. Age-specific fertility rates for 1895, 1900, 1905, 1910, and 1915 are estimates.

Sources: Henripin (1972): 27, Fig. 2.5; Statistics Canada (2006c, 2002i, 1997); Wadhera and Strachan (1993).

Study Questions

1. Why have some developing countries advanced through the fertility transition fairly quickly and others more slowly? Under what social structural and demographic conditions are long-term fertility declines most likely to occur? Discuss the role of family planning programs in fertility transition in developing countries. What other factors are important?

2. Why did our grandmothers have more children than have more recent generations of Canadian women? Write an essay on this topic.

3. With modernization, the proximate determinants of natural fertility change operate to increase rather than to decrease fertility. Explain this seemingly puzzling relationship, and why in general modernization is associated with fertility declines.

4. For about three decades, fertility in many Western societies and Japan has been at below-replacement level. Explain the social, cultural, and demographic factors underlying this phenomenon. Are there any uniform explanations? Are there any countries in the developed world that are experiencing fertility rates at around the replacement level? What is different about such societies? What is the future of fertility in Western societies?

5. Assume that you are an expert on population dynamics and that a developing country in sub-Saharan Africa experiencing very high fertility and mortality has asked you to advise officials on what they can do to achieve significant fertility reductions over the decade. What would you tell them?

6. Assume that you are a family counsellor and that a young, recently married couple has consulted you about the best strategy for having children and how to space them, given the dual demands of career and family on women and men today. What would you advise this couple? Consider relevant microeconomic theories of fertility decision-making and pertinent research.

7. In Canada today, a few sub-groups maintain relatively high fertility. What explains this fact? Review relevant theories on this subject. Are sub-groups in the population bound to eventually assimilate the fertility patterns of the larger society?

Additional Reading

Agyei-Menshah, Samuel. 1999. *Fertility Decline in Developing Countries, 1960–1997.* Westport, CT: Greenwood.

Bledsoe, Caroline H., Susana Lerner, and Jane I. Guyer. 2000. *Fertility and the Male Life-Cycle in the Era of Fertility Decline.* Oxford: Oxford University Press.

Dalla Zuanna, Gianpiero, and Giuseppe A. Micheli, eds. 2004. *Strong Family and Low Fertility: A Paradox? New Perspectives in Interpreting Contemporary Family and Reproductive Behaviour.* Dortrecht: Kluwer Academic/Springer.

Derosas, Renzo, and Frans van Poppel, eds. 2006. *Religion and the Decline of Fertility in the Western World*. Dortrecht: Springer.

Douglass, Carrie B. 2005. *Barren States: The Population 'Implosion' in Europe*. Oxford: Berg.

Gustafsson, Siv, and Adriaan Kalwij, eds. 2006. *Education and Postponement of Maternity: Economic Analyses for Industrialized Countries*. Dortrecht: Kluwer Academic/Springer.

Harris, Fred. 2006. *The Baby Bust: Who Will Do the Work? Who Will Pay the Taxes?* Lanham, MD: Rowman & Littlefield.

National Research Council . 2001. *Diffusion Processes and Fertility Transition: Selected Perspectives*. Committee on Population. John B. Casterline, ed., Division of Behavioral and Social Sciences and Education. Washington, DC: National Academy.

———. 2003. *Offspring: Human Fertility Behavior in Biodemographic Perspective*. Panel for the Workshop on the Biodemography of Fertility and Family Behavior. Kenneth W. Wachter and Rodolfo A. Bulatao, eds, Committee on Population, Division of Behavioral and Social Sciences and Education. Washington, DC: National Academy.

Rodgers, Joseph L., David C. Rowe, and Warren B. Miller, eds. 2000. *Genetic Influences on Human Fertility and Sexuality*. Boston: Kluwer Academic.

Web Resources

Fertility and other reproductive health data are available for the countries that have been participating in the Demographic and Health Surveys (DHS). Statistical tables and maps can be produced based on data from over 200 surveys in over 75 countries: www.measuredhs.com.

The United Nations Population Division has produced a useful data sheet regarding worldwide contraceptive use. The 2005 wall chart is available at the following address: www.un.org/esa/population/publications/contraceptive2005/WCU2005.htm. Other reports and data on fertility for the countries of the world can also be obtained from the United Nations Population Division website.

Annual birth statistics for Canada may be obtained from the Statistics Canada website: http://statcan.ca/. The annually published *Births* may be downloaded from the following website: www.statcan.ca/english/freepub/84F0210XIE/84F0210XIE2005001.htm.

The Vienna Institute of Demography is an important centre for demographic research and analysis in Europe. The Institute publishes studies on a variety of demographic topics, including fertility: www.oeaw.ac.at/vid/index.html.

Chapter 7

Mortality and Population Health

Introduction

This chapter is concerned with the main concepts, basic measures, and theories of the demographic study of mortality and offers a survey of health and mortality conditions in developed and developing countries. In the most advanced countries, life expectancy is approaching what some scholars believe is the biological limit. Mortality has fallen to such low levels that newborns can expect to live well into their eighth decade of life. Mortality rates for children and for adults under 65 are so low that any improvement in life expectancy relies almost completely on the decline of mortality at older ages.

These low rates of mortality are all the more significant when we consider how recent it was that the average person would not live much beyond his or her twenty-fifth birthday (Acsadi and Nemeskeri, 1970; Coale, 1974). In Sweden, France, and England, mortality rates remained high until the mid-1800s and then fluctuated wildly with outbreaks of disease and famine and with other major societal disruptions. In 1750, the average length of life in these populations ranged between just 25 and 35 years; not until the fourth decade of the twentieth century did life expectancy reach 65 years (Vallin, 2006: 43). Major declines in mortality since then are the product of a general rise in standards of living and advances in modern medicine. Between 1950–5 and 1965–70, the average worldwide life expectancy increased by 9.5 years, from 46.5 to 56.0. This included an increase of 11.3 years, from 40.9 to 52.2, in the less developed regions (Heuveline, 1999: 681).

Indeed, the widespread declines in mortality worldwide since the start of the twentieth century must be considered one of humankind's most important accomplishments. Yet paradoxically, under the generally favourable mortality conditions of today, a portion of the world's population has struggled to keep up in the fight against early death, and in some regions the gains in life expectancy have stagnated or even reversed as a result of massive epidemics of infectious disease exacerbated by widespread poverty and deteriorating living conditions. Two regions stand out in this regard: Africa, where the continuing HIV/AIDS epidemic has reached crisis proportions; and the former Soviet Union, where socioeconomic crises have helped to reverse earlier trends of rising life expectancy.

Determinants of Population Health

Demographers using aggregate-level analyses have carried out extensive research in the area of mortality and health disparities (see, for example, Antonovsky, 1967; Benjamin, 1965; Kitagawa and Hauser, 1973). The more recent literature has tended to emphasize individual observations through cross-sectional and longitudinal surveys (Young, 1999). Both approaches converge on the general assumption that death rates and other mortality measures provide an accurate indication of a population's overall health. The discussion in this chapter adopts this point of view within the context of a *population health perspective*.

The population health perspective recognizes the complex interactions of individual and structural factors in determining health, including the interplay of individual characteristics (including genetics) with social and economic factors (including culture) and physical environments (family, neighbourhood, work, the community, and other important spheres of life). Based on the premise that determinants of health do not exist in isolation from each other, it takes the view that strategies to improve population health must address the entire range of factors that determine health. The population health framework also assumes that societal disparities in health are closely related to disparities in income and wealth, and that health gains can be achieved by focusing interventions not only on the entire population but also on disadvantaged minorities within the larger society (Evans and Stoddart, 1990; Marmot and Wilkinson, 2006; Young, 1999).

Figure 7.1 represents determinants of population health as consisting of structural and individual factors: the physical environment; the social environment; personal health-enhancing or health-eroding behaviours; individual capacity to cope with disease and life challenges; access to and use of health services; and the economic and social well-being of society overall. The factors in this figure are arranged in temporal order, though in reality there are complex

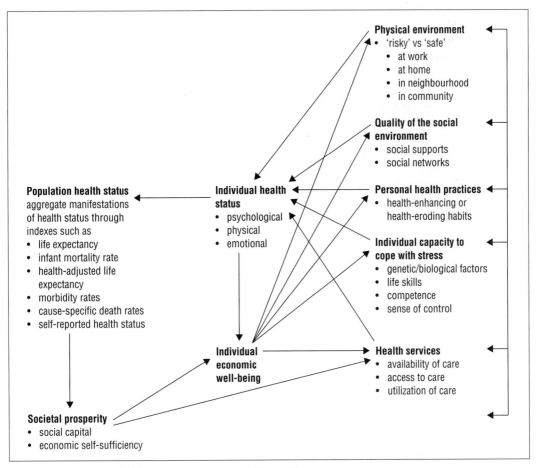

Figure 7.1 A framework of the determinants of population health

Note: Arrows at the right-hand side of the model indicate that all factors are highly correlated.

interactions among them that cannot be easily displayed in graphic form. For example, the stresses associated with living in poverty can lead to unpleasant experiences at work. This in turn can impair one's ability to cope at work and in daily life, leading potentially to unemployment and deeper poverty, with severe consequences for mental and physical health.

A population's health is a crucial determinant of a society's economic prosperity and overall standard of living. Better health, for example, translates into a more productive workforce and thus higher levels of affluence. Societal affluence in turn is key to a society's ability to maintain good health. Having access to economic resources means governments are in a better position to turn wealth into social services like education and health care. An affluent society is also better equipped to provide its citizens with work and opportunities, through which it fosters well-being and better health for the average citizen.

Socioeconomic status is also a key factor in individual health. It is a proven determinant of many conditions that affect individual well-being, including the quality of the physical environment, the extent to which a person has access to social and medical support in times of need, the lifestyle choices one makes (whether they be health-enhancing or health-eroding), and one's capacity to cope with stress and adversity. There is increasing evidence that powerful biochemical and physiological pathways link an individual's socioeconomic experience to vascular conditions over the course of a lifetime, beginning perhaps as early as childhood or even the prenatal period. Unsurprisingly, children born to low-income families are more likely than those born to high-income families to have low birth weights, to eat less-nutritious foods, and to have more difficulty in school. This explains why poor people are likely to get sick more frequently and to die earlier on the average (Caspi et al., 1998; Dong et al., 2004; Duncan et al., 1998; Feinstein, 1993; Finch, 2003; Gortmaker and Wise, 1997; Hayward and Gorman, 2004).

Social environments that support healthy lifestyles have a considerable bearing on health. Support from families, friends, and communities is associated with better health and well-being, while lack of emotional support and low participation in society have negative effects on health. Social stability, social involvement, good working relationships, and belonging to a cohesive community can provide a supportive social context that minimizes exposure to life-threatening risks (Berkman and Breslow, 1983; Egolf et al., 1992; House et al., 1988; Marmot and Wilkinson, 2006; Syme and Berkman, 1976, Berkman and Syme, 1979; Yen and Syme, 1999; Wilkinson, 2005).

The physical environment in which individuals live and work is another important determinant of health. It is well known that poor air and water quality, pollution, and exposure to toxic materials on the job or at home will compromise one's health. Conditions in the human-built environment—homes, workplaces, neighbourhoods, communities, even our roads—play a role as well in either promoting or undermining health (Feinstein, 1993). Clearly, poorly built or badly designed physical environments predispose people to greater risks and adverse conditions through, for example, accidents, abuse, and violence.

To this configuration of factors that affect health we can add biological and genetic endowments. Genetic predispositions can condition a wide range of individual responses to conditions that affect health status (Booth and Neufer, 2005; McIlroy, 2004; Valente et al., 2004). Some people, for instance, are genetically prone to alcoholism and may die prematurely as a result. Evidence of genetic predispositions can in some cases be seen early in life. For example, an infant's birth weight is partly dependent on the family's birth weight history (as a measure of genetic predisposition).

Services designed to maintain and promote good health, prevent disease, and restore health in all sectors of the population, including infants, children, and adults, are essential to the overall health of a population. A robust health care system is at its best when it operates in tandem with a broader framework of health determinants, such as environmental conditions conducive to good health and individual responsibility for limiting risky lifestyle choices (Evans and Stoddard, 1990: 41–5).

Finally, although they are not shown in Figure 7.1, culture and gender are important background factors that may condition the interrelationships shown in this model. Gender is an important determinant because it encompasses an array of socially determined roles, personality traits, attitudes, behaviours, and values, conditioned by primary and secondary socialization (Umberson, 1987); its role as a factor in nearly every other determinant in this figure cannot be underestimated. Like gender, culture can be a predisposing factor in differential health, morbidity, and mortality (MacLachlan, 1997; Masi, 1995; Moore et al., 1987).

Demographic and Sociological Dimensions of Mortality

In demographic terms, mortality refers to the number of events ('deaths') taking place in a given interval in a specific population. The medical definition of 'death' is quite specific: it is the postnatal cessation of vital functions without possibility of resuscitation. Since death can occur only after a live birth, it does not encompass miscarriage, stillbirth, or abortion. Demographers operationally define death as the event described in the medical definition above and verified in writing by a death certificate signed by a licensed physician or medical examiner (or coroner). This means that a person on life-support systems is considered to be alive. Moreover, a person who is missing is assumed to be alive until his or her death has been confirmed (Pressat, 1985: 151).

Sociologically, the decline of the death rate has engendered profound changes across all spheres of the social world. In fact, many of us might not be alive today were it not for novel developments in public health, medicine, and

It has been suggested that the nearness and frequency of death in pre-modern societies contributed to religious belief and fascination with ghosts and communities of the dead. Conversely, the reduced social significance of death in modern society has led to the 'disappearance' of ghosts and belief in an afterlife (Blauner, 1966; Goldscheider, 1971).

standards of living that were introduced in the industrialized world at the start of the twentieth century. White and Preston (1996) determined that about half of the current population would never have been born were it not for significant progress in health and disease prevention made in the early 1900s.

Socially, too, life today would be vastly different had mortality remained at the high levels of the past. For many of us living in post-industrial societies, death is something that occurs only among those in advanced old age, and the experience of losing intimate family members early in one's life is a relatively uncommon occurrence (Uhlenberg, 1980). Try to imagine how, in the past, family life would have been disrupted frequently by the death of an infant, a child, or other loved ones (Ariès, 1974; Gottlieb, 1993; Preston and Haines, 1991). From an individual point of view, the expectation of a long life encourages us to plan for the future, especially for our old age (Preston, 1977). On the other hand, it also encourages feelings of invincibility and complacency. As Ariès (1974) explains,

The certainty of death and the fragility of life are foreign to our existential pessimism. On the contrary, the man of the late Middle Ages was very acutely conscious that he had merely been granted a stay of execution, that this delay would be a brief one, and that death was always present within him, shattering his ambitions and poisoning his pleasures. And that man felt a love of life which we today can scarcely understand, perhaps because of our increased longevity. . . . [Today], [t]echnically, we admit that we might die; we take out insur-

ance on our lives to protect our families from poverty. But really, at heart we feel we are non-mortals. (44–5, 106)

Why Are You Alive?

You have a better chance of living longer today than ever before in human history. It's a fact of modern life that we all take for granted. But have you ever considered your chances of never having been born? What if Mom had died of typhoid as a baby? What if Dad had never been born because *his* father had died young?

Your chances of being here at all were about 50–50. If death rates at the beginning of the [twentieth] century had not changed and all other factors had remained the same, we would be a nation of 139 million people instead of 270 million, say Kevin M. White and Samuel H. Preston, demographers at the University of Pennsylvania. 'Half of the population owes its existence to twentieth-century mortality improvements,' White and Preston wrote. The demographers reached this conclusion by using 'counterfactual projections'. That is, they set up a *what-if* experiment. Think of it as a demographist history of the United States that never happened. What if no significant progress had been made in American public health and medicine after 1900? White and Preston calculated that fully half the people now alive would have died young or would be absent because one of their parents would not have survived to reproductive age.

The increase in American life expectancy in this [the twentieth] century has been amazing. Life expectancy at birth in 1900 was 47.3 years; in 1994, it was 75.6 years. In 1900, fewer than 60 per cent of women could expect to reach the age of 50. In 1992, it was calculated that 95 per cent of women would reach age 50. The baby boomers may now be in the throes of 50-something angst, but they should consider the alternative to suffering through an 'over the hill' party.

In their counterfactual history of the United States, White and Preston recalculated population growth across the century in five-year increments, using the real improvements in lifespan that occurred. The big impacts came early in the century, and the younger age groups experienced the greatest benefits. Since 1950, improvements in survival rates have been slower and have had the greatest impact on the elderly. If the US mortality rate had remained stuck at the 1950 level, the US population would nevertheless be 94 per cent of its size today.

Researchers have made great advances in medicine over the past 100 years, but at least half of us owe our very lives to one big breakthrough: Preston credits the acceptance of the germ theory of disease and the changes it brought to the practice of medicine, the handling of food, and the treatment of water. Simple sanitation was the innovation with the greatest impact on human life in the past century, indeed the past 1,000 years. Knowledge of germ theory is the mighty lever that opened a new philosophy of life for most of us. We can expect to live. We can expect our children to live. The instruments of that optimism are all around us.

Source: Adapted from Fleischman (1999): 230–1.

Basic Measures of Mortality

Crude Death Rate

The crude death rate (CDR) is defined as the number of deaths in a given interval, usually a year, divided by the midpoint population (or an estimate of the mid-year population for non-census years); it is typically expressed per 1,000 population:

$$CDR = \frac{D}{P} \times 1,000$$

where D is the number of deaths observed in the interval, and P refers to the mid-year population.

Demographers commonly compute a three-year average crude death rate to ensure greater stability in the measure by eliminating unusual yearly fluctuations in the number of deaths:

$$CDR = \frac{(D_1 + D_2 + D_3)}{P_2} \times \frac{1}{3}$$

where D_1, D_2, and D_3 represent the number of deaths in three successive years, with year two being the central year. The population at risk is P_2, the mid-year population for the central year.

To illustrate the interpretation and the range of crude death rates, let us consider Table 7.1, which includes death rates for selected countries in 2005. The Canadian rate of 7 per 1,000 population tells us that in 2005 in Canada, there were 7 deaths for every 1,000 people. You will see that there is a wide variation in crude death rates across countries. Countries like Canada, Japan, the United Kingdom, Sweden, and other highly industrialized countries have relatively low rates. The highest crude death rates are found in countries of sub-Saharan Africa—notably Botswana (28 per 1,000) and Sierra Leone (24 per 1,000)—and in parts of Asia.

An interesting fact revealed in this table is that the CDRs of the developed countries are

Table 7.1   Crude death rates per 1,000 population, selected countries (2005)

Country	CDR
Egypt	6
Libya	4
Ghana	10
Nigeria	19
Sierra Leone	24
Zambia	23
Botswana	28
Mexico	5
Canada	7
United States	8
Argentina	8
Brazil	8
Israel	6
Saudi Arabia	3
Afghanistan	22
Thailand	7
China	6
Japan	8
Sweden	10
United Kingdom	10
France	8
Italy	10
Hungary	13
Russia	16

Source: Population Reference Bureau (2005).

actually higher than those of some of the developing countries. For example, Canada's CDR of 7 is higher than Mexico's CDR of 5. This may be surprising, given the vast difference in the two countries' socioeconomic conditions. Similarly, Saudi Arabia shows a lower CDR than Canada and other western European countries included in this table. What this tells us is that these comparisons cannot be taken as a definitive indication of each country's level of mortality. The crude death rate simply measures the total number of deaths divided by the total population; it is insensitive to the effects of age composition, which play an important role in mortality. Consider the fact that the older one is, the greater the likelihood of dying; conversely, the younger one is, the lower the risk of death. As a result, some developing countries have lower crude birth rates because their age compositions are younger than those of more developed countries. Age structure must be taken into account if we are to obtain a clear picture of the true level of mortality in a country or any population of interest, and this leads us to the age-specific death rate.

Age-Specific Death Rate

The age-specific death rate helps us circumvent the confounding effects of age composition on any cross-country comparison of mortality. It is defined as the number of deaths to persons of a given age divided by the mid-year population at risk in that same age category. Age-specific death rates can be calculated for separate age categories. The general formula takes the following form:

$$M_x = \frac{D_x}{P_x} \times 1,000$$

where M_x stands for age-specific death rate, the letter x indexes a given age category, and the terms D_x and P_x correspond to the deaths and the mid-year population for age category x, respectively.

Although it is customary to multiply the age-specific death rates by 1,000, this is not absolutely necessary. In fact, in some applications it is preferable to express the rates per person.

It is important to recognize that the age-specific death rate and the crude death rate are related. The crude death rate is essentially the weighted average of a set of age-specific death rates, where the weights are the proportions of the total population at each age. Stated differently, the crude death rate is the cumulative product of a set of age-specific death rates and an age distribution for a given population. This can be shown using the same definitions of terms as before, except that M_x here refers to age-specific death rate per person.

The numerator of the crude death rate is the

$$CDR = \frac{D}{P} \times 1,000 \qquad (1)$$

$$= \frac{\sum D_x}{P} \times 1,000 \qquad (2)$$

$$= \frac{\sum M_x P_x}{P} \times 1,000 \qquad (3)$$

$$= 1,000 \times \sum \frac{P_x}{P} \times M_x \qquad (4)$$

$$= 1,000 \times \sum w_x M_x \qquad (5)$$

sum (indicated by the Greek letter sigma, Σ) of age-specific deaths divided by the total population (equation 2), which can also be derived by taking the sum of the products of age-specific death rates multiplied by the age-specific populations, as in equation 3. Dividing this sum by the total population produces the crude death rate. The last two expressions say the same thing using different notation (P_x/P is the proportion of population in a given age category). If each age-specific proportion is multiplied by its corresponding death rate, the sum of these products would yield the crude death rate (i.e., equation 4). Equation 5 is the same as 4 but expressed as the sum of products—i.e., the sum of age-specific population weights (w_x) multiplied by age-specific death rates.

Age Pattern of Mortality

The risk of death varies markedly with age (Emlen, 1970; Horiuchi, 2003; Kasteloot and Huang, 2003). If plotted on a graph, the age-specific death rates will form a distinct pattern that is general across all human populations. The pattern is so universal that it may be considered a 'law-like phenomenon'.

It is important to recognize the difference between the *age pattern* of mortality and the *level* of mortality for a population. The former refers to the shape of the pattern of death rates over age, while the latter corresponds to the overall death rate of a population (or some other indicator of mortality, such as life expectancy at birth). The level of mortality is generally lower for advanced countries than it is for poorer nations. This means that if we were to plot the age-specific death rates of an industrialized population and those of a poor developing country, the former would show relatively low age-specific death rates compared to the latter, yet the two lines would, for the most part, have the same basic shape.

According to this age pattern of mortality that is common to all populations, the risk of death is high in the first month after birth but declines during the rest of infancy and childhood and remains low throughout adolescence; it rises in young adulthood but then stabilizes, increasing only slightly until past middle age, when the risk of death begins to intensify with advancing age. These fluctuations in mortality over the lifespan reflect to a large extent changes in human physiological conditions and resistance to disease from early childhood through adulthood.

While the age pattern of mortality applies across all human populations, it does differ in one important respect for pre-transitional and post-transitional populations. Age-specific death rates for pre-transitional societies tend to follow a U-shaped pattern, reflecting exceptionally high mortality in infancy and early childhood, and also in old age. With increasing modernization, the incidence of infant mortality declines. This helps to produce the J-shaped pattern of mortality now common in advanced societies (Horiuchi, 2003: 649; Olshansky and Ault, 1986; Petersen, 2000: 82, 1995).

Figure 7.2a displays the pattern of age-specific mortality for Canadian men and women. Although the two rates follow a similar pattern, mortality rates for men are higher than those for women. On the arithmetic scale this is difficult to distinguish in the ages between early childhood and middle age; for this reason, it is often useful to plot age-specific death rates on the natural logarithm scale (Figure 7.2b).

Infant Mortality Rate and its Components

Infant mortality is defined as death occurring between birth and the end of the first year of life. For analytical purposes, infant deaths are often subdivided into three categories:

- *Early neonatal mortality* includes deaths that occur between birth and the end of the first week of life.

DeMoivre (1667–1754), in his *Treatise of Annuities on Lives*, was the first to propose a mathematical 'law' of mortality. His work, according to Henderson (1915), was a starting point for Gompertz (1825), who developed a mathematical model to trace the physiological process of aging. Observing that the same age patterns of mortality were found in all subgroups of the human population, Gompertz proposed a common underlying biological force. His formula assumed that past the age of 15, mortality increases in geometric progression with advancing age, in effect implying that there is an exponential increase in the probability of dying with age. This relationship, Gompertz reasoned, corresponds to the organism's growing 'inability to withstand destruction' as it ages. Gompertz specified his formula as $q_x = Bc^x$, where q_x is the probability of dying at age x, and B and c are constants to be estimated empirically.

Makeham (1860, 1867) took this formula a step further by adding a constant term to represent causes of death that were not dependent on physiological aging. Thus, $q_x = A + Bc^x$, where A is the risk of dying from 'external' causes of death, such as accidents, violence, and self-inflicted death. Makeham suggested that the term A was especially dominant among wild animal populations and in primitive human societies (Caughley, 1966; Emlen, 1970; Fries and Crapo, 1981: 149; Kormondy, 1969).

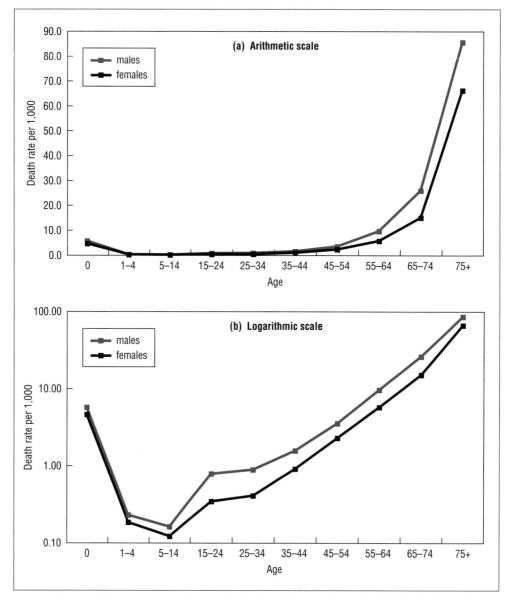

Figure 7.2   Age pattern of mortality for Canadian men and women in 2000, expressed on the arithmetic (a) and logarithmic (b) scales

Source: Based on data from the World Health Organization (2006b).

- *Late neonatal mortality* includes deaths that occur from the eighth day after birth to the end of the twenty-seventh day after birth.

- *Post-neonatal mortality* includes deaths from the twenty-eighth day after birth to the end of the first year.

Early neonatal and late neonatal deaths are sometimes combined under the heading *neonatal mortality*. When calculating infant mortality it is customary to include late fetal deaths (explained below) with early neonatal deaths to form a fourth category of infant mortality, *perinatal mortality*.

Vital statistics agencies in developed countries also collect information on *fetal deaths*. Fetal death is the death of a fetus (or 'product of conception') prior to its complete removal or expulsion from the mother, regardless of the length of the pregnancy. Fetal death includes miscarriages, abortions, and stillbirths. The last of these is often synonymous with the term *late fetal death*, which refers to a death that occurs late in a pregnancy, usually in the twenty-eighth week of gestation or later. 'Miscarriage' is the spontaneous or accidental termination of fetal life early in pregnancy. 'Abortion' is any termination of pregnancy—spontaneous or induced—before the twenty-

eighth week of gestation. An induced abortion is carried out with the intention of terminating a pregnancy; all other abortions are considered spontaneous (McGehee, 2004: 266). The World Health Organization, recognizing that the spontaneous loss of a fetus can occur prior to the twenty-eighth week of gestation, recommends that fetal deaths be classified according to the period of gestation during which they occur:

- **Early fetal mortality** occurs prior to the twentieth week of gestation.
- **Intermediate fetal mortality** occurs between the twentieth and twenty-seventh week of gestation.
- **Late fetal mortality** occurs in the twenty-eighth week of gestation or later. (Gourbin, 2006: 435–6)

Figure 7.3 clarifies the components of infant

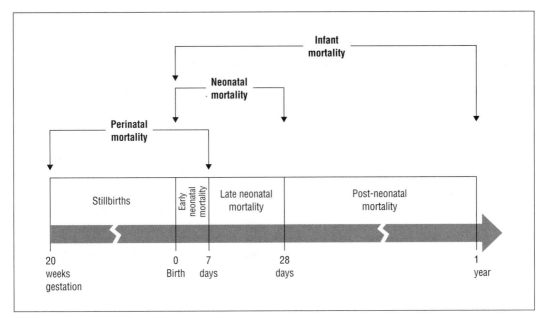

Figure 7.3 Infant mortality and its components

Note: In Canada, stillbirths are fetal deaths that occur after at least 20 weeks of gestation or after attaining a weight of 500 grams.

Source: Adapted from Statistics Canada publication *Demographic and Health Indicators: Presentation and Interpretation*, by Yves Péron and Claude Strohmenger. Catalogue no. 82-543E, p. 195.

mortality. While all of this may sound excessively specific, it is worth noting that not all countries apply a uniform definition of fetal death, and this can cause problems when infant mortality rates are compared (see Chase, 1969; Frisbie, 2005; Gourbin, 2006; Lamb and Siegel, 2004).

The infant mortality rate (IMR) is calculated as the number of infant deaths in a given year divided by the number of live births in the same year; it is usually multiplied by 1,000. Thus, an infant mortality rate of 20 would indicate that for every 1,000 live births in a population, there are 20 infant deaths. The formula is expressed as follows:

$$IMR = \frac{D_0}{B} \times 1,000$$

where D_0 is the number of infant deaths in a given year, and B is the number of live births during the same year.

A drawback of this formula is that it overlooks the fact that a proportion of the infant deaths that occur during a given year are deaths of infants who were born during the preceding year and hence are not part of the same 'universe' of births used to compute the rate. It is possible to make adjustments for this problem (see Barkley, 1958; Shryock and Siegel, 1976). One adjustment relies on having complete information on the number of live births occurring over three calendar years around a central year (i.e., y_{-1}, y, and y_{+1}, where y is the central year) as well as data on all infant deaths taking place over these same three years in accordance with their year of birth (i.e., y_{-1}, y, and y_{+1}). This data layout makes it possible to separate the different infant deaths occurring in the central year y into two parts: those deaths that belong to the birth cohort of one year ago (i.e., y_{-1}), and those that belong to the birth cohort of the current year y. Infants born in year y who die in the next year, y_{+1}, can then be linked to the birth cohort of year y. Typically, if the numbers of infant deaths

Component-specific infant mortality rates can also be computed. The *early neonatal death rate* can be obtained by dividing the infant deaths that occur in the first week of life by the total number of live births in the year. The *late neonatal death rate* is derived by dividing the infant deaths that occur between the end of the first week of life and the end of the first month of life by the total number of live births in the year. The post-neonatal mortality rate is obtained by dividing the number of infant deaths between the end of the first month of life and the end of the first year of life by the total number of live births in the year.

and births are not changing radically from one year to the next, the infant mortality rates computed with the usual and the more refined methods give very similar results.

As Table 7.2 shows, there are wide variations in IMRs across the world, ranging from 172 for Afghanistan to 2.8 for Japan. Barring some notable exceptions (such as Cuba), the developing countries as a whole have higher rates of infant mortality than do the more developed countries. Worldwide, the IMR for 2005 was 54 per 1,000. Among the more developed countries, the rate was just 6 infant deaths per 1,000 live births; among the less developed countries, the IMRs are about 10 times greater on average.

Causes of Death in Infancy

Bourgeois-Pichat (1981 [1951], 1952) proposed that infant deaths could be classified into two major categories, depending on whether they are *endogenous* or *exogenous*. *Endogenous* infant deaths are related to complications arising in the neonatal period. These include congenital anomalies (chromosomal abnormalities, malformations of the heart and central nervous system, deformities of the musculoskeletal system, etc.), complications during delivery, and low birth weight (Kalter, 1990). Because endogenous deaths stem from complications with the newborn's constitu-

Table 7.2 Infant mortality rates per 1,000 live births, selected countries, 2005

Country or region	IMR in 2005
World	54
More developed countries	6
Less developed countries	59
Less developed countries—excl. China	64
Sierra Leone	165
Niger	153
Liberia	142
Angola	139
Canada	5.4
USA	6.6
Mexico	30
Cuba	5.8
Haiti	80
Argentina	16.8
Brazil	27
Saudi Arabia	23
Afghanistan	172
Nepal	64
Philippines	29
China	27
Japan	2.8
Sweden	3.1
United Kingdom	5.2
France	3.9
Germany	4.7
Romania	16.7
Russia	12
Italy	4.8
Spain	3.8
Australia	4.5
New Zealand	5.6

Source: Population Reference Bureau (2005).

tion, they are difficult to control (though advances in medicine are helping to reduce these rates). *Exogenous* deaths occur mainly in the post-neonatal period. They are strongly associated with external factors or situations in the socio-economic environment of the infant, such as exposure to cold or excessive heat, infection, inadequate care, malnutrition, accidents, and even violence (Antonovsky and Bernstein, 1977). Exogenous mortality also accounts for a significant number of deaths to children between the ages of 1 and 4, especially in the developing countries (Pebley, 2003). Poston and Rogers (1985) have shown that endogenous mortality rates predominate during the first 18 days of life, and that curves representing the patterning of day-specific endogenous and exogenous mortality rates converge at around the eighteenth day. This is a significant finding, as it suggests that one cannot safely assume that all infant deaths in the post-neonatal period are exogenous (see also Galley and Woods, 1999; Sowards, 1997).

Antonovsky and Bernstein (1977) have observed that for populations undergoing socioeconomic modernization, declining mortality rates in the general population are typically accompanied by major improvements in mortality rates for post-neonatal infants and for children aged 1–4, yet not for infants in the neonatal period. This differential pattern of mortality decline indicates that improvements to public health, which tend to occur with modernization, have a greater bearing on the causes of post-neonatal and early childhood mortality than on neonatal causes of death, which are mostly endogenous in nature (Gortmaker and Wise, 1997; Kliegman, 1995; Klinger, 1985; Wise, 2003). However, once the infant mortality rate in a population falls to the range of about 20 deaths per 1,000 live births, infant mortality tends to become less clustered in the neonatal period as a result of improved care in the pre-natal, delivery, and postnatal stages (Pebley, 2003).

One of the major causes of deaths in neonates is *low birth weight*, which is usually associated with prematurity. There are different categories of low birth weight:

• **Low birth weight infants** are those whose weight at birth falls between 500 and 2,499 grams.

- *Very low birth weight infants* weigh less than 1,500 grams.
- *Extremely low birth weight infants* are those whose weight at birth is less than 1,000 grams. (Philip, 1995)

Over the past several decades there have been great improvements in the survival rates for low birth weight babies in the industrialized countries, mainly owing to the development of neonatal intensive care units and *exogenous surfactant therapy*, which helps restore normal pulmonary activity in infants with pulmonary functioning complications, a potentially lethal condition in premature or low birth weight babies (*Dorland's Pocket Medical Dictionary*, 1977: 641). In a comprehensive study of changing survival rates for infants of various birth weights in the United States, Philip (1995) discovered that during the 1980s, the gestational age at which there was a 50 per cent survival rate fell from 26 weeks to 24 weeks; this was accompanied by a marked increase in the survival rate for very low birth weight infants.

Despite these very positive outcomes, our success in lowering the mortality probabilities of neonates may be reaching a limit. For any dramatic reduction in neonatal mortality rates to occur, it would be necessary to lower even further the death rate for very low and extremely low birth weight babies. Whether this is possible and to what extent remain open questions (Kliegman, 1995; Philip, 1995).

Cause-Specific Death Rate

A very wide range of diseases, events, and conditions contribute to a population's mortality. In industrialized nations, for instance, two of the deadliest killers are heart disease and cancer, although a large portion of all deaths in these countries can also be attributed to accidents and violence. This kind of information is usually made public by central statistical agencies of individual countries. Globally, the World Health Organization (WHO) regularly collects and publishes mortality statistics by cause of death for each country.

These tabulations are based on a classification system called the *International Classification of Diseases* (ICD), which involves a detailed listing of all known diseases and medical conditions that can result in death. Each disease or condition is assigned a letter and a numerical code. For example, under the latest ICD revision (ICD-10), the code for breast cancer is C50, for prostate cancer C61. Suicide, because it can be committed by several different means, encompasses codes X61 to X88. The letter in front of the code represents a 'chapter', or category, of fatal disease or event. For instance, the first chapter in the ICD-10 is 'Certain Infectious and Parasitic Diseases', which covers cholera, typhoid fever, and other related viral and bacterial illnesses that can cause death. In all, the ICD-10 revision contains 22 chapters, each corresponding to a particular type of disease or external condition. Table 7.3 lists the 22 chap-

Table 7.3 ICD-9 and ICD-10 chapter titles and category ranges

Chapter: ICD-9	Title	Category range	Chapter: ICD-10	Title	Category range
I	Infectious and parasitic diseases	001–139	I	Certain infectious and parasitic diseases	A00–B99
II	Neoplasms	140–239	II	Neoplasms	C00–D48
III	Endocrine, nutritional, and metabolic diseases and immunity disorders	240–279	III	Diseases of the blood and blood-forming organs and certain disorders involving the immune mechanism	D50–D89

(continued)

Table 7.3 (*continued*)

Chapter: ICD-9	Title	Category range	Chapter: ICD-10	Title	Category range
IV	Diseases of blood and blood-forming organs	280–289	IV	Endocrine, nutritional, and metabolic diseases	E00–E90
V	Mental disorders	290–319	V	Mental and behavioural disorders	F00–F99
VI	Diseases of the nervous system and sense organs	320–389	VI	Diseases of the nervous system	G00–G99
VII	Diseases of the circulatory system	390–459	VII	Diseases of the eye and adnexa	H00–H59
VIII	Diseases of the respiratory system	460–519	VIII	Diseases of the ear and mastoid process	H60–H95
IX	Diseases of the digestive system	520–579	IX	Diseases of the circulatory system	I00–I99
X	Diseases of the genitourinary system	580–629	X	Diseases of the respiratory system	J00–J99
XI	Complications of pregnancy, childbirth, and the puerperium	630–679	XI	Diseases of the digestive system	K00–K93
XII	Diseases of the skin and subcutaneous tissue	680–709	XII	Diseases of the skin and subcutaneous tissue	L00–L99
XIII	Diseases of the musculoskeletal system and connective tissue	710–739	XIII	Diseases of the musculoskeletal system and connective tissue	M00–M99
XIV	Congenital anomalies	740–759	XIV	Diseases of the genitourinary system	N00–N99
XV	Certain conditions originating in the perinatal period (excluding stillbirths)	760–779	XV	Pregnancy, childbirth, and the puerperium	O00–O99
XVI	Symptoms, signs, and ill-defined conditions	780–799	XVI	Certain conditions originating in the perinatal period	P00–P96
XVII	external causes, injury, and poisoning	800–999	XVII	Congenital malformations, deformations and chromosomal abnormalities	Q00–Q99
No chapter number	Supplementary classification of external causes of injury and poisoning	E800–E999	XVIII	Symptoms, signs, and abnormal clinical and laboratory findings, not elsewhere classified	R00–R99
No chapter number	Supplementary classification of factors influencing health status and contact with health services	V01–V82	XIX	Injury, poisoning and certain other consequences of external causes	S00–T98
No corresponding chapter			XX	External causes of morbidity and mortality	V01–Y98
No corresponding chapter			XXI	Factors influencing health status and contact with health services	Z00–Z99
No corresponding chapter			XXII	Codes for special purposes	U00–U99

Source: Adapted from Statistics Canada publication *Comparability of* ICD-10 *and* ICD-9 *for Mortality Statistics in Canada.* Catalogue no. 84-548-XIE, pp. 44–5.

ters and the 17 chapters contained in the previous revision, ICD-9.

Since mortality data are usually tabulated by age and sex, it is possible to compute not just cause-specific death rates but also age–sex–cause-specific death rates. The general form of the cause-specific death rate is

$$\text{cause-specific death rate} = \frac{D_c}{P} \times 100{,}000$$

where D_c is deaths due to a particular disease or 'cause' c, occurring in the population during a specified interval, and P is the mid-year population exposed to the risk of dying from disease or condition c in the interval; the constant 100,000 is used by convention when computing cause-specific death rates.

In some circumstances it may be necessary to compute a *cause-specific death ratio* in the form

$$\frac{D_c}{D} \times 100$$

where the numerator is the number of deaths from a given cause, and the denominator is the total number of deaths.

The constant value of 100 allows us to calculate this as a true percentage (i.e., the percentage of deaths out of the total number of deaths that is attributable to cause c). Thus, unlike the cause-specific death rate, which is a measure of incidence (how many deaths from cause c occur per 100,000 population), the cause-specific death ratio tells us what percentage of all deaths are attributable to cause c. For instance, in Canada, about 37 per cent of all deaths in a given year are due to diseases of the circulatory system, and another 27 per cent are caused by cancer; this means that the remaining causes account for about 36 per cent of all deaths.

The cause-specific death rate is really just a crude death rate for a given cause of death. It can easily be expanded to include age, sex, and other characteristics. To illustrate, in Canada in 1995, the number of people aged 55–64 who died from suicide and self-inflicted injury was 378, including 284 men and 94 women. The total mid-year population for this age group was 2,510,000, including 1,240,000 men and 1,270,000 women. So the suicide-specific death rates for men and women separately and for the age category overall would be as follows:

$$\text{suicide death rate}_{\text{men 55–64 in 1995}}$$
$$= \frac{284}{1{,}240{,}000} \times 100{,}000 = 22.90$$

$$\text{suicide death rate}_{\text{women 55–64 in 1995}}$$
$$= \frac{94}{1{,}270{,}000} \times 100{,}000 = 7.40$$

$$\text{overall suicide death rate}_{\text{age 55–64 in 1995}}$$
$$= \frac{378}{2{,}510{,}000} \times 100{,}000 = 15.06$$

Figure 7.4 shows that the age pattern of mortality varies by cause of death. Compare, for example, the graphs of neoplasms (cancers) with suicide and motor vehicle accidents. They are quite different.

The Life Table

Basic Description of the Life Table

Life tables are used frequently in the biological and social sciences and in many applied industrial situations. For demographers, the life table is a tool for describing a population's mortality using period cross-sectional, age-specific death rates. In this sense, the life table describes the survival experience of a fictional (or *synthetic*) cohort subjected to the current age-specific death rates of an actual population over the cohort's imagined lifetime. This is generally referred to as the *period life table*. A *cohort* (or *generational*) *life table* is computed from historical data for a birth cohort that was born many years ago and is now extinct (see, for

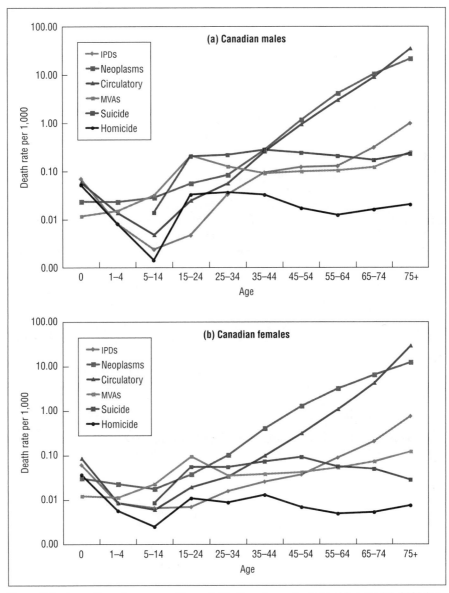

Figure 7.4   Age pattern of cause-specific mortality, Canadian males (a) and females (b), 2000 (logarithmic scale)

Note: IPDs are infectious-parasitic diseases.

Source: Author's computations based on data from the World Health Organization (2006b).

example, Bourbeau, Legaré, and Émond, 1997).

In technical terms, a life table is a hypothetical population of 100,000 newborn babies, exposed to the prevailing age-specific mortality schedule of an actual population. We can trace the lives of the 100,000 from birth to death, and in this way we are able to see how the hypothetical population experiences age-specific prob-

The life table was introduced by John Graunt (1620–74) in his *Natural and Political Observations Made upon the Bills of Mortality*, published in 1662. Early refinements of Graunt's model (made by Gottfried Leibniz (1646–1716), Edmund Halley (1656–1742), William Kersseboom (1691–1771), Nicolaas Struyck (1686–1769), and Antonie Déparcieux (1703–68), among others) were all based simply on the numbers of deaths by age, as the total population at risk was not known. The first modern life table using age-specific death rates was devised by Peter Wargentin (1717–83) in 1766 (Guillot, 2003b: 601).

contains the life tables for men and women in Canada in 2001, arranged by *single years of age.* We can also compute *abridged life tables*, which divide the population into five-year age groups, except for infants, those aged 1–4, and those in the terminal open-ended age group (95+). (Abridged life tables are featured in the exercise section at the end of this chapter.) As a period life table, Table 7.4 applies only to the period from which the age-specific death rates were taken (i.e., 2000–2).

One of the most frequently used measures derived from the life table is *life expectancy*. Life expectancy is the average number of years of life remaining for someone aged x, where x may represent any age category in the life table, from birth to some upper limit (for example, 110). Let's suppose we wanted to determine the life expectancy of a newborn baby boy. Using

abilities of death and survival as it passes through age and calendar time (see Figure 7.5). Table 7.4

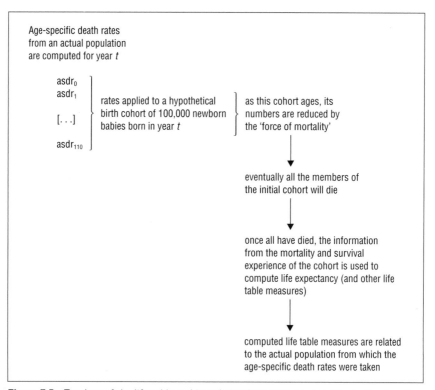

Figure 7.5 Typology of the life table and its relationship to the age-specific death rates of an actual population

Table 7.4 Life table for Canadian males and females, 2000–2

Age (x)	Proportion of persons alive at beginning of age interval dying during interval (q_x)		Of 100,000 born alive: Number living at beginning of age interval (l_x)		Number dying during age interval (d_x)		Stationary population (person-years lived): In the age interval (L_x)		In this and all subsequent age intervals (T_x)		Average number of years of life remaining at beginning of age interval (e_x^0)	
	Male	Female	Male	Female	Male	Female	Male	Female	Male	Female	Male	Female
0	0.005770	0.004670	100,000	100,000	577	467	99,486	99,589	7,691,802	8,203,072	76.92	82.03
1	0.000350	0.000350	99,423	99,533	35	35	99,405	99,514	7,592,316	8,103,483	76.36	81.41
2	0.000210	0.000200	99,388	99,498	21	20	99,376	99,486	7,492,911	8,003,969	75.39	80.44
3	0.000210	0.000150	99,367	99,478	21	15	99,356	99,471	7,393,535	7,904,483	74.41	79.46
4	0.000200	0.000120	99,346	99,463	20	12	99,336	99,456	7,294,179	7,805,012	73.42	78.47
5	0.000170	0.000100	99,326	99,451	16	10	99,318	99,445	7,194,843	7,705,556	72.44	77.48
6	0.000130	0.000080	99,310	99,441	13	9	99,303	99,437	7,095,525	7,606,111	71.45	76.49
7	0.000090	0.000070	99,297	99,432	9	7	99,293	99,429	6,996,222	7,506,674	70.46	75.50
8	0.000080	0.000070	99,288	99,425	8	7	99,284	99,421	6,896,929	7,407,245	69.46	74.50
9	0.000080	0.000070	99,280	99,418	8	7	99,276	99,415	6,797,645	7,307,824	68.47	73.51
10	0.000100	0.000090	99,272	99,411	10	9	99,267	99,407	6,698,369	7,208,409	67.48	72.51
11	0.000100	0.000090	99,262	99,402	10	8	99,257	99,398	6,599,102	7,109,002	66.48	71.52
12	0.000150	0.000130	99,252	99,394	15	13	99,244	99,387	6,499,845	7,009,604	65.49	70.52
13	0.000230	0.000160	99,237	99,381	23	15	99,225	99,374	6,400,601	6,910,217	64.50	69.53
14	0.000340	0.000200	99,214	99,366	34	20	99,197	99,356	6,301,376	6,810,843	63.51	68.54
15	0.000460	0.000240	99,180	99,346	45	24	99,158	99,333	6,202,179	6,711,487	62.53	67.56
16	0.000570	0.000280	99,135	99,322	56	28	99,107	99,308	6,103,021	6,612,154	61.56	66.57
17	0.000660	0.000310	99,079	99,294	65	31	99,047	99,278	6,003,914	6,512,846	60.60	65.59
18	0.000720	0.000330	99,014	99,263	72	33	98,978	99,246	5,904,867	6,413,568	59.64	64.61
19	0.000780	0.000340	98,942	99,230	76	33	98,904	99,214	5,805,889	6,314,322	58.68	63.63
20	0.000820	0.000340	98,866	99,197	81	34	98,825	99,180	5,706,985	6,215,108	57.72	62.65

(continued)

Table 7.4 (continued)

| Age (x) | Proportion of persons at beginning of age interval dying during interval (q_x) | | Of 100,000 born alive: | | | | | | Stationary population (person-years lived): | | | | Average number of years of life remaining at beginning of age interval (e^0_x) | |
| | | | Number living at beginning of age interval (l_x) | | Number dying during age interval (d_x) | | In the age interval (L_x) | | In this and all subsequent age intervals (T_x) | | | | | |
	Male	Female	Male	Female	Male	Female	Male	Female	Male	Female			Male	Female
21	0.000850	0.000340	98,785	99,163	85	33	98,742	99,146	5,608,160	6,115,928			56.77	61.68
22	0.000870	0.000340	98,700	99,130	85	33	98,658	99,114	5,509,418	6,016,782			55.82	60.70
23	0.000870	0.000330	98,615	99,097	86	33	98,571	99,080	5,410,760	5,917,668			54.87	59.72
24	0.000850	0.000330	98,529	99,064	85	33	98,487	99,047	5,312,189	5,818,588			53.92	58.74
25	0.000830	0.000330	98,444	99,031	81	32	98,404	99,015	5,213,702	5,719,541			52.96	57.76
26	0.000810	0.000330	98,363	98,999	79	33	98,323	98,982	5,115,298	5,620,526			52.00	56.77
27	0.000800	0.000330	98,284	98,966	79	33	98,244	98,950	5,016,975	5,521,544			51.05	55.79
28	0.000820	0.000350	98,205	98,933	81	34	98,164	98,916	4,918,731	5,422,594			50.09	54.81
29	0.000840	0.000370	98,124	98,899	82	36	98,083	98,881	4,820,567	5,323,678			49.13	53.83
30	0.000880	0.000390	98,042	98,863	86	39	97,999	98,843	4,722,484	5,224,797			48.17	52.85
31	0.000910	0.000420	97,956	98,824	90	42	97,911	98,803	4,624,485	5,125,954			47.21	51.87
32	0.000960	0.000460	97,866	98,782	94	45	97,819	98,760	4,526,574	5,027,151			46.25	50.89
33	0.001000	0.000500	97,772	98,737	97	50	97,724	98,711	4,428,755	4,928,391			45.30	49.91
34	0.001050	0.000550	97,675	98,687	102	54	97,623	98,660	4,331,031	4,829,680			44.34	48.94
35	0.001100	0.000610	97,573	98,633	108	60	97,519	98,603	4,233,408	4,731,020			43.39	47.97
36	0.001160	0.000670	97,465	98,573	113	66	97,409	98,539	4,135,889	4,632,417			42.43	46.99
37	0.001230	0.000730	97,352	98,507	120	72	97,293	98,471	4,038,480	4,533,878			41.48	46.03
38	0.001320	0.000790	97,232	98,435	128	78	97,168	98,397	3,941,187	4,435,407			40.53	45.06
39	0.001410	0.000850	97,104	98,357	137	83	97,035	98,315	3,844,019	4,337,010			39.59	44.09
40	0.001520	0.000920	96,967	98,274	147	91	96,893	98,229	3,746,984	4,238,695			38.64	43.13
41	0.001640	0.000990	96,820	98,183	159	97	96,740	98,134	3,650,091	4,140,466			37.70	42.17
42	0.001780	0.001090	96,661	98,086	173	107	96,575	98,033	3,553,351	4,042,332			36.76	41.21
43	0.001950	0.001200	96,488	97,979	187	117	96,395	97,920	3,456,776	3,944,299			35.83	40.26

(continued)

Table 7.4   (continued)

Age (x)	Proportion of persons alive at beginning of age interval dying during interval (q_x)		Of 100,000 born alive: Number living at beginning of age interval (l_x)		Number dying during age interval (d_x)		Stationary population (person-years lived): In the age interval (L_x)		In this and all subsequent age intervals (T_x)		Average number of years of life remaining at beginning of age interval (e^0_x)	
	Male	Female	Male	Female	Male	Female	Male	Female	Male	Female	Male	Female
44	0.002130	0.001320	96,301	97,862	205	129	96,198	97,797	3,360,381	3,846,379	34.89	39.30
45	0.002330	0.001450	96,096	97,733	224	142	95,984	97,662	3,264,183	3,748,582	33.97	38.36
46	0.002550	0.001600	95,872	97,591	244	156	95,750	97,513	3,168,199	3,650,920	33.05	37.41
47	0.002790	0.001760	95,628	97,435	267	171	95,495	97,350	3,072,449	3,553,407	32.13	36.47
48	0.003040	0.001930	95,361	97,264	290	187	95,216	97,170	2,976,954	3,456,057	31.22	35.53
49	0.003310	0.002100	95,071	97,077	314	204	94,914	96,975	2,881,738	3,358,887	30.31	34.60
50	0.003600	0.002290	94,757	96,873	341	222	94,587	96,761	2,786,824	3,261,912	29.41	33.67
51	0.003940	0.002510	94,416	96,651	372	243	94,230	96,530	2,692,237	3,165,151	28.51	32.75
52	0.004340	0.002760	94,044	96,408	408	266	93,840	96,275	2,598,007	3,068,621	27.63	31.83
53	0.004810	0.003050	93,636	96,142	450	293	93,411	95,996	2,504,167	2,972,346	26.74	30.92
54	0.005330	0.003370	93,186	95,849	497	323	92,938	95,687	2,410,756	2,876,350	25.87	30.01
55	0.005900	0.003720	92,689	95,526	547	355	92,415	95,349	2,317,818	2,780,663	25.01	29.11
56	0.006540	0.004100	92,142	95,171	603	390	91,841	94,976	2,225,403	2,685,314	24.15	28.22
57	0.007260	0.004510	91,539	94,781	665	427	91,207	94,568	2,133,562	2,590,338	23.31	27.33
58	0.008050	0.004940	90,874	94,354	731	466	90,508	94,121	2,042,355	2,495,770	22.47	26.45
59	0.008900	0.005380	90,143	93,888	803	505	89,742	93,636	1,951,847	2,401,649	21.65	25.58
60	0.009820	0.005870	89,340	93,383	877	548	88,901	93,109	1,862,105	2,308,013	20.84	24.72
61	0.010850	0.006410	88,463	92,835	960	595	87,983	92,538	1,773,204	2,214,904	20.04	23.86
62	0.011980	0.007040	87,503	92,240	1,048	649	86,979	91,915	1,685,221	2,122,366	19.26	23.01
63	0.013210	0.007740	86,455	91,591	1,142	709	85,884	91,236	1,598,242	2,030,451	18.49	22.17
64	0.014510	0.008500	85,313	90,882	1,239	772	84,693	90,496	1,512,358	1,939,215	17.73	21.34
65	0.015930	0.009330	84,074	90,110	1,339	841	83,405	89,689	1,427,665	1,848,719	16.98	20.52
66	0.017520	0.010260	82,735	89,269	1,449	915	82,010	88,812	1,344,260	1,759,030	16.25	19.70

(continued)

Table 7.4 (continued)

Age (x)	Proportion of persons alive at beginning of age interval dying during interval (q_x)		Of 100,000 born alive: Number living at beginning of age interval (l_x)		Number dying during age interval (d_x)		Stationary population (person-years lived): In the age interval (L_x)		In this and all subsequent age intervals (T_x)		Average number of years of life remaining at beginning of age interval (e^0_x)	
	Male	Female	Male	Female	Male	Female	Male	Female	Male	Female	Male	Female
67	0.019300	0.011310	81,286	88,354	1,570	999	80,501	87,854	1,262,250	1,670,218	15.53	18.90
68	0.021240	0.012430	79,716	87,355	1,693	1,086	78,870	86,812	1,181,749	1,582,364	14.82	18.11
69	0.023290	0.013620	78,023	86,269	1,817	1,175	77,115	85,682	1,102,879	1,495,552	14.14	17.34
70	0.025550	0.014930	76,206	85,094	1,947	1,271	75,232	84,458	1,025,764	1,409,870	13.46	16.57
71	0.028100	0.016450	74,259	83,823	2,086	1,378	73,216	83,134	950,532	1,325,412	12.80	15.81
72	0.031040	0.018230	72,173	82,445	2,240	1,503	71,053	81,694	877,316	1,242,278	12.16	15.07
73	0.034290	0.020190	69,933	80,942	2,398	1,635	68,734	80,124	806,263	1,160,584	11.53	14.34
74	0.037790	0.022300	67,535	79,307	2,552	1,768	66,258	78,423	737,529	1,080,460	10.92	13.62
75	0.041650	0.024670	64,983	77,539	2,707	1,913	63,629	76,582	671,271	1,002,037	10.33	12.92
76	0.045990	0.027420	62,276	75,626	2,864	2,074	60,844	74,589	607,642	925,455	9.76	12.24
77	0.050910	0.030660	59,412	73,552	3,025	2,255	57,899	72,425	546,798	850,866	9.20	11.57
78	0.056310	0.034240	56,387	71,297	3,175	2,441	54,799	70,076	488,899	778,441	8.67	10.92
79	0.062100	0.038070	53,212	68,856	3,305	2,621	51,560	67,546	434,100	708,365	8.16	10.29
80	0.068460	0.042400	49,907	66,235	3,417	2,809	48,198	64,830	382,540	640,819	7.67	9.67
81	0.075550	0.047480	46,490	63,426	3,512	3,011	44,734	61,920	334,342	575,989	7.19	9.08
82	0.083530	0.053540	42,978	60,415	3,590	3,235	41,183	58,798	289,608	514,069	6.74	8.51
83	0.092140	0.060680	39,388	57,180	3,629	3,470	37,573	55,445	248,425	455,271	6.31	7.96
84	0.101290	0.068720	35,759	53,710	3,623	3,691	33,948	51,865	210,852	399,826	5.90	7.44
85	0.111350	0.077550	32,136	50,019	3,578	3,879	30,347	48,080	176,904	347,961	5.50	6.96
86	0.122680	0.087030	28,558	46,140	3,504	4,015	26,806	44,132	146,557	299,881	5.13	6.50
87	0.135660	0.097040	25,054	42,125	3,398	4,088	23,355	40,081	119,751	255,749	4.78	6.07
88	0.150050	0.107670	21,656	38,037	3,250	4,095	20,031	35,990	96,396	215,668	4.45	5.67

(continued)

Table 7.4 (continued)

Age (x)	Proportion of persons alive at beginning of age interval dying during interval (q_x)		Of 100,000 born alive: Number living at beginning of age interval (l_x)		Number dying during age interval (d_x)		Stationary population (person-years lived): In the age interval (L_x)		In this and all subsequent age intervals (T_x)		Average number of years of life remaining at beginning of age interval (e^o_x)	
	Male	Female	Male	Female	Male	Female	Male	Female	Male	Female	Male	Female
89	0.165580	0.118990	18,406	33,942	3,047	4,039	16,882	31,922	76,365	179,678	4.15	5.29
90	0.182640	0.130880	15,359	29,903	2,806	3,914	13,956	27,946	59,483	147,756	3.87	4.94
91	0.201600	0.143220	12,553	25,989	2,530	3,722	11,288	24,128	45,527	119,810	3.63	4.61
92	0.222830	0.155880	10,023	22,267	2,234	3,471	8,906	20,532	34,239	95,682	3.42	4.30
93	0.220860	0.170870	7,789	18,796	1,720	3,212	6,930	17,190	25,333	75,150	3.25	4.00
94	0.238670	0.186800	6,069	15,584	1,448	2,911	5,344	14,129	18,403	57,960	3.03	3.72
95	0.257540	0.203760	4,621	12,673	1,190	2,582	4,026	11,382	13,059	43,831	2.83	3.46
96	0.277510	0.221770	3,431	10,091	952	2,238	2,954	8,972	9,033	32,449	2.63	3.22
97	0.298580	0.240830	2,479	7,853	741	1,891	2,109	6,908	6,079	23,477	2.45	2.99
98	0.320770	0.260940	1,738	5,962	557	1,556	1,460	5,184	3,970	16,569	2.28	2.78
99	0.344060	0.282090	1,181	4,406	406	1,243	977	3,784	2,510	11,385	2.13	2.58
100	0.368460	0.304250	775	3,163	286	962	632	2,682	1,533	7,601	1.98	2.40
101	0.393960	0.327400	489	2,201	193	721	393	1,841	901	4,919	1.84	2.23
102	0.420530	0.351510	296	1,480	124	520	234	1,220	508	3,078	1.71	2.08
103	0.448150	0.376510	172	960	77	361	133	779	274	1,858	1.60	1.94
104	0.476780	0.402370	95	599	45	241	72	478	141	1,079	1.48	1.80
105	0.506370	0.429020	50	358	26	154	38	281	69	601	1.38	1.68
106	0.536870	0.456380	24	204	13	93	17	158	31	320	1.29	1.57
107	0.568220	0.484390	11	111	6	54	9	84	14	162	1.20	1.46
108	0.600360	0.512960	5	57	3	29	3	43	5	78	1.11	1.36
109	0.633200	0.542000	2	28	1	15	1	20	2	35	1.04	1.27

Note: The function p_x is not shown because it is easily derivable from the q_x column by taking $1-q_x$ for each age category.
Source: Adapted from Statistics Canada publication *Life Tables: Canada, Provinces and Territories, 2000 to 2002*. Catalogue no. 84-537-XIE.

Assumptions of the Life Table

There are five inherent assumptions underlying life tables:

1. The life table is a hypothetical population that is closed to migration; as a result, births and deaths are the only demographic processes in this population.
2. Because the life table does not take migration into account, the crude death rate and the crude birth rate are identical in this population, and therefore the rate of natural increase will always be zero (because 100,000 people are born, and the same 100,000 people will eventually die). The life table is thus a *stationary population*, meaning that it has stable, unchanging annual age-specific mortality rates, with unchanging numbers of births (i.e., 100,000).
3. The number of births in the life table population is conventionally set at 100,000; this is called the *radix* of the life table.
4. The birth cohort of 100,000 dies according to a predetermined schedule of age-specific death rates, taken from an actual population.
5. In most practical cases, it is assumed that the distribution of deaths is uniform within every age category except for infancy, early childhood, and very old age, where the distribution of deaths is clearly not uniform.

Source: Chiang (1984); Shryock and Siegel (1976).

Canada's mortality rates for 2005, we would first compute the 2005 age-specific death rates for males, and then from these rates generate the corresponding life table. We could then consult the life table for the life expectancy figure corresponding to male infants. We might find that, on the basis of 2005 death rates, the life expectancy for a newborn baby boy in Canada is 77 years (Population Reference Bureau, 2005). This tells us that on the average, a male born in 2005 can expect to live 77 years, assuming that current death rates remain unchanged.

It is important to note that although it is an artificial construct, the life table tells us something very useful about the population upon which it is based. Life tables are particularly useful for comparing mortality across populations or sub-groups within a population having different age–sex compositions. In fact, because all life tables start out with the same number of hypothetical babies (i.e., 100,000), the life table

standardizes for age-compositional differences, which allows for better cross-population comparison of mortality and survival probabilities.

Life Table Functions

As we have seen, age-specific death rates are used to generate the life table. Once we have computed age-specific death rates for a population (usually denoted as m_x), we can derive a number of life table functions (i.e., columns) mathematically:

- q_x, the conditional probability of dying within a given age interval, or the proportion of persons alive at the beginning of an age interval who will die during the interval before attaining the next birthday;
- p_x, the probability of those at age x surviving to their next birthday (i.e., $1 - q_x$);
- l_x, the number, out of 100,000 hypothetical people born alive, of persons alive at the

beginning of age interval x (this column of the life table is called *the survivorship function*);

- d_x, the number, out of 100,000 hypothetical people born alive, of deaths during age interval x;
- L_x, the combined number, out of 100,000 hypothetical people born alive, of person-years lived in the age interval x;
- T_x, the number, out of 100,000 hypothetical people born alive, of person-years lived in the age interval x and subsequent age intervals (this essentially measures the number of person-years left to be lived by the cohort, given its current age, x); and
- e^0_x, expectation of life, or the average number of years of life remaining at the beginning of age interval x (i.e., T_x/l_x).

Figure 7.6 illustrates four stylized life table functions: q_x, l_x, e^0_x, and d_x.

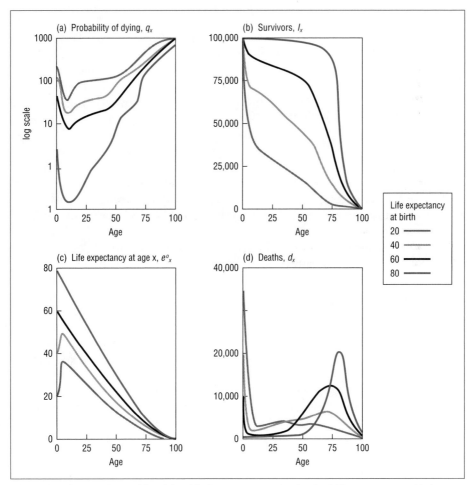

Figure 7.6 Stylized shape of four life table functions at varying levels of life expectancy at birth

Note: Values are plotted for four life tables from the Coale-Demeny series (region West) for females with life expectancies at birth of 20, 40, 60, and 80 years (see Coale and Demeny, 1983).

Source: Pressat (1985): 127. Reprinted by permission of Blackwell Publishing.

Mortality Change through History

For much of human history, life was punctuated by famine, war, and repeated waves of epidemic diseases (Galloway, 1986; Schofield, Reher, and Bideau, 1991; Vallin, 2006). However, since the mid-1700s, apart from periodic setbacks, life expectancy has continued to rise since the mid-1700s, and in virtually all parts of the world the gains in life expectancy made over the twentieth century have exceeded all earlier gains that had been achieved since prehistoric times (Acsadi and Nemeskeri, 1970: 97; Fogel, 2004a; Preston, 1977: 165; Schultz, 1993). The dramatic increases in life expectancy over the course of the twentieth century can be attributed to the fact that degenerative causes of death have largely replaced deaths caused by infectious and pathogenic diseases.

Epidemiological Transition

In 1971, Omran presented a systematic account of the shifting historical pattern of disease and mortality experienced in the West. His theory described the complex change in patterns of health and disease, and focused on the interactions between these patterns and their demographic, economic, and sociological determinants and consequences (Omran, 1971: 510). According to Omran's theory, societies as they modernize experience a gradual change in their patterns of disease and mortality. Typically they move from a long period in which infectious and parasitic diseases (such as cholera, typhus, and smallpox) along with famine, pestilence, and war are the dominant agents of premature death, to a stage in which chronic and degenerative diseases (such as cancer and heart disease) become the leading killers. Omran (1971) identified three stages of epidemiological change, outlined in Figure 7.7 and described below.

The Age of Famine and Pestilence (Prehistory to c.1750)

From prehistory until roughly the mid-eighteenth century, the pattern of population growth was cyclic, with minute net increases. Mortality and fertility rates, fluctuating radically from year to year, were both very high, accounting for very little natural increase. The population during this period was predominantly rural, with a 'few crowded, unsanitary, war-famine-epidemic ridden cities of small and medium size' (Omran, 1971). Society was traditional, with a fatalistic orientation sustained by rigid, hierarchical sociopolitical structures. The economy, based on an agrarian system, was heavily dependent on manual-labour-intensive production that was susceptible to interruptions caused by debilitative diseases. The standards of living were very low. Public and private spaces were fouled by grossly unsanitary conditions, and most of the population depended on food of poor quality and frequently in very short supply.

Children and women in the fertility years were most adversely affected by these conditions. Life expectancy at birth fluctuated between 20 and 40 years, and infant and childhood mortality was very high (200–300 infant deaths per 1,000 births). Women in their adolescent and reproductive years were at higher risk of death than were men, but at lower risk in older ages. Mortality was higher in urban than in rural areas, and the leading causes of death were wars; epidemic scourges; endemic, parasitic, and deficiency diseases; pneumonia-diarrhea-malnutrition complex in children; and tuberculosis-puerperal-malnutrition complex in females. Widespread famine and severe malnutrition underlay disease and death from most other causes. The primary community health problems—epidemics, famine, malnutrition, childhood diseases, and maternal death (death as a consequence of pregnancy and/or childbirth)—were all aggravated by environmental problems, including contaminated

Demographic Transition	Epidemiological Transition
Stage 1: Age of Pestilence and Famine	
High death rate High birth rate Low growth rate	(a) High and fluctuating mortality (b) Dominance of infectious and parasitic diseases as causes of mortality (c) Low life expectancy
Stage 2: Age of Receding Pandemics	
Low death rate High birth rate High growth rate	(a) Accelerated declines in mortality (b) Shifts from infectious and parasitic diseases mortality to degenerative disease mortality (c) Rising life expectancy
Stage 3: Age of Degenerative and Man-Made Diseases	
Low death rate Low birth rate Low growth rate	(a) Continuation of mortality declines and its eventual approach to stability at low levels (b) Dominance of degenerative disease mortality, caused by aging, changing lifestyle, and deteriorating environment (c) Further rise in life expectancy

Figure 7.7 Demographic-epidemiological transitions: A brief description of the stages

Source: Dhruva Nagnur and M. Nagrodski (1990), 'Epidemiological Transition in the Context of Demographic Change: The Evolution of Canadian Mortality Patterns' *Canadian Studies in Population* 17, 1: 1–24.

water and food, poor housing, disease-carrying insects and rodents, and lack of personal hygiene. There was no health care system and few decisive therapies; people relied mainly on indigenous healing and witchcraft.

The Age of Receding Pandemics (*c.*1750 to the early 1920s)

Omran (1971) saw the second stage, characterized by receding pandemics, divided into early and late phases. The early phase ushered in the preconditions for mortality decline and improved health in society. Improvements in agriculture and land use were coupled with modest developments in transportation and communication networks, which encouraged the process of early industrialization. Standards of living remained quite low but began to improve as more effective agricultural methods (e.g., crop rotation and new technology to enhance yields) contributed to better nutrition and reduced death from starvation. Mortality remained high but showed signs of declining as fluctuations became less pronounced. Overall life expectancy rose to the mid-20s and early 30s, though women were still at high risk of dying in the adolescent and fertile years. Infant and childhood mortality were also still high, and urban mortality remained higher than rural. The leading causes of death were epidemic scourges, childhood and maternal complexes (especially smallpox in children), and endemic, parasitic, and deficiency diseases. Tuberculosis peaked with industrialization and was especially virulent in young women. Heart disease remained low. There was still no proper health care system, and hospitals were seen as 'death traps'. However, people began to benefit from gradual improvements in personal hygiene and nutrition.

The late part of this period was marked by explosive population growth due to a sustained pattern of mortality decline coupled with high fertility and a predominantly young population concentrated more and more in cities. Continued improvement in agriculture practices meant greater availability of food and better nutrition, while advances in sanitation and hygiene (including water filtration and garbage removal) and recognition of the importance of workers' health created healthier conditions everywhere except in city slums. The life expectancy at birth gradually rose to 30 or 40 years. Declines in mortality favoured children under 15 and women in the reproductive ages, while infant mortality dropped below 150 per 1,000 births. Proportionate mortality of those aged 50 or over increased to close to 50 per cent. Pandemics of infection, malnutrition, and childhood diseases receded, and plagues largely disappeared, in spite of outbreaks of cholera. The introduction of the smallpox vaccine for children in the late 1800s meant that adults became the primary sufferers of this illness. Infection remained the leading cause of death, but non-infectious diseases, including heart disease and cancer, began to become more significant. Death from starvation became rare, and many deficiency diseases such as scurvy began to disappear.

The Age of Human-Made and Degenerative Causes of Death (early 1920s to the 1960s)

In sharp contrast to earlier stages, populations in the third stage of the epidemiological transition enjoyed relatively high life expectancy (in the range of 70 years or more), low infant mortality rates (below 25 per 1,000 live births), low maternal death rates, and high conditional probabilities of survival by age. Crude death rates declined rapidly to below 20 per 1,000 population, though the rate of decline slowed with time. Similarly, fertility dropped to below 20 per 1,000 with the occasional rise (e.g., dur-

ing the post-war baby boom). A progressive aging of the population meant that more people—especially women—survived to middle and old age.

This period saw cancer, heart disease, and stroke emerge as the leading killers, as infectious and parasitic diseases accounted for relatively few deaths (though pneumonia, bronchitis, influenza, and some viral diseases continued to be significant problems). Polio rose and then tapered off, and scarlet fever began to disappear. Tuberculosis remained low but persistent, especially in slum populations and among older, disadvantaged individuals, particularly men. Smallpox was now rare.

The population during this phase had become predominantly urban, with excessive growth of cities due to rural-to-urban migration, international migration, and urban natural increase. Economically, scientific progress and technology helped produce substantial growth and a consumerist society. Public welfare and leisure spending rose, and society became organized according to rational bureaucratic principles. Large segments of the population enjoyed progressive rises in living conditions, and the nuclear family became the dominant family form. Smaller families allowed women to strive for more options in their social roles, including higher education and careers.

In this societal context, people became extremely conscious of nutrition, especially that of children and mothers. However, increasing consumption of rich and high-fat foods heightened the risk of heart and metabolic diseases. Morbidity—rates of disease—began to overshadow mortality as an index of health, as degenerative and chronic illnesses became more prominent, along with mental illness, addiction, accidents, radiation hazards, and environmental conditions. Health systems gradually became oriented to preventive care, in spite of high medical costs. Improvements in survival selectively began to favour the young more than the old, women more than men, and the privileged more than the poor (Omran and Roudi, 1993).

Opinions vary about the causes of western Europe's epidemiological transition. For instance, what caused the plague to virtually disappear by the start of the twentieth century after recurring outbreaks since the eleventh?[1] One school of thought focuses on the introduction of the smallpox vaccine in the late 1800s and the role of improved hygiene (Mercer, 1985, 1986, 1990; Razzel, 1974). Another hypothesis attributes the remarkable declines in Europe's death rate to the recession of virulent epidemic diseases, thanks to major improvements in standards of living and improved nutrition, which enabled people to withstand infections and live longer. This hypothesis, advanced by McKeown and colleagues and known as the *standards of living thesis* (McKeown, 1976; McKeown, Brown, and Record, 1972), appears to be a plausible explanation. McKeown's analysis of historical data for England and Wales led him to a series of interesting conclusions, which form the basis of the standards of living thesis:

1. Declines in mortality during the eighteenth and early nineteenth centuries was associated primarily with a decline in deaths from infectious diseases, and secondarily with a decrease in deaths from two non-infective causes, infanticide and starvation.
2. Although some infectious diseases declined as a result of a change in the relationship between organism and host, this alone cannot account for the enormous reduction of mortality and growth of population during this time.
3. Mortality was not greatly affected by immunization before 1935. The decrease in deaths from infections with effective medical treatments before 1935—smallpox, syphilis, tetanus, diphtheria, and diarrheal diseases—made only a small contribution to the decline in deaths after 1838.

4. Given the second and third conclusions, the only other explanation for the reduction of mortality is improvements in the socioeconomic environment.
5. Beginning in the second half of the nineteenth century, new hygienic measures (water purification, sewage disposal, proper treatment of food) led to a substantial reduction of mortality from intestinal infections.
6. The most acceptable explanation for the reduction of mortality and growth of population that preceded advances in hygiene is an improvement in nutrition due to greater food supplies.
7. The decline of mortality from non-infective causes (infanticide and starvation in the eighteenth and nineteenth centuries and a large number of conditions in the twentieth) was due mostly to contraceptive use and improved nutrition. In particular, new measures designed to avoid unwanted pregnancies likely played the greatest role in the decrease of deaths from non-infective conditions.

In short, historical evidence suggests that modern medicine could not have had a major impact on mortality declines until well into the first half of the twentieth century, when germ theory was advanced, leading to the invention of antibiotics to help fight major diseases such as polio, tetanus, and tuberculosis (Porter, 1997).

Extensions to Epidemiological Transition Theory

The Age of Delayed Degenerative Diseases

In the United States, death rates from heart disease declined by more than 30 per cent between 1968 and 1982, with most of this decline occurring among middle-aged and older segments of the population. Researchers have observed this same trend in other industrialized countries (Caselli, Meslé, and Vallin, 2002; Mackenzie, 1987; Salomon and Murray, 2002; Vallin, 2006; White, 2002), leading Olshansky and Ault (1986) to suggest that advanced society is now

---

[1] For further insights on the history of plague and its impact on society, see Herlihy (1997); Scott and Duncan (2001).

in a fourth stage of epidemiological transition, the *age of delayed degenerative diseases*. This fourth stage is characterized by continuing slow and often fluctuating mortality declines, which are increasingly concentrated in the later stages of life, and a variable pattern of change in the average onset and duration of major chronic ailments, notably cardiovascular diseases and, to a lesser degree, cancer. In other words, chronic and degenerative diseases continue to dominate, but the onset of major disability from these diseases is occurring later in life.

The Hybristic Stage

Although Omran (1971) speculated that environmental and lifestyle factors could be key to an account of disease and mortality in the advanced stage of epidemiological transition, this idea was not central to his theory. So, in addition to the trends identified by Olshansky and Ault (1986) for populations in the fourth stage, Rogers and Hackenberg (1987) identified a number of epidemiological features of post-industrial societies, mostly linked to lifestyle and health behaviours, including smoking, alcohol and drug use, diet, exercise, and so on. Societies in the fourth stage have also seen, particularly among disadvantaged subgroups of the population, a resurgence of some lethal infectious diseases thought to have been long conquered, including new antibiotic-resistant strains of tuberculosis. HIV is among the deadliest and most widely known of these lethal new viruses, which, Rogers and Hackenberg (1987) argue, are largely related to behavioural factors (e.g., profligate sexual behaviours and intravenous drug use). For Rogers and Hackenberg (1987), post-industrial societies have entered a *hybristic* epidemiological stage, characterized by a prominence of both chronic and communicable diseases, which in combination account for an increasing portion of deaths.

Recent evidence supports these theories. Mokdad and colleagues (2004) determined that the 'real' causes of death today are related mainly to lifestyle behaviours that compromise good health and longevity, specifically smoking, overeating, maintaining an unhealthy diet, and avoiding exercise. In the United States, tobacco use accounts for 18 per cent of all deaths, poor diet and physical inactivity are responsible for 16.6 per cent of all deaths, and alcohol use contributes 3.5 per cent to the total. In Canada, over 15,000 people lose their lives annually to lung cancer, a disease connected to tobacco use. A recent report by the World Health Organization (2005a) predicts that more than one million Canadians will suffer needless deaths over the next 10 years because they have smoked too much, exercised too little, and eaten unhealthy foods. Deaths from diabetes, a condition closely connected to obesity, are projected to increase by 44 per cent over current levels.

A number of other causes of death can be linked to the lifestyle behaviours Mokdad and colleagues (2004) identified. Many deaths are caused each year by unsafe driving, the misuse of firearms, risky sexual behaviours, and illegal drug use. Suicide and homicide remain significant causes of premature death, particularly among young and middle-aged adults (Stack, 2000a, 2000b).

The extensions of epidemiological transition theory presented by Olshansky and Ault (1986) and by Rogers and Hackenberg (1987) may be viewed as complementary dimensions of the epidemiological context of post-industrial societies. The two sets of authors differ mainly in emphasis: Olshansky and Ault emphasize chronic and degenerative diseases and improved survival rates in the older ages, while Rogers and Hackenberg stress the importance of lifestyle factors and individual behaviours as causes of premature death.

Exceptions to Epidemiological Transition Theory

Although we might expect the developments outlined in the classical form of the epidemiological transition theory to apply generally across all populations, the empirical evidence shows some notable exceptions.

Live Fast, Die Young

What do Elvis Presley, Otis Redding, Buddy Holly, Sid Vicious, Freddie Mercury, Brian Jones, Kurt Kobain, and Joe Ramone have in common? They were all famous rock stars who died young. In fact, according to research by Bellis and colleagues (2007), early death is not uncommon among famous rock stars. The study shows that rock stars are three times more likely to die young than the rest of the population. Of over 1,000 European and American musicians who had their first chart success between 1956 and 1999, 100 are dead. Forty per cent of the Americans and 28 per cent of the Europeans died from overdoses, accidents, or chronic diseases related to the use of alcohol and illegal drugs. The average age at death for the Americans was 42, and for the Europeans just 35.

Notwithstanding these dire statistics, it must be mentioned that there are honourable exceptions of European and North American rock starts still performing today in their 60s. Notable examples include Mick Jagger and Keith Richards of the Rolling Stones, the Guess Who's Burton Cummings and Randy Bachman, and Bob Dylan.

Cause of death	American rock stars (% deaths)	European rock stars (% deaths)
Suicide	2.8	3.6
Violence	6.9	3.6
Drug/alcohol overdose	15.3	28.6
Accident (drug/alcohol-related)	2.8	7.1
Chronic disorder (drug/alcohol)	9.7	3.6
Cancer	19.4	21.4
Cardiovascular disease	18.0	3.6
Other accident	13.9	21.4
Other	11.1	7.1
Total	100.0	100.0

Source: Bellis et al. (2007).

For instance, studies by Caldwell (1986), among others (Gauri and Khaleghian, 2002; Gjonca, 2001; Gjonca, Wilson, and Falkingham, 1997; Heuveline, Guillot, and Gwatkin, 2002), cast doubt on the generality of a central tenet of the epidemiological theory: that decreased mortality results from socioeconomic advancement, because modernization paves the way to better health care and public health systems. These studies have found that in some poor countries major health improvements are possible without large-scale economic growth.

Notkola, Timaeus, and Siiskonen (2000) studied mortality change in the Ovamboland region of Namibia in southern Africa, where they found the main agent of health transition was not economic change or sociopolitical intervention but the Church. After analyzing parish registers of Namibia's Evangelical Lutheran Church from 1930 to 1990, the authors of the study discovered that between the early 1950s and the early 1960s, adult mortality fell at a rate far greater than one would predict from life table models. Among many developments that contributed to

Ovamboland's overall decline in mortality, the most important factor was the establishment of a Western system of health care by Lutheran missionaries from Finland. Regrettably, the recent surge of the HIV/AIDS epidemic in Namibia (and other parts of the African continent) has reversed the favourable trends achieved decades earlier.

Another flaw in epidemiological theory is its implicit assumption of a linear—and irreversible—progression through the various stages. Caselli and colleagues (2002) have identified a number of cases of retrogressions in mortality improvements. Among the examples they cite are some of the former Soviet Bloc countries, which have seen reductions in life expectancy over recent decades, a situation not at all envisioned by the classical version of the epidemiological theory. In Russia, life expectancy gains achieved between 1965 and the late 1990s have fluctuated between periods of decline, stagnation, and partial recovery (Anderson, 2003; Anderson and Silver, 1989; Kucera et al., 2000; Nierenberg, 2005: 94). Vallin, Meslé, and Valkonen (2001: 137) have shown that life expectancy for men in Russia declined between 1965 and 1984, increasing slightly until 1987, and then dropping again over the next six years until 1994; since then, the evidence indicates an upturn in male life expectancy, though as of 1996, it remained well below what it had been in 1965. The trend for women is similar, but the fluctuations are nowhere near as extreme as those for men. Con-

The Puzzling Origins of AIDS

Where did HIV/AIDS come from, and how was the virus first transmitted to and spread among humans? Several explanations have been offered, though no one theory has been universally accepted. Moore (2004) has identified four leading theories.

The Tainted Polio Vaccine
According to this theory, the progenitor virus, which in the case of HIV-1 is found in chimpanzees, crossed into humans through a large-scale trial of an experimental oral polio vaccine, carried out between 1957 and 1960 in three countries that today form the epicentre of the HIV/AIDS epidemic in Africa: the Democratic Republic of the Congo (Belgian Congo before independence), Burundi, and Rwanda. It is thought that the oral polio vaccine became contaminated by a then-unknown *simian immunodeficiency virus* (SIV) carried by African green monkeys (themselves immune to the virus), whose kidney cells were used as a substrate to grow viruses for research on vaccine production. More than 900,000 people may have been infected, laying the groundwork for the current HIV/AIDS epidemic.

The tainted polio vaccine theory is not fully accepted by medical scientists because a number of independent confirmatory analyses on existing samples of the vaccine have been inconclusive or have turned up negative for traces of chimpanzee DNA or SIV. Sequence analyses aimed at determining the initial date of the HIV virus in humans indicate that HIV began earlier than the period in which the oral polio vaccine trials were conducted.

The Cut-Hunter Hypothesis
The second explanation suggests a simian progenitor virus was passed on to humans through cuts as someone was hunting or butchering a chimpanzee (or, in the case of HIV-2, a type of

West African monkey called the sooty mangabey). According to this view, the virus, which is typically cleared in its human host, managed to survive on at least several times during the twentieth century and became established as HIV. The sudden spread of HIV in the middle part of the twentieth century can be explained by urbanization and the population's increased geographic mobility, which helped in the spread of sexually transmitted diseases. The problem with this theory is that it cannot explain why HIV did not appear earlier, given that Africans began moving to colonial capitals and ports as early as the nineteenth century.

The Contaminated Needles Theory

A third theory, related to the cut-hunter hypothesis, points to the widespread reuse of disposable syringes in Central Africa during the 1950s as part of a campaign to eradicate several diseases through immunization. It was customary for medical workers to use the same needle—which was plastic and so could not be sterilized in boiling water—on different subjects in order to reduce costs. The practice of reusing needless may have helped the spread of human viruses, including viruses from monkeys or chimpanzees acquired by hunters. With each transfer via contaminated needle, the simian virus finds a fresh host and an opportunity to proliferate before the infected person can mount an immune response. Chance mutations accumulate, and eventually the SIV adapts, becoming HIV (Moore, 2004: 544).

The Heart of Darkness Thesis

Moore himself is credited with the fourth explanation, named after the famous novel by Joseph Conrad. It focuses on the disruptive, often brutal effects of colonialism on the populations of Central Africa. According to Moore (2004), the number of Africans who died as a result of colonial practices in French Equatorial Africa and neighbouring Belgian Congo between 1880 and the onset of World War II surpasses the number of Africans taken as slaves over the preceding 400 years. The major mortality crises throughout the colonial reign and the large-scale displacements of the population took place while the colonial powers forced many of their subjects to undergo medical treatments. One of these was immunization against polio, which unfortunately involved the use and reuse of unsterilized syringes. Colonial authorities also frequently subjected the indigenous population, particularly those in forced labour camps, to inoculations against diseases such as smallpox, dysentery, and sleeping sickness (or trypanosomiasis). Multiple injections were given to tens or hundreds of workers with only a handful of syringes, making the transfer of pathogens virtually inevitable. Moore writes that a 1916 expedition to control sleeping sickness treated some 89,000 people in Ubanghi Shari, now the Central African Republic, using just six syringes.

These four theories cannot provide a definitive answer to the question of what sparked the HIV epidemic in humans, but they do help us understand that the origin of HIV was not fundamentally natural. The emergence of the virus can clearly be traced to major social changes that include, in Moore's words, 'the abuses carried out at the hand of an invading foreign power; abrupt urbanization overwhelming the ability of medical and political authorities to manage the process; the under-supervised transfer of medical technology and half-measures in development programs; doctors taking liberties in distributing medicines without adequate precautions' (Moore, 2004: 547).

sequently, the male disadvantage in life expectancy has been as large as ten years or more in Russia, and just as high in Estonia, Belarus, Lithuania, and Ukraine. These drops in life expectancy are driven largely by a high incidence of premature death among middle-aged adults, particularly males, mainly from cardiovascular diseases, poisonings, and injuries. Key contributing factors to these trends are excessive use of alcohol and tobacco and poor diet (Bobadilla and Costello, 1997; Haynes and Husan, 2003; Leon et al., 1997; Shkolnikov, Meslé, and Vallin, 1997).

According to the epidemiological transition theory, infectious diseases are supposed to play a minor role in mortality during the most advanced stages of epidemiological transition. Yet in recent years the world has seen the emergence of lethal new viruses that pose serious threats to population health. The appearance of HIV/AIDS in the developed countries in the early 1980s is a clear case in point. The latest threat is the so-called avian flu, or H5N1 virus, which could, if it spreads to humans, cause the next major world pandemic, potentially far deadlier than the Spanish influenza of 1918–19. The return of some old infectious diseases, like antibiotic-resistant strains of tuberculosis, also attests to the inability of the theory to anticipate new epidemiological developments in modern industrial society.

A final problem with the theory is its implied assumption of homogeneity in the health conditions of a population within any stage of epidemiological development. The theory fails to allow for the possibility of health and mortality inequalities among disadvantaged subpopulations, whose overall health lags far behind that of the larger society. Canada's First Nations are just one example of a population whose epidemiological condition is much worse than that of the dominant population; the cases of indigenous populations in the United States and Australia are similar (Hogg, 1992; Kunitz, 1994, 1990; Trovato, 2001; Young, 1994).

Health Transition

Recent demographic literature has broadened in scope to examine ideas surrounding *health transition* (Caldwell, 1991; Frenk et al., 1991; Johansson, 1991; Riley, 2001, 2005a, 2005b). As a theoretical perspective, health transition theory describes the improvements in life expectancy and overall health of populations over the historical spectrum, going beyond the scope covered by epidemiological transition theory. Health transition theorists concentrate on explaining how the health of a population changes as a result of change in social organization, environment, health care institutions, and prevention systems, as well as genetic and biological factors, lifestyles and behaviour, and culture. In particular, they focus on several interacting sets of factors viewed as playing a role in the health of populations:

- *systemic factors*, including those related to the environment and social organization
- *societal factors*, including structural determinants such as stratification and inequality in the population
- *institutional/household-level factors*, including proximate factors like working conditions, living conditions, health care systems, and lifestyles
- *individual factors*, such as health status and risk factors (Cutler and Miller, 2005; Frenk et al., 1991: 23; Nathanson, 1996)

Health transition theory examines the role that these cultural, social, and behavioural determinants of health play in the rising life expectancy at birth (the mortality transition) and the decreasing proportion of deaths caused by infectious diseases (the epidemiological transition). Caldwell (1991), the originator of this idea, has argued that health transition can help demographers and other social scientists focus on how people stay healthy while alive instead of simply how long they live (Johansson, 2003: 479).

Epidemiological and health transition theories both emphasize the prevalence of chronic diseases in the most advanced stages of social and economic development. Where they differ most is in their views of how social systems produce good health. Epidemiological transition theory is less explicit in recognizing this aspect of societal change, while health transition theory explicitly argues that socioeconomic modernization plays a key role in changing population health. Health transition theorists point to the contributions of the state and its health care system, and also to individuals, in health and disease change, adding that economic development is not the only factor—nor necessarily the most important—in the epidemiological change. In doing so, health transition theorists stress the exceptional experience of poor countries in attaining relatively good health at relatively low levels of economic development, a point elaborated in greater detail later.

Aging and Health Dynamics in Advanced Societies

Early in the twenty-first century, life expectancy at birth in high-income countries is approaching—and in some cases has surpassed—the eighth decade of life, leading some analysts to suggest that life expectancy may be approaching an upper limit in these societies (Coale, 1996; Fries, 1980). High life expectancy is coupled with increasing rates of demographic aging as a result of decades of subreplacement fertility. Infant, childhood, and young adulthood mortality have fallen to historically low levels in advanced societies, and the vast majority of deaths are now concentrated in the ages above 65 (Beaver, 1975; Berry, 1977; Hogberg, 2004; Kannisto et al., 1994; Klinger, 1985; Mertens, 1994; Meslé and Vallin, 2006; Valent et al., 2004; Robine, 2001; Singh and Yu, 1995).

Given these trends, researchers have increasingly shifted their attention to issues of health and longevity in the older ages and the possible societal implications of increased survival rates. One of the questions being debated in this context is what maximum average human lifespan could be attained (Aarssen and de Haan, 1994; Bongaarts, 2006b; Bongaarts and Feeney, 2002; Caselli and Lopez, 1996; Lopez, Caselli, and Valkonen, 1995; Manton, Gu, and Lamb, 2006). Scientific work in this area is wide-ranging and includes laboratory molecular studies on mice and other organisms, computer simulations of the effects of cause-of-death elimination or life expectancy improvements, and epidemiological follow-up studies of cohorts as they pass through life (e.g., Allard et al., 1998; Arking, 2002; Carey and Judge, 2001a; Dreifus, 2004; Finch and Tanzi, 1997; Hekimi and Guarente, 2003; Karousu et al., 2005; Miller, 2005; Olshansky, Carnes, and Cassel, 1990; Perls and Fretts, 2002; Reaney, 2003; Schriner et al., 2005). In the section that follows we will look at the concept of lifespan and how it has generated speculations on the future course of longevity in societies of the world that are at the most advanced stages of epidemiological transition.

The Concept of Lifespan

Lifespan is a characteristic of life history that is the product of evolution. For an individual, it refers to the period between birth and death. At the cohort level (as represented in a life table), it is the average age at death, or the life expectancy at birth; thus, it may be called *average human*

Born in Arles, France, on 21 February 1875, Jeanne Calment was 122 years and 164 days old when she died in a French nursing home on 4 August 1997. Her total lifespan of an astonishing 44,724 days is the longest confirmed human lifespan in history. She led a remarkable life that spanned the rule of 20 French presidents. As a child she met Vincent Van Gogh, who often frequented her father's art supply store in Arles. Among the many tributes to her life is a CD titled *Time's Mistress*, which features her voice set to funk-rap, techno, and dance music. For more on Jeanne Calment, see Allard et al. (1998).

Two variables that have strong positive correlations with lifespan for humans and other primates are body mass and relative brain size. Regression analyses using these two variables have yielded predicted lifespans for humans through different periods in evolutionary history. Scientists have estimated that the lifespan for *Homo habilis* was in the range of 52 to 56 years, and for *Homo erectus*, 60 to 63 years. From such studies scientists have concluded that a major increase in longevity between these two ancestors of *Homo sapiens sapiens* must have occurred some 1.7 to 2 million years ago (Carey, 2003a, 2003b). Of course, for much of human history, to live as long or longer than the predicted lifespan must have been extremely rare.

lifespan. Biologists refer to the highest verified age at death in a particular population, cohort, or species as the *maximum observed lifespan*, and the overall highest verified age for a species is its *record lifespan*. Jeanne Calment, who died at the age of 122, currently represents the record lifespan for the human population (Allard et al., 1998). All sexually reproducing species are assumed to have a theoretical highest attainable age, known as *maximum potential lifespan* (Carey, 2003a, 2003b), but it is not known what that 'maximum' might be for humans, because there is no 'identifiable age for which some select individuals can survive but beyond which none can live' (Carey, 2003b: 1).

For the modern period there is evidence, based on Swedish death records, that the record age at death in humans has been increasing for well over a century (Carey, 2003a, 2003b; Wilmoth et al., 2002). The rise of maximum human lifespan to over 120 years is believed to have been brought about by two phenomena. The first is Darwinian natural selection, which is thought to have extended the human lifespan to somewhere in the range of 72 to 90 years. The second, post-Darwinian phenomenon is 'artifactual' growth resulting from 'improved living conditions of modern society' (Carey, 2003a: 593). This second aspect of human longevity improvement may have set in motion a self-perpetuating system of longevity extension through incremental societal improvements that have translated into better health and increased longevity. Fogel and Costa (1997) have referred to this phenomenon as a *techno-physio evolution*.

Rectangularization of Survival

For populations in the advanced stages of epidemiological and health transitions, the survival curve in the life table has become increasingly rectangular, reflecting gradual improvements in age-specific survival probabilities (Cheung et al., 2005; Horiuchi and Wilmoth, 1998; Paccaud et al., 1998; Robine, 2001). The increasing rectangularization of the survival curve in the life table has resulted from two important changes in mortality and survival probabilities by age over time. The first is the significant improvement in survival rates for infants, then children and later young adults, over the course of the twentieth century, as society passed through the epidemiological transition. The second is the continued improvement in survival chances for these same age groups in conjunction with significant mortality gains late in the century among those over the age of 65. As survival probabilities among the younger ages have tended to level off, survival rates for the elderly have been improving faster, producing a greater degree of rectangularization in the life table curve for the population 65 and over, beginning in the last quarter of the twentieth century (Nagnur, 1986a; Nagnur and Nagrodski, 1990).

Canada's rectangularization trends can be observed in the life table survival curves shown in Figure 7.8. As the figure shows, conditional survival probabilities have improved substantially since the late nineteenth century; however, between successive periods, the survival curves have become less distant from each other. In other words, recent improvements in mortality are not as great as the improvements made in earlier periods. The term *entropy of the life table* describes the tendency for the survival probabilities in the life table to attenuate once a population reaches a high level of life expectancy.[2]

---

[2] Technically, entropy in the context of the life table is the percentage improvement in the expectation of life at age x, if a 1 per cent improvement in mortality takes place at age x and above (Keyfitz, 1977).

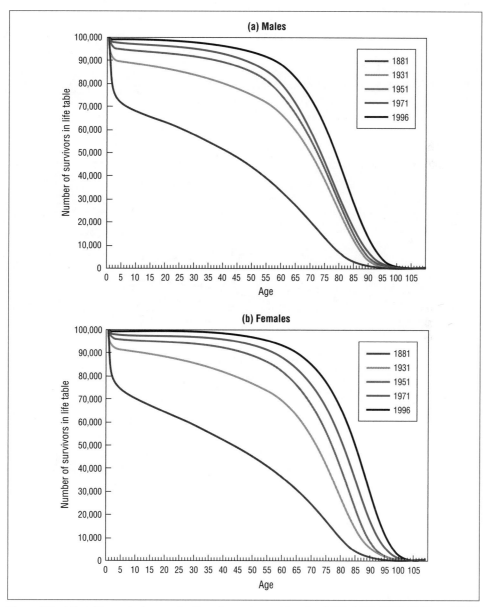

Figure 7.8   Life table survival curves for Canadian males and females, 1881, 1931, 1951, 1971, and 1996

Sources: Dominion Bureau of Statistics (1947, 1960); Statistics Canada (1974); Bourbeau, Légaré, and Émond (1997).

Compression of Morbidity and Mortality

In 1980, James Fries proposed a theory that relies in part on the concept of survival rectangularization. He reasoned that the future pattern of mortality and morbidity in advanced societies would be affected by a 'compression' phenomenon, in which major disability and sickness would be increasingly 'compressed' into fewer and fewer years occurring in advanced age, close to the time of 'natural death'. Fries (1980, 1983) argued that the rectangularization of survival probabilities in the life table over the past century is a reflection of the tendency for each new generation to be generally healthier than the preceding one. Fries (1980) projected a future in which most individuals would remain relatively healthy for most of their lives; only once they approach the maximum average age at death (which, Fries esti-

mated, would reach 85 by about 2050) would individuals experience the onset of major disability and illness, soon followed by natural death.[3] Thus, under Fries' scenario, the onset of major disability would occur later and later in life, and the period of debilitating infirmity would be relatively short for the average citizen—compressed, as it were, into a few years, close to the time of death (see Figure 7.9).

There is some research to support the view that a life expectancy much beyond age 85 may

---

[3] Fries (1980) prepared his estimate of average maximum human life using a linear model assuming that life expectancy at birth and life expectancy at age 65 would at some point in the future converge. That point of convergence should occur, according to Fries' calculations, around the year 2050.

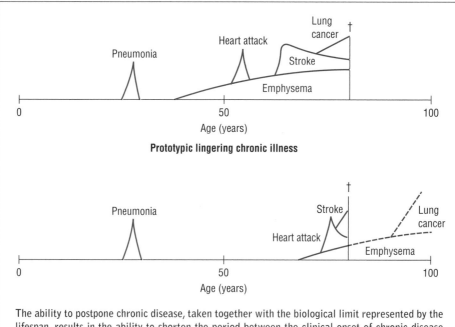

Prototypic lingering chronic illness

The ability to postpone chronic disease, taken together with the biological limit represented by the lifespan, results in the ability to shorten the period between the clinical onset of chronic disease and the end of life. Infirmity (morbidity) is compressed into a shorter and shorter period near the end of the lifespan.

Figure 7.9 Stylized form of the compression of morbidity and mortality concept
Source: Fries and Crapo (1981): 92.

not be feasible—at least given current medical and technological knowledge (see Olshansky and Carnes, 2001; Olshansky, Carnes, and Cassel, 1990; Olshansky, Carnes, and Hayflick, 2004). It has been estimated, for example, that in order for life expectancy in the United States to surpass 85 years, adults late in life would need to attain the mortality profile of teens—in other words, a 55-year-old man would have to have the death rate of a 15-year-old boy (Olshansky, Carnes, and Cassel, 1990). If we accept 85 as the average age at death, with the standard deviation of 10 years around this parameter and a more or less normal distribution of deaths, then most people in the population would die between the ages of 75 and 95, and only about 2.5 per cent of the population would cross this upper limit, with very few surviving past 100.

Fries' assumption that each generation is generally healthier than the preceding one has received substantial, though not unequivocal, support in the literature. In general, it appears that the typical 65-year-old of today is 'younger', in terms of vitality and health, than was the typical 65-year-old a century or even as recently as a quarter-century ago (Chen and Millar, 2000; Fogel, 2004b; Fogel and Costa, 1997; Fries and Crapo, 1981; Rice and Fineman, 2004; Unal et al., 2005). Yet recent analyses suggest that society may be facing a looming health care crisis.

In Canada, Wister (2005) documented alarming rates of obesity and health problems linked to smoking and other lifestyle habits and warned that the situation is likely to worsen over the next three to six decades, as the baby boomers pass through old age and into their final years. According to Wister, even though the generation born during the 20-year period after the Second World War is smoking less, drinking less, and exercising more than earlier generations, obesity in this sector of the population continues to rise. The problem is that obesity is linked to a host of health complications, including life-threatening conditions such as diabetes. Obesity among Canadian baby

boomers in 2001 was at 16.2 per cent, nearly double the 1985 rate of 8.2 per cent; in the same year, Canada's baby boomers showed a 77 per cent higher rate of diabetes than the same age group in 1978–9. Currently more than half of this population do not exercise regularly; nearly one in three are obese, and one in five is a smoker.

American studies reveal similar health trends in the adult population. If the impact of obesity on health conditions—notably cardiovascular complications and certain cancers—takes about two decades to materialize, then the continuation of these trends in North American obesity suggest that a major health crisis is on the horizon (*The Economist*, 2003d; Flegal et al., 2005; Fontaine et al., 2003; Haveman-Nies et al., 2002; Mason, 2005; Mokdad et al., 2004; Peters et al., 2003; Picard, 2006a, 2006b, 2004; Tao et al., 2005). Moreover, rising obesity levels among North American children could contribute to a decrease in life expectancy by as much as two years (Lalasz, 2005; Moore, 2004; Olshansky et al., 2005).

Perhaps these projections are excessively gloomy. While obesity remains a major health concern, Preston (2005) offers evidence of positive influences on future longevity among young people. Not only are younger cohorts better educated, but their lives have been less scarred by infectious diseases, which influence the development of many chronic diseases of adulthood. Preston adds that younger cohorts have, at given ages, consumed fewer cigarettes than older cohorts have, suggesting that these younger cohorts will have lower morbidity from cardiovascular disease, emphysema, and arthritis. Preston believes that the US population is already taking positive steps in addressing its obesity problem, with many people modifying their lifestyles to reduce a variety of health risks through better diet and medication.

Life table analyses of *disability-free life expectancy* (the years of life when an individual's health does not affect the ability to perform normal activities) indicate that the average number of years people now spend in a state of disability and infirmity in old age diminished over the course of the twentieth century, especially since the early 1970s (Cambois, Robine, and Hayward, 2002; Costa, 2000; Crimmins, Saito, and Ingegneri, 1997; Crimmins et al., 2006; Fogel, 2004b; Manton and Singer, 1994; Martel and Belanger, 2000; Olshansky and Ault, 1986; Wilkins and Adams, 1983). Manton, Gu, and Lamb (2006) show that between 1982 and 1999 in the United States, *active life expectancy* (i.e., life expectancy free of major disability) increased among those aged 65 and older, and also among those aged 85 and older. In 1999, for instance, a 65-year-old could expect to live almost 14 out of an average of almost 18 years of life remaining in a state free of major disability. For an 85-year-old, almost 50 per cent of expected remaining life could be spent free of major disability. Projections to 2022 and 2080 by these authors and other researchers suggest further improvements in active life expectancy among the elderly are to come (Friedman, Martin, and Schoeni, 2002; Perenboom et al., 2004; Shoeni et al., 2006).

Demographers use four measures of disability:

1. *Prevalence* tells us how many cases of physical disability there are at a given time.
2. *Disability-free life expectancy* tells us how many years an average person is expected to live without major disability.
3. *Disability-free life expectancy with different levels of severity* is essentially disability-free life expectancy computed for varying degrees of disability.
4. *Disability-adjusted life expectancy* assigns weights to the different levels of severity to provide more detail about the influence of these disabilities on personal functioning; it estimates the number of years of good health a person is expected to experience. (Perenboom et al., 2004)

Expansion of Survival

Not everyone agrees with Fries' assertion that the maximum average age at death for human populations is 85 (e.g., Bongaarts, 2006b; Kannisto, 1996, 1994, 1988; Kannisto et al., 1994; Lynch and Brown, 2001; Manton, 1982; Manton and Singer, 1994; Manton and Vaupel, 1995; Mertens, 1994; Oeppen and Vaupel, 2002; Vallin, Meslé, and Valkonen 2001; Vaupel et al., 1998; Wilmoth et al., 2002). In fact, there are indicators to suggest that survival probabilities in the older ages have been expanding, and that this trend is likely to continue into the foreseeable future. Bongaarts (2006), for instance, has found that gains in senescent mortality (mortality associated with aging) since the mid-twentieth century have outpaced improvements in both juvenile mortality and background mortality (i.e., deaths caused by accidents, violence, and infectious/parasitic diseases). Bongaarts's (2006) findings—essentially, that older people are living longer—confirm the optimists' view that there is no evidence of an upper limit to human longevity. On the downside, Bongaarts's calculations show that the pace of improvement in senescent life expectancy over the last half century has been somewhat slower than anticipated (0.15 years per year, versus the predicted rate of 0.25 years per year). Nonetheless, since this trend has been generally linear, it is likely that there will be further improvements in senescent life expectancy, and that life expectancy at birth should increase by an average of about 7.5 years over the next half century. These anticipated improvements in longevity imply rapid population aging. With the accumulated evidence of an improving trend in seniors' health, gerontologists now speak of a *healthy aging paradigm* (Perls and Silver, 1999; Rice and Fineman, 2004; Wilmoth and Ferraro, 2006). While few could expect to attain the 122-year longevity of Jeanne Calment, the healthy aging paradigm suggests that the average human lifespan in the future could surpass the presumed upper limit to human average life suggested by Fries and his associates.

As active life expectancy keeps improving, there has been a significant growth in the number of centenarians—hundred-year-olds—worldwide. In the 14 developed countries with the most reliable statistics, the proportion of centenarians has risen from 5 per million inhabitants in 1960 to 50 per million inhabitants in 1990 (Jeune and Skytthe, 2001: 75). More than two-thirds of this increase is due to a considerable reduction of mortality among eighty- and ninety-year-olds. Also important is that survival probabilities for those over 90 have been increasing, and there may be a deceleration in mortality rates in this segment of the elderly population (Horiuchi and Wilmoth, 1998; Lynch and Brown, 2001; Manton and Yashin, 2006; Vaupel et al., 1998). Again, taken together, these positive trends seem to contradict the idea that upper maximum average age at death for humans is all but fixed at 85 years.

Health Patterns in Low- and Middle-Income Countries

Life Expectancy Trends

By looking at life expectancy trends over the last 150 years or so, and particularly over the last century, we can identify three waves of improvement worldwide. The first wave began in western Europe in the late 1800s and spread to North America soon thereafter. Although the upward trend in life expectancy in the West was interrupted by the two world wars and a major economic depression, the rate of longevity has been generally upward, especially since 1950. In fact, for each calendar year between 1940 and 1950, life expectancy in the West increased by an average of 0.43 of a year (Gwatkin, 1980: 616). Shortly after the acceleration of mortality decline began in the West, a second wave of even greater progress began in eastern and southern Europe. According to Gwatkin (1980), this region experienced gains of between 0.50 and 1.0 years of life expectancy per calendar year between the 1920s and 1950s, in spite of

periodic interruptions due to the wars and the 1930s depression. By the 1960s, eastern and southern Europe had nearly closed the gap in life expectancy with the countries of northern and western Europe.

The third wave pertains to the mortality decline in the developing countries, which began shortly after World War II, though even earlier in regions such as Latin America (1900) and India (early 1920s) (Gwatkin, 1980: 616). Most impressive were the mortality gains recorded immediately after the end of World War II in such countries as Taiwan, Malaysia, Sri Lanka, Mauritius, Jamaica, and Mexico. For example, in Mauritius and Sri Lanka, the increase in life expectancy exceeded two years annually: life expectancy rose from 33.0 to 51.1 in Mauritius between 1942–6 and 1951–3 and from 42.7 to 56.7 in Sri Lanka between 1946 and 1953. As Gwatkin remarks, 'Many developing countries recorded life expectancy gains three or more times as large as those achieved in Western Europe at a comparable stage in its mortality transition' (Gwatkin, 1980: 617).

The second half of the twentieth century saw a marked convergence in the length of human life between the world's rich and poor countries. Schultz (1993), drawing on United Nations estimates, summarized life expectancy trends by region for the period 1950–90. He concluded that during this period life expectancy increased in high-income countries from 55 to 75 years (or by 19 years), while in the low-income countries it increased by 21 years, from 42 to 63. Latin America was the healthiest low-income region in 1950, with a life expectancy of 51, and gained 16 years during this 40-year period. In Southeast Asia and East Asia, life expectancy grew by 26 years, from 44 to 70, and in South Asia and western Asia it increased 20 years, from 40 to 60. The least progress was made in Africa, where life expectancy rose by just 16 years, from 38 to 54. Table 7.5 summarizes regional trends in life expectancy from the early 1950s to 2005.

Over recent years these regional trends have continued their rise, though at a much reduced

Table 7.5 Life expectancy at birth by region and selected countries, 1950–2005

Region/country	1950–5	1960–5	1970–5	1980	1990	2000	2005
World	46.5	52.4	58.0	61	64	66	67
MDCs	66.2	69.7	71.4	73	74	75	76
LDCs	41.0	47.7	54.7	58	61	64	65
Africa	37.8	42.1	46.3	49	52	52	52
North Africa	41.8	46.3	51.2	54	59	64	68
West Africa	35.5	39.3	43.4	46	48	51	47
East Africa	36.5	41.0	45.1	47	50	46	47
Middle Africa	36.0	39.6	43.9	45	50	49	48
South Africa	44.2	49.2	53.1	59	62	54	50
Asia	41.3	48.4	56.3	58	63	66	68
Southwest Asia	45.2	52.1	57.9	61	64	68	68
Middle South Asia	39.3	45.5	50.1	54	57	61	62
India	38.7	45.5	50.3	55	57	61	62
Southeast Asia	41.0	46.7	51.8	56	61	65	69
East Asia	42.9	51.4	63.0	66	69	72	73
China	40.8	49.5	63.2	64	68	71	72
Japan	63.9	69.0	73.3	75	79	81	82
North America	68.9	70.2	71.7	73	74	77	78
Canada	69.1	71.4	73.2	73	77	79	80
USA	68.9	70.0	71.5	73	75	77	78
Mexico	50.6	58.3	62.4	65	68	72	75
Latin America	51.4	56.8	60.9	64	67	70	72
Central Latin America	49.2	56.4	61.1	64	68	71	74
Caribbean	52.1	58.5	63.1	66	68	69	69
Tropical South America	57.1	62.8	66.0	68	69	70	72
Temperate South America	61.2	63.9	66.3	68	70	71	72
Europe	65.7	69.6	71.0	72	74	74	75
Northern Europe	69.2	71.2	73.0	75	76	77	78
Western Europe	67.6	70.8	72.5	74	76	78	79
Eastern Europe	64.3	68.7	69.8	71	71	69	69
Southern Europe	63.3	68.6	71.5	73	75	77	79
USSR/Russia	64.6	67.9	69.7	70	69	67	66
Oceania	60.9	64.0	66.1	69	72	74	75

Note: Temperate South America comprises Argentina, Chile, and Uruguay. Tropical South America comprises Bolivia, Brazil, Colombia, Ecuador, Guyana, Paraguay, Peru, Suriname, and Venezuela.

Sources: Data for 1950–5 to 1970–5 are from United Nations Department of Economic and Social Affairs Population Division (2002a); data for 1980, 1990, 2000, and 2005 are from the Population Reference Bureau, World Population Data Sheets (indicated years).

pace compared to the 1950–90 period. By 2005, the more developed countries had reached a life expectancy of 76, and less developed countries 65 (63 years if China is excluded). Among the less developed regions, Latin America has the best life expectancy at 72 years, followed by East Asia and the Pacific (73 years). The Arab states and South Asian regions trailed with life expectancies of 68 and 62, respectively. Two exceptional cases stand out: those of sub-Saharan Africa and of Russia and eastern Europe (essentially, the former Soviet Bloc countries). In both of these cases there were notable setbacks in average length of life after 1980 or 1990. The situation seems most precarious for sub-Saharan Africa, where life expectancy has dropped since the early 1990s by as much as 8 years.

The conditions responsible for declines in life expectancy in the two regions are quite different. In the former Soviet Union, as we have already seen, alcoholism and its negative ramifications has been the prime culprit, exacerbated by other unhealthy trends such as smoking and by accidents and violence. In sub-Saharan Africa the key factor has been the devastating HIV/AIDS epidemic, although there have been other notable problems, including famine, conflict, and war.

Health-Achieving Poor Nations

The term *low- and middle-income countries* (LMICs) has come into vogue recently as a synonym for 'developing countries'. By implication this terminology signifies the existence of a global stratification system (Ebrahim and Smeeth, 2005), in which variations in national wealth are linked to cross-national differences in population health and well-being. Given their limited resources, an ongoing concern for low- and middle-income countries is how to improve the health of their populations at relatively low cost. Caldwell (1986) looked at countries in Asia and Latin America, including China, Cuba, Sri Lanka, and the Indian state of Kerala, to see if there were common factors that differentiated

nations with respect to life expectancy gains. Typically, the beginning of a health transition is associated with a decade or two successive decades marked by sustained gains in survival, as measured by life expectancy and infant mortality (Riley, 2005a, 2005b). Caldwell (1986) discovered that even in some countries where per capita income is not very high, significant improvements in life expectancy have been attained over a relatively short period of time. According to Caldwell, these health-achieving, relatively poor nations share a number of common features:

- Their societies afford women a relatively high status, which entitles them to enjoy high levels of education and autonomy.
- There is a determination on the part of these governments to intervene in the areas of health and nutrition for the benefit of the population.
- They have relatively small populations.
- They have isolated populations with a strong European outlook.
- They have maintained major cash export crops (e.g., coffee) since the nineteenth century.
- They have well-established rural economies.

Taken together, these features imply that the governments of 'health-overachieving nations' have been able to translate national resources into universal social programs, notably education and health care. Poor nations can learn from these examples and hasten their health transitions in spite of having modest levels of per capita income. It is also worth noting that some high-income developing countries (for instance, some oil-producing nations in the Arab world) have higher rates of infant mortality and lower rates of life expectancy than might be expected. Clearly, as Caldwell suggests, it takes more than high income for societies to attain high levels of population health. The importance of political will cannot be underestimated. A nation must utilize wealth and resources for the betterment of its citizens first if it is to achieve major improvements in health.

Burden of Disease

The Continuing Threat of HIV/AIDS

Acquired immunodeficiency syndrome, more commonly known as AIDS, is caused by the human immunodeficiency virus (HIV), which is spread through blood, semen, vaginal secretions, and breast milk. The most common method of transmission is unprotected sexual intercourse with a partner who is HIV-positive. Other practices that can lead to infection include transfusions of HIV-infected blood or blood products; tissue or organ transplants; use of contaminated needles, syringes, or other skin-piercing equipment; and mother-to-child transmissions during pregnancy, birth, or breast-feeding (Lamptey, Johnson and Khan, 2006: 3).

Many experts have called HIV/AIDS the most deadly epidemic of our time. Over 22 million people have already lost their lives, and more than 40 million are thought to be currently living with the disease (United Nations Department of Economic and Social Affairs Population Division, 2004a). As Table 7.6 shows, most of the reported HIV/AIDS cases in the world are in sub-Saharan Africa (UNAIDS, 2005b), although Asia—especially China and India—and eastern Europe are currently experiencing the most rapid growth in the number of new HIV infections (Lamptey, Johnson, and Khan, 2006; Thompson, 2005). Given that these regions are so populous, the situation will most certainly worsen over the foreseeable future (Walker et al., 2004).

Figure 7.10 shows the trend in the number of people living with HIV/AIDS by world region between 1986 and 2004. It is abundantly clear that the number of HIV cases has risen exponen-

---

Table 7.6 HIV and AIDS indicators by region, 2005

Region	People living with HIV	People newly infected in 2005	Prevalence (% of adults infected)	Deaths due to AIDS in 2005
World	40,300,000	4,900,000	1.1	3,100,000
Sub-Saharan Africa	28,800,000	3,200,000	7.2	2,400,000
North Africa/Middle East	510,000	67,000	0.2	58,000
South/Southeast Asia	7,400,000	990,000	0.7	480,000
East Asia	870,000	140,000	0.1	41,000
Oceania	74,000	8,200	0.5	3,600
Latin America	1,800,000	200,000	0.6	66,000
Caribbean	300,000	30,000	1.6	24,000
Eastern Europe/Central Asia	1,600,000	270,000	0.9	62,000
Western/Central Europe	720,000	22,000	0.3	12,000
North America	1,200,000	43,000	0.7	18,000

Note: Estimates represent the midpoint of a range. The world total, for example, ranges from 36.7 million to 45.3 million. Prevalence rate refers to the percentage of adults ages 15 to 49 infected with HIV.

Source: Lamptey, Johnson, and Khan (2006): 3. (See also UNAIDS, 2005b: 3.)

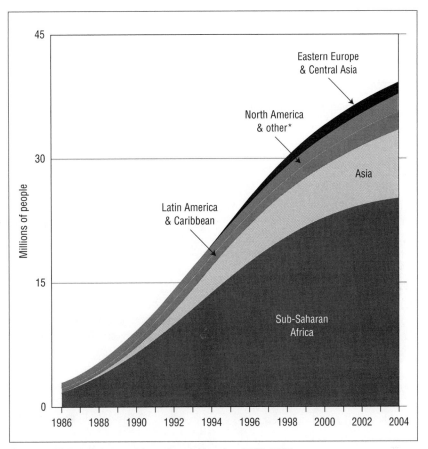

Figure 7.10 People living with HIV by world region, 1986–2004

*North American, Europe (except eastern), North Africa, and the Middle East.

Source: Lamptey, Johnson, and Khan (2006): 7.

tially in the world. No region has been spared. At the end of 2004, most of the roughly 40 million people infected with HIV were living in sub-Saharan Africa and in Asia. Yet while the number of infections is lower in Latin America, eastern Europe, and North America, the trend in these regions is increasing.

There remains a huge unmet burden of treatment of HIV infections worldwide. Of the 20 countries with the highest unmet need, 16 are in Africa (see Table 7.7). Lamptey, Johnson, and Khan (2006) report that while some areas have managed to slow the epidemic, it is surging in others. Only about 15 per cent of the 6.5 million AIDS sufferers in developing countries have access to the antiretroviral drugs required for treatment. In the most affected regions, hard-earned improvements in health care over the last 50 years have been overwhelmed by death and disability from AIDS. The disease is crippling progress at the personal, family, community, and national levels; it is also threatening economic growth and political stability in the most severely affected nations.

Table 7.7   Estimated range of treated and yet untreated HIV cases for the 20 countries with the highest unmet need in 2005

Country	Estimated range of treated cases so far	Amount of original treatment target that is unmet
South Africa	97,000–138,000	866,000
India	33,000–67,000	735,000
Nigeria	28,000–48,000	598,000
Zimbabwe	9,500–16,000	308,000
Tanzania	5,500–9,500	307,000
Ethiopia	15,000–19,000	261,000
Kenya	33,000–46,000	233,000
Mozambique	11,000–13,000	204,000
Democratic Republic of Congo	5,000–6,000	203,000
Zambia	26,000–33,000	153,000
Malawi	18,000–23,000	159,000
Ivory Coast	11,000–19,000	96,000
Russia	4,000–6,500	94,000
Cameroon	12,000–20,000	92,000
Uganda	52,000–64,000	90,000
China	11,000–14,000	65,000
Sudan	500	62,000
Thailand	67,000–82,000	60,000
Ghana	2,500–3,000	58,000
Lesotho	2,500–3,000	55,000

Source: Nolen (2005): A15. (Data are from the World Health Organization.)

The Growing Burden of Non-Communicable Diseases

Some of the world's poorest countries, while fighting rising epidemics of infectious diseases such as HIV, malaria, and tuberculosis, are also facing increasing levels of non-infectious illnesses, such as heart disease, diabetes, and cancer, creating a sort of double-punch (Ebrahim and Smeeth, 2005). To make things worse, mal-

nutrition remains a major problem, especially among young children and mothers (Caldwell, Caldwell, and Quiggin, 1989; Kibirige, 1997; Lindstrom and Berhanu, 1999; Mosley and Chen, 1984; Olshansky et al., 1997; Quinn, 1995).

Estimates prepared by the World Health Organization and summarized by Ebrahim and Smeeth (2005: 962), shown in Table 7.8, indicate that the three leading causes of death in the developed countries are ischemic heart disease (accounting for 22.6 per cent of all deaths), cerebrovascular disease (13.7 per cent), and cancers of the lung, trachea, and bronchus (4.5 per cent). In the developing countries the leading causes are ischemic heart disease (9.1 per cent), cerebrovascular disease (8.0 per cent), lower respiratory infections (7.7 per cent), HIV/AIDS (6.9 per cent), and perinatal conditions (5.6 per cent). Projections for the year 2020 see the developed and developing countries becoming increasingly similar in their cause-of-death distributions, with ischemic heart disease and cerebrovascular complications becoming, respectively, number one and number two in both cases. The proportion of annual deaths due to these two diseases is expected to be 24 and 13 per cent respectively in the developed countries; and 14 and 11 per cent respectively in the developing countries.

One notable difference in the sets of data for developed and developing countries concerns lung cancer. In the developed countries, it is forecast to become the third leading cause of premature mortality; in the developing countries, it is projected to be the seventh leading cause. The early onset of the smoking epidemic in the industrialized countries, now spreading rapidly in the developing countries, explains the different rank order of this disease. It seems that the developing countries may not be heeding the lesson of the developed countries concerning the health risks associated with cigarettes (Dodu, 1984).

The World Health Organization (2005a) estimates that 25 per cent of chronic disease occurs among people below the age of 60, placing

HIV/AIDS: A Regional Breakdown

In 2005, 38 million of those infected with HIV/AIDS worldwide were adults; 17.5 million were women and 2.3 million were children under the age of 15. Of the 3.1 million people who died of AIDS that year, about 2.6 million were adults and just over half a million were children (Kim and Watts, 2005; Quinn and Overbaugh, 2005; UNAIDS, 2005b). A regional breakdown of the HIV/AIDS epidemic as of 2005 by UNAIDS (2006, http://www.unaids.org/en/Regions_Countries/default.asp) reveals the following:

- Sub-Saharan Africa is home to more than 60 per cent of all people living with HIV (25.8 million). An estimated 3.2 million people in the region are newly infected, while 2.4 million adults and children died of AIDS in 2005. The prevalence rate of HIV infection was 7.2 per cent.
- In Asia, roughly 8.3 million people are living with HIV, including 1.1 million people who became newly infected in 2004. AIDS claimed some 520,000 lives in 2005.
- The number of people infected with HIV in eastern Europe and central Asia has reached an estimated 1.6 million. Around 62,000 adults and children died of AIDS-related illnesses in 2005, and approximately 270,000 people were newly infected with HIV. Around 75 per cent of the reported infections between 2000 and 2004 affected people younger than 30.
- AIDS claimed an estimated 24,000 lives in the Caribbean in 2005, making it the leading cause of death among adults aged 15–44. A total of 300,000 people in the region are currently living with HIV, including 30,000 who became infected in 2005.
- The number of people living with HIV in Latin America has risen to an estimated 1.8 million. In 2005, approximately 66,000 people died of AIDS, and 200,000 were newly infected. Among people 15–24 years of age, an estimated 0.4 per cent of women and 0.6 per cent of men were living with HIV in 2005.
- The number of people living with HIV in North America and western and central Europe rose to 1.9 million in 2005, with approximately 65,000 people having acquired HIV in the previous year. Wide availability of antiretroviral drugs helped to limit the number of AIDS-related deaths in 2005 to 30,000.
- Recent estimates show that 67,000 residents of the Middle East and North Africa became infected with HIV in 2005. Approximately 510,000 people are living with HIV in the region, and an estimated 58,000 adults and children died of AIDS-related illnesses in 2005.
- Roughly 74,000 people in Oceania are living with HIV. Although fewer than 4,000 people are believed to have died of AIDS-related illnesses in 2005, about 8,200 are thought to have become newly infected with HIV. Among those aged 15–24, an estimated 1.2 per cent of women and 0.4 per cent of men were living with HIV in 2005.

tremendous socioeconomic burdens on individuals, families, and society as a whole. Long-term morbidity and premature death in this age group—the most productive segment of the population—is not desirable. For many families, the death of a family member of this age leads to poverty and destitution. On a national scale, rising levels of chronic disease combined with increasing communicable illnesses can mean huge economic setbacks (Sachs, Mellinger, and

Table 7.8 Estimated 10 leading causes of death in the world, developed and developing countries, 2005 and projected for 2020

	World		Developed countries		Developing countries	
2000 rank	**Causes**	**% total**	**Cause**	**% total**	**Cause**	**% total**
1	ischemic heart disease	12.4	ischemic heart disease	22.6	ischemic heart disease	9.1
2	cerebrovascular disease	9.2	cerebrovascular disease	13.7	cerebrovascular disease	8.0
3	lower respiratory infections	6.9	trachea, bronchus, and lung cancers	4.5	lower respiratory infections	7.7
4	HIV/AIDS	5.3	lower respiratory infections	3.7	HIV/AIDS	6.9
5	chronic obstructive pulmonary disease	4.5	chronic obstructive pulmonary disease	3.1	perinatal conditions	5.6
6	perinatal conditions	4.4	colon and rectal cancers	2.6	chronic obstructive pulmonary disease	5.0
7	diarrheal diseases	3.8	stomach cancer	1.9	diarrheal diseases	4.9
8	tuberculosis	3.0	self-inflicted injury	1.9	tuberculosis	3.7
9	road traffic accidents	2.3	diabetes	1.7	malaria	2.6
10	trachea, bronchus, and lung cancers	2.2	breast cancer	1.6	road traffic accidents	2.5
2020 rank						
1	ischemic heart disease	16.3	ischemic heart disease	24.1	ischemic heart disease	14.3
2	cerebrovascular disease	11.2	cerebrovascular disease	12.7	cerebrovascular disease	10.9
3	chronic obstructive pulmonary disease	6.9	trachea, bronchus, and lung cancers	5.9	chronic obstructive pulmonary disease	7.7
4	lower respiratory infections	3.7	chronic obstructive pulmonary disease	4.1	tuberculosis	4.1
5	trachea, bronchus, and lung cancers	3.5	lower respiratory infections	3.2	road traffic accidents	3.9
6	road traffic accidents	3.4	colon and rectal cancers	2.7	lower respiratory infections	3.7
7	tuberculosis	3.4	stomach cancer	2.4	trachea, bronchus, and lung cancers	2.9
8	stomach cancer	2.3	self-inflicted injury	1.8	stomach cancer	2.3
9	HIV/AIDS	1.8	diabetes	1.6	diarrheal diseases	2.2
10	self-inflicted injury	1.8	road traffic accidents	1.7	HIV/AIDS	2.1

Source: Shah Ebrahim and Liam Smeeth (2005), 'Non-Communicable Disease in Low and Middle-Income Countries: A Priority or a Distraction?', *International Journal of Epidemiology* 34: 961–6. (Estimates are from WHO). Reprinted by permission of the authors and OUP Journals.

Gallup, 2001; Stuckler, 2008) while overstressing health care systems of countries that cannot cope with the rising burden of disease. China, for example, stands to lose close to $558 billion (US) in national income over the next 10 years as a result of premature deaths caused by heart disease, stroke, and diabetes (World Health Organization, 2005a).

Why are rates of chronic disease growing in the developing countries? There are many interrelated causes, ranging from demographic aging due to recent fertility declines to the failure of governments to promote appropriate economic and social policies and make health care more available to their rapidly growing populations. Apart from these structural issues, one of the most important culprits is the so-called *nutrition transition*. With increasing globalization, the traditional diets of the developing countries, like other aspects of life, have been changing. Whereas in the past a traditional diet was based largely on homegrown fruits and vegetables, people are now consuming more energy-dense foods high in sugar, saturated fats, and salt, as well as more processed foods. Compounding the problem are falling rates of physical activity (World Health Organization, 2005b). These trends explain why more than 1 billion people worldwide are overweight and another 300 million are clinically obese (World Health Organization 2005a, 2005b). Altogether, the changes in diet contribute to many of the chronic diseases now being experienced in greater numbers in the developing countries. Without vigorous education and public health campaigns aimed at discouraging unhealthy eating practices, the increase in chronic disease is likely to continue (World Health Organization, 2005a, 2005b).

Canadian Mortality: Trends, Patterns, and Differentials

Mortality Trends before 1921

Most of the mortality statistics for Canada are available dating back to 1921, when the Canadian vital statistics registration system came into effect. Estimates for earlier periods are available but are typically based on regional data. Pelletier and colleagues (1997), for instance, prepared an estimate of Quebec mortality in the early nineteenth century, calculating a crude death rate of 26.43 per 1,000 population for the year 1810. Wadhera and Strachan (1994) estimated early mortality statistics for Canada as a whole. Their estimated crude death rate for the mid-1800s was in the range of 22 per 1,000 population, declining slightly to 21 for the decade 1861–71. From this point until close to the time of vital registration, the crude death rate dropped steadily to around 12 per 1,000 in 1921. In a comparative sense, the level of mortality in Canada during this time is thought to have been lower than that of the American States (McInnis, 2000a).

Concerning infant mortality, Pelletier and colleagues (1997) estimated that in Quebec in 1851–2 the rate ranged between 93 infant deaths per 1,000 live births for the province as a whole to 197 in Quebec City and 232 in Montreal. In 1860–1, Quebec's infant mortality increased to 104 per 1,000, largely as a function of the increases experienced by Montreal, where the rate soared to nearly 272 infant deaths per 1,000 live births. Pelletier and colleagues (1997) have attributed Montreal's higher infant mortality rates to the fact that the city was a major port of entry for an immigrant population at greater risk of contracting major infectious diseases. In fact, between 1831 and 1841, the province of Quebec, and the city of Montreal in particular, did experience outbreaks of cholera and typhus. In general, however, mortality during the nineteenth century was higher in the towns and cities than in rural areas. It would not be until after the late 1800s—and especially after the start of the twentieth century, as cities adopted sanitation systems and better ways of treating the water supply—that urban and rural death rates would begin to converge (Pelletier, Legaré, and Bourbeau, 1997).

Prior to the start of the twentieth century, tuberculosis was the leading killer in Canada. In

1880–1, when the population of Canada was just over 4 million, some 6,695 people perished from this disease (McVey and Kalbach, 1995a: 204). McInnis (2000a: 570) has estimated that the death rate from tuberculosis was likely around 180 per 100,000 at that time.

Mortality Trends since 1921

With vital registration data from 1921 on, we are in a more secure position to outline the broad contours of Canadian mortality over the last eight decades.

In 1921, Canada's crude death rate of 11.9 per 1,000 population was already low by global standards, and well below the current rates of many of today's developing countries. Then, as Table 7.9 shows, large declines in mortality took place until midway through the twentieth century, with the age-standardized death rate dropping from almost 13 per 1,000 in 1921 to 9.0 in 1951. Since then, the decline in overall mortality has been steady, with notable improvements during the 1960s and 1970s, though on the whole less dramatic than the declines of earlier periods. In 2001, the age standardized death rate reached its lowest point in history, at 5.1 per 1,000 population.

Early in the twentieth century, infectious and parasitic diseases—especially influenza and pneumonia—were the dominant killers (see Table 7.10), although diabetes (a chronic disease) and violence also accounted for a significant share of deaths. Over time, particularly since the early 1950s, influenza and pneumonia have receded and have become relatively minor forces in Canadian mortality trends. The leading causes of death today are not infectious and parasitic diseases but circulatory and neoplastic diseases, including myocardial infarction and other forms of heart disease; cancers of the trachea,

Table 7.9 Total number of deaths, crude death rates, and standardized death rates (per 1,000 population), Canada, 1921–2001

Period	Deaths	Male death rates**	Female death rates**	Total crude death rates	Male standard-ized death rates***	Female standard-ized death rates***	Total standard-ized death rates***	% change standardized death rate from previous period
1921	104,531*	11.9	11.2	11.6	13.3	12.4	12.9	—
1931	108,446	10.5	9.6	10.2	12.7	11.7	12.8	−0.8
1941	118,797	10.9	9.1	10.1	12.0	10.2	11.2	−12.5
1951	125,823	10.1	7.8	9.0	10.0	8.0	9.0	−19.6
1961	140,985	9.0	6.5	7.7	9.0	6.3	7.6	−15.6
1971	157,272	8.5	6.1	7.3	8.4	5.2	6.7	−11.8
1981	171,029	8.0	6.0	7.0	7.2	4.3	5.8	−13.4
1991	195,568	7.8	6.5	7.2	6.8	4.1	5.4	−6.9
2001	219,114	7.3	6.8	7.1	6.6	4.0	5.1	−5.6

*Excludes the Yukon and Northwest Territories.

**Excludes Newfoundland prior to 1949 and the Yukon and Northwest Territories prior to 1928.

***Excludes Quebec prior to 1926, Newfoundland prior to 1949, and the Yukon and Northwest Territories prior to 1950.

Note: Rates standardized to Canada's 1956 population.

Sources: Adapted from McVey and Kalbach (1995a): 184; Trovato (1994): 22–64; Statistics Canada Health Statistics Division (1999); World Health Organization (2006b).

Table 7.10 Numerical and percentage distribution of selected causes of death, Canada, 1921 and 2000

Causes of death	1921		2000	
	Numerical	%	Numerical	%
Infectious and parasitic diseases	9,346	13.8	3,112	1.4
Diseases of the circulatory system	9,142	13.5	76,426	35.0
Diseases of the respiratory system	8,668	12.8	17,744	8.1
Diseases of the digestive system	6,840	10.1	8,148	3.7
Perinatal diseases	6,230	9.0	898	0.4
Malignant neoplasms	5,011	7.4	62,672	28.7
External causes of death	4,199	6.2	8,758	4.0
Subtotal	49,436	72.8	177,758	81.3
All causes of death	67,722	100.0	218,061	100.0

Note: Data for 1921 excludes Newfoundland.

Sources: McVey and Kalbach (1995a): 206; World Health Organization Mortality Data Base, http://www3.who.int/whosis/mort/table1.cfm? path=whosis,mort,mort_table1&language=english (accessed June 28, 2006).

lung, and bronchus; and cerebrovascular complications. Indeed, over two-thirds of all annual deaths in Canada are now attributable to either heart disease or cancer. Significant reductions in accidental mortalities did not occur until the mid-twentieth century, and even today this category of premature death, which includes automobile fatalities, remains a serious public health problem.

Infant Mortality

Like the overall death rate, infant mortality in Canada had declined considerably by the second decade of the twentieth century (see Figure 7.11). Around 1921, 88.1 of every 1,000 babies born in Canada would perish before reaching their first birthday. By midway through the century this rate had dropped to 38.5, falling even further to 17.6 by 1971. By the beginning of the 1980s, infant mortality had decreased to below 10 per 1,000 live births, and in 2006, the rate stood at 5.3 per 1,000 (Population Reference Bureau, 2006). Another way to illustrate the dramatic decline of infant mortality is to compare the actual number of infant deaths earlier in the century with the figure today. In 1921,

there were 27,051 infant deaths. By 1951, this number had been cut by almost half, to 14,673. In 2000, the number of infant deaths was just 1,736 (World Health Organization, 2006b).

In the past, tuberculosis and influenza headed a list of infectious diseases that figured prominently in infant and early childhood mortality. Measles, mumps, chicken pox, whooping cough, and scarlet fever, though not quite as deadly as TB and influenza, all contributed to high rates of death among infants and children (King, Gartrell, and Trovato, 1994). Mothers were also at high risk of dying from infectious diseases. But by the middle of the century, there had been significant improvements in the areas of obstetric medicine and pre- and postnatal care of infants. After 1930, new and effective medical therapies, most notably blood transfusion and antibiotics, greatly improved the survival chances of infants and mothers (Berry, 1977; Mitchinson, 2002). Early-age mortality from communicable diseases dropped considerably after the third decade of the twentieth century, when water chlorination and pasteurization of milk were added to the list of important public health developments (Beaver, 1975).

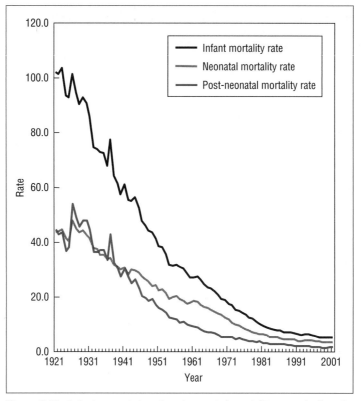

Figure 7.11 Infant, neonatal, and post-neonatal mortality rates in Canada, 1921–2001

Source: Wadhera and Strachan (1993): 22–3; Statistics Canada Health Statistics Division (1999); Statistics Canada Health Statistics Division, *Deaths* (various years).

Infectious diseases today are responsible for less than 1 per cent of infant deaths.

The pattern of change in neonatal and post-neonatal mortality rates over the twentieth century parallels the pattern noted for infant mortality in general. Early in the century, neonatal and post-neonatal rates fluctuated very closely together, from approximately 43 deaths per 1,000 live births in 1921 to close to 58 per 1,000 in the mid-1920s. From that point, both rates have followed a generalized pattern of decline. The two rates began to diverge in the early 1940s, and since then neonatal death rates have been consistently higher than post-neonatal rates, which have for the most part fallen faster. In 2000, the neonatal and post-neonatal death rates were 3.64 and

1.7 per 1,000 live births, respectively. Thus, the significant reductions in early-life mortality in Canada have been accompanied by a gradual shift in the preponderance of deaths from the post-neonatal to the neonatal phase. While approximately 27 per cent of all infant deaths in 1921 were neonatal, this proportion has risen to about 70 per cent in recent years.

A large part of the success in saving neonates must be attributed to medical innovations such as the introduction, in the 1980s, of exogenous surfactant therapy to fight respiratory complications in newborns and the establishment of neonatal intensive care units (Kliegman, 1995). By far, the most prevalent causes of premature death among infants today, accounting for nearly three-quarters of all infant deaths in Canada, are congenital anomalies and complications originating in the perinatal period, including low birth weight. Early in the twentieth century such problems accounted for less than 10 per cent of all neonatal cases and approximately 4.0 per cent of post-neonatal mortality (King, Gartrell, and Trovato, 1994).

Further reductions in perinatal, neonatal, and post-neonatal mortality are possible through a combination of medical and behavioural interventions. Ongoing research is being directed toward perfecting therapies and surgical techniques to help reduce mortality at both the perinatal and neonatal stages. Growing attention is also being given to the prenatal environment as a risk factor in perinatal and neonatal mortality risk (Behrens, 2003; Priest and Harding, 2006; Smith, 2004; Smith et al., 2004). Increased education and public health knowledge can help expectant mothers avoid certain risks that compromise the well-being of

the fetus, most importantly smoking, alcohol and substance abuse, and excessive distress during pregnancy (Dole et al., 2003; Phung et al., 2003; Henriksen et al., 2004; Ponce et al., 2005; Wisborg et al., 2001).

Childhood Mortality

Children Aged 1–4

By today's standards, the probability of death for a child between the ages of 1 and 4 at the start of the twentieth century was exceptionally high— 79 per cent for boys and 76 per cent for girls, according to Bourbeau and colleagues (1997). By 1921, these conditional death probabilities had declined to 39 and 36 per cent, respectively. By the end of the century, the chance of death for children aged 1–4 was approaching zero, with estimated rates of 1.26 per cent for boys and 0.95 per cent for girls in 1996 (Bourbeau, Legaré, and Émond, 1997). As Figure 7.12 shows, the largest improvements in death prob-

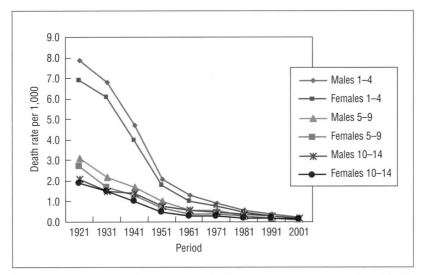

Figure 7.12 Time trend in age-specific death rates in Canada, ages 1–4 to 10–14, 1921–2001

Source: Peron and Strohmenger (1985): 195; Wadhera and Strachan (1993); World Health Organization, Mortality Data Base: http://www3.who.int/whosis/mort/table1.cfm?path=whosis,mort,mort_table1&language =english; World Health Organization, Life Tables: http://www3.who.int/whosis/life/life_tables/life_tables_ process.cfm?path=life_tables&language=english.

abilities for boys and girls took place around the halfway mark of the century.

During the first half of the twentieth century, the leading causes of death in boys and girls were infectious diseases like influenza, bronchitis, pneumonia, tuberculosis, diarrhea, diphtheria, whooping cough, and meningitis. Diarrhea and enteritis alone were responsible for the deaths of 92 boys for every 100,000 population in 1931; influenza, bronchitis, and pneumonia took the lives of 190 out of every 100,000 1- to 4-year-old girls, while diarrhea and enteritis were the second leading cause of death for girls in this age group. Fortunately, today these scourges of the past have receded to a considerable degree. Deaths of boys and girls from influenza, bronchitis, and pneumonia fell from 59 and 160 per 100,000 in 1931 to just 1 and 2 per 100,000 by the mid-1980s, and diarrhea and enteritis have virtually disappeared as causes of death to children (King, Gartrell, and Trovato, 1994). One disturbing trend remains, however: the rate of death from accidents and violence, which was the second leading cause of death among young boys in 1931, continues to be relatively high for children, especially for boys.

Children Aged 5–14
Large-scale mortality improvements since the 1930s have also been recorded for Canadian children between the ages of 5 and 14. From 1931 to 1951, the death rate for boys dropped from 185 to 89 per 100,000 while the death rate for girls declined from 162 to 59 per 100,000. Reductions since 1951, though modest by comparison with those of the earlier two decades, continue to be significant. Success in reducing child death rates can be attributed largely to the implementation of effective vaccines and other medical interventions that have helped to cut down children's exposure to infections.

Young Adulthood through Old Age

Young Adults Aged 15–24
Young people between the ages of 15 and 24 are particularly prone to accidental or violent death. This is especially so for men, whose rates of accidental or violent death have been approximately three to five times greater than those of women since the 1930s. This differential has not changed by much over time. As Table 7.11 shows, the leading cause of death among 15- to 24-year-olds in 1931 was tuberculosis, which killed more women than men earlier in the century. By the mid-1900s, motor vehicle accidents had surpassed TB as the leading cause of death among men in this aged group. Overall, the dramatic improvement in young adult mortality can be attributed in large part to the dramatic decline of tuberculosis.

An encouraging trend is the reduction in motor vehicle fatalities among young adults, especially since the early 1970s. Among the factors involved in this trend are laws making the use of seat belts mandatory, stiffer penalties for impaired driving, better and safer vehicle construction, and, perhaps, a greater awareness overall of road safety fostered through public health campaigns. Unfortunately, motor vehicle accidents, along with violence and suicide, continue to claim a disproportionate number of young lives. Meanwhile, cancer and cardiovascular disease remain rare among young adults, and death rates associated with these causes have been declining.

Adults Aged 25–44
In 1931, the overall death rate for men between the ages of 25 and 44 was 410 per 100,000; the rate for women was 440 per 100,000. By the end of the century these rates had dropped to 126 and 68 for men and women, respectively (see Table 7.11). The higher overall rate for women in 1931 was the result of a combination of conditions, including higher rates of tuberculosis, cancer, cardiovascular disease, and nephritis, and complications associated with childbirth. But as conditions improved for women midway through the century, death rates for men surpassed those for women in every major cause category except cancer. At the same time,

Table 7.11 Death rates (per 100,000 population) for Canadian men and women by broad age category, cause of death, and period, 1931–2000

Age and cause of death	Males							Females						
	1931	1951	1971	1981	1986	1991	2000	1931	1951	1971	1981	1986	1991	2000
Age 1–4														
Diarrhea/enteritis	92	41	1	0	0	0	0	70	9	1	0	0	0	0
Accidents/violence	81	48	41	28	23	13	7	50	61	28	19	14	7	4
Influenza/bronchitis/pneumonia	59	98	8	2	1	0	0	160	40	10	2	2	0	0
Tuberculosis	51	31	0	0	0	0	0	45	14	0	0	0	0	0
Diphtheria	36	11	0	0	0	0	0	34	1	0	0	0	0	0
Whooping cough	21	16	0	0	0	0	0	32	3	0	0	0	0	0
Total	679	399	91	59	49	39	23	612	205	78	46	41	28	18
Age 5–14														
Accidents/violence	46	45	34	24	15	11	7	15	16	17	12	9	5	4
Tuberculosis	23	6	0	0	0	0	0	28	8	0	0	0	0	0
Appendicitis	17	2	2	0	0	0	0	16	2	2	0	0	0	0
Influenza/bronchitis/pneumonia	14	5	0	0	1	0	0	16	5	0	0	1	0	0
Diphtheria	11	1	1	0	0	0	0	12	1	1	0	0	0	0
Total	185	89	53	37	27	23.2	16	162	59	35	24	18	17	12
Age 15–24														
Tuberculosis	71	18	0	0	0	0	0	118	24	0	0	0	0	0
Motor vehicle accidents (MVAs)	22	37	73	66	48	38	22	5	10	23	18	14	12	9
Other accidents/violence	67	41	40	35	20	19	14	9	5	9	8	4	4	4
Influenza/bronchitis/pneumonia	19	5	2	1	1	0	0	13	4	2	1	1	0	0
Cardiovascular	14	8	4	3	3	3	2	16	7	3	2	2	2	2
Cancers	7	10	9	6	6	6	6	5	6	6	4	4	4	4
Suicide	6	6	18	28	27	29	21	4	2	4	5	5	4	5
Total	284	161	158	150	126	110	78	269	92	57	46	41	37	34

(continued)

Table 7.11 (continued)

Age and cause of death	Males							Females						
	1931	1951	1971	1981	1986	1991	2000	1931	1951	1971	1981	1986	1991	2000
Age 25–44														
Tuberculosis	86	28	1	0	0	0	0	110	26	1	0	0	0	0
Motor vehicle accidents (MVAs)	27	41	39	39	27	19	21	5	6	12	10	8	7	4
Other accidents/violence	54	120	59	24	19	11	19	7	20	10	7	5	5	5
Cardiovascular	43	59	46	32	25	20	16	48	34	18	12	9	8	7
Influenza/bronchitis/pneumonia	31	6	4	1	2	2	1	26	5	3	1	1	1	1
Cancers	25	25	29	23	24	21	19	53	45	37	28	30	29	26
Suicide	19	12	24	26	30	28	25	7	4	9	9	8	8	6
Total	**410**	**252**	**218**	**174**	**158**	**153**	**126**	**440**	**183**	**118**	**87**	**77**	**76**	**68**
Age 45–64														
Cardiovascular	352	687	597	454	368	272	171	319	376	199	160	102	98	62
Cancer	202	243	286	309	327	305	227	267	266	238	250	269	240	207
Tuberculosis	90	48	6	2	1	1	0	61	21	3	1	1	0	0
Influenza/bronchitis/pneumonia	89	35	34	17	20	17	15	71	25	14	8	12	10	12
Nephritis/nephrotis	86	30	5	5	0	4	4	89	27	4	4	0	4	2
Motor vehicle accidents (MVAs)	39	44	35	32	20	14	10	12	10	14	11	9	7	5
Other accidents/violence	58	49	52	37	27	24	23	13	10	17	13	11	8	8
Suicide	37	25	32	29	27	25	22	8	9	14	12	10	8	8
Total	**1,249**	**1,336**	**1,208**	**1,044**	**928**	**804**	**591**	**1,118**	**868**	**599**	**552**	**529**	**449**	**364**

(continued)

Table 7.11 *(continued)*

Age and cause of death	Males							Females						
	1931	1951	1971	1981	1986	1991	2000	1931	1951	1971	1981	1986	1991	2000
Age 65–74														
Cardiovascular	1,754	2,488	2,271	1,827	1,606	1,243	1,228	1,532	1,862	1,201	986	764	599	586
Cancer	763	783	1,034	1,073	1,147	1,127	907	698	618	566	610	652	659	732
Influenza/bronchitis/pneumonia	332	170	193	100	129	110	153	366	127	60	42	64	50	93
Nephritis/nephrotis/renal failure	329	105	15	25	33	28	34	338	97	12	16	9	19	20
Accidents/violence (−MVAs)	155	141	111	105	47	33	34	82	56	58	42	32	25	20
Tuberculosis	107	72	14	5	4	2	2	85	35	6	2	1	1	1
Total	4,352	4,309	4,174	3,703	3,543	3,135	2,603	3,835	3,207	2,215	1,901	1,845	1,679	1,505
Age 75+														
Cardiovascular	5,247	7,456	7,025	5,749	4,997	4,237	3,454	5,302	7,085	5,662	4,514	4,097	3,466	2,884
Cancer	1,186	1,446	1,880	2,074	2,185	2,247	1,279	1,016	1,137	1,088	1,084	1,188	1,190	2,044
Influenza/bronchitis/pneumonia	1,142	890	836	593	739	663	863	1,136	808	453	326	430	433	507
Senility	1,021	234	40	23	13	8	6	1,205	273	45	27	26	4	40
Nephritis/nephrotis/renal failure	945	335	50	124	200	156	170	824	357	38	79	134	101	114
Accidents/violence (−MVAs)	316	331	259	216	183	102	104	458	376	217	172	183	254	268
Hernia/intestinal obstruction	128	74	55	47	39	37	33	85	57	48	41	44	40	41
Diabetes	93	101	206	160	195	197	37	132	140	207	170	187	180	40
Diarrhea/enteritis	81	24	13	9	1	0	0	97	31	9	10	3	2	1
Suicide	35	31	27	32	36	18	14	5	6	4	12	6	7	5
Total	11,881	12,169	11,446	10,410	10,206	9,531	8,567	11,635	11,059	8,329	7,190	7,030	6,863	6,617

Notes: Death rates have been rounded to whole numbers. MVAs = motor vehicle accidents.

Source: Trovato (1994): 22–64; data for 1991 and 2000 from World Health Organization, http://www3.who.int/whosis/menu.cfm?path=whosis,mort&language=english (accessed 10 April 2006).

some of the most lethal diseases of earlier periods—tuberculosis, appendicitis, ulcers of the stomach and duodenum, and intestinal obstruction—began to recede to the point where they no longer constituted major risks.

For both men and women in this age category, death from cardiovascular disease rose until the early 1970s and has been declining ever since, following a pattern that has been observed in other industrialized countries, including the United States. Most scholars agree that reductions in cigarette smoking, the introduction of new treatments to control hypertension, increased consciousness of the importance of diet in health maintenance, and the control of cholesterol levels through medication, as well as better management of lifestyles, all helped reduce vascular disease mortality (Bonita and Beaglehole, 1989; Breslow, 1985; Epstein, 1989; Kaplan et al., 1988; Levy, 1981; Martikainen et al., 2005; Muir and Sasco, 1990; Ragland, Selvin, and Merrill, 1988; Rothenberg and Koplan, 1990; Thom, 1989; Tuck, 2003). Declines in cancer mortality have been less impressive, though major improvements in treatment are likely to be reflected in changing rates (Rothenberg and Koplan, 1990; Collins and Barker, 2007). Cancer is the number-one cause of death for women in this age category.

Suicide, despite declining rates since around the mid-1980s, remains a leading cause of premature death for people aged 25–44, especially men. Declines in the suicide rate have not prevented it from replacing motor vehicle accidents as the principal cause of death among 24- to 44-year-old men. The prevalence of suicide among men is not unique to Canada, but is common in other high-income countries as well (Ahlburg and Schapiro, 1984; Pampel, 1996, 1998; Stack, 2000a, 2000b). Pampel has observed that suicide rates for young adult males are highest in societies characterized by a high degree of individualism versus collectivism. Suicide rates are lower in societies where the social system protects those in need (the unemployed, the disad-

vantaged, etc.). Pampel notes that the situation is worst in individualistically oriented social contexts where young men experience high rates of unemployment and belong to a large birth cohort (which reduces chances for the individual in gaining access to jobs under difficult economic conditions).

Adults Aged 45–64

In 1931, the overall death rate for men aged 45–54 was 1,249 per 100,000, while that for women was 1,118 per 100,000 (see Table 7.11). These rates have plummeted over the course of the century, to 591 and 364, respectively, as of 2000. Mortality in this age group is now caused mainly by chronic and degenerative diseases, especially cardiovascular ailments and cancers. This pattern of disease contrasts sharply with the trends that characterized the earlier part of the twentieth century, when the major killers were influenza, bronchitis, and pneumonia (and, to a lesser degree, complications such as nephritis and nephrosis). By the late twentieth century these and other causes (tuberculosis, syphilis, hernias, and stomach ulcers) had declined to insignificance.

Adults Aged 65–74

Large-scale improvements in mortality among older adults between the ages of 65 and 74 have been gained over the twentieth century. In 1931, men and women had death rates of 4,352 and 3,835 per 100,000, respectively. By the midway mark of the century, these rates had declined to 4,309 and 3,207, respectively, and further decreases over subsequent decades brought these rates to 2,603 and 1,505 as of the start of the twenty-first century (see Table 7.11). In the early 1900s, a mix of infectious and chronic diseases (in order, cardiovascular disease, cancer, influenza/bronchitis/pneumonia, nephritis, accidents, and tuberculosis) claimed many lives of seniors in this age category. Today, cardiovascular disease and cancer pose the greatest threats to people in this age category, accounting for over 44,000 lives annually and just over 20 per cent of all deaths in Canada (World Health Organization, 2006b).

Mortality rates associated with cancer and cardiovascular disease are key to understanding why women in this age group have enjoyed lower rates of mortality overall. Cardiovascular mortality rates have been declining for both sexes since the mid-1900s, but fell faster for women from the 1950s until the 1980s, when the declining female rate was overtaken by the falling male rate. At the same time, cancer death rates in this age group have always been higher for men, even though male rates have levelled off and begun to decline in recent decades, while female cancer rates have been rising since the 1970s. This divergent trend between male and female cancer mortality rates means that the overall mortality advantage for women aged 65–74 is now diminishing. This interesting topic is examined later in the context of the changing sex differential in life expectancy.

Adults Aged 75 and Older
Mortality rates for Canadians aged 75 and older have been declining since early in the twentieth century. Between 1931 and the mid-1980s, the overall death rate for women in this age group fell by 37 per cent, from 11,635 per 100,000 to 7,030. Over the same period, the male mortality rate dropped from 11,881 to 10,206 per 100,000, for a 14 per cent decline. These trends repeat the pattern, evident in other age groups, of more precipitous declines in the death rate for women. It is worth noting, however, that between 1991 and 2000, the male death rate dropped by 10 per cent, while female mortality declined by just 3.5 per cent, indicating somewhat larger mortality improvements by men recently.

As with adults aged 65–74, cardiovascular disease and cancer are the leading causes of death in this age group. Nonetheless, it is interesting to note the declines in cardiovascular mortality for both men and women. In 1931, the cardiovascular mortality rates for men and women aged 75 and over were 5,247 and 5,302, respectively. These rates peaked in the early 1950s and have been following a downward trend ever since, to 4,997 and 4,097, respectively, in the mid-1980s and 3,454 and 2,884 by 2000. The same declines have not been matched by cancer rates for this age group. Men's cancer rates rose throughout most of the twentieth century, beginning to decline only recently in the 1990s. Women's rates rose between 1931 and 1951, declined from 1951 through 1981, and have been rising since then. Between 1981 and 2000, the female cancer death rate has risen faster than the corresponding male rate, owing largely to increased rates of lung cancer mortality among women stemming from increased smoking in the post-war years.

Mortality from influenza, bronchitis, pneumonia, senility, and nephritis (including renal failure), which were leading killers earlier in the century, have declined significantly over time for adults 75 years of age and over. Likewise, hernia and intestinal obstructions, diarrhea, and enteritis are now minor causes of death. However, diabetes has risen in importance. Suicide for elderly Canadian men and women has followed two trends: a decline between the early 1930s and the early part of the 1970s, and a rise thereafter until the mid 1980s, from which point the trend has been downward. Accidental and violent deaths have declined over time.

Inequalities in Health and Mortality

The Sex Differential in Mortality
The female advantage in mortality and life expectancy is one of the most entrenched differentials in human populations (Luy, 2003; Madigan, 1957; Stolnitz, 1955; Vallin, 1983). At the international level, only a few exceptions to this have been noted (Das Gupta and Shuzhuo, 2000; D'Souza and Chen, 1980; El-Badry, 1969; Mishra, Roy, and Retherford, 2004; Murphy, 2003; Nadarajah, 1983).

Preston (1976) found that the sex differential in mortality tended to favour men until the period of large-scale modernization in the late nineteenth century, when the balance swung in favour of women and then began to widen over most of the twentieth century. Indeed, historical evidence for western Europe confirms that during the late 1800s, at a time when life expectancy was much below what it is today, women's life expectancy exceeded men's by about two or three years (Acsadi and Nemeskeri, 1970; Preston, 1976). This small female advantage could have been greater had it not been for high rates of maternal mortality (Henry, 1989). With gradual improvements in socioeconomic conditions and public health during the nineteenth and twentieth centuries, the rate of pregnancy-related deaths decreased, helping women to gain considerable numbers of years of life expectancy. Stolnitz (1955) established that the sex differential in mortality started to widen after about the second decade of the twentieth century, and that by the 1940s, women outlived men by about 4 years on average. By the 1950s,

the sex gap in the industrialized countries had grown to approximately 5 or 6 years, reaching 7 or 8 years by the 1970s (Lopez, 1983; Vallin, 1983).

The general trend in men's and women's mortality is illustrated in Figures 13a and 13b, which focus on the experience of Canada and Austria. In both countries, the difference between men's and women's longevity ranged between 3 and 4 years early in the twentieth century. The sharp drop and recovery of the differential during the early 1920s in Canada may reflect problems with the estimated life expectancy figures, or possibly some event that produced a temporary narrowing of the sex gap in life expectancy at birth. One possible explanation is the influenza pandemic of 1918–19. Noymer and Garenne (2000) have shown that during the pandemic, female mortality in the young adult ages exceeded male mortality in the United States; in fact, women lost a substantial portion of their mortality advantage over men for a temporary period (see also Smith, 1993: 83). Since the US, like Canada, saw a sharp drop

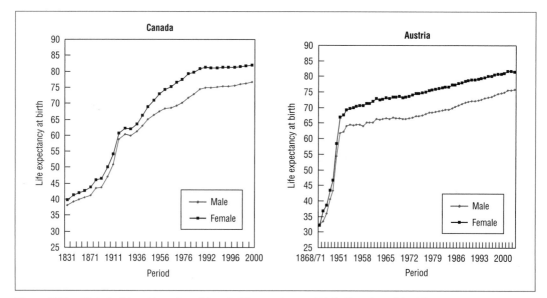

Figure 7.13a Historical trend in male and female life expectancy at birth, Canada and Austria

Source: Adapted from Peron and Strohmenger (1985): 115; Bélanger (2003: 17); Nagnur (1986b); Statistik Austria (2005:79).

in women's mortality advantage in the early 1920s, it's reasonable to speculate that the pandemic had similar effects on mortality differences in both countries, and that this may explain the temporary drop in the sex differential in men's and women's life expectancy in Canada during the early 1920s.

By the middle of the twentieth century, the Canadian gender gap in life expectancy had risen to about 4.5 years, and to just over 5 years in Austria. Around the same time, the differential stood at almost 6 years in the United States and ranged between 2 and 7 years across the other industrialized countries (Lopez, 1983; Peron and Strohmenger, 1985: 121; Smith, 1993: 83). The difference reached nearly 7 years in both Canada and Austria during the early part of the 1970s. Today, the gender gaps in life expectancy for the two countries are virtually identical to those recorded in the mid-1950s (around 5.5 years). This pattern of gender difference in average longevity is not unique to Canada and Austria: it has been observed across a large number of industrialized countries also. A significant exception is Japan, where the difference, in favour of women, has continued to grow (Pampel, 2002; Trovato and Hayen, 2005; Trovato and Lalu, 1996a; Waldron, 1993).

In spite of the recent narrowing of the mortality differential, many experts believe the gap will never close completely. This raises two important questions: why should we expect an indefinite mortality advantage for women, and why did the differential narrow at all after increasing in favour of women over much of the twentieth century? Biological and genetic differences between the sexes help us to answer the first question; the rest of the puzzle may be explained in terms of differences in acquired risks due to behavioural differences.

Males' greater vulnerability to death begins very early in life—from the moment of conception. Kramer (2000), after a careful review of the literature, arrived at the conclusion that males are, on most relevant measures, inherently more vulnerable owing to 'the biological fragility of the male fetus' (1609). In other words, maleness seems to have some intrinsic risks that are genetic/biological in origin (Madigan, 1957; Perls and Fretts, 2002; Verbrugge, 1976, 1989b; Waldron, 1976). Studies conducted on primates and humans reinforce the possibility of a hor-

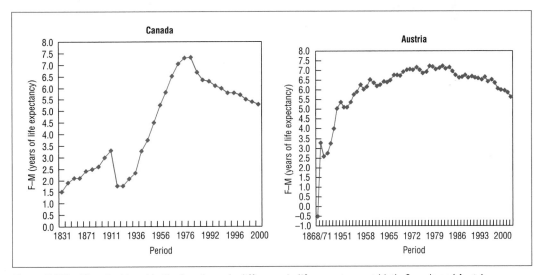

Figure 7.13b   Historical trend in the female–male difference in life expectancy at birth, Canada and Austria

Source: Source: Adapted from Peron and Strohmenger (1985): 115; Bélanger (2003: 17); Nagnur (1986b); Statistik Austria (2005:79).

monal basis for the higher mortality of males. Among other things, it is believed that low *immunocompetence*—an organism's all around ability to avoid the harmful effects of parasites—in male mammals is due to the effect of testosterone, which is an immunosuppressant (Owen, 2002). The resulting differences in immunocompetence may underlie male-biased mortality from parasitic infections as well as from some other conditions. Exactly how testosterone is linked to immunosuppression is not yet fully known, but one theory is that testosterone alters the way in which males allocate resources among competing physiological needs. Males may be unable to mount an effective immune response because they face a trade-off between allocating resources to fending off disease and allocating resources to other metabolic activities (Owen, 2002). Women's stronger immune system gives them an advantage in longevity over males (Pido-Lopez, Imami, and Aspinall, 2001).

As we have seen, men have higher death rates than women do from vascular diseases, especially coronary heart disease. As this is a leading cause of death, this sex differential would account for a significant portion of the overall male disadvantage in mortality risk (Rogers, Hummer, and Nam, 2000). In both men and women the mortality rate from coronary heart disease increases exponentially with age, starting at about age 35, but the rise in the age-related rate for women lags behind that for men by 5 to 10 years (Smith, 1993: 89). Figure 7.14a illustrates this situation in both Canada and the US. It's worth noting that this lagged pattern, which contributes significantly to the gender gap in overall mortality, is not evident in the case of cancer, where the rise in death rates for men and women begins more or less at the same time at around the age of 35 (see Figure 7.14b).

The female relative advantage in vascular disease has been ascribed to the protective effects prior to menopause of the female hormone

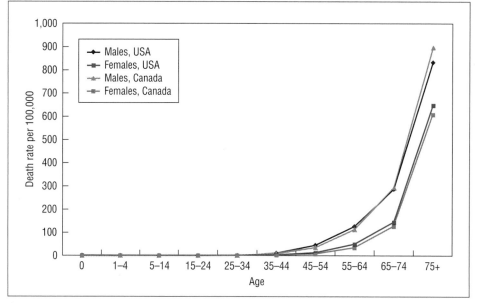

Figure 7.14a   Age-specific death rates from acute myocardial infarction by sex, Canada and the United States, 2000

Source: Author's computations based on data from the World Health Organization (2006b).

estrogen, which plays a role in the modulation of cholesterol (Smith, 1993). The incidence of cardiovascular disease in women rises sharply after the menopausal transition, when female hormones, most notably estrogen, decline. It has also been observed that with menopause the levels of HDL cholesterol drop while LDL cholesterol increases, creating a situation that is conducive to an increased risk of vascular disease. Hormone replacement therapy appears to lower women's risk of this disease, suggesting that estrogen plays an important protective role in women (Mendelsohn and Karas, 2005).

In addition to these possible biological differences, the sex differential in health and longevity may be attributed to differences in modifiable risk factors associated with lifestyle and behaviour (Case and Paxson, 2005; DesMeules et al., 2004; Kramer, 2000; Veevers and Gee, 1986; Verbrugge, 1976; Waldron, 1976, 2000). Roughly 75 per cent of the mortality discrepancy between men and women during adult-

hood can be accounted for by differences between the sexes in death from lung cancer, cirrhosis of the liver, suicide, homicide, motor vehicle accidents, heart disease, and stroke, all of which have strong behavioural components (such as stress, safety, diet, and substance abuse). In the United States, Waldron (1986) calculated that male mortality from coronary heart disease exceeded female mortality by a ratio of 2 to 1; for lung cancer the ratio was 6 to 1. Male mortality from emphysema was five times greater than women's mortality, and men were three times as likely as women to suffer motor vehicle fatalities and suicides. As Table 7.12 shows, the calculated cause-specific death rate ratios for Canada and the United States tend to be above 1.0 (signifying higher male mortality).

Many deaths from cancer, especially lung cancer, are associated with the long-term effects of cigarette smoking (Bartecchi et al., 1994; Doll and Peto, 1981; Peto et al., 2000; Ravenholt, 1990). Even though the differential

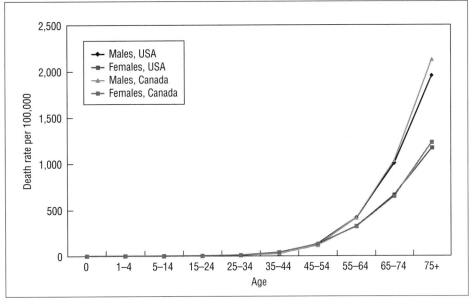

Figure 7.14b   Age-specific death rates from malignant neoplasms by sex, Canada and the United States, 2000

Source: Author's computations based on data from the World Health Organization (2006b).

Table 7.12   Male and female crude death rates for selected causes of death and corresponding male-to-female ratios of death rates, Canada and the United States, 2000

Cause of death	Canada			United States		
	Male	Female	Male:Female	Male	Female	Male:Female
Infectious/parasitic	11.3	8.9	1.30	23.0	19.0	1.21
Malignant neoplasms	218.8	188.6	1.16	207.2	186.2	1.11
Lung cancer	63.3	41.7	1.52	65.5	45.4	1.44
Acute myocardial infarction	74.2	55.6	1.33	72.7	64.6	1.13
Other ischemic heart disease	79.0	67.1	1.18	116.1	113.0	1.03
Bronchitis/emphysema/asthma	35.8	27.1	1.32	43.3	42.8	1.01
Liver disease and cirrhosis	10.1	5.0	2.02	13.8	7.4	1.86
Motor vehicle fatalities	11.0	5.2	2.12	20.6	9.5	2.17
Suicide	18.4	5.2	3.54	17.1	4.0	4.28
Homicide	2.2	0.8	2.75	9.2	2.7	3.41

Source: Author's computations based on data from the World Health Organization (2006b).

between men and women has been narrowing lately, men have a significantly higher death rate from lung cancer. In the United States, Retherford (1975) estimated that an astonishing 47 per cent of the sex gap in life expectancy can be attributed to differences in men's and women's smoking habits. Valkonen and von Poppel (1997), in a similar study of five northern European nations, found that between 1970 and 1974, about 40 per cent of the sex gap in mortality was due to sex differences in smoking, a figure that dropped to about 30 per cent between 1985 and 1990. Men with smoking-related illnesses also tend to suffer more severely than women do, leading Case and Paxson (2005) to hypothesize that a part of the sex gap in mortality can therefore be explained by the fact that men are more likely to experience major chronic conditions related to smoking.

Figure 7.15 shows the year 2000 age-specific death rate ratios for Canada and the United States in several categories, including overall mortality, homicide, motor vehicle accidents, and suicide. The age patterns of these rate ratios are remarkably similar for both countries, suggesting that common forces may be at work in

the higher mortality of males. The ratio of male-to-female death rate is most pronounced among 15- to 24-year-olds, and then for those aged 25 to 34. Expert opinion is unified in support of the proposition that, in general, the greater tendency for men to die from such causes arises largely from sociocultural conditioning, which induces greater risk-taking and aggressiveness in men (Kramer, 2000; Veevers and Gee, 1986; Verbrugge, 1976; Waldron, 1976, 2000). One of the factors underlying the propensity for young men to die from violence and accidents is a phenomenon that Hannerz (2001) has termed the 'manhood trials'—dangerous rites of passage, common in most societies in various forms among boys passing into adulthood, that carry 'an added mortality risk' (189).

Returning to the question of why the longevity gap between men and women has been narrowing recently, we can look for the answer in behavioural changes between the sexes and how these changes have affected the survival probabilities of men and women. The recent literature in this area has focused on the changing role of women in industrialized societies and how it is linked to the narrowing sex difference in mort-

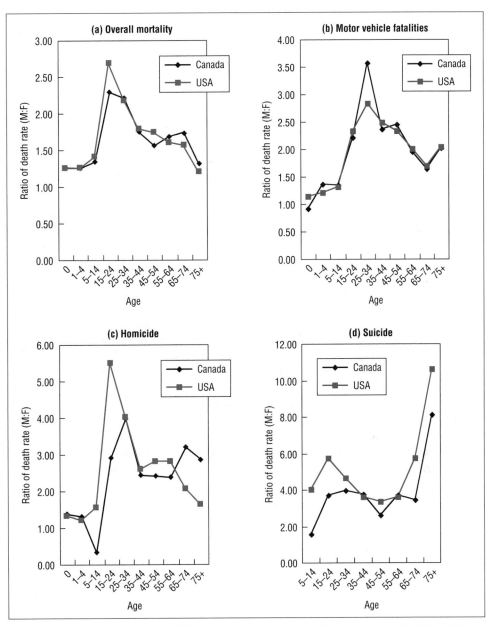

Figure 7.15   Sex ratios of mortality (M:F) for (a) overall mortality, (b) motor vehicle fatalities, (c) homicide, and (d) suicide, by age group, Canada and United States, 2000

Source: Author's computations based on data from the World Health Organization (2006b).

ality. Other studies have examined changing patterns of smoking in men and women and their long-term effects on male and female death rates.

Nathanson (1995) has hypothesized that in countries with relatively high levels of gender equality there are high levels of smoking prevalence among women, which would result in slower gains in life expectancy for women aged 40. Nathanson's cross-national analysis revealed that increased female labour force participation is inversely associated with change in female life expectancy at age 40, and that in countries where female smoking prevalence in 1970 was relatively high, women's life expectancy gains between 1970 and 1988 were slower than in those countries characterized by low smoking prevalence. Japan, for example, with very low female smoking rates, showed the largest increases in female life expectancy between 1970 and 1988; by contrast, Denmark, with the highest smoking prevalence, had the slowest gain in female life expectancy during this period. Nathanson's results suggest that change in some aspects of the behaviour of women (in this case, increased rates of smoking) may have adversely affected their longevity gains over recent decades.

Pampel (2002, 2003) took a different perspective on women's changing attitudes towards smoking, attributing it instead to a diffusion phenomenon. Women who increasingly over the latter part of the twentieth century took up smoking were essentially following the pattern of smoking established earlier in the century by men, establishing a trend whose effects would be felt decades later, in the form of diminishing longevity gains (Lopez, Caselli, and Valkonen, 1995). Women's smoking began to rise significantly in the 1960s, at a time when men were abandoning the habit in response to intensive public health campaigns warning of the health dangers of tobacco. Owing to the differential timing of smoking initiation and cessation in men and women, the trends in lung cancer mortality (and other smoking-related diseases) for men and women have diverged. While lung cancer mortality in men peaked and levelled off in the early 1980s and has shown a downward trend recently, the corresponding rates for women have been rising rapidly. This differential pattern of change has contributed significantly to the recent narrowing of the sex gap in mortality and life expectancy.

As Figure 7.16 shows, the most important contributors to the narrowing of the sex difference in life expectancy in Canada have been faster declines for men in rates of death from heart disease, lung cancer, and other cancers, all of which are strongly connected to cigarette smoking. As well, men's death rates with respect accidents and violence (excluding suicide) have been falling faster in recent years, and this is another important contributor to the declining sex difference in life expectancy.

Glei and Horiuchi (2007) have identified another significant cause of the narrowing sex differential in life expectancy. For populations in the most advanced stage of epidemiological transition, life table survival probabilities have become increasingly rectangular over time. The degree of rectangularization has been noticeably greater for females, which means that an increasing proportion of female deaths are concentrated in the older ages. For men, the degree of rectangularization is less, and therefore deaths are more dispersed across age categories. This also implies that men have greater room for further improvements in survival probabilities as compared to women. Thus, as Glei and Horiuchi point out, this varying distribution of deaths in male and female life tables is responsible for some of the decline in sex differences in life expectancy at birth because under this circumstance the same rate of mortality decline would produce a smaller life expectancy gain for women than for men. This in turn translates into larger life expectancy gains for men than for women, serving to reduce the female–male difference in life expectancy.

The Aboriginal Disadvantage in Health and Survival

Aboriginal minorities in Canada and other parts of the world have a long history of socioeconomic disadvantage, social isolation, and relatively poor health (Hayward and Heron, 1999; Kunitz, 1990, 2000; Leonard and Crawford, 2002; Pool, 1991, 1994; Ross and Taylor, 2002; Sandefur, Rindfuss, and Cohen, 1996; Taylor, Bampton, and Lopez, 2005). Many of Canada's

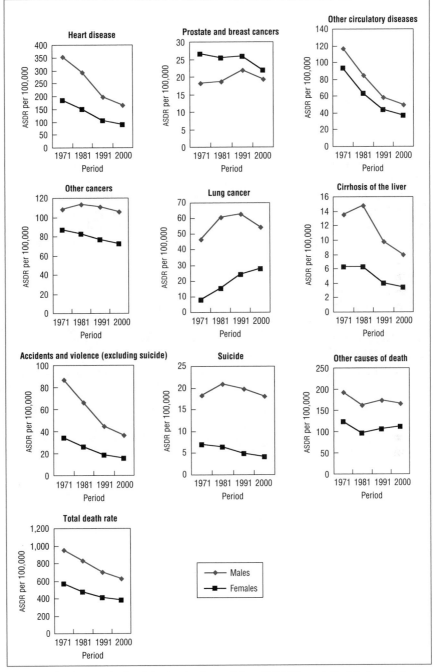

Figure 7.16 Age standardized death rates (ASDRs) (per 100,000 population) in Canada by sex, cause of death, and total death rate, 1971–2000

Note: The standard population is the European standard million (World Health Organization, 1998).

Source: Trovato and Lalu (2007): 112–13. Reprinted by permission of the publisher.

Aboriginal people experience social, economic, and epidemiological conditions that can only be described as deplorable (Anderssen, 1998; Pfeiff, 2003). In many communities, especially those that are more remote, housing is generally substandard, and basic services such as fresh water, proper sewage disposal, and essential health care are unavailable (Royal Commission on Aboriginal Peoples, 1995; Young, 1994). In combination, poverty and isolation have fostered pernicious social pathologies that have been exacerbated over time by high rates of alcoholism and substance abuse (Whitehead and Hayes, 1998). The devastating effects of alcohol abuse and its role in the high incidence of family violence, crime, and violent deaths among Aboriginal people has been extensively documented in Canada and other parts of the world (Bachman, 1992; Broudy and May, 1983; De Wit, De Wit, and Embree, 2000; Gray, 1990; Hayward and Heron, 1999; Hisnanick, 1994; Hogg, 1992; Jarvis and Boldt, 1982; Kunitz, 1983, 1990, 1994; Levy and Kunitz, 1971; Pool, 1991; Young, 1988a, 1988b, 1994).

It is often difficult to gain a comprehensive view of Canada's Native population, as official vital statistics data are not readily available for Inuit and Métis peoples. We know more about the demography of Registered Indians because their lives are closely monitored by government institutions. Evidence shows that the crude death rate for Registered Indians has decreased by 21 per cent between 1979 and 1993, from 7.0 to 5.5 per 1,000 (Health Canada, 1996b: 17). A more accurate picture of mortality differentials is obtained from an examination of life expectancy at birth. Table 7.13 shows that the average length of life for Aboriginal people in Canada, in the United States, in Australia, and in New Zealand falls well below the respective national populations. The deficit is astonishingly large for Australian Aborigines, whose lives are on average 20 years shorter than those of non-Aboriginal Australians. In the other three nations, the disadvantage in life expectancy ranges between 6 and 7 years.

Canada's Aboriginal populations are currently undergoing the epidemiological transition, though they are lagging substantially with

Table 7.13   Life expectancy at birth by sex and corresponding national populations for Registered Indians in Canada, Indigenous People in Australia, Maori population in New Zealand, and American Indian and Alaska Native population of the United States (selected years)

Sex and population	Canada, 1996–2000	Australia, 1997–9	New Zealand, 1995–7	United States, 1996–8
Aboriginals				
Male	68.3	55.6	67.2	67.0
Female	74.5	56.3	71.6	74.0
Larger society				
Male	75	75	73	73
Female	81	81	79	79
Aboriginals – larger society				
Males	−6.7	−19.4	−5.8	−6.0
Females	−6.5	−24.7	−7.4	−5.0

Source: Verma, Michalowski, and Gauvin (2004): 197–235; Population Reference Bureau, *World Population Data Sheets* 1997 and 1998.

respect to the larger Canadian population. This has brought on a new challenge, in addition to the existing problems of poverty and high levels of social pathologies: a rising epidemic of chronic and degenerative diseases. As a function of long-term adaptations to Western ways of living, Canadian Aboriginal people have all but lost their traditional ways of life, which once centred on hunting, fishing, and agriculture. They have become a predominantly sedentary population, and partly because of this change they now experience an increased prevalence of chronic and degenerative diseases. In the late 1990s, the four leading causes of death among Canada's First Nations were injuries and poisonings (107.2 per 100,000), followed by circulatory disease (84.6), cancer (58.8), and respiratory ailments (16.5) (Health Canada, 2003: 26–7). Additional evidence suggests that rates of heart disease and diabetes among Canada's Native people are increasing faster than in the non-Aboriginal Canadian population (Health Canada, 2003; Narayan, 1997; Ng, 1996; Young, 1997).

Table 7.14, comparing a number of health status indicators for Registered Indians and for the rest of Canada's population, highlights two other areas of particular concern: the greater incidence of sudden infant death syndrome (SIDS) and infant deaths from 'other or unknown' causes in the Registered Indian population. While it is impossible to say precisely what is included in the category of 'other or unknown' causes, it is reasonable to assume that it includes cases that reflect poor pre- and postnatal care for mothers and infants and high incidence of high birth weight babies, which can threaten both babies and mothers with serious complications (Luo et al., 2004).

Death from injuries and poisonings is nearly three times as common in the Registered Indian population as in the non-Indian population of Canada. Digestive diseases and endocrine disorders are also substantially more prevalent. The lower portion of Table 7.14, which charts potential years of life lost due to different causes of death, illustrates another notable statistic: that with the exception of four causes of death (circulatory disease, cancer, nervous disorders, and blood disorders), premature death results in a much higher number of potential life years lost in the Indian population compared with Canada's non-Indian population. This points to the need to eradicate the epidemics of violence, abuse, neglect, and injuries that so frequently claim the lives of Aboriginals in Canada.

Socioeconomic Disparities in Health and Mortality

Closely tied to racial disparities in health are disparities in socioeconomic status (SES), which in industrialized societies is usually based on measures of income, education, and occupation. Disparities in health and mortality by socioeconomic status have been observed for a long time in the industrialized countries, with one of the key findings in this literature being the existence of an inverse socioeconomic gradient in mortality risk: as socioeconomic status increases, mortality declines, and as socioeconomic status decreases, mortality rates increase (Antonovsky, 1967; Cambois, 2004; Cardano, Costa, and Demaria, 2004; Feinstein, 1993; Hertzman, 2001; Hummer, Rogers, and Eberstein, 1998; Kitagawa and Hauser, 1973; Marmot, 1995, 2005; Pensola and Martikainen, 2004; Steenland, Henley, and Thun, 2002; Valkonen, 1993; Wilkinson, 1996, 2005).

Observations in Canada are consistent with these general findings. Wilkins (1980), using the occupations of men aged 25–64 as the index of SES, investigated disparities in life expectancy at birth across districts of Montreal. He computed mortality ratios of five occupational classes (class 1 being the highest ranked and class 5 the lowest), and, using the overall average death rate across all classes as the standard, found clear evidence of an inverse gradient: the highest occupational class had the lowest relative mortality, and the lowest class showed the highest relative mortality.

Table 7.14 Comparative mortality indicators for Registered Indians and Canada, 1999

	Indians	Canada	Indians: Canada
Infant mortality rate (per 1,000)	8.0	5.5	**1.45**
Stillbirth rate (1985–8)	10.6	5.1	**20.8**
Perinatal death rate	14.5	7.9	**1.83**
Cause of death in infancy (%)			
Congenital anomalies	25	28	.89
Conditions originating in the perinatal period	27	45	.60
SIDS	11	9	**1.22**
All other and unknown	37	18	**2.06**
Birth weight			
Low (<2,500 grams)	6.0	5.6	**1.07**
High (≥ 4,000 grams)	22.0	12.2	**1.80**
Age-standardized death rate: Leading causes of death			
Circulatory disease	213.6	231.8	.92
Cancer	141.5	186.5	.76
Injury and poisoning	123.9	42.2	**2.94**
Respiratory diseases	63.6	64.4	.99
Digestive diseases	33.0	23.8	**1.39**
Endocrine and immune disorders	32.6	22.0	**1.48**
Potential years of life lost by cause of death (per 100,000 population)			
Injury	4,909	1,271	**3.86**
Circulatory	900	961	.94
Cancer	770	1,617	.48
Perinatal	329	211	**1.56**
Ill-defined	294	130	**2.26**
Congenital	293	178	**1.65**
Digestive	280	177	**1.58**
Respiratory	247	201	**1.23**
Endocrine	225	148	**1.52**
Mental	142	60	**2.37**
Nervous	137	144	.95
Musculoskeletal	70	16	**4.38**
Genitourinary	45	39	**1.15**
Blood	10	17	.59

Source: Health Canada (2003): various pages; for perinatal and stillbirth rates, Canadian Institute for Child Health (1994):143; World Health Organization (2006e).

More recently, Wilkins, Berthelot, and Ng (2002) looked at how differences in income-related mortality had changed in Canada between 1971 and 1996. They based their study on population data for residents of census metropolitan areas (CMAs), excluding those residents who were institutionalized at the time. Within each CMA, neighbourhoods were grouped into income quintiles based on what percentage of each neighbourhood's residents were living below Canada's low-income cut-offs. The researchers reported both promising and discouraging results. On the positive side, differences in life expectancy at birth between the richest and poorest quintiles diminished from 6.3 to 5.0 years for men, and from 2.8 to 1.6 years for women. During this same period, the infant mortality differential between the wealthiest and poorest categories declined by 76 per cent, and the rate of income-related potential years of life lost before age 75 dropped by 35 per cent. Socioeconomic disparities for most causes of death—particularly ischemic heart disease, most injuries, cirrhosis of the liver, and perinatal conditions—had diminished markedly between 1971 and 1996. However, the researchers also found that the socioeconomic gradient for some causes of death—including lung cancer, prostate cancer, suicide (for men), and breast cancer (for women)—showed little change over time. A few causes of death—namely lung cancer for women, and infectious diseases, mental disorders, and diabetes for both sexes—showed widening disparities across income quintiles.

As for the causal mechanisms that link socioeconomic status to health status, the importance of income is well understood: more money usually affords individuals and their families greater access to health care and insurance, as well as a host of other health-conferring benefits (Canadian Institute for Health Information, 2002: 32).

In his extensive review of the literature, Wilkinson (2005: 25) identified three key social risk factors underlying differences in health in a population, all tied to socioeconomic inequality:

- low social status
- poor social affiliations
- poor quality of early childhood experiences

Poor socioeconomic conditions predispose a person to a life of physical, mental, and economic difficulties. Research has shown that infants and children who grow up in poor and disorganized socioeconomic contexts are more likely to be abused and neglected. The effects of abuse on the neural development of a child are thought to be permanent; they cannot be erased by therapy or other medical interventions (Teicher, 2003). Further, as the child grows to become an adult, he or she passes these effects on to the next generation of children, thereby perpetuating a cycle of poverty and hardship (see also Barker, 2003; Finch, 2003; Hayward and Gorman, 2004; Khoury, Little, and Burke, 2003).

Feinstein (1993) developed a useful framework for understanding how socioeconomic disadvantage relates to poor health. Feinstein's typology (see Table 7.15) emphasizes four sets of factors (represented by the four cells) that affect the ways that health inequalities are produced and maintained by socioeconomic status. For instance, cell 1 indicates that health inequality, as measured by differences over the lifespan, is fostered by discrepancies in material conditions such as housing, availability of sanitation facilities in the home, overcrowding, and exposure to health hazards at work. Cell 2 indicates that the class differential in health is a function of long-term behaviours associated with diet, smoking, exercise, alcohol and substance use, and risk-taking. Cell 3 shows how differences in material resources affect access to and use of health care services. In countries where health care is not universally available, the ability to purchase medical services and pharmaceuticals, and make regular physician visits, is largely determined by income. Finally, cell 4 illustrates

Table 7.15 Typology of socioeconomic discrepancies by type of explanation and source of health inequality

		Source of inequality in health	
		Lifespan (average length of life)	Access to and use of health care services
Type of explanation	**Materialistic causes** (having to do with access to material resources)	(1) • housing • overcrowding • sanitation • transit mode • occupational hazards • environmental hazards	(3) • ability to purchase health care • ability to purchase pharmaceuticals • regular access to and ability to consult a family physician
	Behavioural/ psychosocial causes (having to do with cultural predispositions to health behaviour)	(2) • diet • smoking • amount of exercise • choice of leisure activities • risk-taking behaviour • alcohol and substance abuse	(4) • access to comprehensive medical information • understanding of how to 'play the system' • ability to follow medical instructions • ability to self-diagnose • awareness of disease recurrence

Source: Adapted from Feinstein (1993): 279–322.

the interaction of behavioural factors with access to and use of health care, showing that differences in health arise from individuals' use or non-use of health care. For example, health is compromised to the degree that one fails to seek proper medical treatment, or fails to follow proper medical regimens after diagnosis; fails to take preventive precautions and to self-diagnose the presence of disease as a precursor to seeking treatment. There is indication in the literature that in this regard the economically disadvantaged fare less well (Feinstein, 1993).

There is also a psychosocial dimension to the socioeconomic gradient in health and mortality. The root causes of disparities in health emanate from the effects of social exclusion and isolation and the stressful life experienced by disadvantaged people, which usually results from lack of education, poor job prospects, unemployment, and low income. A sense of fatalism and powerlessness often accompanies these conditions, leading to smoking and alcohol as means of easing stress. Add to this configuration of poor material conditions the poor nutrition and diet that are typical of impoverished socioeconomic status and it is not difficult to see how, over the long term, a majority of socioeconomically disadvantaged individuals develop compromised immune systems through reduced resistance to communicable and non-communicable illness, which, combined with their susceptibility to accidental and violent death, greatly increases their mortality risk (Berkman and Breslow, 1983; Cassel, 1976; Cobb, 1976; House, Landis, and Umberson, 1988; Marmot, Kogevinas, and Elston, 1987; Robert, 1999; Syme and Berkman, 1976; Wilkinson, 2005; Wilkinson and Marmot, 2003).

Canadian Mortality in Comparative Perspective

Table 7.16 compares Canada with five other wealthy nations—the United States, Japan, Sweden, the United Kingdom, and France—across several indicators of population health. These include age-standardized death rates (using Canada as the standard population), age-specific death rates, life expectancy at birth, and health-adjusted life expectancy (the average number of years a person can expect to live free of major disability). The differences in overall age-standardized death rates across the six countries are not particularly large, although the rates for the United States and the United Kingdom stand out as being relatively high, close to 8.5 per 1,000. Since Canada was used as the standard in this part of the analysis, its crude death rate will be equal to its standardized death rate, which is 7.08 per 1,000. Next to Japan's rate of 5.93, this is the lowest among the six countries. Looking at the age-specific death rates, Canada appears to have a mortality advantage over the other countries across most of the age categories, except when compared to Japan, whose death rates by age are, with one or two exceptions, consistently lower than Canada's. The worst age profiles of mortality among these countries belong to France and the United States, where

Table 7.16 Population health indicators for Canada and 5 other high-income countries, 2000

Indicator	Country					
	Canada	US	Japan	Sweden	UK	France
Crude death rate per 1,000	7.08	8.54	7.66	10.54	10.19	9.01
Age-standardized death rate per 1,000	7.08	8.46	5.93	7.40	8.27	7.40
Infant mortality rate per 1,000	5.3	6.9	3.3	3.4	5.6	4.4
Age-specific death rates per 1,000						
<1	5.2	7.4	3.3	3.5	5.5	4.5
1–4	0.2	0.3	0.3	0.1	0.2	0.3
5–14	0.1	0.2	0.1	0.1	0.1	0.1
15–24	0.6	0.8	0.4	0.4	0.5	0.6
25–44	0.9	1.5	1.7	0.8	1.0	1.3
45–64	5.3	4.1	9.4	4.7	6.0	5.7
65–74	20.2	24.0	15.8	19.1	24.1	18.4
75+	73.5	81.8	61.5	83.9	87.1	75.8
Life expectancy at birth (both sexes)	79.4	76.8	81.1	79.6	77.8	79.0
Healthy life expectancy at birth (both sexes)	68.6	62.2	76.5	62.4	61.2	62.3
Healthy life as % of life expectancy	86.4	81.0	94.3	78.4	78.7	78.9
Expenditure on health as % of country GDP	9.9	15.2	7.9	9.4	8.0	10.1

Note: The standard population for the computation of age-standardized death rate is the Canadian population in 2000.

Source: Author's computations based on data from the world Health Organization's Mortality Data Base, http://www3.who.int/whosis/menu.cfm?path=whosis,mort&language=english (accessed 7 March 2006); life expectancy at birth and disability-free life expectancy from World Health Organization (2006d): 22–9; total expenditure on health (in 2003) figures are from the World Health Organization (2006d): 58–61.

age-specific death rates are notably greater in infancy and in old age. In an overall sense, the health of Canada's population seems quite strong, falling somewhere between those of Japan and Sweden.

In terms of life expectancy at birth, Canada ranks third, behind Japan and Sweden. Also significant is the fact that next to Japan, Canada has the highest healthy life expectancy. Canadians can expect to live free of major disabilities for almost 69 years out of a total 79.4, or about 87 per cent of overall life expectancy. The corresponding rate in Japan is 94 per cent, while the healthy life expectancy of the other countries accounts for about 80 per cent of total life expectancy. These wealthy countries spend between 15 (USA) and 8 (Japan) per cent of their GDP on health care. Higher spending does not necessarily translate into best overall performance in terms of population health, as evidenced by the US, which has the highest expenditure yet does not have the best mortality profile (see also Kunitz, 2007; Kunitz and Pesis-Katz, 2005; Torrey and Haub, 2004). Japan, meanwhile, spends the least on health care as a proportion of GDP but shows the best population health profile. Canada's situation is somewhere in the middle.

Healthy Life Expectancy (HALE)

One of the most widely used indexes of a population's overall health status is life expectancy at birth, which measures the average number of years a newborn is expected to live. A key component of the average length of life is the proportion of life that one can expect to live free of major disability. An empirical measure that takes this into account is the *health-adjusted life expectancy* (HALE). By specifying the portion of overall life expectancy spent in good health, this measure is a valuable indicator of population health. HALE takes into account the average number of years the population spends in good health free of major disability, given its overall life expectancy at birth. Table 7.17 shows life expectancy at birth for men and women, and the associated HALE values for the World Health Organization health regions and for the world as a whole (World Health Organization, 2007).

As the table shows, Africa has the lowest life expectancy at birth (less than 50 years) and also the lowest HALE scores (between 40 and 42 years). Thus, African people can expect to live, on average, 84 per cent of their relatively short lives free of major disability. The Region of the Americas enjoys the highest life expectancy at birth (72 years for men and 77 years for women), and the proportion of life expectancy in good health is close to 90 per cent. On the average, then, people in the Americas not only live longer than people in Africa, but can expect to spend a greater proportion of their lives in good health.

The regional figures mask wide variations in both life expectancy and HALE across specific countries. The highest life expectancy is in Japan, where the average man lives 77 years and the average woman 86. Japan also has the highest HALE scores (72 for men, 78 for women); thus, Japanese men and women spend just over 90 per cent of their relatively long lives in good health. By contrast, the most disadvantaged country in the world is Sierra Leone, where male life expectancy is just 37 years and female life expectancy just 40. HALE values for Sierra Leone are 27 years for men and 30 years for women. So, a Sierra Leonean man can hope to live about 73 per cent of his relatively short life free of major disability, while a woman can expect her disability-free life to be 75 per cent of her life. In other words, in Sierra Leone, about one-quarter of the average citizen's life—short as it is—would be spent in a state of ill health. Many countries in sub-Saharan Africa share life expectancies below 50 years, with correspondingly low HALE values (World Health Organization 2007: 22–30).

Table 7.17   Life expectancy at birth and health-adjusted life expectancy in years, by WHO region

Life expectancy at birth (e_0) or Healthy Life Expectancy at Birth (HALE)	WHO region						
	African Region	Region of the Americas	South-east Asia Region	European Region	Eastern Mediter-ranean Region	Western Pacific Region	Global
e_0 males	48	72	62	69	62	71	64
e_0 females	50	77	65	77	64	75	68
e_0 female − e_0 male	2	5	3	8	2	4	4
HALE male	40	63	54	62	53	63	56
HALE female	42	67	55	68	54	66	59
HALE (male) − HALE (female)	−2	−4	−1	−6	−1	−3	−3
% of life in good health, given e_0 (males)	83.3	87.5	87.1	89.7	84.5	88.7	87.5
% of life in good health, given e_0 (females)	84.0	87.0	84.6	88.3	84.4	88.0	86.8

Source: World Health Organization (2007): 30.

Future Prospects

So what is the most likely course of Canada's mortality over the twenty-first century? One encouraging trend, noted earlier, is the declining rate of cardiovascular mortality among adults and the elderly since the 1960s. A key to the decline of heart disease (which is the most important component of cardiovascular mortality) has been a reduction in cigarette smoking and the move towards healthier diets and greater participation in physical exercise, all of which contribute to a reduction in hypertensive complications. There are still gains to be made in the fight against heart disease. Less optimistic are the trends for cancer. As the average age of the population rises, the incidence of cancer is bound to increase over the foreseeable future (Roterman, 2006). Prospects for hope rest with continuing research, which is bound to produce favourable results (Collins and Barker, 2007; Wigle et al., 1986), and with strategies for prevention, namely the eradication of risk factors including tobacco, alcoholism, high-fat diets, and inactivity (Rothenberg and Koplan, 1990; Muir and Sasco, 1990).

Compared with those of a few decades ago, current rates of death from suicide, homicide, and motor vehicle accidents are lower and show promise of further declines. Of some concern is the large number of Canadians that perish on an annual basis as a result of respiratory conditions and, among infants, the large proportion of deaths due to congenital anomalies and other complications of the perinatal period, largely associated with low birth weight. Although Canada's infant mortality rate is one of the lowest in the world, the lower rates of Japan and Sweden demonstrate that further progress in this area is possible.

As for reducing health and mortality disparities within Canada itself, further success will likely depend on greater public health efforts aimed at reducing inequalities along socioeconomic lines. Recent findings by James and associates (2007) shed considerable light on this problem. Their investigation of mortality disparities by neighbourhood showed that gaps have narrowed for causes of death considered amenable to medical treatment, such as breast cancer, cervical cancer, testicular cancer, Hodgkin's disease, leukemia, diabetes, cerebrovascular disease, influenza, and perinatal conditions. Wide gaps remained, however, for causes of death that are presumed to be largely amenable to greater public health interventions—for example, HIV, lung cancer, skin cancer, chronic obstructive pulmonary disease, cirrhosis of the liver, and motor vehicle accidents. The findings suggest that greater public health efforts are required to reduce the socioeconomic gaps in Canadian health and mortality.

Conclusion

A population's overall health status is a function of a complex set of factors—environmental, institutional, socioeconomic, and genetic, among others. The epidemiological transition theory states that societies pass through several stages of development with respect to the major causes of premature death, from an early stage in which pestilence and famine predominate, to an intermediary stage of receding pandemics, to a final stage of human-caused and degenerative diseases. Recent scholars have proposed extensions to this typological explanation, including a fourth stage characterized as the age of delayed degenerative diseases. During this stage there is a tendency for the most advanced countries to experience notable improvements in medical therapies that help to postpone not only the onset of major disabilities, such as cardiovascular disease and cancers, but also death for those afflicted with those diseases. An important point raised in the recent literature concerns the key role of lifestyle and health habits in understanding why there is so much chronic disease and premature death in today's most advanced countries. In recent years, parts of the developing world have suffered major setbacks in the fight against disease and premature death; the most dramatic of these setbacks are associated with the HIV/AIDS epidemic. At the same time, the burden of disease due to non-communicable diseases such as cancer and circulatory conditions is bound to worsen with time as these societies pass through the different stages of the epidemiological transition.

Notes for Further Study

Standardization of Death Rates

Age composition has a strong effect on mortality. If a relatively young population is compared to a relatively old population, the young population might actually show a lower crude death rate. To circumvent this problem, it is advisable, when comparing mortality across two or more populations, to apply statistical standardization to remove differences in age compositions of the populations being compared. There are two methods of standardization used in demographic analysis: *direct standardization* and *indirect standardization*.

Direct Standardization

In this type of standardization, an appropriate 'standard population' is selected and then used to derive age-standardized death rates for the populations being compared. Essentially, the age-specific death rates of the study populations are applied to the standard population to obtain the number of expected deaths that would occur in the standard population if it had the age-specific death rates of a study population.

Standardization allows us to examine populations in a *relative* sense, even though in absolute terms the standardized rates have no real meaning. Standardization merely allows the researcher to make relative types of comparisons. A standardized death rate, for instance, is a fictitious rate obtained through a statistical procedure under a restrictive assumption: that the study population experiences the same age distribution as the standard population.

Table 7.18 below illustrates the application of direct standardization to Canada and Mexico for the year 2000. For the purpose of this example, the overall population of Canada in 2000 is used as the standard.

The age structures of Canada and Mexico are very different: Canada's is considerably older. In 2000, the crude death rates for Mexican men and women were lower than those for Canadian

Table 7.18 Direct standardization of death rates for Canada and Mexico, 2000

	Age-specific death rates per person				Standard	Canada		Mexico	
	Canada		Mexico		Canada	Males	Females	Males	Females
Age (1)	Males (2)	Females (3)	Males (4)	Females (5)	2000 (6)	$(2) \times (6)$ $= (7)$	$(3) \times (6)$ $= (8)$	$(4) \times (6)$ $= (9)$	$(5) \times (6)$ $= (10)$
0	0.005716	0.004583	0.019050	0.015342	336,189	1,922	1,541	6,404	5,158
1–4	0.000230	0.000184	0.000817	0.000741	1,446,080	332	266	1,181	1,071
5–14	0.000162	0.000122	0.000388	0.000274	4,097,595	663	499	1,591	1,121
15–24	0.000784	0.000343	0.001249	0.000491	4,162,089	3,262	1,428	5,197	2,045
25–34	0.000889	0.000406	0.002054	0.000710	4,404,726	3,917	1,790	9,046	3,126
35–44	0.001565	0.000907	0.003590	0.001525	5,306,541	8,307	4,815	19,049	8,093
45–54	0.003534	0.002286	0.006392	0.003739	4,363,765	15,421	9,973	27,895	16,318
55–64	0.009647	0.005722	0.013488	0.009439	2,814,615	27,154	16,106	37,963	26,567
65–74	0.026031	0.015049	0.029385	0.021996	2,143,223	55,789	32,254	62,979	47,141
75+	0.085677	0.066169	0.093585	0.077296	1,716,011	147,022	113,547	160,593	132,640
Total					30,790,834	263,789	182,219	331,898	243,280
CDR per 1,000	7.33	6.84	4.99	3.87					
SDRs per 1,000						8.57	5.92	10.78	7.90

Note: Figures in columns 6–10 are rounded to whole numbers. The age compositions for the two countries are shown below:

Age group	Canada %	Mexico %
<15	20.23	35.50
15–64	67.75	60.22
65+	12.02	4.28
Total population	30,790,834	98,872,000

The overall national standardized death rates per 1,000 population are 7.08 for Canada and 9.23 for Mexico. The corresponding national crude death rates are 7.08 and 4.42, for Canada and Mexico, respectively.

Source: Author's computations based on data from the World Health Organization (2006b).

men and women. This seems counter-intuitive, given Canada's more advanced social structure. Around the year 2003, Canada's gross national income per purchasing parity was $26,530; Mexico's was $8,240. Infant mortality rates were 7 per 1,000 live births in Canada and 25 per 1,000 in Mexico. By all relevant indicators, Canada should have lower mortality than Mexico.

In Table 7.18, columns 2, 3, 4, and 5 list the age-specific death rates (per person) for Canadian and Mexican men and women in 2000. Column 6 shows the age-specific population of Canada for 2000, and columns 7–10 include the expected deaths by age and sex, obtained by multiplying the appropriate age-specific death rates in the study population by the corresponding standard population in each age. The steps required to compute the standardized death rates are outlined below, using Canadian men as an example:

1. Multiply each age-specific death rate for Canadian men by the corresponding standard population in column 6; the results are shown in column 7.
2. Sum all values in column 7.
3. Divide the total from step 2 by the total standard population.

And so, the directly standardized death rate (DSDR) for Canadian males is:

$$\text{DSDR} = \frac{\text{sum of male expected deaths}}{\text{total standard population}} \times 1,$$

$$\text{DSDR} = \frac{263,789}{30,790,834} \times 1,000 = 8.57$$

In formal terms, this can be written as

$$\text{DSDR} = \frac{\sum M_x P_x}{P}$$

where x is the age for a given group, M_x is the age-specific death rate of the popula-

tion being studied, P_x is the age-specific population of the standard, and P is the total standard population.

The other computations (for Canadian women and for Mexican men and women) are executed in the same way.

Once we have calculated the directly standardized death rate, we can compare it with the crude death rate. The DSDR for men in Canada is 8.57 per 1,000, which is higher than the corresponding CDR of 7.33. The DSDR of 5.92 for Canadian women is substantially lower than the corresponding CDR of 6.84. The DSDRs for Mexican men and women are, respectively, 10.78 and 7.90, both higher than their corresponding CDRs of 4.99 and 3.87.

So how do we interpret a standardized death rate? As we noted earlier, this is in essence a fictitious figure: it does not exist anywhere in the real world. What it tells us is the number of deaths that would occur in the standard population if it were exposed to the actual age-specific death rates of the study population.

The standardized death rate really just allows us to compare two or more populations being studied. Looking at the directly standardized death rate for Mexican men (10.78), we can see that it is substantially higher than the rate for Canadian men (by a difference of 2.21 deaths per 1,000 population). Similarly, the standardized death rate for Mexican women (7.90) exceeds the DSDR for Canadian women by 1.98 deaths per 1,000 population. These comparisons make it quite clear that Canada has lower mortality than does Mexico.

The standardization procedure can be easily applied to cause-specific death rates as well. First, age–sex–cause-specific death rates are computed for a population, and then these age–sex–cause-specific death rates are applied to a standard population to derive the expected deaths by cause. Finally, the total expected deaths for each cause and for each sex would be divided by the total standard population to obtain the cause-specific age-standardized death rates.

Indirect Standardization

Indirect standardization is applied under different circumstances to accomplish the same objective as direct standardization. The problem presented below illustrates when and how indirect standardization is used.

Table 7.19 includes information about the Canadian-born and foreign-born populations in 1991. Age-specific death rates are available for Canada as a whole, but the information is not available for the Canadian-born and foreign-born subpopulations. For these two groups, all we have is the age-specific populations for men and women, obtained from the census. We do not have information on the number of deaths by age and sex, which means that we cannot calculate the age-specific death rates for those born in and outside of Canada.

This is the sort of situation in which indirect standardization is typically used. While direct standardization depends on having the age-

Table 7.19 Age-specific death rates in 1991 for Canada, and the population distributions of Canadian-born and foreign-born populations

Age	Age-specific death rates (per person), Canada, 1991	Canadian-born population, 1991	Foreign-born population, 1991
0	0.006387	325,724	3,581
1–4	0.000324	1,252,398	45,284
5–9	0.000182	1,579,411	102,969
10–14	0.000212	1,554,553	135,237
15–19	0.000660	1,546,791	190,975
20–24	0.000806	1,623,847	283,499
25–29	0.000858	1,966,184	388,377
30–34	0.000936	2,061,771	416,710
35–39	0.001209	1,890,790	443,484
40–44	0.001697	1,727,301	502,914
45–49	0.002745	1,358,081	413,755
50–54	0.004354	1,097,075	351,229
55–59	0.007309	1,012,185	321,673
60–64	0.011898	973,854	311,367
65–69	0.018941	888,005	293,010
70–74	0.029585	679,977	184,315
75–79	0.049726	508,529	135,043
80–84	0.086686	311,589	104,789
85+	0.232103	234,201	763,84
Total Population		22,592,264	4,704,595
CDR per 1,000	7.152		
Total deaths		139,879	55,338

Source: Custom tabulation from Statistics Canada and author's computations.

specific death rates of a study population, the indirect method is used when this information is not available. Instead, the indirect method applies the age-specific death rates of a standard population to the age distribution of the study population to derive the number of deaths that could be expected in the study population if it experienced the age-specific death rates of the standard. The formula for the indirectly standardized death rate is

$$\text{ISDR}_j = \frac{O}{E} \times \text{CDR}_s$$

where ISDR_j is the indirectly standardized death rate for study population j, E is the number of expected deaths in the study population, O is the number of observed deaths in the study population, and CDR_s is the crude death rate of the standard population.

Exercises

1. Table 7.20 shows age–sex-specific populations and deaths by cause for Canada in 1971 and 1998. The corresponding crude death rates (per 100,000) are also listed. Use these data to complete direct standardization of male and female cause-specific death rates for Canada in 1971 and 1998. Use the total Canadian population in 1971 as the standard. Before carrying out the standardization, examine how the population age distributions of males and females may have changed over time. Look as well at the male and female crude death rates for each cause of death. Do the directly standardized death rates differ substantially from the crude death rates? Interpret your results. Has the sex differential in cause-specific mortality changed over time?

Table 7.20 Populations, deaths, and death rates by cause for Canada, 1971 and 1998

1971	Population	Heart disease	Other circulatory	Lung cancer	Other cancers	Suicide	Other external	Other causes	Total deaths
Males									
0	186,400	5	6	0	17	0	204	3,575	3,807
1–4	769,100	4	3	0	76	0	329	314	726
5–14	2,345,500	12	9	0	184	14	765	270	1,254
15–24	1,981,100	40	30	1	181	358	2,357	295	3,262
25–34	1,400,200	132	54	11	190	300	1,209	291	2,187
35–44	1,298,100	910	171	124	452	344	1,031	713	3,745
45–54	1,119,200	3,247	478	563	1,124	335	986	1,502	8,235
55–64	829,300	6,687	1,236	1,322	2,363	256	779	2,625	15,268
65–74	481,700	8,747	2,554	1,535	3,267	122	551	3,866	20,642
75+	275,400	12,821	5,991	891	4,043	67	675	6,237	30,725
Total	10,686,000	32,605	10,532	4,447	11,897	1,796	8,886	19,688	89,851
CDR per 100,000		305.12	98.56	41.62	111.33	16.81	83.16	184.24	840.83

(continued)

Table 7.20 (*continued*)

1971	Population	Heart disease	Other circulatory	Lung cancer	Other cancers	Suicide	Other external	Other causes	Total deaths
Females									
0	177,200	6	6	0	13	0	130	2,604	2,759
1–4	730,800	2	4	0	66	0	198	288	558
5–14	2,241,600	10	6	0	130	4	374	243	767
15–24	1,929,400	24	28	2	111	91	596	238	1,090
25–34	1,390,600	52	68	6	209	125	328	270	1,058
35–44	1,267,600	217	184	43	730	150	323	516	2,163
45–54	1,143,800	731	373	149	1,796	159	346	898	4,452
55–64	842,000	2,102	779	230	2,563	97	317	1,527	7,615
65–74	548,800	4,833	1,887	215	2,882	50	305	2,272	12,444
75+	366,100	12,768	7,210	164	3,570	19	745	5,049	29,525
Total	10,637,900	20,745	10,545	809	12,070	695	3,662	13,905	62,431
CDR per 100,000		195.01	99.13	7.60	113.46	6.53	34.42	130.71	586.87
1998									
Males									
0	175,258	14	6	1	8	0	29	943	1,001
1–4	786,841	8	2	0	20	0	84	103	217
5–14	2,093,593	10	6	0	49	30	159	109	363
15–24	2,091,297	29	13	0	108	457	853	280	1,740
25–34	2,302,083	90	30	16	254	568	867	500	2,325
35–44	2,609,915	576	142	127	649	713	1,007	1,094	4,308
45–54	2,028,899	1,779	293	732	1,727	513	677	1,611	7,332
55–64	1,305,844	3,558	672	1,938	3,562	296	495	2,577	13,098
65–74	987,407	7,779	2,000	3,743	6,938	201	531	6,466	27,658
75+	600,064	16,893	6,042	3,459	9,624	147	1,258	17,541	54,964
Total	14,981,201	30,736	9,206	10,016	22,939	2,925	5,960	31,224	113,006
CDR per 100,000		205.16	61.45	66.86	153.12	19.52	39.78	208.42	754.32
Females									
0	167,160	13	8	0	13	0	15	760	809
1–4	746,253	7	1	0	24	0	52	87	171
5–14	1,988,231	7	4	0	51	16	98	90	266
15–24	1,993,166	16	13	2	60	105	266	158	620
25–34	2,250,342	32	28	9	212	133	256	249	919
35–44	2,596,641	165	110	186	946	182	328	561	2,478
45–54	2,037,567	490	239	635	2,103	159	267	898	4,791
55–64	1,343,982	1,169	460	1,190	3,275	70	216	1,703	8,083
65–74	1,138,227	3,987	1,515	2,105	5,480	59	329	4,476	17,951
75+	1,004,021	21,897	9,286	2,122	10,359	50	1,776	23,506	68,996
Total	15,265,590	27,783	11,664	6,249	22,523	774	3,603	32,488	105,084
CDR per 100,000		182.00	76.41	40.94	147.54	5.07	23.60	212.82	688.37

Source: World Health Organization, http://www3.who.int/whosis/mort/table1.cfm?path=whosis,mort,mort_table1&language=english.

2. Using the data in Table 7.19 (page 321), compare the age distributions of the populations born in and outside of Canada. How do the distributions differ? Which population is older? Compute indirectly standardized death rates for the Canadian-born and the foreign-born populations. What do your computations indicate about the mortality differential between the Canadian-born and non-Canadian-born? Would the results of indirect standardization be identical to those obtained through direct standardization? Explain.

3. The questions below are to be worked out from data contained in the Canadian life tables for 1901 (tables 7.21 and 7.22) and 2000–2 (see table 7.4 on page 261). The male and female life tables for 1901 are examples of 'abridged' life tables, whereas the 2000–2 tables are single-year life tables. In the abridged tables, age is grouped into 5-year categories starting from age 5. Note that infancy (age 0) and ages 1–4 are grouped differently because of the unique mortality pattern in these ages: in infancy, the death rate is relatively high, while from ages 1 to 4 the probability of death drops significantly. In other words, the beginning of these age intervals has considerably higher chances of death than the end points. In the age ranges between 5 and 85, it can be safely assumed that deaths are distributed more or less evenly. However, in extreme old age the even distribution assumption may not hold.

After examining the 1901 and 2000–2 life tables, answer the following questions. All of the questions rely on the information contained in the survivorship (i.e., l_x) columns of these life tables. You will compute a series of probabilities. The first question is worked out to illustrate the computations.

a) What is the probability of a newborn boy surviving to age 5 in 1901 and in 2001?

Answer
The probability of an infant boy surviving to age 5 in 1901 is obtained by dividing the l_x value for age 5 by the l_x value for age 0:

$$\frac{78,772}{100,000} = 0.78772$$

This tells us that in 1901, the probability of survival to age 5 for a newborn baby boy was almost 79 per cent. How does this compare to 2000–2? In 2000–2, the probability of a boy infant surviving to age 5 is:

$$\frac{99,326}{100,000} = 0.99326$$

The chance of survival to age 5 for a newborn boy in 2000–2 is over 99 per cent, which is a significant improvement over the survival probability in 1901. These computations can be executed for an infant girl surviving to age 5 over the same two periods.

b) What is the probability of a boy aged 5 in 1901 surviving to age 65? Calculate this probability for a girl. Calculate these probabilities for 2001. Calculate the percentage change in these probabilities over time for males and females separately. Interpret the results.

c) What is the probability of a man aged 65 in 1901 surviving to age 80? What is the probability in 2001? Answer the same question for a woman. Calculate the percentage change in these probabilities over time. Interpret the results.

d) What is the probability of a 15-year-old male in 1901 surviving to his 25th birthday? What is this probability for a 15-year-old female? Calculate the same probabilities for 2001. Interpret your results.

e) For these two periods, is the probability of a 10-year-old boy surviving to age 85 greater or smaller than the probability of a 65-year-old male surviving to age 85? Calculate these probabilities and interpret your results.

Table 7.21   Abridged life table for Canadian males, 1901

| Age (x) | Proportion of persons alive at beginning of age interval dying during interval (q_x) | Of 100,000 born alive: | | Stationary population (years lived): | | Average number of years of life remaining at beginning of age interval (e^0_x) |
		Number living at beginning of age interval (l_x)	Number dying during age interval (d_x)	In the age interval (person-years lived) (L_x)	In this and all subsequent age intervals (T_x)	
0	0.14398	100,000	14,398	90,353	4,714,155	47.14
1–4	0.07979	85,602	6,830	324,455	4,623,808	54.02
5–9	0.02246	78,772	1,769	388,730	4,299,353	54.58
10–14	0.01492	77,003	1,149	382,225	3,910,623	50.79
15–19	0.02190	75,854	1,661	375,389	3,528,398	46.52
20–24	0.03004	74,193	2,229	365,563	3,153,009	42.50
25–29	0.03473	71,964	2,499	353,630	2,787,446	38.73
30–34	0.03739	69,465	2,597	340,867	2,433,816	35.04
35–39	0.04107	66,868	2,746	327,570	2,092,949	31.30
40–44	0.04856	64,122	3,114	313,032	1,765,379	27.53
45–49	0.06227	61,008	2,799	295,887	1,452,347	23.81
50–54	0.08471	57,209	4,846	274,420	1,156,460	20.21
55–59	0.11892	52,363	6,227	246,853	882,040	16.84
60–64	0.16857	46,136	7,777	211,854	635,187	13.77
65–69	0.23752	38,359	9,111	169,437	423,333	11.04
70–74	0.32877	29,248	9,616	122,148	253,896	8.68
75–79	0.44219	19,632	8,681	75,755	131,748	6.71
80–84	0.57029	10,951	6,265	37,916	55,993	5.11
85–89	0.70465	4,686	3,302	14,065	18,077	3.86
90–94	0.82225	1,384	1,138	3,478	4,012	2.90
95–99	0.91057	246	224	501	534	2.17
100+	1.00000	22	22	33	33	1.50

Note: The function p_x is not shown because it is easily derivable from the q_x column by taking $1 - q_x$ for each age category.

Source: Adapted from Statistics Canada publication *New Birth Cohort Life Tables for Canada and Quebec, 1801–1991*. Catalogue no. 91F0015MIE.

Table 7.22   Abridged life table for Canadian females, 1901

Age (x)	Proportion of persons alive at beginning of age interval dying during interval (q_x)	Of 100,000 born alive:		Stationary population (years lived):		Average number of years of life remaining at beginning of age interval (e^0_x)
		Number living at beginning of age interval (l_x)	Number dying during age interval (d_x)	In the age interval (person-years lived) (L_x)	In this and all subsequent age intervals (T_x)	
0	0.12389	100,000	12,389	91,947	5,010,903	50.11
1–4	0.07690	87,611	6,737	332,791	4,918,960	56.15
5–9	0.02177	80,874	1,761	399,285	4,586,169	56.71
10–14	0.01546	79,113	1,223	392,608	4,186,884	52.92
15–19	0.02175	77,890	1,694	385,443	3,794,276	48.71
20–24	0.02865	76,196	2,183	375,676	3,408,833	44.74
25–29	0.03309	74,013	2,449	364,004	3,033,157	40.98
30–34	0.03553	71,564	2,543	351,483	2,669,153	37.30
35–39	0.03770	69,021	2,602	338,635	2,317,670	33.58
40–44	0.04163	66,419	2,765	325,283	1,979,035	29.80
45–49	0.04955	63,654	3,154	310,602	1,653,752	25.98
50–54	0.06431	60,500	3,891	293,153	1,343,150	22.20
55–59	0.08974	56,609	5,080	270,919	1,049,997	18.55
60–64	0.13099	51,529	6,750	241,523	779,078	15.12
65–69	0.19451	44,779	8,710	202,906	537,555	12.00
70–74	0.28695	36,069	10,350	154,937	334,649	9.28
75–79	0.41160	25,719	10,586	101,794	179,712	6.99
80–84	0.56261	15,133	8,514	53,089	77,918	5.15
85–89	0.71718	6,619	4,747	19,645	24,829	3.75
90–94	0.83921	1,872	1,571	4,550	5,184	2.77
95–99	0.91694	301	276	593	635	2.11
100+	1.00000	25	25	42	42	1.66

Note: The function p_x is not shown because it is easily derivable from the q_x column by taking $1 - q_x$ for each age category.

Source: Adapted from Statistics Canada publication *New Birth Cohort Life Tables for Canada and Quebec, 1801–1991*. Catalogue no. 91F0015MIE.

4. Table 7.23 shows life expectancies at birth for males and females for selected countries between 1971 and 2000. From this information, compute the sex differentials in life expectancy at birth for each period (female minus male) for each country. Then compute the absolute sex differences in life expectancy at birth between successive periods for each country (i.e., take the difference of the differences across successive periods). Finally, compute the absolute change in these differences across successive periods for each country (i.e., difference in period 2 minus difference in period 1, etc.). What can you conclude from these calculations about the change in the sex gap in life expectancy at birth across these populations between the early

1970s and the late 1990s or the year 2000? Consider sociological reasons for the observed changes in the sex differentials in life expectancy over time across the selected countries.

Table 7.23   Trend in the sex differential in life expectancy at birth in selected high-income countries; early 1970s to late 1990s/2000

Country	Early 1970s Male	Female	D1	Early 1980s Male	Female	D2	Early 1990s Male	Female	D3	Late 1990s/2000 Male	Female	D4
Canada	69.48	76.65		71.92	79.24		74.44	81.00		76.14	81.79	
Austria	66.73	73.80		69.23	76.46		72.75	79.36		76.06	81.88	
USA	67.23	74.73		70.30	78.00		71.91	78.97		74.08	79.47	
England & Wales	69.30	75.60		71.18	77.18		73.52	79.18		75.92	80.68	
West Germany	67.60	74.04		70.28	77.03		73.02	79.50		—	—	
Germany	—	—		—	—		72.06	78.60		74.89	81.01	
Italy	68.82	75.05		71.58	78.24		73.73	80.47		76.27	82.58	
France	69.14	76.85		71.03	79.27		73.58	81.99		75.10	82.75	
Sweden	72.18	77.58		73.16	79.33		75.14	80.82		77.08	82.01	
Japan	70.22	75.66		74.08	79.64		76.28	82.71		77.20	84.08	

Notes: The actual time points for the countries are as follows: Canada (1971, 1981, 1991, 1998); Austria (1970, 1980, 1990, 2001); USA (1970, 1980, 1990, 1999); England and Wales (1971, 1980, 1991, 2000); West Germany (1970, 1980, 1991); Germany (1990, 1999); Italy (1970, 1980, 1990, 1999); France (1970, 1980, 1990, 1999); Japan (1970, 1981, 1990, 1999); Sweden (1970, 1980, 1990, 1999). East and West Germany were reunited in 1990; data after this date is reported for Germany as a whole.

The symbol '—' means data not available.

D1, D2, D3, and D4 are the female–male differences in life expectancy at birth in each time period, to be computed.

Source: World Health Organization, http://www3.who.int/whosis/mort/table1.cfm? path=whosis,mort,mort_table1&language=english. Reprinted by permission of the publisher.

Study Questions

1. Discuss the health and epidemiological transitions of high-income nations and how these are similar to or different from the situation in developing countries.

2. The epidemiological transition theory has been criticized as being a linear model of health and mortality change. What does this mean? What evidence is there to support this criticism?

3. Discuss competing theories of senescence and aging in countries in the fourth stage of epidemiological transition. Based on these theories, what are the long-term implications for societies' future burden of disease?

4. Outline the general pattern of mortality change in Canada since the early part of the twentieth century. What factors are responsible for this pattern of change? What are the implications of current mortality conditions for further gains in life expectancy in Canada?

5. Notwithstanding universal health care in Canada, there are significant discrepancies in health and mortality across different sectors of the population. Discuss the factors responsible for these persisting differentials and how existing health disparities can be minimized or eliminated over the course of the twenty-first century.

6. Would further increases in health care spending be effective in raising the overall health status of Canadians? Why or why not?

7. Explain why there are inequalities in health and mortality across countries in the more developed world, in the developing world, and between more developed and less developed countries. What can be done to reduce the inequalities in mortality within and across these different categories of countries?

8. What are the sociological and biological bases for the sex differential in mortality and life expectancy? How has this differential changed in the most advanced countries since the later stages of the twentieth century? Speculate on the long-term future of this differential in Canada. What age groups in Canada contribute the most to the sex gap in mortality? What possible interventions would help reduce the male disadvantage in mortality in relation to women?

9. Married people have been found to have better health and lower death rates than single, widowed, and divorced people. Why do you think this is so? Can you think of any exceptions to this differential? Will this differential diminish or even disappear in the long term given the significant changes in family patterns and marriage in highly developed nations over recent decades?

Additional Reading

Bengtsson, Tommy, Cameron Campbell, and James Z. Lee, et al., eds. 2004. *Life Under Pressure: Mortality and Living Standards in Europe and Asia, 1700–1900*. Cambridge, MA: MIT Press.

Doblhammer, Gabriele. 2004. *The Late Life Legacy of Very Early Life*. Berlin: Springer.

Haggett, Peter. 2000. *The Geographical Structure of Epidemics*. Oxford: Clarendon Press.

Johansen, Hans Christian. 2002. *Danish Population History: 1600–1939*. Odense: University Press of Southern Denmark.

Marks, Geoffrey, and William K. Beatty. 1976. *Epidemics: The Story of Mankind's Most Lethal and Elusive Enemies—From Ancient Times to the Present*. New York: Charles Scribner's Sons.

Marmot, Michael G., and Richard G. Wilkinson, eds. 2006. *The Social Determinants of Health*. Oxford: Oxford University Press.

Murphy, Barbara. 2002. *Why Women Bury Men: The Longevity Gap in Canada*. Winnipeg, MB: J. Gordon Shillingford.

Raphael, Dennis. 2007. *Poverty and Policy in Canada: Implications for Health and Quality of Life*. Toronto: Canadian Scholars' Press.

Szreter, Simon. 2005. *Health and Wealth: Studies in History and Policy*. Rochester: University of Rochester Press.

Tabeau, Eva, Anneke van den Berg Jeths, and Christopher Heathcote. 2001. *Forecasting Mortality in Developed Countries: Insights from a Statistical, Demographic and Epidemiological Perspective*. Dordrecht: Kluwer Academic.

Timaeus, Ian M., Juan Chackiel, and Lado Ruzicka, eds. 1996. *Adult Mortality in Latin America*. Oxford: Clarendon.

Wunch, Guillaume, Michel Mouchart, and Josianne Duchene, eds. 2002. *The Life Table: Modelling Survival and Death*. Dordrecht: Kluwer Academic.

Web Resources

The World Health Organization (WHO) is an easy-to-access source for country-specific mortality data: www.who.int/whosis/database/mort/table1.cfm.

The United Nations Development Program produces an annual *Human Development Report*, which outlines important social, political, sociologic, economic, demographic, and environmental trends for the world's countries. The focus is on development issues, including health concerns across developed and developing countries: http://hdr.undp.org/reports/global/2005/.

UNAIDS is, along with the World Health Organization, the authority in charting global and regional trends of the HIV/AIDS epidemic: www.unaids.org/en/CountryResponse/default.asp.

HNPStats is the World Bank's Health, Nutrition, and Population data platform, an important data source for indicators from various national and international data sources. It provides direct access to more than 100 indicators, with time series for countries and country groups from 1960 to the most recent year, where data are available. The website is continuously updated as new information becomes available: http://devdata.worldbank.org/hnpstats/.

Two interesting websites that feature current research and issues related to aging and longevity are BlueZones, which is headed by Dan Buettner, an award-winning journalist (www.bluezones.com/) and Thomas Perls's *Long Life Family Study* website (www.bumc.bu.edu/Dept/Home.aspx?DepartmentID=361).

An important website that features demographic research, including mortality, is the Max Planck Institute for Demographic Research: http://www.demogr.mpg.de/. (See also this institute's journal, *Demographic Research*, at http://demographic-research.org.)

PART FOUR

Demographic Processes II:
Internal and International Migration

Chapter 8

Internal Migration

Introduction

Migration is the third key component of population change, after fertility and mortality. Most of us will relocate at some point in our lives. Some will move to a different country from the one where we were born or raised; this is international migration, the subject of Chapter 9. Many more will relocate within Canada, however. Some will move from one end of the country to the other; others will move to a different place within their home region; some will move more than once—perhaps several times. A recent publication by Statistics Canada points to the ubiquity of migration in our lives. Between 1996 and 2001, four in ten Canadians picked up and moved. Many headed for the Prairies or British Columbia; young adults opted mainly for large metropolitan areas, while seniors generally left the big cities for smaller towns or rural areas (Statistics Canada, 2002c). What all these types of internal migration have in common is the fact that they are motivated by the movers' desire for improvement, whether in their economic situation or in their overall sense of well-being.

Basic Concepts

Defining Terms

Migration

What counts as migration? Does a move from one neighbourhood to another within the same community qualify? Is a visit to another country a migration? What about the daily movement from home to workplace and back? While all these examples involve *geographic mobility*, none of them would count as an instance of migra-

tion. In demography, *migration* is usually understood to have three main components: the crossing of administrative boundaries, long-distance travel, and a permanent or semi-permanent change in residence (Yaukey and Anderton, 2001: 271–2). As we shall see, however, not every migration meets the long-distance criterion. The duration dimension may also be problematic, since it is not always possible to determine individuals' intentions (Goldscheider, 1971; Morrison, Bryan, and Swanson, 2004; Newell, 1988; Ritchey, 1976; Shaw, 1975). In practice, therefore, most studies of migration use an operational definition based on change in place of usual residence from one administrative area to another.

Scale of Analysis

The first step in any investigation of migration is to classify the study population into two groups: those who have changed address during a specified interval and those who have not. A subset of the 'movers' will be *migrants*: people who not only changed address but who moved to a different administrative jurisdiction (community, town, city, or province). Another subset will consist of people who changed their address but stayed within the same administrative area or jurisdiction. People in this category are called *non-migrants*; examples include individuals who move house within the same community and students who move away from their usual community but only for a limited period of time, to attend college or university. 'Transients', who may move from one jurisdiction to another but have no fixed address and whose movements therefore cannot be easily traced, are also treated as non-migrants. These sorts of temporary and transient moves are generally not considered to fall within the definition of migration (Hinde, 1998: 191). Researchers studying the people involved treat transients as unique subpopulations in the sociological sense.

As Figure 8.1 shows, geographic mobility is analyzed at a variety of geopolitical scales, from local to international. Demographers use parallel terms to refer to migration into and out of a locality within a country or between countries.

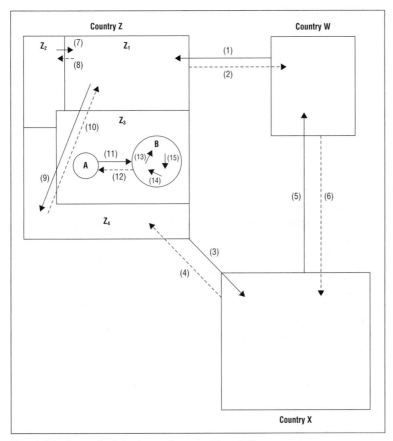

Figure 8.1   Conceptualizing types of geographic mobility

   (1) immigration to country Z (emigration from country W)
   (2) immigration to country W (emigration from country Z)
   (3) immigration to country X (emigration from country Z)
   (4) immigration to country Z (emigration from country X)
   (5) immigration to country W (emigration from country X)
   (6) immigration to country X (emigration from country W)
   (7) in-migration to area Z1 (out-migration from area Z2)
   (8) in-migration to area Z2 (out-migration from area Z1)
   (9) in-migration to area Z4 (out-migration from area Z1)
(10) in-migration to area Z1 (out-migration from area Z4)
(11) in-migration to city B in area Z3 (out-migration from city A)
(12) in-migration to city A in area Z3 (out-migration from city B)
(13), (14), (15) local mobility within city B

In the case of *international migration*, the term *immigrant* refers to a citizen or permanent resident of a country who moves into another country. The parallel term in cases of internal migration is *in-migrant*, denoting a person who migrates into one administrative area from another area within the same country. The corresponding terms referring to outward movement are *emigrant* and *out-migrant*. The former pertains to people who leave one country and relocate to a different one; the latter refers to those who leave one administrative area for another within the same country.

The Uniqueness of Migration

Migration, as we noted at the outset, is one of three key components of population change. It differs from the other two—fertility and mortality—in a number of ways, some fairly obvious, others less so. For instance, birth and death are once-in-a-lifetime events, whereas an individual can—and many individuals do—experience migration many times. Migration is not a biological process, and so it is not subject to biological restrictions, as fertility is: anyone can migrate, whatever their age or gender. Yet migration, unlike fertility and mortality, is not common to all societies: it is theoretically possible for a society to have no experience of migration. Finally, whereas virtually all countries require that births and deaths be reported to governmental statistical bureaus, this is not the case with migration. As we shall see in the next section, this makes collecting data on migration uniquely challenging.

Sources of Migration Statistics

Many countries (including Denmark, Finland, Sweden, Japan, the Netherlands, Bahrain, Kuwait, and Singapore) require that changes of residence be reported, and China demands that officials approve every such move in advance; but many others have no such regulations (Bryan, 2004: 32; Shryock and Siegel, 1976: 353). In practical terms this means that migration data tend to be less complete than data on

births, deaths, and nuptiality. For this reason, migration studies often depend on estimates produced using indirect methods.

The ideal migration data set would include, at a minimum, the following:

- data on the origins and destinations of migrants
- data disaggregated by age, sex, and other characteristics (marital status, occupation, income, race/ethnicity)
- data available in one-year age groups
- data available annually for a large number of time periods
- data produced in a timely manner
- data consistent with the relevant population base for calculating migration rates

Ideally, these data would be available for all the major geographic units in a country, from provinces or states down through the smaller units such as counties and subcounty divisions. Unfortunately, it is not always possible to obtain such a detailed data set, and therefore many analyses of migration must be based on less extensive information. Where do we obtain migration data? There are a number of potential sources, including population registers, sample surveys, and administrative files (income tax returns, family allowance records, and so on). The most comprehensive data source, however, is the census.

Typically, the census will ask respondents to state their address at two points in time: on census day and at some earlier date (usually five years before). (A one-year mobility question is often included as well.) By juxtaposing respondents' addresses at the time of the census and at some earlier date, the census can tell us a good deal about respondents' movements. Table 8.1 shows the various types of geographic mobility in Canada over several census periods from 1956 to 2006. The overall consistency of these figures is remarkable. Just over half of Canadians aged five years and older do not change their place of residence in each census interval. Of

Table 8.1 Population 5 years and over by mobility status and census period, Canada, 1956–61 to 2001–6 (percentages and total population aged 5 and over at the time of the census)

Mobility status	Census period						
	1956–61	1966–71	1976–81	1986–91	1991–6	1996–2001	2001–6
Non-migrants							
Non-movers	54.6	52.6	52.4	53.2	56.7	58.1	59.1
Local (residential) movers	25.4	23.5	24.9	23.2	23.0	22.4	22.0
Migrants							
Within same province	13.5	14.0	15.1	15.9	13.4	12.8	12.1
Different province	3.4	4.3	5.1	3.9	3.4	3.2	2.9
From abroad	3.1	4.2	2.5	3.7	3.5	3.5	3.9
Not stated[1]	0.2	1.4					
Total population aged 5+	15,302,621	19,717,210	22,280,095	24,927,870	26,604,135	27,932,590	29,544,485

[1] Until 1981, 'not stated' responses were identified as such; since then, imputation methods have been used to allocate the 'not stated' cases to the various categories of mobility.

Source: Adapted from McVey Jr and Kalbach (1995a): 123, Table 5.2; Statistics Canada (2007h, 2004a, 2004b).

those who do move, approximately half stay within the same community. This means that within any census interval, roughly one-quarter of all Canadians aged five years and older qualify as migrants, and most of them relocate within the same province (i.e., *intraprovincially*).

As important as this information is, census-based data collection is unsatisfactory for at least three reasons. First, the census question cannot detect multiple moves within the specified period. In fact, it is possible to move many times in the census period and still not be counted as having moved at all, if one happens to have returned to the original residence by the time of the next census. For this reason, census data generally underestimate the true extent of migration during a five-year period. A second problem is sampling error. The mobility question is not asked of all census respondents—only of the 20 per cent of households that receive the long census form. As a result, the reliability of the estimated migration levels for relatively small

subpopulations (e.g., ethnic and racial groups) and geographic subunits below the level of the county (towns, municipalities, villages) is questionable. A third weakness of relying on censuses for migration data is that they cannot tell us anything about emigration (i.e., movement *from* Canada to another country; see Chapter 9). The clear advantage of census data is that they cover the entire country and make it possible to cross-classify movers by a host of individual characteristics. So, for example, analysts can classify interprovincial movers during a census interval with respect to age, sex, marital status, and education. Many other demographic characteristics can be included in a multivariate analysis (using multiple regression, for example) to ascertain the relative importance of background characteristics in explaining geographic mobility (see Long, 1988; Stone, 1978).

Migration data can also be obtained from administrative records, such as annual income tax returns. Finnie (1999a), for example, used

The Longitudinal Administrative Database (LAD) is a 10 per cent representative sample of Canadian tax filers, followed over time and matched into family units on an annual basis. It provides individual- and family-level information on incomes, taxes, and basic demographic characteristics, including province of residence. Because the rate of tax filing in Canada is very high, the LAD's coverage of the adult population is considered to be very good (Finnie, 1999b: 231–2).

the Longitudinal Administrative Database (LAD) developed by Statistics Canada, which links individuals' income tax files over time, to categorize individuals as stayers, one-time movers, returnees, or multiple movers. He was also able to address some important questions about migration in Canada and its effects on individuals' earnings. He found, for instance, that interprovincial migration usually brings some improvement in income, though an average migrant's income may not be at par with that of the receiving population. Finnie (1999a) also noted that the size of the increase in income for interprovincial migrants depends on a number of factors, including age, gender, and the province of destination, since some provinces are more bountiful than others in terms of job opportunities and wage scales; the amount of time spent in the destination province is also important (presumably income rises with duration of residence in a new province).

Basic Measures of Migration

In most studies of migration the objective is, as Shaw (1975: 8) put it, 'to describe migration in terms of distributions by age, sex, education, occupation, etc.' in order to 'examine variations in the degree of intensity with which sending or receiving populations lose or gain migrants [in relation to] their varying socioeconomic con-

texts.' To do this, analysts need to be able to compare migration rates. The problem is that the data needed to compute those rates—namely, the actual numbers of in- and of out-migrants for a given area—are frequently not available. This difficulty is generally resolved by using the demographic components equation to estimate net migration without direct knowledge of in- and out-migration frequencies (Hinde, 1998; Plane and Rogerson, 1994; Yaukey and Anderton, 2001; see page 343 for an illustration).

Migration Rates

Like marriage, divorce, or childbirth, a change of residence may be seen as a transition between two different states: a non-mover in the population of origin becomes a migrant in the population of destination. This means that changes of residence in the population are the numerators when computing rates of migration. A general migration rate can be calculated as follows:

$$\text{migration rate} = \frac{\text{number of persons moving in a given period}}{\text{population at risk of moving in the period}} \times 1,000$$

This equation treats migration no differently from any other demographic rate. But in fact, as we noted earlier, migration is different, because—unlike fertility or mortality—it is not irreversible. Rather, migration operates in two directions: for any given area, some people will move in and others will move out. This makes it necessary to calculate two rates for any given area: a rate of in-migration and a rate of out-migration. Let us look first at out-migration:

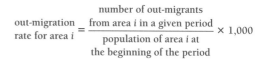

$$\text{out-migration rate for area } i = \frac{\text{number of out-migrants from area } i \text{ in a given period}}{\text{population of area } i \text{ at the beginning of the period}} \times 1,000$$

This formula calculates the out-migration rate for area i as the number of persons that leave area i during a given period, divided by the population of area i at the beginning of the period. In fact, since census data are usually based on the mid-year population, the denominator is usually the mid-year census population. For example, if in a given year there are a certain number of out-migrants from area i (O_i) and the population at mid-year for this same area is given (P_i), then we can compute a central out-migration rate for area i:

$$\text{out-migration rate for area } i = \frac{O_i}{P_i} \times 1{,}000$$

where O_i is the number of out-migrants from area i in the period, and P_i is the mid-year population at risk of leaving area i.

By convention, the rates are expressed as per 1,000 population.

Although it might seem that the in-migration rate could be calculated in parallel fashion, a complication arises when we try to identify the 'population at risk'. In theory, the population at risk should be everyone who is *not* living in area i at the beginning of the period—in other words, the population of all regions in the system being studied other than area i (Hinde, 1998: 193; Plane and Rogerson, 1994: 97; Yaukey and Anderton, 2001: 273–4). This information is often difficult to determine. Instead, in practice the in-migration rate is calculated using the same denominator used for the out-migration rate. So, if the number of in-migrants to area i in a given period is defined as I_i, then,

$$\text{in-migration rate for area } i = \frac{I_i}{P_i} \times 1{,}000$$

The use of the same denominator in the in- and out-migration rate is problematic. On the one hand, out-migration rates make sense because the total resident population in an area at least bears some resemblance to the number of people who could move out. But this is not the case when it comes to the in-migration rate, since the resident population by definition cannot move

into the area it already resides in, and its size has no direct bearing on the number of people who could move there.

On the other hand, using the same denominator for both the in- and out-migration rates does have an important advantage, in that it allows us to compute two additional rates commonly used in the literature: the *gross migration rate* (GMR) and the *net migration rate* (NMR):

$$\text{GMR}_i = \frac{I_i + O_i}{P_i} \times 1{,}000$$

$$\text{NMR}_i = \frac{I_i - O_i}{P_i} \times 1{,}000$$

The *gross migration rate* is a sum of two migratory flows for a given area: in-migration plus out-migration. In other words, it is the sum of the in-migration to area i plus the out-migration from area i, divided by the mid-year population of area i. The usefulness of this measure is that it provides an indication of the extent of migration turnover in a given locality during a specified period. Usually, areas that attract a large number of migrants also experience substantial out-migration: in addition to those leaving the area for the first time, there are many migrants returning to their places of origin, creating a large volume of *counterstream migration*. In such cases the gross migration rate would be substantial.

The *net migration rate* is simply the difference between the numbers of in- and out-migrants for a given area during a given period, divided by the population of the area. It is a useful indicator of the regional gains and losses produced by the interplay between in-migration and out-migration, and gives a good sense of the relative impact of migration on the extent of a region's overall population change. A positive net migration rate means that the population is gaining people through migratory exchanges; a negative rate means that the population is losing people. Underdeveloped regions tend to experience net losses, while more prosperous areas enjoy net

It is often assumed that areas with high in-migration rates will have low rates of out-migration. In fact, such regions typically have higher-than-average rates of out-migration as well. For example, Alberta has consistently been the most popular destination province for internal migrants since 1996, averaging between 25,000 and 30,000 in-migrants per year. However, Alberta also loses large numbers of residents to other provinces. Between 1 July 2006 and 30 June 2007, for instance, a total of 131,441 persons moved to Alberta—by far the largest in-flow recorded by any province. During the same time, however, 80,272 individuals left Alberta to go to other provinces; this was the second-largest outflow (Ontario, with 107,590 out-migrants, had the largest). The net result of this exchange was a gain of 51,169 residents for Alberta. All the other provinces except British Columbia (+10,646) experienced net losses. It is interesting to note that during the third quarter of 2007, Alberta continued to receive the largest number of interprovincial migrants (29,690), but at the same time experienced the largest outflow of all the provinces (32,690); this was the first time Alberta had experienced negative net migration since 1994 (Statistics Canada Demography Division, 2007a, 2007b).

gains. In this sense, the net migration rate is a good reflection of geographical disparities in socioeconomic opportunities.

Table 8.2 looks at the net balance of inter-provincial migration in Canada from 1951–60 to 2001–6. Historically there has been a directional bias in favour of Ontario, British Columbia, and Alberta. This is the same pattern discussed in Chapter 3 in terms of 'core–periphery' relations: economic deprivation causes the underdeveloped peripheral regions to export people, while the economically developed core must import people in order to meet its economic objectives. Core–periphery systems reflect unequal regional development processes and the relative abundance or lack of the natural

and human capital resources that stimulate economic growth. Since 1945 in Canada, the Atlantic region—especially Newfoundland and Labrador—has been a net loser, in terms of net migration, while Ontario, British Columbia, and Alberta (with some periodic exceptions) have been net gainers (Bélanger, 2002; Dumas, 1990; George, 1970; Stone, 1969). However, as economic conditions fluctuate, the balance of migration can change from positive to negative (or vice versa), sometimes from one year to the next. During the early to mid-1990s, for instance, Ontario's economy suffered a downturn, while Alberta enjoyed sustained economic growth; not surprisingly, Alberta gained a substantial number of people from elsewhere in Canada, while Ontario experienced a net loss of internal migrants. Although British Columbia experienced a net loss between 1996 and 2001, over the longer term (1991–2001) it actually gained roughly 135,000 new residents from other parts of Canada. Alberta's migratory dominance is also clearly evident in the most recent period of observation, 2001–6.

Since the middle of the 1990s, Alberta has once again become (as it was in the 1970s) the top destination for internal migrants, attracting workers from virtually all parts of Canada, but especially BC, Ontario, Saskatchewan, Manitoba, and Newfoundland/Labrador. These five provinces accounted for almost 206,000 in-migrants to Alberta between 1996 and 2001. Ontario also recorded net gains in this period, following a five-year interval of net losses. At the same time, BC dropped in rank preference for potential migrants and lost almost 34,000 residents through net migration.

A significant limitation of the net migration measure becomes apparent when it is analyzed on its own, because it tells us nothing directly about the magnitudes of the two component parts that give rise to it. For example, a net migration rate of 10 for a given area could reflect any number of combinations of in- and out-migration (20–10, or 150–140, or 1,180–1,170, etc.). Moreover, there is no such thing as a 'net migrant' in the real world—just people who are

Table 8.2 Interprovincial migratory balance (net migration) in Canada over 5 decades, 1951–60 to 2001–6

Province/territory	Period 1951–1960	1961–1970	1971–1980	1981–1990	1991–2001	2001–2006
Newfoundland and Labrador	−9,816	−34,537	−20,840	−30,626	−55,784	−15,114
Prince Edward Island	−7,938	−5,732	2,927	378	2,162	−407
Nova Scotia	−28,851	−43,521	4,165	3,331	−11,056	−7,225
New Brunswick	−25,360	−45,277	6,441	−5,915	−12,178	−8,382
Quebec	−72,877	−142,594	−234,163	−122,143	−130,642	−21,375
Ontario	148,036	236,081	−96,391	184,649	26,516	−29,617
Manitoba	−40,587	−64,161	−68,977	−37,968	−51,833	−24,892
Saskatchewan	−87,938	−123,492	−50,603	−67,475	−60,009	−35,080
Alberta	32,858	30,022	244,991	−61,203	165,249	128,962
British Columbia	93,075	192,713	216,486	144,345	135,834	15,286
Yukon and NWT[1]	−600	519	−4,036	−7,373	−8,279	−2,156
Total movements	**2,962,004**	**3,660,061**	**3,849,741**	**3,168,426**	**3,257,874**	**1,398,181**

[1]Data for Nunavut (established as a separate territory in 1992) are included with Yukon and Northwest Territories.
Sources: Dumas (1990): 106; Bélanger (2003): 73; Bélanger (2002): 58; Statistics Canada Demography Division (2007a): 17–21, Table 2-4.

arriving at places or leaving them (Plane and Rogerson, 1994: 98).

Table 8.3, based on 2006 census data, focuses on interprovincial migration between 2001 and 2006. This table allows for a more complete analysis of interprovincial migration as it contains migration inflows and outflows between all pairs of provinces, as well as the summary balances of in-, out-, and net-migration for each province (the Canada totals across the table represent out-migration counts from each province; the Canada column is the in-migration to each province). During this time interval, Alberta and BC, and to a lesser extent, Prince Edward Island, were the only provinces to experience positive net migration (88,175, 22,135, and 610, respectively). The most substantial losses were for Ontario (−26,920), Saskatchewan (−25,380) and Manitoba (−20,715).

Patterns of interprovincial migration can change abruptly over shorter time intervals. For instance, commenting on the situation for the interval between 2001 and 2002, Bélanger

(2003: 72) noticed that Newfoundland and Labrador and Quebec both reduced their migratory losses. In addition, for the first time in 25 years, more Ontarians moved to Quebec than vice versa (*National Post*, 2004: A3). This pattern was repeated between 1 July 2006 and 30 June 2007, when nearly 21,000 people moved from Ontario to Quebec while just under 17,000 left Quebec for Ontario (Statistics Canada Demography Division, 2007a). It is likely that many of those moving to Quebec are francophones returning to their home province. In fact, Quebec has recently been attracting increasing numbers of francophones from other parts of Canada. Statistics Canada (2007g) reports that between 1996 and 2001 the French-speaking population outside Quebec grew by nearly 10,000, primarily because of migration from Quebec. Between 2001 and 2006, however, the francophone population outside Quebec declined by 5,000, largely because of return movement to Quebec (Statistics Canada, 2007g: 16–17).

Table 8.3 Interprovincial migration in Canada, 2001–2006 (population 5 years and over as of 2006 census)[1]

Province/ territory 2006	Canada	NL	PE	NS	NB	QC	ON	MB	SK	AB	BC	YT	NT	NU
							Province/territory 2001							
Canada	852,580	32,020	7,690	56,040	42,180	85,200	212,705	57,330	64,310	138,690	142,575	4,015	7,045	2,770
NL	25,780	0	365	3,635	2,895	760	10,160	1,750	240	4,115	1,385	50	135	275
PE	8,300	455	0	1,930	1,325	420	2,680	205	90	630	500	0	45	0
NS	48,035	4,260	1,520	0	8,005	2,665	19,245	1,275	830	5,295	4,330	125	300	180
NB	31,575	1,345	1,170	6,290	0	5,345	11,200	805	380	3,175	1,685	35	110	35
QC	73,550	975	475	3,445	6,750	0	44,535	1,805	1,220	5,890	7,880	135	125	310
ON	185,785	9,060	2,125	19,450	11,395	52,770	0	13,975	7,060	29,800	38,120	355	900	775
MB	36,585	705	100	1,200	985	1,815	11,125	0	5,670	7,745	6,580	100	390	165
SK	38,930	605	55	675	570	945	6,050	5,855	0	16,635	7,000	145	295	105
AB	226,865	11,355	1,345	12,625	7,765	9,750	49,455	19,595	37,430	0	72,680	1,455	3,105	310
BC	164,710	2,220	470	5,960	2,165	10,070	56,035	11,455	10,700	62,795	0	1,480	1,165	195
YT	3,665	35	0	120	40	195	545	150	125	750	1,380	0	295	35
NT	6,360	610	45	465	190	280	1,090	230	480	1,655	820	110	0	365
NU	2,425	405	15	235	100	180	580	225	80	195	215	20	185	0
Net migration	0	−6,240	610	−8,005	−10,605	−11,650	−26,920	−20,715	−25,380	88,175	22,135	−350	−685	−345

[1]Data generated from a 20% sample of the population of Canada, taken during the 2006 census.

Source: Statistics Canada, 2006 Census of Population, Statistics Canada catalogue no. 97-556-XCB2006010. Accessed 8 July 2008.

Stream-specific Migration Rates

In many cases analysts are interested in the exchange of migratory flows or streams between two places. The intensity of migration between origin place i and destination place j (MR_{ij}) can be computed as

$$MR_{ij} = \frac{M_{ij}}{P_i} \times 1{,}000$$

where M_{ij} is the number of people moving from place i to place j, and P_i is some measure of the population at risk of moving away from place i (ideally the population at the start of the interval).

The intensity of migration in the opposite direction—from place j to place i—would then be

$$MR_{ji} = \frac{M_{ji}}{P_j} \times 1{,}000$$

where M_{ji} is the number of people moving from place j to place i, and P_j is some measure of the population at risk of moving away from place j (ideally the population at the start of the interval).

Analysis of Migration Frequencies

Where absolute numbers—or 'frequencies'—are available, they are preferable to estimates. By showing exactly how many people are moving into or out of a given area during a given interval, they give us a concrete sense of migration's impact on both sending and receiving populations.

Migration Efficiency

Internal migration essentially redistributes a nation's population through flows and counterflows between its various geographical subunits. An important measure of migration that reflects this principle is *migration efficiency* (also referred to as *migration effectiveness*). Closely connected to the gross and net migration concepts discussed earlier, migration efficiency is measured as the ratio of net migration to total migration (in + out), denoted below as MER (migration efficiency ratio):

$$MER_i = \frac{I_i - O_i}{I_i + O_i} \times 100$$

This formula is specific to a single geographic area. It says that the efficiency of migration to area i is the *net migration for that area* (the sum of total inflow to area i from all other areas minus total outflow for area i) divided by the *gross migration for this same area* (the sum of total inflows to area i from all other areas plus the sum of total outflow from area i). As Stillwell and colleagues (2000: 19) explain, migration efficiency

measures the degree of imbalance, or asymmetry, between a pair, a set, or system of migration flows and counterflows. Symmetrical flows suggest that migration operates primarily as an exchange process which serves to maintain the settlement system in dynamic equilibrium. Significant population exchanges take place because individual areas that perform specific roles within the settlement system (such as cities) attract migrants at certain life course stages, or with particular motivations, from other areas. But these flows are often balanced, to a greater or lesser degree, by other migrants drawn in the reverse direction by a different set of needs, motives, opportunities, or aspirations. In this situation, migration therefore acts as a mechanism for rejuvenation and renewal of population structures, and restores imbalances brought about by other demographic processes such as aging and mortality, but may bring about little if any net redistribution of population.

By convention, migration effectiveness ratios are expressed as percentages, so in the case of an area-specific ratio the MER will range between -100 and $+100$. High negative or positive values would indicate that net migration is an efficient mechanism for population redistribution, generating a large net effect for the given volume of movement. Conversely, values closer to zero indicate that inter-area flows are more balanced and migration serves to maintain a dynamic equilibrium in terms of population distribution across geographic areas.

If 100 people migrate to a given area i and 100 individuals leave it, the efficiency of migration to area i is zero, since

$$\frac{100 - 100}{100 + 100} = \frac{0}{200} = 0$$

In this case, where equal numbers of migrants were received and sent out by area i there is equilibrium. However, if 100 people move into area i and only 10 leave, the efficiency ratio increases substantially:

$$\frac{100 - 10}{100 + 10} \times 100 = \frac{90}{110} \times 100 = 81.82$$

In this case, for every 100 people received and sent out, area i receives a net inflow of 82 individuals. This indicates a very high degree of efficiency. If we were to turn this example around, so that area i sends 100 out-migrants to other places and receives only 10 in-migrants, the efficiency ratio would be -81.82 (i.e., $[10 - 100]/[10 + 100] \times 100 = -81.82$), meaning that for every 100 migrants it gains or loses, area i sends a net outflow of 82 persons to other places; here, too, the degree of efficiency is very high, but this time it operates in the opposite direction, redistributing migrants to other regions. Migration effectiveness can be measured at different levels—for a specific area (as above), between two or more regions, for pairs of origin and destination areas, or for an entire system.

In some applications analysts may be interested in studying the effectiveness of individual migration streams (M_{ji}) and counterstreams (M_{ij}) between pairs of origin and destination areas (i.e., *stream-specific effectiveness ratios*). The migration effectiveness ratio (MER$_{ij}$) for any two pairs of origin and destination areas i and j can be expressed as:

$$\mathrm{MER}_{ij} = \frac{M_{ji} - M_{ij}}{M_{ji} + M_{ij}} \times 100$$

where M_{ji} is the migration from j to i (the stream), and M_{ij} is the migration in the opposite direction (the counterstream).

An MER$_{ij}$ value of zero would imply equilibrium in the migratory exchanges between the two places i and j. A positive value would indicate that for every 100 movements between i and j, area i would be the net gainer (meaning that area i is the more attractive area), and therefore this particular migratory stream is efficient in redistributing population from j to i. A negative MER$_{ij}$ value would suggest the opposite: that area j is a net gainer in relation to area i (or that area j is the more attractive place), and that this stream is efficient in redistributing population from area i to area j.

If all the area-specific, or stream-specific, efficiency ratios are summed for a given geographical system (e.g., summing province-specific MERs to derive an overall migration efficiency value for Canada) we can obtain an overall *migration efficiency index* (MEI) for the system as a whole. To do so, we sum the *absolute* values of the net migration balances for all the geographical sub-units in the system, and then divide this sum by the sum of all the gross inflows and outflows for all the subunits in the system:

$$\mathrm{MEI} = \frac{\sum_i \left| M_{ji} - M_{ij} \right|}{\sum_i M_{ji} + M_{ij}} \times 100$$

Whereas the two efficiency measures outlined above had a broad range (between -100 and $+100$), this overall migration efficiency index has a more limited range, with values between 0 and 100. High positive values in this case would indicate that inter-area migration is an efficient factor for population redistribution, generating a substantial net effect in relation to the total volume of movement in the system as a whole. This index can be compared over time periods in order to gauge the extent of migration efficiency in a particular geographical system. For instance, Stillwell et al. (2000, 2001) discovered that the migration efficiency declined in magnitude in both Australia and the United Kingdom between 1976–81 and 1991–6. Changes in the migration efficiency index may reflect demographic changes (e.g., differential population aging across regions), shifts in economic opportunities across regions, or innovations (e.g., new communication and transportation technologies) that serve to either increase or decrease net shifts in population across geographic areas. For example, a declining rate of population growth may have the effect of reducing inter-area migration. On the other hand, trends towards population aging and early retirement may serve to increase movement towards locations attractive to seniors. Structural changes in the economy can produce asymmetries in inter-area migration, as some regions enjoy economic booms while others suffer downturns. Technological innovations might encourage urban-to-rural migration, either by making it easier for people to commute long distances to work or by allowing them to 'telework' from home.

A system-wide migration efficiency measure summarizes the extent to which migration is transforming the pattern of human habitation, while reflecting 'the human response to spatial variations in opportunities and constraints' and the degree of 'equilibrium or disequilibrium in the flows between geographical areas that constitute the migration system' (Stillwell et al., 2000: 19). The calculation of migration effi-

ciency for different levels of analysis is best illustrated with actual data. The Notes for Further Study at the end of this chapter and the exercise section include further information as well as worked-out examples at the levels of individual provinces, pairs of provinces, and the Canadian system as a whole.

Estimating Migration Using Residual Methods

We have already noted that the data necessary to compute actual rates of migration are not always available. In such circumstances we must rely on estimates produced using indirect or 'residual' methods. There are several ways of doing this. One approach is to use the *demographic components equation*, based on the numbers of births and deaths during the period in question, along with the total population sizes at the beginning and the end of the period. With such data net migration can be worked out by rearranging the components equation as follows:

$$\text{net migration} = (P_2 - P_1) - (B - D)$$

where B and D represent the number of births and deaths during the interval, and P_1 and P_2 are the population totals at the start and the end of the period, respectively.

To illustrate, we'll apply this formula to the population of Nunavut for the period 1992–6 (data in Bélanger, 2003: 104). Nunavut's net migration for this period is calculated to be $-1,300$:

$$\text{NM}_{\text{Nunavut, 1992-6}} = (25,300 - 22,500) \\ - (3,600 - 500) = -1,300$$

This procedure can be extended to subgroups in the population (e.g., employed, unemployed, single, married, etc.) and for specific combinations of age and sex categories (e.g., males aged 20–24; females aged 20–24), assuming that the necessary information is available. In such cases we need to know the populations at the beginning and end of a specific period for a given age–sex group, and how many people in that group have died during the interval in question, taking into account the fact that everyone will be *n* years older at the second point in time. (Note that except in the youngest age groups, births do not figure into the calculation.) Unfortunately, it is not always possible to know the exact number of deaths within an age cohort over *n* years during a given time interval. This problem is particularly acute in the case of smaller administrative units, such as counties or municipalities, for which the required data are typically unavailable. In such cases analysts usually rely on a residual method called the *survival rate method*. This is an advanced topic in formal demographic analysis, but some explanation and a rudimentary example may be found in the Notes for Further Study and in the exercise section at the end of this chapter (see also Morrison, Bryan, and Swanson, 2004; Siegel and Swanson, 2004).

Explanations of Migration

Why does population movement take place? Why are some locations within a geographical system more attractive to migrants than others? What is the relationship between socioeconomic modernization and geographical mobility? How do individual and societal factors influence migration? A number of explanatory frameworks and models have been proposed to address these and other migration-related questions.

The 'Laws' of Migration

In the late 1800s, E.G. Ravenstein (1885, 1889) outlined a number of propositions that he called 'laws of migration'. Here is a summary of those 'laws':

1. *Migration and distance.* (A) Most migrants travel short distances, and the volume of migration from one area to another decreases as the distance between them increases. (B) People who travel long distances tend to gravitate towards the largest urban centres, where the economic opportunities are greatest.

2. *Migration by stages.* Urban expansion tends to have a gradual effect on migration. People living close to the city move there to take up newly created jobs, then migrants from more remote areas of the country move in to take up jobs in the places that have been vacated.

3. *Stream and counterstream.* For every stream of migration in one direction there is a corresponding counterstream of migration.

4. *Urban–rural differences in propensity to migrate.* Migration is more likely among rural than urban populations.

5. *Predominance of women among short-distance migrants.* Women tend to outnumber men in short-distance migration, and men outnumber women in long-distance migration.

6. *Technology and migration.* Technological development, to the extent that it reflects economic growth and related developments (e.g., improvements in transportation), tends to stimulate migration.

7. *Dominance of economic motives.* Economic considerations are the most important determinants of migration.

Many surveys have supported the last of these propositions (see, for example, Brown and Neuberger, 1977; Cadwallader, 1992; Cebula, 1979; Lansing and Mueller, 1973; Lewis, 1982; Ritchey, 1976; Shaw, 1975; Smith, Tayman, and Swanson, 2001; Stone, 1974; Tobler, 1995). For instance, a review by Frey (2003) of US survey data found that 47 per cent of intercounty movers with post-college education said the reason for their change of residence was work-related (job transfer, new job, etc.). Summarizing a large number of survey studies, Lewis (1982: 118) concluded that 'taking a job' and 'looking for work' were the most frequent responses when migrants were asked about their motivations (see also Shaw, 1985: 17). For a study of the economic benefits of interprovincial migration in Canada, see the following box.

Does It Pay to Migrate?

Do migrants gain economically from moving? According to Shin and Ram (2001) the answer depends in part on the characteristics of the migrants themselves and in part on the characteristics of their regions of origin and destination. Given that migrants tend to be relatively young, well educated, and productive, those moving from less prosperous to more prosperous regions can be expected to gain economically in relation to those who stay behind. But what happens when migrants travel in the opposite direction? Table 8.4 summarizes the findings of two analyses conducted by Shin and Ram for out-migrants and in-migrants. The unadjusted results do not take into account the influence of age and education, while the adjusted ones do. In general, the results indicate that in-migrants to economically disadvantaged provinces also gain in income when compared to non-migrants in the destination provinces, but that the income gains are greatest for those moving from disadvantaged provinces to more affluent ones.

Table 8.4 Average total income ratios, interprovincial migrants to non-migrants: Canada, provinces and territories, 1991 and 1996 censuses

| | Out-migrants compared to non-migrants | | | |
| | 1991 | | 1996 | |
Province/territory	Unadjusted	Age–education adjusted	Unadjusted	Age–education adjusted
Canada	1.034	0.961	0.987	0.937
Newfoundland and Labrador	1.257	1.122	1.124	1.097
Prince Edward Island	1.232	1.137	1.162	1.100
Nova Scotia	1.242	1.132	1.211	1.133
New Brunswick	1.197	1.106	1.120	1.072
Quebec	1.178	1.040	1.147	1.009
Ontario	0.971	0.890	0.935	0.872
Manitoba	1.158	1.047	1.097	1.025
Saskatchewan	1.135	1.057	1.121	1.068
Alberta	1.028	0.962	0.918	0.881
British Columbia	0.948	0.919	0.898	0.898
Yukon	0.881	0.864	0.841	0.850
Northwest Territories	1.149	0.839	1.030	0.787

(continued)

Table 8.4 *(continued)*

| Province/territory | Comparison of in-migrants to non-migrants | | | |
| | 1991 | | 1996 | |
	Unadjusted	Age–education adjusted	Unadjusted	Age–education adjusted
Canada	1.034	0.961	0.987	0.937
Newfoundland and Labrador	1.193	1.017	1.182	0.983
Prince Edward Island	1.153	1.008	1.089	1.019
Nova Scotia	1.162	1.037	1.116	1.041
New Brunswick	1.213	1.046	1.156	1.013
Quebec	1.182	1.055	1.080	0.986
Ontario	1.022	0.945	0.988	0.923
Manitoba	1.104	1.029	1.052	0.999
Saskatchewan	1.108	1.012	0.944	0.900
Alberta	0.924	0.932	0.932	0.966
British Columbia	0.973	0.921	0.915	0.871
Yukon	1.039	1.015	0.939	0.918
Northwest Territories	1.455	1.025	1.316	1.029

Note: Ratios greater than 1.0 imply above average income gain. Ratios below 1.0 imply the opposite.
Source: Shin and Ram (2001).

The Mobility Transition

Another important contribution to our understanding of migration is the theoretical framework developed by Zelinsky (1971, 1979), who looked at geographic mobility as both a consequence and a cause of broader societal changes. Starting from the proposition that socioeconomic modernization over the last two centuries has produced a 'mobility transition' paralleling the demographic transition of the Western world, Zelinsky identified seven types of geographic mobility (see Figure 8.2) and charted their evolution through five numbered 'phases' representing different degrees of socioeconomic complexity. Phase I represents the most primitive, pre-transitional type of society, while phase V represents the most advanced, in which economic activity is largely post-industrial (i.e., a tech-

nologically advanced service- and information-based economy).

In the first phase, the *pre-modern traditional* society, people live in small communities and rely on the land for sustenance. There is little genuine residential migration in this type of society and only limited movement (for purposes such as agriculture, social visits, commerce, warfare, or religious observance). The next phase, the *early transitional*, is characterized by massive rural-to-urban relocation (sparked in western Europe by the Industrial Revolution) and internal migration to 'colonization frontiers'. In addition, as the population expands rapidly, this phase may be marked by massive emigration to foreign lands. In the *late transitional* phase, rural-to-urban migration levels off and the population movement becomes increasingly

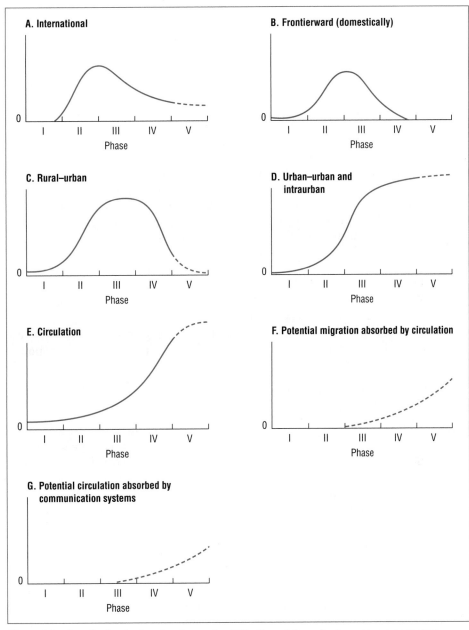

Figure 8.2 Changing levels of various forms of mobility through time: A schematic representation

Source: Zelinsky (1971). Copyright © American Geographical Society 1971.

urban-to-urban, though there may also be increasing movement of international migrants in response to labour demand. The direction and volume of these international migrations depend on economic circumstances and conditions in the receiving nations. In the *advanced society* (phase IV), the majority of the population lives in urban areas. Accordingly, rural-to-urban migration is further reduced, and city-to-city mobility becomes the most important type of movement. In this phase, a country in need of workers may attract significant numbers of unskilled and semi-skilled immigrants from underdeveloped areas of the world. However, in the more advanced stages of development, Zelinsky assumes that international migration will decline gradually as levels of socioeconomic development rise and states begin to impose strict controls on immigration. Advanced societies will experience high levels of 'circulation mobility'—any form of territorial movement that involves at least one night away from home but does not entail a permanent change of residence (Bell, 2001: 5; Prothero and Chapman, 1984); this pattern is typically associated with economic and leisure activity. Finally, in the *super advanced society*, sophisticated communication technologies, such as the Internet, that allow people to work from home eliminate the need for much day-to-day circulation mobility, including the journey to and from work.

Typological Models of Migration

So many factors—individual and societal, personal and psychological, economic and structural—play a role in migration that it may not be possible to formulate an overarching theory. Nevertheless, among the many explanations, various typologies of migration have been proposed. Typologies are conceptual schemata that describe a phenomenon—in this case, migration—in relation to selected factors deemed relevant toward an understanding of it. The advantage of the typological approach is that it offers a way to impose conceptual order on sets of factors presumed to be involved in generating migration. A disadvantage of this approach is that it may oversimplify an inherently complex process, since typologies do not deal directly with causal structure, but only with associations among factors.

Conservative vs Innovating Migration

Petersen (1958) developed a complex typology based on the various forces that may trigger migration and the two fundamentally different states of mind that may be associated with two types of movement: *innovating* (motivated by the desire to improve one's socioeconomic status) and *conservative* (motivated by the desire to escape a situation that poses a significant threat to the well-being of the individual, such as a war or systematic persecution by a dominant group toward a minority). Specifically, Petersen arrived at his typology by juxtaposing the type of migration—whether innovating or conservative—with three factors:

- the type of interaction involved: nature and humans, state (or equivalent) and humans, humans and their norms, collective behaviour
- the migratory force assumed: ecological push, migration policy, higher aspirations, social momentum
- the class of migration: primitive, impelled, forced, free, mass

Petersen's typology is reproduced in Table 8.5.

To interpret this typology we need to think about the interplay of the factors cross-classified with the type of migration. For example, Petersen defines 'primitive migration' as a migration stimulated by the interaction of nature and humans and impelled by 'ecological push'; in other words, primitive migration is a response to humans' inability to cope with natural forces. But this is only one level in Petersen's scheme. In addition, he maintains that primitive migration can be classified as either 'conservative' or 'innovating'. Within the 'conservative' category is another division, between 'wandering' and 'gatherers and nomads'. In prehistoric times the earliest humans were more or less constantly compelled to relocate for environmental reasons (e.g., fire, flood, drought, seasonal shortages of food); for these early humans, movement was a

Table 8.5 Petersen's typology of migration

General typology of migration				'Conservative'				'Innovating'			
Type of interaction	Migratory force	Class of migration	Type of migration	Type of migration	Destination	Migratory selection	Comments/examples	Type of migration	Destination	Migratory selection	Comments/examples
1. Nature and man	Ecological push	Primitive	Wandering	Wandering of peoples / Marine wandering	None	Survival of the fittest	Prehistoric migrations	Flight from the land	Move for land (or towns)	?	Malthusian pressure
			Gatherers and nomads	Gathering nomads	Greener pastures	None	Migratory way of life				
2. State (or equivalent) and man	Migration policy	Impelled	Flight	Flight	Place of safety	None or minority groups	Émigrés and refugees	Coolie trade	Site of work, usually plantations	Young males	Large remigration
		Forced	Displacement	Displacement	Any place		Population exchanges	Slave trade	Site of work	Young males	Mercantile or industrial
3. Man and his collective norms	Higher aspirations	Free	Group	Group	New lands	Dissident groups	Social momentum	Pioneer	Pioneer lands	Young males	Individually motivated
4. Collective behaviour	Social momentum	Mass	Settlement	Settlement	Rural areas	Young males predominate	Social momentum	Urbanization	Towns	Young females predominate	

Sources: Petersen (1958); Kosinski and Prothero (1975): 8.

way of life. Another form of primitive migration, however, Petersen classifies as 'innovating': for example, an agrarian population that, for reasons of drought or overcrowding (because of high population growth rates), would leave to find other agricultural lands. In modern times, some 'innovative' migrants have set out for urban areas within national borders; others have moved overseas (e.g., the wave of Irish immigration to North America during and after the Great Famine of 1846–52).

'Impelled' and 'forced' migration, according to Petersen, can also be classified as either conservative or innovating. The activating force in such cases is the state or some equivalent institution. To illustrate the distinction between the two types of movement, Petersen used the example of Nazi Germany: between 1933 and 1938 the state enacted a variety of anti-Semitic laws in an effort to encourage Jews to emigrate. The decision to leave at that time was 'impelled' in that it was made under pressure, but it still involved some degree of volition. Eventually, however, the Jews had no power to decide one way or the other and were 'forced' to move—transported to extermination camps—against their will.

In the contemporary context, Petersen's framework can be applied to internal or external (international) migration. Although the majority of migrations worldwide over the past half century have typically been voluntary (motivated primarily by socioeconomic considerations), forced migration in the form of refugee movements and large-scale displacements still occur all too frequently today in certain regions of the world. On the other hand, Petersen's typology does not explicitly account for several important dimensions of migration, such as the *time* factor (whether the move is temporary or permanent); the *distance* travelled (long, short); the types of *boundaries* crossed (internal, external); the geographical *area units* involved (between communities, counties, states, countries); and the *numbers* involved in migration (Krishnan and Odynak, 1987).

Spatial Models of Migration

Another class of explanatory frameworks emphasizes the interaction of structural forces on a macro scale. Typically, such models include relatively few variables, and distance plays a major role. Models of this kind explicitly stress the importance of aggregate relationships: for example, the relationship between interregional wage differentials and migration rates.

The Distance–Gravity Model

Ravenstein (1885, 1889) suggested that most immigrants move only a short distance, and that long-distance moves are relatively infrequent. Many of the migration models developed since his time explicitly incorporate the idea that distance is a deterrent to migration (Bogue, 1969; Cadwallader, 1992; Goldscheider, 1971; Lee, 1966; Ritchey, 1976; Shaw, 1975). One important model in this tradition also incorporates the notion that different places within some defined geographical system (e.g., cities within a country) exert differential gravitational pull in the sense of attracting potential migrants. (The idea of distance–gravity developed by Zipf [1946] was inspired by Sir Isaac Newton's proposition that the gravitational force between two objects is directly proportional to their masses and inversely proportional to the square of the distance between them.) In accordance with this formulation, Zipf (1946) proposed that the gross migration (M_{12}) between two places (e.g., cities) whose populations are P_1 and P_2, and the distance between them D, would be given by the equation

$$M_{12} = \frac{P_1 P_2}{D}$$

which says that the volume of migration between any two places is a function of the differential force of attraction between each locality, divided by the linear distance separating the two places. Empirically, the relationship between distance and the probability of migration between places is not linear, but negatively exponential: there is a great deal of migration close to the point of origin, but as distance increases from the origin the volume of migration drops abruptly to low levels. The version of the distance–gravity model frequently applied in empirical studies takes this into account:

$$M_{12} = K\frac{P_1P_2}{D^a}$$

where M_{12} is the gross migration between any two places (i.e., the sum of in- and out-migration), and K and a are constants.

The latter term measures the exponential deterrent effect of distance on migration, while the former is an overall average value of the number of migrants. If the size of a is large, this implies that distance has a strong deterrent effect on migration: the majority of people will migrate to places that are relatively close to the point of origin, and relatively few will travel to distant locations. If a is small (or statistically insignificant) then distance is of minor importance, and the key determinant of migratory moves between places would be the relative population sizes of destinations (i.e., their relative 'pull', or 'gravity', in attracting migrants).

The distance–gravity model is intuitively appealing, as it corresponds to the basic notion of 'least effort': the idea that when people are required to migrate—for example, to look for work—they would generally prefer to travel as short a distance as possible.

Why is distance so critical? As a general principle, the psychological and financial costs of migration vary in direct proportion to the distance between the places of origin and destination: the longer the distance, the greater the financial, psychological, and social costs of migration are likely to be. Viewed in this way, it is not difficult to see why distance can be a deterrent to migration. In most circumstances the psychological costs of relocation (e.g., separation from family and friends) will be greater

for long-distance migrants than for those who travel only a short distance from their community of origin. In the same way, immigrants to a new country will usually face greater social and psychological adjustments than people moving within the boundaries of their home country.

The Intervening Opportunities Model

For Stoufer (1940, 1960), by contrast, the most important factor explaining migration between places was not distance but opportunity. He proposed that the number of people moving a given distance is directly proportional to the number of opportunities at that distance and inversely proportional to the number of opportunities that intervene between places—in other words, the number of opportunities a migrant would encounter (and might decide to take up) on the way from one place to the other. In essence, Stoufer argued that for any pair of geographic places, the number of migrants from one place to the other will be determined by how many opportunities exist between the two areas. A frequent operationalization of the term in the empirical literature has been the number of jobs between places or the number of housing vacancies (see Plane and Rogerson, 1994: 206–11; Shaw, 1975: 49). However, Stoufer also pointed out that in any given destination area there would be other migrants competing for the same opportunities. Expressed mathematically, Stoufer's intervening opportunities equation is as follows:

$$M_{ij} = a\frac{(P_iP_j)^{b1}}{(O_{ij})^{b2}(C_{ij})^{b3}}$$

where M_{ij} is the number of migrants between places i and j, P_i and P_j are the population sizes of the two places, O_{ij} is the number of intervening opportunities between places i and j, and C_{ij} is the number of competing migrants seeking opportunities in place j, the destination.

The terms a, b_1, b_2, and b_3 are unknown parameters to be estimated empirically. Verbally, the model can be stated as follows: migration between i and j = a direct function of (opportunities at place j) + inverse function of (opportunities intervening between places i and j) + inverse function of (number of other migrants competing for opportunities at place j) (Shaw, 1975: 4). Stoufer's formulation has the advantage of recognizing that migrants, as rational actors, generally seek 'opportunities', (i.e., work) and that this is a prime motivation for relocation.

Evidence from Canada seems generally consistent with the basic postulates of both the Zipf and the Stoufer models. For example, we saw in Table 8.1 that the majority of Canadians do not relocate at all between census periods, and that of those who do move, the majority remain within the same municipality; only a small proportion of people travel long distances (i.e., interprovincially). This suggests that distance is in fact a deterrent to migration, consistent with the distance–gravity model. Also supporting that model is the fact that the provinces with the largest populations tend to attract the largest volumes of both internal and international migrants (Shaw, 1985: 6).

A further test of the distance–gravity model might consider interurban migration patterns. Again, the evidence here is consistent with the basic postulates of the model. Canada's largest census metropolitan areas (CMAs) are Toronto, Vancouver, Montreal, Ottawa–Gatineau, Calgary, and Edmonton. These centres attract the largest shares of internal and international migrants (Shaw, 1985); thus at face value there appears to be a direct correlation between population size and the volume of in-migration to a CMA. It also appears to be the case that smaller urban centres generally lose more people than they gain through migratory exchanges.

Under the postulates of the distance–gravity model, it would not be surprising to find that the migratory flows between urban centres often take a step-like form, with migrants from smaller centres generally gravitating towards larger urban localities that are relatively close to the sending areas. For instance, the number of migrants moving from St John's to Halifax would be expected to exceed the number of migrants moving from St John's to Quebec City. And the volume of migration between Edmonton and Calgary would likely be much larger than the volume moving between Calgary and Thunder Bay, Ontario.

Extending this principle, we would expect to see fewer people migrating from St John's to Edmonton, or Calgary, or Vancouver, than to Toronto, since Toronto (1) is the largest urban centre in Canada, (2) is closer geographically to St John's, and (3) offers many more 'opportunities' than St John's does. In fact, historically there have been large migratory flows from Newfoundland and Labrador, and the Atlantic region generally, to Toronto and other parts of Ontario. Nevertheless, sizeable migratory streams have developed between St John's and Calgary, Edmonton, and Vancouver, in spite of the long distance involved. The intervening opportunities model would say that the relative frequency of long-distance migration in this case is largely a function of fewer intervening opportunities in eastern and central Canada. In fact, Alberta has received many migrants from Newfoundland—people attracted by the large number of jobs available in Alberta as compared to the intervening provinces.

The Neoclassical Macroeconomic Model

In 1966, Lowry formulated a model that incorporates indirectly some of the ideas inherent in the distance–gravity and intervening opportunity models. He wanted to test the proposition that the labour market works to allocate people more or less where they belong in terms of (a) their skills and training and (b) the various regions' demand for specialized labour (Plane and Rogerson, 1994). The underlying premise is that differential economic opportunity structures across geographical areas are the key determinants of interregional migration patterns, and that structural conditions in the areas of origin and destination can either promote or discour-

Newfoundlanders in Fort McMurray, Alberta

. . . Anyone who has moved away from a place they were fond of knows this feeling of displacement—a homesickness for the place left behind, no matter how eagerly the new home was anticipated. Fort McMurray, with its abundant oil sands employment opportunities, has become a new home for many. While it has attracted immigrants from around the world, a significant proportion have come from Newfoundland. . . .

Most Newfoundlanders who move to Fort McMurray know someone who's already working there—a cousin, an uncle, or an aunt who reported back to family at home, 'Hey, there's lots of work here—why don't you come?' The large community perpetuates itself and generates a sense of home away from home. Doug Faulkner, the mayor of Fort McMurray, came from Newfoundland in 1980 after his cousin told him about the job opportunities. Faulkner claims Newfoundlanders are the 'most resilient people in the world and bounce right back. . . . They go wherever they can find work and feel at home, and a lot of them feel much at home here.' Faulkner says that somewhere between 13,000 and 18,000 Newfoundlanders live in Fort McMurray—about a third of the population. 'We have a saying here, a joke, that we're Newfoundland's third largest city.'. . .

Newfoundlanders in Fort McMurray have almost identical answers about what they miss from home. First, they miss family. 'It took me almost three years to get used to being away from Newfoundland,' says a cook at the Newfoundland Club. 'And even to this day when I talk to my mom on the phone I get lonely for Newfoundland.' Second, they miss the ocean. Paulette Dobbin, the president of the McMurray Newfoundland Club sums this up: 'I miss the ocean, I really miss the salt water. When I go home, that's the first thing I do—take a walk along the waterfront and breathe in the salt air.'

But there is also a deeper sense of longing for a way of life left behind. Tana Adams, from Robert's Arm, Newfoundland, writes a weekly column called 'From the Rock', for the *Fort McMurray Today* newspaper. She says, 'Newfoundland represents a feeling. A lot of Newfoundlanders have this feeling in their gut—a sense of longing, of homesickness to a way of life, things we took for granted when we were growing up.' This feeling is especially strong among those who have children. Luther Bowers wrote a letter to Newfoundland's *Downhomer* magazine expressing concern about his two-year-old son: 'If he does grow up here [in Fort McMurray], I can't help but think of how different it will be compared to how I grew up. The peace and quiet of small-town Newfoundland, playing around the beaches, ice pans, and "badicaters" [layers of ice and snow that form along shorelines], playing hockey on the frozen harbour, mummering at Christmas, and in summer, swimming over in the brook, out in the boat for a jig, fish'n'brewis on the rocks, and being awed by huge icebergs as they drift by and sometimes "founder" with a thunderous noise, much to our delight. I know we can bring him back and show him some of these things, but you can't have the same appreciation and feeling if you speak of this kind of creative outdoor play and freedom that we remember from our childhood in Newfoundland outports.' Their children in Fort McMurray play in designated parks or organized sports and spend many hours in front of the TV.

For many, though, Alberta has become home in spite of the longing they feel for Newfoundland. Those who have been in Alberta for 20 years or more, whose children—and even grandchildren—have grown up in Alberta, no longer think about returning to Newfoundland; the presence of family makes Alberta home for them now. 'The oddest thing is when your children grow up, they are Albertans,' says Catherine Davis-Herbert, an education instructor at Keyano College. 'They do not think of themselves as being Newfoundlanders. Newfoundland might be a place they visit occasionally, but they are Albertans.'

Newfoundlanders have also made Fort McMurray feel like home. In the city's grocery stores, you can buy cod tongues and Purity biscuits. Cable TV offers Newfoundland Television. There are two 'Mary Brown's Chicken' franchises. You can walk almost into any store or business and hear someone speaking with a Newfoundland accent. And the McMurray Newfoundland Club provides hospitable surroundings for Newfoundlanders (and guests) to gather for music and conversation.

Nearly everyone in Fort McMurray is from somewhere else. . . . The Newfoundlanders stand out, though, because of their numbers and their active involvement with the community at large. Mike Rogers, an organization development adviser for Syncrude, describes them as 'culturally significant to this community'. He says: 'They are here as a presence and I think it's a positive presence. They are friendly, generous, fun-loving, caring people, and they have their own unique brand of humour. They have a culture from the island. They brought it with them, and they've maintained it.' And they share this culture not just with other Newfoundlanders but with the whole community. According to Davis-Herbert, 'People get involved, get networked in the community, through the sense of fun and positive outlook brought by the Newfoundlanders.' . . .

Many Newfoundlanders believe their move to Fort McMurray will be temporary—a few years of good wages to help get them on their feet to set up a business or establish themselves more securely back home. Often, they find they can't save enough to move back. The wages sound good, but much of their paycheques are consumed by the high cost of housing, food and other necessities. . . .

Others hope their work experience in Fort McMurray will help them land a job in Newfoundland. Lee Dehann, a young Newfoundlander, has been in Fort McMurray for only 10 months, and he's already looking for a job back home. 'I'm going home for a holiday, and when I go up there I'm going to check around Bull Arm and Come by Chance. They've got oil up there, and I've got a bit of experience at it. A lot of people recognize Syncrude. So hopefully when I get back there I can get a full-time job. Up here is not a long-term plan, hopefully. I'll ride it out while I can. The ultimate goal is to go back home.'

But the economic future of Newfoundland remains uncertain, and it's unlikely the oil industry there will become a sustaining force for the locals. According to Calgary-based offshore oil analyst Ian Doig (creator of *Doig's Digest*), oil companies are hesitant to embark on business projects in Newfoundland, because offshore pursuits are expensive, especially with the climate and iceberg-laden waters off the coast. The hope for new jobs that arose from Husky Oil's and PetroCan's decision to proceed with the White Rose offshore project was muted, as the decision came shortly after Chevron pulled out from the Hebron/Ben Nevis project. And White Rose anticipates employing only 1,000 people—a small number considering that Fort McMurray alone is home to more than ten times that many Newfoundlanders.

The classified columns in Newfoundland's local papers have numerous advertisements for oil industry and service industry jobs in Alberta—strong encouragement for locals to leave. The long-term effects of the continuing employment exodus are unknown for New-foundlanders at home and in Fort McMurray. Will they ever be able to return home? Will they retain their strong sense of identity and culture? Will a sense of displacement remain? . . .

Source: Excerpts from Kay Burns (2003), 'Far from Home: Newfoundlanders Find Work and Heartache in Fort McMurray', *Alberta Views* 6, 2 (March–April): 48–51. Reprinted by permission of the author.

age migration. Lowry (1966: 12) specified the following equation:

$$M_{ij} = k\left[\frac{U_i}{U_j} \cdot \frac{W_j}{W_i} \cdot \frac{L_i L_j}{D_{ij}}\right]$$

where M_{ij} is the number of migrants from place i to place j; k is an overall average migration rate; L_i and L_j are the number of persons in the non-agricultural labour force at i and j, respectively; U_i and U_j are unemployment as a percentage of the civilian non-agricultural labour force at i and j, respectively; W_i and W_j are the hourly manufacturing wages, in dollars, at i and j, respectively; D_{ij} is the airline distance from i to j, in miles.

Under the log transformation, Lowry's model become linear, easily estimated with multiple regression:

$\log M_{ij} = \log k + \log U_i - \log U_j - \log W_i + \log W_j + \log L_i + \log L_j - \log D_{ij}$

For an interesting application and extension of this model, see Barsotti (1985).

The economic rationale of this model is consistent with the principle that more migrants will move from low-wage to high-wage areas than vice versa, and that unemployed people in areas with a surplus of labour should seek out opportunities where labour is in short supply. Similarly, regions with high wages will tend to retain more people than places with relatively low wages.

What factors besides size, distance, and socioeconomic opportunities influence migratory flows? Shaw (1985) studied this question with reference to Canadian intermetropolitan migration. Among the additional factors that he identified were aspects of the labour market and the business cycle—i.e., industrial wage rate, unemployment, rate of residential building construction—as well as conditions such as weather, climate, and crime levels. Shaw (1985) suggests also that the role of economic factors as determinants of internal migration is diminishing in the post-industrial age. In rich countries, concerns about social amenities and security become almost as important as labour market mechanisms in explaining differential migration patterns across regions. This might be particularly true of highly educated and highly skilled workers, who enjoy an exceptionally broad range of options and locational alternatives (Florida, 2002, 2005). On the whole, Shaw's analysis (see Table 8.6) suggests several generalizations:

1. Distance has declined as a deterrent to migration in Canada (though it is still important), probably because of reductions in the cost of transportation and telecommunications. 'Declining transport costs are relevant to reduced "fixed costs" of relocation whereas declining telecommunications costs are relevant to reduced "psychic costs" of moving away from, say, friends and relatives' (Shaw, 1985: 21).

Table 8.6   Determinants of Canadian intermetropolitan migration

Variable	Empirical measure
Labour market component	
Earnings opportunities	Industrial wage composite
Employment opportunities	Industrial composite employment growth
Unemployment	Unemployment rate
The business cycle	Residential building construction
Government transfers	
Unemployment Insurance	UIC benefits; availability
Government fiscal policy	Federal transfers to provinces
Natural resource revenues	Resource revenues
Additional economic factors	
Home ownership	Ownership, 25–34-year-olds
Housing costs	Cost of new housing units
Dual income-earning households	Female labour force participation
Immigration	Immigration of foreign born
Information and psychic costs	
Distance	Distance between places
Language	Commonality of
Social and amenities considerations	
Crime	Crimes of violence
Climate severity	Total snowfall
Selectivity considerations	
Education	Proportion of highly educated

Source: Davis (1995): 73. Reprinted with permission of the Publisher from *Demographic Projection Techniques for Regions and Smaller Areas: A Primer* by H. Craig Davis © University of British Columbia Press 1995. All rights reserved by the Publisher.

2. Areas with high proportions of highly educated people are more likely to send out migrants than are places with lower proportions of highly educated people. This is likely a reflection of the fact that people with more education have greater access to information regarding the prospects for economic gain through migration.

3. By itself, a higher incidence of violent crime in a particular CMA is not likely to deter migrants from going there; this suggests that other factors override crime as a consideration.

4. With some exceptions, places that normally experience harsh winter conditions do not attract as many migrants as CMAs that are situated in more moderate locations (e.g., Vancouver or Victoria).

5. A CMA that attracts many immigrants from abroad is also likely to attract many internal migrants, probably because it offers greater social and economic opportunities than other areas.

The 'Rational Actor' Model of Migration

All of the models outlined so far take a macro-level perspective, emphasizing spatial dynamics and macrostructural factors that influence the volume of migration. Implicitly, these models assume that migration is governed by microeconomic rationality, in which individuals make their rational choices based on available options (Burch, 1979; Da Vanzo, 1981; De Jong, 1999; Taylor, 2003; Walmsley and Lewis, 1993). Push and pull factors associated with the places of origin and destination are taken into account and are generally represented as economic costs and benefits, calculated according to the individual's own values. An influential model that explicitly incorporates this premise is Lee's (1966); see page 358.

The foundations of the 'rational actor' explanation of migration decision-making can be traced to a seminal work by Sjaastadt (1962), who proposed that the decision to move is based on assessment of the long-term benefits of relocation in relation to the long-term costs (psychological and material). What values and goals are most important in motivating rational actors to migrate? What is it that migrants seek? In Table 8.7, De Jong (1999: 283) offers a systematic list of goals in migration decision-making. Essentially, people who move are searching for a better life: they are looking to improve their incomes, their standards of living,

Another 'rational actor' approach to migration decision-making is *place utility theory*, which focuses on migrants' perceptions of the advantages anticipated at the new location, usually in the context of local residential mobility (Bach and Smith, 1977; Deane, 1990; Landale and Guest, 1985; Lee, Oropesa, and Kanan, 1994; Speare, 1972; Wolpert, 1965a, 1965b). Individual actors are considered to have enough information to form a realistic picture of the chances of success in achieving their objectives. Actual behaviour (i.e., the decision to move) is contingent on the 'worked out' probabilities with respect to the perceived gains and losses attached to each option (migration versus non-migration), plus considerations related to satisfaction with the current residence and neighbourhood. It is possible to incorporate into this type of decision-making model both the influence of significant others (e.g., spouse, colleague, parents) and the experience of cognitive dissonance—the tendency to hold to a decision even in the face of information that would argue against a move (see Burch, 1979: 284).

Table 8.7   Values and goals in migration decision-making: Some concepts from empirical research

Values	Goals
Income/wealth	Attaining desired income, affiliation, stable income, high standard of living, and employment stability
Comfort	Living in a pleasant, healthful, and socially and morally acceptable community and home environment
Stimulation	Gaining entertainment and educational opportunities and variety in interpersonal relations
Affiliation	Living near family and friends, being with a spouse, and having family and friend support available
Easier lifestyle	Attaining a less strenuous and more peaceful life
Environmental quality	Having clean air and water, scenic landscapes, and low noise and pollution
Health	Preserving or improving one's physical or mental well-being
Functional independence	Attaining or maintaining self-reliance
Political and economic freedom	Having choices in economic and political behaviors

Source: De Jong (1999): 283, Table 13.2.

their access to opportunities for themselves and their children, and their lives overall.

Lee's Theory of Migration

Lee (1966) focused on the role played by structural factors in either 'pushing' or 'pulling' the individual to migrate. For instance, a high unemployment rate in the home community would be considered a 'push' factor, compelling the individual to seek employment elsewhere. The presence of family and friends in the local area, on the other hand, would constitute a 'pull', deterring out-migration. 'Push' and 'pull' factors, as perceived by the individual prospective migrant, also operate with respect to the area of intended destination. For instance, a 'pull' factor would be any feature of the destination community that would offer the migrant an important relative gain or advantage, such as a greater number of jobs in the migrant's occupational class, and therefore a greater likelihood of finding employment. A 'push' factor in the intended destination might be a geographical location associated with harsh winter conditions.

Lee considered four sets of factors:

1. factors associated with the area of origin
2. factors associated with the area of destination
3. intervening obstacles
4. personal factors

The prospective migrant's decision about whether or not to migrate is thus based on an assessment of the pluses and minuses in both the place of origin and the potential destination. For instance, someone might perceive that relocation would mean a gain in economic opportunities, while remaining in the community of origin would limit the opportunities for a better life. At the same time, he or she might perceive that moving would entail major difficulties, such as the need to search for a new job, or to adapt to an unfamiliar social environment—perhaps even a new language. The possibility of avoiding such difficulties by staying home could be an important pull factor. Finally, personal factors can also play a role in promoting or discouraging migration. Age, for instance, can be an important consideration: a plus for a young adult, but a minus for someone older. Figure 8.3 is a schematic representation of Lee's decision-making theory.

When the positives outweigh the negatives, the decision shifts heavily in favour of migration. Nevertheless, the individual must still be able to overcome what Lee (1966) calls 'intervening obstacles'. These intervening obstacles can take many forms, including the financial cost of moving, the emotional cost of geographic separation from family and friends, and the psychological insecurities associated with starting a new life in a new environment. For interna-

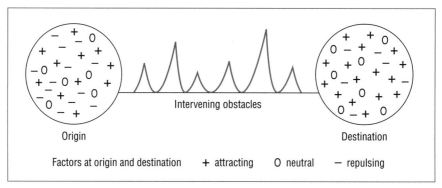

Origin   Intervening obstacles   Destination

Factors at origin and destination   + attracting   O neutral   − repulsing

Figure 8.3 Lee's rational actor model of migration

Source: Lee (1966): 50 (Chart 1). Reprinted by permission of the Population Association of America.

tional migrants, one obvious obstacle would be the legal hurdles that must be cleared before gaining permission to enter a new country. Even if the pluses of migration outweigh the minuses, the intervening obstacles may still prevent the individual from moving.

Todaro's Model of Rural–Urban Migration in Developing Countries

One of the fundamental questions regarding migration in the developing countries is why large cities attract rural migrants even when the socioeconomic prospects they offer are not necessarily any better than the prospects in the rural countryside—for example, when unemployment rates in the city are high. According to Todaro (1969), what matters is the perception of a significant wage differential between rural and urban areas. Non-economic factors are also important, including

- *social factors* (the desire to break away from traditional constraints or social organizations);
- *physical factors* (climate and natural disasters like floods and droughts);
- *demographic factors* (rural population growth);
- *cultural factors* (the security of urban 'extended family' relationships; the allure of 'bright city lights'); and
- *communication factors* (improved transportation, urban education systems, and the 'modernizing' impact of media such as radio, television, and film).

As important as these non-economic factors may be, rural–urban migration in rapidly urbanizing countries largely reflects urban–rural differences in *expected*—not *actual*—earnings. According to Todaro, migrants consider the various labour market opportunities available to them in the rural and urban sectors and choose the one that maximizes their expected gains from migration to the city. (*Expected gains* can be measured by the difference in *real incomes*

between rural and urban sectors and the *probability* of a new migrant obtaining an urban job.) In essence, Todaro assumes that members of the labour force, both actual and potential, compare their *expected incomes* for a given *time horizon* in the urban sector (i.e., the difference between the gains and the costs of migration) with the prevailing *average rural incomes*, and will migrate to the city if the former exceeds the latter. In other words, people from the countryside migrate to the cities because they expect that the economic opportunities there will far exceed the opportunities in the rural sector. This helps to explain the high rates of rural–urban migration in developing countries even though the job prospects in the city may in fact be poor.

Social Demographic Aspects of Migration

Selectivity of Migrants

Migration is a selective process because migrants generally do not represent a random sample of the population. Rather, they differ in their background characteristics from both the populations they leave behind and the populations they enter. Migration can therefore significantly alter the population compositions of both sending and receiving areas. Thus, from a sociological perspective, migration selectivity affects the distribution of characteristics such as age, sex, marital status, education, and occupation in both sending and receiving populations (Bedard and Michalowski, 1997; Ram and Shin, 2007). The degree of selectivity in a given migration stream, however, depends on a variety of circumstances. Lewis (1982: 97), in his survey of the literature, found several common patterns in migration stream selectivity:

1. Migration stimulated by economic growth and technological improvements attracts the better educated. Conversely, areas tending towards economic stagnation lose their better educated and more skilled persons first.

2. If the migration stream between two populations tends to be of equal size in both directions, then the composition of those streams tends to be of minimum selectivity, as measured by indicators such as education and occupational skills of the migrants. If the stream flowing in one direction is greater than the stream flowing in the other direction, there is a greater selectivity in both streams. But the place showing a net gain would have a greater proportion of men, young adults, and single, divorced, and widowed people, while the place showing a net loss would have high proportions of 'migration failures' (returnees), employees of new establishments, local migrants, migrants 'passing through' on their way to bigger centres, and retired migrants returning to their place of origin.

3. Where the 'push' factor is very strong—as in the case of refugee movements or people fleeing ecological disasters, famine, or drought—origin selectivity is minimal. This is generally the case because a large segment of the population is typically affected by the 'push' conditions.

4. In modern technological societies, major migration streams between metropolitan centres tend to show very little selectivity.

This last observation is especially interesting. Other scholars, writing before and after Lewis, have also suggested that advanced societies, having reached a very high degree of industrialization and technological sophistication, tend to become increasingly homogeneous with respect to characteristics such as education and occupation, and therefore exhibit less selectivity in those variables. As the overall level of migration in industrialized nations has tended to increase with increasing industrialization over the twentieth century and the expansion of commercial activity, simultaneously the selectivity in the occupational and educational characteristics of migrants has been declining or weakening (Long, 1973; Shaw, 1985; Williamson, 1965).

This is not to say that selectivity has become totally irrelevant for industrialized countries. In Canada, Liaw and Qi (2004) analyzed 1996 census data to study Canadian-born persons aged 60 and older who, at the time of the census, resided in a province other than that of their birth. Among the strong selective forces they identified was mother tongue: specifically, the exchange of lifetime migrants between the province of Quebec (which is predominantly French-speaking) and the rest of Canada (predominantly English-speaking) had the effect of making Quebec more French—that is, Quebec gained more French-speaking people than it lost. According to Liaw and Qi (2004), instead of leading to a melting pot, the lifetime migration somewhat aggravated the spatial polarization between the two language groups. Newbold (1996a) reached a similar conclusion based on his analysis of 1986 census data.

Recently, Ram and Shin (2007) examined the educational selectivity of migration streams across the Canadian provinces between the 1981 and 2001 censuses. They found an education gradient associated with out-migration from all regions of Canada, with the highly educated being more geographically mobile than the less educated. Interestingly, this pattern was most pronounced among the regions with persistently poor economic conditions and therefore net migratory losses over the years, namely the Atlantic region, Manitoba/Saskatchewan, and Quebec. By contrast, the three high-income provinces of Ontario, Alberta, and British Columbia not only experienced lower overall net losses, but were also less likely to lose their better-educated residents, even during bad economic times. Hou and Beaujot (1995) reached a similar conclusion in their investigation of interprovincial migration between Ontario and the Atlantic provinces between 1981 and 1991. The sociological implications of this educational selectivity are far-reaching, since the migration of highly educated and highly skilled persons to a few well-off provinces at the expense of the less well-off provinces will exacerbate longstanding regional socioeconomic inequalities.

An investigation by Hunt (2004) of internal migration in West Germany from 1984 to 2000 is consistent with the Canadian literature on the selective nature of migration. One-fifth of all internal migrants in Germany moved as a result of relocation within the same firm (i.e., same employer). These migrants tended to be highly skilled and educated, and their pre-move wages were significantly higher than those of non-migrants. Other internal migrants were found to be quite heterogeneous in occupational and background characteristics and not necessarily more skilled than the non-migrants. Consistent with the general selectivity literature, Hunt (2004) also observed that in West Germany those who travelled long distances were generally more skilled than short-distance migrants, and that return migrants were more representative of a mix of successes and failures (i.e., a mix of people who succeed or fail to realize their aspirations through migration).

Age Pattern of Migration

Age is one of a few variables that strongly affect migration probabilities; the others are education, occupation, sex, marital status, and income (Johnson et al., 2005; Ravenstein, 1885, 1889; Rogers, 1984; Shaw, 1975; Thomas, 1938). The importance of age as a determinant of migration is that it is strongly correlated with stage in the life cycle (Greenwood, 1985). For example,

entry into the workforce is typically linked to the end of formal schooling, generally between the late teens and mid-twenties. Graduation usually implies the start of a search for work, often in a location other than one's community of origin. Retirement is another example of the interconnectedness of age, life cycle stage, and migration probabilities. For most people in the industrialized world, the official retirement age is set at 60 or 65. Upon retirement, many people migrate to locations that are geographically attractive to seniors, with a warm climate, many amenities, and so on.

So consistent is the correlation of age with migration probabilities that it has taken on the status of a general 'law' in the demographic literature (Greenwood, 1985; Rees et al., 2000; Tobler, 1995). Rogers and Castro (1986) have summarized this relationship mathematically (see also Rogers, Castro, and Lea, 2005). There are three main segments assumed in the age pattern of migration:

1. *the pre-labour force years* (childhood)
2. *the labour force stage* (adulthood)
3. *the post-labour force phase* (retirement and beyond)

The mathematical specification of this model includes a term for the overall average level of migration, which is assumed to be constant across all age categories (see Figure 8.4).

In childhood the chance of migration is rela-

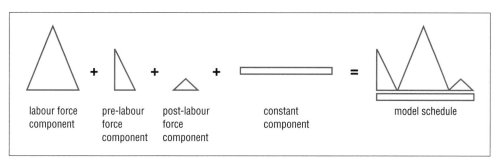

Figure 8.4   The age pattern of migration and its components
Source: Rogers and Castro (1986): 157–208. Reprinted with kind permission from Springer Science and Business Media.

tively low and strictly tied to the family. Young adulthood typically brings a number of events: the start of university or college; entry into the labour force; marriage or co-residence with a partner; and so on. Because of all these life cycle changes, the probability of moving is highest in young adulthood, between the ages of 18 and 24. After young adulthood the likelihood of migration diminishes, dropping precipitously past the late thirties. By the early forties most people are relatively settled in the mundane routines of work, family, and household maintenance, and the likelihood of migration is accordingly low.

A rise in the likelihood of migration in the post-retirement ages, especially after about age 75, has been identified as a characteristic feature of advanced societies (Warnes, 1992). Some of the literature concerning that rise in this area describes it as part of a general tendency among retirees to favour 'sunny' regions such as Florida and California in the United States, and British Columbia in Canada (Bergob, 1992; Biggar, 1979; Chevan and Fisher, 1979; Gober, 1993; Krout, 1983; Martin et al., 1987; Northcott, 1988; Rogers, 1992; Serow, 1987; Sullivan, 1985; Sullivan and Stevens, 1982; Warnes, 1992). However, in Australia, Britain, and Canada, as Figure 8.5 shows, the more pronounced rise in migration probabilities at more

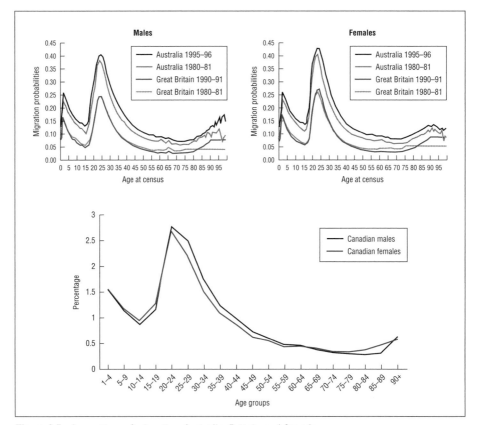

Figure 8.5 Age pattern of migration: Australia, Britain, and Canada

Source: Rees, Bell, Duke-Williams, and Blake (2000): Figure 1, migration probability profiles for Australia and Britain, various years; Ram, Shin, and Pouliot (1994): 14 (figure: interprovincial migration rates for population aged 1 year and over by age group and sex, Canada, 1990–91).

advanced ages suggests the influence of factors associated with late life conditions.

The post-retirement period is, in fact, not a unitary phase. Silverstein (1995) has identified several sub-stages in those years. With retirement many people embark on a 'journey to rest', which typically means travelling to some place with a more comfortable climate than the place of origin. Eventually, the aging migrants begin to experience debilitating health problems. As they become increasingly frail, they seek either to return to their community of origin or to relocate close to children or other relatives who may offer help and support. The final move, to a hospital or nursing home, occurs when aging parents become so incapacitated that their children can no longer care for them.

Gender, the Family, and Migration

Ravenstein's (1885) early proposition that women were less likely than men to migrate over long distances and more likely to migrate short distances may no longer hold in the indus-

trialized countries, where women are active in the labour force. As a result, sex can be expected to play a less significant role in migration today than it did in the past. One way to assess the relevance of gender in migration is by looking at indicators of long- and short-distance moves. An indirect indicator for long-distance travel is interprovincial migration. The 1991 Canadian census counted 413,060 male and 406,600 female interprovincial migrants during the five-year interval between 1986 and 1991. This is not a large differential (McVey and Kalbach, 1995: 137). Data from the 2001 Canadian census suggest a similar conclusion: as Tables 8.8 and 8.9 show, out of 905,665 interprovincial migrants in the period 1996–2001, there were only 3,975 more males than females.

Some areas of the country received more males than females, most notably Alberta (6,940); but for the most part the sex differences in in-migration to each province are not large. More men than women migrated from Prince Edward Island, Nova Scotia, New Brunswick,

Table 8.8   Male–female difference in net balance of interprovincial migration, 1996–2001 (population 5+), by province/territory

Province/territory	In-migrants males–females	Out-migrants males–females
Newfoundland and Labrador	20	1,400
Prince Edward Island	−340	65
Nova Scotia	−1,700	980
New Brunswick	−545	410
Quebec	235	−2,380
Ontario	−765	−1,015
Manitoba	585	−545
Saskatchewan	220	−690
Alberta	6,940	1,705
British Columbia	−725	3,668
Yukon Territory	−180	155
Northwest Territories	180	60
Nunavut	50	165
Total M−F difference	3,975	3,975

Source: Adapted from Statistics Canada (2004d).

Table 8.9 Interprovincial migration in Canada, 1996–2001, by sex (population 5 years and over, 2001 Census—20% sample data)

	Canada	NL	PE	NS	NB	QC	ON	MB	SK	AB	BC	YT	NT	NU
Males														
Canada	454,815	24,250	3,910	27,635	20,735	58,680	94,795	30,320	33,420	62,255	89,500	3,320	4,485	1,505
NL	8,040	0	130	1,345	400	405	3,320	160	105	1180	780	40	105	75
PE	3,780	425	0	795	505	160	1,170	50	50	300	250	0	55	15
NS	25,650	3,225	915	0	3,990	1,495	8,505	815	585	2,685	3,140	70	140	90
NB	16,045	1,090	520	3,155	0	2,705	5,105	495	230	1,410	1,120	70	60	85
QC	31,335	475	125	1,590	3,105	0	18,005	965	515	2,130	4,125	55	70	175
ON	120,865	8,980	1,140	11,465	7,025	39,300	0	7,395	4,390	16,215	23,605	445	655	260
MB	21,590	370	45	745	555	935	6,490	0	3,330	4,560	4,145	70	225	120
SK	21,415	450	50	500	300	485	2,620	3,595	0	8,220	4,710	125	300	70
AB	124,585	7,455	795	5,325	3,600	6,035	22,515	10,545	18,615	0	46,300	1,095	2,070	230
BC	75,495	1,240	180	2,395	1,110	6,860	26,150	5,995	5,260	24,325	0	1,265	575	145
YT	1,780	65	0	50	15	75	260	35	110	280	770	0	95	20
NT	2,960	280	15	155	70	95	405	175	175	820	465	75	0	215
NU	1,285	195	10	115	55	135	260	95	50	125	90	15	140	0
Females														
Canada	450,855	22,850	3,845	26,655	20,325	61,060	95,810	30,865	34,110	60,555	85,835	3,165	4,425	1,340
NL	8,020	0	170	1,330	495	450	3,230	205	115	1,000	815	50	100	65
PE	4,120	485	0	945	610	235	1,180	40	55	270	240	10	55	10
NS	27,350	3,525	940	0	4,150	1,845	9,715	900	395	2,620	2,920	85	130	115
NB	16,590	1,125	570	3,775	0	2,925	4,835	415	180	1,370	1,215	85	55	45
QC	31,100	530	140	1,445	3,115	0	18,690	975	450	1,830	3,620	90	75	135
ON	121,630	8,575	1,235	10,670	7,055	41,210	0	7,830	4,460	16,060	23,350	335	545	300
MB	21,005	350	40	770	430	920	6,310	0	3,520	4,195	4,115	70	200	85
SK	21,195	340	35	390	250	480	2,680	3,685	0	8,035	4,825	145	285	40
AB	117,645	6,300	510	4,580	3,005	5,780	21,535	10,235	19,030	0	43,385	1,030	2,035	220
BC	76,220	1,125	195	2,425	1,105	6,850	26,680	6,290	5,560	24,010	0	1,190	690	110
YT	1,960	65	0	60	10	95	310	55	120	300	835	0	95	10
NT	2,780	270	15	145	50	125	365	155	180	775	435	70	0	195
NU	1,235	170	10	115	35	145	285	95	45	90	80	10	160	0

Source: Statistics Canada (2004d). Adapted from Statistics Canada website. Catalogue no. 97F0008XCB01005. Accessed 12 September 2004.

British Columbia, and the Yukon Territory. But four provinces lost more women than men: Quebec, Ontario, Manitoba, and Saskatchewan. Overall, therefore, gender seems to have made little difference in terms of long-distance migration differentials. Analysis of intraprovincial migration and local mobility, however, does support Ravenstein's proposition that women tend to be more mobile than men over short distances (see Table 8.10).

Census data cannot tell us what percentage of the Canadians who relocate do so as part of a family, but the proportion is probably substantial. In single-earner families the decision to move can be relatively straightforward, based on a rational assessment of the costs and benefits (monetary and psychic) of migrating as opposed to staying put. Things are not so simple for dual-earner couples, however. Mincer (1978) has suggested that in most such cases the wife is a 'tied' or 'trailing' migrant. In other words, wives move because it is expected that husbands stand to gain more from relocating than wives stand to lose. Even in cases where the woman has a well-

paying job, it is usually expected that the man's economic gains will compensate for her economic losses.

On the other hand, in cases where the potential gains from migration would be greater for the wife, the husband may well be the trailing migrant. According to Mincer, however, in many such cases the wife becomes a 'reluctant stayer', forgoing migration and its potential rewards in order to keep the family together. In short, traditional gender roles may still constrain married women's ability to influence family migration decisions.

Although modern industrial society is thought to be generally egalitarian in promoting economic opportunities for men and women, much of the evidence uncovered in the context of family migration research indicates that women are more likely than men to subordinate their careers to those of their partners. In fact, the empirical evidence indicates that the economic gains of migration tend to be substantially lower for wives than for husbands (Bonney, McCleery, and Forster, 1999; Boyle,

Table 8.10 Male–female differences in intraprovincial migration, 1996–2001 (population 5+), by province/territory

Province/territory	Males	Females	Total	% male	% female	Diff: M–F
Newfoundland and Labrador	19,165	21,800	40,965	1.10	1.19	−2,635
Prince Edward Island	4,765	5,345	10,110	0.27	0.29	−580
Nova Scotia	26,585	29,555	56,140	1.52	1.61	−2,970
New Brunswick	30,490	33,185	63,675	1.75	1.81	−2,695
Quebec	530,025	560,355	1,090,380	30.36	30.60	−30,330
Ontario	648,520	675,350	1,323,870	37.15	36.88	−26,830
Manitoba	39,875	42,920	82,795	2.28	2.34	−3,045
Saskatchewan	49,430	54,315	103,745	2.83	2.97	−4,885
Alberta	152,250	154,245	306,495	8.72	8.42	−1,995
British Columbia	241,780	251,435	493,215	13.85	13.73	−9,655
Yukon Territory	805	775	1,580	0.05	0.04	30
Northwest Territories	1,100	1,140	2,240	0.06	0.06	−40
Nunavut	925	970	1,895	0.05	0.05	−45
Total	1,745,715	1,831,390	3,577,105	100	100	−85,675

Source: Adapted from Statistics Canada (2003f).

Halfcree, and Smith, 1999; Cooke and Bailey, 1999; Green, Hardill, and Munn, 1999; Halfcree and Boyle, 1999; Lim, 1993; Shihadeh, 1991).

Migration decisions are further complicated for couples who have children or aging parents to consider. Bailey, Blake, and Cooke (2004), for instance, describe how 'linked lives' may either enable or constrain family migration. As we have seen, some migrants return to their former communities in order to care for parents in need of assistance (Bailey, Blake, and Cooke, 2004; Silverstein, 1995). In some cases three generations may live together in the same household (Knodel et al., 2000), although recent research based on the United States indicates that the incidence of co-residence of adult children and their elderly parents has actually declined over time (Grundy, 2000; Kobrin, 1976).

Migration and 'Social Disorganization'

The 'social disorganization' school of sociology (Durkheim, 1897 [1951]; Merton, 1964; Shaw and McKay, 1942; Wirth, 1938) has sometimes associated high rates of migration with rapid social and economic change. A central proposition in this literature is that geographic areas characterized by high rates of population mobility experience weakening of normative controls against deviant behaviours and 'social pathologies'. It has also been found that rates of divorce show a strong correlation with measures of migration in both the United States and Canada (Fenelon, 1971; Canon and Gingles, 1956; Glenn and Supancic, 1984; Makabe, 1980; Pang and Hanson, 1968; Wilkinson et al., 1983; Trovato, 1986a), perhaps in part because of the strains that migration can introduce to a relationship. The correlation between migration and crime may be a reflection of the fact that migration is highly selective of young adult males (Hartnagel and Lee, 1990; Hirschi, 1969; Kennedy and Forde, 1990; Kennedy and Veitch, 1997; Steffensmeir, Streifel, and Shihadeh, 1992).

Other factors may also be involved, however. For instance, an economic boom might attract an influx of migrants to an area while at the same time contributing to a rise in social disorganization and a weakening of established traditions, resulting in increased rates of crime, family dissolution, and suicide (Trovato, 1986b, 1992). On the other hand, high crime rates in a particular place might also lead to an increase in out-migration (Liska, Logan, and Bellair, 1998; Massey, Gross, and Shibuya, 1994).

Internal Migration Patterns and Differentials in Canada

The Regional Basis of Internal Migration in Canada

As we've noted already, to the extent that migrants self-select in terms of demographic and socioeconomic characteristics, high-volume migration can have significant social and economic impacts on both sending and receiving areas. Potentially, geographical mobility can help to reduce the overall level of income inequality within the larger system insofar as it allows individuals and their families to get ahead economically (Wilson, 2003). Given the selective nature of migration, however, interregional migration may actually help sustain inequalities at the regional level because underdeveloped regions will tend to lose their most skilled and productive people to more prosperous parts of the country.

Canada's history and geography have given rise to notable regional differences in economic wealth and resources. These regional differences reflect the regions' differential endowments of natural resources, proximity to natural and man-made major transportation routes, political influence, and success in promoting capital investments (Sitwell and Seifried, 1984). Industrial activity has been concentrated in Ontario and Quebec, the industrial core of the nation, leaving other regions to rely mainly on natural resources and, in the case of the Prairie provinces, also agriculture as the main bases of economic growth and development. One consequence of uneven economic development has been the formation of asymmetric patterns of migration across the regions (Anderson, 1966; Barnes et al., 2000; George, 1970; Ledent, 1988; Sitwell and Seifried, 1984; Wallace, 2002; Warkentin, 1999).

In general, migrants in Canada, as elsewhere, seek to move to locations that offer good economic prospects. Areas that fail to generate sufficient employment opportunities will tend to lose many of their most skilled workers to areas that offer greater socioeconomic opportunities. Over time this pattern of migration serves to shift the geographic concentration of specialized skills and labour in accordance with supply and demand principles (Bourne and Rose, 2001). In other words, as was explained earlier, internal migration acts as an efficiency mechanism by which workers with specialized skills are attracted to the regions where those skills are in demand and consequently will pay higher wages to workers. In this sense, internal migration plays an important redistribution function helping to enhance the efficiency of the national economic system. But at the same time, those provinces that cannot provide sufficient economic incentives to skilled workers will progressively fall behind in their economic growth and development.

Reinforcing this idea, Liaw and Qi's (2004) analysis of lifetime interprovincial migration in Canada indicates there are substantial net transfers of migrants from the 'have not' provinces (Newfoundland and Labrador, Nova Scotia, New Brunswick, Prince Edward Island, Manitoba, Saskatchewan) to the 'have' provinces (Alberta, Ontario, British Columbia, Quebec), and that migrants moving to these wealthier provinces generally achieve long-term income improvements (though generally not large enough to compensate for the disadvantages of being born in a 'have not' province. In other words, being born in a disadvantaged region is a factor in terms of the bundle of human capital (measured, for example, in education and occupational qualifications) one is able to acquire.

Ram and Shin (2007) identify another important mechanism that reinforces regional inequalities through differential patterns of internal migration in Canada. They have found that migrants are positively selected even when migration is stimulated by economic stagnation. The unemployment rate, they argue, does not necessarily influence the out-migration of less educated and less skilled persons, even though these people are typically among those with the highest rates of unemployment. Rather, it appears that unemployment actually serves as a push factor that encourages people to move if they are well educated and skilled (131). What this means in practical terms is that those regions of the country that tend toward economic stagnation will also lose much of their younger, better-educated, and more skilled population first, which on the whole produces an unfavourable effect, not only in term of demographic composition (i.e., helping to increase population aging) but also in the sense of reduced economic productivity.

It is important to note that interprovincial migration in Canada is not unidirectional, in other words predominantly from less developed to more developed regions. In fact, provinces that have traditionally lost out through net migration also tend to experience a significant amount of return migration. Recall Ravenstein's proposition that for every dominant stream of migration in a given direction there is typically a less dominant flow in the opposite direction. This tendency is evident in the Canadian context. For instance, historically Ontario has been the recipient of migrants from all other provinces in Canada; but for each province that sends migrants to Ontario there is a counterflow in the opposite direction, albeit usually smaller in volume. The same point can be made with regard to Alberta and British Columbia (George, 1970; Grant and Vanderkamp, 1984; McInnis, 1971; Rosenbaum, 1988; Stone, 1969, 1974, 1978; Vanderkamp, 1971).

So does return migration in any way help to compensate 'have-not' provinces economically? Vanderkamp (1968), in an early study, showed that the most common reasons for return migration were difficulties either in finding work or in holding onto a job in the new location. He concluded that return migration in Canada accounted for a substantial proportion of total migration, particularly during periods of economic recession. This return movement, which is positively related to unemployment, tends to be directed predominantly to regions that experience net out-migration (i.e., less prosperous regions). To the extent that this tendency prevails on a wide scale, it may be taken as indirect evidence in support of the proposition that for many, return migration represents some kind of 'failure', be it in finding employment or in adjusting to life in the new province. These migrants may experience a strong longing for a more familiar social environment; others may have difficulty adjusting to a new way of life or unfamiliar workplace demands. Young single people are perhaps especially prone to these types of problems (Grant and Vanderkamp, 1985; Rosenbaum, 1988). Thus, the effects of return migration to relatively underdeveloped areas of the country may not have significant impacts on the economic development of such regions.

It should also be noted that not all cases of return migration reflect negative experiences. Young people who return to their home regions after attending university or college elsewhere are also counted as return migrants, as are older people who return to their home provinces after retiring from the labour force. These migrant categories may in fact help stimulate economic improvements in the economically disadvantaged areas. Thus, the net effect of return migration on economic growth in such regions may be negligible, as these two types of tendencies effectively cancel each other out. It thus appears that the crucial factor in economic development is the extent to which the highly educated and skilled components of the labour force leave for other regions (Ram and Shin, 2007).

Geographic Mobility of Immigrants

Interurban Mobility

Excluding the contribution of natural increase, massive immigration from the early twentieth century to the present is the factor most responsible for the growth of North America's largest cities. The early immigrants from Europe crowded into cities, where they could most readily get jobs while establishing and maintaining their ethnic associations and ethnic-based economies (Thompson, 1983; Ward, 1971; Yancey, Ericsen, and Juliani, 1976). These ethnic communities effectively sheltered newcomers from the disruptive effects of immigrating and adapting to a new land (Clark, 1972: 97).

The process of ethnic community development must be understood in the context of immigration and urbanization history. For example, the largest Italian communities in this country are concentrated in the metropolitan areas of Ontario and Quebec (namely Toronto and Montreal) because Italian immigration early in the twentieth century was largely determined by the economic exigencies of these prosperous regions—specifically, the rising demand for labour in the construction and manufacturing sectors in a context of post-war economic boom. Immigrants from Italy, as well as other parts of Europe, found jobs in construction and helped power the massive growth of Toronto as a global city. These initial settlers blazed the trail for immigrants who subsequently came to Toronto and contributed to the growth of both the city and its ethnic communities. This process has been repeated in every one of Canada's major cities, even though the principal nationalities involved may differ, depending on the region of the country. In the Prairies, for example, many of the initial settlers in Calgary, Edmonton, and Winnipeg were from eastern Europe, especially Ukraine, Germany, and Poland. Consequently, their presence in this part of Canada is still highly noticeable.

Immigrants today continue to gravitate to Canada's largest metropolitan centres, which have become home to a large proportion of the country's total foreign-born population. In contrast, the Canadian-born population is more widely dispersed across a broad range of settlement size categories, and it is much better represented in small urban settlements (Trovato, 1988). This differential pattern of concentration across urban settlements of varying size may be reinforced, in part, by interurban mobility flows among immigrants. For instance, Trovato (1988) noted that the percentage of established immigrants in the largest cities is lower than the percentage of recently arrived immigrants. This difference could be attributed to differences in the out-migration rates of more established immigrants. More recent immigrants, if they do engage in interurban mobility, are more inclined to exchange one large city for another large city, or perhaps leave smaller cities for larger ones. In fact, Trovato's (1988) analysis indicates that the most dominant migration stream of foreign-born Canadians is between large urban centres, and that there is considerably less movement away from large cities toward smaller ones.

Hou's (2004) recent investigation of the Canadian 'gateway cities' of Toronto, Montreal, and Vancouver reveals that during the 1970s and 1980s, the redistribution or relocation of foreign-born citizens after immigration tended to occur on just a small scale. This fact, combined with continued immigration from abroad and some internal relocation to these cities from elsewhere in Canada, produced an increasing concentration of immigrants in the three cities. In all, roughly 44 per cent of the immigrants who arrived in Canada between 1970 and the early 1980s were located in regions outside Toronto, Montreal, and Vancouver; just 10 years later, this proportion had fallen to 39 per cent, suggesting a small amount of internal redistribution had taken place in favour of the gateway cities. Among more recent immigrants to Canada, internal relocation after immigration has had a much smaller impact on the changing concentrations of immigrants. Hou (2004)

observed that about 31 per cent of immigrants arriving between 1986 and 1990 settled initially in places other than Toronto, Montreal, and Vancouver, and that this share remained constant a decade later.

The propensity of foreign-born people to leave the place of initial settlement is closely linked to two related factors: the size of the city and the region in which the city is situated. Metropolitan centres in prosperous parts of the country offer widespread social and economic opportunities, making out-migration less of a priority. Furthermore, ethnic communities in large cities have a dampening effect on out-migration probabilities because they are made up of strong social networks joining relatives and friends of the same nationality. These communities typically support well-developed enclave economies in which many of their members are gainfully employed, which also helps to discourage out-migration (Darroch and Marston, 1988; Kobrin and Speare, 1983; Trovato, 1988).

All things considered, it appears that once immigrants settle in cities like Toronto, Montreal, Vancouver, Ottawa, Calgary, Edmonton, and Winnipeg, the likelihood of relocation out of these metropolitan centres is slight (Breton, 1964). Immigrants to Canada generally replicate the settlement preference of earlier generations of immigrants, taking up residence in the country's metropolises and, once established, showing little inclination to leave. While certainly many immigrants do move from their initial destinations to other parts of Canada, the majority move to Toronto, Montreal, or Vancouver, or else to some of the larger non-gateway cities like Ottawa, Calgary, Edmonton, Winnipeg, and Hamilton. The situation of refugees to Canada differs only slightly. While many are settled initially in non-gateway cities and small communities, they demonstrate an even stronger tendency to resettle in Toronto and Vancouver, although many do remain and integrate fully in their initial settlements (Hou, 2004; Krahn, Derwing, and Abu-Laban, 2005).

Interprovincial Migration

Early studies of interprovincial migration indicated that those born outside of the country change provinces slightly more frequently than Canadian-born people do (see, for example, Liaw and Ledent, 1988). Research by Newbold (1996b), based on data for 1981–6, confirms that among persons in the labour force (aged 20–64), the foreign-born have higher interprovincial migration rates than do those born in Canada.

As we might expect, given what we know about the bearing regional economic development has on selective migration, interprovincial migration rates among those born outside of Canada tend to reflect regional differences in economic growth. Thus, Newbold (1996b) noted that foreign-born residents of Ontario, British Columbia, and Quebec had relatively low out-migration rates, whereas these three provinces were likely to draw foreign-born residents from poorer parts of the country (Atlantic Canada, Saskatchewan, and Manitoba). (At the time of the study, Alberta was in the midst of an economic bust and therefore showed high rates of out-migration among both Canadian-born and foreign-born people.) We can conclude, then, that immigrants to Canada and those born in this country engage in interprovincial migration for the same reasons: they are attracted to provinces that offer employment and relatively high wages, and are dissuaded by distance, cold climate, and high unemployment rates (Newbold, 1996b).

It is important to recognize that although we have been treating 'foreign-born Canadians' as a category, it is far from homogeneous. As a result, there are differences, based on nationality, language, and ethnicity, in the likelihood of internal migration among this population. Among the non-economic factors governing interprovincial migration among those born outside the country are variations in comfort and familiarity with Canada's official languages and community-level ethnic influences that may either encourage or discourage out-migration (Newbold, 1999; Nogle, 1994; Rebhun, 2003; Uhlenberg, 1996;

Zavodny, 1999). Interprovincial migration rates among English-speaking immigrants to Canada are higher than among French-speaking immigrants—no doubt because there are relatively few French-speaking communities outside Quebec in which to settle. Among immigrants who speak neither English nor French there is low probability of internal migration (Stone, 1969, 1974). This could help to explain why geographic mobility within Canada is relatively low among southern European and East Asian immigrants (Ram and Shin, 2000a, 2000b; Trovato and Halli, 1983), who, if they do not have English or French in addition to their native language, are handicapped by a linguistic deficit.

Geographic Mobility of Aboriginal Peoples

Indigenous minorities in New World countries—Canada, the US, Australia, and New Zealand—differ significantly from mainstream populations, both socioeconomically and demographically. The dire conditions in which many indigenous people live led Young (1995) to describe the Aboriginal populations in these societies as representing a 'Third World in the First'. It is generally agreed that Aboriginal peoples' relative deprivation is a legacy of colonialism. Not surprisingly, they lag considerably in the demographic transition.

Indigenous populations share some distinctive patterns of geographic mobility. Taylor and Bell (2004) explain that as a consequence of colonization, indigenous groups in New World nations have experienced significant territorial displacement and have been pushed to reserves or to isolated geographic areas away from the majority population. However, since the end of the Second World War, the settlement and geographic mobility patterns of Aboriginal people have changed: they are no longer confined to remote reserve communities but dispersed across a wide variety of settings, both urban and rural. In addition, Taylor and Bell cite five other features common to indigenous populations of New World countries since the second half of the twentieth century:

1. *high levels of geographic mobility* compared with the majority population, particularly in rates of short-term circulatory movements between reserve communities and the city. This reflects unique features of Aboriginal populations, namely their participation in seasonal work; their extensive kin networks, which link individuals to both the city and the reserve; the problems they have experienced in finding adequate housing in the city; and their difficulty adjusting to the urban setting.
2. *high regional variability in geographic mobility*, reflecting the range of Aboriginal responses to regional variations in socioeconomic conditions.
3. *sustained presence in non-metropolitan residential areas*, including reserves both close to and far removed from large urban centres.
4. *rising post-war migration from the rural areas* (i.e., reserves) to the city, intensifying in the 1970s. Migration to urban centres has abated since the 1980s.
5. *significant return migration to places of Aboriginal cultural significance*, such as reserves. (Taylor and Bell, 2004: 2)

The geographic mobility patterns of Aboriginal people in Canada have been documented extensively (see, for example, Frideres, Kalbach, and Kalbach, 2004; Maxim, Keane, and White, 2002; Norris, 1990, 1996; Norris et al., 2004). Detailed analyses of 1996 and 2001 census data by Norris and Clatworthy (2002) and Clatworthy and Norris (2006) point to a higher overall level of geographical mobility—local and migratory combined—among Aboriginal Canadians than among the general population. Between 1996 and 2001, 20.1 per cent of Aboriginal people aged five and older had been involved in migration; the figure for the general population was 16.5 per cent. During this same interval, roughly 30 per cent of Aboriginal people had changed residence locally, compared to about 22 per cent for the general population. The 2006 census gives further indication of the difference in mobility rates between Aboriginal and other Canadians. Eight of 10 First Nations people (81 per cent) lived at the same address in 2006 as they did one year before the census, compared with 86 per cent of the non-Aboriginal population. The Aboriginal population was

Table 8.11 Mobility status of Aboriginal identity population, 1991–1996 and 1996–2001, by subgroup (population aged 5+)

	Registered Indians	Non-status Indians	Métis	Inuit
1991–1996				
Local movers	40.0	26.0	23.0	14.0
Migrants	20.6	48.0	46.3	54.0
Sub-total	60.6	74.0	69.3	68.0
Non-movers	39.7	26.0	30.7	32.0
Total	100.0	100.0	100.0	100.0
1996–2001				
Local movers	29.5	32.4	31.5	36.2
Migrants	19.3	23.7	24.4	16.0
Sub-total	48.8	56.1	55.9	52.24
Non-movers	51.3	43.9	44.1	47.8
Total	100.0	100.0	100.0	100.0

Sources: Adapted from Norris and Clatworthy (2003): 59, 69.

slightly more likely than others to have either moved within the same community (11 per cent versus 8 per cent) or to have relocated to their current address from another community (8 per cent versus 5 per cent).

To gain an accurate overview of the mobility patterns of Canadian Aboriginal people, we must look at the sub-groups that make up this category. Table 8.11 looks at the mobility status of Registered Indians, non-status Indians, Métis, and Inuit during the 1991–6 and 1996–2001 census periods. Registered Indians and non-status Indians are members of First Nations bands that have negotiated land treaties with the Crown. Many of these treaties established reserve lands where members of these groups have historically lived. Non-status Indians are those who are not officially registered under Canada's Indian Act; many of them are of mixed Native and non-Native parentage, and relatively few of them live on reserves. The Métis are also of mixed Aboriginal and non-Aboriginal (typically French-Canadian) ancestry, and trace their roots to the historical Red River community in western Canada. The Inuit are indigenous to northern Quebec, the Northwest Territories, Nunavut, and Labrador (Norris and Clatworthy, 2002).

During the 1991–6 census period, Registered Indians (40 per cent) were far more likely than non-status Indians (26 per cent), Métis (23 per cent) and Inuit (14 per cent) to make residential moves within the same municipality. Curiously, in the subsequent five-year interval (1996–2001) this order is reversed, as the Inuit were the most locally mobile, followed by non-status Indians, Métis, and then Registered Indians. In terms of migration across administrative boundaries, 54 per cent of the Inuit population aged five and older had made this type of move between 1991 and 1996, while the Métis and non-registered Indians had similarly high rates of migration (46 per cent and 48 per cent, respectively) during the same interval. If local moves and migration are added together, non-

status Indians exhibited the highest overall level of geographical mobility (74 per cent) across the sub-groups between 1991 and 1996; during the 1996–2001 period, all four groups had similar levels of overall mobility, ranging between 49 per cent for Registered Indians and 56 per cent for non-status Indians and Métis.

The tendency for Aboriginal people to be involved in some form of geographic mobility may reflect a number of underlying factors. It may indicate that Canada's Aboriginal people find it difficult to settle down because of problems they face due to their minority status. On the other hand, it may indicate a growing tendency for Aboriginal people to integrate into urban communities while maintaining strong attachments to their indigenous cultures. Over time, more and more Aboriginal people have set up residence in urban areas, and today fewer First Nations people live on reserve than off reserve (40 per cent versus 60 per cent, as of 2006). According to 2006 census data, the off-reserve population is most likely to live in urban areas of varying population size, including large metropolitan centres (Statistics Canada, 2008a). A unique feature of Aboriginal people's pattern of geographical movement is their tendency to move back and forth between the city and the reserve, often described as *circular mobility* (Norris et al., 2004; Taylor and Bell, 2004). As Table 8.12 shows, circular mobility is most pronounced among Registered Indians.

Further analysis of recent census data by Clatworthy and Norris (2006) shows that reserve lands were the only geographic areas to see net migration gains among Aboriginal people. In terms of their Aboriginal populations, all other residential localities—rural areas, small urban areas, and large metropolitan centres—witnessed net migration losses. Reserves experienced a net inflow of about 14,400 in 1991–6 and almost 11,000 in 1996–2001, mostly at the expense of urban metropolitan and non-metropolitan areas. The greatest net losers were rural areas (−6,385 in 1991–6 and −6,430 in 1996–

Table 8.12 Distribution of Aboriginal migrant flows by origin, destination, and Aboriginal identity group, 1991–1996 and 1996–2001 (population aged 5+)

Migration stream	Registered Indians	Non-status Indians	Métis	Inuit	Total
1991–1996					
Urban to reserve	19.6	2.3	1.4	0.3	23.6
Reserve to urban	6.9	1.2	0.4	0.6	9.1
Sub-total	26.5	3.5	1.8	0.9	32.7
Rural to reserve	4.8	0.7	0.5	0.8	6.8
Reserve to rural	1.4	0.4	0.2	2.1	4.1
Sub-total	6.2	1.1	0.7	2.9	10.9
Reserve to reserve	3.1	0.2	0.0	0.0	3.3
All other streams	64.2	95.2	97.5	96.2	46.9
Total migrants aged 5+	87,340	20,130	37,460	4,760	149,690
	100.0	100.0	100.0	100.0	100.0
1996–2001					
Urban to reserve	18.2	2.3	1.2	1.8	23.0
Reserve to urban	10.7	1.5	1.2	2.7	16.1
Sub-total	28.9	3.8	2.4	4.5	39.1
Rural to reserve	5.7	0.7	0.4	2.0	9.0
Reserve to rural	1.7	0.2	0.5	1.4	3.8
Sub-total	7.4	0.9	0.9	3.4	12.8
Reserve to reserve	3.5	0.3	0.2	1.8	5.0
All other streams	60.2	95.0	96.4	90.4	43.1
Total migrants aged 5+	93,150	22,300	53,815	5,520	171,420
	100.0	100.0	100.0	100.0	100.0

Sources: Adapted from: Norris and Clatworthy (2003: 59, 69); Clatworthy and Norris (2006): 214.

2001) and urban non-metropolitan places (−4,405 in 1991–6 and −4,095 in 1996–2001). Large urban centres, even though they received a substantial number of migrants (mainly from rural areas and non-metropolitan places), still experienced net migratory deficits of −3,295 in 1991–6 and −430 in 1996–2001 (Clatworthy and Norris, 2006: 215; Norris et al., 2004: 142–3). These data make it clear that the focal points of recent Aboriginal migration have been urban areas and reserves, and that

large inflows to urban locations have been overshadowed by much larger outflows of urban population.

Figure 8.6 tracks the net migratory patterns for the largest of the four Aboriginal subgroups—Registered Indians—and reveals a picture consistent with what has been presented so far. Rural communities are the greatest net losers, and reserve communities the major net gainers. Metropolitan centres have witnessed an irregular pattern of ups and downs in net migration, but

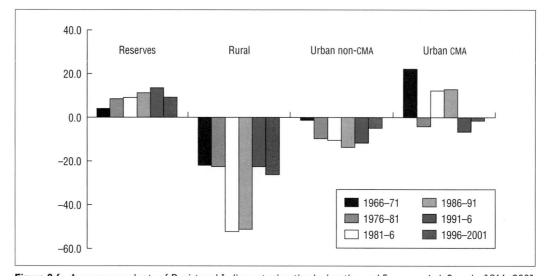

Figure 8.6 Average annual rate of Registered Indian net migration by location and 5-year period, Canada, 1966–2001

Source: From 'Registered Indian Mobility and Migration in Canada: Patterns and Implications', by M.J. Norris, M. Cooke, E. Guimond, D. Beavon, and S. Clatworthy, in *Population Mobility and Indigenous Peoples in Australasia and North America*, J. Taylor and M. Bell, eds. Copyright © 2004. Published by Routledge. Reproduced by permission of Taylor & Francis Books, UK.

during the 1991–6 and 1996–2001 census periods, the net balance has been clearly negative. Urban non-metropolitan areas have also, since the mid-1960s, lost more Registered Indians than they have gained. Again, from these trends it is evident that the reserves have enjoyed consistent growth as a result of the redistribution of the Registered Indian population.

The observed pattern of net gains and losses across different residential areas since 1966 contradicts much of the early literature on Aboriginal mobility, which pointed to massive out-flows of Aboriginal people from reserves and rural areas to the cities (see, for example, Dosman, 1972; Hawthorne, 1966; Royal Commission on Aboriginal Peoples, 1995: 89). Some of this literature went as far as predicting an eventual extinction of many reserves. Certainly, as many scholars have noted, there was significant out-movement from reserves to cities between the 1950s and the early 1970s (Frideres and Gadacz, 2008: 163). How can we account for the marked change in Aboriginal migration trends?

One hypothesis for the reported rise in city-ward migration in the two decades after the Second World War is that small levels of reserve-to-city migration were exaggerated by the fact that many Aboriginal people in the cities were, for the first time, declaring their Native ancestry on the census. Some researchers mistakenly interpreted this rise in urban Aboriginal numbers as having been generated by migration from reserves (Norris et al. 2004). In reality, as Norris and associates (2004) argue, there was—as there continues to be—a great deal of return migration from the city to the reserve. Further, they argue that from the 1950s through the 1970s, the most significant migration streams were from rural non-reserve places to reserves, and from rural non-reserve areas to urban areas. Thus, far from there having been a unidirectional flow from reserves to cities, both reserves and urban areas were involved as net migration gainers during the post-war years (Norris et al., 2004; Clatworthy and Norris, 2006). In fact, then, Aboriginal migration to the reserve is not a new trend but one that has been going on since the 1950s.

Factors in Aboriginal Geographic Mobility

In examining the factors behind Aboriginal geographic mobility it is important to remember that although this is a marginalized population, Aboriginal people are not completely isolated from mainstream Canadian people and institutions. They face many of the same life situations that other Canadians do, and many of the factors that stimulate mobility in the general population—such as opportunities for employment and education—are of equally great importance to Aboriginal people. That said, there are important differences between the experiences of Aboriginal Canadians and those of the majority population, and these bear particularly on Aboriginal circular mobility and return to reserve communities.

Many Aboriginal people return to their home reserves after struggling to find jobs or adapt generally to life in the city. Many also have difficulty finding affordable housing, which serves as a major push factor out of the city. Those Aboriginal people who do take up residence in cities tend to be disproportionately concentrated in the poorest and most run-down neighbourhoods, where crime and other social problems abound. The social context of the reserve community, where conditions are far more welcoming, affords these individuals a reprieve from the chronic problems and stress of city life. In fact, data from the Aboriginal Peoples' Survey, reviewed by Norris and associates (2004), indicates that 'family reasons' are the most frequently cited motives for moving back to the reserve, which reinforces the idea that social networks play a key role in the circular movements of Aboriginal people.

Some of the net migration gains by reserve areas may be attributed to legislative changes associated with Bill C-31, which provided a mechanism for restoring official Indian status lost through marriage. Prior to 1985, when the bill was introduced, Registered Indian women who married non-Native or non-status Indian men lost their own status, as did their children. Bill C-31 may have prompted reinstated Registered Indians living in the city to seek residence on reserves, where they could enjoy certain legal benefits not available to those living off-reserve (such as free housing and education).

Finally, many reserves are located close to a major city, which allows Aboriginal people to move conveniently from reserve to city on a regular basis. Many Aboriginal people live on reserve for part of the year and then move to the city to gain seasonal employment, returning to the reserve once the work is no longer available. This phenomenon contributes to the high degree of circular migration characteristic of the Aboriginal population (Trovato, Romaniuc, and Addai, 1994; Norris et al., 2004).

In summary, the city and the reserve present a series of 'pulls' and 'pushes' that affect decisions about where to live. Difficulties of integration and adjustment may 'push' many Aboriginal people from the city, while the more congenial social context of the reserve may be a strong 'pull factor'. Then again, many Aboriginal people have friends and relatives in the city, representing a strong pull factor. Reserves that show a greater degree of socioeconomic development offer pull factors in the form of opportunities for work and social resources. On the other hand, a disproportionately high sex ratio (i.e., a greater number of men than women) can be a push factor. LaRocque (1994) has identified physical and sexual abuse among Aboriginal women within their reserve communities as a powerful factor pushing them to leave the reserve for the city. Figure 8.7 presents an assemblage of conceivable push and pull factors for Aboriginal migration. It lists individual characteristics such as age, sex, marital status, employment status, and education, as well as larger structural factors, such as the proximity of a reserve to a city (Gerber, 1984).

Conclusion

Internal migration—as distinct from local or residential mobility—is an important subject of demographic analysis. This chapter has

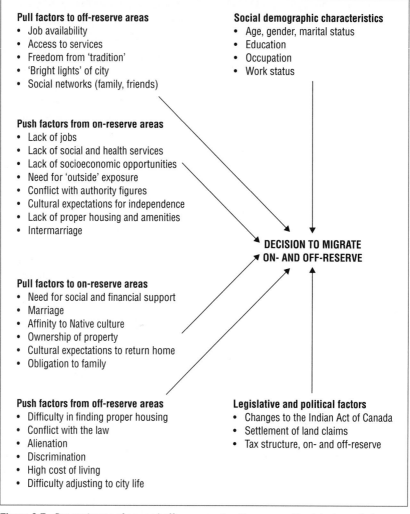

Figure 8.7 Determinants of on- and off-reserve migration among Aboriginal people in Canada

explained various measures of migration and introduced several typologies and models of geographic mobility. The last section of the chapter focused on sociological aspects of migration, including the selectivity of migrants, patterns of mobility among immigrant communities, the relevance of gender to family migration, and the association of migration with social disorganization. In Canada, broadly speaking, interregional migration patterns have changed little since the mid-twentieth century. Regions with prosperous economies have tended to attract a large share of internal migrants from the poorer regions, deepening longstanding regional inequalities in socioeconomic development. Finally, differentials in geographic mobility, nationality, ethnicity, and language reflect a host of factors, some economic and others non-economic, that can either enhance or reduce internal migration probabilities.

Notes for Further Study

Migration Efficiency

Tables 8.13a, b, and c contain worked-out examples of how migration efficiency is calculated at the level of the province, the migration stream, and at the systemic level. The information is confined to Alberta, Ontario, and British Columbia over the one-year interval 1 July 2006–30 June 2007. For illustrative purposes we may view these three provinces as comprising a single migration system. The elements in

all three sub-tables are interprovincial migration flows; therefore all diagonal cells are blank.

In Table 8.13a, the elements in the cells can be read as follows. Over the study period under consideration, 31,189 persons left Alberta to go to British Columbia, and 14,474 Albertans went to Ontario. Alberta received 29,213 people from British Columbia and another 45,144 from Ontario. British Columbia welcomed 19,128 migrants from Ontario, while 14,099 British Columbians moved east to Ontario. Also shown in this sub-table, for each province, are the following:

Table 8.13a Interprovincial migration matrix: Alberta, British Columbia, and Ontario; 1 July 2006 to 30 June 2007

Origin (out)	Destination (in)		
	Alberta	British Columbia	Ontario
Alberta		31,189	14,474
British Columbia	29,213		14,099
Ontario	45,114	19,128	
Migration measures for each province			
In-migration	74,327	50,317	28,573
Out-migration	45,663	43,312	64,242
Net migration	28,664	7,005	−35,669
Gross migration	119,990	93,629	92,815
Migration efficiency ratio*	23.89	7.48	−38.43

$$\text{Migration efficiency index for the system} = \frac{|28,664| + |7,005| + |-35,669|}{119,990 + 93,629 + 92,815} \times 100$$

$$= \frac{71,338}{306,434} \times 100$$

$$= 23.28$$

Note: *Refer to the text for the migration efficiency formulas and their description.

Table 8.13b Net migration between pairs of provinces (stream analysis)

Origin (out)	Destination (in)		
	Alberta	British Columbia	Ontario
Alberta	0	1,976*	−30,640**
British Columbia		0	−5,029***
Ontario			0

Notes: *net gain for BC in its exchange with Alberta; **net loss for Ontario in its exchange with Alberta; ***net loss for Ontario in its exchange with BC.

Table 8.13c Gross migration between pairs of provinces (stream analysis)

	Destination (in)		
Origin (out)	Alberta	British Columbia	Ontario
Alberta	0	60,402*	59,588**
British Columbia		0	33,227***
Ontario			0

Notes: *total migratory exchange between Alberta and BC; **total migratory exchange between Alberta and Ontario; ***total migratory exchange between BC and Ontario.

Table 8.13d Calculation of stream-specific migration efficiency ratios based on pairs of provinces and overall index of migration efficiency for the system

	Destination (in)		
Origin (out)	Alberta	British Columbia	Ontario
		(1)	(2)
Alberta	0	$\dfrac{1,976}{60,402} \times 100 = 3.27$	$\dfrac{-30,640}{59,588} \times 100 = -51.42$
			(3)
British Columbia		0	$\dfrac{-5,029}{33,227} \times 100 = -15.14$
Ontario			0

$$\text{Migration efficiency index for the system} = \frac{|1,976| + |-30,640| + |-5,029|}{60,402 + 59,588 + 33,227} \times 100$$

$$= \frac{35,669}{153,217} \times 100$$

$$= 23.28$$

Notes: The interpretation of cells (1) to (3): (1) for every 100 migrants BC receives from and sends to Alberta, BC gains net 3.27 migrants from Alberta; (2) for every 100 migrants Ontario receives from and sends to Alberta, Ontario loses net 51.42 migrants to Alberta; (3) for every 100 migrants Ontario receives from and sends to BC, Ontario loses net 15.14 migrants to BC.

Data source: Statistics Canada Demography Division. 2007(a). Annual Demographic Estimates: Canada, Provinces and Territories, 2007. Ottawa: Minister of Industry (Cat. No. 91-215-XIE), p. 41, table 5.

- in-migration
- out-migration
- net migration
- gross migration
- the efficiency of migration

The overall index of migration efficiency for the system is shown at the bottom of this sub-table.

Sub-table 8.13b derives from the information in Table 8.13a; it is a migration stream analysis, showing the net migratory exchanges between pairs of provinces. Sub-table 8.13c lists the gross migration frequencies between each pair of provinces. Sub-table 8.13d lays out the calculations for the computation of migration efficiency measures for each of the individual migration streams based on the figures in sub-tables 8.13b and 8.13c.

The computed efficiency ratios in sub-table 8.13a indicate that in a comparative sense there is greater migration efficiency to Ontario and Alberta than to British Columbia. The efficiency of migration to Alberta is 23.9, and to Ontario it is −38.4; it is 7.5 in the case of British Columbia. Thus, for every 100 migrants Alberta receives and sends out, it gains net almost 24 people, redistributed there from the other two provinces. This also indicates a notable level of asymmetry in terms of migratory exchanges involving Alberta and the other provinces, with Alberta as a net beneficiary. By comparison, for every 100 people Ontario receives and sends out, it suffers a net loss of about 38 persons. This indicates that Ontario is an important agent in redistributing migrants elsewhere in the system. The case of British Columbia is one of almost dynamic equilibrium: for every 100 people it receives and sends out, it gains net only 7 migrants from elsewhere. (Note that these results would differ considerably if all the Canadian provinces were included in the analysis.)

The overall efficiency of migration index encompassing the three provinces as a system is calculated by dividing the *absolute value* of all three provinces' net migration by the total gross migration across these same provinces, and then multiplying this quotient by 100. The efficiency of migration for this system is 23.3 per cent, meaning that for every 100 migrants received and sent out within this system, 23 persons are redistributed. This indicates a fair degree of asymmetry in the migratory flows between the provinces that constitute this system.

Sub-table 8.13d shows the computation of migration efficiency ratios for individual migration streams (shown within the cells), and the overall migration efficiency index for the system as a whole. Note that the value of the index is identical to the value obtained in sub-table 8.13a, as it should be.

Survival Rate and Census Survival Methods of Migration Estimation

Survival Rate Method

In the absence of explicit information on births and deaths, the expected population of each age group at the end of a particular period can be estimated on the basis of survival rates. The difference between the expected population at the end of the period and the actual population recorded by the census is taken to represent migration. Two versions of this method have been devised: *forward survival* and *reverse survival*. The first of these is the one most commonly applied. Using this method, net migration for a given age group can be estimated (using the notation suggested by Smith, Tayman, and Swanson, 2001: 117), as

$$NM_{x,x+n} = {_nP_{x+y,l}} - {_nS_x}({_nP_{x,b}})$$

where ${_nP_{x,b}}$ is the population age x to $x+n$ in year b (i.e., at the start of the interval), ${_nP_{x+y,l}}$ is the population age $(x + y)$ to $(x + n + y)$ in some later year l, y is the number of years between b and l, and ${_nS_x}$ is the y-year survival rate for age group x to $x+n$.

The y-year survival rate can be obtained from an appropriate life table for the area being investigated. For example, if the estimation is for a province, a suitable life table would be the life table for the province; but if this is not available, the life table of the nation could be substituted, on the assumption that it adequately describes survival probabilities in the province.

A brief example can help clarify the application of this formula. Suppose the census showed Alberta had 265,268 residents aged 40–44 in 1991 and 457,378 residents aged 50–54 in 2001, and the 10-year survival rate for this age cohort was 0.9621 (i.e., a 96.21 per cent 5-year survival probability for those aged 40–44 in 1981): the estimated net migration between 1991 and 2001 for this age cohort would be

$$NM = 457,378 - [0.9621 \times 265,268]$$
$$= 202,164$$

Census Survival Method

The *census survival* method is similar, except that the survival term is derived not from a life table but from information from two sequential censuses corresponding to the start and end points of a specified time interval for an age cohort. Thus, using the same notation as before, we write:

$$NM_{x,x+n} = {}_nP_{x+y,l} - {}_nR_x({}_nP_{x,b})$$

The terms here are identical to those used earlier, the only difference being the form of the survival ratio ${}_nR_x$, which now is $({}_nP_{x+y,l}/{}_nP_{x,b})$. In this version of survival ratio, the two populations come from the two censuses for time points l and b (i.e., 1991 and 2001 censuses in the Alberta example).

Assume again that Alberta had 265,268 residents aged 40–44 in 1991, and 457,378 residents aged 50–54 ten years later, in 2001. For the nation as a whole, the two censuses counted 1,563,780 persons aged 40–44 in 1991 and 1,638,938 persons aged 50–54 in 2001. Using the national counts, the 10-year survival ratio for this age cohort is expected to be 1,628,938 / 1,563,780, or 1.048062. This ratio says that for the nation as a whole, the population for the cohort enumerated at the time of the second census is about 4.8 per cent greater than expected.

Theoretically, a survival rate should have an upper limit of 1.000. However, under certain circumstances it is possible for a survival ratio computed with census data to exceed 1.000, as is the case in this example. This outcome arises when there has been significant immigration from abroad in the age cohort under consideration during the period (Shryock and Siegel, 1976). The estimated net migration in this example is the difference between the population actually enumerated by the second census and the expected population for that point in time. That is,

$$NM = 457,378 - [1.048062 \times 265,268]$$
$$= 179,361$$

As these two examples show, the survival rate method and the census survival approach do not yield identical results, though the differences should not be extremely large. The advantage of using the census survival ratio method is that the sum of net migration estimates for a given age cohort across all regions of a country will be zero (or very close to zero). The reason is that if some areas gain migrants, other areas must necessarily lose out migrants, and vice versa; thus, on balance the sum at the national level should be zero (or very close to it).

Common to both approaches is their strict dependence on accurate census and life table data. Any errors in these data sources would necessarily translate into errors in the estimates of net migration. In practice, however, the advantages of these residual techniques tend to outweigh the potential problems inherent in using censuses or life tables as data sources. The major advantage of residual estimates of migration is that they do not require direct knowledge of actual in- or out-migration for a given geographic locality. This is particularly useful in population estimates for local areas (e.g., the country or the municipality) for which data are either unavailable or difficult to obtain (see Lee and Goldsmith, 1982; Smith, Tayman, and Swanson, 2001).

Exercises

Table 8.14 shows the numbers of in- and out-migrants, by province of origin and destination in Canada, for the period 1999–2000. Using this data, execute the following calculations and answer the corresponding questions.

Table 8.14   Number of interprovincial migrants by province of origin and destination, Canada, 1999–2000

Province/territory in 1999 (origin)	Province/territory in 2000 (destination)												
	NL	PE	NS	NB	QC	ON	MB	SK	AB	BC	YT	NT	NU
NL	0	430	2,198	809	138	6,492	187	120	2,769	619	56	178	123
PE	167	0	610	501	45	652	10	22	182	174	9	8	2
NS	1,520	694	0	3,232	772	6,902	444	251	2,331	1,612	30	103	94
NB	546	658	3,091	0	2,255	4,137	239	127	1,511	892	42	49	38
QC	362	123	1,073	2,184	0	30,300	704	269	2,524	3,642	42	72	81
ON	4,672	841	6,106	4,528	16,215	0	5,459	2,434	11,208	19,211	201	425	229
MB	191	41	517	246	568	6,135	0	3,491	5,044	3,898	25	50	38
SK	167	42	436	108	174	3,413	3,871	0	14,475	4,134	58	149	52
AB	2,763	264	2,694	1,673	1,992	13,196	4,214	10,236	0	22,331	374	1,047	108
BC	1,066	264	1,755	766	2,759	19,437	3,542	3,576	30,707	0	738	341	68
YT	26	4	35	0	29	234	92	81	688	965	0	145	22
NT	79	0	80	43	33	279	98	142	1,142	341	90	0	243

Source: http://www.statcan.ca/english/Pgdb/demo02.htm.

1. Identify the five most dominant interprovincial migration streams (i.e., the largest migration flows in absolute numbers). For each of these five streams determine the net exchanges between the provinces of origin and destination. Discuss how different theoretical models of migration might lead to different interpretations of the observed net migration losses and gains.
2. Calculate the in-, out-, net-, and gross migration figures for each of the provinces. Are there any patterns that emerge from these data? Is there any discernible relationship between in- and out-migration across the provinces? Which provinces and regions gain and lose through net migration? Why do some provinces experience relatively high gross migration levels and yet end up losing through net migration?
3. Calculate the efficiency of migration measures for: (a) each of Ontario, Quebec, Alberta, and British Columbia; (b) the whole system, consisting of these four provinces. Interpret your results.
4. Table 8.15 shows percentage distribution of mobility in Canada between 1991 and 1996 by type of move and broad age categories. Describe the age pattern of mobility for each of the four categories of moves across the two census periods. (It may be useful to graph the percentages.) What may account for the observed patterns? Comment on the changes in age-specific mobility and overall mobility for each type of move between the two census periods.
5. Table 8.16 includes interprovincial migration streams for 25–34-year-old men and women in Canada, based on the 1996 census. What can you conclude on the basis

Table 8.15 Percentage distribution of mobility in Canada, 1991–6, by type of move and age in 1996

	Movers, non-migrants	Intraprovincial migrants	Interprovincial migrants	Immigrants from abroad
1986–91				
5–14	17.86	15.32	16.11	16.12
15–24	15.62	16.84	17.20	18.98
25–34	28.79	30.42	31.92	30.04
35–44	18.07	17.44	18.53	18.89
45–54	8.57	8.43	7.43	7.25
55–64	5.30	5.73	4.46	4.61
65+	5.79	5.81	4.34	4.11
Total	5,776,215	3,970,600	977,050	913,320
1991–6				
5–14	16.31	14.68	15.24	14.50
15–24	14.82	16.07	17.00	19.85
25–34	26.83	28.51	29.91	25.94
35–44	20.32	18.81	19.29	19.02
45–54	10.58	10.07	9.22	9.61
55–64	5.25	5.89	4.72	6.04
65+	5.89	5.97	4.64	5.04
Total	6,130,740	3,575,025	890,270	928,690

Sources: Statistics Canada (1993a, 2004b).

Table 8.16 Interprovincial migration 1991–6, Canadian males and females aged 25–34 in 1996

Province/territory in 1996	Province/territory in 1991											
	NL	PE	NS	NB	QC	ON	MB	SK	AB	BC	YT	NT
Males 25–34												
NL	0	45	490	205	80	1,365	60	30	170	95	0	60
PE	125	0	245	160	45	360	20	10	65	55	0	10
NS	760	315	0	1,025	515	2,470	190	115	610	740	0	55
NB	355	140	1,245	0	780	1,635	110	50	300	255	10	30
QC	135	55	590	970	0	7,470	380	205	815	1,130	0	40
ON	2,465	305	3,185	1,860	8,705	0	2,140	1,005	4,070	4,055	70	155
MB	145	0	220	175	350	2,070	0	905	1,380	900	25	25
SK	10	30	150	75	200	1,030	1,065	0	3,035	1,135	40	120
AB	1,115	105	1,205	780	1,090	6,375	2,425	4,335	0	6,025	115	425
BC	1,100	90	1,935	835	3,435	15,535	2,835	2,130	11,600	0	365	240
YT	65	0	25	10	35	125	85	60	195	245	0	25
NT	160	10	110	45	70	325	75	110	435	125	15	0
Females 25–34												
NL	0	35	570	195	95	1,555	55	20	170	110	0	45
PE	85	0	315	185	45	335	10	0	120	25	0	0
NS	885	385	0	970	580	2,785	200	100	620	560	10	25
NB	435	140	1,230	0	920	1,765	100	35	320	165	0	20
QC	130	70	480	800	0	7,460	330	140	705	845	20	50
ON	2,330	340	3,315	1,680	10,030	0	2,225	985	4,320	3,990	45	130
MB	85	30	330	100	325	1,935	0	1,025	1,325	795	15	55
SK	10	30	110	70	180	1,005	1,010	0	3,020	985	45	95
AB	850	135	1,090	590	1,060	5,925	2,285	4,240	0	5,715	155	425
BC	825	110	1,635	475	3,015	14,115	2,750	2,025	11,730	0	410	265
YT	50	0	40	25	30	170	50	60	190	260	0	30
NT	140	20	115	40	60	295	95	115	430	135	25	0

Source: Adapted from Statistics Canada publication *Five-Year Mobility Data, 1996 Census* (1999). [CD-ROM].

of the overall pattern of interprovincial migration in Canada for men and women aged 25–34? Does the level of interprovincial migration vary by sex? Do the results of your observations differ substantially from the pattern of interprovincial migration observed in Table 8.14? Explain.

6. Using the forward survival method to estimate net migration means assuming that the difference between the population counted by the census at the end of an interval and the expected population for that point in time based on survival probabilities during the interval is due to the difference between in- and out-migration. Table 8.17 contains hypothetical data arranged to facilitate the computation of net migration using the forward survival procedure. Follow the procedures indicated in each column. What is the net migration for each of the age cohorts over the 10-year interval? What is the total net migration for the interval?

Table 8.17 Estimation of net migration using the forward survival method (hypothetical data)

(1)	(2)	(3)	(4)	(5) = (2)×(3)	(6)	(7) = (6)−(2)
Age at first census (t)	Population at first census (t)	10-year life table survival rate	Age at second census (t+10)	Expected population at second census (t+10)	Actual population at second census (t+10)	Net migration between t and t + 10 = actual − expected
15–19	1,074,430	0.99387	25–29	1,067,876	1,182,575	
20–24	941,775	0.99339	30–34	935,559	1,237,690	
25–29	800,710	0.99345	35–39	795,425	1,133,670	
30–34	660,875	0.99274	40–44	656,051	1,042,185	
35–39	645,045	0.99032	45–49	638,788	824,200	
40–44	640,765	0.98556	50–54	631,538	663,285	
45–49	613,415	0.97368	55–59	597,282	608,085	
50–54	518,895	0.95691	60–64	496,531	571,940	
55–59	472,415	0.93080	65–69	439,724	492,505	
Total						

Note: The population data are actually for 1971 and 1991 Canada, while the life table survival ratios are based on the Canadian male life table for 1986. These data are used only for illustrative purposes.
Sources: Statistics Canada (2002g, 1992b, 1973b).

7. Table 8.18 shows the number of internal migrants (five years of age and older) by census metropolitan area (CMA) of residence five years ago and CMA of residence at the time of the 2006 census. From these figures it is possible to compute the in-, out-, and net migration between any pair of CMAs.

Select a reference CMA (e.g., Edmonton) and then compute the net migration (in − out) between this CMA and each of the other CMAs listed below (excluding the reference CMA you have chosen):

- Victoria
- Vancouver
- Calgary
- Edmonton
- Saskatoon
- Winnipeg
- Thunder Bay

- Sudbury
- London
- Toronto
- Ottawa–Gatineau
- Montreal
- Quebec City
- Halifax

- Saint John (New Brunswick)
- St John's (Newfoundland and Labrador)

Repeat the same computations, but this time use a different CMA (e.g., St John's, Newfoundland and Labrador) as the reference point. Graph your results for

(a) in-migration
(b) out-migration
(c) net migration

(Note: it is possible to graph in- and out-migration counts in the same graph.) You may use a spreadsheet program such as Excel to execute these computations. What geographical patterns of migration can you discern from these computations? What theories/models of internal migration might be useful in the interpretation of your results? Explain.

Execute the following computations and then interpret your results:

(d) all the possible pair-wise migration efficiency ratios (MERs) for the following CMAs: Toronto, Montreal, Vancouver, Ottawa–Gatineau, Edmonton, Calgary
(e) the migration efficiency index (MEI) for the system made up of these six CMAs

Table 8.18   Internal migrants 5 years and over by CMA of residence in 2006 and 2001 (20% sample)

CMA 2006	Canada	Abbotsford	Barrie	Brantford	Calgary	Edmonton	Greater Sudbury	Guelph	Halifax	Hamilton	Kelowna	Kingston	Kitchener	London	Moncton	Montréal	Oshawa
Canada	2,184,075	22,695	21,905	12,230	91,860	78,540	14,910	18,590	41,415	60,450	17,860	21,730	42,460	41,585	13,140	186,605	31,365
Abbotsford	23,245	0	10	0	730	490	0	65	35	125	430	35	50	105	0	130	55
Barrie	38,045	25	0	180	165	230	765	165	235	875	10	180	510	400	25	175	505
Brantford	15,155	15	125	0	90	120	65	315	10	3,505	15	70	2,035	390	0	100	100
Calgary	119,105	890	315	170	0	12,380	325	440	2,115	995	2,080	480	795	1,215	385	2,595	530
Edmonton	109,330	690	200	150	10,445	0	210	185	1,450	475	1,010	560	445	550	365	1,910	230
Greater Sudbury	14,725	30	305	105	160	145	0	85	65	285	20	105	225	355	35	260	215
Guelph	18,645	10	135	225	135	120	125	0	85	1,065	10	135	2,195	515	45	560	230
Halifax	39,735	50	165	25	975	685	75	125	0	575	0	490	380	495	1,240	880	155
Hamilton	60,370	45	540	1,685	765	330	345	790	565	0	60	590	2,165	1,545	115	1,255	560
Kelowna	30,140	785	55	40	2,940	1,810	15	40	90	210	0	40	100	100	20	210	35
Kingston	21,550	30	215	70	340	575	250	140	510	440	10	0	360	540	115	825	185
Kitchener	47,250	85	425	1,230	470	335	540	3,125	300	2,590	65	450	0	1,970	55	810	540
London	41,510	25	375	490	580	405	445	560	340	1,475	55	530	1,745	0	30	675	345
Moncton	16,235	0	60	65	280	130	25	90	945	135	10	45	120	35	0	565	40
Montréal	144,155	135	120	100	1,510	930	175	150	1,205	705	90	450	570	745	545	0	290
Oshawa	50,215	20	305	100	295	145	325	165	310	715	25	300	580	630	85	630	0
Ottawa–Gatineau	90,305	50	470	120	1,640	1,935	1,610	680	3,110	1,480	85	2,840	1,245	1,450	545	11,650	765
Ottawa–Gatineau (Ont. part)	69,525	50	440	100	1,470	1,670	1,370	675	2,945	1,345	85	2,590	1,230	1,420	440	6,165	735
Ottawa–Gatineau (Que. part)	20,780	0	25	15	170	265	240	10	165	135	0	255	10	30	110	5,480	35

Ottawa–Gatineau	Ottawa–Gatineau (Ont. part)	Ottawa–Gatineau (Que. part)	Peterborough	Québec	Regina	Saguenay	Saskatoon	Sherbrooke	St. Catharines–Niagara	St. John's	Saint John	Thunder Bay	Toronto	Trois-Rivières	Vancouver	Victoria	Windsor	Winnipeg	Non-CMA
85,585	70,010	15,575	12,995	51,985	22,400	15,505	31,035	19,665	25,985	14,490	11,580	10,270	283,820	15,020	129,390	35,470	20,750	53,010	627,760
160	155	10	0	0	115	0	160	0	75	25	25	70	495	0	12,480	405	10	245	6,700
615	610	10	285	45	40	0	55	10	350	110	50	140	20,315	0	270	55	110	210	10,945
210	195	15	100	0	0	15	30	0	540	40	15	110	2,365	0	105	25	140	50	4,440
2,345	2,270	80	95	305	3,445	25	4,160	65	510	865	520	825	8,260	45	10,900	2,230	505	5,505	52,785
2,225	1,950	270	110	400	1,605	85	2,820	130	320	1,055	455	565	5,020	15	6,020	1,545	405	3,875	63,815
735	675	60	60	35	10	0	35	15	150	75	0	185	1,965	0	175	30	105	75	8,680
305	300	0	165	15	85	0	45	0	390	25	25	95	6,190	10	205	65	150	90	5,200
2,295	2,195	100	60	295	90	45	185	65	345	1,060	1,140	55	3,430	10	1,045	655	170	460	21,995
1,635	1,590	45	235	125	125	0	90	105	4,275	110	160	190	29,260	15	1,120	180	630	340	10,400
515	515	0	45	35	300	10	430	35	60	10	10	155	1,005	0	6,120	750	35	875	13,260
2,115	2,080	30	330	305	40	20	80	60	305	100	45	145	3,210	15	500	215	135	270	9,045
1,500	1,405	100	255	60	80	0	75	10	1,110	320	85	125	14,150	10	805	120	615	410	14,510
1,180	1,105	70	265	40	60	20	180	35	875	105	125	165	8,245	20	810	180	1,490	500	19,110
505	490	15	10	140	10	30	10	50	75	105	1,020	15	675	0	155	20	35	70	10,775
9,320	4,900	4,420	70	15,945	205	4,550	235	5,985	255	445	200	95	10,525	4,825	3,555	420	405	820	78,575
920	890	30	1,050	120	20	0	20	25	510	155	80	105	33,240	0	415	155	380	155	8,215
0	0	0	715	3,365	425	700	420	450	855	650	255	400	11,700	505	3,005	1,235	820	1,535	33,580
0	0	0	720	885	410	55	400	145	745	610	255	370	11,115	35	2,825	1,110	730	1,395	24,995
0	0	0	0	2,480	15	650	20	305	115	35	0	25	580	470	180	125	90	145	8,590

(continued)

Table 8.18   (*continued*)

CMA 2006	Canada	Abbotsford	Barrie	Brantford	Calgary	Edmonton	Greater Sudbury	Guelph	Halifax	Hamilton	Kelowna	Kingston	Kitchener	London	Moncton	Montréal	Oshawa
Peterborough	15,550	0	160	100	160	95	60	90	50	400	40	315	155	350	0	120	1,500
Québec	57,610	0	15	0	185	155	15	15	290	25	25	235	20	35	165	13,105	0
Regina	18,590	40	60	10	990	555	0	55	90	130	80	30	40	20	0	140	0
Saguenay	10,760	0	0	0	0	40	0	0	100	10	0	20	0	20	10	2,020	0
Saskatoon	26,745	70	15	0	1,575	935	25	115	145	60	115	70	50	110	0	150	50
Sherbrooke	21,425	10	10	0	50	25	0	0	60	25	15	0	0	10	70	6,000	10
St. Catharines–Niagara	25,580	50	285	255	235	215	295	310	160	4,490	80	165	635	690	85	305	420
St. John's	17,865	10	80	15	570	410	10	10	865	155	15	145	295	90	65	200	70
Saint John	8,265	10	25	115	345	110	10	80	635	95	10	75	100	105	465	170	65
Thunder Bay	9,895	25	25	25	150	240	140	30	55	145	55	65	130	90	10	75	90
Toronto	179,060	430	6,215	1,400	4,975	2,835	2,175	4,110	4,005	19,070	170	3,960	9,205	8,955	445	16,170	10,600
Trois-Rivières	14,235	0	0	0	0	20	0	0	10	0	0	0	10	0	15	3,250	0
Vancouver	107,575	7,845	295	225	7,795	5,665	125	430	1,215	1,195	3,300	480	730	1,300	135	4,205	335
Victoria	43,040	460	240	55	2,890	1,945	90	130	845	400	930	320	235	445	20	730	100
Windsor	17,815	0	140	85	330	205	190	115	160	585	25	115	445	1,310	20	635	160
Winnipeg	42,000	240	40	50	1,915	1,390	80	60	405	225	275	135	275	290	125	785	115
Non-CMA	688,325	10,610	10,480	5,130	48,160	42,925	6,395	5,895	20,950	17,785	8,735	8,295	16,595	16,695	7,880	115,285	13,060

Note: Data exclude incompletely enumerated Indian reserves.

Source: Adapted from Statistics Canada publication *2006 Census*. Catalogue no. 97-556-XCB2006012.

Ottawa–Gatineau	Ottawa–Gatineau (Ont. part)	Ottawa–Gatineau (Que. part)	Peterborough	Québec	Regina	Saguenay	Saskatoon	Sherbrooke	St. Catharines–Niagara	St. John's	Saint John	Thunder Bay	Toronto	Trois-Rivières	Vancouver	Victoria	Windsor	Winnipeg	Non-CMA
565	555	0	0	40	0	0	10	0	150	30	30	40	4,215	0	120	45	80	40	6,585
1,975	600	1,380	0	0	20	3,160	0	1,480	10	40	10	0	585	1,590	185	115	15	110	34,005
270	270	10	15	55	0	10	2,470	0	35	60	45	15	455	0	705	130	20	630	11,400
150	40	105	0	1,590	0	0	0	155	0	0	0	0	35	85	40	10	0	70	6,405
190	180	10	0	35	2,140	10	0	0	105	15	35	65	785	10	850	210	50	710	18,055
390	130	260	0	1,185	30	440	0	0	10	0	10	0	160	400	40	20	25	45	12,410
770	760	15	220	60	50	0	135	40	0	70	15	165	7,470	15	505	175	345	345	6,520
420	405	20	0	20	25	0	25	10	80	0	840	0	1,560	0	320	75	40	640	10,795
205	205	0	0	40	0	0	25	0	30	40	0	35	445	0	160	50	30	50	4,720
465	455	10	75	0	10	0	60	10	135	20	0	0	875	0	405	155	55	410	5,870
11,675	11,410	265	2,310	510	565	75	615	180	5,745	1,170	510	1,140	0	95	11,585	1,360	4,365	3,210	39,215
255	25	230	0	1,230	10	190	0	265	10	0	0	10	70	0	35	15	0	15	8,800
3,555	3,430	120	205	390	930	20	1,145	140	560	685	205	340	13,715	15	0	7,905	695	3,715	38,075
1,335	1,285	50	85	80	415	20	480	15	225	175	45	125	2,645	30	7,935	0	110	915	18,565
455	435	20	90	55	70	0	75	0	315	70	90	50	3,595	0	415	20	0	160	7,820
1,055	965	90	50	175	800	30	680	40	145	195	90	575	2,185	0	2,470	490	130	0	26,475
35,255	27,530	7,725	6,090	25,295	10,665	6,040	16,280	10,280	7,425	6,660	5,445	4,270	84,945	7,315	55,920	16,425	8,650	26,450	0

Additional Reading

Brown, Lawrence A. 1991. *Place, Migration and Development in the Third World: An Alternative View*. London: Routledge.

Frey, William H., and Alden Speare, Jr. 1988. *Regional and Metropolitan Growth and Decline in the United States*. New York: Russell Sage Foundation.

Greenwood, Michael J. 1981. *Migration and Economic Growth in the United States: National, Regional and Metropolitan Perspectives*. New York: Academic.

Hochstadt, Steve. 1999. *Mobility and Modernity: Migration in Germany, 1820–1989*. Ann Arbor, MI: University of Michigan Press.

Khatun, Hafiza. 2003. *Dhakaiyans on the Move*. Dhaka: Academic.

Kono, Shigemi, and Mitsuru Shio. 1965. *Inter-Prefectural Migration in Japan, 1956 and 1961: Migration Stream Analysis*. Bombay: Asia Publishing House.

Mangalam, J.J., with Cornelia Morgan. 1968. *Human Migration: A Guide to Migration Literature in English 1955–1962*. Lexington, KY: University of Kentucky Press.

Pieke, Frank N., and Hein Mallee, eds. 1999. *Internal and International Migration: Chinese Perspectives*. Surrey, UK: Curzon.

Stillwell, J., and P. Congdon, eds. 1991. *Migration Models: Macro and Micro Approaches*. London: Belhaven.

Weidlich, W., and G. Haag, eds. 1988. *Interregional Migration: Dynamic Theory and Comparative Analysis*. Berlin: Springer-Verlag.

Web Resources

The Institut National de la Recherche Scientifique (INRS) is a network of four research centres within the Université du Québec. For research on internal migration visit the site dedicated to 'Urbanisation, Culture et Societé': www.inrs-ucs.uquebec.ca.

Alberta Finance provides updated figures on interprovincial migration in Canada for each quarter of each year: www.finance.gov.ab.ca/aboutalberta/population_reports/2007_1stquarter.pdf.

The Development Research Centre on Migration, Globalisation and Poverty at the University of Sussex, England, conducts research on migration, including internal migration, in poor countries, with the aim of promoting new policy approaches that will help to maximize the potential benefits of migration for poor people, while minimizing its risks and costs: www.migrationdrc.org/index.html.

Chapter 9

International Migration

Introduction

In 2006 more than 190 million people around the world were living in a country other than the one in which they were born. Just over 115 million of these migrants were in the more developed countries, and about 85 million in less developed areas of the world. International migrants represented just under 3 per cent of the world's population, but almost 10 per cent of the population of the more developed countries, taken together (United Nations Department of Economic and Social Affairs Population Division, 2006f). A host of intersecting social, economic, political, and demographic dimensions continue to produce and sustain large-scale migrations today. The number of countries involved in migration, either as sources or as receivers, continues to grow, and societies that once exported many of their nationals to other countries now receive significant numbers of immigrants themselves. Meanwhile, in countries with longer immigration histories, the foreign-born populations are growing rapidly, and their societies are being transformed as a result (Parsons and Smeeding, 2006).

The intensification of migration (including refugee movements) beginning in the latter half of the twentieth century can be partly attributed to political upheavals, including the collapse of the Soviet Empire in the late 1980s and the civil unrest that has occurred in parts of Africa, Asia, and eastern Europe (Castles and Miller, 2003). Economic globalization has played a part as well by freeing up the movement both of work and of workers, which has spurred international migration—sometimes permanent, sometimes temporary—to and from all parts of the globe.

Moreover, clandestine migration remains an ongoing concern for the receiving societies, especially the United States and countries in southern and western Europe.

This chapter begins with an overview of international migration. An introduction to basic concepts and measures is followed by a brief outline of human migratory patterns from prehistory to the post-industrial age, a review of prominent theories of international migration, and a survey of Canadian immigration history and associated social demographic features, in particular the changing nature of immigration and its impact on the social demographic composition of the country. The chapter concludes with a look at the philosophical questions around international migration that the world's liberal democracies now face.

The Complex Nature of International Migration

Migration usually represents a response to 'push' and 'pull' factors in the countries of origin and destination, respectively. In both cases, there will be demographic, economic, political, and social consequences associated with migration (see Figure 9.1). As with internal migration, the decision to emigrate is usually made on the basis of rational cost–benefit principles: people will move if there is something important to be gained (Lee, 1966). Probably the most striking example of voluntary migration was the movement from Europe to the New World, which saw, in the course of a century (c.1850–1950) some 60 million people leave their homelands

The United Nations Convention Relating to the Status of Refugees was drawn (1951) in response to the European refugee crisis created by the Second World War and expanded (1977) to address the plight of refugees worldwide. Specifically, it defines refugee as: 'A person who is outside his or her country of nationality or habitual residence; has a well-founded fear of persecution because of his or her race, religion, nationality, membership of a particular social group or political opinion; and is unable or unwilling to avail himself or herself of the protection of that country, or to return there, for fear of persecution.' The United Nations High Commissioner for Refugees (UNHCR) is the UN agency entrusted to protect refugees from being forcibly returned to countries where they might face persecution or death. As well, UNHCR seeks ways to help refugees restart their lives, either through local integration, voluntary return to their homeland, or, if neither of these is possible, through resettlement in 'third' countries. Although internally displaced persons (people displaced within their own countries because of sociopolitical crises or unrest) are not explicitly covered by the UN Convention on Refugees, the UNHCR today is heavily involved in protecting this category of people, which as of 2007 was thought to number in the range of 24.5 million people worldwide.

was close to 9.9 million. When internally displaced persons are also taken into account, the number of people of concern to the UN agency responsible for the welfare of refugees (the United Nations High Commissioner for Refugees, or UNHCR) was closer to 33 million (United Nations High Commissioner for Refugees, 2007: 11). A separate agency, the United Nations Relief and Works Agency for Palestine Refugees in the Near East, was formed in 1949 to provide education, health care, and social services to the refugees—now numbering more than 4 million—in Jordan, Lebanon, Syria, the West Bank, and the Gaza Strip, approximately one-third of whom still live in camps.

The largest number of refugees and internally displaced persons is found in Asia (about 8 million), followed by Africa (3 million). Worldwide, the number of refugees, which increased in the 1980s and 1990s a result of major regional crises (the breakup of Yugoslavia, for example), has actually declined in the new millennium (from 10.3 million in 1983 to 17.4 million in 1991 to 9.9 million in 2007), despite the sense among the citizens of many countries—especially those in western Europe—that they are being overwhelmed by asylum seekers (United Nations Department of Economic and Social Affairs Population Division, 2005a: 25; United Nations High Commissioner for Refugees, 2007: 11, 15).

In addition to those people recognized as refugees are unknown numbers of undocumented migrants. It is virtually impossible for a receiving country to know precisely how many of these people may be living within its borders. For instance, official estimates of 'illegal aliens' in the United States put the number at roughly 5 million as of 1996 (Borjas, 1999: 41), and it is thought that approximately 300,000 illegal migrants enter the country each year, mostly from Mexico (Bean, Edmonston, and Passel, 1990; Massey and Espana, 1987; Massey et al., 1987). Massey and Singer (1995) have suggested that undocumented entries into the United States from Mexico between 1965 and

in search of socioeconomic opportunities in North America (Petersen, 1975: 279).

But history is also full of migrations that have been involuntary—forced or coerced (Crépeau et al., 2006). International movement resulting from persecution and conflict is known as *asylum migration*; those involved in asylum migration are *refugees*, defined by the United Nations as persons who have been forced to flee their country because of a real threat of persecution or death for reasons of race, religion, nationality, or political opinion. It is estimated that as of 2007, the number of refugees around the world

MACRO-LEVEL DETERMINANTS ('push' and 'pull' factors)	INTERNATIONAL MIGRATION	MACRO-LEVEL CONSEQUENCES
Country of origin factors demographic economic political social	**Voluntary** (various classes, e.g., permanent settlers, temporary workers, visitors, etc.)	**For receiving country** demographic economic political social
Country of destination factors demographic economic political social	**Forced** (refugees, displaced people) **Illegal** (undocumented; clandestine movements)	**For sending country** demographic economic political social

Figure 9.1   Macro-level determinants and consequences of international migration

1990 likely totalled approximately 36.5 million; with return migration to Mexico taken into account, it is quite possible that the net inflow of undocumented Mexican migrants amounted to about 5.2 million.

Temporary migration is another important phenomenon today (Castles and Miller, 2003; Edmonston and Michalowski, 2004: 458). Temporary migrants maintain a particular place of residence but spend varying amounts of time working or studying in another country. In western Europe, laws allow citizens free movement among the countries that form the European Union, enabling many temporary migrants to cross borders on a daily, weekly, or seasonal basis. Segments of the Canada–US border are also crossed daily by people who live on one side and work on the other; this is the case for many auto workers in the neighbouring cities of Windsor and Detroit, for example. Similarly, many Mexicans find seasonal work in the US agricultural sector. In some cases, temporary migrants may be permitted to settle permanently in the host country if, for example, political circumstances in their country of origin mean that returning there would put them at risk of persecution or death (Castles and Miller, 2003).

Basic Concepts

Of the components of population change, international migration is the one that is most directly affected by legal restrictions and government planning. According to the United Nations, *international migrants* are people who change their country of abode (i.e., the country in which they spend most of their sleeping hours over the course of a year) (Edmonston and Michalowski, 2004: 456). Countries impose strict border controls and attempt to ensure that all immigrants are genuinely committed to making their lives in the new society. For this reason, governments make a strict differentiation between permanent and temporary migrants. Applicants may be refused admission on many grounds, including lack of desired occupational skills, a history of criminal offences, or adherence to an ideology that the state considers subversive.

Classification of International Migrants

International migration can be broken down into various categories. Some moves are voluntary; others are forced or compelled by war or persecution. Instances of migration may also be classified according to whether they are peaceful or non-peaceful, civilian or military, and work- (or study-) related as opposed to optional, for purposes such as tourism (Edmonston and Michalowski, 2004: 456). The following box contains a detailed classification of international migrants.

Legal Categories of International Migrants

Bilsborrow and colleagues (1997: 36–9) offer a useful classification of international migrants. From the point of view of a receiving country, the people seeking entry fall into two general groups: citizens returning home and foreigners (the latter consisting of various sub-categories, including regular immigrants, asylum migrants, and undocumented migrants).

A   Citizens

1. *Returning migrants* are persons who have been abroad as migrants in a country other than their own and who return to their own country to settle in it. Among persons entering their own country, returning migrants should be distinguished on the basis of the time that they have spent abroad and the time that they intend to spend in their country of citizenship. A year is a reasonable cut-off point in both cases, so that returning migrants are citizens who have been abroad for at least a year and who intend to remain in their own country for more than a year.

B   Foreigners

2. *Returning ethnics* are persons who are admitted by a country other than their own because of their historical, ethnic, or other ties with that country, and who are immediately granted the right of permanent abode in that country or who, having the right to citizenship in that country, become citizens within a short period after admission.

3. *Migrants with the right to free movement* are persons who have the right to enter, stay, and work within the territory of a state other than their own by virtue of an agreement or treaty concluded between their state of citizenship and the state in which they reside.

4. *Foreigners admitted for special purposes*:

    (a) *Foreign students* are persons admitted by a country other than their own for the specific purpose of following a particular program of study. In some countries, foreign students are allowed to work under certain conditions.

    (b) *Foreign trainees* are persons admitted by a country other than their own to acquire particular skills through on-the-job training. Foreign trainees are therefore allowed to work only in the specific institution providing the training and are allowed to stay for a limited period.

    (c) *Foreign retirees* are persons beyond retirement age who are allowed to stay in the territory of a state other than their own provided that they do not become a charge to that state. They are generally allowed to be accompanied by their spouses.

5. *Settlers* are persons who are granted the right to stay indefinitely in the territory of a country other than their own and to enjoy the same social and economic rights as the citizens of that country. Settlers are usually accorded the opportunity to become naturalized citizens of the receiving state once minimum requirements have been met. (The terms *permanent migrants* or *immigrants* are often used to refer to settlers.)

6. *Migrant workers* are persons admitted by a country other than their own for the explicit purpose of exercising an economic activity:

   (a) *Seasonal migrant workers* are persons employed in a state other than their own for only part of a year because the work they perform depends on seasonal conditions.

   (b) *Project-tied migrant workers* are workers admitted to the state of employment for a defined period of work solely on a specific project carried out in that state by the migrant workers' employer. The employer is responsible for providing the inputs needed to complete the project, including labour. The employer of an agent who may have acted as an intermediary must ensure that project-tied migrant workers leave the country of employment once the work is completed.

   (c) *Contract migrant workers* are persons working in a country other than their own under contractual arrangements that set limits on the period of employment and on the specific job held by the migrant. Once admitted, contract migrant workers are not allowed to change jobs and are expected to leave the country of employment upon completion of their contract, irrespective of whether the work they do continues or not. Although contract renewals are sometimes possible, departure from the country of employment may be mandatory before the contract can be renewed.

   (d) *Temporary migrant workers* are persons admitted by a country other than their own to work for a limited period in a particular occupation or a specific job. Temporary migrant workers may change employers and have their work permits renewed without having to leave the country of employment.

   (e) *Established migrant workers* are migrant workers who, after staying some years in the country of employment, have been granted the permission to reside indefinitely and work without major limitations in that country. Established migrant workers need not leave the country of employment when unemployed and are usually granted the right of being joined by their immediate family members, provided certain conditions regarding employment and housing are met.

   (f) *Highly skilled migrant workers* are migrant workers who, because of their skill, are subject to preferential treatment regarding admission to a country other than their own and are therefore subject to fewer restrictions regarding length of stay, change of employment, and family reunification.

7. *Economic migration* covers persons who move internationally in connection with the exercise of an economic activity that is either not remunerated from within the country of destination or demands a certain investment from the migrant concerned:

   (a) *Business travellers* are foreigners admitted temporarily for the purpose of exercising an economic activity remunerated from outside the country of destination.

(b) *Immigrating investors* are foreigners granted the right to long-term residence on the condition that they invest a minimum amount in the country of destination or start a business employing a minimum number of persons in the country of destination.

8. *Asylum migration* covers the whole spectrum of international movements caused by persecution and conflict. Specific types of migrants that are part of asylum migration are listed below:

   (a) *Refugees* are persons who, owing to a well-founded fear of being persecuted for reasons of race, religion, nationality, membership of a particular social group, or political opinion, are outside of their country of nationality and are unable or, owing to such fear, are unwilling to avail themselves of the protection of that country. Persons recognized as refugees under this definition are sometimes called *Convention refugees* and are usually granted an open-ended permission to stay in the country of asylum. When they are admitted by another country for resettlement, they are called *resettled refugees*.

   (b) *Persons admitted for humanitarian reasons* are persons who, being outside of their country of nationality, are in refugee-like situations because they cannot avail themselves of the protection of the State in which they find themselves. Sometimes such persons are characterized as *refugees type B* because they do not fully meet the criteria stipulated in the 1951 Convention. They usually receive treatment equal to that of Convention refugees.

   (c) *Asylum seekers* are persons who file an application for asylum in a country other than their own. They remain in the status of asylum seeker until their application is considered and adjudicated.

   (d) *Persons granted temporary protected status* are persons who are outside their country of nationality and cannot return to that country without putting their lives in danger. The temporary protected status granted to them by the country in which they find themselves allows them to stay for a limited though often open-ended period (as long as return to their country is considered detrimental to their security).

   (e) *Persons granted stay of deportation* are persons who have been found not to qualify for refugee status or to be in an irregular situation and who are under deportation orders but who have been granted a temporary reprieve from being deported because their lives would be in danger if they returned immediately to their country of nationality.

9. *Irregular migrants* are persons in a state other than their own who have not fully satisfied the conditions and requirements set by that state to enter, stay, or exercise an economic activity in that state's territory.

10. *Migrants for family reunification* are persons admitted by a country other than their own for the purpose of accompanying or joining close relatives migrating to that country or already living in that country. Because most migrants for family reunification are relatives of other migrants, they should be considered as a distinct sub-category of that to which the primo-migrant belongs.

The Canadian Immigration System

The Canadian immigration program offers a specific example of how international migration is codified and controlled by a receiving country. It also illustrates the legal complexities involved in immigration. There are two main ways for foreigners to legally enter Canada for periods longer than those allowed under short-term tourist and business-travel arrangements: (1) with *permanent residence* status granted through the permanent immigration program, and (2) on a *temporary residence* basis as students, refugee claimants, or temporary workers. It is possible, under certain conditions, for temporary residents to gain permanent status as *landed immigrants*. Permanent resident status may be granted to three main categories of migrants (see Figure 9.2):

- *family class* (people with close relatives in Canada)
- *independents* (which comprises two subgroups: skilled workers and investors/entrepreneurs)
- *refugees*

Each entry class has its own requirements. Family-class applicants must be sponsored by someone who is either a Canadian citizen or a permanent resident. Skilled workers must pass a point-based test designed to assess the likelihood that they will become successfully established in Canada. Business-class applicants are required either to make a minimum investment in a Canadian business or to establish, purchase, or invest in a designated business that will create employment for others (Citizenship and Immigration Canada, 2005a). Finally, people who qualify as refugees under the criteria of the UN Convention are always admitted, and those who do not qualify as Convention refugees may still be admitted on humanitarian grounds as judged by the appropriate government authorities. Under the general heading of 'refugee' are three sub-categories: (1) *government-assisted refugees*, selected abroad; (2) *privately sponsored refugees*, also selected abroad; and (c) *asylum seekers*, who first arrive in the country and then claim refugee status. Among the latter group, only those whose claims are subsequently found to be valid

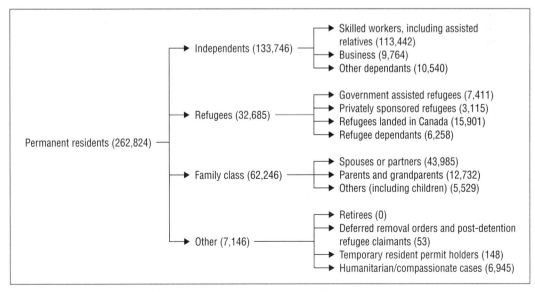

Figure 9.2   Permanent residents in Canada by immigration category, 2004

Source: Adapted from Citizenship and Immigration Canada (2005a).

in the eyes of officials (i.e., the members of a refugee board) are allowed to remain in the country.

Data Sources and Basic Measures

Data on internal migration, as we have seen, can be obtained from a variety of sources, including administrative records and the census. The situation with international migration is more complicated because, though virtually all countries collect information on in-bound migration, most do not systematically monitor out-bound migration. Countries may co-operate bilaterally by trading information about the number of nationals they exchange as a result of cross-border moves. Canada and the United States, for example, share information on the numbers of the other country's nationals crossing their respective borders. This type of co-operation allows such countries to produce annual estimates of emigration.

Edmonston and Michalowsky (2004: 458) identify five classes of international migration data:

1. statistics collected at the points where people move across international borders (i.e., at border crossings, seaports, and airports)—these data are gathered mostly from border-control operations and lists of passengers on sea or air transport manifests
2. statistics regarding passports and applications for passports, visas, work permits, and other documents for international migration
3. statistics obtained through population registers recording movement into and out of a country as well as births, deaths, and internal movements (most countries do not have population registers)
4. statistics obtained from censuses or periodic national population surveys through inquiries regarding previous residence, place of birth, nationality, or citizenship

5. statistics collected through various special or periodic inquiries (e.g., surveys, registration of aliens, and enumeration of citizens overseas)

Unfortunately, the most accessible data source, the census, does not distinguish between the different categories of immigrants. Nor do censuses usually identify the legal status of immigrants (e.g., illegal or undocumented, as opposed to legal permanent residents, refugees or asylum seekers, and temporary immigrants). Numbers of illegal migrants are usually estimated using indirect methods based on a combination of data sources (e.g., administrative, census, and even survey data). For example, administrative records provide data on individuals who may have entered a country legally but stayed longer than the regulations permit. It is also possible to obtain information based on decedents who are later determined to have been in the country illegally. Border-crossing data can be used to identify visitors who have not left within the allotted time. Censuses and current population surveys can be used to estimate the size of the illegally resident population by subtracting the legally resident 'foreign-born' population, adjusted for census undercount, from the total foreign-born population (Yaukey and Anderton, 2001: 279). The margin of error associated with indirect methods such as these can be quite substantial, however.

Estimating International Migration

In the absence of actual statistics, countries can produce estimates of net international migration using a variety of demographic methods outlined below.

Vital Statistics Method
One such approach to estimating net migration is called the *vital statistics method*. Let us recall the growth equation, $P_{t2} - P_{t1} = (B_{t1, t2} - D_{t1, t2})$

+ $(IN_{t1, t2} - OUT_{t1, t2})$. This equation can be rearranged to obtain an estimate of net international migration between two time points $(NM_{t1, t2})$:

$$NM_{t1, t2} = (IN_{t1, t2} - OUT_{t1, t2})$$
$$= (P_{t2} - P_{t1} - B_{t1, t2} - D_{t1, t2})$$

Thus, net international migration equals the difference between two population counts from two censuses $(P_{t2} - P_{t1})$, minus the difference between the number of births and deaths that occurred in the interval $(B_{t1, t2} - D_{t1, t2})$. Table 9.1 illustrates how this *vital statistics method* has been applied for the world and the major regions between 1995 and 1999. Column 1 shows the population at the end of the period, while the next two columns display estimated numbers of births and deaths in the preceding year. Column 4 is the natural increase, obtained by subtracting column 3 from column 2. Column 5 is the population growth between 1995 and 1999. The last column is the estimate of net migration derived by subtracting column 4 from column 5. The table shows that three regions experienced net migratory gains: Europe,

It is possible to apply the vital statistics method to specific age–sex combinations. If we know (a) the size of a given age–sex cohort at the beginning and the end of the interval, and (b) the number of deaths that occurred in the cohort, then we can obtain an estimate of net migration for this cohort. This approach to estimating net migration generalizes to any additional factors (e.g., net migration for age–sex–regional categories).

Northern America, and Oceania. On the whole, the developing regions (especially Asia) lost more population than they gained through migration.

This type of indirect estimation is far from satisfactory. Beside the potential for error in the components parts of the equation (i.e., births, deaths, and population), which could affect the derived net migration estimate, net migration measured in this way is a residual figure that cannot differentiate between the two migration streams—those entering the country and those leaving it. All it can tell us is the net balance of

Table 9.1 Net migration into world regions, 1995–1999, estimated by the vital statistics method (figures in thousands)

Region	P_2 1999 Population (1)	B Births (2)	D Deaths (3)	$B - D$ Natural increase (4)	$P_2 - P_1$ Total growth (5)	M Net migration (6)
World	5,978,401	129,810	52,072	77,738	77,738	0
More developed regions	1,185,174	13,224	11,951	1,273	3,243	1,971
Less developed regions	4,793,227	116,586	40,121	76,465	74,494	−1,971
Africa	766,623	28,115	10,331	17,784	17,496	−287
Asia	3,634,279	77,953	27,492	50,461	49,254	−1,207
Europe	728,934	7,493	8,248	−755	195	950
Latin America/Caribbean	511,345	11,554	3,245	8,309	7,838	−471
Northern America	307,202	4,172	2,528	1,644	2,574	930
Oceania	30,018	527	227	300	381	81

Source: United Nations Department of Economic and Social Affairs Population Division (1999): 9. Reprinted with the permission of the United Nations.

migration. Thus, we have no way of knowing whether a net balance of zero means equal numbers of immigrants and emigrants or no migration at all. Nevertheless, residual measures are frequently used in some contexts because direct information on immigration—and especially emigration—is lacking. This problem is most in evidence at the sub-national level.

Residual Method of Estimating Emigration

Most countries collect immigration data from their periodic censuses and annual administrative records of new arrivals. (In Canada the agency responsible for collecting this information is Citizenship and Immigration Canada.) The more difficult aspect of measuring net international migration is the emigration component, for which direct information is often difficult to obtain. As most countries do not routinely collect information on emigration, for an accurate account we would need to know how many people leave the country, when they leave, and where they go. Knowledge of whether emigrants are native- or foreign-born would also be useful.

The *residual method of estimating emigration* uses population data from two successive censuses, plus the numbers of births, deaths, and persons entering the country in the interval between the two censuses. To illustrate, let us recall the components of growth equation cited above. Population growth between two points in time is a function of the interplay of births and deaths during the interval, plus the difference between in-migration (immigration) and out-migration (emigration). In practice, of course, the numbers of emigrants are usually not known. Therefore we need to derive an indirect estimate of emigration ($E_{t1,t2}$), as follows:

$$E_{t1,\,t2} = [P_{t2} - P_{t1}] - [B_{t1,\,t2} - D_{t1,\,t2} + I_{t1,\,t2}]$$

where $E_{t1,\,t2}$ is the estimated number of emigrants between two time points, t_1 and t_2;
P is the census population at two time points, t_1 and t_2;

B is the number of births between t_1 and t_2;
D is the number of deaths between t_1 and t_2;
I is the number of immigrants between t_1 and t_2;
t_1 is the the start of the interval; and
t_2 is the the end of the interval.

The census populations at the beginning and end of the interval are included in this equation. But since the census is seldom a wholly accurate count of the population, the estimate produced by this formula is usually adjusted for census undercoverage. In Canada over last several censuses the undercoverage error has been in the range of 2 to 3 per cent.

Other Methods

In practical applications, estimating emigration (and net international migration) is much more complicated. Statistics Canada's estimates of emigration have three components: emigration of Canadian citizens and alien permanent residents, return of emigrants, and net emigration of Canadian residents temporarily abroad. The first two components are estimated using a model based on administrative data, extracted by the Canada Customs and Revenue Agency from the federal Canada Child Tax Benefit program. Information is provided only on families that are entitled to the benefit (based on income and the presence of children under the age of 18). Statistics Canada also uses data collected by the US Immigration and Naturalization Service on Canadian residents admitted to the United States for permanent residence. The third component, Canadians temporarily abroad, is estimated using a technique called the reverse record check (Edmonston and Michalowski, 2004: 482).

Statistics Canada, in its estimate of emigration, takes into account the following flows:

- the emigration of permanent citizens and landed immigrants;
- the return migration of permanent citizens and landed immigrants;
- the number of new immigrants coming into the country in a given interval;

- the number of non-permanent residents that leave the country; and
- the number of non-permanent residents that return to Canada.

Non-permanent residents are foreigners in Canada for a limited stay and who are expected to leave after their stay expires. This category includes people claiming refugee status and others on student or work visas; non-permanent residents may eventually become landed immigrants.[1] The data used to produce estimates of the number of non-permanent residents are obtained from Citizenship and Immigration Canada. Statistics Canada also distinguishes between permanent and temporary migration. (Permanent leaves may be taken by citizens, landed immigrants, and temporary residents who exit the country permanently.)

Once all these data have been assembled, a total emigration component is calculated to reflect the net flows of permanent, returning, and temporary emigrants, all of this representing a net loss of population through emigration. The formula developed by Statistics Canada Demography Division (2003: 85) is

$$E_{(t, t+i)} = PE_{(t, t+i)} - RE_{(t, t+i)} + \Delta TE_{(t, t+i)}$$

where $E_{(t, t+i)}$ is the number of total emigrants over the period $(t, t+i)$;

t is the start of the interval and $t + i$ is the end point of the interval;

$PE_{(t, t+i)}$ is the number of permanent emigrants over the period $(t, t+i)$;

$RE_{(t, t+i)}$ is the number of returning emigrants over the period $(t, t+i)$; and

$\Delta TE_{(t, t+i)}$ is the change in the number of temporary emigrants over the period $(t, t+i)$.

Once immigration is measured from official statistics and emigration has been estimated in this way, net migration is computed by taking the difference between these two components.

Table 9.2 breaks down Canada's population growth from 1991–2 to 2004–5 into its individual components, including natural increase and the various aspects of immigration and emigration, as well as net international migration. Note that the net migration column (column 12) is derived as follows: net migration = (number of immigrants − number of emigrants − number of net temporary emigrants + number of return emigrants + number of net non-permanent residents).

Migration in History: An Overview

Migration has been a feature of the human experience ever since our earliest ancestors began moving out of Africa and into Asia and Europe, eventually spreading to Oceania and, most recently, the Americas (Balter, 2001; Cavalli-Sforza and Cavalli-Sforza, 1995; Diamond, 1999; Manning, 2005). Many of these movements have been forced by humans' desire to expand beyond their territory; by wars, conquest, and persecution; and by the strong tendency among peoples of diverse civilizations to establish contacts with others through trade and exploration (Fairchild, 1925; McNeill, 1984; Hoerder, 2002). In the more recent history of international migration, labour and settlement movements have figured prominently as well.

Figure 9.3 shows Diamond's (1999: 37) interpretation of the prehistoric migratory experience of *Homo*. It is generally agreed that *Homo erectus* had moved out of Africa by about 1 million years ago, first to the Middle East and parts

[1] In addition to the categories listed, non-permanent residents include people in Canada who hold a Minister's permit and non-Canadian-born dependants of (a) people claiming refugee status or (b) people holding student authorization, employment authorization, or a Minister's permit. Children born in Canada to parents of non-permanent resident status are considered Canadian by birth and have all rights and privileges associated with citizenship (Statistics Canada Demography Division, 2003: 31, 65).

Table 9.2 Components of population growth in Canada, 1991–2 to 2004–5

(1) Period	(2) Population[1]	(3) Non-permanent residents	(4) Births	(5) Deaths	(6) Natural increase	(7) Immigrants	(8) Emigrants[2]	(9) Net temporary emigrants	(10) Returning emigrants	(11) Net non-permanent residents[3]	(12) Net migration	(13) Residual[4]	(14) Total growth[5]
1991–2	28,031,394	395,077	403,107	196,967	206,140	244,281	45,633	19,741	15,899	−42,919	151,887	−22,684	335,343
1992–3	28,366,737	352,158	392,181	201,808	190,373	266,890	43,993	19,744	15,279	−71,185	147,247	−22,681	314,939
1993–4	28,681,676	280,973	386,159	206,464	179,695	235,360	49,456	19,746	16,358	−22,196	160,320	−22,685	317,330
1994–5	28,999,006	258,777	381,998	209,389	172,609	220,738	52,069	19,745	18,388	−14,152	153,160	−22,684	303,085
1995–6	29,302,091	244,625	372,453	209,766	162,687	217,478	48,396	19,745	19,035	−826	167,546	−21,567	308,666
1996–7	29,610,757	243,799	357,313	217,221	140,092	224,857	52,815	25,564	18,956	182	165,616	−9,293	296,415
1997–8	29,907,172	243,981	345,123	217,688	127,435	194,459	51,816	25,563	18,671	−3,983	131,768	−9,293	249,910
1998–9	30,157,082	239,998	338,295	217,632	120,663	173,194	48,008	25,567	17,491	18,317	135,427	−9,294	246,796
1999–2000	30,403,878	258,315	336,912	217,229	119,683	205,710	48,089	25,564	17,680	25,032	174,769	−9,295	285,157
2000–1	30,689,035	283,347	327,107	219,114	107,993	252,533	47,766	25,563	17,910	35,627	232,741	−8,518	332,216
2001–2	31,021,251	318,974	328,155	220,494	107,661	256,334	38,928	25,560	18,079	33,750	243,675	–	351,336
2002–3	31,372,587	352,724	330,523	224,702	105,821	199,212	34,825	25,558	15,785	36,128	190,742	–	296,563
2003–4	31,669,150	388,852	335,701	231,260	104,441	239,116	35,535	25,564	15,785	6,970	200,772	–	305,213
2004–5	31,974,363	395,822	337,856	234,645	103,211	244,579	35,866	25,563	15,786	−6,003	192,933	–	296,144
2005	32,270,507	389,819	–	–	–	–	–	–	–	–	–	–	–

[1]Population at the beginning of the period.

[2]Emigration figures are estimated by Statistics Canada.

[3]Net non-permanent residents' is estimated separately by Statistics Canada, and then it is added into the net migration estimate (i.e., net migration = immigrants − emigrants − net temporary emigrants + returning emigrants + net non-permanent residents).

[4]The 'residual' column is an adjustment by Statistics Canada (the error of closure) used to reconcile the population estimates at the end of each period with the population at the beginning of the interval, once growth due to net migration and natural increase have been taken into account. Values for beyond 2001 not yet available, as they can only be derived once the next round of postcensal population estimates has been undertaken based on the population data from the 2006 census.

[5]The 'total growth' column is the sum of columns (6) and (12) plus column (13).

Source: Adapted from Statistics Canada publication *Annual Demographic Statistics 2005*. Catalogue no. 91-213-XIB, p.23, Table 1.2.

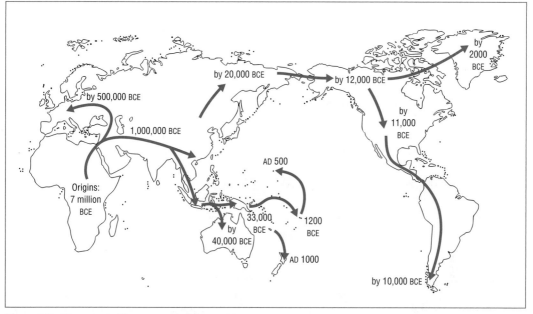

Figure 9.3 The spread of humans around the world

Source: Diamond (1999): 37. 'The Spread of Humans Around the World', from *Guns, Germs and Steel: The Fates of Human Societies*, by Jared Diamond, copyright © 1997 by Jared Diamond. Used by permission of W.W. Norton & Company, Inc.

of Southeast Asia, and by 500,000 BCE (possibly much earlier) to the European continent. *Homo sapiens* had occupied all of Eurasia, as well as Australia and New Guinea, by about 30,000 years before the present, and probably arrived in North America around 12,000 BCE, crossing from northern Asia to the region that is now Alaska either by boat or on foot across the narrow land bridge that at that time connected the two continents. Migrations southward to the temperate areas of North America were followed by further southward movements to the tropical regions of North and South America, the Caribbean, and finally the temperate regions of South America and its highlands.

Among the forces that provoked primitive migrations, the quest for food must have been of central importance. People moved nomadically out of necessity, whether following game or seeking more favourable environmental conditions. With the development of agriculture and the domestication of animals, beginning

around 8000 BCE, humans started forming settled communities, some of which would eventually develop into cities. The rise of cities marked the beginning of what we call civilization. At that point in history, as competition for territory and resources increased, the reasons for migration expanded to include forcible relocation by invading armies. Ongoing exploration and colonization led to new migrations, and trade and commerce helped to spread knowledge and skills across civilizations (McNeill, 1984: 4).

Historians generally place the beginning of the 'modern era' around the year 1500 (Barzun, 2001: xxi). Immigration history since that time can be subdivided into four distinct phases:

1. the mercantile period
2. the industrial period
3. a period of limited migration between the two world wars
4. the post-industrial period (since the 1960s)

The earliest date for the presence of *Homo erectus* on European soil has been the subject of some debate. Before the 1990s, scientists believed there had been no humans in Europe earlier than 500,000 years ago, but recent discoveries suggest that hominids may have been in Europe as far back as 1 million years ago. Recent literature has also speculated about the disappearance of *Neanderthals*, which are believed to have coexisted at one time with *Homo sapiens*. Balter (2001) suggests that *Homo erectus* was present in Europe before dividing into two populations: the *Neanderthals* and the *Homo sapiens*. The latter, having the larger brain, became dominant, and the *Neanderthals* became extinct. Whether there was any interbreeding between early *Homo sapiens* and *Neanderthals* is uncertain (see Manning, 2005: 51; Diamond, 1999: 41). According to another scenario that has been proposed, the ancestors of modern humans remained in Africa until roughly 100,000 years ago, when modern humans began moving out of Africa and into Europe, pushing the *Neanderthals* and other remaining hominids aside. (For additional insights on this question, see Finlayson, 2004).

Migration during the Mercantile Period

The main impetus for transnational movements during the mercantile period (1500–1800) was European colonization of the New World: the Americas, parts of Africa, Asia, and Oceania. As these areas were settled, their new economies required abundant labour. According to Massey (1999), emigrants from Europe during this period generally fell into three categories: a relatively large number of agrarian settlers; a smaller number of administrators and artisans; and an even smaller number of entrepreneurs who established plantations to produce raw materials (sugar and rubber, for example) for Europe's growing mercantile economies. The rise of plantations meant that an outside source of cheap labour had to be found to sustain colonial economies. It was in response to this need that

the slave trade and system of indentured labour developed. Over the course of three centuries, approximately 10 million West Africans were forcibly taken to the Americas.

Migration during the Industrial Period

The industrial period (1800–1914) was an especially important part of modern migration history. During the nineteenth century, New World nations—particularly Canada, the United States, Australia, New Zealand, Argentina, and South Africa—were eager for European migrants to help populate their lands and develop their economies. The migratory flow that took place during this period is not likely ever to be matched for magnitude, intensity, or impact on sending and receiving areas. According to Petersen (1975: 279), some 60 million Europeans settled in the Americas between 1800 and 1950, and perhaps another 7 million relocated to Australia and New Zealand. The key sending countries were Britain, Italy, Norway, Portugal, Spain, and Sweden. Between 1850 and 1914, emigration accounted for a cumulative loss of more than one-tenth of Europe's population (Easterlin, 1961a).

The European migration to the New World was propelled by interrelated demographic, economic, and social forces, both within Europe and between Europe and the New World. Among the forces identified by Easterlin (1961a) were increased population pressures in Europe and relatively low wages there compared with what could be earned in the emerging nations of the New World. The economic prosperity of the New World, most notably of the United States, was a strong 'pull' factor enticing many immigrants from various parts of Europe. The Industrial Revolution, which destabilized Europe's rural economies, also played a major role: while some of those who were left out of work during the shift to manufacturing managed to find jobs in the factories, many others decided to seek opportunities overseas (Hatton and Williamson, 1994, 1998; D. Thomas, 1941; B. Thomas, 1954). Once these settlers became established in their adoptive countries, they encouraged other family members to join them. For prospective migrants, this type of social networking helped to reduce the financial and psychological costs of migration and settlement in a new land. By the late 1800s, however, demographic and economic pressures within Europe were diminishing in strength as stimulants of emigration. Emigration became less desirable as wages and living conditions in Europe began to catch up with those in the New World. As a result, the European attraction to the New World waned, and emigration rates fell sharply even before the outbreak of the First World War. It is interesting to note that emigration contributed somewhat to this convergence of wages and living standards between Europe and the New World by effectively transferring socioeconomic inequalities from Europe to the New World. Once in the new country, newcomers would take their place at the bottom of the receiving country's income and occupational hierarchy.

Migration during the Interwar Period

Together, the two world wars (1914–18 and 1939–45) and the Great Depression of the 1930s severely limited international migration during the first half of the twentieth century. Major receiving countries like the United States and Canada, believing that nationals should have priority access to whatever work was available, set legal restrictions on immigration. Some governments, including those of the US and France, even encouraged foreign residents to return to their own countries (Taft, 1936). In Canada, the number of newcomers in 1931 was just 27,530, down from 135,982 in 1926, and by the start of World War II, in 1939, the annual total was a mere 9,329—the lowest in Canadian history (see Figure 9.4).

Although voluntary migration was limited during this period, the two world wars uprooted and displaced massive numbers of people from their homelands, in Europe and elsewhere. For instance, in Asia Minor, the Russian Empire, and the Balkans, the deportation of entire peoples after the First World War amounted to a kind of ethnic cleansing. The Ottoman-led expulsion of Armenians from Turkey, in what is known as the Armenian Holocaust, is but one instance that occurred during this time. This kind of forced

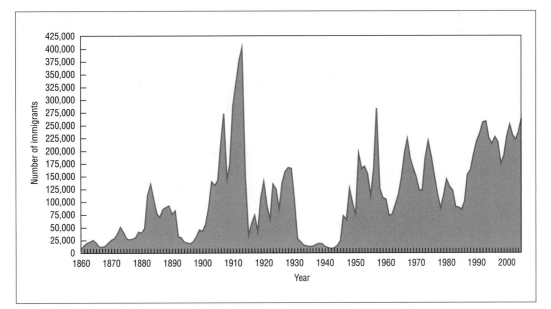

Figure 9.4

(continued)

Where immigrants came from (top 10)

1913		1957		1974		1991		2001	
Origin	%	Origin	%	Origin	%	Origin	%	Origin	%
UK	37.4	UK	38.6	UK	17.6	Hong Kong	9.7	China	16.1
US	34.5	Hungary	11.2	US	12.1	Poland	6.8	India	11.1
Russian	4.6	Germany	10.0	Portugal	7.4	China	6.0	Pakistan	6.1
Ukrainian	4.3	Italy	9.8	India	5.8	India	5.6	Philippines	5.2
Italian	4.1	Netherlands	4.2	Hong Kong	5.8	Philippines	5.3	Rep. Korea	3.8
Chinese	1.8	US	3.9	Jamaica	5.1	Lebanon	5.2	US	2.4
Hebrew Russian	1.5	Denmark	2.7	Philippines	4.3	Vietnam	3.9	Iran	2.3
German	1.2	France	2.0	Ireland	2.3	UK	3.3	Romania	2.2
Bulgarian	1.1	Austria	2.0	Haiti	2.2	El Salvador	3.0	Sri Lanka	2.2
Polish Russian	1.1	Greece	1.9	Trinidad&Tobago	2.2	Sri Lanka	3.0	UK	2.1
Total	**404,432**	**Total**	**282,164**	**Total**	**218,465**	**Total**	**228,557**	**Total**	**250,346**

Where immigrants settled (region)

Region	%	Region	%	Region	%	Region	%	Region	%
BC	14.8	BC	13.3	BC	15.7	BC	13.8	BC	15.3
Prairies	35.3	Prairies	13.1	Prairies	10.9	Prairies	10.9	Prairies	9.2
Ontario	31.1	Ontario	52.1	Ontario	55.0	Ontario	51.4	Ontario	59.3
Quebec	14.9	Quebec	19.5	Quebec	15.3	Quebec	22.4	Quebec	15.0
Atlantic	3.7	Atlantic	1.8	Atlantic	2.8	Atlantic	1.3	Atlantic	1.2

Figure 9.4 Immigration to Canada, 1867–2005 (*continued*)

Source: *The Globe and Mail* (1992, 2003); Citizenship and Immigration Canada (2002, 2005b, 2006).

displacement, representing a systematic attempt to exterminate an entire ethic community, has unfortunately been seen, both previously and since, in many other times and in many different contexts (see Charny, 1999). In the 1930s, the Japanese invasion of Manchuria forced many Chinese to flee. In the 1940s, following the Fascist victory in the Spanish Civil War, large numbers of Spaniards were forced to leave the country. And during Stalin's regime in the Soviet Union, there were large-scale deportations of different categories of peoples, like the close to 2 million kulaks (land owners, viewed as the enemies of the workers), who were moved to labour camps in Siberia (Polian, 2004). In the context of the Second World War, an estimated 7 million people threatened by the Nazi regime fled their homes, many of them Jews, the population that, at the hands of the Third Reich, suffered the worst genocide in history (Charny, 1999; Kraft, 2005).

Migration in the Post-industrial Period

Migration history since the Second World War may be divided into two periods. First, from 1945 to roughly 1970, the countries of the Western world needed migrant labour to help rebuild their economies. During this period, many people from peripheral areas of the Mediterranean region (Italy, Spain, Portugal, Greece, Turkey) migrated to the industrialized north, particularly to countries such as West Germany, Belgium, France, Austria, Switzerland, the Netherlands, England, and Wales, which had recently established 'guestworker' systems. These countries also saw a large influx of workers from their former colonies. During this time there was also a heavy amount of permanent settlement migration to Canada, the United States, and Australia (Castles and Miller, 2003).

The second period may be said to have begun in 1973, when a severe oil shortage sparked a major economic recession that subsequently led to a fundamental restructuring of the world economy. Castle and Miller identify a number of ways in which this development significantly altered migratory movements, including

- changes in global investment patterns, with increased capital exports from developed countries and the establishment of manufacturing industries in some previously underdeveloped areas;
- the micro-electronic revolution, which reduced the need for manual workers in manufacturing;
- the erosion of traditional skilled manual occupations in highly developed countries;
- the expansion of the service sector, with increased demand for both highly skilled and low-skilled workers;
- the growth of informal sectors in the economies of developed countries;
- the 'casualization' of employment, with increasing part-time work and less secure employment conditions; and
- increased differentiation of labour forces on the basis of gender, age, and ethnicity, through mechanisms that have pushed many women, young people, and members of ethnic minorities into casual or informal-sector work while forcing workers with outmoded skills into early retirement.

To adapt to this configuration of globalizing forces, corporations throughout the industrialized world have tried to restructure and to find ways to reduce costs—notably by exporting manufacturing operations to the developing countries, where growing populations with minimal economic prospects are eager to be given factory work, even at very low wages. In some developing regions, this has had important transformative effects, leading to rapid industrialization and economic development; the development of the Organization of Petroleum Exporting Countries in the Gulf Region is an early example. In other developing regions, such as Africa, the pace of economic growth has been less impressive.

In western Europe, the dawn of globalization in the post-industrial period had a devastating effect on the migrant workers of the 1950s and 1960s, who for the most part had limited education and few skills beyond those required for their work, mainly in manufacturing and construction. Rates of unemployment among these immigrants increased significantly, and many older workers became permanently jobless (Therborn, 1987). To cope with demographic aging and a labour force that was shrinking during the 1970s, 1980s, and 1990s, many of these western European countries adopted a second generation of policies designed to entice workers from abroad to settle on a temporary basis.

Overall, immigration has intensified dramatically since the early 1970s, thanks largely to globalization, with all regions of the globe (and a far broader range of both sending and receiving areas) participating in one way or another. The increasing global demand for labour and the relative ease of modern transportation make it possible for people in many parts of the world beyond Europe to emigrate. The majority of immigrants to major receiving countries, including Canada, the US, Germany, France, Belgium, Switzerland, Sweden, and the United Kingdom, now come from the developing world: Africa, Asia, Latin America, and the former Soviet Bloc countries of eastern Europe. At the same time, nations that traditionally exported immigrants—countries like Italy, Spain, Greece, and Portugal—are now receiving immigrants themselves (Coleman, 2002; Therborn, 1987). Oil-rich countries like Saudi Arabia and Kuwait have been importing labour, much of it from developing countries, to work in their growing oil-based economies. And since the 1980s, there has been much more active migration to, from, and within the newly industrializing centres of Asia—South Korea, Taiwan, Hong Kong, Singapore, Malaysia, and Thailand. Figure 9.5 shows the major migratory flows since the 1970s.

The major features of international migration since the late twentieth century can be summarized as follows (Castles and Miller, 2003):

1. Migration has become a global process as opposed to a localized regional phenomenon.
2. The volume and pace of international migration have reached unprecedented levels.
3. Migration has become increasingly differentiated, as migrants to receiving countries are ethnically and racially heterogeneous.
4. Immigration no longer is male-dominated, as women are increasingly participating in transnational movements (owing in part to the growing demand for female labour in

French lawmakers recently passed a controversial bill calling for language exams and potential DNA testing for prospective immigrants to France. The DNA amendment, which is meant to ensure that claims of family ties are true, was added as a way to guard against visa-seekers using fraudulent papers, a practice that is common in some African countries. While the expensive test is optional, critics fear it may be viewed as mandatory by those hoping to join family members in France. Opponents of French President Nicolas Sarkozy's conservative government argue that the new legislation is actually a sop to France's extreme right-wing movement, headed by Jean-Marie Le Pen, an ardent anti-immigration spokesperson (Schuck, 2007). This example shows how immigration has become highly politicized since the late twentieth century.

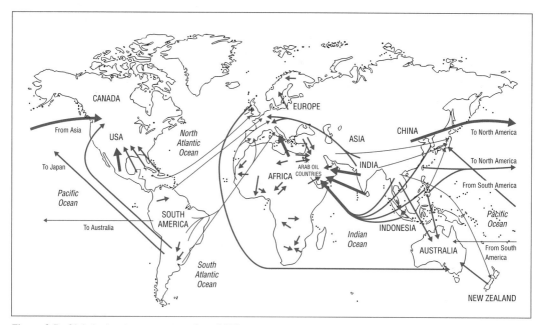

Figure 9.5 Global migratory movements from 1973

Note: Arrow dimensions give only a rough indication of the size of the movement.

Source: Castles and Miller (2003): 6, Figure 10. From Stephen Castles and Mark J. Miller, *The Age of Migration: International Population Movements in the Modern World*, published in 2003 by Palgave Macmillan. Reproduced by permisison of Guilford Press and Palgrave Macmillan.

certain economic sectors and to family reunification policies implemented by some major receiving countries).

5. Immigration has become highly politicized, especially in the major receiving countries, where the public hold perceptions that immigration threatens national security and challenges host nations' sense of nationhood. Some European countries have taken controversial measures to curb immigration, partly in response to such fears.

Theories of International Migration

Systems Perspective

Kritz, Lim, and Zlotnik (1992) point out that the world today is characterized by a number of *migration systems*: ongoing patterns of migratory exchange in which some countries and regions function as core immigration magnets and others as peripheral sending areas. In the North American migration system, for instance, the United States, and to a lesser extent Canada, are the core receiving countries, while Mexico, parts of Central and South America, and a number of countries in Asia and Europe are the primary sending areas, with relatively minor counterstreams from the two core countries to these other parts of the world. This particular system has existed for some time and is likely to continue indefinitely.

Massey and associates (1998) identify four principal systems, in addition to the North American one, centring on Europe, the Gulf states, the Asia–Pacific region, and South America. Each system has its own unique dynamics, but there are some common features as well. How did these systems develop? What are the root causes of international migration today? Though no single theory explains everything, different theories focusing on different dimensions can provide valuable insight into the complex nature of international migration, its determinants, and its consequences.

Kritz, Lim, and Zlotnik (1992: 3) note that each migration system is situated within particular contexts (social, political, demographic, economic). These contexts, conditioned largely by previous migrations and policies in the core and peripheral countries, dictate the extent of migratory flows in a system. For example, immigration laws may be restricted and then relaxed under conditions of economic downturns and upturns in the core nation. Historical links between core and periphery, such as those that exist among many European nations and their former colonies, will have some bearing on migration flows. The demographic context becomes particularly important when labour shortages in the core nations spark a demand for workers from countries in the periphery, especially those with labour surpluses.

Economic and Sociological Perspectives

In their review of migration theories, Massey and colleagues (1993) begin with *neoclassical economics*, according to which migration decisions are driven primarily by differences in economic opportunities between sending (peripheral) and receiving (core) countries. The idea that workers in peripheral countries are motivated by the desire for employment in countries that offer higher wages implies that international migration will continue if wage differentials persist and diminish if they decrease. Theorists in the neoclassical economics tradition (e.g., Harris and Todaro, 1970: Sjaastad, 1962; Todaro, 1969) believe that the possibility exists for migration between the established sending and receiving countries to cease at some point in the future, since the intensification of migration over time will result in lower wages in the destination country while at the same time reducing the supply of labour in the sending country. Meanwhile, wages in the sending country will gradually rise as a result of remittances (that is, money sent home by those who have emigrated) and economic development. Over time, wage levels in the two countries will converge, and the need for emigration will diminish accordingly. In general, then, migration as seen from this perspective is the consequence of uneven economic development across countries and therefore uneven distribution of capital and labour. Although this explanation is usually developed at the macro level, it can also be used at the micro level to explain how individuals, perceiving differences between countries or regions, understand the potential gains and losses associated with moving or not moving.

Essentially, the neoclassical economics theory is the one used earlier in this chapter to explain the course of the great European migration to the New World. But it has some limitations. First, given the wide income disparities that exist between regions, it suggests that migration rates around the world ought to be much higher than they are; but as we have already noted, only about 3 per cent of the world's people are migrants. Second, it does not take into account non-economic factors such as state policies that prevent the free movement of labour across borders. In fact, it says nothing at all about the role of the state. And although it implies that governments in sending and/or receiving countries can control immigration by influencing labour markets, it does not specify how this might be done (Massey et al., 1998). Nor does it recognize the role played by earlier emigrants who persuade other family members and friends to join them and facilitate their migration by providing information and assistance.

A more recent take on this theory (Stark, 1997) shifts the emphasis from the macro level of core–periphery differences to the micro level of the family seeking to diversify its sources of income and minimize its exposure to risk—a particular concern in developing countries, where insurance to safeguard against calamities such as crop failure or unemployment is either non-existent or too costly for the majority of people. One way of reducing risk is to have some family members working in the local economy and others working in foreign labour markets. A family using this strategy might be able to ride out a period of economic difficulty at home with the help of remittances from abroad. At the same time, financial support from abroad might enable a family to improve its situation without having to borrow money from a bank; this strategy might be especially useful in countries where capital markets are weak, access to banking may be difficult, and a family may not have adequate collateral to secure a loan.

In emphasizing 'push' factors such as the need to reduce risk and the desire for institutional features such as insurance and bank loans, the 'new economics' perspective suggests that migration could well continue even if wage differentials between sending and receiving countries were eliminated. It also suggests that immigrant remittances could tend to accentuate socioeconomic inequalities in the local community, as receiving families would use the income to raise their standard of living and invest in livestock, equipment, schooling, and so on. One consequence of this process might be to generate feelings of relative deprivation among other households in the community. This in turn would generate further waves of immigration, as other families seek to close the wealth gap between themselves and the families of previous migrants (Zlotnik, 2006).

A related perspective focuses on the social networks that link migrants to family and friends back home. *Network theory* defines networks as interpersonal ties based on commonality of background, relations, and obligations (Boyd, 1990). As the numbers of international migrants increase, so do the numbers of social networks in operation, creating strong synergetic forces that promote additional migration. In this process, known as *cumulative causation*, each act of migration from the local community alters the social context within which subsequent migration decisions are made, typically in ways that make additional movement more likely.

By contrast, *dual labour market theory* focuses on the 'pull' side of the equation, specifically capitalist societies' chronic need for foreign labour (Piore, 1979). For proponents of this theory, immigration is due primarily to pull factors in the receiving societies rather than push factors in the sending areas. It is the inescapable need for foreign labour in wealthy nations that stimulates immigration.

One of the key reasons for this need is the demography of advanced capitalist societies. As the average age of these populations continues to rise, certain sectors of their workforce will shrink over time. This is especially true of the entry level, where wages are typically below average. In the past, industrial economies could rely on teenagers and women to fill those low-paying jobs, because work for these social categories was typically transient. In recent decades, however, the pool of entry-level workers has shrunk considerably as a result of two factors: first, the long-term decline in fertility and the extension of formal schooling, both of which have reduced the number of teenagers entering the labour force; and, second, the urbanization of society, which has virtually eliminated rural areas as a source of entry-level labour. The imbalance between demand and supply at this level increases the long-term demand for foreign workers in industrial societies.

According to dual labour market theory other structural features of advanced economies that serve to promote reliance on immigration include the following:

1. *Structural inflation.* Highly skilled workers wish to maintain their pay superiority in relation to those in the middle and lower ranks of the occupational hierarchy. This means that a rise in wages at the lower levels of the workforce would necessitate a wage increase at the upper levels. Employers get around this problem by hiring foreign workers who are willing to accept low wages. Similarly, immigrants may be more willing than others to accept low-status jobs.
2. *Economic dualism.* Advanced economies are characterized by variable demand for and supply of goods. When demand is high, employers can hire temporary or seasonal workers; then, when demand falls, these seasonal workers can be laid off. Thus, a dual economy develops in which workers in the capital-intensive part of the economy have stable jobs, and those at the seasonal end of the labour force have unstable jobs. Workers in the stable sector tend to be unionized, which means that they cannot be easily laid off, and employers typically have invested heavily in their training. Under sub-optimal market conditions, therefore, employers will lay off those in the lower ranks, the seasonal workers and the non-unionized workers, many of whom are immigrants.
3. *Ethnic enclaves.* Over time, advanced capitalist societies with large immigrant populations have seen the development of *ethnic enclaves* that foster ethnic economies within the larger economy. Ethnic entrepreneurs establish businesses and hire successive waves of immigrants from the same country. This process tends to reproduce itself: once established, some immigrants from the ethnic enclaves go on to launch their own ethnic businesses, generating new demand for immigration.

The dual labour market theory assumes that international labour migration is largely demand-based, initiated by employers in developed societies, or by governments acting on their behalf. Therefore the governments of advanced societies are unlikely to promote international migration policies that might disrupt the wage or employment structures in their countries.

Finally, *world systems theory* explains international migration as a response to the expansion of the capitalist economy into the 'peripheral' (i.e., developing) regions of the world. World systems theorists maintain that this process has been under way and gaining in intensity since the sixteenth century (Braudel, 1979; Wallerstein, 1974). Driven to constantly increase their profits and wealth, capitalist firms enter ('penetrate') poor countries on the periphery of the world economy in search of raw materials, labour, and new consumer markets. In the past this market penetration was facilitated by colonial regimes that co-operated with the colonizing powers. Today multinational firms exert influence through their investments in developing economies, and are assisted by neocolonial governments and national elites who in return for their co-operation receive development assistance and in some cases personal gain.

With the spread of capitalism from its centres in western Europe, North America, Oceania, and Japan, an increasing proportion of the world's population is being incorporated into the global market economy. And as those people in peripheral regions leave rural agricultural areas for the cities in search of work in the new economy (thus contributing to over-urbanization and urban poverty), others are drawn abroad. In the process, an uprooted proletariat is created that then becomes a part of the international movement of labour to the core capitalist economies. And as we have already seen in connection with migration systems, cultural and historical linkages between core and peripheral regions also facilitate migration, so that many developing nations and one-time colonies of Western countries have linkages that promote migration to the former imperial powers.

In short, the world systems theory sees the core countries' domination (*hegemony*) of the peripheral regions as a multidimensional phenomenon involving past as well as present political, economic, and cultural influences. Seen in this context, international migration has little to do with wage rates or employment differentials between countries. Rather, it is a product of the expansion of markets within a global political and economic hierarchy. One weakness of the world systems explanation is its vast scope. In this sweeping perspective, migration is only a small (though important) part of the picture, and some of the finer points highlighted by other theories are inevitably missed. Finally, the world systems theory does not differentiate between the var-

Hegemony is a concept closely associated with the Italian political scientist Antonio Gramsci (1891–1937). It refers to a particular kind of dominance that one social group or system exerts over another, in which the ruling group or system (the *hegemon*) acquires some degree of consent from the subordinate, rather than having to exert dominance purely by force.

ieties of international migration. Thus, it does not recognize the fact that transnational migration today can take a number of forms besides the one associated with capitalist penetration of peripheral regions.

Other Factors

The State

Each of the theories reviewed here has something of value to say about the determinants of international migration. None of them, however, directly or systematically addresses the role that the state plays in migration. If it were not for modern states' regulation of migration (through their immigration policies), the numbers of international migrants around the world would be significantly larger than they are. We noted earlier that, despite the inequalities that exist around the globe, fewer than 3 per cent of the world's people took part in international migration in 2005 (United Nations Department of Economic and Social Affairs Population Division, 2006b). According to Zolberg (1981), the reason this percentage is so low is that the world is organized into mutually exclusive and legally sovereign states. As sociopolitical entities, states try to maximize the well-being of their citizens both by forging trade and immigration agreements with one another and by controlling the flow of outsiders across their borders and determining who will and will not be allowed to gain citizenship. In fact, every modern state has laws and regulations stipulating the conditions under which foreigners will be allowed entry.

Transnationalism

Transnationalism is the name given to the relatively new tendency among immigrants to retain multiple national identities. Together, the reality of globalization, the ease of travel, and the speed of communication technologies, combined with the desire of many immigrants to maintain social, cultural, and even economic ties to their countries of origin, have fostered a strong sense of belonging to two (or more) worlds simultaneously. One of the terms used to refer to this phenomenon is *diaspora*.

In English, the term *diaspora* originally referred specifically to the dispersion of the Jewish people, beginning about the sixth century BCE. More recently it has been applied to the Africans who were forcibly transported to the New World as slaves, and to the Armenians who were driven from their homes in the Ottoman Empire during and immediately after the First World War (Cohen, 1997: ix; Sheffer, 2003). The displacement of Palestinians following the creation of Israel in 1948 may be viewed as a further example of diaspora.

Common to all diasporic communities is the experience of displacement, forcible or voluntary, from an 'old country' that retains some claim on the loyalty and emotions of those displaced, as well as 'a sense of co-ethnicity with others of a similar background' (Cohen, 1997: xi).

In the contemporary literature *diaspora* generally refers to ethnic minorities that maintain strong sentimental and material links with their countries of origin while gradually adopting a new identification with the host society. The persistence of an emotional attachment to the homeland is not new, of course. What is different today is the ease with which emigrants are able to maintain their connections not only with their home countries but with their fellow emigrants living in other host countries. Immigrants seeking economic advancement and social recognition are typically active in a variety of spheres—cultural, social, economic, political—and may pursue those interests in both their original and adopted countries. In this way dense networks are created across political borders by people who live a kind of dual life, moving easily between cultures and in some cases even maintaining homes in two countries.

This concept of *transnationalism* defies the usual notion of immigration as a matter of leaving one's own country to settle permanently in a new society. It also raises the question whether transnational migrants can be described as citizens at all in the usual sense of the term—as persons who participate in one particular society and identify with one particular state. Closely related to the contemporary concept of *diaspora* is the notion of *transnational communities* whose members live between nations and may not feel much allegiance to any one nation as such. If the trend towards transnationalism and multiple citizenship continues, the sense of attachment to any one country may become increasingly instrumental rather than emotional. Ultimately, it may become necessary to rethink what it means to be a citizen in a globalizing world. (For further insights into transnationalism, see Braziel and Mannur, 2003; Levitt, DeWind, and Vertovec, 2003; Satzewich and Wong, 2006.)

The term *diaspora* has had several meanings through history. Cohen (1997) notes that the term is derived from the Greek verb *speiro* (to sow), and the preposition *dia* (over). The ancient Greeks thought of diaspora in the context of migration and colonization. For the Jewish people, Africans, Armenians, and Palestinians, however, Cohen suggests that the term has more sinister connotations of collective trauma, banishment, and exile. In recent years some other peoples who have also maintained strong collective identities despite being scattered around the world have adopted the term *diaspora* for themselves, even though they have been neither agents of colonization nor victims of persecution.

Immigrant Integration in Host Societies

Another important aspect of migration not addressed in the theories reviewed so far is the reception that immigrants receive in their new countries and the process by which they become integrated, both as individuals and as groups. Some receiving societies have opted for full integration, allowing newcomers equal access to all the benefits enjoyed by the native-born population and making it relatively easy to gain full citizenship. Others are not so accommodating. Different citizenship rules reflect different national ideologies and may have little or nothing to do with the origins or characteristics of migrants themselves.

There are two basic principles that citizenship ideologies—hence models of immigrant integration—may follow: the 'law of the blood' (*jus sanguinis*) and the 'law of the land' (*jus soli*). According to the first of these ideologies, what matters is ethnicity—common descent or blood ties. According to the second, what matters is the territory in which one is born (Castles and Miller, 2003; Koser, 2007).

In practice, as Table 9.3 shows, most modern states combine these two principles, although one or the other tends to be dominant. An exception is Israel, where *jus sanguinis* is the only principle of citizenship. This means that in awarding Israeli citizenship, preference is given to Jews over members of all other ethnic or religious groups. Israel's Law of Return, in conjunction with its citizenship law, grants automatic citizenship to Jewish immigrants to the country. Through these laws, Israel gives priority to Jews over the many Palestinians who fled or were driven from the country during wars in 1948 and 1967. In addition, Israel's marriage law treats Israeli citizens of Palestinian origin (i.e., Israeli Arabs) as second-class citizens. Israeli Arabs who marry Palestinian residents of the West Bank or Gaza must abandon Israel to live with their families, since the law does not permit the reunification of families split between Israel and the occupied territories. This makes it very difficult for Palestinians in the occupied territories to join their spouses in Israel, but promotes the movement from Israel of Israeli Arabs

Table 9.3   Citizenship rules in selected countries

Country	Principle underlying citizenship	Period of residence for naturalization	Dual nationality allowed
Australia	Combination	3 years	Yes
Austria	*Jus sanguinis*	10 years	No
Belgium	Combination	5 years	Yes
Canada	*Jus soli*	3 years	Yes
France	*Jus sanguinis*	5 years	No
Germany	*Jus sanguinis* until 2000, combined with *jus soli* thereafter	8 years	No
Israel	Open to any resident Jew	0	Yes
Netherlands	*Jus sanguinis*	5 years	Yes
Sweden	*Jus sanguinis*	5 years	No
United Kingdom	Combination	5 years	Yes
United States	*Jus soli*	5 years	Yes

Source: Adapted from Koser (2007): 24. Reprinted by permission of Oxford University Press.

who wish to join their spouses and families in the occupied territories (Mariner, 2003).

An interesting example is that of Germany, which has recently changed its citizenship laws to include *jus soli* as a basis for obtaining citizenship. Prior to 2000, the country's citizenship laws were based on the *jus sanguinis* principle of descent. As a result, before the new law was passed, the children and grandchildren of post-war migrant workers (many of whom were from Turkey) were excluded from citizenship, even though most of them had been born and raised in Germany. The *jus sanguinis* principle also meant that when East and West Germany were reunified after the fall of the Berlin Wall, ethnic Germans who had lived outside the country for generations (mostly in eastern Europe and the former Soviet Union) were automatically granted German citizenship. By contrast, in countries such as Canada, the United States, Australia, and the United Kingdom—all of which follow the *jus soli* principle—a child born to a legal immigrant is automatically entitled to full citizenship. With its new law, Germany joins these and many other countries in granting citizenship based on the *jus soli* principle.

Most countries allow migrants who have been legally resident for a certain number of years to become 'naturalized' citizens. The principle behind this practice is known as *jus domicile*. In Canada and Australia, the residence requirement is three years; elsewhere (e.g., in Austria and Germany) it may be as long as eight or ten years. Some countries (like Canada) permit dual nationality, but others (Austria, for instance) demand that migrants give up their original nationality as a condition for acquiring citizenship.

The extent to which immigrants are expected to assimilate to their new society varies. In some countries, newcomers are expected to give up their original cultures and adopt the host culture as their own. In others, immigrants are legally permitted to pursue and maintain their own languages and cultures. These two very different situations correspond to two opposite models of immigrant integration: *assimilation* and *multiculturalism*. In *assimilationist* contexts, immigrants are expected to give up their distinctive linguistic, cultural, and social characteristics in order to blend in with the majority host population. A variation on this theme is the *republican* model, which sees the nation based on a constitution and a system of laws defining citizenship, and which is therefore willing to accept newcomers as long as they abide fully by the political rules and are prepared to adopt the culture of the receiving nation (Castles and Miller, 2003; Koser, 2007: 23). The *multicultural* model differs from the republican model in that it does not demand assimilation from immigrants; instead, it accepts and promotes existing cultural differences among subgroups in the population (Castles and Miller, 2003).

Historically, Canada, the US, and Australia have relied on immigration as part of their nation-building strategy, and have generally encouraged permanent settlement, at least among immigrants from 'desirable' countries of origin. Therefore, the official policies of these countries have shifted over time away from assimilation and towards multiculturalism. By contrast, countries that do not seek immigrants

In 2000, Germany adopted the *jus soli* principle and reformed its citizenship policy so that the German-born children of immigrants would automatically become German citizens. This reform was a long-overdue response to the fact that more than seven million foreigners had been living in Germany on a long-term basis—half of them had been German residents for at least 20 years. The new law also reduced the mandatory waiting period for naturalization. The principal intention behind these reforms was to facilitate the integration of immigrants into the civic community (German Embassy, London, 2007).

and whose laws make it difficult or impossible for immigrants to attain citizenship status have tended to foster the development of marginalized ethnic enclaves as opposed to fully integrated ethnic communities (Castles and Miller, 2003; Therborn, 1987).

Canadian Immigration History

In 2006, almost 20 per cent of Canada's population was foreign-born—the highest that figure has been in 75 years. The corresponding percentage in the United States is significantly lower (12.8 per cent), even though the US has the world's largest immigrant population in absolute terms (38.4 million) (see Table 9.4). Immigration has made Canada an ethnically and racially diverse society, consisting of three 'charter groups' (English, French, and Aboriginal) and a multitude of other nationalities.

Immigration and Nation-Building

Immigration has featured prominently in Canada's development as a nation. In its first century alone (1867–1967) it admitted an estimated eight million immigrants (Hawkins, 1988). Table 9.5 outlines the connections between

Table 9.4 The 20 countries or areas with the most international migrants in 2005

Country or area	Number of migrants (in millions)	Migrants as % of total migrants worldwide	Migrants as % of receiving country/ area's population
United States	38.4	20.2	12.8
Russian Federation	12.1	6.4	8.5
Germany	10.1	5.3	12.3
Ukraine	6.8	3.6	14.5
France	6.5	3.4	10.6
Saudi Arabia	6.4	3.3	26.6
Canada	6.1	3.2	18.7
India	5.7	3.0	0.5
United Kingdom	5.4	2.8	9.4
Spain	4.8	2.5	5.5
Australia	4.1	2.2	10.7
Pakistan	3.3	1.7	2.0
United Arab Emirates	3.2	1.7	65.3
Hong Kong, SAR[1] China	3.0	1.6	42.9
Israel	2.7	1.4	37.5
Italy	2.5	1.3	4.2
Kazakhstan	2.5	1.3	16.3
Côte d'Ivoire	2.4	1.2	6.1
Jordan	2.2	1.2	21.4
Japan	2.0	1.1	1.6
Total migrants worldwide	**191**	**3.0**	**100.0**

[1] Semi-autonomous region.

Source: Adapted from United Nations Department of Economic and Social Affairs Population Division (2006b): 3.

Table 9.5 Immigration and Canadian nation-building: sociopolitical, demographic, and economic contexts, pre-1850–present

Features	Pre-1850 period	1850–1950	1950–70	1970–present
Sociopolitical	English–French dualism; French and British seen as 'founding' ('charter') groups, Aboriginal people treated as subordinate. British and French define Canada as a Nation.	English–French dualism (the 'two solitudes'); Canada established as a nation (Confederation).	Canada as a democratic welfare state. Multiculturalism and bilingualism become official policies. Widening regional economic inequalities. British–French dualism; threat of Quebec separation.	English–French dualism continues, but with increasing recognition of Aboriginal people, the injustice done to them in the past, and the need to settle outstanding land claims and establish some form of self-government.
Social demographic	Ethnic composition mainly British and French.	British and French backgrounds still dominate, followed by other European origins (German, Italian, etc.).	British and French still dominate, but ethnic composition becomes increasingly diverse; Canada is increasingly seen as a land of immigrants and their descendants. In the 1960s 16 per cent of the total population was foreign-born.	Increasing ethnic diversity. 'Visible minority' becomes an official social category. Sustained low fertility in the post-baby boom years and increasing aging of the population.
Economic	Staples-based economy (e.g., fur trade) gives way to industrialization.	With industrialization, central Canada becomes economic centre. Increasing demand for labour attracts large-scale immigration from Europe. Settlement of the West (mass migration of Europeans).	Post-war economic recovery; rapid economic growth, periodic recessions starting in the early 1970s.	Annual immigration targets raised. Policy changes emphasize humanitarian principles (family reunification and refugees) and qualifications such as education and skills are central features of policy. Growing concerns of increased concentration of immigrants in the largest cities; post-9/11 security issues.
Immigration	Immigrants come from Britain, the US, north-western Europe.	British immigrants continue to dominate until after World War II. Active exclusion of some categories of immigrants. Significant wave of immigrants from southern Europe in the 1950s.	Immigration from southern Europe slows in the late 1960s as 'New Wave' immigration (non- European origins) begins. Non-discriminatory point system introduced in 1967. New policy emphasizes economic/demographic sustainability and humanitarian principles.	Most immigrants now come from Asia, Latin America, Africa, and the Caribbean. Refugees come from all regions of the world, including eastern Europe (breakup of Soviet Empire).

immigration and the major stages in Canada's economic and sociopolitical development. Conditions in the nineteenth century were particularly favourable to immigration, as the spread of industrialization created a rapidly growing demand for labour, and the new nation formed in 1867 sought to populate the vast territories to the west of Upper Canada. But interest in western settlement was limited: in 1891 the population living west of Ontario amounted to roughly 350,000—just 7.2 per cent of the country's population. It was not until the turn of the century, when the Laurier government began offering free land for homesteading, that prospective settlers flocked to the Prairies and British Columbia. According to McInnis (2000b: 533), this was one of the most important episodes in Canadian history, helping to trans-

Canada Immigration: Historical Highlights

Period	Development
1896–1905	The settlement of the West with an offer of free land results in large numbers of immigrants from the United Kingdom, Europe, and the United States
1906	Immigration Act
1910	Immigration Act
1913	400,000 immigrants arrive in Canada
1914–18	Immigration slump during World War I
1928	Opening of Halifax's Pier 21, the Atlantic gateway to Canada
1930s	Extremely low levels of immigration during the Depression years
1940s	During and after World War II, approximately 48,000 war brides and their 22,000 children arrive in Canada
1950s	Canada receives about one-and-a-half million immigrants from Europe
1952	Immigration Act
1956–7	Canada accepts 37,500 Hungarian refugees
1962	New immigration regulations are tabled to eliminate all discrimination based on race, religion, and national origin
1967	The government amends Canada's immigration policy and introduces the point system for the selection of skilled workers and business immigrants
1968–9	Canada takes in 11,000 Czechoslovakian refugees
1972	Canada resettles more than 6,175 Ugandan Asians
1973	Canada accepts more than 6,000 Chileans
1975–8	Canada resettles almost 9,000 Indochinese
1976	Immigration Act
1979–80	Refugees—'boat people'—from Vietnam, Cambodia, and Laos (137,000) arrive in Canada
1999	Canada accepts more than 7,000 Kosovars
2002	Immigration and Refugee Protection Act (IRPA)

Source: Citizenship and Immigration Canada website: http://www.cic.gc.ca/english/pub/index-2.html#statistics (accessed 15 Nov. 2005). Reproduced with the permission of the Minister of Public Works and Government Services Canada, 2007.

form Canada into a fully continental economy. As part of this movement, in 1913 alone Canada welcomed more than 400,000 immigrants—an annual total that remains unmatched to this day (see Figure 9.4 on page 405).

It is interesting to note that the periods with the highest volumes of immigration to Canada have not necessarily been the periods with the highest net migration figures. Between 1901 and 1921, for instance, immigration reached unprecedented levels, but emigration was also very high. Thus, net migration, while substantial, was actually lower than it has been in more recent years, when emigration rates have been much lower (McVey and Kalbach, 1995a: 100). The volume of emigration declined from over 66,000 in 1970–1 to just under 36,000 in 2004–5 (Verma, 2006; Statistics Canada, 2006a: 23).

As a consequence of the decline in fertility rates since the 1970s, international immigration has played an increasingly important role in Canada's population growth in recent years. Whereas net migration accounted for 37.1 per cent of total population growth between 1971 and 1976, its contribution between 1996 and 2001 was more than 60 per cent. In 2004–5, net international migration was responsible for more than 65 per cent of the country's population growth (Statistics Canada, 2006a: 2).

Change in the National Origins of Immigrants

In 1913, more than 70 per cent of the immigrants admitted to Canada came from the United Kingdom and the United States; the rest came mainly from Russia, Ukraine, Italy, China, Germany, Bulgaria, and Poland (see Figure 9.4). Europe would continue to account for the great majority of immigrants through to the 1960s.

The return of peace following the end of the Second World War brought an increase in immigration to Canada. In the context of a booming economy, over 430,000 immigrants were admitted between 1946 and 1950, exceeding the numbers in the preceding 15 years. Legislative amendments to the Immigration Act provided for the admission of people who had been displaced during the war, and the toll taken on Europe's economy by the heavy costs of waging war meant that people from different parts of Europe were seeking to emigrate; Canada was an attractive destination.

During the 1950s, European immigrants continued to come to Canada in large numbers, including many from southern Europe. The peak year for immigration was 1957, when Canada received over 282,000 immigrants. More than 31,000 Hungarians were admitted, mostly on humanitarian grounds, after the uprising of 1956. Italians, Germans, Dutch, and Portuguese continued to arrive in large numbers until the early 1970s.

By the late 1980s, western Europe and the United States together accounted for only about one-third of Canada's immigrants; another third came from Asia, and the remaining third from the rest of the world, especially South America, the Caribbean, Central America, and eastern Europe. At the root of this shift was the new Immigration Act adopted in 1967, which introduced a new point system for assessing applicants. Potential immigrants were to be judged and assigned a score on the basis of their education and skills, rather than on characteristics such as ethnicity or national background, which had been used as immigration criteria in the past. The official policy of multiculturalism, introduced just four years later, in 1971, was designed to promote equality among Canada's three founding cultures (Aboriginal, French, and English) and the growing number of groups of other ethnic backgrounds. Further revisions to the Immigration Act, in 1990, reflected the growing sense that immigration numbers had to increase if Canada was to avoid significant labour shortages in the future. Currently, annual immigration targets are in the range of 250,000—a significant increase over the target of 100,000 set in 1967, when Canada's population was just over 20 million as compared to 33 million today.

During the first two decades of the twentieth century, Canada passed a number of immigration Acts that were clearly discriminatory. They were meant to bar entry to nationalities or races that the government at the time considered undesirable. Two examples illustrate the racist elements inherent in Canadian immigration law during this time.

The first case concerns immigrants from China. After the Canadian Pacific Railroad was completed in 1885, the many Chinese workers that had been recruited to help build the railway were no longer wanted in Canada. The Chinese Immigration Act of 1885, which imposed a $50 fee on any Chinese person entering Canada, was part of an effort to restrict further immigration of settlers from China, including spouses and children of those already in the country. When the new fee failed to stem Chinese immigration, it was raised, in 1900, to $100, and just three years later to $500. (By comparison, today's Right of Landing fee is only $490.) Because some Chinese immigration continued in spite of these prohibitive entry fees, the Canadian government in 1923 passed the Chinese Exclusion Act, which banned Chinese immigration altogether; it was not repealed until 1947, when, in the aftermath of World War II, the Canadian government felt it could no longer abide by such a discriminatory policy directed against a specific nationality.

The second case that illustrates the government's orientation to 'undesirables' involved immigrants from India. The *Komagata Maru* was a Japanese steamliner that in 1914 arrived in Vancouver from Hong Kong via Shanghai and a number of other ports along the way. Among the passengers were 342 Sikhs, 24 Muslims, and 12 Hindus, all subjects of the British Empire. After two months of deliberation, during which the ship's passengers suffered deteriorating conditions in limbo offshore, Canadian authorities barred the immigrants from landing, and the ship was turned back. This shameful incident is viewed by many historians of a prime example of Canada's early-twentieth-century 'White Canada' policy.

In 1967, Canada's new Immigration Act struck down all references to 'preferred nationalities, ethnicities or races', heralding a new era of immigration policy driven mainly by Canada's desire to expand demographically while espousing humanitarian principles.

Meanwhile, the range of sending areas has continued to become more varied. In 1991, Hong Kong contributed almost 10 per cent of all immigrants to Canada. The only 'traditional' sending country in the top ten was the United Kingdom, which ranked eighth that year, just ahead of El Salvador and Sri Lanka. By the turn of the new millennium, the majority of immigrants came from Asia, Africa, and Latin America. The top four source countries in 2006 were China, India, the Philippines, and Pakistan (Citizenship and Immigration Canada, 2006: 19).

These figures notwithstanding, immigration has had a relatively minor impact on the ethnic composition of Canada's population as a whole. In 2001, with one or two notable exceptions, the rank order of the top ten ethnic groups had not changed appreciably over past censuses since 1951: British and French continued to rank first and second among the reported ethnic backgrounds, followed by Scottish, Irish, German, and Italian (see Table 9.6). The shift in the major source countries of immigrants in recent decades has changed the composition of the foreign-born population, however. One of the most important developments in this regard has been the growth of visible minorities in Canada.

Geographic Distribution of Immigrants

In 2001, roughly 60 per cent of all immigrant arrivals went to Ontario; Quebec and British Columbia each attracted about 15 per cent, the

Table 9.6   Top 10 ethnic origins[1], Canada, 2001 and 1996

	2001			1996			% change 1996– 2001[2]
Ethnic origin	Population	%	Ethnic origin	Population	%		
Canadian	11,682,680	39.4	Canadian	8,806,275	30.9		32.7
English	5,978,875	20.2	English	6,832,095	23.9		−12.5
French	4,668,410	15.8	French	5,597,845	19.6		−16.6
Scottish	4,157,215	14.0	Scottish	4,260,840	14.9		−2.4
Irish	3,822,660	12.9	Irish	3,767,610	13.2		1.5
German	2,742,765	9.3	German	2,757,140	9.7		−0.5
Italian	1,270,369	4.3	Italian	1,207,475	4.2		5.2
Chinese	1,094,700	3.7	Ukrainian	1,026,475	3.6		4.3
Ukrainian	1,071,055	3.6	Chinese	921,585	3.2		18.8
North American Indian	1,000,890	3.4	Dutch (Netherlands)	916,215	3.2		
Total	29,639,030	100	Total	28,528,125	100		3.9

[1] Table shows total responses. Because some respondents reported more than one ethnic origin, the sum is greater than the total population or 100 per cent.

[2] Calculated on the basis of the difference between population figures for 1996 and 2001.

Source: Statistics Canada (2003b). Adapted from Statistics Canada publication *2001 Canada's Ethnocultural Portrait: The Changing Mosaic.* Catalogue no. 96F0030XIE2001008, p. 45.

Prairies about 9, and the Atlantic provinces just a little over 1 per cent (see Figure 9.4). This uneven distribution reflects longstanding regional discrepancies in economic development (Sitwell and Seifried, 1984). Ontario's dominance as a destination was firmly established by the second decade of the twentieth century.

In every region, newcomers generally choose to settle in large urban centres. Two reasons in particular account for this pattern. First is the strong 'pull' of established ethnic communities in the city, where others of the same national background can assist in the settlement process; second is the wide availability of jobs, amenities, and resources, both within the ethnic economy itself and within the larger context of the city (Fong, 2005; Fong and Shibuya, 2005; Hou, 2004).

Table 9.7 shows the distribution of immigrants, by period of immigration, across the census metropolitan areas of Toronto, Montreal, and Vancouver in 2001. Roughly 37 per cent of all immigrants in Canada lived in Toronto, just over 11 per cent in Montreal, and just under 14 per cent in Vancouver. Together these three CMAs were home to approximately 62 per cent of Canada's foreign-born population. The majority of those born in Europe arrived before 1980. In Toronto, 53 per cent of European immigrants arrived before 1971, while the majority of those from Central and South America, the Caribbean, Africa, and Asia came as part of the post-1970 wave. The same general patterns can be seen in Montreal and Vancouver. These data confirm the ethnic diversity of Canada's major urban centres.

The 2006 census shows that these three cities together are home to nearly 3.9 million immigrants, an increase of almost 15 per cent from 2001. The total number of immigrants in Canada in 2006 was 6.18 million. Together,

Table 9.7　Distribution of immigrants by period of immigration to Canada in the CMAs of Toronto, Montreal, and Vancouver, 2001

CMA and region of birth	Total immigrants	<1961	1961–70	1971–80	1981–90	1991–2001	1991–95	1996–2001
Toronto total	**2,032,960**	11.0	12.4	16.9	20.8	39.0	18.5	20.4
United States	37,790	11.6	18.4	22.2	17.8	30.0	10.8	19.2
Central and South America	135,725	1.0	5.5	23.6	32.7	37.3	21.9	15.4
Caribbean and Bermuda	167,420	1.6	14.7	31.1	23.0	29.5	17.4	12.1
Europe	716,245	28.8	24.1	15.3	13.1	18.7	8.9	9.8
United Kingdom	142,985	33.4	27.8	21.2	10.3	7.4	4.0	3.4
Other north and west Europe	75,180	52.7	19.1	10.8	8.6	8.9	3.9	5.0
Eastern Europe	182,680	18.7	6.3	6.8	23.8	44.3	19.5	24.8
Southern Europe	315,405	26.9	33.9	18.6	9.3	11.3	6.1	5.2
Africa	98,975	1.1	6.1	20.0	25.1	47.7	24.7	23.0
Asia	869,510	0.8	3.7	13.8	24.5	57.2	25.8	31.4
West Central Asia & Middle East	111,415	1.0	4.2	8.6	24.0	62.3	24.2	38.1
Eastern Asia	299,865	1.5	4.4	13.3	24.2	56.7	26.2	30.5
Southeast Asia	178,820	0.2	2.9	21.1	33.1	42.7	25.7	17.1
Southern Asia	279,420	0.3	3.3	11.7	19.6	65.0	26.2	38.8
Oceania and other	7,295	8.4	19.9	21.5	19.6	30.6	15.3	15.4
Montreal total	**621,890**	13.3	14.4	17.1	20.6	34.6	16.2	18.4
United States	15,180	15.7	14.2	23.4	20.3	26.3	11.1	15.2
Central and South America	47,385	0.7	3.4	16.5	34.3	45.1	27.1	18.0
Caribbean and Bermuda	65,940	2.1	9.2	31.2	27.5	30.0	17.4	12.6
Europe	240,530	30.9	25.5	14.6	10.7	18.2	8.0	10.2
United Kingdom	14,480	39.2	23.0	18.5	10.1	9.3	4.7	4.7
Other north and west Europe	57,515	26.4	19.2	14.7	12.9	26.8	9.8	17.0
Eastern Europe	49,745	26.4	7.5	6.2	17.1	42.8	19.3	23.5
Southern Europe	118,790	34.0	36.4	17.6	7.1	4.8	2.7	2.1

(continued)

Table 9.7 (continued)

CMA and region of birth	Total immigrants	<1961	1961–70	1971–80	1981–90	1991–2001	1991–95	1996–2001
Africa	73,510	2.0	13.9	14.4	16.6	53.2	17.0	36.2
Asia	178,065	1.5	4.5	15.9	29.5	48.7	24.2	24.5
West Central Asia & Middle East	62,950	1.7	5.6	12.3	34.4	46.0	24.9	21.1
Eastern Asia	32,855	4.0	5.4	10.1	20.3	60.3	25.1	35.2
Southeast Asia	47,120	0.3	2.2	27.9	38.5	31.0	19.2	11.9
Southern Asia	35,140	0.3	4.6	11.4	17.1	66.5	28.8	37.7
Oceania and other	1,280	16.8	24.2	27.7	10.2	21.1	8.6	12.9
Vancouver total	**738,550**	**10.0**	**9.9**	**16.8**	**19.3**	**44.0**	**21.0**	**23.0**
United States	23,070	9.9	19.2	26.5	17.5	27.0	11.8	15.2
Central and South America	20,585	2.3	5.6	16.7	30.9	44.5	20.1	24.5
Caribbean and Bermuda	5,955	5.7	22.5	36.6	16.5	18.6	12.3	6.3
Europe	186,640	32.9	22.2	15.8	11.5	17.7	8.2	9.4
United Kingdom	69,110	31.6	26.5	22.2	10.7	9.0	5.0	4.0
Other north and west Europe	45,125	49.2	20.9	13.2	8.1	8.7	4.1	4.6
Eastern Europe	36,285	21.2	8.6	7.5	23.2	39.6	16.1	23.4
Southern Europe	36,130	26.6	29.1	15.3	5.4	23.6	11.8	11.8
Africa	24,700	1.9	6.3	33.6	18.8	39.5	18.7	20.8
Asia	455,110	1.7	4.5	15.0	22.0	56.8	27.1	29.7
West Central Asia & Middle East	27,700	0.8	2.2	6.8	24.5	65.7	21.1	44.6
Eastern Asia	262,815	2.3	4.4	11.8	18.5	63.0	30.7	32.3
Southeast Asia	88,645	0.4	3.1	21.7	30.9	43.9	22.6	21.4
Southern Asia	75,945	1.5	7.0	21.0	23.1	47.4	22.3	25.0
Oceania and other	22,490	4.1	13.5	29.6	21.9	30.9	18.9	11.9
Total Canada	**5,448,480**	**16.4**	**13.7**	**17.2**	**19.1**	**33.6**	**15.9**	**17.7**

Source: Statistics Canada (2005a). Adapted from Statistics Canada website. Catalogue. no. 95F0358XCB2001004.IVT. Accessed 18 January 2005.

therefore, these three CMAs shared about 63 per cent of Canada's immigrant population in 2006. Approximately half of the foreign-born residents of these three metropolitan centres in 2006 were recent immigrants who had arrived between 1991 and 2006 (see Table 9.8).

In 2001, 13 per cent of Canada's people identified themselves as belonging to a visible minority (Statistics Canada, *The Daily*, 22 March 2005). *Visible minorities* is an official designation based on either self-designation in the census or cross-classification of birthplace, ancestry, language, and religion. Most members of a visible minority in Canada today are first-generation immigrants, but their Canadian-born descendants may also qualify for the 'visible minority' designation.

The Employment Equity Act defines *visible minorities* as persons, other than Aboriginal people, who are non-Caucasian in race or non-white in colour. The ten groups in this category are Chinese, South Asian, Black, Filipino, Latin American, Southeast Asian, Arab, West Asian, Japanese, and Korean (Statistics Canada, *The Daily*, 2005b). The visible minority population today is growing much faster than the overall population. As Table 9.9 shows, visible minorities increased by 25 per cent between 1996 and 2001, while the total population of Canada grew by only 4 per cent. Projections indicate that by

2017 roughly one in five people in Canada—between 19 and 23 per cent of the nation's population—could be a member of a visible minority (Statistics Canada, 2005b). Under the various scenarios considered for these projections, Canada would have between 6.3 million and 8.5 million visible minorities by 2017. By contrast, the estimated increase for the rest of the population is between 1 and 7 per cent. Almost 95 per cent of visible minorities in 2017 would live in metropolitan areas, almost 75 per cent in the three largest CMAs: Vancouver, Montreal, and—above all—Toronto, which was expected to be home to 45 per cent of the total visible minority population.

It is sometimes suggested that immigrants in general, and visible minority immigrants in particular, experience some occupational discrimination that results in a loss of income (Samuel, 1987). This is a difficult proposition to test directly. Still, the literature on inequality leaves little doubt that economic integration is a serious problem for recent immigrants in general. Ever since Porter's (1965) analysis revealed the extent of Canada's social stratification on the bases of race and ethnicity, sociologists using a variety of measures have found that immigrants generally and certain minorities in Canada do not fare as well as the larger Canadian society. For instance, the average earnings of immigrants

Table 9.8 Immigrant populations in 2006 in Toronto, Montreal, and Vancouver CMAs, by period of immigration

Period of immigration	Immigrant population				Percentage distribution			
	Total	Toronto	Montreal	Vancouver	Total	Toronto	Montreal	Vancouver
Before 1961	326,785	189,925	63,665	73,195	8.40	8.19	7.66	9.89
1961–70	386,225	232,635	69,385	84,205	9.92	10.03	8.35	11.37
1971–80	545,470	324,150	119,670	101,650	14.02	13.97	14.40	13.73
1981–90	666,760	405,340	136,025	125,395	17.13	17.47	16.36	16.94
1991–2000	1,201,585	720,185	290,830	190,570	30.87	31.04	34.99	25.74
2001–06	764,970	447,930	151,695	165,345	19.66	19.31	18.25	22.33
Total	3,891,795	2,320,165	831,270	740,360	100.00	100.00	100.00	100.00

Source: Statistics Canada (2007i).

Table 9.9 Visible minorities, Canada, Montreal, Toronto, and Vancouver, 1981–2001[1]

Canada	Total population	Visible minority	%
1981	24,083,495	1,131,825	4.7
1986	25,021,915	1,577,715	6.3
1991	26,994,040	2,525,480	9.4
1996	28,528,125	3,197,480	11.2
2001	29,639,030	3,983,845	13.4
Montreal			
1981	2,798,040	146,365	5.2
1986	2,887,855	204,740	7.1
1991	3,172,005	349,415	11.0
1996	3,287,645	401,425	12.2
2001	3,380,640	458,330	13.6
Toronto			
1981	2,975,495	404,790	13.6
1986	3,399,680	586,500	17.3
1991	3,868,875	997,500	25.8
1996	4,232,905	1,338,095	31.6
2001	4,647,955	1,712,530	36.8
Vancouver			
1981	1,250,610	173,300	13.9
1986	1,362,445	230,845	16.9
1991	1,584,195	379,480	24.0
1996	1,813,935	564,600	31.1
2001	1,967,480	725,655	36.9

[1]1981 and 1986 data for the census metropolitan areas are not adjusted for 2001 census boundaries.

Source: Statistics Canada (2003b): 44. Adapted from Statistics Canada publication *2001 Canada's Ethnocultural Portrait: The Changing Mosaic*. Catalogue no. 96F0030XIE2001008, p. 45.

have fallen in recent decades. A study by Picot, Hou, and Coloumbe (2007) showed that in 2002 immigrants during their first year in Canada were 3.5 times more likely than those born in Canada to fall below the low-income cut-off.

That recent arrivals are worse-off than longer-established immigrants may be attributed, at least in part, to the time of their arrival, since employment opportunities vary from year to year, depending on the state of the economy. But such findings are not easily explained by one or two factors alone (see, for example, Aydemir and Borjas, 2006). Part of the problem may be that some professions make it difficult for recently arrived practitioners to gain the necessary accreditation in Canada; this is the reason, for example, that many medical doctors, lawyers, and engineers must resort to low-paying jobs. This remains an important social policy concern. Making accreditation easier to obtain would help to close the income gap between immigrants and the larger society. Immigrants with lower occupational skills generally cannot expect to experience any significant upward mobility until they have lived in Canada for several years. It is but a small consolation that in this respect Canada's situation appears to be better than that of the United States.

Other research suggests that many visible minority immigrants work within in their ethnic enclaves, where jobs are generally not as well-paying as jobs in the larger economy. A study by Li and Dong (2007) based on 2001 census data found that immigrants working in the Chinese ethnic enclave were less well paid than their counterparts in the mainstream economy, even when the analysis controlled for factors such as urban location, type of job, and years of work experience. These researchers found that the types of jobs filled by immigrants in the ethnic enclave largely explained their lower wages, though language was also a factor: workers in the Chinese enclave tend not to speak English or French. Therefore most had jobs in lower-paying non-professional sectors such as manufacturing, wholesaling and retailing, accommodation, and food services. By contrast, Chinese workers in the mainstream economy are concentrated in the higher-paying financial and professional sectors. These findings suggest that part of the immigrant disadvantage in earnings may be explained by the very features that make the presence of an ethnic enclave attractive to new immigrants: 'a common minority language and an ethnic consumer based economy' (93).

Immigrants and Wages

Few Canadians would be surprised to learn that immigrants pull down the wages of the domestic workers whom they challenge for jobs. That has been the law of supply and demand since humans first scrabbled to make a living. What is surprising, as a new Statistics Canada study makes clear, is that immigrants to Canada have narrowed the gap between the country's highest-paid workers and lowest-paid workers, reducing income inequality. In the United States, it's the opposite: the presence of immigrants increases the gap between the rich and the poor.

The contrast underlines the differences between the US and Canadian approaches to immigrant selection. The study found that a 10-per-cent change in labour supply from international migration is associated with a 3- to 4-per-cent change in weekly earning in the opposite direction. It does not draw the inevitable conclusion that Canadian policy, which favours more highly skilled immigrants, is better for social peace and general prosperity than US policy, even if it unfortunately leads to lower wages for more educated workers.

To catalogue the workers and their wages, a Statscan researcher and a Harvard University economics professor scrutinized census data for male labour-market participants over several decades in the US, Mexico and Canada. Since the 1960s, American immigration policy has emphasized family reunification, which has led to the entry of a high proportion of low-skilled workers. In 2001, only 20 per cent of US immigrants had more than an undergraduate university degree compared with roughly 40 per cent of Canadian immigrants.

Although neither nation's immigration policy is a resounding success, their different approaches to immigrant selection have affected different income groups. In Canada, the study says, immigration 'played a role' in the 7-per-cent drop in real weekly wages between 1980 and 2000 for workers with more than a university undergraduate degree. However, largely because Canada did not import huge numbers of low-skilled immigrants, the wages of low-skilled workers rose. As a result, immigration has moderated the growing gap between the wages of low-skilled and high-skilled workers. In contrast, US immigrants have depressed the wages of all low-skilled workers while barely affecting the wages of more highly skilled workers. Real weekly wages for more highly skilled US workers grew by 20 per cent between 1980 and 2000. In effect, immigration magnified the wage inequality.

Good immigration policies should not foster the creation of large pools of low-skilled workers who compete ferociously with each other and drive down wages. Immigrants in that US underclass have far less hope of improving their fortunes than well-educated Canadian immigrants—even those who may be struggling to get their credentials recognized. Canada's immigration policy, while imperfect, correctly gives preference to the highly qualified.

Source: *The Globe and Mail*. 2007. 'Immigrants and Wages' (Editorial). Monday, May 28: A12. Reprinted with permission from The Globe and Mail.

International Migration: The Future

Aging Western societies are being transformed by the immigrants they depend on to sustain their labour forces. Ultimately, these societies may have to renounce the idea of the nation as a singular homogeneous cultural entity and revise their self-concept to embrace ethnic diversity.

Imagined Futures

Can theories of international migration help immigrant-receiving nations respond to this challenge? Of the theories outlined earlier in this chapter, none in itself can adequately cover the diversity of issues pertaining to the formulation of immigration policy. For example, the economic and dual labour market theories focus exclusively on economic considerations; they have nothing to say about issues of national self-determination or national identity.

Simmons (1999) has proposed that immigrant-receiving countries (liberal democracies) can adopt what he calls an 'imagined futures' approach to designing immigration policy. Under the imagined futures approach, a country would set immigration policy in light of its economic goals and its ideas about its cultural identity (see Figure 9.6). A nation would also consider its sociopolitical and economic position in the international context and then develop appropriate policies regarding not only trade and commerce with other nations but also immigration in general and immigration targets specifically. This would require that national leaders have a clear image of their country's future, specifically whether or not that future includes immigrants as fully integrated citizens. According to Simmons, once an imagined future has been formulated, immigration policies consistent with this vision can be designed.

To some extent, this approach resembles Canada's perspective on immigration since the 1967 reforms. The nation's view of itself is clearly multicultural, and its immigration policy has helped bring about this reality. At the same time, Canada is a leading economic player in the world economy, and its immigration targets are set with an eye to ensuring that its economic needs are satisfied over the long term. By contrast, countries like Japan and those of western Europe have taken a different approach. These countries, historically, have not been countries of immigration, seeing themselves as distinct and rather homogeneous nations. But in the light of continued immigration and their undeniable ethnic diversity, they could perhaps benefit from an *imagined futures* perspective.

Immigration as Demographic Salvation?

Immigration has been proposed as a possible solution to combat the effects of demographic aging and below-replacement fertility levels in advanced societies. The United Nations report *Replacement Migration* (United Nations Department of Economic and Social Affairs Population Division, 2000) suggested that immigration could be used by countries as a strategy to avoid population decline in the near future. We can think of *replacement migration* as the number of immigrants needed for a country to maintain its current size of the labour force population (aged 15–64) over an indefinite period of time.

Viewed in this way, immigration can be seen as a means of stalling population decline, so long as countries are willing to dramatically increase their immigration targets. For example, under one of the scenarios presented in the UN report, Italy, in order to maintain the size of its year 2000 labour force population for 50 years, would need to raise its annual number of net migrants to 7,000 per 1,000 inhabitants; Germany would require a migration rate of 6,000 per 1,000 population, and Japan a rate of about 5,000.

A related question is whether immigration can be adjusted to stave off the effects of demographic aging. Research on this question demonstrates that it could, but that the number of immigrants needed to offset declines in the

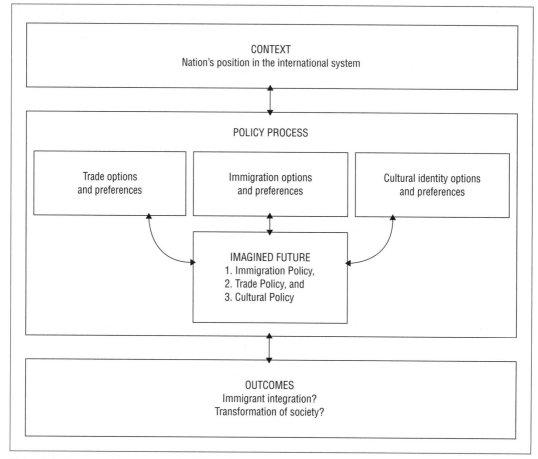

Figure 9.6 Imagined futures and immigration policy

Source: Simmons (1999): 35, Fig. 2.1. Reproduced by permission of the University of Toronto Press.

working-age population are significantly larger than those needed to offset total population decline. The UN concluded that the levels of migration needed to offset population aging (i.e., to maintain the current balance of dependents to workers in the population) would be extremely large, and in all cases entail vastly more immigration than occurred in the past. Scholars such as Coleman (2002) and McNicoll (2000) have estimated that immigration can only prevent population aging at unprecedented, unsustainable, and increasing levels that would generate rapid

population growth and eventually displace the original population from its majority position. It seems doubtful, therefore, that increased immigration in Japan and the rich countries of western Europe can be viewed as a viable remedy to demographic aging.

Open Borders?

A number of scholars (see, for example, Carens, 1987, 1999; Hayter, 2000; Legrain, 2006; Moses, 2006) have argued that migration is a fundamental human right, and that immigration controls should therefore be abolished. The issue of 'open borders', they argue, strikes at the heart of what is morally just in a world that is increasingly divided along socioeconomic lines. Is it a violation of a fundamental human right—the freedom to choose where to live—for a privileged nation to deny someone from a less privileged country the opportunity to immigrate? Is there any moral objection to the adoption of an 'open borders' policy?

Having examined three theories of moral justice (Rawlsian, Nozichean, and utilitarian), Carens (1987) found that even though they differed on some critical issues, they all concurred that states have an obligation to respect all human beings as free and equal moral persons, and that part of that commitment should entail 'open borders'. To prohibit people from entering a territory because they do not hold citizenship there is no part of any state's legitimate mandate (Carens, 1987: 255).

On the other hand, proponents of the communitarian perspective (Isbister, 2000; Meilaender, 1999; Walzer, 1992) have suggested that unrestricted immigration would restrict a nation's right to self-determination and its citizens' right to economic well-being, while threatening not only the national cultures of receiving societies but possibly even liberal democratic values and liberties. To these arguments, proponents of open borders would respond that the real purpose of immigration controls is to protect the privileges that the affluent societies of Europe and North America enjoy over the less fortunate societies of Africa and Asia—in short, that border controls have less to do with restricting people than with controlling economic resources. Advocates of open borders would acknowledge that such a policy would require that the society relinquish some control over its cultural and demographic compositions; however, they contend, open borders would in no way prevent such a state from functioning. These theorists would therefore insist that moral justice requires open borders. Critics of the open borders idea (Isbister, 2000; Meilaender, 1999; Walzer, 1992) would agree that liberal states have a moral obligation to aid poor countries in need, but only so long as the 'costs' to the providers of assistance are not too high. These critics do not advocate abolition of immigration to Western liberal democracies, but they do insist that states have a moral obligation to place the interests of their own citizens first.

Whether open borders would be a practical option for liberal states remains a question for further debate (see Coleman, 2002; Golini, 2003; Keely, 2001; Romellón, 2001). Carens (1987) himself has acknowledged that on practical grounds and issues of national sovereignty and security, liberal democracies are not likely to accept free migration to all as a policy option. This view would seem applicable today and into the foreseeable future. Liberal democracies are bound to stay the course with their immigration policies, emphasizing a balance between national self-interest and the promotion of humanitarian principles (i.e., regarding asylum seekers, refugees, and family reunification). In any event, under existing conditions, immigrant-receiving liberal democracies cannot avoid the kinds of challenges associated with the integration of an increasing number of newcomers and the resultant ethnic diversity.

Notes for Further Study

If appropriate data are available, it is possible to compute rates and various ratios of international migration.

International Migration Ratios and Rates

Ratios

A set of migration measures may be based solely on frequencies. Edmonston and Michalowski (2004: 484) present six migration ratios, expressing relations among immigration, emigration, and net migration:

$$\frac{\text{emigration}}{\text{immigration}} = \frac{E}{I} \qquad (1)$$

$$\frac{\text{net immigration}}{\text{immigration}} = \frac{I - E}{I} \ (\text{where } I > E) \qquad (2)$$

$$\frac{\text{net emigration}}{\text{immigration}} = \frac{E - I}{I} \ (\text{where } E > I) \qquad (3)$$

$$\frac{\text{immigration}}{\text{gross migration}} = \frac{I}{I + E} \qquad (4)$$

$$\frac{\text{emigration}}{\text{gross migration}} = \frac{E}{I + E} \qquad (5)$$

$$\frac{\text{net migration}}{\text{gross migration}} = \frac{I - E}{I + E} \qquad (6)$$

Which of these ratios is most appropriate depends on the purpose of the analysis and the migration characteristics of the area or country under study. For instance, in the case of a country that receives large waves of immigration, it may be useful to compute the ratio of immigration to gross migration (equation 4): this would measure the proportion of immigration that is effectively added to the population. On the other hand, if there is a high level of emigration in a country, then it would be especially informative to compute the ratio of net emigration to immigration (equation 3): this would give an indication of the proportion of the emigration that is effectively lost. Equation 6 measures the effectiveness of migration. It is the relative difference between the effective addition or loss through migration and the overall gross movement. The ratio varies from negative one to positive one. The higher or lower the ratio from zero, the fewer the moves required to produce a net gain or loss in population for a particular country.

Despite their seeming simplicity, these ratios should be treated with some caution. As Edmonston and Michalowski (2004: 485) explain, it is important to understand the logic of possible negative values in these ratios and

the possibility of small values in both the numerator and denominator:

A negative sign may simply be taken to indicate that emigration exceeds immigration. Extremely large ratios resulting from very small denominators must ordinarily be interpreted with special care. Extremely small ratios resulting from very small numerators simply indicate that the effective addition or loss is small in relation to gross migration or migration turnover.

Rates

Migration rates have a general form that can apply to either internal or external types of movement. We will look at five migration rates, all crude rates. For the sake of simplicity and data access, the denominator in these rates is usually the mid-year population of a country at the end of a specified interval, typically the census population. If population estimates are available for the beginning of the year, these can be used as the denominator. Below, the symbols I and E represent the volume of immigration and emigration, respectively, during the interval:

$$\text{crude immigration rate} = \frac{I}{P} \times 1{,}000 \qquad (7)$$

$$\text{crude emigration rate} = \frac{E}{P} \times 1{,}000 \qquad (8)$$

$$\text{crude net migration rate} = \frac{I - E}{P} \times 1{,}000 \qquad (9)$$

$$\text{crude gross migration rate} = \frac{I + E}{P} \times 1{,}000 \qquad (10)$$

Table 9.10 shows cross-national examples of each of these migration rates around 1995. Note the variations across the countries. Israel and Ecuador for instance, have relatively high net migration rates (especially Israel) while the other countries are far behind in this measure. The reason for this is readily seen in the emigration rates, where the other countries have rela-

Table 9.10 Various rates of migration for selected countries, c.1995

Country and year (1995 unless noted otherwise)	Immigration[1] (1)	Emigration[1] (2)	Population[2] (in thousands) (3)	Immigration rate (1)/(3) × 1,000 = (4)	Emigration rate (2)/(3) × 1,000 = (5)	Net migration rate [(1) − (2)]/(3) × 1,000 = (6)	Gross migration rate [(1) + (2)]/(3) × 1,000 = (7)
South Africa	5,064	8,725	41,244	0.1	0.2	−0.1	0.3
Zimbabwe	2,901	3,282	11,526	0.3	0.3	<0.05	0.5
Canada	300,313	165,725	29,615	10.1	5.6	+4.5	15.7
US[3]	878,288	263,232	262,765	3.3	1.0	+2.3	4.3
Ecuador	471,961	348,845	11,221	42.1	31.1	+11.0	73.1
Venezuela	62,482	77,388	19,787	3.2	3.9	−0.8	7.1
Indonesia	218,952	57,096	194,755	1.1	0.3	+0.8	1.4
Israel (1990)	197,533	14,191	4,660	42.4	3.0	+39.3	45.4
Japan	87,822	72,377	125,197	0.7	0.6	+0.1	1.3
South Korea	101,612	403,522	45,093	2.3	8.9	−6.7	11.2
Belgium	62,950	36,044	10,137	6.2	3.6	+2.7	9.8
Germany	1,096,048	698,113	81,661	13.4	8.5	+4.9	22.0
Italy (1994)	99,105	65,548	57,204	1.7	1.1	+0.6	2.9
Poland (1994)	6,907	25,904	38,544	0.2	0.7	−0.5	0.9
Russian Fedn (1994)	1,146,735	337,121	147,968	7.7	2.3	+5.5	10.0
Sweden	45,887	33,984	8,831	5.2	3.8	+1.3	9.0
Switzerland	90,957	69,357	7,041	12.9	9.9	+3.1	22.8
UK	245,452	191,570	58,606	4.2	3.3	+0.9	7.5
Australia	253,940	149,360	18,049	14.1	8.3	+5.8	22.3

[1] Long-term immigrants: non-residents, or persons who have not continuously lived in the country for more than one year, arriving for a length of stay of more than one year. Long-term emigrants: residents, or persons who have resided continuously in the country for more than one year, who are departing to take up residence abroad for more than one year.

[2] Estimated mid-period population.

[3] United States Census Bureau estimate: immigration includes refugees and illegal entrants as well as legal permanent residents; emigration includes departures of legal foreign-born and native residents.

Source: Adapted from Edmonston and Michalowski (2004), 487.

tively high emigration rates, which substantially lower their net migration rates. Notice as well the gross migration rates, which combine immigration and emigration into one measure. This rate may be viewed as an overall indication of population turnover in a country. On this account, Ecuador surpasses Israel, though this is clearly a function of Ecuador's much higher rate of emigration: while a lot of people move into Ecuador, a significant number also leave the country. By contrast, most of Israel's high gross migration rate can be accounted for by its high immigration rate combined with its low emigration figure.

Age-Specific International Migration Rates

Rates specific to age, sex, nationality, or any other characteristic may be computed as well. The general form of such rates can be illustrated with the age-specific net migration rate (NM_x) shown below, where I_x and E_x represent immigration specific to a given age category x, and P_x represents the mid-year population for the age group.

$$NM_x = \frac{I_x - E_x}{P_x} \times 1{,}000 \qquad (11)$$

International Migration as a Component of Population Growth

How much of total population growth is due to international net migration? One way to answer this question is to compute measures that relate the net migration in a given interval to the natural increase in the same interval. This gives the amount of net migration (NM) as a percentage of the amount of natural increase (NI). Thus:

$$\frac{NM}{NI} \times 100 \qquad (12)$$

Another possibility is to express net migration as a proportion of the total growth (i.e., natural increase + net migration) in a given interval:

$$\frac{NM}{NI + NM} \times 100 \qquad (13)$$

The relative contribution of natural increase to total population growth can also be computed, and then compared to the relative contribution of net migration:

$$\frac{NI}{NI + NM} \times 100 \qquad (14)$$

Exercises

1. Use the data in Table 9.2 (page 402) to compute for each period:

    (a) all possible migration ratios
    (b) the contribution of net migration to total population growth
    (c) the amount of net migration as a percentage of the amount of natural increase
    (d) the contribution of natural increase to total population growth

    Interpret your results.

2. Collect similar information for four other immigrant-receiving countries of your choice and carry out the same computations. Compare your results to those obtained for Canada. Is the contribution of net international migration different across the countries? If so, explain why.

3. The period since the 1960s has been described by some as the 'age of migration'. Others have referred to 'worlds in motion'. In the same context, it has been written that in comparison to earlier modern history, there has been 'an acceleration of migration'; and that 'migration is 'highly differentiated' and increasingly 'politicized'. Write an essay on how global migration patterns, causes, and consequences have been altered in the post-World War II years and the possible future of immigration for liberal democracies.

4. Receiving societies can be located along a continuum of 'exclusiveness–inclusiveness' with respect to their reception of and treatment of immigrants. Discuss this idea in relation to different countries in the world that receive a substantial number of immigrants. What are the immigration policy challenges for societies at different locations on the continuum?

5. Write a critical essay on the role that ethnic communities play in the integration of immigrants into North American society.

Additional Reading

Adler, Leonore Loeb, and Uwe P. Gielen, eds. 2003. *Migration: Immigration and Emigration in International Perspective*. Westport, CT: Praeger.

Cohen, Jeffrey H. 2004. *The Culture of Migration in Southern Mexico*. Austin, TX: University of Texas Press.

Crépeau, François, Delphine Nakache, Michael Collyer, N.H. Goetz, A. Hansen, R. Modi, N. Nadig, S. Spoljar-Vrzina, and L.H.M. van Willigen, eds. 2006. *Forced Migration and Global Processes: A View from Forced Migration Studies*. Lanham: Lexington.

Francis, Diane. 2002. *Immigration—The Economic Case*. Toronto: Key Porter.

Hatton, Timothy J., and Jeffrey G. Williamson. 2005. *Global Migration and the World Economy: Two Centuries of Policy and Performance*. Cambridge, MA: MIT Press.

Hoerder, Dirk. 2002. *Cultures in Contact; World Migrations in the Second Millennium*. Durham, NC: Duke University Press.

Marfleet, Philip. 2006. *Refugees in a Global Era*. New York: Palgrave Macmillan.

Parsons, Craig A., and Timothy M. Smeeding, eds. 2006. *Immigration and the Transformation of Europe*. Cambridge: Cambridge University Press.

Waldinger, Roger, ed. 2001. *Strangers at the Gates: New Immigrants in Urban America*. Berkeley: University of California Press.

Waters, Mary C., and Reed Ueda (with Helen B. Marrow). 2007. *The New Americans: A Guide to Immigration Since 1965*. Cambridge, MA: Harvard University Press.

Web Resources

The Migration Policy Institute (MPI) is a non-partisan, non-profit think tank dedicated to the study of the movement of people worldwide: www.migrationpolicy.org/.

The Migration Information Source, MPI's award-winning online resource, presents the most current migration data in user-friendly interactive forms, along with incisive analysis from prominent scholars in the migration and refugee fields. To select specific regions for analysis, go to www.migrationinformation.org/Resources/.

'Facts and Figures' is an annual statistical publication on immigration to Canada, available from Citizenship and Immigration Canada (CIC): www.cic.gc.ca/english/resources/statistics/menu-fact.asp.

For up-to-date information on refugees, go to the United Nations High Commissioner for Refugees (UNHCR) website: www.unhcr.org/cgi-bin/texis/vtx/home.

PART FIVE

Population Change and Societal Interrelationships

Chapter 10

Urbanization

Introduction

Four decades ago, Kingsley Davis (1970: 4) remarked that before 1850 no society could be described as predominantly urbanized, and that by 1900 only Great Britain could be seen as being more urban than rural. Today, the urbanization process in industrialized countries has come to a virtual halt, with many urban areas having attained a point of almost complete saturation. Since the mid-twentieth century, urbanization has occurred rapidly in the developing countries, where migration to the cities is widespread, motivated by the combination of rapid population growth and extreme poverty and hardship in the countryside. As these countries industrialize, there is great unevenness in the extent and pace of economic development, and of urbanization. In many parts of the developing world, large primate cities are growing faster than other urban settlements, and the rural areas have fallen behind in development as a result of inattention by governments focused on promoting the urban sector of their economies. Given this uneven development, large urban centres are often viewed by rural dwellers as attractive places, where they can establish a better life for themselves and their families. In many respects, this situation in the world's poorer countries is reminiscent of the experience nearly 200 years ago of countries in the West as they underwent the upheavals associated with a rapidly changing economy brought on by the Industrial Revolution and rapid urbanization.

Basic Concepts and Measures

Urbanization is a complex process of change affecting both the population and the geography of a country or region. It is characterized particularly by three developments:

1. a progressive concentration of people and economic activity in cities and towns, which alters the general scale of population settlement;
2. a shift in the national economy, in which the non-agricultural mode of production, situated predominantly in areas of the country designated as 'urban', becomes dominant; and
3. an increasing diffusion of technological innovation spreading from larger to smaller urban centres and eventually to rural areas, so that in the advanced stages of urbanization the urban and the rural become similar in the extent and intensity of technological adoption as well as in certain social-psychological aspects, including lifestyles, values, and attitudes.

The homogenizing social-psychological effect of urban living on the population is what defines *urbanism*, a term referring to the style of life found in urban areas. The sociological implications of urbanism have preoccupied scholars for well over a century; notable contributions to the study of urbanism have come from such eminent sociologists as Tönnies (1883 [1995]), Weber (1905 [1958]), Simmel (1903 [1969]), Burgess (1925), and Park (1916, 1929 [1959]). In social-psychological terms, as well as in demographic and economic terms, urbanization is a transforming process. In the initial stages of urbanization there are sharp sociological differences between the urban and the rural populations. Early theorists tended to characterize life in the city as impersonal and isolating, detached from the traditional forms of living characteristics of the rural folk community. Simmel, for example, viewed urban life as psychologically overwhelming—so much so that it drove city-dwellers to detach themselves from others and compartmentalize their lives in order to make them more manageable (Sennett, 1969: 8–9).

As countries in the West have become predominantly urban, sociologists have developed new conceptions of urbanism. One view sees the city as a culturally heterogeneous place whose benefits outweigh the characteristically urban disadvantages of crime, deviancy, and poverty. Jacobs (1967), for instance, championed cities—especially neighbourhoods—as places that provide close affiliation for their citizens and, in this way, a natural form of protection against crime. Moreover, in the anonymous environment of the city it is possible for people of like orientations to form associations for the purposes of promoting activities of common interest; this is what makes cities places of innovation and cultural creativity (Fischer, 1975, 1976). Still, the darker aspects of city life cannot be ignored, and it is fair to say that urbanization is a process that produces both negative and positive results in a country: on the one hand, it creates problems associated with socioeconomic inequalities, such as poor housing and urban crime, and promotes congestion, encroachment on agricultural land, and environmental degradation; on the other hand, it engenders, for many people, a better standard of living, material and social progress, and greater cultural diversity.

Having progressed through a century or more of sustained industrialization, most Western countries and Japan have reached what appears to be a peak level of urbanization, and the pace of additional urban growth is occurring at a slower and slower rate. Currently, the proportion of the population living in urban areas of Europe, North America, and Latin America exceeds 75 per cent (Jones, 2003: 952), and few substantial differences in lifestyle, values, and attitudes remain between the urban and the rural sectors. Indeed, we can question the degree to which urban and rural populations really differ at all with respect to these sociological dimensions in an age in which television, radio, the Internet, computers, wireless communication networks, and interconnected systems of transportation are commonplace (Small and Witherick, 1986: 225). The same cannot be said of the developing countries, where large segments of the population are rural and without ready access to advanced communication technologies. Nevertheless, as urbanization intensifies through the urban hierarchy and diffuses to the rural areas of these countries, a blurring of urban–rural lifestyle differences, similar to what has occurred in the industrialized countries of the West, seems inevitable.

What is 'Urban'?

The term *urban* is used frequently in the popular media and in everyday conversation, though its precise meaning is elusive. This is the case even in demography. For instance, what exactly constitutes an *urban area*? Variations in the definition of 'urban' across countries make this seemingly simple question difficult to answer, and make international comparisons of urbanization challenging to carry out (United Nations Department of Economics and Social Affairs, 2002c: 20).

In Canada, the country's urban population comprises all incorporated places that have a population of at least 1,000 and a density of at least 400 persons per square kilometre; all remaining areas are classified as rural (Statistics Canada, 2003c: 104). In the United States and in Mexico, a place must have a population of at least 2,500 to qualify as urban. These definitions of urban, though they are not consistent, are straightforward compared with how the term is defined in other countries. In India, for example, an urban area is any place with 5,000 or more inhabitants, a density of no fewer than 1,000 persons per square mile (or 390 per square kilometre), and at least three-quarters of the adult male population employed in pursuits other than agriculture. In China, an urban population is designated according to its role in the country's economy or political administration: any area in which the dominant economic activity is agriculture is considered rural, while administrative centres and places that are pre-dominantly industrial are considered urban (Brockerhoff, 2000: 6). Table 10.1, which includes definitions of 'urban' for selected countries, shows clearly that despite attempts by the United Nations to standardize the use of 'urban', wide variations exist in how the term is applied in different countries.

Table 10.1 Urban population of selected countries in 2001 and definition of 'urban'

Country	Percentage urban	Total population (in thousands)	Definition of urban
Albania	42.9	3,145	towns and industrial centres with a population of 400 or more
Angola	34.9	13,527	localities with a population of 2,000 or more
Argentina	88.3	37,488	localities with a population of 2,000 or more
Bahrain	92.5	652	localities with a population of 2,500 or more
Benin	43.0	6,446	localities with a population of 10,000 or more
Brazil	81.7	172,559	cities and towns as defined by municipal law
Canada	80.0	31,021	places of 1,000 or more inhabitants and a population density of 400 or more per square kilometre
Costa Rica	59.5	4,112	administrative centres of canton, including adjacent areas with clear urban characteristics
Czech Republic	74.5	10,260	localities with a population of 5,000 or more
Denmark	85.1	5,333	capital city plus provincial capitals
Dominica	71.4	71	cities and villages with a population of 500 or more
Finland	58.5	5,178	urban communes
Gambia	31.3	1,337	capital city of Banjul
Germany	87.7	82,007	localities with a population of 5,000 or more
Greece	60.3	10,623	municipalities and communes in which the largest population centre has 10,000 or more inhabitants, plus 18 urban agglomerations
Iceland	92.7	281	localities with a population of 200 or more
Jordan	78.7	5,051	localities with a population of 10,000 or more
Kuwait	96.1	1,971	agglomerations of 10,000 or more
Laos	19.7	5,403	five largest towns
Madagascar	30.1	16,437	centres with more than 5,000 inhabitants
Mauritius	41.6	1,171	towns with proclaimed legal limits
Mongolia	56.6	2,559	capital city and district centres
Nigeria	44.9	116,929	towns with 20,000 inhabitants whose occupations are not mainly agrarian

(continued)

Table 10.1 (*continued*)

Country	Percentage urban	Total population (in thousands)	Definition of urban
Norway	75.0	4,488	localities with a population of 200 or more
Oman	76.5	2,622	two main towns of Muscat and Matrah
Pakistan	33.4	144,971	places with municipal corporation, town committee, or cantonment
Papua New Guinea	17.6	4,920	centres with 500 inhabitants or more
Peru	73.1	26,093	population centres with 100 dwellings or more grouped contiguously and administrative centres of districts
Romania	55.2	22,388	cities, towns, and 183 other localities having certain socioeconomic characteristics
Saint Kitts/Nevis	34.2	38	cities of Basseterre and Charlestown
Suriname	74.8	419	capital city of Greater Paramaribo
United States	81.0	281,422	places with a population of 2,500 or more and urbanized areas
Uruguay	92.1	3,361	cities as officially defined
Vietnam	24.5	79,175	places with a population of 4,000 or more
Zimbabwe	36.0	12,852	nineteen main towns

Sources: McKibben and Faust (2004): 105–23; United Nations Department of Economic and Social Affairs Population Division (2002c).

The Urban–Rural Dichotomy: An Obsolete Concept?

The diffusion of lifestyles, values, and attitudes from urban to rural areas through urbanization has erased many of the once widely accepted differences that distinguished cities from smaller communities (see Table 10.2). For this reason, the rural–urban dichotomy, once commonly used to describe the social, demographic, economic, and spatial dimensions of urban and rural areas, is too simplistic for modern contexts and should probably be abandoned. Significant changes in communication technologies, transportation, and economic activity have brought about new forms of urbanization that are best studied using a multidimensional rather than a unidimensional conceptualization of settlement systems (Hugo, Champion, and Lattes, 2003). Consider some of the ways in which urban and rural functions are increasingly intermixed. To cite just one example, advances in transporta-tion and communication technologies have enabled many people to commute daily from homes in rural areas to jobs in the nearby city.

Many parts of the world today are experiencing changes to settlement patterns that cannot be observed through the traditional measure of urbanization, the 'per cent urban'. For example, in Europe, the traditional monocentric form of the urban region is disappearing. It is being replaced by a variety of polycentric urban configurations, ranging in scale from individual metropolitan areas in which centres subsidiary to the main core can be identified along the lines of the city's edge, to much wider urban fields that incorporate several polynuclear metropolitan regions to form even larger urban systems, or *megalopolises*. Similar changes are taking place in the developing countries. For instance, the Philippines and Thailand are witnessing the growth of extended metropolitan regions characterized by a mixture of urban and rural features

Table 10.2 Some widely accepted differences between urban and rural populations

Dimension	Urban	Rural
Economy	dominated by secondary and tertiary activities	predominantly primary industry and activities supporting it
Occupational structure	manufacturing, construction, administration, and service activities	agriculture and other primary industry occupations
Education levels and availability	higher than national averages	lower than national averages
Accessibility to services	high	low
Accessibility to information	high	low
Demography	low fertility and mortality	high fertility and mortality
Politics	greater representation of liberal and radical elements	conservative, resistance to change
Ethnicity	varied	more homogeneous
Migration levels	high and generally net in-migration	low and generally net out-migration

Source: Hugo, Champion, and Lattes (2003): 279, Table 1. Reprinted by permission of Blackwell Publishing.

and linked by urban development along major transport routes. New spatial forms such as these challenge the usual conception of what constitutes a city (Hugo, Champion, and Lattes, 2003).

Basic Measures of Urbanization

In this section we look at some of the more widely used measures of urbanization. None of the simple measures reviewed here can tell us anything about the causes and consequences of urbanization, or even why levels of urbanization change; these measures are but a starting point to a more substantive analysis of the phenomenon of urbanization.

Urban population change is usually described in terms of three commonly adopted measures:

- the urban proportion and its change over time
- the distribution of population in accordance with size of settlement and change in these distributions
- the urban growth rate and its change over time

While considering the usefulness and applicability of these measures, it is important to keep in mind the preceding discussion of the limits to unidimensional measures of urbanization and the conceptual problems of defining 'urban'.

Urban Proportion

Urban proportion refers to the percentage of a country's population that resides in areas that are designated as 'urban'. That is,

$$\% \text{ urban} = \left[\frac{\text{urban population}}{\text{urban population} + \text{rural population}} \right] \times 100$$

The data required to compute this measure is easy to obtain for countries that take periodic censuses of their populations. Usually, tabulations are compiled showing the distribution of population according to the type of residence, rural or urban. For example, the UN's *2000 Demographic Yearbook* (United Nations Department of Economic and Social Affairs Population Division, 2002c) gives Ireland's total population for 1996 as 3,626,087, of which 2,107,991 lived in urban areas, and 1,518,096 resided in rural localities. Therefore the urban proportion for Ireland in 1996 was

$$\frac{2,107,991}{3,626,087} \times 100 = 58.13\%$$

The most recent UN report on world urbanization uses the urban proportion measure to show that in 2003, the population of the world was just over 48 per cent urbanized. In that year, there were 3.04 billion people living in urban places and 3.26 billion living in rural areas. In the same year, the population of the more developed regions (as defined by the United Nations) was estimated to be 1.20 billion, and that of the less developed regions 5.10 billion. As Table 10.3 shows, the urban proportion was 74.1 per cent for the more developed countries, and 42.9 per cent for the less developed countries (United Nations Department of Economic and Social Affairs Population Division, 2004c: 4).

A drawback of this measure is the wide variation, noted earlier in the chapter, in how *urban* is defined internationally. This can make it difficult to compare rates of different nations. However, the index can be used unambiguously to measure the extent to which a country's population resides in urban areas, and it can be applied without complication to measure levels of urbanization within countries—across provinces, states, and so on.

Percentage Change in Urban Proportion

In many applications the analyst is interested in looking at the extent of change over time in the percentage of the population that lives in urban areas. The *percentage change in urban proportion* measures (in percentage terms) the magnitude of increase or decrease, between any two points in time, of the population living in urban areas. The formula for this index of urbanization is

$$\text{\% change in urban proportion} = \left[\frac{\text{\% urban population, } t_2 - \text{\% urban population, } t_1}{\text{\% urban population, } t_1} \right] \times 100$$

We'll continue with the example of Ireland. In 1978, Ireland was 52.00 per cent urbanized (Population Reference Bureau, 1978). As we saw earlier, by 1996, the percentage had grown to 58.13. Thus, the percentage change in the urban proportion over this period was

$$\frac{58.13 - 52.00}{52.00} \times 100 = 11.79\%$$

We can also apply this measure on a global scale. In 1950, the world's urban and rural proportions were 29.1 and 70.9 per cent, respectively. By the year 2000, the proportions were

Table 10.3   Urban and rural population by major world area, 2005

Region	Population (in billions)			Percentage		
	Urban	Rural	Total	Urban	Rural	Total
World	3.15	3.31	6.46	48.7	51.3	100.0
More developed countries	0.90	0.31	1.21	74.1	25.9	100.0
Less developed countries	2.25	3.00	5.25	42.9	57.1	100.0

Source: Adapted from United Nations Economic and Social Affairs Population Division (2006d): 9.

47.1 per cent urban and 52.9 per cent rural (United Nations Department of Economic and Social Affairs Population Division, 2004c: 5). The percentage change in the urban proportion was therefore

$$\frac{47.1 - 29.1}{29.1} \times 100 = 61.86\%$$

and the corresponding change in the rural proportion was

$$\frac{52.9 - 70.9}{70.9} \times 100 = -25.39\%$$

Rate of Growth of Urban Population

In many cases the analyst wishes to examine the rate of growth in the actual number of people that live in urban areas over some specified interval, rather than looking at change in the urban proportion. To do this, he or she would take the difference between *actual* population counts for the urban population. There are three different growth rates that can be computed: the *arithmetic*, the *exponential*, and the *geometric*. If the time interval is relatively short, the arithmetic average is adequate. However, if the interval is long—say five years or longer—then either the exponential or the geometric would be more appropriate (see the discussion of population growth models in Chapter 3).

The *arithmetic rate of growth of urban population* between two points in time, t_1 and t_2, can be computed as

$$\frac{\left[\dfrac{\text{urban population, } t_2 - \text{urban population, } t_1}{\text{urban population, } t_1}\right]}{n}$$

where n is the number of years in the interval between t_1 and t_2.

This formula gives the arithmetic average annual rate of change (either positive or negative) of the urban population over an interval between t_1 and t_2, but the rate can also be expressed as a percentage by multiplying the quotient by 100.

As an illustration, let's consider the case of Canada over the 30-year interval 1871–1901. The census of 1871 counted 722,343 Canadians living in urban areas. In 1901, the number of Canadians living in urban areas was 2,014,222 (Basavarajappa and Ram, 1983: A67–74). The arithmetic average rate of growth of the urban population during this interval was

$$\frac{\left[\dfrac{2,014,222 - 722,343}{722,343}\right]}{30} = 0.05962/\text{year}$$

Expressed in percentage terms, this translates into an average annual growth rate of 5.96 per cent over the 30-year interval.

If the change of the urban population is assumed to follow an *exponential* progression over time, the formula can be reworked using natural logarithms of the populations divided by the number of years in the interval. The exponential average growth rate of urban population between t_1 and t_2 is

$$\frac{\ln P_2 - \ln P_1}{n}$$

where ln stands for 'natural logarithm'.

Using the information from the example above, this works out to:

$$\frac{\ln 2,014,222 - \ln 722,343}{30} = 0.0342$$

This tells us that the annual average exponential growth rate of the urban population between the two time points is 3.42 per cent.

If growth between periods is thought to follow a *geometrical* progression, then the formula changes as follows:

$$\left[\frac{P_2}{P_1}\right]^{1/n} - 1$$

Using the same population data as before, this formula yields an average annual growth rate of urban population of 3.48 per cent per year. That is,

$$\left[\frac{2,014,222}{722,343}\right]^{1/30} - 1 = 0.0348, \text{ or } 3.48\%/\text{year}$$

As we can see, the exponential and geometric rates are quite similar.

Distribution of Urban Population by Size of Settlement

In spatial terms, urbanization implies (among other things) a rise in the extent to which the population of a nation or region is concentrated in towns and cities (Davis, 1973: 47). In order to measure this aspect of urbanization, we need to incorporate categories of urban settlement defined by population size. The first step would be to create size categories of settlements (e.g., small, medium, large), and then classify the population according to these categories. This approach requires us to define what we mean by 'small urban', 'medium urban', 'large urban', and so on. The way these categories are defined would depend on the country and also the historical period being analyzed. In a country with a population of, say, 200 million, 'small' settlements might be localities with populations of less than 5,000. In a country with a much smaller population, this designation might apply to places with populations of less than 1,000.

By classifying the urban population according to settlement size, it is possible to see how uniformly the population is distributed across settlements of different size. In some regions, for instance, the urban population may be heavily concentrated in the largest urban centres of a country, with a relatively small proportion of the people living in smaller settlements. In other cases, the distribution may be more even. An analyst could use this measure to study the extent to which the overall urban population of a particular country is concentrated in, say, cities of one million population or greater, or cities with less than 500,000 people, and so forth. As a general formula we may write

$$\text{\% urban population living in settlements of size } k \text{ at time } t = \frac{N_{k,t}}{\sum N_{k,t}} \times 100$$

where $N_{k,t}$ is the number of people residing in urban places of size k at time t, and $\sum N_{k,t}$ is the total number of people across all k categories of urban population size (i.e., the total urban population of the country) at time t.

Table 10.4 World population distribution by area of residence (urban, rural) and size class of urban settlement, 1975 and 2005

Area and urban size class	Population (in millions)		Percentage (based on total urban population)	
	1975	2005	1975	2005
Total world population	4,068	6,460		
Urban population	1,516	3,150	100.00	100.00
10 million or more	65	293	4.29	9.30
5 million to 10 million	131	204	8.64	6.48
1 million to 5 million	333	713	21.97	22.63
500,000 to 1 million	179	318	11.81	10.10
Fewer than 500,000	808	1,622	53.30	51.49
Rural population	2,552	3,310		

Source: Adapted from United Nations Economic and Social Affairs Population Division (2006d): 19

Table 10.4 shows that just over half of the world's urban population resides in places with fewer than 500,000 inhabitants. Between 1975 and 2003, however, the proportion of the urban population living in places of this size declined, from 53.30 to 51.74 per cent. In 2005, about 23 per cent of the world's urban population lived in settlements of between 1 and 5 million residents. In proportionate terms, this settlement size increased slightly from 21.97 per cent in 1975. Urban places of 10 million or more inhabitants (known as *megacities*) have seen their share of the world's urban population increase over this interval from 4.29 per cent to 9.30 per cent, the largest gain over this period across all five urban size classes. And although the population in settlements of between 5 and 10 million grew in absolute terms (from 131 million to 175 million) over the interval, the share of population for this urban size category declined in proportionate terms from 8.64 to 5.75 per cent.

Change in the Number of Settlements of a Given Population Size

The data in Table 10.4 show how the global population changed, over a 30-year interval, for five categories of urban settlement classed according to population size. Another way to chart these changes would be to look at the increase and decrease in the number of settlements of each size. So, for example, we could look at the change in the number of cities exceeding a population of 100,000 across several time periods. The percentage change in the number of settlements of size k between t_1 and t_2 can be computed as follows:

$$\left[\frac{\begin{array}{l}\text{number of settlements of size } k, t_2 \\ - \text{ number of settlements of size } k, t_1\end{array}}{\text{number of settlements of size } k, t_1}\right] \times 100$$

As we discussed earlier, we can obtain an arithmetic average annual rate of change for this measure by dividing the percentage by n, the number of years in the interval between t_1 and

t_2. For example, Davis (1972) determined that between 1950 and 1960, the number of cities worldwide with 125,000 or more inhabitants grew from 757 to 1,071. Thus, for urban settlements of this size, the absolute change was 314. The corresponding percentage change in the number of settlements of this size over the ten-year interval was

$$\frac{1{,}071 - 757}{757} \times 100 = 41.48\%$$

The annual arithmetic average rate of growth for cities over 125,000 between 1950 and 1960 was thus

$$\frac{41.48}{10} = 4.15\%/\text{year}$$

On a global level, the United Nations Department of Economic and Social Affairs Population Division (2004c: 14) reports that in 1975 the world contained 21 'urban agglomerations' with 5 million or more inhabitants. By 2003 that number had risen to 46, for an absolute change of 25 and a corresponding percentage growth of 119 per cent. The average arithmetic annual percentage change in the number of cities with populations of 5 million or more over the 28-year interval was therefore 4.25 per cent per year. Most of this increase may be attributed to growth in the world's less developed regions, which were home to 33 of the 46 urban agglomerations of this size in 2003 (United Nations Department of Economic and Social Affairs Population Division, 2004c: 14).

Components of Urbanization

As a demographic process, urbanization is driven by changes in fertility and mortality (natural increase) and in internal and external migration (net migration). In general, the greater the rate of growth of the national population, the faster the rate of urbanization (Davis, 1955). But urbanization is also a spatial phenomenon, and an administrative one. *Annexation* is the process in which a city artificially expands its geographical boundaries and also its population size by appropriating adjacent land or territory that typically contains sparsely or densely populated smaller settlements. *Incorporation* of new places is a legal/administrative process that formalizes the establishment of settlements as towns or cities. Incorporation essentially increases the number of towns and cities in a country.

The relative contribution of natural increase and net migration to urban growth has varied over history. Prior to the Industrial Revolution, from the thirteenth century through the seventeenth century, European cities grew mostly through migration rather than through natural increase. These cities were generally characterized by high mortality rates that would typically exceed birth rates by a significant margin, thus accounting for negative rates of natural increase. The high mortality was due to underdeveloped socioeconomic conditions and widespread infectious diseases, including the notorious pandemic known as the Black Death, which wiped out about a quarter of western Europe's population during its most devastating period, between 1348 and 1350 (Langer, 1973). The population levels of cities subject to such adverse demographic conditions could be maintained by migration from the countryside (Davis, 1973: 102–3; de Vries, 1984: 199–200; United Nations Department of Economics and Social Affairs, 1973: 196).

Cities in Europe did not reach self-maintenance (in terms of population growth through natural increase) until the eighteenth and nineteenth centuries. Paris and London achieved self-maintenance by the close of the eighteenth century, while a number of German and Swedish cities gained this status during the first half of the nineteenth century (United Nations Department of Economics and Social Affairs, 1973: 196). Between 1841 and 1911, towns and cities in England and Wales grew more by natural increase than by net in-migration. In urban areas as a whole, net migration was responsible for only one-sixth of the overall population growth in England and Wales. The city of London grew from 2.3 million to 7.3 million during this time, with natural increase accounting for 3.8 million of this growth and net migration 1.3 million (or roughly 33 per cent) (Hinde, 2003: 251).

In general, we can say that over the nineteenth and twentieth centuries, natural increase replaced migration as the main factor in urban growth. This is particularly true of the industrialized countries, where urbanization has peaked and the rural populations are relatively small. Today, mortality and fertility rates in the urban and rural populations of industrialized countries are no longer very different (both being generally low), and it is fair to conclude that future urban population growth will occur mainly through natural increase. In major immigrant-receiving nations like Canada and the United States, urban growth through natural increase will be supplemented by significant international migration.

Natural increase is responsible for a large portion of urban population growth in most contemporary developing countries, accounting for over half of urban population growth in some cases. It is also true that the contributions to urban growth of natural increase and net migration are not uniform across regions in the developing world (Beier, 1976; Gugler, 1988; National Research Council, 2003; Preston, 1979). McGee and Griffith (1998) have shown that between 1980 and 1990, natural increase explained about half of urban growth in the less developed regions (taken as a whole), with the remaining half attributable to the combined effects of net migration and reclassification (e.g., annexation). In Africa and Latin America specifically, natural increase was responsible for between 60 and 73 per cent of urban growth over this 10-year interval. In Asia, by contrast, more than half of the urban growth could be credited to rural-to-urban migration and reclassification of settlement boundaries. McGee and

Griffith (1998) concluded that as fertility rates continue to decline in developing countries, internal migration may play a greater role in the projected population growth of urban centres. However, it seems reasonable to suggest that, in general, high rates of urban growth are at least as much a function of natural increase as of rural-to-urban migration. The National Research Council (2003) has confirmed recently that in an overall sense, about 60 per cent of urban growth in the developing countries can be attributed to the effect of natural increase, and the balance left to migration and reclassification.

Urbanization History

Early Origins of Cities

Urbanization as a historical process cannot be understood in isolation from the development of early cities in the ancient world. The very concept of human civilization is inextricably tied to the development of cities (De Coulanges, n.d.; Faris, 1963: 341; Hall, 1998; Mumford, 1961; Scott, 1988; Weber, 1905 [1958]). Civilization in its etymology means urbanization, cities being the points of political and cultural progress through history, and the places where modern economies developed (Keyfitz, 1996b: 269).

The oldest village known is thought to have been a place just outside of present-day Jericho, in Palestine. It is believed that it may have sprung up around a shrine used by roving bands of hunter-gatherers; by about 10,500 years ago, it had evolved into a small farming village. Many millennia passed before the first undisputed cities were established, about 5,500 years ago (Balter, 1998). The expansion of these early settlements coincided with the rise of farming, during the Neolithic Revolution, also known as the Agricultural Revolution (Cipolla, 1967; Gist and Favia, 1974). The fertile agricultural lands in the valleys of the Tigris and Euphrates rivers of Mesopotamia, in a region that has been described as the 'Fertile Crescent'

In 1958, excavations in southern Anatolia (Turkey), led by the British archaeologist James Mellaart, revealed the remains of an 8,000-year-old settlement, Catal Huyuk, which dates to about 6500 BCE. Once hailed as the earliest city, with a population of about 10,000, Catal Huyuk is thought to be the largest and best preserved site of the Neolithic age, the age in which agriculture developed. Among the many findings uncovered in this prototypical Neolithic village is evidence that the people of Catal Huyuk were among the world's first farmers and artisans, and that they buried their dead under the plastered floors of their houses. In fact, skeletal evidence has led archaeologists to surmise that the people of Catal Huyuk must have had elaborate burial rituals that likely reflected deep expressions of emotional ties to their departed (Balter, 1998, 2005).

(i.e., the hilly uplands of present-day Israel, Lebanon, Jordan, Syria, northern Iraq, and western Iran), served as an ideal setting for the beginnings of urban life in the Old World. The surplus food produced in these alluvial regions would sustain a number of prospering cities, including Ur, Uruk, Susa, Sialk, Mashkan-shapir, Babylon, Nippur, Kish, and Tepe Yahya (Kenoyer, 2005; Lamberg-Karlovsky and Lamberg-Karlovsky, 1971 [1973]; McDowell, 2005; Stone and Zimanky, 2005). By 2500 BCE, cities had also emerged in the Indus valley of present-day Pakistan and, by 1800 BCE, in the middle reaches of the Yellow River in northern China (Sjoberg, 1965 [1973]: 20). These and other urban communities may have diffused outward from Mesopotamia. In the New World, the ancient Mayas, the Zapotecs, the Mixtecs, and the Aztecs of Central America developed urban communities on a major scale long before the arrival of European explorers (Gist and Favia, 1974; Sjoberg, 1965 [1973]).

There appears to have been three essential requirements for the first cities to emerge:

- an ecological base conducive to the development of viable agriculture (i.e., with favourable climate and soil and an abundant supply of water);
- gradual improvements in technology to produce surplus food and distribute it to the population; and
- a complex, socially stratified mode of organization (i.e., with specialization and coordination of economic activities) (Cipolla, 1967; Sjoberg, 1960: 27–31).

Abundant food production allowed people to form settlements that would, in time, become densely populated. These settlements developed complex stratified forms of social organization, as the production and distribution of food required a social system beyond that of the family and the kin group (Boserup, 1965).

Many of the early cities eventually disappeared as a result of warfare, epidemic diseases, and other catastrophic developments; a number of them were rediscovered and resettled, only to disappear under conditions of war, invasion, disease, natural disaster, neglect, and mass aban-

donment. Cities such as Babylon, Ur, Uruk, Nippur, Kish, and Mashkan-shapir all became extinct (Johnson, 1954 [1973]; Proskouriakoff, 1955 [1973]; Stone and Zimansky, 2005). Others, though, including Rome, Athens, and Istanbul, have managed to survive through periods of decline and ascendancy. What distinguished this latter group of cities was their ability to reconstruct, adapt and innovate, and ultimately flourish as centres of commerce, culture, knowledge, religion, and political influence (Hall, 1998; Sjoberg, 1965 [1973]: 24–5).

Sjoberg (1960) has classified cities through history into four major categories:

- the folk-preliterate society
- the feudal town
- the pre-industrial city (e.g., in the Roman Empire and medieval Europe)
- the urban-industrial city after the Industrial Revolution

Sjoberg's classification places cities on a continuum, reflecting the nature of their societies at each stage of their development. For instance, the feudal European city was typically small, not larger than a town, with unpaved streets and small houses surrounding the landlord's imposing estate, and usually a monastery. The medieval era in Europe brought early signs of the rise of pre-industrial European cities, where political power became consolidated in impressive complexes of technological, cultural, religious, and governmental structures. Later, as Europe entered the industrial age in the eighteenth and nineteenth centuries, financial and commercial organizations took over as the dominant urban forms alongside these other institutions (Hall, 1998; Mumford, 1961; Sjoberg, 1960).

Industrialization and Urbanization
Urbanization progressed gradually over most of human history but has accelerated significantly during the last two centuries, driven largely by industrialization. The Industrial Revolution began in the mid-1800s in England and Wales,

The Neolithic Revolution was a turning point in human history. The origins of civilization as we know it today evolved during this part of our collective historical existence. Agriculture, as we have seen, began during the Neolithic age, but we can also trace our understandings of science and technology to the early architects of the Neolithic, who devised ways to build the first houses using the most basic of elements: stone, mud, and timber. '[A]ll the blessings and features of modern civilization'—including art, organized religion, architecture, writing, cities, and even humanity's darker features, such as war, social inequality, and exclusion—'can be traced to that seminal moment in human prehistory when people decided that they wanted to live together in communities' (Balter, 2005: 3).

before spreading to other areas of northern, western, and southern Europe and eventually to the New World (Canada, the US, Latin America, Australia, New Zealand) and Japan. Why does industrialization lead to rising levels of urbanization? To answer this question we must look at the important role of rural-to-urban migration.

During the early stages of the population explosion in Europe, from the mid-nineteenth century to the early twentieth century, the majority of the population lived on farms in rural communities. Sustained high rates of natural increase during this part of European history sparked unprecedented levels of population growth in the then largely rural sector. The effect of population growth on rural communities soon became evident to the people, for every time two or more children came of age within a family, the land had to be divided in order for the young to establish themselves. As a result, parcels of farmland became smaller and smaller, and people in the countryside began to look toward the towns and cities, where jobs in factories were becoming abundantly available (Davis, 1963; Friedlander, 1969; Kennedy, 1973). It was this shift to an economy based on urban industrial manufacturing that sparked the rural exodus in Europe during the nineteenth and twentieth centuries, and we can argue that the spread of urbanization in the modern demographic history of the Western world can be attributed largely to the destabilizing effects of the Industrial Revolution on the agrarian system of economic production. And as was discussed earlier, only later, once the majority of a country's population has become concentrated in its cities and towns, does natural increase take over as the leading factor in urban population growth.

Worldwide, urbanization is proceeding at differential rates, with some regions growing rapidly and others nearing a saturation point. The United Nations has kept records of urbanization for all countries since 1950. According to the 2005 revision of their *World Urbanization Prospects*, the percentage of the world's urban population rose from 29.0 in 1950 to 48.7 in 2005 (United Nations

Department of Economic and Social Affairs Population Division, 2006d). This accounts for a change in the absolute number of people living in urban areas from 0.73 billion in 1950 to 3.15 billion in 2005. Although currently there are more people living in rural than in urban areas throughout the world, this situation is projected to reverse in the very near future. In fact, as of 2007, the world's urban and rural percentages had practically converged, with the urban proportion reaching nearly 50 per cent (49.4 per cent) (United Nations Department of Economic and Social Affairs Population Division, 2008a). Figure 10.1 shows the historical and projected trends in urban and rural populations for the world and major development regions.

According to the UN's estimates, the annual rate of urbanization worldwide between 1950 and 2005 was 0.94 per cent per year. Between 2005 and 2030, this rate is expected to drop to 0.83 per cent per year. This slowdown in the overall rate of urban growth has to do with the declining pace of urbanization in the more developed countries, where urbanization is reaching a limit, and the contribution of the developing countries, where rates of urbanization, though greater than in the more developed countries, are expected to follow a declining trend over time. By 2030, the urban share of the world's population is projected to reach 60 per cent, and will likely grow to almost 70 per cent by the year 2050 (United Nations Department of Economic and Social Affairs Population Division, 2008a: 7). In spite of the anticipated slowdown in the rate of urbanization, these projections, together with past trends, point to the inescapable conclusion that our planet is becoming increasingly urbanized, and that most of the world's population will soon be living in urban areas (see Figure 10.2).

Urban Systems

Within countries or regions, urbanized human settlements tend to naturally arrange themselves

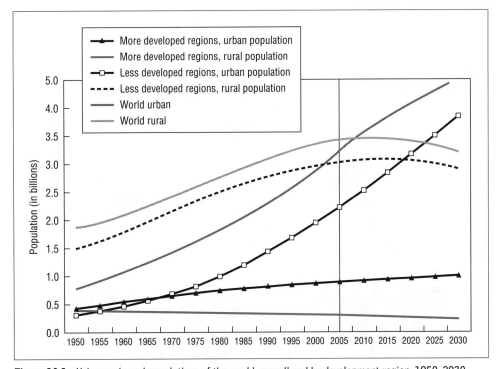

Figure 10.1   Urban and rural populations of the world, overall and by development region, 1950–2030

Source: United Nations Department of Economic and Social Affairs Population Division (2006d): 9, 15. Reprinted with the permission of the United Nations.

in what geographers call *urban systems*. These are networks consisting of cities, towns, and smaller urban settlements connected by roads, communication systems, and social and economic activity. The constituent parts of an urban system are interdependent: no one town or city in the system is wholly self-sufficient, and each one relies in varying degrees on the goods and services produced by other centres within the system. Urban systems are also characterized by a high level of social interaction among the constituent centres as a result of their interconnectedness in economic, sociological, and geographic terms.

Urban Hierarchy

Geographers typically view the urban system as constituting a hierarchical arrangement of settle-

ments of varying sizes within a defined geographic space, such as a country or a province (Christaller, 1933 [1966]; Losch, 1954). In strictly demographic terms, urban places tend to arrange themselves according to population size, from largest to smallest (or *vice versa*). Strongly correlated with population size (in direct proportion) is the primacy and centrality of urban centres in social and economic terms, especially in the production and distribution of goods and services. Compared to smaller urban centres, a large city will typically produce a greater variety of goods and services for its own population and for those of its surrounding areas and hinterlands. Thus, its sphere of social and economic influence extends well beyond that of smaller urban places. Geographers have coined the term *urban hierarchy* to describe these interrelated

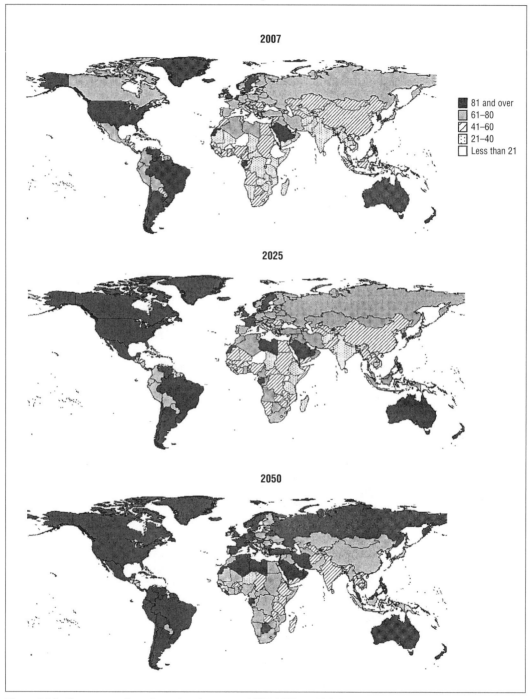

Figure 10.2 Percentage of population in urban areas, 2007, 2025, and 2050

Source: United Nations Department of Econonmic and Social Affairs Population Division (2008a): 8, Figure 1. Reprinted with the permission of the United Nations.

aspects of urban systems. A conceptual perspective of this is shown in Figure 10.3.

A *primate city* is a city that accounts for a dis-

proportionate share of the overall population of a country. Jefferson (1939) specified that cities are primate if they are at least twice as large as

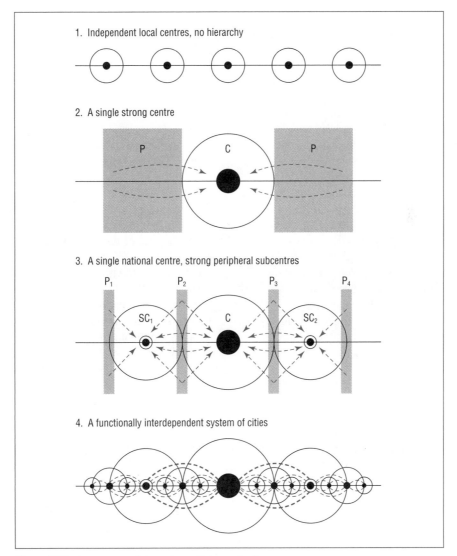

Figure 10.3 A sequence of stages in spatial organization

Note: C = Dominant centre; P = Periphery; SC_1 and SC_2 = Secondary centres; P_1 to P_4 = Peripheral regions between centres. The arrows can be thought of as indicating the direction of migratory attraction of a centre and therefore its political and economic geospatial dominance. In (3) the peripheral areas exert pressures on the centres for economic and political integration. In (4) a complex interdependent urban system evolves, with some centres being dominant and others less dominant in economic and political influence.

Source: Gilbert and Gugler (1992): 39.

A city may become primate because of its favourable location in a productive region. In the late 1930s, Jefferson (1939: 227) coined the term *primate city* to describe the demographic and economic bases that favoured certain cities over others. Jefferson pointed to the cases of Chicago (field crops), Seattle (forests), and Pittsburgh (minerals) as American examples of cities whose rise to prominence had been fuelled by favourable natural factors. It is also possible that a city may become dominant because of its advantageous situation on lines of communication or transportation, as in the cases of New Orleans and New York. In other cases, a dominant city emerges because a successful entrepreneur has chosen it as a site of manufacturing (as with Detroit, home to Henry Ford's automobile empire). These kinds of forces—natural, social, economic—often act together. And once a city becomes larger than any other in its country or region, this fact alone gives it an impetus to grow even more. It draws people from surrounding cities and gains character by virtue of being the best market for exceptional products and ideas.

the next largest city and more than twice as significant in terms of economic, political, social, and cultural influence on the nation or region. Jefferson added that a primate city, as a country's leading city, is always disproportionately expressive of national capacity and feeling, making it both a product and a reflection of its nation's culture. For example, Paris (with a population of 2.2 million) is definitely the focus of France and has a population more than double that of the country's second largest city (Marseilles, population 800,000). The United Kingdom's primate city, London, has a population nearly seven times as great as that of the second largest city, Birmingham (6.9 million versus 1 million). Similarly, Mexico City (population 9.8 million in

the city; 16.6 million in the metropolitan area) outshines Guadalajara (1.7 million), and a huge divide exists between Bangkok (population 5.9 million) and Thailand's second largest city, Nakhon Ratchasima (278,000) (United Nations Department of Economic and Social Affairs Population Division, 2002c).

Based solely on the demographic criterion for primacy (i.e., having a disproportionately large population) not every country has a primate city. India's most populous city, Mumbai (formerly Bombay), with its population of 9.9 million, is not significantly larger than Delhi, which is home to 7 million; Kolkata (formerly Calcutta) is the country's third-largest city with 4.4 million inhabitants, and Chennai (formerly Madras) is fourth, with 3.8 million. China, Canada, Australia, Brazil, and the United States are other examples of countries without primate cities; in none of these countries is there a vast difference between the top city and the second- and third-ranked cities.

Besides having large populations and embodying their national cultures, primate cities are major centres of economic and social activity; they dominate the country—and, in some cases, the areas beyond their national boundaries. Size and influence are strong pull factors that attract additional residents, causing the primate city to grow at a much greater rate than the smaller cities in the country. A primate city is often also a capital city and thus a centre of political power. In this respect it is important to note that primacy is not simply a matter of population size (Small and Witherick, 1986: 170). If one applies the size and rank criteria alone to define primacy, then some of the largest metropolitan areas of the world—including, for example, New York, Karachi, and Mumbai (Bombay)—are not primate. However, if one considers primacy in its broader sense, as embodying a nation's culture and dominant influence in social, political, cultural, and economic matters, then these cities are clearly primate cities.

Based solely on population size and rank criteria, McKibben and Faust (2004: 115) indicate that of the 20 cities in the world with the highest degree of primacy in 2000, only one (Lisbon) was in a developed country (Portugal); the remaining 19 were all in developing countries, beginning with Conarky, which makes up 74.9 per cent of the total population of Guinea:

Conarky (Guinea), 74.9%
Panama City (Panama), 73%
Guatemala City (Guatemala), 71.8%
Beirut (Lebanon), 69.8%
Brazzaville (Congo), 67.1%
Santo Domingo (Dominican Republic), 65.1%
Kuwait City (Kuwait), 61.8%
Luanda (Angola), 60.8%
Port-au-Prince (Haiti), 60.3%
Lisbon (Portugal), 60.1%
Ndjamena (Chad), 57.3%
Phnom Penh (Cambodia), 55.4%
Bangkok (Thailand), 54.9%
Yerevan (Armenia), 52.2%
Kabul (Afghanistan), 52.1%
San Jose (Costa Rica), 51.3%
Quagadougou (Burkina Faso), 51.3%

Three cities had the highest primacy in the world in 2000 by virtue of their containing 100 per cent of their nations' populations: Hong Kong, Gaza Strip, and Singapore (McKibben and Faust (2004:115).

Running counter to the principle of primacy is a view of urban hierarchy known as the *rank-size rule of cities*. Empirical studies have shown that in a set of statistical observations (such as incomes, population sizes, housing prices) there will be a few very large values or objects, and that as the value decreases, the number of items or cases increases in a fairly regular way. In 1949, Zipf devised the theory of rank-size rule as an expression of this fundamental principle.[1]

His goal was to explain that with respect to population size, a country's cities follow a general rule based on a relationship between the size of the largest city and the relative rank of cities of lesser size. In general, the number of small towns in a country exceeds the number of medium-sized towns, which outnumber the large towns.

Based on the rank-size rule, Zipf (1949) devised a general theory of how settlements develop within a region. Settlement patterns, he argued, are determined by the opposing forces of *diversification* and *unification*. Diversification tends to promote the establishment of small communities scattered over territory in locations best situated for gathering raw materials for economic production. Under these conditions, communities are widely spread and largely autonomous. Unification operates in an opposite manner. As economic activity becomes more diversified and complex it becomes more efficient for production and consumption to take place in one big city. Unification tendencies minimize the costs and difficulties associated with transporting manufactured goods. Optimum population distribution is thought to occur when both forces, diversification and unification, are operating in a geographical system, so that the ratio of large to medium and small settlements remains consistent as the overall population grows.

Figure 10.4 is early evidence that the urban hierarchy of some countries fits Zipf's model fairly well. However, there are in some cases notable deviations from the expected distribution (Clarke, 1970). Indeed, most geographers now expect deviations to occur in any empirical application of the Zipf equation, and as a result it is now commonly viewed as a probability

[1] Clarke (1970: 51) points out that even though the rank-size rule is attributed to Zipf, often others preceded Zipf in developing this 'rule', most notably Auerbach (1913) in Germany, and Lotka (1925) in the United States.

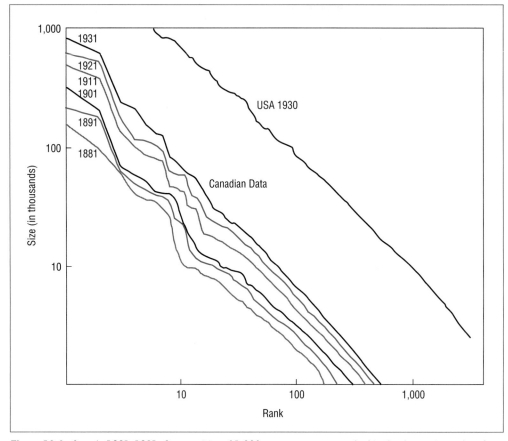

Figure 10.4 Canada 1881–1931: Communities of 1,000 or more persons, ranked in the decreasing order of population size

Note: The Canadian urban system has conformed fairly consistently to the rank-size rule. As urbanization brought increased populations to cities at every level in the urban hierarchy, the rank-size graph has shifted to the right.

Source: Zipf (1949): 417.

model rather than a 'law' (Brackman et al., 1999; Reed, 1988). (Please refer to the exercise section of this chapter for more on this point.)

An important category of cities today is the *global city*. Global cities have large populations, though they are not necessarily among the world's largest cities, nor are they necessarily primate in their own countries, as defined strictly in terms of population size. They are distinguished by their specialized functions, which give them a wide sphere of influence in the global arena (Hall, 1996; Sassen, 2000, 2001a,

2001b). London, Amsterdam, Genoa, Lisbon, and Venice have all been global cities at some point in history. These were important centres that gained this distinction by virtue of their centrality with respect to trade, commerce, and political influence worldwide. Paris, Rome, and Vienna became world cities in the eighteenth century, just as others, like Genoa, were becoming much less influential. Over the course of the nineteenth century, Berlin, Chicago, Manchester, and New York emerged as leading global cities, while Venice receded in importance.

In the contemporary world, with the acceleration of economic globalization, world cities are associated less with the concentration of imperial power and the orchestration of trade than with key features of today's global economy, such as transnational corporate organizations, international banking and finance, international non-governmental agencies, and supranational governance. The global cities of today may be thought of as command centres for the world's flow of scientific, technological, and cultural information, the production of new knowledge, the dissemination of global culture, and the control of finance and investing. Cities like New York, Miami, Los Angeles, London, Brussels, Paris, Tokyo, Hong Kong, Singapore, and Johannesburg are highly interconnected along these critical dimensions, and in this sense they provide an interface linking the global to the local. In other words, they feature the economic, cultural, and institutional structures that, on the one hand, help channel national and provincial resources into the global economy, and on the other, transmit the impulses of globalization back to the national and provincial centres. Chase-Dunn and Jorgensen (2003) have ranked world cities in three categories according to extent of global influence (see Figure 10.5). Although all three categories of world cities are important and are highly interconnected, alpha cities are the most central in terms of global influence; beta cities are of intermediate impact, and gamma cities are of least influence globally.

As we have discussed, not every country has a primate city or a global city. In most countries, the urban landscape is made up of *urban agglomerations*, which are clusters of interconnected cities and towns, smaller urban centres, and even rural areas within a specified region. From a sociological standpoint, agglomerations in North America are useful units of study, since they tend to be highly integrated socially and

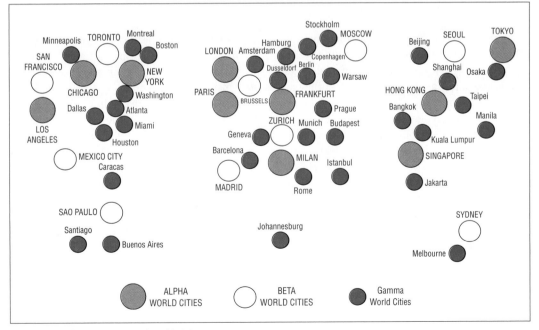

Figure 10.5 Globalization and world cities

Source: Chase-Dunn and Jorgenson (2003): 142. Reprinted with permission of Gale, a division of Thomson Learning: www.thomsonrights.com. Fax 800 730-2215.

Seven Key Features of Global Cities

In their review of the global city, Knox and Marston (2004: 404) list a number of key functional characteristics of world cities:

1. They are the sites of most of the leading global markets for commodities, commodity futures, investment capital, foreign exchange, equities, and bonds.
2. They are home to clusters of specialized advanced business services, especially those that are international in scope and that are attached to finance, accounting, advertising, property development, and law.
3. They house concentrations of corporate headquarters—not just of transnational corporations but also of major national firms and large foreign firms.
4. They house concentrations of national and international headquarters of trade and professional associations.
5. They are sites of leading non-governmental organizations (NGOs) and intergovernmental organizations (IGOs) that are international in scope.
6. They are headquarters for the most powerful and internationally influential media, news and information services, and culture industries (including art and design, fashion, film, and television).
7. They attract, because of their importance and visibility, many terrorist acts.

economically, with commuter populations travelling daily between the home community and the urban core. However, the urban agglomeration is essentially a statistical construct: they are intended to impose a relative degree of homogeneity on a given geographic area with respect to demographic, economic, social, historical, or cultural characteristics (Plane, 2004: 86).

The concept of agglomeration is associated with an important urban designation: the *metropolitan area*. The nomenclature and criteria used to define a metropolitan area vary from country to country. For instance, in Canada these areas are called census metropolitan areas, or CMAs. In the United States, they are called metropolitan statistical areas (MSAs) and are distinguished from micropolitan statistical areas, which are smaller. It is important to note that as with urban agglomerations, the metropolitan area is a statistical construct created by national bureaus of statistics for ease of collecting and comparing data.

In Canada, the metropolitan area is a statistical construct that includes both *census metropolitan areas* (CMAs) and *census agglomerations* (CAs). Both of these units, as defined by Statistics Canada, are formed by one or more adjacent municipalities centred on a large urban area, known as the *urban core*. The urban core may be thought of as a city, and the city typically gives its name to the census agglomeration or census metropolitan area. For example, the Montreal CMA encompasses nearly 100 municipalities, including Laval, Longueuil, La Prairie, and Mirabel; the city of Montreal, on the island of Montreal, is the central municipality for which the CMA is named. A census agglomeration must have an urban core population of at least 10,000. A census metropolitan area must have a total population of at least 100,000, of which 50,000 or more live in the urban core. For a municipality to be considered part of an adjacent CMA or CA, it must have a high degree of integration with the urban core, as measured by commuting flows derived from census place of work data. A census agglomeration can lose its designation if its urban core population falls below 10,000, but a census metropolitan area retains its status even if its total population or urban core population falls below the minimum requirements. Finally, the *urban fringe* consists of any urban areas in the CMA or CA that are not contiguous to the urban core; rural areas of a CMA or CA make up its *rural fringe* (Statistics Canada, 2006f).

Megacities are urban agglomerations of 10 million persons or more. The proportion of people around the world living in megacities is actually quite small: as of 2005, only about 4.5 per cent of the world's population lived in a megacity, though this is expected to rise to 5 per cent by 2015 (United Nations Department of Economics and Social Affairs Popula-

tion Division, 2004c: 2; 2006d: 19). In 1950, there were just two megacities in the world— New York (12.3 million) and Tokyo (11.3 million). Twenty-five years later, the list of megacities had doubled, with Shanghai (11.4 million) and Mexico City (10.7 million) joining Tokyo and New York, whose populations had risen to 26.6 million and 15.9 million, respectively. By 2005, the number of megacities worldwide had grown to 20, and this figure is expected to rise to 24 by 2015 and to 27 by 2025 (United Nations Department of Economics and Social Affairs Population Division, 2004c; 2006d). Table 10.5 lists the world's megacities and their changing growth trends from 1950 and projected to 2015.

Some urban systems extend beyond metropolitan urban agglomerations to form a *megalopolis*. Gottman (1964) coined this term based on her observations of the almost continuous and densely populated urban and suburban area

The Grave Plight of Cairo's Homeless

The megacities of the developing world face major challenges. Population growth is occurring at a rapid pace as a result of high rates of natural increase and high net migration from the countryside, and city officials are struggling to provide and maintain basic infrastructures, such as piped water, sanitation, drainage, roads, accessible health care, and affordable housing. The last of these is an especially difficult challenge. Evidence of inadequate housing is visible in the shanty towns that are common in many large cities of the developing world.

The problem is so bad that in some cases, people have resorted to setting up residence in urban cemeteries owing to the lack of proper, accessible housing in their cities. For decades, Cairo's Northern Cemetery—a walled Mamluk-era necropolis better known as the City of the Dead—has been home to tens of thousands of people who have made their homes inside the often extensive tombs that sometimes hold centuries-old bodies. They are but some of the Egyptian capital's many urban poor, forced to live among the dead by conditions of overcrowding and unemployment that plague this city of 11 million. No one knows just how many people live in the City of the Dead, since Cairo's government officials effectively ignore the cemetery's residents, who are forced to steal electricity from adjacent neighbourhoods. Water is easier to come by since most of the mausoleums have their own wells. (MacKinnon, 2006).

Table 10.5 Population of urban agglomerations with 10 million inhabitants or more in 2005 and their average annual rates of change; selected periods, 1950–2015 (projected)

Urban agglomeration	Population (in millions)					Average annual rate of change (%)[c]	
	1950	1975	2000	2005	2015	1975–2000	2000–2015
Tokyo, Japan	11.3	26.6	34.4	35.2	35.5	0.93	0.08
Mexico City, Mexico	2.9	10.7	18.1	19.4	21.6	1.99	1.05
New York, USA[a]	12.3	15.9	17.8	18.7	19.9	0.55	0.60
Sao Paulo, Brazil	2.3	9.6	17.1	18.3	20.5	2.15	1.13
Mumbai (Bombay), India	3.0	7.3	16.1	18.2	21.9	3.15	1.84
Delhi, India	—	4.4	12.4	15.0	18.6	4.08	2.12
Shanghai, China	5.3	11.4	12.9	14.5	17.2	2.28	1.72
Kolkata (Calcutta), India	4.4	7.9	13.1	14.3	17.0	1.98	1.73
Jakarta, Indonesia	—	4.8	11.1	13.2	16.8	3.37	2.41
Buenos Aires, Argentina	5.0	9.1	11.8	12.6	13.4	1.20	0.65
Dhaka, Bangladesh	—	2.2	10.2	12.4	16.8	5.81	3.04
Los Angeles, USA[b]	4.0	8.9	11.8	12.3	13.1	1.07	0.63
Karachi, Pakistan	—	4.0	10.0	11.6	15.2	3.56	2.67
Rio de Janeiro, Brazil	2.9	7.6	10.8	11.5	12.8	1.39	1.07
Osaka-Kobe, Japan	4.1	9.8	11.2	11.3	13.3	0.45	0.04
Cairo, Egypt	2.4	6.4	10.4	11.1	13.1	1.82	1.66
Lagos, Nigeria	—	1.9	8.4	10.9	16.1	5.84	3.94
Beijing, China	3.9	8.5	10.8	10.7	12.9	1.91	1.82
Moscow, Russian Federation	5.4	7.6	10.1	10.7	11.0	1.12	0.34
Metro Manila, Philippines	—	5.0	10.0	10.7	12.9	2.53	1.90

Notes: Urban agglomerations are ordered according to their population size in 2005. Blank lines denote data not available.

[a] Refers to the New York–Newark urbanized area.

[b] Refers to the Los Angeles–Long Beach–Santa Ana urbanized area.

[c] Rates calculated by the exponential growth formula.

Source: United Nations Department of Economic and Social Affairs Population Division (2004c): 8, 120; United Nations Department of Economic and Social Affairs Population Division (2006d): 21.

stretching from Boston to Washington, DC, in the United States. In a more general sense, the concept refers to the growing together and integration of large urban agglomerations into a higher order of urban structure or complex. Megalopolitan areas are discernible in highly urbanized countries. Examples include the Axial Belt of Britain; the Pacific coastlands of Honshu, Japan; the Rhone valley of France, between Lyons and Marseilles; the region of California between Los Angeles and San Diego; and the Pearl River Delta in China (Knox and Marston, 2004; Small and Witherick, 1986).

Figure 10.6 shows the megalopolitan system of North America, which extends through parts of eastern and western Canada and the United States. In Canada, the St Lawrence River and Great Lakes urban system encompasses some of the country's oldest and largest urban centres. It begins in the easternmost Atlantic region with Halifax and St John's, extends down through the many cities, towns, and villages along the shores

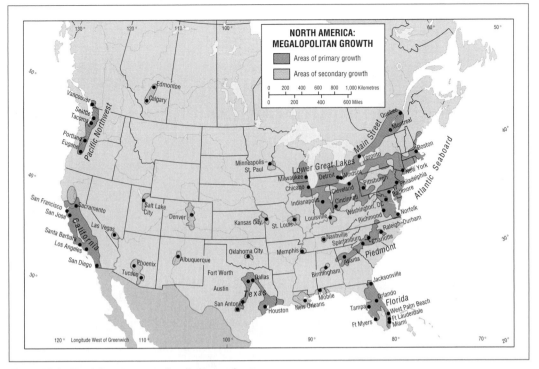

Figure 10.6 North American megalopolitan growth

Source: de Blij and Murphy (2003): 356. Copyright © 2002. Reprinted with permission of John Wiley & Sons, Inc.

of the St Lawrence River between Quebec City and Montreal, and reaches across the densely populated cities and surrounding urban areas of Ontario, including Kingston, Ottawa, Toronto, Hamilton, London, Saint Catharines–Niagara, and Windsor, among other localities. Approximately 13.5 million people—almost 45 per cent of Canada's population—live in this megalopolitan system.

Canadian Urbanization

Urbanization History

Canada's history traces a transformation brought about by the combined forces of industrialization and urbanization. The country has passed through several economic regimes, from the mercantilist era prior to 1800 to the current post-industrial age, characterized by rapid eco-

nomic globalization. As part of its transformation, the country has witnessed major interrelated demographic, technological, and social changes (see Table 10.6). Broadly speaking, Canada's urbanization history can be divided into five stages:

1. Pre-Confederation
2. Confederation to 1900
3. The early 1900s to 1931
4. The 1930s to 1951
5. The 1950s to the present

1. Pre-Confederation

In the early stages of Canada's development, population growth was largely a rural phenomenon, as most people lived and worked on farms. In the early period of colonization, during the seventeenth century, the process of settlement formation was in its incipient phase. The prior-

Table 10.6 Canada's population by urban and rural residence and various measures of change, 1871–2006

Period	Population			% change from previous period: total population	% urban	% rural	% change from previous period		% change in urban and rural proportions (change from previous period)	
	Total	Urban	Rural				Urban	Rural	Urban	Rural
1871	3,689,257	723,094	2,966,163		19.6	80.4				
1881	4,324,810	1,111,476	3,213,334	17.2	25.7	74.3	53.7	8.3	31.1	-7.6
1891	4,833,239	1,536,970	3,296,269	11.8	31.8	68.2	38.3	2.6	23.7	-8.2
1901	5,371,315	1,874,589	3,496,726	11.1	34.9	65.1	22.0	6.1	9.7	-4.5
1911	7,206,643	3,012,377	4,194,266	34.2	41.8	58.2	60.7	19.9	19.8	-10.6
1921	8,787,949	4,165,488	4,622,461	21.9	47.4	52.6	38.3	10.2	13.4	-9.6
1931	10,376,786	5,447,813	4,928,973	18.1	52.5	47.5	30.8	6.6	10.8	-9.7
1941	11,506,655	6,409,207	5,097,448	10.9	55.7	44.3	17.6	3.4	6.1	-6.7
1951	14,009,429	8,811,931	5,197,498	21.8	62.9	37.1	37.5	2.0	12.9	-16.3
1956	16,080,791	10,709,807	5,370,984	14.8	66.6	33.4	21.5	3.3	5.9	-10.0
1961	18,238,247	12,803,249	5,434,998	13.4	70.2	29.8	19.5	1.2	5.4	-10.8
1966	20,014,880	14,690,922	5,323,958	9.7	73.4	26.6	14.7	-2.0	4.6	-10.7
1971	21,568,310	16,521,325	5,046,985	7.8	76.6	23.4	12.5	-5.2	4.4	-12.0
1976	22,992,605	17,566,350	5,426,255	6.6	76.4	23.6	6.3	7.5	-0.3	0.9
1981	24,343,000	18,549,366	5,793,634	5.9	76.2	23.8	5.6	6.8	-0.3	0.8
1986	25,309,000	19,412,003	5,896,997	4.0	76.7	23.3	4.7	1.8	0.7	-2.1
1991	27,297,000	21,073,284	6,223,716	7.9	77.2	22.8	8.6	5.5	0.7	-2.1
1996	28,847,000	22,644,895	6,202,105	5.7	78.5	21.5	7.5	-0.3	1.7	-5.7
2001	30,007,094	23,915,654	6,091,440	4.0	79.7	20.3	5.6	-1.8	1.5	-5.6
2006	31,612,897	25,290,318	6,322,579	5.4	80.0	20.0	5.8	3.8	0.4	-1.5

Notes: Definitions of 'urban' and 'rural' have changed over the censuses as follows: from 1871 to 1941, 'urban population' means population living in incorporated villages, towns, and cities regardless of size; all remaining population is 'rural'. In 1951, the definition of 'urban' was changed to all persons living in cites, towns, and villages of 1,000+, whether incorporated or not, plus the urban fringes of census metropolitan areas; 'rural' included the remaining population. In 1956, 'urban population' was defined as the population living in cities, towns, and villages of 1,000+, whether incorporated or not, plus the urban fringe of major urban areas (cities with a population of 25,000–50,000); 'rural' included the remaining population. For 1961 and 1971, 'urban' was defined as: (1) population of incorporated cities, towns, and villages with a population of 1,000 and over, plus (2) unincorporated places of 1,000 and over having a population density of at least 1,000 per square mile, plus (3) built-up fringes of (1) and (2) having a minimum population of 1,000 and a density of at least 1,000 per square mile. For 1976 and beyond, 'urban population' is population living in an area having a population concentration of 1,000 or more and a population density of at least 400 per square kilometre; 'rural' is the remaining population (Leacy, 1983: A54–93).

The urban and rural populations for 2006 were estimated based on the assumption that the urban population represents 80 per cent of the total population of Canada in 2006.

Source: Leacy (1983); Statistics Canada (2002d); Statistics Canada (2000): 702–3, Table A.4; Haines and Steckel (1995a): 149; McVey and Kalbach (1995a): 149; Statistics Canada website (2005b); Statistics Canada (2007b).

ity for early settlers was to establish safe settlements near natural transportation routes (rivers, lakes, oceans) that would facilitate trade with Europe. In the period from about 1760 to 1849, known as the pre-industrial stage or staples economy stage (Innis, 1930),[2] urbanization proceeded gradually. By the first quarter of the nineteenth century, Quebec (then Lower Canada) had two cities of over 20,000 (Montreal and Quebec City) that comprised more than 5 per cent of the entire colonial population of British North America; this made Canada one of the most urbanized regions of the world at that time.

Urbanization gained momentum in the latter half of the nineteenth century (from roughly 1849 to 1896) as the nation reoriented itself toward an industrial-based economy. With the construction of the Canadian Pacific Railway, completed in 1885, the interior hinterland of the country (Manitoba and the rest of the Prairies, and the westernmost province of British Columbia) attracted increasing numbers of settlers, many from western, northern, and eastern Europe. Although this settlement of the West involved a great deal of movement to farms and homesteads in rural areas, increases in agricultural production combined with a gradual shift toward a service economy did, in time, stimulate significant urban growth, as more and more people relocated to the towns and cities. Taken together, the early urban settlements of Upper and Lower Canada (i.e., Quebec and Ontario) and the easternmost areas of the country, plus the emerging settlements in the interior, accounted for an urbanization level of roughly 16 per cent by 1861 (McVey and Kalbach, 1995a: 146–7; Stone, 1969: 29).

2. Confederation to 1900

By 1867, the year of Confederation, the number of urban settlements in the country had grown steadily, so that in 1871, the proportion of the population living in urban locations (at that time mostly in Ontario, Quebec, and the Maritimes) had risen to nearly 20 per cent (see Table 10.7 and Figure 10.7). The scale and speed of urbanization during this part of Canada's history was quite dramatic.[3] Indeed, the decade after Confederation can be seen as marking the nation's 'take-off' toward higher levels of urbanization (Stone, 1969). The large-scale shift toward a concentration of the population in medium- and large-sized cities, away from the rural areas and smaller towns, had truly begun, and by 1901, out of a population of approximately 5.4 million, roughly 35 per cent of Canadians were urban dwellers.

Census figures for 1891 give an indication of how Canada's population was distributed among cities of various size. In that year, Canada's census recorded a total of 4.8 million inhabitants, of whom nearly 30 per cent were living in urban settlements (Leacy, 1983: A67–74; Stone, 1969: 39). Out of an overall urban population of about 1.5 million living in incorporated centres of at least 1,000 persons, about 30 per cent of Canadians were located in places with a population of between 1,000 and 4,999. An almost equal proportion were settled in incorporated places of over 100,000 (27.6 per cent) and places of between 5,000 and 29,999 (27.1 per cent); another 16 per cent resided in localities of between 30,000 and 99,999 population (Leacy, 1983: A67–74).

3. The Early 1900s to 1931

Although urbanization was well underway by the start of the twentieth century, the majority of Canadians still lived a life centred on the land, the homestead, the village, and the parish. Life was in many respects regulated by the seasons: the spring and summer months were typically spent cutting down trees to clear new land for

---

[2] See Watkins (1963) and Bertram (1963) for extensions of the ideas of Innis (1930).

[3] For a useful overview of the historical evolution of the Canadian settlement system see Dahms (1990).

Table 10.7 Canadian society and urban evolution

Period	Pre-1900	1900–45	1945–75	1975–2000+
Regime	Mercantile	'Great Transformation'; early industrial capitalism, early industrial society	Post-war economic boom; advanced capitalism	Post-industrial shift; globalization
Prevailing technology	Sail, horse and cart, water, early steam power	Steel, rail, early automobiles, telephone, telegraph	Auto, aviation, television	Expressways, telecommunications
Urban system	Small number of port cities acting as entrepôts; hierarchy of service centres develops as agriculture expands	Industrial core (Windsor to Quebec City) and resources-based periphery; incipient decline in eastern provinces	Metropolitan dominance; rapid increase in proportion of urban population	Toronto gains primacy; shift to the West; Quebec's system becomes more autonomous, some centres decline
Urban economy	Staples-based	Early corporate capitalism; Fordism	Advanced corporate capitalism; late Fordism	Deindustrialization; shift to service economy
Urban demographics	Immigration (primarily European) is major input to population growth	Urbanization growth slowed by World War I, Great Depression, and World War II	Baby boom; high rates of post-war immigration	Baby bust; population growth becomes a function of immigration (mainly from non-traditional sending areas)
Political agenda	From colonies to Confederation	Nationalism: transportation, protective tariffs, regional support	Keynesian policies; federal transfers; regional economic development	Federalism under siege; NAFTA; multiculturalism; retrenchment of welfare agenda
Canadian distinction	Colonialism	Staples base	Welfare state	Multiculturalism

Source: Adapted from Bunting and Filion (2000): 54; Bourne (2000): 32.

planting, tilling the soil and preparing it for seeding, and, later on in the season, harvesting crops. Much of the rhythm of daily activity was directed to the production of basic necessities to last through the long and harsh winter months (Fingard, 1974). But these conditions were changing, and over the early decades of the new century, Canada, in the throes of rapid urban-

ization, began its inexorable move from being a folk society to becoming an urban industrial nation.

It was not until the early 1920s that the share of Canada's population living in urban localities reached 48 per cent (Stone, 1969). At that time, there were just six cities in Canada with populations in excess of 100,000. But it was during this

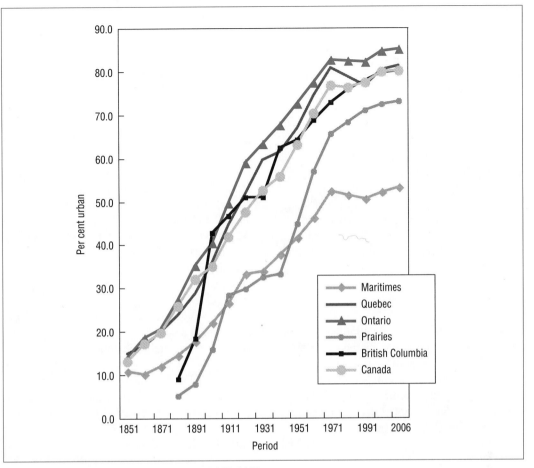

Figure 10.7 Urban trends by region, Canada, 1851–2006

Notes: For Canada total prior to 1951, Newfoundland is excluded. Nunavut came into existence in 1998 (formerly part of the North-west Territories). From 1851 to 1911 the urban population figures refer to incorporated cities, towns, and villages of 1,000 and over only. From 1921 to 1951 the percentages are estimates of the percentages that would have been reported in the respective censuses had the 1961 census definition and procedures been used. For the regions, percent urban in 2006 was extrapolated based on the his-torical series. For changes in the definition of 'urban' since 1871, refer to the note under Table 10.6 (page 460).

Source: Haines and Steckel (2000): 702–3, Table A.4; Kubat and Thornton (1974): Table P1; Leacy (1983); McVey and Kalbach (1995a): 149; Statistics Canada (2002d); Statistics Canada website (2005a, 2005b); Stone (1969): 29. United Nations Department of Economic and Social Affairs Population Division (2007).

period that the process of urbanization picked up momentum. By 1931, over 45 per cent of Canadians had their homes in cities of 100,000 and over, and a declining proportion (about 16 per cent) of the people were situated in the smaller settlements of between 1,000 and 4,999

population (Leacy, 1983: A67–74). The census of 1921 recorded a total population of about 8.8 million, representing an increase of 22 per cent over the previous decade and a dramatic rise of 63 per cent from the population enumerated in 1901 (5.4 million). Between 1901 and 1911, the

For an interesting account of life during Quebec's frontier society in the early 1900s, see Louis Hémon's novel *Maria Chapdelaine* (1916). The ongoing struggle to tame the harsh farmland is the backdrop to this classic of world literature, which is set in Quebec's Lac Saint-Jean region. When the heroine of the novel rebuffs a wealthy American suitor to marry a French-Canadian farmer, she effectively chooses to continue the same difficult life she and her family have always known. Her devotion to traditional values, writes Paul Socken (1997), 'symbolizes Quebec's determined struggle to secure a foothold for rural, Catholic, French society away from the onslaught of modern, urban, English-dominated life'.

urban share of the total population had risen to about 42 per cent, reaching, by the early 1920s, about 47 per cent. Significant during this part of the nation's history was the massive immigration from the European continent, particularly eastern Europe. A large share of the immigrants settled in rural areas, but many others ended up in the growing cities (McVey and Kalbach, 1995a).

By the start of the Great War of 1914–17, Canada's shift to an industrial-based economy had been firmly imprinted, and by the start of the Great Depression of 1929–39, the composition of today's Canadian urban system had been established (McInnis, 2000b). We can make this claim based on three criteria:

- the timing at which the current census metropolitan areas reached 25,000 people;
- the degree of growth of centres of 25,000 people; and
- the evolution of places with populations of 2,500 or more. (McInnis, 2000b)

By 1901, ten of the current census metropolitan areas of Canada had passed the 25,000

mark in population. One-fifth of the nation's population resided in those ten centres, the five largest of which were Montreal (368,000), Toronto (240,000), Quebec City (104,000), Ottawa–Hull (98,000), and Halifax (51,000). Edmonton and Calgary were among the cities that had not yet surpassed 25,000 inhabitants, whereas Winnipeg had already reached a population of 48,000 people. In 1901, Vancouver was still comparatively small, with just 33,000 people. (By comparison, in 1901 the United States had 160 cities with populations over 25,000, together accounting for 26 per cent of its national population.) By 1931, all but one (Sudbury) of the CMAs listed in Table 10.8 (page 468) had passed the 25,000 mark in population, and the portion of the Canadian population living in these centres had reached just over 39 per cent.

In terms of the second criterion, by 1931 Canada had added 14 cities of 25,000 or more, bringing the overall percentage of the population living in CMAs to just over 42 per cent. As for the third and broadest of the three criteria of urbanization, population in places of 2,500 or more, the proportion of the Canadian population that could be considered 'urban' had, by the third decade of the twentieth century, risen to almost 50 per cent (McInnis, 2000b: 558–64). Stone's analysis (1969: 39), based on the percentage of the population classified as urban, confirms that, indeed, 1931 was the turning point at which Canada's population attained a 50 per cent level of urbanization.

4. The 1930s to 1951

Based on all reasonable indicators, by the early 1930s Canada's population had crossed the 50 per cent threshold of urbanization. Yet during the 1930s and 1940s, urbanization proceeded at a slower pace than in earlier decades. The depression of the 1930s brought high levels of unemployment and a crisis in the agricultural economy (owing in part to draught and dust-bowl conditions on the Prairies and in the plains of the US), which slowed internal migration from the countryside to the city considerably. Stone (1969: 21) points out that the period from the start of the Great Depression up to the Second World War was marked by an enormous dampening of the factors promoting urbanization. Immigration and population growth decelerated markedly, as did the demand for the products of non-primary activities; the rate of investments in new technologies also dropped.

Faced with the harsh realities of the day, many city-dwellers returned to the countryside, seeking refuge with family and relatives in the rural areas. As a result, city growth slowed. According to McInnis (2000b: 566), the Atlantic region, which had been an area of heavy emigration in the 1920s, ceased to lose people. Cities in Quebec barely retained their natural increase, and Toronto, Hamilton, and London—the major urban centres of Ontario—probably did not retain their natural increase. Winnipeg's population kept constant, and Vancouver grew by barely 10 per cent. Rural-to-urban migration had essentially stopped, and interregional migration dropped to a low level. Many Prairie residents, driven off their farms during the severe draught, had nowhere promising to go. Only British Columbia grew substantially, with gains derived from both natural increase and net international migration.

During the Second World War, Canada entered a recovery phase of unprecedented industrialization. New industries developed to meet the wartime demand for such items as synthetic rubber, roller bearings, diesel engines, antibiotics, high-octane gasoline, aircraft, ships, and other industrial products. The steel industry boomed. This new wave of industrialization caused heavy declines in the agricultural working force in the 1940s, and these changes, combined with a period of unprecedented prosperity following the war, were tied to a marked upsurge in urbanization. By 1951, the national level of urbanization had surpassed the 60 per cent mark (Stone, 1969: 22).

5. The 1950s to the Present

Aided by the high fertility of the baby boom years (1946–66) and augmented by large waves of immigrants from all over the world, Canada in the 1950s and 1960s underwent another period of intense urbanization. By 1961, almost three-quarters of the population was classified as urban. The prosperous post-war urban economy played a major role in this trend, as the rural sector underwent significant depopulation through large outflows of migrants headed for the country's metropolitan centres. By the early 1960s, nearly 8 million people, out of a national population of just over 18 million, lived in 18 urban places with populations of 100,000 or more, and by 1971, the number of CMAs in Canada had grown to 23, increasing to 27 in 1996.

The 1960s brought a significant development in Canada's urbanization: the 'flight to suburbia'. Canada's inner cities underwent decline as the growth of industry in the urban fringes, combined with the development of efficient systems of roadways and transportation routes linking the core and surrounding areas, enabled people to commute between the suburbs and other sections of the metropolitan system on a daily basis. People could live in the suburbs, where real estate properties were more affordable, and commute fairly easily to work either in the city or in other surrounding urban localities.

In the 1970s and 1980s, Canada went through two successive economic recessions. The first one, sparked by the oil crisis of 1973, hit the economies of central Canada (Ontario and Quebec) particularly hard. Meanwhile, the discovery of abundant oil reserves in Alberta promoted staggering economic growth in this part of the country. The economic boom in Alberta during the 1970s drew internal migrants from virtually every part of Canada, and while urban centres in the east were experiencing a slowdown in population growth, cities such as Calgary and Edmonton grew rapidly, aided by the significant endowments of a resource-based economy. Further west, Vancouver was also benefiting from rapid population growth.

In the early 1980s, when the census recorded a 76 per cent level of urbanization, Canada was hit with another economic downturn. Immigration to Canada slowed considerably, and fertility rates, which had been dropping since the early 1960s, continued to fall. Unlike the 1970s economic downturn, which favoured western Canada, the recession of the 1980s hurt the economies of the western provinces (particularly Alberta's), forcing many people to the urban areas of central Canada to look for work opportunities. Most immigrants coming to Canada likewise headed to metropolitan areas like Toronto, Ottawa–Hull, and Hamilton in the east, and to Vancouver in the west. Population growth in Calgary and Edmonton therefore slowed considerably. In Quebec, Montreal continued to experience net migratory losses that began in the aftermath of the separatist Parti Québécois's win in the 1976 provincial election (Shaw, 1985); Montreal would not see net migration gains until the early years of the new millennium (Statistics Canada, *The Daily*, 2004b: 11). By 1981, Toronto had replaced Montreal as the leading metropolis in the country, with Vancouver forming the third-largest population across Canadian metropolises (Statistics Canada, 2002d).

The 2001 census showed that approximately 80 per cent of Canada's population was urban. Moreover, of the total population of just over 30 million, about one-third lived in just three urban centres: Toronto, Montreal, and Vancouver. Since the mid- to late 1990s, Alberta has been experiencing another significant economic upturn, which has drawn people from centres—particularly in eastern Canada—whose economies are not as strong (Statistics Canada, 2002d). Both Calgary and Edmonton, the province's largest cities, have seen their populations grow significantly. Between 1996 and 2001, Calgary's population grew by almost 16 per cent to just below 1 million, a mark it

surpassed the following year (Statistics Canada, 2006a). Edmonton's growth rate of just under 9 per cent accounted for a population size of 937,000 in 2001. On the west coast, Vancouver grew by 8.5 per cent to almost 2 million people at the end of this period. Significant growth was not restricted to Canada's western cities. Oshawa grew by 10.2 per cent and Toronto by 9.8 per cent (Statistics Canada, 2002d). Among those urban areas that experienced population declines between 1996 and 2001 are Regina, St John's, Trois-Rivières, Saint John, Chicoutimi–Jonquière, Thunder Bay, and Sudbury. As we will see, some of these CMAs experienced recoveries in population growth between 2001 and 2006, while some among those that had experienced population gains between 1996 and 2001 lost population in the interval between 2001 and 2006 (see Figure 10.9, page 472).

Canada's Metropolitan System

It has already been mentioned that throughout most of its history, Canada has not had a single, dominant primate metropolis (McInnis, 2000b). However, there is little doubt that, overall, Montreal and Toronto have shared dominance in terms of population growth and economic centrality to Canada. As early as 1871, Montreal, with 153,516 residents, and York (Toronto), with 115,974, had populations well above the third-ranked Canadian City (Quebec). By the turn of the century, Montreal's population had risen to just over 371,000, while Toronto's was notably smaller, at 272,663 (Dominion Bureau of Statistics, 1953: 6-25, 6-54). Between 1901 and 1931, Toronto grew more rapidly than Montreal, yet its population at the end of this period was still just 80 per cent of Montreal's. It was not until the mid-twentieth century that Montreal and Toronto (with 1.1 million people and 1.4 million people, respectively) had roughly equal populations. By the time of the 1981 census, Toronto had gained supremacy, reaching close to 3 million as compared to Montreal's population of 2.8 million (McInnis,

Figure 10.8 The Canadian Urban System—census metropolitan areas and census agglomerations

Source: Bourne (2000): 27.

2000b: 560, 597). The 2001 census counted Toronto's population as being almost 4.7 million, and that of Montreal just over 3.4 million.

It is clear that the population gap between Canada's two largest CMAs has stretched quite substantially over the last quarter of the twentieth century, and it is even greater today (see Table 10.8). In 2001, the population of Toronto CMA exceeded that of Montreal's by approximately 1.2 million people, and as of 2006, the difference had grown to 1.5 million. There are several factors to consider in regards to this development.

The first, noted earlier, is the rise of the Quebec separatist movement, beginning with Parti Québécois's victory in the 1976 provincial election, which sparked heavy out-migration flows from the province of Quebec generally and the

city of Montreal in particular. Many of those who left Quebec—including many English-speaking Canadians—ended up in Ontario, mostly in Toronto. A second factor favouring Toronto has been the much heavier volume of international migration it has received since the early 1970s. Finally, part of Toronto's growth may be attributed to its amalgamation of several municipalities surrounding the metropolitan region.

Following Toronto and Montreal in Canada's metropolitan system is the CMA of Vancouver, with a population of close to 2 million in 2001. The combined CMA of the National Capital Region, comprising Ottawa and Gatineau, held just over 1 million people in 2001. Calgary and Edmonton would be the next largest CMAs, though as of 2001 neither had yet attained a

Table 10.8 Populations of the metropolitan areas of Canada in 2001, traced back to 1901

CMA	1901	1931	1951	1961	1971	1981	1991	2001
Toronto	240,000	828,000	1,117,000	1,824,000	2,628,043	2,999,000	3,893,045	4,682,897
Montreal	368,000	1,040,000	1,395,000	2,110,000	2,743,208	2,828,000	3,127,240	3,426,350
Vancouver	33,000	333,000	531,000	790,000	1,082,352	1,268,000	1,602,500	1,986,965
Ottawa–Gatineau	98,000	188,000	282,000	430,000	602,510	718,000	920,855	1,063,664
Edmonton		84,000	173,000	337,568	495,702	657,000	839,920	937,845
Calgary		84,000	139,000	279,062	403,319	593,000	754,030	951,395
Winnipeg	48,000	289,000	354,000	475,989	540,262	585,000	652,355	671,274
Quebec City	104,000	188,000	275,000	357,568	480,502	576,000	645,550	682,757
Hamilton	68,000	175,000	260,000	395,189	498,523	542,000	599,760	662,401
St Catharines–Niagara	35,000	100,000	162,000	150,226	303,429	304,000	364,550	377,009
London	43,000	78,000	122,000	181,283	286,011	284,000	381,525	432,451
Kitchener		53,000	63,000	154,864	226,846	288,000	356,420	414,284
Halifax	51,000	79,000	134,000	183,946	222,637	278,000	320,500	359,183
Victoria		61,000	104,000	154,152	195,800	233,000	287,900	311,902
Windsor		115,000	158,000	193,365	258,643	246,000	262,075	307,877
Oshawa		34,000	52,000	80,918	112,093	154,000	240,105	296,298
Saskatoon		44,000	55,000	95,526	126,449	154,000	210,025	225,927
Regina		57,000	71,000	112,141	140,734	164,000	191,695	192,800
St John's			68,000	90,838	131,814	155,000	171,855	172,918
Sudbury		25,000	71,000	110,694	155,424	150,000	157,610	155,601
Chicoutimi–Jonquière (Saguenai)*		31,000	56,000	105,009	133,703	135,000	754,030	154,938
Sherbrooke		37,386	62,166	70,253	84,570	115,983	139,195	153,811
Abbotsford								147,370
Kingston**				53,526	59,047	109,000	136,401	146,838
Trois-Rivières		50,000	68,000	83,659	97,930	111,000	136,300	137,507
Saint John		50,000	78,000	95,563	106,744	114,000	124,980	122,678
Thunder Bay		46,000	66,000	110,920	112,093	121,000	124,430	121,986
Total population of Canada	5,371,000	10,377,000	14,009,000	18,238,247	21,568,310	24,343,185	27,296,860	30,007,094
Total CMAs population	1,088,000	4,069,386	5,916,166	9,026,259	12,228,388	13,825,599	17,394,851	19,296,926
CMAs as % of total population	20.3	39.2	42.2	49.5	56.7	56.8	63.7	64.3

*Since 2002, Chicoutimi–Jonquière CMA has been renamed Saguenai CMA.

**Figures for Kingston in 1961 and 1971 pertain to the central city (urban core) of Kingston.

Notes: To be included in 1901, 1931, and 1951, the population must have been at least 25,000.

Source: Adapted from McInnis (2000b): 597–8; McVey and Kalbach (1995a): 71, 163; Stone (1969): 175; Dominion Bureau of Statistics (1953, 1962); Statistics Canada (1973a, 1982, 1992); Statistics Canada website (2005c).

population of 1 million (both have since reached that milestone). The remaining CMAs, as of 2001, had populations well below these numbers, the smallest being Thunder Bay, with a population of 121,986.

A number of interrelated factors account for the noted patterns of metropolitan development in Canada. The location of the nation's initial settlements and economic specialization in certain kinds of industries in different parts of the country figure prominently. Most important, according to McInnis (2000b), is the fact that the Canadian urban system has historically divided economic functions in a way that has precluded the emergence of a single dominant metropolis. Canada's major cities have essentially been ports. In the nineteenth century, Toronto was an inland port, on the same lake and river system as Montreal, which was the leading commercial centre of Canada. In the latter half of the nineteenth century, Montreal reinforced its position as the country's leading Atlantic port even though it was more than a thousand miles from the ocean. Quebec City, prior to the middle of the nineteenth century, had been the principal Atlantic port, but Montreal took over that role after the river channel was dredged to allow ocean ships to reach it. Had Montreal been the leading port from the outset and not had to share economic functions with Quebec City, it might have established a position of dominance earlier. Toronto, meanwhile, became the leading urban centre and eventually the metropolitan focus of industrial Canada. Vancouver, initially, was less a port city than a commercial centre for BC's logging industry; however, with the opening of the Panama Canal in 1914, Vancouver's position as a port city was greatly enhanced, and it remained the only major city on Canada's Pacific coast (McInnis, 2000b: 560–1).

The 2001 census saw the addition of Abbotsford, BC, and Kingston, Ontario, as census metropolitan areas, bringing the number of CMAs to 27 and furthering the trend of Canada's popula-

tion gravitating towards its largest urban areas. The combined population of the 27 CMAs made up over 60 per cent of the nation's total population. As Table 10.9 shows, the population of these CMAs tends to be concentrated in the urban cores; the portion of residents living in the urban and rural fringes tends to make up a small portion of the overall population of CMAs. So, for example, 96 per cent of Toronto's population lives in the urban core; Greater Sudbury has the lowest portion of urban core population among CMAs, at 67 per cent of its overall population. Halifax, Kingston, and Saint John are exceptional cases: in each of these cities, the rural fringe makes up over a quarter of the population.

Looking at the nation as a whole, about 92 per cent of the population living in CMAs in 2001 lived in an urbanized core; only 2.7 per cent of CMA residents lived in an urban fringe, and just 5.8 per cent lived in the rural fringe of their CMA. In the census agglomerations—urban areas with populations between 10,000 and 99,999—the urban core is also dominant, though to a lesser degree.

Recent Developments: The 2006 Census

Early data released from the 2006 census confirms that most of Canada's population growth continues to take place in urban areas, especially in the suburbs and areas surrounding the suburbs of the largest census metropolitan areas. Most rural areas grew at a slower pace than the country as a whole, and some experienced population decline. Generally, these rural areas are in remote locations, far from the country's large urban centres (Statistics Canada, 2007a: 21).

The 2006 census shows that growth rates higher than the national average were concentrated largely in four large regions that have major metropolitan centres: southern Ontario, southeastern Quebec, BC's lower mainland, and the Calgary–Red Deer–Edmonton corridor. Between 2001 and 2006, southern Ontario's 'Golden Horseshoe' experienced high popula-

Table 10.9 Canadian CMAs and CAs, showing urban core, urban fringe, and rural fringe populations in 2001 (CMAs arranged in alphabetical order)

CMA	Population, 2001				Percentages			
	Total	Urban core	Urban fringe	Rural fringe	Urban core	Urban fringe	Rural fringe	Total
Abbotsford	147,370	129,475	0	17,895	87.9	0.0	12.1	100.0
Calgary	951,395	899,659	20,159	31,577	94.6	2.1	3.3	100.0
Chicoutimi–Jonquière*	154,938	123,588	2,778	28,572	79.8	1.8	18.4	100.0
Edmonton	937,845	814,031	36,448	87,366	86.8	3.9	9.3	100.0
Greater Sudbury	155,601	103,879	33,874	17,848	66.8	21.8	11.5	100.0
Halifax	359,183	276,221	7,116	75,846	76.9	2.0	21.1	100.0
Hamilton	662,401	618,820	2,180	41,401	93.4	0.3	6.3	100.0
Kingston	146,838	108,158	0	38,680	73.7	0.0	26.3	100.0
Kitchener	414,284	387,319	13,018	13,947	93.5	3.1	3.4	100.0
London	432,451	385,981	6,561	39,909	89.3	1.5	9.2	100.0
Montreal	3,426,350	3,312,045	27,691	86,614	96.7	0.8	2.5	100.0
Oshawa	296,298	234,779	40,011	21,508	79.2	13.5	7.3	100.0
Ottawa–Hull	1,063,664	848,881	101,118	113,665	79.8	9.5	10.7	100.0
Quebec City	682,757	635,184	1,922	45,651	93.0	0.3	6.7	100.0
Regina	192,800	178,225	6,610	7,965	92.4	3.4	4.1	100.0
Saint John	122,678	90,762	2,724	29,192	74.0	2.2	23.8	100.0
Saskatoon	225,927	196,816	10,601	18,510	87.1	4.7	8.2	100.0
Sherbrooke	153,811	127,354	0	26,457	82.8	0.0	17.2	100.0
St Catharines–Niagara	377,009	315,038	22,006	39,965	83.6	5.8	10.6	100.0
St John's	172,918	140,613	7,790	24,515	81.3	4.5	14.2	100.0
Thunder Bay	121,986	103,215	0	18,771	84.6	0.0	15.4	100.0
Toronto	4,682,897	4,485,055	62,962	134,880	95.8	1.3	2.9	100.0
Trois-Rivières	137,507	117,758	3,296	16,453	85.6	2.4	12.0	100.0
Vancouver	1,986,965	1,829,854	103,498	53,613	92.1	5.2	2.7	100.0
Victoria	311,902	288,346	6,118	17,438	92.4	2.0	5.6	100.0
Windsor	307,877	274,053	1,316	32,508	89.0	0.4	10.6	100.0
Winnipeg	671,274	626,685	4,143	40,446	93.4	0.6	6.0	100.0
Total CMAs	19,296,926	17,651,794	523,940	1,121,192	91.5	2.7	5.8	100.0
Total CAs	4,542,160	3,505,068	170,080	867,012	77.2	3.7	19.1	100.0
Total CMAs + CAs	23,839,086	21,156,862	694,020	1,988,204	88.7	2.9	8.4	100.0

Notes: The populations counts for some CMAs (i.e., Victoria and Montreal) and CAs are incomplete owing to the exclusion of census data for one or more incompletely enumerated Indian reserve or settlement.

The CMA of Chicoutimi–Jonquière was renamed Saguenai CMA in 2002.

Source: Statistics Canada website (2005c). Adapted from Statistics Canada publication 'Population Counts, for Census Metropolitan Areas and Census Agglomerations, by Urban Core, Urban Fringe and Rural Fringe', 2001 Census, http://www12.statcan.ca/english/census01/products/standard/popdwell/Table-CMA-UR.cfm?T=1&SR=126&S=1&O=A. Accessed 14 January 2005.

tion growth for the zone from Peterborough to London, including Oshawa, Toronto, Hamilton, and Kitchener. Quebec's high rate of population growth occurred in a large area surrounding the island of Montreal, encompassing Montérégie, the Eastern Townships, and the Lower Laurentians. Alberta saw growth rates above the national average in a north–south corridor running from Edmonton to Medicine Hat, including Red Deer and Calgary. In BC, the lower mainland and southern Vancouver Island area, which contains three of the province's four CMAs (Victoria, Vancouver, and Abbotsford), accounted for most of the province's growth (Statistics Canada, 2007a: 21). In addition to those four major urban zones, there were other urban areas that underwent significant growth between 2001 and 2006. Notable among these are the Ottawa–Gatineau region, Moncton, Quebec City, Winnipeg, and the Grande Prairie and Wood Buffalo areas of northern Alberta.

As of the 2006 census, Canada has 33 census metropolitan areas, up from 27 in 2001. The six added since 2001 are Kelowna, BC; Barrie, Brantford, Guelph, and Peterborough, in Ontario; and Moncton, New Brunswick. Table 10.10 shows the 2006 populations of all 33 CMAs. Since 2001, Canada's CMAs grew by 1.4 million, which represents nearly 90 per cent of the country's overall population increase of 1.6 million between 2001 and 2006. The largest CMAs—Toronto, Montreal, Vancouver, Ottawa–Gatineau, Calgary, and Edmonton, all with populations above 1 million—grew by 6.9 per cent, well above the national average growth rate.

Figure 10.9 charts the growth rates of the 33 CMAs over the two census periods of 1996–2001 and 2001–6. The fastest-growing CMA during both periods was Barrie, followed by Calgary, Oshawa, and Edmonton. In 2006, more than two-thirds (68 per cent) of the Canadian population—21.5 million people—lived in one of these 33 urban centres, 14.1 million of them in the six largest CMAs. But as Figure 10.9 shows, growth across the CMAs was uneven, and some

Table 10.10 Population of Canada's census metropolitan areas in 2006

Order	CMA	Province	Population
1	Toronto	ON	5,113,146
2	Montreal	QC	3,635,571
3	Vancouver	BC	2,116,581
4	Ottawa–Gatineau	ON/QC	1,130,761
5	Calgary	AB	1,079,310
6	Edmonton	AB	1,034,945
7	Quebec City	QC	715,515
8	Winnipeg	MB	694,668
9	Hamilton	ON	692,911
10	London	ON	457,720
11	Kitchener	ON	451,235
12	St Catharines–Niagara	ON	390,317
13	Halifax	NS	372,858
14	Oshawa	ON	330,594
15	Victoria	BC	330,088
16	Windsor	ON	323,342
17	Saskatoon	SK	233,923
18	Regina	SK	194,971
19	Sherbrooke	QC	186,952
20	St John's	NL	181,113
21	Barrie	ON	177,061
22	Kelowna	BC	162,276
23	Abbotsford	BC	159,020
24	Greater Sudbury	ON	158,258
25	Kingston	ON	152,358
26	Saguenay	QC	151,643
27	Trois-Rivières	QC	141,529
28	Guelph	ON	127,009
29	Moncton	NB	126,424
30	Brantford	ON	124,607
31	Thunder Bay	ON	122,907
32	Saint John	NB	122,389
33	Peterborough	ON	116,570

Source: Statistics Canada (2007a). Adapted from Statistics Canada publication 'Portrait of the Canadian Population in 2006', *2006 Census, Population and Dwelling Counts.* Catalogue no. 97-550-XIE, p. 22.

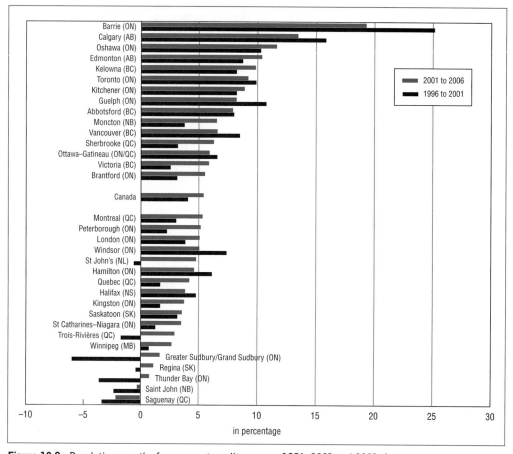

Figure 10.9 Population growth of census metropolitan areas, 1996–2001 and 2001–6

Source: Statistics Canada (2007a): 24. Adapted from Statistics Canada publication 'Portrait of the Canadian Population in 2006', 2006 Census, *Population and Dwelling Counts*. Catalogue no. 97-550-XIE.

centres (Saint John, Saguenay) experienced population declines over the two periods; others (St John's, Trois-Rivières, Sudbury, Regina, Thunder Bay) experienced population declines in the earlier census period but recovered with population gains between 2001 and 2006.

Another important trend that shows up in the 2006 census data is the significant growth within census metropolitan areas of smaller urban places outside of the CMA's central municipality. This pattern of urban development, which has been going on since the mid-twentieth century, is a product of urban sprawl,

which occurs when sustained population growth in a municipality sparks rapid development of the lands surrounding the municipality, which become suburban communities. Statistics Canada (2007a: 22) reports that between 2001 and 2006, the growth rate of peripheral municipalities within the 33 CMAs —11.1 per cent—was double the national average. During the same period, the central municipalities of the CMAs grew more slowly, at the rate of over 4.2 per cent (see Table 10.11).

Alberta's two CMAs, Calgary and Edmonton, are good illustrations of this trend. From 2001

Table 10.11 Population growth of central municipalities and peripheral municipalities for the 33 census metropolitan areas, 2001 to 2006

Region	2001	2006	Growth (%)
Central municipalities	12,230,443	12,739,103	4.2
Peripheral municipalities	7,891,108	8,769,472	11.1
Total of census metropolitan areas	20,121,461	21,508,575	6.9

Source: Statistics Canada (2007a). Adapted from Statistics Canada publication 'Portrait of the Canadian Population in 2006', 2006 Census, *Population and Dwelling Counts*. Catalogue no. 97-550-XIE, p. 31.

to 2006, Calgary's population increased by 12.4 per cent. This growth occurred along the McLeod Trail to the south and the Crowchild Trail to the north, skirting such obstacles as the Nose Hill Natural Environment Park and the Foothills Industrial Park. The municipalities around Calgary, including Cochrane, Chestermere, Airdrie, and Crossfield, grew at a torrid pace of 29.2 per cent. In Edmonton, extensive urban sprawl has occurred along the Calgary Trail to the south of the municipality, in the districts north of the municipality, and around the West Edmonton Mall. Similar growth patterns are evident in Canada's three largest CMAs: Toronto (see Figure 10.10), Vancouver, and Montreal (Statistics Canada, 2007a: 31–2).

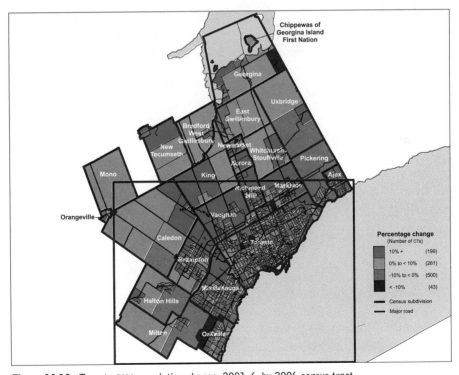

Figure 10.10 Toronto CMA population change, 2001–6, by 2006 census tract

Source: Statistics Canada (2007a). Adapted from Statistics Canada publication 'Portrait of the Canadian Population in 2006', *2006 Census. Population and Dwelling Counts*. Catalogue no. 97-550-XIE.

Some of Canada's smaller towns situated on the fringes of the metropolitan areas, beyond the suburbs, experienced rapid expansion between 2001 and 2006. Heading the list of Canada's fastest-growing *exurbia* (as they are referred to by urban planners) in Table 10.12 is Okotoks, Alberta, population 17,145, which experienced an astonishing growth rate of 46.7 per cent between 2001 and 2006. Three other places in Alberta—Wood Buffalo, Grande Prairie, and Red Deer, all three within the influence of Calgary and Edmonton CMAs—enjoyed growth rates of between 24 and 22 per cent. Near Montreal CMA, St-Jean-sur-Richelieu, with a population of almost 88,000 in 2006, grew by almost 10 per cent. The rapid growth of such small towns and rural areas on the outskirts of metropolitan centres is a testament to the importance of modern communications systems and efficient roadways that facilitate

Table 10.12   Mid-size urban centres with the fastest population growth or decline, 2001–6

Mid-sized urban centres with the fastest population growth

Order	Centre	Province	Population in 2001	Population in 2006	% change
1	Okotoks	Alberta	11,689	17,145	46.7
2	Wood Buffalo	Alberta	42,581	52,643	23.6
3	Grande Prairie	Alberta	58,787	71,868	22.3
4	Red Deer	Alberta	67,829	82,772	22.0
5	Yellowknife	Northwest Territories	16,541	18,700	13.1
6	Lloydminster	Saskatchewan/Alberta	23,964	27,023	12.8
7	Canmore	Alberta	10,792	12,039	11.6
8	Medicine Hat	Alberta	61,735	68,822	11.5
9	St-Jean-sur-Richelieu	Quebec	79,600	87,492	9.9
10	Joliette	Quebec	39,720	43,595	9.8
11	Chilliwack	British Columbia	74,003	80,892	9.3
12	Fort St John	British Columbia	23,007	25,136	9.3
13	Parksville	British Columbia	24,285	26,518	9.2
14	Lethbridge	Alberta	87,388	95,196	8.9
15	Courntenay	British Columbia	45,205	49,214	8.9
16	Granby	Quebec	63,069	68,352	8.4
17	Nanaimo	British Columbia	85,664	92,361	7.8
18	Collingwood	Ontario	16,039	17,290	7.8
19	Kawartha Lakes	Ontario	69,179	74,561	7.8
20	Vernon	British Columbia	51,530	55,418	7.5
21	Centre Wellington	Ontario	24,260	26,049	7.4
22	Drummondville	Quebec	72,778	78,108	7.3
23	Ingersol	Ontario	10,977	11,760	7.1
24	Whitehorse	Yukon	21,405	22,898	7.0
25	Woodstock	Ontario	33,269	35,480	6.6

(continued)

Table 10.12   *(continued)*

Mid-sized urban centres with the fastest population decline

Order	Centre	Province	Population in 2001	Population in 2006	% change
1	Kitimat	British Columbia	10,285	8,987	−12.6
2	Prince Rupert	British Columbia	15,302	13,392	−12.5
3	Quesnel	British Columbia	24,426	22,449	−8.1
4	Terrace	British Columbia	19,980	18,581	−7.0
5	Williams Lake	British Columbia	19,768	18,760	−5.1
6	Campbellton	New Brunswick/Quebec	18,820	17,888	−5.0
7	North Battleford	Saskatchewan	18,590	17,765	−4.4
8	Kenora	Ontario	15,838	15,177	−4.2
9	Elliot Lake	Ontario	11,956	11,549	−3.4
9	Bathurst	New Brunswick	32,523	31,424	−3.4
11	Edmundston	New Brunswick	22,173	21,442	−3.3
12	Cape Breton	Nova Scotia	109,330	105,928	−3.1
13	La Tuque	Quebec	15,725	15,293	−2.7
14	Thetford Mines	Quebec	26,721	26,107	−2.3
15	Dolbeau-Mistassini	Quebec	14,879	14,546	−2.2
16	Prince George	British Columbia	85,035	83,225	−2.1
16	Miramichi	New Brunswick	25,274	24,737	−2.1
16	Amos	Quebec	18,302	17,918	−2.1
19	Baie-Comeau	Quebec	30,401	29,808	−2.0
20	Prince Albert	Saskatchewan	41,460	40,766	−1.7
21	Timmins	Ontario	43,686	42,997	−1.6
22	Estevan	Saskatchewan	11,297	11,135	−1.4
23	New Glasgow	Nova Scotia	36,735	36,288	−1.2
24	Alma	Quebec	32,930	32,603	−1.0
24	Matane	Quebec	16,597	16,438	−1.0

Source: Statistics Canada (2007a): 34, 35. Adapted from Statistics Canada publication 'Portrait of the Canadian Population in 2006', 2006 Census, *Population and Dwelling Counts*. Catalogue no. 97-550-XIE, p. 34–5.

commuting between the larger municipalities of a CMA system and its remoter places. It is clear, too, that the growth of these smaller centres is contingent on their proximity to urban centres where jobs are abundant. Most of the mid-sized urban centres whose population declined between 2001 and 2006 are located in regions where the economy depends partly or completely on the exploitation of natural resources, most notably forests. Many, for instance, are in remote areas of British Columbia, which have been hurt by the Canada–US softwood lumber dispute, although clearly this is not the sole cause of decline.

We can observe similar patterns of growth and decline among Canada's rural areas. Table 10.13, which lists the rural towns and areas with the fastest population increases and decreases between 2001 and 2006, distinguishes two types of rural places: those that are close to urban centres and those that are more remote. In rural areas that are close to urban centres, more than 30 per cent of the labour force commutes to work in the urban centre. The growth rate of these places between 2001 and 2006 was 4.7 per cent, which was just below the national growth rate of 5.4 per cent. Key to this growth in rural areas is the existence of highway access to and from the nearby urban centre (Statistics Canada, 2007a: 36). By contrast, the 25 small towns and rural communities that experienced the fastest population declines between 2001 and 2006—Crowsnest Pass in Alberta, Marystown in Newfoundland and Labrador, Flin Flon, Manitoba, to name just a few—were all located far from large urban centres.

Table 10.13   Small towns and rural communities with the fastest increase or decrease in population between 2001 and 2006

Small towns and rural communities with the fastest population growth

Order	Small towns and rural communities	Proximity to an urban centre	Province	Population in 2001	Population in 2006	% change
1	Sylvan Lake	Adjacent	Alberta	7,503	10,208	36.1
2	Strathmore	Remote	Alberta	7,621	10,225	34.2
3	Stanley	Remote	Manitoba	5,122	6,367	24.3
4	Prévost	Remote	Quebec	8,280	10,132	22.4
5	Shelburne	Adjacent	Ontario	4,213	5,149	22.2
6	Chertsey	Adjacent	Quebec	4,112	5,006	21.7
7	Wasaga Beach	Adjacent	Ontario	12,419	15,029	21.0
8	Galway-Cavendish and Harvey	Adjacent	Ontario	4,372	5,284	20.9
9	Nanaimo F	Adjacent	BC	5,546	6,680	20.4
10	Lakeland County	Remote	Alberta	5,306	6,365	20.0
11	Steinbach	Remote	Manitoba	9,227	11,066	19.9
12	Saint-Hyppolyte	Adjacent	Quebec	6,039	7,219	19.5
13	Tiny	Adjacent	Ontario	9,035	10,784	19.4
14	Foothills No. 31	Adjacent	Alberta	16,602	19,736	18.9
15	Capital G	Remote	BC	4,307	5,101	18.4
16	Iqualuit	Remote	Nunavut	5,236	6,184	18.1
17	Rawdon	Remote	Quebec	8,648	10,058	16.3
18	Saint-Calixte	Adjacent	Quebec	4,912	5,687	15.8
19	Shefford	Adjacent	Quebec	5,133	5,941	15.7
20	Sainte-Sophie	Adjacent	Quebec	8,966	10,355	15.5
21	Sainte-Adèle	Remote	Quebec	9,215	10,634	15.4
22	Wilmot	Adjacent	Ontario	14,866	17,097	15.0
23	Winkler	Remote	Ontario	7,943	9,106	14.6
24	Lacombe	Remote	Alberta	9,384	10,742	14.5
25	Saint-Lin-Laurentides	Adjacent	Quebec	12,379	14,159	14.4

(continued)

Table 10.13 *(continued)*

Small towns and rural communities with the fastest population decline

Order	Small towns and rural communities	Proximity to an urban centre	Province	Population in 2001	Population in 2006	% change
1	Crowsnest Pass	Remote	Alberta	6,262	5,749	−8.2
2	Marystown	Remote	NL	5,908	5,436	−8.0
3	Kapuskasing	Remote	Ontario	9,238	8,509	−7.9
4	Kenora, unorganized	Remote	Ontario	7,631	7,041	−7.7
5	Stephenville	Remote	NL	7,109	6,588	−7.3
6	Bulkley-Nechako A	Remote	BC	5,696	5,290	−7.1
7	Inverness, subd. B	Remote	NS	5,769	5,369	−6.9
8	Flin Flon (part)	Remote	Manitoba	6,000	5,594	−6.8
9	Melfort	Remote	Saskatchewan	5,559	5,192	−6.6
10	Labrador City	Remote	NL	7,744	7,240	−6.5
11	Algoma, unorganized N. part	Remote	Ontario	6,114	5,717	−6.5
12	Alnwick	Remote	NB	6,566	6,152	−6.3
13	Banff	Remote	Alberta	7,135	6,700	−6.1
14	Kimberley	Remote	BC	6,484	6,139	−5.3
15	Yarmouth	Adjacent	NS	7,561	7,162	−5.3
16	La Sarre	Remote	Quebec	7,728	7,336	−5.1
17	Parry Sound	Remote	Ontario	6,124	5,818	−5.0
17	Oromocto	Remote	NB	8,843	8,402	−5.0
17	Happy Valley–Goose Bay	Remote	NL	7,969	7,572	−5.0
20	Antigonish, subd. B	Remote	NS	6,819	6,509	−4.5
20	Chibougamau	Remote	Quebec	7,922	7,563	−4.5
20	Trail	Remote	BC	7,575	7,237	−4.5
23	Chandler	Remote	Quebec	8,278	7,914	−4.4
24	Castelgar	Remote	BC	7,585	7,259	−4.3
24	Kirkland Lake	Remote	Ontario	8,616	8,248	−4.3

Source: Statistics Canada (2007a). Adapted from Statistics Canada publication 'Portrait of the Canadian Population in 2006', 2006 Census, *Population and Dwelling Counts*. Catalogue no. 97-550-XIE, p. 38–9.

The Effects of Urbanization on Rural and Small-Town Canada

In a nation that is becoming increasingly urbanized, Canada's small towns and rural villages face an uncertain future. As the 2006 data shows, some of these places thrive, others decline, and still others undergo slumps and recovery in cycles. The reasons for this are linked mainly to the changing nature of the rural economy. Unlike past times, when rural areas relied almost exclusively on the products of independent family farms and rural communities were essentially isolated from urban centres, conditions today dictate a very high degree of spatial interdependence when it comes to social and economic activity. Rural-based processing and manufacturing has become almost fully amalgamated into the larger urban economy (Beckstead et al., 2003; Coffey, 1994; Wallace, 2002).

There are those who argue that the fondly held image of rural Canada as a blend of farmland, mining towns, mill towns, and railroad towns is more a product of nostalgia than a realistic portrayal of life outside of Canada's largest cities. The remnants of resource-based industries are still found in rural areas and small towns, but the way they are organized is not the same as it once was. Large corporations have replaced small agricultural producers. Small woodlots, sawmills, and bush camps of the forestry sector have been overtaken by vast timber reserves, and there is long-haul trucking of timber to large, centralized pulp- or sawmills. Multinational corporations buy and sell materials. Small fishing boats are less commonly found in the pictur-

We Have Seen the Future, and It's Sprawl and Emissions

This week's census told us what we already knew: Canada, the world's second-largest land mass, is an urban country.

Actually, Canada is increasingly a suburban country, since the suburbs of the large cities are growing faster than the urban cores.

Beyond suburbia lies what planners call exurbia: cities within striking distance of the big ones, connected to them by highways and sprawl. Places such as Barrie, Whitby, and Brampton in Ontario; Maple Ridge, Surrey, and Port Moody in British Columbia; Vaudreuil, Mirabel, and Blainville near Montreal; and Okotoks, south of Calgary.

Taken together, 'peripheral municipalities' (the Statistics Canada term) grew by 11 per cent from 2001 to 2006, compared with 4.2 per cent for central cities. Put another way, the periphery grew by about 900,000, central cities by 500,000.

The consequences of suburbanization, therefore, will intensify. Sprawl will define the future, just as it has the past. With sprawl comes more automobile use, since suburban densities mock public transit with its point-to-point routes.

With more automobile use, and more mileage driven, will come more greenhouse-gas emissions. Add more car use to Canada's growing population, throw in solid economic development, and we have a recipe for faster, not slower, GHG growth.

Nothing the Harper government has suggested will reverse these trends, just as nothing the Liberals did had positive results.

Public transit, useful in and of itself, cannot be the principal answer to GHG-induced buildup from suburbanization. Commuter trains will serve market niches, such as those between Barrie and Toronto, the South Shore and Montreal, and Calgary and Edmonton through Red Deer.

Only economic regulations that force changes in fleet composition, and taxes that change the price and kinds of fuels, will allow more automobiles and fewer emissions. Nothing else will do, since people aren't going to hop on their bikes from, say, Whitby to Scarborough.

Only new building codes with much stricter insulation requirements and inducements/ requirements for new forms of heating (solar, heat pumps) can combat GHG buildup in new suburbs. But which government is far-sighted enough to see this necessity? Suburban politicians tend to be growth-oriented types who grew up amid sprawl, like it, and want the municipal revenues from more development.

Cities, suburbs, and exurban areas are increasing largely from net immigration. It remains the social phenomenon most responsible for changing Canada, and it is driven by federal policies (although some provinces are becoming more active) that push up the number of immigrants.

Immigration is not working as it should, as study after study shows. More immigrants than ever are landing in poverty and staying there. Fewer than before are reaching the average incomes of the population within 10 years. Do you hear a debate about this issue? It's too risky for most politicians.

A huge mismatch has opened between the nominal qualifications of arrivals and their ability to use these qualifications in the workforce. Meantime, some parts of Canada (read Alberta, but other places, too) are crying for skilled labour.

The drift to urban/suburban/exurban areas mocks the electoral system. Legislatures remain weighted toward rural areas or, in the case of Parliament, toward Atlantic Canada (and Saskatchewan), where the population remains steady while other areas grow.

Someday, someone will bring a Charter of Rights argument against the existing electoral maps. They will claim that the maps discriminate (as they clearly do) against urban/suburban voters by according them less representation than equality merits. You might think a court would refuse to hear the case on the ground the issue is political. Under the Charter, courts are wont to rule on just about anything.

Immense and costly efforts have been made to resist the population movement from rural Canada: regional development programs; farm, fish, and forestry subsidies; industrial inducements; favourable treatment of mining shares. Look at the Quebec election. Half the population lives in and around Montreal; most of the promises are for the development of the 'regions'.

The best that can be said for these costly efforts might be that they have slowed down the movement. The political pressure remains intense on all governments to defend and, where possible, enrich these programs, aided by outdated political maps.

Source: Jeffrey Simpson, 2007, 'We have seen the future, and it's sprawl and emissions', *The Globe and Mail* (17 March): A12. Reprinted with permission from The Globe and Mail.

esque harbours of Canada's east and west coasts, and sea products are caught, cleaned, and frozen at sea on large vessels, or else farmed in pens according to a business model typically controlled and administered by large conglomerate corporations (Reimer, 2005: 79–80).

These widespread changes have dramatically altered many rural settlements and small towns, in some cases quite negatively. For instance, as many of the traditional rural jobs are taken over by highly efficient new technologies, young men and women must look for employment in the city. Depopulation and economic stagnation are the too-often inevitable outcomes of all such changes. Regions that have been hit especially hard include parts of Newfoundland and Labrador, Cape Breton Island, northern New Brunswick, the Gaspé region of Quebec, and rural Saskatchewan (Beshiri and Bollman, 2001; Bollman, 2000; Catto, 2003; Dale, 1988; Hodge and Qadeer, 1983; Reimer, 2005).

On the other hand, some parts of rural Canada have not fared as badly. Parts of the North, central British Columbia, southwestern

Quebec, and rural regions surrounding larger cities in the Atlantic provinces have experienced population growth over the last 20 years. Recognizing the diversity of rural and small-town Canada, Hawkins and Bollman (1994: 78–80) have suggested a seven-category typology of settlements:

1. *primary settlements* – census divisions containing the largest cities in Canada; these areas have growing populations and high levels of net migration
2. *urban frontier* – rural areas strongly integrated into the economic activities of urban regions, with characteristics similar to primary settlements, though less pronounced
3. *rural nirvana regions* – areas that have positive population growth, especially as a result of the in-migration of young workers; these rural areas do relatively well economically and socially, and are typically situated near large urban centres
4. *agro–rural* – small, dispersed, agriculture-based settlements in the Prairies, southern Quebec, the Annapolis Valley region of Nova Scotia, and parts of British Columbia
5. *rural enclave* – rural areas, mainly in the Atlantic provinces and the Gaspé region of Quebec, that have low rates of economic activity and high rates of unemployment; they are highly dependent on government social transfer payments
6. *resource areas* – areas rich in forests and in mineral and petroleum resources, located in northern regions of the western provinces and territories, northern Ontario, and Labrador; these areas have a high proportion of young people and low percentage of elderly
7. *the Native North* – areas of the subarctic and arctic regions of Canada that have growing populations, relatively low education, and low economic activity

Two elements seem particularly important in the success of rural places and small towns: proximity to urban centres, and availability of natural amenities and resources, such as raw materials, natural attractions for tourism, and natural transport routes like rivers and lakes (Biggs and Bollman, 1994; Bollman and Biggs, 1992; Bryant and Joseph, 2001; Hamilton, 2002, 2004; Holubitsky, 2005; Reimer, 2005). Rural communities that lie relatively close to large urban centres benefit from a wider range of goods and services for their residents, and from a regular influx of city-dwellers and tourists in search of recreational properties and nature parks outside the city.

Conclusion: Urban Change in the Future

In general, countries pass through three stages of urbanization: an initial stage, followed by a stage of acceleration, and then a stage of maturity (see Figure 10.10). What lies beyond this third stage is a question of considerable interest, especially for the advanced countries, where the level of urbanization has reached or is fast approaching a plateau. These societies may be moving into a fourth but uncertain stage of urban development.

Between the 1960s and the 1990s, three unexpected urbanization trends took place in the high-income countries. First, following widespread urbanization in the post-war years, these societies underwent a period of 'counterurbanization', characterized by the growth of small centres at the expense of the large urban areas. Second, by the late 1970s and early 1980s, the counterurbanization trend had slowed and seemingly reached an end; it was then followed by a third development, a return to the traditional pattern of urbanization, referred to in the literature as 'reurbanization' (Champion, 2001; Fielding, 1989 [1996]; Frey, 1987, 1989, 1990; 1993; Frey and Speare, 1992; Geyer and Kontuly, 1993 [1996]; Glaeser and Shapiro, 2003; Morrison and Wheeler, 1976; Vining and Kontuly, 1978 [1996]).

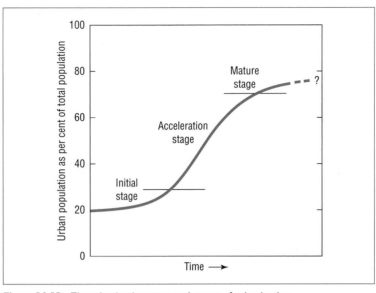

Figure 10.11   The urbanization curve and stages of urbanization

Source: Small and Witherick (1995): 235.

The counterurbanization phenomenon was first observed in the United States, where it lasted for about a decade beginning in the early 1970s. It was later recognized in western Europe, Japan, Australia and New Zealand, parts of eastern Europe, and some of the more developed industrializing countries, like South Korea (see Fielding, 1989 [1996]; Vining and Kontuly, 1978 [1996]). The rise of counterurbanization as the dominant force shaping American settlement systems was seen by many as a turning point. Berry (1976 [1996]) characterized it as a movement from a state of more concentration to a state of less concentration. He showed that American metropolitan regions grew slower than the nation as a whole and lost, through net migration, about 1.8 million people to non-metropolitan areas between March 1970 and March 1974. This development stood in sharp contrast to what had occurred during all proceeding decades dating as far back as the early nineteenth century. What was more, it was the largest metropolitan areas in the country—those exceeding populations of 3 million, including New York, Boston, Los Angeles, Chicago, Philadelphia, San Francisco, and Washington— that accounted in greatest measure for the decline in metropolitan growth. In contrast, rapid growth had taken place in smaller metropolitan areas, particularly those situated in the state of Florida; in the South and the West; in exurban counties beyond metropolitan areas, with large commuter populations; and in counties not tied to metropolitan labour markets (Beale, 1975, 1977 [1996]; Frey, 1990; Gordon, 1979 [1996]; Morrison and Wheeler, 1976; Richter, 1985 [1996]; Vining and Strauss, 1977 [1996]; Wardwell, 1977; Zelinsky, 1978).

Outside of the US, Vining and Kontuly (1978 [1996]) studied the time trend of net migration across settlements of varying size in a number of European and non-European countries, covering the period between 1950 and the mid-1970s. They noted rising levels of net migration to the cities during the 1950s and 1960s, followed by a general pattern of declining net migration in the 1970s. This development could not be explained by changes to the boundaries of metropolitan areas. One country where this trend was pronounced was Japan.

Historically, Japan had seen a general flow of population from the peripheral areas of the country into the core region of Hanshu, stretching back from the port cities of Tokyo, Osaka, and Nagoya, and the Tokkaido megalopolis (the Kanto, Toakai, and Kinki regions). The growth of these centres was particularly strong in the 1960s: in certain years of that decade, these regions gained over half a million people through net migration. But this general and sustained movement of population towards the Pacific coast of central Honshu came to an end in the 1970s. In 1971, for instance, the region's net migration gain was around 430,000 persons; in 1976, the net gain was just 9,000. Statistics for Italy, Norway, Denmark, New Zealand, Belgium, France, West Germany, East Germany, and the Netherlands confirmed the counterurbanization trend. These countries all showed either a reversal in the direction of net population flow from periphery to core or a drastic reduction in the level of this net flow.

What caused the population turnaround? The literature highlights a number of possible explanations, ranging from a desire to 'get back to nature' and a renewed appreciation of rural life to the far-reaching effects of regional economic restructuring (Frey, 1990). Counterurbanization may have represented a response to the increasingly hectic way of life associated with city living. Morrison and Wheeler (1976) found evidence of this mindset among the American people, and argued that with the rise of affluence and better means for commuting daily from a rural home to a job in the city, many Americans were able to realize this preference by moving to smaller urban settlements and rural areas. Innovations in communication and transportation technology have made access to the city and its amenities possible without necessarily living in the city (Long, 1981).

Regional economic restructuring is another compelling explanation for counterurbanization. The economic dislocations that occurred during the 1970s, sparked in part by the oil crisis, led to deindustrialization and the develop-

ment of a new geography of production based predominantly on advanced service delivery, high-tech research, and recreation and leisure-time activities. Those metropolitan areas that failed to adapt to the post-industrial circumstances experienced population decline. At the same time, better roads and highways helped to increase the geographic range of rural towns, linking them together and making possible a new territorial division of labour in the non-metropolitan areas. These efficiencies of communication and transportation effectively reduced the constraints of distance.

By the early 1980s the counterurbanization trend had slowed considerably. The pattern that was so prevalent during the 1970s began to reverse, and metropolitan areas again experienced significant population growth, mostly through net migration. Following a decade of shifting population trends in favour of peripheral regions within countries of the more developed Western world, the early 1980s marked the recovery of core regions (Champion, 1988 [1996]). This new tendency was apparent in parts of western Europe and especially in the United States, where the annual average rate of growth for central cities was 0.64 per cent, up from 0.09 per cent in the 1970s (Cochrane and Vining, 1988 [1996]; Vining and Pallone, 1982). American metropolitan areas with one million or more people in the 1980s had grown by 12 per cent over the previous decade, with much of this growth occurring in the southern and the western states, and in certain larger centres of the north, notably New York and Boston (Frey and Speare, 1992).

Compared with the extensive urban growth that occurred in the US, the phenomena of counterurbanization and reurbanization were relatively minor developments in Canada (Keddie and Joseph, 1991). Even so, the 1980s saw a significant return of population gains to the central province of Ontario, most notably the census metropolitan area of Toronto, which grew by almost one million people between 1981 and 1991 (a 30 per cent growth rate); this was twice the city's growth rate during the 1970s (Champion, 2001: 156). Though it was the outer urban areas that contributed most of these gains to Toronto CMA, Bourne and Olvet (1995) have noted that there was an inner-city recovery during this time. The urban centre of Toronto, which experienced a 16 per cent decline in population during the 1970s, saw a gain of 6 per cent in the 1980s. Other Canadian investigators have documented similar inner-city growth rates (see Champion, 2001; Ley, 1992; Ram, Norris, and Skof, 1989).

The counterurbanization phenomenon and subsequent reurbanization may suggest that urban systems in the advanced countries simply went through a temporary deviation in the general pattern of urbanization established over the past century and are now back on track. Yet it is far from certain what the future holds. The industrialized world may currently be passing through a transitional period, moving perhaps toward some new development, with no clear outcome in sight (Champion, 2001).

Today, most advanced societies are undergoing a mixture of urbanization trends. Many regions are experiencing suburbanization or reurbanization, and others are experiencing both processes simultaneously. Some urban centres are losing population to the smaller settlements while others are gaining. In assessing this situation, Champion (2001: 158) has remarked that 'if there is one certainty to be drawn from this review of urban population trends, it is that nothing is the same as it was in those apparently straightforward days when "urbanization" meant greater population concentration in any geographical framework used.' Contemporary suburbanization processes appear to be very different from those that shaped the 'dormitory-style' bedroom communities of the past. Suburbs are increasingly becoming 'urbanized' in the sense that they are home to occupational and resource facilities traditionally associated with the inner city. This suggests that the advanced economies have moved recently into a situation 'beyond urbanization' (Champion, 2001: 159).

Canada, like all other major industrialized nations, is now at an uncertain juncture in its urbanization process. There cannot be much more rural-to-urban migration, as the proportion of rural inhabitants has essentially bottomed out. On the other hand, as shown by the 2006 census, suburban expansion is bound to continue. It would seem inconceivable that the suburbs would falter in continuing to attract urban dwellers, given that they now offer many of the functional properties and amenities that were once the purview of the urban core, including places to shop and work, leisure facilities, and arts centres (Smith, 2000). In all likelihood Canada will also continue to see an increasing concentration of its population in the largest metropolitan areas, with some peripheral growth among the surrounding zones of the larger urban centres due to urban sprawl. The ability of the large urban centres to attract migrants will, of course, fluctuate in response to economic periods of boom and bust in different regions of the country (Bourne and Rose, 2001; Coffey, 2000; Keil and Kipfer, 2003; Wallace, 2002). As the metropolitan areas increase in size, their infrastructures will require constant maintenance and upgrading (Henderson, 2003; Ley, 2000; Zolnik, 2004). City planners will face enormous challenges from a list of growing concerns that includes, among other items,

- increased congestion,
- the need to provide housing for the poor,
- the need to revitalize older neighbourhoods,
- the possibility of escalating crime rates, and
- rising health concerns associated with pollution and the spread of communicable diseases (Gillis, 2005; Kazemipur and Halli, 2000; Peressini, 2005).

On a global scale, the most striking feature of urbanization over the past fifty years and, projected, over the first half of the twenty-first century is the pronounced difference in the pace and magnitude of growth in the world's more and less developed areas. The United Nations

2007 *Revision of World Urbanization Prospects* (United Nations Department of Economic and Social Affairs Population Division, 2008c: 1–12), in its forecast for world population growth to 2050, has made the following observations and predictions:

1. The world urban population is expected nearly to double by 2050, increasing from 3.3 billion in 2007 to 6.4 billion in 2050.
2. By mid century the world urban population will likely be the same size as the world's total population in 2004.
3. Virtually all of the world's population growth will be absorbed by the urban areas of the less developed regions, whose population is projected to increase from 2.4 billion in 2007 to 5.3 billion in 2050.
4. The urban population of the more developed regions is projected to increase modestly, from 0.9 billion in 2007 to 1.1 billion in 2050.
5. Globally, the level of urbanization is expected to rise from 50 per cent in 2008 to 70 per cent in 2050. More developed regions are expected to see their level of urbanization rise from 74 per cent to 86 per cent over the same period. In the less developed regions, the proportion urban will likely increase from 44 per cent in 2007 to 67 per cent in 2050.
6. There are marked differences in the size of the urban population and the proportion of urban dwellers among the major areas of the world. By 2050, Asia and Africa will each have more urban dwellers than any other major area, with Asia alone accounting for over half of the urban population of the world.
7. As of 2007, the combined number of urban dwellers in Europe, Latin America and the Caribbean, Northern America, and Oceania (1.28 billion) was smaller than the number in Asia (1.65 billion).
8. Latin America and the Caribbean are highly urbanized, with 78 per cent of the region's population living in urban settlements as of 2007. This proportion is twice as high as those for Africa (39 per cent) and Asia (41 per cent).
9. In Europe and Northern America, the percentages of the population living in urban areas are expected to rise from 72 per cent and 80 per cent, respectively, in 2007, to 84 and 90 per cent in 2050. The proportion of urban inhabitants of Oceania is likely to rise from 71 percent to 76 per cent over this period.

The social, economic, and environmental implications of these projected trends are far-reaching. Approximately 2 per cent of the earth's total land area is occupied by urbanized places (Redman and Jones, 2004); however, as urbanization continues, the densely populated core urban areas encroach inexorably on the low-density city fringes and the countryside surrounding cities. Urban population growth in most countries is now outstripping overall population growth. As urbanized areas expand into the hinterlands, where the land is primarily agricultural or 'natural' (i.e., forests, wetlands, grasslands), urbanization will impose significant challenges on ecosystems, hydrological systems, and local climates. These challenges may, in turn, affect human health. Compounding these potentially adverse environmental scenarios is people's increasing reliance on automobiles for transportation, which add pollutants to the environment while necessitating the construction or expansion of roads and highways (Redman and Jones, 2004).

To maintain order and essential services in the growing urban centres of the developing world, exceptional resources and planning will be required. Urbanization unfolds fairly smoothly in the developed countries, but the same cannot be expected in the developing world, where expanding cities lack the means to provide essential services like housing, education, health care, police protection, and affordable transportation (Jones, 2002). Health care is particularly important, since the higher population density of cities helps the spread of lethal communicable diseases (Aguirre, Pearl, and Patz, 2004; Dyson, 2003b; Nsiah-Gyabaah, 2004; Redman and Jones, 2004). Yet many of the world's poorest countries have issues of greater concern to contend with, including collapsing economies, civil war, and anarchy (Linden, 1996). The large-scale flow of rural migrants into the cities adds an almost unmanageable level of complexity to these problems, as many among the growing numbers of poor rural migrants are forced to set up makeshift urban shantytowns in the face of extreme poverty and severe housing shortages.

Notes for Further Study

Zipf's Rank-Size Rule and Zipf's 'Law'

The literature distinguishes between Zip's 'law' and Zipf's rule. Zipf's 'law' is, in essence, a special case of Zipf's rank-size rule.

Zipf's rule states that if all settlements of a country or region are ranked, from largest to smallest, according to their population size, the population (P_n) of the nth settlement in the list will be 1/nth that of the largest settlement (P). So, the population of a given city (P_n) is determined by $P(1/r)$, where r is the rank of the given city in relation to the largest city. For example, if the largest city in a country contained one million citizens, the second city would contain half (1/2) as many as the first, or 500,000 people; the third would contain one-third (1/3) the population of the largest, or 333,333; the fourth would hold a quarter (1/4), or 250,000; and so forth. When graphed, this equation produces an inverted J-shaped curve between rank (x axis) and population size (y axis). However, if rank and population size are transformed to logarithms, the graph becomes a straight line.

Fundamentally, Zipf's 'law' can be explained as follows. Consider a set of data values, ordered

as $x(1) \geq x(2) \geq \ldots \geq x(n)$, in the reverse of the conventional arrangement (i.e., with the largest value ranked first). We may think of r as the rank and $x(r)$ as the absolute size of the rth data value in the ordered set. Zipf noticed that the relationship $rx(r)$ was a constant, and that this seemed to hold for various kinds of objects, including cities by population, books by number of pages, and biological genera by number of species (Reed, 1998: 674). From this equation it is possible to derive the rank-size distribution: $rx(r)$ = a constant. Under Zipf's 'law', the parameter $q = 1$. So, the rank-size 'law' is actually a special case of the rank-size distribution. If in empirical study the value of the parameter q differs from unity, then we have a 'rank-size function', or 'rank-size distribution' as opposed to Zipf's 'law'.

In empirical applications, it is customary to use the log-linear version of Zipf's 'law':

$$\log (\text{population size}) = \log (\text{constant}) - q\,[\log (\text{rank})]$$

If q is 1, then the plot of log (population size) against log (rank) will be a strong inverse relationship (as depicted in Figure 10.4, page 454). If q is less than 1, the slope of the curve would be flatter, with a more even distribution of city sizes than predicted by Zipf's 'law'. If q is greater than 1, then large cities are larger than predicted under Zipf's 'law', and there will be a wider dispersion of city sizes.

It is interesting to note that Gabaix (1999: 740) computed for the metropolitan areas of the United States in 1991 a value of $q = 1.005$. For the Netherlands, Brackman et al. (1999) reported values of $q = 0.55$ for 1600, $q = 1.03$ for 1900, and $q = 0.72$ for 1990. This suggests that the value of q is not always constant over time, meaning that in some cases urban growth is not proportional. Sometimes, the urban population becomes more concentrated in the larger cities (which increases the value of q) whereas during other periods the urban population becomes more evenly distributed across the various cities (which decreases q). (Gossman and Odynak [1983] provide additional insights into the applicability of Zipf's 'law' to Canadian data.)

The Dissimilarity Index

Urban researchers have applied a number of indexes to study the unequal distribution of ethnic and minority groups across neighbourhoods or other geographic sections of cities, such as the census tract. A host of such indexes have been proposed in the literature, each having their strengths and weaknesses (for a review, see Kazemipur and Halli, 2000). One of the most commonly used indexes of residential segregation is the dissimilarity index (DI). Table 10.14 shows a hypothetical data set (proposed by Lieberson, 1981), which can be used to construct this index for two ethnic groups (blacks and whites) across four sections of a hypothetical city.

The formula for the dissimilarity index (DI) is:

$$DI = \frac{1}{2} \sum_{i=1}^{n} \left| \frac{N1_j}{N1} - \frac{N2_j}{N2} \right|$$

where
$N1_j$ is the population of group 1 (i.e., blacks) in the jth census tract;
$N2_j$ is the population of group 2 (i.e., whites) in the jth census tract;
$N1$ is the total population of group 1 in the given city; and
$N2$ is the total population of group 2 in the given city.

(The solid bars call for the absolute difference between the two terms inside the bars.)

The value of DI ranges between 0 (in which case there is no segregation because the percentage distribution is identical for each group) and 100 (signifying maximum segregation: in the present example, blacks would be found only in subareas of the city where whites where absent, and vice versa). Stated differently, the value of DI is equal to the proportion of the minority (or majority) population that would have to be redistributed to each portion of the city (neighbourhoods, city blocks, etc.) in order to produce a completely even distribution of the two groups among the subareas of the city.

Table 10.14 Hypothetical data for computing the index of segregation (DI) for blacks and whites in a hypothetical city

Subareas	Number of blacks	Number of whites	Total	Percentage black	Percentage white	Black proportion of subarea total
A	60	370	430	30	37	0.140
B	20	290	310	10	29	0.065
C	0	300	300	0	30	0.000
D	120	40	160	60	4	0.750
Sum	200	1,000	1,200	100	100	

Source: Adapted from Lieberson (1981).

Exercises

1. Table 10.15 shows the Canadian CMAs in 2001, 1996, and 1986 along with their corresponding population sizes and population size ranks (1 = largest population). The logarithms of the populations and the ranks are also included in this table. Examine the data and then address the following:

   a) Plot the populations of the CMAs (y-axis) against their corresponding ranks (x-axis) for each period (all on one graph). Exclude Abbotsford and Kingston CMAs.

   b) Plot the log of population (y-axis) against the log of the ranks for each period (x-axis). Exclude Abbotsford and Kingston CMAs.

   c) Discuss these two graphs from the point of view of the concept of the rank-size rule (note: no calculations required). Is the graphical evidence for the Canadian CMAs consistent with this 'rule' for the periods under observation? Explain.

2. Analysts will often present the population distribution of urban places according to broad categories of population size. For instance, one could group the CMAs in Table 10.15 as follows:

   • CMAs with populations of 4 million or greater
   • CMAs with populations between 1 and 3.99 million
   • CMAs with populations between 500,000 and 999,999
   • CMAs with populations between 250,000 and 499,999
   • CMAs with populations between 100,000 and 249,999

   Using these categories, derive the frequency distributions (i.e., the number of CMAs that fall into each population size category) for each period. Describe the resulting frequency distributions. Has there been any change over time in the distributions of urban size categories? What percentage of the total CMA population is situated in each urban size class? Which urban size class contains the most population?

3. Visit the United Nations website http://esa.un.org/unup/ and look for the UN's *World Urbanization Prospects: The 2007 Revision Population Database*. Click on Panel 1 and select three countries: a highly developed country, a developing country, and a least developed country. Execute a comparative analysis of the chosen countries with respect to the following measures of urbanization over the period 1950–2000:

   a) total population
   b) rural population
   c) urban population
   d) per cent urban
   e) per cent rural
   f) urban annual growth rate
   g) rural annual growth rate
   h) total annual growth rate
   i) annual rate of change of percentage urban
   j) annual rate of change of percentage rural

Table 10.15 Distribution of Canadian CMAs according to population size and rank, 1986, 1996, and 2001

CMA	2001 Population	2001 Rank	1996 Population	1996 Rank	1986 Population	1986 Rank	Log of population 2001	Log of population 1996	Log of population 1986	Log of rank 2001	Log of rank 1996	Log of rank 1986
Toronto	4,682,897	1	4,263,759	1	3,427,168	1	6.53	6.63	6.67	0	0	0
Montreal	3,426,350	2	3,326,447	2	2,921,357	2	6.47	6.52	6.53	0.30	0.30	0.30
Vancouver	1,986,965	3	1,831,665	3	1,380,729	3	6.14	6.26	6.30	0.48	0.48	0.48
Ottawa–Hull	1,063,664	4	998,718	4	819,263	4	5.91	6.00	6.03	0.60	0.60	0.60
Calgary	951,395	5	821,630	6	671,326	6	5.83	5.91	5.98	0.78	0.78	0.78
Edmonton	937,845	6	862,600	5	785,465	5	5.90	5.94	5.97	0.70	0.70	0.70
Quebec City	682,757	7	671,889	8	603,267	8	5.78	5.83	5.83	0.90	0.90	0.90
Winnipeg	671,274	8	671,274	7	625,304	7	5.80	5.83	5.83	0.85	0.85	0.85
Hamilton	662,401	9	624,360	9	557,029	9	5.75	5.80	5.82	0.95	0.95	0.95
London	432,451	10	416,546	11	342,302	11	5.53	5.62	5.64	1.04	1.04	1.04
Kitchener	414,284	11	382,940	12	311,195	12	5.49	5.58	5.62	1.08	1.08	1.08
St Catharines–Niagara	377,009	12	372,406	10	343,258	10	5.54	5.57	5.58	1.00	1.00	1.00
Halifax	359,183	13	342,966	13	295,990	13	5.47	5.54	5.56	1.11	1.11	1.11
Victoria	311,902	14	304,287	14	255,547	14	5.41	5.48	5.49	1.15	1.15	1.15
Windsor	307,877	15	286,811	15	253,998	15	5.40	5.46	5.49	1.18	1.18	1.18
Oshawa	296,298	16	268,773	16	203,543	16	5.31	5.43	5.47	1.20	1.20	1.20
Saskatoon	225,927	17	219,056	17	200,665	17	5.30	5.34	5.35	1.23	1.23	1.23
Regina	192,800	18	193,652	18	186,521	18	5.27	5.29	5.29	1.26	1.26	1.26
St John's (NL)	172,918	19	174,051	19	161,901	19	5.21	5.24	5.24	1.28	1.28	1.28
Sudbury	155,601	20	165,618	20	148,877	21	5.17	5.22	5.19	1.30	1.30	1.32
Chicoutimi–Jonquière	154,938	21	160,454	21	158,468	20	5.20	5.21	5.19	1.32	1.32	1.30
Sherbrooke	153,810	22	147,380	22	129,960	22	5.11	5.17	5.19	1.34	1.34	1.34
Abbotsford (BC)	147,370	23	136,480	25	na	na	na	5.14	5.17	1.36	1.40	na
Kingston	146,838	24	144,528	23	na	na	na	5.16	5.17	1.38	1.36	na
Trois-Rivières	137,507	25	139,956	24	128,888	23	5.11	5.15	5.14	1.40	1.38	1.36
Saint John	122,678	26	125,705	27	121,265	24	5.08	5.10	5.09	1.41	1.43	1.38
Thunder Bay	121,986	27	126,643	26	122,217	25	5.09	5.10	5.09	1.43	1.41	1.40
Total Canada	30,007,095		28,846,760		27,296,859		7.44	7.46	7.48			

Notes: 'na' means locality not a CMA in that period. The logarithms are base 10.

Chicoutimi–Jonquière CMA has since 2002 been renamed Saguenai CMA.

Source: Statistics Canada (2002d). Adapted from Statistics Canada publication *A Profile of the Canadian Population: Where We Live*. Catalogue no. 96F0030XIE010012001

Graph each of these measures for the three countries.

- What differences and patterns do you observe in these figures?
- Which of the three countries is the most urbanized?
- What is the projected level of urbanization to the year 2050 for these countries?
- Discuss possible demographic, economic, and sociological implications of urbanization across the three countries over the first half of the twenty-first century.

4. Work through the example with the data in Table 10.14 (page 486). What can we conclude from these results concerning the distribution of blacks and whites in this hypothetical city?

5. Table 10.16 below shows pairs of computed DI values for four ethnic/racial groups in Toronto, Montreal, and Vancouver in 1991. Study the DI values in this table before addressing the following questions:

   a) Does the level of DI vary across cities? If so, describe how.
   b) Why would the city have an effect on the value of DI?
   c) Which two groups are least segregated from each other within each city?
   d) Which two groups are most segregated from each other within each city?
   e) Discuss the reasons underlying your observations for (c) and (d).

Table 10.16 Dissimilarity indexes (DI) for 4 ethnic groups in Toronto, Montreal, and Vancouver, 1991

	French	British	Aboriginal	Black
Toronto				
French	0	0.22	0.53	0.49
British		0	0.56	0.52
Aboriginal			0	0.63
Black				0
Montreal				
French	0	0.47	0.34	0.61
British		0	0.54	0.54
Aboriginal			0	0.66
Black				0
Vancouver				
French	0	0.21	0.50	0.44
British		0	0.54	0.48
Aboriginal			0	0.59
Black				0

Source: Adapted from Kazemipur and Halli (2000): 82–7.

Study Questions

1. Describe the urbanization process from prehistory to the present. What is the future of urbanization for the developed and the developing countries?

2. Why do some cities get very large and others do not? What are the factors responsible for this differential growth?

3. What are some of the most pressing challenges that cities in the developing world face today and over the course of the twenty-first century? Can you propose some solutions?

4. What are some of the most pressing policy issues facing Canadian cities today?

5. Write an essay on the social and demographic conditions facing rural Canada today. How are rural localities to cope with increasing urbanization on the one hand and the tendency for rural youth to flock to the cities on the other?

Additional Reading

Dutt, Ashok K., Allen G. Noble, G. Venugopal, and S. Subbiah, eds. 2006. *Challenges to Asian Urbanization in the 21st Century*. Dordrecht: Klewer Academic.

Gugler, Joseph. 2004. *World Cities Beyond the West: Globalization, Development and Inequality*. Cambridge: Cambridge University Press.

Jacobs, Jane. 2004. *Dark Age Ahead*. New York: Random House.

Luloff, A.E., and R.S. Krannich. 2002. *Persistence and Change in Rural Communities: A 50-Year Follow-up to Six Classic Studies*. CABI Publishing.

National Research Council. 2003. 'Cities Transformed: Demographic Change and Its Implications in the Developing World'. Panel on Urban Population Dynamics, in M.R. Montgomery, R. Stren, B. Cohen, and H.E. Reed, eds, *Committee on Population, Division of Behavioral and Social Sciences and Education*. Washington, DC: The National Academies Press.

Osada, Susumu. 2003. 'The Japanese Urban System 1970–1990'. *Progress in Planning* 59: 125–231.

Savitch, H.V., and Paul Kantor. 2002. *Cities in the International Marketplace: The Political Economy of Urban Development in North America and Western Europe*. Princeton: Princeton University Press.

Taylor, Peter J., Ben Derudder, Pieter Saey, and Frank Witlox, eds. 2007. *Cities in Globalization: Practices, Policies and Theories*. London: Routledge.

Worldwatch Institute. 2007. *State of the World 2007: Our Urban Future*. Washington, DC: Worldwatch Institute.

Web Resources

The Worldwatch Institute website posts information on a variety of topics, including urbanization and the environment. See, for example, its recent report, *State of the World 2007: Our Urban Future*: www.worldwatch.org.

One of the most authoritative sources for information on world urbanization is the United Nations Population Division: www.un.org.

The United Nations Human Settlements Programme, UN-HABITAT, is the United Nations agency for human settlements. It is mandated by the UN General Assembly to promote socially and environmentally sustainable towns and cities with the goal of providing adequate shelter for all: www.unchs.org/.

The Canadian Urban Institute (CUI) is a non-profit organization dedicated to enhancing the quality of life in urban areas across Canada and internationally. Through its website you can access information about the institute's upcoming events and its various research publications: www.canurb.com/.

The European Academy of the Urban Environment is an excellent resource for information on issues pertaining to sustainable urban development: www.eaue.de/.

The World Bank features authoritative research and study reports on aspects of urbanization and development in developing countries: www.worldbank.org/.

Chapter 11

Population and Resources

The idea that human population growth must be controlled in the interest of societal well-being has been a subject of attention and controversy for centuries, and the debate is no less heated now than it was in the past. This chapter examines two opposing views on the importance of population to environmental and societal well-being. The chief spokesmen for the opposing viewpoints are Thomas Malthus and Karl Marx (with Frederick Engels). The chapter will also look at some of the predecessors of Malthus and Marx, as well as a number of the authors who have followed in their footsteps—the Neo-Malthusians and the Neo-Marxists. Other perspectives on the possible impact of population growth on ecological sustainability are discussed in the context of contemporary research and theorizing in this area.

Population: The Ongoing Debate

A Sampling of Views from the Mid-1700s to the Twenty-First Century

'The Almighty will bless, protect, and maintain a people that obey His Command to multiply and populate the Earth.'
> (Peter Suessmilch, 1741, from *The Divine Order in the Transformation of the Human Race as Demonstrated through Birth, Death, and the Multiplication of the Same*)

'The power of population is indefinitely greater than the Power in the Earth to produce subsistence in men.'
> (Thomas Malthus, 1798, from *An Essay on the Principle of Population; or a View of Its Past and Present Effects on Human Happiness, with an Inquiry into our Prospects respecting the Future Removal or Mitigation of the Evils which it Occasions*)

'Is it necessary for me to give any more details of the vile and infamous doctrine [Malthus's population theory], this repulsive blasphemy against man and nature, or to follow up its consequences any further? Here, brought before us at last, is the immorality of the economists in its highest form.'
> (Frederick Engels, 1844, from *Outlines of a Critique of Political Economy*)

'Malthus, that master in plagiarism (the whole of his population theory is a shameless plagiarism . . . quite commonplace and known to every schoolboy).'
> (Karl Marx, 1867, from *Das Kapital*)

'In terms of the practical problems that we must face in the next few generations . . . it is clear that we will greatly increase human misery if we do not, during the immediate future, assume that the world available to terrestrial human population is finite. "Space" is no escape.'

(Garret Hardin, 1968, from 'The Tragedy of the Commons', *Science* 162, 3859 (13 December 1968): 1243–8)

'Suppose you own a pond on which a water lily is growing. The lily plant doubles in size each day. If the lily were allowed to grow unchecked, it would completely cover the pond in 30 days, choking off the other forms of life in the water. For a long time the lily plant seems small, and so you decide not to worry about cutting it back until it covers half the pond. On what day will that be? On the twenty-ninth day, of course. You have one day to save your pond.'

(Donella H. Meadows et al., 1972, from *The Limits to Growth: A Report for the Club of Rome's Project on the Predicament of Mankind*)

'One hears that "we" have more people than "we" have "need" of, though "we" inevitably goes undefined. What amazing arrogance and self-centredness!'

(Julian Simon, 1990, from *Population Matters*)

'Contemporary academic economists . . . find that although population growth and density can have bad effects on development, these will only be severe with wrong economic policies. Technical advance and substitution in free markets avoid major difficulties. . . . But ecologists see the poor cutting trees for firewood, the rich pouring carbon into the atmosphere, and doubt the capacity of the environment to absorb the effects of dense and growing populations and their present technologies.'

(Nathan Keyfitz, 1991, from 'Population and Development within the Ecosphere: One View of the Literature', *Population Index*)

'Scarcities of renewable resources are already contributing to violent conflicts in many parts of the developing world. These conflicts may foreshadow a surge of similar violence in coming decades, particularly in poor countries where shortages of water, forests and, especially, fertile land, coupled with rapidly expanding populations, already cause great hardship.'

(Thomas F. Homer-Dixon, J.H. Boutwell, and G.W. Rathjens, 1993, from 'Environmental Change and Violent Conflict', *Scientific American* 268, 2 (February): 38–45)

'We are not running out of energy or natural resources. There will be more and more food per head of the world's population. Fewer and fewer people are starving. . . . Mankind's lot has actually improved in terms of practically every measurable indicator.'

(Bjorn Lomborg, 2001, from *The Skeptical Environmentalist*)

'We believe it self-evident that Earth is finite, that the human population cannot grow indefinitely without compromising our terrestrial home.'

(John Firor and Judith Jacobsen, 2002, from *The Crowded Greenhouse: Population, Climate Change and Creating a Sustainable World*)

Thomas Robert Malthus (1766–1834)

Thomas Robert Malthus was born in 1766 in Surrey, England, the sixth of eight siblings. After four years at Cambridge University (1784–8) he took holy orders in the Church of England, and from 1793 served as a curate in Surrey. Five years later, in 1798, his *Essay on the Principle of Population as it Affects the Future Improvement of Society, with Remarks on the Speculations of Mr. Godwin, M. Condorcet, and other Writers* was published anonymously. The subtitle Malthus attached to subsequent editions—*A view of its past and present effects on human happiness, with an inquiry into our prospects respecting the future removal or mitigation of the evils which it occasions*—gives a good indication of the tone of the work.

Based on his observations and analysis of the relationship between population growth and resources across a variety of national settings, Malthus concluded that population tends to *grow geometrically* while resources (especially those used for food) follow an *arithmetical*, or linear, pattern of change. If left unchecked, he warned, the population would become so large that it would eventually surpass humans' ability to produce food in sufficient quantities.

Malthus believed the human population was capable of doubling itself, on average, every 25 years if 'reducing effects' such as plagues, wars, and disease did not occur. Yet according to what he identified as the *principle of population*, these very events, which he considered 'positive checks' on population growth, would be inevitable results of allowing population growth to continue unabated. The ensuing rise in the death rate would eventually reduce human numbers to an equilibrium, at which point there would be an adequate supply of food and resources available to sustain the population.

Malthus believed that the only way to prevent successive cycles of population growth and collapse—which, he argued, had already characterized much of human history—was to implement 'preventive checks' on population to curtail the birth rate and hence the rate of population growth. Malthus was thinking particularly of celibacy and late marriage, both of which he saw as expressions of 'moral restraint'. For Malthus, these personal choices, in conjunction with restrained sexuality, coincided perfectly with the moral codes of a Christian life, and their diligent application would help humanity avoid collapsing under the weight of over-population.

Yet Malthus openly expressed pessimism in humans' ability to apply moral restraint, even to avert catastrophe. Moreover, he feared that any attempts to remove the conditions that cause ill health and poor living standards would have the effect of promoting even greater population growth. Grounded on this supposition, he was most reluctant to support the passage of laws intended to assist the poor, as institutionalized aid would only lead to a situation in which there were more mouths to feed, the ranks of the poor swollen to higher and higher levels.

Responses to the *Essay*, together with additional observations, led Malthus to publish a revised edition under his own name in 1803; another four revisions were to follow in 1806, 1807, 1817, and 1826 (as well as a posthumous edition in 1872). Malthus also issued, in 1830, an abbreviated version of his thesis, *A Summary View of the Principle of Population*, in order to make his argument more accessible to the public. The *Essay* brought Malthus both recognition and notoriety. In 1805 he was offered the post of Professor of General History, Politics, Commerce, and Finance at the East India College in Hertfordshire, a position he held until his death in 1834, and in 1819 he was elected a Fellow of the Royal Society (Flew, 1970; Petersen, 1979).

Several momentous events took place during Malthus's lifetime, including the American Revolution (1776–9), the French Revolution (1789–99), and a significant portion of the Industrial Revolution (c.1740–1850). The latter in particular profoundly altered the traditional economic order, forcing large segments of the rural population in England and Wales to leave the countryside for the cities in search of work in the factories. Both living and working conditions were poor, the latter often dangerous; child labour was common and poverty widespread. Sensitive to these realities, Malthus recognized that the plight of the poor would only be compounded as their numbers increased, and this awareness undoubtedly helped to shape his thinking about population. At the same time, he was strongly critical of previous schools of thought on population matters, most notably the mercantilist writers of the seventeenth and eighteenth centuries, who emphasized the positive aspects of population growth for the good of the state, and the revolutionary utopian philosophers of the Enlightenment period, who believed in the inherent goodness of humankind and the corrupting nature of the institutions that governed and shaped society. As we will see, two influential utopian thinkers with whom Malthus was deeply at odds were William Godwin and the Marquis de Condorcet.

Pre-Malthusian Thought on Population
Theories of population had been expressed as early as the classical periods of ancient Greece, Rome, and China. Stangeland (1904: 14), in his authoritative study of population thought, claims that 'as a matter of historical fact, [population] has occupied the attention of thoughtful men in nearly all ages.' To this he adds that Malthus himself recognized that others long before him, including the early Greek philosophers Plato (c.424–348 BCE) and Aristotle (384–322 BCE), had proposed remedies of various kinds to avert the human misery associated with overpopulation.

Stangeland (1904: 16–17) identified seven pre-Malthusian perspectives on population. Some are pronatalist, while others advocate restraint in matters of procreation and sexuality. The importance of marriage as a vehicle to promote population growth is prominent in these early writings, just as it was central to Malthus's own theory. Another recurring theme is the

quandary states would face under conditions of excess population on the one hand and deficits on the other, and the appropriate means to intervene under these radically different conditions. Finally, some of the early thoughts on population are highly embedded in moral religious arguments and the tension these moral arguments posed for state and individual, whose interests are not always in harmony.

1. *The primitive attitude, usually expressed in religious veneration of the procreative powers.* Many ancient pagan rituals began as ways to encourage humans to procreate (examples include phallic cults and bacchanalia festivals in the ancient world). Perhaps these rituals represented a way for early societies to stimulate population growth in the light of recurrent epidemics of disease and war that decimated their numbers.

2. *The Greek view, which saw procreation as a civic duty, hence something to be regulated according to the needs of the city state.* In Ancient Greece, both public sentiment and written law punished celibacy. Frequent wars and epidemics had to be countered by population growth, which was best achieved through early marriage and procreation. In this context, Plato expressed the view that all personal ends had to be subordinated to the common good, and therefore marriage, as a means to propagate the race, was a personal duty to the state. On the other hand, Plato maintained that if a city state grew beyond a certain limit, which he estimated to be a population of 5,040, it would be morally acceptable for couples to resort to infanticide and abortion.

3. *The Roman policy of promoting continuous population growth, with a view to the indefinite expansion of the Roman state.* Like the ancient Greeks, the Romans viewed marriage primarily as a vehicle for rearing offspring and therefore a duty owed to the state. Heavy taxes were imposed on bachelors, while laws like the *lex Papia Poppaea* were passed to pro-

mote marriage and fecundity. In accordance with Roman law, widows and divorced women had to remarry within one or two years. Childless couples were accorded a low status in Roman society, while those with children enjoyed important privileges (such as the succession of property to their off-spring). In addition to marriage and procreation, the Romans saw the conquest of new lands as an important mechanism for avoiding underpopulation within their territories.

4. *The Medieval Christian conception of sexual relations, which emphasized the moral superiority of celibacy*. Unlike the Ancient Greeks and Romans, who favoured marriage and procreation, the Medieval Christian writers advocated celibacy and the ascetic life, which they considered more consistent with Christian morality. In fact, this view may have developed as a reaction to the immoral conditions that prevailed in the early Roman Empire. Thus, Christian scholars such as Saint Paul (d. AD 64/67), Saint Augustine (354–430), and, later, Saint Thomas Aquinas (1225–74) abhorred marriage and preferred chastity as a path bringing them closer to Christ. But though they considered celibacy the superior lifestyle, they acknowledged that marriage played a salutary role in society.

5. *The attitude of the humanists, who echoed the Greeks in emphasizing the need to regulate population*. During the Renaissance, a number of humanist scholars endorsed the view that population should be controlled. Among those was Sir Thomas More (1478–1535), who, in his work *Utopia*, which presented a model of the ideal city-state, suggested that cities be composed of small groups of people, not to exceed 6,000. Families, he recommended, should have no fewer than 10 members and no more than 16.

6. *The individualistic and anti-ascetic attitude of the Reformation (1517–1648)*. In reaction to the asceticism of the Medieval Christian scholars, the Reformation period, which began with Martin Luther's (1483–1546) criticism of Church doctrine in 1517, promoted the view that virtuosity and marriage are not incompatible. Luther himself advocated that young men should marry not later than the age of 20, and women no later than 18.

7. *The mercantilist attitude, favouring population growth as a way of maintaining national economic and political power*. The mercantilist writers believed that the wealth of the nation was more important than the good of the individual. The greater the population, they reasoned, the greater the state's productivity and, hence, prosperity. They believed that population could be increased by imposing taxes on celibates, by excluding unmarried men from public office, and by rewarding those who married with tax exemptions. An early and well-known proponent of mercantilist thought was Niccolò Machiavelli (1469–1527), who championed the idea that population growth, in conjunction with agriculture, industry, and trade, would guarantee tangible socioeconomic benefits to a city-state. He warned, however, that population could at some point increase beyond the capacity of the city state's limited territory, and that war, want, and disease would be the likely results of this situation. His insight became a key theme of Malthus's own writings.

Precursors to Malthusian Thought

Given the many scholars who studied and wrote about population matters before Malthus's time, one has to wonder how original Malthus's principle of population really was. Indeed, the Renaissance writer Giovanni Botero (1543–1617) is known to have espoused elements of this theory long before Malthus. Stangeland (1904: 106) writes that Botero's work contained the essentials of the Malthusian doctrine that populations tend to grow faster than the resources available to sustain them, a view that was also put forth by the philosopher Thomas Hobbes (1588–1679). Botero argued that the *virtus generativa* (the biological drive to reproduce) is stronger than the *virtus nutriva* (the human need for sustenance), and that ultimately the limits to population growth are imposed by limits in the means of subsistence in addition to the misery imposed by war and disease. Meanwhile, the idea that population tends to increase in geometric progression had been suggested by the English political arithmetic scholars John Graunt (1620–74) and William Petty (1623–87) (McNicoll, 2003a; Stone, 1986). And a number of eighteenth-century writers prior to Malthus had advanced the notion that a population would increase up to the limits set by the available means of subsistence; notable among these was the French economist Victor de Riquetti, marquis de Mirabeau (1715–89), who stated bluntly that 'men will multiply to the limits of subsistence like rats in a barn' (Stone, 1986: 44).

It appears that Malthus may not have been aware of these early works when he produced the first edition of his *Essay* (Petersen, 1979), though he did explicitly acknowledge that his main argument was certainly not new; in fact, he singled out four scholars whose thinking had influenced his own: Adam Smith (1723–90), David Hume (1711–76), Robert Wallace (1694–1771), and Richard Price (1723–91). But while these writers—and several who preceded them—gave attention to the subject of population, they all fell short of developing a systematic theory of population change and its effects on resources and the overall well-being of humanity. In a sense, Malthus's main contribution was incorporating into his own way of thinking the principal ideas of these four influential precursors to develop an explicit theory of population and resources.

Malthus, Condorcet, and Godwin

Although they disagreed on many issues, some of the principal figures of the eighteenth-century Enlightenment shared a utopian outlook on the nature of humanity. In particular, Voltaire (1694–1778), Rousseau (1712–78), and the Marquis de Condorcet (1743–94) believed that humans were inherently good but that social institutions were problematic and needed to be brought in line with the inherent goodness of humans (these thoughts would later influence the thinking of Karl Marx, whose ideas are discussed in the second part of this chapter). In the opening lines of *The Social Contract*, Rousseau clearly reflects this perspective: 'Man is born free, and everywhere he is in chains' (Petersen, 1979: 6). Similarly, the English philosopher William Godwin (1756–1836), best known for his *Enquiry Concerning the Principle of Political Justice* (1793), denounced society's established institutions as 'obstacles to human development' (Petersen, 2003a: 468). Like Godwin, Condorcet, in his *History of Human Progress from Its Outset to Its Imminent Culmination in Human Perfection*, expressed his belief in the perfectibility of humankind and society. He foresaw a day when social and economic inequalities would be eliminated, along with war, crime, and disease, through the application and elevation of human reason over emotion and instincts. He also believed it to be an immutable principle of human society that population would never exceed the means of subsistence. If population growth should ever threaten to outpace the growth of the means of subsistence, social institutions would be to blame, and the problem could be solved by society through the application of reason (Petersen, 2003b). Godwin, in his study *Of Population* (1820), took a similar view, arguing that the growth of population could not exceed the growth of the means of subsistence. This was precisely the sort of utopian thinking that Malthus set out to refute in his *Essay*.

Malthus was also critical of the mercantilists, who favoured population growth as a stimulus for economic growth and, especially, expansion of the state, which needed a substantial army if it was to conquer new lands. For the mercantilists, the goal of economic activity was to enhance the glory and power of the state: for them the welfare of the individual 'was never considered as an end, only as a means' (Overbeek, 1974: 28).

Condorcet's rosy view of humanity is neatly summarized by Petersen (1979: 42) as follows:

[M]ankind has moved upward through a series of evolutionary stages (somewhat like those later delineated by Comte, or in a different context, by Marx), starting with a mode of existence not dissimilar from that of other animal species, proceeding through social patterns like those of American Indians and other surviving primitives, and developing further through the advances of historical societies. The French Revolution had started the last stage of this progress and soon the human race, freed from the chains of error, crime, and injustice, would attain universal truth, virtue, and happiness. All inequalities of wealth, of education, of opportunity, of sex, would disappear. Animosities between nations and races would be no more. All persons would speak the same language. The earth would be bountiful without stint. All diseases would be conquered, and if man did not become immortal, the span of his life would be no assignable upper limit. In this rational age to come, everyone would recognize his obligation to those not yet born and to the general well being both of his own society and of all humanity, and not to the puerile idea of filling the earth with useless and unhappy beings.

By contrast, the classical economists gave priority to the welfare of the individual. Although Adam Smith (1723–90), one of the central figures of classical economics, saw population growth as inherently desirable, he recognized that it could not continue indefinitely. In *The Wealth of Nations* (1776), Smith argued that larger populations would not only expand markets but also encourage the specialization of economic activity in society. Larger populations would produce economies of scale, which in turn would produce greater wealth and well-being for the individual and his society. But Smith understood that resource constraints ultimately impose limits on population growth. (As noted earlier, Malthus openly acknowledged Smith for this insight.)

The Principle of Population

In 1798, Malthus dismissed as overly optimistic Godwin and Condorcet's opinion that humankind and society were perfectible. He then proposed his principle of population:

I think I may fairly make two postulata. First, that food is necessary to the existence of man. Secondly, that the passion between the sexes is necessary, and will remain nearly in its present state. . . . Assuming then, my postulates as granted, I say, that the power of population is indefinitely greater than the power in the earth to produce subsistence for man. Population, when unchecked, increases in a geometrical ratio. Subsistence increases only in an arithmetical ratio. A slight acquaintance with numbers will show the immensity of the first power in comparison of the second (Malthus, 1798 [1960], 9/12; vol. 1 in Wrigley and Souden, 1986a: 8).

In the sixth and final edition of the *Essay*, Malthus sets out three key conclusions:

(1) Population is necessarily limited by the means of subsistence. (2) Population invariably increases where the means of subsistence increase, unless prevented by some very powerful and obvious checks. (3) These checks, and the checks which repress the superior power of population, and keep its effects on a level with the means of subsistence, are all resolvable into moral restraint, vice, and misery

(Malthus, 1826, 22/4, vol. 1 in Wrigley and Souden, 1986a: 20–1).

In short, Malthus argued that population growth will tend to surpass the means available to sustain humanity, and that unchecked population increases geometrically (1, 2, 4, 8, 16, 32, etc.), while the food supply increases only arithmetically (1, 2, 3, 4, 5, 6, 7, etc.) (see Figure 11.1).

Malthus argued that in the long run the difference in growth rates between population and food would produce its own remedies in the forms of what he called 'misery' (including famine, war, disease, and pestilence) and 'vice' (including all the ways that humans had then discovered to avoid unwanted conceptions and children, notably abortion and infanticide) (see Table 11.1). Malthus described the 'miseries' as *positive checks* on population growth because they all contributed to increasing mortality, thereby helping to lower population to the point where the resources available would once again

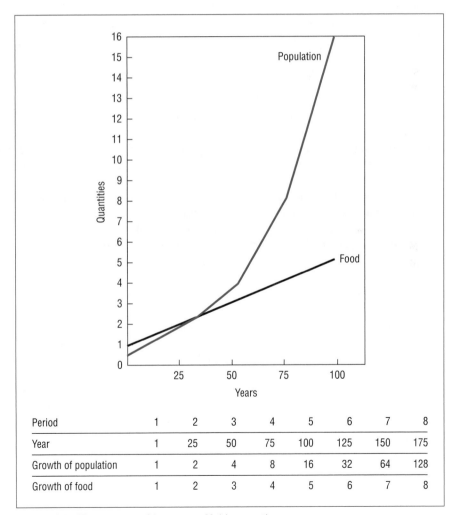

Period	1	2	3	4	5	6	7	8
Year	1	25	50	75	100	125	150	175
Growth of population	1	2	4	8	16	32	64	128
Growth of food	1	2	3	4	5	6	7	8

Figure 11.1 The two rates of increase as Malthus saw them

Source: Adapted from Overbeek (1974): 43.

Table 11.1   Malthusian checks on population

Positive checks – conditions that increase the death rate (*misery*)	*Preventive checks* – behaviours that act on the birth rate	
	Illicit (*vice*)	Licit (*moral restraint*)
• unwholesome occupations • severe labour • exposure to the seasons • bad and insufficient food and clothing arising from poverty • bad nursing of children • excesses of all kinds • famine • pestilence • disease • war • infanticide	• all forms of contraception and 'unnatural acts that prevent the consequences of irregular connections' • abortion	• permanent celibacy or late marriage • 'strictly moral conduct toward sex'

Source: Adapted from Flew (1970).

be sufficient to sustain it. The 'vices' he described as *preventive checks*, as they all served to lower the birth rate. It is clear that Malthus disapproved strongly of these behaviours, which he considered illicit and immoral. His preferred remedy to reduce fertility was the voluntary adoption of preventive checks more consistent with a moral and Christian way of life—specifically sexual abstinence outside of marriage and the postponement, or even avoidance, of marriage itself.

As a preventive approach, Malthus preferred 'moral restraint' because it represented the application of morally sound actions toward a desirable societal goal. Moreover, he reasoned, by postponing marriage until the people concerned were capable of supporting a family, individuals and society would both benefit. And by working longer before establishing a family, people would be able to save more of their income, thus helping to reduce poverty and raise the overall level of well-being. In this sense, Malthus's theorizing has helped to raise awareness that effective population control in rapidly growing societies—where the balance between

population and resources may be precarious ultimately rests on the private decisions of individuals.

Malthus elaborated on this relatively simple system through several revisions of his *Essay*. The basic Malthusian principles—that population growth will always tend to outpace growth in the means of subsistence and must be held in check one way or the other—remained central, but he later outlined a more complex model in which population change in any particular society depends on a variety of factors specific to that society. These factors—the level of technology; the level of available natural resources; the rates of usurpation of productive surplus by centres of political power; the competitiveness of markets; and, implicitly, the normative standards of living that influence how much each member consumes and, hence, what is available for consumption by others (Turner, 1995: 12)—are outlined in Figure 11.2.

Modern Criticism of Malthus
Modern critics have faulted Malthus for not anticipating how the worst consequences of

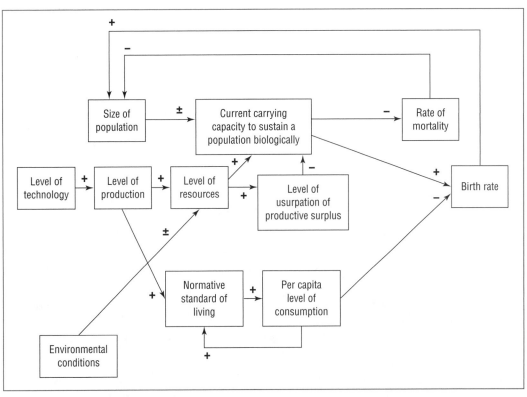

Figure 11.2 Malthus's model of population dynamics

Source: Jonathan H. Turner. 1995. Macrodynamics: Toward a Theory on the Organization of Human Populations. Copyright © 1995 by Jonathan H. Turner. Reprinted by permission of Rutgers University Press.

overpopulation might be mitigated. For example, some say that he failed to take full account of human resilience in the face of difficult predicaments. Throughout history, humans have been remarkably good at problem-solving. Simon (1995, 1996) has suggested that progress in science, technology, and socioeconomic well-being has moved in tandem with population growth. Similarly, Fogel and Costa (1997) have argued that the exponential rise of population in modern times has been accompanied by exponential advances in scientific understanding and technological innovation (see Figure 11.3). In fact, Boserup (1965, 1981) proposed a thesis that in a sense reverses the Malthusian causal order: whereas Malthus argued that an increase in the food supply would translate into

increased birth rates and lower mortality, hence population growth, Boserup argued that, historically, increasing population density was itself the driving force behind agricultural and technological innovations that increased the food supply, promoted economic growth, and raised standards of living.

Malthus suggested that population and food supply must be in balance. But what constitutes optimum population size is difficult to specify. It depends not only on the resources available but on the culture's standards regarding the appropriate level of subsistence for individuals. Social standards vary from society to society and from one historical period to another. The more developed the society, the higher its expectations. As material aspirations rise, so do levels of

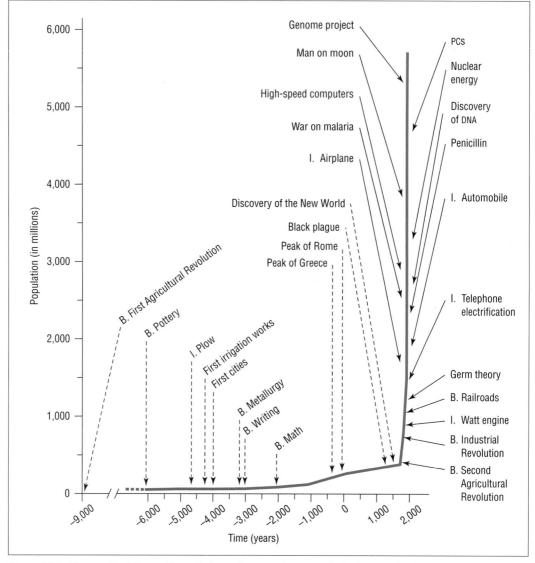

Figure 11.3 The growth of the world population and some major events in the history of technology

Notes: I = invention; B = beginning. There is usually a lag between the invention of a process or a machine and its general application to production. 'B' is intended to identify the beginning, or earliest stage, of this diffusion process.

Source: Fogel and Costa (1997), 50. Reprinted by permission of the Population Association of America.

consumption. Increased consumer demand for material goods means greater economic activity, but increases in economic activity also heighten the risk of environmental damage, increased pollution, and resource depletion (Cohen, 1995, 2003; Ehrlich and Ehrlich, 1990). Consider that even the most useful technological innovations often have undesirable by-products or side-effects. For example, the automobile has transformed society by allowing people to move about faster and more efficiently than ever before; yet over the years since its invention, automobile emissions have contributed significantly to environmental pollution. It is true that technologies have been developed to counteract harmful side-effects; thus, it has become standard practice among car manufacturers to install catalytic converters to reduce carbon emissions. This technology is just one example of the measures that wealthy, highly industrialized countries have relied on to limit automobile-related pollution. Poorer countries, however, may not be able to afford such costly techno-fixes. In other words, sustainability and optimum population size are so closely interrelated that it is virtually impossible to say at what point a certain population has reached the limits to its growth.

Because Malthus rejected birth control as a way of curbing rapid population growth, he is often regarded as more of a moralist than a scientist. Yet it may be unfair to accuse Malthus of excessive moralism. His recommendation that people delay marriage and save their money before starting a family seems, by today's standards, like perfectly sound advice consistent with the modern idea of family planning. Malthus's opposition to birth control and sex outside of marriage was in many ways justifiable given his background as an Anglican deacon and the traditional conservative environment in which he recorded his ideas.

Critics have also noted that although he did address the role of migration in population change, Malthus failed to anticipate the use of large-scale emigration by European society in the nineteenth century to relieve population pressure. Between 1800 and 1950, some 60 million people left Europe for the New World (Kennedy, 1993a: 6; Petersen, 1975: 279). This massive exodus served as a 'safety valve' during the stage of the Western demographic transition when western Europe faced a prolonged period of rapid population growth. Having said that, it is

highly unlikely that emigration on such a scale will be an option for the less developed countries that are undergoing the transition today.

Finally, if economic growth is equated with overall well-being and prosperity in the human population, then Malthus's dire predictions were once again off the mark. Since the Industrial Revolution, global production of goods and services has expanded to a degree that few, if any, in his time could have imagined. The International Monetary Fund (2000) has estimated that between 1750 and the early 1900s population growth exceeded world gross domestic product (GDP); yet from the early 1900s onward, real GDP has outstripped world population growth by a significant degree. The world's economic productivity is sustaining a larger population than ever seen in the history of humanity, and standards of living around the world are higher than ever before (United Nations Department of Economic and Social Affairs Population Division, 2001: 8–9).

The Importance of Malthus to Population Studies

Malthus explained clearly and forcefully how rapid population growth could be detrimental to humanity. Through his insistence on the application of moral restraint, he also emphasized the responsibility of the individual. His work has sparked much research on the question of optimum population and its relationship to social and economic development and questions pertaining to environmental sustainability.

Recently, scholars have questioned the value of Malthusian theory in the light of (a) the contemporary demographic outlook for an increasing number of countries facing demographic maturity and low or even declining annual rates of natural increase, and (b) the improvements achieved in food production, health, and standards of living since his time. So, should Malthus be retired? No. Moral objections to birth control may have no place in the twenty-first century, but many of the issues Malthus raised are still relevant in a world characterized by unequal population growth across regions, ecological and environmental instability, and wide socioeconomic inequalities across and within nations. We shall return to some of these issues later.

It may be too early to dismiss Malthus altogether. We must remind ourselves that in spite of advancements in overall standards of living, a significant portion of the global population—perhaps a billion of the earth's inhabitants—still live in abject poverty under precarious circumstances, besieged by war, famine, disease, and other calamities (Barro and Sala-i-Martin, 2004; Livi-Bacci and De Santis, 1998). The battle to extirpate poverty and human suffering is far from over. In the poorest countries of the world—particularly those of Tropical Africa and Central Asia—poverty is a cause of rapid population growth, and rapid population growth compounds these societies' ability to reduce poverty. A vicious cycle prevails, producing a 'poverty trap' from which these countries cannot seem to escape (Sachs, 2007).

In addition, we may credit Malthus with laying the foundations of modern demography (Winch, 2003: 619). For Pressat (1985: 133), Malthus was 'unquestionably one of the most influential figures in the development of population studies as well as an economist of the first rank'. Through his writings Malthus helped to develop optimum population theory—the area of the field concerned with determining the population size that is best suited to a given environment. Along with the demographic transition theory, Malthusian theory represents the starting point of any serious analysis of population dynamics (Petersen, 1975: 144; Singer, 1971; Zimmerman, 1989). The classical sociological theorists—Auguste Comte (1798–1857), Herbert Spencer (1820–1903), and Émile Durkheim (1858–1917)—found many of their

The Logistic Equation and the Concept of 'Carrying Capacity'

Another example of the Malthusian influence on the study of population is the development of the logistic equation. The logistic equation is a way of calculating the growth rate of a population by taking into account its current size; in this respect it differs from the geometric and exponential models, both of which assume a constant rate of growth.

The logistic equation was formulated in 1838 by Pierre François Verhulst (1804–49) in response to Malthus's description of population growth as indefinitely exponential. Exponential growth cannot actually proceed indefinitely, and so Verhulst sought a more realistic description of population growth over time, one that would take into account how populations adjust under the combined pressures of crowding and resource depletion (Lesthaeghe, 2003).

In 1920, without prior knowledge of Verhulst's early work, Raymond Pearl (1879–1940) and Lowell Reed (1886–1966) produced the same mathematical model. Like Verhulst, Pearl and Reed saw the logistic equation as an expression of a natural, self-regulating process whereby human populations undergo three successive stages of growth: first slow, then rapid, and finally slow again as the populations' numbers approach some upper limit. Pearl (1927) suggested that as a population approached the limits of the resources available to sustain it, certain controls would kick in to reduce the rate of growth. This kind of reaction to population growth may be thought of as a *density-dependent effect*. For example, in animal populations in the wild, a prolonged period of high growth and increased density usually leads to a period of increased death rates, which then reduces the population to levels consistent with the food supply. Lotka (1925) and Volterra (1926) independently expressed this idea in mathematical form to describe the rise-and-fall sequences of two species in the wild characterized by a predator–prey relationship.

This type of mechanism was precisely what concerned Malthus, with the exception that humans, unlike animals, have the ability to regulate population growth through preventive checks, and thus avoid the positive checks (Cohen, 1995; Sibly and Hone, 2002; Lutz and Qiang, 2002). Thus, in the logistic equation, exponential rate of growth and the absolute size of a population change in inverse proportion over time: as population size increases, the rate of exponential growth declines. And it is this pattern that gives the logistic curve its characteristic elongated S-shape.

These thoughts about the logistic equation bear some resemblance to the more recent concept of *carrying capacity*—the sustainability of the earth's ecosystem given the food, habitat, water, and other ecosystem necessities required to support the human population. Underlying the concept is a fundamental question: what is the number of persons that the earth can support without significant negative impacts to both humans and the planet? Arriving at an answer is not straightforward. For one thing, unlike animal species, whose relationship to the ecosystem entails mainly their interactions for food and habitable space, humans bring many more complex variables to the equation. For instance, along with our tendency to take resources from the earth, we also try to replace what we have removed (for instance, by planting seedlings to replenish forests). And as self-reflexive agents, humans are capable of considering how our behaviours may be damaging the environment and take steps to modify our behaviour to avert potential disaster in the long-run. Whether we are succeeding remains an important question subject to further study (see, for example, Meadows, Randers, and Meadows, 2005; Stern, 2007).

insights on the sociological significance of population size and density in Malthus (Bogardus, 1968). Clearly, there were others, some of whom have been mentioned already, whose contributions to the development of population studies cannot be denied—William Petty, John Graunt, Gregory King, Edmund Halley, and Peter Sussmilch are but just a few. What distinguishes Malthus, however, is that he went so far as to develop a system of thought on population and its interactions with biology, social structure, and resources, thus laying the foundation of a long-standing debate on population matters, which no serious scholar can overlook.

Karl Marx (1818–83)

Karl Marx was born in Trier, Germany, and received his doctorate in philosophy in 1841. As a young man he worked as a journalist and edited a newspaper that was suppressed by the authorities because of its overly liberal content. Throughout his life, Marx combined scholarly research and writing with political activism. He moved to Paris in 1842 to continue his editorial work, but was expelled from the city in 1845 at the request of the Prussian government. He then sought refuge first in Brussels and eventually in London, where he settled with his family in 1849 and lived until his death in 1883.

In the mid-1840s, Marx found a close friend and collaborator in Frederick (Friedrich) Engels (1820–95). Together, Marx and Engels published a booklet that was to become one of the most frequently cited works in the history of social thought: the *Communist Manifesto* (1847). Among the goals it set out were the following:

- abolition of property in lands (i.e., an end to private landownership);
- abolition of all rights of inheritance;
- introduction of a progressive (graduated) income tax;
- nationalization of the means of transportation and commerce;
- compulsory labour for all; and
- free education, and an end to child labour. (Bogardus, 1960: 252)

Marx's magnum opus, however, was *Das Kapital*, an analysis of the evolution of capitalism. The first volume was published in 1867; the remaining two volumes, still incomplete at his death, were edited by Engels and published in 1885 and 1895. Marx argued that under advanced capitalism, wealth becomes increasingly concentrated in fewer and fewer hands. In order to survive, those without the capital assets needed to produce wealth themselves— the 'proletariat'—are forced to sell their labour power, and to do so in a marketplace in which competition for jobs is ensured by the constant presence of what Marx called the 'industrial reserve army' of the unemployed. This competition allows employers to keep wages below what they would be if workers were paid the

full value of their labour. It is in this way—by appropriating to themselves the 'surplus value of labour'—that capitalists exploit the working class. Yet this exploitation cannot continue forever, according to Marx: for as capitalism advances, so too will the workers' 'class consciousness'. Awareness of their common suffering and exploitation will lead to class action through powerful labour organizations, and the proletariat will eventually win the class struggle, overthrowing the capitalists and seizing control of the means of production.

Marxist thought offers no systematic theory of population (Bogue, 1969, 16–17; Linder, 1997). The closest Marx comes to considering population dynamics is in his discussion of the 'reserve army' of labour—but this is a feature of advanced capitalism, not of human populations in general. Whereas Malthus proposed a general principle of population, a universal natural law applicable in all places and times, Marx insisted that the population of any society is determined by the prevailing social and economic conditions. Each specific societal stage (or *mode of production*) creates its own law of population. As Marx put it (1867 [1967]: 631–2):

> The laboring population . . . produces, along with the accumulation of capital produced by it, the means by which [it] itself is made relatively superfluous, is turned into a relative surplus-population; and it does this to an always increasing extent. This is a law of population peculiar to the capitalist mode of production; and in fact every special historic mode of production has its own special laws of population, historically valid within its limits alone. An abstract law of population exists for plants and animals only, and only in so far as man has not interfered with them.

In other words, for Marx the 'reserve army' of unemployed labour is not the inevitable product of biological urges—what Malthus called 'the passions between the sexes'. Rather, it is generated primarily by capital itself as the capitalist class invests in new machinery, which displaces workers from their jobs and adds them to the 'reserve army'. The ongoing process of capital investment serves to maintain a reserve army of labour large enough to keep workers' wages low and employers' profits high.

Believing that society's greatest problem was not population at all but the capitalist system, Marx did not propose any alternative to Malthus's theory. Engels, like Marx, believed that the Malthusian principle of population was terribly mistaken, arguing that there was no proof that productivity of land increases in arithmetical progression, as Malthus believed. Moreover, he added, even if population grows geometrically, as Malthus claimed, science is just as limitless and grows at least as rapidly as population. For Engels, science and technology could easily solve any problems that might result from population growth (Engels, 1844 [1971]).

Nevertheless, Marx's theory of capitalism clearly included a demographic component, for in his view the size and strength of the industrial reserve army depended not only on the displacement of workers from the industrial production process by new technology but on rural-to-urban migration and high fertility rates

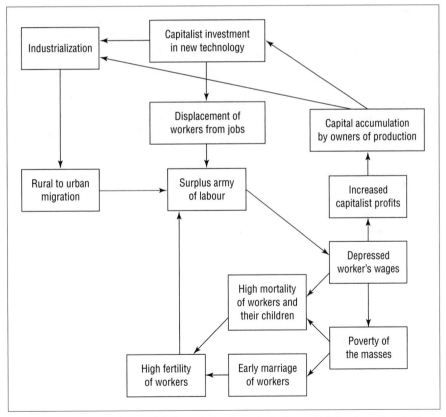

Figure 11.4 Marx's implicit model of population dynamics in the capitalist system of production

Source: Author's rendition.

among the poor (who tended both to marry earlier than the wealthy and to produce more children). These demographic realities, Marx suggested, helped to perpetuate the surplus of workers in the capitalist system despite the high mortality rates characteristic of the working class. Figure 11.4 is a rendition, based on Marx's comments, of the connections between demography and capitalism.

Modern Perspectives on Marx's View of Population

Marx's analysis of socioeconomic inequality is an outstanding contribution to our understanding of society. With respect to demography, however, his views have been largely set aside. Even China—a communist state—recognized decades ago that slowing population growth is, in the long term, essential to societal well-being. With few exceptions, developing countries around the world have abandoned the Marxist perspective and adopted organized family planning.

Just as Malthus has been criticized for rejecting contraception on moral grounds, Marx has been criticized for failing to recognize that uncontrolled population growth can be detrimental to human well-being. In their classic study, Coale and Hoover (1958) identified three ways in which rapid population growth has hampered economic development in India and Mexico. First, the larger a population becomes, the more resources it needs for health care, education, and other important services; this will make it difficult for a government with limited resources to meet its service obligations. Second, the more rapidly a population grows, the more resources it will need in order to achieve a given standard of living. Third, a rapidly growing population will typically have a sizable burden of dependent children and youths (as a result of persistently high birth rates) and a relatively small working-age population to carry it. A society with a relatively large working-age population will generally enjoy higher per capita income 'as a direct result

of having a higher fraction of its population eligible on account of age for productive work' (Coale and Hoover, 1958: 24). It is no coincidence that the fastest-growing populations in the world tend to have relatively low rates of economic growth and high rates of social and political instability. Population may not be the only cause of such problems, but it seems clear that rapid population growth will exacerbate whatever other structural difficulties a society may face.

As for Marx's prediction that the capitalist system would be overthrown, in reality capitalism appears to be stronger than ever. Instead of increasing misery and discontent, the working classes have experienced significant improvements in their lives as a result of the scientific and technological advances promoted by capitalism. In fact, it has been argued that economic growth has been more beneficial to the poor than the rich in society by increasing their chances of employment and hence their socioeconomic opportunities (Hayek, 1998: 296).

Among the other societal benefits associated with industrialization and capitalism, Simon (1995) notes the dramatic decline in infant mortality, longer life expectancy, good health and nutrition, better education, more money, more leisure time, and greater individual freedom and happiness (see also Leisinger, Schmitt, and Pandya-Lorch, 2002: 4–5).

Finally, some analysts have attributed the socioeconomic difficulties experienced by the less advantaged regions of the world to their historical experience of colonialism and peripheral capitalism (e.g., Frank, 1969, 1991; Myrdal, 1957). Yet for such nations, capitalism may not be the main problem at all. In fact, what these societies really need may be more, not less, capitalism, in order to provide meaningful productive work, a better standard of living, and greater individual freedom (Bhagwati, 2000). The collapse of the Soviet system strongly suggests that communism is not a viable solution for poor countries (Rusmich and Sachs, 2003). Of course, capitalism alone, in the absence of major developments in other spheres of a society, will not solve the problems of poor countries. Above all, together with capitalism there must be democratic governance and political stability. In addition, human rights and individual freedoms must be promoted and protected to allow people the confidence to explore profitable enterprises that help to stimulate economic growth and overall well-being.

The Importance of Marxist Thought to Population Studies

As we have seen, there is actually very little demography in Marx. Perhaps his most important contribution to the field has been his insistence that socioeconomic inequality is inherent in the nature of capitalism itself. Even in the most advanced societies, overall income may rise without diminishing the relative gap between the wealthy and the poor (Fischer, 2003; Galbraith, 2002; Sarin, 2003). Marx's penetrating analysis helps to bring into focus the fact that the rise of wealth and socioeconomic well-being around the world has not occurred equitably. This is significant because as the developing countries modernize—some faster than others—many may enjoy an increase in their overall national wealth, yet this rise in national wealth will not necessarily translate into a more equitable distribution of income within society. It is possible for within-country income inequality to increase even as between-country inequality diminishes (see Firebaugh, 2003).

Malthus and Marx Contrasted

Table 11.2 juxtaposes Malthus and Marx on several issues related to population: their views of humanity; their basic theses regarding the role of population in societal problems; the contemporary schools of thought based on their theories;

Table 11.2   A summary of Malthusian and Marxist perspectives

Dimension	Malthusian	Marxist
View of humanity	Pessimistic: humans will always live at the edge of subsistence because—contrary to utopian visions of their perfectibility—the majority will not exercise the self-restraint necessary to control 'the passion between the sexes'.	Optimistic: the capitalist system is unjust, but it will eventually be overthrown through a revolution of the proletariat.
View of population	Population grows geometrically, while the food supply grows arithmetically; therefore, a rapid increase in population promotes poverty. Population and resources (i.e., food supply) must be in balance.	Population, as a problem, is secondary to the poverty and inequality on which the capitalist system depends. Capitalism produces an oversupply of workers, and this helps capitalists keep wages in check. This relationship reinforces the capitalist system of production and exploitation of the working classes: the larger the number of workers, the larger the supply of labour, which in turn has the effect of keeping workers' wages lower than they should be.

(continued)

Table 11.2 (*continued*)

Dimension	Malthusian	Marxist
Evidence	That rapid population growth is detrimental to economic growth is a proposition that has been supported by Coale and Hoover (1958) and by more recent evidence showing that countries that grow rapidly tend to have relatively young populations and also significant social and economic problems and political instability. At the same time, population growth contributes to rapid urbanization, increased pollution, and deforestation.	In many contexts (i.e., in poor developing countries) poverty has been shown to be associated with high fertility, which in turn accounts for explosive rates of population growth. Marxists essentially turn Malthus upside down by arguing that it is poverty that causes high birth rates and therefore high rates of population growth, not the other way round.
Intervention	Responsibility for solving the 'population problem' lies with the individual. The licit 'preventive checks' of moral restraint (i.e., celibacy and late marriage) are preferable to 'positive checks' associated with misery (famine, pestilence, disease, war) and vice (abortion, infanticide, contraception—i.e., illicit 'preventive checks').	Capitalism must be overthrown through a revolution of the proletariat. If population grows exponentially, 'necessity' provokes among humans a search for solutions through the application of science and technology.
Criticism	• Too pessimistic about humans' ability both to practise self-restraint and find innovative solutions to address the subsistence problem. • Objected, on moral grounds, to the use of contraceptive devices. • Failed to foresee that advances in agriculture, etc. could extend the bounds of subsistence or that migration could relieve population pressures. • Did not foresee the population decline in contemporary industrialized nations, where the problem is not that population is pressing on resources, but that the economy presses on a slowly growing (even declining) population (i.e., a Malthusian inversion situation).	• Underestimated the problems associated with overpopulation. • Failed to foresee that even communist societies (e.g., China) would reject the Marxist view and adopt a plan to curb population growth consistent with Malthusian principles. • Perhaps underestimated the positive aspects of capitalism, such as its tendency to promote innovation and create the jobs necessary to raise standards of living of poor countries.

(continued)

Table 11.2 (*continued*)

Dimension	Malthusian	Marxist
Contemporary Schools	• *Neo-Malthusians* believe that population is a key factor in social, economic, and environmental matters; most demographers implicitly or explicitly agree. • They advocate population control through family planning and believe that to avert global ecological breakdown, immediate action must be is taken to curb population growth and consumption. Among their recommended interventions are (a) family planning; (b) development aid and debt relief to poor countries. • Some Neo-Malthusians see globalization as a positive force to the extent that it helps developing countries attain higher standards of living. Others—especially environmentalists—oppose globalization because it promotes excessive economic growth through the exploitation of resources (oil, forests, fresh water, etc.). • Environmentalists argue that population growth is a multiplier: more people means a greater demand for goods; increasing demand increases resource depletion, pollution, global warming, etc.	• *Neo-Marxists* (including dependency/ world systems theorists and anti-globalists) blame the capitalist system for economic and political inequalities around the world. • They believe overpopulation is not a cause of human suffering but a consequence of poverty; eliminating world regional inequality—a legacy of colonialism and unequal political and economic relations between the super-powers and the rest of the world—will take care of the population problem. • Today's multinationals control an increasing share of global wealth, while populations in developing countries represent both a source of cheap labour and an expanding consumer market. • Neo-Marxists are generally wary of globalization because it increases inequality and helps rich countries exploit poor countries.
Impact on population policy	Significant: neo-Malthusian ideas underlie family planning and reproductive health programs across the developing world.	Minimal: although Marxist doctrine was reflected in some aspects of population policy under the communist regimes of the former Soviet Bloc (i.e., antagonistic to contraception but liberal with respect to abortion), today most developing countries (e.g., China) have abandoned Marxism and actively promote family planning to curb population growth.

and their impact on population policy. From the works of these two scholars, Malthus appears to have been somewhat pessimistic about the future of humanity, while Marx perhaps was more optimistic. Unlike Malthus, Marx felt the capitalist system could be changed for the better

through a revolution of the proletariat; Malthus was less sanguine about humanity's ability to overcome what he saw as biological tendencies that drive humankind to live at the brink of subsistence. Nevertheless, undoubtedly both thinkers have offered important insights on the human condition. In terms of impact on population policy, however, Malthus comes out on top; few if any countries today outwardly accept Marxism as a guiding doctrine toward the solution of population problems—certainly not China with its one-child policy. In recent decades virtually all developing countries have embraced one key element of the neo-Malthusian remedy as a means of tackling rapid population growth, most notably through a combination of family planning, reproductive health campaigns, and increased education for boys and girls—interventions that have been quite effective in reducing fertility rates on the one hand, and lowering mortality on the other.

Contemporary Perspectives on Population

Contemporary perspectives on population can be classified under three headings: Neo-Malthusianism, Neo-Marxism, and Revisionism.

Neo-Malthusianism

Neo-Malthusians—contemporary scholars following in the footsteps of Malthus—believe that the earth's human population is too large to be sustainable. Paul Ehrlich (1995: 3), a prominent population ecologist, exemplifies the Neo-Malthusian position:

> I predict that the most important demographic development in the next 50 years will be the worldwide recognition that there is an intimate connection between the size of the human population and the state of earth's life support systems. This will be accompanied by a realization that current levels of overpopulation greatly increase the vulnerability of humanity to catastrophe, and that it is in the common interest of both rich and poor to work together to solve the human predicament. That should lead to a determined effort to: (1) gradually and humanely reduce

human population size (especially in the rich countries which have disproportionate per-capita impacts); (2) limit wasteful consumption among the rich to make room for needed growth among the poor; (3) transition to much more efficient, environmentally benign technologies and cultural practices. Whether this can be accomplished in time to avoid an enormous increase in death rates from widespread loss of agricultural productivity and/or deterioration of the epidemiological environment is inherently unpredictable at the moment.

Two decades earlier, Meadows and colleagues (1972) carried out a massive computer simulation designed to project future environmental and resource sustainability. They concluded that if the then-current trends 'in world population, industrialization, pollution, food production, and resource depletion' were to continue, the 'limits to growth' on earth would be reached within a century: 'The most probable result', in their view would be 'a rather sudden and uncontrollable decline in both population and industrial capacity. Ultimately, continuing human population growth, excessive consumption, and incessant economic production would together usher in ecological breakdown. Implicit in the neo-Malthusian view is the belief that the world would be a better place if it contained fewer people. In contrast to Malthus himself, however, neo-Malthusians promote contraception and family planning as crucial elements in the control of population growth.

Figure 11.5 is a conceptual model of the basic neo-Malthusian view of the links between population growth, resources, and environment. According to this view, population growth is not a proximate cause but an exogenous one: it exerts *indirect* pressure on resources and environment through its effects on other variables in the system. Note also that these effects actually feed back to population, through a series of intervening variables. When neo-Malthusians attribute environmental and resource problems to population, therefore, what they are really referring to are the sorts of mechanisms depicted in Figure 11.5.

Has the situation reached a critical point? What is the causal connection from population size and growth rates to social and ecological conditions? From the point of view of the industrialized countries it may be that the real problem is not population but over-consumption (Schumacher, 1974). Woolmington (1985) has inverted the Malthusian scenario in which population presses on resources, suggesting instead that it is the economy that presses on the population because consumption and production are required in order to maintain economic growth. In this case (which is known as *Malthusian inver-*

sion) population decline could make the spiral of consumption and production unsustainable over the long term; it is not inconceivable that at some point the system will collapse.

Beyond Malthus

Contemporary scholars in the Malthusian tradition recognize the complexity of the interaction between population, environment, and resources. As Pebley (1998) notes, there have been three waves of concern, in the scientific literature and in society in general, regarding the environment and resources. In the first wave (1940s–1950s) the principal concern was over the classic Malthusian scenario: the threat that population growth would eventually lead to inadequate food production and exhaustion of

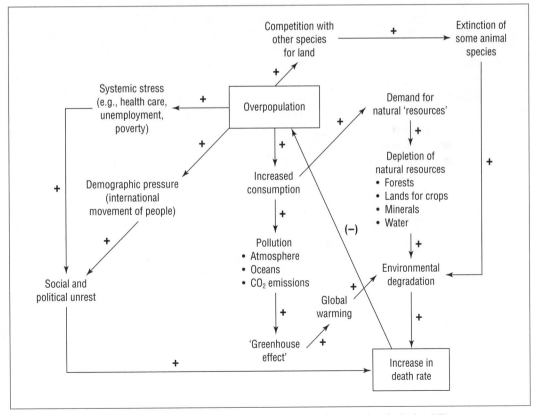

Figure 11.5 A neo-Malthusian model of the relationship between population and ecological stability

Source: Author's rendition.

non-renewable resources. In the second wave (1960s–1970s) the concern shifted to the by-products of increased production and consumption (e.g., pesticide and fertilizer use; waste disposal; noise, air, and water pollution; radioactive and chemical contamination). The third wave, which began in the 1980s and continues today, has focused mainly on issues such as acid rain, the depletion of the ozone layer, and global climate change, all of which have some relationship, if indirect, to population. Lester Brown and colleagues (1999) at the Worldwatch Institute have analyzed the complex interrelationships between population, environment, and resources. Their findings are outlined below.

Impact of Population Growth

The population of the world in 2007 was 6.6 billion. Medium-range projections prepared by the United Nations indicate that by the year 2050 the global population could soar to as high as 9.2 billion, representing a growth of about 2.6 billion people. Such an increase is likely to exacerbate existing problems of unemployment, land depletion, and water shortages, to a greater extent in some parts of the world (e.g., India, China) than in others. The amount of grain land per person has been diminishing and is expected to continue its fall over the next 50 years. In general, consumption of both renewable and non-renewable resources is on the rise worldwide; therefore, the impact of a growing population on the environment has intensified.

Jobs

The number of people of working age worldwide grew from 1.2 billion to 2.7 billion between 1950 and 1997. However, this growth, according to Brown, Gardner, and Halweil (1999: 53), outstripped the growth in job creation during this period. In more recent years global labour force trends have improved. However, a number of important challenges remain, largely associated with inadequate job income for a large number of workers and a significant number of unemployed adults, especially in the poorest regions of the globe (i.e., sub-Saharan Africa, the Middle East, and South Asia). According to the International Labor Organization (2008), in 2007 there were 3 billion workers in the world aged 15 and older (an increase of 17.4 per cent from 1997), of which nearly 190 million were unemployed (an increase from nearly 165 million in 1997). Although the number of working poor earning less than $1 US per day declined since 1997 (612.6 million), the number of such individuals in 2007 was substantial, which stood at 486.7 million. And if the definition of working poor is extended to earnings of less than $2 US per day, this number swells to 1.3 billion persons. Thus depending on the definition of working poor applied, the proportionate share of such individuals worldwide in 2007 was in the range of 16.4 per cent ($1 per day) and 43.5 per cent ($2 per day). Based on this trend, the International Labor Organization (2008: 10) affirmed that in order for the world to make a long-term inroad into unemployment and working poverty, 'it is essential that periods of high growth are better used to generate more decent and productive jobs. Reducing unemployment and working poverty through creation of such jobs should be viewed as a precondition for sustained economic growth.'

Infectious Diseases

The specific causes of any epidemic—whether of HIV/AIDS, SARS, Ebola, dengue, malaria, or drug-resistant TB (to name just a few)—are complex and multivariable. It is clear, however, that factors such as high population density, crowding, deforestation, dam-building, and migration may all play contributing roles. Governments that choose to divert financial resources away from health care and into military buildup contribute to this problem by underfunding systems to detect and prevent these diseases.

Climate Change

Over the past 50 years the earth's climate has been undergoing a warming trend. There is growing—and some say indisputable—evidence that human activity has contributed to this phenomenon. Population increases, which have caused higher levels of consumer demand for raw materials, industrial production to meet this demand, and carbon emissions, are assumed to have contributed to this trend. It has recently been suggested that in some respects even the Intergovernmental Panel on Climate Change may have underestimated the extent of the climate change that has taken place since the mid-twentieth century (Rahmstorf et al., 2007). Recent models of climate change suggest that the degree of global warming since the 1950s is even greater than the amount of warming expected to occur. Scientists generally agree that our planet is heating up, and we are beginning to see real signs of this: Arctic sea ice is melting unexpectedly fast (at 9 per cent a decade); glaciers are melting surprisingly swiftly; and a range of natural phenomena (e.g., hurricanes) that were once thought to be unrelated to climate change are now being linked to global warming (Stern, 2007).

Grain Production and Food

Around the world, cropland per capita has declined since the 1950s. Between 1950 and 1984, the amount of grain grown increased from 247 to 342 kilos per person, but since 1984 that output has fallen by 9 per cent. The trend varies across countries, however: China, for instance, is doing relatively well, but Pakistan has been experiencing a decline in grain production per person since 1981. In general, the main reasons for a slowdown in grain production are lack of new land for growing grain; slower growth in irrigation facilities; and slow growth of fertilizer use.

Today, some regions of the globe are experiencing serious food shortages. Estimates of the number of chronically hungry people worldwide are in the range of 815 million, which is a modest decline from the 956 million estimated in 1970 (Halweil, 2003: 28). Most of those are in India and Asia, although the most acute hunger crises are localized in sub-Saharan Africa, where in 2002 approximately 40 million people were in desperate need of food aid, according to Halweil (2003: 28). These are regions that have experienced years of poor grain harvests, exacerbated by drought, civil conflict, and HIV/AIDS. At the same time, grain and flour prices have increased beyond the reach of much of the population, and imports and international relief have been insufficient to stem the crisis. The situation points to the serious impediments to growing sufficient food and providing adequate nutrition in some parts of the world.

Fresh Water

Water levels have been falling in some of the world's major rivers (e.g., the Colorado River, the Yellow River in China, and the Nile in Egypt). Part of the reason is the growth of industries that require water. It is projected that by 2050 there will be scarcely one-fourth as much fresh water per person worldwide as there was in 1950.

Biodiversity

'Biodiversity' in the broadest sense refers to the number and variety of species within a given ecosystem. The earth is home to millions of distinct biological species, terrestrial and marine, and their ecosystems. Maintaining this diversity is important for the overall well-being of the planet and its inhabitants: for instance, the vast variety of natural compounds found in plant and biological species allows medical scientists to produce important drugs to save lives, and a significant portion of the food supply for humans comes from many varieties of plants and animals.

Lately it has been estimated that the pace of species extinction is 100 to 1,000 times the natural rate. Many, if not most, of the factors responsible can be attributed to human activity: population pressure and human encroachment on wild habitats, over-hunting, deforestation, and increased pollution.

Energy

Around the world, energy consumption per capita is increasing, and demand continues to rise. Currently, energy consumption is highest in the industrialized countries, where population growth rates are the lowest in the world. Per capita consumption in the US, for example, is more than 13 times that in the developing countries. In the next 50 years, the greatest growth in energy demand is expected to come from the regions where economic activity is intensifying—in particular Asia (where consumption is expected to grow by 361 per cent, though population itself will grow by only 50 per cent), Latin America, and Africa.

Oceanic Fish Catch

In 1950, average fish consumption worldwide was 8 kilograms per person; by 1984, the rate had grown to 17 kilos per person. Although that figure has since fallen slightly (to 16 kilos in 1999–2001), over-fishing is pushing certain species to the limit, and we can expect to see some disappear altogether in the near future. One contributing problem is the use of vast trawl nets that scoop up everything in their paths. Another is the growth of fish farming, which—though in part a response to the depletion of wild stocks—can also threaten wild populations by exposing them to infectious diseases and parasites.

Deforestation

Around the world, deforestation increases housing pressures as a consequence of the rising cost of wood for building material. This problem is especially acute in poor nations, where population growth rates are high.

Rapid Urbanization

The world has become increasingly urbanized over the past half century. The global urban population is expected to increase from 3.3 billion in 2007 to 4.6 billion in 2025, when the urban population will represent nearly 60 per cent of the total global population (United Nations Department of Economic and Social Affairs Population Division, 2008c: 1–5). Among the most obvious consequences of rapid urbanization in the developing countries are rampant urban poverty, rising crime rates, air pollution, and the rapid spread of communicable diseases because of overcrowding and, in many cases, underdeveloped sanitary systems. In this sense, rapid urbanization in some parts of the developing world can be seen as bringing about the kind of misery that Malthus predicted would ultimately serve as a 'positive check' on population growth (World Bank, 2003).

Resource Scarcity and Insecurity

In some parts of the planet rapid population growth exacerbates existing conflicts between states competing for scarce resources. As resources like fresh water and arable land become increasingly scarce, interstate violence becomes more likely (Homer-Dixon, Boutwell, and Rathjens, 1993). Poor countries are particularly vulnerable to this kind of conflict because they lack both the material and the human capital resources to buffer themselves against the effects of such environmental scarcities. Homer-Dixon (1999: 5) outlines five possible conflict types for such nations:

1. disputes arising directly from local environmental degradation caused, for instance, by factory emissions, logging, or dam construction;
2. ethnic clashes arising from population migration and deepened social cleavages due to environmental scarcity;
3. civil strife (including insurgency, banditry, and coups d'état) caused by environmental scarcity that affects economic productivity and, in turn, people's livelihoods, the behaviour of elite groups, and the ability of states to meet these changing demands;
4. scarcity-induced interstate war over resources such as water; and

5. conflicts between the developed and developing worlds over mitigation of, adaptation to, and compensation for global environmental problems such as climate change, ozone depletion, threats to biodiversity, and decreases in fish stocks.

The most common types of these conflicts, according to Homer-Dixon (1999: 5), are ethnic clashes and civil strife. In these circumstances, population growth may be an exogenous factor leading countries to resort to violence as a way of either obtaining or protecting the scarce resources (e.g., fresh water and arable land).

Neo-Marxism

Whereas neo-Malthusian scholars see the world's growing human population as central to environmental problems, neo-Marxist writers maintain that to fixate on overpopulation as the root cause of human suffering is to obscure the reality that the world is divided into wealthy and relatively poor regions, and that this divide is widening. Neo-Marxists argue that the population predicament of poor developing nations, for instance, is largely a function of their relative economic deprivation and continued dependency on the industrialized nations. They view the source of the problem as economic inequality, not overpopulation.

There are entrenched and persisting imbalances in economic and political power across nations, with some nations enjoying inordinate influence in the global arena and others almost none. The globalization of capital—seen by many writers as offering the developing nations the opportunity to emulate the 'success story' of the West—is seen by neo-Marxists as exacerbating rather than diminishing socioeconomic disparities within and across societies (Wimberly, 1990).

As we saw in Chapter 3, it was the neo-Marxist scholar Andre Gunder Frank (1991) who coined the phrase 'underdevelopment of development' to refer to the chronic dependence of the developing regions in a world where the great economic powers exercise overwhelming influence and control. Development—or, more precisely, underdevelopment—serves the interests of powerful nations (see also Wallerstein, 1974, 1980). The aid that poor nations receive comes at the cost of persistent dependence on the aid providers. Imbalances in the distribution of wealth, resources, and political influence have exacerbated socioeconomic inequality, poverty, and other social problems. From this perspective, therefore, overpopulation is not the prime cause of human suffering, as the neo-Malthusians contend, but the result of a complex chain of causation arising from power imbalances in international political and economic relations (Myrdal, 1957).

The challenge, as the neo-Marxists see it, is to distribute the benefits of progress equitably among the peoples of the world. The consumerism of wealthy regions and their overwhelming economic and political influence over the less advantaged nations is one of the impediments to this goal.

Revisionism

Beginning in the early 1950s, the literature on the population question was increasingly dominated by the neo-Malthusian perspective. In the 1980s, however, some of this literature (e.g., *The Limits to Growth*; *The Population Bomb*) came to be seen as overly alarmist. By the end of the twentieth century, the industrialized world—especially western Europe, North America, Japan, and Oceania—had seen several decades of near-zero population growth, with fertility at sub-replacement levels. In these regions, depopulation has replaced overpopulation as the primary concern. Moreover, following sharp declines in reproductive levels in many developing countries during recent decades, the global rate of natural increase has been declining since the early 1970s. There is also recent evidence that the poorest developing countries have embarked on a path of sustained fertility

The Ecological Footprint

The overall impact of human activities on the environment can be estimated by calculating the so-called 'ecological footprint' developed by Wackernagel and Rees (1996). The exercise is designed to answer the question *How much of the regenerative capacity of the biosphere is occupied by human activities?* The result is an account like the GDP or a bank statement, but rather than money, it adds up how much land and water is necessary to provide the resources we consume and to absorb the waste we generate (Global Footprint Network, 2008: http://www.footprint network.org/gfn_sub.php?content=europe2005).

The World Wildlife Fund and the Global Footprint Network's *Living Planet Report 2006* shows that humanity's ecological footprint has increased to the point where the earth is unable to replace resources at the rate at which humans are consuming them; our footprint now exceeds the world's ability to regenerate by about 25 per cent. This means that the world is currently in a state of 'overshoot'.

Any particular country or region may have either an ecological surplus or a deficit. In Figure 11.6a, the difference between a region's footprint (solid bar) and its *biocapacity* (dotted line) is shown as its *ecological reserve*, which can be positive or negative. North America, even with its considerable biocapacity, has the largest per capita deficit, with the average person using 3.7 global hectares more than the region has available. The European Union (EU) is next: with a person deficit of 2.6 global hectares, the region is using over twice its own biocapacity. At the other extreme is Latin America: with ecological reserves of 3.4 global hectares per capita, the average person's footprint in the region is only about a third of the biocapacity available in the region per person. Figure 11.6b shows the footprint by national average per person income. As these graphs illustrate, high-income regions show an average per capita footprint significantly greater than those of middle- and low-income regions. The *Living Planet Report 2006* notes three implications of these ecological trends:

1. The human population has, over the past several decades, been exceeding the earth's ability to support our increasing rates of consumption and resource use.
2. The biggest single contributor to the human population's footprint is energy generation and use. As a result of our growing reliance on fossil fuels to meet our energy needs, climate-changing emissions now make up 48 per cent, or almost half, of our global footprint.
3. What we currently accept as 'high development' is a long way away from 'sustainable development': as countries improve their overall standards of living, they are bypassing the goal of sustainability and are using more resources than the planet produces. This is bound to hinder socioeconomic development among poor countries, while threatening the high standards of living already attained in wealthy countries.

As to what to do about these trends, the report calls for people to adopt a more sustainable way of living by

- promoting technologies that lighten our footprint, especially those that can reduce climate-threatening carbon dioxide emissions;
- safeguarding ecosystems, especially fisheries and forests; and
- stemming biodiversity loss by protecting vital natural habitats in the earth's ecosystem.

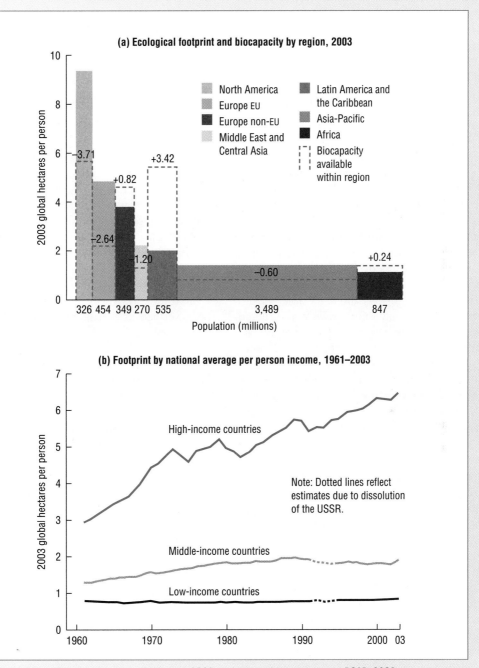

Figure 11.6 Ecological footprint by region, 2003, and national income groups, 1961–2003

Source: World Wildlife Fund and Global Footprint Network, 2006, Living Planet Report 2006 (WWF International, Gland: Switzerland): 18, Figs 20 & 21. Copyright © 2000 WWF (panda.org). Some rights reserved.

decline. As noted already, as the 'population crisis' of the 1950s, 1960s, and 1970s has subsided, the focus of the literature has shifted to sustainability and ecological balance.

In this general context, a new revisionist perspective has emerged. Revisionists (many of whom are neoclassical economists) subscribe neither to neo-Marxism nor to neo-Malthusianism, although elements of their thinking at times comes seemingly close to both perspectives (see Ahlburg, 1998; Birdsall, Kelley, and Sinding, 2001; Cincotta and Engelman, 1997; Clarke, 1996; Evans, 1998; Furedi, 1997; National Research Council, 1986; Preston, 1998). They are principally concerned with examining empirical evidence to assess its fit in terms of their conceptual models, which specify various causal mechanisms of population growth and economic, social, and ecological change. They base their conclusions about the role and importance of population growth and demographic structure on empirical observation, and from these observations, population policy implications are possible.

The analyses of revisionist scholars can be wide-ranging: sometimes population is found to be central to some specific problem; sometimes it turns out to be relatively unimportant. Revisionists are open to the possibility that population change can have benefits for society, and some of their views have sparked controversy (see, for example, *Scientific American*, January 2002). Some revisionists have argued that the presumed negative effects of population on the environment are minimal at most; they are generally quite skeptical of the environmental movement (see, for example, Aligica, 2007; Lomborg, 2001). The late economist Julian Simon (1995, 1996), who was known for his polemical attacks on the Malthusian view of population growth as harmful, maintained that population growth, on balance, has brought benefits to humankind: in his view, people are the ultimate resource. MacKellar (2003: 888) summarized Simon's critique of Malthusianism

along the following lines. First, he took a utilitarian view on the matter of population, arguing that individuals might rationally prefer to have many children rather than higher levels of material wealth or a clean environment; this is a matter of values, in Simon's view. Second, he contended that Malthusians generally underemphasize the positive contribution of population pressure to technological innovation. Third, he pointed to time series data as evidence that, in general, standards of living have improved. This view accords with the argument, outlined earlier in this chapter, that throughout human history, population growth has been associated with progress, innovation, specialization of economic activity, rising incomes, and improved standards of living (Boserup, 1965, 1981; Fogel and Costa, 1997). This view has been reasserted most recently by Aligica (2007).

In some ways, the revisionist perspective can be described as 'cornucopian' in orientation because of its often explicitly positive assessments of the state of the human condition and its plentiful resources (see, for example, Lomborg, 2001). In this context, a report by the United States National Research Council (1986) marked a turning point in the literature. Based on its expert assessment, the committee responsible for the report proclaimed that population might have no discernible relationship to the dangers that were once attributed to it. In other cases, it conceded that population may be an important—though not necessarily the most important—indirect determinant of societal and environmental problems. Nevertheless, it found that on balance slower population growth would be beneficial to economic development for most developing countries.

The same report suggested that the relationship between population growth and the depletion of non-renewable resources is statistically weak and often exaggerated. It found income growth and excessive consumption to be more important factors, reasoning that a world with a rapidly growing population but slow income growth might deplete its resources more slowly than one with a stationary population but rapidly increasing income. However, it also found that reducing population growth rates would increase the rate of return to labour (i.e., average wages and productivity) and thus help to reduce income inequality in a country.

The report suggested that while population is directly related to the growth of large cities in the developing world, its role in urban problems is likely secondary; ineffective or misguided government policies tend to play a more important role. Moreover, although the literature often assumes that reducing population growth leads to reductions in poverty and income inequality, in fact this relationship holds up only to a certain point. For instance, if the population of Bangladesh were halved, its status as a poor nation would not change appreciably; it would move from the second poorest nation to thirteenth poorest in the world. This suggests that other factors besides population growth rates contribute to a country's level of poverty.[1]

The impact of rapid population growth on economic growth is an important area of investigation. Between the mid-1960s and the early 1990s, economic demographers tended to emphasize the deleterious effects of rapid population growth on a country's ability to generate sufficient economic growth. The standard explanation for this effect is the Coale and Hoover (1958) model mentioned earlier, in which rapid population growth causes the age structure to widen in the youthful age groups, thus posing a serious youth dependency problem for governments attempting to raise average incomes. Lately, following further scrutiny, this model has been amplified in terms of the causal mechanisms involved (see Birdsall, Kelley, and Sinding, 2001). A country's GDP can take a turn for the better if a period of sustained fertility

increases is followed by a rapid fertility decline. As we noted in Chapter 4, this scenario can represent a 'window of opportunity' for developing countries currently in the final stage of demographic transition (Birdsall, Kelley, and Sinding, 2001): for these countries, earlier high fertility has created a bulge in the current working-age population, while the recent drop in fertility reduces the youth dependency ratio. These two coincident demographic conditions can create a significant economic benefit for a country. But revisionist scholars are quick to point out the crucial role of social and political institutions in taking full advantage of this one-time 'demographic bonus' (Bloom, Canning, and Sevilla, 2003; Cincotta and Engelman, 1997). If economic success is to follow, a government must provide adequate education and training for its labour force and find ways to create jobs for an expanding, youthful working-age population.

Towards a Synthesis

However deeply their economic and political ideologies may differ, Marxists and free-market cornucopians share a basic optimism with regard to the future. Most environmentalists, by contrast, share the Malthusian view. The economists believe that population growth can fuel economic growth, hence well-being, and that problems such as vanishing resources and environmental degradation can be solved through technical and scientific innovation. The environmentalists are not so confident.

Keyfitz (1993) has asked why economics and the natural sciences (biology, ecology, etc.) generally differ so radically in the ways they conceptualize issues pertaining to population, environment, and resources. He suggests that more progress would be made in formulating an appropriate population policy if the two camps could agree on the nature of the problems involved and their urgency. But biologists/ecologists and economists perceive the world in very different ways. As Keyfitz explains it, part of the problem is that economists tend to see humans

---

[1] Additional reviews based on the National Research Council report are found in the World Bank's *World Development Report for 1992* (World Bank, 1992).

as the central fact of life on earth, whereas ecologists and biologists see humans as just one species among many in the web of life. Economics has a time scale of years or decades at most, whereas biology and ecology are accustomed to thinking about evolutionary processes operating over millennia. Economics is concerned with inputs and outputs within a particular human economy; biology and ecology are concerned with the biosphere that sustains all life. Economics deals with two parts of a truncated commodity cycle—production and consumption; biology and ecology look at the much longer cycle of production, consumption, and waste, and how all these affect the ecosystem.

As it turns out, the data these two disciplines have generated on the effects of population on the environment are far from conclusive. Keyfitz recognizes how difficult it is to relate population growth to rising income in the world: 'does population drive the economy . . . or does the improving economy lead to fewer deaths, and hence to rising population?' (1993: 6898). Statistical correlations cannot provide definitive answers to such complex questions. Biologists and ecologists see no need for a general law to prove the harm that would be done if the earth's human population were to continue growing. On the other hand, the data compiled by economists, though plentiful, are not well suited to developing any sort of general law of population and resources, primarily because economists take a comparatively short-term view.

Clearly, the field is far from monolithic. Is a conceptual synthesis possible? Twenty-one years after the publication of *The Limits to Growth*, the lead author of that report, Donella H. Meadows, described four groups with competing perspectives on population and ecological sustainability. Meadows (1993) identified each of these groups with a colour:

1. The 'blues' see economic growth as the key to solving human problems. Capital and technology, they say, must grow faster than population.

2. The 'reds' follow the Marxist idea that a radical change in the social system is needed to eradicate inequality and human suffering in the world.
3. The 'greens' are environmentalists, concerned above all with sustaining the planetary ecosystem for all the earth's species. They believe that the global economy is too big and growing too fast, promoting overconsumption, and that long-term survival depends on reducing consumption and production as well as human population growth.
4. The 'whites' emphasize self-reliance and put the local community ahead of the larger social system. They object to elite experts telling the people what they must do to deal with problems. Whites focus their efforts on making their local communities self-sufficient.

As different as these schools of thought appear, Meadows (1993) urged that they be reconciled, since each is correct in some respects and has something valuable to contribute to our greater understanding of the complex issues surrounding population, environment, and resources (see also Bandarage, 1997).

The blues, for instance, emphasize the importance of economic growth to human welfare. Growth promotes well-being by creating jobs and raising incomes. People around the world need to have meaningful and productive work in order to live a good life and provide for their families, and as long as economic progress continues, the population can enjoy a rising standard of living. The people of the developing countries, with the help of economic globalization, can share in the benefits of economic progress and rising socioeconomic conditions.

The reds, for their part, represent the collective social conscience. They call attention to the plight of the poor and marginalized, and they insist that socioeconomic inequalities must be eliminated. Once this task is accomplished, the pace of population growth in the poor countries will slow and stabilize in line with the world average.

The greens focus on the environment and its fragility in the face of economic growth and globalization. But economic progress and environmental sustainability need not be opposing goals (Demeny, 1998). The world community should be able to achieve both objectives: increasing economic growth and ecological sustainability alike.

Finally, the whites emphasize the value of smallness and reliance on local community to find co-operative solutions to human challenges (e.g., Schumacher, 1974). If human communities can become more self-sufficient, the need for widespread economic production will be reduced, and, with it, the overuse of natural resources.

Conclusion

This chapter has looked at the Malthusian and Marxist perspectives on population and resources and the contemporary manifestations perspectives, as well as some recent revisionist views. The point that emerges most clearly is that rapid population growth can, and often does, have very serious consequences for society, resources, and the environment, even though its role is often indirect through other factors. Yet, as we have seen, there are cases where population plays a minor or even inconsequential role. The pressures exerted on the environment by the industrialized countries, for instance, have much more to do with affluence than with population numbers. Less developed countries with rapidly growing but relatively poor populations have had much smaller ecological footprints. On the other hand, we might reasonably expect wealthy nations to do more than poor ones to mitigate the damage they do. Transitional societies undergoing rapid industrialization—such as China and India, both population billionaires—will play an increasingly significant role in terms of pollution and

resource depletion in the future, unless of course they find ways to avoid excessive damage to the environment during their rapid industrialization. Thus, the challenge for these societies is to promote economic growth while also accepting the costs of limiting the environmental damage that growth entails. In summary, population does play a role in some ecological and resource problems, but its effects are primarily synergetic or indirect, produced in interaction with other factors such as societal affluence and consumption patterns, rapid economic growth, and the willingness and ability of governments to promote appropriate solutions to societal and environmental problems.

Notes for Further Study

Malthusian theory implies that population growth is a key determinant of societal well-being. It assumes that for a given habitat there is a positive correlation between population growth rate, absolute population size, and population density, and that unless population growth is checked by moral restraint, at some point density will increase to such an extent as to cause depletion of the food supply and other resources like water and arable land; this will in turn cause mortality to rise. We have already looked at measures of population growth (geometric, exponential, and logistic models). Below we examine the concept of population density in its elemental forms. Population density measures provide an indication of the balance between population and resources in a given habitat.

The simplest measure of population density is the ratio of people to all land in a given habitat (e.g., country or territory). This simple measure expresses density in terms of persons per unit of area (usually persons per square kilometre). In 2003, the Population Reference Bureau calculated that the world's people-to-land ratio was 122 persons per square mile. There is a notable disparity in this measure between the developed and developing countries. The more developed areas of the world as a whole had a population density of 61 persons per square mile, compared to 160 for the less developed countries. The relative difference between these two figures is 2.62, meaning that the population pressure on resources is almost three times greater in the developing countries than in their more developed counterparts.

There are two main problems with the people-to-land ratio, however. First, it does not take into account the portions of any given geographic territory that are not habitable—mountains, rivers, lakes, oceans, deserts, and so forth. Second, as Ehrlich, Ehrlich, and Holdren (1977: 717) have pointed out, population density itself does not take into account the fact that it takes more than physical space to support a population. A shortage of fresh water or fertile soils, or a climate unsuitable for agriculture, for instance, 'may make it difficult to supply even a sparse population in a given area with the necessities of existence. Large parts of Africa, North and South America, and Australia are or could quickly become overpopulated in this respect despite their low densities because over large areas they lack sufficient dependable water, good soils, or a moderate climate.'

From the Malthusian point of view, the real concern is the number of people in a given area in relation to the means of subsistence in that area. The people-to-land ratio should therefore be refined to

$$\frac{\text{population of geographic area } i}{\text{means of subsistence in geographic area } i}$$

A ratio greater than 1 would indicate 'overpopulation'—the greater the ratio, the greater the degree of overpopulation. A ratio below 1 would denote overabundance of land or subsistence in

relation to the number of people in that habitat.

In societies that rely mainly on agriculture, 'means of subsistence' would include, at a minimum, the amount of land suitable for agricultural production, or the amount of the land area that is occupied by fresh water and other resources essential for the production of food. In an industrial economy, agricultural land remains essential, but other types of resources are also important: for instance, the raw materials and energy sources needed for technological development and economic productivity; education and health services for the labour force; capital investment; and so forth. Thus, as Ehrlich, Ehrlich, and Holdren (1977: 716) argue,

[T]he physical necessities—food, water, clothing, shelter, a healthful environment—are indispensable ingredients of well-being. A population too large and too poor to be supplied adequately with them has exceeded the optimum, regardless of whatever other aspects of well-being might, in theory, be enhanced by further growth. Similarly, a population so large that it can be supplied with physical necessities only by the rapid consumption of nonrenewable resources or by activities that irreversibly degrade the environment has also exceeded the optimum. . . .

An important problem in such measures of population density is how to identify the 'essential resources' for a given population in a given geographic area, and then to clearly specify measureable indicators of 'essential resources'. Various refinements to the measure of population density are presented by Plane and Rogerson (1994) and also by Shryock and Siegel (1972: 71).

Exercises

1. Using data from the *United Nations Demographic Yearbooks*, or issues of the *World Population Data Sheet* from the Population Reference Bureau, locate the 10 countries with the largest populations in 2007 and, for the same year, the 10 countries with the smallest populations. For these 20 populations, record (a) the population density ratios from 1991 to 2007 and (b) the corresponding decennial gross national product (GNP) (or gross national income per purchasing parity, GNI PPP).
2. For the 10 largest populations in 2007, graph the time trends of both the population density variable and the GNP/GNI PPP variable.
3. Graph the same trends for the 10 smallest populations.
4. Explain the time trends in these variables for the two sets of countries. What is the association between population density and GNP/GNI PPP for these countries? Can you explain the association from the point of view of the Malthusian principle of population? Do these data support the Malthusian theory? Explain.
5. Suggest ways in which the population density measures presented above could be improved. Assume that you would have access to any information that might be necessary for your refinements. Are the concepts of 'density-dependence' and 'carrying capacity' relevant to human populations? Explain.
6. Write a brief essay on the applicability of Malthusian theory to today's population and resource situation in regard to the more developed and less developed countries. What new issues do we face today that Malthus could not have foreseen? Suggest interventions to help solve identified concerns.
7. Examine the Marxist theory of population and write a brief essay on its present and possible future applicability towards explaining the population and resources problems faced by the contemporary least developed nations (i.e., the poorest nations in the world). Is a Marxist analysis of the situation of any value from the point of view of population policy in these poor societies?

Additional Reading

Bailey, Ronald. 2002. *Global Warming and Other Eco-Myths: How the Environmental Movement Uses False Science to Scare Us to Death*. Roseville, CA: Prima Publishing/Forum.

Cartledge, Bryan, ed. 1995. *Population and the Environment*. Oxford: Oxford University Press.

Coleman, David, and Roger Schofield, eds. *The State of Population Theory: Forward from Malthus*. Oxford: Basil Blackwell.

Davis, Kingsley, and Mikhail S. Bernstam, eds, 1991. *Resources, Environment, and Population: Present Knowledge, Future Options*. Supplement to Population and Development Review No. 16. New York: Oxford University Press.

Jensen, An-Magritt, Torbjorn Knutsen, and Anders Skonhoft, eds. 2003. *Visiting Malthus: The Man, His Times, the Issues*. Oslo: Abstrakt Forlag AS.

Kondratyev, Kirill Y., Alexei A. Grigoryev, and Costas A. Varotsos. 2002. *Environmental Disasters: Anthropogenic and Natural*. Chichester, UK: Springer and Praxis.

Linner, Bjorn-Ola. 2003. *The Return of Malthus: Environmentalism and Post-War Population-Resources Crises*. Strond, Isle of Harris, UK: White Horse.

Lutz, Wolfgang, Alexia Prskawetz, and Warren C. Sanderson, eds. 2002. *Population and Environment: Methods of Analysis*. Supplement to Population and Development Review Volume 28.

McKee, Jeffrey K. 2002. *Sparing Nature. The Conflict Between Human Population Growth and Earth's Biodiversity*. New Brunswick, NJ: Rutgers University Press.

Pullen, John, and Trevor Hughes Parry, eds. 1997. *T.R. Malthus: The Unpublished Papers in the Collection of Kanto Gakuen University*. Vols 1 and 2. Cambridge: Cambridge University Press for the Royal Economic Society.

Ramphal, Shridath, and Steven W. Sinding, eds. 1996. *Population Growth and Environmental Issues*. Westport, CT: Praeger.

Rose, J., ed. 2000. *Population Problems: Topical Issues*. Amsterdam: Gordon and Breach.

Simon, Julian, ed. 1998. *The Economics of Population: Classic Writings*. New Brunswick, NJ: Transaction.

Slack, Paul, ed. 1999. *Environments and Historical Change*. Oxford: Oxford University Press.

Weart, Spencer R. 2003. *The Discovery of Global Warming*. Cambridge, MA: Harvard University Press.

Web Resources

For information on economic history, including other eighteenth-century thinkers, such as David Ricardo and John Stuart Mills, whose views helped to shape social and economic policy, visit the History of Economic Thought website. This site provides historical background to the social economic context of some of the theorists discussed in this chapter: http://cepa.newschool.edu/het/home.htm.

The French Revolution was a turning point in the history of the West. This formative event was mentioned in this chapter as part of the historical context of Thomas Robert Malthus. Interested readers can visit: www.angelfire.com/va/frenchrev/.

Another useful website is The World Population: A Guide to the WWW, maintained by David Jensen of Excelsior College, New York: http://tigger.uic.edu/~rjensen/populate.html.

The following websites are devoted to environmental sustainability and population issues:

- World Energy Assessment: Energy and the Challenge of Sustainability. United Nations Development Programme, United Nations Department of Economic and Social Affairs, and World Energy Council, 2001: www.undp.org/energy/activities/wea/drafts-frame.html.
- Intergovernmental Panel on Climate Change: www.ipcc.ch/.
- Population Action International : www.populationaction.org.
- Population Environment Research Network: www.populationenvironmentresearch.org/.

- PopPlanet: http://popplanet.org/.
- World Resources Institute: www.wri.org/index.html.
- The United Nations Population Fund (UNFPA): www.unfpa.org.
- The UN Chronicle: www.un.org/chronicle.
- The Worldwatch Institute: www.worldwatch.org.
- The World Bank: www.worldbank.org.
- The Club of Rome: www.clubofrome.org.
- The Sierra Club: www.sierraclub.org/education/.
- Global Footprint Network: www.footprintnetwork.org.

Chapter 12

Demographic Change and Policy Concerns

Introduction

The twenty-first century could well be a volatile century, punctuated by periods of major global instability. As Smil (2005a, 2005b) has noted, change can come about both because of sudden, catastrophic events and because of the more gradual unfolding of fundamental demographic, social, economic, strategic, and environmental trends. Crises are likely to arise from factors that are increasingly undermining the stability of societies, including human devastation of the earth's environment, advancing uncontrollable diseases, dwindling energy supplies, and the growing gap between rich and poor nations (Cincotta, Engelman, and Anastasion, 2003; Homer-Dixon, 2006; Kawachi and Wamala, 2007; Meadows, Randers, and Meadows, 2005; Nichiporuk, 2000; Stern, 2007).

Adding to these sources of potential global instability is the problem of uneven population growth, which threatens to exacerbate the disparities in wealth between developed and developing countries. It is well established that most of the growth over this century will take place in the developing countries, which will only worsen the dire socioeconomic conditions of these societies (Birg, 1995a; Bongaarts, 1994, 1998; Demeny, 2003a; Lutz, Sanderson, and Scherbov, 2008). At the same time, the world's population will increasingly get older, but aging will be most intense in the most advanced societies, where demographic maturity and below-replacement fertility rates have taken central stage as societal issues of concern

(Vaupel and Lochinger, 2006; Wattenberg, 2004).

But while the developing and developed countries are facing opposite challenges of population growth and population decline, respectively, it is wrong to view their fates separately. Deteriorating standards of living in developing countries cannot be seen as a problem restricted solely to the developing countries. For instance, rapid population growth in developing countries is one of the main reasons behind the rising waves of illegal and asylum-seeking migrations to some of the wealthy nations of the West, which, paradoxically, must rely increasingly on immigration to help combat their growing demographic deficit and supplement a dwindling native workforce. Yet for some receiving countries in the West, immigration (legal and illegal) has come to be viewed as both a problem and a solution: immigrants are increasingly needed, though not necessarily wanted as citizens (Castles and Miller, 2003; Marfleet, 2006).

How can the world's developed countries cope with their shortfall in fertility and consequent demographic maturity over the long term? Is increased immigration the most viable solution? What can poor developing countries do to help themselves out of the poverty trap? Is reduced population growth the answer? In this chapter we shall address these questions through a discussion of population policy and its relationship to broader sociological and socioeconomic trends. We will begin by examining population policy as a concept, before making an overview of current demographic policy concerns among developed and developing countries, and concluding with a discussion of population policy issues from the point of view of Canadian society.

Population Policy

Population policy may be defined as an objective plan formulated by government to reduce, increase, or stabilize population growth rates over some specified period of time. Usually, the aim of population policies is to effect *quantitative change* through one or more of the three major demographic variables—fertility, mortality, migration—in order to reduce or increase the rate of population growth. Less often, governments may implement policies directed at changing the composition of their population, thus effecting *qualitative demographic change*. For example, a country's immigration policy may be modified to encourage immigration from certain areas of the world with the goal of changing the county's racial or ethnic composition.

Policies with a direct bearing on fertility, mortality, or migration are called *direct population policies*. There is a long history of such policies in the developing countries. Family planning programs are a good example. Aimed at affecting birth rates, family planning programs are designed to bring about fertility decline by giving women access to effective contraceptives and education about fertility so that they may gain greater control over their reproductive lives, particularly in terms of the number and spacing of children they have.

Indirect policies are programs designed to influence non-demographic variables that have an indirect impact on the key demographic variables. Indirect policies include programs aimed at improving population health, such as immunization programs and anti-malaria campaigns in poor countries. These types of programs, if successful, can reduce rates of infant, childhood,

and maternal mortality. Over the long term, these same programs may cause, indirectly, a decline in parents' demand for children, because as child survival probabilities improve, parents will desire fewer offspring. Policies aimed at improving the status of women could be expected to have a similar indirect effect on fertility rates: as women's status improves, women gain greater autonomy over their personal lives, which we would expect to translate into delayed marriage and later timing of childbearing (National Research Council and Institute of Medicine, 2005).

Figure 12.1 summarizes the stages of population policy creation. Typically, population policy is formulated on the basis of past and current trends in fertility, mortality, and migration; rate of natural increase and age structure; and the anticipated future trajectory of these variables. Population projections over some specified period (usually 25 or 50 years) are computed by taking the central demographic variables of fertility, mortality, and migration and applying different assumptions about whether, when, how, and to what extent current trends might change. Projections are usually executed under 'high', 'medium', 'low', and 'no change' scenarios to account for varying degrees of change in the variables. These scenarios provide a good indication of the extent of population growth that could be expected as well as what changes in age structure may result from the forecasted interplay of natural increase and net migration.

Governments tend to take very seriously the projection exercise and the possible socioeconomic ramifications of the projected demographic futures. Attention then turns to what policy or policies may be implemented to alter the projected increase/decrease in population and age structure. For example, in populations where fertility has been below replacement for many years, population projections could forecast eventual deficits in the working-age population. Officials might wish to respond to such a prognosis by introducing policies to increase

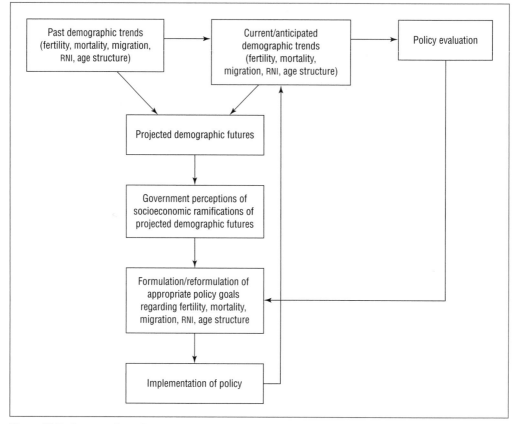

Figure 12.1 Demographic policy process

birth rates. The opposite scenario could prevail in poor developing countries, where persisting high birth rates might lead to predictions of continued population growth and a superabundance of workers. In such circumstances, officials would likely recommend policies aimed at fertil-ity reduction. Once a policy has been devised and implemented, governments need to monitor the demographic trends over time in order to gauge the effectiveness of the policy, which may need to be adjusted or replaced if it fails to produce the desired demographic changes.

Using Population Projection to Address Policy Questions

One of the most important demographic developments in Canada over the past 15 years is the increasing contribution of net international migration to population growth. Since 1993, Canada's population has grown more from net international migration than from natural increase, with immigration contributing between 64 and 69 per cent of total growth since 2001. It seems very likely that natural increase will soon become negative, leaving international migration as the sole source of population growth. The Canadian government's current immigration targets are set at around 250,000 per year. Can increasing this figure really be the solution to Canada's impending demographic deficit and inexorably aging population?

George and Loh (2007) set out to answer this question through a series of population projections starting in 2005 and ending in 2056. They actually began with two questions:

- In the absence of migration, when and to what extent would the size of the population decline?
- How great would be the impact of migration on population aging?

Table 12.1 (page 532) outlines the various fertility, mortality, and migration assumptions that went into George and Loh's population projections. One scenario assumed an initial continuation of migration to Canada at 2004 levels followed by a change over the projection period, as specified in the table. Another scenario assumed no international migration and emigration whatsoever, which left fertility and mortality as the only variables bearing on population change over the projection period.

As Table 12.2 (page 533) shows, in the absence of migration, Canada's population would peak at 33.1 million around 2026 and then begin to decline, reaching 28.8 million in 2056. If some international migration is assumed, the population in 2056 may be over 42 million. Yet even in this latter scenario, although population growth would remain positive throughout the projection period, the rate of growth would begin to decline between 2026 and 2031, falling to just 0.2 per cent by 2056. With no migration, population growth would be negative, −0.7 per cent, by 2051–6.

A key finding of George and Loh's investigation is that assumed increases in net international migration over the projection period would have only a negligible effect on lowering the extent of population aging in Canada. While immigration would help to slow down the increase in total support ratios (i.e., the ratio of young and elderly dependents to those of working age, 15–64), it would not avert significant increases in this measure in the future, with older people making up the bulk of the dependent population. In the absence of international migration, the increase in overall support ratios would be even greater. The median age of the population and the proportion of people aged 65 and over would also increase appreciably over the projection period, regardless of whether or not international migration is assumed. In 2006, the average Canadian was approximately 39 years old; by 2050, this will be substantially higher: 47 if migration is assumed, 51 if no migration is assumed.

In summary, George and Loh's (2007) population projection analysis suggests that either with reasonable increases in international migration or with no immigration at all, Canada's population will get substantially older over the next half century. Therefore, while increasing immigration to reasonable levels beyond the present 250,000 annual targets would help to increase the population to about 43 million by 2056, such immigration increases cannot reverse the population aging trend in Canada, at least over the next 50 years or so.

Table 12.1 Summary of assumptions, by component, used in George and Loh's population projections for Canada, 2005–56: medium growth scenario

Component	Projection with international migration	Projection without international migration
Fertility	A constant fertility of 1.5 children per woman throughout the projection period.	A constant fertility of 1.5 children per woman throughout the projection period.
Mortality	Life expectancy would reach 81.9 years for males and 86.0 years for females in 2031 and remain constant thereafter.	Life expectancy would reach 81.9 years for males and 86.0 years for females in 2031 and remain constant thereafter.
Immigration	The 2004 immigration rate would reach 7.0 per 1,000 population in 2010 and remain constant until 2031; the projected number in 2031 would remain constant thereafter.	Zero immigration after 2004 (i.e., no immigration at all).
Emigration: returning emigrants and persons temporarily abroad	A constant emigration rate of 1.5 per 1,000 throughout the projection period; 38 per cent of emigrants return each year; a net annual figure of 26,000 persons reside temporarily abroad from 2005 to 2006, which will be reduced linearly to 22,000 in 2011 and kept constant thereafter.	Zero emigration after 2004 (i.e., no emigration at all).
Non-permanent residents	A constant stock of 390,000 persons per year; a zero balance is assumed between persons entering this population and those leaving it.	A constant stock of 390,000 persons per year; a zero balance is assumed between persons entering this population and those leaving it.

Source: Adapted from George and Loh (2007).

Table 12.2 Summary of population projections for Canada to the year 2056 (base year 2005)

Population growth (in millions) by period	With international migration	Without international migration
2006	32.5	32.4
2011	33.9	32.8
2026	37.9	33.1
2031	39.0	32.9
2056	42.5	28.8
Average rate of population growth (%) by period		
2005–6	0.9	0.3
2011–16	0.8	0.2
2021–6	0.7	0.0
2031–6	0.5	−0.3
2041–6	0.3	−0.6
2051–6	0.2	−0.7
Median age by period		
2006	38.8	38.9
2011	40.1	40.8
2026	43.3	45.5
2031	44.3	47.0
2056	46.9	51.1
Number of dependents per 100 workers by period		
2006	43.9	44.0
2011	43.7	43.9
2026	56.8	60.8
2031	61.3	68.0
2056	68.7	80.9

Age structure by period	% <15	% 15–64	% 65+	% <15	% 15–64	% 65+
2006	17.3	69.5	13.2	17.3	69.5	13.3
2011	16.0	69.6	14.4	15.7	69.5	14.8
2026	15.0	63.8	21.2	14.1	62.2	23.7
2031	14.6	62.0	23.4	13.6	59.5	26.9
2056	13.5	59.3	27.2	12.2	55.3	32.5

Source: Adapted from George and Loh (2007).

Population Policy–Societal Interrelationships

The process of formulating and implementing population policy always takes place within a broader societal context. No policy is ever implemented without first having some idea of the socioeconomic and environmental implications of current and projected population trends (Birg, 1995). In this sense, population policy is but one part of a broader societal configuration involving—beside demographic considerations—social structure, economy, polity, and culture.

Figure 12.2 is intended to map out, broadly, the complex interrelationship between population policy and the key government and societal factors that shape it. The diagram assumes a close connection (though not necessarily a per-

fect correlation) between type of government (i.e., democratic or otherwise) and other societal forces that either promote or fail to promote the overall well-being of citizens. This sketch implies that societal well-being is an important determinant of a country's demographic regime—in other words, whether it is post-transitional, transitional, or delayed transitional. In turn, the prevailing demographic conditions and those projected into the future, as understood and perceived by a ruling government, will influence the type of population policy that is promoted and implemented. Governments in liberal democracies tend to promote policies that are consistent with the basic principles of democracy: freedom, equality, and dignity of the individual. These principles are not always upheld by non-democratic governments, which, as a result, may be much more assertive in the kinds

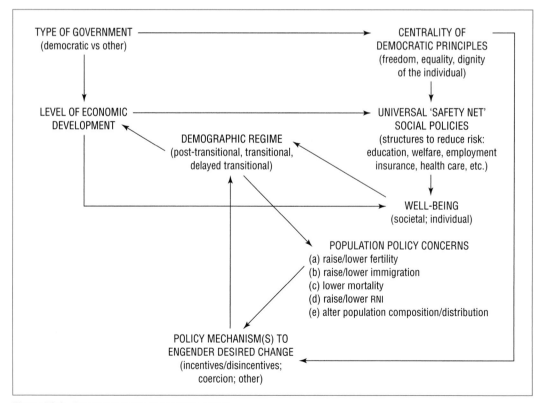

Figure 12.2 Population policy in societal context

of policies they introduce into their societies. For example, officials in non-democratic regimes would see the principle of individual freedom as secondary to what the state perceives as most important.

Depending on how they perceive the demographic and socioeconomic conditions of their country, government officials—democratically elected or not—will devise policies according to four different aims:

1. to raise the rate of natural increase
2. to reduce the rate of natural increase
3. to maintain the current rate of natural increase
4. to achieve population growth through immigration

There are numerous impediments to population policy in liberal democracies. These include the lack of a political basis for long-term planning (since elected politicians typically hold office for just a few years), the emphasis on individual freedom and welfare as paramount to broader societal objectives, and the difficulty of addressing environmental concerns in any policy aimed at promoting population growth rather than decline in the future. Apart from these obstacles, there is a tendency for government officials in democratic societies to see their constituencies only in terms of organized groups, and so the government's role becomes one of arbitrating competing claims. The interests of organized groups in democratic societies may relate less to the population as a whole than to specific concerns, such as family, feminism, the environment, health, multiculturalism, refugees, and so forth. Furthermore, demographic policy matters seldom receive widespread attention from the public in democratic societies (McNicoll, 1995).

Non-democratic regimes have significantly greater leeway in the realm of population policy. For example, China's family planning program, with its one-child policy as its centrepiece, was introduced in 1979 amid a belief among govern-

ing officials that it was necessary for the good of the nation to curb population growth rates. Chinese officials wanted to actualize a predictable trajectory of population growth with the goal of eventually stabilizing population at about 1.2 billion by the end of the twentieth century (Bongaarts and Greenhalgh, 1985; Greenhalgh, 1986). To do this, they devised a set of regulations governing family size, the timing of marriage and childbearing for women, and the spacing of children in cases where a second child is permitted. With some exceptions, all Chinese couples in urban areas and all government employees must opt for a one-child limit or else they will face a variety of penalties administered by family planning committees at the provincial and local levels. Couples who wish to have more than one child may be allowed to pay a large fine (known as a 'social maintenance fee') over many years; the funds generated by these fines are used by the government to cover costs of education and other basic services for 'extra' children (Greenhalgh, 1986; Winckler, 2002).

China's one-child policy is not applied universally across the country. Instead, the Chinese government has divided the country into three regions, each with its own fertility targets and, accordingly, its own degree of flexibility in how

The term 'one-child policy' is a misnomer because the Chinese government, over the years, has relaxed this rule. Allowable exceptions to the one-child limit have been given to couples in the countryside whose first born is a daughter or is disabled; however, second children are subject to birth spacing rules, which means that parents typically have to wait three or four years between births. When two children have been approved by officials, any additional children born to a couple are subject to heavy fines and penalties, just as is the case for those who fail to abide by the one-child directive (Attané, 2002).

the policy is applied. In the first region, only 20 to 50 per cent of childbearing women are permitted to have a second child. Among the provinces in this group are Hubei and those lying along a narrow coastal strip running from Heilongjiang to Zhejiang, where about a third of China's population lives. A second region, which comprises roughly 55 per cent of China's population, includes the central and southern provinces. Here, parents are allowed a second child if the first is a girl or if the parents are experiencing significant hardship because they have only one child. The local cadres are left the task of judging what constitutes 'significant hardship'. Under these conditions, 50 to 70 per cent of the women in this region would be allowed to have a second child. The third group of provinces, which includes Guizhou, Hainan, Nei Menggu, Ningxia, Qinghai, Tibet, Xinjiang, and Yunnan, contains the greatest proportion of ethnic minorities. Here, the rules are more permissive: at least 70 per cent of women are allowed to have a second child, and in Xinjiang, approximately 40 per cent of women are allowed a third (Attané, 2002: 104).

In recent years the one-child policy has been relaxed somewhat, but there is little doubt that it remains a policy based on incentives and penalties, with a certain element of coercion. It is clear that the Chinese population policy would be inconceivable in a democratic society, not only because of its punitive dimensions, but because it violates a fundamental principle of democracy: freedom of the individual, in this case freedom to make personal choices about the number of children one wants to have.

In strictly demographic terms, China's one-child policy has been highly successful. In 1975, China's rate of natural increase was one of the highest in the world (1.7 per cent); by 1985, after several years of the one-child policy, it had declined to 1.1 per cent. In 2006, China's rate of natural increase stood at 0.6 per cent, well below the world rate of 1.2 per cent (Population Reference Bureau, 1975, 1985, 2006). From a human rights perspective, however, the one-child policy has some distinct problems (see Aird, 1990; Berelson and Lieberson, 1979; Lim, 2006; McLarty, 2006; Potts, 2006; Smith, 2006). Most notably, it has created a certain disdain for female infants, and as a result, there has been an increase in the level of sex-selective abortions in the country and more reported cases of neglect, abandonment, and even infanticide of newborn

Baby Boom a Perk that Only Elite Can Afford

The rich and famous are paying exorbitant fines to bypass China's controversial one-child policy

China's controversial one-child policy, which has led to forced abortions and sterilizations, is facing a new assault from an unexpected group: the rich and famous.

The *nouveaux riches*, an increasingly powerful class in China, are paying big money to be exempted from the one-child limit, and this could jeopardize efforts to control the growth of the world's most populous nation, a Chinese official warned yesterday.

Some wealthy families and show-business celebrities are paying $20,000 or more in official penalties for evading the one-child limit, and they see it as a small price to pay for the privilege, Chinese media have reported.

The latest revelations will fuel the outrage of the ordinary masses, already bitterly resentful of the perks and privileges of the wealthy. The widening gap between the rich and poor has sparked fears among government officials who worry that the gap will destabilize Chinese society and trigger class conflict.

The one-child policy was introduced in 1979 to restrain China's fast-rising population, which has reached 1.3 billion today. Most urban couples are limited to one child, and most rural couples are limited to two children.

The policy, enforced with ruthless zeal in some parts of the country, has managed to moderate the growth of China's population over the past two decades. But now there is a growing risk of a 'population rebound', according to the latest warning.

Zhang Weiqing, the top Chinese family-planning official, said the widening gap between rich and poor is threatening the one-child policy, since wealthy families often 'disdain' the policy and simply 'pay to have as many children as they like', the state-run Xinhua news agency reported yesterday.

The gulf between China's rich and poor grows wider every year. In 2005, the most recent data available, the top 10 per cent of urban dwellers were earning 9.2 times more than the bottom 10 per cent. The gap had increased from the previous year, when the richest were earning 8.9 times more than the poorest.

At the same time, the average urban resident is earning 3.2 times more than the average farmer, an 'alarming' gap in comparison to other countries, another Chinese official said in February.

While this widening income gap is dangerous enough, some of the most extreme anger is aimed at business tycoons and wealthy showbiz personalities who seem to consider themselves above the law.

'We found out that most celebrities and rich people have two children, and 10 per cent have three,' Yu Xuejun, a senior official of China's population and family planning commission, said in an interview with a Beijing newspaper in March.

'This phenomenon must be stopped,' he said.

The government vowed that any celebrities or tycoons who violate the one-child policy will be prohibited from receiving awards or honours in the future. The idea is to hit the celebrities in their public image, rather than just their pocketbook. 'They will have a dear price to pay,' Mr Yu declared.

But it's unclear whether the penalties are working. One affluent Beijing woman said she and her husband had happily paid $13,000 for the right to have a second child. 'This sum of money is nothing to our family,' she said to a reporter from China Youth Daily.

Some wealthy families have reportedly paid more than $100,000 for the right to have a second child.

Earlier this year, an opinion survey of almost 8,000 people on a Chinese website found that the vast majority were outraged that wealthy families could violate the one-child policy.

One professor at a Beijing university commented that the exemption is the same as allowing a wealthy person to drive through the red lights at traffic intersections.

Other commentators have criticized celebrities such as basketball star Yao Ming and Hollywood actress Zhang Ziyi, both of whom have casually remarked in interviews that they might decide to have several children.

Source: Geoffrey York, 2007. 'Baby boom a perk that only elite can afford', *The Globe and Mail* (8 May): A3. Reprinted with permission from The Globe and Mail.

girls. As a consequence of almost three decades of imbalanced sex ratios, young Chinese men today are having difficulty finding young marriageable brides. The rapid decrease in fertility rates in conjunction with improved mortality conditions has led to an increased proportion of elderly people in the population. With the lack of adequate pension coverage, more and more young Chinese couples will be solely responsible for the care of one child and four parents, a situation that has been called the 4:2:1 problem (Hesketh, Lu, and Xing, 2006).

We can compare policies aimed at curbing population growth in China with similar efforts in India, the world's largest democracy. With its 1.7 per cent rate of natural increase in 2006—well above the world level of 1.2 per cent (Population Reference Bureau, 2006)—India maintains one of the highest rates of natural increase among transitional societies. Jones and Leete (2002) point out that even though the total fertility in India has declined—from 5.97 in 1950–5 to 2.93 in 2000—its level of fertility is still very high by comparative standards. (In 2000, the TFR in Asia as a whole was 2.52.) Since gaining independence in 1947, India's population has trebled in size, and projections by Dyson, Cassen, and Visaria (2004) indicate that India's 2006 population of 1.1 billion will likely reach 1.4 billion in 2026 and somewhere between 1.5 and 1.7 billion by 2050.

In its implementation of population policies, India has been less successful than might have been expected. One of the reasons stems from challenges in implementing its family planning program. In the early days of the program, Indian government officials tried to promote the rhythm method and the widespread use of condoms. It soon became clear that this approach was not working. In desperation, the government began a campaign of wide-scale sterilization. Mass vasectomy 'camps' were established in the early 1970s, and in some parts of the nation large incentives were offered to men who agreed to the procedure. The campaign resulted in more than 2 million sterilizations in 1972 and

over 3 million in 1973. A year later, however, the program was abandoned owing to a combination of problems, including funding cuts, a large incidence of health complications related to the procedure, and rising doubts among officials about the effectiveness of this policy intervention. The government also attempted to reformulate the abortion law to make the procedure more accessible to women, but with limited success.

In 1976, a new sterilization campaign was initiated. New laws made sterilization mandatory for couples with three or more children. Though these laws were never actually accepted by the Indian president, many local administrators adopted the policy of compulsory sterilization and attempted to achieve the 'targets' set by government officials by relying on police and bully squads to round up men for the operation (Potts and Selman, 1979: 318). Ultimately, the excesses of this campaign helped to bring down the government of Indira Ghandi and set back the progress of family planning.

Dyson, Cassen, and Visaria (2004) conclude that in spite of the many problems that India has faced in applying its family planning policies over the years, there is undeniable evidence that these policies have had some effect in lowering fertility: 'In short', they write, 'the programme has facilitated the country's fertility decline' (348). Undoubtedly, China's relative success in meeting demographic goals through family planning policy can be attributed to the Chinese government's much greater freedom to impose tough policies without the risk of popular rebellion.

Figure 12.2 (page 534) suggested that a country's demographic regime—whether post-transitional, transitional, or delayed transitional—is closely linked to the level of societal well-being: the greater the level of well-being, the greater the likelihood that birth and death rates will be under control, keeping population growth rates low. The historical experience of Western societies fits this proposition. The West's fertility transition occurred as standards of living improved. Better socioeconomic conditions brought lower rates of

Population Policy in Romania

A famous piece of population policy was put into effect in Romania by the country's totalitarian leader Nicolae Ceauşescu. In 1957, Ceauşescu's communist government issued a decree making abortion available, on request, to Romanian women. Given that birth control was then unavailable, this became the principal means of fertility control in Romania. In 1965, for example, 80 per cent of all conceptions ended in abortion (Berelson, 1979; Frejka, 1983; Pop-Eleches, 2006).

As the birth rate fell to low levels, Ceauşescu and his officials began to worry that population declines, were they not to reverse, would jeopardize the country's economic progress. Thus, in 1966, the government changed its policy, making abortion available only under certain restrictive conditions, such as risk to the life of the mother, risk of deformity to the fetus, and rape. With the sudden withdrawal of abortion on demand, the birth rate jumped, in 1967, to an unprecedented rate of 27.4 per 1,000 population. Fertility rates would eventually level off and, by the late 1970s, return to 'normal' levels. However, the boost in fertility brought about by the draconian abortion policy actually created a baby boom of a magnitude similar to the one experienced in the United States after the Second World War (Berelson, 1979).

infant and childhood mortality, which meant that couples, confident that their children would reach adulthood, could plan to have fewer children. Mortality improvements have helped promote the small-family ideal, keeping fertility levels low in Western societies. By contrast, fertility rates and rates of natural increase are typically high in settings characterized by high levels of poverty, where having a large family is seen as a way to minimize risk and uncertainty. In countries frequently afflicted by famines, droughts, and other natural calamities, children are long-term investments that help reduce risk for families and ensure security for parents in old age (Cain, 1982, 1983, 1985, 1987; Dercon, 2005).

Social Policy and Its Connection to Population Policy

As we noted earlier, population policy cannot be viewed in isolation from the broader societal context within which it is formulated and imple-

mented. In general, the idea behind population policy is to intervene in demographic matters to ultimately enhance the well-being of the population. Closely related to population policy is social policy. *Social policy* refers to the legal structures created and maintained by a government to ensure minimum standards of well-being for the population. It typically operates through one of two principles: (1) the mitigation of risk for individuals and their families under conditions of loss (examples include employment insurance, health insurance, welfare, etc.), and (2) the maintenance of equity standards in access to socioeconomic opportunities and human rights (such as rights and freedoms of the individual, universal education, old-age security, safety standards on the road and in the workplace, etc.). Social policy has an indirect bearing on the demography of a society because it aims to reduce insecurity and hardship among the people while enhancing their overall socioeconomic well-being; in these conditions, there is a greater likelihood that fertility rates may be controlled.

Democratic societies are often called 'welfare democracies' because they are based on the principle of the social contract—the idea that the people agree to be governed by elected individuals who, in turn, are expected to act in the best interests of the electorate and society at large. It is understood that citizens are to help pay for the services and benefits received from government (universal health care, education, public pensions, and so on); as a result, workers pay a portion of their wages or salary to the government, which in turn uses the revenues for the wider benefit of the society. Those with greater income are expected to contribute more so as to maintain equity. Democratic governments may also generate revenue by collecting corporate taxes and by taking interest from government investments. All of these funds are used to help maintain societal well-being through the provision of 'safety nets' (social security systems) designed to protect the citizen who, by virtue of misfortune or circumstance, suffers a setback in life (e.g., disability, illness, unemployment).

Not all governments can or are willing to exercise the degree of political will required to implement the extensive social security systems found in most Western democracies. This is often true of despotic regimes whose main interests lie in preserving power and achieving (through corruption) financial gain. In other cases, where the political will is present, the cost of building up an extensive 'safety net' is prohibitive. This situation characterizes many poor developing countries today.

To use statistical terms, the correlation between type of government and level of socioeconomic development is certainly not perfect. However, as measured in Human Development Index (HDI) scores, it is true that liberal democratic regimes provide greater social and economic stability than do authoritarian regimes (United Nations Development Programme, 2002b). Notwithstanding their difficulties in the arena of population policy, democratic countries are generally more successful at promoting economic growth while maintaining individual freedoms. The greater a government's ability to generate wealth, the greater its ability to implement and maintain safety net structures for the benefit of its citizens. It is partly because of their success in achieving wealth that many welfare democracies enjoy a level of well-being and prosperity that is unmatched by the developing countries.

China may prove to be an example of a non-democratically governed society that experiences significant economic growth. However, it remains, in important respects, a problematic exception to the principle that democratic countries have healthier economies. Economic development in the country is occurring very unevenly. Certainly, as a by-product of the country's 'economic miracle', wages have risen, and the middle class is getting larger. But while millions of Chinese people have become richer, hundred of millions of others have not. More than 60 per cent of the Chinese population still toils in agriculture, living in abject poverty. With the country undergoing a transition to a market economy, the program of lifetime employment once guaranteed to all Chinese citizens is now eroding fast. Millions of workers have lost their jobs in the wake of economic restructuring. All the while human rights in China exist only on paper; there has been no significant liberalization of political freedoms in China to speak of.

Demographic Concerns: A Global Perspective

The Demographic Divide

As we mentioned at the outset of the chapter, there exists a vast demographic divide between the developed and developing countries. On one side are the impoverished Third World countries with relatively high birth and death rates and low life expectancies; on the other are the mostly wealthy countries characterized by low birth rates and high life expectancies, population decline and demographic aging. Of major concern is the strong correlation between these divergent demographic trends and growing disparities between the two worlds' standards of living, health conditions, and socioeconomic well-being (Sutcliffe, 2001; Therborn, 2006). While this regional divide is undeniable, it's worth noting that within each of these two 'worlds' there are notable exceptions, making the notion of a developed and a developing world somewhat incomplete in describing the broad contours of the world's demography. For example, in some developed regions (such as eastern Europe) population decline is already underway, while in others (the United States, for instance) population continues to grow with no sign of imminent decline. At the same time, some countries of the developing world (such as South Korea) have been experiencing below-replacement birth rates for quite some time and are facing the prospect of population decline in the near future.

Kent and Haub (2005: 9) are among those who have asked what caused the demographic divide. Among the world's underdeveloped nations, some factors we can point to are widespread poverty, populations that are predominantly rural, high rates of illiteracy, limited family planning efforts by governments, and the absence of 'safety nets' for the people. Given these prevailing conditions, high fertility and rapid population growth are bound to persist in poor countries. At the other end of the spectrum, argue Kent and Haub (2005), the persistence of sub-replacement fertility in wealthy countries may be attributed to a combination of sociological and economic factors, including the disjuncture between material expectations and rising economic uncertainty among young couples, the inhibiting effects of this condition on marriage and childbearing, the difficulty for young people of securing permanent employment, and the problem of securing independent housing as a result of the rising cost of living. Clearly, the conditions giving rise to high or low fertility are quite different. It follows, therefore, that the population policies for the two sets of societies described here would be vastly different.

As a way to help poor countries improve their standards of living and their levels of social and economic development, the United Nations in 2000 initiated a multi-year program that would provide tangible benchmarks for measuring progress in eight areas. The UN's eight Millennium Development Goals, designed to be achieved by 2015, are as follows:

1. Eradiate extreme hunger and poverty by halving the number of people living on less than $1 a day and halving the number of people suffering from malnutrition.
2. Make primary education universal by ensuring that all children are able to complete primary schooling.
3. Eliminate gender disparities in primary and secondary schooling, preferably by 2005 and no later than 2015.
4. Reduce child mortality by cutting the under-five death rate by two-thirds.
5. Improve maternal health by reducing the maternal mortality rate by three-quarters.
6. Halt and reverse the spread of HIV/AIDS, malaria, and other deadly diseases.
7. Reduce by half the number of people living without access to safe drinking water and sanitation.
8. Develop a global partnership for development by reforming aid and trade programs, with special treatment for the poorest countries. (Cheru and Bradford, 2005; Sacks and McArthur, 2005; United Nations Development Programme, 2005: 39)

As of 2007—the midpoint between the adoption of the Millennium Development Goals and the 2015 target date—the program had achieved mixed success (United Nations, 2007). There have been some gains in the eight key areas, but more work is needed to achieve the targets by 2015. Among the positives are some success in reducing poverty from 1990 levels. That year, almost 32 per cent of people in the developing world lived on less than a dollar a day; as of 2004, that figure had fallen to 19.2 per cent, and it is expected to fall below 16 per cent by 2015. Part of this decline in poverty can be attributed to growing economic prosperity in China and India, the two most populous countries in the world. But extreme poverty has also fallen in sub-Saharan Africa, a region that has seen some recent economic growth and advances in children's education. Africa's extreme-poverty rate has fallen from approximately 46 per cent in 1999 to 41 per cent in 2004. Unfortunately, this pace of poverty reduction is considered slow and not sufficient to meet the 2015 goal of 22 per cent. The region is also plagued by other problems, most notably hunger and malnutrition. The proportion of children under the age of 5 who are underweight has declined only marginally since 1990, from 33 per cent that year to 29 per cent in 2005. Rapid population growth has exacerbated these problems. This means, among other things, that although more African children are attending school today, many more are not; this is a problem that is likely only to worsen in the future. In 1990, there were 237 million Africans under the age of 14; today, that figure is 348 million, and by 2015, the number is expected to reach 400 million. Governments in Africa will find it increasingly difficult to provide for such a large population of children.

Poverty Reduction in the Developing Countries

Worldwide, the number of people in developing countries living on less than $1 a day fell to 980 million in 2004—down from 1.25 billion in 1990. The proportion of people living in extreme poverty fell from nearly a third to 19 per cent over this period. If progress continues, the MDG [Millennium Development Goals] target will be met. However, success is inequally shared, since the decline in global poverty is mostly due to rapid economic growth in Asia. Eastern and South-Eastern Asia, in particular, experienced impressive reductions in poverty, and accelerating growth in India has also put Southern Asia on track to achieve the goal.

In contrast, poverty rates in Western Asia more than doubled between 1990 and 2005. Extreme poverty rose sharply in the early 1990s in the Commonwealth of Independent States (CIS) and the transition countries of South-Eastern Europe. Poverty rates in those regions are now dropping, however, and approaching the levels of the 1980s.

In sub-Saharan Africa, the proportion of people living in extreme poverty fell from 46.8 per cent in 1990 to 41.1 per cent in 2004. Most of this progress was achieved since 2000. The number of people living on less than $1 a day is also beginning to level off, despite rapid population growth. The per capita income of seven sub-Saharan countries grew by more than 3.5 per cent a year between 2000 and 2005; another 23 had growth rates of more than 2 per cent a year over this period, providing a degree of optimism for the future.

In most developing regions, the average income of those living on less than $1 a day has increased. The poverty gap ratio, which reflects the depth of poverty as well as its incidence, has decreased in all regions except Western Asia, where the rising poverty rate has caused the poverty gap to increase, and in the transition countries in Europe and the CIS, where there has been marginal deterioration or no change. In contrast, the poor in Eastern and South-Eastern Asia have made important gains. In spite of some improvement, the poverty gap ratio in sub-Saharan Africa remains the highest in the world, indicating that the poor in that region are the most economically disadvantaged in the world.

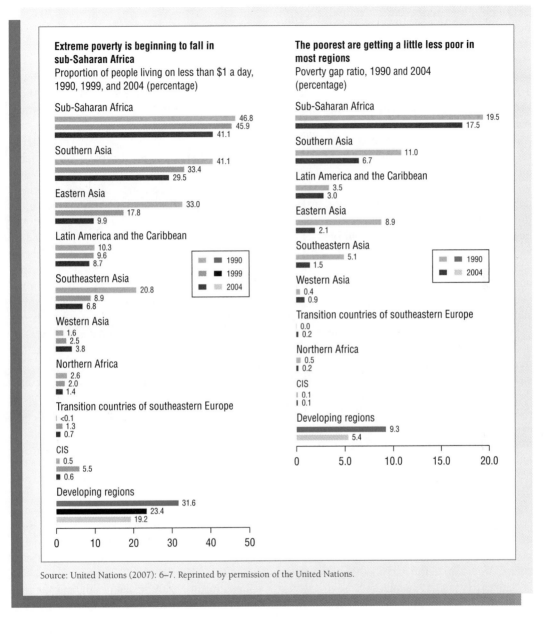

Extreme poverty is beginning to fall in sub-Saharan Africa
Proportion of people living on less than $1 a day, 1990, 1999, and 2004 (percentage)

Sub-Saharan Africa
46.8
45.9
41.1

Southern Asia
41.1
33.4
29.5

Eastern Asia
33.0
17.8
9.9

Latin America and the Caribbean
10.3
9.6
8.7

Southeastern Asia
20.8
8.9
6.8

Western Asia
1.6
2.5
3.8

Northern Africa
2.6
2.0
1.4

Transition countries of southeastern Europe
<0.1
1.3
0.7

CIS
0.5
5.5
0.6

Developing regions
31.6
23.4
19.2

0   10   20   30   40   50

1990
1999
2004

The poorest are getting a little less poor in most regions
Poverty gap ratio, 1990 and 2004 (percentage)

Sub-Saharan Africa
19.5
17.5

Southern Asia
11.0
6.7

Latin America and the Caribbean
3.5
3.0

Eastern Asia
8.9
2.1

Southeastern Asia
5.1
1.5

Western Asia
0.4
0.9

Transition countries of southeastern Europe
0.0
0.2

Northern Africa
0.5
0.2

CIS
0.1
0.1

Developing regions
9.3
5.4

0   5.0   10.0   15.0   20.0

1990
2004

Source: United Nations (2007): 6–7. Reprinted by permission of the United Nations.

From Bucharest to Cairo and Beyond: Shifts in Global Population Policy Orientations

In the 1960s and 1970s, the leading demographic issue from a global perspective was rapid population growth. The world's population had grown to three billion, and rates of natural increase had risen to their highest levels in history at just over 2 per cent per annum. Neo-Malthusians sounded the alarm over the devastating long-term effects of rapid population growth on the environment and on socio-economic well-being. Among the many well-publicized studies that took this perspective and gained widespread attention in the late 1960s and early 1970s were *The Population Bomb* (Ehrlich, 1968) and *The Limits to Growth* (Meadows et al., 1972).

Shortly after the publication of these influential studies, the demographic community gathered in 1974 at the World Population Conference in Bucharest, Romania. As expected, issues and debates surrounding world population growth dominated the agenda. Representatives of the developed countries argued in favour of vigorous family planning programs as a means to curb the developing world's explosive rates of population growth. Representatives of the developing world countered that family planning could not possibly work in the context of poor underdeveloped nations; instead, they argued, these developing countries would benefit most from increased economic development and assistance from the wealthy countries. The belief was that economic development would enable poor countries to get out of the poverty trap. Mortality rates would fall as a consequence, to be followed, eventually, by diminishing fertility rates, all leading to lower rates of population growth. Among professional demographers, Kingsley Davis (1967) and Judith Blake (1969) were two of the fiercest critics of organized family planning programs. They criticized the multi-billion-dollar-a-year establishment for promoting a naive approach to population control, since family planning, they argued, would do nothing to alter the motivation of couples to want large families.

At subsequent conventions, in Mexico City in 1984 and in Cairo in 1994, opposition to family planning programs was considerably milder. A number of studies based on empirical evidence from the 1970s and 1980s left little doubt about the effectiveness of family planning programs in those countries in which they had been adopted (see Berelson, 1969; Berelson et al., 1990; Mauldin and Berelson, 1978; Mauldin and Ross, 1991; Potts and Selman, 1978: 215; Rathor, 2004; Ross and Mauldin, 1996; Tsui, 2001). At the 1984 conference, most representatives of the developing countries expressed strong acceptance of family planning programs in recognition of the successes achieved by those countries that had adopted such programs during earlier decades.

By the early 1990s, rates of population growth in the world had dropped considerably from the high levels of the 1960s and early 1970s. With the exception of some nations of sub-Saharan Africa and parts of Asia, most developing countries had progressed to advanced stages of the fertility transition, and by the 1990s, many African countries were beginning to see some fertility declines as well. Consequently, the focus of the 1994 International Conference on Population and Development had shifted to issues of reproductive health and women's autonomy as new policy concerns.

What was especially significant about the issue of reproductive health was that it was viewed primarily as a human rights issue and only secondarily as a demographic concern (Chasteland, 2006; Kantner and Kantner, 2006; Locoh and Vandermeersch, 2006; McNicoll, 2001). Many experts attending the Cairo conference believed that women should have access not just to family planning measures but to pre- and postnatal care and to health education, all to help reduce the risk of infections and illness among mothers and their children. Reproductive health, as it was embraced by the United Nations Fund for Population Activities (UNFPA) at the Cairo conference, encompassed family planning, maternal and infant health, sexual health, and the prevention of AIDS (Haberland and Measham, 2002; Sai, 2002). Fertility programs since Cairo have increasingly been designed with the view that family planning and reproductive health are both integral aspects of population health policy that, along with the goal of controlling the spread of HIV/AIDS, should be pursued in developing countries (Kantner and Kantner, 2006; Locoh and Vandeermeersch, 2006).

Current Population Policy Concerns through the Eyes of Government Officials

The United Nations routinely surveys national governments to gauge their perceptions of population change in their countries. Specifically, officials in each country are asked to comment on the following variables:

- population size and growth
- population age structure
- spatial distribution
- fertility
- mortality
- migration

For each of these variables, officials are asked to discuss whether the level or trend is acceptable/satisfactory in relation to other social and economic conditions in the country. Officials are also asked whether it is the government's policy to raise, lower, or maintain current levels of each variable, and whether (and, if so, by what means) there has been any active intervention to influence the variable.

As one might expect, the population policy concerns differ significantly between developing and developed countries. On a global level, HIV/AIDS is considered the most significant population issue, as Table 12.3 shows; however, it

Table 12.3   Major population concerns of governments in 2007: Issues of significance to at least one half of governments in 2007 by level of development

Region	Issue	Percentage of governments reporting it as significant
World	HIV/AIDS	90
	Infant and child mortality	73
	Maternal mortality	70
	Size of the working-age population	66
	Adolescent fertility	58
	Low life expectancy	57
	Population aging	55
	Pattern of spatial distribution	51
More developed regions	HIV/AIDS	81
	Population aging	81
	Low fertility	61
	Size of the working-age population	61
Less developed regions	HIV/AIDS	93
	Infant and child mortality	86
	Maternal mortality	83
	Size of the working-age population	69
	Adolescent fertility	65
	Low life expectancy	64
	Pattern of spatial distribution	56
	High fertility	54
	High rates of population growth	50

Source: United Nations Department of Economic and Social Affairs Population Division (2008b): 8. Reprinted with the permission of the United Nations.

was cited by 93 per cent of officials in developing countries and just 81 per cent of officials from the developed regions. The second and third leading population policy concerns among less developed countries were high infant and child mortality and maternal mortality. These developing countries are also concerned about the large size of their working-age population, which presents a problem of providing sufficient work for a rapidly expanding labour force brought on by a history of high fertility rates.

In this section, we will look at some of the prevailing concerns and implications addressed in developed and less developed regions of the world.

Population Age Structure

The demographic transition from high to low fertility and from high to low mortality inevitably produces dramatic shifts in a country's age structure, from relatively young to increasingly old. In the more developed regions, population aging has been a steady trend for some time. The United Nations has estimated that by 2050, one in three people in the developed world will be aged 60 or older, and that there will be two older persons for every child. But population aging is also underway in the developing countries, where the percentage of the population aged 60 or older is expected to rise from 8 per cent in 2005 to almost 20 per cent by 2050 (United Nations Department of Economic and Social Affairs Population Division, 2006a).

The rate at which a population ages is of great importance to government officials and policymakers, particularly those who are primarily responsible for providing adequate pensions and health care for the population. Anticipating periods of rapid change in demographic aging is vitally important if appropriate adjustments are to be made in a timely manner. Recent estimates based on a variety of new indicators of population aging developed by Lutz, Sanderson, and Scherbov (2008) indicate that by any measure, demographic aging worldwide is increasing

rapidly; it is likely to peak sometime between 2020 and 2030 before slowing down. But in spite of the anticipated decline, Lutz, Sanderson, and Scherbov predict that there will be further increases in demographic aging throughout the twenty-first century. When it hits its ultimate peak will depend on past fertility trends in each global region. For instance, in the United States and parts of western Europe, the progression through the age structure of the post-war baby boom generations will be a significant factor, while in China the introduction of the one-child policy in the late 1970s will play a defining role.

Change in the age structure occurs at the bottom, at the top, and in the middle of the age pyramid. With regards to aging at the middle, an issue of critical importance is the size of the working-age population. Given their demographic history, the developed countries are concerned about impending labour force shortages. In contrast, the developing countries are worried about having working-age populations that are too large, a situation that threatens to cause high unemployment rates. While developed countries are trying to find ways to reduce the consequences of aging in the middle and at the top by increasing the legal retirement age, eliminating early retirement incentives, and encouraging more women to enter the labour force (Vaupel and Loichinger, 2006), the developing countries have fewer available measures for minimizing the projected influx of young adults in the labour force. However, some developing societies, if they are able to generate jobs for an expanding labour force, will soon be in a position to take advantage of the so-called 'demographic bonus' that results from past high fertility rates (Birdsall, Kelley, and Sinding, 2001; Bongaarts, 2004; Cleland, 1996; Leahy et al., 2007; United Nations Department of Economic and Social Affairs Population Division, 2006a).

Fertility and Family Planning

As we have seen in earlier chapters, fertility worldwide has been declining for well over three decades. In 1970–5, the average number of children born to women globally was 4.5; by 2000–5, the total fertility rate had fallen to 2.6 (United Nations Department of Economic and Social Affairs Population Division, 2006c). Below-replacement fertility now characterizes much of the developed world and also some developing countries, including South Korea, Singapore, Taiwan, and Thailand (Bongaarts, 1998). Countries in sub-Saharan Africa maintain characteristically high fertility, well above the world average.

According to the latest United Nations report on population policies, one of the most significant population policy developments during the second half of the 1990s was the rise in the number of African governments that implemented policies to reduce their fertility. In the mid- to late 1980s, only 41 per cent of African governments had policies aimed at reducing fertility. By 2005, the proportion of African countries that had policies directed at lowering fertility had risen to 74 per cent (United Nations Department of Economic and Social Affairs Population Division, 2006a). In countries that did not adopt such policies (e.g., Gabon, Angola), fertility rates remain generally above 4 births per woman. In response, a variety of measures have been implemented to directly and indirectly affect fertility rates.

Further declines in fertility among the world's poorest countries are possible, especially in those countries where total fertility rates remain above the world average. From a global perspective, further reductions in fertility would significantly help diminish the impact of population momentum on global population growth over the next several decades. Bongaarts (1994) has proposed that further investments in family planning programs would help speed up the fertility transition in such countries, but he has also argued that other policy options should be considered. In particular, he suggests that governments of poor countries should introduce measures to reduce the high demand for children, the large number of unwanted births (especially to teen mothers), and the gap between desired and actual family size (Casterline and Sinding, 2000; Potts, 2006).

In spite of the success achieved in implementing family planning and reproductive health programs over the past four decades, there remains an unfinished family planning agenda in the poorest countries. Cleland and associates (2006) note that although family planning programs have raised contraceptive use from less than 10 per cent to 60 per cent while reducing fertility in the developing countries from 6 to about 3 births per woman over the past 40 years, contraceptive practice remains low in half of the 75 largest low-income and lower middle-income countries (mainly in Africa), where fertility, population growth, and an unmet need for family planning are high. As we noted earlier, international funding and promotion of family planning has faded since the 1990s. Cleland and colleagues maintain that even though most poor countries have some family planning programs in place, they receive too little international encouragement and funding to implement these programs with vigour.

At the other end of the demographic divide, some developed countries are faced with a low-fertility problem. As a whole, this group of countries showed a total fertility of just 1.6 children per woman in 2000–5, according to the United Nations report on world population policies (United Nations Department of Economic and Social Affairs Population Division, 2006c). In 1976, only one-quarter of European countries expressed concerns over low fertility; by 2005, however, about two-thirds of these countries cited low fertility as an issue that needed to be addressed. Of the 46 countries that in 2005 viewed fertility as being too low, more than three-quarters had put in place 'pronatalist' policies aimed at raising the birth rate. These include baby bonuses, family allowances, extended maternal and parental leaves from work, subsidized childcare, tax breaks, subsidized housing, flexible work schedules, and promotion of shared parenting and household duties between spouses (Corman, 2002;

Douglass, 2005; Gauthier, 2005; Gauthier and Hatzius, 1997).

There is some doubt about whether pronatalist policies actually work in Western societies. A recent review of the evidence by Kohler, Billari, and Ortega (2006) suggests that policies such as the ones just mentioned have at best only a moderate effect on fertility. Specifically, the authors of the study found that family cash benefits ('baby bonuses') have minor positive effects on the total fertility rate in most countries. Tax policies, in the United States and Canada, have some positive effects, but mostly on the timing of childbearing rather than on completed fertility. In other words, as a result of the tax policies, couples may have their children earlier but won't necessarily end up having more children. The effect of 'family-friendly' policies appears mixed: the evidence indicates that more flexible work schedules have a positive effect on the TFR, but the effects of extended parental leave are weak and contradictory. Finally, the availability of childcare has been shown to have a positive influence on the TFR, but this influence is generally weak. Overall, the evidence offers mixed conclusions about the effects of pronatalist policies in Western countries; on balance, the best that can be said is that the impact of these policies on fertility is positive but not very strong (Calot, 2006; De Santis, 2006).

If pronatalist policies are not the key to raising fertility, what is? Kohler, Billari, and Ortega (2006) suggest it is crucial for countries that wish to raise their birth rates to implement policies designed to make childbearing compatible with labour force participation, and to devise strategies aimed at reducing the anxiety young adults face regarding high unemployment. Others have expressed the view that the key to raising fertility levels in high-income nations depends on effecting a change of outlook regarding the gendered division of labour in the home. Torr and Short (2004), for instance, argue that too many women are burdened by what they refer to as 'the second shift'—the tendency for women to work outside the home and to then handle the raising of children as well as routine domestic chores without much assistance and support from their male partners. In other words, there remains in Western societies an unfinished gender-role revolution. Women have made significant advances toward gaining 'institutional' equality (i.e., in opportunities for education and work) but have had less success in gaining equality in the home (McDonald, 2000).

Health and Mortality

From a humanitarian standpoint, one of the most important demographic goals is the extension of life expectancy across the more deprived populations of the world. In global terms, health trends in general over much of the past century have been positive, with the exception of some temporary setbacks due to war. In recent decades, life expectancy has improved substantially in the developing countries as a result of major improvements in preventing infant and child mortality, while in most of the developed world already low death rates continue to decline.

Unfortunately, against the backdrop of general improvements in global mortality rates, some regions have experienced unexpected life expectancy declines. Notable among these regions are sub-Saharan Africa, where the HIV/AIDS epidemic still rages on, and parts of the former Soviet Union, although North Korea, the Bahamas, Haiti, Fiji, and Iraq have also recorded recent declines in life expectancy (McMichael et al., 2004). McMichael and associates (2004) have divided the world's countries into three groups with respect to life expectancy change between 1950 and 2000:

1. national populations that have undergone rapid gains in life expectancy (i.e., transitional developing countries such as Chile, Mexico, Tunisia, India, Senegal, and Mali);
2. countries that have experienced slower, and perhaps plateauing, gains in life expectancy (i.e., highly developed countries that had already attained high levels of life expectancy in 1950); and

3. countries that have seen reversals in life expectancy (such as North Korea, Zimbabwe, Botswana, Kenya, Uganda, Rwanda, and Ethiopia).

McMichael and colleagues view the existence of these three groups as disproving any notion of a global convergence in health and mortality trends predicted by classical theories of population and epidemiological change. They argue that there are three major impediments to convergence in global population health:

1. the persistence of health gradients both within and among countries, reflecting unequal access to adequate health care;
2. the rise or return of various highly virulent infectious diseases, usually associated with poverty and deteriorating living standards (such as malaria, tuberculosis, and HIV/AIDS); and
3. the growing number of deaths in poor countries related to violence from conflict and war and, increasingly, to ecological disasters. (McMichael et al., 2004)

Spatial Distribution and Internal Migration
Since the 1970s, governments in developing countries have introduced various policies aimed at changing the spatial distribution of their populations. Some of these policies are meant to redirect growth from large urban agglomerations to small and medium-sized cities or to establish sustainable rural development; others have created regional development zones and imposed internal migration controls. Unfortunately, these kinds of policies have typically been minimally effective. Consequently, there is a growing concern among officials in some countries that rapid and unchecked urbanization will hamper their ability to service an expanding urban population with safe drinking water, proper sanitation, public transportation, and—most of all—employment and affordable housing (see National Research Council, 2003).

In the developed countries, where the issues are different, spatial distribution policies have in general not been vigorously pursued. According to the UN's report on policies, the policies undertaken in this part of the world have generally focused on achieving balanced regional development, for instance by recognizing the interdependence of rural and urban areas and by promoting an integrated rural and urban economy through the diversification of economic activity in rural areas.

International Migration
The complex nature of contemporary international migration has been treated at length in Chapter 9. It suffices to say that this remains an extremely sensitive yet important policy domain. Key policy concerns for both sending and receiving countries include, among others, controlling the extent to which countries experience 'brain drain' (the loss of highly educated and skilled people to other countries) and 'brain gain' (the increasing competition among the more developed countries for highly educated and skilled immigrants from the developing countries); monitoring the circulation of seasonal migrants; increasing pressures on the more developed countries to provide asylum for refugees; and policing the illegal trafficking and the undocumented movement of people. All of these issues intersect with national demographic concerns, particularly over low fertility and population aging in the major receiving countries.

Added to these kinds of policy issues is the major challenge of integrating a growing and diverse immigrant population into the social fabric of the major receiving countries of the world. This is a matter that has been complicated in recent years by mounting concerns over national security and rising levels of xenophobia, especially among some sectors of the population in the receiving countries of western Europe (see, for example, Semyonov, Rijman, and Gorodzeisky, 2006; Wilkes, Guppy, and Farris, 2007). The UN's report on world population policies (United Nations Department of Economic and

Social Affairs Population Division, 2006c: 32) notes that since the 'Programme of Action' was adopted at the 1994 International Conference on Population and Development in Cairo, there has been growing recognition that international migration and development are inexorably linked and are vitally important to the global agenda. The UN warns that greater levels of international co-operation and policy coherence are essential to minimizing the adverse consequences of international migration while maximizing its benefits for both sending and receiving countries. This will require, according to the United Nations Department of Economic Affairs Population Division (2006a: 332), the practice of 'safe, orderly and rule-governed migration within a framework where States understand their obligations and protect the rights of migrants, and migrants recognize their rights and responsibilities, as well as respect for national and international laws.'

The challenge for national governments is how to achieve the needed policy coherence with other governments given the radically divergent interests—economic, social, and demographic—of the major receiving countries and the growing number of sending countries (Massey and Taylor, 2004). Unsurprisingly, the immigration policies of receiving countries are very selective, favouring the admission of people who meet specific labour needs or who have skills considered to be in short supply. According to the United Nations report on world population policies (United Nations Department of Economic and Social Affairs Population Division, 2006c), in 2005 some 30 out of 134 countries with available data had policies in place promoting the migration of highly skilled workers.

Canadian Population Policy Concerns

Each census in Canada's history provides a unique snapshot of the prevailing social demographic conditions at the time. For instance, the census of 1901 testifies to the dominance of English and French ethnic origins yet also reveals considerable diversity in the rest of the population, reflecting widespread immigration from western Europe (Kralt, 1990). One hundred years later, the census of 2001 reveals a Canadian population that is getting older, with a dependency ratio that is getting larger. It also shows that the population is unevenly distributed, with a disproportionately large share living in the largest metropolitan areas of Toronto, Montreal, Vancouver, and Ottawa–Gatineau. Concerning population growth, the census confirms that in recent years the country has been relying increasingly on net international migration as the principal source of growth, compensating for declining rates of natural increase. The results imply that the low fertility and aging of the population will, should these trends continue, lead to significant labour force shortages about midway into the twenty-first century.

Canada's Population in the Twenty-First Century

Recent projections by Statistics Canada (Bélanger, Martel, and Caron-Malenfant, 2006; Statistics Canada, *The Daily*, 2006) indicate that the population of Canada could reach 40 million in about 25 or 30 years, and possibly close to 43 million by 2056. These projections are based on the medium-growth scenario, which assumes a continuation in the most recent trends in fertility, mortality, and immigration. The high- and low-growth scenarios involve high and low estimates of changes in fertility, mortality, and immigration levels. The low-growth scenario projects a decline in Canada's population, beginning in 2040. In all the scenarios considered, natural increase would eventually become negative—in 2020 under the low-growth scenario, in 2030 under the medium-growth scenario, and in 2046 under the high-growth scenario. As a result, international net migration would become the country's only source of population growth. Since the fertility rate is assumed to remain below replacement levels in all scenarios considered, the forecasted population growth, in all three projections, depends heavily on immigration levels.

As for the projected trends in regional population growth, Ontario, Alberta, and British Columbia are the only provinces predicted in more than one scenario to achieve average annual growth rates exceeding the growth rate for Canada as a whole. Between now and 2031, each of these provinces would see an increase in its population share, while Newfoundland and Labrador, New Brunswick, and Saskatchewan could have smaller populations by 2031. These differences result from the cumulative long-term effects of fertility, immigration, and interprovincial migration, which vary widely from province to province.

As we would expect, given the declines in fertility over the past four decades, Statistics Canada projects Canada's population to age rapidly. Currently the median age is 39; by 2031, according to projections, it would reach somewhere between 43 and 46, and by 2056 it is expected to be between 45 and 50. Demographic aging is inevitable because of the age structure of the current population. Although Canada's population today is young by comparison with other countries in the West, it will age more rapidly as a result of the fertility declines that began after the peak years of the post-war baby boom. According to Statistics Canada projections, senior citizens will outnumber children in about ten years. By about 2031, the number of people aged 65 and over will range between 8.9 million and 9.4 million (depending on the scenario selected), while the number of children would range between 4.8 million and 6.6 million.

As the baby boom generation quickly nears retirement age, many people of this generation will soon be leaving the workforce. This has important implications in terms of labour force renewal. The proportion of working-age population is projected to decline over the next 30 years. Currently, the working-age population represents 70 per cent of the total population;

by 2030, it would decline to 62 per cent, and then level off at about 60 per cent. This means that the demographic dependency ratio (the number of children aged less than 15 and seniors over 65 for every 100 working-age people) will also increase until 2031. As of 2005, there are 44 children and seniors for every 100 working-age people. According to the medium-growth scenario, this ratio is predicted to grow to about 61 by 2031. However, in absolute numbers, the growth in the working-age population depends on the type of scenario. In the medium-growth scenario, the working-age population would grow more and more slowly until 2020, then remain steady for a decade, and eventually resume growing. Under the low-growth scenario, it would start decreasing in 2017. Under the high-growth scenario, it would increase continuously through the projection period.

Policy Challenges

Concern over Canada's current and projected demographic trends has sparked debate over what may be the most effective policies to reverse low fertility and population aging or else mitigate their long-term consequences for society. Grant and colleagues (2004) identify three broad policy approaches that demographically mature societies have considered at various times:

1. policies that encourage childbearing among younger couples
2. policies that increase immigration of working-age people
3. public policies aimed at improving the negative effects of the demographic trends

The last category includes measure such as raising the age of retirement, encouraging more women to enter the workforce, guaranteeing flexible work hours for parents of young children, ensuring the availability of childcare, and extending parental leave.

Most of the attention in the policy literature has been directed toward the second of these three policy orientations: immigration. With the exception of Quebec, where a baby bonus was introduced in 1988 to help boost fertility (and then abandoned in 1992, when it was deemed unsuccessful) (Milligan, 2002), Canada has had no pronatalist policies. There are several possible reasons for this. First, as we've seen earlier, it is difficult for governments of liberal democracies to affect private behaviour, most especially reproduction (Demeny, 2003a). Leaders of liberal democracies also prefer to emphasize social policies that, unlike direct demographic policies, tend to work (when they do work) over the long term. As well, population change is a slow process, and the results of a policy implemented now could take many years to bear fruit. Policies aimed at increasing fertility in order to ensure a viable future labour force would take at least one generation before society would see any real change in the number of new labour force entrants. From a political standpoint, these kinds of policies are not appealing. As a result, public policy has usually focused on programs designed to generate more immediate change in society, by altering immigration policy to either increase or decrease the number of newcomers admitted, by introducing incentives for businesses to hire more entry-level workers, by increasing labour force participation rates, and by modifying the laws regarding legal age of retirement from the labour force, and other similar strategies (Grant et al., 2004).

Policies That Can Affect Fertility

Persistent low fertility in Canada and other Western societies (and also Japan) is primarily the result of delays in family formation among young people (Kent and Haub, 2005). This makes union formation (or marriage) one of the most important proximate determinants of fertility, along with contraceptive use, abortion, and breastfeeding. Any pronatalist policy, if it is to be effective, must operate through these proximate determinants. For obvious practical and ethical reasons, democratic governments cannot

possibly reduce access to contraception and abortion as a way to boost birth rates. Thus, if fertility in Canada is to increase above its current rate of 1.5 children per woman, it will be necessary to introduce policies that in the least would help young couples attain a more balanced work and family life. Canada can implement 'family-friendly' social policies that, first, remove workplace and career impediments to childrearing and, second, promote union formation among young adults (Beaujot, Ravanera, and Burch, 2005; Grant et al., 2004).

The review by Grant and colleagues (2004) reinforces the view that fertility rates in liberal democracies respond positively when governments implement social policies that benefit families. For instance, Grant and Milne (1991) found that 1 per cent increase in real value of unemployment insurance maternity benefits could produce an increase in the total fertility rate of between 0.09 and 0.26 per cent. This is not a large effect, but it is noteworthy, and it can be achieved by paying more into social programs that economically benefit couples who have children. This is of crucial importance because even a small increase in the total fertility rate could help to slow down the pace of demographic aging while boosting natural growth of the population (Beaujot, 1990; Beaujot, Ravanera, and Burch, 2005). Perhaps some of Canada's existing social programs could be modified with these goals in mind. The tax system could be altered to substantially increase tax breaks for couples with young children; family allowance benefits could be made universal for all low- and middle-income families with young children; young parents could be provided with more generous parental leaves from work; and quality daycare could be made available with government subsidies to working parents. It is likely that many young adults today are postponing union formation and childbearing because of economic insecurity. Alleviating this type of insecurity among young adults should be made a priority. Social and economic policies and programs such as these would provide a more economically secure foundation for both young families just starting out and those who already have children. While social policies of this nature would be costly, the costs may be viewed as an investment in the future of the country. Even if the period TFR could be raised by 0.3 of a child to a constant birth rate of 1.8, this would have significant long-term benefits to Canadian society. This rate would boost natural population growth and slow the rate of demographic aging, and at this level of fertility, immigration targets could be raised to more socially acceptable levels.

In addition to the need to stimulate union formation among young couples, there are other important societal issues that can be addressed through family-friendly policies. One of the implications of demographic aging is the growing need for elder care. How families will cope with this challenge of caring for aging parents remains a timely social policy concern. A related matter is the need to support lone parents in an era of 'birth dearth'. Today there are many lone parents—especially mothers—having or choosing to raise children. Given the very low fertility levels in Canada today, family-friendly policies should also be directed at lone parents.

The Immigration Option
There will never be a shortage of immigrants hoping to establish residence in this country. Therefore Canada can manage long-term demographic change by periodically altering its immigration policy. Immigration targets can be raised to grant entry to more workers as needed.

Yet this solution is not problem-free. Some critics have taken exception to the idea that immigration can solve Canada's demographic and economic challenges (see, for example, Francis, 2002; Green and Green, 1999). Among the problems they raise is the uneven geographic distribution of immigration. Most immigrants choose to settle in Ontario, Quebec, and BC, specifically in the largest census metropol-

itan areas of these provinces, Toronto, Montreal, and Vancouver. This uneven settlement pattern accentuates existing disparities in regional economic development and amplifies problems of population density and congestion in the largest cities. Another concern with increased immigration is the growing costs of integrating newcomers into Canadian society.

On demographic considerations alone, it is doubtful that increased immigration could substantially raise the prevailing low levels of fertility in Canada. It is true that, generally speaking, immigrants have higher fertility than Canadian-born citizens, but the difference is small (Bélanger, 2006). Immigration levels could be adjusted annually to affect population size and growth, but the number of immigrants needed would be very large, and they would have to be predominantly young if this measure were to appreciably slow demographic aging in Canada (Seward, 1986; George and Loh, 2007). Further, Denton, Feaver, and Spencer (2002) indicate that even if immigration numbers were increased from their current levels of about 200,000–250,000 annually to 450,000 per year by 2011, the impact on the age distribution of Canada's population would be minor. For immigration to have an appreciable impact on the age composition, the annual number of newcomers to Canada would have to exceed half a million. Given these large numbers, immigration as a means of solving the country's demographic challenges seems like a difficult option, and one not likely to receive widespread acceptance by the public.

Other Policy Concerns
Finally, attention must be given to policies addressing the impact of demographic change on non-demographic features of society. For example, the changing age–sex distribution has broad implications for crime rates, military service, education, childcare, elder care, and the costs and accessibility of health care. The increasing congestion of Canada's cities is also a matter of concern for policy analysts, some of

whom have asked whether it might be feasible—and desirable—to offer new immigrants incentives that might encourage them to settle in smaller centres and less populated regions (Krahn, Derwing, and Abu-Laban, 2005; Hawkins, 1977; Trovato, 1988b). Should this question be viewed as a policy matter? Furthermore, urban sprawl across Canada's largest cities is progressing unabated: should this not be another matter of concern for demographic policy analysts?

Conclusion

A principal responsibility of any government is the implementation of effective policies aimed at improving the level of security, comfort, and well-being of its population. In some respects governments are constrained in their ability to implement policies designed to alter demographic behaviours such as childbearing, which most citizens consider a private matter. In liberal democracies, the basic principles of freedom, equality, and dignity of the individual must be upheld; government policies cannot violate these tenets. Governments of liberal democracies, then, face considerable obstacles in any attempt to promote directly pronatalist policies. And even if such policies were truly effective, the financial costs would be exceptionally large. As a result, many liberal democracies look to a combination of public policies directed at easing

the dual responsibilities of work and family life for young adults, which hold promise as indirect mechanisms to boost period total fertility rates. The challenge is not as great for non-democratic governments, which have much greater leeway in the type of policies they can implement.

Canada's population policy concerns and challenges overlap with those of other demographically mature countries of the West and Japan, which are likewise facing low fertility and rapid population aging. Canada's main demographic policy concerns boil down to two challenges: how to boost the country's below-replacement fertility level, and how to cope with the impending negative effects of demographic aging and labour force shortages. A modest and achievable goal would be an increase in period total fertility to 1.8 children per women. Policy mechanisms for actualizing this target would likely include programs aimed at helping young couples—and especially women, who take on a disproportionate share of the burden known as the 'double shift'—achieve a better balance between work and family life. Canada could continue to rely solely on immigration as a demographic policy option, but this is not a problem-free solution. Immigration levels, even if they were to be increased substantially from their current targets, would bring only minor change to the age distribution of Canada's population. Immigration policy should be exercised in conjunction with social policies along the lines suggested, not in isolation.

Study Questions

1. *Population policy cannot be viewed independently of other aspects of the social system.* Elaborate on this statement. Explain how population policy and social policy are interrelated.

2. Evaluate the claim that the most successful population policies have been implemented in non-democratic societies. How would one define 'successful' in this case? Give examples of some success stories and also of some failed policies. Should governments have any role at all in affecting demographic behaviour?

3. What would be the justification for wanting to raise fertility in liberal democracies when most of the world's population is faced with serious population pressures? Would it not be more sensible for low-fertility societies to increase their immigration targets as a means to avert long-term population decline? Isn't immigration a relatively 'easy' solution to demographic aging for low-fertility societies? Discuss and critically evaluate these questions.

Additional Reading

Cromartie, Michael, ed. 1995. *The Nine Lives of Population Control*. Washington, DC, and Grand Rapids, MI: Ethics and Public Policy Center and William B. Eerdmans Publishing Co.

Demeny, Paul, and Geoffrey McNicoll, eds. 2006. *The Political Economy of Global Population Change, 1950–2050*. Supplement to *Population and Development Review* 32. New York: The Population Council.

Eager, Whaley Paige. 2004. *Global Population Policy: From Population Control to Reproductive Rights*. Gower House, England: Ashgate.

Greenhalgh, Susan, and Edwin A. Winckler. 2005. *Governing China's Population: From Leninist to Neoliberal Biopolitics*. Stanford, CA: Stanford University Press.

Jones, Gavin W., and Mehtabl S. Karim, eds. 2005. *Islam, the State and Population*. London: Hurst and Company.

Perrin, Andrew. 2006. *Citizen Speak: The Demographic Imagination in American Life*. Chicago: University of Chicago Press.

Poston, Dudley L. Jr, Che-Fu Lee, Chiung-Fang Chang, Sherry L. McKibben, and Carol S. Walther, eds. 2006. *Fertility, Family Planning, and Population Policy in China*. London: Routledge.

Rathor, Anupurna. 2004. *Family Planning Practices in Third World Countries*. Delhi: Adhyayan.

Sadik, Nafis, ed. 2002. *An Agenda for the People: The UNFPA Through Three Decades*. New York: New York University Press.

Tobin, Kathleen A. 2004. *Politics and Population Control*. Westport, CT: Greenwood.

Websites of Interest

Population Action International (PAI) is an independent policy advocacy group working to strengthen worldwide political and financial support for population programs grounded in individual rights. As a private, non-profit group, it focuses on research and public policy strategic initiatives, with a mission to work toward the improvement of individual well-being and preserve global resources by mobilizing political and financial support for population, family planning, and reproductive health policies and programs: www.populationaction.org.

The United Nations Social and Economic Affairs Population Division is the authoritative source on population policies across the countries of the world: www.un.org/esa/population/.

Examples of Canadian Census and Vital Registration Documents

Canadian Census Questionnaire

The following is an excerpt of the long questionnaire used to conduct the 2006 Canadian census. The excerpt here contains just the first 15 pages; the full document, which is 40 pages long, is available from the Statistics Canada website.

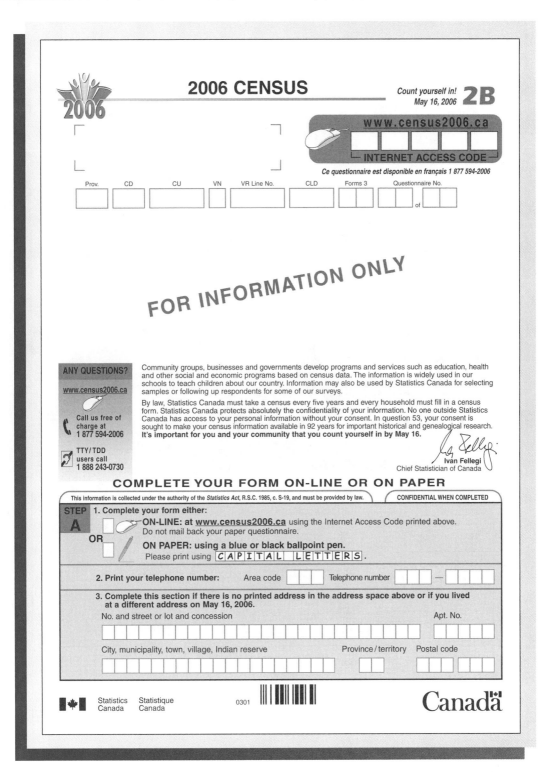

2006 CENSUS

Count yourself in!
May 16, 2006 **2B**

www.census2006.ca

INTERNET ACCESS CODE

Ce questionnaire est disponible en français 1 877 594-2006

Prov.	CD	CU	VN	VR Line No.	CLD	Forms 3	Questionnaire No.

of

FOR INFORMATION ONLY

ANY QUESTIONS?

www.census2006.ca

Call us free of
charge at
1 877 594-2006

TTY/TDD
users call
1 888 243-0730

Community groups, businesses and governments develop programs and services such as education, health and other social and economic programs based on census data. The information is widely used in our schools to teach children about our country. Information may also be used by Statistics Canada for selecting samples or following up respondents for some of our surveys.

By law, Statistics Canada must take a census every five years and every household must fill in a census form. Statistics Canada protects absolutely the confidentiality of your information. No one outside Statistics Canada has access to your personal information without your consent. In question 53, your consent is sought to make your census information available in 92 years for important historical and genealogical research. **It's important for you and your community that you count yourself in by May 16.**

Ivan Fellegi
Chief Statistician of Canada

COMPLETE YOUR FORM ON-LINE OR ON PAPER

This information is collected under the authority of the *Statistics Act*, R.S.C. 1985, c. S-19, and must be provided by law.   CONFIDENTIAL WHEN COMPLETED

STEP A

1. Complete your form either:

ON-LINE: at www.census2006.ca using the Internet Access Code printed above.
Do not mail back your paper questionnaire.

OR

ON PAPER: using a blue or black ballpoint pen.
Please print using C A P I T A L   L E T T E R S .

2. Print your telephone number: Area code   Telephone number   —

3. Complete this section if there is no printed address in the address space above or if you lived at a different address on May 16, 2006.

No. and street or lot and concession   Apt. No.

City, municipality, town, village, Indian reserve   Province/territory   Postal code

Statistics   Statistique
Canada   Canada

0301

Canada

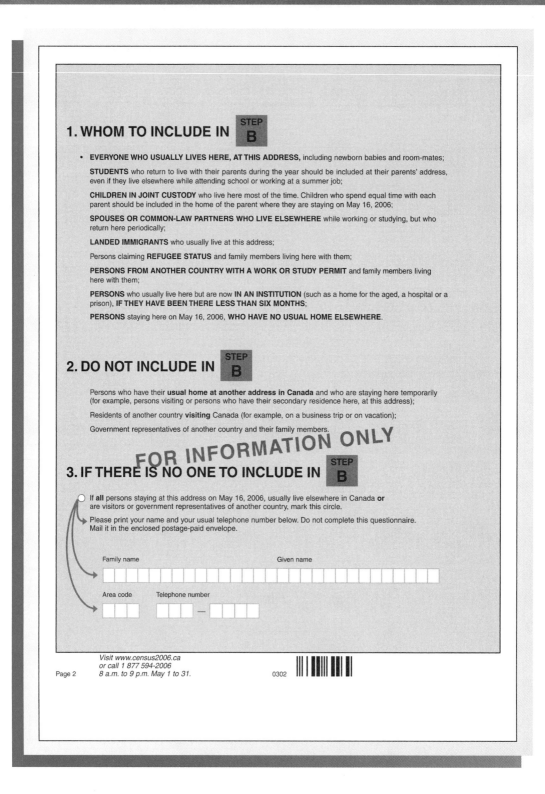

1. WHOM TO INCLUDE IN STEP B

- **EVERYONE WHO USUALLY LIVES HERE, AT THIS ADDRESS,** including newborn babies and room-mates;

  STUDENTS who return to live with their parents during the year should be included at their parents' address, even if they live elsewhere while attending school or working at a summer job;

  CHILDREN IN JOINT CUSTODY who live here most of the time. Children who spend equal time with each parent should be included in the home of the parent where they are staying on May 16, 2006;

  SPOUSES OR COMMON-LAW PARTNERS WHO LIVE ELSEWHERE while working or studying, but who return here periodically;

  LANDED IMMIGRANTS who usually live at this address;

  Persons claiming **REFUGEE STATUS** and family members living here with them;

  PERSONS FROM ANOTHER COUNTRY WITH A WORK OR STUDY PERMIT and family members living here with them;

  PERSONS who usually live here but are now **IN AN INSTITUTION** (such as a home for the aged, a hospital or a prison), **IF THEY HAVE BEEN THERE LESS THAN SIX MONTHS**;

  PERSONS staying here on May 16, 2006, **WHO HAVE NO USUAL HOME ELSEWHERE**.

2. DO NOT INCLUDE IN STEP B

Persons who have their **usual home at another address in Canada** and who are staying here temporarily (for example, persons visiting or persons who have their secondary residence here, at this address);

Residents of another country **visiting** Canada (for example, on a business trip or on vacation);

Government representatives of another country and their family members.

3. IF THERE IS NO ONE TO INCLUDE IN STEP B

If **all** persons staying at this address on May 16, 2006, usually live elsewhere in Canada **or** are visitors or government representatives of another country, mark this circle.

Please print your name and your usual telephone number below. Do not complete this questionnaire. Mail it in the enclosed postage-paid envelope.

Family name   Given name

Area code   Telephone number

Visit www.census2006.ca or call 1 877 594-2006 8 a.m. to 9 p.m. May 1 to 31.

Page 2   0302

STEP B

1. Including yourself, how many persons usually live here, at this address, as of **May 16, 2006?** *Include all persons who usually live here, even if they are temporarily away.*

→ ☐☐

2. Including yourself, list below, using CAPITAL LETTERS, all persons who usually live here. *Begin the list with an adult followed, if applicable, by that person's* **spouse** *or* **common-law partner** *and by their children who usually live here. Continue with all other persons who usually live here.*

	FAMILY NAME	GIVEN NAME
Person 1		
Person 2		
Person 3		
Person 4		
Person 5		
Person 6		
Person 7		
Person 8		
Person 9		
Person 10		

FOR INFORMATION ONLY

STEP C

Did you leave anyone out of Step B because you were not sure the person should be listed?

For example:
• *a person living at this address who has another home;*
• *a person temporarily away.*

○ No

○ Yes → Specify the name, the relationship and the reason.

Name(s)

Relationship/ Reason

STEP D

1. Is anyone listed in Step B a farm operator who produces at least one agricultural product **intended for sale?** (crops, livestock, milk, poultry, eggs, greenhouse or nursery products, Christmas trees, sod, honey, bees, maple syrup products, furs, etc.)

○ No → **Go to Step E**   ○ Yes

2. Does this farm operator make the day-to-day management decisions related to the farm?

○ No   ○ Yes

STEP E

Copy the names in Step B to Question 1, on top of page 4. Keep the same order.

If more than five persons live here, you will need an extra questionnaire; call 1 877 594-2006.

0303

Page 3

1 NAME

In the spaces provided, copy the names in the same order as in **Step B**. Then answer the following questions for **each** person.

PERSON 1

Family name

Given name

PERSON 2

Family name

Given name

2 SEX

PERSON 1
- ○ Male
- ○ Female

PERSON 2
- ○ Male
- ○ Female

3 DATE OF BIRTH

Day	Month	Year

Example: | 1 3 | 0 2 | 1 9 5 0 |

If exact date is not known, enter best estimate.

PERSON 1

Date of birth

Day	Month	Year

PERSON 2

Date of birth

Day	Month	Year

4 MARITAL STATUS

Mark "⊗" one circle only.

PERSON 1
- ○ Never legally married (single)
- ○ Legally married (and not separated)
- ○ Separated, but still legally married
- ○ Divorced
- ○ Widowed

PERSON 2
- ○ Never legally married (single)
- ○ Legally married (and not separated)
- ○ Separated, but still legally married
- ○ Divorced
- ○ Widowed

5 Is this person living with a common-law partner?

Common-law refers to two people of the opposite sex or of the same sex who live together as a couple but who are not legally married to each other.

PERSON 1
- ○ Yes
- ○ No

PERSON 2
- ○ Yes
- ○ No

6 RELATIONSHIP TO PERSON 1

For **each** person usually living here, describe his / her relationship to Person 1.

Mark "⊗" or specify one response only.

Stepchildren, adopted children and children of a common-law partner should be considered sons and daughters.

If none of the choices apply, use the "Other" box to indicate this person's relationship to Person 1.

Examples of "Other" relationships to Person 1:
- *cousin*
- *niece or nephew*
- *lodger's husband or wife*
- *room-mate's son or daughter*
- *employee*
- *same-sex married spouse*

FOR INFORMATION ONLY

PERSON 1
- ⊗ PERSON 1

PERSON 2
- ○ Husband or wife of Person 1
- ○ Opposite-sex common-law partner of Person 1
- ○ Same-sex common-law partner of Person 1
- ○ Son or daughter of Person 1
- ○ Son-in-law or daughter-in-law of Person 1
- ○ Grandchild of Person 1
- ○ Father or mother of Person 1
- ○ Father-in-law or mother-in-law of Person 1
- ○ Grandparent of Person 1
- ○ Brother or sister of Person 1
- ○ Brother-in-law or sister-in-law of Person 1
- ○ Lodger or boarder
- ○ Room-mate

Other — *Specify*

Visit www.census2006.ca or call 1 877 594-2006 8 a.m. to 9 p.m. May 1 to 31.

Page 4

0304

| ○ Male | ○ Male | ○ Male |
| ○ Female | ○ Female | ○ Female |

| Date of birth | Date of birth | Date of birth |
| Day   Month   Year | Day   Month   Year | Day   Month   Year |

○ Never legally married (single)	○ Never legally married (single)	○ Never legally married (single)
○ Legally married (and not separated)	○ Legally married (and not separated)	○ Legally married (and not separated)
○ Separated, but still legally married	○ Separated, but still legally married	○ Separated, but still legally married
○ Divorced	○ Divorced	○ Divorced
○ Widowed	○ Widowed	○ Widowed

| ○ Yes | ○ Yes | ○ Yes |
| ○ No | ○ No | ○ No |

FOR INFORMATION ONLY

○ Son or daughter of Person 1	○ Son or daughter of Person 1	○ Son or daughter of Person 1
○ Son-in-law or daughter-in-law of Person 1	○ Son-in-law or daughter-in-law of Person 1	○ Son-in-law or daughter-in-law of Person 1
○ Grandchild of Person 1	○ Grandchild of Person 1	○ Grandchild of Person 1
○ Father or mother of Person 1	○ Father or mother of Person 1	○ Father or mother of Person 1
○ Father-in-law or mother-in-law of Person 1	○ Father-in-law or mother-in-law of Person 1	○ Father-in-law or mother-in-law of Person 1
○ Grandparent of Person 1	○ Grandparent of Person 1	○ Grandparent of Person 1
○ Brother or sister of Person 1	○ Brother or sister of Person 1	○ Brother or sister of Person 1
○ Brother-in-law or sister-in-law of Person 1	○ Brother-in-law or sister-in-law of Person 1	○ Brother-in-law or sister-in-law of Person 1
○ Lodger or boarder	○ Lodger or boarder	○ Lodger or boarder
○ Room-mate	○ Room-mate	○ Room-mate
Other — Specify	Other — Specify	Other — Specify

ACTIVITIES OF DAILY LIVING

7 Does this person have any **difficulty** hearing, seeing, communicating, walking, climbing stairs, bending, learning or doing any similar activities?

- ○ Yes, sometimes
- ○ Yes, often
- ○ No

- ○ Yes, sometimes
- ○ Yes, often
- ○ No

FOR INFORMATION ONLY

8 Does a physical condition **or** mental condition **or** health problem **reduce the amount or the kind of activity** this person can do:

(a) at home?

- ○ Yes, sometimes
- ○ Yes, often
- ○ No

- ○ Yes, sometimes
- ○ Yes, often
- ○ No

(b) at work or at school?

- ○ Yes, sometimes   ○ No
- ○ Yes, often   ○ Not applicable

- ○ Yes, sometimes   ○ No
- ○ Yes, often   ○ Not applicable

(c) in other activities, for example, transportation or leisure?

- ○ Yes, sometimes
- ○ Yes, often
- ○ No

- ○ Yes, sometimes
- ○ Yes, often
- ○ No

SOCIOCULTURAL INFORMATION

9 Where was this person born?

Specify one response only, according to present boundaries.

Born in Canada

- ○ Nfld.Lab.   ○ Manitoba
- ○ P.E.I.   ○ Sask.
- ○ N.S.   ○ Alberta
- ○ N.B.   ○ B.C.
- ○ Quebec   ○ Yukon
- ○ Ontario   ○ N.W.T.
- ○ Nunavut

Born outside Canada
Specify country

Born in Canada

- ○ Nfld.Lab.   ○ Manitoba
- ○ P.E.I.   ○ Sask.
- ○ N.S.   ○ Alberta
- ○ N.B.   ○ B.C.
- ○ Quebec   ○ Yukon
- ○ Ontario   ○ N.W.T.
- ○ Nunavut

Born outside Canada
Specify country

10 Of what country is this person a citizen?

*Indicate **more than one** citizenship, if applicable.*

*"**Canada, by naturalization**" refers to the process by which an immigrant is granted citizenship of Canada, under the Citizenship Act.*

- ○ Canada, by birth
- ○ Canada, by naturalization

Other country — *Specify*

- ○ Canada, by birth
- ○ Canada, by naturalization

Other country — *Specify*

Visit www.census2006.ca or call 1 877 594-2006 8 a.m. to 9 p.m. May 1 to 31.

0306

FOR INFORMATION ONLY

○ Yes, sometimes	○ Yes, sometimes	○ Yes, sometimes
○ Yes, often	○ Yes, often	○ Yes, often
○ No	○ No	○ No

○ Yes, sometimes	○ Yes, sometimes	○ Yes, sometimes
○ Yes, often	○ Yes, often	○ Yes, often
○ No	○ No	○ No

○ Yes, sometimes	○ No	○ Yes, sometimes	○ No	○ Yes, sometimes	○ No
○ Yes, often	○ Not applicable	○ Yes, often	○ Not applicable	○ Yes, often	○ Not applicable

○ Yes, sometimes	○ Yes, sometimes	○ Yes, sometimes
○ Yes, often	○ Yes, often	○ Yes, often
○ No	○ No	○ No

Born in Canada

○ Nfld.Lab.	○ Manitoba	○ Nfld.Lab.	○ Manitoba	○ Nfld.Lab.	○ Manitoba
○ P.E.I.	○ Sask.	○ P.E.I.	○ Sask.	○ P.E.I.	○ Sask.
○ N.S.	○ Alberta	○ N.S.	○ Alberta	○ N.S.	○ Alberta
○ N.B.	○ B.C.	○ N.B.	○ B.C.	○ N.B.	○ B.C.
○ Quebec	○ Yukon	○ Quebec	○ Yukon	○ Quebec	○ Yukon
○ Ontario	○ N.W.T.	○ Ontario	○ N.W.T.	○ Ontario	○ N.W.T.
	○ Nunavut		○ Nunavut		○ Nunavut

Born outside Canada
Specify country

[ ][ ][ ][ ][ ][ ][ ][ ][ ][ ][ ] [ ][ ][ ][ ][ ][ ][ ][ ][ ][ ][ ] [ ][ ][ ][ ][ ][ ][ ][ ][ ][ ][ ]

○ Canada, by birth	○ Canada, by birth	○ Canada, by birth
○ Canada, by naturalization	○ Canada, by naturalization	○ Canada, by naturalization
Other country — *Specify*	Other country — *Specify*	Other country — *Specify*

[ ][ ][ ][ ][ ][ ][ ][ ][ ][ ] [ ][ ][ ][ ][ ][ ][ ][ ][ ][ ] [ ][ ][ ][ ][ ][ ][ ][ ][ ][ ]

0307

11 Is this person now, or has this person ever been, a **landed immigrant**?

A "landed immigrant" (permanent resident) is a person who has been granted the right to live in Canada permanently by immigration authorities.

- ○ No → Go to Question 13
- ○ Yes

- ○ No → Go to Question 13
- ○ Yes

FOR INFORMATION ONLY

12 In what year did this person first become a landed immigrant?

Year
☐☐☐☐ *If exact year is not known, enter best estimate.*

Year
☐☐☐☐ *If exact year is not known, enter best estimate.*

13 Can this person speak English or French well enough to conduct a conversation?

Mark "⊗" one circle only.

- ○ English only
- ○ French only
- ○ Both English and French
- ○ Neither English nor French

- ○ English only
- ○ French only
- ○ Both English and French
- ○ Neither English nor French

14 What language(s), **other than English or French**, can this person speak well enough to conduct a conversation?

- ○ None
  OR
  Specify other language(s)
  ☐☐☐☐☐☐☐☐☐☐☐☐
  ☐☐☐☐☐☐☐☐☐☐☐☐

- ○ None
  OR
  Specify other language(s)
  ☐☐☐☐☐☐☐☐☐☐☐☐
  ☐☐☐☐☐☐☐☐☐☐☐☐

15 (a) What language does this person speak **most often** at home?

- ○ English
- ○ French
  Other — *Specify*
  ☐☐☐☐☐☐☐☐☐☐☐☐

- ○ English
- ○ French
  Other — *Specify*
  ☐☐☐☐☐☐☐☐☐☐☐☐

(b) Does this person speak any other languages **on a regular basis** at home?

- ○ No
- ○ Yes, English
- ○ Yes, French
  Yes, Other — *Specify*
  ☐☐☐☐☐☐☐☐☐☐☐☐

- ○ No
- ○ Yes, English
- ○ Yes, French
  Yes, Other — *Specify*
  ☐☐☐☐☐☐☐☐☐☐☐☐

16 What is the language that this person **first learned** at home **in childhood** and **still understands**?

If this person no longer understands the first language learned, indicate the second language learned.

- ○ English
- ○ French
  Other — *Specify*
  ☐☐☐☐☐☐☐☐☐☐☐☐

- ○ English
- ○ French
  Other — *Specify*
  ☐☐☐☐☐☐☐☐☐☐☐☐

FOR INFORMATION ONLY

| ○ No → **Go to Question 13** | ○ No → **Go to Question 13** | ○ No → **Go to Question 13** |
| ○ Yes | ○ Yes | ○ Yes |

| Year | Year | Year |
| ▢▢▢▢ *If exact year is not known, enter best estimate.* | ▢▢▢▢ *If exact year is not known, enter best estimate.* | ▢▢▢▢ *If exact year is not known, enter best estimate.* |

○ English only	○ English only	○ English only
○ French only	○ French only	○ French only
○ Both English and French	○ Both English and French	○ Both English and French
○ Neither English nor French	○ Neither English nor French	○ Neither English nor French

○ None	○ None	○ None
OR	**OR**	**OR**
Specify other language(s)	*Specify other language(s)*	*Specify other language(s)*

○ English	○ English	○ English
○ French	○ French	○ French
Other — *Specify*	Other — *Specify*	Other — *Specify*

○ No	○ No	○ No
○ Yes, English	○ Yes, English	○ Yes, English
○ Yes, French	○ Yes, French	○ Yes, French
Yes, Other — *Specify*	Yes, Other — *Specify*	Yes, Other — *Specify*

○ English	○ English	○ English
○ French	○ French	○ French
Other — *Specify*	Other — *Specify*	Other — *Specify*

The census has collected information on the ancestral origins of the population for over 100 years to capture the composition of Canada's diverse population.

17 What were the ethnic or cultural origins of this person's **ancestors**?

An ancestor is usually more distant than a grandparent.

For example, Canadian, English, French, Chinese, Italian, German, Scottish, East Indian, Irish, Cree, Mi'kmaq (Micmac), Métis, Inuit (Eskimo), Ukrainian, Dutch, Filipino, Polish, Portuguese, Jewish, Greek, Jamaican, Vietnamese, Lebanese, Chilean, Salvadorean, Somali, etc.

Specify as many origins as applicable using capital letters.

Specify as many origins as applicable using capital letters.

FOR INFORMATION ONLY

18 Is this person an Aboriginal person, that is, North American Indian, Métis or Inuit (Eskimo)?

If "Yes", mark "⊗" the circle(s) that best describe(s) this person now.

○ No → **Continue with the next question**

○ Yes, North American Indian

○ Yes, Métis

○ Yes, Inuit (Eskimo)

Go to Question 20

○ No → **Continue with the next question**

○ Yes, North American Indian

○ Yes, Métis

○ Yes, Inuit (Eskimo)

Go to Question 20

19 Is this person:

Mark "⊗" more than one or specify, if applicable.

This information is collected to support programs that promote equal opportunity for everyone to share in the social, cultural and economic life of Canada.

○ White

○ Chinese

○ South Asian *(e.g., East Indian, Pakistani, Sri Lankan, etc.)*

○ Black

○ Filipino

○ Latin American

○ Southeast Asian *(e.g., Vietnamese, Cambodian, Malaysian, Laotian, etc.)*

○ Arab

○ West Asian *(e.g., Iranian, Afghan, etc.)*

○ Korean

○ Japanese

Other — *Specify*

○ White

○ Chinese

○ South Asian *(e.g., East Indian, Pakistani, Sri Lankan, etc.)*

○ Black

○ Filipino

○ Latin American

○ Southeast Asian *(e.g., Vietnamese, Cambodian, Malaysian, Laotian, etc.)*

○ Arab

○ West Asian *(e.g., Iranian, Afghan, etc.)*

○ Korean

○ Japanese

Other — *Specify*

Visit www.census2006.ca or call 1 877 594-2006 8 a.m. to 9 p.m. May 1 to 31.

0310

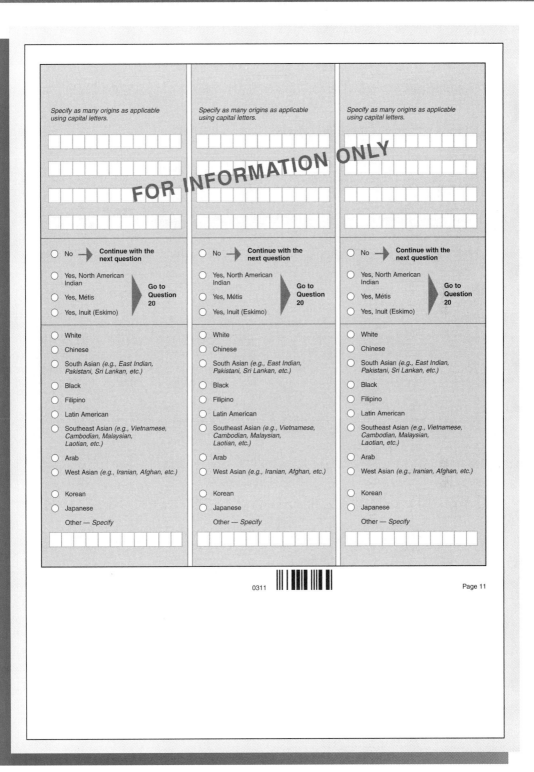

Specify as many origins as applicable using capital letters.

○ No → **Continue with the next question**

○ Yes, North American Indian
○ Yes, Métis → **Go to Question 20**
○ Yes, Inuit (Eskimo)

○ White
○ Chinese
○ South Asian *(e.g., East Indian, Pakistani, Sri Lankan, etc.)*
○ Black
○ Filipino
○ Latin American
○ Southeast Asian *(e.g., Vietnamese, Cambodian, Malaysian, Laotian, etc.)*
○ Arab
○ West Asian *(e.g., Iranian, Afghan, etc.)*
○ Korean
○ Japanese
Other — *Specify*

Specify as many origins as applicable using capital letters.

FOR INFORMATION ONLY

○ No → **Continue with the next question**

○ Yes, North American Indian
○ Yes, Métis → **Go to Question 20**
○ Yes, Inuit (Eskimo)

○ White
○ Chinese
○ South Asian *(e.g., East Indian, Pakistani, Sri Lankan, etc.)*
○ Black
○ Filipino
○ Latin American
○ Southeast Asian *(e.g., Vietnamese, Cambodian, Malaysian, Laotian, etc.)*
○ Arab
○ West Asian *(e.g., Iranian, Afghan, etc.)*
○ Korean
○ Japanese
Other — *Specify*

Specify as many origins as applicable using capital letters.

○ No → **Continue with the next question**

○ Yes, North American Indian
○ Yes, Métis → **Go to Question 20**
○ Yes, Inuit (Eskimo)

○ White
○ Chinese
○ South Asian *(e.g., East Indian, Pakistani, Sri Lankan, etc.)*
○ Black
○ Filipino
○ Latin American
○ Southeast Asian *(e.g., Vietnamese, Cambodian, Malaysian, Laotian, etc.)*
○ Arab
○ West Asian *(e.g., Iranian, Afghan, etc.)*
○ Korean
○ Japanese
Other — *Specify*

20 Is this person a member of an Indian Band / First Nation?

○ No

○ Yes, member of an Indian Band / First Nation

⤷ Specify Indian Band / First Nation (for example, Musqueam)

[ ][ ][ ][ ][ ][ ][ ][ ][ ][ ][ ][ ]

○ No

○ Yes, member of an Indian Band / First Nation

⤷ Specify Indian Band / First Nation (for example, Musqueam)

[ ][ ][ ][ ][ ][ ][ ][ ][ ][ ][ ][ ]

21 Is this person a Treaty Indian or a Registered Indian as defined by the *Indian Act* of Canada?

○ No

○ Yes, Treaty Indian or Registered Indian

○ No

○ Yes, Treaty Indian or Registered Indian

22 Answer Questions 23 to 52 for each person aged 15 and over.

Continue only for each person aged 15 years and over (born before May 16, 1991).

Continue only for each person aged 15 years and over (born before May 16, 1991).

MOBILITY

23 Where did this person live **1 year ago**, that is, on **May 16, 2005**?

Mark "⊗" one circle only.

Note:

For those who mark the third circle:

Please give the name of the city or town rather than the metropolitan area of which it is a part.

For example:

- *Saanich rather than Victoria (metropolitan area);*
- *St. Albert rather than Edmonton (metropolitan area);*
- *Laval rather than Montréal (metropolitan area).*

○ Lived at the **same** address as now

○ Lived at a **different** address in the **same** city, town, village, township, municipality or Indian reserve

○ Lived in a **different** city, town, village, township, municipality or Indian reserve **in Canada**

⤷ Specify name of:

City, town, village, township, municipality or Indian reserve

[ ][ ][ ][ ][ ][ ][ ][ ][ ][ ][ ][ ]

[ ][ ][ ][ ][ ][ ][ ][ ][ ][ ][ ][ ]

Province / territory

[ ][ ][ ][ ][ ]

Postal code

[ ][ ][ ] [ ][ ][ ]

○ Lived **outside Canada**

⤷ Specify name of country

[ ][ ][ ][ ][ ][ ][ ][ ][ ][ ][ ][ ]

○ Lived at the **same** address as now

○ Lived at a **different** address in the **same** city, town, village, township, municipality or Indian reserve

○ Lived in a **different** city, town, village, township, municipality or Indian reserve **in Canada**

⤷ Specify name of:

City, town, village, township, municipality or Indian reserve

[ ][ ][ ][ ][ ][ ][ ][ ][ ][ ][ ][ ]

[ ][ ][ ][ ][ ][ ][ ][ ][ ][ ][ ][ ]

Province / territory

[ ][ ][ ][ ][ ]

Postal code

[ ][ ][ ] [ ][ ][ ]

○ Lived **outside Canada**

⤷ Specify name of country

[ ][ ][ ][ ][ ][ ][ ][ ][ ][ ][ ][ ]

FOR INFORMATION ONLY

○ No	○ No	○ No
○ Yes, member of an Indian Band/First Nation	○ Yes, member of an Indian Band/First Nation	○ Yes, member of an Indian Band/First Nation
Specify Indian Band/First Nation (for example, Musqueam)	*Specify Indian Band/First Nation (for example, Musqueam)*	*Specify Indian Band/First Nation (for example, Musqueam)*

○ No	○ No	○ No
○ Yes, Treaty Indian or Registered Indian	○ Yes, Treaty Indian or Registered Indian	○ Yes, Treaty Indian or Registered Indian

Continue only for each person aged 15 years and over (born before May 16, 1991).	**Continue only for each person aged 15 years and over (born before May 16, 1991).**	**Continue only for each person aged 15 years and over (born before May 16, 1991).**

○ Lived at the **same** address as now	○ Lived at the **same** address as now	○ Lived at the **same** address as now
○ Lived at a **different** address in the **same** city, town, village, township, municipality or Indian reserve	○ Lived at a **different** address in the **same** city, town, village, township, municipality or Indian reserve	○ Lived at a **different** address in the **same** city, town, village, township, municipality or Indian reserve
○ Lived in a **different** city, town, village, township, municipality or Indian reserve **in Canada**	○ Lived in a **different** city, town, village, township, municipality or Indian reserve **in Canada**	○ Lived in a **different** city, town, village, township, municipality or Indian reserve **in Canada**
Specify name of:	*Specify name of:*	*Specify name of:*
City, town, village, township, municipality or Indian reserve	City, town, village, township, municipality or Indian reserve	City, town, village, township, municipality or Indian reserve
Province/territory	Province/territory	Province/territory
Postal code	Postal code	Postal code
○ Lived **outside Canada**	○ Lived **outside Canada**	○ Lived **outside Canada**
Specify name of country	*Specify name of country*	*Specify name of country*

FOR INFORMATION ONLY

0313

Page 13

Remember, these questions are only for persons aged 15 and over.

24 Where did this person live **5 years ago**, that is, on **May 16, 2001**?

Mark "(✗)" one circle only.

Note:

For those who mark the third circle:

Please give the name of the city or town rather than the metropolitan area of which it is a part.

For example:

- *Saanich rather than Victoria (metropolitan area);*
- *St. Albert rather than Edmonton (metropolitan area);*
- *Laval rather than Montréal (metropolitan area).*

○ Lived at the **same** address as now

○ Lived at a **different** address in the **same** city, town, village, township, municipality or Indian reserve

○ Lived in a **different** city, town, village, township, municipality or Indian reserve **in Canada**

▼ *Specify name of:*

City, town, village, township, municipality or Indian reserve

[ ][ ][ ][ ][ ][ ][ ][ ][ ][ ][ ][ ][ ][ ]

[ ][ ][ ][ ][ ][ ][ ][ ][ ][ ][ ][ ][ ][ ]

Province / territory

[ ][ ][ ][ ]

Postal code

[ ][ ][ ]   [ ][ ][ ]

○ Lived **outside Canada**

▼ *Specify name of country*

[ ][ ][ ][ ][ ][ ][ ][ ][ ][ ][ ][ ][ ][ ]

○ Lived at the **same** address as now

○ Lived at a **different** address in the **same** city, town, village, township, municipality or Indian reserve

○ Lived in a **different** city, town, village, township, municipality or Indian reserve **in Canada**

▼ *Specify name of:*

City, town, village, township, municipality or Indian reserve

[ ][ ][ ][ ][ ][ ][ ][ ][ ][ ][ ][ ][ ][ ]

[ ][ ][ ][ ][ ][ ][ ][ ][ ][ ][ ][ ][ ][ ]

Province / territory

[ ][ ][ ][ ]

Postal code

[ ][ ][ ]   [ ][ ][ ]

○ Lived **outside Canada**

▼ *Specify name of country*

[ ][ ][ ][ ][ ][ ][ ][ ][ ][ ][ ][ ][ ][ ]

PLACE OF BIRTH OF PARENTS

25 Where was **each of** this person's parents born?

(a) **Father**

Mark "(✗)" or specify country according to present boundaries.

Father

○ Born in Canada

Born outside Canada
Specify country

[ ][ ][ ][ ][ ][ ][ ][ ][ ][ ][ ][ ][ ]

Father

○ Born in Canada

Born outside Canada
Specify country

[ ][ ][ ][ ][ ][ ][ ][ ][ ][ ][ ][ ][ ]

(b) **Mother**

Mark "(✗)" or specify country according to present boundaries.

Mother

○ Born in Canada

Born outside Canada
Specify country

[ ][ ][ ][ ][ ][ ][ ][ ][ ][ ][ ][ ][ ]

Mother

○ Born in Canada

Born outside Canada
Specify country

[ ][ ][ ][ ][ ][ ][ ][ ][ ][ ][ ][ ][ ]

FOR INFORMATION ONLY

*Visit www.census2006.ca
or call 1 877 594-2006
8 a.m. to 9 p.m. May 1 to 31.*

Page 14   0314

Remember, these questions are only for persons aged 15 and over.

○ Lived at the **same** address as now	○ Lived at the **same** address as now	○ Lived at the **same** address as now
○ Lived at a **different** address in the **same** city, town, village, township, municipality or Indian reserve	○ Lived at a **different** address in the **same** city, town, village, township, municipality or Indian reserve	○ Lived at a **different** address in the **same** city, town, village, township, municipality or Indian reserve
○ Lived in a **different** city, town, village, township, municipality or Indian reserve **in Canada**	○ Lived in a **different** city, town, village, township, municipality or Indian reserve **in Canada**	○ Lived in a **different** city, town, village, township, municipality or Indian reserve **in Canada**
↓ *Specify name of:*	↓ *Specify name of:*	↓ *Specify name of:*

City, town, village, township, municipality or Indian reserve

Province / territory

Postal code

○ Lived **outside Canada**

↓ *Specify name of country*

FOR INFORMATION ONLY

Father

○ Born in Canada

Born outside Canada
Specify country

Mother

○ Born in Canada

Born outside Canada
Specify country

0315

Page 15

Vital Registration Forms

The following four legal documents are registration forms used to record vital statistics —death, birth, stillbirth, and marriage—in the Province of Alberta.

Registration of Death

Registration of Birth

Alberta

Registration No.	
Amendment No.	Pre-Registration No.

Please **PRINT** clearly in **black** ink only.

This is a legal document

Registration of Birth

1. CHILD'S Last Name (*restrictions apply - see Information Guide*)
▶

2. CHILD'S Full Given Name(s) (*first and all middle names*)
▶

3. Sex of Child ☐ Male ☐ Female

4. Date of Child's Birth month by name   day   year

5. Time of Child's Birth (*use 12 hour clock*) Hour :   Minutes   ☐ AM ☐ PM

6. Place of Child's Birth
a) In Hospital ☐ Yes ☒ No
b) Name of Hospital (*if not in hospital, give exact location*)
c) City/Town/Village (*if rural, give nearest city/town/village*)

7. Kind of Birth ☐ Single ☐ Twin ☐ Triplet ☐ Other

8. If this was a multiple birth, state if this child was born: ☐ 1st ☐ 2nd ☐ 3rd ☐

9. Birth Weight (*in grams*)

10. Duration of Pregnancy (*completed weeks*)

Children born to this Mother (include this birth)
11. Number of Live Births
12. Number of Stillbirths (*excluding miscarriages*)

13. (a) Type of Birth Attendant ☐ Physician ☐ Midwife ☐ Other: (*specify*)
(b) Name of Birth Attendant

14. Mother's Usual Home Address at the time of this child's birth (*If rural, give exact location e.g. Township, Section, Meridian*)
Street/Apt. No.   City/Town/Village   Province/State   Country   Postal/Zip Code
Telephone No. (daytime) Area Code ( )

15. Complete Mailing Address (*if different than No. 14*) Street Address/Apt. No./PO Box No./RR No.   City/Town/Village   Province/State/Country   Postal/Zip Code

16. Mother's Marital Status - DEFINITIONS: (*read carefully before checking one of the boxes below*)
For the purpose of registering this birth, a married woman is a woman who was legally married at any time between the conception and birth of this child. Common-Law is not considered legally married. If the mother is separated, she is still legally married.

Check **ONE** only:

1. ☐ Legally married and **husband is** the natural father of this child - check this box, then go to No. 17 below.

2. ☐ Legally married and **husband is not** the natural father of this child - check this box, then go to the attached "Statutory Declaration" and read the instructions. Return to complete the parent(s) information below.

3. ☐ Not legally married (*includes: Never Married, Widowed or Divorced*) - check this box, then go to No. 17 below, if applicable

Father Of This Child

17. Legal LAST Name of Father (of this child) See the definition on the first page of the Information Guide.
▶

18. All Legal GIVEN Name(s) of Father (of this child) (as shown on birth certificate)
▶

19. Date of Birth of Father (of this child) month by name day year
▶
20. Present Age of Father (of this child)

21. Place of Birth of Father (of this child) City/Town/Village Province/Country
▶

22. I acknowledge that I am the natural father and jointly request, with the mother, that the name of this child be registered as shown above in Numbers 1 and 2.

Signature of the Father (of this child)
X _____

Mother Who Gave Birth To This Child

23. MAIDEN LAST Name of Mother (of this child) This is your last name before you were married. See the definition on the first page of the Information Guide.
▶

24. All Legal GIVEN Name(s) of Mother (of this child) (as shown on birth certificate)
▶

25. Date of Birth of Mother (of this child) month by name day year
▶
26. Present Age of Mother (of this child)

27. Place of Birth of Mother (of this child) City/Town/Village Province/Country
▶

THIS BOX MUST BE COMPLETED TO REGISTER YOUR CHILD.
28. PRINT the LAST name that you are currently using.
▶

29. I certify the above is correct and request, jointly with the father listed (if applicable), that the name of this child be registered as shown above in Numbers 1 and 2.

Signature of the Mother (of this child) Date Signed
X _____   mm / dd / yyyy

30. Informant (only required when the mother is incapable of completing this form). I certify the above is correct to the best of my knowledge.
X _____
Signature of Informant   Relationship to Child

FOR HOSPITAL REGISTRAR USE ONLY

31. Hospital Certification
I certify this registration was accepted by me at _____
Name of Hospital   City/Town/Village
Alberta, on _____ ( )
Date (month by name, day, year)   Hospital Telephone Number   Signature of Hospital Registrar

32. Hospital Notes

33. Vital Statistics Notes

This information is being collected for the purposes of Vital Statistics records in accordance with the Vital Statistics Act. Questions about the collection of this information can be directed to the Freedom of Information and Protection of Privacy Coordinator for Alberta Registries, Box 3140, Edmonton, Alberta T5J 2G7, (780) 427-7013.

REG 3216 (2005/07)

Registration of Stillbirth

| Registration No. |
| Amendment No. |
| Service Request No. | Pre-Registration No. |

Alberta

- This is a permanent legal record.
- Type or print clearly in black ink only.
- Do not sign until this form is completed in full.

Registration of Stillbirth

Child

1. Last Name of Child (*restrictions apply - see Information Guide before completing*)

Full Given Name(s)

2. Sex
☐ Male
☐ Female

3. Date of Stillbirth (*month name, day, year*)

5. Place of Stillbirth a) Name of Hospital (*if not in hospital give exact location*)   b) City/Town/Village (*if rural, give nearest city/town/village*)

6. Kind of Birth
☐ Single ☐ Twin
☐ Triplet
☐ Other: ___

7. Order of Birth
(*multiple births only*)
☐ 1st ☐ 2nd
☐ 3rd

8. Birth Weight
(*in grams*)

9. Duration of Pregnancy
(*completed weeks*)

Children born to this Mother (*include this birth*)
10. Number of Live Births ___
11. Number of Stillbirths ___
(*excluding miscarriages*)

12. a) Type of Birth Attendant
☐ Physician ☐ Midwife ☐ Other: (*specify*)

b) Name of Birth Attendant

See Information Guide ▶

13. Are parents married to each other (*at conception, birth, or any time in between*)? ☐ Yes ☐ No

14. If parents are **not** married to each other, indicate **Mother's** marital status
☐ Never Married ☐ Divorced ☐ Widowed ☐ Married

Mother

15. Currently Used Last Name of Mother

16. Legal Maiden Last Name

Full Legal Given Name(s)

17. Alberta Personal Health Number

18. Date of Birth (*month name, day, year*)

19. Place of Birth   City/Town/Village   Province/Country

20. Usual Residence   Street Address   City/Town/Village

Province/State   Country   Postal/Zip Code   Telephone No. (*daytime*)

(if different than Usual Residence)

21. Mailing Address   Street Address/PO Box No.   City/Town/Village

Province/State   Country   Postal/Zip Code

22. **I certify** the above to be correct to the best of my knowledge and request jointly with the father listed (if applicable), the last name of the child be registered as named above.

X ___
Signature of Mother   Date (*month name, day, year*)

or Informant: I certify the above to be correct to the best of my knowledge.

X ___
Signature of Informant   Relationship to Child

Father

See Information Guide before completing

23. Legal Last Name of Father

Full Legal Given Name(s)

24. Alberta Personal Health Number

25. Date of Birth (*month name, day, year*)

26. Place of Birth   City/Town/Village   Province/Country

27. **I acknowledge** that I am the natural father of this child and request jointly with the mother, the last name of the child be registered as named above.

X ___
Signature of Father   Date (*month name, day, year*)

Disposition Information
To be completed by Funeral Director/Hospital

28. Method of Disposition
☐ Burial ☐ Cremation ☐ Department of Anatomy
☐ Mausoleum ☐ Fetal/Infant Death (*disposition by hospital*)

29. Proposed Date of Disposition (*month name, day, year*)

30. Name of Cemetery, Crematorium or Place of Disposition

Address

31. Name of Funeral Home, Hospital, or Person in Charge of Remains

Address

Telephone Number

Hospital/District Registrar Certification

Burial Permit Issued by (*name of facility*)

Date Issued
(*month name, day, year*)

I certify this registration was accepted by me at (*name of facility*)

at ___, Alberta

dated ___

X ___
Signature of Hospital/District Registrar

Notations (*Vital Statistics Use Only*)

This information is being collected for the purposes of Vital Statistics records in accordance with the Vital Statistics Act. Questions about the collection of this information can be directed to the Freedom of Information and Protection of Privacy Coordinator for Alberta Registries, Box 3140, Edmonton, Alberta T5J 2G7, (780) 427-7013.

REG 3218 (05/07)

Registration of Marriage

Alberta

| Registration No. |
| Amendment No. |
| Service Request No. | Pre-Registration No. |

Please do not bend or **fold** this document.
Type or print clearly in **black ink only.**

- The **marriage ceremony cannot take place** unless both the Registration (top) and License (bottom) sections of this form **are presented to the marriage officiant.**
- This is a **permanent legal record**; certificates are prepared according to this information and in compliance with legislation.
- **Do not sign** this registration **prior to the marriage.**

Registration of Marriage

Groom
1. Legal Last Name and Full Legal Given Name(s)

2. Marital Status   ☐ Never Married ☐ Widowed ☐ Divorced   Sex

3. Date of Birth   4. Religious Denomination

5. Place of Birth   City/Town/Village   Province/Country

6. **Mother's** Legal Maiden Last Name and Full Legal Given Name(s)

7. Place of Birth   City/Town/Village   Province/Country

8. **Father's** Legal Last Name and Full Legal Given Name(s)

9. Place of Birth   City/Town/Village   Province/Country

10. **Signature**   X

Witness
11. Full Legal Given Name(s) and Last Name of **Witness**

12. Complete Mailing Address

13. **Signature** of Witness   X

Bride
18. Legal Last Name and Full Legal Given Name(s)

19. Marital Status   ☐ Never Married ☐ Widowed ☐ Divorced   Sex

20. Date of Birth   21. Religious Denomination

22. Place of Birth   City/Town/Village   Province/Country

23. **Mother's** Legal Maiden Last Name and Full Legal Given Name(s)

24. Place of Birth   City/Town/Village   Province/Country

25. **Father's** Legal Last Name and Full Legal Given Name(s)

26. Place of Birth   City/Town/Village   Province/Country

27. **Signature**   X

Witness
28. Full Legal Given Name(s) and Last Name of **Witness**

29. Complete Mailing Address

30. **Signature** of Witness   X

OFFICIANT'S CERTIFICATION

I certify that I performed the marriage ceremony of the couple named above at the place and on the date stated.

14. **Marriage Licence No.**

15. Date of Marriage (month by name, day, year) ▶

16. Place of Marriage (City/ Town/ Village) ▶ , ALBERTA

17. Name of church or address where marriage was held ▶

31. Name of Officiant (print)

32. Officiant's Certification No.   Religious Denomination
☐ MC
☐ Clergy   X   Signature of Officiant

Registrar's Certification
I certify this registration was accepted by me on _____
at _____ , Alberta.
X   Signature of District Registrar

Notations - For Vital Statistics Use Only

This information is being collected for the purposes of Vital Statistics records in accordance with the Vital Statistics Act. Questions about the collection of this information can be directed to the Freedom of Information and Protection of Privacy Coordinator for Alberta Registries, Box 3140, Edmonton, Alberta T5J 2G7, (780) 427-7013.

REG 3215a (2005/09)

Glossary

Below is a select list of terms and definitions that appear in this book. For a more complete list of demographic terms see *The Dictionary of Demography*, by Roland Pressat (edited by Christopher Wilson, 1985, Oxford University Press), and the 'Technical Notes on the Statistical Tables' in *United Nations 2004 Demographic Yearbook* (UN Department of Economic and Social Affairs, New York, [ES/ESA/STAT/SER.R/35], http://unstats.un.org/unsd/demographic/products/dyb/dybsets/2004%20DYB.pdf). A more extensive list of terms used in the Canadian census appears in Statistics Canada's *Census Dictionary*, found at www12.statcan.ca/english/census06/ reference/dictionary/index.cfm.

abortion The termination of a pregnancy, either voluntarily (i.e., *induced abortion*) or involuntarily (i.e., *spontaneous abortion*).

age The interval of time, expressed in completed years, between the date of birth and the present. Age is a fundamental characteristic of population structure.

age pattern As used in demography, *age pattern* refers to the way in which the incidence of a phenomenon, such as births, deaths, and migration, varies with age. For example, the timing of childbearing varies such that most births occur to women between the ages of 20 and 34, with many fewer births occurring before age 20 and after age 35.

age–sex pyramid The graphic representation (e.g., a histogram or vertical bar chart) portraying the relative number of males and females in the population in accordance with age category. Because of the interplay of fertility and mortality, and to a lesser extent migration, such a chart often assumes the shape of a pyramid (or triangle). In fact, however, the shape of the age distribution of a population can take on a variety of forms that can deviate substantially from a pyramid.

age–sex structure The composition of the population according to the number or percentage of males and females in each age category. This distribution is often represented as an age–sex pyramid chart.

age-specific rate A measure of the incidence of a demographic event (e.g., death) within a given age group in relation to the overall population in the same age category at risk of experiencing the event (e.g., age-specific death rate).

aging For an individual, *aging* refers to the biological process of getting older. For a population, it refers to the increasing prevalence of 'older persons' as denoted by some statistical indicator, such as the proportion over the age of 65.

baby boom A significant surge in the number of births taking place in a population over a protracted period (e.g., the post-WWII baby boom in Europe, North America, Australia, and New Zealand between 1946 and 1966, with its peak around 1960). The sharp decline in births after a baby boom is often referred to in the literature as a *baby bust*.

balancing equation An expression of the change in population as a function of change in births, deaths, and migration. This equation is often referred to as the *components equation* because it expresses population change as a function of two components: natural increase (births − deaths) and net migration (in migration − out migration).

birth The complete expulsion or extraction, from the mother, of a product of conception, regardless of the length of pregnancy, that, after such separation, breathes or shows any other evidence of life, such as beating of the heart, pulsation of the umbilical cord, or definite movement of voluntary muscles.

birth cohort A group of individuals born during a specified period of time, usually a given calendar year or a given five-year interval. The term is often used interchangeably with the term *generation*.

birth control Planned behaviour by couples aimed at preventing sexual intercourse from leading to a birth; examples include the use of *contraception*.

birth interval The interval between successive births, or between marriage (or cohabitation) and the first birth.

birth order The classification of a birth according to the number of previous births to the same mother or according to the number of previous births within a single marriage or sexual union.

brain drain The emigration of highly skilled persons from a country to other countries offering better socioeconomic opportunities. This term is often applied to the loss of skilled people by developing countries to the more developed countries.

breastfeeding The practice (also known as lactation) of feeding a baby with milk from the mother's breast. This behaviour is important to demographic analysis because its extent and duration in a population has a bearing on the birth rate: the greater the average duration of breastfeeding in a population, the lower the population's birth rate, all other things being equal.

cardiovascular disease Diseases of the heart and blood vessels. Along with cancer, this category of disease accounts for most deaths on an annual basis in the developed countries.

carrying capacity The maximum population sustainable by a given territory under specific conditions, such as a given level of land use and consumption of natural resources.

cause of death An illness, injury, or condition that leads to or contributes to a person's death. Causes of death are categorized according to the *International Classification of Diseases* (ICD), a detailed system of all known diseases, medical conditions, and types of injuries.

cause-specific death rate A *death rate* computed for a specific cause of death.

census The process of collecting, compiling, and publishing data on the demographic, social, and economic situation of all persons in a specified territory at a particular point in time. Governments usually undertake censuses every decade or every five years. The census may be thought of as giving a snapshot of the population at one point in time.

census metropolitan area A statistical construct describing a large agglomeration of urban centres that show a high level of economic integration with a central city, from which the metropolitan area derives its name (e.g., Toronto metropolitan area). Different countries have different statistical criteria to define a metropolitan area. In Canada, a census metropolitan area must have a population size of at least 100,000, and the majority of the population in the agglomeration must be involved in non-agricultural economic activity.

central death rate The *death rate* obtained by dividing the number of deaths in a specified period by the mid-year population at risk. This type of rate is commonly computed in the study of age–sex specific demographic rates.

children ever born The number of children ever born to a woman. Usually this refers to the number of live children.

child–woman ratio A ratio that expresses the number of children aged 0–4 to the number of women aged 15–49 (or 15–44), commonly expressed per 1,000. This ratio, which can be computed with census data, is often used as a rough indicator of fertility in countries where more refined measures of fertility are not available.

circulation A term used by geographers to refer to short-term, repetitive, or cyclical movements that do not lead to a permanent change of residence for an individual.

citizenship The official, legal recognition of an individual's right to be a citizen of a given state. States confer citizenship to their people through various legal criteria, including birth in the country and, for immigrants, duration of residence in the country. In sociological terms, citizenship pertains to rights (e.g., the right to vote) and obligations (allegiance to the adopted state by an immigrant's renunciation of citizenship to his or her country of birth).

cohabitation A type of conjugal union involving two persons of the opposite sex or (since 2001) of the same sex living together, possibly with children. This kind of union, often referred to as either a *consensual union* or *common-law marriage*, is not formalized though legal or religious marriage rites.

cohort A group of persons beginning their experience of a significant event at the same time; examples include a *birth cohort* (persons born in the same year) and a *marriage cohort* (couples married in the same year).

cohort fertility The reproductive experience of a particular birth cohort of women or of women belonging to a specific marriage cohort, as observed at the end of the cohort's childbearing years (i.e., cohort completed fertility). This type of fertility is often contrasted with *period fertility*, which measures the reproductive experience at one point in time as produced by different cohorts at different stages in their childbearing years passing though the given point of observation together (this yields the *period total fertility rate*).

coitus interruptus As a form of birth control, this refers to the withdrawal of the penis during sexual intercourse before ejaculation in order to avoid the possibility of conception.

common-law marriage See *cohabitation*.

consensual union See *cohabitation*.

contraception The application of a variety of means (condom, birth control pill, IUD, etc.) by couples in order to prevent conception when sexual intercourse has taken place.

cornucopians A label used to describe members of a particular school of thought with an optimistic view of future population trends. Unlike *neo-Malthusians*, cornucopians do not view population growth as detrimental to the future of humanity; rather, they consider population growth as potentially beneficial to overall societal well-being.

counterurbanization A phenomenon, observed during the 1970s in the United States and some other industrialized countries, in which rural areas and smaller urban settlements grew faster than large urban centres, largely as a function of net migration stimulated by economic restructuring, and partly because of a general preference among some people to reside away from the city. This development was facilitated by the existence of effective systems of roadways linking city and countryside.

crude rate Any rate that measures the incidence of a phenomenon in relation to the total population (the crude birth rate, the crude death rate, the crude marriage rate, the crude divorce rate, etc.). Such rates are called 'crude' because they overlook age, which is an important factor in demographic phenomena. Thus, while they are easily computed, these rates are generally considered poor indicators of the phenomena they measure. Besides overlooking the age effect, crude rates, being based on the total population, include in the denominator irrelevant subsets of the population that may have nothing in common with the process being measured. For example, the denominator of the crude birth rate includes men, as well as women under the age of 15 and over the age of 50.

death As defined by the World Health Organization and the medical profession, *death* is the permanent disappearance of all evidence of life at any time after birth. This definition excludes stillbirths and abortions, which are considered categories of *fetal mortality*.

death rate The number of deaths in a given time interval divided by the mid-interval population at risk.

de facto **population** In the context of a census, this refers to the population enumerated according to where persons happen to be staying on census night, rather than according to their usual place of residence. The opposite of *de facto* population is *de jure* population. On a worldwide basis, *de facto* censuses are more common than *de jure* ones.

de jure **population** In the context of a census, this refers to the population normally resident in a specified area. It includes those who are temporarily absent but excludes visitors or transients (compare *de facto population*).

demand for children On the aggregate level, this refers to the number (and sometimes also sex) of children that couples would choose under prevailing socioeconomic conditions and demographic conditions, including the level of infant and childhood mortality. Various theories of change in the demand for children by parents have been proposed in the demographic literature.

demographic transition A systematic description of the historical shift in birth and death rates for a population. A population undergoing demographic transition moves from an early stage of high birth and death rates with low rates of natural increase, to an intermediate stage of declining death rate and continued high fertility and high rates of natural increase, to a final stage of low birth and death rates and therefore low rates of natural increase.

demography The scientific study of population. The field of demography encompasses formal (mathematical) and social demographic (population studies) subspecialties.

dependency ratio Conceptually, a dependency ratio is intended to indicate the balance between the sectors of a population that are not economically productive and those sectors of the population that are economically productive. In practice, the dependency ratio is calculated on the basis of population below age 15 plus population above age 65, divided by the population in the age range of 15 to 64 (the *working-age population*). The dependency ratio for a population can be broken down into a *youth dependency ratio* (population below age 15 divided by population aged 15–64) and an *old age dependency ratio* (population aged 65 and over divided by population aged 15–64). Since both ratios are based on the same denominator, they can be added together to form the overall dependency ratio.

depopulation A reduction of the size of a population resulting from negative natural increase and/or negative net migration sustained over a period of time, or even indefinitely. Depopulation has been frequent throughout human history. In the past, famines, disease pandemics, natural disasters, and wars all contributed to depopulation of certain areas of the world. Some of these populations recovered while others eventually became extinct.

divorce The legal dissolution of a marriage.

divorce rate The rate at which couples legally dissolve their marriages in a given population. There are a variety of divorce rates, the crude divorce rate being the most basic. More refined measures include the age-specific divorce rate and the duration-specific divorce rate.

doubling time The number of years it takes a population to double its size, given the current rate of growth and assuming it remains constant. A quick approximation of doubling time is $70/r$, where r is the rate of growth of the population expressed as a percentage.

early neonatal mortality See *infant mortality*.

ecological footprint A measure of the impact of human activity on Earth's natural ecosystem.

emigration The migration of persons out of a country.

endogenous mortality See *exogenous mortality*.

epidemic A mass outbreak of a communicable disease in a particular locality, typically spreading slowly at first, then rapidly, and eventually disappearing, all within a relatively brief period of time. When this phenomenon spreads over a wide area it is referred to as a *pandemic*.

epidemiological transition A systematic description of the historical shift in disease and mortality patterns coinciding with societal modernization and demographic transition. The explanation—often described as a theory—includes three stages: the age of pestilence and famine, the age of receding pandemics, and the age of man-made and degenerative diseases. The generality of this description has been challenged in the recent demographic literature.

epidemiology The scientific study of the distribution and incidence of disease within and across populations and the factors that cause disease and its distribution.

exogenous mortality Deaths due to conditions external to the organism, including accidents, violence, and parasitic diseases. In contrast, *endogenous mortality* results from causes associated with aging and congenital defects—i.e., conditions originating within the organism itself at the genetic and molecular level that lead to deterioration or breakdown of vital organs and their functions. Exogenous causes are easier to prevent than are endogenous ones.

exponential growth A mathematical model that assumes a population is subject to a constant rate of growth, and that if the rate is positive the population will therefore increase without limit, while if the rate is negative, the population will decrease steadily. In actuality, no real population can sustain exponential growth indefinitely, and other mathematical models of growth (e.g., the logistic growth model) have been developed to take this into account.

family Two or more people related by birth, marriage, or adoption sharing a common residence. There are many types of families, two of which are the *nuclear family* (husband, wife, children) and the *extended family* (husband, wife, children, plus other kin).

family planning In a general sense, this is the exercise of conscious effort by couples or individuals to control the number and spacing of births. At the societal level, *family planning* refers to organized efforts by governments to provide the necessary means and services for couples to achieve the family size they desire and at the same time for the population to reduce its fertility rate.

fecundity The physiological capability of a woman, a man, or a couple to produce a live birth.

fertility In contrast to *fecundity*, *fertility* is the actual reproductive performance of an individual, a group, or a population. At the population level, fertility can be measured through a variety of indexes, including the crude birth rate, the gross reproduction rate, and the total fertility rate.

fertility transition A description of the pattern of a society's birth rate as it passes through socioeconomic modernization. Fertility transition theory is a subset of *demographic transition* theory.

fetal mortality The death of a fetus prior to its complete removal or expulsion from the mother, regardless of the length of the pregnancy. Fetal death includes miscarriages, abortions, and stillbirths.

gender The sociological significance and role expectations associated with being male or female in a society.

generation See *birth cohort*.

gravity model A mathematical description of the tendency for migration to decline with distance from a given origin and to be influenced by differential population sizes of places in a geographical system.

gross migration The total movement of migration for a specified territory (i.e., in-migration plus out-migration). In contrast, *net migration* is the difference between in- and out-migration for a given territory.

gross reproduction rate The average number of daughters born to a hypothetical cohort of mothers that experience the prevailing age-specific fertility rates of the population.

growth rate A rate that describes the change in population size between two points in time. There are several such rates, including the annualized percentage change, the geometric, and the exponential.

health transition A complementary explanation of *epidemiological transition*. While epidemiological transition focuses mostly on the shift in disease patterns over time, *health transition theory* incorporates a broader set of factors as responsible for epidemiological change, including the role of public health, government intervention, and medical and lifestyle changes at the population level.

Human Development Index An empirical measure developed by the United Nations to assess the level of overall well-being for a country's population. The index consists of three components: life expectancy, literacy, and national income per capita. The index ranges between 0 (no human development) and 1 (perfect human development). No country has ever scored 0 or 1, although some are close to these two extremes.

immigration The movement of people into a country for purposes of either permanent or temporary settlement.

infant mortality The death of live-born infants occurring in the first year of life. Infant mortality can be subdivided into three components: *early neonatal* (mortality in the first week of life); *late neonatal* (mortality in the first month of life) and *post-neonatal* (mortality in the first year of life). Demographers sometimes consider a fourth component, called *perinatal mortality*, consisting of late fetal deaths and early neonatal deaths.

infecundity The complete inability of a woman to conceive because of physiological impairments.

infertility The reduced ability to conceive and/or to carry a conception to term.

in-migration The movement of people into a receiving territory.

intermediate variables In fertility analysis, *intermediate variables* are those that are assumed to affect fertility directly and are intermediate to the influence of societal factors. For example, an increase in a society's average income may affect the birth rate only through one or more of the intermediate variables, which include the timing and extent of marriage of women, the extent to which contraception is used, the extent to which abortion is practised, and the duration of breastfeeding. The term has been replaced recently by an alternative term, the *proximate determinants of fertility*.

internal migration Migration within a given territory but involving the crossing of significant administrative boundaries (e.g., those of a city or province).

International Classification of Diseases A systematic list of diseases and causes of death established by the World Health Organization, used as a standard classification system throughout the world.

international migration The movement of people across national borders; these people are called *immigrants* by the receiving country.

intrinsic rate of natural increase A population that has been subjected to constant age-specific schedules of mortality and fertility over many years and that is closed to migration will eventually converge to a stable population. The difference between the stable birth and death rates in this population is the intrinsic rate of natural increase (or intrinsic growth rate).

late neonatal mortality See *infant mortality*.

life expectancy The average number of remaining years to live for a group of persons reaching a certain age, subject to a set of specified death rates at each age.

life span   The maximum number of years a person can be expected to live under ideal circumstances. This is different than the average life span, which is a measure of the longevity of a population (e.g., life expectancy at birth). Life span is a variable concept in the sense that it is not fixed. Currently, the maximum life span for humans is 122, the age at death of Jeanne Calment, who is known as the longest-lived human.

life table   A statistical table that displays the mortality and survival probabilities of a population by age. A number of measures are derived from the life table, including *life expectancy*.

logistic growth   A mathematical model of population growth characterized by an S-shaped curve, denoting slow population growth initially, followed by a period of rapid growth and then finally, once the population approaches a maximum level, decreasing rates of growth.

marital status   The status of individuals with regard to marriage, as measured in the census and vital statistics system.

marriage cohort   See *cohort*.

maternal mortality   Deaths to women arising from conditions and causes connected with pregnancy and childbearing.

mean age of population   The arithmetic average age of the population. This measure is usually not the ideal indicator of average age of population because of its sensitivity to extreme values.

median age   The age that is greater than the age of one half of the population and lower than the other half. This measure is usually preferred to the mean, or arithmetic average, age because it is not affected by extreme values.

megacity   An urban agglomeration of 10 million persons or more.

megalopolis   A large, almost contiguous, and densely populated urban system that extends beyond metropolitan urban agglomerations. In a more general sense, the term refers to the integration of large urban agglomerations into an even higher order of urban structure and complexity. An example of megalopolis is the Eastern Seaboard and St Lawrence–Great Lakes urban system that straddles eastern United States and eastern Canada.

metropolitan area   A term used to describe a very large interconnected urban settlement. Specific definitions and criteria as to what exactly constitute a metropolitan area vary across countries.

mid-year population   The size of the population at the midpoint of a calendar year. The mid-year population is used as the denominator in the computation of central rates of demographic processes.

migration   The movement of individuals or groups of people involving a permanent or semi-permanent change of residence. The general term *mobility* is used to denote all forms of geographical movements, irrespective of whether they are permanent or temporary.

momentum of population   The increase or decrease in population size that would ultimately occur if fertility in a population changed immediately to the level at which it would just ensure the replacement of the generations.

morbidity   The state of illness and disability in a population as reflected by statistics based on causes of death and other health status indicators. Several epidemiological measures are used to study the frequency, duration, and severity of illness in a population (e.g., prevalence, disability, and case fatality rates, among others).

mortality   The aggregate incidence and number of deaths in a population at specified periods.

natural fertility   Fertility that prevails in underdeveloped societies (e.g., pre-industrial) characterized by the absence of conscious planning of births by couples.

natural increase   The excess of births over deaths in a population.

neo-Malthusians   Contemporary followers of Malthus, who believe that population growth must be controlled; unlike Malthus himself, they advocate the use of birth control (including contraception and even induced abortion) to reduce population growth rates.

neo-Marxists Contemporary followers of Marx, who believe that population growth is an issue of secondary concern to such problems as poverty and inequality in the world.

neonatal mortality Deaths to live-born babies during the first month of life (see *infant mortality*).

net migration The difference between in- and out-migration for a given territory (compare *gross migration*).

net reproduction rate It is the same as the gross reproduction rate, but it further assumes that there is some risk of mortality to women in the reproductive ages.

nuclear family See *family*.

nuptiality A sub area of demographic study that focuses on the frequency, characteristics and dissolution of unions (e.g., marriages) in a population. The close connection between nuptiality and fertility makes this an important area of demographic analysis.

old age dependency ratio See *dependency ratio*.

optimum population The ideal size of population that would make it possible for a society to achieve a particular set of objectives (e.g., economic growth, social stability, etc.).

out-migration The movement of people out of a given territory.

overpopulation A concept referring to an excess of population in a given territory in relation to the level of resources available.

pandemic An epidemic that spreads beyond a local area to a very wide area or territory, for example the 1918–19 influenza pandemic, thought to have been responsible for the deaths of between 20 and 50 million people worldwide.

perinatal mortality According to the World Health Organization, deaths that occur during the last stage of pregnancy (late fetal deaths) plus deaths in the first week of life (see *infant mortality*).

period fertility See *cohort fertility*.

period total fertility rate See *cohort fertility*.

population A collectivity of people in a particular geographic territory at a particular point in time.

population aging The transformation of a population's age structure over time such that there is an increasing proportion of people in the older age categories and a declining proportion in the younger age categories.

population density The relative concentration of population in specified geographic areas.

population explosion A term used to describe the dramatic rise of the world's population in modern history.

population growth The increase or decrease of the population over time as a result of the interplay of births, deaths, and migration.

population policy An objective plan devised and implemented by governments to affect population change in a desired direction.

population projection The estimate of population trends into the future, produced under varying assumptions regarding changes in fertility, mortality, and migration.

population pyramid See *age–sex pyramid*.

population register A form of continuous data collection maintained at a community level in some countries for the purposes of tracking demographic events in the population (births, deaths, migration, marriages, divorces) as well as the socioeconomic characteristics of the population. Relatively few countries maintain population registers. Most countries have vital statistics registration systems to record births, deaths, marriages, and divorces, as well as periodic censuses.

post-neonatal mortality See *infant mortality*.

prevalence of a disease The percentage of people in the population who have a particular disease at a specified point in time.

primary sterility See *sterility*.

probability of dying The conditional risk of death, given one's age, sex, and other characteristics (e.g., marital status) under prevailing mortality rates as reflected in the population's life table.

proportion A type of ratio in which the denominator includes the numerator (e.g., the ratio of males to the total population).

proximate determinants of fertility See *intermediate variables*.

rate A measure used (in demography) to quantify the intensity of a demographic event, such as the frequency of death or birth over a specified interval of time in relation to the population at risk of experiencing the event in question (typically the mid-year population).

ratio A statistic expressing the relative size of numbers in a numerator (e.g., the number of males) and a denominator (e.g., the number of females), the two being unrelated to each other.

replacement fertility The fertility level that a population must achieve, given its mortality level, to replace itself in the long term. The usual replacement rate is 2.1 children per woman, but this figure would need to be adjusted upwards in contexts where female death rates are high.

secondary sterility See *sterility*.

sex ratio The balance of men to women in a population or within an age category, expressed as the ratio of males to females multiplied by 100.

stable population A population closed to migration and with unchanging age-specific death and fertility rates, which ultimately converges to an unchanging age–sex structure, thus either increasing or decreasing in size at a constant rate (i.e., the intrinsic rate of natural increase).

standardization A technique applied to allow data to be compared across different populations. This method involves making adjustments for the confounding effects of compositional differences (e.g., age composition) across the study populations. In the analysis of mortality, there are two types of standardization: direct and indirect. Although they assume different conditions, both direct and indirect standardization adjust crude death rates in order to remove the confounding effect of differences in age composition in order to allow a comparison of death rates across the different study populations.

stationary population A stable population that has a constant intrinsic rate of natural increase equal to zero. In the life table, the L_x column is a stationary population.

sterility The inability of a woman, a man, or a couple to conceive. In the case of *primary sterility*, a woman has never been able to conceive; *secondary sterility* occurs after a woman has given birth to at least one child.

total fertility rate The average number of children born to women in the childbearing ages at a specific point in time. It is the sum of age-specific fertility rates for a given period over the whole range of reproductive ages (15–49). This measure can be interpreted as the number of children a woman would have during her lifetime is she were to experience the age-specific fertility rates in the given period of observation.

urbanization The process by which the population concentration intensifies in localities defined by a country as 'urban'. The criteria for what constitutes urban vary considerably across countries: in Canada an urban area is a territory with a population of at least 1,000 and a population density of at least 400 persons per square kilometre; in the United States, 'urban area' includes any densely populated places of 2,500 or more.

vital statistics system Also known as a vital registration system, this is a legal structure established by a government for the continuous registration of births, deaths, marriages, and divorces in a country. These data are routinely published by the official statistical bureaus of countries.

working-age population See *dependency ratio*.

youth dependency ratio See *dependency ratio*.

References

Aarssen, Karin, and Laurens de Haan. 1994. 'On the Maximal Life Span of Humans', *Mathematical Population Studies* 4, 4: 259–81.

Aarssen, Lonnie W. 2005. 'Why Is Fertility Lower in Wealthier Countries? The Role of Relaxed Fertility-Selection', *Population and Development Review* 31, 1: 113–26.

Abley, Mark, ed. 1999. *Stories from the Ice Storm*. Toronto: McClelland and Stewart.

———. 1998. *The Ice Storm*. Toronto: McClelland and Stewart.

Agadjanian, Victor, and Ndola Prata. 2002. 'War, Peace, and Fertility in Angola', *Demography* 39, 2: 215–31.

Agnihotri, Satish Balram. 2001. 'Rising Sons and Setting Daughters: Provisional Results of the 2001 Census', in Vina Masumdar and N. Krishnaji, eds, *Enduring Conundrum: India's Sex Ratio: Essays in Honour of Asok Mitra*. Noida, Uttar Pradesh, India: Rainbow.

———. 2000. *Sex Ratio Patterns in the Indian Population: A Fresh Exploration*. New Delhi: Sage.

Aguirie, A. Alonso, Mary C. Pearl, and Jonathan Patz. 2004. 'Urban Expansion Impacts on the Health of Ecosystems, Wildlife and Humans', <http://www.populationenviron mentresearch.org> (29 November–15 December 2004).

Ahlburg, Dennis A. 1998. 'Julian Simon and the Population Growth Debate', *Population and Development Review* 24, 2: 317–27.

———, Allen C. Kelley, and Karen Oppenheim Mason. 1996. 'Editors' Introduction', in Dennis A. Ahlburg, Allen C. Kelley, and Karen Oppenheim Mason, eds, *The Impact of Population Growth on Well-Being in Developing Countries*. Berlin: Springer.

———, and M.O. Schapiro. 1984. 'Socioeconomic Ramifications of Changing Cohort Size: An Analysis of US Postwar Suicide Rates by Age and Sex', *Demography* 21, 1: 97–108.

Aird, John. 1990. *Slaughter of the Innocents*. Washington, DC: American Enterprise Institute.

Akers, Donald S. 1967. 'On Measuring the Marriage Squeeze', *Demography* 4: 907–24.

Albert, Mark. 1998. 'Where Have all the Boys Gone?', *Scientific American*, <http://www.sciam.com> (17 July).

Aligica, Paul Dragos. 2007. *Prophecies of Doom and Scenarios of Progress: Herman Kahn, Julian Simon, and the Prospective Imagination*. New York: Continuum International.

Allan, B.B., R. Brant, J.E. Seidel, et al. 1997. 'Declining Sex Ratios in Canada', *Canadian Medical Association Journal* 156, 1: 37–41.

Allard, Michel, Victor Lebre, Jean-Marie Robine, and Jean Calment. 1998. *Jeanne Calment: From Van Gogh's Time to Ours: 122 Extraordinary Years*. New York: W.H. Freeman.

Alter, George. 2004. 'Height, Frailty, and the Standard of Living: Modelling the Effects of Diet and Disease on Declining Mortality and Increasing Height', *Population Studies* 58, 3: 265–79.

Anderson, Barbara A. 2003. 'Russia Faces Depopulation? Dynamics of Population Decline', *Population and Environment* 23, 5: 437–64.

———, and Brian D. Silver. 1989. 'Patterns of Cohort Mortality in the Soviet Population', *Population and Development Review* 15, 3: 471–502.

Anderson, I.B. 1966. *Internal Migration in Canada, 1921–1961*. Economic Council of Canada, Staff Study no. 13. Ottawa: Queen's Printer.

Anderson, Margo J. 2003. 'Census', in Paul Demeny and Geoffrey McNicoll, eds, *Encyclopedia of Population*, vol. 1. New York: Macmillan Reference USA/Thomson Gale.

———, and Stephen E. Fienberg. 1999. *Who Counts? The Politics of Census-Taking in Contemporary America*. New York: Russell Sage Foundation.

Anderssen, E. 1998. 'Canada's Squalid Secret: Life on Native Reserves', *The Globe and Mail* (12 October): A1, A3.

Andorka, Rudolph. 1978. *Determinants of Fertility in Advanced Societies*. London: Methuen.

Antonovsky, Aaron. 1967. 'Social Class, Life Expectancy and Overall Mortality', *The Milbank Quarterly* 45, 4: 151–93.

———, and Judith Bernstein. 1977. 'Social Class and Infant Mortality', *Social Science and Medicine* 11: 453–70.

Ariès, Philippe. 1980. 'Two Successive Motivations for Declining Birth Rates in the West', *Population and Development Review* 6: 645–50.

———. 1974. *Western Attitudes Toward Death: From the Middle Ages to the Present*. Trans. Patricia M. Ranum. Baltimore, MD: Johns Hopkins University Press.

———. 1960. 'Interprétations pour une histoire des mentalités', in Hélène Berques et al., *La Prévention des naissances dans la famille: ses origines dans les temps modernes*. National Institute for Demographic Studies, monograph no. 35. Paris: Presses Universitaires de France.

Arking, Robert. 2002. 'Aging: A Biological Perspective', *American Scientist* 91 (November–December): 508–15.

Attané, Isabelle. 2002. 'China's Family Planning Policy: An Overview of its Past and Future', *Studies in Family Planning* 33, 1.

Audette, Trish. 2007. 'Census 2006. Mini Baby Boom on Base Mirrors Rest of Alberta: Province Retains Title as Country's Top Baby Producer', *Edmonton Journal* (13 September): A2.

Auerbach, Felix. 1913. 'Das Gesetz der Bevoelkerungskoncentration', *Petermanns Geographische Mitteilungen* 59: 74–6.

Aydemir, Abdurrahman, and George J. Borjas. 2006. 'A Comparative Analysis of the Labor Market Impact of International Migration: Canada, Mexico, and the United States'. National Bureau of Economic Research, Working Papers, <http://www.nber.org/papers/w12327.pdf>.

Bach, R.L., and J. Smith. 1977. 'Community Satisfaction, Expectations of Moving, and Migration', *Demography* 14: 147–67.

Bachman, Ronet. 1992. *Death and Violence on the Reservation: Homicide, Family Violence, and Suicide in American Indian Populations*. New York: Auburn House.

Bagozzi, Richard P., and M. Frances Van Loo. 1978a. 'Toward a General Theory of Fertility: A Causal Modeling Approach', *Demography* 15: 301–20.

———, and ———. 1978b. 'Fertility as Consumption: Theories from the Behavioral Sciences', *Journal of Consumer Research* 4 (March): 199–228.

Bailey, Adrian J., Megan K. Blake, and Thomas J. Cooke. 2004. 'Migration, Care, and the Linked Lives of Dual-Earner Households', *Environment and Planning A* 36: 1617–32.

Balakrishnan, T.R., George E. Ebanks, and Carl F. Grindstaff. 1979. *Patterns of Fertility in Canada, 1971*. Cat. no. 99-759. Ottawa: Statistics Canada.

———, Karol J. Krotki, and Evelyn Lapierre-Adamczyk. 1993. *Family and Childbearing in Canada: A Demographic Analysis*. Toronto: University of Toronto Press.

Balter, Michael. 2005. *The Goddess and the Bull*. New York: Free Press.

———. 2001. 'In Search of the First Europeans', *Science* 291, 5509 (2 March): 1722–5.

———. 1998. 'Why Settle Down? The Mystery of Communities', *Science* 282 (20 November): 1442–7.

Bandarage, Asoka. 1997. *Women, Population and Global Crisis: A Political Economy Analysis*. London: Zed Books.

Banister, Judith, and Ansley J. Coale. 1994. 'Five Decades of Missing Females in China', *Demography* 31: 459–79.

Barash, David P., and Judith Eve Lipton. 2001. *The Myth of Monogamy: Fertility and Infertility in Animals and People*. New York: W.H. Freeman.

Barker, D.J.P. 2003. 'Editorial: The Developmental Origins of Adult Disease', *European Journal of Epidemiology* 18: 733–6.

Barkley, George W. 1958. *Techniques of Population Analysis*. New York: John Wiley & Sons.

Barnes, Trevor J., John H. Britton, W.J. Coffey, et al. 2000. 'Canadian Geography at the Millennium', *The Canadian Geographer* 44, 1: 4–24.

Barro, Robert J. 1997. *Determinants of Economic Growth: A Cross-Country Empirical Study*. Cambridge, MA: MIT Press.

———, and Sala-i-Martin. 2004. *Economic Growth*, 2nd edn. Cambridge, MA: MIT Press.

Barsotti, Odo. 1985. 'Cause e Effetti Della Immigrazione Regionale', in Alberto Bonaguidi, ed., *Migrazioni e Demografia Regionale in Italia*. Milano: Franco Angeli.

Bartecchi, Carl F., Thomas D. MacKenzie, and R.W. Schrier. 1994. 'The Human Costs of Tobacco Use: Part I', *New England Journal of Medicine* 330, 13: 907–12.

Bartel, A.P. 1989. 'Where Do New Immigrants Live?', *Journal of Labor Economics* 7: 371–91.

Barzun, Jacques. 2001. *From Dawn to Decadence: 500 Years of Western Cultural Life 1500 to the Present*. New York: Harper Perennial.

Basavarajappa, K.G., and Bali Ram. 1983. 'Population and Migration', in F.H. Leacy, ed., *Historical Statistics of Canada*. Ottawa: Statistics Canada.

Beale, Calvin L. 1977 [1996]. 'The Recent Shift of United States Population to Nonmetropolitan Areas, 1970–75', in H.S. Geyer and T.M. Kontuly, eds, *Differential Urbanization: Integrating Spatial Models*. London: Edward Arnold.

———. 1975. 'The Revival of Population Growth in Nonmetropolitan America', ERS 605. Washington, DC: United States Department of Agriculture.

Bean, Frank D., Barry Edmonston, and Jeffrey S. Passel. 1990. 'Introduction', in Frank D. Bean, Barry Edmonston, and Jeffrey S. Passel, eds, *Undocumented Migration to the United States: IRCA and the Experience of the 1980s*. Santa Monica, CA: RAND Corporation.

Beaujot, Roderic. 2000. *Earning and Caring in Canadian Families*. Toronto: Broadview.

———. 1995. 'Family Patterns at Mid-Life (Marriage, Parenting and Working)', in Jean Dumas, ed., *Family Over the Life Course: Current Demographic Analysis*. Cat. no. 91-543-E. Ottawa: Statistics Canada.

———. 1990. 'The Challenge of Changing Demographics', *Policy Options/Options Politiques* (December): 19–22.

———. 1978. 'Canada's Population: Growth and Dualism', *Population Bulletin* 33, 2. Washington, DC: Population Reference Bureau.

———, and Don Kerr. 2004. *Population Change in Canada*, 2nd edn. Don Mills, ON: Oxford University Press.

———, Karol J. Krotki, and P. Krishnan. 1978. 'Socio-Cultural Variations in the Applicability of the Economic Model of Fertility', *Population Studies* 32, 2: 319–25.

———, and Kevin McQuillan. 1982a. *Growth and Dualism: The Demographic Development of Canadian Society*. Toronto: Gage.

———, and ———. 1982b. 'The Population of Canada Before Confederation', in Roderic Beaujot and Kevin McQuillan, *Growth and Dualism: The Demographic Development of Canadian Society*. Toronto: Gage.

———, Zenaida Ravanera, and Thomas K. Burch. 2005. 'Toward an SDC (Social Development Canada) Family Research Framework'. Issues Paper for Social

Development Canada Roundtable on Families (1–2 December 2005).

Beaver, M.W. 1975. 'Population, Infant Mortality and Milk', *Population Studies* 27, 2: 243–54.

Becker, Gary S. 1992. 'Fertility and the Economy', *Journal of Population and Economics* 5: 185–201.

———. 1991. *A Treatise on the Family*, enlarged edn. Cambridge, MA: Harvard University Press.

———. 1974. 'A Theory of Marriage: Part II', *Journal of Political Economy* 82: S11–26.

———. 1973. 'A Theory of Marriage: Part I', *Journal of Political Economy* 81, 4: 813–46.

———. 1960. 'An Economic Analysis of Fertility', in *Demographic and Economic Change in Developed Countries*. A Conference of the Universities, National Bureau Committee for Economic Research, Special Conference Series 11. Princeton, NJ: Princeton University Press.

———, Elisabeth M. Landes, and Robert T. Michael. 1977. 'An Economic Analysis of Marital Instability', *Journal of Political Economy* 85, 6: 1141–87.

Beckstead, Desmond, Mark Brown, G. Gellatly, and C. Seaborn. 2003. *A Decade of Growth: The Emerging Geography of New Economy Industries in the 1990s*. The Canadian Economy in Transition Research Paper Series 11-622-MIE2003003. Analytical Studies Branch. Ottawa: Statistics Canada.

Bedard, Mario, and Margaret Michalowski. 1997. *Advantages of the One Year Mobility Variable for Breaking Down Interprovincial Migration by Age, Sex and Marital Status*. Cat. no. 91F0015MIE1997004. Ottawa: Statistics Canada.

Beenstock, M. 1999. 'Internal Migration by Immigrants in the Short-Run: Israel 1992–1994', *International Migration Review* 33, 4: 1098–1106.

Behiels, Michael D. 1986. *Prelude to Quebec's Quiet Revolution*. Montreal and Kingston: McGill-Queen's University Press.

Behrens, T. 2003. 'Allergic Disease and the Pre- and Perinatal Environment', *European Journal of Epidemiology* 8: 739–741.

Beier, George J. 1976. 'Can Third World Cities Cope?', *Population Bulletin* 31, 4. Washington: Population Reference Bureau.

Bélanger, Alain. 2006. *Report on the Demographic Situation in Canada: 2003 and 2004*. Cat. no. 91-209-XIE. Ottawa: Statistics Canada.

———. 2003. *Report on the Demographic Situation in Canada: 2002*. Cat. no. 91-209-XPE. Ottawa: Statistics Canada.

———. 2002. *Report on the Demographic Situation in Canada: 2001*. Cat. no. 91-209-XPE. Ottawa: Statistics Canada.

———, and Eric Caron-Malenfant. 2006. 'The Fertility of Visible Minority Women', in Alain Bélanger, ed., *Report on the Demographic Situation in Canada 2003 and 2004*. Cat. no. 91-209-XIE. Ottawa: Statistics Canada.

———, and Jean Dumas. 1998. *Report on the Demographic Situation in Canada: 1997*. Cat. no. 91-209-XPE. Ottawa: Statistics Canada.

———, Laurent Martel, and Eric Caron-Malenfant. 2006. *Population Projections for Canada, Provinces and Territories 2005–2031*. Cat. no. 91-520-XIE. Ottawa: Statistics Canada.

———, and Geneviève Ouellet. 2002. 'A Comparative Study of Recent Trends in Canadian and American Fertility, 1980–1999', in Alain Bélanger, *Report on the Demographic Situation in Canada in 2001*. Cat. no. 91-209-XPE. Ottawa: Statistics Canada.

Bell, Martin. 2001. 'Understanding Circulation in Australia', *Journal of Population Research* 18, 1: 1–18.

Bellis, Mark A., Tom Hennell, Clare Lushey, et al. 2007. 'Elvis to Eminem: Quantifying the Price of Fame Through Early Mortality of European and North American Rock and Pop Stars', *Journal of Epidemiology and Community Health* 61: 896–901.

Benjamin, B. 1965. *Social and Economic Factors Affecting Mortality*. The Hague and Paris: Mouton.

Berelson, Bernard. 1979. 'Romania's 1966 Abortion Decree: The Demographic Experience of the First Decade', *Population Studies* 33, 2: 205–22.

———. 1969. 'Beyond Family Planning', *Studies in Family Planning* 38 (February): 1–16.

———, Shireen J. Jejeebhoy, Allen C. Kelly, et al. 1990. 'The Great Debate on Population Policy: An Instructive Entertainment', *International Family Planning Perspectives* 16, 4: 126–48.

———, and Jonathan Lieberson. 1979. 'Government Efforts to Influence Fertility: The Ethical Issues', *Population and Development Review* 54, 4: 581–614.

Bergeron, Leandre. 1975. *The History of Quebec: A Patriot's Handbook*. Toronto: NC Press.

Bergob, Michael J. 1992. 'Where Have all the Old Folks Gone? Interprovincial Migration of the Elderly in Canada: 1981–1986', *Canadian Studies in Population* 19, 1: 17–25.

Berkman, Lisa F., and Lester Breslow. 1983. *Health and Ways of Living: The Alameda County Study*. New York: Oxford University Press.

———, and Leonard S. Syme. 1979. 'Social Networks, Host Resistance and Mortality: A Nine Year Follow-up Study of Alameda County Residents', *American Journal of Epidemiology* 109, 2: 186–204.

Bernhardt, Darren. 2004. 'NHL Lockout Could Spawn a Baby Boom', *National Post* (26 November): A2.

Bernhardt, Eva. 2003. 'Cohabitation', in Paul Demeney and Geoffrey McNicol, eds, *Encyclopedia of Population*. New York: Macmillan Reference USA/Thomson Gale.

Berry, Brian J.L. 1976 [1996]. 'The Counterurbanisation Process: Urban America Since 1970', in H.S. Geyer and T.M. Kontuly, eds, *Differential Urbanization: Integrating Spatial Models*. London: Edward Arnold.

Berry, Linda G. 1977. 'Age and Parity Influences on Maternal Mortality: United States, 1919–1969', *Demography* 14, 3: 297–310.

Berton, Pierre. 1971. *The Last Spike: The Great Railway 1881–1885*. Toronto: McClelland and Stewart.

Bertram, Gordon W. 1963. 'Economic Growth in Canadian Industry, 1870–1915: The Staple Model and the Take-Off Hypothesis', *The Canadian Journal of Economics and Political Science* 29, 2: 159–84.

Beshiri, R., and Ray D. Bollman. 2001. 'Population Structure and Change in Predominantly Rural Regions', *Rural and Small Town Canada Analysis Bulletin*. Cat. no. 21-006-0XIE, no. 2.

Bezanson, Kate. 2006. *Gender, the State, and Social Reproduction*. Toronto: University of Toronto Press.

Bhagwati, Jagdish. 2002. *Free Trade Today*. Princeton, NJ: Princeton University Press.

———. 2000. *The Wind of the Hundred Days*. Cambridge, MA: MIT Press.

Bhat, Mari P.N., and Shiva S. Halli. 1999. 'Demography of Brideprice and Dowry: Causes and Consequences of the Indian Marriage Squeeze', *Population Studies* 53, 2: 129–48.

Bielby, W.T., and D.D. Bielby. 1992. 'I Will Follow Him: Family Ties, Gender-Role Beliefs, and Reluctance to Relocate for a Better Job', *American Journal of Sociology* 97, 5: 1241–67.

Biggar, Jeanne C. 1979. 'The Sunning of America: Migration to the Sunbelt', *Population Bulletin* 34, 1. Washington: Population Reference Bureau.

Biggs, Brian, and Ray D. Bollman. 1994. 'Urbanization in Canada', *Canadian Social Trends*, 2: 67–72. Toronto: Thompson.

Billari, Francesco, and Hans-Peter Kohler. 2004. 'Patterns of Low and Lowest-Low Fertility in Europe', *Population Studies* 58, 2: 161–76.

Bilsborrow, R.E., ed. 1996. 'The State of the Art and Overview of the Chapters', in Richard E. Bilsborrow, ed., *Migration, Urbanization, and Development: New Directions and Issues*. New York: United Nations Population Fund and Kluwer Academic Publishers.

———, G. Hugo, A.S. Oberai, and H. Zlotnik. 1997. *International Migration Statistics: Guidelines for Improving Data Collection Systems*. Geneva: International Labour Office.

Biraben, Jean Noel. 2003a. 'The Rising Numbers of Humankind', *Population and Societies* 394 (October). Also available at <http://www.ined.fr/englishversion/publications/pop_et_soc/index.html>.

———. 2003b. 'World Population Growth', in Paul Demeny and Geoffrey McNicoll, eds, *Encyclopedia of Population*. New York: Macmillan Reference USA/Thomson Gale.

———. 1979. 'Essai sur l'Évolution du nombre des hommes', *Population* 34, 1: 13–25.

Birdsall, Nancy, Allen C. Kelley, and Steven Sinding, eds. 2001. *Population Matters: Demographic Change, Economic Growth, and Poverty in the Developing World*. Oxford: Oxford University Press.

———, and Steven W. Sinding. 2001. 'How and Why Population Matters: New Findings, New Issues', in Nancy Birdsall, Allen C. Kelley, and Steven W. Sinding, eds, *Population Matters: Demographic Change, Economic Growth, and Poverty in the Developing World*. Oxford: Oxford University Press.

Birg, Herwig. 1995. *World Population Projections for the 21st Century: Theoretical Interpretations and Quantitative Simulations*. Frankfurt and New York: Campus Verlag and St Martin's.

Blake, Judith. 1969. 'Population Policy for Americans: Is the Government Being Misled?', *Science* 164, 3879: 522–9.

———. 1968. 'Are Babies Consumer Durables?', *Population Studies* 22, 1: 5–25.

Blankenhorn, David. 2007. *The Future of Marriage*. New York: Encounter Books.

Blauner, Robert. 1966. 'Death and Social Structure', *Psychiatry* 29: 378–394.

Bloom, David E., and David Canning. 2001. 'Cumulative Causality, Economic Growth, and the Demographic Transition', in Nancy Birdsall, Allen C. Kelley, and Steven W. Sinding, eds, *Population Matters: Demographic Change, Economic Growth, and Poverty in the Developing World*. Oxford: Oxford University Press.

———, ———, and Jaypee Sevilla. 2003. 'The Demographic Dividend: A New Perspective on the Economic Consequences of Population Change', *Population Matters: A RAND Program Policy-Relevant Research Communication*. Santa Monica, CA: RAND Corporation.

———, and Jeffrey G. Williamson. 1998. 'Demographic Transitions and Economic Miracles in Emerging Asia', *The World Bank Economic Review* 12,3: 419–55.

Bobadilla, José Luis, and Christine A. Costello. 1997. 'Premature Death in the New Independent States: An Overview', in José Luis Bobadilla, Christine A. Costello, and Faith Mitchell, eds, *Premature Death in the New Independent States*. Washington, DC: National Academies Press.

Bobak, Martin, and Arjan Gjonca. 2001. 'The Seasonality of Live Birth is Strongly Influenced by Socio-Demographic Factors', *Human Reproduction* 16, 7: 1512–17.

Bogardus, Emory S. 1960. *The Development of Social Thought*, 4th edn. New York: David McKay.

Bogue, Donald J. 1969. *Principles of Demography*. New York: John Wiley.

Bollman, Ray D. 2000. *Rural and Small Town Canada: An Overview*. <http://www.statcan.ca:8096/bsolc/english/bsolc?catno=21F0018X&CHROPG=1>.

———, and Brian Biggs. 1994. 'Rural and Small Town Canada: An Overview', in Ray D. Bollman and Brian Biggs, eds, *Rural and Small Town Canada*. Toronto: Thompson.

———, and ———, eds. 1992. *Rural and Small Town Canada*. Toronto: Thompson.

Bonaguidi, Alberto, ed. 1985. *Migrazioni e Demografia Regionale in Italia*. Milano: Franco Angeli.

Bongaarts, John. 2006a. 'Late Marriage and the HIV Epidemic in Sub-Saharan Africa'. Policy Research Division, Working Papers, 2006, no. 216. New York: Population Council.

———. 2006b. 'How Long Will We Live?' *Population and Development Review* 32, 4: 605–28.

———. 2004. 'Population Aging and the Rising Cost of Public Pensions', *Population and Development Review* 30, 1: 1–24.

———. 2003. 'Proximate Determinants of Fertility', in Paul Demeny and Geoffrey McNicoll, eds, *Encyclopedia of Population*. New York: Macmillan Reference USA/ Thomson Gale.

———. 1998. 'Demographic Consequences of Declining Fertility', *Science* 282 (16 October): 419–20.

———. 1994. 'Population Policy Options in the Developing World', *Science* 263 (11 February): 771–6.

———. 1978. 'A Framework for Analyzing the Proximate Determinants of Fertility', *Population and Development Review* 4, 1: 105–32.

———. 1975. 'Why High Birth Rates Are so Low', *Population and Development Review* 1, 2: 289–96.

———, and Rodolfo A. Bulatao, eds. 2000. *Beyond Six Billion: Forecasting the World's Population*. Washington, DC: National Academies Press.

———, and Susan Cotts Watkins. 1996. 'Social Interactions and Contemporary Fertility Transitions', *Population and Development Review* 22, 4: 639–82.

———, and Griffith Feeney. 2002. 'How Long Do We Live?', *Population and Development Review* 28, 1: 13–29.

———, and ———. 1998. 'On the Quantum and Tempo of Fertility', *Population and Development Review* 24, 2: 271–92.

———, and Susan Greenhalgh. 1985. 'An Alternative to the One-Child Policy in China', *Population and Development Review* 11, 4: 585–618.

———, W. Parker Mauldin, and James F. Philips. 1990. 'The Demographic Impact of Family Planning Programs', *Studies in Family Planning* 21, 6: 299–310.

———, and Robert G. Potter. 1983. *Fertility, Biology, and Behavior: An Analysis of the Proximate Determinants*. New York: Academic Press.

Bonita, Ruth, and Robert Beaglehole. 1989. 'Increased Treatment of Hypertension Does Not Explain the Decline in Stroke Mortality in the United States, 1970–1980', *Hypertension* 13 (Supplement I): I-69–I-73.

Bonney, Norman, Alison McCleery, and Emma Forster. 1999. 'Migration, Marriage and the Life Course: Commitment and Residential Mobility', in Paul Boyle and Keith Halfcree, eds, *Migration and Gender in the Developed World*. London: Routledge.

Booth, Alan, David R. Johnson, Lynn White, et al. 1984. 'Women, Outside Employment, and Marital Instability', *American Journal of Sociology* 90: 567–83.

Booth, Frank W., and P. Darrell Neufer. 2005. 'Exercise Controls Gene Expression', *American Scientist* 93 (January–February): 28–35.

Borjas, George J. 1999. *Heaven's Door: Immigration Policy and the American Economy*. Princeton, NJ: Princeton University Press.

Boserup, Ester. 1981. *Population and Technological Change: A Study of Long-Term Trends*. Chicago: The University of Chicago Press.

———. 1965. *The Conditions of Agricultural Growth*. Chicago: Aldine.

Bourbeau, Robert, Jacques Légaré, and Valerie Émond. 1997. *New Birth Cohort Life Tables for Canada and Quebec, 1801–1991*. Current Demographic Analysis no. 3. Cat. no. 91F0015MPE. Ottawa: Statistics Canada.

Bourgeois-Pichat, Jean. 1986. 'The Unprecedented Shortage of Births in Europe', *Population and Development Review* 12 (supp.): 3–25.

Bourgeois-Pichat, M.J. 1952. 'Essai sur la mortalité "biologique" de l' homme', *Population* 3 (July–September): 381–94.

———. 1951 [1981]. 'Measuring Infant Mortality'. *Population* (Selected Papers no. 6). Paris: National Institute of Population Studies.

Bourne, Larry S. 2000. 'Urban Canada in Transition to the Twenty-First Century: Trends, Issues, and Visions', in Trudi Bunting and Pierre Filion, eds, *Canadian Cities in Transition: The Twenty-First Century*. Don Mills, ON: Oxford University Press.

———, and A.E. Olvet. 1995. *New Urban and Regional Geographies in Canada: 1986–91 and Beyond*. Major Report 33. Toronto: Centre for Urban and Community Studies.

———, and Damaris Rose. 2001. 'The Changing Face of Canada: The Uneven Geographies of Population and Social Change', *The Canadian Geographer* 45, 1: 105–19.

Boyd, Monica. 1990. 'Family and Personal Network in International Migration: Recent Developments and New Agendas', *International Migration Review* 23, 3: 638–70.

———, and Michael Vickers. 2000. '100 Years of Immigration in Canada', *Canadian Social Trends* (pp. 2–12). Cat. no. 11-008. Ottawa: Statistics Canada.

Boyle, Paul, Keith Halfcree, and Dareen Smith. 1999. 'Family Migration and Female Participation in the Labour Market: Moving Beyond Individual-Level Analyses', in Paul Boyle and Keith Halfcree, eds, *Migration and Gender in the Developed World*. London: Routledge.

Bozon, Michel. 2003. 'At What Age do Women and Men Have Their First Sexual Intercourse? World Comparisons and Recent Trends', *Population & Societies*, no. 391 (June): 3. INED <http://www.ined.fr/english version/pop_et_soc/index.html>.

Brackman, S., H. Garretsen, C. Van Marrewijk, et al. 1999. 'The Return of Zipf: Towards a Further Understanding of the Rank-Size Distribution', *Journal of Regional Science* 39: 183–213.

Braudel, Fernand. 1979. *Civilization and Capitalism, 15th–18th Centuries*. 3 vols. Trans. Siân Reynolds. Vol. 1: *The Structures of Everyday Life*; vol. 2: *The Wheels of Commerce*; vol. 3: *The Perspective of the World*. New York: Harper and Row.

———. 1966. *The Mediterranean and the Mediterranean World in the Age of Philip II*, vol. 1. Berkley: University of California Press.

Braziel, Jana Evans, and Anita Mannur, eds. 2003. *Theorizing Diaspora: A Reader*. Malden, MA: Blackwell.

Breslow, Lester. 1985. 'The Case of Cardiovascular Diseases', in Jacques Vallin and Alan D. Lopez, eds, *Health Policy, Social Policy and Mortality Prospects*. Paris: Institut National d'Etudes Demographiques and International Union for the Scientific Study of Population.

Breton, Raymond. 1964. 'Institutional Completeness of Ethnic Communities and the Personal Relations of Immigrants', *American Journal of Sociology* 70: 193–205.

Brewis, Alexandra, and Mary Meyer. 2005. 'Marital Coitus Across the Life Course', *Journal of Biosocial Science* 37: 499–518.

Brian, Eric, and Marie Jaisson. 2007. *The Descent of Human Sex Ratio at Birth: A Dialogue Between Mathematics, Biology and Sociology*. Dordrecht: Springer.

Brockerhoff, Martin P. 2000. 'An Urbanizing World', *Population Bulletin* 55, 3. Washington, DC: Population Reference Bureau.

———, and Ellen Brennan. 1998. 'The Poverty of Cities in Developing Regions', *Population and Development Review* 24, 11: 75–114.

Broudy, D.W., and P.A. May. 1983. 'Demographic and Epidemiologic Transitions Among the Navajo Indians', *Social Biology* 30:1–16.

Brown, Alan A., and Egon Neuberger. 1977. 'Comparative Analysis of Internal Migration: An overview', in Alan A. Brown and Egon Neuberger, eds., *Internal Migration: A Comparative Perspective*. New York: Academic Press.

Brown, Lester, Gary Gardner, and Biran Halweil. 1999. *Beyond Malthus: Nineteen Dimensions of the Population Challenge*. New York: W.W. Norton.

Bryan, Thomas. 2004. 'Basic Sources of Statistics', in Jacob S. Siegel and David Swanson, eds, *The Methods and Materials of Demography*, 2nd edn. San Diego, CA: Elsevier.

Bryant, Christopher R., and Alun E. Joseph. 2001. 'Canada's Rural Population: Trends in Space and Implications in Place', *The Canadian Geographer* 45, 1: 132–7.

Budinski, Ron, and Frank Trovato. 2005. 'The Effect of Premarital Cohabitation on Marital Stability Over the Duration of Marriage', *Canadian Studies in Population* 32, 1: 69–95.

Bulatao, Rodolfo A. 2001. 'Introduction', in Rodolfo A. Bulatao and John B. Casterline, eds, *Global Fertility Transition*, supp. to *Population and Development Review* 27. New York: Population Council.

———, and John B. Casterline, eds. 2001. *Global Fertility Transition*, supp. to *Population and Development Review* 27. New York: Population Council.

———, and Ronald D. Lee. 1983. *Determinants of Fertility in Developing Countries*, vols 1–2. New York: Academic Press.

Bumpass, Larry L., James A. Sweet, and Andrew Cherlin. 1991. 'The Role of Cohabitation in Declining Rates of Marriage', *Journal of Marriage and the Family* 53: 913–27.

Bunting, Trudy, and Pierre Filion, eds. 2000. *Canadian Cities in Transition: The Twenty-First Century*, 2nd edn. Don Mills, ON: Oxford University Press.

Burch, Thomas K. 2003. 'The Life Table as a Theoretical Model: Demography in a New Key'. Session 13: Innovative Applications to Enhance Use of Secondary Data. Paper presented at Population Association of America 2003 Annual Meeting (1–3 May), Minneapolis.

———. 2002a. 'Teaching the Fundamentals of Demography: Ten Principles and Two Rationales', *Genus* LVIII, 3–4: 21–34.

———. 2002b. 'Teaching the Fundamentals of Demography: A Model-Based Approach to Family and Fertility', *Genus* LVIII, 3–4: 73–90.

———. 1987. 'Age-Sex Roles and Demographic Change: An Overview', *Canadian Studies in Population* 14, 2: 129–46.

———. 1979. 'The Structure of Demographic Action', *Journal of Population* 2, 4: 279–93.

———. 1966. 'The Fertility of North American Catholics: A Comparative Overview', *Demography* 3, 2: 174–87.

Bureau de la Statistique du Quebec. 1997. *La Situation démographique au Québec: édition 1997*. Quebec City: Les Publications du Québec.

Burgess, Ernest W. 1925. 'The Growth of the City', in Robert E. Park, Ernest W. Burgess, and R.D. MacKenzie, *The City*. Chicago: Chicago University Press.

Butz, William P., and Michael P. Ward. 1979a. 'The Emergence of Countercyclical US Fertility', *The American Economic Review* 69, 3: 318–28.

———. 1979b. 'Will US Fertility Remain Low? A New Economic Interpretation', *Population and Development Review* 5, 4: 663–88.

Cadwallader, Martin. 1992. *Migration and Residential Mobility: Micro and Macro Approaches*. Madison, WI: The University of Wisconsin Press.

Cai, Yong, and Wang Feng. 2005. 'Famine, Social Disruption, and Involuntary Fetal Loss', *Demography* 42, 2: 301–22.

Cain, Mead. 1993. 'Patriarchal Structure and Demographic Change', in Nora Federici, Karen Oppenheim Mason, and Solvi Sogner, eds, *Women's Position and Demographic Change*. Oxford: Clarendon.

———. 1987. 'The Consequences of Reproductive Failure: Dependence Mobility and Mortality Among the Elderly of Rural South Asia', *Population Studies* 40, 3: 375–88.

———. 1985. 'On the Relationship Between Landholding and Fertility', *Population Studies* 39: 5–15.

———. 1983. 'Fertility as an Adjustment to Risk', *Population and Development Review* 9, 4: 688–702.

———. 1982. 'Perspectives on Family and Fertility in Developing Countries', *Population Studies* 36, 2: 159–75.

Caldwell, Gary, and Daniel Fournier. 1987. 'The Quebec Question: A Matter of Population', *Canadian Journal of Sociology* 12, 1–2: 16–41.

Caldwell, John C. 2006. 'On Net Intergenerational Wealth Flows: An Update', in John C. Caldwell, *Demographic Transition Theory*. Dordrecht: Springer.

———. 2001. 'The Globalization of Fertility Behavior', in Rodolfo A. Bulatao and John B. Casterline, eds, *Global Fertility Transition*, supp. to *Population and Development Review* 27. New York: Population Council.

———. 1991. 'Introductory Thoughts on Health Transition', in John C. Caldwell, et al., eds, *What We Know About Health Transition: The Cultural, Social and Behavioural Determinants of Health*, 2 vols. Proceedings of an International Workshop (May 1989). Canberra: Australian National University.

———. 1986. 'Routes to Low Mortality in Poor Countries', *Population and Development Review* 12, 2: 171–220.

———. 1982. *Theory of Fertility Decline*. London: Academic Press.

———. 1976. 'Toward a Restatement of the Demographic Transition Theory', *Population and Development Review* 2, 3–4: 321–66.

———, and Pat Caldwell. 1997. 'What Do We Know About the Fertility Transition?', in Gavin W. Jones, et al., eds, *The Continuing Demographic Transition*. Oxford: Clarendon.

———, and ———. 1990. 'High Fertility in Sub-Saharan Africa', *Scientific American* (May): 118–125.

———, ———, and Pat Quiggin. 1989. 'The Social Context of AIDS in Sub-Saharan Africa', *Population and Development Review* 15, 2: 185–234.

———, James F. Phillips, and Barkat-e-Khuda. 2002. 'Family Planning Programs in the Twenty-first Century', Special Issue of *Studies in Family Planning* 33, 1 (March).

———, and Thomas Schindlmayr, 2003. 'Explanations of the Fertility Crisis in Modern Societies: A Search for Commonalities', *Population Studies* 57, 3: 241–63.

Calot, Gérard. 2006. 'The Effect of Pronatalist Policies in Industrialized Countries', in Graziella Caselli, Jacques Vallin, and Guillaume Wunsch, eds, *Demography: Analysis and Synthesis*. Amsterdam: Elsevier.

Cambois, Emannuelle, 2004. 'Careers and Mortality in France: Evidence on How Far Occupational Mobility Predicts Differentiated Risks', *Social Science and Medicine* 58: 2545–58.

———, Jean-Marie Robine, and Mark D. Hayward. 2002. 'Social Inequalities in Disability-Free Life Expectancy in the French Male Population, 1980–1991', *Demography* 38, 4: 513–24.

Campbell, Kenneth L., and James W. Wood, eds. 1994. *Human Reproductive Ecology: Interactions of Environment, Fertility, and Behavior*, vol. 709. New York: The New York Academy of Sciences.

Campisi, Domenico, Agostino La Bella, and Giovanni Rabino. 1982. *Migration and Settlement 17. Italy.* Laxenburg, AT: International Institute for Applied Systems Analysis.

Canadian Broadcasting Corporation (CBC). 2004. 'Chechnya', *The Passionate Eye* (aired 15 November).

Canadian Institute for Child Health. 1994. *The Health of Canada's Children: A CICH Profile*, 2nd edn. Ottawa: CICH.

Canadian Institute for Health Information. 2002. *Health Care in Canada*. Ottawa: CIHI.

Canon, Kenneth L., and Ruby Gingles. 1956. 'Social Factors Related to Divorce Rates for Urban Counties in Nebraska', *Rural Sociology* 21: 34–40.

Cardano, Mario, Giuseppe Costa, and Moreno Demaria. 2004. 'Social Mobility and Health in the Turin Longitudinal Study', *Social Science and Medicine* 58: 1563–74.

Carens, Joseph H. 1999. 'Reconsidering Open Borders', *International Migration Review* 33, 4: 1082–97.

———. 1987. 'Aliens and Citizens: The Case for Open Borders', *Review of Politics* 49, 2: 251–73.

Carey, James R. 2003a. 'Life Span', in Paul Demeny and Geoffrey McNicoll, eds, *Encyclopedia of Population*. New York: Macmillan Reference USA/Thomson Gale.

———. 2003b. 'Life Span: A Conceptual Overview', in James R. Carey and Shripad Tuljapurkar, eds, *Life Span: Evolutionary, Ecological, and Demographic Perspectives*, supp. to *Population and Development Review* 29. New York: Population Council.

———, and Debra S. Judge. 2001a. 'Principles of Biodemography with Special Reference to Human Longevity', *Population: An English Selection* 13, 1: 9–40.

———, and ———. 2001b. 'Life Span Extension in Humans Is Self-Reinforcing: A General Theory of Longevity', *Population and Development Review* 27, 3: 411–36.

———, and Shripad Tuljapurkar, eds. 2003. *Life Span: Evolutionary, Ecological, and Demographic Perspectives*, supp. to *Population and Development Review* 29. New York: Population Council.

Carlson, Gosta. 1966. 'The Decline in Fertility: Innovation or Adjustment Process', *Population Studies* 20: 149–74.

Carr-Saunders, A.M. 1964. *World Population: Past Growth and Present Trends*, 2nd edn. London: Frank Cass.

Case, Anne, and Christina Paxson. 2005. 'Sex Differences in Morbidity and Health', *Demography* 42, 2: 189–214.

Caselli, Graziella, and Alan D. Lopez. 1996. 'Health and Mortality Among the Elderly: Issues for Assessment', in Graziella Caselli and Alan D. Lopez, eds, *Health and Mortality among Elderly Populations*. Oxford: Clarendon.

———, F. Meslé, and J. Vallin. 2002. 'Epidemiologic Transition Theory Exceptions', *Genus* LVIII, 1: 9–52.

Caspi, Avshalom, Bradley, R. Entner Wright, T.E. Moffitt, et al. 1998. 'Early Failure in the Labor Market: Childhood and Adolescent Predictors of Unemployment in the Transition to Adulthood', *American Sociological Review* 63, 3: 424–51.

Cassel, J. 1976. 'The Contribution of the Social Environment to Host Resistance', *American Journal of Epidemiology* 104: 107–23.

Casterline, John B. 2001. 'The Pace of Fertility Transition: National Patterns in the Second Half of the Twentieth Century', in Rodolfo A. Bulatao and John B. Casterline, eds, *Global Fertility Transition*, supp. to *Population and Development Review* 27. New York: Population Council.

———, and Steven W. Sinding. 2000. 'Unmet Need for Family Planning in Developing Countries and Implications for Population Policy', *Population and Development Review* 26, 4: 691–723. New York: Population Council.

Castles, Steven, and Mark J. Miller. 2003. *The Age of Migration: International Population Movements in the Modern World*, 3rd edn. New York: Guilford.

Catto, Susan. 2003. 'A Slow Death', *Time* (Canadian edn) 13 October: 49–59.

Caughley, Graeme. 1966. 'Mortality Patterns in Mammals', *Ecology* 47, 6: 906–918.

Cavalli-Sforza, L., and W.F. Bodmer. 1971. *The Genetics of Human Populations*. San Francisco: W.H. Freeman.

———, and Francesco Cavalli-Sforza. 1995. *Great Human Diasporas: The History of Diversity and Evolution*. Trans. Sarah Thorne. New York: Addison-Wesley (Helix Books).

Cebula, Richard J. 1979. *The Determinants of Human Migration*. Lexington, MA: Lexington Books.

Chahnazarian, Anouch. 1988. 'Determinants of the Sex Ratio at Birth: Review of Recent Literature', *Social Biology* 35: 214–35.

Champion, Anthony H. 2001. 'Urbanization, Suburbanization, Counterurbanization and Reurbanization', in Ronald Paddison, ed., *Handbook of Urban Studies*. London: Sage.

———. 1988 [1996]. 'The Reversal of the Migration Turnaround: Resumption of Traditional Trends?', in H.S. Geyer and T.M. Kontuly, eds, *Differential Urbanization: Integrating Spatial Models*. London: Edward Arnold.

———, and Graham Hugo. 2004. *New Forms of Urbanization: Beyond the Urban-Rural Dichotomy*. London: Ashgate.

Chappell, Neena L., Ellen M. Gee, L. MacDonald, and M. Stones. 2003. *Aging in Contemporary Canada*. Canada, Toronto: Prentice-Hall.

Charbonneau, Hubert. 1977. 'Les Regimes de Fecondite Naturelle en Amerique du Nord: Bilan et Analyse des Observations', in Henri Leridon and Jane Menken, eds, *Natural Fertility*. International Union for the Scientific Study of Population. Liege: Ordina Editions.

———. 1975. *Vie et mort de nos ancêtres*. Montreal: Les Presses de l'Université de Montréal.

———, Bertrand Desjardins, Jacques Legare, and Hubert Denis. 2000. 'The Population of the St Lawrence Valley, 1608–1760', in Michael R. Haines and Richard H. Steckel, eds, *A Population History of North America*. Cambridge: Cambridge University Press.

Charles, Enid. 1948. *The Changing Size of the Family in Canada,* Census Monograph no. 1, *Eighth Census of Canada, 1941*. Ottawa: King's Printer.

Charny, Israel W. 1999. *The Encyclopedia of Genocide*. Santa Barbara, CA: ABC-CLIO.

Charon, Joel M. 1998. *The Meaning of Sociology*, 6th edn. Upper Saddle River, NJ: Prentice Hall.

Chase, Helne C. 1969. 'Registration Completeness and International Comparisons of Infant Mortality', *Demography* 6, 4: 425–33.

Chase-Dunn, Christopher, and Andrew Jorgenson. 2003. 'Systems of Cities', in Paul Demeny and Geoffrey McNicoll, eds, *Encyclopedia of Population*. New York: Macmillan Reference USA/Thomson Gale.

Chasteland, Jean-Claude. 2006. 'World Population Growth and the International Community From 1950 to Present Day', in Graziella Caselli, Jacques Vallin, and Guillaume Wunsch, eds, *Demography: Analysis and Synthesis*. Amsterdam: Elsevier.

Chen, Jiajian, and Wayne J. Millar. 2000. 'Are Recent Cohorts Healthier Than Their Predecessors?', *Health Reports* 11, 4: 9–23.

Cherlin, Andrew J. 2004. 'The Deinstitutionalization of American Marriage', *Journal of Marriage and the Family* 66: 848–61.

———. 2003. 'Family Demography', in Paul Demeny and Geoffrey McNicoll, eds, *Encyclopedia of Population*. New York: Macmillan Reference USA/Thomson Gale.

———. 1981. *Marriage, Divorce, and Remarriage*. Cambridge, MA: Harvard University Press.

Cheru, Fantu, and Colin Bradford, eds. 2005. *The Millennium Development Goals: Raising the Resources to Tackle World Poverty*. London and New York: Zed Books.

Chesnais, Jean-Claude. 1992. *The Demographic Transition: Stages, Patterns and Implications*. Trans. Elizabeth and Philip Kreager. Oxford: Clarendon.

Cheung, Siu Lan Karen, Jean-Marie Robine, Edward J.C. Tu, et al. 2005. 'Three Dimensions of the Survival Curve', *Demography* 42, 2: 243–58.

Chevan, A., and L.R. Fischer. 1979. 'Retirement and Interstate Migration', *Social Forces* 57: 1365–80.

Chiang, Chin Long. 1984. *The Life Table and Its Applications*. Malabar, FL: Robert E. Krieger.

Chitose, Yoshimi. 2001. 'The Effects of Ethnic Concentration on Internal Migration in Peninsular Malaysia', *Asian and Pacific Migration Journal* 10, 2: 241–72.

Christaller, Walter. 1933 [1966]. *Central Places in Southern Germany*. Trans. Carlisle Baskin. Englewood Cliffs, NJ: Prentice Hall.

Chui, Tina W.L., and Frank Trovato. 1989. 'Ethnic Variations in Fertility: Microeconomic and Minority Group Status Effects', *International Review of Modern Sociology* 19, 1: 80–92.

Cincotta, Richard P., and Robert Engelman. 1997. 'Economics and Rapid Change: The Influence of Population Growth', Occasional Paper no. 3 (October). Washington, DC: Population Action International.

———, ———, and Daniele Anastasion. 2003. *The Security Demographic: Population and Civil Conflict after the Cold War*. Washington, DC: Population Action International.

Cipolla, Carlo M. 1962. *The Economic History of World Population*. Harmondsworth, UK: Penguin.

Citizenship and Immigration Canada. 2006. *Annual Report to Parliament on Immigration 2006*. Cat. no. C&I-831-10-06.

———. 2005a. *Annual Report to Parliament on Immigration 2005*. Cat. no. C&I-572-10-05.

———. 2005b. *Facts and Figures 2004: Immigration Overview: Permanent and Temporary Residents*. Cat. no. C&I-743-08-05E. <http://www.cic.gc.ca/english/pub/facts2004/overview/1.html> (accessed 30 September 2005).

———. 2002. <http://www.cic.gc.ca/english/pub/facts2001/1imm-05.html>.

Clapson, Mark. 2003. *Suburban Century: Social Change and Urban Growth in England and the USA*. Oxford: Berg.

Clark, S.D. 1972. 'Rural Migration and Patterns of Urban Growth', in Edward B. Harvey, ed., *Perspectives on Modernization: Essays in Memory of Ian Weinberg*. Toronto: University of Toronto Press.

Clark, Warren. 2003. 'Pockets of Belief: Religious Attendance Patterns in Canada', *Canadian Social Trends* 68 (Spring): 2–5.

Clarke, Alice L., and Bobbi S. Low. 2001. 'Testing Evolutionary Hypotheses with Demographic Data', *Population and Development Review* 27, 4: 633–60.

Clarke, John I. 2003. 'Sex Ratio', in Paul Demeny and Geoffrey McNicoll, eds, *Encyclopedia of Population*. New York: Macmillan Reference USA/Thomson Gale.

———. 2000. *The Human Dichotomy: The Changing Numbers of Males and Females*. Amsterdam: Pergamon.

———. 1997. *Predictions: The Future of Population*. London: Phoenix.

———. 1996. 'The Impact of Population Change on Environment: An Overview', in Bernardo Colombo, Paul Demeny, and Max F. Perutz, eds, *Resources and Population: Natural, Institutional, and Demographic Dimensions of Development*. Oxford: Clarendon.

———. 1970. *Population Geography*. Oxford: Pergamon.

———, Peter Carson, S.L. Kayastha, and P. Nag, eds. 1989. *Population and Disaster*. Oxford: Basil Blackwell.

Clatworthy, Stewart, and Mary Jane Norris. 2006. 'Aboriginal Mobility and Migration: Trends, Recent Patterns, and Implications: 1971–2001', in Jerry P.

White, Susan Wingert, Dan Beavon, and Paul Maxim, eds, *Aboriginal Policy Research: Moving Forward, Making a Difference*, 4: 207–34. Toronto: Thompson.

Cleland, John. 2001. 'The Effects of Improved Survival on Fertility: A Reassessment', in Rodolfo A. Bulatao and John B. Casterline, eds, *Global Fertility Transition*, supp. to *Population and Development Review* 27. New York: Population Council.

———. 1996. 'Population Growth in the 21st Century: Cause for Crisis or Celebration?', *Tropical Medicine and International Health* 1, 1: 15–26.

———, Stan Bernstein, Alex Ezeh, et al. 2006. 'Family Planning: The Unfinished Agenda', *The Lancet* 368 (18 November): 1810–27.

———, and John Hobcraft. 1985. *Reproductive Change in Developing Countries: Insights from the World Fertility Survey*. Oxford: Oxford University Press.

———, and Christopher Wilson. 1987. 'Demand Theories of the Fertility Transition: An Iconoclastic View', *Population Studies* 41, 1: 5–30.

Coale, Ansley J. 1996. 'Age Patterns and Time Sequence of Mortality in National Populations with the Highest Expectation of Life at Birth', *Population and Development Review* 22, 1: 127–36.

———. 1991. 'Excess Female Mortality and the Balance of the Sexes', *Population and Development Review* 17: 517–23.

———. 1986. 'The Decline of Fertility in Europe since the Eighteenth Century as a Chapter in Demographic History', in Ansley J. Coale and Susan Cotts Watkins, eds, *The Decline of Fertility in Europe*. Princeton, NJ: Princeton University Press.

———. 1983. 'Recent Trends in Fertility in Less Developed Countries', *Science* 221: 828–32.

———. 1974. 'The History of the Human Population', *The Human Population*, special issue of *Scientific American*. San Francisco: W.H. Freeman.

———. 1973. 'The Demographic Transition Reconsidered', in *Proceedings of the International Population Conference*. Liege, BE: Liege International Union for the Scientific Study of Population.

———. 1972. *The Growth and Structure of Human Populations: A Mathematical Investigation*. Princeton, NJ: Princeton University Press.

———. 1969. 'The Decline of Fertility in Europe from the French Revolution to World War II', in S.J. Behrman, Leslie Corsa Jr, and Ronald Freedman, eds, *Fertility and Family Planning: A World View*. Ann Arbor, Michigan: The University of Michigan Press.

———. 1964. 'How a Population Ages or Grows Younger', in Ronald Freedman, ed., *Population: The Vital Revolution*. Garden City, NY: Doubleday (Anchor Books).

———. 1957a. 'How the Age Distribution of a Human Population is Determined', *Cold Spring Harbor Symposia on Quantitative Biology* 22: 83–9.

————. 1957b. 'A New Method for Calculating Lotka's *r*— The Intrinsic Rate of Growth in a Stable Population', *Population Studies* 11, 1: 92–4.

————. 1955. 'The Calculation of Approximate Intrinsic Rates', *Population Index* 21, 2: 94–7.

————, and Susan Cotts Watkins, eds. 1986. *The Decline of Fertility in Europe*. Princeton, NJ: Princeton University Press.

————, and Paul Demeny. 1983. *Regional Model Life Tables and Stable Populations*, 2nd edn. New York: Academic Press.

————, and Edgar M. Hoover. 1958. *Population Growth and Economic Development in Low-Income Countries*. Princeton, NJ: Princeton University Press.

Cobb, S. 1976. 'Social Support as a Moderator of Life Stress', *Psychosomatic Medicine* 38: 300–14.

Cochrane, S.G., and D.R. Vining Jr. 1988 [1996]. 'Recent Trends in Migration Between Core and Peripheral Region in Developed and Advanced Developing Countries', in H.S. Geyer and T.M. Kontuly, eds, *Differential Urbanization: Integrating Spatial Models*. London: Edward Arnold.

Coffey, William J. 2000. 'Canadian Cities and Shifting Fortunes of Economic Development', in Trudy Bunting and Pierre Filion, eds, *Canadian Cities in Transition: The Twenty-First Century*, 2nd edn. Don Mills, ON: Oxford University Press.

————. 1994. *The Evolution of Canada's Metropolitan Economies*. Montreal: The Institute for Research on Public Policy.

Cohen, Joel E. 2003. 'Human Population: The Next Half Century', *Science* 302 (14 November): 1172–5.

————. 1995. *How Many People Can the Earth Support?* New York: W.W. Norton.

Cohen, Robin. 1997. *Global Diasporas: An Introduction*. Seattle: University of Washington Press.

Cohn, Samuel Jr. 2003. 'Black Death', in Paul Demeny and Geoffrey McNicoll, eds, *Encyclopedia of Population*. New York: Macmillan Reference USA/Thomson Gale.

Coleman, David. 2002. 'Replacement Migration, or Why Everyone is Going to Have to Live in Korea: A Fable for Our Times from the United Nations', *Philosophical Transactions of the Royal Society of London B*: 357: 583–98.

————. 2001. 'Why Borders Cannot be Open', International Union for the Scientific Study of Population General Conference. San Salvador de Bahia, Brazil. August 24, 2001.

Collins, Francis S., and Anna D. Barker. 2007. 'Mapping the Cancer Genome', *Scientific American* 296, 3 (March): 50–7.

Coltrane, S. 1996. *Family Man: Fatherhood, Housework and Gender Equity*. New York: Oxford University Press.

Columbia Encyclopedia, 6th edn. 2003. Columbia University Press. <http://www.bartleby.com/65/>.

Conley, Dalton, and Neil G. Bennett. 2001. 'Birth Weight and Income: Interactions across Generations', *Journal of Health and Social Behavior* 42: 450–65.

Cook, Ramsey. 2002. 'The Triumph and Trials of Materialism (1900–1945)' in Craig Brown, ed., *The Illustrated History of Canada*. Toronto: Key Porter.

Cooke, Thomas, and Adrian Bailey. 1999. 'The Effect of Family Migration, Migration History, and Self-Selection on Married Women's Labour Market Achievement', in Paul Boyle and Keith Halfcree, eds, *Migration and Gender in the Developed World*. London: Routledge.

Corman, Diana. 2002. 'Family Policies, Work Arrangements and the Third Child in France and Sweden', in Erik Klijzing and Martine Corijn, eds, *Dynamics of Fertility and Partnership in Europe: Insights and Lessons from Comparative Research*, vol. 2. New York and Geneva: UN.

Costa, Dora L. 2000. 'Understanding the Twentieth-Century Decline in Chronic Conditions among Older Men', *Demography* 37, 1: 53–72.

————. 1998. *The Evolution of Retirement: An American Economic History 1880–1990*. Chicago: The University of Chicago Press.

Courchene, Thomas J. 1970. 'Interprovincial Migration and Economic Adjustment', *Canadian Journal of Economics* 3: 550–76.

Cowgill, Donald O. 1971. 'The Use of the Logistic Curve and the Transition Model in Developing Nations', in Ashish Bose, P.B. Desai, and S.P. Jain, eds, *Studies in Demography*. Chapel Hill, NC: The University of North Carolina Press.

Cowling, Ellis B. 1991. 'Acid Rain and Other Airborne Pollutants: Their Human Causes and Consequences', in Kingsley Davis and Mikhail S. Bernstam, eds, *Resources, Environment, and Population: Present Knowledge, Future Options*, supp. to *Population and Development Review* 16. New York: Oxford University Press.

Crenshaw, Edward M., Ansari Z. Ameen, and Matthew Christenson. 1997. 'Population Dynamics and Economic Development: Age-Specific Population Growth Rates and Economic Growth in Developing Countries', *American Sociological Review* 62, 6: 974–84.

Crépeau, Francois, Delphine Nakache, Machale Collyer, et al., eds. 2006. *Forced Migration and Global Processes: A View from Forced Migration Studies*. Lenham, UK: Lexington Books.

Crimmins, Eileen M. 1990. 'Are Americans Healthier as well as Longer-Lived?', *Journal of Insurance Medicine* 22, 2: 89–92.

————, Melanie L. Johnston, Mark Hayward, and Teresa E. Seeman. 2006. 'Age Differences in Allostatic Load: An Index of Frailty', in Zeng Yi, et al., eds, *Longer Life and Healthy Aging*. Dordrecht: Springer.

————, Yasuhiko Saito, and D. Ingegneri. 1997. 'Trends in Disability-Free Life Expectancy in the United States,

1970–90', *Population and Development Review* 23, 3: 555–72.

Croll, Elisabeth J. 2000. *Endangered Daughters*. London: Routledge.

Crompton, Susan, and Michael Vickers. 2000. 'One Hundred Years of Labour Force', *Canadian Social Trends* 57 (Summer): 2–13.

Cummings, David R. 2003. 'The Influence of Latitude and Cloud Cover on the Seasonality of Human Births', *Social Biology* 50, 1–12: 23–41.

Cutler, David, and Grant Miller. 2005. 'The Role of Public Health Improvements in Health Advances: The Twentieth Century United States', *Demography* 42, 1: 1–22.

D'Souza, Stan, and Lincoln C. Chen. 1980. 'Sex Differential in Mortality in Rural Bangladesh', *Population and Development Review* 6, 2: 257–70.

Da Vanzo, Julie. 1981. 'Microeconomic Approaches to Studying Migration Decisions', in G.G. De Jong and R.W. Gardner, eds, *Migration Decision Making*. New York: Pergamon.

Dahms, F.A. 1990. 'The Evolution of Settlement Systems: A Canadian Example, 1851–1970', in Gilbert A. Stelter, ed., *Cities and Urbanization: Canadian Historical Perspectives*. Toronto: Copp Clark Pitman.

Daily, Gretchen C., and Paul R. Ehrlich. 1992. 'Population, Sustainability, and Earth's Carrying Capacity', *BioScience* 42, 10: 761–71.

Dale, Edmund H, ed. 1988. *The Future of Saskatchewan Small Town*. Victoria, BC: Department of Geography, University of Victoria.

Dalla Zuanna, Gianpiero. 2006. 'Induced Abortion', in Graziella Caselli, Jacques Vallin, and Guillaume Wunsch, eds, *Demography: A Treatise in Population Studies*, vol. 1. Amsterdam: Elsevier and Academic Press.

Darroch, G.A., and W.G. Marston. 1988. 'Patterns of Urban Ethnicity: Toward a Revised Ecological Model', in N. Iverson, ed., *Urbanism and Urbanization: Views, Aspects, and Dimensions*. Leiden: E.J. Brill.

Das Gupta, Monica, and Lee Shuzhuo. 2000. 'Gender Bias in China, South Korea and India 1920–1990: Effects of War, Poverty and Fertility', in Shahra Razavi, ed., *Gendered Poverty and Well-Being*. Oxford: Blackwell.

Daugherty, Helen L., and Kenneth C.W. Kammeyer. 1955. *An Introduction to Population Studies*. New York: Guildford.

David, Henry P. 1992. 'Abortion in Europe, 1920–91: A Public Health Perspective', *Studies in Family Planning* 23, 1: 1–22.

———, and Joanna Skilogianis, eds. 1999. *From Abortion to Contraception: A Resource to Public Policies and Reproductive Behavior in Central and Eastern Europe from 1917 to the Present*. Westport, CT: Greenwood Press.

Davis, Craig H. 1995. *Demographic Projection Techniques for Regions and Smaller Areas: A Primer*. Vancouver: University of British Columbia Press.

Davis, D.L., M.B. Gottlieb, and J.R. Stampnitzky. 1998. 'Reduced Ratio of Male to Female Births in Several Industrialized Countries: A Sentinel Health Indicator?', *Journal of the American Medical Association* 279: 1018–23.

Davis, Hugh, Heather Joshi, and Romana Peronacci. 2000. 'Forgone Income and Motherhood: What do Recent British Data Tell Us?', *Population Studies* 54, 3: 293–305.

Davis, Kingsley. 1986. 'Low Fertility in Evolutionary Perspective', in Kingsley Davis, Mikhail S. Bernstam, and Rita Ricardo-Campbell, eds, *Below-Replacement Fertility in Industrial Societies: Causes, Consequences, Policies*, supp. to *Population and Development Review* 12.

———. 1984a. 'Wives and Work: The Sex Role Revolution and its Consequences', *Population and Development Review* 8, 3: 495–511.

———. 1984b. 'Declining Birth Rates and Growing Populations', *Population Research and Policy Review* 3: 61–75.

———. 1973. 'The Evolution of Western Industrial Cities', *Readings from Scientific American*, in Kingsley Davis, ed., *Cities: Their Origins, Growth and Human Impact*. San Francisco: W.H. Freeman.

———. 1970. 'The Urbanization of the Human Population', *Scientific American*. New York: Alfred Knopf.

———. 1967. 'Population Policy: Will Current Programs Succeed?', *Science* 158, 3802 (10 November): 730–9.

———. 1963. 'The Theory of Change and Response in Modern Demographic History', *Population Index* 29, 4: 345–66.

———. 1955. 'The Origin and Growth of Urbanization in the World', *American Journal of Sociology* 60 (March): 429–37.

———. 1948. *Human Society*. New York: Macmillan.

———. 1945. 'The World Demographic Transition', *The Annals of the American Academy of Political and Social Science* 235: 1–11.

———, and Judith Blake. 1956. 'Social Structure and Fertility: An Analytical Framework', *Economic Development and Cultural Change* 4, 4: 211–35.

———, and Pietronella van den Oever. 1982. 'Demographic Foundations of New Sex Roles', *Population and Development Review* 8, 3: 495–512.

Day, Lincoln H. 1992. *The Future of Low-Birthrate Populations*. London: Routledge.

———. 1985. 'Illustrating Behavioral Principles with Examples from Demography: The Causal Analysis of Differences in Fertility', *Journal for the Theory of Social Behaviour* 15, 2: 189–201.

———. 1978. 'What Will a ZPG Society Look Like?', *Population Bulletin* 33, 3. Washington: Population Reference Bureau.

———. 1968. 'Natality and Ethnocentrism: Some Relationships Suggested by an Analysis of Catholic-Protestant Differentials', *Population Studies* 22: 27–50.

Deane, Glenn D. 1990. 'Mobility and Adjustments: Paths to the Resolution of Residential Stress', *Demography* 27, 1: 65–77.

de Blij, H.J., and Alexander B. Murphy. 2003. *Human Geography: Culture, Society, and Space*, 7th edn. New York: John Wiley.

De Coulanges, Fustel. N.D. *The Ancient City: A Classic Study of the Religious and Civil Institutions of Ancient Greece and Rome*. Garden City, NY: Doubleday (Anchor Books).

De Jong, Gordon F. 2000. 'Expectations, Gender and Norms in Migration Decision-Making', *Population Studies* 54: 307–19.

———. 1999. 'Choice Processes in Migration Behavior', in K. Pandid and S. Davis Withers, eds, *Migration and Restructuring in the United States: A Geographic Perspective*. Lanham, MD: Rowman and Littlefield.

Demeny, Paul. 2003a. 'Population Policy Dilemmas in Europe at the Dawn of the Twenty-First Century', *Population and Development Review* 29, 1: 1–28.

———. 2003b. 'Population Policy', in Paul Demeny and Geoffrey McNicoll, eds, *Encyclopedia of Population*. New York: Macmillan Reference USA/Thomson Gale.

———. 1998. 'Population Size and Material Standards of Living', in Paul Demeny and Geoffrey McNicoll, eds, *The Earthscan Reader in Population and Development*. London: Earthscan.

———. 1974. 'The Populations of the Underdeveloped Countries', in *The Human Population*, special issue of *Scientific American*. San Francisco: W.H. Freeman.

———. 1968. 'Early Fertility Decline in Austria-Hungary: A Lesson in Demographic Transition', *Daedalus* 97: 502–22.

———, and Jeoffrey McNicoll, eds. 1998. *The Earthscan Reader in Population and Development*. London: Earthscan.

Denton, T. 1975. 'Canadian Indian Migrants and Impression Management of Ethnic Stigma', *Canadian Review of Sociology and Anthropology* 12, 1: 65–71.

———. 1972. 'Migration from a Canadian Indian Reserve', *Journal of Canadian Studies* 7: 54–62.

Denton, Frank T., Christine H. Feaver, and Byron G. Spencer. 2002. 'Alternative Pasts, Possible Futures: A "What if" Study of the Effects of Fertility on the Canadian Population and Labour Force', *Canadian Public Policy* 28, 3: 443–59.

———, ———, and ———. 2000. 'The Future Population of Canada and its Age Distribution', in Frank T. Denton, Deborah Fretz, and Byron G. Spencer, eds, *Independence and Economic Security in Old Age*. Vancouver: University of British Columbia Press.

———, and Byron G. Spencer. 1995. 'Demographic Change and the Cost of Publicly Funded Health Care', *Canadian Journal on Aging* 14, 2: 147–92.

———, and ———. 1975. *Population and the Economy*. Lexington, MA: Saxon House/Lexington Books.

Dercon, Stefan. 2005. 'Risk, Insurance, and Poverty: A Review', in Stefan Dercon, ed., *Insurance Against Poverty*. Oxford: Oxford University Press.

De Santis, Gustavo. 2006. 'Pronatalist Policy in Industrialized Nations', in Graziella Caselli, Jacques Vallin, and Guillaume Wunsch, eds, *Demography: Analysis and Synthesis*. Amsterdam: Elsevier.

———. 2003. 'The Demography of an Equitable and Stable Intergenerational Transfer System', *Population* 58, 6: 587–622.

DesMeules, Marie, Douglas Manuel, and Robert Cho. 2004. 'Mortality: Life and Health Expectancy of Canadian Women', *BioMed Central (BMC) Women's Health* 4 (supp. 1): S9. <http://www.biomedcentral.com/1472-6874/4/SI/S9>.

de Vries, Jan. 1984. *European Urbanization 1500–1800*. Cambridge, MA: Harvard University Press.

De Wit, Margaret L., David J. De Wit, and Brian G. Embree. 2000. 'Natives' and Non-Natives' Relative Risk of Children's Exposure to Marital Dissolution: The Role of Family Volatility and Implications for Future Nuptiality in Native Populations', *Canadian Studies in Population* 27, 1: 107–33.

Diamond, Jared. 1999. *Guns, Germs, and Steel: The Fates of Human Societies*. New York: W.W. Norton.

Diamond, Larry. 1993. 'The Globalization of Democracy', in Robert O. Slater, Barry M. Schutz, and Steven R. Dorr, eds, *Global Transformation and the Third World*. Boulder, CO: Lynne Rienner.

Dickinson, John, and Brian Young. 2003. *A Short History of Quebec*, 3rd edn. Montreal and Kingston: McGill-Queen's University Press.

Dixon, Ruth B. 1978. 'Late Marriage and Non-Marriage as Demographic Responses: Are They Similar?', *Population Studies* 32: 449–66.

———. 1971. 'Explaining Cross-Cultural Variations in Age at Marriage and Proportions Never Marrying', *Population Studies* 25: 215–33.

Dodds, L., and B.A. Armson. 1997. 'Is Canada's Sex Ratio in Decline?', *Canadian Medical Association Journal* 156, 1: 46–8.

Dodu, Sila R.A. 1984. 'Coronary Heart Disease in Developing Countries: The Threat Can Be Avoided', *WHO Chronicle* 38, 1: 3–7.

Dole, N., D.A. Savitz, I. Hertz-Picciotto, et al. 2003. 'Maternal Stress and Preterm Birth', *American Journal of Epidemiology* 157, 1: 14–24.

Doll, R., and R. Peto. 1981. 'The Causes of Cancer: Quantitative Estimates of Avoidable Risks of Cancer in the United States Today', *Journal of the National Cancer Institute* 66: 1191–1308.

Dominion Bureau of Statistics. 1962. 'Population: Incorporated Cities, Towns and Villages', *Census of Canada, 1961* 1: 1–6.

———. 1960. *Canadian Life Tables, 1950–1952, 1955–1957*. Cat. no. 84-510.

———. 1953. *Ninth Census of Canada, 1951,* vol. 1: *Population: General Characteristics.* Ottawa: The Queen's Printer.

———. 1947. *Life Tables for Canada and Regions, 1941 and 1931.* Cat. no. 84-515.

———. 1923. *Vital Statistics, 1921.* First Annual Report.

Donaldson, Loraine. 1991. *Fertility Transition: The Social Dynamics of Population Change.* Cambridge, MA: Basil Blackwell.

Dong, Maxia, Wayne H, Giles, Vincent J. Felitti, et al. 2004. 'Insights into Causal Pathways for Ischemic Heart Disease: Adverse Childhood Experiences Study', *Circulation* 110: 1761–6.

Dorland's Pocket Medical Dictionary, 22nd edn. 1977. Philadelphia: W.B. Saunders.

Dosman, E.J. 1972. *Indians: The Urban Dilemma.* Toronto: McClelland and Stewart.

Douglass, Carrie B. 2005. *Barren States: The Population 'Implosion' in Europe.* Oxford: Berg.

Dreifus, Claudia. 2004. 'Unlocking Anti-Ageing Secrets', *National Post* (2 March): A14.

Drolet, Marie. 2003. 'Motherhood and Paycheques', *Canadian Social Trends* 68 (Spring): 19–21.

Dublin, Louis I., and Alfred J. Lotka. 1925. 'On the True Rate of Natural Increase', *Journal of the American Statistical Association* 20, 151: 305–39.

———, and Mortimer Spiegelman. 1949. *Length of Life,* revised edn. New York: Ronald.

Dufor, Desmond, and Yves Person. 1979. *Vingt Ans de mortalité au Québec: les causes des décès, 1951–1971.* Montreal: Les Presses de l'Université de Montréal.

Dumas, Jean. 1990. *Report on the Demographic Situation in Canada: 1990.* Cat. no. 91-209E. Ottawa: Statistics Canada.

Duncan, Greg J., W. Jean Yeung, Jeanne Brooks-Gunn, et al. 1998. 'The Effects of Childhood Poverty on the Life Chances of Children', *American Sociological Review* 63, 3: 406–23.

Durand, John D. 1977. 'Historical Estimates of the World Population: An Evaluation', *Population and Development Review* 3, 3: 253–96.

———. 1974. 'Historical Estimates of the World Population' *Analytical and Technical Reports*, no. 10. University of Pennsylvania, Population Center.

Durkheim, Emile. 1897 [1951]. *Suicide: A Study in Sociology.* New York: Free Press.

———. 1893 [1933]. *The Division of Labor in Society.* New York: Free Press.

Dyson, Tim. 2003a. 'Famine in Asia', in Paul Demeny and Geoffrey McNicoll, eds, *Encyclopedia of Population.* New York: Macmillan Reference USA/Thomson Gale.

———. 2003b. 'HIV/AIDS and Urbanization', *Population and Development Review* 29, 3: 427–42.

———, Robert Cassen, and Leela Visaria, eds. 2004. *Twenty-First Century India: Population, Economy, Human Development, and the Environment.* Oxford: Oxford University Press.

———, and Mike Murphy. 1985. 'The Onset of Fertility Transition', *Population and Development Review* 11, 3: 399–440.

Easterlin, Richard A. 1999. *Growth Triumphant: The Twenty-First Century in Historical Perspective.* Ann Arbor: University of Michigan Press.

———. 1987. *Birth and Fortune,* 2nd edn. Chicago: University of Chicago Press.

———. 1983. 'Modernization and Fertility: A Critical Essay', in Rodolfo A. Bulato and Ronald D. Lee, eds, *Determinants of Fertility in Developing Countries,* vol. 2. New York: Academic Press.

———. 1980. *Birth and Fortune: The Impact of Numbers on Personal Welfare.* New York: Basic Books.

———. 1978a. 'The Economics and Sociology of Fertility: A Synthesis', in C. Tilly, ed., *Historical Studies of Changing Fertility.* Princeton, NJ: Princeton University Press.

———. 1978b. 'What Will 1984 Be Like? Socioeconomic Implications of Recent Twists in Age Structure', *Demography* 15, 4: 397–432.

———. 1975. 'An Economic Framework for Fertility Analysis', *Studies in Family Planning* 6, 3: 54–63.

———. 1969. 'Towards a Socio-Economic Theory of Fertility: A Survey of Recent Research on Economic Factors in American Fertility', in S.J. Berham, et al., eds, *Fertility and Family Planning: A World View.* Ann Arbor: University of Michigan Press.

———. 1961a. 'Influences in European Overseas Immigration Before WWI', *Economic Development and Cultural Change* 9: 331–51.

———. 1961b. 'The American Baby Boom in Historical Perspective', *American Economic Review* 51: 869–911.

———, Christine Macdonald, and Diane J. Macunovich. 1990. 'Retirement Prospects of the Baby Boom Generation: A Different Perspective', *The Gerontologist* 30, 6: 776–83.

Eaton, J.W., and A.J. Mayer. 1953. 'The Social Biology of Very High Fertility among the Hutterites: The Demography of a Unique Population', *Human Biology* 25: 206–64.

Eberstadt, Nicholas. 1997. 'World Population Implosion?', *The Public Interest* 129: 3–20.

Ebrahim, Shah, and Liam Smeeth. 2005. 'Non-Communicable Disease in Low and Middle-Income Countries: A Priority or a Distraction?', *International Journal of Epidemiology* 34: 961–6.

Economist, The. 2007. 'Suddenly, the Old World Looks Younger', <http://economist.com/PrinterFriendly.cfm?story_id=9334869> (14 June).

———. 2004a. 'Forever Young: A Survey of Retirement' (27 March).

———. 2004b. 'Japan: A Shrinking Giant' (8 January): 38.

Economist, The. 2004c. 'Population Aging Threatens Countries' Credit Standing; (3 April): 78.

———. 2003a. 'Congo's War: Waiting to be Rescued' (17 May): 40–1.

———. 2003b. 'Sudan's War: Peace, the Unimaginable' (17 May): 41–2.

———. 2003c. 'The Battles to Come' (5 September).

———. 2003d. 'Capitalism and Democracy' (28 June–4 July): 3–18.

Edmonston, Barry, and Margaret Michalowski. 2004. 'International Migration', in Jacob S. Siegel and David A. Swanson, eds, *The Methods and Materials of Demography*, 2nd edn. Amsterdam: Elsevier.

Egolf, Brenda, Judith Lasker, S. Wolf, et al. 1992. 'The Roseto Effect: A 50-Year Comparison of Mortality Rates', *American Journal of Public Health* 82, 8: 1089–92.

Ehrlich, Paul R. 1995. 'Our Demographic Future: Predictions for the Next 50 Years', *Population Today* 23: 2–3.

———. 1973. 'Playboy Interview', in Edward Pohlman, ed., *Population: A Clash of Prophets*. New York: New American Library (Mentor Book).

———. 1968. *The Population Bomb*. New York: Ballantine Books.

———, and Ann H. Ehrlich. 1990. *The Population Explosion*. London: Hutchinson.

———, ———, and John P. Holdren. 1977. *Ecoscience: Population, Resources, Environment*. San Francisco: W.H. Freeman.

El-Badry, M.A. 1969. 'Higher Female than Male Mortality in Some Countries of South Asia: A Digest', *Journal of the American Statistical Association* 64: 1234–44.

Elliot, Jean Leonard, and Augie Fleras. 1992. *Unequal Relations: An Introduction to Race and Ethnic Dynamics in Canada*. Scarborough, ON: Prentice Hall.

Emlen, Merritt J.1970. 'Age Specificity and Ecological Theory', *Ecology* 51, 6: 588–601.

Engelhardt, Henriette, Thomas Kogel, and Alexia Prskawetz. 2004. 'Fertility and Women's Employment Reconsidered: A Macro-Level Time Series Analysis for Developed countries, 1960–2000', *Population Studies* 58, 1: 109–120.

Engels, Frederick. 1844 [1971]. 'Outlines of a Critique of Political Economy', in Ronald L. Meek, ed., *Marx and Engels on the Population Bomb*. Trans. Dorothea L. Meek and Ronald L. Meek. Berkeley, CA: Ramparts.

Epp, Jack. 1986. 'Achieving Health For All: A Framework for Health Promotion'. Cat. no. H39-102/1986E. Ottawa: Health and Welfare Canada.

Epstein, Frederick H. 1989. 'The Relationship of Lifestyle to International Trends in CHD', *International Journal of Epidemiology* 18, 3: S203–9.

Ermisch, John F. 2003. *An Economic Analysis of the Family*. Princeton, NJ: Princeton University Press.

———. 1981. 'Economic Opportunities, Marriage Squeezes, and the Propensity to Marry: An Economic Analysis of Period Marriage Rates in England and Wales', *Population Studies* 35: 347–56.

Espenshade, Thomas J. 1985. 'Marriage Trends in America: Estimates, Implications, and Underlying Causes', *Population and Development Review* 11, 2: 193–245.

Evans, L.T. 1998. *Feeding the Ten Billion: Plants and Population Growth*. Cambridge: Cambridge University Press.

Evans, Robert G., and G.L. Stoddart. 1990. 'Producing Health, Consuming Health Care', *Social Science and Medicine* 31: 1347–63.

Fair, Martha M. 1994. 'The Development of National Vital Statistics in Canada: Part I—From 1605 to 1945', *Health Reports* 6, 3: 356–7.

Fairchild, Henry Pratt. 1925. *Immigration*. New York: Macmillan.

Faitosa, M.F., and H. Krieger. 1992. 'Demography of the Human Sex Ratio in Some Latin American Countries, 1967–1968', *Human Biology* 64, 4: 523–530.

Faris, Robert E.L. 1963. 'Interrelated Problems of the Expanding Metropolis', *The Canadian Journal of Economics and Political Science* 5, 3: 341–7.

Faust, Kimberly. 2004. 'Marriage, Divorce and Family Groups', in Jacob A. Siegel and David A. Swanson, eds, *The Methods and Materials of Demography*, 2nd edn. Amsterdam: Elsevier.

Fawcett, James T. 1983. 'Perceptions of the Value of Children: Satisfactions and Costs', in Rodolfo A. Bulatao and Ronald D. Lee, eds, *Determinants of Fertility in Developing Countries*, vol. 1: *Supply and Demand for Children*. New York: Academic Press.

Feinstein, Joseph. 1993. 'The Relationship Between Socio-Economic Status and Health: A Review of the Literature', *The Milbank Quarterly* 71: 279–322.

Fenelon, Bill. 1971. 'State Variations in United States Divorce Rates', *Journal of Marriage and the Family* 33: 321–7.

Festy, Patrick. 2006. 'Analysis of Couple Formation and Dissolution', in Graziella Caselli, Jacques Vallin, and Guillaume Wunsch, eds, *Demography: Analysis and Synthesis: A Treatise in Demography*. Amsterdam: Elsevier and Academic Press.

Field, Alexander J. 1984. 'Microeconomics, Norms and Rationality', *Economic Development and Cultural Change* 32, 4: 279–93.

Fielding, A.J. 1989 [1996]. 'Migration and Urbanization in Western Europe Since 1950', in H.S. Geyer and T.M. Kontuly, eds, *Differential Urbanization: Integrating Spatial Models*. London: Edward Arnold.

Finch, Brian Karl. 2003. 'Early Origins of the Gradient: The Relationship between Socioeconomic Status and Infant Mortality in the United States', *Demography* 40, 4: 675–99.

Finch, Caleb E., and Rudolph E. Tanzi. 1997. 'Genetics of Aging', *Science* 278 (17 October): 407–11.

Fingard, Judith. 1974. 'The Winter's Tale: The Seasonal Contours of Pre-Industrial Poverty in British North America', *Canadian Historical Association, Historical Papers*: 65–94.

Finlayson, Clive. 2004. *Neanderthals and Modern Humans: An Ecological and Evolutionary Perspective*. New York: Cambridge University Press.

Finnie, Ross. 2001. 'L' Incidence de la mobilité interprovinciale sur les gains des particuliers: estimations de modèles par panel pour le Canada'. Documents de Recherche, Direction des Études Analytiques no. 163 (October 2001). Ottawa: Statistics Canada.

———. 1999a. 'The Patterns of Inter-Provincial Migration in Canada 1982–95: Evidence from Longitudinal Tax-Based Data', *Canadian Studies in Population* 26, 2: 205–34.

———. 1999b. 'Inter-Provincial Migration in Canada: A Longitudinal Analysis of Movers and Stayers and the Associated Income Dynamics', *Canadian Journal of Regional Science* 22, 3: 227–62.

Firebaugh, Glenn. 2003. *The New Geography of Global Income Inequality*. Cambridge, MA: Harvard University Press.

Fischer, Claude S. 1976. *The Urban Experience*. New York: Harcourt Brace Jovanovic.

———. 1975. 'Toward a Subcultural Theory of Urbanism', *American Journal of Sociology* 80: 1319–41.

Fischer, Stanley. 2003. 'Globalization and its Challenges', *The American Economic Review* 93, 2: 1–30.

Fishbein, Martin. 1972. 'Toward an Understanding of Family Planning Behaviors', *Journal of Applied Social Psychology* 2: 214–27.

Flegal, Katherine M., Barry I. Graubard, David F. Williamson, and M. H. Gail. 2005. 'Excess Deaths Associated With Underweight, Overweight, and Obesity', *Journal of the American Medical Association* 293, 1 (20 April): 1861–1867.

Fleischman, John. 1999. 'Why Are You Alive?', *Old Farmer's Almanac*. Dublin, NH: Yankee Publishing Inc.

Flew, Anthony, ed. 1970. *Malthus: An Essay on the Principle of Population*. Harmondsworth, UK: Penguin.

Florida, Richard. 2005. *The Flight of the Creative Class: The New Global Competition for Talent*. New York: Harper Business/HarperCollins.

———. 2002. *The Rise of the Creative Class: And How It's Transforming Work, Leisure, Community, and Everyday Life*. New York: Basic Books.

Fogel, Robert W. 2004a. *The Escape from Hunger and Premature Death, 1700–2100*. Cambridge: Cambridge University Press.

———. 2004b. 'Changes in the Process of Aging during the Twentieth Century: Findings and Procedures of the Early Indicators Project', in Linda J. Waite, ed., *Aging, Health, and Public Policy: Demographic and Economic Perspectives*, supp. to *Population and Development Review* 30. New York: Population Council.

———, and Dora L. Costa. 1997. 'A Theory of Technophysio Evolution, with Some Implications for Forecasting Population, Health Care Costs, and Pension Costs', *Demography* 34, 1: 49–66.

Folbre, Nancy. 1988. 'The Black Four of Hearts: Toward a New Paradigm of Household Economics', in Daisy Dwyer and Judith Bruce, eds, *A Home Divided: Women and Income in the Third World*. Stanford, CA: Stanford University Press.

———. 1983. 'Of Patriarchy Born: The Political Economy of Fertility Decisions', *Feminist Studies* 9: 261–84.

Fong, Eric. 2005. 'Immigration and the City', in Harry H. Hiller, ed., *Urban Canada: Sociological Perspectives*. Don Mills, ON: Oxford University Press.

———, and Kumiko Shibuya. 2005. 'Multiethnic Cities in North America', *Annual Review of Sociology* 31: 1–20.

Fontaine, Kevin R., David T. Rodden, C. Wang, et al. 2003. 'Years of Life Lost Due to Obesity', *Journal of the American Medical Association* 289, 2 (8 January): 187–93.

Foot, David, and Daniel Stoffman. 1998. *Boom, Bust & Echo 2000: Profiting from the Demographic Shift in the New Millennium*. Toronto: Stoddart.

Forster, Peter, and Shuichi Matsumura. 2005. 'Did Early Humans Go North or South?', *Science* 308 (13 May): 965–6.

Foster, Caroline. 2000. 'The Limits to Low Fertility: A Biosocial Approach', *Population and Development Review* 26, 2: 209–34.

Fox News. 2006. 'Japan's Birth Rate Drops to Record Low of 1.25 Babies per Woman', <http://www.foxnews.com/story/0,2933,197866,00.html> (1 June).

Francis, Diane. 2002. *Immigration: The Economic Case*. Toronto: Key Porter.

Frank, Andre Gunder. 1991. 'The Underdevelopment of Development', *Scandinavian Journal of Development Alternatives* 10, 3: 5–72.

———. 1984. 'Political Ironies in the World Economy', *Studies in Political Economy* 15 (Fall): 119–49.

———. 1969. *Capitalism and Underdevelopment in Latin America*. New York: Monthly Review Press.

Frejka, Tomas. 2004. 'The Curiously High Fertility of the USA', *Population Studies* 58, 1: 77–92.

———. 1983. 'Induced Abortion and Fertility: A Quarter Century of Experience in Eastern Europe', *Population and Development Review* 9, 3: 494–520.

———, and G. Calot. 2001. 'Cohort Reproductive Patterns in Low-Fertility Countries', *Population and Development Review* 27: 103–32.

———, and John Ross. 2001. 'Paths to Subreplacement Fertility: The Empirical Evidence', in Rodolfo A. Bulatao and John B. Casterline, eds, *Global Fertility Transition*, supp. to *Population and Development Review* 27. New York: Population Council.

———, and Jean-Paul Sardon. 2004. *Childbearing Trends and Prospects in Low-Fertility Countries: A Cohort Analysis*. Dordrecht: Kluwer Academic Publishers.

Frenk, Julio, Louis Bobadilla, Claudio Stern, et al. 1991. 'Elements for a Theory of the Health Transition', *Health Transition Review* 1: 21–38.

Freud, Sigmund. 1930 [2005]. *Civilization and its Discontents* (*Unbehagen in der Kultur*). Trans. James Strachey. New York: Norton.

Frey, W.H. 2003. 'Internal Migration', in Paul Demeny and Geoffrey McNicoll, eds, *Encyclopedia of Population* vol. 2 (pp. 545–8). New York: Macmillan Reference USA/Thomson Gale.

———. 1993. 'The New Urban Revival in the United States', *Urban Studies* 30, 4–5: 741–74.

———. 1990. 'Metropolitan America: Beyond the Transition', *Population Bulletin* 45, 2. Washington: Population Reference Bureau.

———. 1989. 'United States: Counterurbanisation and Metropolis Depopulation', in A.G. Champion, ed., *Counterurbanisation: The Changing Pace and Nature of Population Deconcentration*. London: Edward Arnold.

———. 1987. 'Migration and Depopulation of the Metropolis: Regional Restructuring or Rural Renaissance?', *American Sociological Review* 52, 2: 240–57.

———, and Alden Speare. 1992. 'The Revival of Metropolitan Population Growth in the United States: An Assessment of Findings from the 1990 Census', *Population and Development Review* 18, 1: 129–46.

Frideres, James S. 1974. 'Urban Indians', in James S. Frideres, ed., *Canada's Indians: Contemporary Conflicts*. Scarborough, ON: Prentice Hall.

———, and René Gadacz. 2008. *Aboriginal Peoples in Canada*, 8th edn. Toronto: Pearson.

———, Madeline A. Kalbach, and Warren E. Kalbach. 2004. 'Government Policy and the Spatial Redistribution of Canada's Aboriginal Peoples', in John Taylor and Martin Bell, eds, *Population Mobility and Indigenous Peoples in Australasia and North America* (pp. 94–114). London: Routledge.

Frieden, Betty. 1963. *The Feminine Mystique*. New York: Norton.

Friedlander, D. 1969. 'Demographic Responses and Population Change', *Demography* 6, 4: 359–82.

Friedman, Debra, Michael Hechter, and Sitoshi Kanazawa. 1994. 'A Theory of the Value of Children', *Demography* 31, 3: 375–401.

Friedman, Vicki A., Linda G. Martin, and Robert F. Schoeni. 2002. 'Recent Trends in Disability and Functioning Among Older Adults in the United States: A Systematic Review', *Journal of the American Medical Association* 288, 24: 3137–46.

Fries, James F. 1983. 'The Compression of Morbidity', *The Milbank Quarterly/Health and Society* 61: 397–419.

———. 1980. 'Aging, Natural Death and the Compression of Mortality and Morbidity', *The New England Journal of Medicine* 303, 3: 130–5.

———, and Lawrence M. Crapo. 1981. *Vitality and Aging: Implications of the Rectangular Curve*. New York: W.H. Freeman.

Frisbie, W. Parker. 2005. 'Infant Mortality', in Dudley Poston and Michael Michlin, eds, *Handbook of Population*. New York: Kluwer Academic Publishers/Plenum.

Furedi, Frank. 1997. *Population and Development: A Critical Introduction*. New York: St Martin's.

Fussell, Elizabeth, and Alberto Palloni. 2004. 'Persistent Marriage Regimes in Changing Times', *Journal of Marriage and the Family* 66, 5: 1201–1213.

Fuwa, Makiko. 2004. 'Macro-Level Gender Inequality and the Division of Household Labor in 22 Countries', *American Sociological Review* 69, 6: 751–67.

Gabaix, X. 1999. 'Zipf's Law for Cities: An Explanation', *Quarterly Journal of Economics* 114: 739–67.

Galbraith, James K. 2002. 'A Perfect Crime: Inequality in the Age of Globalization', *Daedalus* (Winter): 11–25.

Galley, Chris, and Robert Woods. 1999. 'On the Distribution of Deaths during the First Year of Life', *Population* 11: 35–60.

Galloway, Patrick R. 1986. 'Long-Term Fluctuations in Climate and Population in the Preindustrial Era', *Population and Development Review* 12, 1: 1–24.

Gauri, Varun, and Peyvand Khaleghian. 2002. 'Immunization in Developing Countries: Its Political and Organizational Determinants', *World Development* 30, 12: 2109–32.

Gauthier, Anne H. 2005. 'Trends in Policies for Family-Friendly Societies', in Miroslov Macura, Alphonse L. MacDonald, and Werner Haug, eds., *The New Demographic Regime: Population Challenges and Policy Responses*. New York and Geneva: United Nations.

———, and Jan Hatzius. 1997. 'Family Benefits and Fertility: An Econometric Analysis', *Population Studies* 51, 3: 295–306.

Gauvreau, Danielle. 1991. *Québec: une ville et sa population au temps de la Nouvelle France*. Montreal: Presses de l'Université du Québec.

Gavrilov, Leonid A., and Natalia S. Gavrilova. 2000. 'Data Resources for Biodemographic Studies on Familial Clustering of Human Longevity', *Demographic Research* 1, 4. http://www.demographic-research.org.

———, and ———. 1991. *The Biology of Life Span: A Quantitative Approach*. Trans. John and Liliya Payne. Chur, CH: Harwood Academic Publishers.

Gee, Ellen M. 1994. 'The Life Course of Canadian Women: An Historical and Demographic Analysis', in Frank Trovato and Carl F. Grindstaff, eds, *Perspectives on Canada's Population: An Introduction to Concepts and Issues*. Don Mills, ON: Oxford University Press.

———, and Gloria M. Gutman, eds. 2000. *The Overselling of Population Aging: Apocalyptic Demography, Intergenerational Challenges, and Social Policy*. Don Mills, ON: Oxford University Press.

Gelbard, Alene, Carl Haub, and Mary M. Kent. 1999. 'World Population Beyond Six Billion', *Population Bulletin* 54, 1. Washington: Population Reference Bureau.

Gendel, Murray. 2002. 'Boomers' Retirement Wave Likely to Begin in Just 6 Years', *Population Today* 3 (30 April): 4–5.

George, M.V. 1970. *Internal Migration in Canada*. 1961 Census Monograph. Ottawa: Statistics Canada.

——, and Shirley Loh. 2007. 'Projected Population Size and Age Structure for Canada and Province: With and Without International Migration', *Canadian Studies in Population* 34, 2: 103–27.

——, ——, Ravi P. Verma, and Y. Edward Shin. 2001. *Population Projections for Canada, Provinces and Territories, 2000–2026*. Cat. no. 91-520-XPB. Ottawa: Statistics Canada.

Gerber, Linda M. 1984. 'Community Characteristics and Out-Migration from Canadian Indian Reserves: Path Analysis', *Canadian Review of Sociology and Anthropology* 21, 2: 145–65.

Gever, John, Robert Kaufmann, Davis S. Kole, et al. 1986. *Beyond Oil: The Threat to Food and Fuel in the Coming Decades*, 3rd edn. Nivot: University Press of Colorado.

Geyer, H.S. 1996. 'Expanding the Theoretical Foundation of the Concept of Differential Urbanization', *Tijdschrift voor Economische en Sociale Geografie* 87, 1: 44–59.

——, and T. Kontuly, eds. 1996. *Differential Urbanization: Integrating Spatial Models*. London: Edward Arnold.

——, and ——. 1993 [1996]. 'A Theoretical Foundation for the Concept of Differential Urbanization', *International Regional Science Review* 17, 2: 157–77.

Giancoli, Douglas C. 1985. *Physics*, 2nd edn. Englewood Cliffs, NJ: Prentice Hall.

Giddens, Anthony. 1992. *The Transformation of Intimacy: Sexuality, Love and Eroticism in Modern Societies*. Stanford, CA: Stanford University Press.

——. 1984. *The Constitution of Society: Outline of the Theory of Structuration*. Cambridge: Cambridge University Press.

Giere, Ronald N. 1999. *Science without Laws*. Chicago: The University of Chicago Press.

Gilbert, Alan, and Joseph Gugler. 1992. *Cities, Poverty and Development: Urbanization in the Third World*, 2nd edn. Oxford: Oxford University Press.

Gillis, Ron. 2005. 'Cities and Social Pathology', in Harry H. Hiller, ed., *Urban Canada: Sociological Perspectives*. Don Mills, ON: Oxford University Press.

Gist, Noel P., and Sylvia Fleis Favia. 1974. *Urban Society*, 6th edn. New York: Thomas Y. Crowell.

Gjonca, Arjan. 2001. *Communism, Health and Lifestyle: The Paradox of Mortality Transition in Albania, 1950–1990*. Westport, CT: Greenwood.

——, Christopher Wilson, and Jane Falkingham. 1997. 'Paradoxes of Health Transition in Europe's Poorest Country, Albania 1950–1990', *Population and Development Review* 23, 3: 585–609.

Glaeser, Edward L., and Jesse M. Shapiro. 2003. 'Urban Growth in the 1990s: Is City Living Back?', *Journal of Regional Science* 43, 1: 139–65.

Glass, David V., and D.E.C. Eversley, eds. 1965. *Population in History*. Chicago: Aldine.

Glei, Dana A., and Shiro Horiuchi. 2007. 'The Narrowing Sex Differential in Life Expectancy in High-Income Populations: Effects of Differences in the Age Pattern of Mortality', *Population Studies* 61, 2: 141–59.

Glenn, Norvall D., and M. Supancic. 1984. 'The Social and Demographic Correlates of Divorce and Separation in the United States: An Update and Reconsideration', *Journal of Marriage and the Family* 46: 563–79.

Globe and Mail, The. 2007a. 'China Battles Army of Unmarried Men: Fearing Explosion of Social Unrest, Country Vows Sex-Selection Crackdown' (23 January): A3.

——. 2007b. 'Immigrants and Wages'. Editorial (28 May): A12.

——. 2003. 'Portrait of Canadian Immigration' (25 January): A5.

——. 2002. 'Canada Facing Age Crunch' (17 July): A1, A3, A6–7.

——. 1992. 'Canadian Immigration Trends' (20 June): A4.

Gober, Patricia. 1993. 'Americans on the Move', *Population Bulletin* 48, 3. Washington: Population Reference Bureau.

Goldscheider Calvin. 1971. *Population, Modernization, and Social Structure*. Boston: Little, Brown.

——, and Peter H. Uhlenberg. 1969. 'Minority Group Status and Fertility', *American Journal of Sociology* 74: 361–72.

Goldscheider, Frances K., and Linda J. Waite. 1991. *New Families, No Families? The Transformation of the American Home*. Berkeley: University of California Press.

——, and ——. 1986. 'Sex Differences in the Entry into Marriage', *American Journal of Sociology* 92: 91–109.

Golini, Antonio. 2003. 'Current Demographic Setting and the Future of Aging: The Experience of Some European Countries', *Genus* LIX, 1: 15–49.

——. 2001. 'Should Borders be Open?', International Union for the Scientific Study of Population General Conference. San Salvador de Bahia, Brazil. August 24, 2001.

Gompertz, Benjamin. 1825. 'On the Nature of the Function Expressive of the Law of Mortality', *Philosophical Transactions* 27: 513–82.

Goode, William J. 1970. *World Revolution and Family Patterns*. New York: Free Press.

Goodkind, Daniel. 1996. 'On Substituting Sex Preferences Strategies in East Asia: Does Prenatal Sex Selection Reduce Postnatal Discrimination?', *Population and Development Review* 22, 1: 111–25.

——, and Loraine West. 2001. 'The North Korean Famine and its Demographic Impact', *Population and Development Review* 27, 2: 219–38.

Goody, Jack. 1996. 'Comparing Family Systems in Europe and Asia', *Population and Development Review* 22, 1: 1–20.

Gordon, P. 1979 [1996]. 'Deconcentration Without a "Clean Break"', in H.S. Geyer and T.M. Kontuly, eds, *Differential Urbanization: Integrating Spatial Models*. London: Edward Arnold.

Gortmaker, Steven L., and P.H. Wise. 1997. 'The First Injustice: Socio-Economic Disparities, Health Services Technology, and Infant Mortality', *Annual Review of Sociology* 23: 147–70.

Gossman, Charles, and David Odynak. 1983. 'The Canadian Census and the Rank-Size Rule', in N. Waters, ed., *Cartography and Physical and Human Geography: The Douglas College Papers*, BC Geographical Series, no. 40. Occasional Papers in Geography. Vancouver, BC: Tantalus Research Limited.

Gottlieb, Beatrice. 1993. *The Family in the Western World from the Black Death to the Industrial Age*. New York: Oxford University Press.

Gourbin, Catherine. 2006. 'Fetal Mortality', in Graziella Caselli, Jacques Vallin, and Guillaume Wunsch, eds, *Demography: Analysis and Synthesis*, vol. 1. Amsterdam: Elsevier.

Gove, Walter R. 1973. 'Sex, Marital Status and Mortality', *American Journal of Sociology* 79: 45–67.

Goyder, John. 1993. 'The Canadian Syndrome of Regional Polarities: An Obituary', *Canadian Review of Sociology and Anthropology* 30, 10: 1–12.

Grant, E. Kenneth, and John Vanderkamp. 1985. 'Migrant Information and the Remigration Decision: Further Evidence', *Southern Economic Journal* 51: 1202–15.

———, and ———. 1984. 'A Descriptive Analysis of the Incidence and Nature of Repeat Migration Within Canada, 1968–71', *Canadian Studies in Population* 11, 1: 61–78.

———, and ———. 1983. 'The Spatial Aspects and Regularities of Multiple Interregional Migration Within Canada: Evidence and Implications', *The Canadian Journal of Regional Science* 6: 75–95.

———, and ———. 1976. *The Economic Causes and Effects of Migration: Canada, 1965–71*. Ottawa: Economic Council of Canada.

Grant, Jonathan, Stijn Hoorens, Suja Sivadasan, et al. 2004. *Low Fertility and Population Ageing Causes, Consequences, and Policy Options*. Santa Monica: RAND Corporation.

Gratton, Michel. 1992. *French Canadians: An Outsider's Inside Look at Quebec*. Toronto: Key Porter.

Gray, Alan. 1990. *A Matter of Life and Death: Contemporary Aboriginal Mortality*. Canberra: Aboriginal Studies Press.

Green, Alan, and David Green. 1999. 'The Economic Goals of Canada's Immigration Policy: Past and Present', *Canadian Public Policy* 24: 425–51.

Green, Anne, Irene Hardill, and Stephen Munn. 1999. 'The Employment Consequences of Migration: Gender Differentials', in Paul Boyle and Keith Halfcree, eds, *Migration and Gender in the Developed World*. London: Routledge.

Greenhalgh, Susan. 1986. 'Shifts in China's Population Policy', *Population and Development Review* 12, 3: 491–516.

Greenwood, Michael J. 1985. 'Human Migration: Theory, Models and Empirical Studies', *Journal of Regional Science* 25, 4: 521–44.

Gregory, Joel W., and Victor Piché. 1983. 'Inequality and Mortality: Demographic Hypotheses Regarding Advanced and Peripheral Capitalism', *International Journal of Health Services* 13, 1: 89–106.

Greksa, Lawrence P. 2003. 'Birth Seasonality in the Old Order Amish', *Journal of Biosocial Science* 36: 299–315.

Grindstaff, Carl F. 1995. 'Canada's Continued Trend of Low Fertility', *Canadian Social Trends* (Winter): 12–16.

———. 1994. 'The Baby Bust Revisited: Canada's Continuing Pattern of Low Fertility', in Frank Trovato and Carl F. Grindstaff, eds, *Canada's Population: Introduction to Concepts and Issues*. Don Mills, ON: Oxford University Press.

———. 1985. 'The Baby Bust Revisited: Canada's Continuing Pattern of Fertility', *Canadian Studies in Population* 12, 1: 103–10.

———. 1981a. *Canada's Population: A Sociological Perspective*. West Hanover, MA: Christopher Publishing House.

———. 1981b. *Population and Society: A Sociological Perspective*. West Hanover, MA: Christopher Publishing House.

———. 1975. 'The Baby Bust: Changes in Fertility Patterns in Canada', *Canadian Studies in Population* 2: 15–22.

———, and Frank Trovato. 1990. 'Junior Partners: Women's Contribution to Family Income in Canada', *Social Indicators Research* 22: 229–53.

———, T.R. Balakrishnan, and David J. Dewit. 1992. 'Educational Attainment, Age at First Birth and Lifetime Fertility: An Analysis of Canadian Fertility Survey Data', *Canadian Review of Sociology and Anthropology* 28, 3: 324–39.

Grossbard-Schechtman, Shoshana. 1995. 'Marriage Market Models', in Mariano Tommasi and Kathryn Ierulli, eds, *The New Economics of Human Behavior*. Cambridge: Cambridge University Press.

Grundy, E. 2000. 'Co-Residence of Mid-Life Children with their Elderly Parents in England and Wales: Changes Between 1981 and 1991', *Population Studies* 54: 193–206.

Gugler, Joseph. 1988. 'The Urban Transition in the Third World: Introduction', in Joseph Gugler, ed., *The Urbanization of the Third World*. Oxford: Oxford University Press.

Guillot, Michel. 2003a. 'The Cross-Sectional Average Length of Life (CAL): A Cross-Sectional Mortality Measure that Reflects the Experience of Cohorts', *Population Studies* 57, 1: 41–54.

———. 2003b. 'Life Tables', in Paul Demeny and Geoffrey McNicoll, eds, *Encyclopedia of Population*. New York: Macmillan Reference USA/Thomson Gale.

———. 2002. 'The Dynamics of the Population Sex Ratio in India, 1971–96', *Population Studies* 56, 1: 51–63.

Guimond, Eric. 2003. 'Changing Ethnicity: The Concept of Ethnic Drifters', in Jerry P. White, Paul Maxim, and Dan Beavon, eds, *Aboriginal Conditions: Research Foundations for Public Policies*. Vancouver: University of British Columbia Press.

———. 1999. 'Ethnic Mobility and the Demographic Growth of Canada's Aboriginal Populations from 1986 to 1996', in Alain Bélanger, *Report on the Demographic Situation in Canada: 1998 and 1999*. Cat. no. 91-209-XPE. Ottawa: Statistics Canada.

———, Don Kerr, and Roderic Beaujot. 2004. 'Charting the Growth of Canada's Aboriginal Populations: Problems, Options and Implications', *Canadian Studies in Population* 31, 1: 55–84.

Guindon, Hubert. 1988. *Quebec Society: Tradition, Modernity, and Nationhood*. Toronto: University of Toronto Press.

Gunderson, Morley. 1998. *Women and the Canadian Labour Market: Transitions Towards the Future*. Ottawa and Toronto: Statistics Canada and ITP Nelson.

Gusfield, Joseph R. 1967. 'Tradition and Modernity: Misplaced Polarities in the Study of Social Change', *American Journal of Sociology* 72: 351–62.

Guttentag, Marcia, and Paul F. Secord. 1983. *Too Many Women? The Sex Ratio Question*. Beverly Hills, CA: Sage.

Gwatkin, Davidson R. 1980. 'Indication of Change in Developing Country Mortality Trends: The End of an Era?', *Population and Development Review* 6, 4: 615–44.

Haberland, Nicole, and Diana Measham, eds. 2002. *Responding to Cairo: Case Studies of Changing Practice in Reproductive Health and Family Planning*. New York: Population Council.

Haines, Michael R., and Richard H. Steckel. 2000. *A Population History of North America*. Cambridge: Cambridge University Press.

Hajnal, John. 1965. 'European Marriage Patterns in Perspective', in D.V. Glass and D.E.C. Eversley, eds, *Population in History: Essay in Historical Demography*. London: Edward Arnold.

Halfcree, Keith, and Paul Boyle. 1999. 'Introduction: Gender and Migration in Developed Countries', in Paul Boyle and Keith Halfcree, eds, *Migration and Gender in the Developed World*. London: Routledge.

Hall, David R., and John Z. Zhao. 1995. 'Cohabitation and Divorce in Canada: Testing the Selectivity Hypothesis', *Journal of Marriage and the Family* 57: 421–7.

Hall, Peter. 1998. *Cities in Civilization*. London: Weidenfeld & Nicolson.

———. 1996. 'The Global City', *International Social Science Journal* 48: 15–23.

Halli, Shiva S. 1990. 'The Fertility of Ethnic Groups', in Shiva S. Halli, Frank Trovato, and Leo Dridger, eds, *Ethnic Demography: Canadian Immigrant, Racial and Cultural Variations*. Ottawa: Carleton University Press.

Halweil, Brian. 2003. 'Grain Production Drops', in *Vital Signs* (pp. 28–9). The Worldwatch Institute. New York: W.W. Norton.

Hamilton, Graeme. 2004. 'Mission Aims to Seduce Students to Gaspé Charms', *National Post* (18 March): A5.

———. 2002. 'People Don't Even Say Hello Anymore', *National Post* (21 September): A3.

Hanawalt, Barbara A. 2001. 'Childrearing among the Lower Classes of Late Medieval Europe', in Robert I. Rotberg, ed., *Population History and the Family: A Journal of Interdisciplinary History Reader*. Cambridge, MA: MIT Press.

Hank, Karsten, and Hans-Peter Kohler. 2003. 'Sex Preferences for Children Revisited: New Evidence from Germany', *Population* 58, 1: 133–44.

Hannerz, Harald. 2001. 'Manhood Trials and the Law of Mortality', *Demographic Research*, vol. 4, art. 7 (May): 185–202, <http://www.demographic-research.org>.

Hardin, Garret. 1968. 'The Tragedy of the Commons', *Science* 162 (13 December): 1243–8.

Hardy, Melissa A., and Linda Waite. 1997. 'Doing Time: Reconciling Biography with History in the Study of Social Change', in Melissa A. Hardy, ed., *Studying Aging and Social Change: Conceptual and Methodological Issues*. Thousand Oaks, CA: Sage.

Harms, Phillip, and Heinrich W. Ursprung. 2002. 'Do Civil and Political Repression Really Boost Foreign Direct Investments?', *Economic Inquiry* 40, 4: 651–63.

Harris, J.R., and M.P. Todaro. 1970. 'Migration, Unemployment, and Development: A Two-Sector Analysis', *American Economic Review* 60, 1: 126–42.

Hartnagel, Tim F., and G.W. Lee. 1990. 'Urban Crime in Canada', *Canadian Journal of Criminology* 32: 591–606.

Hatt, P.K. 1946. 'The Concept of Natural Area', *American Sociological Review* 11: 423–8.

Hatton, Timothy J., and Jeffrey G. Williamson. 1998. *The Age of Mass Migration: Causes and Economic Impact*. New York: Oxford University Press.

———, and ———. 1994. 'What Drove the Mass Migrations from Europe in the Late Nineteenth Century?', *Population and Development Review* 20, 3: 503–31.

Haub, Carl. 2002. 'How Many People Have Ever Lived on Earth?', *Population Today* (November–December): 3–4.

———. 1995. 'How Many People Have Ever Lived on Earth?', *Population Today* (February): 3–4.

———. 1987. 'Understanding Population Projections', *Population Bulletin* 42, 4. Washington: Population Reference Bureau.

Haugrud, Barry. 2007. Alberta Vital Statistics, personal communication (15 November).

Haveman-Nies, Annemien, Lisette P.G.M. de Groot, Jan Burema, et al. 2002. 'Dietary Quality and Lifestyle Factors in Relation to 10-Year Mortality in Older Europeans', *American Journal of Epidemiology* 156, 1: 962–8.

Hawkins, Freda. 1977. 'Canada and Immigration: A New Law and a New Approach to Management', *International Migration Review* 12: 77–94.

Hawkins, Liz, and Ray D. Bollman. 1994. 'Revisiting Rural Canada: It's Not All the Same', *Canadian Agriculture at a Glance* (pp. 78–80). Ottawa: Statistics Canada. Cat. no. 96-301.

Hawthorne, H.B., ed. 1966. *A Survey of the Contemporary Indians of Canada: Report on the Economic, Political, Educational Needs and Policies.* Two Volumes. Ottawa: Indian Affairs Branch.

Hayek, F.A. 1998. 'The Extended Order and Population Growth', in Paul Demeny and Geoffrey McNicoll, eds, *The Earthscan Reader in Population and Development.* London: Earthscan.

Haynes, Michael, and Rumy Husan. 2003. *A Century of State Murder? Death and Policy in Twentieth-Century Russia.* London: Pluto.

Hayter, Teresa. 2000. *Open Borders: The Case Against Immigration Controls.* London: Pluto.

Hayward, Mark D., and Bridget K. Gorman. 2004. 'The Long Arm of Childhood: The Influence of Early-Life Social Conditions on Men's Mortality', *Demography* 41, 1: 87–107.

———, and Melonie Heron. 1999. 'Racial Inequality in Active Life among Adult Americans', *Demography* 36, 1: 77–92.

Hazelrigg, Lawrence. 1997. 'On the Importance of Age', in Melissa A. Hardy, ed., *Studying Aging and Social Change: Conceptual and Methodological Issues.* Thousand Oaks, CA: Sage.

Health and Welfare Canada. 1986. 'Achieving Health for All'. Ottawa: Department of National Health and Welfare.

Health Canada. 2003. *A Statistical Profile on the Health of First Nations in Canada* (various pages).

———. 1996a. 'Towards a Common Understanding: Clarifying the Core Concepts of Population Health'. Cat. no. H39-391/1996E.

———. 1996b. 'Trends in First Nations Mortality 1979–1993'. Cat. no. 34-79/1993E.

———. 1995. 'Mortality Data and Population Counts for the Registered Indians of Canada for 1979 to 1992'. Special tabulation.

———. 1994. 'Strategies for Population Health: Investing in the Health of Canadians'.

Heilig, Gerhand, Thomas Buttner, and Wolfgang Lutz. 1990. 'Germany's Population: Turbulent Past, Uncertain Future', *Population Bulletin* 45, 4. Washington: Population Reference Bureau.

Hekimi, Siegfried, and Leonard Guarente. 2003. 'Genetics and the Specificity of the Aging Process', *Science* 299 (28 February): 1351–4.

Held, David, Anthony McGrew, David Goldblatt, et al. 1999. *Global Transformations: Politics, Economic and Culture.* Stanford, CA: Stanford University Press.

Heligman, L., and H.H. Pollard. 1980. 'The Age Pattern of Mortality', *Journal of the Institute of Actuaries* 107: 49–80.

Hemon, Louis. 1914 [1965]. *Maria Chapdelaine.* Toronto: Macmillan.

Hempel, Carl G. 1966. *Philosophy of Natural Science.* Englewood Cliffs, NJ: Prentice Hall.

Henderson, Robert. 1915. *Mortality Laws and Statistics.* New York: John Wiley.

Henderson, Vernon. 2003. 'The Urbanization Process and Economic Growth: The So-What Question', *Journal of Economic Growth* 8: 47–71.

Henricksen, Tine Brink, Niels Henrik Hjoullund, Tina Kold Jensen, et al. 2004. 'Alcohol Consumption at the Time of Conception and Spontaneous Abortion', *American Journal of Public Health* 160, 7: 661–667.

Henripin, Jacques. 2003. *La métamorphose de la population canadienne.* Montreal: Les Éditions Varia.

———. 1994a. 'From Acceptance of Nature to Control: The Demography of the French Canadians since the Seventeenth Century', in Frank Trovato and Carl F. Grindstaff, eds, *Perspectives on Canada's Population: An Introduction to Concepts and Issues.* Don Mills, ON: Oxford University Press.

———. 1994b. 'The Financial Consequences of Population Aging', *Canadian Public Policy* 20, 1: 78–94.

———. 1972. 'Trends and Factors of Fertility in Canada', *1961 Census Monograph.* Ottawa: Statistics Canada.

———. 1954. *La population canadienne au début du XVIIIè siècle.* Paris: Institut National d'Études Démographiques.

———, and Yves Péron. 1972. 'The Demographic Transition of the Province of Quebec', in D.V. Glass and Roger Revelle, eds, *Population and Social Change.* London: Edward Arnold.

Henry, Louis. 1989. 'Men's and Women's Mortality in the Past', *Population*, vol. 44 (English selection no. 1): 177–201.

———. 1961. 'Some Data on Natural Fertility', *Eugenics Quarterly* (now *Social Biology*) 8: 81–91.

Henshaw, Stanley K. 2003. 'Abortion: Prevalence', in Paul Demeny and Geoffrey McNicoll, eds, *Encyclopedia of Population* (pp. 529–31). New York: Macmillan Reference USA/Thompson Gale.

Herlihy, David. 1997. *The Black Death and the Transformation of the West.* Cambridge, MA: Harvard University Press. (Edited and with an introduction by Samuel K. Cohn Jr.)

Hertig, Jerald R., David B. Grusky, and Stephen E. Van Rompaey. 1997. 'The Social Geography of Interstate Mobility and Persistence', *American Sociological Review* 62, 2: 267–87.

Hertzman, Clyde. 2001. 'Health and Human Society', *American Scientist* 89 (November–December): 538–45.

Hesketh, Therese, Li Lu, and Zhu Wei Xing. 2006. 'The Effect of China's One-Child Family Policy After 25 Years', *New England Journal of Medicine* 353 (15 September): 1171–6.

Hess, Gregory. 2004. 'Marriage and Consumption Insurance: What's Love Got to Do With It?', *Journal of Political Economy* 112, 2: 290–318.

Heuveline, Patrick. 1999. 'The Global and Regional Impact of Mortality and Fertility Transitions, 1950–2000', *Population and Development Review* 25, 4: 681–702.

———, Michel Guillot, and Davidson R. Gwatkin. 2002. 'The Uneven Tides of the Health Transition' *Social Science and Medicine* 55: 313–22.

———, and Jeffrey M. Timberlake. 2004. 'The Role of Cohabitation in Family Formation: The United States in Comparative Perspective', *Journal of Marriage and the Family* 66: 1214–30.

Hiedemann, B., O. Suhomlinova and A.M. O'Rand. 1998. 'Economic Independence, Economic Status, and Empty Nest in Midlife Marital Disruption', *Journal of Marriage and the Family* 60: 219–31.

Hill, Allan G. 2003. 'Famine in Africa', in Paul Demeny and Geoffrey McNicoll, eds, *Encyclopedia of Population* (pp. 385–8). New York: Macmillan Reference USA/Thomson Gale.

———. 1990. 'Understanding Recent Fertility Trends in the Third World', in John Landers and Vernon Reynolds, eds, *Fertility and Resources* (pp. 146–63). Cambridge: Cambridge University Press.

Hill, Kenneth. 2004. 'War, Humanitarian Crises, Population Displacement, and Fertility: A Review of Evidence'. Roundtable on the Demography of Forced Migration Committee on Population. National Research Council of the National Academies. Washington: The National Academies Press.

Himes, Norman E. 1936. *A Medical History of Contraception*. Baltimore: Williams and Wilkins.

Hinde, Andrew. 2003. *England's Population: A History Since the Domesday Survey*. New York: Oxford University Press.

———. 2002a. 'Demographic Perspectives on Human Population Dynamics', in Helen Macbeth and Paul Collinson, eds, *Human Population Dynamics: Cross-Disciplinary Perspectives* (pp. 17–40). Cambridge: Cambridge University Press.

———. 2002b. 'Population Momentum', in Helen Macbeth and Paul Collinson, eds, *Human Population Dynamics: Cross-Disciplinary Perspectives*. Cambridge: Cambridge University Press.

———. 1998. *Demographic Methods*. London: Edward Arnold.

Hirschi, Travis. 1969. *Causes of Delinquency*. Berkley, CA: Free Press.

Hirschman, Charles. 1994. 'Why Fertility Changes', *Annual Review of Sociology* 20: 203–33.

Hisnanick, John J. 1994. 'Comparative Analysis of Violent Deaths in American Indians and Alaska Natives', *Social Biology* 41, 1–2: 96–109.

Hobcroft, John N. 2004. 'Method, Theory, and Substance in Understanding Choices about Becoming a Parent: Progress or Regress?' *Population Studies* 58, 1: 77–92.

Discussion of the paper by John Caldwell and Thomas Schindlmayer in *Population Studies* 57, 3 (2003).

———. 1987. 'The Proximate Determinants of Fertility', in John Cleland and Chris Scott, eds, *The World Fertility Survey: An Assessment* (pp. 796–837). Oxford: Oxford University Press.

Hodge, Gerald, and Mohammad A. Qadeer. 1983. *Towns and Villages in Canada: The Importance of Being Unimportant*. Toronto: Butterworths.

Hoerder, Dirk. 2002. *Cultures in Contact: World Migrations in the Second Millennium*. Durham: Duke University Press.

Hoffman, Lois Wladis, and Martin L. Hoffman. 1973. 'The Value of Children to Parents', in James T. Fawcett, ed., *Psychological Perspectives on Population* (pp. 19–76). New York: Basic Books.

Hogberg, Ulf. 2004. 'The Decline of Maternal Mortality in Sweden: The Role of Community Midwifery', *American Journal of Public Health* 94, 8: 1312–20.

Hogg, Robert. 1992. 'Indigenous Mortality: Placing Australian Aboriginal Mortality Within a Broader Context', *Social Science and Medicine* 35, 3: 335–46.

Hollander, Samuel. 1997. *The Economics of Thomas Robert Malthus*. Toronto: University of Toronto Press.

Holubitsky, Jeff. 2005. 'Tiny Alberta Village Turns its Fortunes Around', *Edmonton Journal* (17 April): A1, A7.

Homer-Dixon, Thomas. 2006. *The Upside of Down: Catastrophe, Creativity, and the Renewal of Civilization*. New York: Knopf, Island Press.

———. 1999. *Environment, Scarcity, and Violence*. Princeton, NJ: Princeton University Press.

———, J.H. Boutwell, and G.W. Rathjens. 1993. 'Environmental Change and Violent Conflict', *Scientific American* 268, 2 (February): 38–45.

Hoogvelt, Ankie. 2001. *Globalization and the Postcolonial World: The New Political Economy of Development*, 2nd edn. London: Palgrave.

———. 1976. *The Sociology of Developing Societies*. New York: Macmillan.

Horiuchi, Shiro. 2003. 'Mortality, Age Patterns', in Paul Demeny and Geoffrey McNicoll, eds, *Encyclopedia of Population* (pp. 649–54). New York: Macmillan Reference USA/Thompson Gale.

———, and John R. Wilmoth. 1998. 'Deceleration in the Age Pattern of Mortality at Older Ages', *Demography* 35, 4: 391–412.

Hou, Feng. 2004. 'The Initial Destinations and Redistribution of Canada's Major Immigrant Groups: Changes Over the Past two Decades', Working Paper series, Business and Labour Market Analysis Division, Ottawa: Statistics Canada.

———, and Rod Beaujot. 1995. 'A Study of Interregional Migration Between Ontario and Atlantic Canada: 1981–1991', *Canadian Journal of Regional Science* 28: 147–60.

House, James S., Karl R. Landis, and Debra Umberson. 1988. 'Social Relationships and Health', *Science* 2441: 540–5.

Hrdy, Sarah Blaffer. 1999. *Mother Nature: A History of Mothers, Infants and Natural Selection*. New York: Pantheon.

Hugo, Graeme, Anthony Champion, and Alfredo Lattes. 2003. 'Toward a New Conceptualization of Settlements for Demography', *Population and Development Review* 29, 2: 277–97.

Hummer, Robert, Richard G. Rogers, and Isaac W. Eberstein. 1998. 'Socio-economic Differentials in Adult Mortality: A Review of Analytic Approaches', *Population and Development Review* 24, 3: 553–78.

Hunt, Jennifer. 2004. 'Innis Lecture: Are Migrants More Skilled than Non-Migrants? Repeat, Return, and Same-Employer Migrants', *Canadian Journal of Economics* 37, 4: 830–49.

Hurd, W. Burton. 1965. 'Ethnic Origin and Nativity of the Canadian People', *1941 Census Monograph*. Ottawa: Queen's Printer.

Hyatt, Douglas E., and William J. Milne. 1991. 'Can Public Policy Affect Fertility?' *Canadian Public Policy* 17, 1: 77–85.

Inglehart, Ronald. 1997. *Modernization and Postmodernization: Cultural, Economic, and Political Change in 43 Societies*. Princeton, NJ: Princeton University Press.

Inkeles, Alex, and David Horton Smith. 1974. *Becoming Modern: Individual Change in Six Developing Countries*. Cambridge, MA: Harvard University Press.

Innis, Harold A. 1930. *The Fur Trade in Canada: An Introduction to Canadian Economic History*. New Haven: Yale University Press.

International Labor Organization. 2008. *Global Employment Trends: January 2008*. Geneva: International Labor Office.

International Monetary Fund. 2000. World Economic Outlook 2000. Washington, DC.

Isbister, John. 2000. 'A Liberal Argument for Border Controls: Reply to Carens', *International Migration Review* 34, 2: 629–35.

Islam, Mazharul M., M. Ataharul Islam, and Nitai Chakroborty. 2003. 'Fertility Transition in Bangladesh: Understanding the Role of the Proximate Determinants', *Journal of Biosocial Science* 36: 351–69.

Jacobs, Jane. 2004. *Dark Age Ahead*. Toronto: Random House.

———. 1967. Death and Life of Great American Cities. Harmondsworth, UK: Penguin.

Jaffe, A.J. 1992. The First Immigrants from Asia: A Population History of the North American Indians. New York: Plenum.

James, Patricia, ed. 1989a. *T.R. Malthus. An Essay on the Principle of Population*, vol. 1. Cambridge: Cambridge University Press.

———, ed. 1989b. *T.R. Malthus. An Essay on the Principle of Population*, vol. 2. Cambridge: Cambridge University Press.

James, Paul D., Russell Wilkins, Allan S. Detsky, et al. 2007. 'Avoidable Mortality by Neighbourhood Income in Canada: 25 Years after the Establishment of Universal Health Insurance', *Journal of Epidemiology and Community Health* 61: 287–96.

James, William H. 1997. 'Sex Ratio, Coital Rate, Hormones and Time of Fertilization Within the Cycle', *Annals of Human Biology* 24, 5: 403–9.

———. 1987a. 'The Human Sex Ratio: Part I. A Review of the Literature', *Human Biology* 59, 5: 721–52.

———. 1987b. 'The Human Sex Ratio: Part II. A Hypothesis and a Program of Research', *Human Biology* 59, 5: 873–900.

Jarvis, George K., and Menno Boldt. 1982. 'Death Styles among Canada's Indians', *Social Science and Medicine* 16:1345–52.

Jasso, Guilliarmina. 1985. 'Marital Coital Frequency and the Passage of Time: Estimating the Separate Effects of Spouses' Ages and Marital Duration, Birth and Marriage Cohorts, and Period Influences', *American Sociological Review* 50: 224–41.

Jefferson, Mark. 1939. 'The Law of the Primate City', *The Geographical Review* 29: 226–32.

Jeffery, Roger, and Patricia Jeffery. 1997. *Population, Gender and Politics: Demographic Change in Rural North India*. Cambridge: Cambridge University Press.

Jencks, Christopher. 1979. 'Heredity, Environment and Public Policy', *American Sociological Review* 45, 5: 723–36.

Jeune, Bernard, and Axel Skytthe. 2001. 'Centenarians in Denmark in the Past and the Present', *Population: An English Selection* 13, 1: 75–94.

Johansson, S. Ryan. 2003. 'Health Transition', in Paul Demeny and Geoffrey McNicoll, eds, *Encyclopedia of Population* (pp. 479–83). New York: Macmillan Reference USA/Thompson Gale.

———. 1991. 'The Health Transition: The Cultural Inflation of Morbidity During the Decline of Mortality', *Health Transition Review* 1, 1: 39–68.

Johnson, Jothan. 1953 [1973]. 'The Slow Death of a City', *Readings from Scientific American*, in Kingsley Davis, ed., *Cities: Their Origin, Growth and Human Impact*. New York: W.H. Freeman.

Johnson, Kay. 1996. 'The Politics of the Revival of Infant Abandonment in China, with Special Reference to Hunan', *Population and Development Review* 22, 1: 77–98.

Johnson, Kenneth M., Paul R. Voss, Roger B. Hammer, Glenn V. Fuguitt and Scott McNiven. 2005. 'Temporal and Spatial Variations in Age-Specific Net Migration in the United States', *Demography* 42, 4: 791–812.

Johnson, Nan E. 1979. 'Minority-Group Status and the Fertility of Black Americans', *American Journal of Sociology* 84: 1386–1400.

———, and Suwen Lean. 1985. 'Relative Income, Race and Fertility', *Population Studies* 39: 99–112.

Johnson, Stanley P. 1994. *World Population: Turning the Tide: Three Decades of Progress*. London: Graham and Trotman.

Johnson-Hanks, Jennifer. 2007. 'Natural Intentions: Fertility Decline in the African Demograhic and Health Surveys', *American Journal of Sociology* 112, 4: 1008–43.

Johnston, Hugh J.M. 1979. The *Voyage of the Komagata Maru: The Sikh Challenge to Canada's Colour Bar*. Delhi: Oxford University Press.

Jones, Gavin W. 2003. 'Urbanization', in Paul Demeny and Geoffrey McNicoll, eds, *Encyclopedia of Population* (pp. 951–4). New York: Macmillan Reference USA/ Thompson Gale.

———. 2002. 'Southeast Asia Urbanization and the Growth of Mega-urban Regions', *Journal of Population Research* 19, 2: 119–36.

———, and Richard Leete. 2002. 'Asia's Family Planning Programs as Low Fertility is Attained', *Studies in Family Planning* 33, 1.

———, and Pravin Visaria, eds. 1997. *Urbanization in Large Developing Countries: China, Indonesia, Brazil and India*. Oxford: Oxford University Press.

Jones, Steve, Robert Martin, and David Pilbeam, eds. 2000. *The Cambridge Encyclopedia of Human Evolution*. Cambridge: Cambridge University Press.

Junhong, Chu. 2001. 'Prenatal Sex Determination and Sex-Selective Abortion in Rural Central China', *Population and Development Review* 27, 2: 259–82.

Kalbach, Warren E. 1987. 'Growth and Distribution of Canada's Ethnic Populations, 1871–1981', in Leo Driedger, ed., *Ethnic Canada: Identities and Inequalities* (pp. 82–110). Toronto: Copp Clark Pitman.

———. 1970. *The Impact of Immigration on Canada's Population*. Ottawa: The Queen's Printer.

———, and Wayne McVey Jr. 1971. *The Demographic Bases of Canadian Society*. Toronto: McGraw-Hill.

Kalter, Harold. 1991. 'Five-Decade International Trends in the Relation of Perinatal Mortality and Congenital Malformations: Stillbirth and Neonatal Death Compared', *International Journal of Epidemiology* 20 , 1: 173–179.

Kannisto, Vaino. 1996. 'The Advancing Frontier of Survival', *Odense Monographs on Population Aging*, 3. Odense, DK: Odense University Press.

———. 1994. 'Development of Oldest-Old Mortality, 1950–1900: Evidence from 28 Developed Countries', *Odense Monographs on Population Aging*, 1. Odense, Denmark: Odense University Press.

———.1988. 'On the Survival of Centenarians and the Span of Life', *Population Studies* 42: 289–406.

———, Jens Lauritsen, A. Roger Thatcher, and James W. Vaupel. 1994. 'Reductions in Mortality at Advanced Ages: Several Decades of Evidence from 27 Countries', *Population and Development Review* 20, 4: 793–810.

———, Mauri Nieminen, and Oiva Turpeinen. 1999. 'Finnish Life Tables Since 1751', *Demographic Research*, vol. 1. (July) <http://www.demographic-research.org/>.

Kantner, John F., and Andrew Kantner. 2006. *The Struggle for International Consensus on Population and Development*. New York: Palgrave Macmillan.

Kaplan, George A., Barbara A. Cohn, Richard D. Cohen and Jack Guralnik. 1988. 'The Decline in Ischemic Heart Disease Mortality: Prospective Evidence from the Alameda Country Study', *American Journal of Epidemiology* 127, 6: 1131–54.

———, and J.E. Keil. 1993. 'Socio-economic Factors and Cardiovascular Disease: A Review of the Literature', *Circulation* 88, 4: 1973–98.

Kasteloot, H., and X. Huang. 2003. 'On the Relationship between Human All-Cause Mortality and Age', *European Journal of Epidemiology* 18: 503–11.

Kastes, W.G. 1993. *The Future of Aboriginal Urbanization in Prairies Cities: Selected Annotated Bibliography and Literature Review on Urban Aboriginal Issues in the Prairies Provinces*. Winnipeg: Institute of Urban Studies.

Kawachi, Ichiro, and Sarah Wamala. 2007. *Globalization and Health*. Oxford: Oxford University Press.

Kazemipur, Abdolmohammad, and S.S. Halli. 2000. *The New Poverty in Canada: Ethnic Groups and Ghetto Neighbourhoods*. Toronto: Thompson.

Keddie, P.D., and A.E. Joseph. 1991. 'The Turnaround of the Turnaround? Rural Population Change in Canada, 1976 to 1986', *The Canadian Geographer* 35, 4: 367–79.

Keely, Charles. 2001. 'Should Borders be Open?', International Union for the Scientific Study of Population General Conference. San Salvador de Bahia, Brazil. August 24, 2001.

Keil, Roger, and Stefan Kipfer. 2003. 'The Urban Experience and Globalization', in Wallace Clement and Leah F. Vosko, eds, *Changing Canada: Political Economy as Transformation* (pp. 335–62). Montreal and Kingston: McGill-Queens University Press.

Kelley, Allen C. 2001. 'The Population Debate in Historical Perspective: Revisionism Revised', in Birdsall, Nancy, Allen C. Kelley, and Steven W. Sinding, eds, *Population Matters: Demographic Change, Economic Growth, and Poverty in the Developing World* (pp. 24–54). Oxford: Oxford University Press.

Kennedy, Leslie W., and David R. Forde. 1990. 'Routine Activities and Crime: An Analysis of Victimization in Canada', *Criminology* 28: 137–52.

———, and David Veitch. 1997. 'Why Are Crime Rates Going Down? A Case Study in Edmonton', *Canadian Journal of Criminology* 97: 51–69.

Kennedy, Paul. 1993a. *Preparing for the Twenty-First Century*. Toronto: HarperCollins.

———. 1988. *The Rise and Fall of the Great Powers*. London: Unwin Hyman.

Kennedy, Robert E. Jr. 1973. *The Irish: Emigration, Marriage, and Fertility*. Berkeley: University of California Press.

Kenoyer, Jonathan Mark. 2005. 'Uncovering the Keys to the Lost Indus Cities', special issue, *Scientific American* 15, 1: 25–35.

Kent, Mary M., and Carl Haub. 2005. 'Global Demographic Divide', *Population Bulletin* 60, 4. Washington: Population Reference Bureau.

Kerr, Don, Melissa Moyser, and Roderic Beaujot. 2006. 'Marriage and Cohabitation: Demographic and Socioeconomic Differences in Quebec and Canada', *Canadian Studies in Population* 33, 1: 83–117.

Kertzer, David I., and Tom Fricke, eds. 1997. *Anthropological Demography: Toward a New Synthesis*. Chicago: University of Chicago Press.

Kettle, John. 1980. *The Big Generation*. Toronto: McClelland and Stewart.

Keyfitz, Nathan. 2003. 'Euler, Leonhard', in Paul Demeny and Geoffrey McNicoll, eds, Encyclopedia of Population (pp. 322–3). New York: Macmillan Reference USA/ Thomson Gale.

——. 1996a. 'Population Growth, Development and the Environment', *Population Studies* 50: 335–59.

——. 1996b. 'Internal Migration and Urbanization', in Bernardo Colombo, Paul Demeny, and Max F. Perutz, eds, *Resources and Population: Natural, Institutional, and Demographic Dimensions of Development* (pp. 269–85). Oxford: Clarendon.

——. 1996c. 'Population', *Grolier Encyclopedia* on CD-ROM.

——. 1993. 'Are there Ecological Limits to Population?', *Proceedings of the National Academy of Sciences of the USA*, 90 (August): 6895–9.

——. 1992. 'Seven Ways of Causing the Less Developed Countries' Population Problem to Disappear—in Theory', *European Journal of Population* 8: 149–67.

——. 1987. 'Canada's Population in Comparative Perspective', in P. Krishnan, Frank Trovato, and Gordon Fern, eds, *Contributions to Demography: Methodological and Substantive*, vol. 1: *Essays in Honor of Dr. Karol J. Krotki* (pp. 95–110). Edmonton: Department of Sociology, University of Alberta.

——. 1986. 'The Family That Does Not Reproduce Itself', in Kingsley Davis, Mikhail S. Bernstam, and Rita Ricardo-Campbell, eds, *Below-Replacement Fertility in Industrial Societies: Causes, Consequences, Policies* (pp.139–55), supp. to *Population and Development Review* 12.

——. 1985. *Applied Mathematical Demography*, 2nd edn. New York: Springer.

——. 1980. 'Population Appearances and Demographic Reality', *Population and Development Review* 6, 1: 47–64.

——. 1977. *Applied Mathematical Demography*. New York: John Wiley.

——. 1975. 'How Do We Know the Facts of Demography?', *Population and Development Review* 1, 2:267–88.

——. 1971. 'On the Momentum of Population Growth', *Demography* 8, 1: 71–80.

——. 1968. *Introduction to the Mathematics of Population*. Reading, MA: Addison-Wesley.

——. 1966. 'How Many People Have Ever Lived on the Earth?', *Demography* 3, 2: 581–2.

——, and Wilhelm Flieger. 1990. *World Population Growth and Aging: Demographic Trends in the Late Twentieth Century*. Chicago: University of Chicago Press.

Khoury, Muin J., Julian Little, and Wylie Burke, eds. 2003. *Human Genome Epidemiology: A Scientific Foundation for Using Genetic Information to Improve Health and Prevent Disease*. New York: Oxford University Press.

Kibirige, Joachim S. 1997. 'Population Growth, Poverty and Health', *Social Science and Medicine* 45, 2: 247–59.

Kim, Julia C., and Charlotte H. Watts. 2005. 'Getting a Foothold: Tackling Poverty, Gender Inequality, and HIV in Africa', *British Medical Journal* 331: 769–72.

King, Margaret, John Gartrell, and Frank Trovato. 1994. 'Early Childhood Mortality: 1926–1986' in Frank Trovato and Carl F. Grindstaff, eds, *Perspectives on Canada's Population: An Introduction to Concepts and Issues* (pp. 136–41). Don Mills, ON: Oxford University Press.

Kinsella, Kevin, and Victoria A. Vlekoff. 2001. *An Aging World: 2001*. Washington, D.C.: U.S. Census Bureau, Series P95/01-1. U.S. Government Printing Office.

Kirk, Dudley. 1996. 'Demographic Transition Theory', *Population Studies* 50: 361–87.

——. 1960. 'The Influence of Business Cycles on Marriage and Birth Rates', in *National Bureau of Economic Research, Demographic and Economic Change in Developed Countries* (pp. 241–57). Princeton, NJ: Princeton University Press.

Kitagawa, Evelyn M., and Phillip M. Hauser. 1973. *Differential Mortality in the United States: A Study in Socio-economic Epidemiology*. Cambridge, MA: Harvard University Press.

Klasen, Stephan. 2003. 'Sex Selection', in Paul Demeny and Geoffrey McNicoll, eds, *Encyclopedia of Population* (pp. 879–81). New York: Macmillan Reference USA/ Thomson Gale.

——, and Claudia Wink. 2002. 'A Turning Point in Gender Bias in Mortality: An Update on the Number of Missing Women', *Population and Development Review* 28: 285–312.

Kliegman, Robert M. 1995. 'Neonatal Technology, Perinatal Survival, Social Consequences, and the Perinatal Paradox', *American Journal of Public Health* 85: 909–13.

Klinger, Andras. 1985. 'The Fight Against Infant Mortality', in Jacques Vallin and Alan D. Lopez, eds, *Health Policy, Social Policy and Mortality Prospects* (pp. 281–97). Paris: Ordina Editions. Proceedings of a Seminar, 28 February–March 4, 1983. Paris: Institut National d'Etudes Demographiques and International Union for the Scientific Study of Population.

Knodel, John. 1977. 'Age Patterns of Fertility and the Fertility Transition: Evidence From Europe and Asia', *Population Studies* 31: 219–50.

——, and Etienne van de Walle. 1979. 'Lessons From the Past: Policy Implications of Historical Fertility Studies', *Population and Development Review* 5: 217–45.

———, Jed Friedman, Truong Si Anh, and Bui The Cuong. 2000. 'Intergenerational Exchanges in Vietnam: Family Size, Sex Composition, and the Location of Children', *Population Studies* 54: 89–104.

Knox, Paul L., and Sallie A. Marston. 2004. 'Places and Regions in Global Context', *Human Geography*, 3rd edn. Upper Saddle River, NJ: Pearson.

Kobrin, Frances E. 1976. 'The Primary Individual and the Family: Changes in Living Arrangements in the United States Since 1940', *Journal of Marriage and the Family* 38: 233–8.

———, and Alden Speare. 1983. 'Outmigration and Ethnic Communities', *International Migration Review* 17, 3: 425–44.

Kohler, Hans-Peter. 2001. *Fertility and Social Interaction: An Economic Perspective*. Oxford: Oxford University Press.

———. 2000. 'Social Interactions and Fluctuations in the Birth Rates', *Population Studies* 54, 2: 223–37.

———, Francesco Billari, and José Antonio Ortega. 2006. 'Low Fertility in Europe: Causes, Implications, and Policy Options', in Fred R. Harris, ed., *The Baby Bust— Who Will Do the Work? Who Will Pay the Taxes?* (pp. 48–109). Lanham, England: Rowman and Littlefield.

———, ———, and ———. 2002. 'The Emergence of Lowest-Low Fertility in Europe During the 1990s', *Population and Development Review* 28, 4: 641–80.

Kormondy, Edward J. 1969. *Concepts of Ecology*. Englewood Cliffs, NJ: Prentice-Hall.

Korousu, Hiroshi, Masaya Yamamoto, Jeremy D. Clark, et al. 2005. 'Suppression of Aging in Mice by the Hormone Klotho', *Science* 309 (16 September): 1829–33.

Koser, Khalid. 2007. *International Migration: A Very Short Introduction*. Oxford: Oxford University Press.

Kosinski, Leszek A. 1970. *The Population of Europe: A Geographical Perspective*. Bristol: Longman.

———, and R. Mansel Prothero, eds. 1975. *People on the Move: Studies on Internal Migration*. London: Methuen.

Kraft, Barbara Sarina. 2005. 'Refugee', *Microsoft Encarta Encyclopedia*. Microsoft.

Krahn, Harvey, Tracey M. Derwing, and Baha Abu-Laban. 2005. 'The Retention of Newcomers in Second- and Third-Tier Canadian Cities', *International Migration Review* 39, 4: 872–94.

Kralt, John. 1990. 'Ethnic Origins in the Canadian Census: 1871–1986', in Shiva S. Halli, Frank Trovato, and Leo Driedger, eds, *Ethnic Demography: Canadian Immigrant, Racial and Cultural Variations* (pp. 13–30). Ottawa: Carleton University Press.

Kramer, Sebastian. 2000. 'The Fragile Male', *British Medical Journal* 321: (23–30 December): 1609–12.

Kreager, Philip. 2003. 'Graunt, John', in Paul Demeny and Geoffrey McNicoll, eds, *Encyclopedia of Population* 1: 472–3. New York: Macmillan Reference USA/Thomson Gale.

Krishnaji, N. 2001. 'The Sex Ratio Debate', in Vina Masumdar and N. Krishnaji, eds, *Enduring Conundrum:*

India's Sex Ratio: Essays in Honour of Asok Mitra (pp. 28–35). Noida, Uttar Pradesh, India: Rainbow.

Krishnan, P., and David Odynak. 1987. 'A Generalization of Petersen's Typology of Migration', *International Migration* 25, 4: 385–97.

Kritz, M., and J.M. Nogle. 1994. 'Nativity Concentration and Internal Migration Among the Foreign-Born', *Demography* 31, 3: 509–24.

———, Lin Lean Lim, and Hania Zlotnik. 1992. 'Global Interactions: Migration Systems, Processes, and Policies', in Mary M. Kritz, Lin Lean Lim, and Hania Zlotnik, eds, *International Migration Systems: A Global Approach* (pp. 1–16). Oxford: Clarendon.

Krotki, Karol J. 1997. 'How the Proportion of Artificial Canadians Varied between and among Regions of Canada and Ethnic Origins between 1991 and 1996', special issue, *Canadian Journal of Regional Science* 20, 1–2: 169–80.

———, ed. 1978. *Developments in Dual System Estimation of Population Size and Growth*. Edmonton, AB: University of Alberta Press.

———, and David Odynak. 1990. 'The Emergence of Multiethnicities in the Eighties', in Shiva S. Halli, Frank Trovato, and Leo Driedger, eds, *Ethnic Demography: Canadian Immigrant, Racial and Cultural Variations* (pp. 415–37). Ottawa: Carleton University Press.

Krout, J. A. 1983. 'Seasonal Migration of the Elderly', *The Gerontologist* 23: 295–9.

Krull, Cathie, and Frank Trovato. 'The Quiet Revolution and Quebec's Suicide Rate: 1931–1986', *Social Forces* 72, 4: 1121–47.

Kubat, Daniel, and David Thornton. 1974. *A Statistical Profile of Canadian Society*. Toronto: McGraw-Hill.

Kucera, Tomas, Olga Kucerova, Oksana Opara, and E. Schaich, eds. 2000. *New Demographic Faces of Europe: The Changing Population Dynamics in Countries of Central and Eastern Europe*. Berlin: Springer.

Kunitz, Stephen J. 2007. *The Health of Populations; General Theories and Particular Realities*. Oxford: Oxford University Press.

———. 2000. 'Globalization, States, and the Health of Indigenous Peoples', *American Journal of Public Health* 90: 1531–9.

———. 1994. *Disease and Diversity: The European Impact on the Health of Non-Europeans*. New York: Oxford University Press.

———. 1990. 'Public Policy and Mortality among Indigenous Populations of Northern America and Australia', *Population and Development Review* 16, 4: 647–72.

———. 1983. *Disease Change and the Role of Medicine: The Navajo Experience*. Berkeley, CA: University of California Press.

———, with Irena Pesis-Katz. 2005. 'Mortality of White Americans, African Americans, and Canadians: The Causes and Consequences for Health of Welfare State

Institutions and Policies', *The Milbank Quarterly* 83, 1: 5–39.

Kuznets, Simon. 1955. 'Economic Growth and Income Inequality', *American Economic Review* 45: 1–28.

Lalasz, Robert. 2005. 'Will Rising Childhood Obesity Decrease U.S. Life Expectancy?', Population Reference Bureau website, <www.prb.org> (4 July, 2005).

Lalonde, Marc. 1974. *A New Perspective on the Health of Canadians*. Ottawa: Department of National Health and Welfare.

Lam, David A., and Jeffrey A. Miron. 1996. 'The Effects of Temperature on Human Fertility', *Demography* 33, 3: 291–305.

———, and ———. 1991. 'Seasonality of Births in Human Populations', *Social Biology* 38, 1–2: 51–78.

Lam, Lawrence, and Anthony Richmond. 1995. 'Migration to Canada in the Post-War Period', in Robin Cohen, ed., *The Cambridge Survey of World Migration* (pp. 263–70). Cambridge: Cambridge University Press.

Lamb, Emmet J., and Sean Bennett. 1993. 'Epidemiological Studies of Male Factors in Infertility', in Kenneth L. Campbell and James W. Wood, eds, *Human Reproductive Ecology: Interactions of Environment, Fertility, and Behavior* (pp. 165–78). New York: The New York Academy of Sciences, vol. 709.

Lamb, Vicki L., and Jacob S. Siegel. 2004. 'Health Demography', in Jacob S. Siegel and David A. Swanson, eds, *The Methods and Materials of Demography*, 2nd edn (pp. 341–70). Amsterdam: Elsevier.

Lamberg-Karlovsky, C.C., and Martha Lamberg-Karlovsky. 1971 [1973]. 'Readings from Scientific American', in Kingsley Davis, ed., *Cities: Their Origins, Growth and Human Impact* (pp. 28–37). San Franciso: W.H. Freeman.

Lamptey, Peter, Jami L. Johnson, and Marya Khan. 2006. 'The Global Challenge of HIV and AIDS', *Population Bulletin* 67, 1. Washington: Population Reference Bureau.

Landale, Nancy, and Avery M. Guest. 1985. 'Constraints, Satisfaction, and Residential Mobility: Speare's Model Reconsidered', *Demography* 22: 199–222.

Landes, David S. 1999. *The Wealth and Poverty of Nations: Why Some Are So Rich and Some So Poor*. New York: W.W. Norton.

Landry, A. 1945. *Traité de Demographie*. Paris: Payot.

———. 1934. *La Révolution démographique*. Paris: Sirey.

Langer, William L. 1973. 'The Black Death', *Readings from Scientific American*, in Kingsley Davis, ed., *Cities: Their Origins, Growth and Human Impact* (pp. 106–11). San Franciso: W.H. Freeman.

Lansing, J. B., and E. Mueller. 1973. *The Geographic Mobility of Labor*. Ann Arbor: The University of Michigan, Survey Research Centre.

Lapierre-Adamcyk, Evelynne, and Carole Charvet. 2000. 'Cohabitation and Marriage: An Assessment of Research in Demography', *Canadian Studies in Population* 27, 1: 239–54.

LaRocque, Emma D. 1994. *Violence in Aborginal Communities*. Ottawa: Royal Commission on Aboriginal Peoples.

Larson, Lyle E., J. Walter Goltz, and Charles W. Hobart. 1994. *Families in Canada: Social Context, Continuities and Change*. Scarborough, ON: Prentice Hall.

Laslett, Peter. 1991. 'The Emergence of the Third Age', in Peter Laslett, *A Fresh Map on Life: The Emergence of the Third Age*. Cambridge, MA: Harvard University Press.

Lavely, William, and R. Freedman. 1990. 'The Origins of the Chinese Fertility Decline', *Demography* 27, 3: 357–68.

———, Jianke Li, and Jianghong Li. 2001. 'Sex Preference for Children in a Meifu Li Community in Hainan, China', *Population Studies* 55, 3: 319–30.

Leacy, F.H. 1983. *Historical Statistics of Canada*, 2nd edn. Ottawa: Minister of Supply and Services.

Leah, Elizabeth, Robert Engelman, Carolyn Gibb Bogel, et al. 2007. *The Shape of Things to Come: Why Age Structure Matters to a Safer, More Equitable World*. Washington: Population Action International.

Leakey, Louis S.B. 1960. *Adam's Ancestors: The Evolution of Man and His Culture*. New York: Harper and Row (Harper Torchbooks).

LeBourdais, Celine, and Evelyn Lapierre-Adamcyk. 2004. 'Changes in Conjugal Life in Canada: Is Cohabitation Progressively Replacing Marriage?', *Journal of Marriage and the Family* 66: 929–42.

———, Ghyslaine Neill, and Pierre Turcotte. 2000. 'The Changing Face of Conjugal Relationships', *Canadian Social Trends* 56 (Spring): 14–17.

Ledent, Jacques. 1988. 'Canada', in W. Weidlich and G. Haag, eds, *Interregional Migration: Dynamic Theory and Comparative Analysis* (pp. 101–30). Berlin: Springer.

Lee, Barret A., R.S. Oropesa, and W. Kanan. 1994. 'Neighborhood Context and Residential Mobility', *Demography* 31, 2: 249–70.

Lee, Everett S. 1966. 'A Theory of Migration', *Demography* 3, 1: 47–57.

———, and Harold F. Goldsmith, eds. 1982. *Population Estimates: Methods for Small Area Analysis*. Beverly Hills, CA: Sage.

Leeuw, Frans, and Mark van de Vall. 1985. 'National Population Policies in Industrial Countries: Praxis or Paradox?', *Comparative Social Research* 7: 351–68.

Legrain, Philippe. 2006. *Immigrants: Your Country Needs Them*. London: Little, Brown.

Lehrer, Evelyn L. 2004. 'Religion as a Determinant of Economic and Demographic Behavior in the United States', *Population and Development Review* 30, 4: 707–26.

Leibenstein, Harvey. 1982. 'Economic Decision Theory and Human Fertility Behavior: A Speculative Essay', *Population and Development Review* 7: 381–400.

Leisinger, Kalus M., Karin M. Schmitt, and Rajul Pandya-Lorch. 2002. *Six Billion and Counting: Population and*

Food Security in the 21st Century. Washington, DC: International Food Policy Research Institute.

Lenski, Gerhard, and Jean Lenski. 1987. *Human Societies: An Introduction to Macrosociology*, 5th edn. New York: McGraw-Hill.

Leon, David A., Laurent Chenet, Vladimir M. Shkolnikov, et al. 1997. 'Huge Variation in Russian Mortality Rates 1984–94: Artefact, Alcohol, or What?', *The Lancet*: 350 (9 August): 383–8.

Leonard, William R., and Michael H. Crawford, eds. 2002. *Human Biology of Pastoral Populations*. Cambridge: Cambridge University Press.

Leone, Tiziana, Zoe Matthews, and Gianpiero Dall Zuanna. 2003. 'Impacts and Determinants of Sex Preference in Nepal', *International Family Planning Perspectives* 29, 2: 76–83.

Leridon, Henri. 2006. 'Natural Fertility and Controlled Fertility', in Graziella Caselli, Jacques Vallin, and Guillaume Wunsch, eds, *Demography: A Treatise in Population Studies*, vol. 1 (pp. 467–77). Amsterdam: Elsevier and Academic Press.

———. 1976. 'Facts and Artifacts in the Study of Intra-Uterine Mortality: A Reconsideration from Pregnancy Histories', *Population Studies* 39, 2: 319–35.

Leslie, Gerald R., and Sheila K. Korman. 1989. *The Family in Social Context*, 7th edn. New York: Oxford University Press.

Lesthaeghe, Ron. 2003. 'Verhulst, Pierre-Francois' in Paul Demeny and Geoffrey McNicoll, eds, *Encyclopedia of Population* (pp. 959–60). New York: Macmillan Reference USA/Thomson Gale.

———. 1998. 'On Theory Development and Applications to the Study of Family Formation', *Population and Development Review* 24, 1: 1–14.

———. 1995. 'The Second Demographic Transition in Western Countries: An Interpretation', in Karen Oppenheim Mason and An-Margrit Jensen, eds, *Gender and Family Change in Industrialized Countries* (pp. 17–62). Oxford: Clarendon.

———. 1983. 'A Century of Demographic and Cultural Change in Western Europe', *Population and Development Review* 9, 3: 411–36.

———, and K. Neels. 2002. 'From the First to the Second Demographic Transition: An Interpretation of the Spatial Continuity of Demographic Innovation in France, Belgium and Switzerland', *European Journal of Population* 18: 325–60.

———, and Johan Surkyn. 1988. 'Cultural Dynamics and Economic Theories of Fertility Change', *Population and Development Review* 14, 1: 1–45.

———, and Chris Wilson. 1986. 'Modes of Production, Secularization, and the Pace of the Fertility Decline in Western Europe, 1870–1930', in Ansley J. Coale and Susan Cotts Watkins, eds, *The Decline of Fertility in Europe* (pp. 261–92). Princeton, NJ: Princeton University Press.

Levitt, Peggy, Josh DeWind, and Steven Vertovec. 2003. 'International Perspectives on Transnational Migration: An Introduction', special issue, *International Migration Review* 37, 3: 565–75.

Levy, J.E., and Stephen J. Kunitz. 1971. 'Indian Reservations, Anomie and Social Pathologies', *Southwestern Journal of Anthropology* 27, 2: 97–128.

Levy, Robert I. 1981. 'The Decline in Cardiovascular Disease Mortality', *Annual Review of Public Health* 2: 49–70.

Lewis, G. J. 1982. *Human Migration: A Geographical Perspective*. London: Croom Helm.

Lewis, H.E., D.F. Roberts, and A.W.F. Edwards. 1972. 'Biological Problems, and Opportunities, of Isolation among the Islanders of Tristan Da Cunha', in D.V. Glass and Robers Revelle, eds, *Population and Social Change* (pp. 383–417). London: Edward Arnold.

Ley, David. 2000. 'The Inner City', in Trudy Bunting and Pierre Filion, eds, *Canadian Cities in Transition: The Twenty-First Century*, 2nd edn (pp. 274–302). Don Mills, ON: Oxford University Press.

———. 1992. 'Gentrification in Recession: Social Change in Six Canadian Cities, 1981–86', *Urban Geography* 13, 3: 230–56.

Li, Nan, and S. Tuljapurkar. 1999. 'Population Momentum for Gradual Demographic Transitions', *Population Studies* 53, 2: 255–62.

Li, Peter S., and Chunhong Dong. 2007. 'Earnings of Chinese Immigrants in the Enclave and Mainstream Economy', *Canadian Review of Sociology and Anthropology* 44, 1: 65–99.

Liaw, Kao-Lee, and Jacques Ledent. 1988. 'Joint Effects of Personal and Ecological Factors on Elderly Interprovincial Migration in Canada', *Canadian Journal of Regional Science* 11: 77–100.

———, and Mingzhu Qi. 2004. 'Lifetime Interprovincial Migration in Canada: Looking Beyond Short-Run Fluctuations', *The Canadian Geographer* 48, 2: 168–90.

Lichtenstein, P., J.R. Harris, and N.L. Pedersen. 1993. 'Socio-Economic Status and Physical Health: How Are They Related? An Empirical Study Based on Twins Reared Apart and Twins Reared Together', *Social Science and Medicine* 36, 4: 441–50.

Lichter, Daniel T., Felicia B. LeClere, and D.K. McLaughlin. 1991. 'Local Marriage Market Conditions and the Marital Behavior of Black and White Women', *American Journal of Sociology* 96, 4: 843–67.

———, Dianne K. McLaughlin, George Kephart, and David J. Landry. 1992. 'Race and the Retreat from Marriage: A Shortage of Marriageable Men?', *American Sociological Review* 57, 6: 781–99.

Lieberson, Stanley. 1981. 'An Asymmetrical Approach to Segregation', in Peach, et al., eds, *Ethnic Segregation in Cities*. Athens, GA: The University of Georgia Press.

Lim, Lin Lean. 1993. 'Effects of Women's Position on their Migration', in Nora Federici, Karen Oppenheim Mason, and Solvi Sogner, eds, *Women's Position and Demographic Change* (pp. 225–42). Oxford: Clarendon.

Lim, Meng-Kin. 2006. 'China's One-Child Policy: Pseudo Economic Rationalizations' (letter), *British Medical Journal* 333 (24 August).

Linden, Eugene. 1996. 'The Exploding Cities of the Developing World', *Foreign Affairs* 75, 1: 52–65.

Linder, Mark. 1997. 'Was Marx a Crypto-Malthusian?', in Mark Linder, *The Dilemmas of Laissez-Faire Population Policy in Capitalist Societies: When the Invisible Hand Controls Reproduction* (pp. 146–70). Westport, CT: Greenwood.

Lindstrom, David P., and Betemariam Berhanu. 1999. 'The Impact of War Famine, and Economic Decline on Marital Fertility in Ethiopia', *Demography* 36, 2: 247–62.

Liska, Allen E., John R. Logan, and Paul E. Bellair. 1998. 'Race and Violent Crime in the Suburbs', *American Sociological Review* 63, 1: 27–38.

Little, Bruce. 2000. 'Female Boomers Led March Into the Paid Work Force', *The Globe and Mail* (14 February): A2.

Livi-Bacci, Massimo. 2000. *The Population of Europe*. Trans. Cynthia De Nardi Ipsen and Carl Ipsen. Oxford: Blackwell.

———. 1997. *A Concise History of World Population*, 2nd edn. Malden, MA: Blackwell.

———. 1986. 'Social Group Forerunners of Fertility Control in Europe', in Ansley J. Coale and Susan Cotts Watkins, eds, *The Decline of Fertility in Europe* (pp. 182–200). Princeton, NJ: Princeton University Press.

———, and Gustavo De Santis. 1998. *Population and Poverty in Developing Countries*. Oxford: Oxford University Press.

Locoh, Thérèse. 2006. 'Factors in Couple Formation', in Graziella Caselli, Jacques Vallin and Guillaume Wunsch, eds, *Demography—Analysis and Synthesis: A Treatise in Demography* (pp. 373–96). Amsterdam: Elsevier and Academic Press.

———, and Céline Vandermeersch. 2006. 'Fertility Control in Third World Countries', in Graziella Caselli, Jacques Vallin and Guillaume Wunsch, eds, *Demography: Analysis and Synthesis* (pp. 95–127). Amsterdam: Elsevier.

Loh, Shirley, and M.V. George. 2003. 'Estimating the Fertility Level of Registered Indians in Canada: A Challenging Endeavour', *Canadian Studies in Population* 30, 1: 117–35.

Lomborg, Bjorn. 2001. *The Skeptical Environmentalist*. Cambridge: Cambridge University Press.

Long, John. 1981. *Population Deconcentration in the United States*. Washington, DC: US Bureau of the Census.

Long, Larry H. 1988. *Migration and Residential Mobility in the United States*. New York: Russell Sage Foundation.

———. 1973. 'New Estimates of Migration Expectancy in the United States', *Journal of the American Statistical Association* 68, 341: 37–43.

Lopez, Alan D. 1983. 'The Sex Mortality Differential in Developed Countries', in Alan D. Lopez and Lado T. Ruzicka, eds, *Sex Differentials in Mortality: Trends, Determinants and Consequences*. Canberra: Australian National University.

Lopez, Allen, Graziella Caselli, and Tapani Valkonen, eds. 1995. *Adult Mortality in Developed Countries: From Description to Explanation*. Oxford: Clarendon.

Lopez, Alvaro. 1961. *Problems in Stable Population Theory*. Princeton: Office of Population Research.

Losch, August. 1940 [1954]. *The Economics of Location*. Trans. William H. Woglam. New York: Yale University Press.

Lotka, Alfred J. 1934 [1998]. *Analytical Theory of Biological Populations*. Trans. David P. Smith and Helene Rossert. New York: Plenum.

———. 1925. *The Elements of Physical Biology*. Baltimore: Williams and Wilkins.

———. 1907. 'Relation Between Birth Rates and Death Rates', *Science*, n.s., 26: 21–22. Reprinted in David P. Smith and Nathan Keyfitz, *Mathematical Demography: Selected Papers*. (1977). Berlin: Springer.

Lowry, Ira S. 1966. *Migration and Metropolitan Growth: Two Analytical Models*. Los Angeles, CA: Institute of Government and Public Affairs, University of California.

Luo, Zhong-Cheng, William J. Kierans, Russell Wilkins, et al. 2004. 'Infant Mortality Among First Nations Versus Non-First Nations in British Columbia: Temporal Trends in Rural Versus Urban Areas, 1981-2000', *International Journal of Epidemiology* 33, 6: 1252–9.

Lutz, Wolfgang, ed. 1994. *The Future Population of the World: What Can We Assume Today?* London: Earthscan.

———, Sylvia Kritzinger, and Vegard Skirbekk. 2006. 'The Demography of Growing European Identity', *Science* 314 (20 October): 425.

———, B. O'Neill, and Sergei Scherbov. 2003. 'Europe's Population at a Turning Point', *Science* 299: 1991–2.

———, and Ren Qiang. 2002. 'Determinants of Human Population Growth', *Philosophical Transactions of the Royal Society of London B*, 357: 1197–1210.

———, Warren Sanderson, and Sergei Scherbov. 2008. 'The Coming Acceleration of Global Population Ageing', *Nature* 461 (7 February): 716–19.

———, ———, and ———. 2004. *The End of World Population Growth in the 21st Century: New Challenges for Human Capital Formation and Sustainable Development*. London: Earthscan.

———, Vegard Skirbekk, and Maria Tira Testa. 2006. 'The Low-Fertility Trap Hypothesis: Forces that May Lead to Further Postponement and Fewer Births in Europe', *Vienna Yearbook of Demographic Research* 2006: 167–92.

Luy, Marc. 2003. 'Causes of Male Excess Mortality: Insights from Cloistered Populations', *Population and Development Review* 29, 4: 647–76.

Lynch, John W., George Davey Smith, G.A. Kaplan, and J. House. 2000. 'Income Inequality and Mortality:

Importance to Health of Individual Income, Psychosocial Environment, or Material Conditions', *British Medical Journal* 320: 1200–4.

Lynch, Scott M., and J. Scott Brown. 2001. 'Reconsidering Mortality Compression and Deceleration: An Alternative Model of Mortality Rates', *Demography* 38, 1:79–95.

Maatikaninen, Tiina, Julia Critchely, Erkki Vartiainen, V. Salomaa, M. Ketonen, and S. Capewell. 2005. 'Explaining the Decline in Coronary Heart Disease Mortality in Finland Between 1982 and 1997', *American Journal of Epidemiology* 162, 8: 764–73.

McDaniel, Susan. 2002. 'Intergenerational Linkages: Public, Family and Work', in David Cheal, ed., *Aging and Demographic Change in Canadian Context, Policy Research: The Trends Project Series* (pp. 22–71). Toronto: University of Toronto Press.

MacDonald, John A., and L.D. MacDonald. 1964. 'Chain Migration, Ethnic Neighborhood Formation and Social Networks', *The Milbank Quarterly* 42: 82–7.

McDonald, Peter. 2000. 'Gender Equity in Theories of Fertility Transition', *Population and Development Review* 26, 3: 427–40.

———. 1985. 'Social Organization and Nuptiality in Developing Societies', in John Cleland and John Hobcraft, eds, *Reproductive Change in Developing Countries: Insights from the World Fertility Survey* (pp. 87–114). Oxford: Oxford University Press.

———, and Rebecca Kippen. 2001. 'Labor Supply Prospects in 16 Developed Countries, 2000–2050', *Population and Development Review* 27, 1: 1–32.

McDowell, Andrea G. 2005. 'Daily Life in Ancient Egypt', *Scientific American* 15, 1: 68–76.

McEvedy, Colin, and Richard Jones. 1978. *Atlas of World Population History*. Middlesex, England: Penguin.

McFalls, Joseph A. Jr. 1990. 'The Risks of Reproductive Impairment in the Later Years of Childbearing', *Annual Review of Sociology* 16: 491–519.

———. 1979. 'Frustrated Fertility: A Population Paradox', *Population Bulletin* 34, 2. Washington: Population Reference Bureau.

McGee, Terrence G., and C.J. Griffith. 1998. 'Global Urbanization: Towards the Twenty-First Century', *Population Distribution and Migration* (pp. 49–65). New York: United Nations Department of Economic and Social Affairs Population Division.

McGehee, Mary A. 2004. 'Mortality', in Jacob A. Siegel and David A. Swanson, eds, *The Methods and Materials of Demography*, 2nd edn (pp. 265–300). Amsterdam: Elsevier.

McIlroy, Anne. 2004. 'Some Brains Are Old at 40', *The Globe and Mail* (10 June): A17.

McInnis, Marvin. 2000a. 'The Population of Canada in the Nineteenth Century', in Michael R. Haines and Richard H. Steckel, eds, *A Population History of North America* (pp. 371–432). Cambridge: Cambridge University Press.

———. 2000b. 'Canada's Population in the Twentieth Century', in Michael R. Haines and Richard H. Steckel, eds, *A Population History of North America*. (pp. 529–99). Cambridge: Cambridge University Press.

———. 1971. 'Age, Education and Occupational Differentials in Interregional Migration: Some Evidence for Canada', *Demography* 8: 195–204.

———. 1969. 'Provincial Migration and Differential Economic Opportunity', in Leroy O. Stone, ed., *Internal Migration in Canada: Regional Aspects* (pp. 131–202). Ottawa: Dominion Bureau of Statistics.

MacKellar, Landis F. 2003. 'Simon, Julian L.', in Paul Demeny and Geoffrey McNicoll, eds, *Encyclopedia of Population* (pp. 888–9). New York: Macmillan Reference USA/Thomson Gale.

———. 2000. 'The Predicament of Population Ageing: A Review Essay', *Population and Development Review* 26, 2: 365–97.

MacKenzie, Betsy. 1987. 'The Decline of Stroke Mortality', *Canadian Social Trends* (Autumn): 34-37.

McKeown, Thomas. 1976. *The Modern Rise of Population*. London: Edward Arnold.

———, R.G. Brown, and R.G. Record. 1972. 'An Interpretation of the Modern Rise of Populating In Europe', *Population Studies* 26, 3: 345–542.

McKibben, Jerome K., and Kimberly A. Faust. 2004. 'Population Distribution: Classification of Residence', in Jacob B. Siegel and David A. Swanson, eds, *The Methods and Materials of Demography*, 2nd edn. (pp. 105–23). Amsterdam: Elsevier.

MacKinnon, Mark. 2006. *The Globe and Mail*. (25 September): A1, A10.

MacLachlan, Malcolm. 1997. *Culture and Health*. Chichester, England: John Wiley.

McLaren, Angus. 1990. *A History of Contraception*. Oxford: Basil Blackwell.

———. 1984. *Reproductive Rituals: The Perception of Fertility in England from the Sixteenth Century to the Nineteenth Century*. London: Methuen.

McLarty, Cameron B. 2006. 'Not a Policy to Emulate' (letter), *British Medical Journal* 333 (26 August).

McMichael, Anthony J., Martin McKee, Vladimir Shkolnikov, and Tapani Valkonen. 2004. 'Mortality Trends and Setbacks: Global Convergence or Divergence?', *The Lancet* 365 (3 April): 1155–9.

McMillen, Marilyn M. 1979. 'Differential Mortality by Sex in Fetal and Neonatal Deaths', *Science* 204, 6 (April): 89–91.

McNeill, William. 1984. 'Human Migration in Historical Perspective', *Population and Development Review* 10, 1: 1–18.

McNicoll, Geoffrey. 2006. 'Policy Lessons of the East Asian Demographic Transition', *Population and Development Review* 32, 1: 1–25.

———. 2003a. 'Petty, William', in Paul Demeny and Geoffrey McNicoll, eds, *Encyclopedia of Population* (pp.

729–30). New York: Macmillan Reference USA/Thomson Gale.

———. 2003b. 'Population', in Paul Demeny and Geoffre McNicoll, eds, *Encyclopedia of Population*, vol. 2 (pp. 730–2). New York: Macmillan Reference USA.

———. 2001. 'Governments and Fertility in Transitional and Post-Transitional Societies', in Rudofo A. Bulatao and John B. Casterline, eds, *Global Fertility Transition* (pp. 129–58), supp. to *Population and Development Review* 27. New York: The Population Council.

———. 2000. 'Reflections on Replacement Migration', *People and Place* 8, 4: 1–13.

———. 1998. 'Malthus for the Twenty-First Century', *Population and Development Review* 24, 2: 309–16.

———. 1995. 'Institutional Impediments to Population Policy in Australia', Australian National University. Working Paper in Demography no. 53.

Macunovich, Diane J. 2002. *Birth Quake: The Baby Boom and Its Aftershocks*. Chicago: The University of Chicago Press.

———. 1999. 'The Role of Relative Cohort Size and Relative Income in the Demographic Transition', *Population and Environment* 21, 2: 155–92.

McVey, Wayne W. Jr., and Warren E. Kalbach. 1995a. *Canadian Population*. Toronto: Nelson.

Madigan, Francis C. 1957. 'Are Sex Mortality Differentials Biologically Caused?', *The Milbank Quarterly* 35, 2: 202–23.

Makabe, Tomoto. 1980. 'Provincial Variations in Divorce Rates: A Canadian Case', *Journal of Marriage and the Family* 42: 171–6.

Makeham, W.M. 1867. 'On the Law of Mortality', *Journal of the Institute of Actuaries* 13: 325–67.

———. 1860. 'On the Law of Mortality and the Construction of Annuity Tables', *Assurance Magazine* 8: 301–10.

Malenfant, Éric Caron, and Alain Bélanger. 2006. 'The Fertility of Visible Minority Women in Canada', in Alain Belanger, ed., *Report on the Demographic Situation in Canada 2003 and 2004* (pp. 79–95). Cat. no. 91-209-XIE. Ottawa: Statistics Canada.

Mamelund, Svenn-Erik. 2004. 'Can the Spanish Influenza Pandemic of 1918 Explain the Baby Boom of 1920 in Neutral Norway?', *Population E* 59, 2: 229–60.

Manning, Patrick. 2005. *Migration in World History*. New York: Routledge.

Manton, Kenneth G. 1991. 'The Dynamics of Population Aging: Demography and Policy Analysis', *The Milbank Quarterly* 69, 2: 309–38.

———. 1982. 'Changing Concepts of Mortality and Morbidity in the Elderly Population', *The Milbank Quarterly/Health and Society* 60, 2: 183–244.

———, Xi Liang Gu, and Vicky Lamb. 2006. 'Long-Term Trends in Life Expectancy and Active Life Expectancy in the United States', *Population and Development Review* 32, 1: 81–105.

———, and Burton Singer. 1994. 'What's the Fuss About Compression of Mortality?', *Chance* 7, 4: 21–30.

———, and Beth J. Soldo. 1992. 'Disability and Mortality Among the Oldest Old: Implications for Current and Future Health and Long-Term-Care Service Needs', in Richard M. Suzman, David P. Willis, and Kenneth G. Manton, eds, *The Oldest Old* (pp. 199–250). New York: Oxford University Press.

———, and James W. Vaupel. 1995. 'Survival After the Age of 80 in the United States, Sweden, France, England and Japan', *New England Journal of Medicine* 333: 1232–5.

———, and Anatole I. Yashin. 2006. 'Inequalities of Life: Statistical Analysis and Modeling Perspectives', in Claudine Sauvain-Dugerdil, Henri Leridon, and Nicholas Mascie-Taylor, eds, *Human Clocks: The Bio-Cultural Meanings of Age* (pp. 145–70). Bern: Peter Lang.

Mao, Yang B., W. Moloughney, R. Semenciw, and H.W. Morrison. 1992. 'Indian Reserve and Registered Indian Mortality in Canada', *Canadian Journal of Public Health* 83, 5: 350–3.

Marcus, M., J. Kiely, F. Xu, M. McGeehin, R. Jackson, and T. Sinks. 1998. 'Changing Sex Ratios in the United States, 1969–1995', *Fertility and Sterility* 70, 2: 270–3.

Marfleet, Philip. 2006. *Refugees in a Global Era*. New York: Palgrave Macmillan.

Mariner, Joanne. 2003. 'Israel's New Citizenship Law: A Separation Wall Though the Heart', FindLaw Legal News and Commentary. <http://writ.news.findlaw.com/mariner/20030811.html >.

Marini, Mooney Margaret, and Pi-Ling Fan. 1997. 'The Gender Gap in Earnings at Career Entry', *American Sociological Review* 63, 4: 588–604.

Markides, Kyriakos S., and Manuel R. Miranda, eds. 1997. *Minorities, Aging, and Health*. Thousand Oaks, CA: Sage.

Marks, Eli S., William Seltzer and Karol J. Krotki. 1974. *Population Growth Estimation: A Handbook of Vital Statistics Measurement*. New York: The Population Council.

Marmot, Michael G. 2005. 'Social Determinants of Health Inequalities', *The Lancet* 365 (19 March): 1099–1104.

———. 1995. 'Social Status and Mortality: The Whitehall Studies', in Alan Lopez, Graziella Caselli, and Tapani Valkonen, eds, *Adult Mortality in Developed Countries: From Description to Explanation* (pp. 243–60). Oxford: Clarendon.

———, and Richard G. Wilkinson, eds. 2006. *The Social Determinants of Health*. Oxford: Oxford University Press.

———, G.M. Kogevinas, and M.A. Elston. 1987. 'Social/Economic Status and Disease', *Annual Review of Public Health* 8: 1111–35.

Martel, Laurent, and Alain Belanger. 2000. 'Dependence-Free Life Expectancy in Canada', *Canadian Social Trends* 58 (Autumn): 26–9.

Martikainen, Pekka, Tujia Martelin, Elina Nihtila, K. Majamaa, and S. Koskinen. 2005. 'Differences in

Mortality by Marital Status in Finland from 1976 to 2000: Analyses of Changes in Martial-Status Distributions, Socio-Demographic and Household Composition, and Cause of Death', *Population Studies* 59, 1: 99–116.

Martin, H.W., S.K. Hoppe, C.L. Larson, and R.L. Leon. 1987. 'Texas Snowbirds: Season Migrants to the Rio Grande Valley', *Research on Aging* 9: 134–47.

Martin, Linda G. 1991. 'Population Aging Policies in East Asia and the United States', *Science* 251 (1 February): 527–31.

———. 1989. 'The Graying of Japan', *Population Bulletin* 44, 2. Washington: Population Reference Bureau.

Marx, Karl. 1867 [1967]. *Capital: A Critical Analysis of Capitalist Production*. Vol. I. Edited by Frederick Engels. New York: International Publishers.

———, and Frederick Engels. 1845–6 [1970]. *The German Ideology, Part 1, with selections from Parts 2 and 3*, ed. C.J. Arthur. New York: International Publishers.

Masi, Ralph. 1995. 'Multicultural Health: Principles and Policies', in Ralph Masi, Lynette Mensah, and K.A. McLeod, eds, *Health and Cultures*, vol. 1: *Policies, Professional Practice and Education* (pp. 11–23). Oakville, ON: Mosaic Press.

Mason, Gary. 2005. 'Obesity Bursting Healthy-Boomer Bubble', *The Globe and Mail* (29 September): A15.

Mason, Karen Oppenheim. 1997a. 'Explaining Fertility Transitions', *Demography* 34, 4: 443–54.

———. 1997b. 'Gender and Demographic Change: What Do We Know?', in Gavin W. Jones, et al, eds., *The Continuing Demographic Transition* (pp. 158–82). Oxford: Clarendon.

———. 1993. 'The Impact of Women's Position on Demographic Change During the Course of Development', in Nora Federici, Karen Oppenheim Mason, and Solvi Sogner, eds, *Women's Position and Demographic Change* (pp. 19–42). Oxford: Clarendon.

———. 1988. 'A Feminist Perspective on Fertility Decline', *University of Michigan Population Studies Center Research Reports*, nos 88–119. Ann Arbor, Michigan.

Massey, Douglas S. 1999. 'Why Does Immigration Occur? A Theoretical Synthesis', in Charles Hirschman, Philip Kasinitz, and Josh DeWind, eds, *The Handbook of International Migration: The American Experience* (pp. 34–53). New York: Russell Sage Foundation.

———, Rafael Alarcon, Jorge Durand, and Humberto Gonzales. 1987. *Return to Aztlan: The Social Process of International Migration from Western Mexico*. Berkeley: University of California Press.

———, Andrew B. Gross, and Kumiko Shibuya. 1994. 'Migration, Segregation, and the Concentration of Poverty', *American Sociological Review* 59, 3: 425–45.

———, Jaoquin Arango, Graeme Hugo, et al. 1998. *Worlds in Motion: Understanding International Migration at the End of the Millennium*. Oxford: Oxford University Press.

———, ———, ———, et al. 1993. 'Theories of International Migration: A Review and Appraisal', *Population and Development Review* 19, 3: 431–66.

———, and J. Edward Taylor, eds. 2004. *International Migration: Prospects and Policies in a Global Market*. Oxford: Oxford University Press.

———, and F.G. Espana. 1987. 'The Social Process of International Migration', *Science* 237: 733–8.

———, and Audrey Singer. 1995. 'New Estimates of Undocumented Mexican Migration and the Probability of Apprehension', *Demography* 32, 2: 203–13.

Masumdar, Vina, and N. Krishnaji, eds. 2001. *Enduring Conundrum: India's Sex Ratio: Essays in Honour of Asok Mitra*. Noida, Uttar Pradesh, India: Rainbow.

Matras, Judah. 1989. 'Demographic Trends, Life Course, and Family Cycle—The Canadian Example: Part I: Changing Longevity, Parenting, and Kin-availability', *Canadian Studies in Population* 16, 1: 1–24.

———. 1965. 'The Social Strategy of Family Formation: Some Variations in Time and Space', *Demography* 2: 349–62.

Mauldin, Parker W., and Bernard Berelson. 1978. 'Conditions of Fertility Decline in Developing Countries', *Studies in Family Planning* (9 May): 89-147.

———, and John A. Ross. 1991. 'Family Planning Programs: Efforts and Ressults, 1982–89', *Studies in Family Planning* 22, 6: 350–67.

Maxim, S. Paul, Carl Keane, and Jerry White. 2002. 'Urban Residential Patterns of Aboriginal People in Canada', in David Newhouse and Evelyne Peters, eds, *No Strangers in These Parts: Urban Aboriginal Peoples* (pp. 79–91). Ottawa: Policy Research Initiative.

Mayer, Peter. 1999. 'India's Falling Sex Ratios', *Population and Development Review* 25: 323–43.

Meadows, Donella H. 1993. 'Seeing the Population Issue Whole', in Laurie Ann Mazur, ed., *Beyond the Numbers: A Reader on Population, Consumption, and the Environment* (pp. 23–32). Washington, DC: Island Press.

———, Dennis L. Meadows, J. Randers, and W.W. Behrens III. 1972. *The Limits to Growth: A Report for the Club of Rome's Project on the Predicament of Mankind*. New York: Universe Books.

———, Jorgen Randers, and Dennis Meadows. 2005. *Limits to Growth: The 30 Year Update*. London: Earthscan.

———, ———, and ———. 1992. *Beyond the Limits: Confronting Global Collapse, Envisioning a Sustainable Future*. Post Mills, VT: Chelsea Green.

Mealey, Linda. 2000. *Sex Differences: Developmental and Evolutionary Strategies*. San Diego: Academic Press.

Meilaender, Peter C. 1999. 'Liberalism and Open Borders: The Argument of Joseph Carens', *International Migration Review* 33, 4: 1062–81.

Mendelsohn, Michael E., and Richard H. Karas. 2005. 'Molecular and Cellular Basis of Cardiovascular Gender Differences', *Science* 308 (10 June): 1583–7.

Mercer, Alex J. 1990. *Disease, Mortality and Population in Transition: Epidemiological-demographic Change in England Since the Eighteenth Century as Part of a Global Phenomenon*. Leicester, England: Leicester University Press.

———. 1986. 'Relative Trends in Mortality from Related Respiratory and Airborne Infectious Diseases', *Population Studies* 40: 129–45.

———. 1985. 'Smallpox and Epidemiological-Demographic Change in Europe: The Role of Vaccination', *Population Studies* 39: 287–307.

Mertens, Walter. 1994. 'Health and Mortality Trends among Elderly Populations: Determinants and Implications', *IUSSP Policy and Research Papers 3*. Liege: International Union for the Scientific Study of Population.

———. 1976. 'Canadian Nuptiality Patterns: 1911–1961', *Canadian Studies in Population* 3: 57–71.

Merton, Robert K. 1964. 'Anomie, Anomia, and Social Interaction', in M.B. Clinard, ed., *Anomie and Deviant Behavior* (pp. 213–42). New York: Free Press.

Meslé, France, and Jacques Vallin. 2006. 'Diverging Trends in Female Old-Age Mortality: The United States and the Netherlands Versus France and Japan', *Population and Development Review* 32, 1: 123–45.

Messner, Steven F., and Robert J. Sampson. 1991. 'The Sex Ratio, Family Disruption, and Rates of Violent Crime: The Paradox of Demographic Structure', *Social Forces* 69, 3: 693–713.

Milan, Anne. 2003. 'Would You Live in Common-Law?', *Canadian Social Trends* (Autumn): 2–6.

Miller, Richard A. 2005. 'The Anti-Aging Sweepstakes: Catalase Runs for the ROSes', *Science* 308 (24 June): 1875–6.

Miller, Warren B. 1992. 'Personality Traits and Developmental Experiences as Antecedents of Childbearing and Motivation', *Demography* 29, 2: 265–86.

———. 1986. 'Proception: An Important Fertility Behavior', *Demography* 23, 4: 579–94.

———, and R. Kenneth Godwin. 1977. *Psyche and Demos: Individual Psychology and the Issues of Population*. New York: Oxford University Press.

———, David J. Pasta, James MacMurray, et al. 2000. 'Genetic Influences on Childbearing Motivation: Further Testing a Theoretical Framework', in Joseph Lee Rodgers, David C. Rowe, and Warren B. Miller, eds, *Genetic Influences on Human Fertility and Sexuality: Theoretical and Empirical Contributions from the Biological and Behavioral Sciences* (pp. 35–66). Boston: Kluwer Academic Publishers.

———, Lawrence J. Severy, and David J. Pasta. 2004. 'A Framework for Modelling Fertility Motivation in Couples', *Population Studies* 58, 2: 193–206.

Milligan, Kevin. 2002. 'Quebec's Baby Bonus: Can Public Policy Affect Fertility?', Toronto: CD Howe Institute.

Mills, Melinda, and Frank Trovato. 2001. 'The Effect of Pregnancy in Cohabiting Unions on Marriage in Canada, the Netherlands and Latvia', *Statistical Journal of the United Nations Commission for Europe* 18: 103–18.

Mincer, Jacob. 1978. 'Family Migration Decisions', *Journal of Political Economy* 86: 749–73.

Mishra, Vionod, T.K. Roy, and Robert D. Retherford. 2004. 'Sex Differentials in Childhood Feeding, Health Care, and Nutritional Status in India', *Population and Development Review* 30, 2: 269–96.

Mitchinson, Wendy. 2002. *Giving Birth in Canada: 1900–1950*. Toronto: University of Toronto Press.

Mitra, Asok. 2001. 'Implications of Declining Sex Ratios in India's Population', in Vina Masumdar and N. Krishnaji, eds, *Enduring Conundrum: India's Sex Ratio: Essays in Honour of Asok Mitra* (pp. 143–98). Noida, Uttar Pradesh, India: Rainbow.

Mokdad, Ali H., James S. Marks, Donna F. Stroup, and Julie L. Gerberding. 2004. 'Actual Causes of Death in the United States, 2000', *Journal of the American Medical Association* (10 March) 291, 10: 1238–45.

Moore, Jim. 2004. 'The Puzzling Origins of AIDS', *American Scientist* 92 (November–December): 540–7.

Moore, Lorna G., Peter W. Van Arsdale, Jo Ann E. Glittenberg, and Robert A. Aldrich. 1987. *The Biocultural Basis of Health*. Prospect Heights, IL: Wavelength.

Moore, Wilbert E. 1974. *Social Change*, 2nd edn. Englewood Cliffs, NJ: Prentice Hall.

Morgan, Philip S. 2003a. 'Is Low Fertility a Twenty-First-Century Demographic Crisis?', *Demography* 40, 4: 589–603.

———. 2003b. 'Baby Boom, Post-World War II', in Paul Demeny and Geoffrey McNicoll, eds, *Encyclopedia of Population* (pp. 73–7). New York: Macmillan Reference USA/Thompson Gale.

Morissette, René, and Anick Johnson. 2005. 'Are Good Jobs Disappearing in Canada?', *Analytical Studies Research Paper Series*. Cat. no. 11F0019MIE-239. Ottawa: Statistics Canada.

Morrison, H.I., R.M. Semenciw, Y.B. Mao, and D.T. Wigle. 1986. 'Infant Mortality on Canadian Indian Reserves', *Canadian Journal of Public Health* 77: 269–73.

Morrison, P.A., and J.P. Wheeler. 1976. 'Rural Renaissance in America?' *Population Bulletin* 31, 3. Washington: Population Reference Bureau.

———, Thomas M. Bryan, and David A. Swanson. 2004. 'Internal Migration and Short-Distance Mobility', in Jacob A. Siegel and David A. Swanson, eds, *The Methods and Materials of Demography*, 2nd edn. (pp. 493–51). Amsterdam: Elsevier.

Moses, Jonathon W. 2006. *International Migration: Globalization's Last Frontier*. London: Zed Books.

Mosher, William D. 1980. 'Demographic Responses and Demographic Transitions: A Case Study of Sweden', *Demography* 17: 395–412.

Mosley, W. Henry, and Lincoln C. Chen. 1984. 'An Analytical Framework for the Study of Child Survival in Developing Countries', in W. Henry Mosley and Lincoln

C. Chen, eds, *Child Survival: Strategies for Research* (pp. 25–45), supp. to *Population and Development Review* 10. New York: The Population Council.

Muir, C.S., and A.J. Sasco. 1990. 'Prospects for Cancer Control in the 1990s', *Annual Review of Public Health* 11: 143–63.

Mumford, Lewis. 1961. *The City in History: Its Origins, Its Transformations, and Its Prospects*. New York: Harcourt (Harbinger Book).

Murphy, Michael. 1993. 'The Contraceptive Pill and Women's Employment as Factors in Fertility Change in Britain 1963–1980: A Challenge to the Conventional View', *Population Studies* 47, 2: 221–44.

Murphy, Rachel. 2003. 'Fertility and Distorted Sex Ratios in a Rural Chinese County', *Population and Development Review* 29, 4: 595–626.

Myrdal, Gunnar. 1957. *Economic Theory and Under-Developed Regions*. London: Duckworth.

Nadarajah, T. 1983. 'The Transition from Higher Female to Higher Male Mortality in Sri Lanka', *Population and Development Review* 9, 2: 317–25.

Nagnur, Dhruva. 1986a. 'Rectangularization of the Survival Curve and Entropy: The Canadian Experience', *Canadian Studies in Population* 13, 1: 83–102.

———. 1986b. *Longevity and Historical Life Tables: 1921–1981* (abridged): *Canada and the Provinces*. Cat. no. 89-506. Ottawa: Minister of Supply and Services Canada.

———, and M. Nagrodski. 1990. 'Epidemiological Transition in the Context of Demographic Change: The Evolution of Canadian Mortality Patterns', *Canadian Studies in Population* 17, 1: 1–24.

Narayan, K.M. 1997. 'Diabetes Mellitus in Native Americans: The Problem and Its Implications', *Population Research and Policy Review* 16: 169–92.

Nathanson, Constance. 1996. 'Disease Prevention and Social Change', *Population and Development Review* 22, 4: 609–38.

———. 1995. 'The Position of Women in and Mortality in Developed Countries', in Lopez, Caselli, and Valkonen, eds, *Adult Mortality in Developed Countries: From Description to Explanation* (pp. 135–57). Oxford: Oxford University Press.

National Post. 2004. 'Quebec Stems Migration to Ontario: 25-Year Trend Reversed', (16 January): A3.

———. 2002. 'Canadians Older than Ever Before', (17 July): A1, A6–A8.

National Research Council. 2004. *Critical Perspectives on Racial and Ethnic Differences in Health in Later Life*, ed. N.B. Anderson, R.A. Bulatao, and B. Cohen. Panel on Race, Ethnicity, and Health in Later Life. Washington, DC: National Academies Press.

———. 2003. *Cities Transformed: Demographic Change and its Implications in the Developing World*, ed. M.R. Montgomery, R. Stren, B. Cohen, and H.E. Reed. Panel on Urban Population. Washington, DC: National Academies Press.

———. 2000. *Beyond Six Billion: Forecasting the World's Population*, ed. John Bongaarts and Rodolfo A. Bulatao. Panel on Population Projections. Washington, DC: National Academies Press.

———. 1986. *Population Growth and Economic Development: Policy Questions*. Committee on Population and Working Group on Population Growth and Economic Development. Washington, DC: National Academies Press.

———, and Institute of Medicine. 2005. *Growing Up Global: The Changing Transitions to Adulthood in Developing Countries*, ed. Cynthia B. Lloyd. Panel on Transition to Adulthood in Developing Countries. Washington, DC: National Academies Press.

Newbold, Bruce K. 1999. 'Evolutionary Immigrant Settlement Patterns: Concepts and Evidence', in K. Pandid and S. Davis Withers, eds, *Migration and Restructuring in the United States: A Geographic Perspective* (Chapter 12). Lanham, MD: Rowman and Littlefield.

———. 1996a. 'The Ghettoization of Quebec: Interprovincial Migration and Its Demographic Effects', *Canadian Studies in Population* 23, 1: 1–21.

———. 1996b. 'Internal Migration of the Foreign-Born in Canada', *International Migration Review* 30, 3: 728–47.

Newell, Colin. 1998. *Methods and Models in Demography*. London: Belhaven.

Ng, Edward. 1996. 'Disability among Canada's Aboriginal Peoples in 1991', *Health Reports* 8, 1: 25–32.

Nichiporuk, Biran. 2000. *The Security Dynamics of Demographic Factors*. Santa Monica, CA: RAND Corporation.

Nierenberg, Danielle. 2005. 'The Challenge of Uncertainty: The Unexpected Occurrence', *Genus* LXI, 3–4: 91–109.

———. 2003. 'Meat Production and Consumption Grow', in *Vital Signs* (pp. 30–1). The Worldwatch Institute. New York: W.W. Norton.

Nogle, J.M. 1994. 'Internal Migration for Recent Immigrants to Canada', *International Migration Review* 28, 1: 31–49.

Noh, Samuel, and William R. Avison. 1996. 'Asian Immigrants and the Stress Process: A Study of Koreans in Canada', *Journal of Health and Social Behavior* 37: 192–206.

Nolen, Stephanie. 2005. 'UN Says it Will Miss AIDS Target', *The Globe and Mail* (Tuesday, June 30): A15.

———. 2002a. 'Empty Grain Bags and Boiled Weeds are Ethiopia's Bitter Harvest', *The Globe and Mail* (28 November): A12.

———. 2002b. 'Starved for Answers', *The Globe and Mail* (21 October): A11.

Norberg-Bohm, Viki, William C. Clark, Bhavik Bakshi, et al. 2001. 'International Comparisons of Environmental Hazards', in Jeanne X. Kasperson and Roger E. Kasperson, eds, *Global Environmental Risk* (pp. 55–147). Tokyo: United Nations University Press and Earthscan.

Norris, Mary Jane. 1996. 'Contemporary Demography of Aboriginal Peoples in Canada', in David Alan Long and

Olive Patricia Dickason, eds, *Visions of the Heart: Canadian Aboriginal Issues* (pp. 179–237). Toronto: Harcourt.

———. 1990. 'The Demography of Aboriginal People in Canada', in Shiva S. Halli, Frank Trovato, and Leo Driedger, eds, *Ethnic Demography: Canadian Immigrant, Racial and Cultural Variations* (pp.33–59). Ottawa: Carleton University Press.

———, and Stewart Clatworthy. 2003. 'Aboriginal Mobility and Migration Within Urban Canada: Outcomes, Factors and Implications'. Paper presented at the Annual Meetings of the Population Association of America. Minneapolis, Minneapolis, May 1–3, 2003.

———, and ———. 2002. 'Aboriginal Mobility and Migration within Urban Canada: Outcomes, Factors and Implications', in David Newhouse and Evelyne Peters, eds, *No Strangers in These Parts: Urban Aboriginal Peoples* (pp. 51–78). Ottawa: Policy Research Initiative.

———, Martin Cooke, Daniel Beavon, et al. 2004. 'Registered Indian Mobility and Migration in Canada', in John Taylor and Martin Bell, eds, *Population Mobility and Indigenous Peoples in Australasia and North America* (pp. 136–60). London: Routledge.

Northcott, Herbert C. 1988. *Changing Residence: The Geographic Mobility of Elderly Canadians*. Toronto: Butterworths.

Notestein, Frank W. 1953. 'Economic Problems and Population Change', in *Proceedings of the Eighth International Conference of Agricultural Economists* (pp. 13–31). London: Oxford University Press.

———. 1945. 'Population: The Long View', in Theodore W. Schultz, ed., *Food for the World* (pp. 36–57). Chicago: University of Chicago Press.

Notkola, Veijo, Ian M. Timaeus, and Harri Siiskonen. 2000. 'Mortality Transition in the Ovamboland Region of Namibia, 1930–1990', *Population Studies* 54, 2: 153–67.

Noymer, Anderew, and Michel Garenne. 2000. 'The 1918 Influenza Epidemic's Effects on Sex Differentials in Mortality in the United States', *Population and Development Review* 26, 3: 565-581.

Nsiah-Gyabaah, Kwasi. 2004. 'Urbanization Processes: Environmental and Health Effects in Africa'. Paper produced for a Population-Environment Research Network cyberseminar, 29 November–15 December 2004. <www.populationenvironmentresearch.org>.

Nuovo Mondo, Il. 1995. 'Record di Nascite A Sarjevo Assediata', vol. 18, no. 3 (February).

Odum, Eugene P. 1971. *Fundamentals of Ecology*, 3rd edn. Philadelphia: W.B. Saunders.

Oeppen, Jim, and James W. Vaupel. 2002. 'Broken Limits to Life Expectancy', *Science* 296 (10 May): 1029–31.

Olinick, Michael. 1978. *An Introduction to Mathematical Models in the Social and Life Sciences*. Reading, MA: Addison-Wesley.

Olshansky, Jay S., and Brian A. Ault. 1986. 'The Fourth Stage of the Epidemiological Transition: The Age of Delayed Degenerative Diseases', *The Milbank Quarterly* 64: 355–91.

———, and Bruce A. Carnes. 2001. *The Quest for Immortality*. New York: W.W. Norton.

———, and ———. 1997. 'Ever Since Gompertz', *Demography* 34, 1: 1–15.

———, ———, and C. Cassel. 1990. 'In Search of Methuselah: Estimating the Upper Limits to Human Longevity', *Science* 250: 634–40.

———, ———, and Leonard Hayflick. 2004. 'No Truth to the Fountain of Youth', in *Scientific American* (special edition), *The Science of Staying Young* 14, 2: 98–102.

———, Douglas J. Passaro, Ronald C. Hershow, et al. 2005. 'A Potential Decline in Life Expectancy in the United States in the 21st Century', *The New England Journal of Medicine* 352, 1: 1138–45.

———, M.A. Rudberg, B.A. Carnes, et al. 1991. 'Trading Off Longer Life for Worsening Health', *Journal of Aging and Health* 3, 2: 194–216.

Olson, Steve. 2002. *Mapping Human History: Genes, Race, and Our Common Origins*. Boston: Mariner Book.

Omran, Abdel R. 1971. 'The Epidemiological Transition: A Theory of Epidemiology of Population Change', *The Milbank Quarterly/Health and Society* 49: 507–37.

———, and Farzaneh Roudi. 1993. 'The Middle East Population Puzzle', *Population Bulletin* 48, 1. Washington: The Population Reference Bureau.

Ono, H. 1998. 'Husbands' and Wives' Resources and Marital Dissolution', *Journal of Marriage and the Family* 60: 674–9.

Oppenheimer, Valerie Kincade. 1997. 'Women's Employment and the Gain to Marriage: The Specialization and Trading Model', *Annual Review of Sociology* 23: 431–53.

———. 1994. 'Women's Rising Employment and the Future of Family in Industrial Societies', *Population and Development Review* 20, 2: 293–337.

———. 1988. 'A Theory of Marriage Timing', *American Journal of Sociology* 94, 3: 563–91.

Organisation for Economic Co-operation and Development (OECD). 2004. *Reforming Public Pensions: Sharing the Experiences of Transition and OECD Countries*. Paris: OECD.

———. 1998. *Maintaining Prosperity in an Aging Society*. Paris: OECD.

Overbeek, Johannes. 1974. *History of Population Theories*. Rotterdam: Rotterdam University Press.

———. 1980. *Population and Canadian Society*. Toronto: Butterworths.

Owen, Ian P.F. 2002. 'Sex Differences in Mortality Rate', *Science* 297 (20 September): 2008–9.

Owram, Doug. 1996. *Born at the Right Time: A History of the Baby Boom Generation*. Toronto: University of Toronto Press.

Oziewicz, Estanislao. 2005. 'Indonesia Prepares for Baby Boom', *The Globe and Mail* (25 April): A11.

Paccaud, Fred, Claudio Sidoti Pinto, Alfio Marazzi, and J. Mili. 1998. 'Age at Death and Rectangularization of the Survival Curve: Trends in Switzerland, 1969–1994', *Journal of Epidemiology and Community Health* 52: 412–15.

Pampel, Fred C. 2003. 'Declining Sex Differences in Mortality from Lung Cancer in High-Income Nations', *Demography* 40, 1: 45–65.

———. 2002. 'Cigarette Use and the Narrowing Sex Differential in Mortality', *Population and Development Review* 28, 1: 77–104.

———. 1998. 'Nation, Social Change, and Sex Differences in Suicide Rates', *American Sociological Review* 63, 5: 744–58.

———. 1996. 'Cohort Size and Age-Specific Suicide Rates: A Contingent Relationship', *Demography* 33, 3: 341–55.

———, and Elizabeth H. Peters. 1995. 'The Easterlin Effect', *Annual Review of Sociology* 21: 163–94.

Pang, Henry, and Sue Mary Hanson. 1968. 'Higher Divorce Rates in Western United States', *Sociology and Social Research* 52: 228–36.

Panter-Brick, Catherine. 1996. 'Proximate Determinants of Birth Seasonality and Conception Failure in Nepal', *Population Studies* 50: 203–21.

Park, Robert E. 1929 [1959]. *Human Communities*. New York: Free Press.

———. 1916. 'The City: Suggestions for the Investigation of Human Behaviour in the Urban Environment', *American Journal of Sociology* 20: 577–612.

Parkin, Andrew. 2003. 'Introduction: How Canada is Changing', Centre for Research and Information on Canada (pp. 2–9). Montreal: CRIC Papers.

Parsons, Craig A., and Timothy M. Smeeding. 2006. 'What's Unique about Immigration in Europe?', in Craig A. Parsons and Timothy M. Smeeding, eds, *Immigration and the Transformation of Europe* (pp. 1–29). Cambridge: Cambridge University Press.

Pearl, Raymond. 1927. *The Biology of Population Growth*. New York: Knopf.

———, and Lowell J. Reed. 1920. 'On the Rate of Growth of the Population of the United States since 1790 and Its Mathematical Representation', *Proceedings of the National Academy of Sciences* 6: 275–88.

Pebley, Anne R. 2003. 'Infant and Child Mortality', in Paul Demeny and Geoffrey McNicoll, eds, *Encyclopedia of Population* (pp. 533–6). New York: Macmillan Reference USA/Thompson Gale.

———. 1998. 'Demography and the Environment', *Demography* 35, 4: 377–89.

Pelletier, Francois, Jacques Legare, and Robert Bourbeau. 1997. 'Mortality in Quebec During the Nineteenth Century: Form the State to the Cities', *Population Studies* 51, 1: 93–103.

Pensola, Tiina, and Pekka Martikainen. 2004. 'Life-Course Experiences and Mortality by Adult Social Class among Young Men', *Social Science and Medicine* 58: 2149–70.

Perenboom, R.J.M., L.M. Van Herten, H.C. Boshuizen, et al. 2004. 'Trends in Disability-Free Life Expectancy', *Disability and Rehabilitation* 26, 7: 377–86.

Peressini, Tracy. 2005. 'Urban Inequality: Poverty in Canadian Cities', in Harry H. Hiller, ed., *Urban Canada: Sociological Perspectives* (pp. 169–89). Don Mills, ON: Oxford University Press.

Perkins, Dwight H, Steven Radelet, and David L. Lindauer. 2006. *Economics of Development*, 6th edn. New York: W.W. Norton.

Perls, Thomas T., and Margery Hutter Silver. 1999. *Living to 100*. New York: Basic Books.

———, and Ruth C. Fretts. 2002. 'Why Women Live Longer than Men', in Frank Trovato, ed., *Population and Society: Essential Readings* (pp. 101–6). Don Mills, ON: Oxford University Press.

Peron, Yves, and Claude Strohmenger. 1985. *Demography and Health Indicators: Presentation and Interpretation*. Cat. no. 82-543E. Ottawa: Minister of Supply and Services Canada.

———, Helene Desrosiers, H. Juby, E. L-Adamcyk, et al. 1999. *Canadian Families at the Approach of the Year 2000*. Census Monograph Series. Cat. 96-321-MPE no. 4. Ottawa: Statistics Canada.

Peters, Anna, Jan J. Barendregt, Frans J. Willekens, et al. 2003. 'Obesity in Adulthood and Its Consequences for Life Expectancy: A Life-Table Analysis', *Annals of Internal Medicine* 138: 28–34.

Petersen, William. 2003a. 'Condorcet, Marquis De', in Paul Demeny and Geoffrey McNicoll, eds., *Encyclopedia of Population* (pp. 167–8). New York: Macmillan Reference USA/Thomson Gale.

———. 2003b. 'Godwin, William', in Paul Demeny and Geoffrey McNicoll, eds, *Encyclopedia of Population* (pp. 468–9). New York: Macmillan Reference USA/Thomson Gale.

———. 2000. *From Birth to Death: A Consumer's Guide to Population Studies*. New Brunswick, USA and London: Transaction.

———. 1989. 'Marxism and the Population Question: Theory and Practice', in M.S. Teitelbaum and J. Winter, eds, *Population and Resources in Western Intellectual Traditions* (pp. 77–101), supp. to *Population and Development Review* 14.

———. 1979. *Malthus*. Cambridge, MA: Harvard University Press.

———. 1978. 'International Migration', *Annual Review of Sociology* 4: 533–75.

———. 1975. *Population*, 3rd edn. New York: Macmillan.

———. 1958. 'A General Typology of Migration', *American Sociological Review* 23: 256–65.

Peterson, Peter G. 1999. 'Gray Dawn: The Global Aging Crisis', *Foreign Affairs* 78, 1: 42–55.

Peto, R., Alan D. Lopez, J. Boreham, et al. 2000. *Mortality from Smoking in Developed Countries 1950–2000: Indirect Estimates from National Vital Statistics*. Oxford: Oxford University Press.

Pfeiff, Margo. 2003. 'Out of Davis Inlet', *Canadian Geographic* 123, 1. (January/February): 42–52.

Philip, A.G. 1995. 'Neonatal Mortality Rate: Is Further Improvement Possible?', *Journal of Pediatrics* 126: 427–33.

Phillips, James F., and John A. Ross, eds. 1992. *Family Planning Programmes and Fertility*. Oxford: Clarendon.

Phung, H., A. Bauman, T.V. Nguyen, et al. 2003. 'Risk Factors for Low Birth Weight in a Socio-Economic Disadvantaged Population: Parity, Marital Status, Ethnicity and Cigarette Smoking', *European Journal of Epidemiology* 18: 235–243.

Picard, Andre. 2006a. 'Boomers' Lifestyle a Ticking Bomb', *The Globe and Mail* (14 February): A1, A5.

———. 2006b. 'Why U.S. Reached a Cancer Tipping Point First: Deaths Decline South of the Border, but Demographics Fuel Continuing Rise in Canada', *The Globe and Mail* (10 February): A1, A11.

———. 2004. 'Study Links Extra Pounds to More Disease: Obesity Tied to 41 Common Health Ailments', *The Globe and Mail* (22 November): A8.

Picot, Garnett, Feng Hou, and Simon Coulombe. 2007. *Chronic Low Income and Low-income Dynamics Among Recent Immigrants*. Analytical Studies Branch Research Paper Series 11F0019MIE, Volume 2007, number 294. Ottawa: Statistics Canada.

Pido-Lopez, J., N. Imami, and R. Aspinall. 2001. 'Both Age and Gender Affect Thymes Output: More Recent Thymes Migrants in Females than Males as They Age', *Clinical Experimental Immunology* 125: 409–13.

Piore, Michael. 1979. *Birds of Passage: Migrant Labor in Industrial Societies*. Cambridge: Cambridge University Press.

Pison, Giles. 2001. 'The Population of France in 2000', *Population and Societies* 366 (March): 3.

Plane, David A. 2004. 'Population Distribution: Geographic Areas', in Jacob B. Siegel and David A. Swanson, eds, *The Methods and Materials of Demography*, 2nd edn. (pp. 81–104). Amsterdam: Elsevier.

———, and Peter A. Rogerson. 1994. *The Geographical Analysis of Population with Applications to Planning and Business*. New York: Academic Press.

Pohlman, Edward, ed. 1973. *Population: A Clash of Prophets*. New York: New American Library (Mentor Book).

Polian, Pavel. 2004. *Against Their Will: The History and Geography of Forced Migrations in the USSR*. Budapest and New York: Central European University Press.

Pollard, A.H., Farhat Yusuf, and G.N. Pollard. 1981. *Demographic Techniques*, 2nd edn. Sydney: Pergamon.

Pollard, J.H. 1973. *Mathematical Models for the Growth of Human Populations*. Cambridge: Cambridge University Press.

Ponce, N.A., K.J. Hoggatt, M. Wilhelm, et al. 2005. 'Preterm Birth: The Interaction of Traffic-Related Air Pollution with Economic Hardship in Los Angeles Neighbor-hoods', *American Journal of Epidemiology* 162: 140–8.

Ponting, Rick J. 1997. *First Nations in Canada: Perspectives on Opportunity, Empowerment and Self-Determination*. Toronto: McGraw-Hill.

Pool, Ian. 1994. 'Cross-Comparative Perspectives on New Zealand's Health', in John Spicer, Andrew Trlin, and Jo Ann Walton, eds, *Social Dimensions of Health and Disease: New Zealand Perspectives* (pp. 16–49). Palmerston North: Dunmore.

———. 1991. *Te Iwi Maori: A New Zealand Population Past, Present and Projected*. Auckland, NZ: Aukland University Press.

Pop-Eleches, Cristian. 2006. 'The Impact of an Abortion Ban on Socioeconomic Outcomes of Children: Evidence from Romania', *Journal of Political Economy* 114, 4: 744–73.

Population Reference Bureau. Various years. *World Population Data Sheets*. Washington, DC: Population Reference Bureau.

Porter, John. 1965. *The Vertical Mosaic*. Toronto: University of Toronto Press.

Porter, Roy. 1997. *The Greatest Benefit to Mankind: A Medical History of Humanity from Antiquity to the Present*. London: HarperCollins.

Portes, Alejandro, and Rubén G. Rumbaut. 2006. *Immigrant America: A Portrait*. Berkeley: University of California Press.

Poston, Dudley L. Jr, and Richard G. Rogers. 1985. 'Toward a Reformulation of the Neonatal Mortality Rate', *Social Biology* 32, (1–2): 1–12.

Potts, Malcom. 2006. 'China's One Child Policy', *British Medical Journal* 333: 361–2.

———, Peter Diggory, and John Peel. 1977. *Abortion*. Cambridge: Cambridge University Press.

———, and Peter Selman. 1978. *Society and Fertility*. London: Macdonald and Evans.

———, and Roger Short. 1999. *Ever Since Adam and Eve: The Evolution of Human Sexuality*. Cambridge: Cambridge University Press.

Prebisch, Raul. 1959. 'Commercial Policy in the Underdeveloped Countries', *American Economic Review, Papers and Proceedings* (May): 251–73.

Pressat, Roland. 1985. *A Dictionary of Demography*, ed. Christopher Wilson. Oxford: Basil Blackwell.

———. 1974. *A Workbook in Demography*. London: Methuen.

Preston, Samuel H. 2005. 'Deadweight? The Influence of Obesity on Longevity', *The New England Journal of Medicine* 352, 11: 1138–45.

———. 1998. 'Population and the Environment: Scientific Evidence', in Paul Demeny and Geoffrey McNicoll, eds, *The Earthscan Reader* (pp. 257–63). London: Earthscan.

———. 1986. 'Changing Values and Falling Birth Rates', in Mickail Kingsley Davis, S. Bernstam, and Rita Ricardo-Campbell, eds, *Below-Replacement Fertility in Industrial Societies: Causes, Consequences, Policies* (pp. 176–95), supp. to *Population and Development Review* 12, 1986.

———. 1980. 'Causes and Consequences of Mortality in Less Developed Countries during the Twentieth Century', in Richard Easterlin, ed., *Population and Economic Change in Developing Countries* (pp. 289–341, 353–60). New York: National Bureau of Economic Research.

———. 1979. 'Urban Growth in Developing Countries: A Demographic Reappraisal', *Population and Development Review* 5, 2: 195–216.

———. 1977. 'Mortality Trends', *Annual Review of Sociology* 3: 163–78.

———. 1976. *Mortality Patterns in National Populations: With Special Reference to Recorded Causes of Death*. New York: Academic Press.

———, and Michael R. Heines. 1991. *Fatal Years: Child Mortality in Late Nineteenth-Century America*. Princeton, NJ: Princeton University Press.

———, Patrick Heuveline, and Michel Guillot. 2001. *Demography: Measuring and Modeling Population Processes*. Malden, MA: Blackwell.

———, and Alan Thomas Richards. 1975. 'The Influence of Women's Work Opportunities on Marriage Rates', *Demography* 12, 2: 209–22.

Priest, Lisa, and Katherine Harding. 2006. 'Hours After Birth, Xander Received a New Heart', *The Globe and Mail* (Saturday, February 18): A1 and A5.

Proskouriakoff, Tatiana. 1955 [1973]. 'The Death of a Civilization', *Readings from Scientific American*, in Kingsley Davis, ed., *Cities: Their Origin, Growth and Human Impact* (pp. 93–7). New York: W.H. Freeman.

Prothero, Mansel R., and M. Chapman, eds. 1984. *Circulation in Third World Countries*. London: Routledge and Kagan Paul.

Pulliam, H. Ronald, and Nick M. Haddad. 1994. 'Human Population Growth and the Carrying Capacity Concept', *Bulletin of the Ecological Society of America* 75 (September): 141–57.

Quinn, Thomas C. 1995. 'Population Migration and the Spread of Types 1 and 2 Human Immunodeficiency Viruses', in Bernard Roizman, ed., *Infectious Diseases in an Age of Change: The Impact of Human Ecology and Behavior on Disease Transmission* (pp. 77–97). Washington, DC: National Academy of Sciences.

———, and Julie Overbaugh. 2005. 'HIV/AIDS in Women: An Expanding Epidemic', *Science* 308 (10 June): 1582–3.

Radio Free Europe Radio Liberty. 2005. 'Romania: Woman Gives Birth at 66 to Become World's Oldest Mother' (17 January), <http://www.rferl.org/featuresarticle/2005/01/57089a2f-8752-4847-ad33-2b83ce1da609.html>.

Ragland, Kathleen E., Steve Selvin, and Deane W. Merrill. 1988. 'The Onset of Decline in Ischemic Heart Disease Mortality in the Untied States', *American Journal of Epidemiology* 127, 3: 516–31.

Rahmstorf, Stefan, Anny Cazenave, John A. Church, et al. 2007. 'Recent Climate Observations Compared to Projections', *Science* 316 (4 May): 709.

Rainwater, L. 1965. *Family Designs: Marital Sexuality, Family Size and Contraception*. Chicago: Aldine.

———. 1960. *And the Poor Get Children*. Chicago: Quadrangle Books.

Ram, Bali. 2004. 'New Estimates of Aboriginal Fertility, 1966–1971 to 1996–2001', *Canadian Studies in Population* 31, 2: 179–96.

———. 2000. 'Current Issues in Family Demography: Canadian Examples' *Canadian Studies in Population* 27, 1: 1–14.

———, Mary Jane Norris, and K. Skof. 1989. *The Inner City in Transition*. Ottawa: Statistics Canada.

———, and Abdur Rahim. 1993. 'Enduring Effects of Women's Early Employment Experiences on Child-Spacing: The Canadian Evidence', *Population Studies* 47, 2: 307–18.

———, and Edward Y. Shin. 2007. 'Education Selectivity of Out-migration in Canada: 1976–1981 to 1996–2001', *Canadian Studies in Population* 34, 2: 129–48.

———, and ———. 2000a. 'The Internal Migration of Immigrants in Canada', in Shiva S. Halli and Leo Driedger, eds, *Immigrant Canada: Ethnic and Cultural Variations*. Toronto: University of Toronto Press.

———, and ———. 2000b. 'Migration of Linguistic Groups Between Quebec and Ontario, 1971–76 to 1991–96'. Paper presented at the annual meetings of the Population Association of America. Los Angeles, CA (23–25 March 2004).

Rathor, Anupurna. 2004. *Family Planning Practices in Third World Countries*. Delhi: Adhyayan.

Ravenholt, R.T. 1990. 'Tobacco's Global Death March', *Population and Development Review* 16: 213–40.

Ravenstein, Ernst Georg. 1889. 'The Laws of Migration' Paper II, *Journal of the Statistics Society* 52, 2: 167–235 (with commentary). Reprinted, 1976, Arno.

———. 1885. 'The Laws of Migration', Paper I, *Journal of the Statistics Society* 48, 2: 167–235 (with commentary). Reprinted, 1976, Arno.

Raymond, Susan. 2003. 'Foreign Assistance in an Aging World', *Foreign Affairs* 82, 2: 91–105.

Razzel, P.E. 1974. 'An Interpretation of the Modern Rise of Population in Europe', *Population Studies* 28: 5–17.

Reaney, Patricia. 2003. 'Protein Could Be Key to Longevity', *National Post* (11 December): A15.

Rebhun, Uzi. 2003. 'The Changing Roles of Human Capital, State Context of Residence, and Ethnic Bonds in Interstate Migration: American Jews 1970–1990', *International Journal of Population Geography* 9: 3–21.

Redman, Charles L., and Nancy S. Jones. 2004. 'The Environmental, Social, and Health Dimensions of Urban Expansion'. Paper produced for a Population-Environment Research Network cyberseminar, 29 November–15 December, 2004. <www.populationenvironment research.org>.

Reed, Campbell B. 1988. 'Zipf's Law', in Samuel Kotz, Norman L. Jonson, and Campbell B. Reed, eds, *Encyclope-*

dia of Statistical Sciences (pp. 674–6). New York: John Wiley.

Rees, Philip, Martin Bell, Oliver Duke-Williams, and Marcus Blake. 2000. 'Problems and Solutions in the Measurement of Migration Intensities: Australia and Britain Compared', *Population Studies* 54: 207–22.

Reimer, Bill. 2005. 'Rural and Urban: Differences and Common Ground', in Harry H. Hiller, ed., *Urban Canada: Sociological Perspectives* (pp. 71–94). Don Mills, ON: Oxford University Press.

Retherford, Robert D. 1975. *The Changing Sex Differential in Mortality*. Westport, CT: Greenwood.

———, and T.K. Roy. 2003. 'Factors Affecting Sex-selective Abortion in India and 17 Major States', *National Family Health Survey Subject Reports*, no. 21. Mumbai: International Institute for Population Sciences, and Honolulu: East-West Center Program on Population.

Rice, Dorothy P., and Norman Fineman. 2004. 'Economic Implications of Increased Longevity in the United States', *Annual Review of Public Health* 25: 457–73.

Richmond, Anthony H. 1994. *Global Apartheid: Refugees, Racism, and the New World Order*. Toronto: Oxford University Press.

Richter, K. 1985 [1996]. 'Nonmetropoltian Growth in the Late 1970s: The End of the Turnaround?', in H.S. Geyer and T.M. Kontuly, eds, *Differential Urbanization: Integrating Spatial Models* (pp. 47–66). London: Edward Arnold.

Ricklef, Robert E. 1990. *Ecology*, 3rd edn. New York: W.H. Freeman.

Riley, James C. 2001. *Rising Life Expectancy: A Global History*. Cambridge: Cambridge University Press.

———. 2005a. 'Estimates of Regional Global Life Expectancy, 1800–2001', *Population and Development Review* 31, 3: 537–43.

———. 2005b. 'The Timing and Pace of Health Transitions Around the World', *Population and Development Review* 31, 4: 741–64.

Riley, Nancy E. 1999. 'Challenging Demography: Contributions from Feminist Theory', *Sociological Forum* 14, 3: 369–97.

———. 2005. 'Demography of Gender', in Dudley L. Poston and Michael Micklin, eds, *Handbook of Population* (pp. 109–41). New York: Kluwer Academic Publishers/Plenum.

Rindfuss, Ronald R. 1991. 'The Young Adult Years: Diversity, Structural Change, and Fertility', *Demography* 28, 4: 493–512.

———, David Guilkey, S. Philip Morgan, et al. 2007. 'Child Care Availability and First-Birth Timing in Norway', *Demography* 44, 2: 345–72.

Risman, B.J., and D. Johnson-Sumerford. 1998. 'Doing It Fairly: A Study of Postgender Marriages', *Journal of Marriage and the Family* 60: 23–40.

Ritchey, Neil P. 1976. 'Explanations of Migration', *Annual Review of Sociology* 2: 363–404.

Robert, Stephanie A. 1999. 'Socio-economic Position and Health: The Independent Contribution of Community Socio-economic Context', *Annual Review of Sociology* 25: 489–516.

Robey, Bryant, Shea O. Rutstein, and Leo Morris. 1993. 'The Fertility Decline in Developing Countries', *Scientific American* 269, 6: 60–7.

Robine, Jean-Marie. 2001. 'Redefining the Stages of the Epidemiological Transition by a Study of the Dispersion of Life Spans: The Case of France', *Population: An English Selection* 13, 1: 173–94.

Robinson, Warren. 1997. 'The Economic Theory of Fertility Over Three Decades', *Population Studies* 51, 1: 63–75.

Robitaille, Norbert, and Robert Choinière. 1987. 'L'accroissement démographique des groupes autochtones du Canada au XXe siècle', *Cahiers Québécois de Démographie* 16, 1.

Rodgers, Joseph Lee, and Hans-Peter Kohler, eds. 2002. *The Biodemography of Human Reproduction and Fertility*. New York: Academic Publishers.

———, Craig A. St John, and Ronnie Coleman. 2005. 'Fertility After the Oklahoma City Bombing', *Demography* 42, 4: 675–92.

Rogers, Andrei. 1992. 'Elderly Migration and Population Redistribution in the United States', in Andrei Rogers, ed., with W.H. Frey, A. Speare Jr., P. Rees, and A.M. Warnes, *Elderly Migration and Population Redistribution: A Comparative Study* (pp. 226–48). London: Belhaven.

———. 1990. 'Requiem for the Net Migrant', *Geographical Analysis* 22: 283–300.

———, ed. 1992. *Elderly Migration and Population Redistribution: A Comparative Study*. London: Belhaven.

———. 1984. *Migration, Urbanization, and Spatial Population Dynamics*. Boulder, CO: Westview.

———, and Luis J. Castro. 1986. 'Migration', in Andrei Rogers and Frans J. Willkens, eds, *Migration and Settlement: A Multiregional Comparative Study*. Boston and Dordrecht: D. Reidel.

———, ———, and Megan Lea. 2005. 'Model Migration Schedules: Three Alternative Linear Parameter Estimation Methods', *Mathematical Population Studies* 12: 17–38.

———, and Kathy Gard. 1991. 'Applications of the Heligman/Pollard Model Mortality Schedule', *Population Bulletin of the United Nations* 30: 79–105.

———, and S. Henning. 1999. 'The Internal Migration Patterns of the Foreign-Born and Native-Born Populations in the United States: 1975–80 and 1985–90', *International Migration Review*: 403–29.

———, and Frans J. Willikens, eds. 1986. *Migration and Settlement: A Multiregional Comparative Study*. Boston and Dordrecht: D. Reidel.

Rogers, Richard G., and R. Hackenberg. 1987. 'Extending Epidemiologic Transition Theory: A New Stage', *Social Biology* 34, 3–4: 234–43.

———, Robert A. Hummer, and Charles B. Nam. 2000. 'Family Composition and Mortality', in *Living and Dying in the USA: Behavioral, Health, and Social Differentials of Adult Mortality* (pp. 77–93). New York: Academic Press.

Rogers, Stacy J. 2004. 'Dollars, Dependency, and Divorce: Four Perspectives on the Role of Wife's Income', *Journal of Marriage and the Family* 66: 59–74.

Rojansky, N., A. Brzezinski, and J.G. Schenker. 1992. 'Seasonality in Human Reproduction: An Update', *Human Reproduction* 7, 6: 735–45.

Romaniuk, Anatole. 2008. 'History-based Explanatory Framework for Procreative Behaviour of Aboriginal People of Canada', *Canadian Studies in Population* 35, 1: 159–186.

———. 2000. 'Aboriginal Population of Canada: Growth Dynamics under Conditions of Encounter of Civilizations', *The Canadian Journal of Native Studies* 20, 1: 95–137.

———. 1984. *Fertility in Canada: From Baby-boom to Baby-bust.* Cat. no. 91-524E. Ottawa: Statistics Canada.

———. 1980. 'Increase in Natural Fertility during the Early Stages of Modernization: Evidence from an African Case Study', *Population Studies* 34, 2: 293–310.

Romellon, Jorge Santibanez. 2001. 'Should Frontiers be Opened to International Migration?', *International Union for the Scientific Study of Population General Conference.* San Salvador de Bahia, Brazil. August 24, 2001.

Rosano, Aldo, Lorenzo D. Botto, Beverley Botting, and P. Mastroiacovo. 2000. 'Infant Mortality and Congenital Anomalies from 1950 to 1994: An International Perspective', *Journal of Epidemiology and Community Health* 54: 660–6.

Rosenbaum, Harry. 1988. 'Return Inter-Provincial Migration: Canada, 1966–1971', *Canadian Studies in Population* 15, 1: 51–65.

Rosenberg, Matt. 2003. 'Your Guide to Geography: "Micropolitan and Metropolitan Areas of the U.S.A."'. <http://geography.about.com/cs/largecities/a/metromicro _p.htm> (18 February 2007).

Ross, John A., and W. Parker Mauldin. 1996. 'Family Planning Programs: Efforts and Results, 1972–94', *Studies in Family Planning* 27, 3: 137–47.

Ross, Kate, and John Taylor. 2002. 'Improving Life Expectancy and Health Status: A Comparison of Indigenous Australians and New Zealand Maori', *Journal of Population Research* and *New Zealand Population Review*, ed. Gordon A. Carmichael, with A. Dharmalingam: 219–38.

Rostow, W.W. 1998. *The Great Population Spike and After: Reflections on the 21st Century.* New York: Oxford University Press.

Roterman, Michelle. 2006. 'Seniors' Health Care Use', *Statistics Canada Health Reports*, supp. to vol. 16: 33–45.

Rothenberg, Richard B., and Jeffrey P. Koplan. 1990. 'Chronic Diseases in the 1990s', *Annual Review of Public Health* 11: 267–96.

Roussel, Louis. 1985. 'Le Cycle de la vie familiale dans la societe post-industrielle', in *International Population Conference* (pp. 221–35), vol. 3. Florence, Italy: International Union for the Scientific Study of Population.

Rowland, Donald T. 2003. *Demographic Methods and Concepts.* Oxford: Oxford University Press.

Royal Commission on Aboriginal Peoples. 1995. *Choosing Life: Special Report on Suicide among Aboriginal People.* Ottawa: Minister of Supply and Services Canada.

Rusmich, Ladislav, and Stephen M. Sachs. 2003. *Lessons from the Failure of the Communist Economic System.* Lanham, MD: Lexington Books.

Ryder, Norman B. 1980. *The Cohort Approach: Essays in the Measurement of Temporal Variations in Demographic Behavior.* New York: Arno.

———. 1965. 'The Emergence of a Modern Fertility Pattern: United States, 1917–66', in S.J. Behrman, Leslie Corsa Jr, and Ronald Freedman, eds, *Fertility and Family Planning: A World View* (pp. 99–123). Ann Arbor, Michigan: University of Michigan Press.

Saarela, Jan, and Fjalar Finnas. 2005. 'Mortality Inequality in Two Native Population Groups', *Population Studies* 59, 3: 313–20.

Sachs, Jeffrey. 2007. 'Breaking the Poverty Trap', *Scientific American* (19 August): <http://www.sciam.com/article. cfm?id=65077B1D-E7F2-99DF-3D5F60313BBC5668& print=true>.

———. 2002. 'Rapid Population Growth Saps Development', *Science* 297 (19 July): 341.

———, Andrew D. Mellinger, and John L. Gallup. 2001. 'The Geography of Poverty and Wealth', *Scientific American* 284 (March): 70–5.

Sacks, Geoffrey D. and J.W. McArthur. 2005. 'The Millennium Project: A Plan for Meeting the Millennium Development Goals', *The Lancet* 365 (22 January): 47–353.

Saether, Arild. 1993. 'Otto Diederich Lutken: 40 Years Before Malthus?', *Population Studies* 47: 511–17.

Sai, Fred T. 2002. 'The Cairo Imperative: How ICPD Forged a New Population Agenda for the Coming Decades', in Sadik Nafis, ed., *An Agenda for People: The UNFPA Through Three Decades* (pp. 113–35). New York and London: New York University Press.

Salomon, Joshua A., and Christopher J.L. Murray. 2002. 'The Epidemiologic Transition Revisited: Compositional Models for Causes of Death by Age and Sex', *Population and Development Review* 28, 2: 205–28.

Samuel, John T. 1987. *Immigration and Visible Minorities in the Year 2001: A Projection.* Ottawa: Carleton University Press.

Sandefur, Gary D., Ronald R. Rindfuss, and Barney Cohen, eds. 1996. *Changing Numbers, Changing Needs: American Indian Demography and Public Health.* Washington: National Academies Press.

Sanderson, Warren C., and Sergei Scherbov. 2005. 'Average Remaining Lifetimes Can Increase as Human Populations Age', *Nature* 435 (9 June): 811–13.

Sardon, Jean-Paul. 2004. 'Recent Demographic Trends in the Developed Countries', *Population E* 59, 2: 263–314.

———, 2002. 'Recent Demographic Trends in the Developed Countries', *Population* (Eng. edn) 57, 1: 111–56.

Sarin, Radhika. 2003. 'Rich-Poor Divide Growing', in *Vital Signs 2003* (pp. 88–9). Worldwatch Institute. New York: W.W. Norton.

Sassen, Saskia. 2001a. *The Global City: New York, London, Tokyo*, 2nd edn. Princeton, NJ: Princeton University Press.

———. 2001b. 'Cities in the Global Economy', in Ronan Paddison, ed., *Handbook of Urban Studies* (pp. 256–72). London: Sage.

———. 2000. *Cities in a World Economy*. Thousand Oaks, CA: Pine Forge Press.

Satzewich, Vic, and Lloyd Wong, eds. 2006. *Transnational Identities and Practices in Canada*. Toronto: University of Toronto Press.

Scardovi, Italo. 2003. 'Botero, Giovanni', in Paul Demeny and Geoffrey McNicoll, eds, *Encyclopedia of Population* (pp. 104–5). New York: Macmillan Reference USA/ Thomson Gale.

Schneider, Edward L. 1999. 'Aging in the Third Millennium', *Science* 283 (5 February): 796–7.

Schoen, Robert. 2004. 'Timing Effects and the Interpretation of Period Fertility', *Demography* 41, 4: 801–19.

———. 1983. 'Measuring the Tightness of a Marriage Squeeze', *Demography* 20: 61–78.

Schofield, R., D. Reher, and A. Bideau, eds. 1991. *The Decline of Mortality in Europe*. Oxford: Clarendon.

Schriner, Samuel E., Nancy J. Linford, George M. Martin, et al. 2005. 'Extension of Murine Life Span by Overexpression of Catalase Targeted to Mitochondria', *Science* 308 (24 June): 1909–11.

Schuck, Nathalie. 2007. 'Contested French Immigration Bill Passes', *AP Associated Press* <http://news.yahoo.com>.

Schultz, Paul T. 1993. 'Mortality Decline in the Low-Income World: Causes and Consequences', *American Economic Association Papers and Proceedings* 83, 2: 337–42.

Schumacher, E.F. 1974. *Small is Beautiful: A Study of Economics as if People Mattered*. London: Abacus Books.

Scott, Allen J. 1988. *Metropolis: From the Division of Labor to Urban Form*. Berkeley, CA: University of California Press.

Scott, Susan, and Christopher J. Duncan. 2001. *Biology of Plagues: Evidence From Historical Populations*. Cambridge: Cambridge University Press.

Scrimshaw, Susan C. M. 1984. 'Infanticide in Human Populations: Societal and Individual Concerns', in Glenn Hausfater and Sarah Blaffer Hrdy, eds, *Infanticide: Comparative and Evolutionary Perspectives* (pp. 439–62). New York: Aldine.

———. 1978. 'Infant Mortality and Behavior in the Regulation of Family Size', *Population and Development Review* 4, 3: 383–403.

Seiver, Daniel A. 1989. 'Seasonality of Fertility: New Evidence', *Population and Environment* 10, 4: 245–57.

———. 1985. 'Trend and Variation in the Seasonality of U.S. Fertility: 1947–1946', *Demography* 22, 1: 79–100.

Seltzer, Judith A., Christine A. Bacharach, Suzanne M. Bianchi, et al. 2005. 'Explaining Family Change and Variation: Challenges for Family Demographers', *Journal of Marriage and the Family* 67: 908–25.

Semyonov, Moshe, Rebeca Rijman, and Anastasia Gorodezeisky. 2006. 'The Rise of Anti-foreigner Sentiment in European Societies, 1988–2000', *American Sociological Review* 71: 426–49.

Sen, Ragini. 2003. *We the Billion: A Social Psychological Perspective on India's Population*. New Delhi: Sage.

Sennett, Richard, ed. 1969. *Classic Essays on the Culture of Cities*. Englewood Cliffs, NJ: Prentice Hall.

Serow, W.J. 1987. 'Determinants of Interstate Migration: Differences between Elderly and Nonelderly Movers', *Journal of Gerontology* 42: 95–100.

Seward, Shirley. 1986. 'More and Younger?', *Policy Options/ Options Politiques* (January): 16–19.

Sharpe, R.R., and Alfred J. Lotka. 1911. 'Problem in Age Distribution', *Philosophical Magazine* 21: 435–38. Reprinted in David P. Smith and Nathan Keyfitz, *Mathematical Demography: Selected Papers*. (1977). Berlin: Springer.

Shaw, Clifford, and Henry D. McKay. 1942. *Juvenile Delinquency and Urban Areas*. Chicago: University of Chicago Press.

Shaw, R. Paul. 1985. *Intermetropolitan Migration in Canada: Changing Determinants Over Three Decades*. Toronto: New Canada Publications.

———. 1975. *Migration Theory and Fact: A Review and Bibliography of Current Literature*. Philadelphia: Regional Science Research Institute.

Sheffer, Gabriel. 2003. *Diaspora Politics: At Home and Abroad*. Cambridge: Cambridge University Press.

Shihadeh, Edward S. 1991. 'The Prevalence of Husband-Centered Migration: Employment Consequences for Married Mothers', *Journal of Marriage and the Family* 43: 432–44.

Shin, Edward Y., and Bali Ram. 2001. 'Does it Pay to Migrate? The Canadian Evidence'. Canadian Population Society: Conference (29–31 May). Laval University: QC.

Shkolnikov, Vladimir M., France Meslé, and Jacques Vallin. 1997. 'Recent Trends in Life Expectancy and Causes of Death in Russia, 1970–1993', in Jose Luis Bobadilla, Christine A. Costello, and Faith Mitchell, eds, *Premature Death in the New Independent States* (pp. 34–65). Washington, D.C.: National Academies Press.

Shoeni, Robert F., Jersey Liang, Joan Bennett, et al. 2006. 'Trends in Old-Age Functioning and Disability in Japan, 1993–2002', *Population Studies* 60, 1: 39–53.

Shorter, Edward. 1975. *The Making of the Modern Family*. New York: McGraw-Hill.

Shryock, Henry S., Jacob Siegel, et al. 1976. *The Methods and Materials of Demography* (condensed edn by Edward G. Stockwell). San Diego, CA: Academic Press.

———, and ———. 1972. *The Methods and Materials of Demography* (condensed edition by Edward G. Stockwell). San Diego, CA: Academic Press.

Sibly, Richard M., and Jim Hone. 2002. 'Population Growth Rate and Its Determinants: An Overview', *Philosophical Transactions of the Royal Society of London B*, 357: 1153–70.

Siegel, Jacob S. 2002. *Applied Demography*. San Diego: Academic Press.

———, and David A. Swanson, eds. 2004. *The Methods and Materials of Demography*, 2nd edn. Amsterdam: Academic Press.

Siggner, Andy. 1992. 'The Socio-Demographic Conditions of Registered Indians', in Robert A. Silverman and M.O. Nielsen, eds, *Aboriginal People and Canadian Criminal Justice* (pp. 19–30). Vancouver: Butterworths.

———. 1986. 'The Socio-Demographic Conditions of Registered Indians', in J.R. Ponting, ed., *Arduous Journey: Canadian Indians and Decolonization* (pp. 57–87). Toronto: McClelland and Stewart.

———. 1980. 'A Socio-Demographic Profile of Indians in Canada', in J.R Ponting and R. Gibbins, eds, *Out of Irrelevance: A Socio-Political Introduction to Indian Affairs In Canada* (pp. 31–65). Toronto: Butterworths.

———. 1977. *Preliminary Results from a Study of 1966–1971 Migration Patterns Among Status Indians in Canada*. Working Paper no. 1, Program Statistics Division, Department of Indian Affairs and Northern Development, Ottawa: Minister of Supply and Services.

———. 1972. 'The Socio-Demographic Conditions of Registered Indians', in R.A. Silverman and M.O. Nielsen, eds, *Aboriginal People and Canadian Criminal Justice* (pp. 19–30). Vancouver: Butterworths.

Silverstein, Merril. 1995. 'Stability and Change in Temporal Distance Between the Elderly and Their Children', Demography 32, 1: 29–46.

Simmel, George. 1903 [1969]. 'The Metropolis and Mental Life', reprinted in Richard Sennett, ed., *Classic Essays on the Culture of Cities* (pp. 47–60). Englewood Cliffs, NJ: Prentice Hall.

Simmons, Alan B. 1999. 'Immigration Policy: Imagined Futures', in Shiva S. Halli and Leo Dridger, eds, *Immigrant Canada: Demographic, Economic, and Cultural Challenges*. Toronto: University of Toronto Press.

Simmons, James W. 1982. 'The Stability of Migration Patterns: Canada 1966–1971', *Urban Geography* 3: 166–78.

Simon, Julian L. 1996. *The Ultimate Resource 2*. Princeton, NJ: Princeton University Press.

———. 1995. *The State of Humanity*. Cambridge, MA: Blackwell.

Simons, John. 1980. 'Reproductive Behaviour as Religious Sacrifice', in Charlotte Hohn and Rainer Mackensen,

eds, *Determinants of Fertility Trends: Theories Re-examined* (pp. 131–46). Liege, Belgium: Ordina Editions.

Simpson, Jeffrey. 2007. 'We Have Seen the Future, and It's Sprawl and Emissions', *The Globe and Mail* (17 March): A12.

Singer, Fred S. 1971. *Is There an Optimum Level of Population?* New York: McGraw-Hill/Population Council Book.

Singh, Gopal K., and Stella M. Yu. 1995. 'Infant Mortality in the United Sates: Trends, Differentials, and Projections, 1950 Through 2010', *American Journal of Public Health* 85: 957–64.

Singh, Susheela, and Renee Samara. 1996. 'Early Marriage among Women in Developing Countries', *International Family Planning Perspectives* 22: 148–157, 175.

Sitwell, O.F.G., and N.R.M. Seifried. 1984. *The Regional Structure of the Canadian Economy*. Toronto: Methuen.

Sjaastadt, Larry A. 1962. 'The Costs and Returns to Human Migration', *Journal of Political Economy* 705: 80–93.

Sjoberg, Gideon. 1960. *The Preindustrial City: Past and Present*. New York: Free Press.

———. 1965 [1973]. 'The Origins and Evolution of Cities', in Kingsley Davis ed., *Cities: Their Origins, Growth and Human Impact* (pp. 19–27). *Readings from Scientific American*. San Franciso: W.H. Freeman.

Skartein, Rune. 1997. *Development Theory: A Guide to Some Unfashionable Perspectives*. Delhi: Oxford University Press.

Small, John, and Michael Witherick. 1995. *A Modern Dictionary of Geography*, 3rd edn. London: Edward Arnold.

Smil, Vaclav. 2005a. 'The Next 50 Years: Fatal Discontinuities', *Population and Development Review* 31, 3: 201–36.

———. 2005b. 'The Next 50 Years', *Population and Development Review* 31, 4: 605–44.

Smith, Adam. 1776 [1904]. *An Inquiry into the Nature and Causes of the Wealth of Nations*, 5th edn, ed. Edwin Cannan. London: Methuen

Smith, David W.E. 1993. *Human Longevity*. New York: Oxford University Press.

Smith, Gordon C., Jennifer A. Crossley, David A. Aitken, et al. 2004. 'First-Trimester Placentation and the Risk of Antepartum Stillbirth', *Journal of the American Medical Association* 292, 18 (November 10): 2249–2254.

Smith, James P. 2004. 'Unraveling the SES-Health Connection', in Linda J. Waite, ed., *Aging, Health, and Public Policy: Demographic and Economic Perspectives*. A supplement to Population and Development Review Volume 30. New York: The Population Council.

Smith, Peter J. 2000. 'Suburbs', in Trudy Bunting and Pierre Filion, eds, *Canadian Cities in Transition: The Twenty-First Century*, 2nd edn. (pp. 303–32). Don Mills, ON: Oxford University Press.

Smith, Stanley K., Jeff Tayman, and David A. Swanson. 2001. *State and Local Population Projections: Methodology and Analysis*. New York: Kluwer Academic Publishers/Plenum.

Smith, T.E. 1960. 'The Cocos-Keeling Islands: A Demographic Laboratory', *Population Studies* 24: 94–130.

Smith, Vaughn P. 2006. 'Rose-Tinted Spectacles' (letter), *British Medical Journal* 333 (22 August).

Sobotka, Tomas. 2004. 'Is Lowest-Low Fertility in Europe Explained by the Postponement of Childbearing?', *Population and Development Review* 30, 2: 195–220.

Socken, Paul. 1997. '*Maria Chapdelaine*', in Eugene Benson and William Toye, eds, *The Oxford Companion to Canadian Literature* (pp. 728–9). Don Mills, ON: Oxford University Press.

South, Scott J. 1988. 'Sex Ratios, Economic Power, and Women's Roles: A Theoretical Extension and Empirical Test', *Journal of Marriage and the Family* 50: 19–31.

———, and K.M. Lloyd. 1995. 'Spousal Alternatives and Marital Dissolution', American Sociological Review 60,1:21–35.

———, and ———. 1992. 'Marriage Opportunities and Family Formation: Further Implications of Unbalanced Sex Ratios', *Journal of Marriage and the Family* 54: 440–51.

Sowards, Kathryn A. 1997. 'Premature Birth and the Changing Composition of Newborn Infectious Disease Mortality: Reconsidering "Exogenous" Mortality', *Demography* 34, 4: 399–409.

Speare, Alden Jr. 1972. 'Residential Satisfaction as an Intervening Variable in Residential Mobility', *Demography* 11, 2: 173–88.

———, and James McNally. 1992. 'The Relation of Migration and Household Change among Elderly Persons', in Andrei Rogers, ed., *Elderly Migration and Population Distribution: A Comparative Study* (pp. 61–76). London: Belhaven.

Spengler, Joseph. 1974. *Population Change, Modernization, and Welfare*. Englewood Cliffs, NJ: Prentice Hall.

Spengler, Oswald. 1947. *The Decline of the West*. Trans. C.F. Atkinson. New York: Oxford University Press.

Spinelli, Angela, Irene Figá Talamanca, L. Lauria, and the European Study Group on Infertility and Subfecundity. 2000. 'Patterns of Contraceptive Use in 5 European Countries', *American Journal of Public Health* 90: 1403–8.

Stacey, Judith. 1990. *Brave New Families*. New York: Basic Books.

Stack, Steven. 2000a. 'Suicide: A 15-year Review of the Sociological Literature. Part I: Cultural and Economic Factors', *Suicide and Life-Threatening Behavior* 30, 2: 145–62.

———. 2000b. 'Suicide: A 15-year Review of the Sociological Literature. Part II: Modernization and Social Integration Perspectives', *Suicide and Life-Threatening Behavior* 30, 2: 163–176.

Stangeland, Charles E. 1904. *Pre-Malthusian Doctrines of Population: A Study in the History of Economic Theory*. New York: Columbia University Press.

Stark, Oded. 1997. *The Migration of Labor*. Cambridge, MA: Basil Blackwell.

Statistics Canada, 2008a. *Aboriginal Peoples in Canada in 2006: Inuit, Metis and First Nations*, 2006 Census. <http://www12.statcan.ca/english/census06/analysis/aboriginal/index.cfm>.

Statistics Canada. 2008b. *Marriages by Province and Territory*. CANSIM, table 053-0001.<http://www40.statcan.ca/l01/cst01/famil04.htm>.

———. 2007a. *Portrait of the Canadian Population in 2006, Population and Dwelling Counts*. 2006 Census. Cat. no. 97-550-XIE. Ottawa.

———. 2007b. *Portrait of the Canadian Population in 2006, by Age and Sex*. 2006 Census. Cat. no. 97-551-XIE.

———. 2007c. *Age and Sex, 2006 Counts for Both Sexes, for Canada and Census Metropolitan Areas and Census Agglomerations: 100% Data* (table). *Age and Sex Highlight Tables*. 2006 Census. Cat. no. 97-551-XWE2006002. Released 17 July 2007.

———. 2007d. *Family Portrait: Continuity and Change in Canadian Families and Households in 2006*. Cat no. 97-553-XIE.

———. 2007e. 'Marriages by Provinces and Territory', CANSIM Table 053-0001. <http://www40.statcan.ca/l01/famil04.htm>.

———. 2007f. *Annual Demographic Estimates. Census Metropolitan, Economic Regions and Census Divisions, Age and Sex, 2001 to 2006*. Cat. no. 91-214-XIE. Table 1.1–1, p. 20.

———. 2007g. *The Evolving Linguistic Portrait*. 2006 Census. Cat. no. 97-555-XIE. Ottawa: Minister of Industry. Statistics Canada Demography Division. 2007a. Annual Demographic Estimates.

———. 2007h. *Population 5 Years and Over by Mobility Status, by Province and Territory*. 2006 Census. <http://www.40.statcan.ca/l01/cst01/demo57g.htm> (12 December 2007).

Statistics Canada. 2007i. *Population by Immigrant Status and Period of Immigration, 2006 Counts, for Canada and Census Metropolitan Areas and Census Agglomerations – 20% Sample Data*. Immigration and Citizenship Highlight Tables. 2006 Census. Cat. no. 97-557-XWE2006002. <http://www12.statcan.ca/english/census06/data/highlights/Immigration/Table403.cfm?Lang=E&T=403&GH=8&SC=1&S=0&O=A> (17 July 2008).

———. 2006a. *Annual Demographic Statistics 2005*. Cat. no. 91-213-XIB.

———. 2006b. *Labour Force Characteristics by Age and Sex: Estimates for 2005*. <http://www40.statcan.ca/l01/cst01/labor20a.htm?sdi=labour> (11 April 2006).

———. 2006c. *Births, 2004*. Shelf Tables. Cat. no. 84-F0210XPB. Ottawa: Minister of Industry.

———. 2006d. *Births: Live Births 2004*. Cat. no. 84F0210XIE. Ottawa.

———. 2006e. *Life Tables, Canada, Provinces and Territories 2000 to 2002*. Cat. no. 84-537-XIE. Ottawa.

———. 2006f. *Census Dictionary* <http://www12.statcan.ca/english/census06/reference/dictionary/geo009.cfm>.

———. 2005a. *Place of Birth of Respondent, Sex and Period of Immigration for Immigrant Population, for Canada, Provinces, Territories, Census Metropolitan Areas and Census Agglomerations: 20% Sample Data.* 2001 Census. Cat. no. 95F0358XCB2001004.IVT. <http://www.statcan.ca> (18 January 2005).

———. 2005b. *Population Projections of Visible Minority Groups, Canada, Provinces and Regions, 2001 to 2017.* Cat. no. 91-541-XIE. Ottawa

———. 2004a. *Population 5 Years and Over by Mobility Status, Provinces and Territories.* 1996 and 2001 Censuses. <http://www.statcan.ca/english/Pgdb/demo58a.htm> (12 September 2004).

———. 2004b. *Migrants 5 Years and Over by Components of Migration, Census Metropolitan Areas.* 1996 Census. <HTTP://WWW.STATCAN.CA/ENGLISH/PGDB/DEMO59A.HTM> (12 September 2004).

———. 2004c. *Annual Demographic Statistics: 2003.* Cat. no. 91-213.

———. 2004d. *Province or Territory of Residence 5 Years Ago, Mother Tongue, Age Groups and Sex for Interprovincial Migrants 5 Years and Over, for Canada, Provinces and Territories: 20% Sample Data.* 1996 and 2001 Censuses. Cat. no. 97F0008XCB01005. <http://www.statcan.ca> (September 2004).

———. 2003a. *2001 Census Analysis Series: Aboriginal Peoples of Canada: A Demographic Profile* (p. 23). Cat. no. 96F0030XIE2001007.Ottawa: Statistics Canada.

———. 2003b. *Canada's Ethnocultural Portrait: The Changing Mosaic.* Cat. no. 96F0030XIE2001008.

———. 2003c. *2001 Census Analysis Series: Profile of Canadian Families and Households: Diversification Continues.* Cat. no. 96F0030XIE2001003. Ottawa.

———. 2003d. *Annual Demographic Statistics: 2002.* Cat. no. 91-213-XIB.

———. 2003e. *A Profile of the Canadian Population: Where We Live.* <http://geodepot.statcan.ca/Diss/Highlights/Tables_e.pdf> (2 June 2003).

———. 2003f. *Components of Migration (In- and Out-), Mother Tongue, Age Groups and Sex for Migrants 5 Years and Over, for Canada, Provinces, Territories, Census Metropolitan Areas and Census Agglomerations: 20% Sample Data.* 2001 Census. Cat. no. 97F0008XCB01009. <http://www.statcan.ca> (26 March 2003).

———. 2003g. *Population and Growth Components.* 1851–2001 Censuses. <http://www.statcan.ca/english/Pgdb/demo03.htm> (9 September 2003).

———. 2003h. <http://www.statcan.ca/english/sdds/4450.htm>.

———. 2003i. <http://www12.statcan.ca/english/census01/Info/history.cfm#2001>.

———. 2003j. *Marriages, 2000.* Cat. no. 84F0212XPB.

———. 2002a. *2001 Census Analysis Series: A Profile of Canadian Families and Households: Diversification Continues.* Cat. no. 96F0030XIE2001003. Ottawa.

———. 2002b. *2001 Census Analysis Series: A Profile of the Canadian Population by Age and Sex: Canada Ages.* Cat. no. 96F0030XIE2001002. <www.statcan.ca> (16 July 2002).

———. 2002c. *2001 Census Analysis Series: A Profile of the Canadian Population by Mobility Status: Canada, a Nation on the Move.* Statistics Canada Census Operations Division. Cat. no. 96F0030XIE2001006. Ottawa: Minister of Industry.

———. 2002d. *2001 Census Analysis Series: A Profile of the Canadian Population: Where We Live.* Cat. no. 96F0030XIE010012001.

———. 2002e. *Annual Demographic Statistics 2001.* Cat. no. 91-213-XIB. Ottawa: Minister of Supply and Services Canada.

———. 2002f. *Changing Conjugal Life in Canada. General Social Survey: Cycle 15.* Cat. no. 89-576-XIE. Ottawa: Minister of Industry.

———. 2002g. *Life Tables, Canada and Provinces, 1985-1987.* Cat. no. 84-532. Statistics Canada, 1989.

———. 2002h. *Age and Sex for the Population of Canada.* 2001 Census. Cat. no. 95F0300XCB01004.

———. 2002i. Births: Live Births, 2000. Cat. No. 84-F0210XIE. Ottawa: Minister of Industry.

———. 2002j. *Divorces, 2000.* Cat. no. 84F0213XZPB.

———. 1999a. *Annual Demographic Statistics 1998.* Cat. no. 91-213-XPB. Ottawa: Statistics Canada. Minister of Industry.

———. 1999b. *Five-Year Mobility Data.* 1996 Census on CD-ROM.

———. 1999c. *Labour Force Historical Review.* CD-ROM. Cat. no. 71F0004XCB. Ottawa: Statistics Canada.

———. 1997. *Births and Deaths, 1995.* Cat. no. 84-210-XMB. Ottawa: Minister of Industry.

———. 1994. *Selected Mortality Statistics, Canada, 1921–1990.* Cat. no. 82-548. Ottawa: Minister of Industry Science and Technology.

———. 1993a. *Mobility and Migration: The Nation.* Cat. no. 93-322.

———. 1993b. *Selected Birth and Fertility Statistics, Canada, 1921–1990.* Cat. no. 82-553. Ottawa: Minister of Industry Science and Technology.

———. 1992a. *Urban Areas.* 1991 Census of Canada. Cat. 93-305. Ottawa.

———. 1992b. *Age, Sex and Marital Status: The Nation.* 1991 Census of Canada. Cat. 93-310.

———.1990. 'Causes of Death 1988', *Health Reports* 2, 1 (supp. 11). Cat. no. 82-03S. Ottawa: Canadian Centre for Health Information.

———. 1983. *Vital Statistics*, vol. 2: *Marriages and Divorces, 1981.* Cat. no. 84-205.

————. 1982. *Geographic Distribution. Census Divisions, Urban Size Groups and Rural, CMAs and CAs, Urbanized Core and Fringe with Components, Census Subdivisions.* 1981 Census of Canada. Cat. 93-901. Ottawa.

————. 1979. *Vital Statistics*, vol. 2: *Marriages and Divorces, 1977.* Cat. no. 84-205 (annual).

————. 1974. *Life Tables, Canada and Provinces 1970–1972.* Cat. no. 84-532. Ottawa.

————. 1973a. *Cities Towns, Villages, CMAs and CAs.* 1971 Census of Canada. Cat. no. 92-708.

————. 1973b. *Population: Age Groups*, vol. 1, part 2. Cat. no. 92-715. (Bulletin 1: 2–3).

Statistics Canada Census Operations Division. 2003a. *2001 Census Handbook: Reference.* Cat. no. 92-379-XIE. Ottawa: Minister of Industry.

————. 2003b. *Annual Demographic Statistics 2002.* Cat. no. 91-213-XPB. Ottawa: Ministry of Industry.

————. 2003c. *2001 Census Dictionary: Reference.* Cat. no. 92-378-XIE. Ottawa: Minister of Industry. <http://www12.statcan.ca/english/census01/Products/Reference/dict/appendices/92-378-XIE02002.pdf> (6 January 2005).

————. 1997. *1996 Census Handbook: Reference.* Cat. no. 92-352-XPE. Ottawa: Statistics Canada Minister of Industry.

Statistics Canada Demography Division. 2007a. *Annual Demographic Estimates: Canada, Provinces and Territories, 2007.* Cat. no. 91-215-XIE. Ottawa: Minister of Industry.

————. 2007b. *Quarterly Demographic Estimates. July to September 2007, Preliminary 21, 3.* Cat. no. 91-002-X. Ottawa: Minister of Industry.

————. 2005. *Projections of the Aboriginal Populations, Canada, Provinces and Territories: 2001 to 2017.* Cat. no. 91-547-XIE.Ottawa: Minister of Industry.

————. 2003. *Population and Family Estimation Methods at Statistics Canada.* Cat. no. 91-528-XIE. Ottawa: Minister of Industry.

————. 2001. *Population Projections for Canada, Provinces and Territories 2000–2026* Cat. no. 91-520-XIB. Ottawa: Ministry of Commerce.

Statistics Canada Health Statistics Division. 2005. *Comparability of ICD-10 and ICD-9 for Mortality Statistics in Canada.* Cat no. 84-548-XIE. Ottawa: Minister of Industry.

————. 1999. *Vital Statistics Compendium 1996.* Cat. no. 84-214-XPE. Ottawa: Minister of Industry.

————. 2003a. *Births 2001. Shelf Tables.* Cat. no. 84F0210XPB. Ottawa.

————. 2003b. *Marriages, 2001.* Cat. no. 84F0212XPB.

————. 2002. *Life Tables: Canada, Provinces and Territories 1995–1997.* Cat. no. 84-537-XIE. Ottawa: Minister of Industry.

————. 2000. *Divorces, 1999.* Cat. no. 84F0213XPB.

Statistics Canada, *The Daily.* 2007a. 'Study: Low Income Rates among Immigrants Entering Canada' (30 January).

————. 2007b. 'Births (2005 Correction)' (21 September).

————. 2007c. '2006 Census: Family, Marital Status, Households and Dwelling Characteristics' (12 September).

————. 2006. (16 December).

————. 2005a. 'Induced Abortions 2002' (11 February).

————. 2005b. 'Study: Canada's Visible Minority Population in 2017' (22 March).

————. 2005c. 'National Population Health Survey: Obesity: A Growing Issue' (7 April).

————. 2005d. 'Canada's Aboriginal Population in 2017' (28 June).

————. 2004a. 'Joint Canada/United States Survey of Health, 2002/03' (2 June).

————. 2004b. 'Migration, 2002/2003' (29 September).

————. 2003a. (25 September).

————. 2003b. 'Homicides 2002' (1 October).

————. 2002. 'Participation and Activity Limitation Survey: A Profile of Disability in Canada' (3 December).

————. 1999. 'Mortality Rates in Census Metropolitan Areas' (18 August).

Statistics Canada website. 2005a. <http://www.statcan.ca/english/freepub/82-221-XIE00502/tables/html/44.htm> (16 January 2005).

————. 2005b. <http://www.statcan.ca/english/freepub/95F0303XIE/tables/html/agpop1303.htm> (16 January 2005).

————. 2005c. *Population Counts, for Census Metropolitan Areas and Census Agglomerations, by Urban Core, Urban Fringe and Rural Fringe: 100% data.* 2001 Census. <http://www12.statcan.ca/english/census01/products/standard/popdwell/Table-CMA-UR.cfm?T=1&SR=126&S=1&O=A> (14 January 2005).

Statistik Austria. 2005. *Statistisches Jahrbuch 2005.* Vienna.

Steenland, Kyle, Jane Henley, and Michael Thun. 2002. 'All-Cause and Cause-Specific Death Rates by Educational Status for Two Million People in Two American Cancer Society Cohorts, 1959–1996', *American Journal of Epidemiology* 156, 1: 11–21.

Steffensmeir, Darrell, Cathy Streifel, and Edward S. Shihadeh. 1992. 'Cohort Size and Arrest Rates over the Life Course: Easterlin Reconsidered', *American Sociological Review* 57, 3: 306–14.

Stern, Michael. 2007. *The Economics of Climate Change: The Stern Review.* Cambridge: Cambridge University Press.

Stiglitz, Joseph. 2003. 'Special Contribution: Poverty, Globalization and Growth: Perspectives on Some of the Statistical Links', *United Nations Population Development Program, Human Development Report* (p. 80). New York: Oxford University Press.

————. 2002. *Globalization and Its Discontents.* New York: W.W. Norton.

Stillwell, J., M. Bell, M. Blake, et al. 2000. 'Net Migration and Migration Effectiveness: A Comparison Between Australia and the United Kingdom, 1976–96. Part I: Total Migration Patterns', *Journal of Population Research* 17, 1: 17–38.

———, ———, ———, et al. 2001. 'Net Migration and Migration Effectiveness: A Comparison Between Australia and the United Kingdom, 1976–96. Part II: Age-Related Migration Patterns', *Journal of Population Research* 18, 1: 19–39.

Stillwell, O.F.G., and N.R.M. Seifried. 1984. *The Regional Structure of the Canadian Economy*. Toronto: Methuen.

Stolnitz, George J. 1955. 'A Century of International Mortality Trends', *Population Studies* 9 and 10: 24–55, 17–52.

Stone, Elizabeth C., and Paul Zimansky. 2005. 'The Tapestry of Power in a Mesapotamian City', *Scientific American* 15, 1: 60–7.

Stone, Leroy O. 1978. *The Frequency of Geographic Mobility in the Population of Canada. Census Analytical Study*. Cat. no. 99-751F. Ottawa: Minister of Supply and Services.

———. 1974. 'What We Know about Migration within Canada: A Selective Review and Agenda for Future Research', *International Migration Review* 8, 2: 267–81.

———. 1969. 'Migration in Canada: Regional Aspects', *1961 Census Monograph*. Ottawa: Dominion Bureau of Statistics.

———, and Susan Fletcher. 1994. 'The Seniors Boom: Dramatic Increases in Longevity and Prospects for Better Health', in Frank Trovato and Carl F. Grindstaff, eds, *Perspectives on Canada's Population: An Introduction to Concepts and Issues* (pp. 96–111). Toronto: Oxford University Press.

Stone, Richard. 1986. 'Robert Malthus: An Appreciation', in David Coleman and Roger Schofield, eds, *The State of Population Theory: Forward from Malthus* (pp. 42–5). Oxford: Basil Blackwell

Stoufer, Samuel A. 1960. 'Intervening Opportunities and Competing Migrants', *Journal of Regional Science* 2: 1–26.

———. 1940. 'Intervening Opportunities: A Theory Relating Mobility and Distance', *American Sociological Review* 5: 845–67.

Strehler, Bernand L., and Albert S. Mildvan. 1960. 'General Theory of Mortality and Aging', *Science* 132: 14–21.

Stremlau, John. 2000. 'Ending Africa's Wars', *Foreign Affairs* 79, 4: 117–32.

Stuckler, David. 2008. 'Population Causes and Consequences of Leading Chronic Diseases: A Comparative Analysis of Prevailing Explanations', The Milbank Quarterly 86, 2: 273–326.

Sullivan, D.A. 1985. 'The Ties That Bind: Differentials between Seasonal and Permanent Migrants to Retirement Communities', *Research on Aging* 7: 235–50.

———, and S.A. Stevens. 1982. 'Snowbirds: Seasonal Migrants to the Sunbelt', *Research on Aging* 4: 159–67.

Sutcliffe, Bob. 2001. *100 Ways of Seeing an Unequal World*. London and New York: Zed Books.

Suzman, Richard M., David P. Willis, and Kenneth G. Manton, eds. 1992. *The Oldest Old*. New York: Oxford University Press.

Syme, Leonard, and Lisa F. Berkman. 1976. 'Social Class, Susceptibility and Sickness', *American Journal of Epidemiology* 104, 1: 1–8.

Taft, Donald R. 1936. *Human Migration: A Study of International Movements*. New York: Ronald Press.

Tang, Zongli. 2006. 'Immigration and Chinese Reproductive Behavior in Canada', *Social Biology*, 51, 1–2: 37–53.

Tao, Meng-Hua, Xiao-Ou Shu, Zhi Xian Ruan, et al. 2005. 'Association of Overweight with Breast Cancer Survival', *American Journal of Epidemiology* (Advance access published 7 December): 1–7.

Tarver, James D., and R. Douglas McLeod. 1973. 'A Test and Modification of Zipf's Hypothesis for Predicting Interstate Migration', *Demography* 10, 2: 259–76.

Taylor, J. Edward. 2003. 'Migration Models', in Paul Demeny and Geoffrey McNicoll, eds, *Encyclopedia of Population*, vol. 2 (pp. 644–9). Macmillan Reference USA/Thomson Gale.

Taylor, John. 1998. 'Measuring Short-Term Population Mobility among Indigenous Australians: Options and Implications', *Australian Geographer* 29, 10: 125–37.

———. 1997. 'The Contemporary Demography of Indigenous Australians', *Journal of the Australian Population Association* 14, 1: 77–114.

———, and Martin Bell. 2004. 'Continuity and Change in Indigenous Australian Population Mobility', in John Taylor and Martin Bell, eds, *Population Mobility and Indigenous Peoples in Australasia and North America* (pp. 13–43). London: Routledge.

———, and ———. 1996. 'Population Mobility and Indigenous Peoples: The View from Australia', *International Journal of Population Geography* 2: 153–69.

Taylor, Richard, Dale Bampton, and Alan D. Lopez. 2005. 'Contemporary Patterns of Pacific Island Mortality', *International Journal of Epidemiology* 34, 1: 207–14.

Teicher, Martin H. 2003. 'Scars That Won't Heal: The Neurobiology of Child Abuse', *Scientific American* (March): 68–75.

Teisch, Jessica, and Alex De Sherbinin. 1995. 'Population Doubling Time: Looking Backward', *Population Today* (February): 3–4.

Teitelbaum, Michael S. 1975. 'Relevance of Demographic Transition Theory for Developing Countries', *Science* 188 (2 May): 420–5.

———. 1972. 'Factors Associated with the Sex Ratio in Human Populations', in G. A. Harrison and A. J. Boyce, eds, *The Structure of Human Populations* (pp. 90–109). Oxford: Clarendon.

———, and Jay M. Winter. 1985. *The Fear of Population Decline*. San Diego, CA: Academic Press.

ter Heide, H. 1963. 'Migration Models and their Significance for Population Forecasts', *The Milbank Quarterly* 41: 56–76.

Thandani, Veena N. 1978. 'The Logic of Sentiment: The Family and Social Change', *Population and Development Review* 4, 3: 457–500.

Therborn, Goran. 2006. 'Meaning, Mechanisms, Patterns, and Forces: An Introduction', in Goran Therborn, ed., *Inequalities of the World: New Theoretical Frameworks, Multiple Empirical Approaches* (pp. 1–60). London: Verso.

———. 1987. 'Migration and Western Europe: The Old World Turning New', *Science* 237: 1183–8.

Thom, Thomas J. 1989. 'International Mortality from Heart Disease: Rates and Trends', *International Journal of Epidemiology* 18, 3 (supp. 1): S20–8.

Thomas, Brinley. 1954. *Migration and Economic Growth*. Cambridge: Cambridge University Press.

Thomas, Dorothy S. 1941. *Social and Economic Aspects of Swedish Population Movements: 1750–1933*. New York: Macmillan.

———. 1938. Research Memorandum on Migration Differentials. New York: Social Science Research Council.

Thomas, William I., and Florian Znaniecki. 1918–20. *The Polish Peasant in Europe and America*. Boston: William Badger.

Thomlinson, Ralph. 1975. *Demographic Problems: Controversy over Population Control*, 2nd edn. Encino, CA: Dickenson.

Thompson, Bryan. 1983. 'Social Ties and Ethnic Settlement Patterns', in William C. McCready, ed., *Culture, Ethnicity and Identity: Current Issues in Research* (pp. 341–56). New York: Academic Press.

Thompson, Drew. 2005. *China Confronts HIV/AIDS*. Washington, DC: Population Reference Bureau.

Thompson, Warren S. 1944. *Plenty of People*. Lancaster: Jacques Cattel.

———. 1929. 'Population', *American Journal of Sociology* 34: 959–75.

Thorbecke, Erik, and Chutatong Charumilind. 2002. 'Economic Inequality and Its Socioeconomic Impact', *World Development* 30, 9: 1477–95.

Thornton, Russell. 2000. 'Population History of Native North Americas', in Michael R. Haines and Richard H. Steckel, eds, *A Population History of North America* (pp. 9–50). Cambridge: Cambridge University Press.

———. 1987. *American Indian: Holocaust and Survival: A Population History Since 1492*. Norman, OK: University of Oklahoma Press.

Tien, Yuan H. 1983. 'China: Demographic Billionaire', *Population Bulletin* 38, 2. Washington, DC: Population Reference Bureau.

Tobias, Michael. 1994. *World War III: Population and the Biosphere at the End of the Millennium*. Santa Fe, NM: Bear.

Tobler, Waldo. 1995. 'Migration: Ravenstein, Thornthwaite, and Beyond', *Urban Geography* 16, 4: 327–43.

Todaro, Michael P. 1969. 'A Model of Labor Migration and Urban Unemployment in Less Developed Countries', *The American Economic Review* 59: 138–48.

Tönnies, Ferdinand. 1883 [1995]. *Community and Society*. New York: Harper and Row.

Torr, Berna Miller, and Susan E. Short. 2004. 'Second Births and the Second Shift: A Research Note on Gender Equity and Fertility', *Population and Development Review* 30, 1: 109–30.

Torrey, Barbara Boyle, and Carl Haub. 2004. 'A Comparison of US and Canadian Mortality in 1998', *Population and Development Review* 30, 3: 519–30.

Toynbee, Arnold. 1935–54. *A Study of History*, 10 vols. Oxford: Oxford University Press.

Tracey, W.R. 1941. *Fertility of the Population of Canada*. Eighth Census of Canada, 1931 Census. Vol. 12, monographs 99–. Ottawa: King's Printer.

Traphagan, John W., and John Knight, eds. 2003. *Demographic Change and the Family in Japan's Aging Society*. Albany, NY: State University of New York Press.

Tremblay, Marc, Helene Vezina, and Louis Houde. 2003. 'Demographic Determinants of the Sex Ratio at Birth in the Saguenay Population of Quebec', *Population* (English edn) 58, 3: 383–94.

Trewartha, Glenn T. 1969. *A Geography of Population: World Patterns*. New York: John Wiley.

Trovato, Frank. 2005. 'Narrowing Sex Differential in Life Expectancy in Canada and Austria: Comparative Analysis', *Vienna Yearbook of Population Research* 2005: 17–52.

———. 2001. 'Comparative Analysis of Aboriginal Mortality in Canada, the United States and New Zealand', *Journal of Biosocial Science* 33: 67–86.

———. 2000. 'The Probability of Divorce in Canada, 1981–1995', *Canadian Studies in Population* 27, 1: 231–38.

———. 1992. 'An Ecological Analysis of Suicide: Canadian CMAs', *International Review of Modern Sociology* 22: 57–72.

———. 1988a. 'A Macrosociological Analysis of Change in the Marriage Rate: Canadian Women, 1921–25 to 1981–85', *Journal of Marriage and the Family* 50: 507–21.

———. 1988b. 'The Interurban Mobility of the Foreign Born in Canada: 1976–1981', *International Migration Review* 22, 3: 59–86.

———. 1987. 'A Macrosociological Analysis of Native Indian Fertility in Canada, 1961, 1971, and 1981', *Social Forces*, 66, 2: 463–85.

———. 1986a. 'The Relationship between Migration and the Provincial Divorce Rate in Canada, 1971 and 1978: A Reassessment', *Journal of Marriage and the Family* 48: 207–16.

———. 1986b. 'Interprovincial Migration and Suicide in Canada', *International Journal of Social Psychiatry* 32, 1: 14–21.

———. 1981. 'Canadian Ethnic Fertility', *Sociological Focus* 14, 1: 57–74.

————, and Carl F. Grindstaff. 1980. 'Decomposing the Urban-Rural Fertility Differential: Canada 1971', *Rural Sociology* 45, 3: 448–68.

————, and Shiva S. Halli. 1983. 'Ethnicity and Migration in Canada', *International Migration Review* 27, 2: 245–67.

————, and Nils B. Heyen. 2006. 'A Varied Pattern of Change of the Sex Differential in Survival in the G7 Countries', *Journal of Biosocial Science* 38, 3: 301–401.

————, and N.M. Lalu. 2007. 'From Divergence to Convergence: The Sex Differential in Life Expectancy in Canada, 1971–2000', *Canadian Review of Sociology and Anthropology* 44, 1: 101–22.

————, and ————. 1995. 'The Narrowing Sex Differential in Mortality in Canada Since 1971', *Canadian Studies in Population* 22, 2: 145–67.

————, and ————. 1996. 'Narrowing Sex Differentials in Life Expectancy in the Industrialized World: Early 1970s to Early 1990s', *Social Biology* 43, 1–2: 20–37.

————, and Dave Odynak. 1993. 'The Seasonality of Births in Canada and the Provinces, 1881–1989: Theory and Analysis', *Canadian Studies in Population* 20, 1: 1–41.

————, Anatole Romaniuc, and Isaac Addai. 1994. *Aboriginal On and Off Reserve Migration in Canada*. Ottawa: Department of Indian and Northern Affairs.

Trudel, Marcel. 1973. *La Population du Canada en 1663*. Montreal: FIDES.

Trussell, James. 2003. 'Fecundity', in Paul Demeny and Geoffrey McNicoll, eds, *Encyclopedia of Population* (pp. 397–9). New York: Macmillan Reference USA/ Thompson Gale.

Tsui, Amy Ong. 2001. 'Population Policies, Family Planning Programs, and Fertility: The Record', in Rudofo A. Bulatao and John B. Casterline, eds, *Global Fertility Transition* (pp. 184–203), supp. to *Population and Development Review* 27. New York: The Population Council.

————, S. Victor de Silva, and Ruth Marinshaw. 1991. 'Pregnancy Avoidance and Coital Behavior', *Demography* 28, 1: 101–17.

Tuck, Simon. 2003. 'Fewer Canadians Smoke, Poll Finds', *The Globe and Mail* (Thursday, July 31): A8.

Tuljapurkar, Shripad, Nan Li, and Carl Boe. 2000. 'A Universal Pattern of Mortality Decline in the G7 Countries', *Nature* 405 (15 June): 789–92.

————, Nan Li, and Marcus W. Feldman. 1995. 'High Sex Ratios in China's Future', *Science* 10 (February): 874–876.

Turcotte, Pierre, and Alain Bélanger. 1997. 'The Dynamics of Formation and Dissolution of First Common-Law Unions in Canada', Ottawa: Statistics Canada.

Turner, Jonathan H. 1995. *Macrodynamics: Toward a Theory on the Organization of Human Populations*. New Brunswick, NJ: Rutgers University Press.

Udry, Richard. 1970. 'The Effect of the Great Blackout of 1965 on Births in New York City', *Demography* 7, 3: 325–6.

————, and R.L. Cliquet. 1982. 'A Cross-Cultural Examination of the Relationship between Ages at Menarche, Marriage, and First Birth', *Demography* 19, 1: 53–64.

Uhlenberg, Peter. 1996. 'Mutual Attraction: Demography and Life-Course Analysis', *The Gerontologist* 36, 2: 226–9.

————. 1980. 'Death and the Family', *Journal of Family History* 5, 3: 313–20.

————. 1973. 'Noneconomic Determinants of Nonmigration: Sociological Considerations for Migration Theory', *Rural Sociology* 38, 3: 296–311.

Ulizzi, L., and L.A. Zonta. 1993. 'Sex Ratio and Natural Selection in Humans: A Comparative Analysis of Two Caucasian Populations', *Annals of Human Genetics* 57: 211–19.

Umberson, Debra. 1987. 'Family Status and Health Behaviors: Social Control as a Dimension of Social Integration', *Journal of Health and Social Behaviour* 28, 3: 306–319.

UN AIDS (2006). 'Regions'. <http://www. unaids.org/en/Regions_Countries/default.asp> (21 March 2006).

————. 2005a. 'Resource Needs for an Expanded Response to AIDS in Low- and Middle-Income Countries'. <http://www.unaids.org/en/Publications/default.asp> (21 March 2006).

————. 2005b. *AIDS Epidemic Update* (December). <http://www.unaids.org/epi/2005/doc/report_pdf.asp> (14 March 2006).

Unal, Belgin, Julia A. Critcheley, Dogan Fidan, and S. Capewell. 2005. 'Life-Years Gained from Modern Cardiological Treatments and Population Risk Factor Changes in England and Wales, 1981–2000', *American Journal of Public Health* 95, 1: 103–8.

United Nations. 2007. *The Millennium Development Goals Report 2007* (pp. 6–7). New York: UN. <http://mdgs.un.org/unsd/mdg/Resources/Static/Products/Progress2007/UNSD_MDG_Report_2007e.pdf>.

————. 2000. *Below Replacement Fertility*, nos 40–1 (1999). New York: Population Bulletin of the United Nations.

United Nations Department of Economic and Social Affairs Population Division. 2008a. United Nations Expert Group Meeting on Population Distribution, Urbanization, Internal Migration and Development. UN/POP/EGM-URB/2008/01. New York: UN.

————. 2008b. *World Population Policies 2007*. ST/ESA/SER.A/272. New York: UN.

————. 2008c. *2007 Revision of World Urbanization Prospects*. New York: UN.

————. 2007. *World Population Prospects: The 2006 Revision*.

———— 2006a. *Challenges of World Population in the 21st Century: The Changing Age Structure of Population and its Consequences for Development*. Panel Discussion by A. Golini, A. Mason, N. Ogawa, and E. Zuniga. 12 October (2006). New York. <http://www.un.org/esa/population/publications/2006Changing_Age/Age_Structure.htm>.

———. 2006b. *Trends in Total Migrant Stock: The 2005 Revision: CD-ROM Documentation*, POP/DB/MIG/Rev. 2005/Doc. New York: UN.

———. 2006c. *World Population Policies*. ST/ESA/SER.A/254. New York: UN.

———. 2006d. *World Urbanization Prospects. The 2005 Revision.* (Executive Summary; Fact Sheets; Data Tables). ESA/P/WP/200 (October). New York: UN.

———. 2006e. *World Population Prospects: The 2004 Revision*, vols 1–3. ST/ESA/SER.A/246. New York: UN.

———. 2006f. *International Migration Wall Chart.* New York: UN.

———. 2005a. *Population Challenges and Development Goals.* ST/ESA/SER.A/248. New York: UN.

———. 2005b. *World Fertility Report: 2003.* ESA/P/WP.189. New York: UN.

———. 2005c. *World Population Prospects: The 2004 Revision: Highlights.* (24 February). New York: UN.

———. 2004a. *The Impact of AIDS.* ST/ESA/SER.A/229. New York: UN.

———. 2004b. *World Population to 2300.* ST/ESA/SER.A/236. New York: UN.

———. 2004c. *World Urbanization Prospects. The 2003 Revision.* (Data Tables and Highlights). ESA/P/WP.190. (24 March). New York: UN.

———. 2003a. *Partnership and Reproductive Behaviour in Low-Fertility Countries.* Revised version for the web. ESA/P/WP.177. New York: UN.

———. 2003b. *World Population Prospects: The 2002 Revision*, vols 1–2 ST/ESA/SER.A/223. New York: UN.

———. 2003c. *World Population Prospects: The 2002 Revision* (Highlights). ESA/P/WP.180. New York: UN.

———. 2002a. *2002 Demographic Yearbook.* ST/ESA/STAT/SER.R/31. New York: UN.

———. 2002b. *2001 Demographic Yearbook.* New York: UN.

———. 2002c. *2000 Demographic Yearbook.* E/F.02.XIII.1. New York: UN.

———. 2002d. *International Migration 2002* (Wall chart). E.03.XIII.3. New York: UN.

———. 2002e. *World Population Ageing, 1950-2050.* ST/ESA/SER.A/207. New York: UN.

———. 2002f. *World Population Prospects: The 2000 Revision* (Highlights). New York: UN.

———. 2001. *Population, Environment and Development: The Concise Report.* ST/ESA/SER.A/202. New York: UN.

———. 2000. *Replacement Migration: Is it a Solution to Declining and Ageing Populations?* ESA/P/WP.160. New York: UN.

———. 1999. *The World at Six Billion.* ESA/P/WP.154. New York: UN.

———. 1973. *The Determinants and Consequences of Population Trends*, vol. 1. ST/SOA/SER.A/50. *Population Studies* no. 50. New York: UN.

United Nations Development Programme. 2005. *Human Development Report 2005.* New York: Oxford University Press.

———. 2003a. *Arab Human Development Report 2003.* New York: Oxford University Press.

———. 2003b. *Human Development Report for 2003.* New York: Oxford University Press.

———. 2002a. *Arab Human Development Report 2002.* New York: Oxford University Press.

———. 2002b. *Human Development Report 2002.* New York: Oxford University Press.

———. 2001. *Human Development Report 2000.* New York: Oxford University Press.

United Nations High Commissioner for Refugees. 2007. *The 1951 Refugee Convention: Questions and Answers.* New York: UN.

———. 2003. *The 1951 Refugee Convention: Questions and Answers.* Geneva: UNHCR Media Relations and Public Information Service.

———. 2001. *50th Anniversary: The Wall Behind Which Refugees Can Shelter.* The 1951 Geneva Convention.

———. 1950. *Statute of the Office of The United Nations High Commissioner for Refugees.* General Assembly Resolution 428 (v) of 14 December 1950. New York: UN.

United Nations Population Fund. 2001. *The State of the World's Population 2001: Footprints and Milestones: Population and Environmental Change.* New York: UN.

United States Bureau of the Census. 2005. *Current Lists of Metropolitan and Micropolitan Statistical Areas and Definitions.* <http://www.census.gov/population/www/estimates/metroarea.html (18 February 2007).

———. 2002. *Total Midyear Population for the World: 1950–2050.* <http://www.census.gov/ipc/www/worldpop.html> (updated 10 October 2002).

United States Homeland Security. 2005. <http://uscis.gov/graphics/shared/statistics/yearbook/2004/table1.xls> (15 November 2005).

Urquhart, M.C. 1983. *Historical Statistics of Canada*, 2nd edn. Ottawa: Statistics Canada and Social Sciences Federation of Canada.

Valent, Francesca, D'Anna Little, Roberto Bertolini, et al. 2004. 'Burden of Disease Attributable to Selected Environmental Factors and Injury among Children and Adolescents in Europe', *The Lancet* 363 (19 June): 2032–9.

Valente, Enza Maria, Patrick M. Abou-Sleiman, Viviana Caputo, et al. 2004. 'Hereditary Early-Onset Parkinson's Disease Caused by Mutations in PINK1', *Science* 304 (21 May): 1158–60.

Valkonen, Tapani. 1993. 'Socio-economic Mortality Differences in Europe', *NIDI Hofstee Lecture Series* no. 1. (March 1993). Amsterdam.

———, and Frans von Poppel. 1997. 'The Contribution of Smoking to Sex Differences in Life Expectancy: Four Nordic Countries and the Netherlands 1970–89', *European Journal of Public Health* 7: 302–10.

Vallin, Jacques. 2006. 'Europe's Demographic Transition, 1740–1940', in Graziella Caselli, Jacques Vallin, and Guillaume Wunsch, eds, *Demography, Analysis and*

Synthesis: A Treatise in Population Studies (pp. 41–66). Amsterdam: Elsevier.

———. 1983. 'Sex Patterns of Mortality: A Comparative Study of Model Life Tales and Actual Situations with Special Reference to the Case of Algeria and France', in Alan D. Lopez and Lado T. Ruzicka, eds, *Sex Differentials in Mortality: Trends, Determinants and Consequences* (pp. 376–443). Canberra: Department of Demography, Australian National University.

———, France Meslé, and Tapani Valkonen. 2001. 'Trends in Mortality and Differential Mortality', *Population Studies* no. 36. Strasbourg: Council of Europe Publishing.

Vance, James E. Jr. 1970. *The Merchant's World: The Geography of Wholesaling*. Englewood Cliffs, NJ: Prentice Hall.

van de Kaa, Dirk. 2004a. 'Is the Second Demographic Transition a Useful Research Concept: Questions and Answers', *Vienna Yearbook of Population Research*. Vienna Institute of Demography. Vienna: Austrian Academy of Sciences.

———. 2004b. 'The True Commonality: In Reflexive Modern Societies Fertility is a Derivative', *Population Studies* 58, 1: 77–92. Discussion of the paper by John Caldwell and Thomas Schindlmayr in Population Studies 57, 3 (2003).

———. 2003. 'Second Demographic Transition', in Paul Demeny and Geoffrey McNicoll, eds, *Encyclopedia of Population* (pp. 872–3). New York: Macmillan Reference USA/Thompson Gale.

———. 1999. 'Europe and Its Population: The Long View', in Dirk J. van de Kaa, Henri Lerido, Giuseppe Gesano, and Marek Okolski, eds, *European Populations: Unite in Diversity*. Dordrecht: Kluwer Academic Publishers.

———. 1996. 'Anchored Narratives: The Story and Findings of Half a Century of Fertility Research', *Population Studies* 50: 389–432.

———. 1987. 'Europe's Second Demographic Transition', *Population Bulletin* 42, 1. Washington: Population Reference Bureau.

Vanderkamp, John. 1971. 'Migration Flows, Their Determinants and the Effects of Return Migration', *Journal of Political Economy* 79: 1012–31.

———. 1968. 'Interregional Mobility in Canada: A Study of the Time Pattern of Migration', *Canadian Journal of Economics* 1: 595–608.

van de Walle, Etienne. 1992. 'Fertility Transition, Conscious Choice and Numeracy', *Demography* 29, 4: 487–502.

Van Heek, F. 1956. 'Roman Catholicism and Fertility in the Netherlands', *Population Studies* 10: 125–38.

Vartiainen, T., L. Kartovaara, and J. Tuomisto. 1999. 'Environmental Chemicals and Changes in Sex Ratio: Analysis over 250 Years in Finland', *Environmental Health Perspectives* 107, 10: 813–15.

Vasudev, Shefalee. 2003. 'Missing Child', *India Today International* (10 November): 10–16.

Vaupel, James W., and Elke Lochinger. 2006. 'Redistributing Work in Aging Europe', *Science* 312 (30 June): 1911–13.

———, James R. Carey, Kaare Kristensen, et al. 1998. 'Biodemographic Trajectories of Longevity', *Science* 280 (8 May): 855–60.

Veevers, Jane E. 1994. 'The "Real" Marriage Squeeze: Mate Selection, Mortality, and the Mating Gradient', in Frank Trovato and Carl F. Grindstaff, eds, *Perspectives on Canada's Population: An Introduction to Concepts and Issues* (pp.260–76). Don Mills, ON: Oxford University Press.

———, and Ellen M. Gee. 1986. 'Playing it Safe: Accident Mortality and Gender Roles', *Sociological Focus* 19, 4: 349–60.

Verbrugge, Lois M. 1989a. 'Comorbidity and Its Impact on Disability', *The Milbank Quarterly* 67, 3–4: 450–84.

———. 1989b. 'The Twain Meet: Empirical Explanations of Sex Differences in Health and Mortality', *Journal of Health and Social Behavior* 30: 282–304.

———. 1984. 'Longer Life but Worsening Health? Trends in Health and Mortality of Middle-Aged and Older Persons', *The Milbank Quarterly/Health and Society* 62, 3: 475–519.

———. 1976. 'Sex Differentials in Morbidity and Mortality in the United States', *Social Biology* 34, 4: 275–96.

Verhulst, Pierre-Francoise. 1844. 'Recherches Mathematiques sur la loi d'accroisement de la population', *Nouveaux Memoires de L'Academie Royale des Sciences et Belles-Lettres de Bruxelles* XVIII: 1–38.

———. 1838. 'Notice sur la loi que la population suit dans son accroissement', *Correspondence in Mathematics and Physics* 10: 113–21.

Verma, Ravi B.P. 2006. *Estimates of Annual Number of Emigrants from Canada, 1971 to 2004*. Personal communication.

———. 2005. 'Evaluation of Projections of Populations for the Aboriginal Identity Groups in Canada, 1996–2001', *Canadian Studies in Population* 32, 2: 229–55.

———. 1990. 'Estimation of Emigration from Canada: An Emerging Issue'. Paper presented at the University of Alberta, Department of Sociology (Population Research Laboratory).

———, and M.V. George. 2002. 'Application of Multiregional Migration Model for Interprovincial Migration Projections in Canada'. Paper presented at the Southern Demographic Association. 10–12 October (2002). Austin.

———, Margaret Michalowski, and Pierre Gauvin. 2004. 'Abridged Life Tables for Registered Indians in Canada, 1976–1980 to 1996–2000', *Canadian Studies in Population* 31, 2: 197–235.

Veron, Jacques, and Jean-Marc Rohrbasser. 2003. 'Wilhelm Lexis: The Normal Length of Life as an Expression of the "Nature of Things"', *Population E* 58, 3: 303–22.

Vienna Institute of Demography. 2007. *European Demography Data Sheet 2006*. Vienna, Austria. <http://www.oeaw.ac.at/vid/popeurope/download/European_Demographic_Data_Sheet_2006_A3.pdf>.

Vining, D.R., and R. Pallone. 1982. 'Migration between Core and Peripheral Regions: A Description and Tentative Explanation of the Patterns in 22 Countries', *Geoforum* 13: 339–410.

———, and T.M. Kontuly. 1978 [1996]. 'Population Dispersal from Major Metropolitan Regions: An International Comparison', in H.S. Geyer and T. M. Kontuly, eds, *Differential Urbanization: Integrating Spatial Models* (pp. 67–89). London: Edward Arnold.

Vining, D.R. Jr, and A. Strauss. 1977 [1996]. 'A Demonstration that the Current Deconcentration of Population in the United States is a Clean Break with the Past', in H.S. Geyer and T.M. Kontuly, eds, *Differential Urbanization: Integrating Spatial Models* (pp. 28–37). London: Edward Arnold.

Volterra, Vito. 1926. 'Fluctuations in the Abundance of a Species Considered Mathematically', *Nature* 118, 558–60.

Wachter, Kenneth W., and Rodolfo A. Bulatao, eds. 2003. *Offspring: Human Fertility Behavior in Biodemographic Perspective*. Washington, DC: National Academies Press.

Wackernagel, Mathis, and William Rees. 1996. *Our Ecological Footprint: Reducing Human Impact on the Earth*. Gabriola Island, BC: New Society Publishers.

Wadhera, Surinder, and Jill Strachan. 1994. *Selected Mortality Statistics, Canada, 1921–1990*. Cat. no. 82-548. Ottawa: Statistics Canada (Canadian Centre for Health Information).

———, and ———. 1993. *Selected Birth and Fertility Statistics, Canada, 1921–1990*. Cat. No. 82-553. Ottawa: Statistics Canada (Canadian Centre for Health Information).

———, and ———. 1992. *Selected Marriage Statistics, 1921–1990*. Cat. no. 82-552. Ottawa: Statistics Canada.

Waldram, James D., Ann Herring, and Kuo T. Young. 2006. *Aboriginal Health in Canada: Historical, Cultural, and Epidemiological Perspectives*, 2nd edn. Toronto: University of Toronto Press.

Waldron, Ingrid. 2000. 'Trends in Gender Differences in Mortality: Relationships to Changing Gender Differences in Behavior and Other Causal Factors', in E. Annandale and K. Hung, eds, *Gender Inequalities in Health* (pp. 150–81). Buckingham: Open University Press.

———. 1993. 'Recent Trends in Sex Mortality Ratios for Adults in Developed Countries', *Social Science and Medicine* 36, 4: 451–62.

———. 1986. 'The Contribution of Smoking to Sex Differences in Mortality', *Public Health Reports* 101, 2: 163–73.

———. 1983. 'Sex Differences in Human Mortality: The Role of Genetic Factors', *Social Science and Medicine* 17, 6: 321–33.

———. 1976. 'Why do Women Live Longer than Men?', *Social Science and Medicine* 10: 349–62.

Walker, Neff, Nicholas C. Grassly, Geoff P. Garnett, et al. 2004. 'Estimating the Global Burden of HIV/AIDS: What Do We Really Know about the HIV Pandemic?', *The Lancet* 363 (26 June): 2180–5.

Wallace, Iain. 2002. *A Geography of the Canadian Economy*. Don Mills, ON: Oxford University Press.

Wallace, Paul. 1999. *Agequake: Riding the Demographic Rollercoaster: Shaking Business, Finance and Our World*. London: Nicholas Brealey.

Wallerstein, Immanuel. 1980. *The Modern World-System II: Mercantilism and the Consolidation of the European World-Economy, 1600–1750*. New York: Academic Press.

———. 1974. *The Modern World-System I: Capitalist Agriculture and the Origins of the European World-Economy in the Sixteenth Century*. New York: Academic Press.

Walmsley, D.J., and G.J. Lewis. 1993. *People and Environment: Behavioral Approaches in Human Geography*, 2nd edn. New York: John Wiley.

Walzer, M. 1992. *Spheres of Justice*. New York: Basic Books.

Ward, D. 1971. *Cities and Immigrants: Geography of Change in Nineteenth Century America*. New York: Oxford University Press.

Wardwell, J.M. 1977. 'Equilibrium and Change in Non-Metropolitan Growth', *Rural Sociology* 42: 156–79.

Wargon, Sylvia T. 2002. *Demography in Canada in the Twentieth Century*. Vancouver: University of British Columbia Press.

Warkentin, John. 1999. 'Canada and Its Major Regions: Bouchette, Parkin, Rogers, Innis, Hutchison', *The Canadian Geographer* 43, 3: 244–68.

Warnes, Anthony M. 1992. 'Age-Related Variation and Temporal Change in Elderly Migration', in Andrei Rogers, ed., with W.H. Frey, A. Speare Jr., P. Rees, and A.M. Warnes, *Elderly Migration and Population Redistribution: A Comparative Study* (pp. 35–55). London: Belhaven.

Watkins, Melville. H. 1963. 'A Staple Theory of Economic Growth', *Canadian Journal of Economics and Political Science* 29, 2: 141–58.

Watkins, Susan Cotts. 1993. 'If All We Knew about Women Was What We Read in *Demography*, What Would We Know?', *Demography* 30: 551–77.

———, Jane A. Menken, and John Bongaarts. 1987. 'Demographic Foundations of Family Change', *American Sociological Review* 52: 346–58.

Wattenberg, Ben J. 2004. *Fewer: How the New Demography of Depopulation Will Shape Our Future*. Chicago: Ivan R. Dee.

Weber, Max. 1958. *The Protestant Ethic and the Spirit of Capitalism*. Trans. Talcott Parsons. New York: Charles Scribner's Sons.

———. 1905 [1958]. *The City*. London: Heinemann.

Weeks, John R. 1999. *Population: An Introduction to Concepts and Issues*, 8th edn. Belmont, CA: Wadsworth.

Weiner, Myron, and Sharon Stanton Russell, eds. 2001. *Demography and National Security*. New York: Berghahn Books.

Weinstein, Jay, and Vijayan K. Pillai. 2001. *Demography: The Science of Population*. Boston: Allyn and Bacon.

Westoff, Charles F. 2003. 'Trends in Marriage and Early Childbearing in Developing Countries', *DHS Comparative Reports* 5: 2–3, 25. Calverton, MD: ORC Macro.

———. 1990. 'Reproductive Intentions and Fertility Rates', *International Family Planning Perspectives* 16, 3: 84–9.

———. 1986. 'Perspectives on Nuptiality and Fertility', in Kingsley Davis, David Bernstam, and Ricardo-Campbell, eds, *Below-Replacement Fertility in Industrialized Societies: Causes, Consequences, Policies* (pp. 155–75), supp. to *Population and Development Review* 12.

———. 1983. 'Fertility Decline in the West: Causes and Prospects', *Population and Development Review* 9: 99–104.

———. 1978. 'Some Speculations on the Future of Marriage and Fertility', *Family Planning Perspectives* 10: 79–83.

White, Kevin M. 2002. 'Longevity Advances in High-Income Countries, 1955–96', *Population and Development Review* 28, 1: 59–76.

———, and Samuel H. Preston. 1996. 'How Many Americans are Alive because of Twentieth-Century Improvements in Mortality?', *Population and Development Review* 22, 3: 415–30.

Whitehead, Paul C., and Michael J. Hayes. 1998. *The Insanity of Alcohol: Social Problems in Canadian First Nations Communities*. Toronto: Canadian Scholars' Press.

Wigle, Donald T., Yang Mao, Robert Semenciw, and Hoard I. Morrison. 1986. 'Cancer Patterns in Canada', *Canadian Medical Association Journal* 134 (1 February): 231–5.

Wilkes, Rima, Neil Guppy, and Lily Farris. 2007. 'Right-Wing Parties and Anti-Foreigner Sentiment in Europe', *American Sociological Review* 72: 831–40.

Wilkins, Russell. 1980. *Health Status in Canada, 1926–1976*. Occasional Paper no. 13. Ottawa: Institute for Research on Public Policy.

———, and Owen Adams. 1983. 'Health Expectancy in Canada, Late 1970s: Demographic, Regional and Social Dimensions', *American Journal of Public Health* 73, 9: 1073–80.

———, ———, and Anna Brancker. 1989. 'Changes in Mortality by Income in Urban Canada from 1971–1986', *Health Reports* 1, 2: 137–74.

———, Jean-Marie Berthelot, and Edward Ng. 2002. 'Trends in Mortality by Neighbourhood Income in Urban Canada from 1971 to 1996', *Health Reports* (supp.) vols 1–28.

Wilkinson, Kenneth, P., R.R. Reynolds, Jr., J.G. Thompson, and L.M. Ostrech. 1983. 'Divorce and Recent Net Migration in the Old West', *Journal of Marriage and the Family* 45: 437–45.

Wilkinson, Richard G. 2005. *The Impact of Inequality*. New York: New Press.

———. 1996. *Unhealthy Societies: The Afflictions of Inequality*. London: Routledge.

———, and Michael Marmot, eds. 2003. *The Solid Facts: Social Determinants of Health*, 2nd edn. Copenhagen, Denmark: World Health Organization Regional Office for Europe.

Williamson, Jeffrey G. 2001. 'Demographic Change, Economic Growth, and Inequality', in Nancy Birdsall, Allen C. Kelley, and Steven W. Sinding, eds, *Population Matters: Demographic Change, Economic Growth and Poverty in the Developing World* (pp. 106–36). Oxford: Oxford University Press.

Williamson, J.F. 1965. 'Regional Inequality and the Process of National Development: A Description of the Patterns', *Economic Development and Cultural Change* 13: 3–84.

Willis, Robert J. 1987. 'What Have We Learned from the Economics of the Family?' *American Economic Review* 77, 2: 68–81.

———. 1973. 'Economic Theory of Fertility Behavior', in Theodore W. Schultz, ed., *Economics of the Family: Marriage, Children, and Human Capital* (pp. 25–75). Chicago: The University of Chicago Press.

Wilmoth, Jane T., and Kenneth F. Ferraro, eds. 2007. *Gerontology: Perspectives and Issues*, 3rd edn. New York: Springer.

Wilmoth, John R., L.J. Deegan, H. Lundstrom, and S. Horiuchi. 2002. 'Increase of Maximum Life-Span in Sweden, 1861–1999', *Science* 289 (29 September): 2366–8.

Wilson, Chris. 2004. 'Fertility below Replacement Level', *Science* 304, 5668: (9 April): 207–9.

Wilson, Leonard S. 2003. 'Equalization, Efficiency and Migration: Watson Revisited', *Canadian Public Policy* 29, 4: 385–96.

Wilson, Sue J. 2005. 'Partnering, Cohabitation, and Marriage', in Maureen Baker, ed., *Families: Changing Trends in Canada* (pp. 145–62). Toronto: McGraw-Hill.

Wimberley, Dale W. 1990. 'Investment Dependence and Alternative Explanations of Third World Mortality', *American Sociological Review* 55, 1: 75–91.

Winch, Donald. 2003. 'Darwin, Charles', in Paul Demeny and Geoffrey McNicoll, eds, *Encyclopedia of Population* (pp. 189–90). New York: Macmillan Reference USA/Thomson Gale.

Winckler, Edwin A. 2002. 'Chinese Reproductive Policy at the Turn of the Millennium: Dynamic Stability', *Population and Development Review* 28, 3: 379–418.

Winkler, Anne E., Timothy D. McBride, and C. Andrews. 2005. 'Women Who Outearn Their Husbands', *Demography* 42, 3: 523–36.

Winsborough, Halliman H. 1978. 'Statistical Histories of the Life Cycle of Birth Cohorts', in Karl E. Taeuber, Larry L. Bumpass, and James A. Sweet, eds, *Social Demography* (pp. 231–59). New York: Academic Press.

Winter, J.M. 1992. 'War, Family, and Fertility in Twentieth-Century Europe', in John R. Gillis, Louise A. Tilly, and

David Levine, eds, *The European Experience of Declining Fertility, 1850–1970: The Quiet Revolution* (pp. 191–309). Cambridge, MA: Blackwell.

Wirth, Luis. 1938. 'Urbanism as a Way of Life', *American Journal of Sociology* 44: 2–24.

Wisborg, Kirsten, Ulrik Kesmodel, Tine Brink-Henriksen, et al. 2001. 'Exposure to Tobacco Smoke in Utero and the Risk of Stillbirth and Death in the First Year of Life', *American Journal of Epidemiology* 154, 4: 315–22.

Wise, Paul. 2003. 'The Anatomy of a Disparity', *Annual Review of Public Health* 24: 341–62.

Wister, Andrew. 2005. *Baby Boomer Health Dynamics: How Are We Aging?* Toronto: University of Toronto Press.

Wolfe, Barbara L. 2003. 'Fertility, Nonmarital', in Paul Demeny and Geoffrey McNicoll, eds, *Encyclopedia of Population*, vol. 1 (pp. 409–12). New York: Macmillan Reference USA/Thomson Gale.

Wolpert, John. 1965a. 'Behavioral Aspects of the Decision to Migrate', *Papers of the Regional Science Association* 15: 159–69.

———. 1965b. 'Migration as an Adjustment to Environmental Stress', *Journal of Social Issues* 22: 92–102.

Wood, James W. 1994. *Dynamics of Human Reproduction: Biology, Biometry, Demography*. Hawthorne, NY: Aldine De Gruyter.

Woods, Robert. 1982. *Theoretical Population Geography*. London: Longman.

Woolmington, Eric. 1985. 'Small May Be Inevitable', *Australian Geographical Studies* 23 (October): 195–207.

World Bank. 2003. *Sustainable Development in a Dynamic World*. New York: Oxford University Press.

———. 1994. *Averting the Old-age Crisis: Policies to Protect the Old and Promote Growth*. Oxford: Oxford University Press.

———. 1993. *The East Asian Miracle: Economic Growth and Public Policy*. Oxford: Oxford University Press.

———. 1992. *World Development Report 1992: Development and the Environment*. New York: Oxford University Press.

World Health Organization. 2007. *World Health Statistics 2007*. Geneva: WHO.

———. 2006a. *History of the International Classification of Diseases*. Geneva: WHO. <http://www.who.int/classifica tions/icd/en/> (February 2006).

———. 2006b. *Number and Rates of Registered Deaths: Canada*. <http://www3.who.int/whosis/mort/table1_ process.cfm> (28 February 2006).

———. 2006c. *Facts Relating to Chronic Diseases*. <http://www.who.int/dietphysicalactivity/publications/fa cts/chronic/en/> (14 March 2006).

———. 2006d. *World Health Statistics 2006*. Geneva: WHO.

———. 2006e. *Infant Mortality Database*. Geneva: WHO. <http://www3.who.int/whosis/mort/table2_process.cfm > (20 April 2006).

———. 2005a. *Preventing Chronic Diseases: A Vital Investment*. Geneva: WHO. <http://www.who.int/chp/ chronic_disease_report/contents/en/index.html>.

———. 2005b. *Health and the Millennium Development Goals*. Geneva: WHO.

———. 2005c. *Child and Adolescent Injury Prevention: A Global Call to Action*. Geneva: WHO. <http:// whqlibdoc.who.int/publications/2005/92414593415_e ng.pdf> (21 March 2006).

———. 2002. *The Injury Chart Book: A Graphical Overview of the Global Burden of Injuries*. Geneva: WHO.

———. 1998. *World Health Statistics Annual, 1996*. Geneva: WHO.

Wrigley, E.A. 1969. *Population and History*. New York: McGraw-Hill.

———, and R.S. Schofield. 1981a. *The Population History of England 1581–1871: A Reconstruction*. London: Edward Arnold.

———, and ———. 1981b. 'English Population History from Family Reconstitution: Summary Results 1600–1799', *Population Studies* 37, 2: 157–8.

———, R.S. Davies, J.E. Oeppen, and R.S. Schofield. 1997. *English Population History from Family Reconstitution, 1580–1837*. Cambridge: Cambridge University Press.

———, and David Souden, eds. 1986a. *The Works of Thomas Robert Malthus*, vol. 1: *An Essay on the Principle of Population*. London: William Pickering.

———, and ———, eds. 1986b. *The Works of Thomas Robert Malthus*, vol. 2: *An Essay on the Principle of Population*. London: William Pickering.

———, and ———, eds. 1986c. *The Works of Thomas Robert Malthus*. Vol. 3: *An Essay on the Principle of Population*. London: William Pickering.

———, and ———, eds. 1986d. *The Works of Thomas Robert Malthus*, vol. 4: *Essays on Population*. London: William Pickering.

Wu, Zhen. 2000. *Cohabitation: A New Form of Family Living*. Don Mills, ON: Oxford University Press.

———, and T.R. Balakrishnan. 1995. 'Dissolution of Pre-marital Cohabitation in Canada', *Demography* 32: 521–32.

———, and Christoph Schimmele. 2005. 'Divorce and Repartnering', in Maureen Baker, ed., *Families: Changing Trends in Canada* (pp. 202–28). Toronto: McGraw-Hill.

Yancey, W.L., E.P. Ericksen, and R.N. Juliani. 1976. 'Emergent Ethnicity: A Review and Reformulation', *American Sociological Review* 41: 391–403.

Yaukey, David. 1969. 'Theorizing about Fertility', *The American Sociologist* 4 (May): 100–4.

———, and Douglas L. Anderton. 2001. *Demography: The Study of Human Population*, 2nd edn. Prospect Heights, IL: Waveland.

Yen, I.H., and S.L. Syme. 1999. 'The Social Environment and Health: A Discussion of the Epidemiologic Litera-ture', *Annual Review of Public Health* 20: 287–308.

Yongping, Li, and Peng Xizhe. 2000. 'Age and Sex Structures', in Peng Xizhe and Zhigang Guo, eds, *The Changing Population of China* (pp. 64–76). Oxford: Blackwell.

Young, E.A. 1995. *Third World in the First: Development and Indigenous Peoples*. London: Routledge.

Young, T. Kue. 1999. *Population Health: Concepts and Methods*. New York: Oxford University Press.

———. 1997. 'Recent Health Trends in the Native American Population', *Population Research and Policy Review* 16, 1–2: 147–67.

———. 1994. *The Health of Native Americans: Towards a Biocultural Epidemiology*. New York: Oxford University Press.

———. 1988a. *Health Care and Cultural Change: The Indian Experience in the Central Subarctic*. Toronto: University of Toronto Press.

———. 1988b. 'Are Subarctic Indians Undergoing the Epidemiologic Transition?', *Social Science and Medicine* 26, 6: 659–71.

———. 1983. 'Mortality Pattern of Isolated Indians in Northwestern Ontario: A 10-Year Review', *Public Health Reports* 98, 5: 467–75.

———, Linda Bruce, J. Elias, et al. 1991. *The Health Effects of Housing and Community Infrastructure on Canadian Indian Reserves*. Ottawa: Indian and Northern Affairs Canada.

Yount, Kathryn M. 2001. 'Excess Mortality of Girls in the Middle East in the 1970s and 1980s: Patterns, Correlates and Gaps in Research', *Population Studies* 55, 3: 291–308.

Zavodny, M. 1999. 'Determinants of Recent Immigrants' Locational Choices', *International Migration Review* 33, 4: 1014–30.

Zelinsky, Wilbur. 1979. 'The Demographic Transition: Changing Patterns of Migration', *International Union for the Scientific Study of Population* (pp. 165–89). Liege, Belgium: IUSSP.

———. 1978. 'Is Nonmetropolitan America Being Repopulated? The Evidence from Pennsylvania's Minor Civil Divisions', *Demography* 15, 1: 13–39.

———. 1971. 'The Hypothesis of the Mobility Transition', *Geographical Review* 61, 2: 219–49.

———. 1966. *A Prologue to Population Geography*. Englewood Cliffs, NJ: Prentice Hall.

Zimmerman, Klaus F., ed. 1989. *Economic Theory of Optimal Population*. London: Springer.

Zipf, George Kingsley. 1949. *Human Behavior and the Principle of Least Effort*. Cambridge, MA: Addison-Wesley.

———. 1946. 'The P_1P_2/D Hypothesis: On the Intercity Movement of Persons', *American Sociological Review* 11: 677–86.

Zlotnik, Hania. 2006. 'Theories of International Migration', in Graziella Caselli, Jacques Vallin, and Guillaume Wunsch, eds, *Demography: Analysis and Synthesis*, vol. 2 (pp. 293–306). Amsterdam: Elsevier.

Zolberg, Aristide R. 1981. 'International Migrations in Political Perspective', in Mary M. Kritz, Charles B. Keely, and Silvano M. Tomasi, eds, *Global Trends in Migration: Theory and Research on International Population Movements* (pp. 3–27). Staten Island, New York: Center for Migration Studies.

———, and Peter M. Benda, eds. 2001. *Global Migrants, Global Refugees: Problems and Solutions*. New York: Berghahn Books.

Zolnik, Edmund J. 2004. 'The North American City Revisited: Urban Quality of Life in Canada and the United States', *Urban Geography* 25, 3: 217–40.

Zuberi, Tukufu, Amson Sibanda, Ayaga Bawah, and Amadou Noumbissi. 2003. 'Population and African Society', *Annual Review of Sociology* 29: 465–86.

Index